Living in the Environment

Living in the Environment
An Introduction to Environmental Science
Fourth Edition

G. Tyler Miller, Jr.
St. Andrews Presbyterian College

Wadsworth Publishing Company
Belmont, California
A Division of Wadsworth, Inc.

Science Editor: Jack Carey
Production Editor: Patricia Brewer
Managing Designer: Cynthia Bassett
Print Buyer: Barbara Britton
Copy Editors: Brenda Griffing and Judith Hibbard
Art Editor: Wendy Calmenson
Illustrators: Darwen and Vally Hennings
       and John and Judith Waller
Cover photograph: Stephen J. Krasemann/
       Aperture PhotoBank

All world maps in this book are based on a modified
Goode's projection used by permission of the University of Chicago, Department of Geography. Copyright
by the University of Chicago, Department of
Geography.

Printed in the United States of America

2 3 4 5 6 7 8 9 10—89 88 87 86 85

ISBN 0-534-04332-1

Library of Congress Cataloging in Publication Data
Miller, G. Tyler (George Tyler), date
  Living in the environment.
  Bibliography: p.
  Includes index.
  1. Human ecology. 2. Environmental policy. I. Title
GF41.M54 1985   304.2   84-15297
ISBN 0-534-04332-1

Books in the Wadsworth Biology Series

Biology: The Unity and Diversity of Life, 3rd, Starr and Taggart
Energy and Environment: The Four Energy Crises, 2nd, Miller
Replenish the Earth: A Primer in Human Ecology, Miller
Oceanography: An Introduction, 3rd, Ingmanson and Wallace

Biology books under the editorship of William A. Jensen,
University of California, Berkeley

Biology: The Foundations, 2nd, Wolfe
Biology of the Cell, 2nd, Wolfe
Botany, 2nd, Jensen and Salisbury
Plant Physiology, 2nd, Salisbury and Ross
Plant Physiology Laboratory Manual, Ross
Plants: An Evolutionary Survey, 2nd, Scagel et al.
Nonvascular Plants: An Evolutionary Survey, Scagel et al.
Introduction to Cell Biology, Wolfe

A study guide has been specially designed to help students master the concepts presented in this textbook.
Order from your bookstore.

The environmental crisis is an outward manifestation of a crisis of mind and spirit. There could be no greater misconception of its meaning than to believe it to be concerned only with endangered wildlife, human-made ugliness, and pollution. These are part of it, but more importantly, the crisis is concerned with the kind of creatures we are and what we must become in order to survive.

Lynton K. Caldwell

This book is dedicated to Mother Earth who sustains us and all other creatures and to my life partner and best friend, Peggy Sue O'Neal, who understands and attempts to live by the message of this book and who has helped me better understand and appreciate the beauty and complexity of nature.

Preface

An Introductory Course in Environmental Studies The purposes of this book are **(1)** to cover the diverse materials of an introductory course on environmental studies or environmental science in an accurate, balanced, and interesting way without the use of mathematics, **(2)** to enable both teacher and student to use the material in a flexible manner, and **(3)** to use basic ecological concepts to highlight environmental problems and to indicate possible ways to deal with them.

Two Texts in One To provide flexibility, this book is really two texts in one. The 22 chapters of the **basic text** provide, as far as possible, a balanced coverage of major ecological concepts, major environmental problems, and some possible solutions to these problems. The 15 **enrichment studies** allow each instructor flexibility in adding more depth and in providing additional examples. Once Chapters 1 through 5 have been studied, the remainder of the text can be covered in almost any order.

Other Major Features The fourth edition, like earlier editions, **(1)** emphasizes the use of fundamental ecological concepts (Chapters 2 through 5) to show how environmental facts, problems, and possible solutions to these problems are related, **(2)** provides balanced discussions of the opposing sides of major environmental issues, **(3)** is based on an extensive review of the literature (from the thousands of references used, key readings for each chapter are listed at the end of the text), **(4)** is based on extensive manuscript review by experts and instructors who have used one or more of the earlier editions (see List of Reviewers), and **(5)** offers a realistic but hopeful view that shows how much has been done since 1965, as well as how much more needs to be done over the next 50 years.

Major Changes in the Fourth Edition Despite extensive use of this textbook throughout the United States and a number of other countries, I examined and updated and, in many cases, rewrote, every chapter, section, and paragraph to make this an even better textbook and to reduce its overall length. Some of the major changes in this edition include:

1. New material on soil resources (Chapter 8), wildlife resources (Chapter 11), and the health and environmental effects of nuclear war (Enrichment Study 3).

2. Expanded treatment of climate (Section 3–6), human metabolism and nutrition (Section 9–2), history of natural resource conservation and environmental protection in the United States (Section 10–2), rangelands (Section 10–7), location, mining, and processing of mineral resources (Section 13–2), groundwater pollution (Section 18–4), acid deposition (Section 19–4), space as a new frontier (Enrichment Study 4), and hazardous wastes (Enrichment Study 13).

3. Reorganization of chapters on energy resources into three chapters covering, respectively, energy concepts (Chapter 14), nonrenewable energy resources (Chapter 15), and renewable energy resources (Chapter 16).

As you and your students deal with the crucial and exciting issues discussed in this book, I hope you will take the time to correct errors and suggest improvements for future editions. Please send such information to me, care of Jack Carey, Wadsworth Publishing Company, 10 Davis Drive, Belmont, CA 94002.

Supplementary Materials Dr. Robert Janiskee at the University of South Carolina has written an excellent student Study Guide and an Instructor's Manual for use with this text. In addition, overhead transparencies of some of the major illustrations are available from the publisher.

Acknowledgments I wish to thank all the teachers who responded to detailed questionnaires evaluating the first three editions. My thanks also go to the many students and teachers who responded so favorably to the first three editions and offered suggestions for improvement. I am also deeply indebted to the prominent environmentalists who wrote Guest Editorials and to the numerous reviewers who pointed out errors and suggested many important improvements. Any errors and deficiencies remaining are mine, not theirs.

It has also been a pleasure to work with many of the talented people at Wadsworth Publishing Company. I am particularly indebted to Pat Brewer for her outstanding job as production editor, to Cynthia Bassett as the managing designer, to Judith Hibbard and Brenda Griffing for their superb and most helpful copyediting, to Wendy Calmenson for her art editing, and to Darwen and Vally Hennings and John and Judith Waller for their outstanding art work. Above all I wish to thank Jack Carey, science editor at Wadsworth, for his superb reviewing system and for his help and friendship.

G. Tyler Miller, Jr.

Guest Editorialists

Hannes Alfvén
Professor of Applied Physics,
University of California, San Diego;
Nobel Laureate, Physics (1970)

Amory B. Lovins
International energy policy consultant

Gus Speth
President, World Resources Institute

Geraldine Watson
Naturalist and environmental activist

Reviewers

Barbara J. Abraham Hampton College
James R. Anderson U.S. Geological Survey
Kenneth B. Armitage University of Kansas
Virgil R. Baker Arizona State University
Ian G. Barbour Carleton College
Albert J. Beck California State University, Chico
Jeff Bland University of Puget Sound
Georg Borgstrom Michigan State University
Arthur C. Borror University of New Hampshire
Leon Bouvier Population Reference Bureau
Michael F. Brewer Resources for the Future, Inc.
Patrick E. Brunelle Contra Costa College
Lynton K. Caldwell Indiana University
Faith Thompson Campbell Natural Resources
Defense Council, Inc.
E. Ray Canterbery Florida State University
Ted J. Case University of San Diego
Richard A. Cellarius The Evergreen State
University
William U. Chandler Worldwatch Institute
R. F. Christman University of North Carolina,
Chapel Hill
Preston Cloud University of California, Santa
Barbara
Bernard C. Cohen University of Pittsburgh
Richard A. Cooley University of California,
Santa Cruz
John D. Cunningham Keene State College

Herman E. Daly Louisiana State College
R. F. Dasmann University of California, Santa
Cruz
Kingsley Davis University of California, Berkeley
Thomas R. Detwyler University of Michigan
W.T. Edmonson University of Washington
Thomas Eisner Cornell University
Paul P. Feeny Cornell University
Nancy Field Bellevue Community College
Allan Fitzsimmons University of Kentucky
George L. Fouke St. Andrews Presbyterian
College
Eville Gorham University of Minnesota
Katherine B. Gregg West Virginia Wesleyan
College
Paul Grogger University of Colorado
J. L. Guernsey Indiana State University
Ralph Guzman University of California, Santa
Cruz
Raymond E. Hampton Central Michigan
University
Ted L. Hanes California State University,
Fullerton
John P. Harley Eastern Kentucky University
Harry S. Hass San Jose City College
Arthur N. Haupt Population Reference Bureau
Denis A. Hayes Environmental consultant
David L. Hicks Whitworth College

Brief Contents

Detailed Contents

Living in the Environment

Prologue

Passengers on *Terra I,* it is time for the annual State of the Spaceship report. As you know, we are hurtling through space at about 107,200 kilometers (66,600 miles) per hour on a fixed course. Although we can never take on new supplies, our ship has a marvelous set of life-support systems that use solar energy to recycle chemicals needed to provide a reasonable number of us with adequate water, air, and food.

Let me summarize. There are more than 4.8 billion passengers on board, living in the 176 nations that are distributed throughout the ship. One-fourth are in the more developed nations, occupying good to luxurious quarters in the first-class section. Each year these passengers use about 80 percent of the supplies on board.

Unfortunately, conditions have not improved much this year for the 75 percent of you in the so-called less developed nations, traveling in the hold of the ship. Half are living in countries where the average annual income is less than $400 per person. More than one-fifth are suffering from hunger, malnutrition, or both, one-sixth do not have adequate shelter, and one-fourth lack clean water. More people starved to death or died from malnutrition-related diseases this year than at any time in the history of our voyage. Such deaths will certainly rise as long as population growth continues to wipe out gains in food supply and economic development.

With the limited supplies and recycling capacity of our craft, many wonder whether they will ever move from the hold to the first-class section. More important, many are asking why they have to travel in the ship's hold in the first place.

The most important fact molding our lives today is that we have gone around the bend of three curves shaped like the letter J that represents the global increases in population, resource use, and pollution over the past hundred years. Although population growth rates have decreased slightly in recent years, if the present rate is maintained, our population will probably grow to at least 6.2 billion by the year 2000 and could reach almost 10 billion in the next 40 years.

Overpopulation of the hold, serious though it is, may not be as threatening to our life-support system as the overpopulation in the first-class section. Both consumption and pollution rise sharply with even a slight increase in the wealthier population. For example, the 234 million citizens of the United States, making up only 5 percent of our total population, use about 35 percent of all supplies and produce more than one-third of all our human-related pollution. Each first-class passenger has about 25 times as much impact on our life-support system as each passenger traveling in the hold. Efforts to conserve matter and energy resources in the rich nations are still grossly inadequate. Pollution control in these nations improves, but there is a long way to go.

In spite of the gravity of the interlocking problems of overpopulation, dwindling resources, and pollution, the single greatest human and environmental threat is that of war—especially nuclear holocaust. It is discouraging that so little progress has been made in reducing the extravagant waste of resources and human talent devoted to the arms race. During the past year we spent 200 times more on military expenditures than on international cooperation for peace and development. The number of nations that develop the ability to produce nuclear weapons continues to increase.

Some say that our ship is already doomed. Others—technological optimists—see a glorious future for everyone. Most experts agree that the ship's situation is serious but not hopeless. They feel that if we begin now, we have about 50 years to learn how to control our population and consumption and to learn to live together peacefully on the beautiful and fragile lifecraft that is our home. Obviously, more of us must act like members of the crew rather than as passengers, particularly those traveling first class.

Just what is spaceship *Terra I?* Where are we going? What problems and opportunities do we face? What is an individual's responsibility for the other passengers and for preserving the various life-support systems? We must look more deeply into these complex questions so that we may convert our understanding into effective individual and group action.

1. Two college students spending the weekend at a Colorado ski resort caught the State of the Spaceship report on television. "I'm sick of hearing about environmental problems and nuclear war," said John as he ripped the tab from his third can of beer. "It's already too late. My motto is, 'Eat, drink, and have a good time while you can.' What's the world done for me?"

"I don't think it's too late at all," observed Susan. "If we can put astronauts on the moon, we can certainly solve our pollution problems. Sure it's going to cost some money, but I'm willing to pay my share. The whole thing is just a matter of money and technology. By the way, John, during Christmas break let's fly to Switzerland. There are too many people here. We always have to wait in line, and all these hideous new ski lodges have spoiled the view. Besides, I want to shop for a new ski outfit."

2. In a tenement room in New York City, Larry angrily switched off the television, even though he usually kept it on to drown out noises around him—particularly the rats scratching. A high school dropout, he's given up looking for work. "This ecology crap is just another whitey trick to keep us from getting a piece of the action. What do I care about pollution when my little sister was bitten by a rat last night, my ma's got emphysema, and we haven't had any heat in this firetrap for months. Tell it to my uncle in Florida who's paralyzed from the waist down from some chemical used on the fruit he was picking. Give me a chance to pollute and then I might worry about it."

3. In Calcutta, Mukh Das, his wife, Kamala, and their children did not hear the broadcast in the street where they live. As Mukh, age 36, watched his 34-year-old wife patting dung into cakes to be dried and used for fuel, he was glad that 7 of his 12 children were alive to help now that he and Kamala were in their old age. Mukh felt a chill, and he hoped the children would soon return from begging and gathering dung and scraps of food. Perhaps they had been lucky enough to meet another rich American tourist today.

4. In a Connecticut suburb, Bill and Kathy Farmington and their three children were discussing the broadcast. David, a college senior, turned away in disgust. "This ecology thing is just a big cop-out by people who don't really know what it's all about. In the commune I'm moving into we're going to get back to nature and away from this plastic, racist society of people who don't care."

"That's the biggest cop-out of all," said Karen, a college sophomore. "The only reason you have the freedom to drop out is that you live in a rich country. Why don't you help rather than trying to escape? The real problem is with the poor people who keep having all those children. Why don't you work on family planning in the slums this summer? I did last year, and I even got college credit for it. "

Bill Farmington, chief engineer for Monarch Power Company, looked at his children irritably. "The problem with all of you back-to-the-woods dropouts and misguided liberals is that you don't understand the hard work it takes to keep the world going. If you're so fired up about pollution, David, why don't you walk to the commune rather than driving the car I gave you? Karen, you might consider turning in that snowmobile you used to recuperate from your hot summer in the ghetto. How do you think I pay for all the things you kids want? I'm all for clean air and water, but we can't stop the economic progress our American way of life is built on.

"Remember last year when we had a lot of ecofreaks and liberal professors trying to stop us from building the new nuclear power plant? In spite of all the talk about conservation, Americans are going to use more and more energy, and we have to give our customers the electricity they want. You're as bad as those college professors who go around making speeches and writing books on ecology, but don't change their own life-styles and don't know what hard physical work is all about. David, cut off that TV and the one in the kitchen too. I'm sick of hearing about pollution, corruption in government, and rioting in India. Linda, it's getting hot in here. Would you please turn on the air conditioning?"

Kathy Farmington slowly shook her head. "I just don't know. We have to do something about pollution and overpopulation. The problem is, I don't know what to do. One scientist says we shouldn't build nuclear plants, another says we should. One says ban pesticides, and another says that if we do, many will die from diseases and starvation. How can we know what to do when experts disagree? I recognize that the population problem is bad in India, Africa, and South America. Remember how horrid it was in Calcutta on our trip last summer? I just couldn't wait to leave. I'm glad we don't have an overpopulation problem in the United States. At least we can afford to have children."

As Linda, a college freshman, got up, she was thinking that no one had listened to the speech. "Don't you realize that we are all connected with one another and that our primary goal must be to preserve—not destroy—the life-support systems that keep us and other species alive? Can't you see that everyone on *Terra I* is a unique human being, entitled to a share of our ship's basic resources? I'm afraid for all of us too, but I don't think it's too late. When I become a public service lawyer, I plan to devote my life to environmental reform."

PART ONE

Introduction

It is only in the most recent, and brief, period of their tenure that human beings have developed in sufficient numbers, and acquired enough power, to become one of the most potentially dangerous organisms that the planet has ever hosted.

John McHale

Humankind still has the time and option to make it. But it's absolutely touch and go whether we are going to make it on this planet.

R. Buckminster Fuller

1

Population, Resources, and Pollution: An Overview

We travel together, passengers on a little spaceship, dependent on its vulnerable resources of air, water, and soil . . . preserved from annihilation only by the care, the work, and the love we give our fragile craft.

Adlai E. Stevenson

1-1 A Crisis of Interlocking Problems

People have always had an impact on the environment. Throughout most of human history, however, this impact was fairly small and localized, because about 90 percent of all humans that ever lived have been hunter-gatherers. They were small in numbers, and their main energy source was their own muscle power. Agriculture was invented 10,000 to 12,000 years ago, but only about 6 percent of the people who have ever lived on this planet have been shepherds and farmers. Only about 4 percent of humans who have lived on earth were in industrial societies. Yet these few, within slightly more than 100 years, have led us to most of the environmental problems we now face.*

Today the world is at a critical turning point. The prospect for humanity is both brighter and darker than at any time in history. Prophets of doom warn that the earth's life-support systems are being destroyed, and technological optimists promise a life of abundance for everyone. We spend billions to transport a handful of humans to the moon, only to learn the importance of protecting the diversity of life on the beautiful blue planet that is our home. We use modern medicine and sanitation to lower death rates from disease, only to be faced with a population explosion. We feed more people than ever before, yet millions die each year from a lack of food or from diseases brought on or made worse by too little food.

As more and more people try to use the earth's resources, increasing stress is placed on the forests, grasslands, croplands, and on the air, water, and soil that support all life. Tropical forests are cleared to provide lumber and fuelwood and land for growing crops and grazing livestock, but this also threatens thousands of plant and animal species with extinction. Some experts say we are running out of certain fuel and mineral resources; others say we will never run out. We hear of successes in cleaning up rivers, lakes, and the air in some parts of the world, but we are bombarded with stories about new pollution threats such as leaking toxic waste dumps, acid rain, radioactive wastes, and threats to the global climate from the carbon dioxide added to the atmosphere when fossil fuels are burned.

The problems associated with increasing population, increasing use of resources, and pollution are all interrelated. The primary aims of this book are to describe major environmental problems, present ecological concepts that connect them, and use these concepts to evaluate the opportunities we have to deal with these problems in coming decades. Let us begin with a brief overview of the related problems of population growth, resource use, and pollution. In later chapters we will look at these problems and proposed solutions in greater depth.

1-2 Population

The J-Shaped Curve of Exponential Growth Population size, resource use, and pollution are increasing at an *exponential* or *geometric rate*—that is, they are growing by doubling: 1, 2, 4, 8, 16, 32, and so on. When this **exponential** (or **geometric**) **growth** is plotted on a graph, the result is an *exponential curve*, or *J-shaped curve*. Exponential growth is deceptive because it starts out slowly. Then suddenly the bend in the J is rounded, and the curve becomes almost vertical.

Enrichment Studies 1, 2, 3, 4, and 7 are related to this chapter.

*This human cultural evolution from hunter-gatherer society to agricultural society to industrial society is discussed in more detail in Enrichment Study 1.

Exponential growth can be illustrated by folding a page of this book. The page is about 0.1 millimeter (about $\frac{1}{254}$ inch) thick, so after one fold its thickness would be doubled, after 12 doublings the page would be about 410 millimeters (1.34 feet) high, and after 20 doublings about 105 meters (340 feet)—still a relatively unspectacular change. However, after the 35th fold, its height would equal the distance from New York to Los Angeles. After 42 doublings the mound of paper would reach from the earth to the moon, 386,400 kilometers (240,000 miles) away. Slightly past the 51st doubling the pile would reach the sun, 149 million kilometers (93 million miles) from the earth's surface! This is what it means to go around the bend on a J-shaped curve of exponential growth.

The J-Shaped Curve of Population Growth   The human population on earth has rounded the bend on such an exponential or J-shaped curve, as shown in Figure 1-1. Notice from Figure 1-1 that it took 2 to 5 million years to add the first billion people; 80 years to add the second billion; 30 years to add the third billion; and only 15 years to add the fourth billion. At present growth rates the fifth billion will be added in the 12 years between 1975 and 1987, and the sixth billion will be added only 11 years later by 1998. One billion people is more than four times the population of the United States. If this many people were lined up side by side they would stretch more than the distance from the earth to the moon and back.

The average number of live births on this planet is now about 253 babies per minute, or approximately 365,000 per day, while the average number of deaths is only 100 persons per minute, or 144,000 per day. In other words, there are about 2.5 times more births than deaths each day. Population growth for the entire planet over a given time period is determined by the difference between births and deaths:

population = births − deaths
increase   = 365,000 people − 144,000 people
                    per day   per day
           = 221,000 people per day

This adds 1.55 million people each week and 81 million people each year to the 4.8 billion passengers already on "spaceship earth." At this rate, it takes less than 5 days to replace a number of people equal to all Americans killed in all U.S. wars; less than 11 months to replace the more than 75 million people killed in the world's largest disaster, the bubonic plague epidemic of the fourteenth century; and one year to replace the 86 million soldiers and civilians who died in all wars fought in this century.

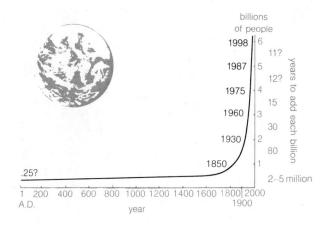

Figure 1-1   J-shaped curve of the world's population growth. Future projections assume that the 1984 growth rate of 1.7 percent will drop to 1.5 percent by 2000.

The good news is that between 1965 and 1984 the annual growth rate of the world's population slowed down from 1.99 to 1.7 percent. The rate of population growth in the United States has slowed down significantly with the average number of children per couple decreasing from 3.8 in 1957 to 1.8 in 1984. By 1984, there were 12 European countries that had reached **zero population growth** (**ZPG**), where the annual number of births equals the number of deaths. Despite these trends in some *more developed countries* (MDCs), by 2000 the world's population is expected to be 6.3 billion, assuming that the annual growth rate has dropped to 1.5 percent by then. About 90 percent of this growth is projected to take place in the *less developed countries* (LDCs), where already the lives and dignity of at least 800 million people—one-sixth of humanity—are degraded by disease, malnutrition, illiteracy, exploitation, fear, and a constant struggle for survival. Even with this further drop in the world's population growth rate, 92 million people are expected to be added in 2000 compared to 81 million in 1984. Based on present trends, United Nations (UN) population experts project that the earliest year the world could reach ZPG is 2040 with 8 billion people. Their more likely projection is the year 2110 with a population of 10.5 billion.

All these new passengers must be fed, clothed, and housed. Each will use some resources and add to global pollution. While some of this population growth is taking place in the MDCs such as the United States and the Soviet Union, most is taking place in the LDCs such as China and India. Currently 75 percent of the people in the world live in the LDCs that have only 20 percent of the world's wealth. As a result, the United Nations estimates

Figure 1-2 One-sixth of the people in the world do not have adequate housing. Lean-to shelters like these are homes for many families in Dacca, Bangladesh.

that at least one-half of the adults on this planet are illiterate; one-fifth of the people are hungry or malnourished; one-sixth have inadequate housing (Figure 1-2); one out of every four lacks clean water; and one out of three does not have access to adequate sewage disposal and effective medical service.

While you ate dinner today, the World Health Organization (WHO) estimates that at least 1,400 people died of starvation, malnutrition, or diseases resulting from or worsened by these conditions. By this time tomorrow, 33,000 will have died from starvation or starvation-related diseases; by next week, 231,000; by next year, about 12,000,000. Half are children under the age of 5. *Those who died were human beings, not numbers or things!* Because this mass starvation of about 12 million a year is spread throughout much of the world instead of being confined to one country or region, it is not even classified as a famine by most officials.

Population growth, however, is not our only problem. We are also faced with the environmental problems of increasing resource use and pollution, both related to population growth.

1-3 Natural Resources

Types of Natural Resources A **resource** or **natural resource** is any form of matter or energy obtained from the physical environment that meets human needs. This definition of natural resources is not as simple as it appears. Most resources are created by human ingenuity. Oil was once a useless fluid until humans learned how to locate it, extract it from the ground, and separate it by distillation into various components such as gasoline, home heating oil, and road tar. Similarly, coal and uranium were once useless rocks. Something may become useful or useless for human needs as a result of changes in the technology of resource extraction and processing, the costs of finding the resource and making it available, cultural changes (for example, it may become unfashionable to wear furs from endangered animal species), and the environmental effects of obtaining and using a resource. Thus, *whether something is classified as a resource depends on technology, economics, cultural beliefs, and the environmental effects of finding and using it.*

Resources can be classified as *renewable* or *nonrenewable* (Figure 1-3). A **renewable resource** is one that either comes from an essentially inexhaustible source (such as solar energy) or that can be renewed and replenished relatively rapidly by natural or artificial processes if managed wisely. Examples include food crops, animals, grasslands, forests, and other living things, as well as fresh air, fresh water, and fertile soil. However, *just because a resource is renewable does not mean that it can never be exhausted.* A renewable resource will not be exhausted only as long as it is used at a rate slower than the one at which its supply can be replenished by natural or human-designed processes. The maximum rate at which a renewable resource can be used without impairing or damaging its ability to be renewed is called its **maximum sustained yield.** If this yield is exceeded a potentially renewable resource is then converted to a nonrenewable resource.

In many parts of the world the maximum sustained yields for renewable resources such as soil, grasslands, forests, and some forms of wildlife are being exceeded. *As a result, we are in greater danger of seriously depleting renewable resource supplies in many parts of the world than of depleting supplies of nonrenewable resources,* as discussed by Gus Speth in his guest editorial at the end of this chapter.

A **nonrenewable resource** is one that is not replaced by natural processes or for which the rate of replacement is slower than the rate of use. It is convenient to divide nonrenewable resources into those that can be recycled or reused and those that cannot. **Recycling** involves collecting and remelting or reprocessing a resource, whereas **reuse** involves using a resource over and over again in the same form. Nonrenewable resources that can be recycled or reused include the nonenergy mineral resources found in the earth's crust in finite amounts. Examples include ore deposits of *metallic*

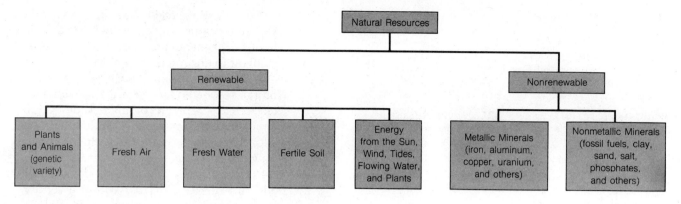

Figure 1-3 Major types of natural resources.

minerals from which metals such as copper, aluminum, and iron can be extracted and deposits of *nonmetallic minerals* such as phosphate rock from which fertilizer nutrients are extracted (Figure 1-3).

Natural geological processes taking place over millions of years have created varying deposits of such metallic and nonmetallic minerals. Once such deposits are mined they are not replaced fast enough to be useful. The easily available and highly concentrated supplies of these nonrenewable minerals are normally depleted first. Then it is necessary to look harder and dig deeper to find the remaining deposits, which usually contain lower concentrations of the desired mineral. This normally costs more, although improvements in resource location and mining technology sometimes reduce costs. Higher costs can stimulate a search for new deposits or make the mining and processing of lower-grade deposits more feasible. However, if the cost of finding, extracting, and concentrating a resource becomes too high, it will no longer be useful even though some supplies remain. Thus, *something is useful as a resource only if it can be made available at a reasonable cost.*

Sometimes a substitute or replacement for a resource that is scarce or too expensive is found. For example, steel is still used to make cars, but much of it is being replaced with aluminum and plastic to make cars lighter and thus conserve gasoline. In many cases aluminum has replaced copper for electrical wiring. Although some resource economists like to talk of infinite substitutability for nonrenewable resources, this is not always the case. Some materials have such unique properties that they cannot be replaced; their replacements may be inferior or too costly. Nothing now known can replace steel and concrete in skyscrapers and dams where strength is needed. In other cases the proposed substitutes are themselves fairly scarce. Such is the case with molybdenum, the main substitute for tungsten.

Recycling and reuse are other ways of stretching the supplies of some nonrenewable minerals. Between 1900 and 1984, the percentage of the copper extracted and concentrated from copper ores each year that was recycled or reused increased from 10 percent to about 40 percent. Large amounts of copper should become available for recycling and reuse as glass fibers replace it in telephone wires. In most LDCs recycling and reuse are necessary for survival. In MDCs, however, economic incentives (such as tax breaks and government price controls) are often used to encourage the use of virgin resources instead of promoting recycling and reuse.

There can also be an economic limit to recycling. Usually recycling is cheaper than mining virgin materials, but only if the material to be recycled is not too widely dispersed. For example, products made from iron and steel, such as cars and toys, are often thrown away, buried, and widely scattered through use. When this happens the labor and energy costs for finding and collecting the objects may be too expensive to make recycling feasible.

Examples of nonrenewable resources that cannot be recycled or reused include nonmetallic mineral energy resources, such as fossil fuels (coal, oil, and natural gas), and uranium, which is used to provide nuclear power. **Fossil fuels** are buried deposits of decayed plants and animals that have been converted to organic matter by heat and pressure in the earth's crust over hundreds of millions of years under specific climatic and geological conditions that no longer exist. We live in a relatively brief period of human history, called the fossil fuel era, in which these deposits are being rapidly depleted in order to provide us with about 84 percent of the energy we use. Once these deposits are used up they will be gone because renewal takes hundreds of millions of years. *There is also no way of recycling the energy in fossil fuels. Once a fossil fuel resource is burned, it is gone forever as a useful source of energy.* The energy released when fossil fuels are

Table 1-1 Average Lifetime (70-Year) Resource Use and Pollution per American

Resource Consumption	Waste
566,000 kilograms (623 tons) of coal, oil, and natural gas	764,000 kilograms (840 tons) of agricultural wastes
557,000 kilograms (613 tons) of sand, gravel, and stone	748,000 kilograms (823 tons) of garbage, industrial, and mining wastes
98,000 cubic meters (26 million gallons) of water	26,000 cubic meters (7 million gallons) of polluted water
80 cubic meters (21 thousand gallons) of gasoline	64,000 kilograms (70 tons) of air pollutants
46,000 kilograms (51 tons) of metals	19,250 bottles
45,000 kilograms (50 tons) of food	19,000 cans
44,000 kilograms (48 tons) of wood	7 automobiles
19,000 kilograms (19 tons) of paper	
4,700 kilograms (5.2 tons) of synthetic plastics, rubber, and fibers	
4,500 kilograms (5 tons) of fertilizer	

Figures assume constant 1983 consumption rates. If average consumption goes up as projected, the figures will be much higher. Figures include direct and indirect uses.

burned is eventually radiated from the earth into outer space as low-grade heat and cannot be used again on earth. Similarly, deposits of uranium will also be rapidly depleted if nuclear power is widely used—unless nuclear breeder reactors are developed that convert some nonusable (nonfissionable) forms of uranium into other forms of uranium or other chemical elements that can be used to produce nuclear power.

Are We Running Out of Natural Resources? Optimists Versus Pessimists   Increasing population causes a rise in resource use, but a rise in the standard of living creates an even greater demand for renewable and nonrenewable natural resources. As income rises people buy, use, and throw away more resources. Thus, affluent nations have gone around the bend on a J-shaped curve of increasing resource use. For example, *the Western affluent nations, Japan, and the Soviet Union together account for only about one-fourth of the world's population but use 80 percent of its natural resources. The United States alone, with about 5 percent of the world's population, produces about 21 percent of the world's goods and services, uses about 30 percent of the world's processed natural resources (Table 1-1), and produces at least one-third of the world's pollution.*

Furthermore, the United States and many other industrialized nations unnecessarily waste as much as one-half of the matter and energy resources they use by failing to encourage and enforce strict programs for the conservation of such resources.

Natural resource use by affluent nations is expected to rise sharply in coming decades. At the same time, poor and moderately affluent nations of the world hope to become more affluent, further increasing resource use. A global economic growth rate of 4 percent a year would expand the output of goods and services fiftyfold within a century, creating enormous pressures on world resource supplies. Nobel Prize-winning economist Wassily Leontief projects that in order for even moderate economic growth to occur between 1975 and 2020, production of food must increase fourfold and that of common minerals fivefold.

This J-shaped curve of increasing resource use raises the question of how long the earth's renewable and nonrenewable resources will last. Great controversy surrounds this question, represented by two distinctly opposing schools of thought. One group called *neo-Malthusians* (or gloom-and-doom pessimists by their opponents) believes that if present trends continue, the world is headed for economic ruin, increased political instability, and threat of global nuclear war because **(1)** the maximum sustained yield of many of the world's renewable resources may be exceeded through overfishing, destruction of habitat for wildlife, overgrazing, deforestation, overpopulation, and pollution; **(2)** there will be shortages of affordable supplies of nonrenewable fossil fuels (especially oil and possibly natural gas) and selected nonrenewable minerals important to economic well-being; and **(3)** the use of some renewable and nonrenewable resources may be limited by the environmental side effects of more and more people using more and more resources, even if supplies are adequate.

Their solutions usually involve recycling, reuse, resource conservation, reducing average per capita consumption primarily by eliminating wasteful use of matter and energy resources, increased pollution control, and slowing world population growth. Several groups of experts have developed global computer models projecting—but not predicting—that if present trends continue global economic collapse could occur within 30 to 50 years (2015 to 2035). One of these models formed the basis of *The Global 2000 Report to the President,* as discussed in Gus Speth's guest editorial at the end of this chapter. Other models are discussed in Enrichment Study 2.

The opposing group, called *cornucopians* (or technological optimists by their opponents), believes that we will never run out of needed renewable and nonrenewable resources and that continued economic growth and technological advances based on human ingenuity will lead to a world of growing affluence and well-being. This group believes that renewable and nonrenewable resources will never be depleted because (1) scarcity will cause prices to rise, which will encourage conservation of renewable resources, enable lower-grade deposits of nonrenewable resources to be mined, and stimulate searches for new deposits and substitutes; and (2) human ingenuity can always develop new forms of technology to mine increasingly lower-grade deposits of nonrenewable resources and when necessary can always find an acceptable substitute for any scarce renewable or nonrenewable resource. Some members of this school of thought also believe that efforts to reduce population growth are not necessary because it will be brought down naturally by economic growth in the LDCs.

The arguments between these two opposing groups have been going on for several decades and will undoubtedly continue. Much of this book is devoted to analyzing this complex debate to help you evaluate each position. As usual, the truth is often found between these two extreme positions. Because natural resources and human beings are so diverse and complex, the answers often differ depending on what resource and what country or group of human beings are being discussed.

1-4 Pollution

What Is Pollution? **Pollution** can be defined as an *undesirable change* in the physical, chemical, or biological characteristics of the air, water, or land that can affect health, survival, or activities of humans or other organisms. Depending on their concentration in the environment, some pollutants such as sulfur dioxide, lead, mercury, and various toxic chemicals may be poisonous or injurious to humans or other organisms. Pollution, however, does not have to cause physical harm. Pollutants such as noise and heat may cause injury but more often cause psychological distress. Forms of aesthetic pollution such as unpleasant sights and foul odors offend the senses. Some forms of pollution may merely interfere with human activities. For example, a lake may be considered polluted if it cannot be used for boating activities.

The problem with defining what is and is not considered pollution is that people often differ in what they believe is an undesirable change. For example, chemicals spewed into the air or water from an industrial plant may be harmful to humans and other organisms living nearby. However, if

expensive pollution controls are required, the plant may be forced to shut down. Workers who would lose their jobs may feel that the risks to them from contaminated air and water are not as great as the benefits of having jobs.

Human value judgments about short-term versus long-term risks also cause controversy. Building a worldwide network of nuclear power plants may provide electricity for the present generation and reduce the use of coal, which produces harmful air pollutants without proper pollution-control equipment. But it compels future generations to handle and store radioactive wastes for thousands of years, even if nuclear power should be abandoned in the future because (1) of economic or safety concerns, (2) the supply of nuclear fuel resources is exhausted, or (3) other, less risky, and perhaps cheaper energy sources are developed. Widespread use of nuclear power can also increase the risk of global nuclear war by increasing the number of countries with nuclear fuel, which can be reprocessed to make nuclear weapons.

Thus, determining which effects of an activity that alters the environment are desirable and which are undesirable is controversial. The nature of tragedy, as the philosopher Hegel pointed out, is the conflict not between right and wrong but between right and right. But despite the difficulties in and controversies over defining pollution, there must be some forms of pollution control to protect humans from their own harmful activities. Thus, we have laws prohibiting or limiting many human acts and activities.

The primary reason economic rewards and laws are needed to help reduce pollution is what biologist Garrett Hardin calls *"the tragedy of the commons."* Officials running a particular industry may voluntarily decide to reduce pollution output by installing expensive pollution control equipment. However, similar industries may refuse to install such equipment primarily because it would reduce profits. Unless the same degree of pollution control is required for these companies, the *common* resources of air, water, and soil used by everyone will continue to be degraded. In addition, the products of the company whose officials voluntarily acted to help protect the environment will cost more than those of their polluting competitors—driving the company that acted responsibly out of business. *The basic issues, then, are in deciding how much pollution is too much and how much we are willing to pay to reduce pollution to levels acceptable by the majority of the people.*

Types of Pollution From a biological viewpoint, there are two major types of pollutants: degradable and nondegradable. A **degradable pollutant** can be decomposed, removed, or consumed and thus reduced to acceptable levels either by natural processes or by human-engineered systems (such as sewage treatment plants), as long as the systems are not overloaded. There are two classes of degradable pollutants: rapidly degradable (nonpersistent) and slowly degradable (persistent). *Rapidly degradable* or *nonpersistent pollutants,* such as human sewage and animal and crop wastes, can normally be biodegraded quickly by decomposing organisms such as bacteria and fungi, if the water, air, or soil system being polluted is not overloaded. For example, a rapidly flowing river can normally cleanse itself of human sewage if it does not receive too much raw sewage from a large city or a number of small cities or farms. Thus, control of rapidly degradable pollutants involves ensuring that natural systems receiving them are not overloaded.

Slowly degradable or *persistent pollutants* remain in the environment for a long time before being broken down or reduced to harmless levels. They include some radioactive materials and synthetic compounds, such as dichlorodiphenyltrichloroethane (DDT), polychlorinated biphenyls (PCBs), and plastics that are resistant to decomposition by heat, light, chemicals, and decomposer organisms. Control of slowly degradable pollutants involves (1) preventing them from reaching the environment either by banning their use or by finding a safe way to store them, (2) learning how to convert or degrade them to a harmless material at a faster rate, or (3) controlling the amount released to the environment so they do not build up to harmful levels.

Nondegradable pollutants are not broken down by natural processes. Examples are mercury, lead, and some of their compounds (Enrichment Study 12) and some plastics. They are controlled in the same ways as slowly degradable pollutants.

Determining Harmful Levels of Pollutants
Determining the amount of a particular pollutant that can cause a harmful or undesirable effect in humans or other organisms is a difficult scientific problem. The amount of a chemical or pollutant in a given volume or weight of air, water, or other medium is called its **concentration.** Concentrations are often expressed as parts per million or parts per billion.

Parts per million (ppm) is the number of parts of a chemical or pollutant found in 1 million parts of a particular gas, liquid, or solid mixture. One part per million is equivalent to 28 grams (1 ounce) of salt in about 28 thousand kilograms (31 tons) of

potato chips or 1 mouthful of food out of all the food consumed during a 70-year lifetime. **Parts per billion** (ppb) is the number of parts of a chemical or pollutant found in a billion parts of a particular gas, liquid, or solid mixture. One part per billion corresponds to 28 grams (1 ounce) of salt in 28 million kilograms (31 thousand tons) of potato chips. Another common way to express the concentration of gaseous pollutants and particulate matter in the air is in micrograms (1 microgram or 1 μg is one millionth of a gram) of pollutant per cubic meter of air (μg/m^3).

One part per million and one part per billion may seem very small, but for some organisms and with some pollutants they represent dangerous levels. Some chemicals, called **nonthreshold pollutants,** are harmful to a particular organism in any concentration (Figure 1-4). Examples include some radioactive substances and mercury, lead, cadmium, and some of their compounds (Enrichment Study 12). Other substances, called **threshold pollutants,** are harmful only above a certain concentration, or *threshold level* (Figure 1-4). For these latter pollutants (DDT and arsenic are examples), the concentration can increase with no effect until the threshold is crossed, when a harmful or fatal effect is triggered—like the straw that broke the camel's back.

Threshold levels and damage potential for a particular pollutant vary widely among different species, among members of the same species, and the environment involved. For example, 1 ppm of phenol in water is lethal to some fish species, 0.2 ppm of sulfur dioxide in the air can increase the human death rate, and 1 ppb of hydrogen fluoride in the atmosphere can injure some plants, such as peach trees. In addition, an organism's sensitivity to a particular pollutant is often different at various times in its life cycle. For most animal species, threshold levels are much lower during the juvenile stage (when body defense mechanisms may not be fully developed) than during the adult stage. One method of indicating the average effect of a pollutant on members of the same species is to determine the concentration required for 50 percent of the population to show some type of nonlethal or lethal response. The amount of exposure to a toxic chemical that results in the death of one-half of the exposed population is called the **LD-50** (for lethal dose-50 percent).

To complicate matters further, pollutants can have both acute and chronic effects. An *acute effect,* such as a burn or death, occurs shortly after exposure, often to fairly large concentrations of a pollutant. A *chronic effect* is one that takes place over a long period of time, often due to continued expo-

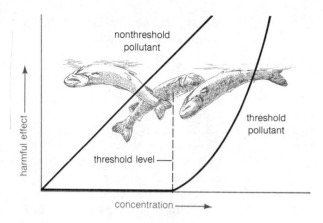

Figure 1-4 Effects of nonthreshold and threshold pollutants.

sure to low concentrations of a pollutant. For example, a person exposed to a large dose of radiation may die within a few days. However, a person receiving the same total dose in small amounts over a long period of time may develop various types of cancer or transfer certain genetic defects to his or her children or grandchildren. Some chronic effects of pollution may not show up for many years, making it difficult to discover which specific pollutants are the villains.

During a lifetime an individual is exposed to many different types and concentrations of potentially harmful pollutants. Thus, the scientific evidence linking a particular harmful effect to a particular pollutant is usually statistical or circumstantial—as is most scientific evidence. For example, so far no one has been able to show what specific chemicals in cigarette smoke cause lung cancer, but an overwhelming amount of statistical evidence links smoking and lung cancer (Enrichment Study 7).

Another problem with identifying the harmful level of a particular pollutant is that certain combinations of pollutants cause more serious problems than exposure to any one pollutant. This is called a *synergistic effect*. For example, asbestos workers and uranium miners who smoke have a much higher chance of getting lung cancer than those who do not. Testing all of the possible synergistic interactions among the thousands of possible pollutants in the environment, even for one type of organism, is essentially an impossible job in terms of both time and money.

Setting Pollution Control Standards and Cost-Benefit Analysis Finding out what level of exposure to a particular pollutant is harmful to most individuals in a particular species is costly, time consum-

ing, and difficult. Most government standards for controlling human exposure to a particular pollutant are set by establishing a level far enough below the statistically projected threshold level to protect the general population but not so low as to cause undue economic hardship for the industries or individuals producing the pollution. Political conflicts occur in making such judgments.

It is tempting to believe that consumers will save money by not having pollution controls or by setting the low pollution control standards often suggested by industry. This, however, is rarely the case. Industries save money by not paying for the *hidden external costs* of pollution such as higher cleaning and maintenance costs because of increased dirt and corrosion from pollution and higher health insurance premiums and medical bills to pay for the costs of illnesses caused or aggravated by pollution. The general public pays for these hidden external costs one way or the other either by paying more for products because of required pollution control or paying higher health insurance and medical bills and maintenance and cleaning costs, and increased taxes. There is no free lunch!

To determine the allowed level of pollution that will protect most of the public and still not force industries out of business, experts on both sides of the controversy often attempt to compare pollution control *costs* with the *benefits* that may occur from pollution control. This procedure is called **cost-benefit analysis.** Industrial officials emphasize the pollution control costs, which are fairly easy to document, while environmentalists and health officials emphasize the pollution control benefits, which are often harder to document and put a price tag on. These problems are discussed further in Chapter 20.

Sources of Pollution Polluting substances enter the environment naturally (volcanoes) or through human activities (burning coal), as shown in Table 1-2. That nature pollutes does not justify humans adding extra pollutants causing threshold-level concentrations to be approached or exceeded. For example, we are exposed to small amounts of radiation from cosmic rays entering the atmosphere and from radioactive minerals in the earth's crust. Nevertheless, this does not mean it is safe to increase the radiation we are exposed to through atomic bomb tests and nuclear power plant accidents. In addition, most natural pollution is not concentrated in a particular area and is normally diluted or degraded to harmless levels. In contrast, the most serious human pollution problems occur in or near urban and industrial areas, where large amounts of pol-

Table 1-2 Pollutants Generated by Natural and Human Activities

Type of Pollutant	Text Discussion
Class 1: Almost completely generated by human activities	
DDT, PCBs, and other chlorinated hydrocarbon compounds	Section 9-9; Enrichment Study 13
Lead in the air (from burning leaded gasoline)	Enrichment Study 12
Solid wastes and litter	Enrichment Study 13
Class 2: Primarily generated by human activities	
Radioactive wastes	Section 15-5
Oil in the oceans	Section 18-5
Sewage (animal and plant wastes)	Chapter 18
Phosphates in aquatic systems	Enrichment Study 14
Waste heat in rivers, lakes, and oceans	Chapter 18
Photochemical smog in the air (from burning gasoline)	Chapter 19
Sulfur dioxide in the air (from burning coal and oil)	Chapter 19
Noise	Enrichment Study 10
Class 3: Primarily generated by natural sources	
Hydrocarbons in the air	Chapter 19
Carbon monoxide and carbon dioxide in the air	Chapter 19; Enrichment Study 5
Solid particles in the air	Chapter 18; Enrichment Study 5
Mercury in the ocean	Enrichment Study 12

lutants are concentrated in relatively small volumes of air, water, and soil. Also, many pollutants from human activities are synthetic chemicals that may not be decomposed by natural processes.

There is little doubt that the biggest overall threat to the environment and to humans and all other forms of life is global nuclear war. *There are already enough nuclear weapons in the world's arsenals to kill 35 times the number of people now living and an average of 10 more nuclear weapons are made each day.* Concern over nuclear power plant safety is also an important issue (Section 15-5), but by early 1984 there were only 82 operating nuclear power plants in the United States and about 35,000 nuclear weapons, each of which poses a greater hazard than a serious nuclear reactor accident. As former presidential science adviser George Kistiakowsky puts it, "When you get emotional about nuclear plants and don't care about nuclear war, it's worrying about a pimple on your cheek when you have a case of cancer." The health and environmental effects of nuclear war are discussed in Enrichment Study 3.

1-5 Relationships Among Pollution, Population, Resources, Technology, and Society

The Roots of Pollution What causes pollution? The obvious answer is people. Thus, we could conclude that pollution increases with population growth. Population growth, however, is not the only cause and is not necessarily the major cause. Pollution occurs when people use matter and energy resources, so a small number of affluent people using matter and energy resources at a high rate can produce more pollution than a much larger number of poor people using such resources at a low rate. But the situation is more complicated. The use of some types of resources creates more pollution than the use of other types. For example, a throwaway aluminum can wastes more resources and creates more pollution than a returnable glass bottle, because making the can requires about three times as much energy as making the bottle. In other words, pollution also depends on the type of technology used.

A crude model has been proposed to estimate the pollution, or harmful environmental impact, caused by people and their consumption activities. In this model, total pollution depends on the product of three factors: the number of people, the amount of resources each person uses, and the pollution resulting from each unit of resource used.

$$
\begin{array}{l}
\text{pollution or} \\
\text{environmental} \\
\text{impact}
\end{array}
=
\begin{array}{c}
\text{population} \\
\text{size}
\end{array}
\times
\begin{array}{c}
\text{resource} \\
\text{use per} \\
\text{person}
\end{array}
$$

$$
\times
\begin{array}{c}
\text{pollution per} \\
\text{unit of} \\
\text{resource used}
\end{array}
$$

Two Kinds of Overpopulation This three-factor model has been used to distinguish between two kinds of overpopulation. One is the result of either too many mouths to feed relative to available food supplies or the inability of poor people to buy food even if it is available. This is called **Malthusian overpopulation,** after Thomas Robert Malthus, who in 1803 warned that population size tends to outrun food production until poor health and death from starvation and disease restore the balance. In this type of overpopulation, the population size factor tends to be much more important than the other two factors. In many LDCs, such as India and Ethiopia, Malthusian overpopulation already means death for an estimated 12 million human beings each year and bare subsistence for hundreds of millions more.

Affluent and technologically advanced countries, such as the United States, the Soviet Union, and Japan, are said to have a second type of overpopulation called **neo-Malthusian overpopulation.** In this type, the resource use and pollution factors are more important than the population size factor. It occurs when a relatively small number of people use resources that produce relatively high levels of pollution at a fast rate. In this case, few people are affected by a lack of food or being too poor to buy food. Instead, they can get sick and in some cases die earlier than necessary from contaminated air, water, and soil. Such rapid resource use by MDCs also makes it difficult—perhaps impossible—for LDCs to become even moderately affluent.

Both the Soviet Union and the United States have made many improvements in environmental quality since 1970. Despite this progress the Soviet Union may be the world's biggest polluter. Of the two-thirds of the land area that is inhabited, an estimated 10 percent already suffers serious soil erosion and poisoning of the land and water from logging, mining, and farming. The Soviet economy is said to produce twice as much air pollution per unit of goods manufactured as the United States. Soviet automobiles are said to pollute the air about four times as much as do American ones, due to more intensive use and poor engine design and maintenance. Water pollution is widespread. In the United States and most industrialized nations, average life expectancy has risen and infant mortality rates have declined since 1970. By contrast, in the Soviet Union the death rates of infants and adults have risen significantly since 1970 presumably from a combination of environmental pollution, industrial accidents, underinvestment in health services, and a high rate of alcoholism.

This does not mean, however, that there is little environmental impact from people in the United States using more of the world's resources each year per person than people in any other nation (Table 1-1). *The average American potentially has a much greater impact on the world's life-support system than a peasant in a less developed country.* For example, the average American consumes 50 times more steel, 56 times more energy, 170 times more synthetic rubber and newsprint, 250 times more motor fuel, and 300 times more plastic than the average citizen of India.

The idea that in neo-Malthusian terms the United States, the Soviet Union, and other industrialized nations are overpopulated, however, is debated. Critics accuse people who warn of the dangers of overpopulation and pollution of being doomsday prophets who oversimplify and overdramatize the problems. They argue that **(1)** several industrialized nations such as Sweden have reached ZPG or are experiencing a population decline (Denmark and West Germany), and most other industrialized nations appear headed for ZPG or declining populations by 2000 to 2020; **(2)** rapid economic growth in MDCs does deplete natural resources and produce pollution, but it also produces industrial products, technology, and knowledge, which in turn can be used to control pollution and to help LDCs improve economically; **(3)** average life expectancy has increased and infant mortality rates have decreased in the United States (but not in the Soviet Union) since 1970, presumably because of a decline in the average levels of many air and water pollutants as a result of pollution control laws, a decrease in cigarette smoking, improved health care, and more individual concern about diet, exercise, and other health factors (Enrichment Study 7); and **(4)** some of the worst forms of environmental abuse occur in LDCs such as China and India, the two most populated nations in the world.

For example, in China government ordered conversion of vast tracts of forests and grasslands into cropland to feed its over 1 billion people has caused serious wood shortages, desertification, soil erosion, and air pollution from dust blown off degraded lands. In most major Chinese cities air pollution is severe because the nation depends on coal for over 80 percent of its energy and drinking water is contaminated primarily because very little of its urban sewage and industrial wastes are treated before being dumped into waterways. The situation in India is similar. More than half of India's agricultural land is threatened by severe erosion, flooding often caused by deforestation, and rivers and lakes filling with eroded soil, waterlogging, and salt buildup in soils. About 70 percent of its rivers and lakes are heavily polluted, mostly with raw sewage but increasingly with toxic wastes.

Neo-Malthusians, however, point out that environmental degradation in China, India, and other LDCs is primarily a result of Malthusian overpopulation. These stresses result from too many people putting too much pressure on renewable resources in their search for wood to burn for heat and cooking and for land to grow food. Throughout this book both sides of this and other major environmental controversies will be considered.

Is Technology the Culprit? Environmentalist Barry Commoner argues that the most important factor in the three-factor model is the pollution per unit of resource used. He suggests that the introduction of environmentally harmful technologies since World War II has been the major cause of pollution in industrialized, affluent nations. These countries have shifted much of their production and consumption from natural products that can be broken down, diluted, or absorbed by natural processes to synthetic products that often cannot be degraded by natural processes (Table 1-3).

The idea that technology is the primary cause of pollution, however, seems too simplistic. New technologies are not always harmful. Since World War II, technologies have been introduced that provide important environmental and resource supply benefits. These benefits include **(1)** substitutes for scarce natural resources, such as rubber; **(2)** improved efficiency and reduced waste in the use of resources such as wood, mercury, and coal; **(3)** development of processes to control and clean up many forms of pollution; and **(4)** the substitution of less harmful products for those previously used. For example, in the early 1900s the major insecticide was lead arsenate—a substance much more toxic and persistent than DDT and most modern insecticides. Decades ago the major red food coloring in the United States was lead chromate—an environmental horror compared with the recently banned red dye no. 2 (Enrichment Study 9).

Our problem and challenge is not to eliminate technology but to decide how to use it more carefully and humanely. As Stuart Chase reminds us, "To condemn technology *in toto* is to forget gardens made green by desalinization of seawater, while to idealize technology is to forget Hiroshima."

Appropriate Technology One attempt to use technology wisely is the increased global emphasis on using *appropriate technology*—also known as intermediate, alternative, frugal, and humane technology—made popular by E. F. Schumacher in *Small Is Beautiful: Economics As If People Mattered* (1973).*

High technology (or *hard technology*) is big, complex, centralized, and expensive and tends to replace people with machines. **Appropriate technology** (or *soft technology*) is small, simple, decentralized, and inexpensive and can preserve meaningful work for people, as summarized in Table 1-4. The use of huge tractors to plow fields in a poor rural village in India is often cited as an example of the use of inappropriate and destructive technology. In such villages the most plentiful resource is human labor. The tractor deprives a number of people of their only means of survival and forces them to migrate to already overpopulated cities, looking for nonexistent jobs. The tractor can also make the people dependent on industrialized nations for expensive gasoline and parts and is normally too complex to be repaired by local people. Instead

---

*To the Student: At the end of this book you will find a list of Readings used as major references for each chapter and which can be used for further information.

Table 1-3 Some Synthetic Products Substituted for Natural Products in Industrialized Nations Since World War II

Natural Product	Modern Substitute
Natural fibers (cotton, silk, and wool), synthetic fibers based on natural cellulose (rayon)	Synthetic fibers (noncellulose)
Lumber	Plastics, aluminum
Soap	Detergent
Natural food	Food with additives
Natural fertilizer	Synthetic fertilizer
Natural predators	Pesticides
Natural rubber	Synthetic rubber
Dyes of plant origin	Synthetic dyes

of a large tractor, a well-designed metal plow, pulled by locally available oxen and made and repaired by a blacksmith, could be used. Another possibility is the two-wheel "walk behind" power tiller.

There are problems, however, with the increased use of appropriate technology in LDCs: **(1)** government officials in India have called it a Western plot to keep India and other LDCs backward by the use of inferior or outdated equipment; **(2)** the poor who need such technology the most cannot afford to buy plows and other forms of appropriate technology even at low prices unless villagers get together and buy equipment for growing more food and for providing water and fuel for the entire village; **(3)** industrialized nations often undermine attempts by LDCs to build and repair forms of appropriate technology locally or regionally by manufacturing, distributing, and marketing such devices before local villagers can raise enough capital and set up small manufacturing businesses; and **(4)** there can be unanticipated and harmful side effects. For example, in India when large landowners began using manure to produce methane (the major component of natural gas) in simple and inexpensive biogas generators, not enough dried animal manure was available to the poor for use as a fuel for cooking.

Using appropriate technology does not mean using outdated or inferior methods. Nor are its advocates opposed to the use of high technology—they are only opposed to its use in situations where people would be better served by soft technology. The use of satellites to improve global communication and genetic engineering to develop improved food crops are examples of the beneficial uses of high technology. Appropriate technology and high technology can also be mixed.

The use of appropriate technology is not confined to LDCs. There are also efforts to scale down

Table 1-4 Characteristics of High and Appropriate Technology

High Technology	Appropriate Technology
Often involves big machines that displace many people	Involves small to medium size machines that don't displace very many people
Is complex and understandable only to highly trained workers	Is simple and understandable to nonspecialized workers
Provides meaningless and uncreative (assembly line) work roles	Provides meaningful and creative (whole product) work roles
Requires much capital to build and maintain	Requires small amounts of capital to build and maintain
Involves machinery that is difficult and expensive to repair	Involves machinery that is easy and cheap to repair
Often depends on imported materials	Emphasizes self-sufficiency and use of local materials
Creates products designed for export	Creates products designed for use in local area
Requires centralized production and control in urban areas	Involves decentralized production under local or regional control in rural areas
Can disrupt local culture	Is compatible with local culture
Produces standardized, short-lasting products that are soon thrown away	Often produces unique, handcrafted products that are durable and easily reused and recycled
Emphasizes use of synthetic materials	Emphasizes use of natural materials
Usually requires large input of matter and energy resources	Requires small input of matter and energy resources
Creates much pollution	Creates little pollution
Usually emphasizes use of nonrenewable energy resources (fossil fuels, nuclear fuels)	Usually emphasizes use of renewable energy resources (sun, wind, water flow, wood)
Is efficient only on a large scale	Is efficient on a small scale
Attempts to disrupt and dominate nature	Attempts to maintain and cooperate with nature

some forms of high technology in industrialized nations. For example, small wind and solar power systems in communities and neighborhoods might replace large, centralized fossil fuel and nuclear power plants (Chapters 14, 15, and 16). Waterless toilets that convert human sewage to fertilizer might be used in place of large sewage systems and treatment plants (Chapter 18). Other examples include solar greenhouses, passive solar homes, compost heaps, and biogas generators. A growing number of Americans are adopting a more self-sufficient, intermediate technology life-style based on voluntary simplicity. Appropriate technology is not a cure for all our environmental problems, but it marks an encouraging trend that should be nurtured.

The Myth of Single Causes for Complex Problems
In the three-factor model presented earlier, no single factor can be ignored. When several factors are multiplied, no factor is insignificant in producing the final result. In addition or subtraction, one number may be so large that the others can be ignored. For example, (193,000 + 2 + 3) is still about 193,000. But leaving out the 2 and 3 in (193,000 × 2 × 3) makes the final answer one-sixth of its actual value. The three-factor model, though useful, is itself far too simple. Other factors need to be considered, for example, the *time-lag factor*. The amount of time needed to change each of the three factors varies. Unless we have nuclear war or catastrophic famines, it should take 70 to 100 years for the world to reach ZPG, even if every family in the world from now on has only two children. This long time lag occurs because a large portion of the people in the world today are under age 15, especially in LDCs. Thus, the total number of people having babies will increase for many decades, even if each couple decides to have fewer children (Chapter 6).

The time-lag factor for reducing average per capita resource use is only about 1 to 5 years, but this would probably require an economic recession or depression. A more gradual and planned reduction in resource use with emphasis on reuse, recycling, and making longer-lasting products can take place in 10 to 20 years. The time lag for reducing the pollution impact of harmful types of technology is about 5 to 10 years with some forms of pollution, but is several decades for slowly degradable pollutants such as radioactive wastes (Section 15-5) and chlorofluorocarbons released from aerosol spray cans and other sources (Section 5-3).

Still other factors need to be added to the three-factor model. Pollution is caused not only by population size but also by *population distribution*. The most severe air and water pollution problems occur when large numbers of people are concentrated in an urban area. Conversely, spreading people out can have a more devastating effect on potentially renewable soil, forest, and grassland resources. Economic, political, cultural, and ethical factors must also be considered. By including the costs of pollution control in the price of all products, we can use the economic system to help control pollution and discourage the use of harmful products (Chapter 20). Similarly, pollution can be controlled politically by enacting and enforcing laws (Chapter 21). Introducing environmentally harmful technologies to other countries can also disrupt cultural values that tend to protect natural resources. Efforts to control pollution by modifying economic and political systems will not occur, however, until a politically active segment of the population (probably 5 to 10 percent, in countries with free elections) realizes that it is both unwise and unethical to abuse the world's life-support systems (Chapter 22). As we examine major environmental problems and their possible solutions in this book, we should be guided by Alfred North Whitehead's motto: "Seek simplicity and distrust it."

1-6 Moving from a Frontier Society to a Sustainable Earth Society

Major Causes of the Environmental Crisis Although experts disagree on their relative importance, the major causes of the environmental crisis have been identified:

1. *Overpopulation:* relative to food or ability to purchase food in less developed countries and relative to resource consumption and pollution in more developed countries (Chapters 6, 7, and 9 and Enrichment Study 2)

2. *Population distribution:* the urban crisis as more and more rural people, especially in the poorer nations, crowd into already overburdened cities looking for work, and the urban sprawl found in many cities in MDCs such as the United States (Chapter 12)

3. *Insufficient pollution control:* increasing pollution of the air, water, and soil in many parts of the world despite efforts at pollution control; failure to enact strict pollution control laws in some countries; failure to enforce existing pollution control laws (Chapters 18 and 19 and Enrichment Studies 2, 5, 7, 10, 12, 13, and 14)

4. *Overconsumption and wasteful patterns of resource consumption:* the throwaway society; making things that fall apart fairly quickly to increase resource use, promote economic growth, and increase profits; failure to distinguish our *wants* from our *needs* in the emphasis on getting

more things not essential for a life of dignity and quality; too little recycling and reuse of vital matter resources; too little emphasis on energy conservation and eliminating wasteful uses of energy resources (Chapters 13, 14, 15, 16, 17, 20, and 22 and Enrichment Study 13)

5. *Unwise use of technology:* failure to consider the short- and long-term environmental and cultural effects of introducing a particular technology on a widespread basis; overemphasis on high technology rather than using appropriate technology or a mix of high and appropriate technology designed to minimize environmental impact; blind faith in technology (Chapter 5)

6. *Oversimplification of the earth's life-support systems:* failure to emphasize preserving the biological diversity found in forests, oceans, grasslands, and wildlife; accelerated extinction or near extinction of plant and animal species; failure to recognize that everything is connected to everything else; failure to preserve cultural diversity (Chapters 5, 8, 9, 10, 11, and 13)

7. *Crisis in management:* emphasis on economic growth at any cost; refusal to establish and enforce short- and long-term priorities to protect the air, water, soil and other renewable and nonrenewable resources that sustain all life on earth (Chapters 20 and 21 and Enrichment Study 14)

8. *Me-first and human-centered behavior:* tragedy of the commons; lack of responsibility for the world's present human population, for future generations, and for plant and other animal species; concentration on satisfying present *wants* (a now-oriented society) instead of present and future *needs*; the-enemy-is-the-other-person mentality; lack of involvement in and caring for the earth and its inhabitants because of self-centeredness, belief that the world is doomed so why not enjoy life while we can, or belief that technology will solve all of our problems (Chapter 22)

The Transition to a Sustainable Earth or Conserver Society Facing this crisis of interlocking problems provides exciting opportunities for change. We have been living by *throwaway* or *frontier rules,* and many environmentalists argue that over the next 50 years we must change to a new set of *sustainable earth* or *conserver rules* designed to maintain the earth's vital life-support systems.

The frontier mentality sees the earth as a place of unlimited room and resources, where ever-increasing production, consumption, and technology inevitably lead to a better life for everyone. If we pollute one area, we merely move to another or eliminate or control the pollution through technology. This mentality is an attempt to dominate nature. Frontier rules can be useful for a population in the initial stages of J-shaped curve of population growth (Figure 1-1), but once we go upward around the bend of the J-shaped curves of increasing population size, resource use, and pollution, such rules can become obsolete and dangerous. Some scientists have proposed that we can help solve the earth's population, resource supply, and pollution problems by creating and populating colonies in space, making space the new "high frontier." Some of the serious limitations of this idea are discussed in Enrichment Study 4.

In contrast to the old or new frontier mentality, a sustainable earth or conserver mentality sees that the earth is a place of limited room and resources and that ever-increasing production and consumption can put severe stress on the natural processes that renew and maintain the air, water, and soil upon which we depend. Sustaining the earth calls for cooperating with nature, rather than blindly attempting to dominate it.

Some Hopeful Signs *Is the achievement of a sustainable earth society over the next few decades a hopeless, idealistic goal? Fortunately, the answer to this important question is no.* There are growing signs that we can make such a transition. Today in the MDCs there is sophisticated awareness of the global problems of population, pollution, and resource depletion and this knowledge is spreading rapidly to the LDCs.

Even more important, this awareness has been translated into action. Today there are over 4,000 organizations worldwide devoted to environmental issues. Most MDCs have passed laws designed to protect the air, water, land, and wildlife, usually after political pressure from nongovernment environmental organizations and concerned citizens. By 1983, environmental protection agencies had been established in 150 of the world's 176 nations—including 111 LDCs, compared to only 11 LDCs in 1972. Since 1970 there has also been an increase in citizen activist environmental organizations in a number of LDCs. In Southeast Asia, tiny and crowded Singapore is one of the world's cleanest cities, thanks to strict antipollution laws and a 5-year $190 million program to clean up waterways.

Nations are also working together to deal with global and regional environmental problems. Such efforts have been encouraged by conferences sponsored by the United Nations and various international environmental organizations, beginning with the United Nations Conference on the Human Environment in Stockholm in 1972. At this conference the United Nations Environment Programme (UNEP) was set up to coordinate actions of governments and international organizations on global environmental issues.

Scientists throughout the world are also hard at work on environmental problems. Their long list of projects includes trying to develop (1) cheaper solar power that would heat dwellings and produce electricity, greatly decreasing dependence on coal and nuclear power; (2) cheaper and more effective ways to remove pollutants from smokestacks, tailpipes, and waterways; (3) genetic engineering techniques for growing food crops and trees faster and with higher yields and increased protection from diseases and pests; and (4) safer and more reliable contraceptives.

Since 1965, 70 U.S. rivers, lakes, and streams have been cleaned up. About 3,600 of the nation's 4,000 major industrial water polluters are meeting federal water pollution cleanup deadlines. In 20 major U.S. cities the air is measurably cleaner than it was before the passage of the Clean Air Act in 1970 and about 90 percent of major U.S. factories are in compliance with federal air pollution regulations. Government and industry are spending $50 billion a year—$220 a year for each American—to reduce pollution. Polls show that public support for using public funds to clean up the environment in the United States has remained strong even during economic hard times.

Other industrialized countries have also made significant progress in pollution control. Smog in London has decreased sharply since 1952, and the river Thames is returning to life. Japan, once regarded as the most polluted country in the world, has dramatically reduced air pollution in most of its major cities and upgraded the quality of its waters since passing antipollution laws in 1967. The Japanese environment, however, is still highly degraded partly because its small size means that most of its people live in crowded cities where pollution levels are concentrated.

The amazing thing is not the lack of progress in dealing with environmental problems in many parts of the world but that so much has been done since 1965. Nevertheless, we should not get carried away with optimism. Environmentalists must constantly struggle to prevent existing environmental laws from being weakened (Section 10-2) and to see that they are enforced. At the same time, many new and serious problems such as hazardous wastes (Enrichment Study 13) and acid deposition (Section 19-4) have been identified. *We have made an important beginning in dealing with the complex environmental problems facing us. But we have a long way to go, as discussed throughout this book.*

Nurturing this hopeful beginning into a new sustainable earth society requires avoiding several traps that prevent people from becoming involved.

First, we must avoid the gloom-and-doom trap, which merely paralyzes us with fear. Second, we must avoid the technological optimism trap. Believing that technology will always provide solutions to our problems and lead to a land of plenty makes people feel that they don't need to be concerned or involved. Even if technology could theoretically solve every problem, it is unlikely that such technology would always be developed. We must remember that 40 percent of all expenditures for research and development, employing over one-half the physical scientists and engineers in the world, are devoted to improving our ability to kill one another (Enrichment Study 3).

Third, we must avoid the good-old-days trap—the romantic idea that all we need to do is to return to the past when life was simpler and better. In the United States the good old days were not so good for most people. The average U.S. life expectancy for adults went up faster in the 1970s than at any other time in recent American history and is 74 years for a baby born in 1984. In 1850 it was only about 35, and in 1900 it was about 45. Around 1800 the work week in the United States averaged 72 hours for men and 98 hours for women. There were no fresh vegetables during the winter, and vitamin-deficiency diseases were common. In 1793 one-fifth of the population of Philadelphia died in a typhoid fever epidemic caused by polluted water. Between 1800 and 1900, epidemics of yellow fever, smallpox, typhus, cholera, and other infectious diseases were common in most U.S. cities.

We don't know all of the new rules needed to sustain the earth, but we are beginning to ask the right questions. What are our responsibilities toward our fellow humans and other forms of plant and animal life on this planet? How close are we to overloading the earth's life-support systems? What are we as individuals willing to do in our own life-styles in order to reduce waste and pollution?

What is the use of a house if you don't have a decent planet to put it on?
Henry David Thoreau

Guest Editorial: The Global 2000 Report

Gus Speth

Gus Speth has been president of the World Resources Institute since 1982. He served as chairman of the President's Council on Environmental Quality (CEQ) between 1979 and 1981, after serving as a member of the council from 1977 to 1979. During his tenure with the CEQ, he was chairman of the Carter administration's Toxic Substances Strategy Committee and a member of the interagency groups that developed the administration's policies on solar energy, nuclear waste management, water conservation, and water resource development. Before his appointment to the CEQ, he was a staff attorney for the Natural Resources Defense Council, a public interest group he helped found in 1970.

During the past decade a number of disturbing studies and reports have been issued by the United Nations, the Worldwatch Institute, the World Bank, and other organizations. These reports have sounded a persistent warning: International efforts to stem the spread of human poverty, hunger, and misery are not achieving their goals; the staggering growth of the human population, coupled with ever-increasing human demands, are beginning to cause permanent damage to the earth's resource base.

The most recent such warning was issued in July, 1980, by the Council on Environmental Quality and the U.S. State Department. Called *The Global 2000 Report to the President,* it was the result of a 3-year effort by more than a dozen agencies of the U.S. government to make long-term projections concerning various population, resource, and environmental concerns. Given the obvious limitations of such projections, the report can best be seen as a reconnaissance of the future. And the results of that reconnaissance are disturbing.

The conclusions of *The Global 2000 Report* indicate the potential for deepening global problems over the next two decades if policies and practices around the world continue as they are today. The next 20 years will see an increasingly crowded world, containing more than 6 billion human beings by 2000. It *could* be a world where growing numbers of people suffer hunger and privation; where losses of croplands and forests mount while human numbers and needs increase; where per capita supplies of fresh water, timber, and fish are diminished; where deterioration of the earth's air and water accelerates; and where plant and animal species vanish at unprecedented rates.

These findings confront the United States and the other nations of the world with one of the most difficult challenges facing our planet during the next two decades. Disturbing as these findings are, however, it is important to stress what the report's conclusions represent: not *predictions* of what will occur, but *projections* of what *could* occur if we do not change our ways. I believe that as the people and governments of the world come to realize the full dimensions of the challenge before us, we *will* take the actions needed to meet it.

The first thing we must do is to get serious about the conservation of resources—renewable and nonrenewable alike. We can no longer take for granted the renewability of our renewable resources. We must realize that the natural systems—the air and water, the forests, the land—that yield food, shelter, and other necessities of life are susceptible to disruption, contamination, and destruction.

In some parts of the world, particularly in the less developed countries, the ability of biological systems to support human populations is being seriously damaged by human demands for grazing land, firewood, and building materials. Nor are these stresses confined to the less developed countries: In recent years, the United States has been losing annually about 3 million acres of rural land—one-third of our prime agricultural land—due to the spread of housing developments, highways, shopping malls, and the like. We are also losing the equivalent, in terms of production capability, of about 3 million more acres a year due to soil degradation, erosion, and salt buildup in irrigated soil.

Achieving the necessary restraint in the use of renewable resources will require new ways of thinking by the peoples and governments of the world. It will require the widespread adoption of a "conserver society" ethic—an approach to resources and environment that, while attuned to the needs of each society, recognizes not only the importance of resources and environment to our own sustenance, well-being, and security, but also our obligation to pass this vital legacy along to future generations.

Fortunately, we are beginning to see signs that people in the United States and in other nations *are* becoming aware of the limits to our resources and the importance of conserving them. Energy problems, for example, are pointing the way to a future in which conservation is the password. As energy supplies go down and prices go up, we are learning that conserving— getting more and more out of each barrel of oil or ton of coal—is the cheapest and safest approach. Learning to conserve nonrenewable resources like oil and coal is the first step toward building a conserver society that values, nurtures, and protects *all* of its resources. Such a society appreciates economy in design and avoidance of waste. It realizes the limits to low-cost resources and to the environment's carrying capacity. It insists that market prices reflect all costs, social as well as private, so that consumers are fully aware in the most direct way of the real costs of consumption.

But the conserver society ethic by itself is not enough. It is unrealistic to expect people living at the margin of existence—people fighting desperately for their own survival—to think about the long-term survival of the planet. When people need to burn wood to keep from freezing, they will cut down trees.

For this reason, an equally important element in an effective strategy to deal with global resource problems must be the *sustainable development* of the less developed nations of the world. Development, far from being in conflict with resource conservation and environmental protection, is essential to achieving these goals. It is only through sound, sustainable economic development that real progress can be made in alleviating hunger and poverty and in erasing the conditions that contribute so dangerously to the destruction of our planet's carrying capacity.

It is clear that the trends discussed in *The Global 2000 Report,* especially the growing disparity in income between the rich and poor peoples of the world, greatly heighten the chances for global instability—for exploitation of fears, resentments, and frustrations; for incitement to violence; for conflicts based on resources. While the humanitarian reasons for acting generously to alleviate global poverty and injustice are compelling enough in themselves, we must also recognize the extent to which poverty and resource problems can threaten the security of nations throughout the world.

These growing tensions can only be defused through a much greater emphasis on *equity*—on a fair sharing of the means to development and the products of growth, not only among nations but also within nations. It should be obvious that the interests of all nations of the world, more developed and less developed alike, are inextricably linked. In helping others, we help ourselves, and in providing generous but effective assistance—grants, loans, technical aid—to nations that are in need, we can make a national investment that will yield important dividends in the future.

Guest Editorial Discussion

1. What specific obligations, if any, do you feel we should have to future generations?

2. How would you define *sustainable development* for the less developed nations of the world? If this goal is adopted, what effects might it have on your life and lifestyle?

3. Do you agree that the means to economic development and the products of economic growth must be shared more fairly not only among nations but also within nations? How would you bring about this greater emphasis on equity?

Discussion Topics

1. How many people would have to die from famine and disease this year for world population to stabilize?

2. Debate the following resolution: High levels of resource use by the United States are necessary because this means (1) purchases of raw materials from poor nations and (2) economic growth in the United States will provide money for foreign aid to LDCs.

3. Should resource use in rich nations be restricted? Which resources, if any, should be restricted? How?

4. Debate the following resolution: The world will never run out of resources because technological innovations will either find substitutes or allow use of lower grades of scarce resources.

5. What is zero population growth? Explain how ZPG in the world could allow average per capita income to rise.

6. What factors could limit the absolute size of the human population on earth? How are these factors related? Which of these factors do you believe are the most important? Why?

7. Should economic growth in the United States and in the world be limited? Why or why not? Is all economic growth bad? Which types, if any, do you believe should be limited? Which types, if any, should be encouraged?

8. Distinguish between two types of overpopulation. Is the world overpopulated? Why or why not? Is the United States overpopulated? Why or why not?

9. Why is pollution so hard to define? Why must it be defined?

10. On the whole, are the substitutes shown in Table 1-3 desirable or undesirable? Which ones would you eliminate? Why? How would these changes affect your life and life-style?

11. Is harmful technology a main cause of pollution? Why or why not? If so, would you be willing to give up automobiles, stereos, central heating, air conditioning, electricity, airplanes, refrigeration, ski lifts, and other conveniences, all of which pollute either in their use or in their making, or both?

12. What might happen to pollution levels if U.S. population size stabilizes but average per capita consumption doubles? What might happen if per capita consumption stabilizes but population size doubles?

13. What forms of existing technology, if any, do you believe should be eliminated? Why? What existing technologies, if any, should be reduced from high to appropriate forms in the United States? Why?

14. You have been appointed to a technology assessment board. What drawbacks and advantages would you list for the following: (a) intrauterine devices for birth control (IUDs); (b) snowmobiles; (c) sink garbage disposal units; (d) trash compactors; (e) portable transistor radios; (f) televisions; (g) electric cars; (h) abortion pills; (i) effective sex stimulants; (j) drugs that retard the aging process; (k) drugs that enable people to get high but are harmless; (l) electrical or chemical methods that stimulate the brain to remove anxiety, fear, and unhappiness; and (m) genetic engineering (manipulation of human genes)? In each case, would you recommend that the technology be introduced?

15. In terms of environmental improvement and the possibility of achieving a sustainable earth or conserver society within the next 50 years, would you classify yourself as a pessimist, an optimist, a pessimistic optimist, or an optimistic pessimist? Why?

16. List ten changes in your life-style that you would be willing to make in order to protect the environment. Which of these changes, if any, do you actually plan to make?

PART TWO

Some Concepts of Ecology

Some Environmental Principles

1. *Everything must go somewhere, or we can never really throw anything away. (Law of conservation of matter)*

2. *You can't get something for nothing, or there is no such thing as a free lunch. (First law of energy, or law of conservation of energy)*

3. *You can't even break even, or if you think things are mixed up now, just wait. (Second law of energy)*

4. *Everything is connected to everything else, but how?*

5. *A thing is right when it tends to preserve the integrity, stability, and beauty of the biotic community. It is wrong when it tends otherwise.*

6. *Natural systems can take a lot of stress and abuse, but there are limits.*

7. *In nature you can never do just one thing, so always expect the unexpected.*

2

Some Matter and Energy Laws

The laws of thermodynamics control the rise and fall of political systems, the freedom or bondage of nations, the movements of commerce and industry, the origins of wealth and poverty, and the general physical welfare of the human race.

Frederick Soddy, Nobel Prize-winning chemist

Look at a beautiful flower, drink some water, eat some food, or pick up this book. The two things that connect these activities and other aspects of life on earth are matter and energy. **Matter,** or anything that has mass and occupies space, is the stuff you and all other things are made of. **Energy** is a more elusive concept. Formally, it is defined as the ability or capacity to do work or produce change by pushing or pulling some form of matter. Energy is what you and all living things use to move matter around and to change it from one form to another. Energy is used to grow your food, to keep you alive, to move you from one place to another, and to warm and cool the buildings in which you work and live. The uses and transformations of matter and energy are governed by certain scientific laws, which, unlike the laws people enact, cannot be broken. In this chapter we begin our study of ecological concepts with a look at one fundamental law of matter and two equally important laws of energy. These laws will be used again and again throughout this book to help you understand many environmental problems and to aid you in evaluating solutions to these problems.

2-1 Law of Conservation of Matter: Everything Must Go Somewhere

We talk about consuming or using up material resources, but actually we don't consume any matter. We only borrow some of the earth's resources for a while—taking them from the earth, carrying

them to another part of the globe, processing them, using them, and then discarding, reusing, or recycling them. In the process of using matter we may change it to another form, but in every case we neither create nor destroy any measurable amount of matter. This results from the **law of conservation of matter:** In any physical or chemical change, matter is neither created nor destroyed but merely changed from one form to another. This law tells us that there is no "away." *Everything we think we have thrown away is still here with us in one form or another.*

We can collect dust and soot from the smokestacks of industrial plants, but these solid wastes must then go somewhere. Most of the larger visible particles and invisible gaseous pollutants in this smoke can be removed. But some of the very tiny particles left can be more damaging than the large solid particles that were removed. We can collect garbage and remove solid wastes from sewage, but these must either be burned (perhaps causing air pollution), dumped into rivers, lakes, and oceans (perhaps causing water pollution), or deposited on the land (perhaps causing soil pollution and water pollution if they wash away or percolate through the soil into underground water supplies).

We can reduce air pollution from the internal combustion engines in cars by using electric cars. However, because the batteries that run these cars must be recharged every day, we would have to build more electric power plants. If these are coal-fired, their smokestacks will add additional and perhaps more dangerous pollutants to the air; more land will be scarred by surface mining and more water polluted by acids leaching from seams in coal mines. We could use nuclear power plants to produce the electricity needed, but then we risk releasing dangerous radioactive substances into the environment through accidents, hijacking of nuclear fuel to make atomic weapons, and leakage of radioactive materials from permanent nuclear waste burial sites.

Although we can certainly make the environment cleaner, the law of conservation of matter says we will always be faced with pollution of some sort.

Enrichment Studies 2 and 5 are related to this chapter.

This means that we must *trade off* one form of pollution for another. This trade-off process involves making controversial scientific, political, economic, and ethical judgments about what is a dangerous pollution level, to what degree a pollutant must be controlled, and what amount of money we are willing to pay to reduce the amount of a pollutant to a harmless level (Section 1-5). Now let's look at energy and the two energy laws to learn more about what we can and cannot do on this planet.

2-2 First Law of Energy: You Can't Get Something for Nothing

Types of Energy   You encounter energy in many forms: mechanical, chemical (food or fuel), electrical, nuclear, heat, and radiant (such as light). Scientists usually classify most forms of energy as either potential energy or kinetic energy (Figure 2-1). **Kinetic energy** is the energy that matter has because of its motion and mass. A moving car, falling rock, speeding bullet, and the flow of electrons or charged particles called electrical energy are all examples. The amount of kinetic energy a sample of matter has depends on both its mass and its velocity (speed). Because of its higher kinetic energy, a bullet fired at a high velocity from a rifle can do more damage than the same bullet thrown by hand at a much lower velocity. Similarly, an artillery shell (with a larger mass) fired at the same velocity as a lighter bullet can do considerably more harm than the bullet.

The energy stored by an object as a result of its position or the position of its parts is called **potential energy.** A rock held in your hand, a bowl of cereal, a stick of dynamite, and a tank of gas are all examples. The rock has stored or potential energy that can be released and converted to kinetic energy (in the form of mechanical energy and heat) if it is dropped. **Chemical energy** is the potential energy stored in the bonds that hold chemicals together. Examples are the energy stored in food and fuel.

Doing work involves changing energy from one form to another. When you rub your hands together rapidly they get warm because the mechanical energy of rubbing is transformed into heat. When you lift this book, chemical energy stored in chemicals obtained from your digested food is converted into the mechanical energy used to move your arm and the book upward and into heat given off by your body.

In an automobile engine, the chemical energy stored in gasoline is converted into mechanical energy that propels the car and into heat. A battery converts chemical energy into electrical energy and heat. In an electric power plant, chemical energy from fossil fuels or nuclear energy from uranium

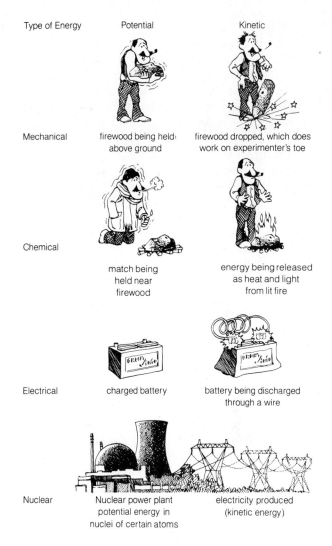

Figure 2-1   Most forms of energy can be classified as either potential energy or kinetic energy.

nuclear fuel is converted into a combination of mechanical energy and heat. The mechanical energy is used to spin a turbine that converts the mechanical energy into electrical energy and more heat. When this electrical energy oscillates through the filament wires in an ordinary light bulb, it is converted into light and still more heat. Note that in all of these energy transformations some energy is always lost as heat that flows into the surrounding environment.

First Energy Law   What energy changes occur when you drop a rock? Because of its higher position, the rock in your hand has a higher potential energy than the same rock at rest on the ground. Has energy been lost or used up in this process? At first glance it seems so. But according to the **law of conservation of energy,** also known as the **first law of thermodynamics,** in any ordinary physical or chemical process energy is neither created nor destroyed but merely changed from one form to another. The energy lost by a *system* or collection of matter under study (in this instance, the rock) must equal the energy gained by the *surroundings* or *environment* (in this instance, air molecules and soil particles moved by the impact of the rock). This energy law holds for all systems, living and nonliving.

Let's look at what really happens. As the rock drops, its potential energy is changed into kinetic energy—both its own and that of the air through which it passes. The friction created when the rock drops through the air causes the gaseous molecules in the air to move faster, so their average temperature rises. This means that some of the rock's original potential energy has been transferred to the air as heat. When the rock hits the ground more of its mechanical energy is transferred to particles of soil. The energy lost by the rock (system) is exactly equal to the energy gained by its surroundings. In studying hundreds of thousands of mechanical processes (such as the rock falling) and chemical processes (such as the burning of a fuel), scientists have found that no detectable amount of energy is either created or destroyed. Energy input always equals energy output.

Although most of us know this first energy law, we sometimes forget that it means that, regarding energy quantity, we can't get something for nothing. In the words of environmentalist Barry Commoner, "There is no such thing as a free lunch." For example, we often hear that we have so much energy available from the world's deposits of oil, coal, natural gas, and nuclear fuels (such as uranium). The first law of thermodynamics tells us that we really have much less energy available than these estimates indicate because *it takes energy to get this energy.* We must use large amounts of energy to find, remove, and process these fuels. The only energy that really counts is the *net energy* or *energy yield* available for use after subtracting the energy needed to make this energy available from the total energy available in the resource (Chapter 14).

2-3 Second Law of Energy: You Can't Break Even

Second Energy Law and Energy Quality Because according to the first energy law energy can neither be created nor destroyed, you might think there will always be enough energy. Yet when you fill a car's tank with gasoline and drive around something is lost. If it isn't energy, what is it? The *second law of energy,* also known as the *second law of thermodynamics,* provides the answer to this question.

Energy varies in its *quality* or ability to do useful work. For useful work to occur energy must move or flow from a level of high-quality (more concentrated) energy to a level of lower-quality (less concentrated) energy. The chemical potential energy concentrated in a lump of coal or a tank of gasoline and the concentrated heat energy at a high temperature are forms of high-quality energy. Because they are concentrated, they have the ability to perform useful work in moving or changing matter. In contrast, dispersed or less concentrated heat energy at a low temperature has little remaining ability to perform useful work.

In investigating hundreds of thousands of conversions of heat energy to useful work, scientists have found that some of the energy is always degraded to a more dispersed and less useful form, usually as heat given off at a low temperature to the surroundings. This is a statement of the **second energy law,** another name for the **second law of thermodynamics.** Thus, because energy quality flows downhill, the supply of concentrated, usable energy available to the earth is being continually depleted.

Let's look at some examples of the second energy law. In an internal combustion automobile engine, only about 20 percent of the high-quality chemical energy available in the gasoline is converted to mechanical energy used to propel the car; the remaining 80 percent is degraded to low-quality heat that is released into the environment. In addition, about half of the mechanical energy produced is also degraded to low-quality heat energy through friction, so that 90 percent of the energy in gasoline is wasted and not used to move the car. When electrical energy oscillates through the filament wires in an ordinary light bulb, it is converted into a mixture of about 5 percent useful radiant energy or light and 95 percent low-quality heat. It is interesting to note that *much of modern civilization is built around the internal combustion engine and the incandescent light that, respectively, waste 90 and 95 percent of their initial energy input.* Some of this waste is due to the energy-quality tax automatically exacted as a result of the second energy law and some is due to technological designs that waste more energy than necessary (Chapter 14).

Another example of the degradation of energy is the conversion of solar energy to chemical energy in food. Photosynthesis in plants converts radiant energy (light) from the sun into high-quality chemical energy (stored in the plant in the form of sugar molecules) and low-quality heat energy. If you eat plant food, such as spinach, its high-quality chemical energy is transformed within your body to high-quality mechanical energy, used to move your muscles and to perform other life processes, and low-quality heat energy. As shown in Figure 2-2, in each of these energy conversions some of the initial high-

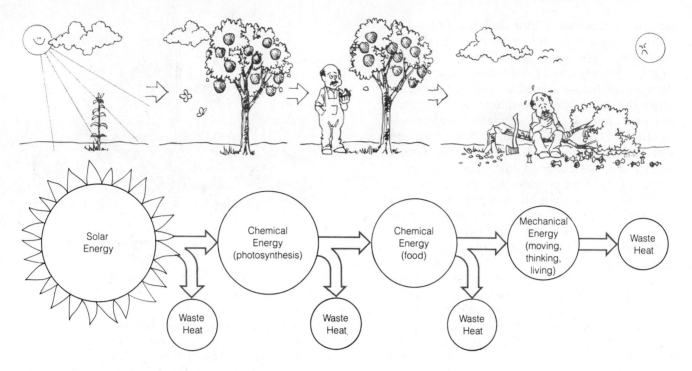

Figure 2-2 The second energy law. When energy is changed from one form to another, some of the initial input of energy is always degraded to low-quality heat that is added to the environment.

quality energy is degraded into low-quality heat that flows into the environment.

Thus, we see that the first energy law governs the *quantity* of energy available from an energy-conversion process, whereas the second energy law governs the *quality* of energy available. According to the first law we will never run out of energy, but according to the second law we can run out of high-quality or useful energy. *Not only can we not get something for nothing (the first law), we can't even break even in terms of energy quality (the second law).*

The second energy law also tells us that high-grade energy can never be used over again. *We can recycle matter but we can never recycle high-quality energy.* Fuels and foods can be used only once to perform useful work. Once a piece of coal or a tank of gasoline is burned, its high-quality potential energy is lost forever. This means that the net useful, or high-quality, energy available from fossil fuels, uranium, or any concentrated energy source is even less than that predicted by the first energy law.

net high-quality = total high-quality energy
   energy   available
            − high-quality energy needed
                to find, get, and process
                the energy (first law)
            − energy quality lost in
                finding, getting, and
                processing the energy
                (second law)

This equation shows that both the first and second energy laws can be used to evaluate our energy options, as discussed further in Chapter 14.

Second Energy Law and Increasing Disorder The second energy law can be stated in a number of ways. One way of looking at this law is to realize that energy tends to flow or change spontaneously from a concentrated and ordered form to a more dispersed and disordered form. Thus, another way of stating the second energy law or **second law of thermodynamics** is that heat always flows spontaneously from hot (high-quality energy) to cold (lower-quality energy). You learned this the first time that you touched a hot stove. A cold sample of matter such as air has its heat energy dispersed in the random motion of its molecules. This is why heat energy at a low temperature can do little if any useful work.

Let's look at other spontaneous changes in the world around us. A vase falls to the floor and shatters into a more disordered state. A dye crystal dropped into water spontaneously dissolves, and the spreading of its color is evidence that its molecules spontaneously tend toward a more dispersed and disordered state throughout the solution. A person dies and the highly ordered array of molecules in his or her body decays to many smaller molecules that become dispersed throughout the environment. Your desk and room seem spontaneously to become more disordered after a few weeks of benign neglect (Figure 2-3). Smoke from a smokestack and exhaust from an automobile disperse spontaneously to a more random or disordered state in the atmosphere, and pollutants dumped into a river spread spontaneously throughout the water. Indeed, until we discovered that the atmosphere and water systems could be overloaded, we assumed that such spontaneous dilution solved the problem of pollution.

These observations all suggest that a *system* of matter spontaneously tends toward increasing randomness or disorder. But is this hypothesis valid? You may have already thought of some examples that contradict this hypothesis. As its temperature decreases to zero degrees Celsius (0°C), liquid water spontaneously increases its order and freezes into ice. What about living organisms with their highly ordered systems of molecules and cells? You are a walking, talking contradiction of the idea that systems tend spontaneously toward disorder. We must look further.

The way out of our dilemma is not to look at changes in disorder or order only in the system but in both the system *and its environment or surroundings*. Look at your own body. To form and preserve its highly ordered arrangement of molecules and its organized network of chemical reactions, you must continually obtain high-quality energy and raw materials from your surroundings. This means that disorder is created in the environment—primarily in the form of low-quality heat. Just think of all the disorder in the form of heat that is added to the environment to keep you alive. Planting, growing, processing, and cooking foods all require energy inputs that add heat to the environment. The breakdown of the chemicals in food in your body gives off more heat to the environment. Indeed, your body continuously gives off heat equal to that from a 100-watt light bulb—explaining why a closed room full of people gets warm.

Measurements show that the total amount of disorder, in the form of low-quality heat, added to the environment to keep you alive is much greater than the order maintained in your body. This does not even count the enormous amounts of disorder added to the environment when concentrated deposits of minerals and fuels are extracted from the earth and burned or dispersed to heat the buildings you use, to transport you, and to make roads, clothes, and shelter.

Thus, *all forms of life are tiny pockets of order maintained by creating a sea of disorder around themselves.* The primary characteristic of modern industrial society is an ever-increasing use or flow of high-

Figure 2-3 The spontaneous tendency toward increasing disorder of a system and its surroundings.

quality energy to maintain the order in our bodies and the pockets of order we call civilization. As a result, today's industrialized nations are creating more environmental disorder than any society in human history.

In considering the system and surroundings as a whole, scientists find that there is always a net increase in disorder with any spontaneous chemical or physical change. For any spontaneous change, either **(1)** the disorder in both the system and the environment increases, **(2)** the increase in disorder in the system is greater than the increase in order created by the environment, or **(3)** the increase in disorder in the environment is greater than the order created in the system. Experimental measurements have demonstrated this over and over again. Thus, we must modify our original hypothesis to include the surroundings. *Any system and its surroundings as a whole spontaneously tend toward increasing randomness or disorder*—or, in other words, if you think things are mixed up now, just wait. This is another way of stating the second energy law, or **second law of thermodynamics.** No one has ever found a violation of this law. In most apparent violations, the observer fails to include the greater disorder (entropy) increase in the surroundings when there is an increase in order in the system.

Scientists frequently use the concept of **entropy,** a measure of relative randomness or disorder. A random system has high entropy, and an orderly system has low entropy. Using this concept, we can state the second energy law as follows: *Any system and its surroundings as a whole spontaneously tend toward increasing entropy.* If you have the feeling that each day the world gets more disordered, you are right. The second law tells us that this is the most fundamental thing going on in the world.

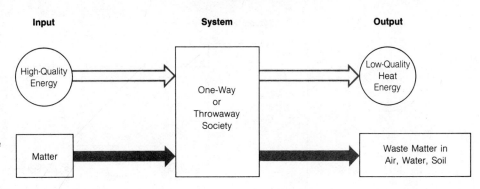

Figure 2-4. The one-way, or throwaway, society found in most industrialized countries is based on maximizing the rates of energy flow and matter flow. This results in a conversion of the world's mineral and energy resources to trash, pollution, and waste heat at a very fast rate. This type of society is sustainable indefinitely only with essentially infinite supplies of mineral and energy resources and an infinite ability of the environment to absorb the resulting heat and matter wastes.

2-4 Matter and Energy Laws and the Environmental Crisis

As discussed throughout this book, the law of conservation of matter and the first and second laws of energy (see box) give us keys for understanding and dealing with environmental problems. The one-

---

Summary of Matter and Energy Laws

Law of conservation of matter: In any ordinary physical or chemical change, matter is neither created nor destroyed but only transformed from one form to another.

Or:

We can never really throw matter away.

First law of thermodynamics (law of conservation of energy): In any ordinary physical or chemical change, energy is neither created nor destroyed but merely changed from one form to another.

Or:

There is no such thing as a free lunch.

Second law of thermodynamics (law of energy degradation): In all conversions of heat energy to work, some of the energy is always degraded to a more dispersed and less useful form, usually heat given off at low temperature to the surroundings.

Or:

Any system and its surroundings (environment) as a whole spontaneously tends toward increasing randomness, disorder, or entropy.

Or:

If you think things are mixed up now, just wait.

---

way or throwaway society found in most industrial countries is based on using more and more of the earth's matter and energy resources at a faster and faster rate (Figure 2-4). The earth receives a constant flow of energy from the sun, but for all practical purposes little matter enters or leaves the earth. *We have all of the matter that we will ever have.*

Technology can help us stretch our supplies of matter resources and perhaps find substitutes (Chapter 13). Some scientists argue that because of the matter and energy laws, sooner or later we must face up to the finiteness of the earth's resource supplies (Enrichment Study 2). Other experts disagree and talk of infinite supplies of resources on earth (Chapter 13) or propose schemes to get new supplies of energy and matter from space (Enrichment Study 4). Others agree that resource supplies on earth are finite but argue that we are not close enough to exceeding any built-in limits to worry about them (Chapter 13).

Some say we should become a *matter-recycling society* so that economic growth can continue indefinitely without depleting material resources. But there is a catch to recycling. In using resources such as iron, we dig up concentrated deposits of iron ore (because they are the cheapest). Then we disperse this concentrated iron over much of the globe as it is fashioned into useful products, discarded, or changed into other chemical substances. To recycle such widely dispersed iron, we must collect it, transport it to central recycling centers or steel mills, and melt and purify it so that it can be used again.

This is where the two energy laws come in. *Recycling matter always requires high-quality energy.* However, if a resource is not too widely scattered, recycling often requires less high-quality energy than that needed to find, get, and process virgin ores. In the long run, a recycling society based on indefinitely increasing economic growth must have an essentially inexhaustible and affordable supply of high-quality energy. And high-quality energy, unlike matter, can never be recycled. Although experts

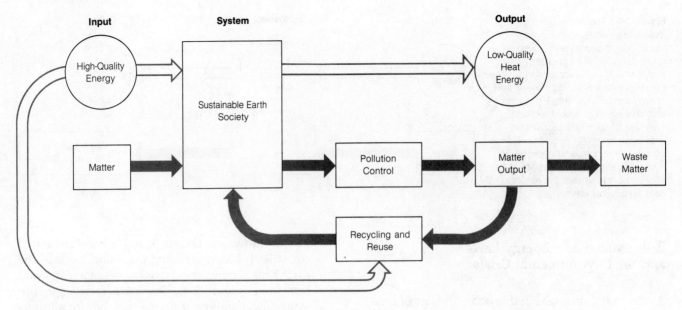

Figure 2-5 A sustainable earth society is based on energy flow and matter recycling. It is based on reusing and recycling renewable matter resources, not using renewable matter resources faster than they are replenished by natural processes, conserving energy (since it cannot be recycled), increasing pollution control, and deliberately lowering the rate at which matter and energy resources are used so that the environment is not overloaded and resources are not depleted.

disagree on how much usable energy we have, it is clear that supplies of nonrenewable fossil fuels and nuclear fuel resources are finite. Indeed, *affordable* supplies of oil, natural gas, and uranium nuclear fuel may last no longer than several decades (Chapters 14 and 15).

"Ah," you say, "but don't we have an essentially infinite supply of solar energy flowing into the earth?" Sunlight reaching the earth is high-quality energy, but the quantity reaching a particular area of the earth's surface each minute or hour is low and is nonexistent at night. Using solar energy to provide hot water and to heat a house to moderate temperatures makes sense (see Chapter 14). However, using solar energy to provide the high temperatures needed to melt metals or to produce electricity in a solar power plant may not make sense. In these cases, solar energy must be collected and concentrated to provide the necessary high temperatures. This requires large amounts of money and high-quality energy to mine, process, and to transport the matter resources needed to make solar collectors, focusing mirrors, pipes, and other materials.

One way to lessen this problem involves the development and widespread use of *solar photovoltaic cells* that convert sunlight directly to electricity in one simple nonpolluting step. If present research increases the efficiency of such cells and decreases their cost, we could be covering entire roofs of houses and buildings with rolls of these cells to provide all the electricity we need. Such a

development could, in a fairly short time, make most large, centralized electric power plants in the world obsolete. Mass production and transportation of solar cells would require energy and matter resources. But most of the matter would come from silicon, one of the most abundant chemicals on earth.

Assume that nuclear fusion energy (still only a technological dream), nuclear fission energy from breeder reactors, solar photovoltaic cells, plant material (biomass), or some other energy breakthrough comes to our rescue (see Chapters 15 and 16). Even with such a technological advance, the *second energy law tells us that as we use more and more energy to transform matter into products and then recycle these products, the disorder in the environment will increase.* Thus, the second energy law tells us that the more we try to order, or "conquer," the earth, the greater the disorder we put into the environment. We will always attempt to order the environment to some extent for our benefit, but the second energy law helps us understand that we should do so with ecological wisdom, care, and restraint.

Why do some think we can avoid the effects of the second energy law? Part of the problem is ignorance. Many people have never heard of the second law of thermodynamics, let alone understood its significance. In addition, this law has a cumulative rather than individual effect. You accept the law of gravity because it limits you and everyone else on a personal level. However, though your individual activities automatically increase the disorder in the environment, this effect seems small and insignificant. But the cumulative impact of the disorder-producing activities of billions of individuals trying to convert more and more of the world's resources to trash and low-quality heat as fast as possible eventually can have a devastating impact on the local and eventually the global life-support systems that sustain us all. *The second energy law tells us that we are all interdependent, whether we like it or not.*

This may seem like a rather gloomy situation, but it need not be. The second energy law, along with the first energy law and the law of conservation of matter, tell us what we *cannot* do. But more importantly, these laws tell us what we *can* do. They show us that one way out is to shift to a *low-entropy-generating or sustainable earth society* (Figure 2-5), based on reducing the rate of using matter and high-quality energy so that local, regional, and global limits of the environment to absorb entropy are not exceeded and vital renewable and nonrenewable resources are not depleted.

Some experts believe that we are so far from exceeding the limits of the earth that there is no urgency to shift from our throwaway society based on ever-increasing use of matter and energy resources (Figure 2-4). Others argue that technology developed by human ingenuity can be used either to extend these limits or to prevent them from being reached. A number of other experts argue, however, that the increasing signs of environmental stress on much of the world's renewable land, wildlife, air, and water resources (Chapter 1 and Enrichment Study 2) and the buildup of pollutants in many areas indicate that we may have only about 50 years to make such a transition.

The law that entropy increases—the second law of thermodynamics—holds, I think, the supreme position among laws of nature . . . If your theory is found to be against the second law of thermodynamics, I can give you no hope; there is nothing to do but collapse in deepest humiliation.

Arthur S. Eddington

Discussion Topics

1. Explain why we don't really consume anything and why there is no such thing as a throwaway society.

2. A tree grows and increases its mass. Explain why this isn't a violation of the law of conservation of matter.

3. Explain why removing odors and large particles from the smoke emitted from smokestacks, while very useful, could be a misleading long-term pollution control strategy. Does this mean it should not be done? Explain.

4. Discuss the line in Genesis 3:19 "You are dust and to dust you shall return" in relation to the law of conservation of matter and the second law of thermodynamics.

5. Describe the energy transformations involved in the flow of water over a dam. How could some of the energy released be used to generate electricity?

6. List six different types of energy that you have used today and classify each as either kinetic or potential energy.

7. According to the first law of energy the world will never run out of energy; therefore, why is there so much talk about an energy crisis?

8. Use the first and second energy laws to explain why the usable supply of energy from fossil and nuclear fuels is usually considerably less than that given by most official estimates.

9. What does it mean to say that electricity is high-quality energy? What is low-quality energy?

10. Use the second energy law to explain why a barrel of oil can only be used once as a fuel.

11. Criticize the statement "Any spontaneous process results in an increase in the disorder of the system."

12. Criticize the statement "Life is an ordering process, and since it goes against the natural tendency for increasing disorder, it breaks the second law of thermodynamics."

13. Explain how the environmental crisis can be considered an entropy crisis.

14. Using the first and second energy laws and the law of conservation of matter, explain the idea "To exist is to pollute." Does this mean that increasing pollution is inevitable? Why or why not? Does it apply to all types of pollution or only to some?

15. a. Use the law of conservation of matter to explain why a matter-recycling society will sooner or later be necessary.

    b. Use the second energy law to explain why there should be more emphasis on reusing than on recycling matter.

    c. Use the second energy law to explain why energy can never be recycled.

3

Ecosystem Structure: What Is an Ecosystem?

And God said, Let there be light; and there was light. . . .
And God said, Let the earth bring forth grass. . . .
Genesis 1:3, 11

Walk into a forest on a warm summer day and look, listen, smell, and feel. A gentle breeze flows over your skin and the air feels cool and slightly damp. Magnificent oak and hickory trees surround you with their beauty. Glimmering sunlight cascades through the canopy of leaves to reveal a varied tapestry of shrubs and herbs growing at your feet. A squirrel scampers noisily up a tree trunk. Looking down you see the tracks of a deer. Turning over a rotting log in your path, you uncover a frenzy of activity as worms, beetles, ants, termites, and other insects scurry in all directions to escape your intrusion into their world. You pick up a handful of soil, knowing that it teems with billions of bacteria and other microorganisms even though you can't see them.

What types of plants and animals live in this forest? How do they get the matter and energy needed to stay alive? How do these plants and animals interact with one another and with their physical environment? What changes will this dynamic system of life undergo with time? Ecology is the branch of science that attempts to answer such questions. In 1866 German biologist Ernst Haeckel coined the term *ecology* from two Greek words: *oikos*, meaning "house" or "place to live," and *logos*, meaning "study of." Literally, then, *ecology* is a study of organisms in their home. In more formal terms, **ecology** is the study of the structure and function of nature or the study of the relationships among living organisms and to the totality of physical and biological factors making up their environment.

Ecologists call a *self-sustaining* collection of living organisms and their environment like the forest just described an *ecological system* or *ecosystem*—a

Enrichment Studies 5 and 6 are related to this chapter.

term first introduced by English botanist A. G. Tansley in 1935. The next three chapters are devoted to a study of ecosystems. This chapter looks at the structures and types of ecosystems. Chapter 4 studies the function of ecosystems, or what happens in them, and Chapter 5 examines some changes that can occur in ecosystems as a result of natural events and human activities.

3-1 The Ecosphere: Our Life-Support System

Hundreds of thousands of species of organisms live on our tiny planet as it hurtles through space at about 107,200 kilometers per hour (66,600 miles per hour). All life exists within a thin spherical shell of air, water, and soil only about 14 kilometers (9 miles) thick. This spherical shell of life is known as the **ecosphere** or **biosphere.** The ecosphere includes all forms of life and every relationship between matter and energy that binds these living things together.

The earth can be divided into three intersecting regions: **(1)** the **atmosphere**—a region of gases and particulate matter extending above the earth; **(2)** the **hydrosphere**—a region that includes all of the earth's liquid water (oceans, smaller bodies of water, and underground deposits called aquifers), frozen water (polar ice caps, floating ice cap, and frozen layers of soil known as permafrost), and the small amounts of water vapor found in the atmosphere; and **(3)** the **lithosphere**—a region of soil and rock consisting of the earth's crust, a mantle of partially molten rock beneath this crust, and the earth's inner core consisting of molten rock called magma. Life is not found throughout all of these regions.

The *ecosphere*, or sphere of life that we and all organisms live in, is found at the intersection of these three areas (Figure 3-1). It consists of three *life zones:* **(1)** above us the lower part of the atmosphere, known as the troposphere that contains 95 percent of the earth's air and extends only 8 to 12 kilometers (5 to 7 miles) above the earth's surface;

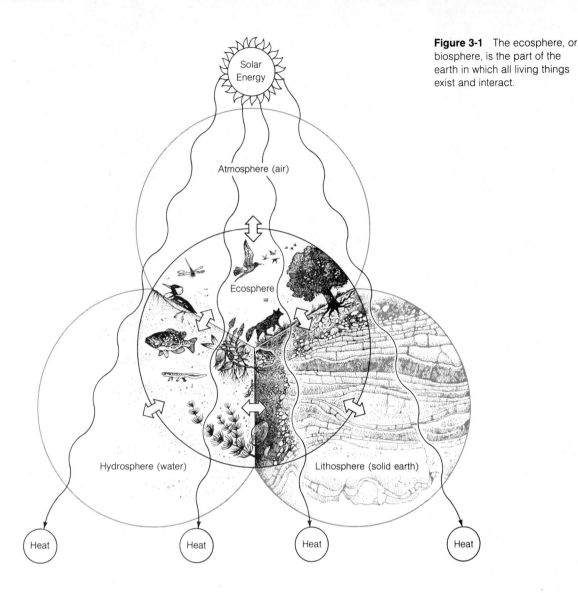

(2) around us, a limited supply of life-supporting frozen water in polar ice caps, floating ice, and permafrost, liquid water in rivers, lakes, oceans, and underground aquifers, and water vapor in the atmosphere; and **(3)** below us, a thin crust of soil, minerals, and rocks extending only a few thousand meters into the earth's interior. This intricate shell of life contains all the water, minerals, oxygen, carbon, nitrogen, phosphorus, and other chemical building blocks essential for life. Because essentially no new matter enters or leaves the earth, these vital chemicals must be recycled again and again for life to continue, as discussed in the next chapter.

If the earth were an apple, the ecosphere would be no thicker than the apple's skin. Everything in this skin of life is interconnected: Air helps purify water and keeps plants and animals alive, water keeps plants and animals alive, plants keep animals alive and help renew the air and soil, and the soil keeps plants and many animals alive and helps purify water. The ecosystems that make up the ecosphere also help to **(1)** moderate the weather, **(2)** recycle vital chemicals needed by plants and animals, **(3)** dispose of our wastes, **(4)** control more than 95 percent of all potential crop pests and causes of human disease, and **(5)** maintain a gigantic genetic pool that we use to develop new food crop strains and medicines.

The ecosphere, then, is a remarkably effective and enduring system—and endure it must, or life will become extinct. It is all we have. Disrupting or stressing the ecosphere in one place often creates unpredictable and sometimes undesirable effects elsewhere, as discussed in Section 5-3. This ecological backlash has been eloquently summarized by the English poet Francis Thompson: "Thou canst not stir a flower, without troubling of a star." *The goal of ecology is to find out just how everything in the ecosphere is related.* Let's begin this study of interrelationships by learning how solar energy sustains all life in the ecosphere and helps determine the earth's climate and weather.

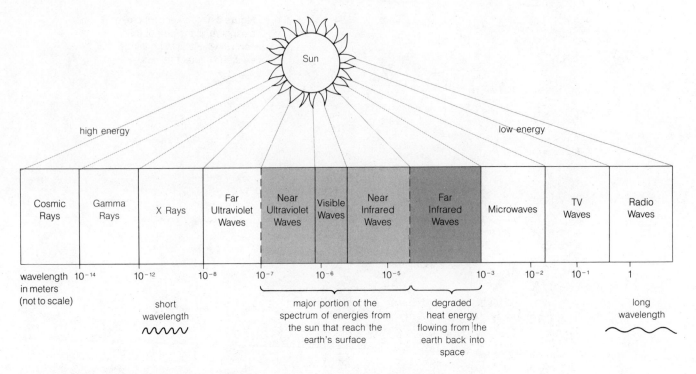

Figure 3-2 The electromagnetic spectrum. The sun radiates a wide range of energies with different wavelengths. Much of this incoming radiation is either reflected or absorbed by earth's atmosphere, so mostly moderate- to low-energy radiation actually reaches the earth's surface.

3-2 The Sun: Source of Energy for Life on Earth

A Nuclear Fusion Reactor Just as an economy runs on money, the ecosphere runs on energy. *The source of the radiant energy that sustains all life on earth is the sun.* It warms the earth and provides energy for photosynthesis in green plants. These plants, in turn, synthesize the carbon compounds that keep them alive and that serve as food for almost all other organisms. Solar energy also powers the water cycle (Section 4-3), which purifies and removes salt from ocean water to provide the fresh water upon which land life depends.

The sun is a medium-sized star composed mostly of hydrogen. At its center, the sun is so hot that a pinhead of its material could kill a person over 161 kilometers (100 miles) away. Under the conditions of extremely high temperatures and pressures found in the interior of the sun, light nuclei of hydrogen atoms are fused together to form slightly heavier nuclei of helium atoms. In this process of *nuclear fusion* some of the mass of the hydrogen nuclei is converted into energy (Section 15-7).

Thus, the sun is a giant *nuclear fusion reactor* 150 million kilometers (93 million miles) away from the earth. Every second the sun converts about 3.7 billion kilograms (4.1 billion tons) of its total mass into

energy. Nevertheless, we need not worry about the sun running out of energy. It has probably been in existence for 6 billion years and estimates are that it has enough hydrogen left to keep going for at least another 8 billion years.

Solar Electromagnetic Radiation The sun's energy comes to us as *radiant energy,* traveling through space as waves of oscillating electric and magnetic fields (∿∿∿) known as **electromagnetic radiation** (Figure 3-2). These electromagnetic waves travel at a speed of 300 thousand kilometers (186 thousand miles) per second. At this speed the light striking your eyes made the 150-million-kilometer (93-million-mile) trip from the surface of the sun to the earth in about 8 minutes. Only about one two-billionth of the sun's total radiated energy is intercepted by the earth, a minute target in the vastness of space.

The visible light rays we call sunlight are only a tiny part of the wide range, or spectrum, of energies given off by the sun, known as the **electromagnetic spectrum,** ranging from high-energy cosmic rays to low-energy radio waves (Figure 3-2). Each type of energy in this spectrum can be treated as a wave with a different **wavelength,** the distance between the crest of one wave and the next.

High-energy electromagnetic waves such as

cosmic rays have short wavelengths (∿∿∿∿), whereas low-energy electromagnetic waves such as radio waves have long wavelengths (⌒⌒⌒⌒) (Figure 3-2). The higher-energy, shorter-wavelength rays—cosmic rays, gamma rays, X rays, and most ultraviolet rays—are harmful to the deoxyribonucleic acid (DNA) molecules that carry the genetic information in most living organisms. Fortunately, most of this harmful electromagnetic radiation is screened out by ozone and water vapor in the earth's atmosphere. Without this screen life on earth could not exist as it does today.

3-3 Ecosystems and Ecosystem Structure

Levels of Organization of Matter Looking at earth from space, we see mostly a blue sphere with irregular green, red, and white patches on its surface. As we zoom closer, these colorful patches appear as deserts, forests, grasslands, mountains, seas, lakes, oceans, farmlands, and cities. Each zone is different, having its own characteristic set of organisms and climatic conditions. Moving in closer, we can pick out a variety of *organisms* or living things. If these plant and animal organisms were greatly magnified, we would find them made up of *cells*—groups of atoms and molecules interacting in an organized way to exhibit what we call life. The *molecules* or *compounds* such as water and proteins found in these cells are chemical combinations of more fundamental building blocks of all matter called *atoms*. All matter on earth is made up of various combinations of atoms of only 108 chemical elements such as hydrogen, carbon, oxygen, nitrogen, and iron. For convenience, each element is given a shorthand symbol such as H for hydrogen, O for oxygen, N for nitrogen, P for phosphorus, Cl for chlorine, and Na for sodium. Atoms in turn are made up of even smaller *subatomic particles* such as electrons, protons, and neutrons. All matter, in fact, can be viewed as being organized in identifiable patterns, or *levels of organization*, ranging in complexity from subatomic particles to heavenly galaxies (Figure 3-3, p. 34).

The Realm of Ecology As Figure 3-3 shows, ecology is primarily concerned with interactions among only five levels of organization of matter—*organisms*, *populations*, *natural communities*, *ecosystems*, and the *ecosphere* or *biosphere*. All organisms of a given kind constitute a **species**. Each species represents a particular array of hereditary material called a *gene pool* that is distinct from the gene pools of other species. Every member of a species is potentially

Table 3-1 System for Classifying Organisms into Different Species

Category	Organisms Included	Example (humans)
Species	Distinctly different kinds of organisms that live together with little or no interbreeding	*Homo sapiens*
Genus	Species that share some but not all features and that are related by descent from a fairly recent, common ancestral form	*Homo*
Family	All genera (plural of genus) related by descent from a more remote common ancestor	Hominoids
Order	All closely related families	Primates
Class	All related orders	Mammals
Phylum	All related classes	Chordates
Kingdom	All related phyla (plural of phylum)	Animals

capable of breeding with all other members of the same species. Normally members of different species do not interbreed. Thus, dogs and cats are separate species because no one has found a hybrid between a dog and a cat. One system used to classify organisms into different species is summarized in Table 3-1.* Members of the animal kingdom can be classified as *vertebrates* if they have backbones and *invertebrates* if they do not. Major types of vertebrates include mammals, birds, reptiles, amphibians, and fishes. Most invertebrates are classified as insects.

Every species in nature is composed of smaller units called populations that tend to live in a particular area or habitat somewhat isolated from other populations of the same species. Thus, a **population** is a group of individual organisms (such as squirrels or oak trees) of the same species that interbreed and that occupy a given area at a given time.

In nature we find several populations of different species living in the same area. The populations of plants and animals living and interacting in a given area at a given time are called a **natural community**. Each organism and population in a natural

*Some biologists group all organisms into two major kingdoms; plants and animals—the simplified scheme used throughout this book. Others divide them into five kingdoms: multicellular plants, animals, fungi, single-celled monera (such as bacteria and blue-green algae), and protista (such as diatoms and amoebas). Some even use a 20-kingdom classification scheme.

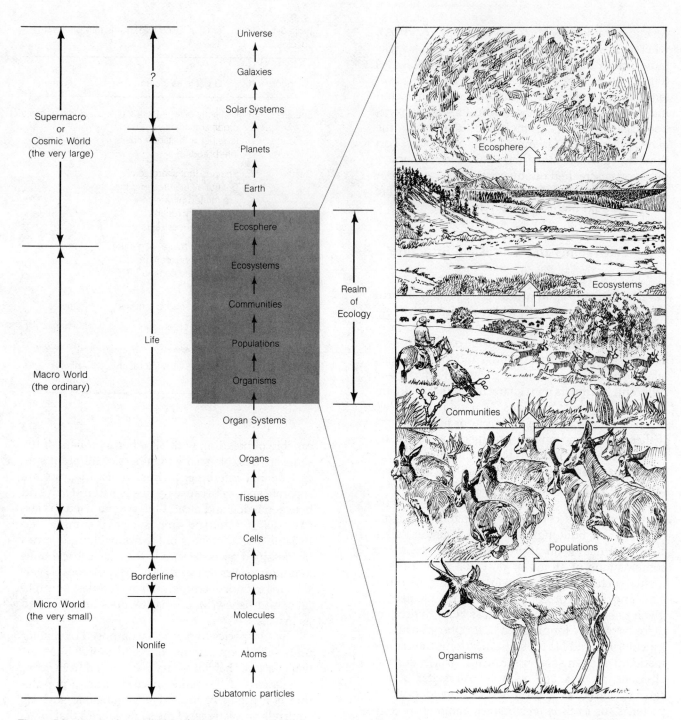

Figure 3-3 Levels of organization of matter.

community has a **habitat,** the place where it lives—its address, so to speak. Habitats vary widely in size from an entire forest to the intestine of a termite. A natural community, such as an oak-hickory forest, is not just a collection of squirrels, trees, plants, bacteria, and other populations living together in the same place. The important aspect of a natural community is that its animals and plants interact with one another. In many natural communities one or two organisms dominate. For example, in an oak-hickory forest natural commu-

nity, oak and hickory trees are the *dominant* species. Other kinds of trees are likely to be scarce. These dominant species modify the environment by providing shade and influencing the soil type, helping determine what types of plants—such as creepers, bushes, and spring flowers—can grow in the forest. These plants in turn provide specific types of habitats and food that influence the kinds of animals that can live there.

The living things in a natural community are surrounded by an **environment** consisting of other living plants and animals, called the *biotic* portion, and a nonliving or *nonbiotic* portion consisting of chemicals and physical factors such as solar energy, temperature, light, wind, and water currents. A natural community of living things that interact with each other (biotic environment) and with their non-biotic environment in a way that perpetuates the community is called an **ecosystem.**

The ecosystem concept was developed by scientists so that a patch of the earth, of any convenient size, could be studied to see how life worked there. The boundaries drawn around ecosystems are arbitrary, selected for convenience in studying each system. An ecosystem can be a planet, a tropical rain forest, an ocean, a fallen log, a puddle of water, or a culture of bacteria in a petri dish. The variation in ecosystems is essentially infinite. But because certain plant and animal species are often found together, it is useful to classify ecosystems according to their similarities in structure.

On a global basis, there are two major classes of *aquatic ecosystems:* **(1)** *marine and estuarine ecosystems,* such as oceans, seas, estuaries (where fresh water from rivers and streams mixes with seawater), and inland bodies of brackish or saline water; and **(2)** *freshwater ecosystems,* consisting of inland bodies of standing freshwater (lentic systems) such as lakes and ponds and inland bodies of flowing water (lotic systems) such as springs, creeks, and rivers, as discussed further in Chapters 17 and 18. On land, the large major types of ecosystems—called *biomes*—are forests, grasslands, and deserts. Each **biome** is a large terrestrial ecosystem with a distinct group of plants and animals, as described in more detail in Section 3-8. All the various ecosystems on the planet, along with their interactions, make up the largest unit, or planetary ecosystem, called the *ecosphere* or *biosphere* shown earlier in Figure 3-1.

The ecosystem approach, however, is not the only way of studying ecology. Some ecologists prefer to approach ecology from the standpoint of biological evolution. Because the evolutionary approach requires a fairly detailed and technical background in biology, the ecosystem approach is used in this book.

Ecosystem Structure   The types of organisms found in a particular ecosystem and the patterns of inter-relationships among these organisms make up the **structure** of that ecosystem. For convenience, scientists divide an ecosystem into two major components: the **abiotic,** or nonliving, components and the **biotic,** or living, components. The *abiotic* parts include **(1)** an outside energy source (usually the sun), **(2)** various other physical factors such as wind and heat that determine the climate and weather of

the ecosystem, and **(3)** all of the chemicals found in the soil, air, and water that are essential nutrients for life and that are obtained by breaking down the matter in dead plants and animals. The type and quantity of various physical and chemical abiotic factors in a given area determine the types of plants and animals that can exist in a particular ecosystem. Merely measuring the value of abiotic factors, however, is not enough to determine which species can thrive in a given ecosystem. Instead, we must know how the temperature, precipitation, or some other abiotic factor varies throughout the year.

The *biotic* or living portion of an ecosystem consists of **(1)** *producers,* green plants and some bacteria that, through photosynthesis, use certain wavelengths of solar energy (Figure 3-2) to produce organic food substances such as glucose from carbon dioxide gas and water obtained from their environment; **(2)** *consumers,* animals called *primary consumers* or *herbivores* (such as deer and grasshoppers) that feed directly on green plants and other animals called *secondary* or *higher-order consumers* or *carnivores* (such as lions and snakes) that feed indirectly on green plants by consuming the tissue of herbivores; and **(3)** *decomposers* or *microconsumers* such as some types of bacteria and fungi that rot, decompose, or otherwise break down organic wastes from live organisms and tissue from dead plants and animals into simpler substances that are returned to the environment for use as nutrients by other living organisms.

Chemical Cycling and Energy Flow in an Ecosystem   Figure 3-4 illustrates the major components of an ecosystem and how they are related by the processes of chemical cycling within the ecosystem and the one-way flow of energy through the ecosystem. Notice that the chemicals (represented by solid arrows in Figure 3-4) that serve as nutrients for living organisms in a ecosystem are *cycled* from the abiotic environment to producers, to consumers, to decomposers, and then back to the abiotic environment for reuse. At the same time solar energy flows into the ecosystem and is used by green plants to produce organic food substances such as glucose. In accordance with the second law of thermodynamics (Section 2-3), much of this input of high-quality solar energy is degraded to low-quality heat energy that flows back into the surrounding environment. This one-way energy flow through an ecosystem is represented by the open arrows in Figure 3-4. These processes of *chemical cycling and one-way energy flow* allow the groupings of producers, consumers, and decomposers found in a particular ecosystem to perpetuate themselves, as discussed in more detail in the next chapter.

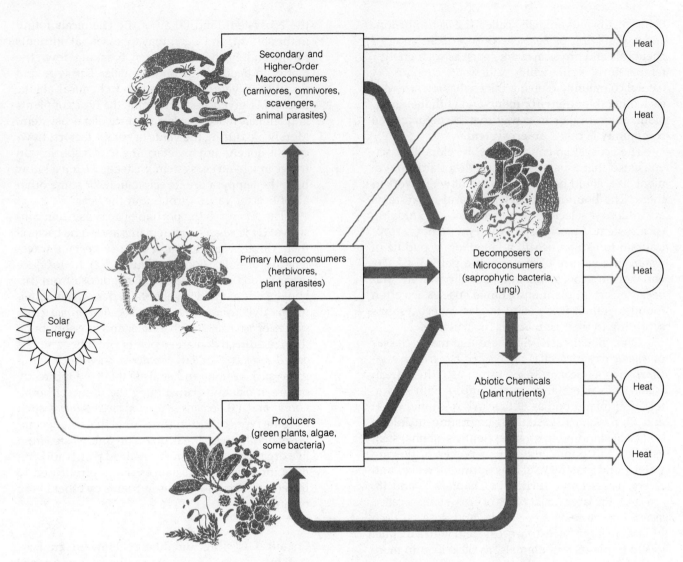

Figure 3-4 The basic components of an ecosystem. Solid arrows represent the cyclical movement of chemicals through the system, and open arrows indicate one-way energy flows.

Any self-sustaining ecosystem must have a mix of producers, consumers, and decomposers. However, as Figure 3-4 shows, it is not necessary for an ecosystem to have secondary and higher-order consumers such as carnivores for the vital processes of chemical cycling and energy flow to take place. Figures 3-5 and 3-6, respectively, show greatly simplified portions of the structure of an ecosystem found in a field and of a freshwater pond ecosystem.

3-4 Abiotic Ecosystem Components: A Closer Look

Physical Factors The major abiotic components of an ecosystem are *physical factors* such as light, temperature, wind, and water currents and *chemicals* that serve as nutrients for the producers, con-

sumers, and decomposers found in an ecosystem. Solar energy normally drives the ecosystem by helping to create climate, to recycle essential chemicals, and to support plant life. Green plants use a tiny fraction of incoming solar energy plus water and carbon dioxide to make carbohydrates such as glucose that store chemical energy. Plants and animals that consume plants or other animals break down (oxidize) these fuel molecules to obtain energy. Other physical factors include conditions such as temperature, light, wind, and water currents, which are created when solar energy interacts with chemicals in the ecosystem and with structural features of the earth's surface.

Chemicals The chemicals found in ecosystems throughout the world are either elements or compounds. **Elements** are chemicals such as iron (Fe),

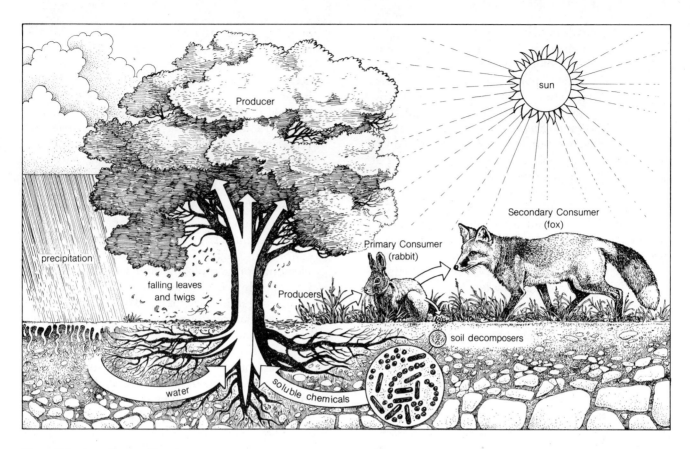

Figure 3-5 A greatly simplified version of the structure of an ecosystem found in a field.

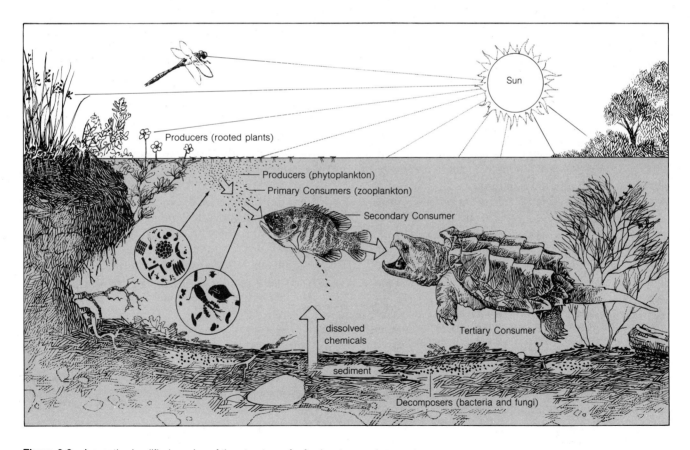

Figure 3-6 A greatly simplified version of the structure of a freshwater pond ecosystem.

sodium (Na), carbon (C), nitrogen (N), and oxygen (O) whose distinctly different atoms serve as the 108 basic building blocks of all matter. Elements exist as *atoms*, which can combine with other atoms to form *molecules*. For example two atoms of hydrogen (H) can combine to form a hydrogen molecule with the shorthand *chemical formula* H_2 (read as *H-two*). Note that the number of atoms (except one) of each kind in a molecule is shown by placing a numerical subscript to the right of the symbol for each element. Similarly, two nitrogen atoms can combine to form a nitrogen molecule represented by the formula N_2 (read as *N-two*). This molecular form of the element nitrogen is a gas that makes up almost 80 percent of the atmosphere. Oxygen gas, which makes up almost 20 percent of the atmosphere, consists of oxygen molecules (O_2) formed by the combination of two atoms of oxygen. Oxygen gas also exists as molecules of ozone, with the formula O_3, formed when three atoms of oxygen combine; it is found primarily in the *ozone layer*, located in the upper region of the atmosphere known as the stratosphere.

Each atom of an element is made up of a tiny center or *nucleus*, consisting of one or more positively charged *protons (p)* and uncharged *neutrons (n)*, and one or more negatively charged *electrons (e)* whizzing around outside the nucleus. For uncharged atoms, the number of positively charged protons in the nucleus equals the number of negatively charged electrons outside the nucleus and this distinguishes one element from another. For example, an atom of the simplest element, hydrogen (H), has one proton in its nucleus and one electron outside its nucleus, and sodium (Na) has 11 protons in its nucleus and 11 electrons outside its nucleus. Atoms or groups of atoms of many of the elements can lose or gain one or more negatively charged electrons outside their nuclei to form positively or negatively charged **ions**. *Positive ions*, such as the sodium ion (Na^+), calcium ion (Ca^{2+}), and ammonium ion (NH_4^+), are formed when an atom or group of atoms loses one or more of its electrons. *Negative ions*, such as chloride ion (Cl^-), nitrate ion (NO_3^-), and phosphate ion (PO_4^{3-}), are formed when an atom or group of atoms gains one or more electrons.

Most matter in the world exists as **compounds**—substances composed of atoms or ions of two or more different elements held together in a fixed ratio by chemical bonds. The basic structural units of compounds are either *molecules* or *formula units* of ions with opposite electrical charges. Water, for example, is a compound composed of H_2O (read as *H-two-O*) molecules, each consisting of two hydrogen atoms chemically bonded to an oxygen atom. Because opposite electrical charges attract one

another, the oppositely charged ions of different elements can attract one another to form compounds made up of formula units rather than molecules. Thus, sodium chloride, the main ingredient in table salt, is composed of extremely large numbers of individual formula units of oppositely charged sodium ions (Na^+) and chloride ions (Cl^-) represented by the formula Na^+Cl^- or more often simply by NaCl (where the electrical charges are not shown).

Compounds are represented in shorthand form by *chemical formulas* in which the number of atoms (except when there is only one) of each type of element present is shown by placing a numerical subscript to the right of the chemical symbol for each element. For example, the chemical formula for carbon dioxide is CO_2 (read as *C-O-two*); that for glucose, a sugar, is $C_6H_{12}O_6$ (read as *C-six-H-twelve-O-six*); and that for ammonium nitrate, an ingredient in some commercial fertilizers, is NH_4NO_3 (read as *N-H-four-N-O-three*).

Compounds are usually classified as either *organic* or *inorganic*. Hydrocarbon compounds containing only atoms of the elements carbon (C) and hydrogen (H) and other compounds derived from hydrocarbons that also contain atoms of one or more elements such as oxygen (O), nitrogen (N), sulfur (S), phosphorus (P), and chlorine (Cl) are called **organic compounds.** Examples include methane (CH_4) (the major component of natural gas), proteins, carbohydrates such as glucose ($C_6H_{12}O_6$) and sucrose or table sugar ($C_{12}H_{22}O_{11}$), lipids (fats), vitamins, and complex molecules such as DNA that carry genetic information in living organisms. Organic compounds are major components of the tissues of living and dead organisms.

Compounds not classified as organic compounds are called **inorganic compounds.** Examples include water (H_2O), ammonia (NH_3), nitrogen (N_2), carbon dioxide (CO_2), sulfur dioxide (SO_2) (an air pollutant produced by volcanoes and by the burning of coal and oil containing sulfur impurities), and sodium chloride (NaCl). Some inorganic compounds are found in the tissues of living and dead organisms; others exist apart from organisms. The critical inorganic and organic chemicals found in the air, water, and soil must be continually recycled through the ecosphere.

Just as words can be combined to make sentences, elements and compounds (the "words" of chemistry) can be combined by *chemical reactions* (the "sentences" of chemistry). A chemical reaction is represented in shorthand form by a *chemical equation* using the chemical formulas for the elements and compounds involved. Formulas of the original starting chemicals, called *reactants*, are placed to the left and formulas of the new chemicals produced, called *products,* are placed to the right. Each different reactant and product is separated by a plus sign (+) and the reactants and products are separate by an arrow, which stands for "produces" or "yields." For example, the combustion (burning) reaction of carbon (C)—the main ingredient in coal—with oxygen gas (O_2) in the atmosphere to produce carbon dioxide gas (CO_2) can be represented by the chemical equation:

$$\text{reactants} \rightarrow \text{products}$$
$$C + O_2 \rightarrow CO_2$$

Because of the law of conservation of matter (Section 2-1), no atoms (matter) can either be created or destroyed in a chemical reaction. Instead, a chemical reaction represents a rearrangement of existing atoms in different forms. Notice that in the chemical equation for the combustion of carbon there are one carbon atom and two oxygen atoms on each side of the equation. A chemical equation that contains the same number of atoms of each element on each side in accordance with the law of conservation of matter is said to be *balanced.*

To balance the atoms on each side of the chemical equation, it is sometimes necessary to put numbers in front of one or more of the formulas for the chemicals involved in the reaction. For example, the chemical equation for the reaction of hydrogen gas (H_2) with oxygen gas (O_2) to form water (H_2O) is balanced as follows:

$$H_2 + O_2 \rightarrow H_2O \qquad \textit{(unbalanced)}$$

This is unbalanced because two hydrogen atoms plus two oxygen atoms does not equal two hydrogen atoms and one oxygen atom. To balance this equation we must have two molecules of H_2 (four atoms of H) reacting with one molecule of O_2 (two atoms of O) to form two molecules of H_2O (four atoms of H and two atoms of O).

$$2H_2 + O_2 \rightarrow 2H_2O \qquad \textit{(balanced)}$$

Balancing an equation is essentially a trial-and-error process carried out until the number of atoms of each element is the same on each side of the equation. For example, the overall balanced equation for the process of *photosynthesis,* in which green plants use sunlight to combine carbon dioxide gas and water to form a sugar such as glucose and oxygen gas, is:

$$\text{carbon dioxide gas} + \text{water} + \text{solar energy} \rightarrow \text{sugars, such as glucose} + \text{oxygen gas}$$

$$6CO_2 + 6H_2O + \text{solar energy} \rightarrow C_6H_{12}O_6 + 6O_2$$

3-5 Biotic Ecosystem Components: A Closer Look

Producers Let's look more closely at the producers, consumers, and decomposers that make up the biotic components of an ecosystem. **Producers** are plants and some types of bacteria that use either solar energy (plants) or chemical energy (bacteria) to convert simple inorganic molecules such as carbon dioxide gas and water obtained from their environment to form complex organic molecules, such as glucose ($C_6H_{12}O_6$) and other nutrient molecules they need to stay alive. Producer plants contain one or more pigments such as chlorophyll that can absorb certain wavelengths (Figure 3-2) of solar energy; they use this energy to combine carbon dioxide and water to form glucose and oxygen gas in a process known as *photosynthesis.* Producer plants range in size from tiny, floating phytoplankton such as algae and diatoms in aquatic ecosystems (Figure 3-6) to large trees in terrestrial ecosystems (Figure 3-5). Because they use either solar energy or chemical energy to synthesize the organic nutrients they need to stay alive, producers are also called *autotrophs* ("self-feeders").

Most producers are green because they contain large amounts of green-colored chlorophyll. In some plants, however, other pigments can overshadow the green color. For example, certain species of trees have reddish leaves and two major groups of algae, red and brown algae, are named for their distinctive colors. It is important to note that *not all plants are producers.* Nonproducer plants that lack chlorophyll or any other pigment capable of absorbing solar energy usually have a whitish color and cannot carry out photosynthesis. Examples include flowering plants such as the Indian pipe and fungi such as mushrooms and molds. Most of these nonproducer plants are decomposers.

Although most producers are plants, a few exist as certain types of bacteria. These bacteria use chemical energy obtained from certain chemicals in their environment instead of light to convert inorganic nutrients such as carbon dioxide and water into organic nutrients in a process called *chemosynthesis.*

Consumers Organisms that feed either directly or indirectly on producers are called **consumers.** Because these organisms cannot manufacture the organic nutrients they need to stay alive and must eat those in other plants and animals, they are also known as *heterotrophs* ("other-feeders"). An organism that feeds directly on a producer is called a

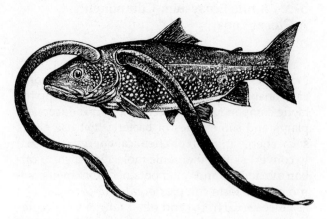

Figure 3-7 The sea lamprey is an ecoparasite that attaches itself to the body of a lake trout or other fish, opens a hole in the skin, and sucks out blood and body fluids.

primary consumer or **herbivore** ("plant-eater"). Examples include whales, deer, rabbits (Figure 3-5), mice, grasshoppers, sheep, and zooplankton (Figure 3-6). They may, like caterpillars, feed on only one species of plant or they may, like rabbits and goats, feed on a variety of plant species. Hooved animals, many of which humans have domesticated, are the best-known herbivores found on the land. Others, such as wild cattle, zebras, and giraffes still live in herds on the grasslands of Africa, Asia, and parts of North America.

An organism that feeds on a primary consumer or herbivore is called a **secondary consumer** or **carnivore** ("meat-eater"). For example, in Figure 3-5 the rabbit that feeds on green plants is a primary consumer and the fox that feeds on the rabbit is a secondary consumer. Other examples include ladybugs, coyotes, frogs, anteaters, cats, and some types of birds and fish. Higher levels of consumers also exist. For example, in Figure 3-6 the fish that feeds on zooplankton primary consumers is a secondary consumer and the turtle that feeds on this fish is a tertiary consumer. Other examples of higher-level consumers include lions, hawks, fleas, and some types of large fish. Organisms such as pigs, rats, cockroaches, and humans that can eat either plants or other animals are called **omnivores** (generalists).

An animal that feeds on another animal is also called a *predator*. The herbivore or carnivore animal that is fed upon by a predator is called the *prey*. These two animals are then said to have a *predator-prey relationship*, as discussed in more detail in Enrichment Study 6. The fox and rabbit in Figure 3-5 have such a relationship: the fox is the predator and the rabbit is the prey.

Another important type of consumer is called a *parasite*. Instead of devouring their prey like other consumers, parasites slowly feed on the exterior or interior of an organism called the *host* in what is called a *host-parasite relationship*. Some, such as tapeworms, live *inside* their host and are called *endoparasites*. Others, such as ticks, fleas, leeches, lice, and the sea lamprey (Figure 3-7) attach themselves to the outside of an organism and are known as *eco*parasites. Bacteria and other microorganisms that cause plant and animal diseases are also examples of specialized endoparasites. Some flowering plants such as mistletoe are parasitic on other plants. Parasites are discussed further in Enrichment Study 6.

Another class of primary, secondary, and higher orders of consumers are known as *detritus feeders*. These are organisms that feed on dead organic material called **detritus** consisting of dead plant material, dead animal bodies, and feces. Although this matter is dead it contains large amounts of organic material that can provide nutrients for large and small detritus feeders such as vultures, earthworms, termites, ants, beetles, and crayfish. Some animals can act as both regular consumers and detritus consumers. For example, when a goat eats grass it acts as a primary consumer and when it eats fallen leaves it acts as a detritus consumer. Some types of flowering plants, such as the Indian pipe, obtain their energy from detritus rather than from photosynthesis and are called *saprophytes* (dead feeders).

Decomposers Most of the dead matter in ecosystems—especially dead leaves and wood—rots, decays, or decomposes instead of being eaten by detritus feeders. Organisms that obtain the nutrients they need to stay alive by breaking down the organic molecules in the remains of dead animals and plants or the waste products of living organisms into simpler substances are called **decomposers.** The two major classes of decomposer organisms are *fungi* and certain types of *bacteria*—microscopic single-celled organisms. Molds, mushrooms, coral fungi, and puffballs are all examples of fungi. Beneath the visible part of a fungus such as a mushroom is a network of tiny rootlike filaments called *mycelia*. These filaments penetrate into detritus and secrete specialized chemicals called *enzymes*. Each enzyme is capable of breaking down a certain type of dead material into simpler organic nutrients, which are then absorbed by the cells of the fungus. Certain types of bacteria can break down dead material into simpler organic nutrients in the same way. These bacteria and fungi in turn are fed upon by other organisms such as protozoans, mites, worms, and insects living in the soil or water.

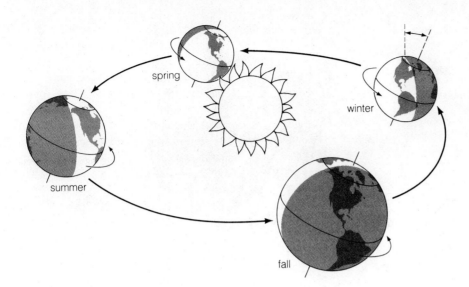

Figure 3-8 The seasons in the northern hemisphere are caused by variations in the amount of incoming solar radiation as the earth makes its annual rotation around the sun. Note that the northern end of the earth's axis tilts toward the sun in summer making the northern hemisphere warmer and away from it in winter making the northern hemisphere cooler.

3-6 Global Patterns of Climate

Weather and Climate **Weather** is the day-to-day variation in atmospheric conditions, such as temperature, moisture (including precipitation and humidity), sunshine (solar electromagnetic radiation), and wind. When the atmosphere thins to nothing, as on the moon or in space, there is no weather. **Climate** is the generalized weather at a given place on earth over a fairly long period of time such as a season, 1 year, or 30 years. Climate involves seasonal and annual averages, totals, and occasional extremes of the day-to-day weather pattern for an area. Climate is the weather you expect to occur at a particular time of the year in your hometown, whereas weather is the actual atmospheric conditions in your hometown on a particular day.

Global Air Circulation Patterns Heat from the sun and evaporated moisture are distributed over the earth as a result of global circulation patterns of atmospheric air masses. Three major factors affecting the pattern of this global air circulation are **(1)** the uneven heating of the equatorial and polar regions of the earth, which creates the driving force for atmospheric circulation; **(2)** the rotation of the earth around its axis, which causes deflection of air masses moving from the equator to the poles and from the poles back to the equator; and **(3)** unequal distribution of land masses, oceans, ocean currents, mountains, and other geological features over the earth's surface.

An *air mass* is a vast body of air in which the conditions of temperature and moisture are much the same at all points in a horizontal direction. A warm air mass tends to rise, and a cold air mass tends to sink. Air in the earth's atmosphere is heated more at the equator where the sun is almost directly overhead than at the poles where the sun is lower in the sky and strikes the earth at an angle. Because of this unequal heating, warm equatorial air tends to rise and spread northward and southward toward the earth's poles as more hot air rises underneath, carrying heat from the equator toward the poles. At the poles the warm air cools, sinks downward, and moves back toward the equator. In addition, because of the earth's annual rotation around the sun, the sun is higher in the sky in summer (July for the northern hemisphere and January for the southern hemisphere) than in winter (January for the northern hemisphere and July for the southern hemisphere). Such annual variations in the duration and intensity of sunlight lead to seasonal variations in the different hemispheres and at the poles (Figure 3-8).

The earth's daily rotation on its axis (Figure 3-8) not only results in night and day; it also produces the major wind belts of the earth. The general tendency for large air masses to move from the equator to the poles and back is modified by the twisting force associated with the earth's rotation on its axis. This force deflects air flow in the northern hemisphere to the right and in the southern hemisphere to the left (Figure 3-9). This distortion of the earth's general air circulation causes the single air movement pattern that would exist in each hemisphere

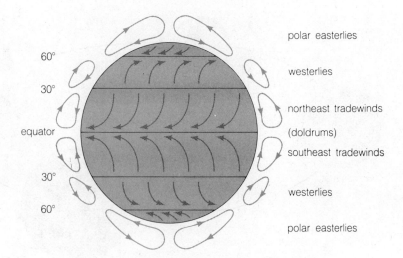

Figure 3-9 The earth's daily rotation on its axis deflects the general movement of warm air from the equator to the poles and back to the right in the northern hemisphere and to the left in the southern hemisphere. This twisting motion causes the air flow in each hemisphere to break up into three separate belts of prevailing winds.

on a nonrotating earth to break up into three separate belts of moving air or *prevailing ground winds:* the polar easterlies, the westerlies, and the tradewinds (Figure 3-9). The equatorial calm is known as the doldrums (Figure 3-9). These three major belts of prevailing winds in each hemisphere contribute to the distribution of heat and moisture around the planet that leads to differences in climate in different parts of the world.

A *front* is the boundary between two colliding air masses. When a warm air mass and a cold air mass collide, the warm air flows up the front slope of the cold air as if it were a mountain slope, and the cold air forms a wedge near the ground. If prevailing winds cause the cold air mass to push the warm air mass back, we have an advancing *cold front.* If the reverse happens, we have an advancing *warm front* and when no motion of the air masses takes place, we have a *stationary front.* An advancing cold or warm front usually brings bad weather because of the rain, snow, and strong winds that are found in the vicinity of its moving air masses.

The boundary where the warm tropical air masses pushed from the south by the prevailing westerlies collide with the cold polar air masses pushed from the north by the polar easterlies (Figure 3-9) is known as the *polar front.* This front is of major importance in determining the weather and climate of the North American continent. Depending on the relative strength of the polar easterlies and the westerlies, the polar front swings northward and southward in a rather unpredictable way. In general, it moves toward the equator during the winter and recedes to the poles during the summer.

The general global circulation pattern of air masses (Figure 3-9) also influences the distribution of precipitation over the earth's surface. A great deal of the sun's heat goes not just into warming the earth's surface but also into evaporating water from

the oceans and other bodies of water that cover about three-fourths of the earth's surface. Evaporation of water from the land and transpiration of moisture from the leaves of plants also contribute water vapor to the atmosphere. A single apple tree, for example, may transpire 6,790 liters (1,800 gallons) of water vapor into the atmosphere during its six-month growing season. The amount of water vapor in the air is called its *humidity.* The amount of water vapor the air is holding at a particular temperature expressed as a percentage of the amount it could hold at that temperature is known as its *relative humidity.* When air with a given amount of water vapor cools, its relative humidity rises; when this same air is warmed, its relative humidity drops. Thus, warm air can hold more water vapor than cold air, explaining why the humidity tends to rise in warmer summer months.

When an air mass rises it cools, which causes its relative humidity to increase. Once the relative humidity of the rising air mass reaches 100 percent, any further decrease in temperature causes tiny water droplets or ice crystals to condense on particles of dust in the atmosphere to form *clouds.* As these droplets and ice crystals in clouds are moved about in turbulent air, they collide and coalesce to form larger droplets and crystals. Eventually they can become big enough to be pulled downward by gravitational attraction toward the earth's surface in the form of *precipitation* such as rain, sleet, snow, or hail. Thus, almost all clouds and forms of precipitation are caused by the cooling of an air mass as it rises. Conversely, when an air mass sinks, its temperature rises and its relative humidity can decrease to the point where it can't release its moisture as rain or snow.

Air rising in the tropics is both hot and moist. As this air rises and cools, some of its water vapor is converted to water droplets, giving up some heat in the process. These droplets form the clouds from which tropical rains fall, helping explain why the tropics are wet and thus covered with lush vegetation. Conversely, areas north and south of the equator where the airflow is mainly downward—such as the deserts of the U.S. Southwest and the Sahara—tend to be dry because sinking air can hold more moisture.

An air mass tends to take on the temperature and moisture characteristics of the surface over which it moves. Thus, the climate and weather of a particular area are also affected by the distribution of land and water over the earth's surface because these surfaces react differently to the incoming rays of the sun. In general, land surfaces are heated rapidly by the sun. Because this heat does not penetrate deeply, land surfaces also cool rapidly. This means that interior land areas not near a large body of water usually have great differences between daily high and low temperatures. Water, however, warms up slowly, holds a much larger quantity of heat than the same volume of land surface, and cools slowly. As a result, the surface layer of air over the oceans is cooler in summer and warmer in winter than that over the continents. Because warm air rises, a net inflow of cool ocean air moves onto the continents in summer, and in winter there is a net outflow of cool air from the continents onto the oceans. Land and sea breezes result from the land being colder than the water at night and early morning but warmer later in the day.

The earth's rotation, prevailing winds, and variations in water temperature give rise to ocean currents such as the Gulf Stream, which carries warm waters from the Florida Straits northward along the Atlantic Coast and on to the British Isles. Such currents affect the climate of coastal areas near their flow. For example, air moving across the warm Gulf Stream acquires heat and moisture and influences the climate and weather along the East Coast. The climate of the East Coast is also affected by the cold Labrador Current, which flows southward as far as Norfolk, Virginia. The cool Japan Current has a major effect on the climate and weather of the West Coast of the United States.

Effects of Topography on Local Climate and Weather Topographical factors can often make local climatic conditions different from the general climate of a region. Such local climatic patterns are called *microclimates*. For example, forests have lower wind speeds and higher relative humidity than open land. Buildings in cities also disrupt wind flow patterns and heat absorption patterns and cause cities to have different microclimates than surrounding nonurban areas (Enrichment Study 5).

Climate is also modified locally by the presence of mountains. An increase in altitude results in a decrease in the density (mass per unit of volume) of the atmosphere, which in turn leads to a decrease in the temperature of the atmosphere. Thus, because of their higher altitudes, mountains tend to be cooler and windier than adjacent valleys. They also act as barriers to interrupt the flow of prevailing winds and the movement of storms. For example, because most U.S. mountain ranges run north and south, they disrupt the flow of the prevailing westerlies.

Mountain ranges also affect precipitation patterns. When prevailing winds reach a mountain range, the air rises and may decrease in temperature to the condensation level (100 percent humidity). When this occurs precipitation may occur on the windward side of the range as the air flows upward. After flowing over the mountain crests, the air flows down the lee side of the range. As this happens, it becomes warmer and its relative humidity can decrease to the point where it can't release its moisture as air or snow. Thus, slopes on the lee side of the mountain range and the land beyond these slopes generally lack abundant precipitation. This *rain shadow effect* is the main reason that arid and semiarid deserts lie to the east of the Coast Ranges and the Cascade and Sierra Nevada ranges of California.

Albedo, Emissivity, and Climate The amount of incoming solar energy reaching the earth's surface also affects climate. Let's look more closely at what happens to the tiny fraction of the sun's total energy output intercepted by the earth. As shown in Figure 3-10, about 34 percent of the incoming solar radiation is immediately reflected back to space by clouds, chemicals and particulate matter in the air, and the earth's surface. This reflectivity of the earth and its atmosphere is called planetary **albedo.** The remaining 66 percent of the incoming radiation is absorbed by the earth's atmosphere, lithosphere, hydrosphere, and ecosphere (Figure 3-10).

About 42 percent of the incoming solar energy heats the land and warms the atmosphere. Another 23 percent is used to evaporate water and cycle it through the ecosphere. A tiny fraction (1 percent) of the incoming solar energy generates winds, which in turn move the clouds and form waves in the ocean. An even smaller fraction, 0.023 percent, is captured by green plants and converted by photosynthesis to carbohydrates, proteins, and other molecules essential for life.

Almost all of the 66 percent of the solar energy that is not reflected away is degraded into longer-wavelength heat or far infrared radiation, in accordance with the second law of thermodynamics (Sec-

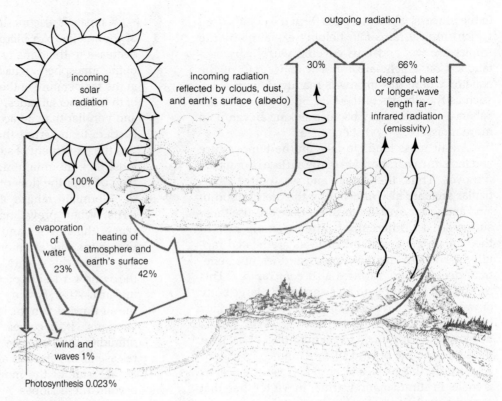

Figure 3-10 The flow of energy to and from the earth.

outgoing radiation

incoming solar radiation

incoming radiation reflected by clouds, dust, and earth's surface (albedo)

30%

66% degraded heat or longer-wave length far-infrared radiation (emissivity)

100%

evaporation of water 23%

heating of atmosphere and earth's surface 42%

wind and waves 1%

Photosynthesis 0.023%

tion 2-3), and flows back into space (Figure 3-2). The total amount of energy returning to space is called the **emissivity** of the earth. Emissivity is affected by the presence of chemicals such as water (H_2O), carbon dioxide (CO_2), ozone (O_3), and particles of matter in the atmosphere. These molecules act as gatekeepers, allowing some of this heat to flow back into space and absorbing and reradiating some of it back toward the earth's surface.

Unless something changes either the albedo or the emissivity of the earth, the average atmospheric temperature for the entire earth remains constant. However, a change of only one- or two-tenths of a percent of the solar radiation reaching the earth's atmosphere and surface can significantly warm or cool the atmosphere and shift global climate patterns. Increasing the albedo of the atmosphere could lead to global cooling, whereas decreasing the atmosphere's emissivity could lead to global heating. For example, a rise of only 2 degrees Celsius in the average global temperature could cause major changes in global weather patterns, and a 3 to 6 degree Celsius rise could eventually melt the polar ice caps, thus flooding a large portion of the world. Similarly, a drop of only a few degrees in the average global temperature could trigger an ice age.

Some climatologists claim that human activities can affect global climate patterns. Increases in the average levels of carbon dioxide in the earth's atmosphere due primarily to the burning of fossil fuels may lead to a *greenhouse effect*, whereby far-infrared radiation (Figure 3-2) that would otherwise escape into space is trapped and raises the average temperature of the atmosphere. On the other hand, it has been theorized that dust from volcanic explosions and particulate matter emitted into the atmosphere from human activities such as land clearing and smokestack, chimney, and automobile emissions could reflect significant amounts of sunlight away from the upper atmosphere and cause global cooling. These possible effects of human activities on global climate patterns are discussed in Enrichment Study 5.

Climate Classification Though climate is affected by a number of variables, the two most important factors determining the climate of an area are average temperature and precipitation. Figure 3-11 (pp. 46–47) shows the global distribution of six major types of climate based on average temperature and precipitation of different areas over 30-year periods: **(1)** tropical humid climates, **(2)** dry climates, **(3)** subtropical humid warm climates, **(4)** temperate humid cold climates, **(5)** cold polar climates, and **(6)** highland (mountain) climates.

Now we are ready to see how these major types of climate based roughly on long-term average temperature and precipitation of different areas are a major factor in determining the distinct and self-sustaining groupings of plant and animal life found on different parts of the earth's surface.

3-7 Limiting Factors in Ecosystems

The Limiting Factor Principle What determines the particular combination of plant and animal species found in a given ecosystem? Why is one area of the earth a desert, another a forest, and another a grassland? Why are there different types of deserts, grasslands, and forests and what determines the variations of plant and animal life found in each of these types?

The structure or type of ecosystem found in a given area depends on various combinations of the abiotic and biotic factors found there. You know that the speed of traffic moving along a one-lane, one-way street filled with bumper-to-bumper traffic is determined by the slowest moving car. Similarly, the overall structure of an ecosystem can often be determined by a single factor such as precipitation or average annual rainfall. Such a factor is called a *limiting factor*. Thus, the structure of an ecosystem is often determined by what is called the **limiting factor principle**: The single factor that is most deficient in an ecosystem is the one that determines the presence or absence of particular plant and animal species.

Precipitation and Temperature as Limiting Factors *Precipitation is the limiting factor that determines whether the biomes found on most of the world's land areas are desert, grassland, or forest.* For example, regardless of the average conditions of temperature and sunlight and the concentrations of certain minerals in the soil, the result will still be a desert if the average amount of precipitation is less than 25 centimeters (10 inches) per year. With so little rainfall, such desert areas typically have sparse vegetation with large areas of bare ground between plants. Similarly, areas with 75 centimeters (30 inches) or more of rainfall a year are generally dominated by a forest ecosystem unless cut down by humans. Regions that have about 25 to 75 centimeters (10 to 30 inches) of precipitation a year are typically grasslands. There is not enough moisture to support large stands of trees, but there is enough moisture to allow grasses to grow over most of the land.

Average precipitation by itself does not determine the particular type of desert, grassland, or forest found in a given area. As shown earlier in Figure 3-11, average precipitation and temperature acting together determine the climate of an area. The combined action of these two abiotic factors also determines the type of desert, grassland, or forest biome found in a particular area, as shown in Figure 3-11. For example, Figure 3-12 shows that

a humid tropical climate with hot temperatures and lots of rainfall produces a *tropical rain forest*, with a wide variety of broad-leaved evergreen trees (species that keep their leaves all year). *Temperate forests* are found in areas with temperate climates with ample precipitation. These forests are dominated by a few species of deciduous trees, such as oak and hickory, that drop their leaves and become dormant during winter when temperatures sometimes drop below freezing. In very cold areas with ample precipitation are *northern coniferous forests*, dominated by a few species of coniferous (cone-bearing), needle-leaved evergreen trees such as spruce and fir.

Figure 3-12 also shows that temperature variations combined with very little precipitation lead to development of tropical, temperate, and cold deserts. Similarly, temperature variations in areas with moderate rainfall leads to tropical grassland (savanna), temperate grasslands, and polar grasslands (tundra). Each of these major types of biomes contains many variations and many smaller ecosystems. Figure 3-13 (pp. 50–51) shows the distribution of the major types of forest, grassland, and desert biomes throughout the world. Correlations between biome type and climate type can be seen by comparing Figure 3-13 with Figure 3-11. The various types of biomes are described in more detail in the next section.

Why do trees in tropical rain forests and temperate forests have broad, flat leaves while those in northern coniferous forests have thin, needlelike leaves? Why should trees in tropical rain forests and in northern coniferous forests keep their leaves all year while trees in temperate forests lose their leaves during winter? Why don't most of the plant species in deserts have leaves? The answers are based on the fact that *the structure of a plant is designed to prevent it from gaining or losing too much heat.*

Trees in a rain forest have broad, flat leaves that provide a large surface area, which helps absorb heat from the sun and cool the trees by evaporation of water obtained from almost daily rains. Trees in temperate forest biomes with fairly mild climates most of the year also have broad, flat leaves to help control their heat input and output. To prevent excessive heat loss during winter when temperatures can drop below freezing, these trees survive by losing their leaves and becoming dormant until spring. Coniferous tree species such as spruce and fir found in the much colder northern coniferous forests have thick clusters of thin, needle-shaped leaves. These leaves lose their heat less rapidly than broad leaves because they have a smaller surface area in relation to their mass. These trees also keep their leaves all year in order to take advantage of brief, warm sunny spells.

Figure 3-11 World climates (Köppen-Geiger classification).

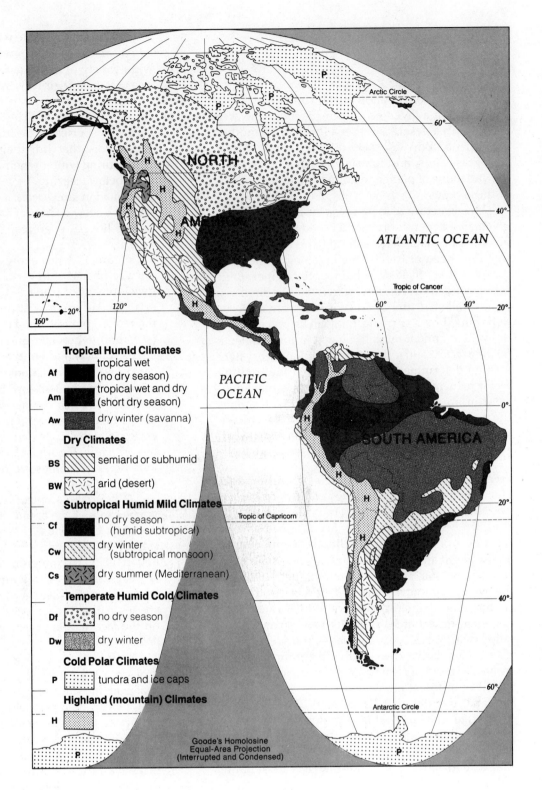

Tropical Humid Climates

Af — tropical wet (no dry season)

Am — tropical wet and dry (short dry season)

Aw — dry winter (savanna)

Dry Climates

BS — semiarid or subhumid

BW — arid (desert)

Subtropical Humid Mild Climates

Cf — no dry season (humid subtropical)

Cw — dry winter (subtropical monsoon)

Cs — dry summer (Mediterranean)

Temperate Humid Cold Climates

Df — no dry season

Dw — dry winter

Cold Polar Climates

P — tundra and ice caps

Highland (mountain) Climates

H

Goode's Homolosine
Equal-Area Projection
(Interrupted and Condensed)

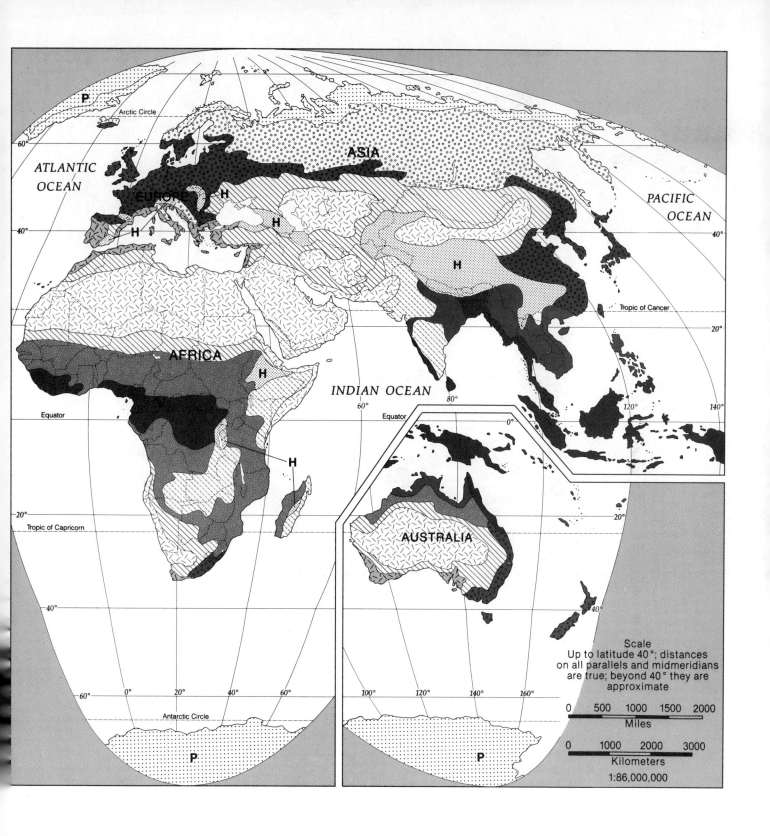

average rainfall (centimeters per year)

120 — 110 — 100 — 90 — 80 — 70 — 60 — 50 — 40 — 30 — 20 — 10 — 0

Northern coniferous forest

Deciduous forest

Tropical rain forest

Polar grassland (tundra)

Temperate grassland

Tropical grassland (savannah)

Cool desert

Temperate desert

Tropical desert

cool   temperate   hot

average temperature

Figure 3-12 The type of desert, grassland, or forest ecosystem found in a particular area is determined primarily by the two abiotic factors, average precipitation and average temperature, that together determine the major climate type of the area.

A different strategy is used by desert plants to balance their heat budget. There is so little water available that desert plants cannot cool themselves by evaporation. Thus, if desert plants had leaves they would heat up during the day, be cooked, and die. The tall sticklike shape of desert plants such as some species of cacti solves this problem by giving the plants the smallest possible surface area exposed to the overhead sun. At the same time, it provides the largest possible surface area away from the sun, used to radiate the heat out.

Other Limiting Factors Light is often the limiting factor that determines the types of trees, bushes, small plants, mosses, fungi, and bacteria found within a forest. The tops of the trees receive most of the light and their leaves provide shade for other species that require less light to grow. Only a fraction of the full light reaches the bushes, still less

reaches the small plants, and even less reaches the mosses. In dense pine and fir forests so little light penetrates that the forest floor contains only an evergreen layer of certain mosses.

In some cases the *soil* that forms a thin layer over much of the land surface of the earth can act as a limiting factor. *Soil* is a complex mixture of small pieces of inorganic rock, gravel, and minerals, and organic compounds, living organisms, air, and water. Soils are formed by the combined action of water, wind, chemical activity, and living organisms on the parent rock. The nature of the parent rock determines the basic composition of the soil. However, climate, topography, time, and various forms of life that live in the soil also determine some of its characteristics, as discussed in Chapter 8. For example, different species of trees are found within a temperate deciduous forest because of differences in the acidity and drainage characteristics of the soil.

3-8 Biomes: A Closer Look at Major Land Ecosystems

Tropical Biomes In "winterless" tropical climates with high temperatures, different types of biomes are found depending on the average amount of precipitation (Figure 3-12). These include tropical rain forests, seasonal forests, thorn scrubs, thorn woodlands, and savannas.

Tropical rain forests are found near the equator (Figure 3-13). Although such a forest has more different kinds of organisms than any other biome, there are fewer individuals of any one species in a given area. This biological diversity is the result of this biome's almost unchanging climate of high but not excessive annual mean temperature of about 28°C (82°F), high humidity, and almost daily and heavy rainfall.

These forests consist of several layers of plant and animal life. The top layer is dominated by tall trees with slender trunks, reaching heights of 30 to 60 meters (100 to 200 feet). Their leathery, evergreen leaves form a canopy overhead so the forest floor below is dark and very humid. With so little sunlight, the ground is relatively free of vegetation except along river banks and clearing edges. Decomposition is rapid, and everything that falls to the ground is quickly carried off, consumed, or decomposed by beetles, termites, ants, and other, often unusually large, insects.

Below the upper canopy a maze of thick, woody vines called *lianas* hang from branches that are covered with thousands of species of ferns, strange pineapplelike plants called bromeliads, and *epiphytes* or air plants (such as orchids). With no underground roots, epiphytes stay alive by getting minerals from falling leaves and animal wastes and by trapping water in their flowers or leaves. These airborne pools of water are miniature ecosystems containing entire communities of insects, spiders, and even tiny frogs.

The animal life in tropical forests is so varied that more different kinds of organisms may be found living in a single tree than in an entire forest to the north. Though relatively few animals are found on the forest floor, many species of huge colorful butterflies and colorful exotic birds, such as parrots, toucans, and macaws, fly around the forest canopy. They are joined by monkeys swinging and hopping about as well as lemurs, snakes, frogs, and other animal species.

Humans have steadily been clearing tropical rain forests to get lumber and to plant crops. If this clearing continues at present rates, within 50 years few of these incredibly beautiful and useful biomes may be left (Section 10-6).

North and south of the equator are the *tropical seasonal forests* where temperatures are fairly high and most of the precipitation occurs during a rainy (monsoon) season (Figure 3-12). Here canopy heights are lower than those in tropical rain forests and there are more deciduous trees that lose their leaves during the dry season.

In tropical climates less humid than those of tropical seasonal forests are *tropical thorn scrub* and *thorn woodland* biomes. There is enough precipitation to support small thorny plants in thorn scrub biomes and a few medium-sized trees in thorn woodland biomes, but not enough to support forests. Grass or dense shrubs grow below the trees. Such areas are found in much of Mexico, parts of Australia, and most of Africa south of the Sahara (Figure 3-13).

The *tropical savanna* biome (Figure 3-12) appears in areas having high temperatures and long dry seasons without enough rainfall to support forests. It is typically covered with grass and scattered groups of small trees and shrubs. During the dry season large areas of savanna often burn—hindering the development of forests. Savannas are found in southern Asia (especially India), Australia, and north and south of the tropical rain forests in Africa and South America (Figure 3-13). Undisturbed tropical savannas are usually populated by large herds of grazing hoofed mammals such as wildebeest, gazelles, zebra, and antelope in Africa and kangaroos and wallabies in Australia. The great herds of such grazing animals and their predators are disappearing rapidly except in protected areas because of ranching, farming, hunting, and other human activities (Chapter 11).

Desert In areas with climates too dry to support grasslands and where evaporation exceeds rainfall you will find the deserts that make up more than one-third of the earth's land surface (Figure 3-12). Global air movements (Figure 3-9) and mountain ranges that create rain shadows also play a role in creating deserts. After months or even years without rain a sudden brief downpour may occur. Unfortunately, most of the water quickly evaporates and runs off the relatively barren soil. There are two general types of deserts: **(1)** *cold deserts* with cold winters (there may even be snow on the ground) and hot summers, like those found in Oregon, Utah, and Nevada, and **(2)** warm deserts with warm to hot temperatures throughout the year. Typical warm deserts are found in Arizona, New Mexico, California, Texas, northern Mexico, Africa (the Sahara), and Saudi Arabia (Figure 3-13).

Though a few hot and very dry deserts like the Sahara consist of endless stretches of barren sand

Figure 3-13 World biomes.

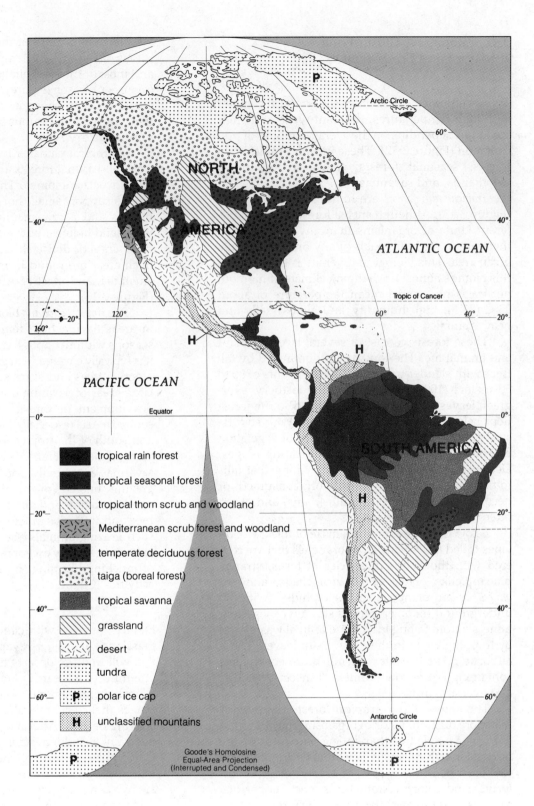

tropical rain forest

tropical seasonal forest

tropical thorn scrub and woodland

Mediterranean scrub forest and woodland

temperate deciduous forest

taiga (boreal forest)

tropical savanna

grassland

desert

tundra

P polar ice cap

H unclassified mountains

Goode's Homolosine
Equal-Area Projection
(Interrupted and Condensed)

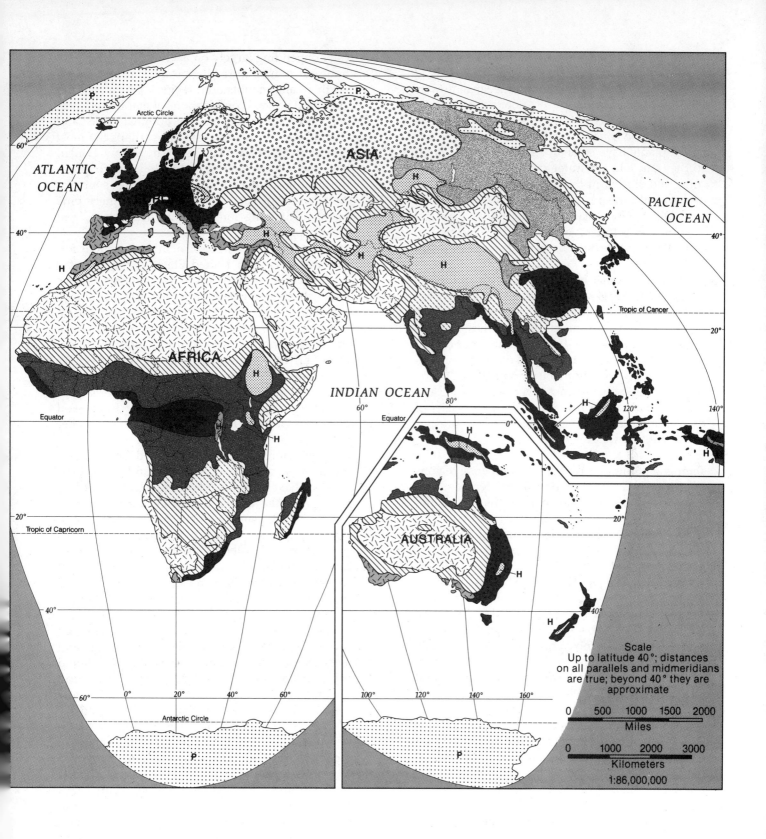

dunes, most consist of widely scattered thorny bushes and shrubs, occasional cacti (especially in the Western Hemisphere), and some small flowers that quickly carpet the desert floor after the brief rains. These desert plants use a number of strategies to get and conserve water. Cacti and other succulent plants have extensive shallow root systems so they can take up water rapidly when the rains come and store it in their fleshy stems. Their lack of leaves also decreases loss of water by evaporation. Other desert plants like mesquite bushes get groundwater with taproots as long as 30 meters (100 feet). The creosote bush has waxy leaves that retard evaporation.

Desert animals include a number of rodents (such as the kangaroo rat), lizards, toads, snakes and other reptiles, owls, eagles, vultures, many small birds, and numerous insects. Most of these animals are small and avoid the heat by coming out only at night especially toward dusk and dawn. Some desert animals get water from the morning dew. Others, such as the kangaroo rat, never drink at all and instead obtain water from their food. The scales of reptiles and the exterior covering of insects prevent evaporation of water.

Temperate Biomes The world's temperate regions on the average experience moderate temperatures and are found north and south of the tropics and their adjacent deserts (Figure 3-13). The major types of temperate biomes include temperate rain forests, evergreen forests, deciduous forests, woodlands, shrublands, and grasslands.

Temperate rain forests are found in cool climates in areas near the sea with abundant rainfall and summer cloudiness or fog (Figure 3-13). Along the Pacific Coast of North America temperate rain forests range from the mixed coastal coniferous forests of Washington, dominated by Douglas fir and several species of pine, to the majestic coastal redwood forests of northern California.

Temperate evergreen forests cover large areas where poor soils and numerous droughts and forest fires favor needle-leaved conifer or broad-leaved evergreen tree species over deciduous tree species. In the western United States large stands of these forests are dominated by spruces, firs, and ponderosa pine.

A somewhat cooler and drier climate produces *temperate deciduous forests* (Figure 3-12), with abundant (but not excessive) precipitation, moderate temperatures that gradually change with the seasons, and a long growing season (4 to 6 months). As temperatures drop in autumn, leaves exhibit a rainbow of colors before falling to the ground. Dominant tree species vary among deciduous for-

ests, depending largely on average local precipitation and temperature. In the moister and colder northern and mountainous regions of New England are found various combinations of maples, birches, and beech. Oak and hickory dominate drier and slightly warmer regions and are perhaps the most typical trees of this biome. Ash, yellow poplar, basswood, black cherry, and walnut are found in the southern deciduous forests (the southern Appalachians). Further south is the southern pine forest, containing longleaf, shortleaf, slash, and loblolly pines.

The dominant herbivore of most deciduous forests in the eastern United States is the whitetail deer. Because its predators (such as the wolf) have largely been eliminated or driven out, the whitetail population can grow out of control, leading to destruction of vegetation and mass starvation of the deer. Other animal species include porcupine (now fairly rare), opossum, raccoon, striped skunk, chipmunk, gray squirrel, shrew, and cottontail rabbit. Hunting and habitat destruction have largely eliminated the wolves, bobcats, gray foxes, and cougars that once fed on many of these smaller mammals.

These forests are also inhabited by an abundance of songbirds, frogs, salamanders, lizards, turtles, snakes, mice, and other rodents including the beaver, the largest rodent in North America. Predator birds, such as owls, hawks, and eagles, play an important ecological role by keeping down populations of small rodents who would otherwise destroy vegetation. As winter approaches, many of the bird species in these forests migrate south, and many of the animal species go into hibernation.

Temperate woodlands are found in areas with climates too dry to support forests but with enough precipitation to support a mixture of grasses and some trees. Such woodlands consisting of scattered oak trees spread across rolling grassland are found in central California and are largely used to grow wheat or barley or as rangeland to feed livestock.

When a temperate area has a so-called Mediterranean climate—mild, damp winters and hot summers with little or no rain—a biome known as *temperate shrubland* (or *chaparral* in Mexico and parts of the southwestern United States) occurs. This biome is found in Europe around the Mediterranean Sea, in southern Australia, at the southern tip of Africa, near the coast of Chile, and in southern and central California (Figure 3-13). The leathery evergreen leaves of many of the shrubby plants found in this biome have waxy coatings that reduce evaporation and help them survive long rainless periods. They also contain volatile and flammable compounds that, combined with dry summers and human activities, lead to periodic fires. These fires play an important ecological role in clearing out dead material and old growth and allowing various plant species that have become adapted to fire to reproduce. But they also destroy homes of residents in areas such as Marin County near San Francisco, who build in chaparral areas to take advantage of the mild year-round climate.

Temperate grasslands are found where rainfall is great enough to keep deserts from forming but low and erratic enough that cycles of drought and fire prevent forests from growing (Figure 3-12). These biomes have carpets of high and low grasses, mixed in some areas with small bushes and shrubs and even a few widely dispersed trees. These grasslands are found all over the world as the Great Plains of the United States, the prairies of Canada, the pampas of South America, the veldts of Africa, and the steppes of Russia and central Asia (Figure 3-13). Here the winters are cold with snow covering the ground at times and summers are hot and dry. The winds blow almost continuously and there are few natural windbreaks to blunt their force. The soils of the tall-grass prairie are among the richest in the world, explaining why most of the grasslands in Canada and the United States have been converted to vast fields of corn and wheat.

At one time the grasslands of the Great Plains of North America were dominated by large herbivores such as the bison, pronghorn antelope, elk, and wild horses. These grazing animals were preyed upon by the wolf, coyote, cougar, grizzly bear and Plains Indians. Today these herds have been replaced by domesticated cattle, sheep, and goats. Because they are confined these animals often overgraze the land, especially in years of severe drought. The exposed soil is quickly blown away and the productivity of the grassland is destroyed, as discussed in more detail in Section 8-5.

Undisturbed temperate grasslands also contain numerous species of small herbivores, such as the prairie dog, ground squirrel, pocket gopher, and jackrabbit. The prairie dog's elaborate tunnels and burrows help aerate the soil and its droppings enrich the soil. Settlers on the North American prairie, however, considered them a nuisance, and the animals have now been largely eliminated and replaced by the ground squirrel.

Taiga (Boreal Forests) Moving north toward the arctic we encounter the *taiga* (from a Russian word meaning "primeval forest") or *boreal forest* biome stretching across the northern portions of North America, Europe, and Asia (Figure 3-13). In this biome winters are long and extremely cold and much of the precipitation falls as snow.

Species diversity is low with these forests being dominated by only a few species of needle-leafed, coniferous (cone-bearing) evergreen trees such as spruce and fir that can survive the extreme winter cold. Lakes, ponds, and bogs are also often found. Decomposition and decay of the carpet of needles and leaf litter on the forest floor are slow because of the cold.

The major large herbivores of these coniferous forests are moose, mule deer, caribou (which migrate down from the tundra during the fall), and elk. Smaller herbivores include the snowshoe hare (which is white in winter and brown during the summer), red squirrels, and a variety of rodents, needle-eating caterpillars, beetles, wasps, mosquitoes, and biting flies. There is relatively little insect diversity, but a single insect pest such as the spruce budworm can cause extensive damage to the huge stands of one or two species of coniferous trees.

Major predators in the taiga are the timber wolf, Canada lynx, and red fox, and to a lesser extent the marten, wolverine, mink, otter, ermine, and short-tailed weasel. Grizzly bears and black bears eat almost anything—leaves, buds, berries, fish, and occasionally mammals and campers' supplies. Because of large-scale killing by farmers and ranchers, the timber wolf, which once inhabited most North American taiga, is now found primarily in Canada and Alaska. When wolf populations are killed off or driven away, the increased populations of moose, caribou, and deer they once controlled can devastate taiga vegetation.

Tundra: Arctic and Alpine Grasslands Few people want to spend much time in the *tundra,* an icy, treeless grassland found between the tree line and the Arctic Circle (*arctic tundra*) and just above the timberline on mountaintops (*alpine tundra*) (Figure 3-13). The limiting factors in this ecosystem are severe cold and a shortage of radiant energy (sunlight).

Only a few hardy plant and animal species can survive in this harsh climate of bitter cold (below $-5°C$, or 23°F) and low precipitation. In many areas the deeper layers of soil remain frozen as *permafrost.* Even if trees could survive the cold air, the permafrost prevents them from putting down deep enough roots to grow. Summers last only a few weeks, just long enough to thaw a thin veneer of soil above the permafrost. During this short thaw, the normally frozen plain turns into a quagmire of puddles, bogs, and shallow lakes because the permafrost retards drainage. Humans and other animals entering this biome during the thaw are attacked by hordes of mosquitoes, deerflies, and blackflies.

The tundra landscape is covered with a mat of low-growing lichens, mosses, grasses, sedges, dwarf woody shrubs, and in alpine tundra some small shrubs and mountain wildflowers. Most of the tundra's permanent animal residents are creatures that burrow under the snow, such as lemmings—small, furry herbivores whose population rises rapidly and then crashes about every 4 years. Large herbivores, such as caribou, reindeer, and musk ox, slowly migrate south during the fall. Carnivores include ermine, snowy owls (which feed on lemmings), white foxes, and lynxes. The white coats of many of these animals help camouflage them from predators during the long winters. This barren biome is also inhabited by omnivores such as the grizzly bear. During the short summer, large numbers of migrating birds, especially waterfowl, nest in the tundra to feed on the swarms of insects.

Because the ground is so cold most of the year, decomposition occurs very slowly. Combined with the shallow soil and slow growth rate of plants, this means that tundra takes a long time to recover when it is destroyed or disrupted—which is why environmentalists are concerned about the long-term ecological effects of running oil and gas pipelines through this type of biome.

In this chapter we have seen how various physical and chemical factors can influence the distribution of plants and animals in an ecosystem. With this background in ecosystem structure, we are ready to learn more about what goes on in an ecosystem as its plant and animal species interact with one another and with their abiotic environment.

We sang the songs that carried in their melodies all the sounds of nature—the running waters, the sighing of winds, and the calls of the animals. Teach these to your children that they may come to love nature as we love it.

Grand Council Fire of American Indians

Discussion Topics

1. Explain what is meant by the statement that the sun is a nuclear fusion reactor.

2. Would you rather be exposed to electromagnetic radiation with a short or a long wavelength? Explain why people who spend a lot of time getting suntans may get skin cancer.

3. Distinguish among *ecosystem, ecosphere, population,* and *community,* and give an example of each. Rank them by increasing complexity or level of organization of matter.

4. List the three major types of biotic components and the three major types of abiotic components of an ecosystem.

5. How can an area have bad weather and a good climate?

6. How is the climate of an area normally affected by the presence of each of the following: (a) mountain ranges, (b) an ocean, (c) a large lake, and (d) warm ocean currents?

7. Does an ecosystem really exist? Explain.

8. Distinguish among herbivores, carnivores, and omnivores, and give two examples of each.

9. Distinguish between parasites and detritus feeders.

10. a. How would you set up a self-sustaining aquarium for tropical fish?

    b. Suppose you had a balanced aquarium sealed with a transparent glass top. Can life continue in the aquarium indefinitely as long as the sun shines regularly on it?

    c. Which of the following will probably be the limiting factor: the oxygen supply in the air above the water, the original oxygen supply dissolved in the water, or the supply of nitrogen in the soil at the bottom?

11. A friend cleans out your aquarium and removes all of the soil and plants, leaving only the fish and water. What will happen?

12. a. A bumper sticker asks "Have you thanked a green plant today?" Give two reasons for thanking a green plant.

    b. Trace back the materials comprising the sticker and see whether the sticker itself represents a sound application of the slogan.

13. a. What is a limiting factor?

    b. Give one possible limiting factor for each of the following: a desert, the open ocean, the arctic tundra, and the floor of a tropical rain forest.

14. What might be limiting factors for the human population on earth? Defend your choice.

15. Use the concept of balanced input and output of heat by plants to explain why there are few, if any, trees on a grassland and why grass has thin, needlelike blades instead of broad, flat leaves.

4

Ecosystem Function: How Do Ecosystems Work?

Earth and water, if not too blatantly abused, can be made to produce again and again for the benefit of all. The key is wise stewardship.

Stewart L. Udall

4-1 Energy Flow and Chemical Cycling

What keeps you, an oak tree, a squirrel, a termite, and other living organisms alive? To survive, you and every other form of life must have an almost continuous *input* of both energy and matter. Merely receiving energy and matter, however, will not keep

Enrichment Studies 5 and 6 are related to this chapter.

you alive. An *output* of degraded energy (heat) and waste matter must also flow from an organism. To remain alive, the input and output of energy and matter must be in balance. Thus, the life of an organism depends on the *one-way flow of both matter and energy.*

In order to be self-sustaining, the ecosphere and any ecosystem depends on *matter cycling*—not matter flow—and *energy flow*, as summarized in Figure 4-1. At the ecosystem and ecosphere levels, life depends on energy flow because, according to the second law of thermodynamics (Section 2-3), *energy quality can never be recycled.* In any ecosystem high-quality energy enters (usually as sunlight), moves through organisms, and eventually escapes to space as low-quality heat energy. Life at the ecosystem and ecosphere levels, however, depends on matter cycling, not on one-way matter flow, because according to the law of conservation of matter

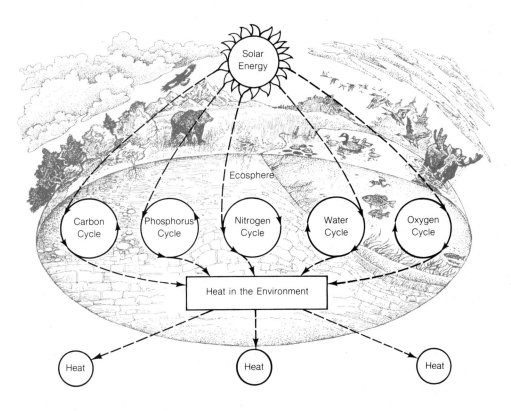

Figure 4-1 Life on earth depends on the cycling of critical chemicals and the one-way flow of energy through the ecosphere. Dashed lines represent energy flow and solid lines represent chemical cycling.

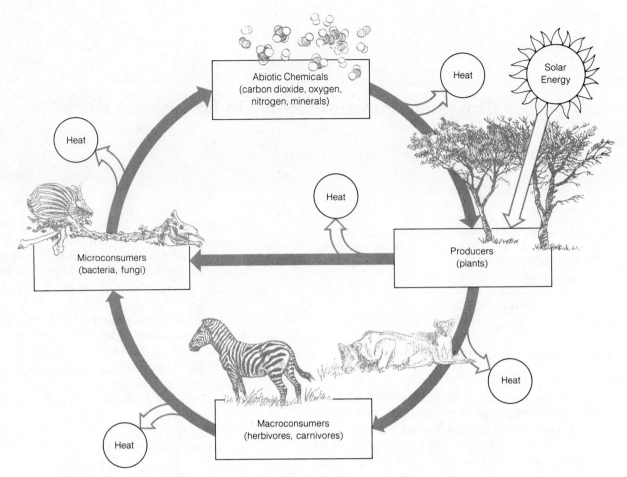

Figure 4-2 A summary of ecosystem structure and function. The major structural components (energy, chemicals, and organisms) of an ecosystem are connected through the functions of energy flow (open arrows) and chemical cycling (solid arrows).

(Section 2-1) matter can neither be created nor destroyed—only changed from one form to another. While the chemicals essential for life must eventually be cycled completely in the ecosphere, chemical cycling in an ecosystem need not be as complete. Most of the matter in a stable ecosystem remains there for a long time. But some of this matter flows from one ecosystem to another because the various ecosystems on earth are interconnected.

Thus, *we can generally answer the question "What happens in an ecosystem?" by saying that energy flows and matter cycles.* These two major ecosystem functions connect the various structural parts of an ecosystem so that life is maintained, as summarized in Figure 4-2.

In the remainder of this chapter we examine these two functional processes in ecosystems. First, we examine energy flow at the ecosystem level. This is followed by a look at how carbon, oxygen, nitrogen, phosphorus, and water are cycled through

ecosystems and the ecosphere in *biogeochemical cycles* (*bio* meaning "living," *geo* for water, rocks, and soil, and *chemical* for the matter that is cycled by being changed from one chemical to another). Then we will look at an organism's *ecological niche*—a concept that summarizes how life forms participate in energy flow and chemical cycling in an ecosystem.

4-2 Energy Flow in Ecosystems: Food Chains, Food Webs, and Energy Productivity

Food Chains In an ecosystem there is almost no such thing as waste matter. One organism's waste or death is another organism's food. A caterpillar eats a leaf; a robin eats the caterpillar; a hawk eats the robin. When the plant, caterpillar, robin, and hawk die, they are in turn consumed by decom-

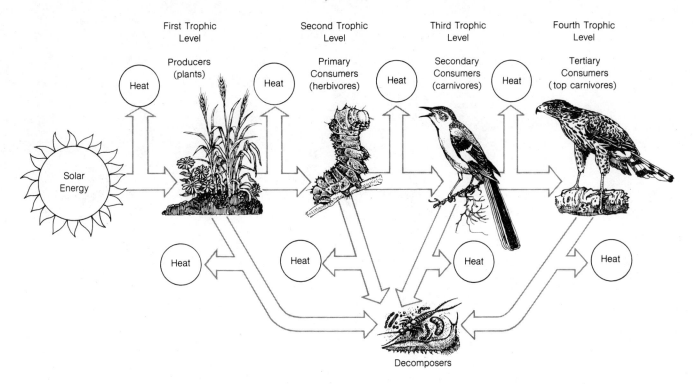

First Trophic Level — Producers (plants)

Second Trophic Level — Primary Consumers (herbivores)

Third Trophic Level — Secondary Consumers (carnivores)

Fourth Trophic Level — Tertiary Consumers (top carnivores)

Solar Energy

Heat

Decomposers

Figure 4-3 A food chain. The arrows show how chemical energy in food flows through various trophic levels, with most of the high-quality chemical energy being degraded to low-quality heat in accordance with the second law of thermodynamics.

posers (Figure 4-3). In general, the flow of energy and the cycling nutrient matter through an ecosystem is the study of what eats or decomposes what. A sequence of transfers of nutrients and energy from one organism to another when one organism eats or decomposes another is called a **food chain** (Figure 4-3).

The various feeding levels of producers and consumers in a food chain are called **trophic levels** (from the Greek *trophikos* for "nourishment" or "food"). As shown in Figure 4-3, all producers belong to the first trophic level, all primary consumers, whether feeding on living or dead producers, belong to the second trophic level, and so on.

Ecologists sometimes distinguish between two major types of food chains in an ecosystem: *grazing food chains* and *detritus food chains* (Figure 4-4). In a **grazing food chain,** green plants are eaten by herbivores, which in turn may be eaten by carnivores. In a **detritus food chain,** decomposers consume the organic waste products and dead organic matter (*detritus*) or partially decomposed tissues of other organisms. These two types of food chains are interrelated (Figure 4-3) because eventually all organisms die and become part of the detritus food chain. Figure 4-4 also shows that aquatic food chains

often have a larger number of trophic levels, or links, than land-based food chains. As omnivores, humans can eat plants and animals. However, *most people on earth function as herbivores in grazing food chains,* getting an average of 89 percent (worldwide) and 64 percent (in the United States) of their food from vegetables, cereals, and fruits.

Food Webs The food chain concept is useful for tracing matter cycling and energy flow in an ecosystem, but it is important to recognize that simple food chains, such as those shown in Figure 4-4, rarely exist by themselves. Many animals feed on several different types of food at the same trophic level. In addition, omnivores, such as humans, bears, and rats, eat several different kinds of plants and animals at several trophic levels. For example, birds that normally eat seeds may switch to insects in the spring. Foxes may gorge themselves on mice when they are abundant, go after rabbits when mice become scarce, eat berries when they are ripe, and switch to grasshoppers and apples in the fall.

Because of these more complex feeding patterns, natural ecosystems consist of interconnected networks of many feeding relationships called **food**

Type of Food Chain	Producer	Primary Consumer	Secondary Consumer	Tertiary Consumer	Quaternary Consumer

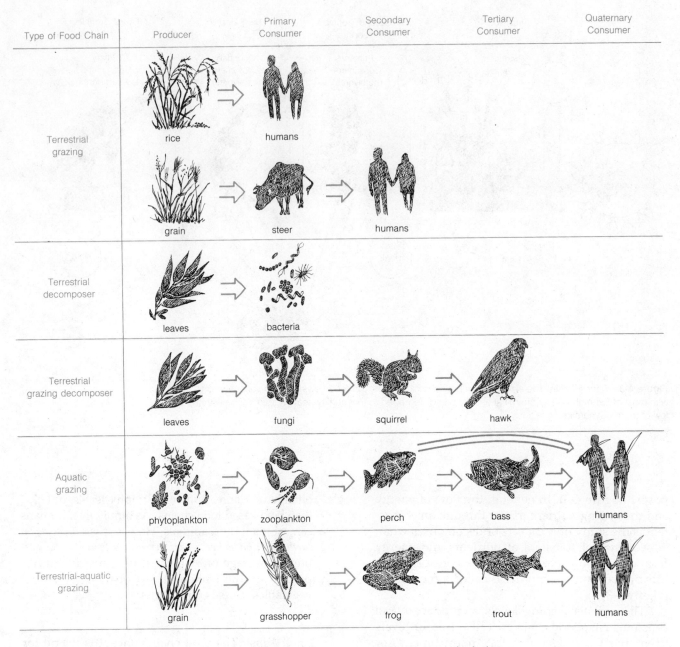

Figure 4-4 Some typical food chains. Upon their death, the plants and consumer animals shown in these simplified chains are broken down by decomposers.

webs, as shown in greatly simplified form in Figure 4-5. For more information on interactions among species in food webs, see Enrichment Study 6.

Food Chains, Food Webs, and the Second Law of Thermodynamics Because of the second law of thermodynamics (Section 2-3), about 90 percent of the high-quality chemical energy stored in food nutrients at one trophic level is *not* transferred to the next trophic in a food chain or web. *Only about 10 percent of the high-quality chemical energy available at one trophic level is transferred and stored in usable form in the bodies of the organisms at the next trophic level. This is sometimes called the* **ten percent rule.***

---

*Actual percentages vary from 2 to 30 percent with species. Typically, only 10 percent of the energy entering the plant population is available to herbivores. For warm-blooded carnivores the conversion efficiency is usually lower than 10 percent, whereas for cold-blooded ones it may be 20 or 30 percent. Ten percent seems an appropriate average.

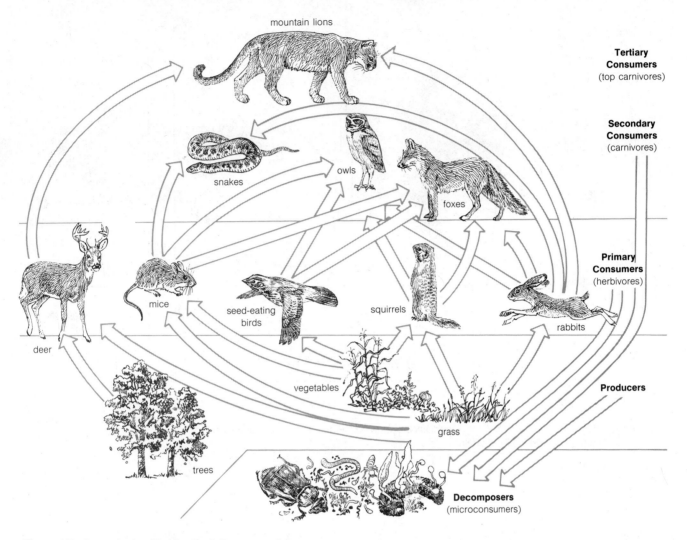

Figure 4-5 A greatly simplified food web for a terrestrial ecosystem.

The remaining 90 percent of the chemical energy transferred from one trophic level to another is degraded and lost as low-quality heat to the environment. Figure 4-6 gives a striking picture of this loss of usable energy at each step in a simple food chain. Such a diagram is known as a *pyramid of energy* because of its shape. Note that the greater the number of steps in a food chain, the greater the loss of usable energy.

We get the same picture by looking at the number of organisms of a particular type that can be supported at each trophic level from a given input of solar energy at the producer trophic level. This *pyramid of numbers* in Figure 4-6 shows that in going from one trophic level up to another the total number of organisms that can be supported decreases drastically. For example, a million phytoplankton producers in a small pond may support 10,000 zooplankton primary consumers. These in turn may

support 100 perch, which might feed one human for a month or so. The pyramid of numbers helps explain why there are more plant-eating rabbits than flesh-eating tigers on the earth—and would be even if humans didn't hunt and kill tigers.

Two important principles emerge from a consideration of the loss of available energy at successively higher trophic levels in the food chains that make up more complex food webs. *First, all life and all forms of food begin with sunlight and green plants. Second, the shorter the food chain, the less the loss of usable energy.* This means that a larger population of humans can be supported if people eat grains directly (for example, rice → human), rather than eating animals that fed upon the grains in a longer food chain such as grain → steer → human. However, a diet based on only one or two plants lacks some of the proteins essential for good health, as discussed in Chapter 9.

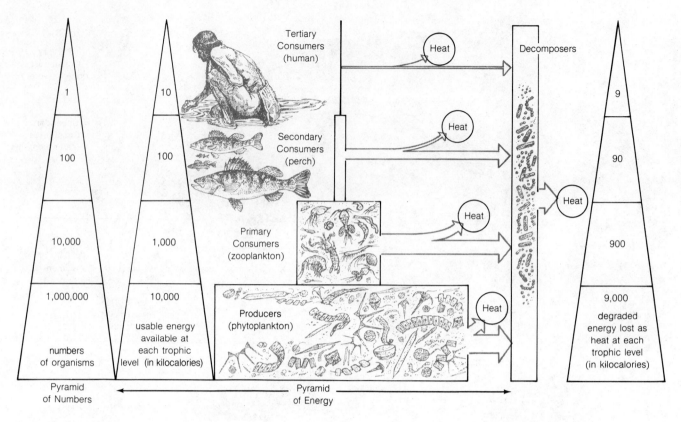

Figure 4-6 Hypothetical pyramids of energy and numbers showing the decrease in usable energy available at each succeeding trophic level in a food chain.

Gross and Net Primary Productivity by Plants The rate at which green plants convert solar energy by photosynthesis into chemical energy is called the **gross primary productivity.** This is the total rate of photosynthesis in a specified area of land over a given time and is usually reported in kilocalories of energy produced per square meter per year.*

Gross primary productivity, however, is not an accurate measure of the amount of energy available to a consumer organism that eats a green plant. Plants and animals must continually break down some of their chemicals to get the energy to stay alive, a process called *cellular respiration.* As high-quality chemical energy is used for cellular respiration, it is degraded to low-quality heat and flows into the environment. Thus, the energy an organ-

ism uses for cellular respiration is not available as food or chemical energy to an animal that consumes the plant. The rate at which plants produce usable food or chemical energy is called **net primary productivity** (also expressed in kilocalories per square meter per year). It is obtained by subtracting the rate at which plants use energy to stay alive (rate of cellular respiration) from the total rate at which they produce energy (gross primary production):

$$\begin{matrix} \text{net primary} \\ \text{productivity} \end{matrix} = \begin{matrix} \text{gross primary} \\ \text{productivity} \end{matrix} - \begin{matrix} \text{rate of cellular} \\ \text{respiration} \end{matrix}$$

Note that both gross and net primary productivity represent rates at which a certain amount of materials that store chemical energy are produced. They should not be confused with the total amount or yield of energy material.

In a given ecosystem, net primary productivity is influenced by such variables as the availability of sunlight and nutrients, temperature, precipitation, duration of the growing season, the occurrence of fires, and the age of producer organisms. For ex-

---

*The joule (abbreviated J and pronounced *jool*) is the standard unit of heat in the metric system of measurement. Other widely used energy units are the kilojoule (kJ), calorie (cal), and kilocalorie (kcal):

$$1 \text{ kJ} = 1{,}000 \text{ or } 10^3 \text{J}$$
$$1 \text{ cal} = 4.186 \text{ J}$$
$$1 \text{ kcal} = 1{,}000 \text{ or } 10^3 \text{ cal} = 4{,}186 \text{ J}$$

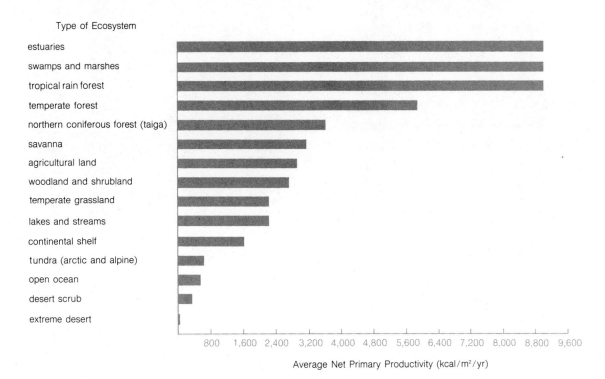

Type of Ecosystem

estuaries
swamps and marshes
tropical rain forest
temperate forest
northern coniferous forest (taiga)
savanna
agricultural land
woodland and shrubland
temperate grassland
lakes and streams
continental shelf
tundra (arctic and alpine)
open ocean
desert scrub
extreme desert

800 1,600 2,400 3,200 4,000 4,800 5,600 6,400 7,200 8,000 8,800 9,600

Average Net Primary Productivity (kcal/m²/yr)

Figure 4-7 Estimated average net primary productivity by plants in major types of ecosystems.

ample, young understory trees in a forest have a high net productivity because much of the energy input is used for growth. However, as they get older and larger, more of their energy input is used to maintain existing plant parts so that net primary productivity decreases.

Net primary productivity is an important concept in food production. Farmers attempt to grow crops yielding the highest net primary productivity in each area of the world. Ecologists have estimated the average annual net primary production per square meter for different major land and water ecosystems throughout the world. Figure 4-7 shows that the highest net productivities are found in estuaries, swamps and marshes, and tropical rain forests and the lowest in tundra, open ocean, and desert ecosystems.

From Figure 4-7 you might conclude that we should clear tropical forests and plant crops there and harvest the estuaries, swamps, and marshes to help feed the growing human population. Such a conclusion is incorrect for two reasons. First, the net primary productivities shown are for plants normally found in such ecosystems. The plants (mostly grasses) in estuaries, swamps, and marshes are not very useful for direct human consumption, although they are extremely important as food sources and spawning areas for many types of fish,

shrimp, and other forms of aquatic life that provide protein for humans. In tropical forests most of the nutrients are stored in the trees and lesser vegetation, rather than in the soil (see Chapter 8). When trees in these forests are cleared the exposed soil is so infertile that food crops can only be grown for a short time without massive and expensive inputs of commercial fertilizers.

The second reason is that the data in Figure 4-7 do not show how much of each ecosystem is available throughout the world. Figure 4-8 shows the world net productivity for major types of ecosystems. Since the total area of estuaries is small, it drops way down the list. Similarly, because so much of the world surface is covered with oceans, the world's open ocean ecosystems now head the list. But we can also misinterpret these numbers. The world net productivity is high for oceans because they cover so much of the globe—not because they have a high productivity per square meter per year. Harvesting widely dispersed algae and seaweeds found in the open ocean requires enormous amounts of energy. Because of the first and second laws of thermodynamics (Sections 2-2 and 2-3), this would take more fossil fuel and energy sources than the food energy we would harvest.

A basic ecological rule is that crops can normally be grown productively in ecosystems that in their natural

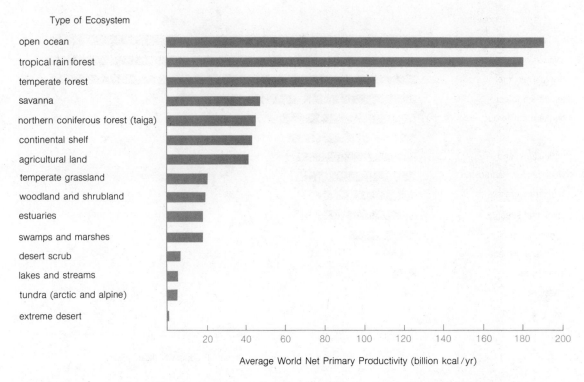

Type of Ecosystem

open ocean	
tropical rain forest	
temperate forest	
savanna	
northern coniferous forest (taiga)	
continental shelf	
agricultural land	
temperate grassland	
woodland and shrubland	
estuaries	
swamps and marshes	
desert scrub	
lakes and streams	
tundra (arctic and alpine)	
extreme desert	

20   40   60   80   100   120   140   160   180   200

Average World Net Primary Productivity (billion kcal / yr)

Figure 4-8 Estimated average world net primary productivity by plants in major types of ecosystems.

state can support a relatively large number of plants similar to the food crop plants. Since most food crops are
grasses or closely related to grasses, the bulk of
agriculture is carried out in temperate grasslands
and on cleared temperate forests. Yet people still
talk about harvesting algae in the oceans and converting tropical forests to vast fields of single crops
to feed large numbers of people.

With this overview of energy flow in ecosystems, we are now ready to look at chemical cycling,
the second major functional process occurring in
ecosystems.

4-3   Chemical Cycling in Ecosystems: Carbon, Oxygen, Nitrogen, Phosphorus, and Water Cycles

Types of Biogeochemical Cycles   In chemical terms,
life can almost be summed up in six words: *carbon,
oxygen, hydrogen, nitrogen, phosphorus,* and *sulfur.*
Although about 40 of the 92 naturally occurring
chemical elements are essential for life, these 6 elements make up over 95 percent of the mass of all
living organisms. These 6 plus a few other required
in relatively large quantities are called **macronutrients.** Iron, manganese, copper, iodine, and other
elements needed in only minute quantities are called
micronutrients.

Because we have a fixed supply of these six
macronutrient elements, they must continuously
cycle from their reservoirs of air, water, and soil
through the food webs of the ecosphere and back
again to their reservoirs in **biogeochemical cycles.**
This means that one of the oxygen molecules you
just inhaled may be one you inhaled 2 years ago or
it may be one inhaled by your grandmother or by
Cleopatra many centuries ago. This movement of
key chemical elements from organism to organism
and from species to species is one of the major factors binding each ecosystem and the world's ecosystems together.

There are three types of these biogeochemical
cycles: gaseous, sedimentary, and hydrologic (water).
The **gaseous cycles,** in which the atmosphere is the
primary reservoir, include the *carbon, oxygen,* and
nitrogen cycles. The **sedimentary cycles** move materials from land to sea and back again. They include
the *phosphorus, sulfur, calcium, magnesium,* and *potassium cycles.* The *hydrologic cycle* represents the cyclical movement of water from the sea to the land
and back to the sea again.

In all chemical cycles, both the nature of the
cycling process and the rate at which critical chemicals are cycled are important. For example, all water
on earth eventually goes through the photosynthesis process in plants, but at a rate estimated to
be once every 2 million years. Similarly, the oxygen
gas produced by green plants through photosyn-

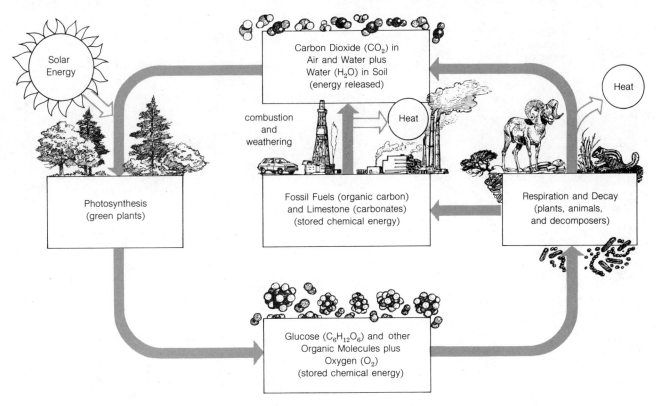

Figure 4-9 A simplified version of the carbon and oxygen cycles, showing chemical cycling (solid arrows) and one-way energy flow (open arrows).

thesis cycles from the atmosphere and back again about every 2,000 years, and the gaseous carbon dioxide given off by all plants and animals when they break down food molecules by cellular respiration cycles about once every 300 years. While vast quantities of critical chemicals remain in their major reservoirs for long periods of time, these chemicals flow fairly rapidly from organism to organism.

Carbon and Oxygen Cycles Carbon is the basic building block of the large organic molecules necessary for life. Most plants found on land get their carbon from the carbon dioxide (CO_2) that makes up 0.03 percent of the atmosphere. The ocean's microscopic floating plants, known collectively as phytoplankton, get their carbon from the much larger amount of carbon dioxide dissolved in the waters that cover three-fourths of the earth's surface. These green plants use solar energy to combine carbon dioxide with water (H_2O) to form organic nutrients such as glucose ($C_6H_{12}O_6$) in the process of **photosynthesis,** summarized as follows:

$$\text{carbon dioxide} + \text{water} + \text{solar energy} \rightarrow \text{sugars, such as glucose} + \text{oxygen}$$

$$6CO_2 + 6H_2O + \text{solar energy} \rightarrow C_6H_{12}O_6 + 6O_2$$

This ability of green plants to synthesize sugars makes most other forms of life possible.

Producers, consumers, and decomposers transform a portion of the carbon in the food they synthesize or eat back into carbon dioxide and water by the process of *cellular respiration.* This **cellular respiration** process provides the energy plants and animals need to live, and can be summarized as follows:

$$\text{sugars, such as glucose} + \text{oxygen} \rightarrow \text{carbon dioxide} + \text{water} + \text{energy}$$

$$C_6H_{12}O_6 + 6O_2 \rightarrow 6CO_2 + 6H_2O + \text{energy}$$

The photosynthesis and cellular respiration processes both consist of a large number (80 to 100) of different chemical reactions operating in sequence. However, from the equations just given, we see that the overall reaction for the sequence involved in respiration is the opposite of that for the photosynthesis process. Thus, photosynthesis and respiration operate together as a closed cycle through which plants produce oxygen needed by animals and absorb the carbon dioxide given off by animals, as shown in greatly simplified form in Figure 4-9. Note from Figure 4-9 that some carbon is tied up in minerals such as fossil fuels and carbonate rock formations (for example, limestone or $CaCO_3$). This

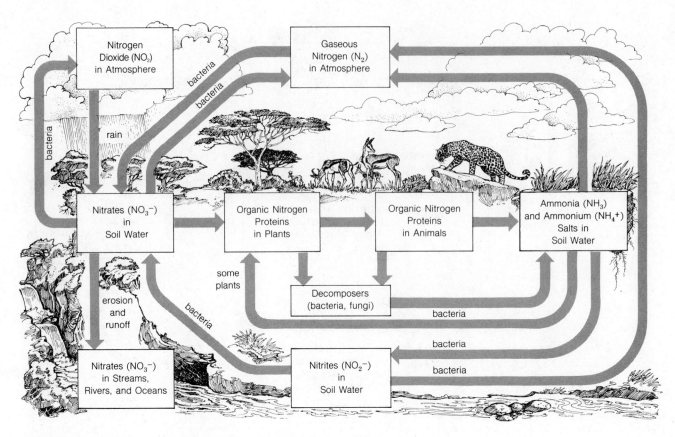

Figure 4-10 A simplified version of the nitrogen cycle (energy flow not shown).

carbon is returned to the cycle as carbon dioxide and water when fossil fuels are burned and when carbonate rock formations slowly weather away.

Nitrogen Cycle Nitrogen is often a factor limiting the growth of plants (Chapter 8). Too little nitrogen can also cause malnutrition in humans (Chapter 9) because many of the body's essential functions require nitrogen-containing molecules, such as proteins, nucleic acids, vitamins, and hormones.

Although molecular nitrogen (N_2) makes up about 78 percent of the earth's atmosphere by volume, it is useless to plants and animals. Fortunately, in the gaseous nitrogen cycle—shown in simplified form in Figure 4-10—nitrogen-fixing bacteria in soil, blue-green algae in water, and symbiotic bacteria in nodules on alfalfa, clover, and other legumes (members of the pea family) convert, or "fix," gaseous nitrogen (N_2) to solid nitrate salts (containing nitrate, or NO_3^-, ions). A small amount of N_2 gas is also fixed by lightning. These nitrate salts dissolve easily in soil water and are taken up by plant roots. The plants then convert the nitrates to large nitrogen-containing protein molecules and other organic nitrogen molecules necessary for life.

Some of these nitrogen-containing protein mol-

ecules are then transferred to plant-eating animals and eventually to other animals that feed on them. When plants and animals die, decomposers break down these large organic nitrogen molecules into ammonia gas (NH_3) and water soluble salts containing ammonium ions (NH_4^+). Ammonia and ammonium are then converted by other groups of soil bacteria into water-soluble nitrite ions (NO_2^-), nitrogen (N_2) gas that returns to the atmosphere, or nitrous oxide (N_2O) gas that also ends up in the atmosphere (Figure 4-10).

Some plants can absorb the ammonium ions from salts dissolved in soil water and convert them to nitrogen-containing protein molecules. Another group of bacteria can add a third oxygen atom to nitrite ions and convert them to nitrate ions, which can be taken up by plants to begin the cycle again. Some nitrogen is temporarily lost from the cycle when soluble nitrate salts are washed from the soil into rivers and streams and eventually into the oceans.

Crop growth can be limited if there is not the right amount of nitrogen in the soil, primarily as nitrate (NO_3^-) and ammonium ions (NH_4^+). During World War I the German chemist Fritz Haber developed an industrial process—now called the *Haber process*—to convert nitrogen gas by reacting

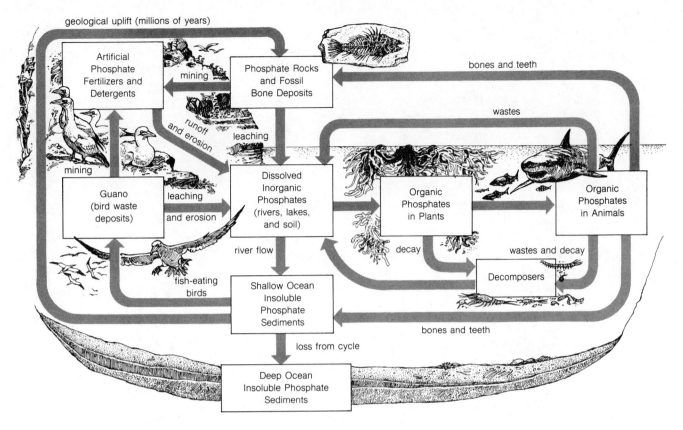

Figure 4-11   A simplified version of the phosphorus cycle (energy flow not shown).

it with hydrogen gas at high temperatures and pressures to produce ammonia gas.

$$\text{Haber process: } N_2 + 3H_2 \rightarrow 2NH_3$$

The ammonia gas can then be converted to ammonium salts and used as commercial fertilizer. Nitrate salts are also mined and used, along with ammonium salts, as artificial fertilizer to increase crop yields in nitrogen-deficient soils.

Phosphorus Cycle   Phosphorus (mainly in the form of phosphate ions, PO_4^{3-}) is an essential nutrient of both plants and animals. It is also a major constituent of the genetic material coded in DNA molecules, the energy storage compound adenosine triphosphate (ATP), and a component of cell membranes, bones, and teeth. Phosphate, together with nitrates and potassium, is a major ingredient in all modern commercial fertilizers.

The *phosphorus cycle*, shown in greatly simplified form in Figure 4-11, is a sedimentary cycle in which the earth's crust is the major reservoir. Phosphorus moves through this cycle primarily in the form of phosphate ions (PO_4^{3-}). The major reservoirs of phosphorus are phosphate rock deposits

on land and in shallow ocean sediments (Figure 4-11). Slowly, through weathering and erosion, the phosphates from these rock deposits are released into the ecosphere. Many of these phosphates wash into rivers and eventually to the oceans where they form insoluble phosphate deposits on the bottom of shallow ocean areas near the coast and in deep ocean sediments.

Fish catches and phosphate-rich waste matter—called *guano*—from fish-eating birds, such as pelicans, gannets, and cormorants, return some of this phosphate to the land. These returns, however, are small compared with the larger amounts of phosphate eroding from the land to the oceans each year as a result of natural processes and human activities. About 1.8 billion kilograms (2 million tons) of phosphates are mined each year in the United States (mostly from shallow ocean deposits in Florida) to produce fertilizers that replace some of the phosphates lost from farmland and lawns and to make phosphate detergents. Most phosphates in detergents are released to rivers as effluents from urban sewage treatment plants and eventually end up in the oceans.

Some of the phosphates released by chemical weathering of phosphate rocks flow fairly rapidly through plants and animals on their way to the

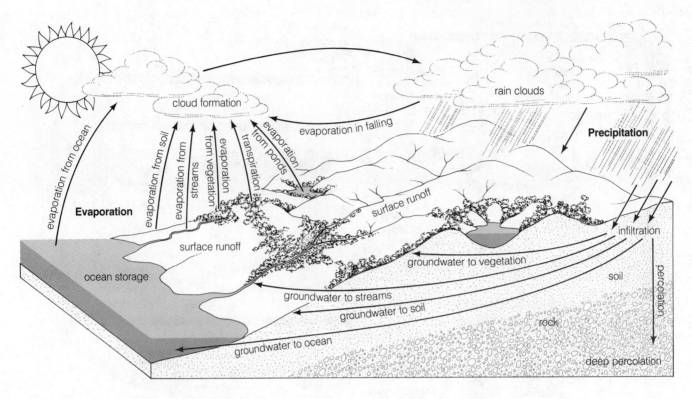

Figure 4-12 The hydrologic cycle. (Source: USDA.)

ocean. This occurs when phosphate rock is dissolved in water in the soil. The roots of plants absorb the phosphate ions and, when the plant is eaten, the phosphorus is passed on to animals. It eventually returns to the soil, rivers, and oceans as animal wastes and decay products.

Phosphorus, more than any other element, can become the limiting factor (Section 3-7) for plant growth in a number of ecosystems. The global consumption of phosphate as fertilizer is growing at 6.3 percent a year. In Asia, for example, it is estimated that between 1975 and 2000 the supply of phosphate fertilizer must increase tenfold to meet food demands. Even at this rate of growth world phosphate supplies are not likely to run out, although local and regional shortages exist and could get worse. These shortages are due primarily to uneven distribution of phosphate deposits and the rising cost of mining, processing, and shipping phosphate fertilizers throughout the world. Most of the world's phosphate rock deposits are not found in the heavily populated areas of the world most in need of phosphate fertilizers. Indeed, 73 percent of the world's phosphate rock is mined by the United States, the Soviet Union, and the Moroccan Sahara. Since 1974 the sharp rise in oil prices has led to a 50 percent increase in the price of phosphate rock,

preventing many LDCs from purchasing the fertilizer they need.

Water or Hydrologic Cycle   The **hydrologic** or **water cycle** (Figure 4-12) is a gigantic water distillation and distribution system. In this cycle, solar energy and gravity continuously move water from the oceans to the atmosphere; from the atmosphere to the land, oceans, other bodies of water; from bodies of water and the soil to living organisms; and from the land back to the oceans.

Incoming solar energy evaporates water from the oceans, lakes, rivers, soil, and plants (evaporation and transpiration) into the atmosphere. As warm air masses rise this water vapor can condense to form tiny droplets or ice crystals that make up clouds. Eventually these droplets or ice crystals coalesce and precipitate out of the clouds as rain, sleet, or snow falling onto the land or back into oceans, rivers, and lakes. Some of this fresh water becomes part of glaciers. Some sinks, or percolates, downward through the soil and ground to form the groundwater system. When rain falls faster than the rate at which water can infiltrate the soil, cement, or other material covering the land, water collects in puddles and ditches and runs off into nearby streams, rivers, and lakes. These streams and rivers carry water back to the oceans, completing the cycle. Water resources provided by this cycle are discussed further in Chapter 17.

4-4 The Niche Concept

Ecological Niches Now that the overall patterns of energy flow and chemical cycling in an ecosystem have been described, let's look more closely at the role that individual species or populations of organisms play in carrying out these processes. The **ecological niche** (pronounced *nitch*) is a description of a species' total functional role in an ecosystem. It describes what a particular species does in the ecosystem—how it transforms matter and energy, and how it responds to and modifies its physical and biotic environment.

The ecological niche, then, includes all of the physical, chemical, and biological factors that a species needs to survive, stay healthy, and reproduce in an ecosystem. To describe a species' niche we must know what it eats and what eats it, where it leaves its wastes, the ranges of temperature, wind, shade, sunlight, and various chemicals it can tolerate, its effects on other species and on the non-living parts of its environment, and what effects other species have on it. Determining the niche of an organism is so complex that we may never know as much as we would like about the niche of most plants and animals.

Ecological niche should not be confused with an organism's *habitat*, the physical location or locations where it lives such as the height above the ground in a forest canopy or the depth in the mud at the bottom of a pond. A common analogy is that an organism's *habitat* refers to its "address" in an ecosystem and an organism's *ecological niche* is its "occupation" and "life-style" in an ecosystem. For example, the habitat of a robin includes such areas as woodlands, forests, parks, pasture land, meadows, orchards, gardens, and yards. In contrast, its ecological niche includes such things as using trees as nesting sites and roosts; eating insects, earthworms, and fruit; and dispersing fruit and berry seeds in its droppings.

Some niches, such as those occupied by producers, are found in every major ecosystem. Others, especially those for some animal and decomposer species, are highly specialized. For example, the niche of some birds such as cattle egrets involves their eating various parasites and ticks found on or near grazing animals such as elephants, cattle, sheep, and deer. Niches can also be limited by physical

conditions. In moist soils, earthworms mix humus, and their burrows loosen and aerate the soil. In dry soils, where earthworms can't exist, this ecological niche is taken over by burrowing ants.

Competitive Exclusion Principle In general, *no two species in the same ecosystem can occupy exactly the same ecological niche indefinitely.* This is known as the **competitive exclusion principle**. The more similar the niches of two species, the more they will compete for the same food, shelter, space, and other critical resources. When two species try to occupy exactly the same niche, one will probably have to relocate, switch its habits, or become extinct, as discussed in more detail in Enrichment Study 6. Thus, each species has a unique niche.

Different species may live together in the same habitat yet have quite different ecological niches. For example, two different species of fish-eating birds, the common cormorant and the shag cormorant, look alike, fish in a similar manner, and live on the same cliffs near the ocean. Careful observations, however, reveal that each species has a different ecological niche. The shag cormorant fishes mainly in shallow water for sprats and sand eels and nests on the lower portion of the cliffs. The common cormorant fishes primarily for shrimp and a few fish farther out to sea and lives nearer the top of the cliffs than the shag cormorant.

Different species, however, occupy similar ecological niches in ecosystems located in diverse places. Such species are called **ecological equivalents**. Grasslands, for example, are found all over the world. The niche of grassland grazers can be occupied by bison and pronghorn antelope in North America, wild horses and antelope in Eurasia, kangaroo in Australia, and antelope and zebras in Africa. In many regions, a number of these ecologically equivalent herbivores have been replaced by domesticated cattle and sheep.

Knowing the niches of species helps ecologists predict what might happen if a new factor is added to, or eliminated from, a given ecosystem—for example, if heated water from a nuclear power plant is added to an aquatic ecosystem or if a new species is introduced to or an existing one eliminated from a habitat.

Ideally, in any ecosystem no foreign species or new physical or chemical factor should be deliberately introduced or eliminated without careful study of the effect of the change on various species in that ecosystem (Chapter 11). Even careful study is not always enough, for in a new habitat an organism may change its nesting or feeding habits. If it has no predators or parasites its population could explode, causing it to become a pest (Section 9-9).

Niche and Population Size The niche concept helps explain why the population size of the various species found in a stable ecosystem remains fairly constant in the long run regardless of the number of offspring a species can have. The **carrying capacity** or maximum number of individuals of each species that can live in a particular ecosystem is set by the number of niche spaces available for that species. Just as there can be no more steelworkers than there are steelworker jobs in a given area of the country, there can be no more mosquitoes than there are mosquito niche spaces (jobs) in a particular ecosystem.

Species like mosquitoes that lay large numbers of eggs may increase their numbers for a short time, but eventually their numbers will be controlled by the numbers of niche spaces available to them in a particular ecosystem. In other words, *the reproductive effort of individuals makes no difference to the eventual size of the population of a species in a stable ecosystem.*

Despite this limitation each individual in most species tries to breed as fast as it can. This is the only way an individual can ensure that its genetic material, in the form of its offspring and subsequent generations of these offspring, successfully occupies as many as possible of the present and future niche spaces in an ecosystem. This is what is meant by "survival of the fittest."

In general, species have developed two approaches to help ensure that their hereditary material occupies as many future niche spaces as possible. Ecologist Paul Colinvaux calls these two breeding strategies "the small egg gambit" and "the large-young gambit." The most common breeding strategy is for an individual in a species such as the housefly, mosquito, or dandelion to produce thousands of tiny eggs or seeds. Because most of these offspring die at an early age, a large number is produced and the chances of a few of the young surviving and reproducing is increased.

Instead of having as many as possible tiny offspring and letting them fend for themselves, other species—such as horses, tigers, white sharks, and people—have a few large offspring and nurse them until they are big and strong. This is the surest method of populating future ecological niches with one's descendants *provided that an individual does not have too many or too few offspring.* If there are too many fairly helpless offspring, the parents may not be able to protect them or to supply them with enough food. If there are too few offspring and they are all killed prematurely (for example, by disease, accident, or predation) the genetic line ends.

Our Ecological Niche What niche do human beings occupy? Most plants and animals are limited to specific habitats in the ecosphere because they can tolerate only a narrow range of climatic and other environmental conditions. But some generalist species—such as flies, cockroaches, mice, and humans—are very adaptable, can live over much of the planet, and eat a wide range of foods.

Humans occupy a generalist niche. In addition to obtaining energy and nutrients by eating a variety of plants and animals, humans also have learned to utilize solar energy stored for millions of years in deposits of coal, oil, and natural gas. With this fossil fuel energy subsidy as well as other forms of energy (draft animals, biomass, nuclear, hydropower, wind, and geothermal), humans have been able to expand their habitat and niche greatly on the globe. This has led to many benefits. At the same time, this ever-increasing use and flow of energy through industrialized societies is a major factor in today's environmental problems (Section 2-4).

In this chapter and the preceding one, we have seen that *the essential feature of the living and nonliving parts of an ecosystem is their interdependence.* In the next chapter we shall see that this interdependence is a key to understanding how ecosystems can change in response to stresses from natural and human sources.

We cannot command nature except by obeying her.
Sir Francis Bacon

Discussion Topics

1. Explain how the survival of an individual organism depends on energy flow and matter flow, whereas the ecosystem in which it lives is able to survive only by energy flow and matter cycling.

2. Why can't energy be recycled in an ecosystem?

3. What effect, if any, can each of the following activities have on the global heat balance, or average temperature of the earth's atmosphere?

   a. operating air conditioning by electricity

   b. driving a car

   c. using a nuclear power plant to produce electricity

4. Using the second law of thermodynamics, explain why there is such a sharp decrease in high-quality energy along each step of a food chain. Doesn't an energy loss at each step violate the first law of thermodynamics? Explain.

5. Using the second law of thermodynamics, explain why many people in LDCs must exist primarily on a vegetarian diet. (A detailed discussion of this topic is found in Chapter 9.)

6. Explain why a balanced vegetarian diet is sound ecological practice. Trace the effects of vegetarianism on the carbon, oxygen, and phosphorus cycles and on global heat balance.

7. Distinguish among a pyramid of numbers, a pyramid of biomass, and a pyramid of energy. How does the inefficiency of energy transfer affect the number of humans that can be supported in a more developed country such as the United States? In a less developed country?

8. What did you have for lunch or supper today? Trace each food item back through various food chains and through the carbon and oxygen cycles. What effect does growing and eating these foods have on the global heat balance?

9. Why don't lions hunt mice?

10. Why would you expect to find more rabbits than coyotes on earth even if humans did not kill and poison large numbers of coyotes?

11. Why is the net primary productivity of a forest lower than its gross primary productivity? Give the two types of ecosystems with the highest net primary productivity and the two with the lowest.

12. a. It has been proposed that we clear the lush tropical rain forests and convert them to modern farmlands. What might happen?

    b. Explain how the extensive draining, filling, dredging, building, and polluting of estuaries, marshes, and swamps can decrease the ability of the planet to support its human population.

    c. Criticize the statement that we can farm the sea to feed the world's increasing population. (See Chapter 9 for a detailed discussion of this question.)

13. What effect does each of the following have on the carbon and oxygen cycles?

    a. using fossil fuels to provide air conditioning

    b. using a light or any electrical appliance (trace electricity from the wall plug back to its source)

    c. driving an automobile or motorcycle

    d. making an automobile

14. When you throw away your trash, where does it go? Trace it through the carbon, oxygen, and nitrogen cycles.

15. What effect does fertilizing a lawn or eating a meat-based diet have on the carbon, oxygen, nitrogen, and phosphorus cycles?

16. Explain how the carbon and oxygen cycles are linked together.

17. Why is phosphorus more often a limiting factor in ecosystems than oxygen, nitrogen, or carbon?

18. How does a species' habitat differ from its ecological niche? Give four examples of ecological equivalents.

19. Compare the ecological niches of humans in a small town and in a large city and that of humans in a more developed country and in a less developed country.

5

Changes in Ecosystems: What Can Happen to Ecosystems?

*When we try to pick out anything by itself we find it
hitched to everything else in the universe.*

John Muir

Some people think "balance of nature" means that
ecosystems do not change. Nothing could be further from the truth. *Ecosystems are dynamic, not static.*
The natural plant and animal communities found
in some ecosystems gradually change their environment in ways that eliminate some species and
make way for invasion by others. The plants and
animals in ecosystems also undergo change as they
attempt to adapt to environmental stresses such as
fires, floods, drought, volcanic eruptions, erosion,
earthquakes, farming, industrialization, pollution,
urbanization, and short- and long-term changes in
climate. Although ecosystems are always changing, they also resist being disturbed and have an
ability to restore themselves after an outside disturbance if it is not too drastic. This ability to adapt
and yet sustain themselves if not pushed too far is
truly a remarkable feature of ecosystems. In this
chapter we will look first at how ecosystems evolve
and change normally without human influence and
then at some human influences on ecosystems.

5-1 Ecological Succession

Types of Ecological Succession   Tropical rain forest, oak-hickory forest, and coral reef ecosystems
do not spring full-blown from the ground or sea.
They develop over decades or centuries, starting
with the colonization of an uninhabited site by a
natural community of *pioneer species* (such as lichens
or weeds)—plants that can grow under harsh conditions such as intense sunlight, wide temperature
swings, or soil poor in nutrients. Typically such
species have short life cycles, must start over each

year, and are small and low-growing. These species
are sometimes called *opportunist (r-selected) species*
because their strategy is to put all of their energy
intake into producing abundant small seeds that
can be scattered widely. These pioneers are slowly
joined and then gradually replaced by other species
to form a new natural community as the ecosystem
matures.

Most of the plants in mature ecosystems such
as perennial herbs and trees do not put most of
their energy into seed production. Instead, they
produce relatively few seeds and develop big roots
for underground storage of some of their energy
input, helping them to last the winter and begin
their seasonal growth the next year early and with
survival advantage over pioneer species. Species
adopting this survival strategy are sometimes called
equilibrium (K-selected) species that are specialized for
life in a narrower range of environmental conditions than opportunist species.

Thus, with time the opportunist species that
first invade a patch of barren ground are eventually
replaced by natural communities with increasing
numbers of equilibrium species. This repeated
replacement of one kind of natural community of
organisms by another over a period of time is called
ecological succession.

If not severely disrupted by natural disasters
or by human activities, most ecosystems eventually
reach a stage that is much more stable than those
preceding. This is sometimes called a **climax ecosystem,** or *climax natural community*. Most climax
ecosystems tend to be self-perpetuating and long-
lived, as long as climate and other major environmental factors remain essentially the same. Some
ecosystems, however, require disturbances such as
fire in order to reach the climax stage of succession.

Ecologists recognize two types of ecological
succession: primary and secondary. When successional changes take place in a soilless area previously devoid of life, this is known as **primary
succession.** Examples of such areas are newly
exposed bare rocks from retreating glaciers, cooled
volcanic lava, newly exposed sand dunes, and surface-mined areas from which all topsoil has been

Enrichment Studies 1, 2, 3, 5, 6, 7, 11, 13, and 14 are related to
this chapter.

exposed rocks

lichens
and mosses

small herbs
and shrubs

heath mat

jack pine,
black spruce,
and aspen

balsam fir,
paper birch, and
white spruce
climax community

Time ⟶

Figure 5-1 Primary ecological succession on a single patch of land on Isle Royale in northern Lake Superior over several hundred years.

removed. On such barren surfaces, primary succession from bare rock to a mature forest may take thousands of years.

A more common form of succession is **secondary succession,** which occurs when successional changes take place in a previously inhabited area that was disturbed and set back to an earlier stage of succession. In this case soil is present, so new vegetation can sprout within a few weeks. Examples include succession on abandoned farmland, forests that have been burned or cut, new ponds that are abandoned, and heavily polluted streams. Let's look at some examples of primary and secondary succession.

Primary Succession   During the early part of this century, William S. Cooper was able to trace the stages of primary succession from bare rock to a balsam, fir, paper birch, and white spruce climax natural community on Isle Royale in northern Lake Superior (Figure 5-1).

First, retreating glaciers exposed bare rock. Wind, rain, and frost weathered the rock surfaces to form tiny cracks and holes. Water collecting in these depressions slowly dissolved minerals out of

the rock's surface. These minerals were able to support hardy pioneer plants, such as lichens and mosses. Gradually these early invaders covered the rock surface, dissolving additional minerals from the rock and depositing organic matter from their dead bodies. Decomposer organisms then moved in to feed on the dead lichens and mosses and were followed by a few small animals such as ants, mites, and spiders. This first combination of plants, animals, and decomposers is called the *pioneer natural community.*

After many years, the pioneer natural community built up enough organic matter in the thin soil to support the roots of small herbs and shrubs such as bluebell, yarrow, bearberry, blueberry, and juniper. These newcomers slowed down the loss of moisture and provided food and cover for new plants, animals, and decomposers. Under these new conditions, the species in the pioneer natural community species were crowded out and gradually replaced with a different type of natural community.

As this new natural community thrived, it added further organic matter to the slowly thickening crust of soil. This led to the next stage of succession, a compact layer of vegetation called a heath mat. This mat, in turn, provided a thicker and richer soil

canopy

lower
canopy trees

understory
trees

tall shrub
understory

low shrub
ground layer

annual   perennial weeds   shrubs   young pine forest   mature oak forest
weeds   and grasses
Time ──────▶

Figure 5-2 Secondary ecological succession on an abandoned farm field over about 150 years.

needed for the germination and growth of trees such as jack pine, black spruce, and occasionally aspen. Over several decades these trees increased in height and density, and the plants of the heath mat were crowded out. The shade and other conditions created by these trees allowed the germination and growth of shade-tolerant climax species such as balsam fir, paper birch, and white spruce. Under the canopy created by these taller climax tree species, most of the earlier shade-intolerant tree species could not reproduce and were eliminated. After several centuries, what was once bare rock became a mature or climax ecosystem (Figure 5-1).

Secondary Succession Figure 5-2 shows a secondary succession that occurs when land in an oak-hickory forest in the eastern United States is cleared for growing corn and then abandoned after harvest. The abandoned field already has a thick layer of soil, so the early stages of primary succession are not necessary. The bare field is quickly covered with crabgrass in the fall. In the spring horseweed takes over, and during the summer the field is invaded by white asters. Within a year the crabgrass is shaded out by these taller plants. After 2 or 3 years, enough organic matter in the soil has built up to support a perennial grass such as broom sedge. As dead plants and other debris accumulate, decomposers thrive

and build up the soil. This prepares the way for the growth of young pine trees, which can thrive in direct sunlight and open fields. Pine seeds are blown in and young pine trees invade the broom sedge, grow within 5 or 10 years to the low-shrub stage, and begin to shade out the broom sedge and other sun-loving weeds and grasses. Over the next 20 years a pine forest develops. The tall pine trees shade out their own seedlings. In the cool shade beneath the pine forest, seedlings of shade-loving hardwood species such as red gum, red maple, black oak, and hickory begin to grow. These new species have long tap roots and can obtain moisture unavailable to the shallow-rooted pines. Over 40 to 120 years these hardwoods, especially oak and hickory, replace the shade-intolerant pines as the latter die out. Other shade-tolerant trees and shrubs, such as dogwood, sourwood, and redbud, fill in the understory below the canopy of oak and hickory trees. We now have a mature oak-hickory deciduous forest (Figure 5-2).

5-2 Stability in Living Systems

What Is Stability? Organisms, populations, communities, and ecosystems all have some ability to withstand or recover from externally imposed

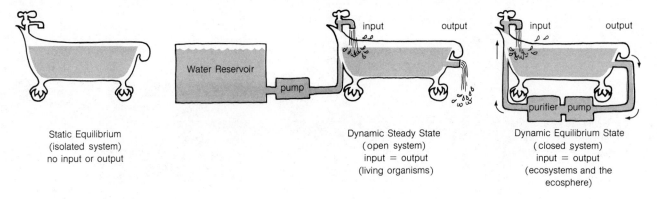

Static Equilibrium
(isolated system)
no input or output

Dynamic Steady State
(open system)
input = output
(living organisms)

Dynamic Equilibrium State
(closed system)
input = output
(ecosystems and the
ecosphere)

Figure 5-3 Three possible states of a bathtub or any system—static equilibrium state, dynamic steady state, and dynamic equilibrium state.

changes or stresses. In other words, they have some degree of *stability*. It is useful to distinguish between two aspects of ecosystem stability, inertia and resilience. *Inertia* is the ability of an ecosystem to resist being disturbed or altered. *Resilience* is the ability of an ecosystem to restore its structure and function following a natural or human-induced stress. Nature is remarkably resilient. For example, human societies survive natural disasters and devastating wars; the genetic structure of insect populations is altered to survive massive doses of deadly pesticides; and plants eventually recolonize areas devastated by volcanoes, nuclear explosions, and being paved for parking lots.

Stability in a system implies persistence of structure over time. This stability is maintained, however, only by constant change. You are continually adding and losing matter and energy, but your body maintains a fairly stable structure over your life span. Similarly, the oak-hickory forest ecosystem in Figure 5-2 will still be recognizable as a deciduous forest 50 years from now unless it is cut, burned, or blown down. Some trees will die; others will take their place. Some species may also disappear, and the numbers of individual species may change. But you will still recognize it as a deciduous forest.

Dynamic Steady States   In real life there are two types of systems, closed and open. In a closed **system,** such as the earth,* energy but not matter is exchanged between the system (earth) and its envi-

---
*Open and closed systems were originally defined by scientists in developing the laws of thermodynamics (Chapter 2). Some people mistakenly call the earth an open system because it receives energy from the sun. It is open to a flow of energy from the sun but in thermodynamic terms it is still defined as a closed system. In thermodynamics, a system in which neither matter nor energy is exchanged between the system and its environment is called an *isolated* system.

ronment (space). In an **open system,** both matter and energy are exchanged between the system and its environment. You are a walking, talking example of an open system. You take energy and matter into your body and then transform and use them to stay alive. At the same time, you put waste matter and degraded heat energy (Section 2-4) into the environment. You and other organisms remain alive only if the input of matter and energy is balanced by an output of matter and energy. When input and output are balanced by a steady flow of both matter and energy through an open system, the system is in a **dynamic steady state.** Thus, *we can describe life as an open system maintained in a dynamic steady state.*

Other terms used to describe a dynamic steady state are *stationary state* and *zero-growth state*. These are unfortunate terms because they give the false impression that a steady state is static and without growth. *The most important thing to remember about a steady state is that it is a very dynamic system. Some things are increasing, some are decreasing, and some remain fairly constant.* All of these ups and downs help keep the system from being destroyed or harmed by exceeding limits of tolerance. In your body, some tissues are growing and the rates of flow of certain chemicals are increasing. At the same time, other tissues are dying and the flow rates of other chemicals are decreasing. Instead of reaching a dynamic steady state, ecosystems and the ecosphere can achieve a **dynamic equilibrium state** based on matter cycling and energy flow (Figure 4-1) rather than matter flow and energy flow.

We can use a bathtub (Figure 5-3) to compare a static equilibrium or true no-growth state (not represented by any form of life) with a dynamic steady state (living organisms) and a dynamic equilibrium state (ecosystems and the ecosphere). A tub filled with water is a static equilibrium system. There is no input or output. By attaching an overflow pipe to the tub, we can convert it to a dynamic steady

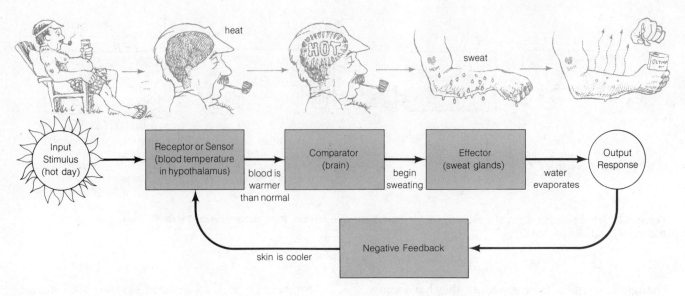

Figure 5-4 Keeping cool on a hot day—a simple homeostatic system based on negative feedback (arrows show flow of information).

state system. By running water in as fast as it flows out, we can keep the water level in a dynamic steady state somewhere below the top of the tub. A number of different steady state levels or different water levels are possible, as long as we don't exceed the limits of the tub. A number of flowthrough rates are also possible, depending on the sizes of input and output pipes, the supply of water, the capacity of the input water pump, and the supply of energy to run the pump. The steady state is a dynamic balance of these variables.

But this open system is still linear, or one way; water is flowing through the system and is wasted. If water is a scarce item, we can run the overflow pipe back into the tub and recycle the water to get a *closed* system in a dynamic equilibrium state. Now we're getting somewhere. We no longer need to worry about running out of water. We just have to get enough energy to run the recycling pump and water purifier. It will take much less energy to pump the water the length of the bathtub than to pump it from the nearest reservoir or river. This system is analogous to an ecosystem, where solar energy is used to recycle water and decomposers are used to break down and purify matter for reuse.

Stability and Negative Feedback All organisms and ecosystems have built-in means of maintaining internal conditions within some tolerable range when external conditions fluctuate—provided these external stresses are not too severe. This tendency for biological systems to resist drastic change by maintaining fairly constant internal conditions is called **homeostasis.**

Constant internal conditions are maintained by *feedback* or flow of information between the network of interconnected parts in organisms and ecosystems. **Feedback** is the return of the output of a system to the system as input. It is a process in which information is fed back into the system that will cause it to change in order to maintain a particular state. The thermostat on a home furnace is an example of control of temperature by information feedback. If the room temperature drops below or rises above the temperature set on the thermostat, this information is fed back into the system to cut the furnace on or off, as appropriate.

There are two types of information feedback: *negative feedback* and *positive feedback*. The most common type of information feedback is **negative feedback**—a flow of information that causes a system to counteract the effects of an input or change in external conditions. The thermostat-furnace system is an example of temperature control through negative feedback. When room temperature falls too low, more heat is supplied; when room temperature becomes too high, less heat is supplied.

Negative feedback also keeps your body temperature at approximately 37°C (98.6°F), as shown in Figure 5-4. This figure shows the common manner in which the homeostatic mechanisms in living organisms operate. An initial input of information, called a *stimulus*, activates a sensing device. For example, a rise in temperature of the environment is sensed by an increase in the temperature of the blood in the hypothalamus of your brain. This negative feedback of information is transmitted over a sensory pathway to a *comparator*—in this case another part of your brain. This information causes your brain to send a signal to *effectors*, which in turn initiate a response. In this case signals are sent to your sweat glands to activate sweating, a cooling mechanism. As the sweat evaporates, it takes heat from your skin. Once your body is cool, this new information output is fed back into the receptors or sensors of the system. If this new information indicates that the temperature of the blood in the hypothalamus has dropped to the desired level, the brain then sends a new message to the effectors to slow or stop the sweating process. Conversely, if the environment is too cold, a similar mechanism stops the sweating, slows blood flow, and may cause shivering so that your body will produce more heat.

Positive feedback—also known as *runaway feedback*—occurs when a change in the system in one direction provides information that causes the system to change in the same direction. For example, suppose the wires on a furnace thermostat were accidentally hooked up backwards. Then when the room got too hot a positive feedback of information would cause the furnace to turn on and make the room even hotter.

Generally, negative feedback tends to keep a system in a fairly constant or stable state and positive feedback tends to disrupt the equilibrium state and cause a system to become unstable. *Thus, organisms and ecosystems are self-regulating homeostatic systems in which control and adaptability are maintained primarily by negative feedback.*

Tolerance Levels and Limiting Factors Run too much or too little electricity through a thermostat-furnace control system and it won't work. Similarly, an organism may die from having too much or too little of a critical nutrient or becoming too hot or too cold. Each organism has a particular **range of tolerance** to variations in certain chemical and physical factors making up its abiotic environment (Figure 5-5). Too much or too little of any single factor may destroy an organism or limit its numbers and distribution. There may be too much moisture or not enough; too high a temperature or too low; too much light or not enough; too many minerals dissolved in the soil or too few. This is summarized in the **limiting factor principle** or *law of tolerance:* The existence, abundance, or distribution of an organism can be determined by whether the levels of one or more limiting factors fall above or below the levels tolerated by the organism (Section 3-7).

The growth of a plant or animal may require many different inputs of matter and energy. However, at any given time only one input is important—the one that is the most limiting factor. For example, suppose a farmer plants corn in a field containing too little phosphorus (as phosphates).

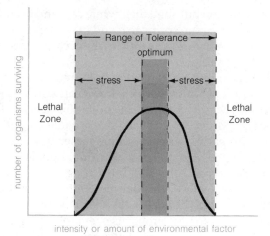

Figure 5-5 Ranges of tolerance for a large number of organisms of the same species to an environmental factor, such as temperature.

Even if the corn's requirements for water, nitrogen, potassium and other chemicals are met, the corn will stop growing when it has used up the available phosphorus. In this case, availability of phosphorus is the *limiting factor.*

Organisms of the same species have the same general range of tolerance to various stresses. Individual organisms within a large population, however, may have slightly different tolerance ranges because of genetic variability. It may take a little more heat or a little more of a poisonous chemical to kill one cat or one human than another. This is why Figure 5-5 is plotted for a large number of organisms of the same species rather than for a single organism.

Normally an organism's sensitivity to a particular stress also varies with its physical condition and with its life cycle. Organisms already weakened by fatigue or disease are usually more sensitive to stresses than healthy individuals. For most animals tolerance levels are much lower in juveniles (where body defense mechanisms may not be fully developed) than in adults. For example, adult blue crabs can tolerate fresh water, but their larvae cannot.

Organism Responses to Stress Organisms have a number of responses to environmental stress: they may **(1)** move away (some birds fly south for the winter), **(2)** wait out the stress period in a less active physiological state (chipmunks, bears, and ground squirrels hibernate in winter), **(3)** change their appearance or certain body functions to counteract the stress (arctic hares are white during the snowy winter season but shed their white coat and become brown during the spring to blend in with the brown tundra vegetation), or **(4)** slowly become used to the new conditions.

This ability to adapt slowly to new conditions is a useful protective device, but it can also be dangerous. Many changes in pollution levels, for instance, occur so gradually that we tolerate them. But with each change we come closer to our limit of tolerance without any warning signals. Suddenly we cross a threshold that triggers a harmful or even fatal effect. This **threshold effect**—the straw that breaks the camel's back—partly explains why so many ecological problems seem to pop up suddenly, even though they have been incubating for a long time (Figure 1-4).

Population Responses to Stress: Natural Selection and Evolution Populations respond in a number of ways to stress. Death rates may increase or birth rates may decrease, reducing the population size to one that can be supported by available resources. Also, the structure of the population may change. The old, very young, and weak members may die, leaving a population more capable of surviving such a stress as a more severe climate or an increase in predators.

Populations are also capable of adapting to environmental changes through *natural selection* and *evolution*. Most organisms in a population produce more offspring than can possibly survive. Because these offspring vary somewhat in their genetic makeup, some are better adapted to survival in the surrounding environment than others. Those individuals better suited to their environment can leave more offspring and thus contribute more of their genetic material to future generations. This increase in individuals in a population with new genetic material that makes them more likely to survive and reproduce in an altered environment is called **natural selection.**

Charles Darwin, who in 1858 first proposed this idea, described natural selection as meaning "survival of the fittest." This has often been misinterpreted to mean survival of the strongest, biggest, or most aggressive. Survival of the fittest means survival of the organisms best adapted to survival and reproduction in the particular environment in which their population exists. Natural selection means different kinds of plants and animals *avoid* competition by occupying different ecological niches (Section 4-4); it is harsh only to an aggressor seeking to occupy the same niche as another. Thus, *survival in nature depends primarily on peaceful coexistence, not harsh struggle.*

Modern research has shown that the hereditary traits of individual organisms are carried in their *genes.* These traits are coded in the sequence of chemical groups in molecules of DNA (<u>d</u>eoxyri-bo<u>n</u>ucleic <u>a</u>cid) found in the genes. In nature, exposure to various environmental factors such as radiation, heat, and certain chemicals subjects DNA molecules to random, spontaneous changes in their chemical makeup called **mutations.** New genetic combinations also arise when genes are separated and recombined through sexual reproduction.

These processes of sexual reproduction and mutation alter the genetic makeup of individual organisms. If a random, new genetic variation detracts from survival and reproduction, organisms with this trait die—eliminating these particular genes from the population. If a particular random variation in genetic makeup enhances the survival and reproduction of an organism, this beneficial genetic variation is passed on to succeeding generations. With time, more and more of the individuals in a population possess the beneficial genetic traits that enhance survival and reproduction in their particular environment. This change in the genetic makeup of a *population* over time through natural selection is called **evolution.**

Two major processes can occur through evolution. One involves a gradual change in genetic makeup within a single species. Populations of species with short generation times and large numbers of offspring, such as bacteria, insects, and rats, can make adaptive evolutionary changes in a relatively short time. For example, in only a few years a number of species of mosquitoes have become genetically resistant to DDT and other pesticides (discussed in Section 9-9). Similarly, species of bacteria can evolve new strains that are genetically resistant to widely used bacteria-killing drugs, such as penicillin. In marked contrast, humans and many other species have long generation times and cannot reproduce a large number of offspring rapidly. For these species, evolutionary adaptation to an environmental stress takes hundreds of thousands and in some cases millions of years. To survive new environmental stresses that last for several decades or centuries, the human race must rely on cultural changes—not biological evolution (see Enrichment Study 1).

In the second evolutionary process, called **speciation,** a single species splits into two species. Recall from Section 3-3 that *species* are distinct kinds of organisms that live together with little or no sign of interbreeding. This splitting of genetic lines of descent has led to the estimated 5 to 10 million different kinds of species found on earth today. Speciation, however, is a very slow process—normally requiring at least 1,000 generations under intensive environmental selection pressure. In some rapidly producing organisms speciation may take place in thousands or even hundreds of years. But in most cases it takes from tens of thousands to millions of years.

Exactly how speciation takes place is not fully understood, partly because it takes place so slowly that biologists have been able to observe only part of the process. In general, speciation occurs when a population of a particular species is distributed over an area that includes several different environments. For example, different populations of the same species may become separated by a mountain, a wide river, or natural occurrences such as floods, hurricanes or a geological process that separates a single land mass into separate islands. If different populations of a single species are isolated from one another over a great many generations, they may begin to diverge genetically in response to their different climates, food sources, soils, and other environmental factors. Eventually enough genetic variations in appearance, structure, behavior, and other characteristics may be produced so that the two populations become different species incapable of interbreeding. For example, the *arctic fox* developed as a species in cold northern regions and the *gray fox* developed in warmer southern regions. The heavier fur and short legs, ears, and nose of the arctic fox represent adaptations to the cold. Similarly, the thinner fur and longer legs, ears, and nose—which give off more heat—of the gray fox represent adaptations to a warmer climate. Different species of plants found going up a mountain slope typically represent different adaptations to altitude. Note that populations and species evolve—not individual organisms.

The incredible genetic diversity created in different populations and species on this planet through evolution is nature's insurance policy against disaster. While species have appeared and disappeared throughout earth's history, every species here today represents stored genetic information that allows these species to adapt to certain changes in environmental conditions. *This genetic information contained in living species along with the cultural information passed along from one human generation to the next is the most valuable resource on this planet.*

Time Delays and Synergistic Effects Another characteristic of homeostatic systems is **time delay**— the delay between the time a stimulus is received and the time the system makes a corrective action by negative feedback. Different feedback loops in a complex system have different response times. Time delays can protect a system for a while. But a time delay between a cause and its effect often means that corrective action is not effective by the time the symptoms finally appear. A pollutant released into the environment may not affect human health or other organisms for years. For example, workers exposed to a cancer-causing (carcinogenic) chemical may not get cancer for 20 to 30 years. By then it is too late for corrective response.

Complex homeostatic systems also can have a property known as a *synergistic effect.* You were taught that 2 plus 2 always equals 4. But in homeostatic systems, two or more factors can interact so that the net effect is greater or less than the sum of the factors acting independently. This is known as a **synergistic effect.**

The effect of two or more factors interacting so that the net effect is less than that from adding their independent effects is called a *negative synergistic* or *antagonistic effect.* This happens when one factor partially counteracts or cancels the effect of another. For example, by themselves the two air pollutants nitrogen dioxide (NO_2) and particulate matter (tiny particles of matter, such as soot and liquid effluent in the air) can harm the lungs. When they act together, however, the effect on the lungs is less than when each acts alone. Negative synergy is one mechanism that helps explain why ecosystems are resilient if not pushed too far.

A *positive synergistic effect* occurs when two or more factors interact so that the net effect is greater than that from adding their independent effects. For example, the two air pollutants particulate matter and sulfur dioxide each do some damage when inhaled into the lungs. Acting together, however, they greatly increase the chances of contracting lung cancer. Another well-known example involves the positive synergistic interaction between alcohol and sleeping pills. Taken alone, each slows down human reflexes, but taken together the two may be fatal.

Biological Magnification Often pollutants are diluted to relatively harmless level in the air or water, or degraded to harmless forms by decomposers and other natural processes. However, some synthetic chemicals, such as DDT (Section 9-9), some radioactive materials (Section 15-5), and some mercury and lead compounds (Enrichment Study 12), for example, are neither diluted nor broken down by natural processes. Instead, they can become more concentrated as they go through various food webs (Section 4-2) in an ecosystem. As a result, organisms at high trophic levels in these food webs receive large doses of such chemicals even though relatively small amounts are in the air, water, or soil.

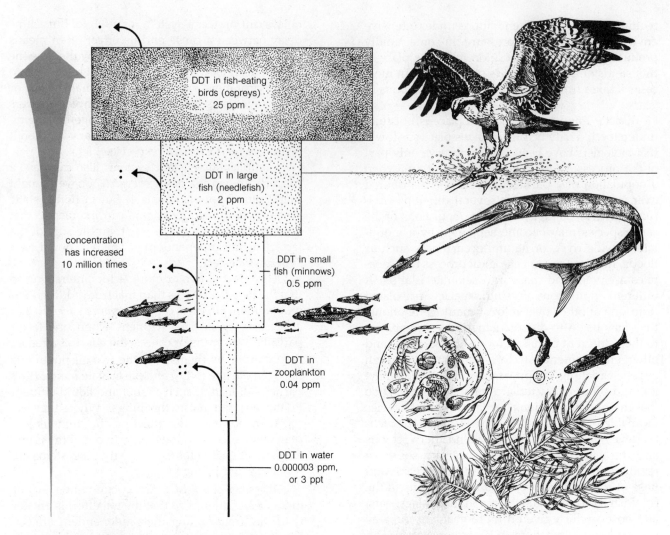

Figure 5-6 The concentration of DDT in organisms is magnified approximately 10 million times in this food chain found in an estuarine ecosystem adjacent to Long Island Sound. Dots represent DDT, and arrows show small losses through respiration and excretion.

Figure 5-6 illustrates this phenomenon of **biological magnification** in an estuarine ecosystem adjacent to Long Island Sound.

Biological magnification in a food chain or web depends on three factors: **(1)** the second law of thermodynamics (Section 2-3), **(2)** chemicals that are soluble in fat but insoluble in water, and **(3)** chemicals that are slowly degraded or broken down in the environment. Since energy transfer at each link in a food chain or web is so inefficient (Figure 4-3), a small fish must eat a great deal of plankton, larger fish must eat a great many small fish, and a pelican must eat a great many larger fish to survive (Figure 5-6). Anything—like DDT—that is not degraded or excreted as it moves through this chain becomes more concentrated, especially if it dissolves in, and remains in, fatty tissues of organisms. If each phytoplankton concentrates 1 unit of DDT from the water, then a small fish eating thousands of phy-

toplankton will store thousands of units of DDT in its fatty tissue. If DDT were water-soluble the fish would excrete it at each level, but it is not. A large fish that eats ten of these smaller fish will receive and store tens of thousands of units of DDT. A bird or human that feeds on several large fish can get hundreds of thousands of units of DDT (Section 9-9).

Maintaining Ecosystem Stability How do ecosystems maintain their stability? Ecologists do not have an answer to this question, although there are many controversial hypotheses. The reason for this lack of knowledge is that ecosystem stability is extremely complex—representing all parts of an ecosystem and the maze of interactions among these parts.

Until recently it was believed that increasing diversity and complexity in ecosystems leads to an increase in their stability. Intuitively it seems that species diversity (the number of different species and their relative abundances) and food web complexity should help stabilize ecosystems. With so many different species and ecological niches, risk is widely spread and the system should have more ways of responding to environmental stress. A complex food web should also promote stability because animals have multiple food sources. If one species is eliminated, many predators can shift to another food source. It seems better for a species not to have all of its eggs in the same basket.

But do diversity and complexity always increase ecosystem stability? If this idea is valid, fairly simple ecosystems such as the tundra (Section 3-8) and agricultural fields consisting of only one crop (monoculture) should be much less stable than more complex and diverse ones, such as tropical rain forests (Section 3-8). Tropical rain forests are indeed stable ecosystems if not cut down, and dramatic fluctuations in the population size of various plant and animal species can occur in tundra. Monoculture food crops are highly vulnerable to destruction from only a single plant disease or pest and must be carefully protected.

Some ecologists point out, however, that the stability of a tropical rain forest may have more to do with its fairly constant year-round climate for millions of years. They also remind us that tropical forests are so unstable when logged or bulldozed that they often cannot regenerate themselves. Similarly, the instability of tundra, indicated by wild fluctuations in their plant and animal population sizes, may be a result of the highly unstable climate found there. Although tundra recover slowly from environmental stress they may eventually recover more fully than a severely damaged tropical rain forest.

These differences between tundra and tropical rain forests, then, are more likely the result of evolution through the process of natural selection. Most of the many different species in a tropical rain forest have become adapted by natural selection to living in an environment that undergoes little change— sharply reducing strategies that would permit survival during times of severe stress such as logging. Similarly, tundra ecosystems are subjected to such harsh changes in climate that they will contain species more adaptable to change. In this sense they have greater long-term stability than more complex tropical rain forests.

There are other problems with the appealing idea that diversity and complexity lead to ecosystem stability. First, most scientific tests that tend to support this hypothesis have been on aquatic ecosystems and simple ecosystems created in the laboratory, rather than on complex terrestrial ecosys-

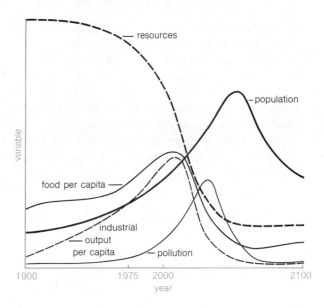

Figure 5-7 A computer model projection of present growth into the future shows worldwide depletion of resources and declining industrial growth. Eventually population declines sharply as death rates rise because of shortages of food and medical services. *These are projections, not predictions.* (Source: D. H. Meadows et al., *The Limits to Growth.* New York: Universe Books, 1972. Used by permission.)

tems. Second, diversity, like stability, has a number of different meanings. It can refer to *species diversity* (the number and distribution of different species in a given area or ecosystem), *food web diversity* (the number and type of food webs in a given area or ecosystem), *genetic diversity* (the existence of different genetic varieties within a given species), *ecological niche diversity* (the variety of niches available in an ecosystem), *biological diversity* (the numbers of species and genetic types within species), and *population distribution diversity* (the ways various populations are distributed in an ecosystem). Thus, *the idea that diversity leads to ecosystem stability may be valid in some cases, but we should be wary of applying this idea to all situations.*

Ecological Modeling Some scientists use mathematical or computer models to attempt a fuller understanding of ecosystems and of the relationships between diversity and stability. In the early 1970s Jay Forrester, and Donella Meadows, Dennis Meadows, and their associates developed a simplified model of the world ecosystem from a human standpoint. In their widely publicized and controversial work *The Limits to Growth* (1972) they tried to simulate the interactions of five major variables: population, pollution, nonrenewable resources, per capita food production, and industrial output. Figure 5-7, adapted from this work, shows one possible outcome if the present rates of growth and industrial pollution continue. This computer model and others that have been developed are evaluated in Enrichment Study 2.

Computer modeling can be a useful tool for helping to project possible consequences of human actions in the ecosphere. However, a computer model is no better than the assumptions and data put into the model; put "garbage in" and you get "garbage out."

5-3 What Can Go Wrong in an Ecosystem?

Effects of Environmental Stress Since ecosystems tend to be self-maintaining and self-repairing, why not drop all of our wastes into the environment and let nature take care of them? By now you realize that there are serious problems with this idea. First, as we have seen, organisms, populations, and ecosystems all have certain limits of tolerance. Second, ecosystems do not have the decomposers and disposal mechanisms for coping with many of the synthetic chemicals produced by humans. Third, populations might evolve so that ecosystems could digest these new chemicals and absorb many of today's environmental insults. However, for most populations—especially the human population—these evolutionary changes would take hundreds of thousands or millions of years, and many people would have to die.

Table 5-1 summarizes what can happen to organisms, populations, and ecosystems if one or more limits of tolerance are exceeded. The stresses that can cause the changes shown in Table 5-1 may result from natural hazards, such as earthquakes, volcanic eruptions, hurricanes, drought, floods, and fires ignited by lightning. Stresses also come from human activities such as industrialization, transportation, agriculture, and other land-clearing activities. Let's examine how such human activities disrupt energy flow and chemical cycling and how they simplify ecosystems.

Disrupting Global Energy Flow: Protecting the Ozone Layer About 20 percent of the air you inhale with each breath consists of oxygen molecules (O_2). Another very important molecule in the atmosphere is *ozone*, the three-atom form of oxygen (O_3). Ozone is a strange chemical. Inhaling a tiny amount of it will kill you, yet it is essential to your life and health.

A few parts per million of ozone are found in the lower stratosphere—a portion of the atmo-

Table 5-1 Some Effects of Environmental Stress

Organism Level

Physiological and chemical changes
Psychological disorders
Fewer or no offspring
Genetic defects (mutagenic effects)
Birth defects (teratogenic effects)
Cancers (carcinogenic effects)
Death

Population Level

Population decrease
Excessive population increase (if natural predators are eliminated or reduced)
Change in age structure (old, young, and weak may die)
Natural selection of genetically resistant individuals
Loss of genetic diversity and adaptability
Extinction

Community-Ecosystem Level

Disruption of energy flow
 changes in solar energy input
 changes in heat output
 changes in food webs and patterns of competition

Disruption of chemical cycles
 leaks (shifts from closed to open cycles)

Simplification
 lower species diversity
 loss of sensitive species
 fewer habitats and ecological niches
 less complex food webs
 lowered stability in some cases
 partial or total collapse of structure and function of the ecosystem
 return to an earlier stage of succession

sphere about 20 to 50 kilometers (12 to 31 miles) above the earth's surface (Figure 19-1). If all the ozone in the stratosphere were compressed by ordinary atmospheric pressure, it would form a layer only about as thick as a dime. Yet this thin shell far above you, called the **ozone layer,** has profound effects. It acts as a shield for life on earth by filtering out about 99 percent of the harmful ultraviolet radiation from the sun (Figure 3-2).

In recent years a number of scientists have become concerned that some human activities, such as nuclear war and supersonic planes that inject reactive nitrous oxide (N_2O) directly into the stratosphere, and the upward movement of chlorofluorocarbons (CFCs, also known as Freons) released from aerosol spray cans and from discarded or leaking refrigeration and air conditioning equipment, could decrease the normal concentration of ozone in the stratosphere. When these chemicals come under the influence of high-energy ultraviolet radiation they can be converted to highly reactive forms that can destroy some of the ozone in the stratosphere in a complicated sequence of chemical reactions. It has been estimated that each 1 percent decrease in ozone would increase the amount of ultraviolet radiation reaching the earth's surface by 1 to 3 percent.

Decreasing the concentration of ozone in the stratosphere could have the following major effects: (1) increasing the number of basal and squamous cell skin cancers that now affect about 450,000 and kill about 1,600 light-skinned people each year in the United States by 2 to 5 percent for each 1 percent decrease in stratospheric ozone; (2) possibly increasing the number of cases of a rarer but often fatal form of skin cancer called malignant melanoma that now kills about 4,000 persons a year in the United States; (3) increasing cases of severe sunburn in unprotected lighter-skinned people; (4) damaging many species of land plants and some aquatic species and possibly decreasing the yields of important food crops such as corn, rice, and wheat; and (5) causing unpredictable changes in world climatic patterns.

At least 192 chemical reactions take place in the stratosphere. Projected effects of various chemicals on the ozone layer are based primarily on theoretical mathematical models of the stratosphere that presently include about 150 or fewer reactions, many of which are poorly understood. Some of the thousands of measurements of ozone concentrations made by weather balloons and orbiting satellites indicate an ozone depletion of about 0.5 percent a year at the 40-kilometer (25-mile) level. These measurements, however, cannot be used to confirm or deny the theoretical models because the amount of ozone in various parts of the stratosphere normally varies by as much as 5 percent a year.

There is general agreement that large-scale nuclear war would probably destroy most of the ozone layer (Enrichment Study 3). Recent research has indicated that N_2O exhausted by supersonic jet planes flying in the stratosphere poses much less threat to the ozone layer than originally projected. In addition, according to a 1984 study by the National Academy of Sciences, the projected release of other nitrogen oxides (NO and NO_2) into the atmosphere by subsonic jets is expected to increase the amount of stratospheric ozone by 1 percent by the year 2000.

By 1983, at least 9.1 billion kilograms (20 billion pounds) of chlorofluorocarbons had been released into the atmosphere. Because CFCs have little tendency to react with other chemicals in the lower atmosphere (troposphere), they remain in the atmosphere from 40 to 110 years depending on the type of CFC. Projections indicate CFCs will rise slowly into the stratosphere in coming decades even if all releases into the atmosphere were banned today. In 1984, a study by the National Academy of Sciences projected a 2 to 4 percent decrease in total global ozone over the next 100 years if CFCs continued to be produced at 1977 rates. However, if usage should rise sharply above the 1977 level, some members of the NAS panel of experts project a 10 to 12 percent reduction in stratospheric ozone over the next 100 years.

In 1978, the United States banned the use of CFCs in aerosol spray cans, but they are still widely used as refrigerants and as foaming agents for various polymers. Manufacturers quickly developed substitutes for CFCs in aerosol spray cans, but virtually nothing else is as efficient and nontoxic as CFCs in refrigeration and air conditioning units. Canada, Sweden, Norway, and Denmark imposed similar bans. Industrial production of CFCs dropped significantly between 1975 and 1980, but worldwide use is now rising again partially due to less pessimistic estimates of ozone reduction by the NAS.

Because protection of the ozone layer is vital for life as we know it on earth, it is hoped that concern over CFCs will serve as warnings that some chemicals added to the atmosphere, even with good intentions, can have serious long-range consequences. Hopefully, this knowledge will cause us to survey present (and future) chemicals released into the atmosphere. Ozone depletion could be caused by any widely used chemicals that (1) exist as a gas in the atmosphere, (2) are unreactive in the lower atmosphere, and (3) are insoluble in water and thus not washed out of the atmosphere by rain.

Additional examples of the potential disruption of global and regional energy flow from burning fossil fuels, land clearing, and other human activities are discussed in Enrichment Study 5.

Disrupting the Oxygen, Nitrogen, and Phosphorus Cycles Let's begin with some good news. In the late 1960s, an ecological horror story was widely circulated that we might use up the earth's oxygen supply by burning fossil fuels. We have many environmental problems, but global suffocation from lack of oxygen is not one of them. The oxygen content of the atmosphere remains essentially constant, with the oxygen consumed by all animals, bacteria, and respiration processes roughly balanced by the oxygen released by land plants and algae in the sea during photosynthesis.

We will not run out of oxygen. But this is not the case for some fish and other oxygen-consuming organisms in some lakes and slow-moving rivers and streams. As part of its natural aging process, a lake receives nutrients such as phosphorus (as

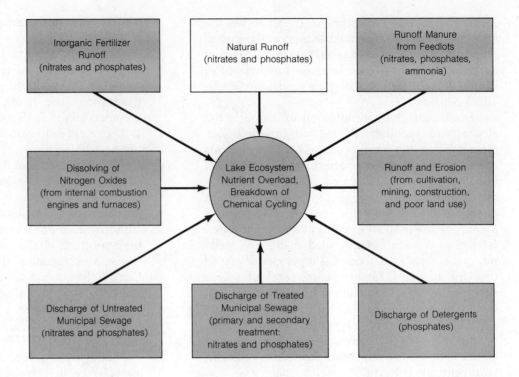

Figure 5-8 Nutrient overload, or cultural eutrophication, from human activities can disrupt the chemical cycles in a lake.

Inorganic Fertilizer Runoff (nitrates and phosphates)

Natural Runoff (nitrates and phosphates)

Runoff Manure from Feedlots (nitrates, phosphates, ammonia)

Dissolving of Nitrogen Oxides (from internal combustion engines and furnaces)

Lake Ecosystem Nutrient Overload, Breakdown of Chemical Cycling

Runoff and Erosion (from cultivation, mining, construction, and poor land use)

Discharge of Untreated Municipal Sewage (nitrates and phosphates)

Discharge of Treated Municipal Sewage (primary and secondary treatment: nitrates and phosphates)

Discharge of Detergents (phosphates)

PO_4^{3-}) and nitrogen (as NO_3^-) by drainage from the surrounding land basin, from bottom sediments, and from organisms living in the lake. This natural erosion and runoff of nutrients from the land into lakes is called **eutrophication** (*eutro* for "well-nourished"). Too many plant nutrients such as phosphates and nitrates can overload the nitrogen and phosphorus cycles (Section 4-3), which in turn can cause a breakdown in the oxygen cycle in the lake. Natural eutrophication can be accelerated by water pollution from a number of human activities—a process known as **cultural eutrophication** (Figure 5-8). The key sources of nutrient overload include **(1)** runoff of commercial fertilizer and animal wastes (manure) from the land; **(2)** increased runoff from mining, construction, and poor land use; **(3)** discharge of municipal sewage and detergents; and **(4)** to a much lesser extent the dissolving in water of nitrogen oxides produced by burning fossil fuels in cars, power plants, and home furnaces (Figure 5-8).

Nitrogen and phosphorus are plant nutrients, and when present in excessive amounts they can set off an explosive growth of green and blue-green algae. These organisms die and fall to the bottom of the lake. Oxygen-consuming bacteria decompose the masses of dead algae and in the process deplete dissolved oxygen from the water. This combined with normal oxygen depletion at night, when algae cannot produce oxygen by photosynthesis, can kill most oxygen-consuming fish. Further oxygen depletion occurs as more bacteria decompose

the dead fish. If nutrient overload continues, the entire chemical cycling system in the lake breaks down; the water becomes foul from gases like hydrogen sulfide (H_2S) produced by anaerobic decomposition and almost devoid of life. Further details on *cultural eutrophication* are given in Enrichment Study 14.

Disrupting Food Webs with Synthetic Chemicals Malaria once infected nine out of ten people on the island of North Borneo, now a state of Indonesia. In 1955, the World Health Organization (WHO) began spraying dieldrin (a pesticide similar to DDT) to kill malaria-carrying mosquitoes.* The program was very successful, almost eliminating this dreaded disease. But other things happened. The dieldrin killed other insects besides mosquitoes, including flies and cockroaches inhabiting the houses. The islanders applauded. But then small lizards that also lived in the houses died after gorging themselves on dead insects. Then cats began dying after feeding on the dead lizards. Without cats, rats flourished and began overrunning the villages. Now people were threatened by sylvatic plague carried by the fleas on the rats. Fortunately, this situation was brought under control when WHO had the Royal Air Force parachute cats into Borneo.

---

*Most versions of this episode report that DDT was the insecticide used. According to a personal communication from A. J. Beck (at one time a medical zoologist at the Institute for Medical Research in North Borneo), dieldrin, not DDT, was used.

On top of everything else, the thatched roofs of some houses began to fall in. The dieldrin also killed wasps and other insects that fed on a type of caterpillar that either avoided or was not affected by the insecticide. With most of their predators eliminated, the caterpillar population exploded. The larvae munched their way through one of their favorite foods, the leaves that made up the roofs. In the end the Borneo episode was a success story in that the terrible disease of malaria and the unexpected side effects of the spraying program were brought under control. But it shows the unpredictable results that may be encountered when we interfere in an ecosystem. More details on the dilemma of using pesticides are found in Section 9-9.

Reducing Variety in Ecosystems by Eliminating and Introducing Species We tend to divide plants and animals into "good" and "bad" species and assume that we have a duty to wipe out the villains. Consider the American alligator. Its marsh and swamp habitats are destroyed to make way for agriculture and industry, and it is hunted for its hide for expensive purses and shoes. Between 1950 and 1960, Louisiana lost 90 percent of its alligators; the population in the Florida Everglades was also threatened.

Why care? The alligator is a key factor in the ecological balance of the Everglades—a balance on which much of the urbanizing state of Florida depends for water. The deep pools, or "gator holes," that alligators dig collect water during dry spells and provide a sanctuary for birds and animals that repopulate the area after droughts. The large alligator nesting mounds are nest sites for birds, including herons and egrets, that are essential to other life cycles. As alligators move from gator holes to nesting mounds, they help keep waterways open. In addition, they preserve game fish balances by consuming large numbers of predator fish, such as gar.

In 1968 the U.S. government placed the American alligator on the endangered species list. Protected from hunters, the alligator population made a comeback by 1975 in many areas. Indeed, they made too much of a comeback. People began finding alligators in their backyards and swimming pools. Now the American alligator has been removed from the endangered species list in most areas, and limited hunting is allowed in some areas (especially Louisiana) to keep its population in check.

Unexpected ecological effects can also occur when a new species is introduced to an ecosystem. In 1948 five cats were brought to an isolated Antarctic island to control the rat population. Today the island still has rats along with about 2,500 feral (wild) cats, who gobble up about 600,000 of the island's birds each year.

In the Sichuan province of China a campaign to catch 200,000 live snakes for medicine and food was so successful that the resulting ecological imbalance allowed soaring rat populations to devour much of the corn crop. For more details on the effects on ecosystems of eliminating and introducing species see Chapter 11.

Hazardous Chemical Dumps: The Love Canal Episode "Out of sight, out of mind" does not always apply. Hazardous industrial wastes buried decades ago can bubble to the surface, find their way into groundwater supplies, or end up in backyards and basements, as residents of a suburb of Niagara Falls, New York, discovered in 1977. Between 1942 and 1953, Hooker Chemicals and Plastics Corporation dumped more than 19 million kilograms (21,800 tons) of chemical wastes (mostly contained in steel drums) into an old canal and then used a clay cap to seal the dump.

In 1953, Hooker Chemicals sold the canal area to the Niagara Falls school board for $1 on the condition that the company would have no future liability for injury or property damage caused by the dump's contents. The company claims that it warned the school board against carrying out any kind of construction at the disposal site. An elementary school and a housing project, eventually with 949 homes, was built in the Love Canal area. Though residents began complaining to city officials about chemical smells and about chemical burns received by children playing in the canal, these complaints were ignored. In 1977 chemicals from badly corroded barrels filled with hazardous wastes began leaking into storm sewers, gardens, and basements of homes adjacent to the canal.

Informal health surveys conducted by alarmed residents revealed an unusually high incidence of birth defects, miscarriages, assorted cancers, and nerve, respiratory, and kidney disorders among residents near the canal. Complaints to local elected and health officials produced little action. After considerable pressure from residents and unfavorable publicity, state officials made a preliminary health survey and tests and found that **(1)** women between the ages of 30 and 34 in one area of the canal had a miscarriage rate four times higher than normal, and **(2)** the air, water, and soil of the canal area and basements of houses nearby were contaminated with a wide range of toxic and carcinogenic chemicals.

In 1978, after local health officials failed to act, the state closed the school and relocated the 239 families whose homes were closest to the dump. In

1980, after protests from the outraged 710 families still living in the area, President Carter declared Love Canal a federal disaster area and had these families temporarily relocated in hotels, motels, and army barracks. Federal and New York State funds were then provided to buy the homes of those who wanted to relocate.

Since that time homes within a block and a half of the canal have been torn down and the state has purchased 550 of the homes; 182 families still live in the area. The dump site has been covered with a clay cap and surrounded by a barrier drain system that includes a permanent water treatment facility for removing contaminants. Local officials have pressed federal officials for a clean bill of health so the state can resell homes it bought from fleeing homeowners and begin rehabilitating the neighborhood. A 1983 study by the U.S. Office of Technology Assessment concluded that an earlier $8 million study by the EPA, which found the area no more contaminated than other industrial areas, was inadequate to determine whether the area was safe to live in. In 1983, the EPA declared that contamination from the toxic dump site was more extensive than originally believed and developed a revised cleanup plan that will postpone decisions on the habitability of various zones in the area to somewhere between 1985 and 1988.

In 1978, over 1,450 residents of the Love Canal area sued Occidental Petroleum, which bought Hooker Chemicals, for a total of $16 billion in health and property damages. In 1983, without admitting any negligence, Occidental Petroleum made an out-of-court settlement expected to total $25 million ($5 to $6 million paid by Occidental and the rest by their insurance companies) with 94 percent of the residents filing claims against the company. By early 1984 Occidental still faced suits from the federal government and New York State, which seek to recover the costs of cleaning up the area and relocating most of its residents.

No definitive study has been made to determine the effects of exposure to these hazardous chemicals on the former Love Canal residents, most now widely scattered. All studies made so far have been criticized on scientific grounds. Even if the effects of exposure to these chemicals should prove to be less harmful than expected, the psychological damage to the evacuated residents is enormous. For the rest of their lives they will wonder whether a disorder will strike and worry about the possible effects of these chemicals on their children and grandchildren.

Regardless of the final outcome, the Love Canal episode vividly reminds us that we can never really throw anything away. It is more frightening when we realize that the EPA estimates that from 1,200 to 2,000 other hazardous chemical dump sites in the United States could pose similar problems. For more details on hazardous wastes, see Enrichment Study 13.

The small number of cases described in this section show that careless uses of technology can cause unexpected side effects. These undesirable effects do not mean that we have to abandon technology; they do mean that we should learn to anticipate possible side effects before introducing a technology on a large scale.

5-4 Humans and Ecosystems

Simplifying Ecosystems In modifying ecosystems for our own use we simplify them. Every dam, cornfield, highway, pipeline, irrigation project, and insecticide use makes an ecosystem simpler. We bulldoze fields and forests containing thousands of interrelated plant and animal species and cover the land with buildings, highways, or single crops. Modern agriculture deliberately keeps ecosystems in early stages of succession, where net productivity of one or only a few plant species (such as corn or wheat) is high.

But such fast-growing, single-crop systems (monocultures) are highly vulnerable. Weeds and a single disease or pest can wipe out an entire crop unless protected with chemicals such as insecticides (insect-killing chemicals) and herbicides (weed-killing chemicals). When quickly breeding insects develop genetic resistance to pesticides, farmers must either use stronger doses or switch to new pesticides. This kills other species that prey on the pests, thus simplifying the ecosystem further and allowing pest populations to grow larger (Section 9-9).

Not only cultivation simplifies ecosystems. Ranchers don't want bison or prairie dogs competing with sheep for grass, so these species are eliminated from grasslands. So too the wolf, coyote, eagle, and other predators that occasionally kill sheep. We tend to overfish and overhunt some species to extinction or near extinction, further simplifying ecosystems, as discussed in Chapter 11.

Achieving a Balance Between Simplicity and Diversity There is nothing wrong with simplifying a reasonable number of ecosystems in order to provide food for the human population. But the price we pay for simplifying, maintaining, and protecting such simplified ecosystems includes time, money, and matter and energy resources, as summarized in Table 5-2.

Table 5-2 Comparison of Properties of a Natural Ecosystem and a Simplified Human System

Natural Ecosystem (marsh, grassland, forest)	Simplified Human System (cornfield, factory, house)
Captures, converts, and stores energy from the sun	Consumes energy from fossil or nuclear fuels
Produces oxygen and consumes carbon dioxide	Consumes oxygen and produces carbon dioxide from the burning of fossil fuels
Creates fertile soil	Depletes or covers fertile soil
Stores, purifies, and releases water gradually	Often uses and contaminates water and releases it rapidly
Provides wildlife habitats	Destroys some wildlife habitats
Filters and detoxifies pollutants and waste products free of charge	Produces pollutants and waste materials, much of which must be cleaned up at our expense
Usually capable of self-maintenance and self-renewal	Requires continual maintenance and renewal at great cost

There is the danger that as the human population grows we may simplify too many of the world's ecosystems to young, productive, but highly vulnerable ones. Simplified human systems depend on the existence of nearby natural ecosystems. For example, simple farmlands on the plains must be balanced by diverse forests on nearby hills and mountains. These forests hold water and minerals, releasing them slowly to the plains below. If the forests are cut for short-term economic gain, then the water and soil washes down slopes in a torrent instead of a nourishing trickle. Thus, forests are valued not only for their short-term production of timber but for their role in protecting watersheds (see Chapter 10).

To preserve a balance between simplified human ecosystems and natural ecosystems we need to know more about how ecosystems work. Biologist Paul Ehrlich has likened the ecosphere to a massive and intricate computer cross-linking a vast array of transistors and other electrical components. Even though we do not really understand it, and even though our lives depend on it, we are busy simplifying this complex network by randomly pulling out transistors and by overloading and disconnecting various parts and circuits. Removing certain species or altering parts of an ecosystem may not be lethal to the system, but we do not know which parts of the system can be safely altered.

As Lewis Mumford put it eloquently:

When we rally to preserve the remaining redwood forests or to protect the whooping crane, we are rallying to preserve ourselves, we are trying to keep in existence the organic variety, the whole span of natural resources upon which our own future development will be based. If we surrender this variety too easily in one place, we shall lose it everywhere; and we shall find ourselves enclosed in technological prison, without even the hope that sustains a prisoner in jail—that someday we may get out.

Some Lessons from Ecology   What can we learn from the brief overview of ecological principles presented in the past few chapters? It should be clear that ecology forces us to recognize five major features of all life: *interdependence, diversity, resilience, adaptability,* and *limits.* Its message is not that we should avoid change, but that we should recognize that human-induced changes can have far-reaching and often unpredictable consequences. Ecology is a call for wisdom, care, and restraints as we alter the ecosphere.

What has gone wrong, probably, is that we have failed to see ourselves as part of a large and indivisible whole. For too long we have based our lives on a primitive feeling that our "God-given" role was to have "dominion over the fish of the sea and over the fowl of the air and over every living thing that moveth upon the earth." We have failed to understand that the earth does not belong to us, but we to the earth.

Rolf Edberg

Discussion Topics

1. Explain how organisms can change local conditions so they become extinct in a given ecosystem. Could humans do this to themselves?

2. Explain how the "balance of nature" is dynamic, not static.

3. Give two examples each of closed systems and open systems not discussed in this chapter. Why is the earth defined as a closed system even though it receives energy from the sun?

4. Criticize the statement by a typical growth-oriented economist that a steady state or no-growth economy would be stagnant and undesirable (see Chapter 20).

5. What does it mean to say that modern farming consists of keeping an ecosystem at an early stage of succession? Why is this necessary? What undesirable effects does this have?

6. Draw a homeostatic diagram (see Figure 5-4) for (a) stopping a moving car and (b) picking up a pencil.

7. Give several examples of negative feedback control in your body, in your room, in your school, and in your community. Analyze a riot with a homeostatic diagram in which the limits of tolerance have been disrupted by positive feedback.

8. Explain why and how 2 plus 2 does not always equal 4 in an ecosystem. Cite specific examples of positive and negative synergistic effects to back up your explanation.

9. Someone tells you not to worry about air pollution because humans through evolution can develop lungs that can detoxify pollutants. How would you reply?

10. Give two examples of time delays not discussed in this chapter. How can time delays be harmful? How can they be helpful?

11. What characteristics must a chemical have before it can be biologically magnified in a food chain or web?

12. It has been said that people live in cities because a city offers more diversity, excitement, and challenge. If so, does this diversity add stability to a city? How do you explain the fact that many large cities seem unstable? How is the term *stability* used here?

13. Should all species be preserved somewhere in their natural habitats? Is this what nature does (see Chapter 11)? Why would you want to preserve the dinosaur? How many? Where?

14. Could the instances of ecological backlash discussed in Section 5-3 have been predicted and avoided? How? Analyze each case separately. Do you think we are learning from these past mistakes? Cite specific evidence, pro or con.

15. Should chlorofluorocarbons be banned from use in refrigeration and air conditioning units? Why or why not?

16. Should the use of commercial fertilizers be banned if it is established that they would deplete the ozone layer over the next 150 years? Why or why not?

17. Should all coyotes and eagles be exterminated from lands where sheep graze? Why or why not? What are the alternatives?

18. Rachel Carson has written, "Most of us walk unseeing through the world, unaware alike of its beauties, its wonders, and the strange and sometimes terrible intensity of the lives that are being lived about us." Relate this sentiment to your own life and the increasing urbanization of the planet. Can you think of moments in your life when nature has suddenly impinged on the plastic bubble that surrounds you?

19. What could happen if we simplify too many ecosystems? Explain to a younger child why we must preserve forests and swamps.

20. Who is most likely to survive a global nuclear war—city dwellers or poor dirt farmers, suburbanites or ghetto residents, people in the more developed or less developed countries? Why? (See Enrichment Study 3.)

21. How does species diversity in an ecosystem differ from diversity in the human population? Is human cultural diversity really necessary? Why? Could we have too much cultural diversity? Could cultural diversity lead to stability or instability in the human population? Relate this to war.

22. What responsibility, if any, do you feel Occidental Petroleum Company, which now owns Hooker Chemicals Company, should have for damages and cleanup costs resulting from the leakage of hazardous wastes from the Love Canal toxic waste dump? Defend your position. The company contends that (1) it sold the land to the Niagara Falls school board only after the board threatened to condemn and take over the site, (2) the school board knowingly and willfully built on the land after being warned by Hooker Chemicals not to construct any buildings over the canal site (a claim the board denies), (3) the dumping was legal at the time, (4) there is no definitive proof that the chemicals are responsible for the illnesses among Love Canal residents, and (5) it was relieved from all legal responsibility by its sales contract with the school board.

PART THREE

Population

We need that size of population in which human beings can most fulfill their potentialities; in my opinion we are already overpopulated from that point of view. Not just in places like India and China and Puerto Rico, but also in the United States and in Western Europe.

George Wald

6

Human Population Dynamics

The present extended period of rapid population growth in the world is unique when seen from a long-range perspective; it has never occurred before and is unlikely to occur again.

Jonas and Jonathan Salk

For about 97 percent of the time since *Homo sapiens* appeared about 300,000 years ago, the human population was under 5 million. World population is now at a record 4.8 billion people and climbing (Figure 1-1). Based on present trends, United Nations (UN) population experts estimate that world population growth will probably reach 6.2 billion by the year 2000 and 8.1 billion by 2020 and not level off until the year 2110 at about 10.5 billion—more than twice the number of people on earth today.

What are the major factors affecting these dramatic changes in the size of the human population? How can the size and growth rate of the human population be controlled? The first question is discussed in this chapter and the second one in the next chapter.

6-1 Major Factors Affecting Human Population Change

Five major factors affect the size and growth rate of the human population:

1. *Birth and death rate.* As long as the birth rate is greater than the death rate, population size will grow at a rate that depends on the difference between birth rate and death rate.

2. *Net migration rate.* If more people *immigrate* (enter) than *emigrate* (leave) a particular country, city, or area during a given period, the population of that area will grow at a rate that depends on the difference between the immigration rate and the emigration rate. This factor does not affect world population but does affect the size and rate of growth in various countries, cities, and areas as people move from one place to another.

3. *Total fertility rate.* World population size can level off only when the average number of children the women in the world have during their reproductive years of ages 15 to 44 stays at or below a replacement level of 2.1 children per woman for a considerable length of time.

4. *Age structure.* The length of time it takes for world population to stabilize after average total fertility rates reach or remain below the replacement level depends on the number or percentage of persons at each age level in the population. The larger the number and percentage of women in their reproductive years (15 to 44) and in their prereproductive years (under age 15), the longer it takes for population size to stabilize.

5. *Average marriage age* or *average age when first child is born:* Normally the later the average marriage age, the lower the average number of children a woman has between ages 15 and 44 (total fertility rate) and the sooner world population size will stabilize.

In the remainder of this chapter we will look more closely at these five factors.

6-2 Birth Rate and Death Rate

Net Population Change The difference between the total number of live births and the total number of deaths throughout the world during a given period of time gives the **net population change.**

$$\text{net population change} = \frac{\text{number of}}{\text{live births}} - \frac{\text{number of}}{\text{deaths}}$$

If there are more births than deaths, population will increase. *Today there are 2.5 births for each death, causing the world's population to increase by 153 people a*

Enrichment Studies 2, 4, 6, 7, and 8 are related to this chapter.

Table 6-1 The World's Ten Most Populous Nations in 1984 with Projections for 2020

Nation	1984 Population (in millions)	Projected 2020 Population (in millions)
China	1,034	1,545
India	746	1,290
Soviet Union	274	364
United States	236	296
Indonesia	162	262
Brazil	134	269
Japan	120	122
Bangladesh	100	245
Pakistan	97	194
Nigeria	88	259

Source: Population Reference Bureau. *1984 World Population Data Sheet.* Washington, D.C.: Population Reference Bureau, and Bouvier, Leon F. 1984. "Planet Earth 1984–2034: A Demographic Vision," *Population Bulletin*, vol. 39, no. 1, 1–39.

Table 6-2 1984 Birth Rates, Death Rates, and Infant Mortality Rates in Nine Geographical Regions

Region	Birth Rate	Death Rate	Infant Mortality Rate
World	28	11	84
More developed nations	16	19	19
Less developed nations	32	11	94
Africa	45	16	119
Asia	29	11	89
Europe	14	10	15
Latin America	31	8	65
North America	15	8	11
Oceania	21	9	42

Source: Population Reference Bureau. *1984 World Population Data Sheet.* Washington, D.C.: Population Reference Bureau.

minute, 9,140 an hour, 221,000 a day, and 81 million a year.

Words like *million* or *billion* often make little impression on us. But suppose you decide to take 1 second to say hello to each of the 81 million persons added during the past year. Working 24 hours a day, you would need almost 2.6 years to greet them, and during that time more than 211 million more persons would have arrived. Table 6-1 shows the world's ten most populous nations in 1984 with their projected population in 2020. By 2020 Japan is projected to be replaced on the list by Mexico with a population of 165 million. Because six of the most populous nations are in Asia, it is not surprising that Asia is by far the most populous continent with 2.8 billion, or 58 percent of the world's population.

Rate of Natural Change Demographers, or population specialists, normally use the **birth rate** and **death rate** (also called *crude birth rate* and *crude death rate*) rather than total births and deaths to describe population change. These rates give the number of births and deaths per 1,000 persons in the population at the midpoint of a given year (July 1) since this should represent the average population for that year. The birth and death rates are calculated as follows:

$$\text{birth rate} = \frac{\text{births per year}}{\text{midyear population}} \times 1,000$$

$$\text{death rate} = \frac{\text{deaths per year}}{\text{midyear population}} \times 1,000$$

In 1984, national birth rates throughout the world varied from a low of 10 in Denmark and West Germany to a high of 53 in the African nation of Kenya. The variation in death rates was lower, from a low of 4 in the Asian nations of Kuwait and Brunei to a high of 28 in the African nation of Gambia. Table 6-2 shows the average birth rates, death rates, and infant mortality rates* in various geographic areas. Notice that death rates do not vary significantly between MDCs and LDCs, whereas there is a sharp difference between the birth rates and infant mortality rates in these two groups of nations.

In LDCs, one-half of all annual deaths are among infants and children under age 5, compared to only 2 to 4 percent of deaths in MDCs. According to the World Health Organization (WHO), about 17 million infants and children under age 5 died each year in the late 1970s and early 1980s—making this the world's single largest health problem. WHO estimates that 15 million of these deaths could be prevented annually if the excellent health conditions found in northern Europe and North America prevailed throughout the world.

The difference between the birth and death rates is the **rate of natural change** (increase or decrease) during a given year.

$$\text{rate of natural change} = \text{birth rate} - \text{death rate}$$

In 1984, the world's birth rate was 28 births per 1,000 population, the death rate was 11 deaths per

*The infant mortality rate is the number of deaths of infants under 1 year of age per 1,000 live births in a given year.

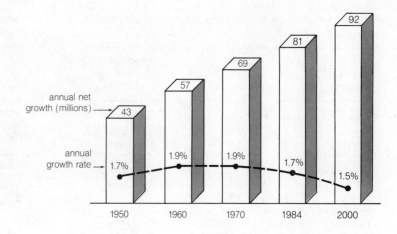

Figure 6-1 Comparison of world net population growth and percent population growth rate per year. Figures for the year 2000 are projected. (Source: Population Reference Bureau. Annual *World Population Data Sheets.*)

1,000 population, and the rate of natural increase was 17 persons per 1,000 population.*

Percentage Growth Rates and Doubling Times
Sometimes the rate of population growth is expressed as a percentage:

$$\frac{\text{percentage annual}}{\text{growth rate}} = \frac{\text{birth rate} - \text{death rate}}{10}$$

$$= \frac{28 - 11}{10} = 1.7\% \text{ in } 1984$$

In the late 1970s, a series of newspaper headlines, such as "Population Time Bomb Fizzles," "Another Non-Crisis," and "Population Growth May Have Turned a Historic Corner," falsely implied that world population growth had almost stopped. What actually happened is that the annual percentage *population growth rate* peaked at about 2 percent in

---

*In 1984 the world population at midyear was 4,763,000,000 or 4.763 billion people. During the year there were about 138.1 million births and 52.4 million deaths. From these figures we can find the birth rate, death rate, and the rate of natural increase:

$$\text{birth rate} = \frac{\underset{\text{(total births)}}{138,100,000}}{\underset{\text{(midyear population)}}{4,763,000,000}} \times 1,000$$

$$= \frac{28 \text{ births}}{\text{per 1,000 population}}$$

$$\text{death rate} = \frac{\underset{\text{(total deaths)}}{52,400,000}}{\underset{\text{(midyear population)}}{4,763,000,000}} \times 1,000$$

$$= \frac{11 \text{ deaths}}{\text{per 1,000 population}}$$

$$\frac{\text{rate of}}{\text{natural increase}} = \text{birth rate} - \text{death rate} = 28 - 11$$

$$= \frac{17 \text{ persons}}{\text{per 1,000 population}}$$

1965 and then began a slow decline to 1.9 percent by 1970 and to 1.7 percent by 1984, as shown in Figure 6-1. Despite this encouraging slowdown in the annual population growth *rate*, as Figure 6-1 shows, the annual *net population growth* increased from 69 million in 1969 to 81 million in 1984. By 2000, the world's population growth rate is projected to decline to 1.5 percent but annual net population growth is projected to increase to 92 million persons a year. Table 6-3 shows the percentage annual growth rates in 1984 and gives UN projections of population increases between 1984 and the years 2000 and 2020 for different geographical regions. The projected growth in population over the 50-year period between 1984 and 2034 for several nations was shown earlier in Table 6-1.

A population growth rate of 1 to 3 percent a year may seem relatively small. However, a population growing at only 1 percent a year will increase by 270 percent in 100 years; one growing by 2 percent a year increases 724 percent in 100 years; and one with a 3 percent annual growth rate increases by 1,922 percent over a century. For example, Nigeria with a population of 88 million and a 3.2 percent growth rate in 1984 is projected to increase to 259 million by 2020 (Table 6-1) and eventually to 623 million, more people than now live in all of Africa.

Another way to indicate the rate at which a population is growing is called **doubling time:** the time it takes for a population to double in size. The approximate doubling time in years can be found by dividing the annual percentage growth rate into 70—using the *rule of 70.*

$$\frac{\text{doubling time}}{\text{(in years)}} = \frac{70}{\text{annual percentage growth rate}}$$

In 1984 the doubling time for the world's population was about 40 years (70/1.7 = 40). Figure 6-2 shows the relationship between annual percentage population growth and doubling times and gives the

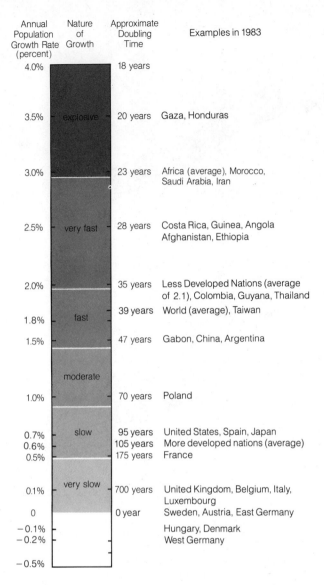

Annual Population Growth Rate (percent)	Nature of Growth	Approximate Doubling Time	Examples in 1983
4.0%	explosive	18 years	
3.5%		20 years	Gaza, Honduras
3.0%		23 years	Africa (average), Morocco, Saudi Arabia, Iran
2.5%	very fast	28 years	Costa Rica, Guinea, Angola Afghanistan, Ethiopia
2.0%		35 years	Less Developed Nations (average of 2.1), Colombia, Guyana, Thailand
1.8%	fast	39 years	World (average), Taiwan
1.5%		47 years	Gabon, China, Argentina
	moderate		
1.0%		70 years	Poland
0.7%	slow	95 years	United States, Spain, Japan
0.6%		105 years	More developed nations (average)
0.5%		175 years	France
0.1%	very slow	700 years	United Kingdom, Belgium, Italy, Luxembourg
0		0 year	Sweden, Austria, East Germany
−0.1% −0.2%			Hungary, Denmark West Germany
−0.5%			

Figure 6-2 Relationship between population growth rate and doubling time (70 divided by annual percentage population growth).

approximate doubling times for the population of selected countries throughout the world. Although doubling time gives a picture of *present* growth rates, it is at best a crude way of estimating *future* population size. This is because it assumes a constant growth rate over decades, whereas growth rates normally change.

Doubling times can also be used to illustrate the dramatic increase in the rate of population growth on earth during the past 300,000 years (Figure 1-1). For 290,000 years the human population grew at an annual rate of only about 0.002 percent, doubling about every 35,000 years. Since the development of agriculture about 10,000 years ago (Enrichment Study 1), population growth began to mushroom—especially during the past 100 years—and now grows at 1.7 percent a year with a doubling time of 40 years.

The rapid growth of the world's population over the past 100 years was not the result of a rise in birth rates but largely due to a decline in death rates—especially in the less developed nations, as shown in Figure 6-3. There are a number of interrelated reasons for this general decline in death rates, including **(1)** an increase in food supplies because of improved agricultural production; **(2)** better food distribution due to improved transportation; **(3)** better nutrition; **(4)** reduction of diseases associated with crowding, such as tuberculosis, because of better housing; **(5)** improved personal hygiene, including the use of soap, which reduced the spread of disease; **(6)** improved sanitation and water supplies, which reduced death rates from plague, cholera, typhus, dysentery, diphtheria, and other fatal diseases; and **(7)** improvements in medical and public health technology through the use of antibiotics, immunization, and insecticides such as DDT, which was used against malaria-carrying mosquitoes.

Table 6-3 Projected Population Growth for Nine Geographical Regions

Region	Annual Growth Rate (%) 1984	Population (in millions)		
		1984	2000	2020
World	1.7	4,762	6,130	7,180
More developed nations	0.6	1,166	1,273	1,342
Less developed nations	2.1	3,596	4,857	6,468
Africa	2.9	531	851	1,399
Asia	1.8	2,782	3,564	4,391
Europe	0.3	491	511	508
Latin America	2.4	397	564	801
North America	0.7	262	302	333
Oceania	1.3	24	29	34

Source: Population Reference Bureau. *1984 World Population Data Sheet.* Washington, D.C.: Population Reference Bureau.

Figure 6-3 Estimated birth and death rates and rates of natural population increase in more developed and less developed countries between 1775 and 1984 and projected rates (dashed lines) to 2000. (Source: Population Reference Bureau. Annual *World Population Data Sheets* and United Nations medium population projections)

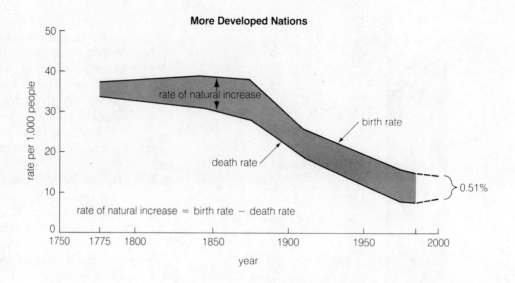

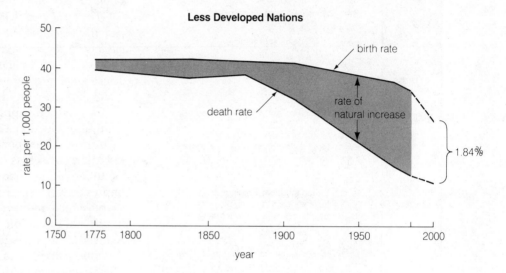

6-3   Migration

Net Migration Rate   For the world, population growth occurs only when there are more births than deaths. For a county, city, or other area, however, we must also consider *immigration* and *emigration* as people migrate from one place to another. For a given place on earth, the **net migration rate** per year is calculated as follows:

$$\text{net migration rate} = \frac{\begin{array}{c}\text{immigrants} \\ \text{per year}\end{array} - \begin{array}{c}\text{emigrants} \\ \text{per year}\end{array}}{\text{midyear population}} \times 1,000$$

If more persons immigrate than emigrate, the net migration rate is positive. If more leave than enter, it is negative.

The **rate of population change** per year for a given country, city, or area is the difference between its birth rate and death rate plus its net migration rate.

$$\begin{array}{c}\text{rate of population} \\ \text{change}\end{array} = \begin{array}{c}\text{birth} \\ \text{rate}\end{array} - \begin{array}{c}\text{death} \\ \text{rate}\end{array} + \begin{array}{c}\text{net migration} \\ \text{rate}\end{array}$$

U.S. Migration Rates   In the eighteenth century the United States was founded by immigrants and their children. Throughout its history the United States has admitted a larger number of immigrants and refugees than any other country in the world. Indeed, the total number is almost twice as large as that received by all other nations combined.

Legal immigrants are those admitted under official U.S. immigration policy according to certain qualifications and based on annual quotas. *Illegal immigrants* are those entering the U.S. without applying for legal immigrant status. *Refugees* are persons fleeing persecution based on race, religion, nationality, political opinion, or membership in a particular social group. Under the terms of the Refugee Act of 1980, the total number of refugees to be admitted each year is determined by the president in consultation with Congress. The maximum annual limit is 50,000 refugees except when justified by the national interest or unforeseen circumstances.

In recent years, it is estimated that about 1.1 million people enter the United States each year as legal or illegal immigrants and refugees, and about 100,000 people emigrate from the United States. Thus, the estimated net migration rate for the United States in 1984 was

$$\begin{aligned}\text{net migration rate} &= \frac{\text{immigrants per year} - \text{emigrants per year}}{\text{midyear population}} \times 1{,}000 \\ &= \frac{1{,}100{,}000 - 100{,}000}{236{,}300{,}000} \times 1{,}000 \\ &= 4 \text{ per } 1{,}000 \text{ population}\end{aligned}$$

In the 1970s legal immigration in the United States averaged about 425,000 per year and refugees averaged about 200,000 per year. Estimates of illegal immigration range from 100,000 to 1,000,000 a year, with 500,000 a year widely used. An estimated 50 to 60 percent of these illegal immigrants come from Mexico. However, accurate estimates of illegal immigrants are very difficult to make. For example, many Mexicans go back and forth across the border several times a year in order to find temporary work and may be counted several times.

Population Growth in the United States Figure 6-4 shows the variation in birth rates, death rates, and rate of natural increase in population (excluding migration) for the United States between 1900 and 1984. Although the rate of natural population increase has declined since 1947 (except for the slight upturn since 1976), the population continues to grow because the birth rate has remained considerably larger than the death rate. In mid-1984, the U.S. population was about 236 million.

In 1984 the birth rate in the United States was 16, the death rate 9, and the net immigration rate (including 1 million legal and illegal immigrants and refugees) was 4 per 1,000 persons. Thus, the rate of population change was

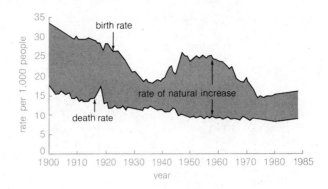

Figure 6-4 Birth and death rates and the rate of natural population increase (migration excluded) in the United States between 1900 and 1984. (Source: Population Reference Bureau. Annual *World Population Data Sheets*.)

$$\begin{aligned}\text{rate of population change} &= 16 - 9 + 4 \\ &= 11 \text{ per } 1{,}000 \text{ persons}\end{aligned}$$

Including migration, the percent annual growth rate in the United States in 1984 was 1.1 percent, with a doubling time of 64 years compared to 100 years when net migration is not included. Thus, *with migration included the U.S. population grew by 7 people a minute, 420 an hour, 10,000 a day, and 3.54 million a year during 1984.*

6-4 Fertility Rate

Total Fertility Rate To improve their ability to understand and project population changes, demographers use the **total fertility rate (TFR),** a *projection* of the average number of live children that would be born to each woman if she were to live through her childbearing lifetime (ages 15 to 44) bearing children at the same rate as other women did in each of these years. The TFR gives us the best idea of the average number of live births per woman for those women who survive to the end of their childbearing age of 44.

Logic suggests that two children should suffice to replace two parents. The actual average number of children needed for replacement, however, is slightly higher than two. In MDCs the *replacement level* is 2.1 children per woman and in the LDCs about 2.7. The two major reasons that both these numbers are above two are **(1)** some female children die before reaching their reproductive years at puberty (especially in LDCs) and **(2)** there is a slightly higher percentage of male children born than female.

In 1984, the average total fertility rate in the world was 3.8 children per woman. The average

Table 6-4 Average 1984 Total Fertility Rates for Nine Geographical Regions

Region	Average Total Fertility Rate
World	3.8
More developed nations	2.0
Less developed nations	4.4
Africa	6.4
Asia	4.0
Europe	1.8
Latin America	4.2
North America	1.8
Oceania	2.5

Source: Population Reference Bureau. *1984 World Population Data Sheet.* Washington, D.C.: Population Reference Bureau.

Table 6-5 United Nations Medium Projections for Stable Populations in Ten Geographical Regions

Region	Stable Population (in millions)	Year of Stabilization
World	10,529	2110
More developed nations	1,390	2080
Less developed regions	9,139	2110
Africa	2,193	2110
East Asia	1,725	2090
South Asia	4,145	2100
Europe	540	2030
Latin America	1,187	2100
North America	318	2060
Oceania	41	2070

Source: United Nations Fund for Population Activities. 1982. *State of World Population: 1982.* New York: United Nations Fund for Population Activities.

rate was 4.4 in the LDCs and 2.0 in the MDCs (Table 6-4). This shows clearly why the world has a long way to go before its population size will level off and begin to decline. It is encouraging that 23 MDCs had TFRs at or below 2.1 and 18 LDCs had TFRs at or below 2.7 by 1984.

Possibilities for World Population Stabilization By 1984 12 European nations **(1)** *were close to zero population growth* (Great Britain, Norway, Belgium, Switzerland, and Italy); **(2)** *had achieved zero population growth* (Austria, Luxembourg, Sweden, and East Germany); or **(3)** *were experiencing decreases in population size because death rates were higher than birth rates* (Denmark, West Germany, and Hungary). Although these nations represent only 5.2 percent of the world's population, this is at least a beginning toward eventual stabilization of world population. If present trends continue, several other more developed European nations should reach ZPG by 1990 and then enter a period of population decrease.

Achieving ZPG in the world, however, is more difficult because the LDCs have a much higher average TFR (Table 6-4). For world population even to begin the transition to ZPG, the average world TFR would have to drop from 3.8 in 1984 to about 2.5 children per woman (2.7 in the LDCs and 2.1 in the MDCs). The year in which this TFR is reached has an important effect on the peak size of the world's population.

According to 1982 estimates by the United Nations, if present trends continue, an average world TFR of 2.5 children per woman could be reached around 2025. Once this TFR is reached and maintained, population would still grow for 70 to 100 years before stabilizing because so many women in the world will still be moving into their reproductive years.

In 1982, the United Nations made three projections of when world population size would reach its peak level (ZPG) followed by a slow decrease in population size. Each projection assumed that an average world TFR of 2.5 would be reached at different times. According to the medium projection, *if the global average total fertility rate declines to 2.5 by 2025 and is maintained, world population should stabilize around 10.5 billion about 85 years later in the year 2110.* If fertility decreases at a faster pace, with a TFR of 2.5 reached around 2005, world population would stop growing much sooner—in 2040 with a peak size of 8 billion. If a TFR of 2.5 is not reached until 2045, world population would not level off until 2130 with a peak population size of 14.2 billion. Table 6-5 shows the projected stable population size and year of stabilization for different geographical regions using the medium UN projection.

Of course, no one knows whether any of these projections will be accurate. All are based on the assumption that there will be adequate supplies of food, energy, and other natural resources. If such supplies are not adequate or if there is a global nuclear war (Enrichment Study 3), then population size could stabilize or be sharply reduced by a sharp increase in death rates rather than a gradual decrease in birth rates. In the next chapter we will look at some of the ways that world population growth can be brought under control.

Possibilities for U.S. Population Stabilization Even with the drop in birth rates (Figure 6-4), U.S. population size is also expected to increase for many decades. One reason is that a decline in the birth rate (assuming death rates remain constant)

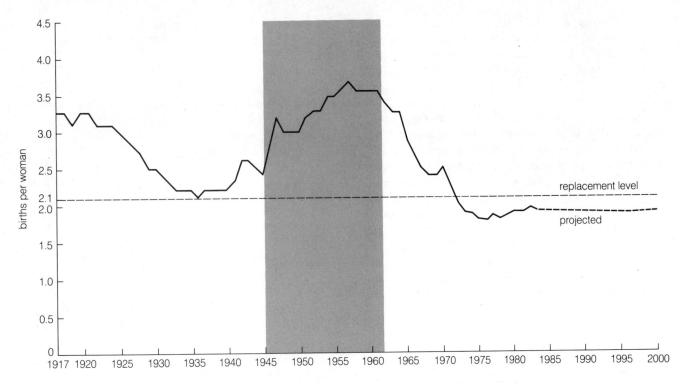

Figure 6-5 Total fertility rate for the United States between 1917 and 1984 and projected rate (dashed line) to 2000. The shaded area shows the peak years of the baby boom. (Source: Population Reference Bureau, 1982. *U. S. Population: Where We Are; Where We're Going*, and 1982 U.S. Bureau of Census medium population projections)

does not tell us whether women are having fewer children on the average or whether there is simply a lower percentage of women in the population who are in their most fertile years.

Such information is provided by the total fertility rate. Figure 6-5 shows that the TFR in the United States oscillates wildly. Note that the peak of the baby boom that took place after World War II, between 1947 and 1964, occurred in 1957 when the average TFR reached 3.7 children per woman. This was followed by a sharp drop to an average of 1.77 children per woman by 1976, with a slight rise to 1.84 between 1976 and 1984 (Figure 6-5)—still considerably below the 2.1 replacement level. Since 1980 there has been an increase in the birth rate of women in their late 20s and 30s who postponed having their first child. This delayed childbearing, however, has caused only a small rise in the overall birth rate and total fertility rate.

Figure 6-5 also shows why birth rates dropped sharply between 1957 and 1976. The average American woman simply had fewer children during her reproductive years. This drop was probably caused by a mixture of several factors including reduction in the number of unwanted and mistimed births because of the widespread use of effective birth control methods (Enrichment Study 8), the availability of legal abortions, changed motivation in favor

of smaller families, rising costs of raising a family, greater social acceptance of childless couples, and increasing numbers of women working outside the home. For example, the birth rate among working women is only one-third of those not working in the labor force.

In the late 1970s some newspapers incorrectly reported that the United States had reached ZPG because the total fertility rate had fallen below the replacement level of 2.1 (Figure 6-5). *It is important to realize that reaching a total fertility rate at or even below replacement level does not mean zero growth of the population has been reached.* Zero population growth occurs in a country or region when, over a period of time, the number of births plus immigrants equals the number of deaths plus emigrants. The United States is a long way from ZPG in spite of the dramatic drop in the TFR. This is due primarily to the age structure of the population, as discussed in the next section.

No one knows whether or how long U.S. total fertility rates will remain below replacement level. The present trend toward smaller families may continue or there could be a swing back toward larger families. The U.S. Bureau of the Census has made several projections for future population growth assuming various TFRs, life expectancies, and net immigration rates. According to the medium projection, usually taken to be the best projection, U.S. population could reach 268 million in the year 2000, peak at 309 million by 2050, and then begin to decrease—assuming an average of 1.9 live births per woman and an annual net migration rate of 450,000 persons.

Some groups such as The Environmental Fund and Zero Population Growth, however, have questioned some of the Census Bureau's assumptions in making these projections. First, they argue that the assumed net migration rate of 450,000 people per year in the medium projection is more likely to be 750,000 to 1,000,000 people per year. Second, they question the assumption that the current fertility rate, the lowest in history, will continue. It may rise for a variety of reasons including some that reflect important changes in the ethnic and racial composition of the population. The proportion of Hispanic and black women in the population is rising, and historically these groups have had higher than average fertility rates. By 1990 some analysts project that Hispanics will surpass blacks as the biggest minority group in the United States.

6-5 Age Structure

Number of Women of Childbearing and Younger Ages Why will world population keep growing for at least 100 or more years (assuming death rates don't rise) even after replacement TFRs are reached? Why do some demographers expect the U.S. birth rate to rise between now and 1993, even though the TFR may drop or stay at low levels?

To answer these questions we must consider a fourth factor in population dynamics. It is the **age structure,** or *age distribution,* of a population—the number or percentage of persons at each age level in a population. A major factor in population growth is the number or percentage of women of child-bearing age—especially the number in the prime reproductive years of ages 20 to 29—and the number or percentage of people in the world below age 15 who will soon be moving into their prime child-bearing years. If a large number of women are of or near childbearing age, births can rise even when women on the average have fewer children. Thus, *any population with a large number of people below age 29, and especially below age 15, will have a powerful, built-in momentum to maintain population growth.*

In 1984 about 35 percent of the people on this planet were under 15 years of age. These young people make up the broad base of the age structure of world population, which explains why population will continue to grow—especially in LDCs—70 to 100 years after replacement level total fertility rates are

Table 6-6 Percentage of Population Under Age 15 and Over Age 64 for Nine Geographical Regions in 1984

Region	Population Under Age 15 (%)	Population Over Age 64 (%)
World	35	6
More developed nations	23	12
Less developed nations	38	4
Africa	45	3
Asia	37	4
Europe	22	13
Latin America	39	4
North America	22	12
Oceania	29	8

Source: Population Reference Bureau. *1984 World Population Data Sheet.* Washington, D.C.: Population Reference Bureau.

reached, unless death rates rise sharply. Table 6-6 shows the percentage of the population under age 15 and over age 64 in various geographic regions. Notice that in the LDCs an average of 38 percent of the population is under 15, while in the MDCs this figure is only 23 percent.

Table 6-6 also shows a significant difference between the percentage of people above age 64 in the MDCs (12%) and the LDCs (4%). The United Nations projects that by the year 2025 there will be almost 1 billion people over 64 who will need to be cared for, with relatively fewer people of working age to care for them. This dramatic shift in population age structure by 2025 is projected to take place because of a combination of fewer children per woman and longer lives. While world birth rates are projected to be cut in half between 1950 and 2025, average life expectancy is expected to rise from 47 to 70. In the LDCs this could mean more old people left to fend for themselves.

Population age structure also explains why it will probably take at least 50 years for the United States to reach ZPG, even if the present historically low TFRs are maintained at 1.7 to 2.0 births per woman (Figure 6-5). It also explains why the number of births each year in the United States could rise between 1984 and 1993. *Even though many U.S. couples are now having smaller families, the number of births could easily rise during the 1980s—not because women will have more babies but because there are more women to have babies.*

The 37 million women born during the baby boom period from 1947 to 1964 will affect U.S. population growth through 1993. Women born at the beginning of the baby boom in 1947 entered their peak reproduction years of 20 to 29 in 1966 and stayed there until 1976. Figure 6-4 shows that the birth rate did not increase as sharply as it could have between 1976 and 1984 after reaching the low-

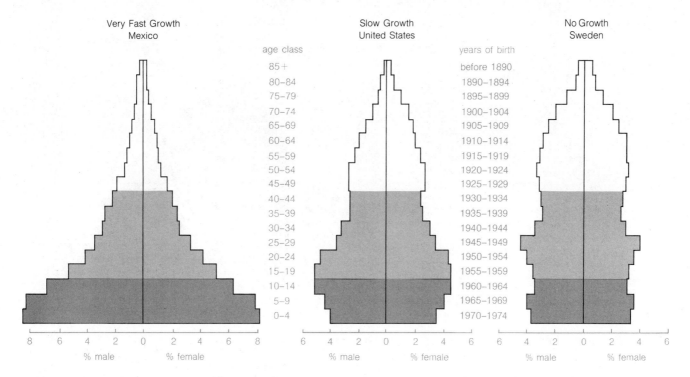

Figure 6-6 Population age structure diagrams for countries with rapid (Mexico), slow (United States), and zero (Sweden) population growth rates. Dark portions represent prereproductive periods (0 to 14), shaded portions represent reproductive years (15 to 44), and clear portions are postproductive years (45 to 85+). (Source: Population Reference Bureau)

est rate in U.S. history in 1976. Women had fewer children during this period for a combination of reasons, including a drop in the marriage rate, steady growth in female employment, and a trend toward delaying having children until education is completed and careers are established.

Women born in 1963, at the end of the baby boom, entered their peak childbearing years in 1984 and will stay there until 1993. The number of women of childbearing age (15 to 44) will reach its high point in 1986 and then slowly fall. Thus, the postwar baby boom can still have an *echo effect* that becomes the *potential* "mother boom" of the late 1980s and early 1990s. A second echo effect with a slight rise in birth rates could begin around 2000 as the increased number of daughters borne by baby boom women will themselves begin reaching childbearing age.

Age Structure Diagrams We can obtain an age structure diagram for the world or for a given country or region by plotting the percentages of males and females in the total population in three age categories: prereproductive (ages 0 to 14), reproductive (ages 15 to 44 with prime reproductive ages 20 to 29), and postproductive (ages 45 to 85+). Figure 6-6 compares the age structure for countries

with rapid (Mexico), slow (United States), and zero (Sweden) population growth rates, and Figure 6-7 compares the age structure diagrams for today's LDCs and MDCs.

The general shape of the age structure diagram is a key to whether a population might expand, decline, or stay the same. A rapidly expanding population has a broad base with a large number already in the reproductive age group (15 to 44) and an even larger percentage of children ready to move into this category during the following 15 years. This is the general shape of the age structure diagrams for LDCs as a whole (Figure 6-7) and for individual LDCs such as Mexico (Figure 6-6)—shapes that are not expected to change before 2000. In 1984 Mexico's population was 77.7 million, with a birth rate of 32 and a death rate of 6. Even though its birth rate is expected to decrease to 25 by the year 2000, Mexico is projected to have a population of 115 million by 2000 and 163 million by 2030. The primary reason for this is that in 1984 44 percent of Mexico's population was under age 15.

Age structure diagrams for nations such as the United States with relatively slow population growth have a small base. Those for nations such as Sweden with zero population growth rate have a shape with almost vertical sides rather than pyramidal sides (Figure 6-6). In such a stabilized age structure, all

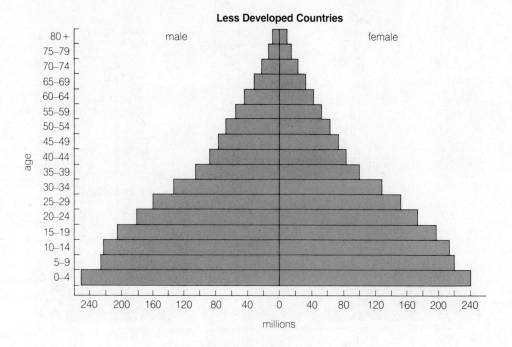

Figure 6-7 Age structure diagrams for LDCs and MDCs in 1984. (Source: United Nations. 1982. *Demographic Indicators of Countries: Estimates and Projections Assessed in 1980.* New York: United Nations.)

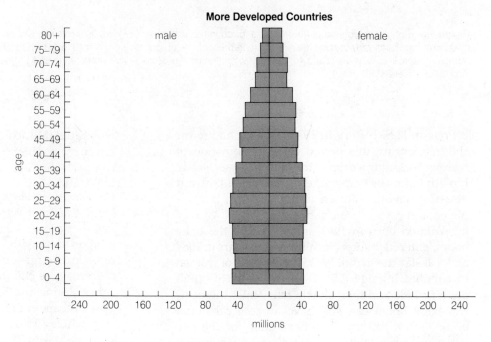

generations and age groups are about the same in number.

Making Future Projections from Age Structure Diagrams   Figure 6-8 shows that the baby boom in the United States between 1947 and 1964 (Figure 6-6) caused a bulge in the age structure, which will move through the prime reproductive ages of 20 to 29 between 1970 and 1987 and through older age groups in later years. This helps explain why the

1960s and 1970s have been called the "generation of youth," the period between 1975 and 1990 could be called the "age of young adults," that between 1990 and 2010 the "age of middle-aged adults," and that between 2010 and 2030 "the age of senior citizens."

As this large baby boom group passes through succeeding age groups, it creates a need for rapid expansion of schools, housing, employment opportunities, medical services, and eventually social security. As economist Robert Samuelson put

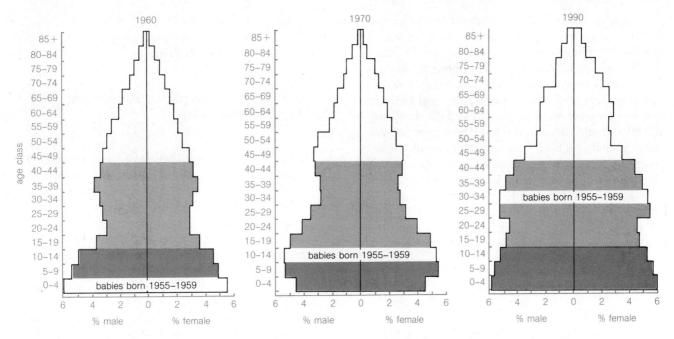

Figure 6-8 Age structure of the U.S. population in 1960, 1970, and 1990 (projected). The population bulge of babies born in 1955 to 1959 will slowly move upward. (Source: Population Reference Bureau)

it, "You cannot understand economics or politics in the United States today without understanding the impact of the baby boom."

Using these diagrams, we can project some of the social and economic changes that may occur in the United States in coming decades. By 1980 there were 40 million more baby boomers between ages 20 and 29 than there were in 1960. In the 1970s and early 1980s large numbers of baby boom adults flooded the job market, causing high unemployment rates for teenagers and adults under 29. This situation won't begin to ease until after 1992, when the last of the people born during the baby boom turn 29. For those with jobs, advancement is likely be much slower than in the present generation, and there will be more cutthroat competition for upper-level jobs. It is estimated that between 1980 and 1990, nearly one-quarter of the baby boom college graduates will be overeducated for the jobs they get—secretaries, store clerks, cab drivers, and factory workers. Even those headed for the seemingly safe occupations of the 1970s—law, medicine, and business schools—will have trouble realizing their aspirations.

In the 1990s the baby boom generation will be settling into middle age: The number of people between ages 35 and 64 is projected to increase from 75 million in 1984 to 94.3 million in 1995 and then to 105 million by 2000. These adults may face relatively little opportunity for advancement unless they somehow force those aged 45 to 59 to retire. We should also see more young leaders in government, politics, and private industry.

Assuming death rates don't rise, the number of people over age 64 will rise from 28 million (11 percent of the population) in 1984 to 35 million (13 percent of the population) by 2000 and 60 million (20 percent of the population) by 2025. The burden of supporting so many retired baby boomers will fall on the shoulders of the much smaller group of babies born in the 1960s, 1970s, and 1980s who make up the work force—primarily those aged 20 to 65 who support children and retired people. This increase in retired citizens could put a severe strain on the U.S. social security and medicare systems. Under the social security system, payments made by the current work force are used to make payments to retired persons. Already, about one-quarter of the federal budget goes to the elderly and their dependents. The United States has two difficult choices for maintaining the social security system: **(1)** raising taxes, which is politically and economically unpopular, or **(2)** reducing benefits either by raising the retirement age or by reducing payments. By the twenty-first century there may be an intense political struggle over how much more of the nation's resources retired baby boomers will command.

The latest baby bust generation, born in the 1970s and early 1980s when total fertility rates were low (Figure 6-5), should have a much easier time than the baby boom generation that preceded them.

Fewer will be competing for education, jobs, and services. Labor shortages should drive up wages for the baby bust generation and the United States could end up relaxing its current immigration laws to bring in new workers. The shortage of young adults means that the armed forces will be hard pressed to meet recruiting levels and the draft may be reinstated. Those in this baby bust group, however, may find it hard to get job promotions as they reach middle age because upper-level positions will be filled by the baby boom group.

From these few projections, we see that any bulge or indentation in the age structure of a population creates a number of social and economic changes that ripple through a society for decades.

6-6 Average Marriage Age

Another factor affecting population size and rate of change is the *average marriage age of women*, or, more precisely, the *average age at which women give birth to their first child*. Because older brides on the average have fewer children, an increase in average marriage age generally leads to a decrease in the total fertility rate.

Although data are lacking for a number of countries, average marriage ages are around 19 in Africa, 21 in Asia and Latin America, 22 in Oceania, and 23 in Europe. Recent studies showed that **(1)** the average age of marriage was rising in most MDCs and in Asia, but not in Africa and Latin America; **(2)** women who delay marriage to age 21 have about as many children as women marrying in their teens; and **(3)** the average marriage age would have to rise to at least 25 in order to lower fertility.

Since 1955 the average marriage age in the United States has been increasing and is now near 23 years of age (24.8 for men and 22.3 for women). This cuts the average childbearing period for American women from ages 15 to 44 to ages 23 to 44. Even more important, the prime reproductive period is almost cut in half from ages 15 to 29 to ages 23 to 29.

We have seen how demographers use five major factors—birth and death rates, migration rate, total fertility rate, age structure, and average marriage age—to make projections of future population changes. Each projection is based on certain assumptions about continuing and future trends in the fertility of couples who have not begun having children and those who have begun but not finished bearing children. Knowing the unpredictability of people, we should recognize that these are not predictions of what will necessarily take place. A line from Shakespeare's play *Macbeth* could be the demographer's motto: "If you can look into the seeds of time/And say which grains will grow and which will not,/Speak then to me."

6-7 The Geography of Population: The Rich-Poor Gap

Comparison of Less Developed and More Developed Nations   The world is polarized into two major groups: one rich and one poor; one literate, the other largely illiterate; one overfed and overweight, one hungry and malnourished; one with a moderate to low rate of population growth, the other with a very high rate. A comparison of LDCs* and MDCs is given in Table 6-7.

The term *rich-poor gap* dramatizes the differences among nations, but it is an oversimplification. That a country is classified as a less developed or poor nation does not always mean that living conditions are hopeless. Many people in LDCs are well fed and live reasonably comfortable lives. At the same time, these regions contain at least 800 million people in dire poverty, characterized by malnutrition, disease, illiteracy, squalid shelter and surroundings, high infant mortality rates, and low life expectancy. In Africa and Asia, almost half of the population exists on an average per capita gross national product of less than $300 per person. Up to 80 percent of this is spent on food.

The Five Worlds   There are some important differences among various LDCs not revealed in Table 6-7. It is useful to divide the nations of the world into five categories:

1. The *first world* indicates the most advanced industrial nations: the United States, Canada, Japan, most noncommunist nations of Europe, Australia, and New Zealand.

2. The *second world* includes the communist nations: the Soviet Union, China, and eastern Europe.

3. The *third world* is made up of a number of states with one or more major resources that should allow them to become more developed nations without significant foreign aid. These include the oil-rich nations such as Saudi Arabia, Mexico, and Iran, Morocco (with reserves of phosphates), Malaysia (tin, rubber, and timber), and Zaire and Zambia (copper).

---

*The terms *less developed nations, developing nations, poorer nations, Third World nations,* and *South* are used to describe nations with nonindustrial economies and average per capita gross national products (GNP) below $3,000 per year.

Table 6-7 Major Characteristics of Less Developed and More Developed Countries in 1984

Less Developed Countries	More Developed Countries
High birth rates (25–50 births per 1,000 population, average 32)	Low birth rates (10–20 births per 1,000 population, average 16)
Low to high death rates (9–25 deaths per 1,000 population, average 11)	Low death rates (9–11 deaths per 1,000 population, average 9)
Low to fairly high average life expectancy (average 58 years)	High average life expectancy (average 73 years)
Rapid population growth (average 2.1%)	Slow population growth (average 0.6%)
Large fraction of population under 15 years old (average 38%)	Moderate fraction of population under 15 years old (average 23%)
Moderate to high infant mortality rate (40–200 deaths of infants under 1 year old per 1,000 live births, average 94)	Low infant mortality (8–20 deaths of infants under 1 year old per 1,000 live births, average 19)
Moderate to high total fertility rate (average 4.4 children per woman)	Low total fertility rate (average 2.0 children per woman)
Low to moderate per capita daily food supply (1,500–2,700 calories per person per day)	High per capita daily food supply (3,100–3,500 calories per person per day)
High illiteracy level (25%–75%)	Low illiteracy level (1%–4%)
Mainly rural, farming population (68% rural, 32% urban)	Mainly urban, industrial population (71% urban, 29% rural)
Low per capita energy use (average 3 million kilocalories per person per year)	High per capita energy use (average 30 million kilocalories per person per year)
Low to moderate average per capita income (widespread poverty) ($90–$3,000 per person per year, average $750)	High average per capita income (widespread affluence) ($3,000–$25,600 per person per year, average $9,190)

4. The *fourth world* consists of nations that have some raw materials and could eventually become more developed, but only with a combination of aid from today's more developed nations and strong government programs for population control and increased self-reliance. This group includes Peru, Liberia, Jordan, and Egypt.

5. The *fifth world* is made up of countries such as Chad, Ethiopia, Somalia, Rwanda, and Bangladesh, which have ample human resources but few natural resources. Without strict population control and massive foreign aid, these countries face mass starvation and continuing poverty.

The countries falling into these five general groups are shown in Figure 6-9. According to the World Bank, economic growth fell behind population growth in 18 fifth world countries, mostly in Africa, between 1970 and 1980.

Life in the Fourth and Fifth Worlds Tables and maps comparing the MDCs and LDCs are useful for their overall patterns, but these abstract statistics translate into hunger, drudgery, and early death for almost one-half of the human beings on this planet. When you walk into a typical rural village or urban slum in one of the fourth and fifth world countries, you smell the stench of refuse and open sewers. Groups of malnourished children sit around wood fires eating breakfasts of bread and coffee. Children and women carry jars or cans of water from a muddy, microbe-infested river, canal, or village water faucet. At night people sleep on the street in the open or under makeshift canopies. Families of 10 or 12 may crowd into single-room shacks, often made from straw, cardboard, or rusting metal. Three or four people may use one bed, but most sleep on dirt floors.

The father and mother and perhaps most of the children may work in the fields or beg for food in the city. If lucky, the parents may make about $200 a year—giving them an average of 55¢ a day to feed their family of eight or nine. The parents, who themselves may die by age 45, know that three or four of their children may die from hunger or routine childhood diseases. The children that survive add to the flood of people in the slums or those heading for cities, hoping to find nonexistent jobs.

Figure 6-9 The five worlds.

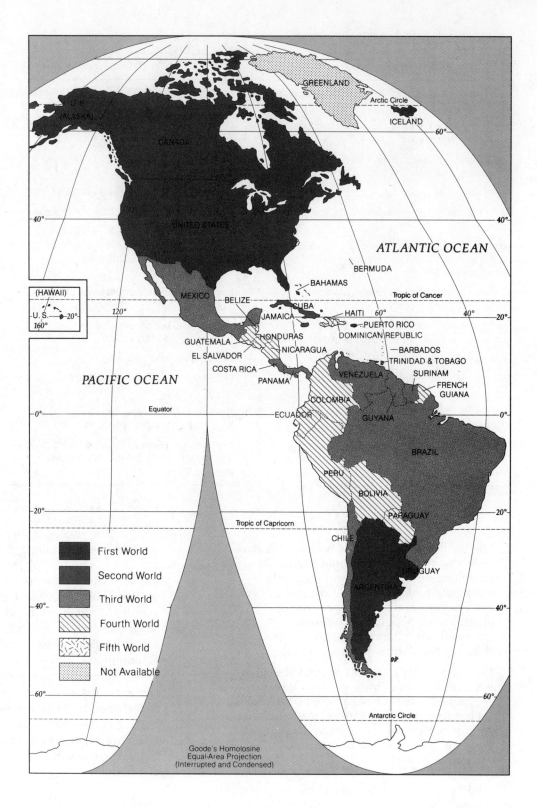

GREENLAND

Arctic Circle

ICELAND

U. S. (ALASKA)

CANADA

60°

ATLANTIC OCEAN

40°

40°

UNITED STATES

BERMUDA

(HAWAII)

BAHAMAS

Tropic of Cancer

U. S. 160°

20°

MEXICO

BELIZE

CUBA

HAITI

60°

40°

20°

120°

JAMAICA

PUERTO RICO

DOMINICAN REPUBLIC

GUATEMALA

HONDURAS

BARBADOS

EL SALVADOR

NICARAGUA

TRINIDAD & TOBAGO

COSTA RICA

SURINAM

PACIFIC OCEAN

PANAMA

VENEZUELA

FRENCH GUIANA

COLOMBIA

ECUADOR

Equator

GUYANA

0°

0°

BRAZIL

PERU

BOLIVIA

20°

PARAGUAY

20°

Tropic of Capricorn

CHILE

First World

URUGUAY

Second World

ARGENTINA

Third World

40°

40°

Fourth World

Fifth World

Not Available

60°

60°

Antarctic Circle

Goode's Homolosine
Equal-Area Projection
(Interrupted and Condensed)

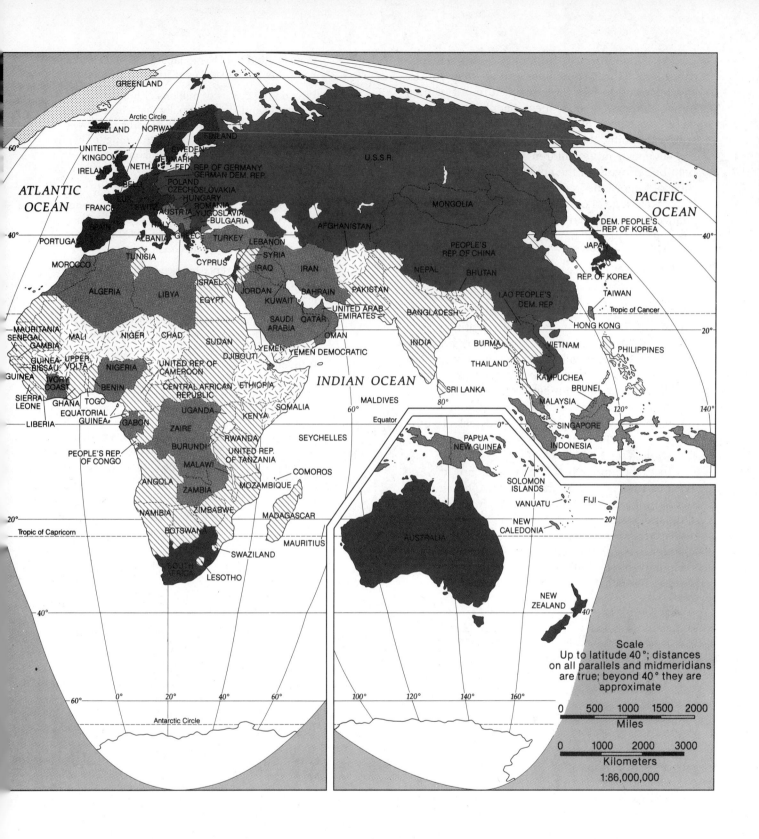

GREENLAND

Arctic Circle

ATLANTIC OCEAN

PACIFIC OCEAN

ICELAND   NORWAY   SWEDEN   FINLAND

60°

UNITED KINGDOM
IRELAND
NETH.   DENMARK
FED. REP OF GERMANY
GERMAN DEM. REP.
POLAND
CZECHOSLOVAKIA
HUNGARY
ROMANIA
AUSTRIA   YUGOSLAVIA
BULGARIA
ALBANIA   GREECE   TURKEY
PORTUGAL
SPAIN
FRANCE
BEL.
LUX.
SWITZ.

U.S.S.R.

MONGOLIA

DEM. PEOPLE'S
REP. OF KOREA

40°

40°

AFGHANISTAN

PEOPLE'S
REP. OF CHINA

JAPAN

REP. OF KOREA

TAIWAN

MOROCCO
TUNISIA
ALGERIA   LIBYA
EGYPT

LEBANON
SYRIA
CYPRUS
ISRAEL
IRAQ   IRAN
JORDAN
KUWAIT
BAHRAIN
SAUDI   QATAR
ARABIA
UNITED ARAB
EMIRATES
OMAN

NEPAL   BHUTAN

PAKISTAN

BANGLADESH

LAO PEOPLE'S
DEM. REP.

Tropic of Cancer

HONG KONG

20°

MAURITANIA
SENEGAL
GAMBIA
MALI
NIGER   CHAD
SUDAN
GUINEA-
BISSAU
UPPER
VOLTA
GUINEA
IVORY
COAST
NIGERIA
SIERRA
LEONE
GHANA   TOGO
LIBERIA
EQUATORIAL
GUINEA
BENIN
GABON
PEOPLE'S REP.
OF CONGO
UNITED REP. OF
CAMEROON
CENTRAL AFRICAN
REPUBLIC
ZAIRE
DJIBOUTI
YEMEN
YEMEN DEMOCRATIC
ETHIOPIA
UGANDA
KENYA
RWANDA
BURUNDI
UNITED REP.
OF TANZANIA
MALAWI
ANGOLA   ZAMBIA

INDIA

BURMA

VIETNAM

PHILIPPINES

KAMPUCHEA

THAILAND

BRUNEI

MALAYSIA
SINGAPORE

120°

140°

INDIAN OCEAN

MALDIVES

SRI LANKA

80°

60°

SOMALIA

SEYCHELLES

Equator

COMOROS

MOZAMBIQUE

0°

INDONESIA

PAPUA
NEW GUINEA

SOLOMON
ISLANDS

VANUATU   FIJI

NAMIBIA   ZIMBABWE

20°

Tropic of Capricorn

BOTSWANA

MADAGASCAR

MAURITIUS

SWAZILAND

NEW
CALEDONIA

NEW
ZEALAND

20°

SOUTH
AFRICA   LESOTHO

AUSTRALIA

40°

40°

60°

0°   20°   40°   60°

100°   120°   140°   160°

Antarctic Circle

Scale
Up to latitude 40°; distances
on all parallels and midmeridians
are true; beyond 40° they are
approximate

0   500   1000   1500   2000
Miles

0   1000   2000   3000
Kilometers
1:86,000,000

When members of affluent societies see such conditions, they sometimes experience culture shock, trying to blot the grim picture out of their minds. Others consider these people ignorant for having so many children. However, from the parents' viewpoint, their survival depends on having six, seven, or more children—especially boys—to help beg or work in the fields and to help them in their old age. One couple in India would have to bear an average of 6.3 children to have a 95 percent chance of one son surviving. For those living near the edge of survival having too many children may cause problems, but having too few can cause death at an early age.

Human Ecology   The past five chapters have introduced you to some fundamental scientific principles used to understand ecology. Throughout the rest of this book we will shift increasingly from classical ecology to human ecology. **Human ecology** is the study of the relations between the human community and its environment. Human ecology crosses traditional academic boundaries and seeks to integrate scientific, behavioral, sociological, political, economic, and ethical factors.

In this complex realm, principles are few and not well understood. Human ecology often involves decision making with insufficient information and little understanding. But the world's problems won't wait until we understand them fully. In the next chapter we begin this emphasis on human ecology by looking at possibilities and methods for bringing world population growth under control.

Not to decide is to decide.

Harvey Cox

Discussion Topics

1. Why are falling birth rates not necessarily a reliable indicator of future population growth trends?

2. Discuss the pros and cons of introducing DDT and modern health and sanitation practices into LDCs. On balance, did the introduction of these practices save more lives? Why? What might be the population situation in LDCs today if DDT and antibiotics had never been discovered? (See Section 9-9.)

3. Why do the deaths of millions of human beings by starvation and famine usually make little impression on many of us, while the deaths of individual human beings by murder, drowning, or being trapped in a coal mine receive nationwide attention and sympathy? Analyze this response in terms of dealing with world population growth.

4. Suppose modern medicine finds cures for cancer and heart disease. What effects would this have on population growth in MDCs and LDCs? On age structure? On social problems?

5. Explain the difference between achieving replacement level and ZPG. Why is the replacement level in LDCs higher than in MDCs?

6. What must happen to the total fertility rate if the United States is to attain ZPG in 40 to 60 years? Why will it take so long? Explain why instant ZPG is for all practical purposes not possible.

7. Explain how the U.S. population has the potential to grow rapidly again through 1993.

8. Project what your own life may be like at ages 25, 45, and 65 on the basis of the present age structure of the U.S. population or that of the country in which you live. What changes, if any, do such projections make in your career choice and in your plans for marriage and children?

9. Explain why raising the average first marriage age to 25 or higher is an effective means of reducing population growth rates.

10. Criticize each of the following headlines or statements. Be specific.
    a. "Baby Boom Replaced by Bust—U.S. in Danger of Instant ZPG."
    b. "Birth Rates Falling—Prophets of Doom Wrong Again."

11. List some basic characteristics of MDCs and LDCs. Which of the characteristics of LDCs do you believe could be changed most rapidly? How?

12. Explain how rapid population growth can lock a country into continued poverty despite an increasing GNP.

13. Explain why it may be rational for a couple in India to have six or seven children. What changes would have to take place for such a couple to think of their behavior as irrational?

14. Do you think the world is more likely to reach the high (14.2 billion), medium (10.5 billion), or low (8 billion) population size projected in 1982 by the United Nations? Explain.

7

Human Population Control

Reproduction is a private act, but it is not a private affair. It has far-reaching social consequences.

Lincoln Day

What factors affect the maximum human population size? Should population growth in the world and in the United States be controlled? What methods are available for controlling the size of the human population? These questions and possible answers are the subjects of this chapter. Let's begin with a discussion of the factors that can limit the population of any species and then relate these ideas to the human population.

7-1   Factors Affecting Maximum Population Size

J Curves and S Curves   The population story for a species can usually be told with two very simple curves—a *J-shaped curve* and an *S-shaped curve*. With unlimited resources and ideal environmental conditions, a species can produce offspring at its maximum rate, called its **biotic potential.** Such growth starts off slowly and then increases rapidly to produce an exponential or J-shaped curve of population growth (Figure 7-1). Bacteria, insects, and rodents have high biotic potentials; larger species, such as lions, elephants, and humans, have relatively low biotic potentials. Since environmental conditions are usually not ideal, a population rarely reproduces at its biotic potential.

Recall from Section 4-4 that organisms use two basic reproductive strategies to assure that their genetic material occupies as many future ecological niche spaces as possible. Some, such as dandelions and houseflies, expend their energies producing thousands of offspring but not caring for them. As

a result, mortality is very high, with only a few individuals reaching reproductive age. Other species such as tigers and people produce a small number of offspring; they then use much energy caring for these few young until they are big and strong enough to fend for themselves.

The population size of a particular species in a given ecosystem is limited by availability of one or more resources that can act as *limiting factors* (Section 3-7). The maximum population size of a given species that a particular ecosystem or area can support indefinitely under a given set of environmental conditions is called the ecosystem's **carrying capacity.** Thus, in an ecosystem with finite resources a J-shaped population growth curve for a particular species cannot go on forever.

All the limiting factors that act together to regulate the maximum allowable size of a population (carrying capacity) are called the population's **environmental resistance.** As a population encounters environmental resistance, the J-shaped curve of population growth bends away from its steep incline

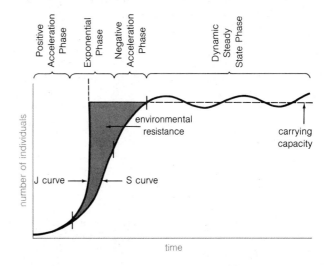

Figure 7-1   The J-shaped curve of population growth is converted to an S-shaped curve when a population encounters environmental resistance caused by one or more limiting factors.

Enrichment Studies 1, 2, 3, 6, and 8 are related to this chapter.

and eventually levels off at a size that typically fluctuates above and below the carrying capacity (Figure 7-1). In other words, environmental resistance opposes the biotic potential of a population and converts a J-shaped curve into a sigmoid, or S-shaped, curve. As environmental conditions change, however, the carrying capacity level for a particular population can be raised or lowered.

Because of a slow time delay, some populations (especially those of insects, bacteria, and algae) may temporarily overshoot their carrying capacity size by a wide margin and then undergo a rapid decrease in population size, known as a **population crash** (Figure 7-2). In some cases a population crash involves a sharp increase in the death rate and in others it can involve a combination of a rise in the death rate coupled with migration of large numbers of individuals to other areas. A population crash can also occur when a change in environmental conditions lowers the carrying capacity level for a population.

Such a population crash occurred in Ireland around 1845 as a result of the Irish potato famine. By the 1700s the Irish people depended heavily on the potato for a major portion of their diet. In 1739, an unusual November freeze destroyed potatoes in the field and in storage. The resulting famine led to the death of an estimated 300,000 people. This was only a temporary setback and the Irish soon became even more dependent on potatoes. More planting and favorable weather helped in allowing the Irish population expand to over 8 million by 1841. In 1845, however, a fungus infection wiped out the entire potato crop in Ireland. The population crashed through a combination of starvation and migration to other countries. Since 1900 the population of Ireland has been about one-half its size in 1845.

Factors Controlling Human Population Size and Growth Rate The populations of most animal species fluctuate in size. According to the Malthusian view (Section 1-5), human population size is controlled by famine, disease, and war. These factors have reduced the population size of certain countries and areas throughout human history, but so far they have had little effect on overall world population growth, as shown in Figure 7-3.

The human population has continued to grow in size because human cleverness, technological and social adaptations, and other forms of *cultural evolution* have extended the earth's carrying capacity for humans. In essence, people have been able to alter their ecological niche (Section 4-4) by increas-

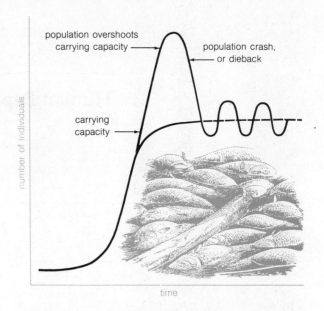

Figure 7-2 A population crash, or dieback, can occur either when a population temporarily overshoots its carrying capacity due to a time lag in negative feedback controls or when a change in environmental conditions lowers the carrying capacity.

ing food production, controlling disease, and using large amounts of energy and matter resources to make normally uninhabitable areas of the earth inhabitable. Figure 7-3 shows that after each major technological change the population has grown rapidly. Then, with the exception of the industrial-scientific revolution we are still experiencing, the J-shaped curve of population growth has leveled off to produce an S-shaped curve representing relatively little population growth for a long period of time.

Projections for the Future The dashed lines in Figure 7-3 show three projections for the human population based on present understanding. No one, of course, knows what the present or future *carrying capacity* for the human population is or what the limiting factor or factors might be—food, air, water, pollution, or lack of space. There are two major reasons for this lack of knowledge. First, there is a wide range of opinion about whether there will be enough affordable supplies of renewable and nonrenewable resources in the future (Section 1-3). Second, there are differences in opinion regarding the average degree of affluence that should be supported by these resources. While 80 percent of the world's people are forced to survive with little or no shelter and minimal supplies of food and water, another 20 percent of the world's population are accustomed to an affluent life-style.

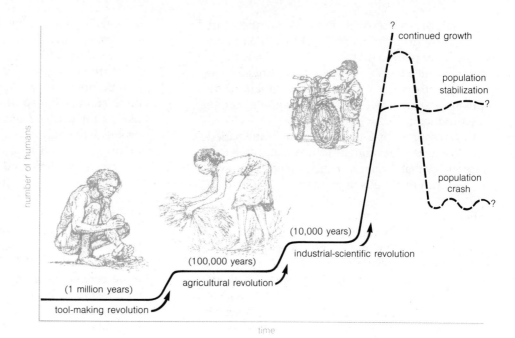

Figure 7-3 So far humans have extended the earth's carrying capacity by technological innovation. After each major technological revolution, the population has grown rapidly and then, with the exception of the industrial-scientific revolution, leveled off for a long period of time. Dashed lines represent different projections for the human population: continued growth, population stabilization, and continued growth followed by a population crash and population stabilization at a much lower level. All curves are suggestive and are not drawn to scale.

Some observers believe we have already gone beyond the carrying capacity point where all of the earth's inhabitants can be adequately fed, sheltered, and supported. H. R. Hulett of Stanford University estimates that present world food production could feed only 1.2 billion people (one-fourth the present world population) based on U.S. dietary standards, and only 600 million (one-eighth of the present world population) at the U.S. rate of energy consumption. Some argue, however, that these rates of food, energy, and resource consumption are wasteful and unnecessarily high (Section 1-5).

At the other end of the spectrum, agricultural economist Colin Clark sees a world in which 45 billion people could have a U.S. type of diet by cultivating all arable land, using nuclear power for energy, and mining much of the earth's crust to a depth of 1.6 kilometers (1 mile). If the human diet were based on grain rather than a mixture of grain and meat, he estimates the earth could support 157 billion people. Bernard Gilland labels such a vision as "a nightmare to be avoided at all costs" and disputes such estimates of potentially arable land.

A second possibility shown in Figure 7-3 is continued growth past the carrying capacity followed by a dieback of billions—perhaps 50 to 80 percent of the world's population—through a combination of famine, disease, nuclear war, and widespread ecological disruption. Some think that this, unfortunately, may be the most likely path to ZPG (Enrichment Study 2).

7-2 Should Population Growth Be Controlled?

Optimum Population Asking how many people the earth could support, however, focuses on the wrong question. Instead, we should be asking how many people the earth could support at a decent standard of living. Thus, a third possibility not shown in Figure 7-3 is stabilization of the world population at some level (perhaps 8 to 15 billion) followed by a gradual decrease to a lower **optimum population** that would allow most, if not all, of the world's population to live with reasonable comfort. Again, no one knows what this optimum population is. Some consider it a meaningless question, some put it at 20 billion, others at 6 billion, and others at a level below today's population level.

World Population Most nations in the world either favor stabilizing the size of their population or at least hope to reduce the rate at which their populations are growing. The problems of war, poverty, racism, disease, pollution, urbanization, ecosystem simplification, and resource depletion won't be solved by population stabilization. But, as *The Global 2000 Report to the President* pointed out, without it each of these problems is very likely to become much worse.

Economist Julian Simon, however, does not favor stabilizing the world population. He argues that **(1)** people are the world's most vital resource, **(2)** the problems of resource depletion and pollution can be solved by human ingenuity and technology so that the more people we have the more likely these problems will be solved, and (3) continued economic growth is not threatened but enhanced by population growth because more people generate more production.

Critics counter that most people are being added in LDCs where education, health, and nutrition levels are so low that continued rapid population growth can condemn hundreds of millions of people to an early death. Technological advances do not necessarily come from people who are well educated or well paid. But encouraging significant increases in births in the *hope* that in the long run a few of these individuals will solve the world's pollution and resource problems condemns hundreds of millions of unique human beings to an early death over the next few decades. Critics argue that this hardly seems like a humane way to preserve and improve the lives of the vital resource of people who already exist. Instead of blindly encouraging births, they argue, providing better education, nutrition, health care, and work opportunities for a smaller population has a better chance of stimulating human ingenuity and technological breakthroughs and preventing unnecessary human misery and deaths. They also point out that poor people are not able to buy many, if any, products and thus do not stimulate production. Instead they represent an economic drain on government and private capital that could be used to stimulate production and technological breakthroughs.

U.S. Population At present the United States has no official population control policy, primarily because population control is a controversial issue. The United States does provide financial support for national and international family planning and for contraceptive and reproductive research, although there are attempts by anti-abortion groups to cut off much of these funds.

Some observers such as Ben Wattenberg argue that the United States should increase its population to maintain economic growth and power throughout the world, pointing out that there are populous nations that are not powerful but no powerful nations that are not populous. Other observers disagree with Wattenberg's idea that numbers equal power in today's information society, where power is based increasingly on brain power. They point to Japan, which, with a relatively small population, has become one of the world's leading industrial nations since 1945, primarily through using brain power rather than sheer numbers. Furthermore, according to the U.S. Commission on Pop-

ulation Growth and the American Future and other studies, the health of the economy, the vitality of business, and individual welfare are not dependent on continued population growth. This commission also pointed out that a good reason for stabilizing population is that adding millions to the U.S. population intensifies many environmental and social problems because increased resource use and pollution are caused by a combination of population growth and increased affluence (Section 1-5). Another reason for setting an official goal to stabilize U.S. population is to set an example for helping persuade other nations to adopt such goals.

Some have argued that population growth in the United States is necessary for continued economic growth and that a ZPG society would be more conservative and less innovative. However, such fears may be unfounded. Sweden has achieved ZPG and is one of the world's more energetic and innovative societies, and the more conservative societies tend to be those LDCs with a youthful age structure and a mostly rural population. South Africa and Portugal, for example, have young populations, but are more conservative than the older populations of Sweden and West Germany. Furthermore, a steady state society is dynamic and diverse (Section 5-2)—not static and dull. Some things grow, some decline, and some remain about the same; in this way the system does not exceed its carrying capacity.

7-3 Methods for Controlling Human Population Growth

Controlling Birth Rates A government can alter the size and growth rate of its population by encouraging a change in any of the three basic demographic variables: births, deaths, and migration. All governments are presumably committed to reducing death rates as much as possible. In addition, most governments restrict emigration and immigration, so migration is a significant factor in only a few countries, such as the United States, Canada, and Australia. Thus, *controlling the birth rate is the only ethically acceptable way of controlling human population growth in the world.*

There are two general approaches to controlling the birth rate of the human population: *economic development* and *family planning* (including abortion). Family planning enables people to have no more than the number of children they desire, whereas economic development changes their motivation for a certain desired number of children. Let's look at these two approaches more closely.

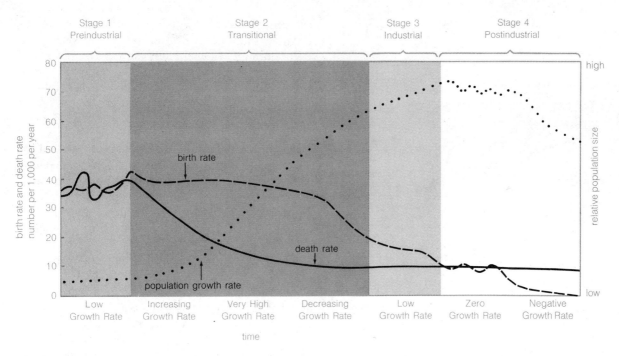

Figure 7-4 A generalized model of the demographic transition.

Economic Development and the Demographic Transition Between 1929 and 1950, demographers began to examine the birth and death rates in western European nations that became industrialized during the nineteenth century. From this analysis they formed a model of population change and control known as the **demographic transition,** based on the hypothesis that population growth decreases with economic development.

Based on analyses of industrialized western European nations, the demographic transition appears to have four distinct phases (Figure 7-4). In the first, or *preindustrial stage,* harsh living conditions lead to high birth rates (to compensate for high infant mortality) and high death rates, with the population stable or growing slowly. In the second, or *transitional stage,* as industrialization spreads and living conditions improve, birth rates remain high but death rates fall sharply. This leads to a temporary but prolonged period of rapid population growth. In the third, or *industrial stage,* industrialization is widespread. Birth rates fall and approach death rates as better educated and more affluent couples (especially in cities) become aware that children hinder them from taking advantage of job opportunities in an expanding economy. Population growth continues but at a slower and perhaps fluctuating rate, depending on economic conditions. According to this hypothesis, the United States, Japan, the Soviet Union, Canada, Australia, New Zealand, and most of the remaining European

nations are in this third phase. A fourth *postindustrial stage* takes place when birth rates decline even further to equal death rates (ZPG) and then possibly continue to fall so that total population size begins slowly to decrease (Figure 7-4). West Germany has entered this fourth stage, if this model is valid.

According to this hypothesis, the LDCs of Africa, Asia, and Latin America should be able to make a similar demographic transition if they receive enough economic aid and technical assistance from the MDCs. Using the demographic transition model, most LDCs today have advanced far enough up the economic ladder that their death rates have fallen, but not far enough that their birth rates have also fallen. In other words, they are still in the transitional phase with high to fairly high population growth rates (Figure 7-5).

There is considerable debate over whether the demographic transition model is valid for most of today's LDCs. First, historical demographers, using new methods and information, have developed a better picture of how the fertility decline began in western Europe, which may modify the classical demographic transition theory. This new evidence suggests that improved and expanded family planning programs may bring about a more rapid decline in the birth rate at a lower cost than economic development alone.

Second, economic development will be more difficult for today's LDCs than it was for the nations that developed a century ago because **(1)** even

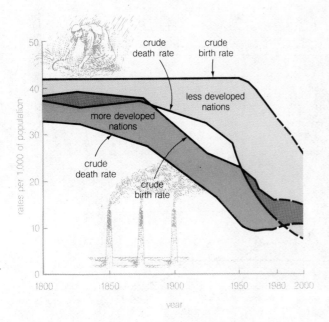

Figure 7-5 Comparison of crude birth rates and crude death rates for more developed and less developed nations between 1800 and 2000 (projected). The LDCs have yet to reach the last stage of the demographic transition and are not expected to do so by 2000.

though many of these nations have a large and growing population they have an underpopulation of the trained workers needed for economic development; **(2)** so many people are below age 15, even with projected fertility declines, that the population of the LDCs is projected to increase from 3.6 billion in 1984 to 4.9 billion in 2000 (equal to the entire world's population in 1984) and 6.7 billion by 2020; **(3)** increases in the production of food and other resources can be wiped out by such large increases in population (doubling food supplies in 30 years does not increase the average amount of food available if the population also doubles in 30 years); **(4)** most low- and middle-income nations lack the capital and resources needed for development and the amount of money being given or loaned to LDCs—already struggling under tremendous debt burdens—has been decreasing rather than increasing recently; **(5)** if future world economic growth averages closer to 2 percent than 4 percent, as it has in the early 1980s, then half of the world's population will soon live in countries where population growth could exceed economic growth; and **(6)** today's LDCs face stiff competition in selling the products on which their growth depends from MDCs and recently modernized LDCs.

These and other factors could prevent most LDCs from completing the demographic transition; they could become caught in the transitional stage

(Figures 7-4 and 7-5) or forced back to the preindustrial stage if death rates rise. According to demographer Michael Teitelbaum of the Ford Foundation, counting only on the demographic transition to reduce fertility in LDCs is wishful thinking.

West Germany and the Postindustrial Phase of the Demographic Transition Most nations in the world are struggling to reduce fertility and birth rates. However, as more nations—especially MDCs—approach ZPG, there may be an increase in programs designed to prevent significant population decreases.

In 1974, West Germany reached ZPG. Since that time its population size has begun to decrease slowly as its birth rate has fallen below its death rate and its total fertility rate has fallen and remained around 1.4 children per woman of childbearing age. Throughout human history various countries have experienced population decreases caused by catastrophic events such as the Black Death in medieval Europe, the Irish potato famine, wars, and political upheavals. West Germany, however, is the first country to experience a population decrease solely because of a fertility rate well below replacement level.

In Section 6-5 you learned that there is a built-in momentum for population growth to continue in a country with a large fraction of its population under age 15. Similarly, there is a built-in momentum for the population of a country to decrease once it achieves and maintains a low fertility rate for 15 years or more: Then there are so few women moving into childbearing ages that these women would have to increase the number of children they have drastically to cause population growth to reverse its decrease and begin rising again. If a low fertility rate of 1.4 is maintained by West Germany and no immigration is allowed, its population will decrease slowly from 61.4 million in 1984 to 59.3 million by 2000 and then more rapidly to 49.3 million by 2020 and 40 million by 2050.

The West German government is already concerned about its population decrease and would like to see birth rates rise again. They fear that there will be too few workers to support continued economic growth and to pay taxes to support the increasing fraction of its population over age 64. Until 1978 West Germany admitted a number of "guest workers" and their families, primarily from Southern Europe and Turkey, to increase their work force. However, the population of these foreign workers and their families have a higher fertility rate than native Germans. As the native population decreases, the 7 percent of the German population of foreign origin could easily double or triple by the early part of the next century. To counter this trend, some pronatalist (probirth) economic incentives such as monthly child allowances and paid maternity leaves are already in effect for German couples. Others such as cash bonuses for each child, better pensions, and health care for people who have more children may be instituted in the future.

The Soviet Union has also recently become concerned about increasing its birth rate in order to ensure the availability of enough workers and soldiers. So far, the experiences of West Germany and other eastern European nations at or near ZPG indicate that trying to raise birth and fertility rates drastically after a long decline is very difficult.

Family Planning Basic **family planning** is a purely voluntary approach whereby information is provided and contraceptives are distributed to help couples have the number of children they want at the time that they want them. Family planning services were first introduced in LDCs in the 1940s and 1950s by private physicians and private groups of self-motivated women. Since that time organizations such as the International Planned Parenthood Federation, the Planned Parenthood Federation of America, the United Nations Fund for Population Activities (UNFPA), the U.S. Agency for International Development (AID), the Ford Foundation, and the World Bank have been helping nations carry out voluntary family planning by providing technical assistance, funding, or both.

By 1982, 72 LDCs with 94 percent of such nations' populations supported family planning programs to reduce population growth rates, for health reasons, or as a fundamental human right. Thus, *by 1982 only 6 percent of the people in LDCs lived under governments that neither supported family planning programs nor aimed to reduce fertility.* Currently, about $1 billion a year is spent on family planning activities in LDCs—two-thirds from the countries themselves and the rest from international aid. More than one-third of this annual international aid is provided by the United States, the undisputed leader in population aid.

Despite the importance of family planning, its official goal is not to lower the birth rate but to help couples have the number of children they want when they want them. Thus, some experts argue that family planning, even coupled with economic development, cannot bring birth and fertility rates down fast enough; recent studies found that most couples in LDCs want to have three to four children—well above the 2.5 average fertility rate needed to bring about eventual population stabilization. The U.S. Agency for International Development (AID) estimates that it will take consistent use of effective contraceptives by 80 percent of women of childbearing age in the LDCs for eventual population stabilization in these countries. Yet, despite family planning efforts since the 1950s, only about one-third of the married women of childbearing age in LDCs are using contraceptives.

The AID estimates that achieving this 80 percent goal would require an immediate investment of $4 billion a year in family planning efforts—four times the current level. This would have to increase to $64 billion per year by 2000, when women of childbearing age in LDCs will have almost doubled in number. Half of these funds would have to come from private organizations and governments of MDCs. In recent years, however, such aid has been decreasing.

Studies so far have shown that the major factors motivating poor couples to want fewer children are (1) increased income through greater equality in the distribution of income and land, (2) more education and work opportunities for women, (3) reductions in infant mortality, (4) availability of pensions and health care for older persons, and (5) widespread availability of free or low-cost health, education, and family planning services (including abortion). In other words, rapid fertility reduction occurs through a combination of economic development with better income distribution among the poor, family planning, and methods that go beyond voluntary family planning. Four of the most widely used of these methods are (1) voluntary abortion, (2) increased rights, education, and work opportunities for women, (3) economic incentives and disincentives, and (4) restricting immigration. Let's look at these approaches in more detail.

Abortion Induced abortion is one of the oldest and most widely used methods of human birth control. The total number of legal and illegal abortions throughout the world each year is estimated at 40 million—about one abortion for every four live births. About half of these are performed illegally and represent a leading cause of death among women of childbearing age.

One of the major social trends throughout the world since 1965 has been the legalization of abortion. *By 1983, only 10 percent of the world's population lived in countries where abortion is prohibited without exception.* Despite this trend hundreds of millions of women are either too poor to afford abortion or live in rural areas where such services are not avail-

Table 7-1 Mortality Risks Associated with Various Obstetrical and Gynecological Procedures

| | Deaths per 100,000 Cases | |
Procedure	United States*	LDCs** (estimated)
Legal abortion	1	4–6
Female sterilization	4	10–100
Live birth delivery	14	250–800
Caesarian section	41	160–220
Hysterectomy	160	300–400
Illegal abortion (non-medical)	50	100–1,000

*Data from U.S. Centers for Disease Control.
**Data from Population Crisis Committee (1982).

able. Where legal abortion is not available, illegal abortion is normally widespread. Table 7-1 shows that illegal abortions cause 50 to 100 times more deaths of women per 100,000 cases than legal abortions and that legal abortions are considerably less risky to women than a live birth and common female surgical procedures such as Caesarian sections and hysterectomies.

Perhaps half of all illegal abortions are self-induced. Women swallow large and dangerous doses of chemicals, such as quinine, sold as home remedies. Should this method fail, these women often resort to back-street abortionists or knitting needles; most poor women abort themselves with sharpened sticks. Infection is understandably a major killer. The most dangerous bacterium, *Clostridium welchii*, kills in only 12 hours unless medical treatment is provided immediately. Antibiotics decrease the risk but must be given quickly; most are often not available in LDCs.

In 1973, the U.S. Supreme Court made the historic decision that during the first 3 months (12 weeks) of pregnancy the decision to have an abortion must be left up to a woman and her doctor. Between 1973 and 1981 the number of legal abortions per year in the United States doubled, increasing from almost 745,000 to over 1.54 million—almost one-third of all pregnancies. Two-thirds of the women getting abortions in 1980 were between ages 15 and 24 and three-fourths were unmarried. An estimated 29 percent of U.S. women who wanted legal abortions during 1980 were unable to obtain them primarily because 80 percent of U.S. counties, mostly in rural areas, are without a clinic or hospital that regularly performs abortions. In addition, a 1977 law passed by Congress banned the use of federal Medicaid funds to pay for abortions. However, by 1984 15 states and the District of Columbia—accounting for about 80 percent of all abor-

tions—were using state funds to provide Medicaid abortions for low-income women.

In 1983 nationwide polls showed that 62 percent of American adults polled support legalized abortion under any circumstances (22 percent) or under certain circumstances (40 percent). In addition, 56 percent of those interviewed in a 1982 Gallup poll believe that federal funds should be used to pay for poor women's abortions. Despite such widespread approval of legalized abortion in the United States, a militant minority, mostly prolife or right-to-life groups, continues to apply intense political pressure against legal abortion. Their strategy involves trying to **(1)** defeat congressional candidates who support the Supreme Court's decision,* **(2)** pass a constitutional amendment banning abortions or allowing each state to establish its own policy, **(3)** pass a law declaring that life begins at fertilization, thus classifying abortion as murder, and **(4)** change the composition of the Supreme Court.

Abortion is a highly emotional issue that does not lend itself to compromise or cool debate. Basically, the argument is between those who regard abortion as murder and those who believe that a woman should have the right to control her body according to her beliefs and needs and not be forced by law to undergo an unwanted pregnancy. Few people are for abortion but most people are for reproductive freedom. They argue that no one should be forced to have an abortion and at the same time no one should be forced to have a baby. Furthermore, they believe that making abortion a crime imposes the religious or moral views of one group on other women who may not hold the same views. Other individuals, however, view abortion as an act of murder—a violent, selfish action that kills the life of one living being by another trying to solve a problem. They argue that the right to life of an unborn child should take precedence over a pregnant woman's right to choose whether to terminate a pregnancy.

The issue is complicated by inconclusive and controversial medical, theological, and legal debate about when life begins—at conception, at birth, or at some difficult-to-define point in between. Many scientists argue that no precise answer is possible. Some argue that life begins when the brain starts functioning, usually 8 weeks after conception. Others make the distinction between an embryo and a viable fetus, arguing that until the fetus can

---

*During the 1982 elections all but one of the senators that prolife groups targeted for defeat were reelected and an additional 20 to 25 members of the House of Representatives were elected who favor legalized abortion.

survive outside the uterus it is not a true person. Because of incubators and modern medical techniques, survival of a fetus is now possible after 28 weeks and in some circumstances after 24 weeks.

No court ruling or law will settle these ethical questions. Indeed, as legal restraints on abortion have been removed, the ethical and moral issues emerge even more strongly for individuals trying to decide whether or not to have an abortion. The absence of legal statutes prohibiting abortion does not prevent people from being faithful to their own religious convictions.

Changes in Women's Roles Studies have shown that increased female education is one of the strongest factors leading to women having fewer children. This occurs because educated women **(1)** are more likely to be employed outside the home rather than stay home and raise children, **(2)** are more likely to marry at a later age, thus reducing their prime fertility years either because they are in school or because they may take more time to find suitable partners, and **(3)** have fewer infant deaths—a major factor in reducing fertility rates.

This means little, however, unless women are offered the opportunity to become educated and to express their lives in meaningful work and social roles outside the home. In most nations women do not have the same access to education as men. About 60 percent of the world's 1.4 billion illiterates are women, and in most cases males are given preference in education and vocational training. Competition between men and women for jobs in many countries should become even more intense by 2000, when there will be another billion people looking for jobs.

In the rural areas of LDCs women typically do all of the housekeeping and child care and more than one-half of the work associated with growing food, gathering firewood, and hauling water. In most cases they are not paid for this vital and exhausting work. These women also suffer the most malnutrition because men and children are given first claim to limited food supplies.

About 50 percent of the world's paid work force in 1980 was female, including 69 percent in Sweden, 68 percent in the Soviet Union, 51 percent in the United States, and 1.8 percent in Algeria. In the United States most women working for pay have clerical and service jobs and in 1983 earned an average of 36 percent less than male workers.

The drive to recognize and guarantee women's rights by law in the United States and several other nations over the past 2 decades is a very significant attempt to reduce sex discrimination and to help decrease birth rates. Cuba, China, and Sweden have made the sharing of housework by men and women an official policy—although all three governments recognize that this policy is almost impossible to enforce. Sweden, France, and East Germany aid women who want to work outside the home by providing preschool care for children over age 3.

These and other efforts are encouraging but there is a long way to go in the MDCs and even further to go in most LDCs where women have few rights. Besides providing better education and work opportunities for women, governments can also help reduce sex discrimination and fertility by guaranteeing women the right to own and inherit property, the right to sue, and increased marriage and divorce rights, including in many countries the right to have a say in the choice of a husband. Eliminating male domination will not be easy and will require women to organize politically and socially. But cultural patterns can change through a combination of political pressure, laws, education, and helping—and when necessary pressuring—males to become more aware of the conscious and unconscious ways in which women's rights are denied throughout most of the world.

Using Economic Incentives and Disincentives An increasing number of countries are using either economic incentives, economic disincentives, or both to help reduce fertility. One-time, relatively small payments to individuals who agree to use contraceptives or become sterilized and payments to doctors and family planning workers for each sterilization they perform and each IUD they insert have been used in about 20 countries, including China and India—the world's two most populous countries. This approach represents the simplest and least expensive kind of payments to promote family planning.

Such payments, however, are most likely to attract people who already have all the children they want. Although such payments are not physically coercive, they have been criticized as being psychologically coercive. In some cases the poor might have little choice but to accept them, even though they strongly want to have more children.

Some countries, such as China, parts of India, and Taiwan have used deferred incentives in the form of old-age pensions and health care, life insurance, education funds, and the like to be paid in the future to people who have succeeded in having a small family. Such schemes leave the choice of birth control to the individual and pose less risk of unfair influence. To help slow down a country's overall birth rate, however, such schemes must be national programs and the people must be confident that the government be able to make such payments in the future. This national social welfare approach is often too expensive for governments of LDCs.

Since the late 1970s, Thailand and Indonesia have had success in using community incentives to reward whole villages that reach certain family planning goals or fertility rates. The government agrees to provide a community with water, livestock, a biogas plant, a school, roads, low-cost loans, or some other desired reward when the community reaches certain goals such as contraception practiced by 60 percent of its couples, an average fertility rate not exceeding one or two children per couple, or increasing the education of women to a certain level. Such an approach works best in small villages where there is a large degree of social cohesion.

Economic disincentives or penalties that impose extra taxes and other costs or that withhold or reduce benefits such as income tax deductions for children, health care, food allotments, and job preference are also ways to reduce fertility. Singapore and China have comprehensive programs of such economic disincentives designed to promote one- or two-child families, which are discussed in the next section.

Like economic incentives, economic disincentives can be psychologically coercive for the poor. Those that withhold food from the poor or increase the cost of raising children can also be unjust and inhumane. They can punish innocent children because parents plan poorly and have more children than they can afford.

Experience has shown that economic rewards and penalties designed to reduce fertility work best when they (1) nudge rather than push people to have fewer children, (2) reinforce existing customs and trends toward smaller families without departing too far from prevailing norms, (3) do not penalize people who have had large families before the new programs were established, and (4) increase a poor family's income or land ownership.

Restricting Immigration Controlling population growth in a particular country by limiting immigration is widely used by most countries in the world. The United States admits approximately twice as many immigrants and refugees each year than all other countries in the world combined. Today about 500,000 legal immigrants and refugees enter the United States each year. In addition an estimated 500,000 illegal immigrants* are added each year to the estimated 3 to 6 million illegal immigrants already in the U.S. This annual addition of about 1 million people now accounts for 40 to 50 percent of U.S. population growth each year.

An estimated 50 to 60 percent of the 500,000 illegal immigrants that enter the U.S. each year come from Mexico, where about 40 percent of the work force is either unemployed or underemployed. Most of the remaining illegal immigrants come from other Latin American countries; many come through Mexico. Most illegal immigrants cross the border at night by scrambling through holes in the few miles of fences the United States has erected, wading the Rio Grande and El Paso rivers, hopping freight trains, or riding in trucks with smugglers ("coyotes") who charge from $100 to $2,000 a head. Only a small fraction are caught because the U.S. Immigration and Naturalization Service (INS) has to patrol an open, easily traversed 3,060-kilometer (1,900-mile) border that is unpatrolled on Mexico's side. Since 1982, when economic conditions in Mexico worsened, there has been a sharp increase in the number of Mexican aliens apprehended at the border while trying to cross into the United States.

In recent years the long tradition of the United States in accepting immigrants and refugees has been challenged. A 1980 Roper poll found that 80 percent of those polled favored reducing legal immigration, and 91 percent favored eliminating or controlling illegal immigration. A 1980 Gallup poll showed 76 percent would ban the hiring of illegal immigrants.

Officials of the INS estimate that illegal immigrants cost the United States $4 billion annually in benefits, lost income taxes, and wages. Another study by the Environmental Defense Fund puts the cost at $14 billion a year. Others point out, however, that many illegal immigrants take menial jobs as farm workers, gardeners, dishwashers, maids, and workers in garment sweatshops that most U.S. workers won't take—mostly because of pay below the minimum wage and worker exploitation. In times when unemployment is high, however, union officials argue that illegal immigrants do take many such jobs away from legal residents looking for any kind of work, especially young people, minorities, and unskilled workers.

Union officials blame not the illegal immigrants but their employers, who exploit illegal aliens by paying them less and often working them under inhumane conditions. Since the wages are often paid in cash, some employers also avoid paying social security taxes and insurance. The INS is convinced that even with a greatly increased number of border patrol agents, they can barely put a dent in the problem unless Congress enacts tougher penalties against employers who hire illegal aliens.

---

*Estimates range from 100,000 to 1 million or more, but 500,000 is commonly used.

With legitimate or easily forged documents, some illegal immigrants get all the benefits of citizenship, including welfare, food stamps, and Medicaid. Studies have shown, however, that in general the social security, income taxes, and other payments made by illegal immigrants fearing deportation far exceed what they take away in benefits. A study showed that over 77 percent of illegal aliens apprehended by the INS had social security taxes withheld from their paychecks, 73 percent had federal income taxes withheld, and 44 percent had made hospitalization payments. Yet numerous studies have shown that small proportions of illegal immigrants use government services: welfare payments, 1 percent; food stamps, 1 percent; have children in schools, 4 percent; unemployment insurance, 4 percent; free medical services, 5 percent; and collected on social security, none. On the other hand, refugees by law are eligible for public services and benefits, and have put a severe strain on locally supported services in cities in Florida and California where most Asian and Latin American refugees settle.

Present U.S. immigration policy has been criticized because it encourages highly trained and skilled scientists, physicians and other persons in LDCs to immigrate to the United States. This "brain drain" policy causes LDCs not only to lose some of their most talented citizens but also the scarce capital that has gone into their training. In effect, such a policy is a reverse form of foreign aid from the LDCs to the United States. Defenders of this policy point out that some of these professionals (1) are unable to get jobs in their own country, (2) send money back to relatives in their native countries, which is a major source of income for these individuals, (3) are more likely to be productive and make contributions that can benefit the world as a whole in a place of their own choosing, and (4) create jobs for other U.S. citizens.

By mid-1984 Congress was considering revisions in U.S. immigration laws that would (1) limit immigration to 425,000 annually, including relatives but excluding refugees, who would continue to be admitted at levels to be determined by consultation between the president and Congress; (2) grant amnesty to all illegal aliens who entered before a specified date but making them ineligible for food stamps, Medicaid, and other federal benefits for a certain number of years; (3) fine employers who hire illegal aliens and send repeated offenders to jail; and (4) provide additional funds for the INS to increase border surveillance, help catch employers who hire illegal aliens, and deport illegal aliens not granted amnesty.

Two major problems involve developing a system such as a counterfeit-resistant Social Security card or a national data bank of registered legal aliens that employers could use to verify applicants as legally eligible for work. Leaders of the increasing number of Hispanics who have become U.S. citizens and employers oppose fines and jail sentences for those hiring illegal aliens. They argue that this would turn employers into law-enforcement officers and fear of breaking the law would inhibit employers from hiring anyone who looks or speaks like a foreigner, thus discriminating against legal immigrants.

7-4 Efforts at Human Population Control

Population Policies In 1960 only two countries—India and Pakistan—had official policies to reduce their birth rates. *By 1983 93 percent of the world's population and 96 percent of the people in LDCs lived in countries where governments had either adopted family planning programs or permitted operation of private programs.* Most population policies involve a combination of economic development and family planning, including abortion. Of course, having a policy to control population growth and providing the financial support and organized efforts to implement such a policy are different. Few governments spend more than 1 percent of their national budgets on family planning services. To get some idea of the success and failure of population control programs, let's look at what has happened in the world's two most populous countries—India and the People's Republic of China.

India India's population problems are staggering. It is the world's second most populous country, with a 1984 population of about 746 million—almost one-sixth of all the people in the world. It contains over three times as many people as the United States even though it is only about one-third the size.

Each year about 27 million Indians are born and 11 million die. This means there are about 16 million more to feed, clothe, and house each year. Because 39 percent of the population is under age 15, India's population is projected to reach 1 billion by 2000, 1.3 billion by 2020, and 1.6 billion before leveling off early in the twenty-second century. In 1984 at least one-third of its population had an annual per capita income of no more than $70 a year, with an average per capita income of only $260. To add to the problem, nearly one-half of India's labor force is unemployed or underemployed. Each *week* 100,000 more people enter the job market, looking mostly for nonexistent jobs.

Recognizing its problem, India started the world's first national family planning program in

1952, when its population was nearly 400 million with a doubling time of 53 years. In 1984, after 32 years of population control effort, India had a population of 746 million and a doubling time of 34 years. In 1952 India was adding 5 million persons to its population each year. In 1984 it added 16 million. Today only about one out of five Indian couples of childbearing age are protected by any method of family planning.

Without its long-standing national family planning program, India's numbers would be growing even faster. But the program has yielded disappointing results primarily because of poor planning, bureaucratic inefficiency, low status of women (despite constitutional guarantees of equality), extreme poverty, and a lack of administrative and financial support until 1965—13 years after the program began.

But the problem is deeper. For one thing, 77 percent of India's people live in 560,000 rural villages, where birth rates are still close to about 40 per thousand. The overwhelming economic and administrative task of delivering contraceptive services and education to its mostly rural population is further complicated by the illiteracy rate of about 71 percent, with 80 to 90 percent of the illiterate being rural women. In spite of years of government information about having fewer children, rural Indian couples have an average of five children. Such couples remain convinced that many children are needed as a source of cheap labor and old age survival insurance. This belief is reinforced by the fact that almost one-third of all Indian children die before age 5. Population control is also hindered by India's diversity: 14 major languages, over 200 dialects, many social castes, and 11 major religions.

To improve the effectiveness of its program, in 1976 Indira Gandhi's government instituted a mass sterilization program, primarily for males with two or more children. The supposedly voluntary program was based on financial incentives. But coercion was allegedly used in a few rural areas to meet sterilization quotas. The resulting backlash played a role in Gandhi's election defeat in 1977 (she was later reelected). In 1978 a new approach was taken, raising the legal minimum age for marriage from 18 to 21 years for males and from 15 to 18 years for females. After the 1981 census showed that the population growth rate between 1971 and 1981 was no lower than that between 1961 and 1971, the government vowed to increase family planning efforts and funding. Whether such efforts will succeed remains to be seen.

China The People's Republic of China is making impressive efforts to bring its population growth under control. In 1984 China had a population of about 1.034 billion, a birth rate of 21 per thousand, a death rate of 8 per thousand, and a doubling time of 54 years. At these rates China's population grows by about 14 million persons each year—a baby being added to its population every 2 seconds. China is about the same size as the United States but has more than four times as many people and approximately one-half as much arable land. With almost one-fourth of the world's people it has only one-twentieth of the world's total continental freshwater resources, one of the lowest per capita averages in the world.

The United Nations projects that the population of China may reach 1.3 billion by 2000 and 1.5 billion by 2020. In the 1970s, however, China established the most extensive and strictest official population control program in the world. Its official goal is to achieve ZPG by the year 2000, in order to stabilize its population at 1.2 billion followed by a slow decline to a population somewhere between 600 million and 1 billion by 2100.

Although China has a long way to go in controlling its population, its drop from an estimated birth rate of 32 per thousand in 1970 to 22 per thousand by 1984 is remarkable. This means that China's population is now growing by about 1 percent a year, comparable to that in some MDCs such as the United States.

China's population control program is built around a number of practices:

1. Strongly encouraging couples to marry at a late age (typically 24 to 28 for women and 26 to 30 for men with a legal minimum marriage age of 20 for women and 22 for men).

2. Indoctrinating couples in family planning techniques at the time of marriage.

3. Strongly encouraging couples to sign pledges to have no more than one child (by 1982, over 15 million couples had signed such pledges) and providing those who sign the pledge with salary bonuses or work points for extra food and supplies, larger old-age pensions, better housing, free medical care and school tuition for their child, and preferential treatment for jobs when the child grows up.

4. Requiring those who break the pledge to return all benefits and using intense peer group pressure on a woman pregnant with a third child to have an abortion.

5. Reducing the salary and old-age pension for couples having more than two children and charging them for each extra child's rations.

6. Requiring one of the parents in a two-child family to be sterilized (instituted in May 1983).

7. Providing free contraceptives and sterilizations for married couples with contraceptives provided either at their place of work or, in rural areas, via home deliveries by barefoot doctors (paramedics).

8. Making abortion freely available.

9. Compensating women and men for time lost from work due to sterilization, abortion, and IUD insertions.

10. Using mobile units to bring sterilization and family planning education to rural areas.

11. Training local people to carry on the program.

12. Encouraging one-child families by showing goals and contraceptive acceptance rates on clinic walls, factory bulletin boards, and through meetings of communes in rural areas and production brigades and resident committees in urban areas.

13. Expecting all leaders to set an example.

Most countries cannot or do not want to exert the same degree of social and political pressure on its population. Some elements of China's program, however, can be transferred to other LDCs. Especially useful is the practice of bringing contraceptives and family planning to the people at little or no cost, rather than making the people come to special centers. Perhaps the best lesson that other nations can learn from China's experience is that countries should not wait to slow population growth until the only answer is the use of compulsory measures. Compulsory approaches can cause a backlash of public resentment and run a high risk of failure. China's population control program has been successful so far. But there are signs of increasing resistance, and whether such a coercive program will work in the long run remains to be seen.

Some population experts emphasize that individuals need to be aware that it is the *quality*, not the *quantity*, of parenthood that is important. Some people have the ability and compassion to provide high-quality parenthood for more than one child, and these rare individuals should not be discouraged from having children. But many couples should stop at two, one, or none.

Short of thermonuclear war itself, rampant population growth is the gravest issue the world faces over the decades immediately ahead.

Robert S. McNamara

Discussion Topics

1. What is an S-shaped population curve? Distinguish between maximum and optimum population size. Do you think we have passed the world's maximum population limit? Have we passed the world's optimum population size? Cite evidence. What do you think the optimum U.S. population is? Why?

2. Should world population growth be controlled? Why or why not?

3. Debate the following resolution: The United States has a serious population problem and should adopt an official policy for stabilizing its population.

4. Is concern about population growth in the world and in the United States diverting attention from other problems, such as war, poverty, and racial, age, and sex discrimination? Give evidence pro and con.

5. Explain why population policy, unlike most other policies, requires a 50- to 70-year plan (see Section 6-5).

6. Describe the demographic transition hypothesis and give reasons why it may or may not apply to LDCs today.

7. Debate one of the following two resolutions: (a) Each woman should have the freedom to use abortion as a means of birth control. (b) Abortion should not be legal because it is an act of murder and denies the unborn child its right to live.

8. Should federal and state funds be used to provide free abortions for the poor in the United States? Defend your position.

9. Debate the following resolution: The unrestricted freedom to reproduce as many children as one wants is a universal human right.

10. What are your beliefs and feelings about the feminist movement and the role of women in U.S. society? Contrast the role of women in the United States with the roles of women in other countries throughout the world such as the Soviet Union, China, and India.

11. What are some of the ways in which women are consciously and unconsciously discriminated against in the United States? On your campus?

12. Make a list of restrictions (for example, stoplights), laws, and other losses in individual freedom that occur as a result of an increase in population and population density. What individual and group freedoms do you gain because of these coercive restrictions and laws?

13. Should the number of legal immigrants allowed into the United States each year be sharply reduced? Why or why not?

14. Should the number of trained or skilled persons admitted as legal immigrants to the United States from LDCs be sharply decreased or halted? Why or why not?

15. Should illegal immigration into the United States be sharply decreased? How would you go about doing this?

16. Debate the following resolution: To help control illegal immigration, every person in the United States should be required to carry a national identification card.

17. Should the United States continue to receive large numbers of refugees? Why or why not?

18. Some people admire China for attempting to come to grips with its population problems. Others criticize China for intruding in the personal lives of its citizens. What is your opinion? If you disagree with its approach, what policies for population control would you institute in China?

19. Survey members of your class and another class or dorm group about what incentives would lead them to limit their family to none, one, or two children. It is important to know the following about each person: age, number of children in his or her family, religious background, number of children he or she already has (if any), and number of children he or she wants.

PART FOUR

Resources

Our entire society rests upon—and is dependent upon—our water, our land, our forests, and our minerals. How we use these resources influences our health, security, economy, and well being.

John F. Kennedy

8

Soil Resources

Like air and water, soil is a basic resource needed to sustain life. **Soil** is a complex mixture of tiny particles of inorganic minerals and rocks, decaying organic matter, water, air, and living organisms. The thin layer of soil—ranging up to several feet thick—on the earth's surface helps provide the food most living things depend on for their survival, the natural fibers used to make clothes, the paper used for writing and packaging, and the lumber used to build houses and furniture.

Despite its importance, throughout human history soil has been one of our most abused resources. Strong evidence exists that entire civilizations collapsed because they failed to prevent depletion and loss of the topsoil that supported them. Unless we wish to relearn the harsh lessons of soil abuse, everyone—not just farmers—needs to be concerned with preserving soil and maintaining its fertility.

In this chapter we will look at the components, formation, properties, and types of soils, soil erosion, and ways to conserve this vital resource. Let's begin by looking at the components of soils.

8-1 Soil Components

Inorganic Minerals Among the 90 chemical elements that occur naturally, the most abundant ones in soils in decreasing order are oxygen (O), silicon (Si), aluminum (Al), iron (Fe), calcium (Ca), sodium (Na), potassium (K), and magnesium (Mg). These and other elements in the earth's crust combine to form compounds such as quartz or silicon dioxide (SiO_2), alumina or aluminum oxide (Al_2O_3), iron oxide (Fe_2O_3), and limestone ($CaCO_3$). Inorganic mineral compounds such as these make up about 45 percent of a typical sample of soil.

Chemical elements required by plants in relatively large amounts for healthy growth and reproduction are called *macronutrients*. Three of the nine elements generally recognized as essential macronutrients for plants—carbon (C), hydrogen (H), and oxygen (O)—are obtained from water (H_2O) and from the atmosphere as O_2 and CO_2. The remaining six plant macronutrients—nitrogen (N), phosphorus (P), potassium (K), calcium (Ca), magnesium (Mg), and sulfur (S)—are obtained from inorganic minerals in the soil. The three most common macronutrients depleted from the soil when crops are grown and harvested are N, P, and K. They are frequently replaced by using organic fertilizers such as manure and compost and inorganic commercial fertilizers, as discussed in Section 8-6.

Seven other elements—iron (Fe), manganese (Mn), molybdenum (Mo), zinc (Zn), copper (Cu), chlorine (Cl), and boron (B)—are also essential nutrients for plants. Large quantities of these elements may be poisonous to plants, but trace amounts are essential for healthy plant growth. Because they are required only at very low levels, they are called *micronutrients* or *trace elements*. If any macronutrient or micronutrient is not present in a sufficient amount in the soil, it becomes a *limiting factor* (Section 3-7) to healthy plant growth.

Organic Matter Ninety percent of all the earth's soils contain a relatively small amount (1 to 7 percent) of organic matter, which serves as a home and source of food for soil microorganisms and acts as a sponge that soaks up and retains moisture. Dead leaves, stems, and roots along with insect remains, animal droppings, and worm secretions accumu-

---

Enrichment Study 14 is related to this chapter.

late as organic matter in the upper portion of soils. Decomposing microorganisms (Section 3-5) break some soil organic compounds into simpler forms, such as nitrate (NO_3^-), phosphate (PO_4^{3-}), potassium (K^+), and sulfate (SO_4^{2-}) ions that are usable by plants.

Some of the organic chemicals in dead organic matter found in soils are not broken down completely by microorganisms. This partially decomposed organic matter is a dark-colored mixture of organic materials called *humus*. Peat moss, for example, is a humus mixture. Because humus is water-insoluble it remains in the soil and helps retain water-soluble ions such as K^+, Mg^{2+}, and NH_4^+ produced by bacterial decomposition in the upper soil layers for use by plants instead of allowing them to dissolve in water and move downward into lower soil layers.

Water A soil's ability to support plant life is influenced by its water-holding capacity. Rain falling on the soil surface percolates downward through the pore spaces of the soil, dissolving minerals and other soluble materials along the way. Some of this water is removed by the plant roots. Through capillary action it is transported upward through the roots, stems, and leaves—carrying nutrients and other materials with it. Some of it may then enter the atmosphere through plant leaves in a process called *transpiration.* Some of the sugars produced by photosynthesis in the leaves are also transported downward to the roots by water.

A soil's water-holding capacity depends primarily on its *porosity*—the amount of pores or open space in the soil. If the soil is too porous it will not hold water. For example, rainwater quickly passes through the large open spaces in sandy soils and sinks deep into the soil. Thus, even in rainy climates sand dunes can be colonized only with widely spaced drought-resistant plants or ones with very deep roots. At the other extreme, clay soils have so few large pores that it is difficult for water and plant roots to penetrate. Even if water eventually soaks in, chemical forces hold it so tightly to the clay particles that it is unavailable to plants.

A fertile soil holds some water but not too much. Such soils have a high humus content that helps retain water. With too much rain or irrigation even fertile soils can become so waterlogged that most useful crops, except rice, cannot grow.

Air About 50 percent of a typical soil's volume is made up of pore spaces. These spaces are filled with water in a waterlogged soil and with air in an extremely dry soil. Most soils fall between these two extremes.

The oxygen gas in the soil air is used by the cells in plant roots to carry out cellular respiration (Section 4-3) to produce carbon dioxide gas (CO_2) and water. The CO_2 given off by the plant roots also concentrates in the soil's pore spaces—reaching concentrations of 10 percent by volume compared to about 0.03 percent in the atmosphere. Some of this CO_2 diffuses into the air, so like humans soil takes in oxygen gas from the atmosphere and gives off carbon dioxide gas.

Living Organisms The upper layer of a fertile soil is teeming with living organisms such as bacteria, fungi, molds, protozoa, mites, nematodes (unsegmented worms ranging from microscopic size to over a foot long), earthworms, small insects, and larger burrowing animals such as moles, gophers, wombats, and badgers. A food web of some of the living organisms in soil is shown in Figure 8-1.

Although these organisms make up only about 0.1 percent or less of the mass of a given amount of soil, they contribute to soil fertility and porosity. Most act as decomposers that break down dead surface material into plant nutrients. Burrowing organisms help maintain soil porosity by churning, mixing, and aerating it and by secreting slimes that help hold soil particles together. In addition, their wastes and dead bodies add inorganic and organic material to the soil.

8-2 Soil Formation

Factors Affecting Soil Development Soil is a dynamic body, ever changing in its response to the environment and at the same time influencing the environment. The development of a soil, its physical and chemical properties, and the characteristics of its layers are determined by a multitude of processes resulting from the interaction of six major factors: **(1)** parent material, **(2)** climate, **(3)** abrasion, **(4)** organisms, **(5)** topography, and **(6)** time.

Soil formation and development can be compared to baking a meat loaf. The parent material is like the hamburger and other basic ingredients. The living organisms can be thought of as the implements used to crumble and mix the ingredients. Abrasion is analogous to the physical forces used to break the ingredients into smaller particles, climate is analogous to the temperature of the oven,

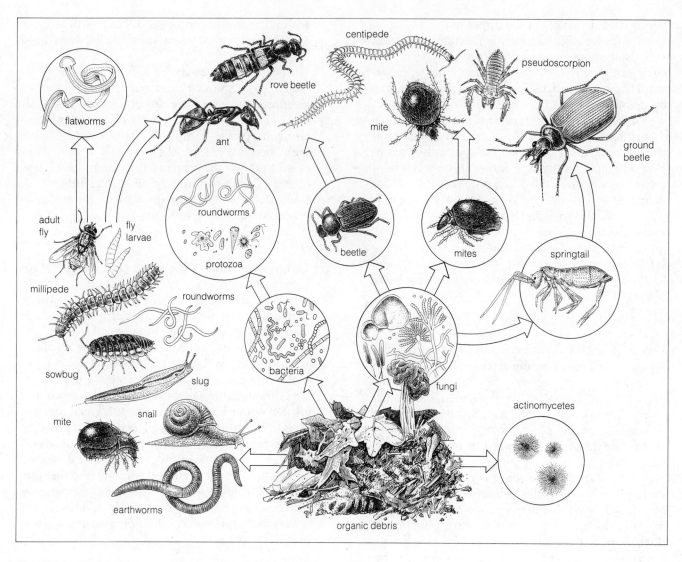

Figure 8-1 Food web of some of the organisms found in soil.

topography to the shape of the baking pan, and time to the length of time the ingredients are baked. The characteristics of the resulting meat loaf depend on the processes resulting from the particular combination of these six factors.

Nature of the Parent Material The main source of the inorganic minerals in soils is the physical and chemical weathering of various types of parent rock. *Physical weathering* involves the breaking down of parent rock into bits and pieces by exposure to temperature changes and the physical action of moving ice and water, growing roots, and human activities such as farming and construction. *Chemical weathering* involves chemical attack and dissolving of par-

ent rock by exposure to rainwater, surface water, oxygen and other gases in the atmosphere, and compounds secreted by organisms.

Residual soils are those that develop in place during the first stages of primary succession (Section 5-1) on outcroppings of bare rocks exposed to physical and chemical weathering. Such soils usually take thousands of years to form and are often thin.

Most soils, however, are *transported soils* formed by the transfer of loose sediments from one area to another by blowing wind, running water, moving glaciers, landslides, or human activities. For example, when major rivers of the world—such as the Nile, Amazon, and Mississippi—periodically overflow their banks, nutrient-rich sediment is deposited on surrounding floodplain areas. Fertile transported soils developed in this way, called *alluvial soils*, are used to grow food crops for almost one-third of the world's population. Transported soils are normally thicker and more fertile than residual soils of the same age and usually require several hundred years to form.

Climate Temperature, wind, rain, and ice are important factors in the physical and chemical weathering of parent material. In the arid climates of desert biomes where it is very hot during the day and cold at night this alternating heating and cooling can cause rocks to expand and contract and eventually crack and shatter. In cold or temperate climates, an important factor in the physical weathering of rocks is the disintegration produced by repeated expansion of water in the pores of parent rock during freezing and contraction when the ice melts—a phenomenon that also helps cause cracks and potholes in highways and city streets.

Unlike physical weathering, chemical weathering changes the chemical composition of the parent material in response to temperature, water, oxygen, and other chemicals. For example, as rainwater falls through the atmosphere it dissolves small amounts of carbon dioxide gas and forms a weak acid solution consisting of hydrogen ions (H^+) and bicarbonate ions (HCO_3^-). The resulting H^+ ions greatly increase the dissolving or leaching power of water on many soil minerals, particularly those containing sodium (Na^+), calcium (Ca^{2+}), chloride (Cl^-), and sulfate (SO_4^{2-}). Other soil minerals, particularly the oxides of silicon (SiO_2), iron (Fe_2O_3), and aluminum (Al_2O_3), are normally resistant to such leaching.

Temperature alters the rate at which chemical weathering takes place. In areas where average temperatures are high these reactions take place more rapidly and in colder regions they take place at a slower rate.

Abrasion Forces that cause rock particles to move and rub against one another contribute to the process of abrasion and the physical breakdown of parent rock. Moving glaciers cause rock particles to grind against one another and break into smaller pieces, which are carried along with the moving glacier and deposited when it retreats.

Ocean waves are powerful rock grinders. Rivers and flowing streams also move rocks and grind them down, which explains the smoothness of most of the rocks and pebbles in a stream or along a shoreline. Rocks on the earth's surface are worn

down by the sandblasting effect of billions of tiny particles carried by the wind.

Living Organisms Plants and animals help in the physical and chemical weathering of parent rock. Growing roots can exert enough pressure to enlarge cracks in solid rock and eventually split the rock. Plants such as mosses and lichens can penetrate between mineral grains and loosen particles of rock. They can also help trap windblown organic debris such as seeds, dead insects, and excrement. Along with bacteria, they secrete acid solutions that slowly can dissolve the parent rock.

The role of plants and animals in producing soil usually increases as disintegrated parent material builds up and is combined with dead organic material to form humus. At this point, plant roots, worms, insects, and other burrowing organisms aerate and move soil particles and add more organic matter to the soil when they die.

Topography and Time The slope of the land has an important effect on the type of soil that can form. When the slope is steep the action of wind, flowing water, and gravity tends to erode the soil constantly. This explains why soils on steep slopes are often thin and in some cases never accumulate to a sufficient depth to support plant growth. By contrast, soils formed on the valleys below steep mountain slopes receive much of the soil particles, nutrients, water, and organic matter from these slopes and thus are often fertile and highly productive if they are not too wet.

Obviously, time affects the nature of a soil. The degree of weathering also affects the time it takes to develop a mature soil. If one soil is developed in a cold northern climate and another in a warm southern climate for the same amount of time, the soil in the south will be more highly weathered and developed than that in the north.

8-3 Soil Properties

Physical Properties Two important physical properties of soil are its *texture* and *structure*. *Soil texture* refers to the size of the soil's individual mineral particles and the proportion in which particles of different sizes are found in the soil. An international classification system defines particles with a diameter less than 0.002 millimeters as *clay*, those with diameters between 0.002 and 0.02 millimeters as *silt*, and those with diameters between 0.02 and

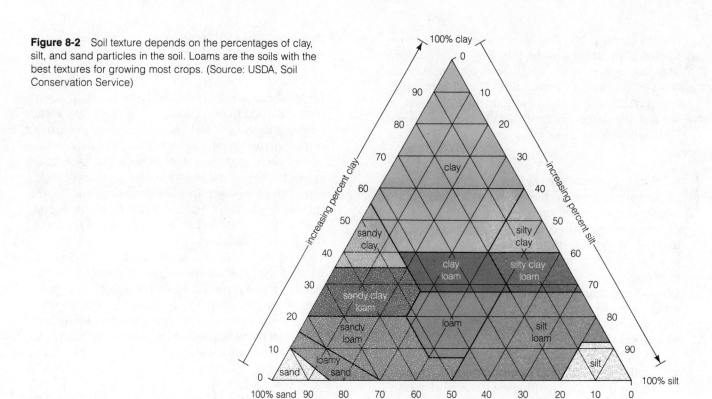

Figure 8-2 Soil texture depends on the percentages of clay, silt, and sand particles in the soil. Loams are the soils with the best textures for growing most crops. (Source: USDA, Soil Conservation Service)

2 millimeters in diameter as *sand*. The mixtures of clay, sand, and silt lead to the various soil textures shown in Figure 8-2. Variations in loam texture are indicated with terms like *sandy loam* and *loamy silt*.

One way to get a rough idea of the texture of a soil is to take about a tablespoon of the soil into the palm of one hand. Work in a little water until the soil is thoroughly wet and firm but not runny. Rub the wet mixture into a thin cake on your palm. Soil with a high clay content feels slippery and may stick to your fingers when compressed. A sandy soil has no shine and feels gritty. A soil with a high silt content feels greasy and slippery but does not have the plastic quality of a clay soil. To confirm this test, roll the damp soil into a clod and drop it on the ground. If the clod holds together completely it is rich in clay; if it completely disintegrates the soil has a high sand content; and if it breaks into a few smaller pieces it is probably a mixture of sand, silt, and clay classified as a loam (Figure 8-2).

Soil texture influences the amount of water a soil can hold and the rate at which water percolates through the soil. In sandy soils, so many relatively large pore spaces exist between the sand particles that water and air flow through rapidly. This reduces surface runoff but such soils drain so well that they retain almost no water. At the other extreme are clay soils in which the particles are so small and so easily packed together that plant roots cannot pen-

etrate. Clay soils with extra small, closely packed particles are poorly aerated and do not drain well—often being too waterlogged to support many plants.

For growing crops the best soil texture consists of almost equal amounts of sand and silt and somewhat less clay—the so-called loams (Figure 8-2). Such soils have a porosity that allows air circulation and good drainage yet retain enough water to support ample plant growth.

The texture of a soil also contributes to *soil structure*—a term describing the way soil particles clump together in larger lumps and clods. The large pores between the clumps allow rapid movement of air and water through the soil. Soil structure depends primarily on the amount of clay and organic material in the soil. Clay soil holds together strongly and when wet can form massive clumps, which is why the clay used by potters holds together and can be molded into any shape.

A good soil for growing plants has a crumbly, spongy quality. When walked on it has a springy feeling. Its particles clump together so that it is about one-half to two-thirds filled with pore space. This abundance of pores provides ample oxygen for plant root cells and retains enough water for roots to absorb without being waterlogged. Since good agricultural soil is easily compacted it is important not to walk or drive heavy machinery on it following rains or irrigation.

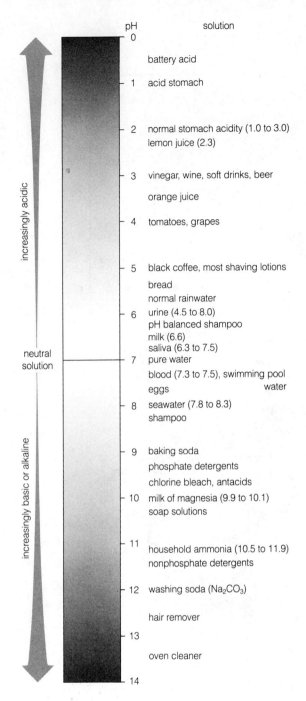

pH	solution
0	
	battery acid
1	acid stomach
2	normal stomach acidity (1.0 to 3.0)
	lemon juice (2.3)
3	vinegar, wine, soft drinks, beer
	orange juice
4	tomatoes, grapes
5	black coffee, most shaving lotions
	bread
	normal rainwater
6	urine (4.5 to 8.0)
	pH balanced shampoo
	milk (6.6)
	saliva (6.3 to 7.5)
7	pure water
	blood (7.3 to 7.5), swimming pool
	eggs water
8	seawater (7.8 to 8.3)
	shampoo
9	baking soda
	phosphate detergents
	chlorine bleach, antacids
10	milk of magnesia (9.9 to 10.1)
	soap solutions
11	household ammonia (10.5 to 11.9)
	nonphosphate detergents
12	washing soda (Na_2CO_3)
	hair remover
13	
	oven cleaner
14	

increasingly acidic

neutral solution

increasingly basic or alkaline

Figure 8-3 The pH scale used to measure acidity and basicity or alkalinity of water solutions. Values shown for common aqueous solutions are approximate.

Chemical Properties The chemical properties of a soil are determined primarily by its oxygen, water, mineral and organic matter content, available plant nutrients, and its pH or relative acidity or alkalinity. All of these properties except pH were discussed in Section 8-1.

The pH or degree of acidity or alkalinity is determined by the relative concentrations of hydrogen ions (H^+) and hydroxide ions (OH^-) in the water found in the soil. Pure water contains equal numbers of H^+ and OH^- ions. It is a *neutral solution*—neither acidic nor basic or alkaline—and has a pH of 7. An *acidic solution* has more H^+ ions than OH^- ions and a pH less than 7; the lower the pH the more acidic the solution. A *basic or alkaline solution* has more OH^- ions than H^+ ions and a pH greater than 7; the higher the pH the more alkaline the solution (Figure 8-3).

A major source of soil acidity is the H^+ ions formed when CO_2 gas in the atmosphere reacts with water to produce H^+ and HCO_3^- ions. Acids (H^+ ions) are also produced by the decomposition of organic matter in the soil and by the addition of ammonium-containing fertilizers.

Crops vary widely in the pH ranges that they can tolerate. Many common food plants such as wheat, spinach, peas, corn, and tomatoes grow best in slightly acidic soils, potatoes and berries in very acidic soils, and alfalfa and asparagus in neutral soils. When soils are too acidic for the crops desired, the acids can be partially neutralized by adding lime (ground up limestone or $CaCO_3$). Adding lime, however, also speeds up the undesirable decomposition of organic matter in the soil. Therefore, when lime is used it is also important to add manure or other organic fertilizer such as crop residues. Otherwise, the first few years of good crop yields will be followed by poor yields. Adding such organic matter to the soil also helps to stabilize soil pH.

In areas of low rainfall, such as the semiarid valleys in the western and southwestern regions of the United States, calcium and other alkaline compounds are not leached away. As a result, soils in these areas may be too alkaline, with a pH above 7.5, for growing some desired crops. If such soils are well drained, they can be made less alkaline by leaching the alkaline compounds away with irrigation water. Soil alkalinity can also be reduced by adding sulfur, which is gradually converted to sulfuric acid (H_2SO_4) by sulfur-loving bacteria.

8-4   Major Types of Soil and Soil Profiles

Classifying Soils According to the U.S. Department of Agriculture, there are about 80,000 different types of soil in the United States and between 500,000 and 600,000 types in the world. Soil maps of areas are made by classifying soils into several major types or *orders*. Each order is broken down into suborders and then into increasingly narrower classifications called great groups, subgroups, families, and series.

Mature soils in different biomes of the world vary widely in the color, physical and chemical properties, and depth of their various layers. These

Figure 8-4 World distribution of major soil orders. (Source: USDA, Soil Conservation Service)

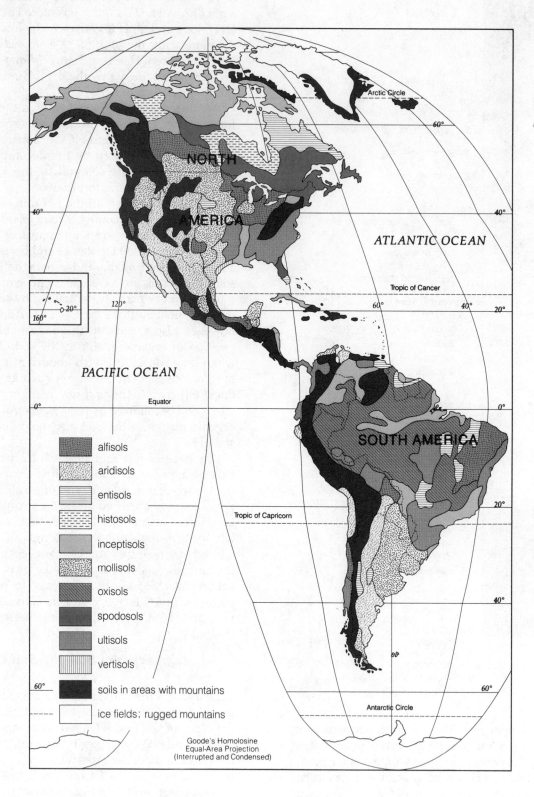

alfisols

aridisols

entisols

histosols

inceptisols

mollisols

oxisols

spodosols

ultisols

vertisols

soils in areas with mountains

ice fields; rugged mountains

Goode's Homolosine
Equal-Area Projection
(Interrupted and Condensed)

NORTH AMERICA

SOUTH AMERICA

ATLANTIC OCEAN

PACIFIC OCEAN

Arctic Circle

Tropic of Cancer

Equator

Tropic of Capricorn

Antarctic Circle

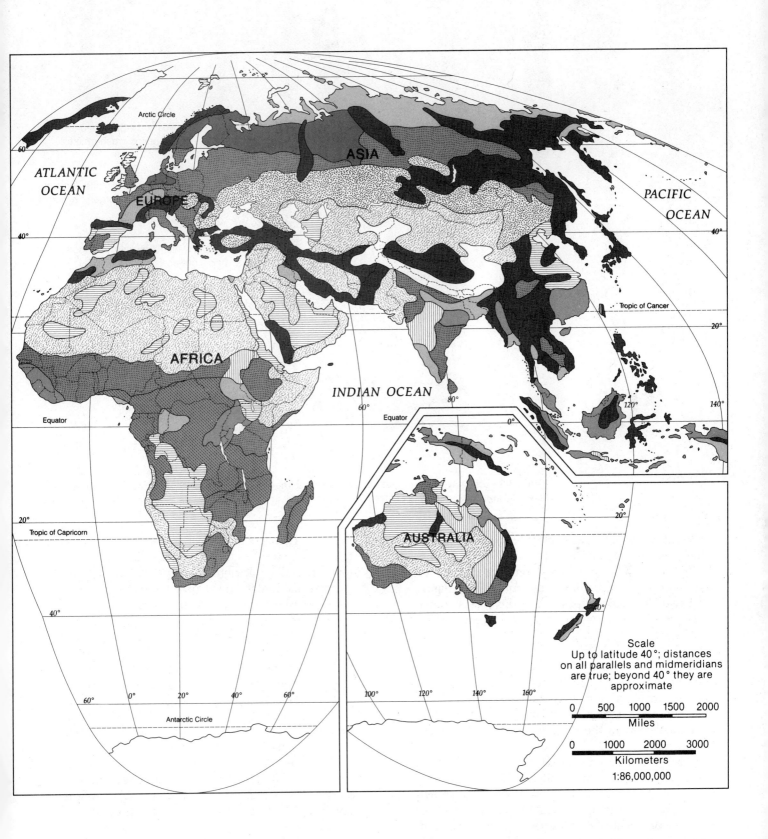

Arctic Circle

ATLANTIC
OCEAN

ASIA

PACIFIC
OCEAN

EUROPE

40°

40°

60°

AFRICA

Tropic of Cancer

20°

Equator

INDIAN OCEAN

80°

60°

Equator

0°

120°

140°

20°

20°

AUSTRALIA

Tropic of Capricorn

40°

40°

40°

0°

20°

40°

60°

100°

120°

140°

160°

Scale
Up to latitude 40°; distances
on all parallels and midmeridians
are true; beyond 40° they are
approximate

60°

0   500   1000   1500   2000
Miles

Antarctic Circle

0   1000   2000   3000
Kilometers
1:86,000,000

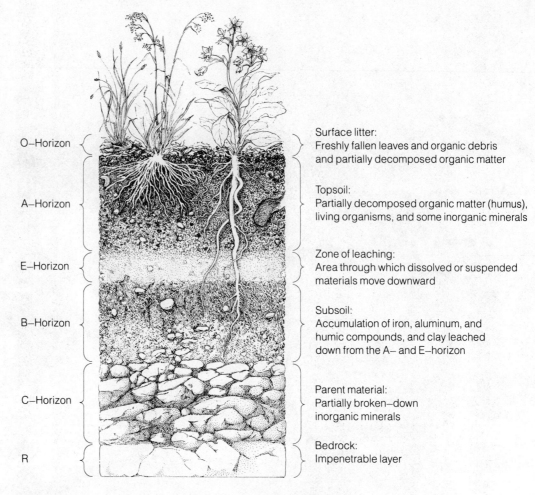

O–Horizon	Surface litter: Freshly fallen leaves and organic debris and partially decomposed organic matter
A–Horizon	Topsoil: Partially decomposed organic matter (humus), living organisms, and some inorganic minerals
E–Horizon	Zone of leaching: Area through which dissolved or suspended materials move downward
B–Horizon	Subsoil: Accumulation of iron, aluminum, and humic compounds, and clay leached down from the A– and E–horizon
C–Horizon	Parent material: Partially broken–down inorganic minerals
R	Bedrock: Impenetrable layer

Figure 8-5 Soil profile showing possible soil horizons. The number, composition, and thickness of these horizontal layers vary with different types of soil, as shown in Figure 8-6.

differences can be used to classify soils throughout the world into ten orders, as shown in Figure 8-4. Correlations among climate, biomes, and these ten soil orders can be seen by comparing Figure 8-4 with the major types of world climates shown in Figure 3-11 and the major types of biomes shown in Figure 3-13.

Soil Profiles Most soils consist of a series of distinctive horizontal layers called **soil horizons,** as shown in Figure 8-5. Each horizon has a distinct thickness, color, texture, and composition. A cross-sectional view of the horizons in a soil is called a **soil profile.**

Most mature soils have three or four of the six major horizons: O (surface litter), A (topsoil), E (zone of leaching), B (subsoil), C, and R (bedrock) shown in Figure 8-5. The uppermost *O-horizon* consists of a layer of freshly fallen leaves, organic litter, and partially decomposed organic debris. Below this horizon is usually found a porous mixture of humus and mineral particles called the *A-horizon,* commonly referred to as *topsoil.* This layer, ranging in

thickness from less than a centimeter on steep slopes to over a meter thick in grassland soils, is the most fertile horizon in the entire soil profile. The O- and A-horizons contain most of a soil's living organisms, organic matter, and plant roots.

In many soils formed in forests, a light-colored *E-horizon* (formerly called the A$_2$-horizon) is found under the O-horizon or under a thin A-horizon. This E-horizon is called the *zone of leaching* because as water percolates through this layer it dissolves water-soluble inorganic and organic matter, carrying it downward to the underlying B-horizon. Most grassland and desert soils do not have E-horizons.

Below the A- or E-horizons is the *B-horizon* or *subsoil,* commonly containing an accumulation of iron, aluminum, and humic compounds and clay leached down from the overlying O-, A- or E-horizons. Although not as fertile as the A-horizon, this horizon provides crucial supplies of water and oxygen for plants with deep roots and for most plants when the A-horizon dries out or does not exist.

Beneath the B-horizon is a zone of relatively undecomposed mineral particles and rock frag-

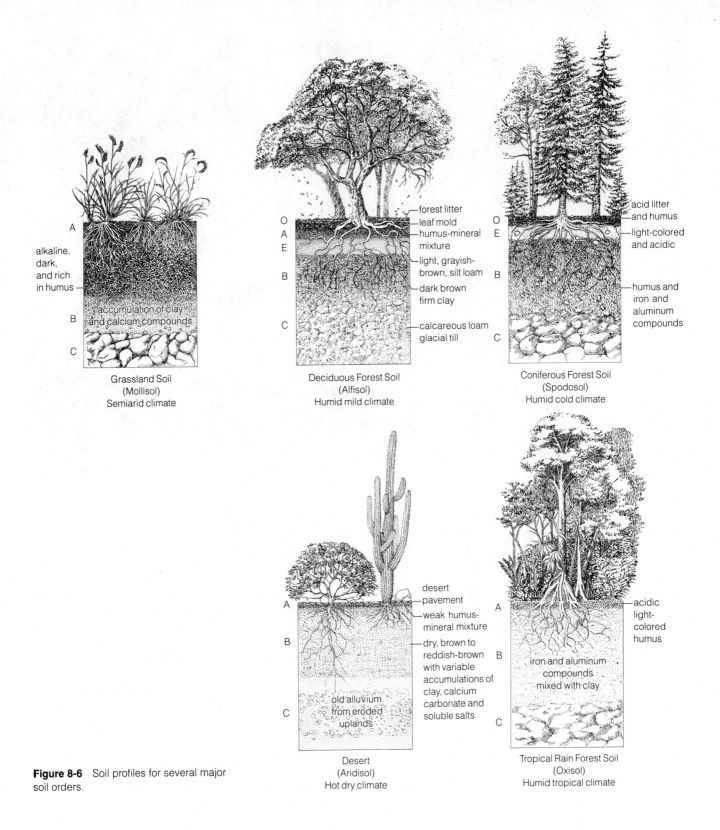

Figure 8-6 Soil profiles for several major soil orders.

Grassland Soil
(Mollisol)
Semiarid climate

alkaline, dark, and rich in humus

accumulation of clay and calcium compounds

Deciduous Forest Soil
(Alfisol)
Humid mild climate

forest litter
leaf mold
humus-mineral mixture
light, grayish-brown, silt loam
dark brown firm clay
calcareous loam glacial till

Coniferous Forest Soil
(Spodosol)
Humid cold climate

acid litter and humus
light-colored and acidic
humus and iron and aluminum compounds

Desert
(Aridisol)
Hot dry climate

desert pavement
weak humus-mineral mixture
dry, brown to reddish-brown with variable accumulations of clay, calcium carbonate and soluble salts
old alluvium from eroded uplands

Tropical Rain Forest Soil
(Oxisol)
Humid tropical climate

acidic light-colored humus
iron and aluminum compounds mixed with clay

ments referred to as the *C-horizon*. In some cases, it contains the same kind of material that has slowly broken down (weathered) to form the minerals in a soil's layers. This horizon contains no organic material. The relatively impenetrable layer of *bedrock*, sometimes encountered within a few feet of the soil surface, is referred to by the symbol R and is often not shown in soil profiles.

Mature soils in different biomes (Section 3-8) have different soil profiles as shown in Figure 8-6 for five of the major soil orders: **(1)** the *mollisols*, highly fertile soils found under the grasslands located

Figure 8-7 Because of poor drainage, white alkaline salts have replaced crops that once bloomed in heavily irrigated Paradise Valley, Wyoming.

USDI Bureau of Reclamation/Lyle C. Axthelm

throughout much of the breadbasket areas of North America, central Asia, central Europe, northern China, and Argentina (Figure 3-13) in semiarid dry climates (Figure 3-11); **(2)** the *alfisols*, found under the deciduous forests (Figure 3-13) in areas with humid, mild climates (Figure 3-11); **(3)** the *spodosols*, found under temperate coniferous forests (Figure 3-13) in areas with humid, cold climates (Figure 3-11); **(4)** the *oxisols*, found under large areas of tropical rain forests and some subtropical forests of Central America, Africa, and Asia (Figure 3-13) mostly in humid, tropical climates (Figure 3-11); and **(5)** the *aridisols*, found in desert areas of northern, central, and southern Africa and South America and in low-elevation areas of the western United States from Wyoming and eastern Oregon to the Mexican border and on into northern Mexico (Figure 3-13) with hot, arid climates (Figure 3-11).

Most of the world's crops are grown on grassland mollisols and alfisols exposed when deciduous forests are cleared. Alfisols, however, are less productive than grassland soils because of their thinner A-horizons and because the higher rainfall in areas where alfisols are formed leaches many of the nutrients from overlying horizons. Unless these nutrients are replaced by fertilizers, soils of cleared temperate deciduous forests will no longer grow satisfactory crops after several years of harvest. Spodosols are not very useful for growing crops when coniferous forests are cleared.

When tropical rain forests with oxisol soils are cleared, the torrential, seasonal rains of the tropics leach most of the nutrients and remaining minerals from their A-horizons. When exposed to the air and sun, the iron oxide that remains can form red rock called *laterite* or *ironstone*—a rock so hard it is used for paving highways. Once laterite forms, the land can be lost to cultivation permanently. It is estimated that laterite-forming oxisols are found close to the surface on about 7 percent of the total land area of the tropics—including 2 percent of tropical America, 11 percent of tropical Africa, and 15 percent of sub-Saharan West Africa (Figure 8-4).

About one-third of the area covered by aridisols is not useful for growing crops because of too little rainfall. With proper soil management and extensive irrigation, soils in certain desert areas, such as the Imperial Valley of California, can produce a variety of valuable crops. Such soils, however, often become unproductive from waterlogging and alkaline salt buildup when they are irrigated without sufficient drainage (Figure 8-7). In general, aridisols are better used as rangelands than as croplands.

Figure 8-8 Extensive soil erosion and gully formation from poor farming practices.

USDA, Soil Conservation Service

8-5 Soil Erosion

Natural and Human-Accelerated Soil Erosion
Soil does not stay in one place indefinitely. The processes by which earthy and rock materials are loosened or dissolved and removed from a place by forces such as wind, water, waves, glaciers, and construction activity and eventually deposited at a new location are called **soil erosion** (from the Latin *erodere*, meaning "to gnaw out"). Blowing wind and flowing water have moved sediments at an extremely slow average rate since the earth formed 4 to 5 billion years ago. Before the rise of agriculture (Enrichment Study 1), this natural erosion was beneficial for the most part because it led to the formation of fertile deltas and valleys. Studies show, however, that the average rate of this natural erosion has been significantly increased by human activities such as poor farming practices, overgrazing, ground clearing for construction, logging, and mining. Some geologists estimate that the overall rate of soil erosion from human activities is over twice the average natural erosion rate over the half-billion years before humans came on the scene.

The destructive human influence on increasing soil erosion rates occurs when the vegetative cover that holds soil particles together is removed through farming, overgrazing, and urbanization. When land is intensively cultivated the rate of erosion is three

or more times what it is when the land is under forest cover (Figure 8-8). Soil is eroded even more rapidly when tracts of land are bulldozed for housing and building construction, leaving large volumes of soil exposed to wind and rain. As this soil is carried away into nearby rivers and lakes the land is robbed of valuable topsoil, and these aquatic systems are polluted with sediment and excess plant nutrients that can accelerate natural eutrophication processes (Enrichment Study 14). After urban construction, the asphalt, cement, and other water-impervious surfaces increase the runoff of rainwater and melting snow even with expensive storm sewers and drainage systems. Thus, the net effect of urbanization is increased soil erosion during construction and often even more soil erosion in the surrounding area after construction is completed.

Global and U.S. Soil Erosion Soil is technically a renewable resource (Section 1-3). However, the average rate of erosion of topsoil per unit of cropland throughout the world greatly exceeds the rate at which it is being formed. In effect, the world is mining much of the world's soil and slowly converting it to a nonrenewable resource to grow crops, to graze animals, and to clear land for logging, construction, and mining. According to 1984 estimates by the Worldwatch Institute, the world is now losing an estimated 21 trillion kilograms (23 billion tons) of soil each year from croplands alone in excess of new soil formation. Each year this amount of valuable topsoil washing and blowing into the world's rivers and oceans would fill a train of freight cars long enough to encircle the entire planet 138 times! At this rate, the world's topsoil is being depleted at 0.7 percent a year—7 percent each decade. This already serious situation is accelerating as cultivation is being extended into ever more marginal areas of land.

The largest amount of excessive soil erosion is occurring in India, followed in order by China, the Soviet Union, and the United States. Altogether the excessive loss of topsoil from these four major food-producing nations, which have 52 percent of the world's cropland and account for over one-half of its production, is estimated at 11 trillion kilograms (11.8 billion tons) a year. Not only does this loss of topsoil reduce soil fertility, it can also reduce irrigation from irrigation ditches filled with sediment, electrical generation from dam reservoirs filling rapidly with silt, and the navigability of waterways clogged with sediment.

This massive loss of the topsoil is not due to a lack of knowledge about how to reduce soil erosion. Instead it results from the political and economic pressures on farmers to produce more in the short run for the world's growing population, with little regard for the long-term consequences. Many of the world's traditional agricultural systems that were ecologically stable as recently as 1950, when there were 2.5 billion people in the world, are breaking down as the world's population approaches 5 billion.

In mountainous areas, such as those in China, Indonesia, Japan, Nepal, and in the Himalayas and the Andes, farmers traditionally constructed elaborate systems of terraces that allowed them to cultivate steeply sloping land that would otherwise rapidly lose its topsoil. In recent decades, however, growing competition for cropland has pushed farmers further up the slopes on more steeply sloped lands. Hastily constructed terraces often give away, causing landslides that sometimes destroy entire villages. In some areas steep slopes are cultivated without building any terraces, causing an irreversible loss of all topsoil within 10 to 40 years. Poor farmers may know that plowing a steep slope causes a rapid loss of topsoil, but they have nowhere else to go to feed their families.

In the tropics—such as parts of Africa south of the Sahara, the Amazon basin, Venezuela, and the outer islands of Indonesia—farmers long ago evolved a system of *shifting cultivation*. A patch of forestland is cleared by cutting and burning the trees, a process that releases nutrients from the trees to the soil. The farmer grows crops for 2 to 4 years, then moves on to another plot. Ideally, the original plot should lie fallow (remain uncultivated) for 10 to 25 years to regenerate the forest and soil nutrients. However, in recent decades mounting population pressures in the tropics have caused farmers in many locales to reduce the fallowing period under shifting cultivation to as little as 2 to 5 years. The result has been a sharp increase in the rate of topsoil erosion.

Overgrazing and poor logging practices (Chapter 10) also cause heavy losses of topsoil. Intense grazing has turned many areas of North Africa from grassland to desert in a process known as *desertification*. Once forested hills in many parts of the world have been stripped bare of trees by peasants looking for firewood for cooking and heating and by timber companies, and the trees are often not replanted (Section 10-6).

Surveys by the USDA's Soil Conservation Service (SCS) show that the average rate of erosion on cultivated land in the United States is about 7 times that at which soil is being reformed. This amounts to an average loss of 2.5 centimeters (1 inch) of soil per acre every 33 years and represents plant nutrient losses worth $18 billion a year in 1979 dollars. This average rate of topsoil loss masks much higher losses of five to eight times this rate in heavily farmed areas with the most severe erosion rates. It is estimated that more than one-third of all U.S. cropland is suffering from losses of topsoil that will gradually decrease crop productivity if soil conservation efforts are not greatly increased. Indeed, according to the SCS, *the United States has already lost about one third of the topsoil on the cropland in use today.*

In the Great Plains of the Midwest, farmers traditionally rotated planting of fields with hay, pasture, and corn every few years and alternated row crops like corn with cover crops like hay to keep the average annual rate of soil erosion to a tolerable level and also add organic matter to the soil. Since 1950, however, most farmers throughout the Midwest, the lower Mississippi Valley, and the Southeast have abandoned crop rotation and alternating row cropping to grow corn, wheat, and soybeans continuously over large areas. Studies have shown that this can increase the annual rate of erosion on such fields from four to seven times the earlier traditional rates, with the higher rate leading to a loss of 2.5 centimeters (1 inch) of topsoil in less than a decade. The shift to large, heavy equipment, large sprinkler irrigation systems (some center-pivot systems have a radius of 0.4 kilometer or a quarter of a mile), and the enlargement of fields, has also eliminated many windbreaking hedgerows and other natural boundaries that helped reduce erosion of topsoil by wind and water.

Heavy and increasingly expensive applications of fertilizers merely temporarily hide the fact that

Figure 8-9 Dust storm approaching Prowers County, Colorado, in 1934.

USDA, Soil Conservation Service/Thomas G. Meier

the natural fertility and productivity of U.S. soils are being depleted at an alarming rate, with the resulting sediment being the single largest source of the nation's water pollution (Chapter 18). Most U.S. farmers are knowledgeable about soil conservation techniques, but choose to ignore them when they conflict with other techniques that offer a higher yield, and a higher profit over the short term.

The Dust Bowl: A Valuable Ecological Lesson   The Great Plains stretch through ten states from Texas through Montana and the Dakotas into Canada. This area is normally dry and very windy and periodically experiences long, severe droughts. Prior to the 1890s, when settlers began planting crops in this region, the extensive root systems of its prairie grasses held its rich grassland soil (Figure 8-6) in place. When the land was planted these perennial grasses were replaced by annual crops with less extensive root systems. In addition, the land was plowed up after each harvest and left bare part of the year.

Thus, the stage was set for severe wind erosion. Crops can be grown in wet years, but unirrigated crops and the soil can be devastated in drought years. Accelerated wind erosion and crop failures occurred during the droughts of 1890 and 1910 and then returned with great severity between 1926 and 1934.

In 1934, after several years of drought, hot, dry windstorms created dust clouds thick enough to

cause darkness in some areas at midday (Figure 8-9); the danger of breathing this dust-laden air was revealed by the rabbits and dead birds left in its wake. During May 1934, the entire eastern half of the United States was blanketed with a dust cloud containing about 318 billion kilograms (350 million tons) of rich topsoil blown off the Great Plains— 2,415 kilometers (1,500 miles) away. Even ships 320 kilometers (200 miles) out in the Atlantic Ocean received deposits of topsoil blown off parts of the Great Plains. This event gave the Great Plains regions a new name, the *Dust Bowl*.

An estimated 3.6 million hectares (9 million acres) of farmland were destroyed and an additional 32 million hectares (80 million acres) were severely damaged. Thousands of displaced farm families from Oklahoma, Texas, Kansas, and other areas migrated westward toward California and to some of the industrial cities of the Midwest and East. Since the nation was still suffering from the Great Depression of the early 1930s, most of these people joined long breadlines of other suffering people. This exodus of Great Plains farmers and the frustration, suffering, and bitterness they encountered is graphically described in John Steinbeck's novel *The Grapes of Wrath*.

In May 1934, Hugh Bennett of the U.S. Department of Agriculture (then one of the world's leading conservationists) was at a congressional hearing pleading for new programs to protect the nation's topsoil. Lawmakers in Washington took action when dust blown from the Great Plains began seeping into the hearing room. In 1935, the United States

Figure 8-10 A combination of contour farming and strip cropping can be used to reduce soil erosion.

USDA, Soil Conservation Service/E. W. Cole

became the first nation to establish a Soil Conservation Service (SCS) as part of the U.S. Department of Agriculture (USDA). With Hugh Bennett as its first head, the SCS began promoting good conservation practices in the Great Plains and then in every state by establishing local soil conservation districts and providing technical assistance to farmers and ranchers. The SCS has since used over $22 billion provided by taxpayers to help preserve millions of acres of soil from erosion and destruction.

Soil Conservation Service efforts, however, did not completely solve the erosion problems of the Great Plains region. From both an economic and ecological viewpoint, much of the Great Plains is better suited for grazing than farming—a lesson its farmers have learned several times since the 1890s and may be forced to learn again. After a moist 1940s, severe drought returned in the 1950s and the government had to provide emergency relief funds.

In 1975 the Council of Agricultural Science and Technology (CAST) warned that severe drought could create another dust bowl in the Great Plains, pointing out that despite large expenditures for soil erosion control topsoil losses today are 2.5 percent worse than in the 1930s. Many of today's debt-ridden farmers are more interested in maximizing short-term crop yields and profits than in long-term soil conservation. A 1977 General Accounting Office (GAO) report noted that many recipients of federal soil conservation funds "did not fully implement suggested or required programs" and spent the

money for other purposes. The GAO also pointed out that follow-up by federal SCS officials to encourage soil conservation programs was practically nil. The stage has been set for another dust bowl as many of the conservation practices described in the next section have been abandoned.

8-6 Soil Conservation

Soil Erosion Control The most important step in soil conservation is to hold the soil in place. Methods used to accomplish this goal include **(1)** *contour farming*, **(2)** *terracing*, **(3)** *minimum tillage farming*, **(4)** *strip cropping*, **(5)** *crop rotation*, **(6)** *gully reclamation*, **(7)** *using windbreaks*, and **(8)** *not planting marginal farming land*.

One simple way to reduce soil erosion up to 50 percent is to use *contour farming*, which involves plowing and planting along the contours of gently sloping land (Figure 8-10) rather than up and down the hills. Each row planted at right angles to the slope of the land acts as a small dam to help hold soil and slow the runoff of water.

Terracing can be used on steeper slopes to reduce soil loss and help retain water. It involves converting a long, steep slope into a series of broad, level terraces running at right angles to the slope of the land. Water running down the slope is retained by each terrace, reducing runoff and soil erosion and providing water for crops. In areas of high rainfall, diversion ditches must be built behind each terrace to permit adequate drainage. Terracing is widely

Figure 8-11 Windbreaks are used to reduce erosion on this farm in Trail County, North Dakota.

USDA, Soil Conservation Service/E. W. Cole

used in China, Japan, and the Philippines (especially for rice), around the Mediterranean, and in the Andes of South America.

In conventional farming the land is plowed, disked several times, and then smoothed to make a planting surface. If plowed in the fall so crops can be planted early in the spring, the soil is left unprotected during the winter and early spring months. In order to lower labor costs, save energy, and reduce soil erosion, this intensive tillage approach is being replaced by *minimum tillage* or *conservation farming* in some MDCs. It involves disturbing the soil as little as possible when crops are planted and keeping crop residues and litter on the ground instead of turning them under by plowing. Special subsurface tillers are used to break up and loosen the soil without turning over previous crop residues and cover vegetation. However, this technique requires increased use of herbicides to control weeds that compete with crops for soil nutrients. Depending on the soil, this approach can be used for 3 to 7 years before more extensive soil cultivation is needed to prevent crop yields from declining. In some cases special planters are used to inject seeds into the soil without plowing at all (known as *no-tillage farming*). By 1984 minimum tillage practices were used on about 35 percent of all U.S. croplands. The USDA estimates that using it on 80 percent of U.S. cropland would reduce soil erosion by 50 percent or more.

Strip cropping involves planting crops in alternating rows or bands of close-growing plants (such

as hay or nitrogen-fixing legumes) and regular crops. The strips of close-growing crops slow water runoff, reduce soil erosion, decrease damage from pests and plant diseases, and help restore soil fertility—especially when legumes are used. This technique can reduce soil losses by up to 75 percent on sloping land when combined with contour farming (Figure 8-10) or terracing.

Crop rotation involves annually rotating areas or strips planted with crops such as corn, tobacco, and cotton that remove large amounts of nutrients from the soil when harvested with legumes that add nitrogen to the soil or with other crops such as oats, barley, and rye. This method improves soil fertility, reduces soil erosion by covering land whose fertility is being improved, and reduces pest infestation and plant diseases by annually switching the plants in each area.

On sloping land not covered by vegetation, deep gullies can be created fairly quickly by water runoff, as shown earlier in Figure 8-8. Thus, *gully reclamation* is an important form of soil conservation. Relatively small gullies can be seeded with quick-growing plants such as oats, barley, and wheat to reduce erosion. For severe gullies (Figure 8-8) small dams of manure and straw, earth, stone, and even concrete can be used to collect silt and gradually fill in the channels. The soil can then be stabilized by planting rapidly growing shrubs, vines, and trees.

Wind erosion from cultivated lands exposed to high winds, such as the Great Plains, can be reduced by using *windbreaks* (Figure 8-11). This is especially

8 Soil Resources **135**

Table 8-1 Land Capability Classification According to the Soil Conservation Service

Land Class	Characteristics	Primary Uses	Secondary Uses	Conservation Measures
Land Suitable for Cultivation				
I	Excellent, flat, well-drained land	Agriculture	Recreation Wildlife Pasture	None
II	Good land, has minor limitations such as slight slope, sandy soil, or poor drainage	Agriculture Pasture	Recreation Wildlife	Strip cropping Contour farming
III	Moderately good land with important limitations of soil, slope, or drainage	Agriculture Pasture Watershed	Recreation Wildlife Urban industry	Contour farming Strip cropping Waterways Terraces
IV	Fair land, severe limitations of soil, slope, or drainage	Pasture Orchards Limited agriculture Urban industry	Pasture Wildlife	Farming on a limited basis Contour farming Strip cropping Waterways Terraces
Land Not Suitable for Cultivation				
V	Use for grazing and forestry, slightly limited by rockiness, shallow soil, wetness, or slope prevents farming	Grazing Forestry Watershed	Recreation Wildlife	No special precautions if properly grazed or logged. Must not be plowed.
VI	Moderate limitations for grazing and forestry	Grazing Forestry Watershed Urban industry	Recreation Wildlife	Grazing or logging may be limited at times.
VII	Severe limitations for grazing and forestry	Grazing Forestry Watershed Recreation Wildlife Urban industry		Careful management required when used for grazing or logging.
VIII	Unsuitable for grazing and forestry because of steep slope, shallow soil, lack of water, too much water	Recreation Watershed Wildlife Urban industry		Not to be used for grazing or logging. Steep slope and lack of soil presents problems.

effective if land not under cultivation is kept covered with vegetation. A large fraction of the windbreaks in the Great Plains have been destroyed to make way for large irrigation systems and farm machinery.

An obvious approach to reducing soil erosion is *not planting crops on marginal lands* that, because of slope, soil structure, presence of high winds and periodic drought (such as much of the Great Plains), or other factors, are subject to high rates of soil erosion.

Though all of these soil conservation practices are well known to farmers throughout the United States, their use has declined (except minimum tillage farming). The net result is an increase in soil erosion.

Land Use Classification To encourage wise land use, the SCS has set up the eight different classes of land summarized in Table 8-1 and illustrated in Figure 8-12. Factors such as soil types and fertility,

LAND CAPABILITY CLASSES

SUITABLE FOR CULTIVATION		NO CULTIVATION-PASTURE, HAY, WOODLAND AND WILDLIFE	
I	REQUIRES GOOD SOIL MANAGEMENT PRACTICES ONLY	V	NO RESTRICTIONS IN USE
II	MODERATE CONSERVATION PRACTICES NECESSARY	VI	MODERATE RESTRICTIONS IN USE
III	INTENSIVE CONSERVATION PRACTICES NECESSARY	VII	SEVERE RESTRICTIONS IN USE
IV	PERENNIAL VEGETATION - INFREQUENT CULTIVATION	VIII	BEST SUITED FOR WILDLIFE AND RECREATION

slope, drainage, and erodibility are used to classify a particular land area into one of these best use categories. After land is classified in this manner, each community has a responsibility to pass laws and use techniques such as zoning to prevent land misuse, as discussed in Section 12-5.

Maintaining Soil Fertility Organic fertilizers and commercial inorganic fertilizers can be applied to soil to restore and maintain plant nutrients lost from the soil by erosion, leaching, and crop harvesting. *Organic fertilizers* include animal manure, green manure, and compost. One important reason for adding organic fertilizers to soil is to stimulate the growth and reproduction of decomposer microorganisms that improve soil fertility by decomposing organic matter. Commercial inorganic fertilizers alone are often not sufficient for this purpose.

Animal manure includes the dung and urine of farm animals such as cattle, horses, and poultry. Application of animal manure improves soil structure, increases organic nitrogen content, and stimulates the growth and reproduction of soil bacteria and fungi. It is particularly useful on rotation crops such as corn, cotton, potatoes, cabbage, and tobacco. The use of animal manure in the United States has decreased for several reasons: **(1)** Most mixed animal- and crop-farming operations have been replaced with separate farms for raising animals (feedlots) and growing crops, **(2)** horses and other draft animals that naturally added manure to the soil have largely been replaced by tractors, **(3)** it is too expensive to use because of high labor costs and high costs for transporting manure from animal feedlots normally located near urban areas to rural crop-growing areas, and **(4)** it has been replaced in most cases by certain commercial fertilizers that can be more easily stored and applied, and to a lesser extent, by green manure.

Green manure is fresh, green vegetation plowed into the soil to increase the organic matter and humus content available to the next crop. It may be weeds that have taken over a field left uncultivated, grasses and clover from a field previously used for pasture, or legumes such as alfalfa or soybeans intentionally grown for use as fertilizer to build up soil nitrogen. The effects of green manure on the soil are similar to those of animal manure. *Compost* is a rich natural fertilizer usually produced by piling up alternating layers of carbohydrate-rich plant wastes such as cuttings and leaves, protein-rich animal manure, and topsoil to provide the microorganisms that aid the decomposition of the plant and animal manure layers.

Today the fertility of most U.S. soils is partially restored and maintained by the application of *commercial inorganic fertilizers*. The most common plant nutrients added with these are nitrogen, phosphorus, and potassium. Such fertilizers are designated by numbers like 6-12-12. This particular combination means that the fertilizer contains 6 percent nitrogen, 12 percent phosphorus, and 12 percent potassium. Other plant nutrients such as magnesium, sulfate, and various micronutrients may also be present. Ideally, the soil is chemically analyzed to determine the particular mix of nutrients that should be added.

Inorganic commercial fertilizers are a concentrated source of nutrients and are relatively cheap and easily stored and applied. There are disadvantages, however, to their use. The natural ability of soil to produce nitrogen in forms usable by plants is apparently decreased by the nitrogen in commercial fertilizers. Consequently, the continued yearly application of commercial nitrogen fertilizers eventually causes crop yields to decrease unless larger amounts are added each year at increasing expense and energy use. Commercial fertilizers also reduce the oxygen content of soil by altering soil porosity, so the added fertilizer is not taken up as efficiently. Another disadvantage is that many of the micronutrients needed by plants are not found in most commercial fertilizers.

Another problem is the movement of rainwater over and through the surface of land. It washes off some of the plant nutrient compounds in commercial fertilizers into nearby streams, rivers, and lakes or leaches them into groundwater supplies. These plant nutrients can poison drinking water and cause overgrowths of algae in lakes and slow-moving bodies of water that can accelerate eutrophication (Section 18-3).

The techniques for sharply reducing soil erosion are well established, but are not being widely used for political and economic reasons even in an agriculturally advanced nation such as the United States. Hopeful trends include the trend toward using minimum tillage farming in the United States and increasing international awareness of the need to reduce topsoil loss. But there is a long way to go.

Though there are occasional localized successes in efforts to conserve soil, there are no national successes, no models that other countries can emulate. In this respect, soil conservation contrasts sharply with oil conservation, where scores of countries have compiled impressive records in recent years.

Lester R. Brown

Discussion Topics

1. Soil is theoretically a renewable resource. Yet in many areas of the world, including the U.S., it is becoming a nonrenewable resource. Explain.

2. Why should urban dwellers, not just farmers, be concerned with soil conservation?

3. Distinguish between plant macronutrients and micronutrients and give three examples of each.

4. Explain how a plant can have ample supplies of N, P, and K and other essential macronutrients and still have stunted growth.

5. Explain the function of soil bacteria and earthworms in increasing soil fertility.

6. List these soils in order of increasing porosity to water: loam, clay, sand, and sandy loam.

7. Why is oxygen gas in soil pores important?

8. Why is the carbon dioxide gas content of soil higher than that in the atmosphere?

9. Discuss briefly how each of the following factors affects the type of soil formed in a given area: (a) parent material, (b) organisms, (c) climate, (d) topography, (e) abrasion, and (f) time.

10. Distinguish between the physical and chemical weathering of a soil and give an example of each.

11. Explain how rainwater can become acidic as it falls through the air and discuss the importance of this in the chemical weathering of soils.

12. What type of soil texture is best for growing crops? Why?

13. What type of soil structure is best for growing crops? Why?

14. If soil pH is too low for growing a particular crop, what can be done to raise its pH? If it is too high, what can be done to lower its pH?

15. Describe briefly what happened in the Dust Bowl of the 1930s and explain how it could happen again. How would you prevent this from recurring?

16. Distinguish among contour farming, terracing, and minimum tillage farming and explain how each can reduce soil erosion.

17. What is strip cropping and crop rotation and how can they be used to reduce soil erosion and help restore soil fertility?

18. Go into rural and semirural areas surrounding your campus and attempt to classify this land into the various land capability classes shown in Figure 8-12 and Table 8-1. Look for examples of land being used for purposes to which it is not suited.

19. What are the major advantages and disadvantages of using commercial inorganic fertilizers to help restore and maintain soil fertility? Why should organic fertilizers also be used on land treated with inorganic fertilizers?

9

Food Resources and World Hunger

Hunger is a curious thing: at first it is with you all the time, working and sleeping and in your dreams, and your belly cries out insistently, and there is a gnawing and a pain as if your very vitals were being devoured, and you must stop it at any cost. . . . Then the pain is no longer sharp, but dull, and this too is with you always.

Kamala Markandaya

In a refugee camp in Bangladesh, several thousand starving Bengalis are near death. Most sit motionless, too weak even to brush away the flies collecting on the sores on their faces. An emaciated 35-year-old woman, who looks 60, clutches an infant whose withered body and peeling skin reveal the signs of severe malnutrition. More than one-half of the world's people spend much of their waking hours and 50 to 70 percent of their income trying to get enough food to keep themselves and their children healthy and alive. In contrast, the affluent one-fourth of the people on earth typically spend a small fraction of their time and from 13 percent (in the United States) to 45 percent of their income on food. While the health of many people throughout the world is threatened by too little food, that of many others is threatened by too much food—making best-sellers out of the latest diet books.

Each day there are 221,000 more mouths to feed. Numerous agricultural experts estimate that world food production must be doubled, if not tripled, between 1980 and 2015 to feed adequately the 8 billion people projected to be living on this planet by 2015. This means that during this 35-year period we must produce as much food as we have since the dawn of agriculture about 12,000 years ago (Enrichment Study 1). How can this be done? Even

if enough food is grown, how can it be made available to those who can't afford to buy it? In this chapter we examine these questions to see how food, soil, water, fossil fuel, and fertilizer resources are interwoven with population growth and pollution.

9-1 Food Supply, Population Growth, and World Food Problems

Population Growth and Food Production Thanks to improved agricultural technologies, practices, and policies, food production has increased since 1950 on all continents except Africa. Despite this success, there are some signs of potential trouble. *First*, although world average per capita food production increased between 1950 and 1980, its rate of increase has been steadily declining each decade, rising 15 percent between 1950 to 1960, 7 percent between 1960 and 1970, and only 4 percent between 1970 and 1980. *Second*, plagued by the fastest population growth of any continent (Tables 6-2 and 6-3), extensive soil erosion and desertification, and underinvestment in agriculture, Africa's average food production per person fell 13 percent between 1970 and 1983—a situation some food experts fear may spread in coming years to other regions such as northeastern Brazil, the Andean countries, Central America, the Indian subcontinent, and the Middle East.

Third, although the *percentage* of the population suffering from hunger and malnutrition has declined by several orders of magnitude since 1950, there are more hungry and malnourished people today than in 1950 because of the large increase in population since that time (Figure 1-1). In 1982 the United Nations estimated that 450 million people—one out of every ten people on earth—were underfed, mostly in Africa and Asia. The World Bank had a higher estimate of 780 million people—one out of six people on earth—either too poor to buy enough food or

Enrichment Studies 1, 2, 5, 7, 9, and 14 are related to this chapter.

lacking sufficient land to grow enough of their own food in 1982.

Finally, 30 to 40 years ago most countries were self-sufficient in food, whereas today most have to import some of their food or are barely self-sufficient. Today's only major food exporting nations are the United States (which provides about 55 percent of all grain exports), Canada, Australia, New Zealand, France, and Argentina. Prolonged bad weather or economic problems in these countries—especially the United States and Canada which together provide about 70 percent of all grain exports—could spell disaster for hundreds of millions of people throughout the world, mostly in many LDCs, who now depend on these food-exporting nations for increasing amounts of food supplies. This increasing dependence on imports drains the national income of these LDCs and reduces opportunities for investments in producing more of their own food.

The Geography of Hunger These general improvements in average per capita food production hide widespread differences in average per capita food supply between and within different nations, and even within a particular family. For instance, although total and per capita food supplies have increased in Latin America, much of this gain has been confined to Argentina and Brazil. Thus, the average per capita food supply in Brazil is high, while that in neighboring Bolivia is fairly low. In more fertile and urbanized southern Brazil, the average daily per capita food supply is high, but in its semiarid and less-fertile northeastern interior many people are badly underfed. In the MDCs too there are pockets of hunger. According to nutrition expert Jean Mayer, during the economic recession of the early 1980s an estimated 22 to 32 million Americans were having difficulty getting enough food because of incomes below the poverty level and cuts in food stamps and other forms of government aid for the needy.

Food is also poorly distributed within families. Among the poor, young children (ages 1 to 5), pregnant women, and nursing mothers are most likely to be underfed because the largest portion of the family food supply goes to working males.

World Food Problems and Proposed Solutions: Producing More Food Is Not Enough Looking at the race between food supplies and population growth as a problem of merely producing more food is misleading. Actually, if all of the grain produced each year were distributed equally among the world's population everyone would have a more than adequate daily diet. And this estimate does not include other foods, such as beans, fruits, nuts, vegetables, and grass-fed beef. The world's supply of grain, however, is not distributed equally among the world's people and is not likely to be in the future. Even if it were, people surviving only on grain would not receive certain essential proteins, vitamins, and minerals. For good health both food *quantity* and *quality* are important.

Furthermore, poor people either do not have enough fertile land to grow their own food or enough money to buy the food they need, regardless of how much is available. Thus, *poverty is the chief cause of hunger and malnutrition for individuals throughout the world.*

In addition, hungry people often won't eat food sent to them by other countries unless it is culturally acceptable. For example, wheat once sent by the United States to relieve starvation in India was not eaten by people used to rice. Despite their hunger people near starvation are often afraid to risk their lives on a strange-looking or strange-tasting food. Many Americans would probably go hungry if grasshoppers—a delicacy in parts of Africa—were the major food available.

In MDCs and LDCs good farmland is often not planted because farmers cannot make enough profit to stay in business. While people go hungry in some parts of the world, U.S. farmers are paid not to grow crops or are given subsidies to guarantee that crop prices do not fall below a certain level. These are designed to prevent crop surpluses that drive prices down, cause some farmers to go bankrupt, and threaten the long-term ability to feed the world's population.

Besides quantity, then, the world's food problem includes a number of complex and interrelated agricultural, economic, social, and ecological problems, as summarized in the accompanying box along with solutions proposed by food experts to deal with these problems.

Many of the world's food and food-related problems and their proposed solutions are discussed in other chapters and enrichment studies (see references in the summary box). The rest of this chapter is devoted to understanding our basic nutritional needs, the world's major types of agricultural systems, and evaluating proposals 1 through 6 in the summary box for wasting less food and producing more food throughout the world.

World Hunger Problems and Possible Solutions

Food and Food-Related Problems

1. *Quantity:* producing enough food to feed the 4.8 billion humans on earth and the world's livestock, poultry, and pets, which require enough food to feed 16 billion people.

2. *Quality:* producing food with enough fats, vitamins, critical minerals, and high-quality protein.

3. *Crop protection:* protecting food before and after harvesting from the pests, diseases, and spoilage that destroy about 45 percent of the food grown each year.

4. *Distribution:* providing the ships, planes, trains, trucks, storage facilities, roads, and marketing systems needed to store, transport, distribute, and sell food.

5. *Poverty:* making sure people can afford to grow or buy the quantity and quality of food they need.

6. *Cultural acceptance:* providing types of food that people with different cultural backgrounds and preferences will buy and eat.

7. *Resource supply:* having enough fertile soil and fertilizers (Chapter 8), pesticides (Section 9-9), water (Chapter 17), fossil fuels (Chapters 14 and 15), and nonmineral resources (Chapter 13) to grow and distribute enough food for the world's human and animal populations.

8. *Economics:* providing incentives for farmers, especially those in LDCS, to produce and sell more food.

9. *Climate and weather:* stockpiling enough emergency food supplies to relieve famine when changes in local and global climate and weather patterns reduce food growing capacity in various parts of the world (Enrichment Study 5).

10. *Population growth:* trying to control population growth (Chapter 7) so that world food production and distribution won't have to be doubled every 32 years in the LDCs.

11. *Ecological effects:* trying to produce, process, and distribute more food without seriously degrading soil (Chapter 8), water (Enrichment Study 14), air (Chapter 19), wildlife (Chapter 11), and forests, rangelands, and estuaries (Chapter 10).

Proposals for Solving World Food Problems

1. *Simplifying diets and using and wasting less food:* shortening the food chain by reducing the use of meat and meat products in MDCs; reducing overnutrition and waste of food in industrialized nations.

2. *Using: new foods* (winged beans, Ye-ed, and insects), *fabricated foods* (simulated meat products made from soybeans), and *unconventional foods* (single-cell protein).

3. *Getting more food from the ocean:* trying to increase the world seafood catch, harvesting ocean plants such as algae and krill, and growing and harvesting fish and shellfish in inland ponds (aquaculture) and in fenced-off coastal areas (mariculture).

4. *Adding new farmland:* cultivating more land by clearing forests, plowing pastures, draining wetlands, and irrigating arid land.

5. *Providing economic incentives:* making credit available to small farmers, providing subsidies and price supports, and trying to control import and export food prices to encourage farmers to cultivate more land and increase crop yields per acre.

6. *Improving crop yields:* Increasing yields per acre by transferring or adapting industrialized agriculture to LDCs.

7. *Applying appropriate agricultural technology:* helping LDCs learn how to grow more food using appropriate agricultural technology (Section 1-5), thus making them less dependent on MDCs for food and aid.

8. *Increasing foreign aid:* having MDCs give money and technical assistance to LDCs that is designed to help these nations grow more of their own food; finding ways to get this aid to poor rural farmers without having it pass first through the hands of the rich and powerful who often prevent much of it from reaching the poor.

9. *Instituting land ownership reform:* encouraging governments in LDCs where land is in the hands of a relatively small number of rich and powerful individuals to distribute more land to the poor.

10. *Controlling population:* limiting world population growth and size (Chapter 7).

Figure 9-1 Summary of metabolism in an
animal cell.

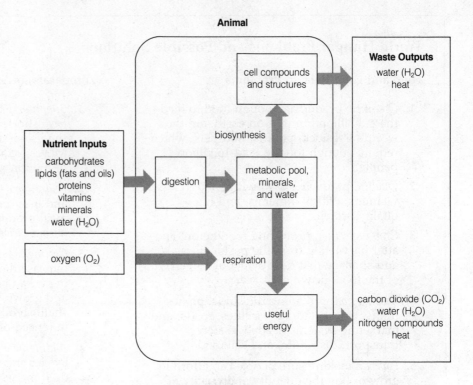

9-2 Human Metabolism and Nutrition: You Are What You Eat

Metabolism and Human Nutrition Figure 9-1 shows that for good health and survival we require inputs of oxygen and six basic groups of nutrients: water, proteins, carbohydrates, fats, vitamins, and minerals. When food is eaten digestive processes break down protein into amino acids, carbohydrates into sugars such as glucose, and fats into glycerol and fatty acids, as summarized in Figure 9-2.

Oxygen is required for cellular respiration, the breakdown of food chemicals in our cells to obtain nutrients, energy, carbon dioxide, and water (Section 4-3). *Water*—which makes up 60 percent of the adult body—regulates body temperature, transports nutrients, and participates in the chemical reactions that keep us alive and healthy.

Proteins give structure to the body and serve as antibodies and hormones, and as enzymes to speed up various metabolic reactions. Once eaten, proteins are broken down into about 22 different amino acid molecules through digestion (Figure 9-2), which are then transported by the blood to cells throughout the body. There the amino acids are linked together like boxcars in a train in various sequences to provide the different large protein molecules we need. Of the 22 amino acids essential for the operation of the human body, 8 cannot be made in the body and must be obtained from protein in the food we eat. If one or more of these **essential amino**

acids are missing or insufficient in the diet, protein malnutrition can result.

Complete proteins, or animal proteins such as meat, fish, eggs, milk, and cheese, provide us with all eight essential amino acids. Plants, however, are **incomplete proteins** lacking one or more essential amino acids; they are also usually low in protein quantity compared to meat and dairy products. However, it is not necessary to have a diet with meat, fish, or dairy products to prevent protein deficiency. The 2 to 3 million strict vegetarians in the United States can get all the essential amino acids they need by eating a proper combination of protein-rich plants such as soybeans, beans, peanuts, and peas and other protein-deficient plants such as wheat, potatoes, corn, cassava, and rice. Most vegetarian diets also need to be supplemented with calcium, iron, and vitamins B_{12} and B_2 (riboflavin). However, the diet of most poor people in the world consists mostly of only one or two protein-deficient plants such as wheat, rice, corn, or cassava. They cannot afford meat, dairy products, and protein-rich plants that would provide them with all the essential amino acids.

Carbohydrates are broken down by digestion into glucose and other simple sugar molecules (Figure 9-2). Through cellular respiration these sugar molecules are broken down to provide the body's main source of energy (Section 4-3). Some of this energy is used for immediate body energy demands and some is stored as chemical energy in molecules of ATP. Without an adequate carbohydrate intake some of the energy needed by the body is obtained by

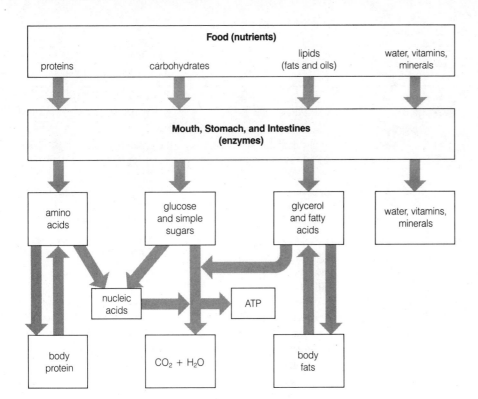

Figure 9-2 Summary of digestion or chemical breakdown of various nutrients in food.

breaking down proteins that are better used for other functions. *Fats* are stored in the body as a reserve source of energy. They also serve as building blocks for some hormones, carry fat-soluble vitamins, provide insulation and protection for important organs and body structures, and are involved in the maintenance of cell membrane structure and function.

There are at least 21 specific organic compounds required in small amounts for life and good health called *vitamins*. Since they cannot be synthesized in the body they must be obtained from certain foods or vitamin supplements. Without a minimum daily intake of these essential vitamins, various nutritional deficiency diseases such as scurvy, beriberi, and rickets can occur, as summarized in Table 9-1. Some vitamins (such as C and the Bs) are water soluble and others (such as A and D) are fat soluble. Some essential vitamins are lost when fruits and vegetables are peeled. Modern food processing also tends to remove vitamins. Heat from cooking breaks down vitamins such as C and B_1. Water-soluble vitamins (Table 9-1) are often drained off when foods are cooked in water. Despite these losses, the individual who eats a varied and well-balanced diet will receive the minimum daily recommended dosage of key vitamins.

But some argue either that many people who live mostly on junk foods and processed foods do not have a well-balanced diet or that the daily minimum recommended dosages are not enough. Some scientists and nutritionists believe that large daily dosages (megavitamin dosages) of vitamins can help prevent or cure a variety of disorders. Other scientists and doctors consider megavitamin dosages of vitamins to be potentially harmful and a waste of money. They are particularly concerned about large daily dosages of vitamins A and D. Because of their solubility in fats (Table 9-1), they tend to be retained in the body and could build up to harmful levels. A basic problem in this controversy is that the effects of large dosages of vitamins on humans are still mostly unknown and are difficult to establish.

Minerals are various inorganic compounds and ions such as sodium chloride (NaCl) and phosphate ions (PO_4^{3-}) that are involved in transmitting electrical impulses in nerves and muscles, formation of bones and teeth, transport of oxygen in blood hemoglobin (iron), and other functions. Six chemical elements (including calcium, sodium, and chlorine) found in inorganic mineral compounds are *macronutrients* needed by the body in relatively large amounts. About 15 others (including iron, copper, iodine, and zinc) are *micronutrients* needed only in trace amounts.

Our food should also contain a seventh type of material, called *roughage*, consisting mostly of the indigestible cell walls of plants. Although it is not a nutrient, it provides bulk that helps the digestive system function properly and prevent constipation. Some researchers have suggested that the 90 percent decrease in roughage in the U.S. diet since 1900 may have contributed to the increased inci-

Table 9-1 Some Important Vitamins

Vitamin	Soluble in	Sources	Possible Deficiency Effects
A	Fat	Fish-liver oils, butter, egg yolks, green and yellow vegetables, milk	Low resistance to infection, night blindness
B_1 (thiamine)	Water	Fruits, cereal grains, milk, green vegetables, nuts, rice polishings	Beriberi
B_2 (riboflavin)	Water	Beef liver, meats, milk, eggs, yeast	Sores on lips, retarded growth in young, bloodshot and burning eyes
B_3 (pantothenic acid)	Water	Cereals, beef liver, milk, eggs, yeast	Retarded growth, emotional instability
B_5 (niacin or nicotinic acid)	Water	Meats, vegetables, rice, fish, eggs	Stunted growth, pellagra
B_6 (pyridoxine)	Water	Eggs, liver, yeast, whole grains, milk, fish	Convulsions in infants, retarded growth, insomnia, eye, nose, and mouth sores
B_{12} (cyanocobalamine)	Water	Meats, eggs, liver, seafood	Degeneration of spinal cord, anemia
C (ascorbic acid)	Water	Citrus fruits, green vegetables, especially tomatoes and green peppers	Scurvy, low resistance to disease; sterility, hemorrhages
D_2* (calciferol)	Fat	Fish-liver oils, yeast, fortified milk, egg yolks	Rickets
E (α-tocopherol)	Fat	Wheat germ oil, cottonseed oil, lettuce, whole grain cereals, egg yolks, soybean oil, beef liver	Sterility? more susceptibility to environmental pollution? more rapid aging?
K_1	Fat	Green leaves, alfalfa, spinach, cabbage, cauliflower	Hemorrhage, slow clotting of blood
Q?	Fat?	Soybeans	Slow clotting of blood

*There are about 10 D vitamins, which have only slight differences in their chemical structures.

dence of heart and circulatory diseases, alimentary tract diseases, obesity, and diabetes.

Food Contaminants and Additives The food we eat can be contaminated with small amounts of radioactive substances (Section 15-5), pesticides (Section 9-9), lead and mercury compounds (Enrichment Study 12), dead insects, and viruses and bacteria such as those that cause food poisoning and dysentery. These **food contaminants** are not deliberately added to food but usually result from poor sanitation, improper food processing or storage, or the widespread, careless use of chemicals such as some pesticides and radioactive substances that can become biologically magnified in food chains and webs (Figure 5-6).

In addition, an increasing number of other chemicals are deliberately added to food when they are processed for sale to retard spoilage, to enhance flavor, color, and texture, and to provide missing amino acids and vitamins. Some of these **food additives** serve useful purposes and help prevent decay and contamination by food poisoning, but most are added to improve appearance and sales. There is controversy over the safety of food additives and the need for those that merely improve sales appeal, as discussed in Enrichment Study 9.

Plants and Animals That Feed the World Of the estimated 350,000 species of plants in the world, perhaps 80,000 are edible. Yet over the course of history people have used only about 3,000 of these

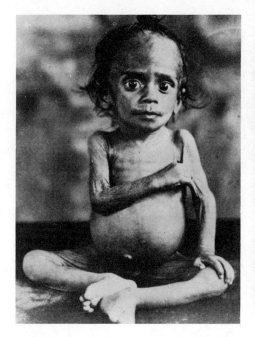

UN Food and Agriculture Organization

Figure 9-3 Most effects of severe protein-calorie malnutrition or marasmus (left photo) can be corrected (right photo). The pictures show a 2-year-old Venezuelan girl before and after 10 months of treatment and proper nutrition.

species for food and cultivated about 175 species. Today only 16 plant species feed the world and provide the poor with almost all of their food energy and over three-fourths of their protein. These plants are (1) five *cereals:* rice, wheat, maize (corn), sorghum, and barley; (2) two *sugar plants:* sugarcane and sugar beets; (3) three *root crops:* potatoes, sweet potatoes, and cassava; (4) three *legumes:* beans, soybeans, and peanuts; and (5) three *tree crops:* coconut, banana, and nuts. Three of these plants—wheat, rice, and maize (corn)—provide people in LDCs with about two-thirds of their daily energy supply and 55 percent of their protein. So important are these three cereal grains that over one-half of the world's cropland is devoted to growing them. These 16 basic food crops are supplemented by about 15 major species of vegetables and a like number of fruit crop species, which supply much of the vitamins and many of the minerals necessary to the human diet.

Plant products make up 93 percent of the human diet, with the remaining 7 percent supplied by animal products obtained indirectly from plants. Even fewer animals have been domesticated than plants. Virtually all of the domestic meat consumed by humans comes from fish and shellfish and just nine groups of livestock: cattle, sheep, pigs, chickens, turkeys, geese, ducks, goats, and water buffalo.

Undernutrition, Malnutrition, and Overnutrition People living mostly on one or more plants such as wheat, rice, maize, or cassava often do not get enough calorie intake and suffer from **undernutrition.** Although needs vary with life-style, an adequate intake of energy is usually defined as 3,000 Calories per day for an adult man and 2,200 Calories per day for an adult woman.

Good nutrition, however, involves more than a daily intake of a certain *quantity* of Calories. People whose diets lack one or more essential amino acids, vitamins, and minerals suffer from **malnutrition.** Those who get neither enough Calories nor enough protein, vitamins, and minerals are said to be suffering from **protein-calorie malnutrition.**

While an estimated one person in ten in LDCs dies from undernutrition, malnutrition, or malnutrition-related diseases, about 15 out of every 100 people in MDCs suffer from **overnutrition**—eating too much of the wrong kinds of food. In the United States, 10 to 12 percent of children and 35 to 50 percent of middle-aged adults are overweight. These overnourished people exist on diets high in Calories, cholesterol-containing saturated fats, salt, sugar, and processed foods and low in unprocessed fresh vegetables, fruits, and fiber. Partly as a result of their overnutrition, these people have high risks of diabetes, hypertension, stroke, heart disease, intestinal cancer, tooth decay, and other health problems.

Nutritional Deficiency Diseases Protein-calorie malnutrition has a devastating effect on children under age 5, who need about twice as much protein and energy in relation to body weight as do adults. Most physical effects of severe protein-calorie malnutrition in infants and young children can be remedied if they get treatment and proper nutrition (Figure 9-3). Brain development, however, begins in the uterus and is usually complete by age 2. Some

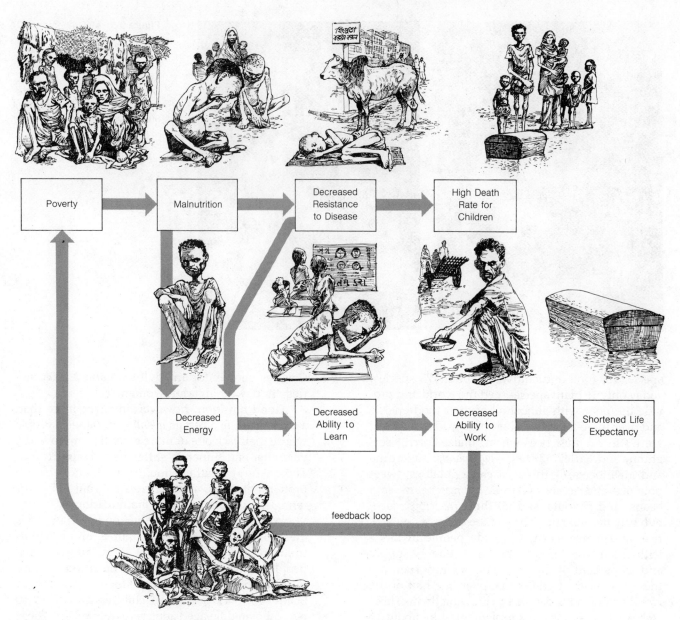

Figure 9-4 The tragic cycle of interactions among poverty, malnutrition, and disease.

nutrition experts believe malnutrition during this period can cause mental retardation that cannot be remedied by later corrective nutritional measures, although this hypothesis is disputed. Whether the damage is permanent or not, many infants and young children in poor families throughout the world today are not getting the type of diet needed to prevent such damage. As a result they may be locked into a tragic cycle of malnutrition, infection, and poverty that can be passed on to their children (Figure 9-4).

The two most widespread nutritional deficiency diseases are *marasmus* and *kwashiorkor*. **Marasmus** (from the Greek "to waste away") occurs when a diet is low in calories and protein. A child suffer-

ing from severe marasmus (Figure 9-3) has a bloated belly, thin body, shriveled skin, wide eyes, and the face of an old person. With marasmus comes diarrhea, dehydration, muscle deterioration, anemia, and a ravenous appetite. It occurs in poor families where a child is not breast-fed or where there is insufficient food after the child is weaned.

Kwashiorkor (a West African word meaning "displaced child") occurs with a diet high in calories but deficient in protein. It is found primarily in infants and young children soon after they are weaned and placed on a starchy diet of cassava, maize flour, or other cereals of low protein quantity and quality. The entire body—not just the stomach—of a child suffering from severe kwashiorkor is bloated because liquids collect under the skin. Other symptoms include hair loss, skin rash and discoloration, and a reddish-orange hair color. This disease leads to brain damage, anemia, digestive disorders, irritability, apathy, and a loss of appetite.

The World Health Organization (WHO) and the UN Food and Agriculture Organization (FAO) estimate that at least *12 million people—one-half of whom are children under age 5—now die each year from undernutrition, malnutrition, and associated diseases, amounting to an average of 33,000 such deaths each day.* Most of these victims do not starve to death. They die because they become more vulnerable to normally minor infections and diseases such as measles, diarrhea, and flu. For example, death rates from measles are typically 180 times higher in Mexico than in the United States, 268 times higher in Guatemala, and 480 times higher in Ecuador. The WHO estimates that diarrhea kills at least 5 million children a year. If made available, a low cost treatment can cut this death toll from diarrhea by using a simple sugar and water drink to rehydrate the body.

Importance of Breast-Feeding   Breast milk is a *free* source of food supplying all of an infant's nutritional needs during its critical first year of life. It also contains antibodies that help protect infants from diarrhea and other infections.

The WHO estimates that each year as many as 10 million serious cases of malnutrition and diarrhea and 1 million infant deaths result from improper use of infant formulas. Many poor mothers using baby formulas lack a source of clean water to prepare the formula, don't know the water should be sterilized because of inability to read instructions, can't afford the fuel needed to sterilize the formula, or dilute the formula because of its high cost.

Breast-feeding also helps decrease birth rates—especially in LDCs where contraceptives and other means of birth control are not widely available or are too costly for the poor. Strong and prolonged suckling can suppress ovulation. This is an important form of birth control that protects nursing women from pregnancy for l0 weeks to 26 months after a birth, depending on the mother's health, diet, and the intensity of suckling.

In MDCS such as the United States only about 30 percent of the babies born each year are breast-fed, although this percentage is gradually increasing. In LDCs the percentage of breast-fed babies is much higher, ranging from 67 percent in Malaysia to 98 percent in Nepal. However, breast-feeding is decreasing in many LDCs, especially in Latin America.

9-3   World Agricultural Systems

Major Types of Agriculture   The three major agricultural systems used in the world today require the input of solar energy used in photosynthesis (Section 4-3) to be supplemented with other forms of energy. These systems are **(1)** *simple (subsistence) agriculture* based on an energy supplement from human labor, **(2)** *animal-assisted agriculture* based on energy supplements from human labor and draft animals, and **(3)** *industrialized agriculture* based on an energy supplement from fossil fuels with an emphasis on replacing most human labor with machines such as tractors and combines.

The first two types of agricultural systems are still widely used in LDCs. Approximately 400 million horses, cattle, oxen, mules, camels, llamas, elephants, and water buffaloes provide about one-third of the energy use in agriculture in LDCs, and in some countries their contribution approaches 90 percent.

MDCs, however, depend primarily on industrialized agriculture, which greatly increases crop yields and productivity per farm worker. To produce one acre of corn by hand requires about 500 hours of human labor compared to 5 hours of human labor using industrialized agriculture. The use of industrialized agriculture explains why only 12 percent of the labor force in MDCs is directly engaged in agriculture, compared to about 60 percent of the work force in LDCs. It has been estimated that agriculture subsidized by fossil fuels provides four times the yield per hectare (2.47 acres) of unindustrialized agriculture, but requires 100 times more energy and mineral resources.

The major components of industrialized agriculture in a country such as the United States are summarized in the box on page 149.

Industrialized Agriculture in the United States   The success of industrialized agriculture when coupled with a favorable climate and fertile soils has been demonstrated by the dramatic increase in food production in the United States (Figure 9-5). Between 1820 and 1983, the percentage of the total U.S. population working on farms declined from about 72 percent to 2.5 percent, but during this same period total U.S. food production approximately doubled and the output per farmer increased eightfold. In 1983 each U.S. farm worker produced enough food and fiber for 77 people or 10 people including all the other agricultural workers involved in the production of farm machinery, fertilizers, and pesticides and in the processing and marketing of food.

Figure 9-5 Some effects of increased use of industrialized agriculture in the United States.

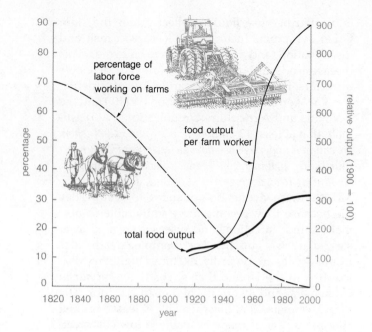

With total assets exceeding $1 trillion, agriculture is the biggest industry in the United States—bigger than the automobile, steel, and housing industries combined. Its annual sales represent about one-fifth of the nation's annual gross national product. It is also the nation's largest employer with 23 million workers—one fifth of all jobs in private enterprise—in some phase of agriculture from growing food to selling it at the supermarket. U.S. farmers, however, received only about $83.5 billion of the nearly $300 billion Americans spent on food during 1982. The remaining $214 billion went to the food processing, packaging, advertising, and retailing industries.

Energy Use and Industrialized Agriculture Making and applying fertilizers, making and running tractors, pumping irrigation water, drying crops, processing food, transporting crops and processed food to markets, and preparing food in restaurants and homes all require energy, mostly from oil and natural gas. Kansas wheat might be shipped to Seattle for milling and processing into cereal, which is then shipped to Boston where it is consumed for breakfast—helping explain why the average food serving in the U.S. travels 2,080 kilometers (1,300 miles) getting from the place where it is grown to the person who eats it.

The energy used to grow food is about 6 percent of total annual energy use in the United States, or 17 percent including the 11 percent of annual energy consumption used to process, package, distribute, and prepare food. Counting the fossil fuel energy inputs used to grow, process, package, transport, refrigerate, and cook all plant and animal food in the United States, *it takes about 9 Calories of fossil fuel to put 1 Calorie of food energy on the table— an energy loss of 8 Calories per Calorie of food energy.*

To feed the world using the U.S. meat-centered diet with food produced by its energy-intensive agriculture would require twice as much global cropland as is now being cultivated, greatly increase environmental pollution and land degradation, consume 80 percent of the world's annual energy use, and wholly deplete the world's known oil reserves in 13 years. If fossil fuels should suddenly become scarce or too expensive, the present agricultural system in industrialized nations would probably collapse, causing a sharp drop in world food production and a corresponding rise in malnutrition and famine.

Organic Farming As fuel prices rise, an increasing number of farmers (about 30,000 in the United States) are resorting to **organic farming,** a method of producing crops and livestock naturally by using only organic fertilizers such as animal manure, green manure, legumes, and compost (Section 8-6) and natural pest control ("good" bugs that eat "bad" bugs, plants that repel bugs, and crop rotation) instead of synthetic chemical pesticides and herbicides (Section 9-9).

A comparison of U.S. organic and nonorganic industrialized farms showed that: **(1)** organic farming provides enough nitrogen for plant growth, but

Components of Modern Industrialized Agriculture

1. *Mechanization:* substituting fossil-fuel-powered machines for manual labor and draft animals. At least two-thirds of the world's cropland is tilled with mechanical power.

2. *Commercial fertilizers:* using commercially produced fertilizers to increase crop yields and restore soil fertility partially (Section 8-6). One-fourth of the world's annual food output is based on the use of commercial fertilizers.

3. *Irrigation:* building dams and canals and using fossil-fuel-powered machines to pump water to croplands (Chapter 17).

4. *Pesticides:* using synthetic chemicals to reduce crop losses due to insect, disease, and weed pests (Section 9-9).

5. *Soil conservation:* establishing sound land use practices to reduce soil erosion (Section 8-6).

6. *Animal feedlots:* shifting from pastures and open rangeland to feedlots where hundreds to thousands of domesticated animals are concentrated and fed in a small space to encourage rapid weight gain and more efficient production (Section 9-4 and Enrichment Study 14).

7. *Genetic selection and hybridization:* using research to select and develop high-yield and disease-resistant crops, livestock, and poultry (Section 9-8).

8. *Large-scale and specialized production:* shifting from small, diversified farms to large, specialized farms.

9. *Storage, processing, distribution, and marketing:* developing storage facilities and extensive transportation, processing, and marketing networks.

10. *Agricultural training and research:* establishing a system of agricultural schools and research centers and using extension services to bring new developments to farmers.

---

may not provide adequate phosphorus and potassium; **(2)** pest control without pesticides is moderately successful and may be more successful with increased use of integrated pest management (Section 9-9); **(3)** some organic farms have 5 to 15 percent higher yields per hectare than nonorganic farms, but this varies by crop and region; **(4)** the net financial returns for both types of agriculture are about equal per hectare of farmland, but the indebtedness of organic farmers is usually lower; and **(5)** organic farms use an average of 40 percent less energy per unit of food produced than do conventional farms. A USDA study indicated that a total shift to organic farming in the United States could meet U.S. food needs, but there would be some decrease in food available for export. Political opposition to such a shift by agricultural chemical industries that sell billions of dollars of fertilizers and pesticides to farmers each year would be intense.

Home Gardening By 1983, 53 percent of all U.S. households were growing some of their own food, amounting to a retail value of at least $19 billion. Increasingly, parts or all of manicured lawns are being replaced with small garden plots and city residents are planting gardens in apartment and condominium grounds, church and school yards, factory and shop lots, public parks, and utility rights-of-way. Window box planters, small greenhouses, and rooftop and patio gardens, where tomatoes and other crops can be grown in small containers, are also widely used. Raised beds are being used to produce high yields of a large variety of vegetables in a small space, a gardening method used for centuries in China. The USDA estimates that a family of four could be well fed without animal products by using high-yield intensive gardening on only one-sixth of an acre.

Environmental Effects of Producing More Food As agricultural expert Lester R. Brown put it, "The central question is no longer 'Can we produce enough food?' but 'What are the environmental consequences of attempting to do so?'" The major environmental effects of food production and some proposed solutions are summarized in Table 9-2. More detailed information on these environmental effects and proposed solutions is found throughout much of this text, as indicated in Table 9-2. With this background in how food is produced, we are ready to evaluate ways of increasing world food production in the future.

Table 9-2 Environmental Effects of Food Production and Proposed Solutions

Effect	Proposed Solutions and Text Discussion
Overfishing	International agreements and laws (Section 11-6); mariculture and aquaculture (Section 9-6)
Overgrazing	Laws and land-use control (Sections 10-7 and 12-5); less dependence on meat in diets (Section 9-4)
Soil erosion and loss of soil fertility	Minimum tillage cultivation, crop rotation, and other well-known practices (Section 8-6); land-use control (Section 12-5)
Salt buildup (salinization) and waterlogging of irrigated soils	Drainage systems, drip-and-trickle irrigation, and higher water prices (Chapter 17)
Waterborne diseases from irrigation	Education of poor people and research to prevent or cure diseases (Enrichment Study 7)
Loss of forests (deforestation)	Replanting forests (Section 10-5); land-use controls (Section 12-5)
Endangered wildlife from loss of habitat	Laws for wildlife protection (Section 11-4); land-use control (Section 12-5)
Loss of genetic diversity	Genetic storage banks for plants (Section 9-8) and wildlife protection (Section 11-4)
Pollution from pesticides	Increased use of biological control and integrated pest management (Section 9-9)
Water pollution from runoff of fertilizer and animal wastes	Preventing soil erosion (Section 8-6) and recycling animal wastes to land (Section 8-6 and Enrichment Study 14)
Climate change from land clearing	Land-use control (Section 12-5 and Enrichment Study 5)
Air pollution from use of fossil fuels	Reduced use of fossil fuels in agriculture (Section 9-4 and Chapter 19)
Health dangers from food additives	Better enforcement of existing laws (Enrichment Study 9)

9-4 Simplifying Affluent Diets and Wasting Less Food and Energy

Human Diets and Food Chain Losses When we eat meat, about 90 percent of the energy available in the meat is degraded and lost to the environment as low-temperature heat because of the second law of thermodynamics (Figures 4-3 and 4-6). This food chain loss of usable energy (Section 4-2) explains why meat is more expensive than grain and why poor people are forced to live primarily on a diet of grain rather than meat. This loss of usable food energy, however, is important only when (1) livestock and poultry animals eat grains or other plants that could be eaten by humans or (2) these animals are grazing on land or being fed from forage crops (such as hay and alfalfa) grown on land that could be used to grow food crops for humans.

As their incomes rise, people begin to consume more grain indirectly, in the form of meat and meat products, than directly in cereal, flour, and other plant products. For example, average per capita meat consumption in the MDCs is 10 to 25 times that in LDCs. Because of this trend toward meat-based diets, about one-third of the world's annual grain production is fed to livestock and poultry to produce meat, eggs, and milk for the affluent. By contrast, only about 3 percent of the available grain supply is fed to livestock in China, India, and most LDCs. Even though there is more hunger and protein malnutrition in Africa than in any other continent, one-third of Africa's protein-rich peanuts end up being fed to European livestock.

In the United States and Canada, about three-fourths of the grain produced each year is fed to livestock, especially those fattened up in feedlots. For example, beef cattle are fed forage (grass) until they reach a certain weight. Then they are moved to a feedlot and, for 2 to 6 months before slaughtering, are fattened using a rich diet of grain mixed with growth-stimulating chemicals and antibiotics. There is growing concern that these antibiotic additives may increase the number of bacteria strains immune to antibiotics in meat-eating humans, thus decreasing our protection against infectious diseases. Animal feedlots also require large inputs of fossil fuel energy. For instance, the fossil fuel input for beef fed grain in feedlots is about twice that for beef fed with forage crops, and about 20 times that for beef feeding on open rangeland.

Altering Affluent Diets to Reduce Food Waste Representatives from LDCs at the 1974 UN Food Conference in Rome and a number of environmentalists and food experts have called for peoples of affluent nations to alter their diets in order to make more food available for export to feed the poor. Major suggestions for reducing food waste are given in the accompanying box.

Some analysts have pointed out that if cattle in the United States were not fattened in feedlots, enough grain would be theoretically available to

Ways to Reduce Food Waste

1. Reduce beef consumption by at least one-half and slightly increase the consumption of fish, chicken, eggs, dried beans, potatoes, and vegetables grown locally or in home gardens.

2. Substitute vegetable protein for animal protein.

3. Replace grain-fed (feedlot) animals with animals eating grass on ranges and eating forage crops grown on marginal agricultural land.

4. Use commercial fertilizer only on food crops and eliminate or sharply reduce its use on lawns, golf courses, and cemeteries, and replace suburban lawns with home gardens and orchards.

5. Use education and financial incentives to encourage people to throw away less food and to reduce the size of portions served. An estimated 20 percent of all food produced in the United States is wasted with enough food thrown away each day theoretically to feed over 50 million people on a U.S. meat-based diet—twice the number of people below the poverty level in the United States.

6. Reduce the use of fossil fuels in industrialized agriculture.

7. Use the sun instead of electricity and natural gas to dry corn and other crops before storage.

8. Control the rapidly growing pet populations, which consume protein that could be used to feed humans.

9. Reduce the weight of overweight people to improve their health and save food.

10. Increase the use of minimum- and no-tillage agriculture to reduce soil erosion, save energy, and increase the soil's ability to hold water (Section 8-6).

---

feed about 400 million people—equal to 80 percent of Africa's population. Even if feedlots were not eliminated, merely decreasing annual meat consumption in the United States by 10 percent could theoretically release enough grain to feed 60 million people. Similarly, commercial fertilizers that are spread each year on U.S. lawns, golf courses, and cemeteries could be used to produce grain for 65 million people.

The pet foods consumed in the United States each year contain enough protein to feed 21 million people. Pets can offset loneliness and help limit population growth by serving as child substitutes. But some experts and animal lovers believe the growth of the pet population in the United States and in many European nations may be getting out of control. The United States has the world's highest ratio of pets to people, followed closely by France and Great Britain. Dogs and cats carry 65 diseases transmittable to humans, litter streets with feces and urine, bite humans, and make noise. Furthermore, U.S. taxpayers pay $600 million a year to dispose of 20 million abandoned dogs and cats.

Suggestions that affluent nations should alter their diets and food production patterns is highly controversial, revealing the complexity of world food problems. Some analysts point out that grain made available by eating less meat, eliminating feedlots, reducing pet populations, and not using fertilizer on lawns and golf courses will not necessarily be made available to the poor in LDCs or in the United States. About 70 percent of U.S. food exports are used to fatten livestock for the meat-based diets of the world's affluent. Others argue that conserving food in affluent nations could actually make less food for the poor because it would lead to food surpluses, price declines, and cuts in production, leading to reductions in exports to other nations. In addition, grain raised to feed animals can be diverted for human use in years of crop failure in parts of the world. This safety net would not exist if there were no demand for grain to be fed to animals.

Furthermore, without feedlots the United States would need to plant more land in forage to keep beef production at the present level. Planting this land would increase energy use up to 5 times the present levels because of the large inputs of fertilizer and water needed to make these marginal lands usable. In addition, hogs and poultry cannot digest grass and thus cannot be raised on either rangeland or forage. The amount of fossil fuels used to produce food crops can be reduced, but energy savings in one area of food production sometimes increases energy use in another area. For example, little fossil fuel is saved by substituting animal manure for commercial fertilizer unless pastures and feedlots are fairly close to the crop fields. Otherwise, most fossil fuel not used to produce fertilizer is needed to haul the manure long distances.

In summary, altering affluent diets and reducing the waste of food and energy in industrialized nations can help ease the world food situation. But this will happen only if such changes are coupled with political, economic, and ethical factors that enable the food and money made available to be given to the poor or used to help them grow their own food.

9-5 Unconventional, Fortified, and Fabricated Foods

Unconventional Foods *Over the next several decades, most of the increase in the world's food supply will result from expanding the supplies of traditional foods—wheat, rice, and maize.* But some suggest that other nontraditional plants could be cultivated to supplement or replace such traditional foods in poor nations. Examples include the *winged bean,* containing as much protein as soybeans; *cocoyam,* a native plant of West Africa and Central and South America as nutritious as the potato; *Ye-ed,* a small bush native to East Africa whose seeds yield a nutritionally balanced diet; and *leucenda,* a tropical legume that can grow 3.6 meters (12 feet) high in 6 months and that, in addition to being a rich source of protein, can be used for firewood and to add nitrogen to the soil.

Some of the insects that compete with us for food crops are important potential sources of protein. In the Kalahari Desert of Africa cockroaches are a diet staple; crickets and locusts are standard fare in several African countries. Lightly toasted butterflies are a favorite food in Bali. French-fried ants are sold on the streets of Bogota, Colombia. Malaysians love deep-fried grasshoppers and New Guinea residents enjoy eating roasted wood spiders, which taste something like peanut butter. Most of these insects are 58 to 78 percent protein by weight—3 to 4 times that of beef, fish, or eggs. In the future you may eat a gourmet meal consisting of fried termites as an appetizer, grasshopper soup, salad with marinated moth sauce, beetle patties as the main course, side orders of cricket quiche and algae with caterpillar sauce, and bumblebee pie for dessert.

Fortifying Existing Foods Adding missing vitamins, minerals, and essential amino acids to conventional food sources such as flour, bread, rice, and salt is relatively easy and inexpensive. In the United States, bread and flour enriched with vitamins, minerals, and missing amino acids has helped to eliminate many nutritional deficiency diseases (Table 9-1), and adding small amounts of iodine to table salt has virtually wiped out goiter. Similarly, Japan has essentially eradicated beriberi since World War II by enriching its rice with vitamin B_1.

A major advantage of enriching existing foods is that people need not change their eating habits. A major disadvantage, however, is that these processed foods are not normally available to rural people in LDCs who grow their own food.

New Protein Supplements and Fabricated Foods In recent years some have suggested that *single-cell protein (SCP)* could be used as a protein supplement for humans and especially in animal feed. This high-protein powder can be produced from oil, natural gas, alcohol, sewage, waste paper, and other organic materials by the action of single-cell organisms such as yeast, fungi, and bacteria. A few small-scale pilot factories, mostly in Europe, are producing SCP for use in animal feed, but there are still a number of problems. If it can be produced economically on a large scale, most feel it is best used as a supplement in animal feed, reducing the use of grain. At present SCP is not useful as a protein supplement for human food because (1) its high ribonucleic acid (RNA) content can cause gout and kidney stone formation, (2) the walls of the cells are indigestible and can cause diarrhea, nausea, and gastric distress, (3) it has a taste many people find unpleasant, and (4) it is fairly costly to produce. Even if these problems can be overcome, some argue that it makes no sense economically or ecologically to use increasingly expensive and dwindling petroleum and natural gas resources to produce SCP.

Another approach is to supplement the protein in foods with meal or flour made from soybeans, cottonseed, peanuts, coconuts, sunflower seeds, rape seeds, and other oil seeds. Soybean meal has been used as a protein supplement for decades along with soybean-based soft drinks. Problems arise, however, in making some of these meal supplements palatable and in removing toxic compounds.

LDCs have had low-cost, high-protein meat substitutes, such as Indonesian *tempeh,* for hundreds of years. To produce tempeh, soybeans are soaked, hulled, partially cooked, and then overgrown with an edible mold that binds the soybean material into a compact cake that can be fried or cut into meatlike chunks. In the United States, oleomargarine and vegetable oils (from soybeans, sunflower seeds, and other plants) have reduced the use of animal products like butter and lard. In MDCs there has been increasing use of imitation bacon, eggs, chicken, ham, and meat extenders that contain spun vegetable protein fibers (SVP), made primarily from soybean concentrate and wheat gluten. If these products are widely accepted, they could dramatically reduce meat consumption in nations such as the United States. Since SVP contains no cholesterol, it could also reduce the incidence of heart disease. To make these products look and taste like meat, a number of dyes, flavors, and other food additives must be used, which some fear might increase risks of cancer and other health hazards (Enrichment Study 9).

If supported by research and development, unconventional, fortified, and fabricated foods such as these could make important contributions to human nutrition. But they are not a cure-all for the serious food problems (Section 9-1) facing the world.

9-6 Catching More Fish and Fish Farming

Trends in the World Fish Catch Fish are the major source of animal protein for more than one-half of the world's people, especially in Asia and Africa. Fish supply about 55 percent of the animal protein in Southeast Asia, 35 percent in Asia as a whole, 19 percent in Africa, about 25 percent worldwide—twice as much as eggs and three times as much as poultry—and 6 percent of all human protein consumption. Two-thirds of the annual fish catch is consumed by humans and one-third is processed into fish meal to be fed to livestock.

Between 1950 and 1970, the marine fish catch more than tripled—an increase greater than that occurring in any other human food source during the same period. To achieve large catches, modern fishing fleets use sonar, helicopters, aerial photography, and temperature measurement to locate schools of fish and lights and electrodes to attract them. Large, floating factory ships follow the fleets to process the catch.

Despite this technological sophistication, the steady rise in the marine fish catch halted abruptly in 1971. Between 1971 and 1976 the annual catch leveled off and rose only slightly between 1976 and 1983. A major factor in this leveling off was the sharp decline of the Peruvian anchovy catch, which once made up 20 percent of the global ocean harvest. A combination of overfishing and a shift in the cool, nutrient-rich currents off the coast of Peru were apparently the major factors causing this decline, which also threw tens of thousands of Peruvians out of work. Meanwhile, world population continued to grow, so between 1970 and 1983 the average fish catch per person declined and is projected to decline even further back to the 1960 level by the year 2000 (Figure 9-6).

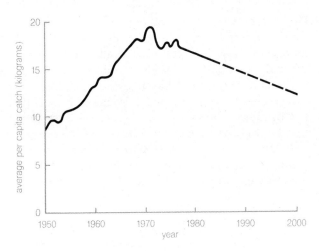

Figure 9-6 Average per capita world fish catch from 1950 to 1983 with projections (dashed lines) to 2000.

Some scientists believe that the world's annual fish catch could be increased by as much as 43 percent by 2000. But others estimate that it may already be at or near its maximum sustainable yield and some fear that even the present annual catch may not be sustainable. To avoid overfishing and to leave enough breeding stock for the next year's catch, no more than 40 percent of the available fish in a species should be harvested in a given year. By 1976 it was estimated that overfishing was causing declines in the annual yields of 30 of the leading species of table fish. Some species have been so overfished that they are in danger of extinction (Chapter 11).

The Sea: A Biological Desert Why can't the yields from ocean fish and shellfish be increased indefinitely if we can somehow control overfishing through international cooperation? The basic reason is that *the open sea, which makes up about 90 percent of the ocean, has such low net primary productivity (Figure 4-7) that it is sometimes called a biological desert.*

Only about 0.06 percent of the annual marine fish catch is taken from the open ocean. The remaining 99 percent of the annual catch, worth more than $50 billion a year, comes from the coastal zone that includes the coastal wetlands and estuaries and coastal waters extending 320 kilometers (200 miles) offshore. Unfortunately, these coastal waters and estuaries receive massive loads of pollutants (Section 18-5). In 1979, 27 percent of U.S. commercial shellfish waters were closed because of dangerous levels of pollution. In France, prime oyster beds face extinction from pollution and a number of shellfish waters off the coast of Japan have been closed because of pollution.

Ocean Food Chains Another reason the sea's food yield is limited is that the most favored food fish tend to be high in ocean food chains and webs—normally in the fourth or fifth trophic level. A typical chain is phytoplankton → zooplankton → mackerel → tuna → humans. Because of the second law of thermodynamics, such species are fewer in number than species in lower trophic levels (Figure 4-6). Thus, catching these fish commercially is a hunting-and-gathering operation taking place over a large area of the world's oceans. This requires so much fuel that inputs of fossil fuel energy for each Calorie of food energy caught are 75 for shrimp, 34 for lobster, 20 for king salmon, 5.3 for flounder, and 1.3 for perch, which helps explain why fish prices have risen significantly along with oil prices since 1973.

Why not go to the base of the marine food chain and harvest phytoplankton, the grass of the sea? Problems of taste and smell aside, the second energy law gets us again. Phytoplankton are so widely dispersed that 3.8 million liters (1 million gallons) of water would have to be filtered to yield 454 grams (1 pound) of phytoplankton. In addition, they have to be processed to remove RNA impurities and to break their cell walls to make them digestible. The extremely large fossil fuel input needed to do all this makes them cost more than they are worth as food.

However, we might increase the protein yield of the sea by going one step above plants in the food chain and harvesting krill—tiny, shrimp-like crustaceans that are plentiful in Antarctic waters. Krill might be particularly useful as a livestock feed supplement. By 1984, at least eight nations were harvesting krill, and Soviet and Japanese scientists believe that each year we could harvest krill equal to the total current annual marine fish catch. But some scientists warn that extensive harvesting could endanger baleen whales, such as the already threatened blue whale (Section 11-6), that feed on krill, along with several kinds of fish, seabirds, seals, and penguins. Furthermore, the energy cost of harvesting krill is very high due to their location in distant Antarctic waters and because these tiny crustaceans must be strained from large quantities of seawater. This has made the economics of krill harvesting and processing less favorable than some of its promoters expected.

Fish and Shellfish Farming: Aquaculture and Mariculture If we have trouble catching more fish and shellfish using our present hunting-and-gathering approach, then why not raise and harvest crops of them in land-based ponds (**aquaculture**) or in fenced in coastal lagoons and estuaries (**mar-**iculture)? These two approaches already supply about 10 percent of the total world aquatic catch—about equal to the annual catch of freshwater fish—and some scientists believe that yields can be increased severalfold by 2000.

Fish farming is not new. In Asia species such as carp (a species of catfish), mullet, tilapia, and milkfish have been raised in ponds, canals, and rice paddies for several thousand years. Catfish farms have been common in many parts of the southern United States since the 1960s and the industry is rapidly expanding. In such land-based aquaculture, a complete ecosystem is set up in a pond or small lake. Commercial fertilizers, animal wastes, fish wastes, and even sewage are used to produce phytoplankton. These are eaten by zooplankton and bottom animals and in turn are eaten by fish.

There is no doubt that aquaculture can be an important source of low-cost, high-quality protein for local consumption in many LDCs—especially those with many lakes, ponds, and marshes. One problem, however, is that the fish can be killed by pesticide runoff from nearby croplands, as has happened in aquaculture ponds in the Philippines, Indonesia, and Malaysia.

Japan, the Soviet Union, and the United States have used mariculture in estuaries to raise fish and shellfish, especially shrimp, lobster, oysters, and salmon. Estuaries are natural sinks for nutrients flowing from the land to the sea. With controlled fertilization they can be used to produce large yields of desirable marine species in fenced-off bays, large tanks, or floating cages.

Although mariculture could be an important source of protein within 20 to 30 years, it seems unlikely. The growing pollution of the sea, particularly along coastal and estuarine zones, threatens both cultivated and wild fish and shellfish (Section 18-5).

In summary, *we can increase the global supply of protein by increasing the fish catch, harvesting krill, and increasing the practices of aquaculture and mariculture. However, instead of increased yields, we may have yields lower than we have today because of overfishing and pollution.* These problems are classic examples of the tragedy of the commons. Each nation takes as much as possible from the ocean and then uses it as a free dump for its wastes—a process that can eventually ruin this common resource for everyone.

9-7 Cultivating More Land

Availability of Arable Land If the sea has limited potential for expanding the world food supply, then what about the land? Why not convert more land to cropland (Figure 9-7)?

Between 1950 and 1980 the total amount of land used to grow crops worldwide increased by about 28 percent. Because of population growth, however, the amount of arable land per person decreased by 21 percent during this same period. Today about 44 percent of all potential cropland is under cultivation, with only about 60 to 70 percent actually harvested each year. The remaining 56 percent of the world's potential cropland consists primarily of tropical forests that could be cleared and planted and arid land that could be irrigated and cultivated (Figure 9-7). Although some of this land is found in North America and parts of the Soviet Union, most of it is found in Africa, South America, and Australia.

Using the classification in Figure 9-7, observers have suggested that we could at least double the world's cropland. Others believe this projection will probably never be realized because of one or more of the following limiting factors: **(1)** remote location and insect infestation, **(2)** poor soils, **(3)** lack of water, **(4)** conversion of existing cropland to other uses, **(5)** excessive costs, and **(6)** lack of economic incentives. Even if more cropland is developed, much of this increase will be used to offset the projected loss of almost one-third of today's cultivated cropland and rangeland through a combination of erosion, overgrazing, waterlogging, salinization, mining, and urbanization. Let's look briefly at each of these limitations.

Remote Location and Insect Infestation as a Limiting Factor   About 83 percent of the world's new potential cropland is in South America's Amazon and Orinoco river basins and in African rain forests. This land is far from population centers—adding to the costs of cultivation and shipping food to places where it is needed. In West Africa, potential cropland equal to five times the area now farmed in the United States cannot be used for grazing or farming because it is infested with tsetse flies which carry sleeping sickness and are essentially impossible to eradicate.

Soil as a Limiting Factor   About 56 percent of the land in the world that can theoretically be converted to cropland (Figure 9-7) is found under the moist jungles and tropical rain forests in Latin America (especially Brazil) and Africa (mostly West Africa). Although blessed with plentiful rainfall and long or continuous growing seasons, the soils under many of these tropical rain forests are not suitable for intensive cultivation (Section 8-4). Once the for-

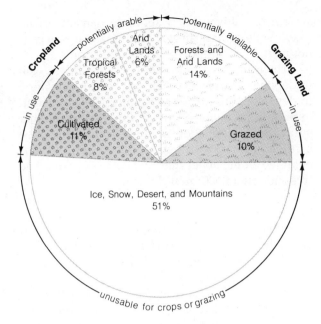

Figure 9-7   Classification of the earth's land. Theoretically, the world's cropland could be doubled in size by clearing tropical forests and irrigating arid lands. But converting this marginal land to cropland would destroy valuable forest resources, cause serious environmental problems, and could cost more than it is worth.

est is cleared the heavy rainfall can cause severe erosion and rapidly wash most of the topsoil away. In addition, an estimated 5 to 15 percent of these soils are oxisols. After clearing, these soils bake under the tropical sun into brick-hard surfaces called laterites that are useless for farming (Section 8-4).

In the Amazon Basin, an estimated 90 percent of the soils are deficient in phosphorus, 73 percent are highly acidic and have too much aluminum for good plant growth (aluminum toxicity), and one-sixth are expected to lose nutrients easily by leaching when vegetation is cleared. Some of these soils can produce up to three crops of grain per year if massive quantities of fertilizer are applied at the right time, but the costs are very high. To make matters worse, the warm temperatures, high moisture, and year-round growing season support large populations of pests and diseases that can wipe out crops. Even if farmers can afford pesticides, most of them are washed away by the heavy rains.

These limitations explain why for centuries tropical forest residents have used shifting (or slash-and-burn) cultivation of small plots (Section 8-4) rather than the extensive clearing found in other areas of the world with more fertile soils. Instead of being backward, shifting agriculture is ecologically sound and well-adapted to tropical rain forests. More than 240 million people in Africa, Asia, and Latin America eke out subsistence using this system of cultivation on about 30 percent of the usable soils in these areas. But unfortunately it cannot be used to support a large population.

The ecology of tropical ecosystems is less well understood than most others and researchers hope to develop methods for more intensive cultivation in these areas. Some scientists, however, argue that agricultural production in these areas should be confined primarily to tree products such as those obtained from rubber trees, oil palms, and banana trees adapted to tropical climates and soils.

Irrigation: Water as a Limiting Factor Irrigated land typically yields from two to four times as much food per hectare as the same land before it was irrigated. About 88 percent of the water used throughout the world each year is for irrigation. Between 1950 and 1984, the area of land irrigated throughout the world more than doubled from about 5 percent to 12 percent. Almost half of the world's food and 30 percent of that in the United States is produced on this irrigated acreage. Half of the world's irrigated cropland is in China and India, where rice is widely grown. Between 1975 and 2000, it is estimated that the amount of irrigated land will have to at least double for food production to keep up with population growth.

Some doubt that such an increase can be accomplished. More than half of the remaining potentially arable land lies in very dry areas (Figure 9-7), where water shortages limit crop growth. Large-scale irrigation in such areas would be very expensive and require large inputs of fossil fuel energy to pump water long distances. Most of the world's accessible rivers are already dammed to provide irrigation water. Those remaining, such as the Mekong and Amazon, are not where the need is greatest. The Amazon's vast width also makes it almost impossible to harness. In addition, the lakes behind dams gradually fill up and provide only temporary supplies of irrigation water.

In some areas irrigation water can be pumped up from deep underground aquifers. However, in addition to incurring high energy costs, this can deplete slowly recharged underground aquifers. This type of groundwater mining is occurring throughout much of the 17 western states in the United States, where 80 percent of all irrigated U.S. cropland is located and 92 percent of all irrigation water is used (Section 17-4). It is estimated that by 2000 about 3.5 million high-yielding, irrigated acres along the Ogallala aquifer, a vast underground lake running through eight states from Nebraska to Texas, will no longer have enough irrigation water to grow cotton and animal feed crops because of a rapidly falling water table and the increased cost of pumping.

To complicate matters further, an estimated one-half of the world's irrigated lands are damaged to some extent by salt buildup on the surface (salinization) and waterlogging and large areas have had to be removed from production (Figure 8-7). From an airplane, glistening white expanses of lands ruined by salinization can be seen in Pakistan, Iraq, India and other countries traditionally dependent on irrigation. Drainage systems that remove excess water and salt from irrigated fields can be installed, but this is expensive. The salt removed from these fields can pollute nearby rivers. For example, in the U.S. Southwest some of this salt ends up in river water eventually used to irrigate Mexican crops. Some people talk of desalinating ocean water for irrigation, but it takes so much energy to remove the salt and to pump the water inland where it is needed that the method would not be cheap enough for agriculture (Chapter 17).

Loss of Existing Cropland as a Limiting Factor There is competition for land to be used for farming and urbanization because both can take place at a lower cost on relatively flat land. The trend in the United States and some LDCs is to take over high-quality farmland for urbanization, transportation, and flooding for water use. Between 1975 and 2000, *The Global 2000 Report to the President* estimated that the world will probably lose an area of cropland to erosion (Section 8-5) and urbanization almost equal to half of the cultivated land in the world today. In Egypt, for example, urbanization has claimed as much fertile land as the massive Aswan Dam has made available through irrigation in the past 20 years.

Each year the United States loses enough cropland and rangeland to highways, shopping centers, airports, housing developments, factories, reservoirs, and other forms of nonagricultural land use to equal a 0.8-kilometer-wide (0.5-mile-wide) strip stretching from New York to San Francisco. Some argue that this is a major crisis because **(1)** such losses of farmland are essentially irreversible and **(2)** the rate may increase because of the urban-to-rural shift in U.S. population (Chapter 12) that spreads people out and puts even more pressure on cropland, rangeland, and forests. Some marginal land in the United States can be converted to farmland to replace that lost by urbanization and erosion, but such conversion is costly and can increase erosion and water pollution.

Others point out that conversion of farmland to other uses amounts to an annual loss of only about 0.18 percent of the nation's potential cropland and less than 0.24 percent of existing cropland. At this rate, the United States would lose only about 3.6 percent of its potential cropland between 1980 and 2000 and still have ample acreage to meet domestic and international demands. It is also argued that this loss of cropland is not nearly as serious as that from soil erosion (Section 8-5) and that such conversions may be desirable from an economic standpoint because factories, shopping centers, housing developments, water reservoirs, and other nonagricultural uses of cropland also have value and contribute to the nation's GNP.

The danger in this economic and environmental tradeoff is that without a plan and land-use laws for preserving a certain fraction of the nation's cropland (especially prime farmland), the ability of the United States to provide food for its population and for export can be eroded. At present less than 4 percent of the existing and potential farmland in the United States is protected under any existing state or local land-use policies.

A new threat to the use of cropland to produce food in the United States and in other nations, such as Brazil, is the increasing interest in growing grain or other crops for conversion to ethyl alcohol to make gasohol (gasoline that contains about 10 to 20 percent ethyl alcohol) to run cars. Fueling all U.S. cars with gasohol would require about 60 percent of the nation's corn crop and could reduce the acreage available for growing food for export. The poor of the world could lose because affluent people can afford to pay more for the grain to be used as fuel, driving world grain prices up.

Money as the Limiting Factor From a technical standpoint, we can farm remote Amazon jungles, irrigate arid lands to grow more food, and at great cost even grow bananas and strawberries at the South Pole. According to agricultural expert Lester Brown, "The people who are talking about cultivating more land are not considering the cost. If you are willing to pay the cost, you can farm the slope of Mt. Everest." Thus, the real questions are how much will it cost to expand the amount of cropland in many parts of the world and how this cost will relate to the ability of the poorest people in the world to pay for the food grown there.

Lack of Economic Incentive as a Limiting Factor Regardless of how much arable land is available it will not be used to produce food for other people unless farmers can make some profit on a year-to-year basis. Because of a lack of economic incentive, much of the potentially arable land in both MDCs and LDCs is not cultivated. Most economists argue the single most important way to increase food pro-

duction is with a system of individual land-owning farmers being able to sell their crops in a free market, without price controls and with price supports to guarantee a reliable market and minimum profit even when the weather leads to poor harvests. To help keep enough farmers in business, governments must also be sure that there is an adequate storage, transportation, and marketing network to distribute the food after it is produced and to store excess food for distribution in years of poor harvests.

Agricultural economics is a tricky business. If a government establishes popular but artificially low food price ceilings and export taxes, farmers have little incentive to produce food to support people living in the cities. For example, Thailand put a heavy export price on rice to help subsidize extremely low prices in the cities. Since there is no incentive for farmers to produce more rice for export, unemployed farmers are moving to cities where they can buy the cheap rice and the country is losing the income it could get from rice exports.

Government price supports, cash subsidies, and import restrictions can be used to stimulate crop production by guaranteeing farmers a certain minimum return on their investment from year to year. For example, despite its population problems (Section 7-4), the average food supply per person in India has been rising for over 2 decades. One reason is the green revolution that has enabled Indian farmers to increase crop yields of wheat per hectare, as discussed in the next section. But the main reason is that the Indian government removed price controls that were keeping wheat prices at artificially low levels and replaced them with price supports that put the price of domestic wheat the same as the import price. With this economic incentive Indian farmers began producing much more wheat. Indian farmers, however, have not made similar gains in rice production because the government put the price support for rice at about half the import price.

On the other hand, if government price supports are too high, people in the city pay high prices to subsidize the rural farming population and with good weather farmers may produce more food than can be stored, transported, and sold. Food prices and profits then drop because of the oversupply and many farmers go bankrupt, as was occurring in the United States in the early 1980s. Between 1952 and 1983, U.S. farm output more than doubled, but net farm income in real terms (1967 dollars) fell from $19 billion in 1950 and $26 billion in 1973 to about $6 billion in 1983. Between 1973 and 1983, the total debt of the 2.4 million U.S. farmers rose over threefold from $60 billion to $210 billion. Record harvests in 1982 pushed prices for major crops so low that many farmers had to sell their products for less than they cost to produce. This loss coupled with high interest rates on borrowed money left many U.S. farmers teetering on the edge of bankruptcy.

Thus, in 1982 when millions around the world were hungry, private and government storage facilities were bulging with so much surplus food that many U.S. farmers were paid not to grow food. Indeed, by 1983 total government subsidies for agriculture almost equalled net farm income and cost taxpayers a record $21.8 billion in 1983—ten times that in 1980. Many U.S. farmers have found that with government subsidies, low crop prices, and high interest rates they can make as much money by not growing crops as by growing them—an offer they find hard to refuse. In California's Central Valley, for example, 2,000 farmers were given crop surplus payments in 1983 for not growing crops on land that was under water because of earlier floods.

Some observers have suggested that the U.S. government should give away more of its surplus food to the needy. The government argues, however, that this could reduce already low food prices by cutting into commercial sales and threaten more farmers with bankruptcy. The government did give away about $1 billion worth of surplus cheese and butter to the needy in 1982, when the government spent $2 billion to purchase dairy products at above-market prices—amounting to an average payment of $10,000 for every U.S. dairy farmer. Most surplus food, however, is in the form of raw crops that cannot be used by most people.

As you can see, encouraging farmers to put idle land into production and produce enough food at a price that consumers—especially poor people—can afford and still keep enough farmers in business is a complex and difficult problem.

9-8 Increasing Crop Yields

The Green Revolution Most experts agree that the quickest and usually the cheapest way to grow more food is to raise the yield per hectare on existing cropland. This is done by cross-breeding wild and existing strains of crops to develop new varieties that are better adapted to climate and soil conditions and can produce higher yields through increased use of fertilizer, water, and pesticides.

Such methods have been used in the United States and most MDCs since the 1950s. The term *green revolution* was coined to describe this approach in 1967 when new high-yield dwarf varieties of rice and wheat, especially selected and bred for tropical and subtropical climates, were introduced into LDCs

Figure 9-8 The green revolution. Scientists compare for two Indian farmers a full, older variety of rice (left) and a new, high-yield dwarf variety (right). The dwarf variety can accept much larger amounts of fertilizer.

such as Mexico, India, Pakistan, the Philippines, and Turkey. The shorter, stiffer stalks of the new dwarf varieties allow them to take up to three times as much fertilizer as conventional varieties without toppling over as long as enough water is available to keep the high levels of fertilizer from killing the crops (Figure 9-8). With sufficient inputs of fertilizer, water, and pesticides at the proper time, wheat and rice yields can be two to three times greater than yields of traditional varieties.

By the 1970s the new wheat varieties had spread to many parts of the world including China and Bangladesh and the new rice varieties were adopted in many parts of Southeast and South Asia. Nearly 90 percent of the increase in world grain output in the 1960s and about 70 percent in the 1970s came from increased yields, mostly as a result of this latest green revolution.

Green evolution is probably a more accurate term for this green revolution because it resulted from 30 years of painstaking genetic research and trials conducted under the joint sponsorship of the Ford and Rockefeller Foundations at two major research centers, the International Maize and Wheat Improvement Center in Mexico, and the International Rice Research Institute in the Philippines. The work in Mexico was led by Norman E. Bourlag who won the 1971 Nobel Peace Prize for his contribution to humanity.

Limitations of the Green Revolution Even with good weather, a lack of water, fertilizer, pesticides, or money can limit the spread of the green revolution in LDCs or cause it to "turn brown." The major factors limiting its more widespread use are: **(1)** Without massive doses of fertilizer and water the new crop varieties produce yields no higher and often less than those from traditional grains; **(2)** the rise in oil and natural gas prices since 1973 has made the price of water and fertilizer so high that many farmers can't afford to use them in large enough quantities to get increased yields; **(3)** some of these new varieties are less resistant to insect pests and various diseases than traditional plants; **(4)** heavy applications of pesticides used on the new crop strains have caused a sharp increase in malaria in many countries because many strains of mosquitoes have developed genetic resistance to insecticides (Section 9-9); **(5)** high yields are jeopardized unless they are planted, irrigated, fertilized, cultivated, and harvested at precise moments in their growth cycle, often requiring technical assistance that may not be available; **(6)** in some countries storage, transportation, and marketing networks have been inadequate to take advantage of the increased yields; **(7)** in some nations market prices and other incentives have been insufficient to motivate farmers to produce more crops; and **(8)** only large landowners and wealthy farmers have the money or can get the credit to buy the fertilizer, irrigation water, pesticides, and equipment that the new seeds require, so its effects have not benefited most of the poor peasant farmers who make up 60 to 90 percent of the population of most LDCs.

However, proponents of the green revolution point out that **(1)** despite its limitations it has helped grow more food per capita, so without it world hunger and malnutrition would be much worse; **(2)** no traditional or new crop variety is perfect and scientists are now working to create a new green revolution by breeding new high-yield strains that do not need as much fertilizer, make their own nitrogen fertilizer like legumes, can thrive in salty soils and withstand periods of drought, make more efficient use of solar energy during photosynthesis, and have greater resistance to insects and disease; **(3)** it was never intended to solve world food and food-related problems, only to buy time for controlling world population growth; and **(4)** it should not be blamed for lack of adequate transportation and marketing networks, poor government policies that do not provide proper economic incentives for growing more food, and the existence of poverty and large land holdings by wealthy elites in poor countries.

Reducing Genetic Diversity Biologist Paul Ehrlich has warned that "aside from nuclear war, there is probably no more serious environmental threat than the continued decay of the genetic variability of crops." When fields of natural varieties are cleared and replaced with monocultures of crossbred varieties, much of the natural genetic diversity essential for developing new hybrids can be reduced or lost forever. There would then be no way to develop crops that would be resistant to climate changes and to the new strains of disease and pests that arise. For example, a perennial variety of wild corn that, unlike cultivated corn, replants itself each year was recently discovered. It is also resistant to a range of viruses and grows well on wet soils. The few thousand plants known to exist were found on a hillside in Mexico that was in the process of being plowed up. Genetic vulnerability was demonstrated in 1970 when most of the corn crop in the U.S. planted mostly in one variety was wiped out by a blight-causing fungus. Seed companies quickly introduced a resistant seed and recovery was rapid, but this episode made farmers aware that genetic diversity is an important form of insurance against disaster.

To preserve genetic variety, the National Academy of Sciences and many other scientists have proposed that naturally growing native plants and strains of food crops throughout the world should be collected and preserved and maintained in genetic storage banks in different areas.

9-9 Reducing Crop Losses from Diseases and Pests: The Pesticide Dilemma

Crop Losses from Pests and Diseases A **pest** is any unwanted organism that directly or indirectly interferes with human activity. It can be an insect that eats crops or bites humans or livestock, rodents that consume crops and stored food, diseases and parasites that can devastate crops and livestock, or weeds—plants growing in the wrong place—that compete with crops for soil nutrients.

Each year pests and disease consume or destroy about 45 percent of the world's food supply; 33 percent of this loss occurs before harvest and 12 percent after harvest. Even in the United States, which uses vast amounts of pesticides and has sophisticated food storage and transportation networks, the total loss due to pests and disease each year is estimated to be 42 percent of potential production—33 percent before harvest and 9 percent after. This leads to annual losses of about $20 billion.

Increasing Use of Insecticides and Herbicides The major revolution in insect pest control occurred in 1939 when Swiss chemist Paul Müller discovered

Table 9-3 Major Types of Insecticides

Type	Examples	Action on Insects	Persistence
Chlorinated hydrocarbons	DDT, DDE, DDD, aldrin, dieldrin, endrin, heptachlor, toxaphene, lindane, chlordane, kepone, mirex	Nerve poisons that cause convulsions, paralysis, and death	High (2 to 15 years)
Organophosphates	Malathion, parathion, Azodrin, Phosdrin, methyl parathion, Diazinon, TEPP, DDVP	Nerve poisons that inactivate the enzyme that transmits nerve impulses	Low to moderate (normally 1 to 12 weeks but some can last several years)
Carbamates	Carbaryl (Sevin), Zineb, maneb, Baygon, Zectran, Temik, Matacil	Nerve poisons	Usually low (days to 2 weeks)

that DDT (short for dichlorodiphenyltrichloroethane), a chemical known since 1874, was a powerful insecticide. Research showed that DDT could be used to kill not only insects that fed on crops but also those that spread diseases such as typhus and malaria. In 1948 Müller was awarded the Nobel Prize for Physiology and Medicine for his discovery.*

Since 1945 fields have been blanketed with a variety of synthetic pesticides to kill insects (*insecticides*), plants (*herbicides*), rodents (*rodenticides*), fungi (*fungicides*), and other organisms humans consider undesirable. By 1984 an average of about 1 pound of pesticides was being used each year for every person on earth. Worldwide use of pesticides is projected to more than double between 1975 and 2000, with usage increasing four- to sixfold in LDCs. In 1984, the LDCs used about 20 percent of the world's total pesticide production, with usage heavily concentrated in three large countries: India, Brazil, and Mexico.

In the United States total pesticide use almost tripled between 1964 and 1983, with the use of insecticides remaining about the same and that of herbicides increasing about sixfold. About 68 percent of the total was used in agriculture, 24 percent by industry and government, and 8 percent in homes and gardens.

Despite the large amounts used, pesticides are not sprayed on every crop and about one-half of U.S. farmers do not use any pesticides. In 1982, about 12 percent of all U.S. cropland (including pastures) was treated with insecticides, 34 percent with herbicides, and 2 percent with fungicides. About two-thirds of all insecticides applied each year in the United States are used on only two crops, cotton (50 percent) and corn (17 percent).

During the past 15 years the use of herbicides has increased more rapidly than any of the other pesticides. Their use is expected to increase even more as farmers switch to minimum-till and no-till farming (Section 8-6), which respectively require 13 percent and 17 percent more herbicides per hectare than conventional tillage farming. About 71 percent of all herbicides used each year in the United States are applied to corn (53 percent) and soybeans (21 percent).

The total use of pesticides is much greater on commercial crops, but suburban lawns and gardens receive the heaviest doses of pesticides per unit of land area. An EPA study showed that 90 percent of all U.S. households use one or more types of pesticides to control insects, weeds, fungi, or rodents and that in 1980 over 250,000 Americans became sick because of pesticides used in the home.

Types and Properties of Insecticides and Herbicides In the United States about 1,200 different chemicals are mixed to make 35,000 different pesticide formulations. For each pesticide marketed, up to 10,000 different compounds may be screened for effectiveness and safety—explaining why it typically costs about $20 million and takes about 11 years to develop, register, and market a single pesticide in the United States.

The three main groups of synthetic insecticides are *chlorinated hydrocarbons* (complex organic compounds that contain carbon, hydrogen, and chlorine), *organophosphates*, and *carbamates* (Table 9-3). A fourth group, compounds made from toxic metals such as arsenic, lead, and mercury (Enrichment Study 12) are little used today. Most chemical insecticides are broad-spectrum nerve poisons that kill

---

*In 1983, biology student Brigette Bollag uncovered documents showing that a critical part of the work on DDT credited to Müller was in fact performed by Swiss entomologist Robert Wiesmann.

most of the target and nontarget insects in the sprayed area by disrupting their nervous systems. Some widely used herbicides are atrazine, alchlor, paraquat, and the phenoxy herbicides, 2,4-D (short for 2,4,5-dichlorophenoxyacetic acid) and 2,4,5-T (short for 2,4,5-trichlorophenoxyacetic acid).

One important property of insecticides and herbicides is their *persistence,* the length of time they remain active in killing insects and weeds. Table 9-3 shows that chlorinated hydrocarbons stay active for 2 to 15 years and are classified as *persistent* or *hard insecticides.* These pesticides accumulate in the soil and in food chains and webs (Figure 5-6). Persistence varies, however, with different climate conditions. For example, it may take 10 to 15 years for one-half of the amount of DDT applied in the United States to break down, while in the tropics one-half of it may break down in 6 months or less. Most organophosphate and carbamate insecticides remain active for a few hours to several months before decomposing to harmless products and are called *nonpersistent* or *soft insecticides.* The lead, mercury, and arsenic insecticides that were once used remain active for hundreds of years and are called *permanent insecticides.* Most herbicides, such as 2,4-D and 2,4,5-T, do not remain active for a long time and are classified as *nonpersistent herbicides.*

The Pesticide Dilemma In 1962, Rachel Carson's book *Silent Spring* (see Readings at the end of the book) dramatized the potential dangers of pesticides to food, wildlife, and humans and set off a controversy between environmentalists and pesticide industry officials that is still going on.*

Since 1970 regulation of pesticides was transferred from the USDA to the EPA and controls have been tightened over their manufacture, distribution, and use. Since 1972 the EPA has banned most uses of DDT and several other persistent chlorinated hydrocarbon pesticides such as aldrin, dieldrin, heptachlor, chlordane, and toxaphene in the United States. As a result, U.S. farmers have switched to less persistent organophosphate and carbamate insecticides (Table 9-3)—some of which are more toxic to humans than the chlorinated hydrocarbons they replaced.

For decades ethylene dibromide (EDB) has been widely used by the citrus and grain industries as a pesticide primarily for fumigating soil, stored grain, and grain milling machinery. Since 1974 studies have shown that relatively low doses of EDB absorbed through the skin or ingested caused stomach cancer and genetic mutations in all test animals in a relatively short period of time. Despite this knowledge, the EPA waited until 1983 to ban its use as a pesticide and establish maximum permissible residue levels in foods already treated with EDB. These actions were taken when alarming levels of EDB were discovered in groundwater supplies in fruit-growing areas of Florida, Texas, Hawaii, California, and Arizona and in grain products, including some cake and muffin mixes on grocery-store shelves.

In 1979, 2,4,5-T and a related herbicide (Silvex) were banned except to control weeds on rice and rangeland because the traces of dioxin found in them may cause miscarriages and birth defects in humans. By 1980, more than 1,200 Vietnam War veterans had filed claims for alleged disabilities caused by exposure to Agent Orange—a mixture of 2,4-D and 2,4,5-T sprayed to defoliate jungles in South Vietnam between 1962 and 1970. A lawsuit against the companies making Agent Orange was settled out of court in 1984.

Most of the pesticides banned for use in the United States or at least their basic ingredients are still made in the United States and shipped to other countries (mostly LDCs) where they have not been banned. In most LDCs over one-half, and in some cases up to 70 percent, of these pesticides are applied to crops such as cotton, coffee, cocoa, and bananas destined for export to consumers in Europe, Japan, and the United States. Thus, much of the food and fiber the United States imports from LDCs is contaminated with these banned pesticides.

The pesticide industry maintains that the evidence upon which these bans were based is inconclusive and that the benefits of using pesticides outweigh their harmful effects. Is this so, and are there other ways to control pests? In the remainder of this section we will take a look at these important and controversial questions by concentrating on the two most widely used types of pesticides: insecticides and herbicides.

The Case for Insecticides and Herbicides The two major benefits from using pesticides are *disease control* and *increased crop yields.* Insecticides can be used to help control the number of cases and the spread of insect-transmitted diseases such as malaria (transmitted by the *Anopheles* mosquito), bubonic plague (rat fleas), typhus (body lice and fleas), sleeping sickness (tsetse fly), and Chagas' disease (kissing bugs) (Enrichment Study 7). Thanks largely to DDT, dieldrin, and several other chlorinated hydrocarbon insecticides (Table 9-3), over 1 billion people have been freed from the risk of malaria and

---

* Although some technical details of Carson's book were shown to be in error by later research, its basic thesis that pesticides can contaminate and cause damage to ecosystems has been established. Unfortunately, her early death from lung cancer came before the book's importance was fully recognized.

the lives of at least 5 million people were saved between 1947 and 1970. Thus, *DDT and other insecticides have probably saved more lives than any other synthetic chemicals since humans have inhabited the earth.*

Although DDT and several other chlorinated hydrocarbons deserve their reputation as givers of life, they are no longer effective in many parts of the world. According to the WHO, by 1980 at least 43 species of malaria-carrying mosquitoes in 62 out of 107 countries where malaria occurs had developed genetic resistance to one or more of the pesticides used to control malaria. As a result between 1970 and 1980 there was a thirty- to forty-fold increase in malaria in a number of countries where it was once almost eradicated. Despite the increasing ineffectiveness of DDT and other insecticides, the WHO points out that a ban on DDT and its substitutes, where they are still useful, would lead to large increases in disease, human suffering, and death.

It is estimated that for each $1 invested in the United States for pesticide control, about $4 is returned in increased crop yields, though some studies put the benefits closer to $2 for each $1 invested. Without the use of insecticides and herbicides in the United States, the USDA and the Office of Technology Assessment estimate that total annual production of crops, livestock, and forests would drop by 25 to 30 percent and food prices could rise by 50 to 75 percent. However, according to entomologist David Pimentel, a total pesticide ban in the United States would increase preharvest losses from pests and crop diseases by only 9 percent (from 33 to 45 percent) and would cause no serious food shortages because there would be only about a 5 percent decrease in the production of foods eaten by humans.

There are alternatives to relying on synthetic chemical insecticides and herbicides to control insects and weeds, as discussed later in this section. But proponents of synthetic pesticides argue that they have several advantages over other approaches: **(1)** A variety of insecticides and herbicides are available to control most insect pests and weeds quickly and at a reasonable cost; **(2)** when genetic resistance occurs in pest insects and weeds, farmers can usually switch to other insecticides and herbicides; **(3)** they have a relatively long shelf life and are easily shipped and applied; **(4)** an increasing number of narrow-spectrum, nonpersistent pesticides, especially herbicides, have been developed to control specific insects, weeds, and diseases without the widespread killing of other nonpest organisms; **(5)** not all pesticides have been shown to have harmful side effects; and **(6)** when properly handled and applied they are safe.

The Case Against Insecticides and Herbicides
Fears persist that some of the pesticides now used and the persistent ones used in the past that are still circulating in global ecosystems may eventually damage wildlife and humans. Some analysts question the value of pesticides. For example, even though insecticide use in the United States has increased tenfold between 1940 and 1980, crop losses from insects have almost doubled from 7.1 percent to 13 percent during the same period. Research has also shown that the widespread use of insecticides and herbicides can cause a number of undesirable and harmful effects in ecosystems and nonpest living organisms, including humans, as summarized in the accompanying box.

Harmful Effects of Widespread Use of Insecticides and Herbicides

1. *Killing of natural enemies:* Broad-spectrum insecticides kill both the target pest species and a host of other organisms, often including the pest's natural predators. Without natural enemies, rapidly reproducing pest insects can make a strong comeback within a few days or weeks, forcing farmers to use heavier doses and more frequent applications of insecticides to keep them under control.

2. *Creation of new pests:* Parasites and insects, especially mites, can become new major pests when their natural predators are killed off by broad-spectrum pesticides.

3. *Development of genetic resistance:* When heavy doses of pesticides are used over and over, the short generation times of most insects, disease organisms, and weeds allow them to adapt and mutate (Section 5-2) so later generations can become highly resistant to being killed by the chemicals within about 5 years and even sooner in the hot and wet tropics, where insects and diseases adapt and mutate even faster. Worldwide, by 1982 at least 432 species of insects, mites, and ticks, 50 species of fungi, and several species of weeds that affect crops, livestock, and humans had strains resistant to one or

more chemical pesticides—more than a fourfold increase since 1960. When genetic resistance or new pests develop, pesticide company representatives recommended more frequent spraying, stronger doses, or switching to a different chemical—putting the farmer on a pesticide treadmill—instead of suggesting crop rotation, biological control, or other methods of keeping populations of pest species below levels that cause economic loss.

4. *Biological magnification of persistent pesticides:* Because DDT and some other persistent pesticides are more soluble in fats than in water, their concentrations can be biologically magnified in food chains and webs to levels thousands to millions of times higher than those in the soil or water (Figure 5-6), threatening the health and survival of species that eat at high trophic levels.

5. *Global mobility of persistent pesticides:* Only about 1 percent of all pesticides applied hit the target pest. The other 99 percent enter local ecosystems and persistent pesticides are transported by wind, rain, snow, and moving water throughout most of the world and are then magnified to higher levels in food chains and webs (Figure 5-6). As a result, there are traces of persistent pesticides such as DDT in food webs just about everywhere in the world, including your body and those of Arctic seals and Antarctic penguins located far from agricultural areas.

6. *Reduction of ecosystem diversity and resilience:* Species and food web diversity can be reduced, which in turn can disrupt the efficiency of energy flow (Section 4-2) and nutrient cycling (Section 4-3) in ecosystems.

7. *Threats to wildlife:* Marine organisms, especially shellfish, can be killed by minute concentrations of chlorinated hydrocarbons. Some bees, necessary for pollination of many vital crops, are extremely susceptible to pesticide poisoning. A breakdown product of DDT, DDE, reduced the populations of the peregrine falcon, brown pelican, osprey, bald eagle, and several other predatory birds that help control populations of rabbits, ground squirrels, and other crop-damaging small mammals. In many cases, sharp population declines occurred because DDE caused shell thinning whereby eggs break before offspring can hatch. Since the U.S. ban on DDT in 1972, the populations of most of these bird species have been increasing.

8. *Threats to human health:* By conservative estimates, about 500,000 farm workers, pesticide plant employees, and children worldwide become seriously ill and about 5,000 die (10,000 according to one estimate) each year from exposure to toxic insecticides—especially organophosphates. In the United States insecticides cause an estimated 45,000 illnesses and 200 deaths each year. Insecticide-related illnesses and deaths are particularly high among farm workers in LDCs, where educational levels are low and control over pesticide use is often lax. Trace amounts of DDT and other persistent pesticides are found in the fatty tissues of almost every person on earth. In 1971 Americans carried an average of about 8 ppm of DDT in their bodies. After the 1972 ban on DDT use in the United States, the average level had dropped to about 2 ppm by 1980. A 1983 study, however, showed that 44 percent of the fruits and vegetables grown in California contained residues of 19 different pesticides, including DDT and other supposedly banned pesticides. Recent National Academy of Sciences studies indicate that 66 percent of the 1,400 different chemicals used in registered pesticides in the United States have not been adequately tested for possible human health hazards and up to 25 percent of these 1,400 chemicals may cause cancer in people. Possible long-term effects, if any, from the trace amounts of DDT and other pesticides in our bodies won't be known for several decades because the oldest people who have carried these chemicals in their bodies since conception only reached age 40 in 1985. Even then it will be almost impossible to determine that a specific chemical such as DDT caused a particular cancer or other harmful effect (Enrichment Study 7).

Alternative Methods of Insect Control The ideal method of insect pest control would **(1)** kill only the target pest, **(2)** be nonpersistent and break down into harmless chemicals, **(3)** not result in genetic resistance in the target organism, and **(4)** be cheap.

Unfortunately, no pest control method meets all these criteria. Fortunately there are a number of alternatives to relying only on conventional chemical insecticides, and they summarized in the box on the next page.

Alternative Methods of Insect Control

Cultural Control

For centuries farmers have modified the crop growth system to reduce damage from insect pests by using rotation to change the crops available to pests, adjusting planting times to avoid certain pests, removing stalks and debris that serve as breeding places for insects, planting hedgerows and alternating rows of different crops as barriers to insect invasion, and growing crops in areas where certain major pests do not exist (Section 8-6). Unfortunately, to increase short-term profits farmers in MDCs such as the United States have abandoned many of these methods.

Biological Control

So far natural predators, parasites, and plant diseases have kept about 90 percent of the potential insect pests from becoming major pests. Because the widespread use of synthetic pesticides has killed off many of these natural predators, scientists have been trying to reintroduce or develop new natural predators, parasites, and pathogens (disease-causing bacteria and viruses) to combat specific insect pests and weeds. Worldwide there have already been about 300 successful biological control projects, especially in China and the Soviet Union. Examples include using ladybugs and praying mantises to control aphids, purple martin birds to control mosquitoes, a bacterial agent (*Bacillus thuringiensis*) to control leaf-eating caterpillars, and viruses to help control the Douglas fir tussock moth, gypsy moth, and the cotton bollworm. Obstacles to widespread use of biological control agents include (1) difficulty in mass production, (2) getting them established in fields, (3) making them work consistently in fields with wide variations in temperature and moisture, (4) protecting them from being killed by pesticides, and (5) being sure that the agents themselves don't become pests.

Genetic Control by Sterilization

Males of an insect species can be raised in the laboratory, sterilized by radiation or chemicals, and then released in an infested area to mate unsuccessfully with fertile females. If sterile males outnumber fertile males by ten to one, pest species in a given area can be eradicated in about four generations, provided reinfestation does not occur. This technique has been used to eradicate the oriental fruit fly in Guam and to control partially the screwworm fly (a major livestock pest)

in the southeastern and southwestern United States. Major problems with this method include (1) providing enough sterile males so they won't be overwhelmed by nonsterile males, (2) having sufficient knowledge of the mating times and behavior of each target insect, (3) the possibility that laboratory-produced strains of sterile males may not be as sexually active as normal wild males, and (4) preventing reinfestation with new nonsterilized males.

Attractants

Sound, light, and sex attractant chemicals can be used to lure pests into traps containing toxic chemicals or to confuse male insects so they can't find mates. Chemical sex attractants such as pheromones are highly specific, active at low concentrations, and have very low persistence. Pheromones are now commercially available for use against 25 major pests, including the pink bollworm, cotton boll weevil, cabbage looper, bark beetle, and oriental fruit fly. Problems with this method are (1) difficulties in identifying and isolating the specific sex attractant for each pest species, (2) knowing the mating behavior of the target insect, (3) coping with periodic reinfestation from surrounding areas, and (4) development of genetic resistance if these chemicals are widely used.

Hormones

Extracted or synthetic chemical insect hormones such as juvenile hormones (JH) and molting hormones (MH) can be used to prevent specific pests from reaching maturity and reproducing. Juvenile hormones (1) are often fairly easy to synthesize, (2) typically break down within a week, (3) aren't poisonous to animals, (4) can be used in small amounts, and (5) can often be tailored to a specific pest. Problems with using hormones are that they (1) take weeks rather than minutes to kill, (2) are often ineffective with a large infestation, (3) sometimes break down chemically in the environment before they can act, (4) must be applied at the right time in the insect's life cycle, and (5) can sometimes affect other nontarget insect species.

Resistant Crop Varieties

New varieties of plants resistant to insects, fungi, and diseases are continually developed by plant breeders. To develop a resistant strain may take

10 to 20 years, however, and new insect pests and plant diseases can arise to which the plants are not resistant.

Integrated Pest Management

In the integrated pest management (IPM) approach, each crop and its major pests are considered as an ecological system, and a control program is developed that integrates a variety of biological, chemical, and cultural methods in proper sequence and timing. The overall aim is not to eradicate but to keep pest populations just below the level of economic loss. Pesticides are used only when absolutely necessary in small amounts and with different chemicals being used to retard development of genetic resistance. Over the past 30 years about three dozen IPM programs have been used successfully. These experiments have shown that a properly designed IPM program can reduce preharvest pest losses by 50 percent, reduce pesticide use and pesticide control costs by 50 to 75 percent, reduce fertilizer and irrigation needs, and at the same time increase yields and reduce costs. Major problems include (1) it is complex and requires expert knowledge about each pest-crop situation; (2) methods developed for a given crop in one area may not be applicable to another area with slightly different growing conditions; (3) although the total costs of IPM are typically lower than those of using conventional pesticides, initial costs may be higher; and (4) highly trained IPM consultants must charge for their services, while pesticide sales representatives offer farmers free advice.

Agricultural experts believe that the use of pesticides in the United States can be reduced sharply by greatly increasing the use of IPM over the next 20 years. However, they point out that so far such a large-scale switch has been prevented by political pressure from powerful agricultural chemical companies that see little profit in such methods. As a result, this approach will have to be developed mostly by greatly increased federal and state financial and technical support. Some environmentalists have pointed out that pesticide use could also be decreased if consumers accepted the fact that a few holes or frayed leaves have nothing to do with the quality of fruits and vegetables. They point out that we may be threatening our own health by forcing growers to use more and more pesticides to provide perfect-looking food that costs us more.

There are two spiritual dangers in not owning a farm. One is the danger of supposing that breakfast comes from the grocery, and the other that heat comes from the furnace.

Aldo Leopold

Discussion Topics

1. Explain how total world food production can keep rising in many countries and regions while average per capita food available drops or rises only slightly.

2. Explain how both of these statements can be true: "We averted the threat of famine in the 1970s and early 1980s" and "We now have the largest annual global famine in history."

3. Explain why most people who die from lack of a sufficient quantity or quality of food do not starve to death.

4. Explain how a decline in breast-feeding can lead to an increase in infant deaths from diarrhea and to a rise in the birth rate in LDCs.

5. Can you get adequate amounts and types of proteins if you don't eat meat and meat products? What precautions would you have to take? Explain why persons in a MDC can get a balanced diet from plant sources alone and why most poor people in LDCs cannot.

6. Debate the following statement: "There really is no world food problem because if the grain produced each year was distributed equally among the world's population, everyone would have an adequate diet."

7. Explain why growing more food is necessary but will not solve world food problems.

8. Should the United States encourage a partial switch to more home gardens and smaller, intensively cultivated organic farms instead of large, energy-intensive farms increasingly owned by large corporations? Why or why not?

9. Explain why the elimination of all livestock animals is not desirable from an ecological and human health standpoint. What changes in the production of livestock animals could be helpful in providing more food for the world?

10. Debate the following resolution: The pet population in the United States and other MDCs should be drastically reduced, and birth control for all pets should be mandatory.

11. Why can more beef be raised on a feedlot than on an open range? Should we do away with animal feedlots? Why or why not?

12. Explain why the use of tractors, crop combines, and other farm machines raises the food output per hour of human labor but sharply decreases the energy efficiency for producing crops. Should we do away with the use of such machinery? Why or why not?

13. Summarize the advantages and limitations of each of the following proposals for increasing world food supplies over the next 30 years: (a) cultivating more land by clearing tropical jungles and irrigating arid lands, (b) catching more fish in the open sea, (c) harvesting algae and krill from the ocean, (d) harvesting fish and shellfish by using aquaculture and mariculture, (e) increasing the yield per hectare of cropland, and (f) shipping the world's excess population to space colonies (see Enrichment Study 4).

14. Should prime U.S. farmland be converted to suburban housing and shopping centers? What are the alternatives?

15. If gasoline prices continue to rise, should the government provide economic incentives for farmers to use more prime farmland for growing grain to produce gasohol for cars? Why or why not?

16. Should price supports and other subsidies paid to U.S. farmers out of tax revenues be eliminated? Why or why not? How would you help ensure that enough farmers make an adequate profit to stay in business?

17. In the United States, farms are becoming larger and are increasingly owned by national and international corporations. Is this a desirable trend? Why or why not? What are the alternatives?

18. Should the United States abandon or sharply decrease the use of pesticides? Explain. What might be the consequences for LDCs? For the United States? For you?

19. Explain how the use of insecticides can actually increase the number of insect pests and threaten some carnivores, including humans.

20. Debate the following resolution: Because DDT and the other banned chlorinated hydrocarbon pesticides pose no demonstrable threats to human health and have probably saved more lives than any other chemicals in human history, they should again be approved for use in the United States.

21. Large quantities of DDT and most other pesticides banned for use in the United States are still manufactured there and shipped to other parts of the world. Should this be halted? Why or why not?

22. Do you agree or disagree with the following suggestions various environmentalists have made concerning pesticide use: (a) Pesticides should be used by prescription only, and (b) licensed IPM advisors should be trained and used by the USDA to provide free information to farmers and approve any use of pesticides. Defend your position.

10

Land Resources: Wilderness, Parks, Forests, and Rangelands

We abuse land because we regard it as a commodity belonging to us. When we see land as a community to which we belong, we may begin to use it with love and respect.

Aldo Leopold

10-1 Land Use in the United States

How Is Land Used? A major portion of the national wealth of the United States is found in its 2.3 billion acres of land. This vital resource supplies food, water, timber, minerals, recreation, vegetation for grazing animals, and wildlife habitats and provides the

Enrichment Studies 1, 5, 11, and 14 are related to this chapter.

spaces on which homes, factories, and roads are built. Figure 10-1 shows how this land is used in the United States.

Notice that small and large urban areas consisting of cities and towns with a population of 2,500 or more people occupy only about 2 percent of the total land area. Although this is a tiny fraction of the total land area, these urban areas must be supported by large cropland, rangeland, watershed, forest, estuary, and other nonurban land regions. Thus, the various uses of urban and nonurban land are all interrelated. Nonurban land use and resources will be discussed in this chapter and urban land use and land use planning will be discussed in Chapter 12. Emphasis is on land use in the United States. The principles developed, however, apply to land areas throughout the world.

U.S. Land Ownership Figure 10-2 shows the ownership of land in the United States: Note that

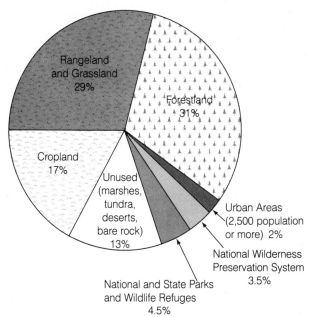

Figure 10-1 Land use in the United States (Source: U.S. Bureau of Commerce and the Conservation Foundation)

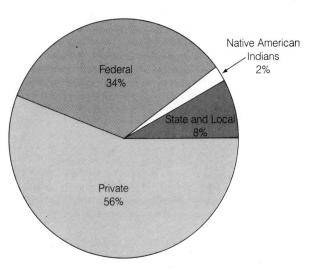

Figure 10-2 Land ownership in the United States. (Source: U.S. Department of the Interior, Bureau of Land Management)

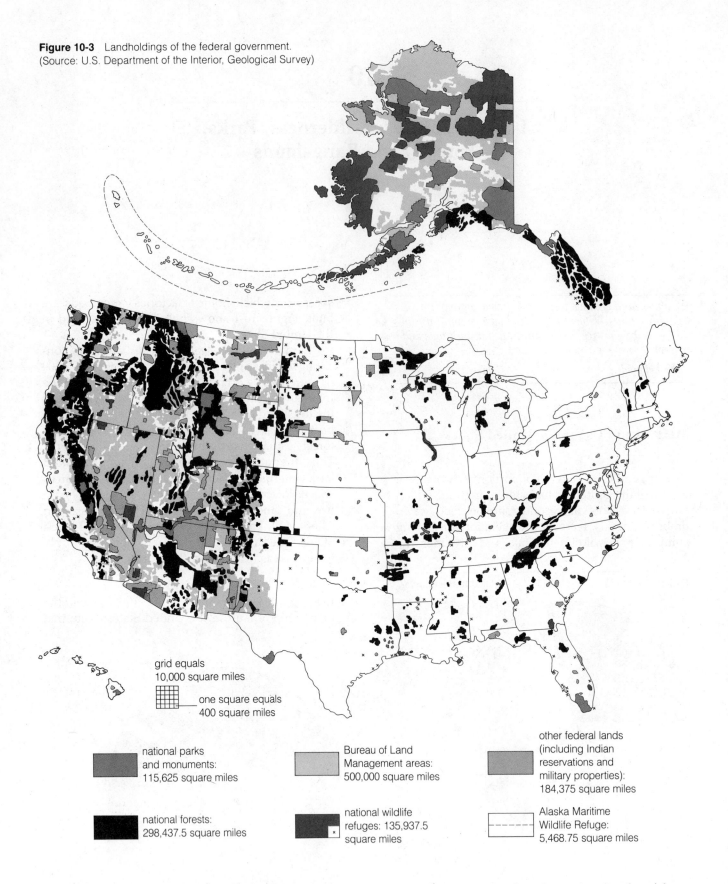

Figure 10-3 Landholdings of the federal government.
(Source: U.S. Department of the Interior, Geological Survey)

grid equals
10,000 square miles

one square equals
400 square miles

national parks
and monuments:
115,625 square miles

Bureau of Land
Management areas:
500,000 square miles

other federal lands
(including Indian
reservations and
military properties):
184,375 square miles

national forests:
298,437.5 square miles

national wildlife
refuges: 135,937.5
square miles

Alaska Maritime
Wildlife Refuge:
5,468.75 square miles

42 percent of the total land area is owned jointly by the nation's citizens and is managed for them by federal, state, and local governments. Federally managed public lands make up more than one-third of the nation's land and consist mostly of large acreages of forest and grassland but also include streets and highways, reservoirs, military reservations, and other holdings. About 95 percent of the

Table 10-1 Land Areas Owned and Administered by Federal Agencies in the United States in 1982

Agency	Name of Landholding	Percentage of All U.S. Land
Bureau of Land Management of the Department of the Interior (DOI)	National Resource Lands	15
U.S. Forest Service of the Department of Agriculture	National Forests	8
Fish and Wildlife Service of the DOI	National Wildlife Refuges	4
National Park Service of the DOI	National Park System	3
Department of Defense	—	1
Other agencies	—	3

federally owned land lies in Alaska and 11 western states, although some is found in nearly every county of every state, as shown in Figure 10-3. Public lands make up more than half of Utah, Idaho, Oregon, and Nevada and nearly 75 percent of Alaska.

Federal public landholdings are distributed unevenly among several departments and agencies as shown in Table 10-1 and Figure 10-3. The Department of the Interior (DOI) alone administers 22 percent of the nation's land. Its National Park Service (NPS) is charged with preserving scenery and wildlife while allowing Americans to visit and enjoy 334 national parks, monuments, seashores, rivers, and recreation areas. Its Fish and Wildlife Service (FWS) supervises 749 wildlife refuges and protects endangered species. Its Water and Power Resources Administration, formerly the Bureau of Reclamation, builds and operates dams to generate electric power, provide flood control, and store water for irrigation, and its Office of Surface Mining (OSM) interprets and enforces federal strip-mining reclamation standards (Section 15-3).

Though little known in the East, Midwest, and South, Interior's Bureau of Land Management (BLM) manages 15 percent of the nation's land, mostly in the western states and Alaska. BLM is responsible for leasing the rights to graze over 3.5 million sheep and cattle on federal rangelands, collecting grazing fees, establishing rules and controls on the use of public rangelands, trying to improve forage and wildlife habitat on land that has been abused by decades of overgrazing, and rounding up 5,000 wild horses and burros a year.

In the Wilderness Act of 1964 and subsequent laws, about one-tenth of all publicly owned land (about 3.5 percent of all U.S. land) has been placed in the National Wilderness Preservation System. These lands are to be managed "for the use and enjoyment of the American people in such a manner as will leave them unimpaired for future use and enjoyment as wilderness." Management of the nation's 257 wilderness areas is distributed among the various federal agencies listed in Table 10-1.

Many of the nation's natural resources are publicly owned but privately used. Individuals use public lands for recreational purposes. Private corporations and individuals cut timber, graze cattle and livestock, and extract oil, natural gas, coal, and other minerals from federal lands. It is estimated that public onshore lands contain 40 percent of the nation's salable timber, 54 percent of the nation's grazing land, 50 percent of its coal, 80 percent of its recoverable shale oil, 4 percent of its known oil reserves, 6 percent of its known natural gas reserves, 55 percent of all geothermal energy resources, 50 percent of known uranium deposits, and most of its copper, silver, asbestos, lead, molybdenum, beryllium, phosphate, and potash.

Land-Use Ethics   Views on how resources on and under publicly owned land should be used fall into four major categories: the *economic ethic*, the *preservationist ethic*, the *balanced multiple-use ethic*, and the *ecological ethic*, as summarized in the accompanying box.

Both the balanced multiple-use ethic and the ecological ethic have the goal of using land resources in ways that leave them undamaged for future generations. The ecological ethic, however, more strongly emphasizes the rights of species of plants and animals to exist unharmed by human activities on certain portions of the earth and places more emphasis on maintaining the natural rather than human-managed self-renewing capacity of land resources.

10-2   Brief History of Natural Resource Conservation and Environmental Protection in the United States

Frontier Versus Conservation Mentality   The history of the ownership and use of federally owned land in the United States provides a look at the ethical conflicts over the use of land resources. When Europeans first settled North America, the entire continent was primitive wilderness little touched by the Native American peoples who lived there. To these landless colonists and pioneers, the vast American wilderness was a hostile country to be conquered, opened up, owned, cleared, and used.

They subscribed to the economic or "use it" ethic. Their lack of concern for the long-term conservation of America's natural resources was reinforced by the belief that the wilderness was too vast to be destroyed.

By the mid-1800s the government owned 80 percent of the total land area of the United States, mostly as a result of the Louisiana Purchase, the Oregon Compromise, the purchase of Alaska, the Mexican Cession, and other acquisitions that ignored the rights of original owners—Native American Indians. At that time the policy of the government was to dispose of these lands as rapidly as possible to encourage settlement and development of the nation and thus strengthen it against its enemies. By 1900 over one-half of this publicly owned land had been sold and given to railroads, timber companies, homesteaders, mining companies, state and local governments, and land-grant colleges.

Early Conservation Efforts (1830–1910) In the first half of the nineteenth century naturalist writers such as Ralph Waldo Emerson and Henry David Thoreau set forth the idea that true progress comes from achieving a harmonious relationship with nature rather than through exploitation. Around 1880 when the nation's frontier was considered closed, George Catlin, John Muir, Frederick Law Olmstead, Charles W. Eliot, Stephen Mather, and others began arguing that America's land resources were finite and were being exploited at an alarming rate through overgrazing, overcutting, and general misuse. They proposed that part of the land owned by the government be withdrawn from public use and preserved for present and future generations in the form of national parks.

George Perkins Marsh, a congressman from Vermont, spearheaded this early conservation movement with the publication in 1864 of his book, *Man and Nature*, still considered one of the greatest American works on the environment. He questioned the idea of the inexhaustibility of natural resources and showed how the rise and fall of past civilizations was linked to their use and misuse of nature. Marsh pointed out that humans, often through ignorance, disrupt the fundamental interconnections in the "web of life." Many of his ideas for federal management of publicly owned forests and watersheds were put into effect in the early 1900s by President Theodore Roosevelt, an ardent conservationist. Marsh's ideas were extended later by Paul B. Sears in 1935 and by Fairfield Osborn in 1948, who tried to alert Americans to some of the environmental problems we face today.

In 1872 President Ulysses S. Grant signed into law a congressional act designating the 2 million acres of the newly discovered Yosemite Forest in northwestern Wyoming for preservation as Yellowstone National Park—the world's first national park. This action marked the first phase of the government's effort to keep and manage public lands rather than to give them away or exploit them.

In the late 1800s Gifford Pinchot, Franklin Hough, Theodore Roosevelt, and other conservationists began efforts to halt the overcutting of publicly owned forestlands. In 1891 Congress designated Yellowstone Timberland Reserve, surrounding Yellowstone Park, as the first federal forest reserve and authorized the president to set aside areas of federal land as national forest reserves. They were to ensure that adequate timber would be available to the nation in the future and to protect the watersheds of the nation's rivers. By 1897 Presidents Benjamin Harrison and Grover Cleveland had set aside 28 forest reserves mostly in the West. Powerful political foes—especially westerners accustomed to using these public lands as they pleased—called these actions undemocratic and un-American.

Effective protection of the national forest reserves did not exist, however, until 1905 when Theodore Roosevelt became president. He transferred administration of the reserves from the Department of the Interior, which had a reputation for lax enforcement, to the Department of Agriculture. In 1905 Congress created the U.S. Forest Service to manage and protect the forest reserves, and President Roosevelt appointed Gifford Pinchot as its first chief. Pinchot pioneered efforts to manage these renewable forest resources according to the principles of *sustained yield* and *multiple use*—policies that still prevail today.

Sustained yield has been achieved when the rate at which timber is removed by cutting, pests, disease, and fire does not exceed the rate at which it is being naturally replenished by new growth. Under **multiple use,** forests are used for a variety of purposes, including timbering, recreation, grazing, wildlife preservation, and water conservation. When there were competing claims on such land resources, Pinchot proposed that the land be reserved for its "highest use." In some areas the highest use was timber cutting; in others it was watershed protection and preservation of natural beauty and wildlife. In 1907 Congress introduced the name "National Forests," implying that these lands could be managed on a multiple-use and sustained-yield basis rather than not being used at all.

These early conservation efforts peaked under President Roosevelt, who added more acres to the national forests than any other president, used the Reclamation Act of 1902 to set up watershed and irrigation districts in the West based on plans presented by John Wesley Powell, protected the Grand Canyon, and established the National Wildlife Refuge System (Sections 11-4 and 11-5).

Preservation Versus Scientific Conservation (1911–1932) After 1910 the conservation movement split into two schools of thought, one emphasizing preservation and the other scientific conservation. Preservationists proposed that large tracts of public lands be set aside as wilderness, protected from all forms of development, and thus *preserved* in their natural state for future generations. By contrast, scientific conservationists believed that public land resources should be managed and used wisely in a manner that would *conserve* them for future generations.

The scientific conservationists were led by Roosevelt, Pinchot, Powell, Charles Van Hise, and others who advocated the use of public land resources on sustained-yield and multiple-use bases. Preservationists were led by California woodsman and nature writer John Muir, who founded the Sierra Club in 1890. After Muir's death in 1914, forester Aldo Leopold became a leader calling for preservation. He proposed an ecological ethic for land use that is best described in his *Sand County Almanac* (1949). According to Leopold, land cannot survive the economic ethic unless it is loved and respected. He proposed that we affirm the right of all species of plants and animals—but not necessarily an individual plant or animal—to continued existence in at least some locations. According to his ecological ethic the role of *Homo sapiens* is that of member, citizen, and protector of the environment—not its conqueror. Another ardent and effective supporter of wilderness preservation was Robert Marshall, an officer in the U.S. Forest Service, who founded the Wilderness Society in 1935. Leopold's land ethic has been continued in more recent years by David Brower, former head of the Sierra Club and founder of Friends of the Earth, Ernest Swift, Stewart L. Udall, and others.

In 1911 Congress passed the Weeks Act, which authorized the Forest Service to buy lands, mostly in the Midwest, South, and East, for use as national forests. Most of these eroding and generally worthless lands were taken back into federal ownership after private owners had stripped them of timber or depleted the soil by farming. In 1912 Congress created the U.S. National Park System, which by 1916 included 16 national parks and 21 national monuments, most of them in the western states. The National Park System Organic Act of 1916 declared that national parks are set aside to conserve scenery, wildlife, and natural and historic objects for the use, observation, health, and pleasure of the people and are to be maintained in a manner that leaves them unimpaired for future generations. This act also created the National Park Service within the Department of the Interior to manage the park system. To carry out these often-conflicting goals the Park Service's first director, Stephen Mather, recruited a corps of professional park rangers to manage the parklands. Mather also began the practice of contracting with private business concessionaires to provide food, lodging, and other services in the parks.

Expanding Federal Role in Land Management (1933–1969) Between 1930 and 1969 the federal government's role in managing the nation's natural resources greatly expanded, especially during the

1930s as President Franklin D. Roosevelt attempted to get the country out of the Great Depression. Shortly after taking office he established the Civilian Conservation Corps (CCC). The CCC hired 2 million unemployed people between the ages of 18 and 25 to work in several thousand camps throughout the country to plant trees, develop parks, improve waterways, provide flood control, develop rangeland, reclaim land, control soil erosion, and protect wildlife. The efforts of the CCC to control soil erosion led to the creation of the Soil Conservation Service under the Department of Agriculture in 1935. Effective soil conservation efforts owe much to the leadership of Hugh H. Bennett, longtime Chief of the Soil Conservation Service.

For many decades public lands, especially in the arid West, had been heavily overgrazed because of the combination of ranchers' ignorance and greed, and periodic drought. The Taylor Grazing Act of 1934 placed 80 million acres of public land outside the national forests and parks into grazing districts to be managed jointly by the Grazing Service established within the Department of the Interior and committees of local ranchers. From the start, however, ranchers resented government interference with their long-established use of public land. Since 1934 they have led repeated efforts to have these lands removed from government ownership and turned over to private cattle and sheep interests. Until 1976, western congressional delegations kept the Grazing Service (which in 1946 became the Bureau of Land Management) so poorly funded and staffed, and without enforcement authority, that many ranchers and miners still misused these lands.

In 1960 conflicts between competing uses of publicly owned land led to the passage of the Multiple Use–Sustained Yield Act. This legislation required the Forest Service and the BLM to attempt to balance outdoor recreation, timber, rangeland, watershed, fish and wildlife habitats, mineral extraction, and other uses of publicly owned land to provide the optimal value to the nation as a whole. Today conflicts continue over what constitutes balanced multiple use of lands managed by these two agencies and what use should have the highest priority when there are competing claims.

In 1964 Congress created the National Wilderness System in which undeveloped tracts of federally owned lands are to be set aside and retained in their natural state unless and until Congress later decides they are needed for the national good. This designation of certain public lands as wilderness is one of the few examples of the preservationist ethic in practice. In this act, **wilderness** is defined as areas where the earth and its community of life have not been seriously disturbed by humans and humans are only temporary visitors. Wilderness areas are open for fishing, hiking, camping, canoeing, and, in some cases, hunting and horseback riding. Roads, timber harvesting, mining, drilling, commercial activities, toilet facilities, man-made structures, motor vehicles, power saws, and other motors are prohibited. Most areas included in the National Wilderness System are undisturbed, but some contain a few abandoned roads, farms, and buildings. Grazing is permitted only where lands were leased before the law was passed. The act allows exploration and identification of mineral, energy, and other resources in wilderness areas as long as such activities do not involve the use of motorized vehicles and other motors. The act also allowed—but did not require—the secretary of the interior to issue energy and mineral development leases in wilderness areas through 1983.

The U.S. concept of setting aside land for protection in the form of national parks, wilderness areas, and so on has been adopted by over 100 other nations. By 1983 about 3 percent of the world's land surface had been set aside for protection from development, overgrazing, and overcutting. The amount of protection actually provided for these designated lands, however, varies widely throughout the world. Despite the warnings of writers such as Marsh, Sears, and Osborn, it was not until 1962 when Rachel Carson published *Silent Spring* that the American public began embracing the notion of environmental protection.

The Environmental Decade (1970–1980) Until the 1970s the role of the federal government in environmental regulation was generally limited to the management of publicly owned land, minerals, timber, and waterways. This situation changed dramatically between 1970 and 1980, a period now known as the *environmental decade*, primarily through extensive media coverage and the writings of such biologists as Paul Erhlich, Barry Commoner, and Garrett Hardin, who helped the general public become aware of the interlocking relationships between population growth, resource use, and pollution (Section 1-5).

During the 1970s two dozen separate pieces of legislation (see Table 20-1) were passed that required the federal government to enforce regulations affecting water quality and drinking water (Chapter 18), air quality (Chapter 19), resource recovery (Section 13-4), pesticides (Section 9-9), endangered species (Section 11-2), noise pollution (Enrichment Study 10), coastal zones (Section 18-5), ocean pollution (Section 18-5), and toxic and hazardous wastes (Enrichment Study 13). In 1970 President Richard Nixon used administrative reorganization to create the Environmental Protection Agency (EPA) to determine environmental standards and see that federal environmental laws are enforced. William D. Ruckelshaus was appointed as its first director.

The National Forest Management Act of 1976 spelled out forest management procedures in more detail with the intent of stopping abuses caused by dominant use of national forests for timber production. In 1976 Congress also passed the Federal Land Policy and Management Act (FLPMA), also known as the Bureau of Land Management Organic Act. It directed the BLM, the nation's largest landowner, to (1) maintain its lands for the most part in public ownership, (2) manage its lands on the principles of multiple resource use and sustained yield, (3) require users of publicly owned resources to pay fair market value for such uses, (4) develop long-range resource management plans with full public involvement, and (5) review all roadless areas and islands of its land containing 5,000 acres or more for possible inclusion in the National Wilderness Preservation System.

At the same time citizen-supported environmental organizations such as the Sierra Club, the Wilderness Society, the National Wildlife Federation, Friends of the Earth, the Environmental Defense Fund (EDF), and the Natural Resources Defense Council (NRDC) lobbied for better protection and management of public lands. They also began taking the government to court to secure enforcement of environmental laws (Section 21-2).

Continuing Controversy: The 1980s The Federal Land Policy and Management Act of 1976 gave the BLM its first real authority to manage its lands. Western ranchers, farmers, miners, off-road motorized vehicle users, and others who had been been doing pretty much as they pleased on BLM lands discovered that this was no longer possible. In the late 1970s western ranchers who had been paying low fees for grazing rights that encouraged overgrazing launched a political campaign that came to be known as the sagebrush rebellion. Its goal, like earlier attempts since the 1930s, was to remove most western public lands, including the national forests, from public ownership, turn them over to the states, and then move them into private ownership or private control. Six western states, led by Nevada, laid claim to federal lands in court, and some western congressional representatives introduced legislation to give public lands to the states. So far these court suits and legislative efforts inspired by the sagebrush rebellion have failed.

In 1980 Ronald Reagan, a declared sagebrush rebel and advocate of less federal government control, was elected president. President Reagan replaced most of the Carter administration's key ap-

pointive environmental and consumer advocates in the Environmental Protection Agency and the Department of the Interior. Environmentalists saw the hard-won environmental protection legislation and policies of the 1970s threatened by such appointments and by the administrative actions and legislative proposals that followed. In 1982 a coalition of 10 environmental groups, led by Friends of the Earth, released a report entitled *Reagan and Environment*. This report and others from the Conservation Foundation entitled *State of the Environment 1982* and *State of the Environment 1984* criticized the environmental and public land-use policies of the Reagan administration. Some of the major charges included the following: (1) relaxing pollution control efforts, (2) increasing the budget for nuclear power and drastically reducing federal budget expenditures for energy conservation and solar energy, (3) cutting drastically the budget, staff, and influence of the White House Council on Environmental Quality (CEQ), which coordinates and advises the president on environmental issues, (4) increasing the budget for a number of dam-building and water-diversion projects (Section 17-3) in the West that according to numerous cost-benefit analyses by the General Accounting Office are environmentally harmful and wasteful, (5) severely reducing the ability of the Interior Department's Office of Surface Mining (OSM) to enforce the 1977 Surface Mining and Control Act (Section 15-4), (6) increasing the amount of coal leased on public lands over 800 percent between 1981 and 1983 at giveaway prices costing taxpayers hundreds of millions of dollars, (7) doubling the amount of public land leased to oil companies for exploration at low royalty rates and putting nearly all 1 billion acres of U.S. coastal waters up for lease by oil companies for exploration (25 times the rate of leasing offered since the program began in 1954), (8) making timber cutting and mineral extraction the dominant uses in national forests by sharply increasing the Forest Service budget for timber sales and mineral management while significantly cutting funds for conservation, (9) changing grazing policy to essentially put ranchers rather than BLM back in charge of grazing policy and encouraging overgrazing and subsidizing ranchers by continuing to offer grazing permits on publicly owned rangelands at a price about one-fifth that on private rangeland, (10) increasing funding for maintenance and restoration of existing national parks but establishing a near 5-year moratorium on the purchase of new national parks or additions to existing ones, (11) attempting to issue mineral and energy leases in wilderness areas before the 1983 moratorium on such leases expired and proposing that the entire wilderness system be opened to mineral and energy development by the year 2000, and **(12)** increasing the budget for maintenance of existing wildlife refuges while proposing no funds for acquiring additional wildlife refuges and wetlands and cutting the budget and staff for endangered species, wildlife habitat preservation, fishery resources, and wildlife research, and **(13)** proposing to sell to other government agencies, state and local governments, and private interests 35 billion acres of publicly owned land and buildings amounting to 5 percent of all federally owned land (equivalent in area to Maine, New Hampshire, Vermont, and Massachusetts combined) to raise cash to decrease the budget deficit.

A number of these proposed legislative changes were blocked by Congress and by court actions brought by environmental organizations. Other proposals such as selling off federal buildings and land were dropped as a result of criticism even from some of the administration's staunchest supporters. Environmentalists, however, suspected that many of these controversial legislative proposals had only been tabled until the results of the 1984 elections were known. Some pros and cons of these Reagan policies are summarized in Table 10-2.

Policies for the Future The history of public land use in the United States has been one of continuing controversy over how much land should be owned by the federal government and how this land should be managed for use by the public. It seems clear that these controversies will intensify in the future because of increased use of publicly owned land and increased demand for the natural resources they contain. Informed citizens will probably insist that public lands be managed more efficiently and without large cash deficits. This means that private corporations and individuals will have to pay more for the use of these resources. With this historical background, we are ready to look more closely at the use of nonurban land resources in the United States.

10-3 Wilderness

Why Preserve Wilderness? It is said that we need places to experience majestic beauty and natural diversity, breathe clean air, drink pure water, and simply get away. Wallace Stegner argues for wilderness philosophically:

Save a piece of country . . . intact and it does not matter in the slightest that only a few people every year will go into it. This is precisely its value . . . we simply need that wild country available to us, even if we never do more than drive to its edge and look in. For it can be a means of reassuring ourselves of our sanity as creatures, a part of the geography of hope.

Still others see important biological and ecological reasons for preserving wild areas and the living species they contain. By preserving wilderness we maintain diverse ecosystems and species that serve as ecological reserves protected from the ravages of an increasingly populated and urbanized world. Wilderness also serves as an ecological laboratory where the natural processes that maintain life on earth may be studied.

No one knows how much wilderness should be preserved. But since it is irreplaceable, preservationists argue that it is best to protect large and diverse areas as an ecological insurance policy against human abuse of the land. In the words of Thoreau: "In wilderness is the preservation of the world."

Expansion of the National Wilderness Preservation System The Wilderness Act of 1964 immediately designated 54 areas to be included in the National Wilderness Preservation System. Since then Congress has designated additional wilderness areas under this act, the Endangered American Wilderness Act of 1978, and the Alaska Lands Act of 1980. As a result, the amount of land in the wilderness system increased from about 10 million acres in 1970 to 80 million acres by 1983. The Alaska Lands Act alone quadrupled the amount of U.S. land officially designated and protected as wilderness, with Alaska now containing 70 percent of all designated U.S. wilderness land. Despite these increases, by 1983 legislated wilderness made up only about 8 percent of government-owned lands, 3.5 percent of all land in the United States, and 1.2 percent of all land in the lower 48 states.

Supporters of wilderness preservation sometimes face a dilemma when new wilderness areas are designated and when organizations such as the Sierra Club publish books and calendars with magnificent photographs of wilderness areas. Many such areas are visited by so many wilderness enthusiasts that their primitive nature is threatened. Federally protected wilderness areas now receive about 8 million visitors a year, almost double the number in 1970. To protect some of the more popular wilderness areas from being damaged by overuse, government agencies have limited the number of people hiking or camping in them at any one time. To prevent overuse, historian and wilderness expert Roderick Nash, in *Wilderness and the American Mind* (3rd ed., 1982), advocates dividing wilderness areas into several categories ranging from **(1)** those fairly accessible, with clearly marked trails, to **(2)** remote areas accessible only to people who qualify for licenses by demonstrating their wilderness skills, to **(3)** areas that should be left undisturbed as a genetic pool of plant and animal resources for earth's future with no human entry allowed.

Table 10-2 Pros and Cons of the Environmental and Land-Use Policies of the Reagan Administration

Administration Position	Environmentalist Position
Budget and staff cuts were necessary to reduce waste and inefficiency and to decrease budget deficits.	There is much unnecessary government waste and inefficiency. But most of the drastic cuts were in environmental programs that protect the public, while most programs that benefit large private corporations were either expanded or cut relatively little.
Increased energy and mineral exploration and development on public lands is necessary to ensure that the country will have enough of these resources to reduce vulnerability to blackmail and resource embargoes. If these resources are developed over the next few decades, crash development programs that would be more environmentally destructive will not be needed later.	Nondestructive identification of resources on public lands is desirable, but it would be wrong to turn over most of the leasing rights on federal lands to private companies, in only a few years, at giveaway prices that can lead to immense corporate profits through speculation.
Low fees and royalties for grazing, oil and gas leasing, mining, and timber harvesting are set by Congress not by the administration.	The administration did not propose price increases for these fees and royalties to Congress, was not obligated to sell these rights at low prices, and seemed intent on leasing public resources to private interests at low fees with undue haste.
It is better to return management decisions and ownership of more federal land to states and private ownership because federal bureaucrats are inept managers and do not put the land to its best use.	The major purpose of federal ownership is to protect public lands from the overgrazing, overcutting, exploitation, and poor management found on much of the nation's privately owned land. The history of state administration of land is primarily one of failure, political scandal, and sale to private corporations and individuals without adequate or reasonable compensation. Many federal lands are badly managed; but as manager of more land than anyone else in the country, the administration should be striving for better management and getting a better return in fees and royalties.
It is better to use limited funds to take better care of the parklands we already have rather than to acquire new units that can't be adequately maintained. These funds should be used to refurbish roads, bridges, hotels, sewers, and tourist facilities in the national parks. A 5-year moratorium should be placed on the purchase of new parklands.	Increased maintenance and protection of existing parks is important but not at the expense of reducing funds for maintaining the irreplaceable land, water, and wildlife resources, which are the park system's major reason for existence. While talking about saving money, the administration abolished the Youth Conservation Corps, which did much of the maintenance in national parks at great savings to taxpayers while also giving valuable work experience to young people. Overcrowding and the increasing number of visits to parklands prove that more units are needed. All units already approved for purchase by Congress could be acquired for the cost of just one nuclear aircraft carrier and should be bought before key areas are lost either to development or to rising prices.
Existing park units near large urban areas should be returned to state and local ownership to reduce the federal budget.	These units were designed to bring parks to the people, especially poor and middle-class people who do not have cars. They are among the most successful and widely used units in the entire park system. State and local governments have neither the desire nor the funds to maintain these units.
Limited funds should be used to protect plants and animals already on the endangered species list and to improve the maintenance of existing wildlife refuges. A 5-year moratorium should be placed on purchasing additional wildlife refuges.	Improved maintenance of existing wildlife refuges is needed, but new units are also needed before satisfactory sites are lost to development and rising prices. Addition of species to the endangered list should not be slowed, because mere designation as an endangered species automatically offers a considerable degree of protection.

Since 1964 the major battle has been over how much land should be added to the wilderness system and whether too much land has already been added to the system. Wilderness enthusiasts have urged Congress to add more areas. They point out that under the guidelines defining wilderness no more than 4 percent of all the land in the United States excluding Alaska could ever be designated as wilderness. Since this land contains only about 1 percent of the nation's onshore oil and gas and only a small percentage of its mineral resources, it is argued that setting aside this much land as a form of ecological insurance would pose no threat to the nation's security and economic health. Political economist John Baden has argued that the best way to protect the National Wilderness Preservation System from eventual development might be to sell or give away the entire system to organizations dedicated to preserving wilderness, such as the Sierra Club, the Wilderness Society, and the National Audubon Society.

Timber and mining industries operating on public lands have opposed wilderness preservation. They accuse preservationists of wanting to lock up the woods for use as parks by the affluent and the physically fit. Timber companies also consider it a waste of the nation's natural resources when the National Forest Service and the National Park Service allow large tracts of timber in wilderness areas to go up in smoke because roads and motorized fire-fighting equipment are not allowed in these areas. Wilderness defenders, however, point out that the periodic fires that are caused by lightning clear out dead wood and underbrush, make room for new growth, and keep more mature trees from being destroyed by much hotter fires when flammable underbrush builds to high levels.

National Wild Rivers System   Another law protecting mostly primitive natural systems is the Wild and Scenic Rivers Act of 1968. Rivers chosen for the system must be outstanding in scenic, recreational, geologic, fish and wildlife, historic, cultural, or similar values. The act recognizes three types of rivers or sections of rivers as suitable for protection: **(1)** *wild river areas* that are primitive, free from impoundments, unpolluted, and generally inaccessible except by trails; **(2)** *scenic river areas* that are free of impoundments, still largely undeveloped and primitive, but possibly accessible in places by roads and railroads; and **(3)** *recreational river areas* that have undergone some impoundment or diversion in the past, are accessible by road or railroad, and may have some shoreline development. By 1984, over 60 rivers and river segments were in the system and a number of others were under consider-

ation. The entire system is administered by the departments of the interior and agriculture in cooperation with state agencies.

10-4   Parks

Park System in the United States   National, state, and local parks are reserved lands that get considerably more use than wilderness areas. They range from small urban street parks to state parks to large national parks such as Yellowstone. Most people think of parks as forested areas, but they include deserts, seashores, lakeshores, zoos, public beaches, monuments, and historic sites.

The national parks provide spectacular scenery on a scale not usually found in state or local parks, preserve wildlife that can't coexist with humans, and serve as buffer zones for wilderness areas. Camping, hiking, fishing, boating, and on-road motorized vehicles are permitted in national parks. However, consumption of resources, as in timbering, hunting, and mining, is not allowed in most Park System units.

Since 1872 the National Park System has grown to include 48 major parks, mostly in the West (Figure 10-3), and 287 national monuments, memorials, battlefields, historic sites, parkways, trails, recreational areas, rivers, seashores, and lakeshores that together make up about 3.5 percent of the nation's total land area. In the 1970s several parks that could be reached by mass transit were established near urban areas. The first two urban park units designed to bring the parks to the people were the Gateway National Recreational Area, which serves more than 20 million people in the Greater New York City area, and the Golden Gate National Recreation Area near San Francisco. Now these facilities are two of the most widely used units in the park system. For thousands of city kids these urban parks provide environmental education, a first overnight camping experience in the woods, and for some a first glimpse of open sea. Opportunities for enjoying nature are also provided for handicapped persons.

Stresses on Parks   The major problems of national and state parks come from their spectacular success. Between 1950 and 1984, annual visits to the almost 4,000 state parks increased from about 100 million to almost 700 million. During the same period visits to National Park System units increased from about 40 million to almost 335 million, with 18 million overnight stays. Most experts expect this trend to continue, putting increasing stress on already overburdened parks.

Under the onslaught of people during the peak summer season, some parks resemble the cities their visitors are trying to escape. The most popular ones are often overcrowded with cars and trailers and plagued by noise, traffic jams, litter, polluted water, drugs, and crimes. Thefts of timber, cacti, and petrified wood chips from national parks are a growing problem. In back country areas, hikers and Park Service rangers are sometimes harassed and assaulted by marijuana growers protecting planted areas with armed guards, patrol dogs, electronic warning systems, and explosive booby traps. Park Service rangers, now trained in law enforcement, must spend an increasing amount of their time acting in their capacity as law enforcement officers.

In some parks limited camping spaces can be reserved in advance through the Ticketron Company. Other sites are allocated on a first-come, first-served basis, with some vacationers waiting in a parking lot for two days for a campsite. People use parks in different ways. Some of the nation's 27 million RV campers arrive in expensive motor homes and enjoy "windshield vacations" by driving through parks and stopping at overlooks. Yet there are 27 million tent campers and 8 million backpackers. Some of the most remote trails in the Rocky Mountain National Park are so heavily traveled that the National Park Service has paved them to prevent erosion. Walkways have also been built over some fragile areas to provide access as well as protection. In some of the heavily used parks the number of hikers and campers in an area at a given time is restricted.

Some people want to turn the most popular and beautiful parks into highly developed recreation and convention centers with luxury hotels, restaurants, golf courses, swimming pools, tennis courts, ski villages, and similar facilities. Others argue that visitor centers and such recreational and housing facilities should be located in private or federally owned areas outside the national parks, as has been done for Arcadia National Park in Maine. They also believe that the use of motorized vehicles in parks should be discouraged by requiring high entry fees for private vehicles or banning them altogether. In parts of some parks such as Yosemite motor vehicles have been banned, and free shuttle buses bring visitors from satellite parking lots to the park interior.

The press of visitors and motor vehicles is not the only stress on national parks. A 1980 survey by the National Park Service revealed that scenic resources were threatened in more than 60 percent of the national parks, while visibility, air and water quality, and wildlife were endangered in about 40 percent of the parks. Some of these threats come from intensive use, but most come from mining, logging, grazing, and land development outside park boundaries. Glacier National Park is polluted by a nearby smelter. Planned geothermal energy development may take the steam out of the geysers in Yellowstone and Lassen National Parks. Nearby electric power plants cause haziness and air and water pollution in Mesa Verde, Zion, Bryce Canyon, Grand Canyon, and Everglades National Parks. Vital water resources are diverted away from Everglades National Park. Underground rivers in Mammouth Caves carry sewage from nearby communities. The list could go on.

As discussed in Section 10-2, government officials and park enthusiasts differ over how increased use of the nation's park system should be handled, and how the new threats should be met. Suggestions include (1) adding new parks or shifting scarce funds to better maintenance and conservation protection of existing parks, (2) transferring ownership of some national parks such as Gateway, Golden Gate, and other recently created urban parks to states and localities, (3) turning more of the management of camping, recreation, and educational activities in the parks to private concessionaires, (4) cutting visitor services to minimal levels at lesser used park units, and (5) sharply increasing entrance, activity, and concessionaire franchise fees to provide more funds for park maintenance and parkland acquisition. Regardless of the options chosen, the National Park Service faces new challenges in the continuing tension between its two basic purposes of providing for visitor enjoyment and conserving our irreplaceable resources for future generations.

10-5 Importance and Management of Forests

Commercial Importance of Forests Forests are renewable resources that normally can regenerate themselves within 10 to 500 years, depending on the species, climate, and soil. Unprotected forests tend to be heavily used for a variety of purposes, including recreation, mining, grazing, and obtaining firewood and lumber.

There are two basic kinds of lumber: hardwood and softwood. Hardwoods such as maple, oak, mahogany, and hickory are used primarily for veneer and furniture. Softwoods such as pine and spruce, often harder than hardwoods, are used as construction lumber and to produce pulp products (paper, rayon, and cellophane). They have more commercial importance than hardwoods because they are easy to harvest, have no large branches, produce long pulp fibers, and are ready for cutting in 10 to 40 years. About one-half of the world's timber cut each year is used as fuel for heating and cooking, one-third goes to sawlogs for construction and veneer, and one-sixth is converted to wood pulp used primarily for paper products.

Ecological Importance of Forests In addition to their commercial value as dead wood, live trees have vital ecological functions. As René Dubos reminds us, "Trees are the great healers of nature." They help control climate by influencing the wind, temperature, humidity, and rainfall. They add oxygen to the atmosphere and assist in the global recycling of water, oxygen, carbon, and nitrogen (Section 4-3). Forested soils absorb, hold, and slowly release water, thus recharging springs, streams, and underground aquifers and regulating the downstream flow of water. This regulation of water flow also helps reduce soil erosion, the amount of sediment washing into rivers and reservoirs (Section 8-6), and the severity of flooding. Forests also provide habitats for organisms that make up much of earth's genetic diversity; they help absorb noise and some air pollutants, and nourish the human spirit by providing solitude and beauty.

Economists typically evaluate forests in terms of their ability to provide firewood, timber, and wood for paper products, without considering the ecological benefits of trees. According to one calculation, a typical tree that lives 50 years provides, free, $196,250 worth of ecological benefits that are only about 0.3 percent of its sale value as dead wood. For example, a single tree produces $31,250 worth of oxygen, $62,500 in air pollution control, $31,250 in soil fertility and erosion control, $37,500 in recycling water and controlling humidity, $31,250 in shelter for wildlife, and $2,500 worth of protein. These important values of trees were recognized long ago in the old English proverb: "Those who plant trees love others besides themselves."

Ecological Factors Affecting Forest Growth and Management Just as agriculture is the cultivation of fields, **silviculture** is the cultivation of forests to produce renewable timber resources. Five major ecological factors affecting forest growth and health are **(1)** the physical environment, **(2)** characteristics of different tree species, **(3)** interrelations among trees and other plants, **(4)** interrelations among trees and animal life, and **(5)** natural ecological succession (Section 5-1).

The major factors in the *physical environment* of a forest are climate (average temperature and precipitation, Section 3-6) and the moisture, physical characteristics, and nutrients of the forest soil (Sections 8-3 and 8-4). Each tree species occurs naturally and grows well within a certain range of tempera-

ture and rainfall (Figures 3-11 and 3-12). Slope steepness and soil depth, type, and drainage determine the size and growth rate of trees, and to some extent the species present. In terms of both growth and forest diversity the most productive sites are those with well-aerated and drained soils on lower north-facing gentle slopes or in bottomlands. Walk along the lower north-facing slope of a mature forest area and you may find red oak, yellow poplar, birch, and sugar maple trees almost 30 meters (100 feet) high. By contrast, dry thin soils on exposed ridge tops or south-facing slopes are the least productive sites and contain dry-site species such as hickory and perhaps some pine.

Some of the major *characteristics of tree species* are **(1)** seeding and germination habits, **(2)** pattern of growth and growth rate in a particular soil and climate, **(3)** tolerance to shade, **(4)** space requirements, **(5)** size at maturity, and **(6)** resistance to damaging agents such as fire, diseases, and weather. One of the most important species characteristics is *tolerance to shade*: the ability of a particular tree species to grow in light that is reduced by the shade of other trees or nonwoody plants. *Shade-intolerant species* thrive in forest openings, while *shade-tolerant* species grow in dim light under the crown cover of larger trees. Most commercial tree species are shade intolerant and do best when grown under full sunlight in *even-aged stands*, where all trees begin growth from seeds or roots planted in the soil during the same year. Examples of shade-intolerant species are black cherry, yellow poplar, sycamore, white birch, black walnut, sweetgum, and loblolly pine. In deep shade these species cannot compete with shade-tolerant species such as sugar maple, beech, white spruce, hemlock, and dogwood. Species with intermediate shade tolerance include yellow birch, hickory, white oak, northern red oak, white pine, and red cedar.

The major factor governing the *interrelations among trees and other plants* is competition for space. Trees growing too close together compete for the same soil nutrients, moisture, and light and thus are small in diameter for their age. Selective thinning can be used to improve the quality and size of tree growth in an overcrowded area. Similarly, a large open area with only one or a few trees can often be seeded with additional trees.

Interrelations between forests and animal life are sometimes critical. For example, birds and squirrels disseminate tree seed. When humans eliminate all natural predators of deer in a forest, deer populations can explode and destroy much of the vegetation. Thus, ecological forestry involves maintaining a diverse array of natural habitats and, where possible, not eliminating animal populations natural to an area.

Natural ecological succession leads to a sequence of tree and other plant species best adapted to the existing climate and soil conditions (Section 5-1). Ideally, it is best to go with, not oppose, natural succession. By selective thinning and the creation of openings, however, it is possible to obtain conditions favorable to pioneer species such as white birch and aspen, which are beneficial to wildlife and have aesthetic appeal. Timber companies try to maintain plantations of even-aged stands of some single commercially desirable pioneer tree species for long periods. This is difficult, however, since it opposes the process of ecological succession.

Forest Management Foresters sometimes have conflicting goals of forest management and harvesting. Some view forests primarily in terms of economics and see themselves as caretakers of forestlands who are meeting the needs of people for timber and pulp products. They tend to emphasize the use of intensive silvicultural methods in which even-aged stands of fast-growing commercially valuable tree species are planted, treated with herbicides and periodically thinned to reduce competition from other species of limited commercial value, treated with pesticides to reduce threats from insects and destructive fungi, harvested in one or several cuts, and then reseeded. This approach is often cheaper than the alternatives and can produce the maximum yield of timber in the shortest time.

Other foresters see the forest as a homeland of diverse forms of plant and animal life, not just a commodity to be harvested with certain production quotas. Instead of planting tree farms they believe in encouraging the growth of tree species and forest types that have already become adapted naturally through geologic time to the climatic and soil conditions in a particular area. They see their role as friends rather than caretakers of the forest and are more concerned with 100- to 500-year tree rotation cycles than with short-term growth and harvesting cycles. This approach preserves the ecological integrity of the forest, works with rather than against natural ecological succession, can be productive and profitable for some species of trees with the proper climate and soil, allows natural controls to reduce susceptibility to attack by disease and insects, and rarely requires the use of expensive and potentially harmful fertilizers, herbicides, or pesticides. Depending on the climate, soil, and tree species being grown and harvested, both these silvicultural methods have a place in forest management.

The major silvicultural systems used for harvesting mature trees are summarized in the accompanying box.

Once an area has been cut by any harvesting method, *reforestation* is necessary if new trees are to be established on the site. Unless they are removed by whole-tree harvesting, some species such as aspen and coastal redwood reseed themselves by quickly sending up new growth from roots and stumps. Areas cut by selection and seed-tree methods can normally reseed themselves. Clearcut and shelterwood-cut areas can be reseeded from the air. For species such as pine it is necessary to plant tree seedlings rather than merely scattering seeds.

Protecting Forests from Fire, Diseases, Pests, and Pollution Protecting forests from fire, diseases, and insects is an important part of forest management. These three threats destroy about one-fourth of the net annual growth of commercially usable saw timber in the United States.

Fires started by a match or by lightning are the best-known threat to forests. According to the U.S. Forest Service, about 85 percent of all forest fires are started by humans, either accidentally or deliberately. The remaining 15 percent, causing about one-half of all damage, are triggered by lightning.

Since fires started by lightning have always been a factor in the environment, many grasses and trees have become adapted to fire. Grasses and pines are protected to some degree from fire because their buds are located deep in the center of leaves or needles. On the other hand, broadleaf species such as oaks are sensitive to fire because their buds are exposed. Redwood and giant sequoia trees are almost fireproof because their bark is very thick and contains no flammable resin. They are also practically immune to insect damage because their bark is loaded with tannin, a natural insect repellent.

In the early 1900s Gifford Pinchot, the first head of the U.S. Forest Service, began a policy of trying to prevent and fight all fires in the national forests. Since the 1950s Smokey the Bear has continued to spread the idea that *all* forest fires are bad. Smokey is credited with saving many lives and much wildlife from destruction, as well as avoiding losses of $20 billion.

It is important, however, to distinguish between two types of forest fire. **Crown fires** are intensely hot fires that can destroy all vegetation, kill wildlife, and accelerate erosion. They tend to occur in forests—especially those in the eastern half of the United States—where all fire has been prevented for several decades. In such areas so much dead wood and ground litter has accumulated that if this natural fuel does become ignited, there will almost certainly be a crown fire. In addition, long-term exclusion of fire alters the composition of forests by allowing fire-sensitive species to replace fire-resis-

Tree Harvesting Methods

Selection Cutting

Mature trees either singly or in small groups in a stand are cut at intervals to encourage younger trees to grow and produce an uneven-aged stand with trees of different species, ages, and sizes (Figure 10-4). If selectively cut openings are not large enough, the net effect is to increase the proportion of shade-tolerant trees such as sugar maple, beech, and redwood in the stand, while reducing the proportion of commercially important shade-intolerant trees such as black cherry, red oak, white birch, and yellow poplar. Although favored by those wishing to use forests for both timber production and recreation, this method can cause excessive erosion in some areas because of the periodic need to reopen logging roads and trails. A related method of cutting that is not considered a reputable forestry practice is called *high grading*. In this approach only the most desired commercial species of trees are cut, leaving only commercially undesirable species for reseeding.

Shelterwood Cutting

Many commercial tree species do best in sunlight, and for economic reasons are usually grown in an even-aged stand with trees of mostly the same species, size, and age. Such even-aged stands of shade-intolerant species are usually harvested by *shelterwood cutting, seed-tree cutting,* or *clearcutting*. Shelterwood cutting involves the removal of all mature trees in an area in a series of cuts over two or three decades. In the first stage unwanted tree species and dying, defective, and diseased trees are removed. Ten to fifteen years later the stand is cut further so that seedlings can receive adequate sunlight and heat and become established under the shelter of a partial canopy of remaining trees. When the seedlings have become well established, a third cut is used to remove the remaining mature canopy trees. This allows the new stand to develop in the open as an even-aged forest. This method leads to very little erosion and is particularly useful for species such as northern red oak, yellow poplar, basswood, hickories, white ash, red pine, and eastern white pine.

Seed-Tree Cutting

Nearly all trees on a site are harvested in one cut, with a few of the better commercially valuable trees left uniformly distributed on each acre to reseed the site. Seed-tree cutting is sometimes used for harvesting the four southern pine tree species (loblolly, longleaf, shortleaf, and slash). It is not used for most species because it has a high potential for erosion and sediment water pollution for a few years after the cut is made; in addition, the seed trees that are left may be brought down by wind or ice, and they may not produce enough seeds to reforest the area.

Clearcutting

All the trees are removed from a given area in a single cutting (Figure 10-5). This is done to establish a new, even-aged stand, usually of a commercially valuable, fast-growing species of shade-intolerant species such as Douglas fir, western white pine, jack pine, loblolly pine, lodgepole pine, black walnut, and black cherry. The clearcut area may consist of a whole stand, a group, a strip, or a series of patches (Figure 10-6). As the new forest grows, thinning and improvement cuts are made periodically to reduce overcrowding and to improve the species composition and quality of the remaining trees. Timber companies prefer clearcutting even-aged stands because it permits rapid and efficient regeneration of shade-intolerant species, reduces harvesting costs and road requirements by concentrating all cutting in a limited area, and permits the use of genetically improved tree planting stock of commercially valuable species. Clearcut areas also improve the forage for many game animals such as deer and elk, and clearcut areas of at least 100 acres provide habitats for various shrubland species of birds. Environmentalists and ecological foresters recognize that clearcutting can be useful in some cases if it is not overdone. However, they have opposed large-scale clearcutting because it is done for purely economic not ecological reasons, is overused on species that could be cut by other less ecologically destructive methods, can lead to severe erosion and sediment water pollution if done in large cuts on steeply sloped land, creates ugly scars (Figure 10-5) that take years to heal, reduces recreational values of the forest for years, destroys habitats for many wildlife species, and replaces a diverse stand of trees with a monoculture of even-aged trees that are often susceptible to damage from insects and diseases.

Whole-Tree Harvesting

After a machine has been used to pull a tree from the ground, the tree is reduced to small chips about half the size of a matchbox by using a large disk with several massive blades. This approach increases productivity and reduces waste by using all the harvested tree. Most ecologists, however, are strongly opposed to this method because by leaving no nutrients for chemical recycling (Section 4-3), it encourages rapid degradation of forest lands.

Figure 10-4   Selective cutting of old trees in a climax forest.

U.S. Forest Service

Figure 10-6   Patch clearcutting.

USDA

Figure 10-5   Clearcutting of redwoods.

Dave Van de Mark

tant species. In such forests Smokey the Bear is right in urging us to help prevent fires.

Ground fires are low-level fires that typically burn only undergrowth and occasionally damage some fire-sensitive trees. They normally do not harm mature trees, and wildlife can generally escape them. Indeed such fires can be beneficial to some forests and wildlife. Ground fires that occur every 3 to 5 years, in areas where a large amount of ground

litter has not accumulated, can help prevent the hotter and more destructive crown fires by burning away this potential fuel. They also help release and recycle valuable nutrients tied up in litter and undergrowth, increase the activity of nitrogen-fixing bacteria, stimulate the germination of certain seeds, and help control disease; in addition, they can wipe out infestations of insects that harm or kill trees. Some conifers such as giant sequoia, lodgepole pine, and jack pine cannot regenerate without fire because their seeds are released only when exposed to the intense heat of a forest fire. Some wildlife species, such as deer, moose, elk, muskrat, woodcock, and quail, depend on periodic ground fires to maintain their habitats and to provide food from the vegetation that sprouts after fires. Many water birds, songbirds, and the endangered California condor (Section 11-2) depend on fire to provide open and treeless spaces for feeding and nesting.

Because of these benefits, ecologists and foresters have increasingly prescribed the use of carefully controlled ground fires as an important tool in the management of some rangelands and forests. Ground fires are particularly useful in forests dominated by conifers such as giant sequoia and Douglas fir. Ground fires that occur in some conifer national forests and park areas in the West are now allowed to burn under supervision, to be sure they do not become crown fires. In other areas the Forest Service and the National Park Service use teams of foresters, wildlife biologists, and scientists to determine where ground fires should be set to clear out ground litter and improve the health of certain areas. Such prescribed fires are carefully controlled and are not started unless the wind speed, temperature, and forest moisture are all at acceptable levels. While such fires are good for some national parks and forests, their thick smoke can ruin summer tourists' views of scenery.

Forest fires get the most publicity, but diseases and insects cause much more forest destruction in the United States and throughout the world. Parasitic fungi cause most diseases that damage trees. These diseases include chestnut blight, Dutch elm disease, white pine blister rust, and oak wilt. Dutch elm disease, carried by insects from tree to tree, has killed more than two-thirds of the elm trees in the United States. It was probably brought to the United States accidentally on a shipment of elm logs from Europe. The best methods for controlling tree diseases include **(1)** banning imported timber that might carry alien parasites, **(2)** treating diseased trees with antibiotics, **(3)** developing disease-resistant species, **(4)** identifying and removing dead, infected, and susceptible trees, and **(5)** reducing air pollution—especially sulfur dioxide, ozone, and nitrogen dioxide—which can damage and kill trees and make them susceptible to disease (Section 19-4). Fungicides may cause more problems than they cure by retarding tree seed germination and also by killing beneficial fungi and earthworms in the soil.

Destruction by insects is another serious problem. Some highly destructive insect pests are the spruce budworm, the gypsy moth, the pine weevil, the larch sawfly, and several species of pinebark beetle. As discussed in Section 9-9, pest control methods include isolating and removing infested trees, introducing other insects that prey on the pests, using sex attractants to lure insects to traps, releasing sterilized male insects to reduce the population growth of pest species, using integrated pest management, and using natural insect control by preserving forest diversity.

A new threat to many of the world's forests, especially in Europe and eastern North America, is *acid deposition*, commonly called acid rain. It occurs when sulfur and nitrogen oxide air pollutants released by the burning of fossil fuels in power plants and cars are transformed chemically in the atmosphere to sulfuric and nitric acids that fall to the earth in rain, snow, or fog, or as dry acidic particulate matter (Section 19-4).

Though the precise mechanism by which acid deposition may be damaging trees is not known,

Table 10-3 Distribution of Forest Areas Throughout the World and Within Continents

Region	Percentage of World's Total Forest Area	Percentage of Continent's Land Area Still Forested
Latin America	34	47
Soviet Union	22	41
North America	17	34
Asia	11	19
Africa	10	27
Europe	4	36
Oceania and Australia	2	22

Source: *The Global 2000 Report to the President* (1980).

evidence is mounting that it is a major threat to forests in Poland, Czechoslovakia, France, the United Kingdom, East and West Germany, the Scandinavian countries, and eastern North America. By 1983, for example, more than one-third of West Germany's forests showed signs of damage. During the early stages, nutrients such as nitrogen added to the soil by acid deposition can increase tree productivity and growth. Eventually, however, it is hypothesized that enough acids can build up in the soil to leach out vital nutrients such as toxic aluminum that can attack the root system of a tree, making it less able to take up moisture and more susceptible to attacks from insects and drought. The major solution to this problem involves using air pollution control devices on fossil-fuel burning plants and cars to reduce emissions of sulfur and nitrogen oxides (Sections 19-5 and 19-6).

10-6 Status of World and U.S. Forests

World Forests Wherever civilization has flourished, forests have been destroyed, reducing the earth's original forested area by at least one-third and perhaps one-half. Today about one-third of the world's land area is covered with forests. Forests are not distributed uniformly among countries or continents, as shown in Table 10-3 and Figure 3-13. North America, Latin America, and the Soviet Union contain about three-fourths of the world's remaining forests. The four countries with the largest forests are, in order, the Soviet Union, Brazil, Canada, and the United States. Most of Africa and Asia and parts of Central and South America have little forest (Figure 3-13). Only about 11 percent of India's land and 9 percent of China's is under adequate tree cover. As a result of clearing for farming and grazing and overcutting for lumber and fuelwood, the world's forests are shrinking by almost 1 percent a year.

Threats to the World's Tropical Moist Forests The two types of tropical moist forests are tropical rain forests and tropical seasonal forests. These forests stretching across parts of Asia, Africa, and Latin America (Figure 3-13) are the world's most diverse, most productive, and least understood biomes (Section 3-8). Tropical moist forests in Latin America contain about one-third of the world's remaining forest area. This includes the Amazon, the world's largest continuous tropical moist forest—equal in size to the continental United States.

At the 1982 meeting of the United Nations Environmental Program (UNEP) in Nairobi, diminution of the world's tropical forests was seen as one of the major environmental problems of the 1980s and 1990s. About one-third of the original expanse of the world's tropical forests has already been cleared or seriously degraded. Africa has lost over 50 percent of its original tropical moist forests, over 42 percent of Asia's have disappeared, and 66 and 37 percent of those in Central America and in Latin America, respectively, are already gone or seriously depleted. Although two-thirds of the original expanse of these irreplaceable forests remains, the present destruction rate of about 0.6 percent a year is expected to increase as tropical LDCs try to develop their resources.

Ecologists have urged tropical nations with such forests to use more responsible tropical forestry practices and have called MDCs to provide funds and technical advice to help tropical LDCs conserve large areas of these vital resources. Otherwise they warn that at least one-half of the world's remaining tropical forests may be gone within the next 50 to 80 years, posing a threat to people in both LDCs and MDCs, as well as to wildlife that inhabit these forests. Ecologists warn that in coming decades, wholesale extermination of many thousands of tropical species through tropical deforestation could greatly hinder efforts to develop new hybrids of food to support future green revolutions (Section 9-8) and new medicines to fight disease (Section 11-1).

Many of the direct causes of the increased rate of tropical deforestation are a result of tropical LDCs trying to become MDCs by partially or completely clearing their forests for growing crops, grazing livestock, gathering firewood, mining, and commercial logging. The indirect causes of such deforestation are poverty, land ownership patterns that favor a few wealthy landowners, unemployment, rapid population growth, and the failure of governments to regulate national and multinational timber companies. The export of lumber cut from tropical forests and beef from cattle grazing on forests converted to pasture can, in the short term, provide a LDC with valuable foreign capital. Without appropriate reforestation and conservation programs, however, the long-term result is forest eradication, with a potentially renewable resource converted into a nonrenewable resource.

When tropical forests are clearcut for timber, agriculture, or grazing they are more difficult to reestablish than temperate forests. Irreversible destruction of these forests is also encouraged because governments seldom require timber companies to replant clearcut areas. In a clearcutting operation in Papua, New Guinea, a company paid the government a royalty for each acre cleared, but the amount was only one-tenth of what it would cost the government to replant each denuded acre.

Timber companies that cut roads into virgin forests are usually followed by poor people looking for land on which to grow subsistence crops. With or without government support, landless farmers cut, burn, and clear a section of the forest, plant crops for several years until the soil is exhausted, and then move deeper into the forest to repeat this shifting slash-and-burn type of cultivation. In Brazil ranchers also clear tropical forest areas or take over soil-depleted areas abandoned by subsistence farmers and transform them into grasslands for grazing. After a few years these areas can no longer be used for grazing without adding large quantities of expensive fertilizer. Ranchers, like slash-and-burn farmers, then find it easier and cheaper to clear new areas for pasture—thus accelerating deforestation.

In 1982 Dr. Ira Rubinoff, director of the Smithsonian Tropical Research Institute, proposed that 1,000 reserves consisting of 250,000 acres each be set aside in the 49 nations that have most of the world's tropical moist forests. This would protect about one-tenth of the world's remaining tropical moist forests from development and destruction. Such a system of reserves would be administered by an international organization such as the World Bank and financed by annual donations or assessments from MDCs.

Suggestions by ecologists and foresters for reducing the destruction of the tropical moist forests not included in this proposed ecological reserve system include: **(1)** securing commitments by governments to plant many more trees; **(2)** requiring timber companies and consumers in MDCs who benefit most from logging these forests to bear a greater share of the costs of reforestation; **(3)** identifying areas in which soils under tropical forests are best suited for various purposes, on a renewable basis, and concentrating each type of use on appropriate patches by zoning areas for their best use; **(4)** using agroforestry techniques by simultaneously planting fast-growing tree crops and food crops on newly cleared forest land, so when the soil is exhausted for growing crops the new trees are well on the way to restoring the forest; and **(5)** greatly increasing the funding for research on tropical soils and development of agriculture, grazing, and silviculture practices more suitable to these areas. The Worldwatch Institute estimates that between 1983 and 2000 the rate of tree planting in tropical areas will have to be increased more than 13 times to meet projected needs.

World Firewood Crisis Over 2 billion people, including 90 percent of the people in the LDCs, depend on wood as their principal fuel for heating and cooking. This use alone accounts for about 80 percent of the wood cut in LDCs and almost one-half of the timber cut in the world. One out of four people on earth lives in areas where the collection of wood for fuel outpaces new growth, and shortages are expected to increase in the future. Many poor people, most of them women, must walk for a full day to collect only several days' supply of fuelwood. The World Bank projects that the rate of firewood planting in LDCs (excluding China) must increase fivefold between 1980 and 2000 to avoid enormous ecological and economic costs.

This scarcity of fuelwood accelerates deforestation especially in areas near villages and cities where commercial markets for firewood and charcoal exist. Food shortages in many LDCs are also made worse by firewood scarcity and increased firewood prices. Crop yields are decreased when families who cannot afford firewood burn dried cow dung instead of returning it to the soil as fertilizer.

Some of the suggestions for dealing with the firewood crisis are: **(1)** promoting government-supported community forestry projects in which representatives from each household form a forestry association to encourage villagers to plant, tend, and harvest local woodlots, with the wood distributed among the households and proceeds from any marketable surplus used to support community development projects, as is being done successfully in South Korea; **(2)** having government foresters act as extension agents who help individuals and communities by providing seed or fuelwood planting stock and giving advice on getting the trees started; **(3)** planting fast-growing fuelwood trees and shrubs in unused patches of land, with emphasis on using local species and introducing new species carefully to ensure that they do not take over large areas of land more suitable for other purposes; **(4)** using

agroforestry to grow both crops and fast-growing fuel trees in certain areas; **(5)** increasing funding for reforestation by government foresters and community forestry groups; **(6)** helping reduce the 90 percent waste of the heat given off when fuelwood is used to cook food over an open fire by using locally produced and efficient wood stoves, solar cookers, and small biogas plants that produce methane gas from organic wastes and leave fertilizer ash as a by-product; and **(7)** population control (Chapter 7).

Forests and National Forests in the United States During the 250 years since the first colonists arrived, the original forested area in the United States has been reduced by about 45 percent. Since 1920, however, the total forested area has remained about the same. Today about one-third of the land area in the United States is forested (Figure 10-7).

About two-thirds of these forests are classified as commerical forest land suitable for growing potentially renewable crops of economically valuable tree species. The remaining third consists of noncommercial forests either reserved for use as parks, wildlife habitat, and wilderness or not capable of producing much commercially valuable timber per acre.

Congress set aside the national forests in the late 1800s to prevent them from being depleted by private timber interests, to set up future reserves of timber for the nation, and to protect watersheds. Today the National Forest System contains 155 individual national forests (mostly in western states: Figure 10-3) and 19 grasslands managed by the U.S. Forest Service in the Department of Agriculture according to the principles of sustained yield and multiple use. The national forests make up only 18 percent of the nation's commercial forestland and about 4 percent of the total U.S. land area. However, they contain 32 percent of the nation's total volume of timber and 51 percent of the softwood sawtimber trees, which provide most of the lumber and plywood used in construction as well as much of the pulp.

In 1900 all the lumber used in the United States was cut from private lands. Until 1950 the Forest Service had a stewardship role as custodian of the timber growing in the national forests. Since 1950, because of the economic boom after World War II and the depletion of many of private commercial forests, timber companies have increasingly looked to the national forests to supply timber for domestic use and export. Between 1950 and 1983 the percentage of lumber that is cut from public lands each year and used domestically increased from 15 to 40 percent.

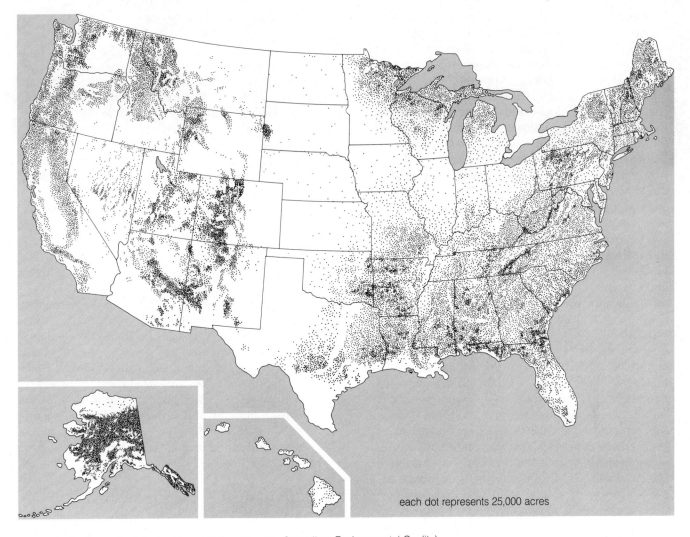

each dot represents 25,000 acres

Figure 10-7 Forest lands in the United States. (Source: Council on Environmental Quality)

National forest areas are also used at little or no charge by an increasing number of picnickers, hikers, campers, hunters, skiers (most commercial ski areas are in national forests), and fishing and boating enthusiasts, having received about 233 million visits for recreational purposes in 1982. Almost every American also uses the national forests indirectly, since they receive, store, and make available most of the nation's water supplies. Increasingly these forests are also being used for illegal purposes such as drug smuggling, marijuana growing, and unauthorized cutting of timber. More than 4 million big-game animals—nearly half the nation's supply—plus numerous species of fish and many of the nation's endangered wildlife species (Section 11-2) also make their homes in the national forests.

Because of these growing and often conflicting demands on national forest resources, the Forest Service has been the subject of heated controversy since the 1960s. Timber company officials complain that the Forest Service does not allow them to buy and cut enough timber on public lands, especially in the national forests of the Pacific Northwest, which contain more than 35 percent of the nation's total inventory of Douglas fir and other softwood species. Most mature trees on land owned by timber companies in this region have already been cut. Company officials argue that restricting the amount of timber they can cut from national forests causes timber shortages and increases the price for houses, furniture, and paper. They also argue that increased cutting in national forests—even if it temporarily violates the principle of sustained yield—is needed over the next few decades if trees replanted on land owned by timber companies are to have a chance to mature.

Environmentalists charge that the allocation of funds in the annual budget of the Forest Service has resulted in timber production and mining becoming the favored uses of the national forests.

Historically the overall volume of timber the Forest Service sells to timber companies for cutting on selected sites has not exceeded the overall rate of growth in the National Forest System. In certain areas, however, the rate of cutting has exceeded the rate of growth. Congress also left a loophole in the National Forest Management Act of 1978 that allows the Forest Service to raise timber harvests beyond the sustained yield in a national forest for a specific number of years. Proposals by the Reagan administration in the early 1980s to abandon the principle of sustained-yield management and a court-blocked attempt to sell some national forest lands to private interests intensified this controversy.

Environmentalists argue that the annual cut in the national forests should not exceed sustained yield and should approach sustained yield only if timber companies are making every effort to reforest lands they own. They point out that much of the land owned by timber companies is not reforested. Instead it is stripped of trees and sold for many times its original cost as building lots and suburban residential developments. Environmentalists fear that as long as these land development operations are more profitable than timber replanting, lumber companies will rely on leases for cutting on federal and state-owned forests to maintain their timber supplies. They also point out that the government encourages excessive timber cutting in the national forests by subsidizing the timber companies' costs of reforestation and building and maintaining roads to areas to be cut. Environmentalists argue that timber companies would be encouraged to reforest and better manage their own lands, and fewer taxpayer dollars would be wasted, if the government (1) decreased rather than increased the annual allowable cut in the national forests, and (2) required timber companies to share in the cost of reforestation and road building in public forests.

Environmentalists have also charged that large-scale clearcutting in the national forests, especially in the 1960s and early 1970s, violated the multiple-use concept by degrading soil and water quality and by making some national forest areas unsuitable for recreation for long periods (Figure 10-6). The argument is not whether clearcutting should be banned in national forests, but how much should be allowed and under what control.

Congress eased this controversy by passing the National Forest Management Act of 1976. This law allows clearcutting in national forests but only under strictly controlled conditions and after trees have reached a minimum age. It is not allowed in large-scale cuts, on steep slopes, on unstable soils, or on lands where the cuts do not blend with the natural terrain. If this law is strictly enforced, it should go a long way toward protecting the national forests.

10-7 Rangelands

Nature of Rangelands Land on which the vegetation is predominantly grasses, grasslike plants, or shrubs such as sagebrush is called **rangeland.** Rangeland provides people and many forms of wildlife with an essential service. Most animals, including people, cannot digest the grasses and shrubs, known as *forage*, that cover these lands. Ruminant animals like sheep and cattle, however, can digest this vegetation and convert it to forms of food that humans can digest. These livestock animals also provide useful nonedible goods such as wool, leather, and tallow.

About one-third of the total land area of the United States consists of rangelands, mostly in the western half of the nation (Figure 10-8).

About 54 percent of all U.S. rangeland is owned and managed by the federal government, mostly by the Forest Service and the BLM. About three-fourths of government and privately owned grassland is actively grazed by domestic animals at some time during each year. Ungrazed rangeland is either too isolated or in too poor condition to support grazing. Mineral and energy resource development—especially oil shale, coal, copper, phosphate, sand, and gravel mining—also take place on publicly owned rangelands.

Characteristics of Rangeland Vegetation Many rangeland weeds and bushes have a single main taproot and can thus be easily uprooted. By contrast, rangeland grass plants have a fibrous taproot system with millions of branches that make such plants very difficult to uproot. This explains why these grasses help prevent soil erosion (Figure 8-6).

For most plants, when the leaf tip is eaten, no further leaf growth occurs. By contrast, each leaf of rangeland grass grows from its base, not its tip. When the upper 50 percent of the stem and leaves of rangeland grass is eaten by livestock or wild herbivores such as deer, antelope, and elk, it can grow back to its original length in a short time. However, the lower 50 percent of the plant, known as the *metabolic reserve*, must be left if the plant is to survive and grow new leaves. As long as only the upper half is eaten, rangeland grass is a renewable resource that can be grazed again and again.

Rangeland Carrying Capacity, Overgrazing, and Desertification Much damage to rangelands has occurred because of failure to realize that each type and area of rangeland has a certain *carrying capacity*—that is, the number of animals that can be sup-

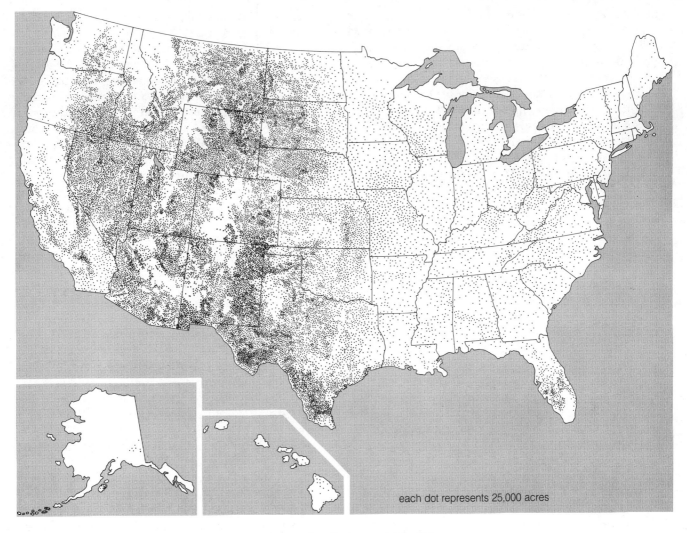

Figure 10-8 Rangelands in the United States. (Source: Council on Environmental Quality)

each dot represents 25,000 acres

ported and kept in good condition in a given area without damage to the range vegetation and soil. Carrying capacity varies with the climate, soil, and type of vegetation.

If the carrying capacity of a rangeland area is exceeded, herbivores start eating the metabolic reserve, often clipping the grass to the bare ground. This *overgrazing* can kill the root system of grass (Figure 10-9). Then either unpalatable weed and shrub invader species take over or all the vegetation disappears, leaving the land barren and vulnerable to erosion. Such overgrazing causes the normal carrying capacity of a rangeland to decrease, sometimes to zero. Restoring overgrazed lands is very difficult and expensive. During the 5- to 10-year period required for restoration, the amount of animals grazing per acre must be decreased or even eliminated.

Climate—especially drought—is also a factor in rangeland damage. Ideally, the number of live-

USDA, Soil Conservation Service

Figure 10-9 Fence separates a highly productive rangeland (left) from an overgrazed area (right).

stock per acre should be reduced in dry years. A widespread drought, however, can cause higher prices for hay or grain used as supplemental feed and lower market prices for livestock. This encourages ranchers to keep excessive numbers of livestock on a range in hopes that the next year will bring more rainfall and higher meat prices.

Sometimes productive rangeland is converted into desert, in a process called *desertification*, through a combination of overgrazing and prolonged drought. The U.S. Agency for International Development has estimated that about 650,000 square kilometers (250,000 square miles) of once productive grazing land along the southern edge of the Sahara have become desert during the past 50 years, and this process is continuing there and in many other arid regions of the world.

According to the U.S. Council on Environmental Quality, one-third of U.S. rangeland (excluding Alaska) is in fair condition and one-third in poor condition; only 15 percent is in high-quality condition. Although much of the overgrazing on public lands took place in the past, the practice continues primarily because of low public land grazing fees. For example, in 1983 grazing fees per animal per month on publicly owned rangeland were about five times less than comparable grazing rates on privately owned rangeland. This means that U.S. taxpayers in effect provide ranchers with federal grazing permits at a subsidy of at least $30 million a year—an average of about $2,110 a year for each rancher using these lands.

Earl Sandvig, who used to run grazing programs for the Forest Service, has suggested the elimination of the grazing permit system and, instead, the sale of grazing rights by competitive bids, as is done for timber cutting rights in national forests. This would also help eliminate complaints by ranchers without federal grazing rights that this economic subsidy is given primarily to ranchers who either have had these permits for many decades or have sold their permit rights to successive owners.

Rangeland Management The major tools used in rangeland management are (1) controlling the number and kinds of grazing animals allowed on a given area of rangeland; (2) controlling the distribution of grazing animals by herding, the use of fences, and rotating stock, and proper placement of supplies of water, salt, and supplemental feed; (3) suppressing the growth of undesirable vegetation and encouraging the growth of desirable vegetation by using herbicides, prescribed burning, and in some cases fertilization and reseeding; (4) using poisons, trapping, and hunting to control herbivores such as jackrabbits and prairie dogs that compete with livestock for forage, and livestock predators such as coyotes.

The first two methods are more widely used because experience has shown that the last two approaches are often too expensive, ineffective, or both. Since cattle, sheep, and wild grazing animals often have different food preferences, the proper number of each type can usually graze on the same rangeland. If certain plants have decreased, grazing animals that feed on these plants must be excluded or reduced until the vegetation recovers.

Some types of livestock and breeds of the same type of livestock are better adapted to one type of rangeland than another. For example, sheep normally do better than cattle on rangeland that is steep and hilly and on which shrubs predominate over grasses. Sheep breeds that tend to band together in herds require a herder to keep them moving to prevent overgrazing and are preferred when ranges are unfenced or predatory animals are common. When there is little danger from predators or on fenced rangelands, breeds of sheep that scatter usually make more even use of rangeland.

Although fencing and herding are expensive, they are very effective in moving livestock from one rangeland area to another to prevent overgrazing or to allow overgrazed areas to recover. Other highly effective and less expensive methods for distributing livestock over rangeland areas involve the strategic location of waterholes and salt blocks. Livestock need both salt and water, but not together. Placing salt blocks in ungrazed areas away from the water sources causes livestock to use these areas rather than congregating and overgrazing vegetation near streams, wet meadows, and waterholes.

Prescribed burning can be used to remove undesirable invader plants and shrubs such as mesquite and to encourage new growth of some desirable grasses. On a long-term basis, however, burning can lead to rangeland degradation by destroying or suppressing the growth of desirable plant species, encouraging invasion by weeds, and promoting soil erosion by destruction of vegetational cover. Herbicides can also be used, normally by aerial spraying, to suppress undesirable plant species. This method, however, is usually too expensive for widespread use over large rangeland areas.

Overgrazed land is invaded not only by pioneer weed species but also by animals such as kangaroo rats, jackrabbits, and ground squirrels, which are considered pests by most ranchers. Numerous studies have shown that the best and cheapest way to allow overgrazed land to recover is to exclude grazing by using barbed-wire fencing rather than spending large amounts of money and time on controlling such pest herbivore species.

Many ranchers still promote the use of poisons, trapping, and shooting to kill off coyotes, foxes, predatory birds, cougars, and other forms of wildlife that sometimes prey on livestock. For example, since 1940 a highly controversial predator control program has been waged primarily by western ranchers against the coyote. As such predator populations are reduced, however, the populations of rodents and rabbits that they prey on and keep under control grow unchecked and compete with livestock for rangeland vegetation. Thus, in the long run extermination or drastic reduction of natural predator populations can reduce rangeland productivity and cause larger economic losses than that from livestock killed by predators.

In 1972 the trapping and poisoning of predatory animals on leased federal grazing lands was banned by executive order of President Nixon. Shortly thereafter the EPA canceled the use of several of the poisons commonly used against predators, even on private land. In 1982 President Reagan, under pressure from western sheep ranchers, revoked the earlier executive ban on the use of the controversial and highly poisonous compound 1080 (sodium fluoroacetate) to kill the small percentage of coyotes that prey on sheep. This deadly compound had been banned because its widespread use by sheep ranchers had killed thousands of nontarget animals, including eagles, hawks, prairie falcons, great horned owls, bobcats, bears, badgers, raccoons, dogs, and many coyotes that had not preyed on sheep. It had also caused 13 proven and 5 suspected deaths of humans before 1963. Environmentalists argue that experiments with llamas and certain breeds of sheep dogs are effective in warding off predator attacks on livestock.

In this chapter you have seen that trying to achieve a balance between the use and preservation of nonurban land resources is a complex, difficult, and controversial process. According to Edmund Burke: "People will not look forward to posterity who never look backward to their ancestors." This suggests that if people are brought up to feel a tie to the past, they can recognize a similar tie to the future, thus becoming more concerned about preserving forests, parks, wilderness, and rangelands for future generations.

The one process ongoing in the 1980s that will take millions of years to correct is the loss of genetic and species diversity by the destruction of natural habitats. This is the folly our descendants are least likely to forgive us.

Edward O. Wilson

Discussion Topics

1. How does the ecological land-use ethic differ from the idea of balanced multiple use of land and from the preservationist ethic?

2. Distinguish between wilderness, national parks, and national forests in terms of purpose and allowed uses.

3. Should more wilderness area be preserved in the United States? Why or why not?

4. Explain why few backpackers are getting back to nature in a fundamental sense. (Hint: Take a look at the technology involved in freeze-dried foods and Dacron-filled sleeping bags.) Should backpacking be encouraged? Why or why not?

5. Conservationists want people to know and appreciate wilderness, but they don't want wilderness areas intruded on and damaged by large numbers of people. How can this dilemma be resolved?

6. Discuss the pros and cons of each of the following suggestions for the use of national parks:
   a. Higher charges should be made for use.
   b. Reservations should be required.
   c. All cars and other private vehicles should be kept out.
   d. Campgrounds, lodges, and other facilities should be moved to nearby areas outside the parks.

7. Discuss the pros and cons of bringing "parks to the people" by establishing more new national and state parks near urban areas. Do you agree with the idea that existing national parks near urban areas should be returned to states and localities? Why or why not?

8. Argue for or against: **(a)** selling national forests and publicly owned rangelands to private interests, **(b)** selling national forests and publicly owned rangelands to state and local governments, **(c)** eliminating future purchases of new land by the federal government for use as wilderness, national parks, national forests, and national wildlife refuges. In each case relate your decision to your own life-style and consumption habits.

9. Outline a program for the management of the small tracts of privately owned woodlands, which make up 59 percent of the forests in the United States. Try to consult a local forester and visit nearby tracts to evaluate their condition and determine how they could be better managed.

10. Should all clearcutting be banned in national forests? Why or why not?

11. In what types of forest can prescribed fires be useful, and what are the benefits from such fires? In what types of forest can they be harmful?

12. What would probably be major characteristics of trees that should be (a) clearcut, (b) selectively cut, and (c) shelterwood cut or seed-tree cut?

13. What are some possible solutions to the firewood crisis that threatens many of the world's forests, especially in LDCs?

14. Because of the rising costs of oil, coal, and natural gas, more and more Americans are switching to wood stoves for heating and cooking. Discuss the pros and cons of this trend.

15. Should trail bikes, dune buggies, snowmobiles, and other off-road vehicles be banned from all national forests, parks, and wilderness areas? Why or why not?

16. Should the total amount of allowed cutting each year in the national forests be increased or decreased? Why?

17. Make a log of your use and consumption of wood and paper products for a single day and relate it to the increased demand for cutting timber in national forests.

18. Explain why you agree or disagree with each of the following statements concerning the use of national forests and wilderness.

   a. "We are not exploiters of a resource, we are harvesters of a resource at the behest of public demand." James R. Turnbull, executive vice-president of American Plywood Association.

   b. "We have the directive from God: 'Have dominion over the earth . . . replenish and subdue it. . . .' God has not given us these resources so we can merely watch their ecological succession." H. D. Bennett, executive vice-president of Appalachian Hardwood Manufacturers, Inc.

   c. "Preservationists are a selfish lot. Only a few are physically able or really want to have a wilderness experience. Ninety-nine percent of the people in New York City are never going to see it." Bernard L. Orell, vice-president of Weyerhauser Lumber and Paper Company.

   d. "If you've seen one redwood, you've seen them all." Ronald Reagan, President of the United States.

19. Explain how you indirectly contribute to the destruction of the world's tropical moist forests. What difference, if any, could the loss of these forests have on your life or on any child you might bring into the world?

20. Do you think that it is better for public land to be owned by the federal government or by state governments? Why?

21. Should private companies cutting timber from national forests continue to be subsidized by receiving federal payments for reforestation and for building and maintaining roads to areas to be cut? Why or why not?

22. Should private companies be allowed to sell for export timber that they cut from publicly owned national forests? Why or why not?

23. Should fees for grazing on federally owned lands be eliminated and replaced with a competitive bidding system? Why or why not? Why would such a change be politically difficult?

24. Explain how elimination of coyotes and other predators that sometimes prey on livestock can lead to a decrease in the number of livestock that can be supported per acre of rangeland.

25. Should the poisoning and hunting of livestock predators be allowed on federal rangelands? Why or why not? Try to have both a rancher and a wildlife scientist present to your class their viewpoints on this controversial issue.

11

Wildlife Resources

It is the responsibility of all who are alive today to accept the trusteeship of wildlife and to hand on to posterity, as a source of wonder and interest, knowledge, and enjoyment, the entire wealth of diverse animals and plants. This generation has no right by selfishness, wanton or intentional destruction, or neglect, to rob future generations of this rich heritage. Extermination of other creatures is a disgrace to humankind.

World Wildlife Charter

In the 1850s Alexander Wilson, a prominent ornithologist, watched a single migrating flock of passenger pigeons darken the sky for over 4 hours. He estimated that this flock of this most numerous bird in North America was 384 kilometers (240 miles) long and 1.6 kilometers (1 mile) wide and contained over 2 billion birds.

By 1914 the passenger pigeon (Figure 11-1) had disappeared forever. How could a species with such vast numbers become extinct in only a few decades? There are probably several reasons, including **(1)** the rapid spread of infectious diseases because these birds nested in dense colonies, **(2)** the inability of the species to recover once flock size was reduced because only one egg was laid per nest, and **(3)** the death of millions of birds in severe storms during their annual fall migration from North America to Central and South America.

Two additional reasons for the extinction of the passenger pigeon involve people. When land clearing for farms and cities destroyed their habitats and food supply, the rigid migration patterns of these birds kept them from moving to other breeding areas. The second human factor was hunting. Passenger pigeons made excellent eating and good fertilizer. They were easy to kill because they congregated in gigantic flocks. People used to capture one pigeon

alive, sew its eyes shut, and tie it to a perch called a stool in a clearing. Soon a curious flock alighted beside this "stool pigeon" and were shot or trapped by nets that might contain more than 1,000 birds. Beginning around 1858 massive killing of passenger pigeons became a big business. Shotguns, fire, traps, artillery, and even dynamite were used. Some live birds served as targets in shooting galleries. In 1878 one professional pigeon trapper made $60,000 by killing 3 million birds at their nesting grounds near Petoskey, Michigan. By 1896 the last massive breeding colony had vanished. In 1914 the last passenger pigeon on earth—a hen named Martha after Martha Washington—died in the Cincinnati Zoo. Her stuffed body is now on view at the National Museum of Natural History in Washington, D.C.

Does it really matter that a wild species such as the passenger pigeon became extinct and the existence of wild species such as the whooping crane and the Bengal tiger is threatened primarily because of human activities? In this chapter we will examine this question by looking at the importance, protection, and management of wildlife resources.

Figure 11-1 The extinct passenger pigeon. The last known passenger pigeon died in the Cincinnati Zoo in 1914.

Enrichment Studies 3, 5, and 6 are related to this chapter.

11-1 Importance of Wildlife and Wildlife Resources

How Many Species Exist? So far about 1.5 million different species of plants and animals have been identified worldwide. Scientists are continually adding to this list as better ways are found to identify and classify species (Table 3-1) and as new lands and waters are explored. Worldwide it is estimated that there may be between 5 and 10 million different species, with insect species far outnumbering all other kinds of life.

An estimated 60 to 80 percent of the world's different plant and animal species live only in the tropics. Although tropical moist forests cover less than 7 percent of the earth's surface (Figure 3-13), biologists estimate that they contain about 40 percent of all plant and animal species on earth.

Distinction Between Wildlife and Wildlife Resources All undomesticated species of plants and animals on earth can be classified as **wildlife** or **wild species**. Although this broad definition is used in this book, "wildlife" is sometimes defined more narrowly to consist only of animals such as mammals and birds, excluding species of plants and the vast number of invertebrate insect animal species.

Wild species that have some useful value to humans are known as **wildlife resources.** These are potentially renewable natural resources (Section 1-3) if not driven directly or indirectly to extinction or near extinction by human activities. Wildlife resources that provide sport in the form of hunting or fishing are classified as *game species.* Many game animals and sport fish are managed by wildlife resource biologists to protect endangered populations and to maintain healthy populations of desired species, as discussed in Sections 11-5 and 11-6.

Why Preserve Wild Species? The four basic arguments for not hastening the extinction of the wild species that inhabit the earth are summarized in the accompanying box. Let's look more closely at each of these arguments concerning the importance of the wild species that share the earth with us.

Economic Importance To most people certain wild species are important because of their actual or potential *economic value.* Most of the 16 plants, except wheat, that produce 90 percent of the world's food today (Section 9-2) were domesticated from species of wild plants, mostly found in the tropics. Existing

---

Reasons for Preserving Wild Species

1. The economic argument

Wildlife resources provide humanity with a wide variety of direct economic benefits as irreplaceable sources of food, medicines, scientific understanding, fuel, fibers, and building and industrial materials. Other wild species not classified as wildlife resources have the potential for producing direct economic benefits. History has shown that some of the most important discoveries of useful wildlife resources have come from unlikely and unpredictable sources.

2. The aesthetic-recreational argument

Many wild species are a never-ending source of beauty, joy, and recreational pleasure for humans.

3. The ecological argument

Wild species provide our own and other species with an array of indispensable ecosystem services that help maintain ecosystem integrity and life on this planet. Because the exact role of a species in an ecosystem may never be known, we cannot predict with certainty how the elimination of a species as a result of our activities may affect other species, including *Homo sapiens.*

4. The ethical argument

All living species on earth have an inherent right to exist. Destroying another species is ethically and morally wrong.

---

wild plant species, many of them still unclassified and evaluated, will be needed by agricultural scientists to develop new crop strains that have higher yields and increased resistance to diseases, pests, heat, and drought (Section 9-8).

On a worldwide basis wild species of fish supply about one-fourth of the animal protein directly consumed by humans. Their use in animal feeds also makes an indirect contribution to human protein consumption (Section 9-6). Wildlife biologists have suggested that African grazing animals such as wildebeest, antelopes, buffaloes, and warthogs could be herded and used as human food sources in Africa. These undomesticated species should produce higher yields of meat with fewer environmental problems than cattle, which are poorly suited to most African environments.

Certain natural predator insects, parasites, and disease-causing bacteria and viruses are increasingly being used for the biological control of various weeds and insect pests (Section 9-9). In Florida, for instance, citrus growers saved about $30 million a year through a one-time outlay of $35,000 for the importation from the tropics of three species of parasitic wasps that live off citrus crop pests. Various hormones and sex attractant chemicals are also extracted from insects and used to control insect pests (Section 9-9). In some parts of the world insects are eaten as a source of protein, and they may become an even more important food source in the future (Section 9-5). Pollination by insects is essential for many food and nonfood plant species.

Since the beginning of recorded history all or part of some wild plant species such as herbs have been used as medicines. Today in China 1,700 plants and in India at least 2,500 plants are used directly for medicinal purposes. About 40 percent of the prescription and nonprescription drugs now on the world market have active ingredients extracted from plants and animals, as shown in Table 11-1.

Nonhuman animal species have been widely used in research and experimentation to increase our understanding of human health and disease. Some examples include the use of (1) elephants under stress to study the origins of heart disease, (2) armadillos to study leprosy, (3) squid to learn how nerves function, (4) cotton-topped marmoset and owl monkeys to search for anticancer vaccines, (5) chimpanzees to test the safety of hepatitis vaccine, (6) rhesus monkeys to test smallpox, measles, mumps, and live polio vaccines, (7) mice, rats, chimpanzees, sponges, and rhesus monkeys to test for possible cancer-causing agents and toxic chemicals, and (8) mice, fruit flies, guinea pigs, wasps, butterflies, and sea urchins to get a better understanding of genetics and embryology.

Trees and plants are also sources of an enormous variety of useful materials such as (1) *wood* for construction, paper products, and fuel, (2) *fibers* (cotton, flax, and hemp), (3) *cooking oils* (safflower, peanut, olive, and soybean), (4) *lubricating oils and waxes* (jojoba oil from a desert shrub may replace sperm oil from sperm whales and thus help save this endangered species from extinction), (5) *oils used in varnishes and paints* (soybean, tung, linseed, and flax), (6) *dyes*, (7) *coffee and tea*, (8) *spices*, (9) *herbs*, (10) *scents* used in perfumes, soaps, and other products, and (11) *natural insecticides* (pyrethrum and rotenone).

Plants and trees not presently classified as wildlife resources may become future sources of energy and paper. Soon fast-growing trees and bushes may be planted in large *biomass energy plantations* and harvested for use as fuel to supplement or replace the world's dwindling oil supplies (Section 16-5). For example, fast-growing tropical *Leucaena* shrubs and trees in the pea family can be planted to provide firewood harvestable every 3 to 10 years. They also produce timber, nutritious forage for cattle, and rich organic fertilizer. Other scientists have suggested planting "petroleum plantations" of plants such as the tropical copaiba tree and some of the 2,000 varieties of plants of the genus *Euphorbia*, which produce an oillike material that could be extracted and either used directly to fuel vehicles or refined to produce gasoline. Less than

Table 11-1 Examples of Drugs Derived from Plants and Animals

Type of Drug or Condition	Examples
Amoebic dysentery	Ipecacuanha from the wild ipecac plant found in Brazil
Antibiotics	Penicillins from fungi; chloromycin, streptomycin, erythromycin, and tetracycline from bacteria, and other antibiotics from sea sponges
Anticancer agents	Vincristine from the rosy periwinkle plant (used with 80 percent success to treat Hodgkin's disease and acute lymphocytic leukemia); other chemicals from a variety of marine animals including segmented worms, clams, sea anemones, corals, mollusks, sea squirts, sharks, and stingrays
Anticoagulants (to stop blood from clotting)	Venom of Malayan pit vipers and extract from some seasnakes
Blood pressure control	Digitalis and related drugs from the purple foxglove flower; reserpine from rauwolfia; an extract from the octopus
Burns, skin irritations, and hemorrhoids	Gel from the aloe plant
Congestive heart failure	Digitalis from purple foxglove; extract from fireflies
Nasal decongestants	Ephedrine from a semidesert shrub
Pain killers	Morphine and codeine from the opium poppy; tetrodotoxins from puffer fish, porcupine fish, and sand fish
Schizophrenia	Mescaline from a spineless cactus plant; reserpine from rauwolfia
Skin wounds	Skin excretion from the Arabian Gulf catfish
Tranquilizers	Reserpine from the rauwolfia shrub

1 percent of the earth's plant species have been thoroughly studied for their possible usefulness to humans. As tropical moist forests are cleared, many potentially useful plant species and any animal species that depend on them will be wiped out forever—much like throwing away a present before removing the wrapping.

Commercially useful materials obtained from animals include silk, glue, leathers, musk (from deer), down feathers from geese and other birds, and fleeces such as wool, cashmere, llama, and vicuña. Some animal species, however, have been driven to extinction or near extinction because of the economic value of their skin (cheetah, tiger, vicuña, jaguar, and snow leopard), horns (rhinoceroses), ivory tusks (elephants), oil (sperm whales), or other parts (Section 11-2).

Aesthetic and Recreational Importance Many different species of plants and animals are a source of beauty, wonder, and joy to people everywhere. It is impossible to place a monetary value on experiences such as observing the leaves change color in autumn, smelling the aroma of wildflowers, or watching an eagle or sea gull soar overhead, or a porpoise glide through the water. A 1980 survey by the Fish and Wildlife Service indicated that nearly 100 million Americans (43 percent of the population) participated in some form of wildlife activity. In the process they spent $40 billion for travel and equipment.

Ecological Importance Some argue that the most important contributions of the wild species result from their roles in maintaining the health and integrity of the world's ecosystems. Ecosystem services provided by wild plant and animal species include provision of food from the soil and the sea, production and maintenance of oxygen in the atmosphere, filtration and detoxification of poisonous substances, moderation of the earth's climate, regulation of freshwater supplies, disposal of wastes, recycling of nutrients essential to agriculture, production and maintenance of fertile soil, control of the majority of potential crop pests and carriers of disease, maintenance of a vast gene pool from which humanity can draw, and storage of solar energy as chemical energy in food, wood, and fossil fuels.

Such ecosystem services are rarely incorporated into cost-benefit decisions regarding development primarily because it is difficult to assign a dollar figure to these services and because most decision makers are unaware how heavily we rely on these services. Because we still know relatively little about the workings of even the simplest ecosystems, we cannot be sure which species play crucial roles today, which ones have genes crucial for our survival and the survival of other species in the future, and how many species can be removed before an ecosystem collapses or suffers serious damage.

Ethical Importance Some believe that it is ethically and morally wrong for humans to hasten the extinction of a species. As environmental historian Roderick Nash (see *Readings* for Chapter 10) put it, "We must be concerned about conservation and environmental responsibility not because it is profitable or beautiful, and not even because it promotes our survival, but because it is *right.*"

Some believe that each individual wild creature has an inherent right to survive without human interference, just as each human being has the inherent right to survive. Such a philosophy, however, is essentially impossible to apply because it would be violated each time a person ate a plant or any kind of meat. Some make distinctions between the survival rights of plants and those of animals. The poet Alan Watts once commented that he was a vegetarian "because cows scream louder than carrots." Others make ethical distinctions between the killing of various types of animal. Most people, for instance, think little about killing a fly or mosquito, catching and killing fish, or having someone else kill hogs, cattle, or chickens to provide them with meat. The same people, however, might deplore the killing by hunters of unendangered game animals such as deer, squirrels, or rabbits.

In practice, most advocates of the ethical position argue that only a *wild* species—not each individual organism—has the inherent right to survive. This is based on the belief that the human species is no more important than any other species on earth. Many Native Americans, who occupied much of North America long before the arrival of white settlers, had such a philosophy. Anthropologist Stan Steiner has summarized the Hopi Indian philosophy of the sacred Circle of Life:

In the Circle of Life every being is no more, or less, than any other. We are all Sisters and Brothers. Life is shared with the bird, deer, insects, plants, mountains, clouds, stars, sun. To be in harmony with the natural world, one must live within the cycles of life.

One problem associated with extending such ethical concerns to all wild species is that in Western culture humans are usually viewed as the most dominant and supremely important species on earth. Under this value system, any other species and individual members of such species have a right to survive only as long as they make a contribution to human well-being. This conflict between human-centered (homocentric or anthropocentric) and earth-centered (ecocentric) value systems is discussed further in Chapter 22.

11-2 How Species Become Endangered and Extinct

Formation and Extinction of Species in Prehistoric Times The earth's present inventory of perhaps 5 to 10 million different species is believed to be the result of two biological processes—*speciation* and *extinction*—taking place over billions of years. It is estimated that 70 to 98 percent of the different species that at one time or another lived on the earth either have become extinct or have evolved into something sufficiently different to be identified as a new species. Speciation may take place when populations of the same species become reproductively isolated from one another by an ocean, a river, a jungle, or a high mountain range for 1000 to 100,000 generations. Then two new and distinct species can arise in response to the different environmental conditions experienced by each population (Section 5-2).

What appears in the fossil records as extinction can represent different processes. In many cases it involves the *development* by natural selection (Section 5-2) of a single species such as the horse over a long period of time. For example, the early equine species, known as the dawn horse, lived in dense semitropical forests and was only about 25 to 50 centimeters (10 to 20 inches) high. As the world's climate and vegetation changed, this early equine species gradually evolved into the much larger species of horse found today. Thus, although the dawn horse is extinct, many of its genetic traits are still present.

In other cases, certain species have gradually evolved, flourished, and suddenly vanished. For example, dinosaurs first evolved about 225 to 250 million years ago. They slowly grew in varieties and numbers for perhaps 25 to 50 million years until they inhabited almost every corner of the world and dominated the planet for about 135 million years—longer than any other order. By contrast, the human species is only a few million years old. About 65 million years ago, for reasons we probably shall never know, these outstanding evolutionary successes disappeared from the earth.

Despite such losses, the fossil records and other studies indicate that throughout most of the earth's history the average rate of new species gain through speciation has been a little faster than the average rate of species loss through extinction. Thus, the total number of living species on earth has generally increased over the ages.

Formation and Extinction of Species Today In contrast to prehistoric times, there is growing concern that the rate of species loss is beginning to run ahead of the rate of species gain. According to a number of biologists, there are two primary reasons for this change. First, human activities have increased the rate of extinction primarily through destruction of habitat, species overexploitation, and pollution. Second, opportunities for geographic speciation, which typically takes thousands to tens of thousands of years, have been reduced by the destruction, degradation, and homogenization of habitat throughout the earth to provide shelter, food, and other resources for the growing number of people.

Species heading toward extinction are often classified as either *endangered* or *threatened*. An **endangered species** is one having so few individual survivors that the species could soon become extinct in all or part of its range. Examples are the black-footed ferret, the eastern timber wolf, the pronghorn antelope, the blue whale, the whooping crane, and the California condor (Figure 11-2), the green turtle, and various species of plants—especially cacti and orchids. **Threatened species**, such as the grizzly bear, the bald eagle, and the American alligator, are still abundant in their range but likely to become endangered within the foreseeable future because of a decline in numbers.

Between 1975 and 2000, conservation specialist Norman Myers warns that at least 1 million of the world's 5 to 10 million species will probably have disappeared, primarily because of extensive clearing of the world's remaining tropical moist forests (Section 10-6). Most of these species will be plants and invertebrate animals such as insects, mites, and nematode worms that have yet to be classified and evaluated.

Although animal extinctions receive most of the publicity, plant extinctions are more important ecologically. Harold Koopowitz, head of the Arboretum at the University of California at Irvine, and other biologists such as Thomas Eisner estimate that about 10 percent of the world's plant species are already threatened with extinction and 15 to 25 percent of all plant species face extinction by the year 2000.

Major Causes of Extinction Today The major human-related factors that can lead to a species becoming threatened, endangered, or extinct are **(1)** *habitat disturbance and elimination,* **(2)** *commercial hunting,* **(3)** *pest and predatory control for protection of livestock and crops,* **(4)** *collecting specimens as pets, for medical research, and for zoos,* **(5)** *pollution,* and **(6)** *accidental or deliberate introduction of a new competing or predatory species into an ecosystem.* Some species

Bureau of Sport Fisheries and Wildlife, U.S. Department of the Interior

Figure 11-2 The whooping crane and the California condor are two endangered species in the United States.

are driven to extinction or near extinction by a single factor such as habitat loss, while others succumb to a combination of factors. Some species also have biological and behavioral characteristics that make them particularly vulnerable to extinction from human-related activities. Let's look more closely at these factors.

Habitat Disturbance and Loss   The greatest threat to plant and animal wildlife is the destruction or alteration of habitat: the area in which species seek food, find shelter, and breed. As the human population grows, it increases its habitat at the expense of the habitats of other creatures. This disruption of natural communities can threaten wild species by destroying migration routes, breeding areas, and food sources. Plant species unique to a small locality can be eliminated from the earth by a single bulldozer, as can the animals that feed on them.

Habitat disturbance has been a major factor in the disappearance of some of America's most magnificent bird species such as the ivory-billed woodpecker and in the near extinction of the whooping crane and the California condor, the largest land-flying bird in North America. The ivory-billed woodpecker formerly inhabited riverbottom hardwood forests in the southeastern United States. As virgin forests have been cut down and replaced by plantations of even-aged trees, the food source for this species (insects on standing dead timber) diminished to the point where no recent sightings of this bird have been reported.

Commercial Hunting   It is important to distinguish between three types of hunting: *commercial hunting, hunting for food,* and *sport hunting primarily for recreation.* At one time commercial hunting in the United States was an important factor in the extermination of species such as the American passenger pigeon and the near extermination of species like the American bison and the snowy egret.

In the late 1800s the snowy egret, which inhabits coastal regions of the southeastern United States, was hunted almost to extinction because the feathers were used to adorn women's hats. Egret plumes sold for $50 an ounce—and each ounce cost the lives of six courting male birds. In 1886 the newly formed Audubon Society began a campaign against this slaughter. Texas and Florida passed laws protecting plumed birds, but the laws were mostly ignored. Then in 1900 Congress passed the Lacey Act, which banned interstate traffic in illegally killed wildlife. This cut off the supply, and these beautiful birds began thriving again as parks, preserves, and refuge areas were established for the protection of wildlife species. The economic incentive for selling products from endangered species has been reduced in the United States by the Endangered Species Act of 1973, which made it illegal to import or to carry on trade in any product made from an endangered species. But U.S. customs officials and those in other nations assign a low priority to the wildlife trade.

Threatened species are supposedly protected by the 1975 Convention on International Trade in Endangered Species (CITES), signed by 81 nations, but enforcement is poor. According to experts at the World Wildlife Fund, illegal trafficking in wild animals and wildlife is flourishing and amounted to a $2 billion to $5 billion business in 1983.

On a worldwide basis commercial hunting threatens species such as the jaguar, the cheetah, the tiger, and the snow leopard (all hunted for their furs), alligators (skins), elephants (ivory tusks), Asian musk deer (musk oil for perfumes and soaps), and rhinoceroses (horns). For example, the number of African rhinos has been reduced from hundreds of thousands in 1950 to about 13,500 today, bringing them to the verge of extinction. Rhinoceros horn—a mass of compact hair—is worth as much as $5000 a pound because it is used to make Arabian dagger handles that certify the manhood of young men and is ground into a powder that is used to reduce fever and is thought by many Asians to be a sexual stimulant. Although 81 nations have agreed not to import or export the rhino horn, the illegal traffic goes on because poacher gangs usually outnumber and sometimes outgun rangers patrolling protected areas.

It is not surprising that Bengal tigers face extinction, since a coat made from their fur sells for $95,000 in Tokyo. Nor is it surprising that poor African villagers become illegal poachers, since the sale of a large pair of elephant tusks can provide them with the equivalent of 10 years' income. In 1978 alone between 100,000 and 400,000 African elephants were killed for their tusks, and in 1983 another 80,000 were slaughtered. Even when illegal wildlife smugglers are caught, the penalties are usually too low to hurt overall profits. In 1979 a Hong Kong fur dealer illegally imported 319 Ethiopian cheetah skins valued at $43,900. The dealer was apprehended, but paid a fine of only $1,540.

At one time *hunting for food* was also a major cause of extinction of some species. In the early 1880s, for instance, the eastern elk became extinct in the United States primarily because it was hunted commercially and privately for food and its hides. Today such hunting has declined in most areas. Species endangered today because of their food value include the giant tortoise (liver and flesh), Steller's albatross (eggs), the green turtle (flesh and eggs), Kemp's Ridley sea turtle (eggs), and several species of whales (mostly for use in pet food) and commercial fish (Section 11-6).

Sport hunting is closely regulated in most nations and endangers a game species only when such regulations don't exist or are not enforced. No animal in the United States, for instance, has ever been seriously reduced in population or exterminated by regulated sport hunting. In some areas, however, sport hunting does endanger some species. For example, hunters from many parts of the world go to West Central Africa to shoot bull giant sable ante-

Figure 11-3 The black-footed ferret is one of the most endangered mammalian species in the United States.

lopes, hoping to bring back their magnificent curved horns as a trophy. As a result, only about 500 to 700 of these animals remain in this portion of Africa.

Predator and Pest Control Extinction or near extinction can also occur because of attempts to exterminate pest and predator species that compete with humans and livestock for food. The Carolina parakeet was exterminated in the United States around 1914 primarily because it fed on fruit crops. Its disappearance was hastened because when one member of a flock was shot, the rest of the birds hovered over its body. Large numbers of endangered African elephants have been killed to keep them from trampling and eating food crops. Carnivore predators that sometimes kill livestock are also shot, trapped, and poisoned. Ranchers, hunters, and government employees involved in predator control programs have wiped out the timber wolf, the grizzly bear, and the mountain lion over most of the continental United States.

Sometimes the extermination of a particular species can upset the food webs and endanger other species. For example, campaigns to protect rangeland for grazing livestock by poisoning prairie dogs and pocket gophers have just about eliminated their natural predator, the black-footed ferret (Figure 11-3), now one of the rarest mammals in North America.

Pets, Medical Research, and Zoos Worldwide over 5.5 million live wild birds are sold each year, most

11 Wildlife Resources **197**

of them ending up in pet-loving nations such as the United States, Great Britain, and Germany. As a direct result of this trade, at least nine bird species are now listed as threatened or endangered. In 1980 over 128 million tropical fish, 2 million reptiles, 1 million other individual animals, and millions of wild plants were legally imported into the United States, mostly for sale as pets. Large numbers of these animals and plants die during shipment. Many others die after purchase or are killed or abandoned by their owners.

Some species of exotic plants such as orchids, lilies, palms, and cacti are also endangered because they are collected (often illegally) and sold to decorate houses, offices, and landscapes. Nearly one-third of the cactus species native to the United States are thought to be endangered because they are collected and sold for use as potted plants.

Medical research makes use of large numbers of animals. According to the Office of Technology Assessment, about 71 million animals are used each year in the United States for toxicity testing, biomedical and behavioral research, and drug development. About 60 million of the animals are mice and rats. The remaining 11 million animals that are poisoned, irradiated, suffocated, blinded, driven insane, dismembered, or otherwise killed or harmed in laboratories each year are dogs, cats, monkeys, birds, frogs, guinea pigs, rabbits, and hamsters. The number of dogs and cats harmed or killed in animal research each year, however, is 100 times less than the number killed (euthanized) each year by humane societies or abandoned by their owners to die of starvation, disease, or accidents (212,000 versus 20 million). Although most species of test animals are not endangered, medical research coupled with habitat loss is a serious threat to endangered wild primates, such as the chimpanzee and the orangutan.

Under intense pressure from animal rights groups, scientists in industry, universities, and government laboratories are trying to find alternative testing methods that either do not subject animals to suffering or—better yet—do not use animals at all. Promising alternatives include the use of cell and tissue cultures, simulated tissues and body fluids, bacteria, and computer-generated mathematical models that can estimate the toxicity of a new compound from its chemical structure and properties.

Public zoos, botanical gardens, and aquariums are under constant pressure to exhibit rare and unusual animals such as the orangutan. For each exotic animal or plant that reaches a zoo or botanical garden alive, many others normally die during capture or shipment. For example, an estimated 50 birds die for each of the brilliant red "Cock of the Rock" birds that arrives at a zoo for display. Since 1967 reputable zoos and aquariums have agreed to no longer purchase endangered species, although there are still some abuses. However, in rare cases where extinction seems imminent efforts may be made to establish a captive breeding stock in the safety of a zoo, as discussed in Section 11-4.

Pollution Chemical pollution is a relatively new but growing threat to wildlife. Industrial wastes, mine acids, and excess heat from electric power plants have wiped out some species of fish, such as the humpbacked chub, in local areas. Oil pollution from tanker and offshore oil rig accidents can affect the survival of some vulnerable marine species such as the black-footed penguin. The Canadian aurora trout now appears to be extinct as a result of an increase in acidity of its freshwater habitat from acid deposition (Section 19-4). Chlorinated hydrocarbon pesticides, especially DDT and dieldrin, have been magnified in food chains (Figure 5-6) and have caused reproductive failure and eggshell thinning of important birds of prey, such as the peregrine falcon, the Eastern and California brown pelicans, the osprey, and the bald eagle (Section 9-9). The banning of such persistent pesticides in North America and Europe has allowed most of the species to recover. Yet these substances are increasingly being exported for use in LDCs.

Species Introduction Accidental or deliberate introduction of a species not normally found in an ecosystem can cause a species to become endangered or even extinct. Island species are especially vulnerable. For example, the dodo bird, which lived only on the small island of Mauritius in the Indian Ocean, became extinct by 1681 after pigs brought to the island consumed its eggs. Other examples are discussed in Section 11-3.

Characteristics of Extinction-Prone Species Some species have certain natural characteristics that make them more susceptible to extinction by human activities and natural disasters than other species, as summarized in Table 11-2. Species such as the California condor with two or more of these characteristics are particularly at risk. This large vulture with a wing span up to 2.7 meters (9 feet) once flourished from Canada to Baja California. By mid-1984 only about 18 of these critically endangered birds remained alive in the wild, living mainly in a relatively small mountainous sanctuary north of Los Angeles, and 9 were being cared for in captivity in the San Diego and Los Angeles Zoos.

Table 11-2 Characteristics of Extinction-Prone Species

Characteristic	Examples
Feed at high trophic levels	Bengal tiger, bald eagle, Andean condor, timber wolf
Large size	Bengal tiger, African lion, elephant, Javan rhinoceros, blue whale, American bison, giant panda
Low reproductive rate	Blue whale, polar bear, California condor, Andean condor, passenger pigeon, giant panda, *Homo sapiens*
Limited or specialized nesting or breeding areas	Kirtland's warbler (nests only in 6- to 15-year-old jack pine trees), whooping crane (depends on marshes for food and nesting), orangutan (now found only on islands of Sumatra and Borneo), green sea turtle (lays eggs on only a few beaches), bald eagle (preferred habitat of forested shorelines), nightingale wren (nests and breeds only on Burro Colorado Island, Panama)
Fixed migratory patterns	Blue whale, Kirtland's warbler, Bachman's warbler
Specialized feeding habits	Ivory-billed woodpecker (beetle larvae in recently dead trees), Everglades kite (apple snail of southern Florida), blue whale (krill in polar upwelling areas), black-footed ferret (prairie dogs and pocket gophers)
Certain behavioral patterns	Passenger pigeon and white-crowned pigeon (nests in large colonies), redheaded woodpecker (flies in front of cars), Carolina parakeet (when one bird is shot, rest of flock hovers over body), Key deer (forages for cigarette butts along highways—it's a "nicotine addict")
Highly intolerant of human presence	California condor, grizzly bear, red wolf, Carolina parakeet
Preys on livestock or humans	Timber wolf, some crocodiles
Valuable for fur, flesh, feathers, or other uses	Cheetah, Bengal tiger, Indian elephant, snow leopard, rhinoceros, green turtle
Found in only one place or region	Woodland caribou, elephant seal, Cooke's kokio, and many unique island species

This decline is the result of loss of habitat, food scarcity, shooting, poisoning, egg collecting, contamination with pesticides, and stress from contacts with humans, coupled with the condor's large size and low reproductive rate. Being big, the con-

dor was an easy target for hunters, who prized its long feathers. Many birds also were killed by ranchers and farmers who incorrectly blamed them for the death of lambs, calves, and chickens. Condors, however, are scavengers that feed on the carcasses of dead animals, especially deer fatally wounded and then lost by hunters, and dead calves on cattle ranges. Condors are monogamous partners for life and usually produce only one offspring every 2 years. Chicks fail to hatch when human activities and noise scare the parents away from the nest during the 42-day incubation period. A newborn chick depends on its parents for up to 2 years and dies if prematurely abandoned. Condors also require a large undisturbed habitat.

11-3 Species Introduction

General Effects A new species that is introduced into an ecosystem, either accidentally or deliberately, can become the dominant species if it has no natural predators and competitors. Such species may then cause a population decrease or even extinction of one or more existing species in an ecosystem by preying on them, competing with them for food, destroying their habitat, or upsetting the ecological balance. It can also cause a population explosion of one or more existing species by killing off their natural predators.

Table 11-3 gives examples of some of the effects of the accidental or deliberate introduction of alien species into the United States. The Department of Agriculture estimates that illegally imported pest species cause at least $10 billion a year in crop damage. This explains why customs officials ask travelers entering the United States, "Do you have any meat, fruit, vegetables, plants, or other agricultural products?" Not all alien species introductions have had harmful effects. Most major U.S. food crops were deliberately imported from other areas.

Examples of Harmful Introductions Mongooses were deliberately introduced into Hawaii in 1883 to control the rodent population, which was destroying much of the valuable sugarcane crop. Unfortunately, mongooses hunt by day and rats tend to hunt by night; thus the two species rarely met. The mongoose population continued to grow, attacking amphibians, reptiles, and some birds that had helped keep the rat population down. With fewer predators, the rat population rose, and the sugarcane crop was in worse trouble than before.

Fire ants stowed away on a Brazilian cargo ship and came ashore in Mobile, Alabama, in 1918. Today

Table 11-3 Damage Caused by Plants and Animals Imported into the United States

Name	Origin	Mode of Transport	Type of Damage
Mammals			
European wild boar	Russia	Intentionally imported (1912), escaped captivity	Destruction of habitat by rooting; crop damage
Nutria (cat-sized rodent)	Argentina	Intentionally imported, escaped captivity (1940)	Alteration of marsh ecology; damage to levees and earth dams; crop destruction
Birds			
European starling	Europe	Intentionally released (1890)	Competition with native songbirds; crop damage; transmission of swine diseases; airport interference
House sparrow	England	Intentionally released by Brooklyn Institute (1853)	Crop damage; displacement of native songbirds
Fish			
Carp	Germany	Intentionally released (1877)	Displacement of native fish; uprooting of water plants with loss of waterfowl populations
Sea lamprey	North Atlantic Ocean	Entered via Welland Canal (1829)	Destruction of lake trout, lake whitefish, and sturgeon in Great Lakes
Walking catfish	Thailand	Imported into Florida	Destruction of bass, bluegill, and other fish
Insects			
Argentine fire ant	Argentina	Probably entered via coffee shipments from Brazil (1918)	Crop damage; destruction of native ant faunas
Camphor scale insect	Japan	Accidentally imported on nursery stock (1920s)	Damage to nearly 200 species of plants in Louisiana, Texas, and Alabama
Japanese beetle	Japan	Accidentally imported on irises or azaleas (1911)	Defoliation of more than 250 species of trees and other plants, including many of commercial importance
Plants			
Water hyacinth	Central America	Intentionally introduced (1884)	Clogging waterways; shading out other aquatic vegetation
Chestnut blight (a fungus)	Asia	Accidentally imported on nursery plants (1900)	Destruction of nearly all eastern American chestnut trees; disturbance of forest ecology
Dutch elm disease *Cerastomella ulmi* (a fungus, the disease agent)	Europe	Accidentally imported on infected elm timber used for veneers (1930)	Destruction of millions of elms; disturbance of forest ecology

From *Biological Conservation* by David W. Ehrenfeld. Copyright © 1970 by Holt, Rinehart and Winston, Inc. Modified and reprinted by permission.

they range across nine southern states, stinging people and livestock and disrupting cultivation of food crops with their 2- to 3-foot-high conical nests. Since 1958 more than $150 million has been spent to eliminate this illegal alien, with little success.

In 1829 the opening of the Welland Canal unintentionally admitted the sea lamprey to the Great Lakes, where it had no natural predators or competitors. The sea lamprey is a primitive, parasitic vertebrate with a slender eellike body and a round, sucking mouth, which enables it to climb rock walls and to prey on fish by attaching itself (Figure 3-9). It rips open wounds in its prey's skin with its rasping tongue and sharp, horny teeth, then sucks out blood and body fluids. If the attacked fish is not killed outright, it may die of bacterial and fungal infections that invade the gaping wounds. Even if the fish survives, the ugly scar makes it unsalable. For a century the sea lamprey spread slowly throughout the lakes. Between 1940 and 1960 the sea lamprey, along with overfishing and pollution, caused a 97 percent decrease in the multimillion-dollar Great Lakes fishing industry, affecting species such as whitefish, sturgeon, and trout.

In the early 1950s, the U.S. Fish and Wildlife Service, the Great Lakes Fisheries Department, and the Canadian government declared war on the lamprey. First, they used electric fences to trap adults in their spawning streams, with very limited success. Then after testing over 6,000 chemicals, scientists discovered the selective poison trifluoromethylnitrophenol (TFM), which in minute amounts destroys sea lamprey larvae within 16 hours but is harmless to trout and sunfish and to the insect larvae, lake clams, and other food species of these game fish. The application of TFM to all lamprey-spawning tributaries to the Great Lakes had cut the sea lamprey population 80 percent by 1962. Restocked with millions of lake trout, coho salmon, and other species since 1960, the Great Lakes fisheries' remaining enemy is pollution.

A Case Study: The Water Hyacinth If you visit Florida you may admire the beauty of mats of leaves and purple flowers that cover many freshwater lakes and streams. These water hyacinths—plants native to Central and South America—were brought to the United States in the 1880s for an exhibition in New Orleans. A woman took one to plant in her backyard in Florida. Within 10 years the colorful plant was a public menace. Unchecked by natural enemies and thriving on Florida's nutrient-rich waters, the fast-growing hyacinth, which can double its population in only 2 weeks, rapidly displaced native aquatic plants and blocked boat traffic in many ponds, streams, canals, and rivers. The water hyacinths have also spread to waterways in other southeastern states, aided by canals that crisscross parts of the region.

In 1898 the U.S. Army Corps of Engineers tried unsuccessfully to use a mechanical cropper to remove these plants from navigable waters. Next they tried sodium arsenite. This chemical was somewhat successful, but it was abandoned in the 1930s because the deadly arsenic found its way into the food of spray boat crews. In the mid-1940s a combination of mechanical removal and the herbicide 2,4-D was used, but the water hyacinth continued to spread.

The Florida manatee, or sea cow, feeds on aquatic weeds and in sufficient numbers can control the growth and spread of water hyacinths in inland waterways more effectively than mechanical or chemical methods. But these gentle and playful mammals, which can weigh up to 1,000 kilograms (2,200 pounds) each, are threatened with extinction—slashing by powerboat propellers and entanglement in fishing gear are the main causes of premature death. As a result, only only about 800 to 1,000 sea cows now exist in Florida.

In recent years, scientists have brought in other natural predators to help control the hyacinth. For example, a species of weevil that feeds only on hyacinths has been imported from Argentina. Results look promising, but it is too early to evaluate this experiment. A species of water snail from Puerto Rico has also been introduced, but it is less effective than the weevil and can also feed on other, more desirable plants.

The grass carp, or white amur, brought in from the Soviet Union, is also being used to control water hyacinths and other undesirable aquatic weeds. The grass carp, which can weigh 45 kilograms (100 pounds), satisfies its huge appetite mostly by eating aquatic vegetation. This introduced fish species may solve the water hyacinth problems, but it could easily become a major pest itself. If its population grows, the grass carp may eat nearly every aquatic plant, including desirable species.

Although the water hyacinth has been extremely troublesome in the southeastern waterways, there is some good news. Preliminary research by the National Aeronautic and Space Administration (NASA) has shown that hyacinths can be used in several beneficial ways: (1) introduced in sewage treatment lagoons to absorb toxic chemicals, (2) converted by fermentation to a biogas fuel similar to natural gas, (3) used as a mineral and protein supplement for cattle feed, and (4) used as a fertilizer and soil conditioner.

11-4 Wildlife Protection

Approaches to Wildlife Protection In general, three main strategies are used to protect endangered and threatened wildlife and to prevent wildlife from becoming endangered: (1) *establishing treaties and passing laws* to protect particular species of endangered and threatened wildlife from being killed and to preserve their critical habitats from destruction and degradation, (2) *using gene banks, zoos, research centers, botanical gardens, and aquariums* to preserve threatened or endangered species and in some cases to breed individuals of critically endangered species in captivity, for eventual return to the wild, and (3) *preserving a variety of unique and representative ecosystems* and the variety of species they contain rather than concentrating on individual species.

The Species Approach: Treaties and Laws On a worldwide basis organizations such as the IUCN, the International Council for Bird Preservation (ICBP), and the World Wildlife Fund (WWF) have identified threatened and endangered species and led efforts to protect them. In 1973, for example, after 10 years of work by the IUCN, representatives from 80 nations drew up the Convention on International Trade in Endangered Species of Wild Flora and Fauna (CITES) treaty and also developed lists of plants and animals needing protection. This treaty is designed to control the international trade in protected species. By 1984, 81 nations had agreed to abide by this treaty. Although implementation and enforcement of this agreement vary from nation to nation, the treaty appears to have contributed to the conservation of a number of plants and animals such as sea turtles and crocodiles. In addition, various nations have entered into a number of other international conservation agreements.

The United States has increased efforts to protect native game and nongame endangered species with the passage of the Endangered Species Conservation Act of 1966, the Marine Mammal Protection Act of 1972, and the Endangered Species Act of 1973 (ESA). With adequate funding and strict enforcement, the 1973 ESA (including amendments in 1978 and 1982) may be the most far-reaching species protection law enacted by any nation and one of the toughest and most controversial environmental laws ever passed by Congress. This act authorizes the National Marine Fisheries Service (NMFS) of the Department of Commerce to identify and list marine species and the DOI's Fish and Wildlife Service (FWS) to identify all other plant and animal species that are endangered (in danger of extinction) or threatened (likely to become endangered) in the United States and abroad. The decision by the responsible government agency (NMFS or FWS) to add or remove a species from the list must be based solely on biological grounds without economic considerations and must be made within one year of the initial proposal for addition or removal. In 1982 the official list of protected species included 682 *endangered species* of plants and animals (238 of them in the U.S.) and 76 *threatened species* (52 of them in the U.S.).

The Endangered Species Act also authorizes the departments of Commerce and Interior to design and conduct programs for the recovery of endangered and threatened species, to assist states and other countries to conserve such species, and to determine, protect, and—when necessary—purchase *critical habitats* in the United States as required for the normal needs and survival of endangered or threatened species. The ESA also prohibits interstate and international commercial trade of endangered or threatened *plant or animal species* (with certain exceptions) or products made from such species, and it prohibits the killing, hunting, collecting, or injuring of any protected animal species. It also directs federal agencies not to carry out, fund, or authorize projects that would jeopardize endangered or threatened species or destroy or modify habitats critical to their survival.

This last provision has been highly controversial. In 1975 conservationists filed suit against the Tennessee Valley Authority (TVA) to stop construction of the $137 million Tellico Dam on the Little Tennessee River because the area to be flooded by the dam reservoir threatened the only known breeding habitat of an endangered species, the snail darter—a 7.6 centimeter- (3-inch-) long minnow. Although the dam was 90 percent completed, construction was halted by the court action including a final appeal by TVA to the Supreme Court.

In 1978 Congress amended the ESA to permit exemptions for federally declared major disaster areas or for national defense; or a seven-member Endangered Species Review Committee could grant an exemption if it believed that the economic benefits of a project would outweigh the potential harmful ecological effects. At their first meeting, the review committee denied the request to exempt the Tellico Dam project on the grounds that it was economically unsound. In 1979, however, Congress passed special legislation exempting the project from the Endangered Species Act and the dam's reservoir is now full of water. The snail darters that once dwelled there were transplanted to nearby rivers. In 1981 snail darter populations were found in several other remote tributaries of the Little Tennessee River. For this reason their status was downgraded by the Fish and Wildlife Service from endangered to threatened in 1983.

In 1982 the ESA was up for reauthorization. Well-funded groups representing mining, timber, and other national and multinational industries attempted to weaken the act primarily by allowing economic factors to be important determinants of whether a species and its critical habitat should be protected and by removing invertebrates from protection. Despite intense pressure by industry lobbyists, the major provisions of the act will remain intact through 1985, the next reauthorization date.

Environmentalists complain that the ESA is not being carried out as intended by Congress because of budget cuts and administrative rules. For example, in 1983 the federal government proposed to spend no more on endangered species than it would cost to buy 12 Army bulldozers. Environmentalists have also complained that DOI rules, coupled with budget cuts, effectively prohibit listing of invertebrate species because species proposed for protection are evaluated in the following unscientific order: mammals, birds, fishes, reptiles, amphibians, vascular plants, insects, mollusks, and other invertebrates.

The Endangered Species Act has been an important tool in preventing a number of species from becoming extinct. No animal or plant species listed as endangered has recovered sufficiently to be completely removed from the protection and recovery plan, and teams have been developed for only about 15 percent of the species already listed. But the numbers of several species such as the American alligator (Section 5-3), the American bison, and the bald eagle have increased enough to change their status in most places from endangered to threatened.

The Species Approach: Wildlife Refuges

The world's largest system of protected wildlife habitats is in the United States. Federal and state governments and private groups have established hundreds of wildlife refuges. Private organizations like the Nature Conservancy, Ducks Unlimited, and the National Audubon Society lease or purchase important tracts of wildlife habitats that might be destroyed by commercial development. The first federal wildlife refuge, Pelican Island in Florida, was established through executive order by President Theodore Roosevelt in 1903. Since that time more than 400 refuges have been designated as part of the National Wildlife Refuge System. These federal refuges are administered by the Fish and Wildlife Service.

The three major types of federal refuges are those designed for game species of migrating waterfowl, for big-game animals such as deer and antelope, and to save endangered species from extinction. Until recently, nearly all state and federal wildlife conservation efforts focused on the protection and management of waterfowl and big-game species, primarily for the 17 million Americans who hunt. A major reason for this emphasis is that funds used for state and federal wildlife conservation come primarily from fees for state and federal hunting and fishing licenses and permits and from taxes on hunting and fishing equipment. These revenues from sport hunting and fishing have supported wildlife research, habitat protection and restoration, and reintroduction of wildlife on depleted ranges. Such efforts have been focused primarily on game species, but many nongame species have also benefited.

In recent years there has been an increase in state and federal efforts to improve the conservation of nongame animals. By 1980, 13 states had enacted tax legislation to provide funds for the conservation of nongame wildlife. Federal wildlife refuges for specific endangered species have helped the endangered Key deer of southern Florida, the trumpeter swan, and the bald eagle to recover.

The Gene Bank–Zoo–Botanical Garden–Aquarium Approach

When the living wild population of a species reaches a certain critical level, the species may become extinct if the normal or accidentally increased death rate among surviving individuals comes to exceed their reproduction rate. A last ditch approach to save such critically endangered species is to preserve in special facilities a certain number of live organisms or samples of their genetic material—such as sperm, seeds, tissues, or fertilized embryos.

Gene banks of most known and many potential varieties of agricultural crops now exist throughout the world, and scientists have urged that many more be established (Section 9-8). Despite their importance, gene banks have significant disadvantages and need to be supplemented by preservation of a variety of representative ecosystems throughout the world. Storage is not possible for many species. Accidents, human error, and vandalism can cause irrecoverable losses. Furthermore, stored species do not continue to evolve and lack the genetic variability found in a species surviving in the wild.

Zoos, botanical gardens, arboretums, and aquariums are also being used increasingly to preserve and study representatives of critically endangered species that would otherwise become extinct. Some species such as Père David's deer, originally native to China, and Cooke's kokio, a small Hawaiian tree, are already extinct in the wild, surviving only in zoos, botanical gardens, and private collections throughout the world. When it is judged that an animal species will not survive on its own, eggs may be collected and hatched in captivity, or captive breeding programs may be established in zoos or private research centers. Other techniques include artificial insemination for species that don't breed well in captivity, using adults of one related species to serve as foster parents to hatch collected eggs and raise offspring, and removing newly laid eggs from captive or wild individuals for incubation elsewhere. This "egg-pulling" approach is designed to induce parents to renest and lay more eggs.

In some but not all cases, captive breeding and egg incubation programs may allow a population to increase sufficiently that the species can be successfully reintroduced into the wild. Captive breeding programs along with habitat protection have saved the elephant seal, down to 20 animals in 1890 and now numbering perhaps 75,000, all living on

Figure 11-4 The Arabian oryx barely escaped extinction in 1969 after being overhunted in the deserts of the Middle East. Captive breeding programs in zoos in Arizona and California apparently have been successful in saving this antelope species from extinction.

San Diego Zoo.

a Mexican island sanctuary. This approach has also been used to increase the almost extinct Hawaiian goose, or nene, Hawaii's state bird, from a wild population of about 35 in 1942 to several thousand today. Once nearly extinct, the Arabian oryx antelope (Figure 11-4) is now being returned in small numbers to the wild as a result of captive breeding programs at zoos in Phoenix, San Diego, and Los Angeles. The number of whooping cranes in the wild has been raised from 15 in 1941 to more than 100 in 1983 by habitat preservation and by captive breeding programs involving egg pulling, artificial insemination, and using wild sandhill cranes as foster parents to hatch and raise whooping crane chicks.

In 1983 scientists from the National Audubon Society and the Fish and Wildlife Service began an egg-pulling program in an attempt to save the critically endangered California condor. So far the strategy has worked. By the end of 1983 four chicks had hatched from captured eggs. Scientists have also been able to capture two live condor chicks and hope to get enough males and females for mating in captivity. If enough chicks survive and mate in captivity, scientists hope to begin returning condors to the wild within 20 to 30 years. This captive breeding approach has been opposed by the Sierra Club, Friends of the Earth, and other environmental groups. Wildlife experts from these groups argue that the best way to save these birds is to increase the size of their habitat, assure them a food supply in all seasons, and rigorously protect the remaining birds from disturbance by all humans, including biologists, photographers, and the public.

Captive breeding can help save some critically endangered species but it has several disadvantages. It is expensive and requires a minimum cap-

tive population of 100 to 150 individuals, half of them born in captivity, to assure long-term survival of a mammalian species in captivity. Most zoos use their limited funds and capacity to display as many different species as possible instead of preserving 100 or more individuals of one or a few endangered species. Thus, today the world's zoos contain only 20 species with populations of 100 or more individual animals. Such relatively small captive animal populations also suffer a loss of genetic variability.

Because of limited funds and scarcity of trained personnel, only a few of the world's endangered and threatened species can be saved by laws and wildlife refuges. At present, efforts to save species are concentrated on animal species that find favor with the general public primarily because they are furry and cuddly (koala bears), beautiful (whooping cranes and Bengal tigers), unique (blue whales), or symbolic (bald eagles). Campaigns centered on such well-known animal species can generate sizable public donations and interest. These funds can also be used to help preserve other species with less popular appeal.

An increasing number of wildlife experts, however, have suggested replacing this haphazard approach to saving endangered species with an environmental form of *triage,* a practice developed by Allied doctors during World War I. In triage, wounded soldiers were sorted into three groups: those likely to die despite medical care, those likely to recover without medical care, and the remainder, who were treated with the limited medical resources available. The proponents of environmental triage suggest that limited funds for preserving threatened and endangered wildlife be concentrated on those species that **(1)** have the best chance for survival, **(2)** have the most ecological value to an ecosystem, and **(3)** are potentially useful for agriculture, medicine, or industry. In effect, the Fish and Wildlife Service has already adopted a triage program, but it is based primarily on economic and political considerations.

The Ecosystem Approach   Most wildlife biologists argue that the major threat to most wildlife species today— namely, the destruction of habitat—cannot be halted using a species-to-species approach. Instead, they believe that wildlife conservation efforts should be concentrated on preserving large reserves all over the globe that contain a representative cross section of the world's ecosystems. In this approach, emphasis is on preserving biological diversity. Adequate and well-protected ecological reserves would help prevent species from becoming endangered by human activities, reduce the need for human intervention to prevent extinction, and provide scientists with opportunities for wildlife research. In addition, it costs less to run such reserves than to manage species one by one.

By 1982, 210 reserves, including 33 in the United States, had been set aside by 55 nations. A few tropical countries, including Brazil, Colombia, Cameroon, Costa Rica, Peru, Thailand, and Venezuela, have established sizable natural reserves. This is an important beginning, but only about one-half the world's biogeographical provinces has been included so far, and the quality of protection and management varies widely. National parks, forests, and wilderness areas also offer some protection to ecosystems and the wildlife they contain. But most of these areas are managed for multiple purposes instead of being set aside to preserve biological diversity.

11-5   Wildlife Management

Management Approaches   Ideally, the goal of a professional wildlife manager is to produce a large population of certain desirable game species that can be harvested each year during hunting season while leaving a strong, healthy reproductive population for the next year. The two major approaches used to manage such species are *population regulation* and *manipulation and protection of habitat.*

Effective management requires an understanding of population dynamics, type and amount of habitat required, natural predators, diseases and parasites, and feeding, mating, and nesting habits for each species. In addition, wildlife managers must know the type or types of *cover* an animal needs to take refuge from the elements, to rest, to breed, to rear young, and to conceal itself from its enemies. Ideally, they should also know how these factors are affected by interactions with populations of other species and by environmental factors such as fire, logging, grazing, and climate.

Population Regulation by Controlled Hunting Game animals such as deer, rabbits, squirrels, quail, and ducks that reproduce rapidly can exceed the carrying capacity of their habitat. For example, a deer population can more than double every 2 years. As the number of deer exceeds the carrying capacity of their range, vegetation is destroyed, the habitat deteriorates, and many animals die of starvation during winter. Since humans have eliminated most natural predators of deer, carefully regulated hunting can be used to keep the deer population within the carrying capacity of the habitat available.

Hunting is usually regulated by game laws. In the United States, for example, populations of game animals such as deer are managed by **(1)** specifying certain times of the year (usually the fall) for the hunting of a particular species, **(2)** restricting the length of hunting seasons, **(3)** regulating the number of hunters permitted in an area, and **(4)** placing limits on the size, number, and sex of animals allowed to be killed. The hunting of most game species is prohibited during the spring and summer, when the young are produced. If the population falls too low, the hunting season is shortened or closed. If the population becomes too large and threatens its food supply, the length of the season and the number of animals that can be killed may be increased. Often the killing of female animals is limited or prohibited for polygamous species such as deer, elk, pheasant, grouse, antelope, moose, and most ducks. This encourages a high reproductive rate during the spring and summer months when hunting is not allowed.

Habitat Protection and Manipulation   Once the food habits, predators, and nesting, mating, and cover requirements of a desired game species are known, a wildlife manager can alter and protect the habitat to encourage adequate production of that species for harvesting during hunting season. This is done primarily by controlling the stage of ecological succession (Section 5-1) of vegetation in various areas. Wildlife can be classified into four major categories according to the stage of ecological succession at which they are most likely to be found: **(1)** wilderness species; **(2)** late-successional species; **(3)** midsuccessional species; and **(4)** early-successional species.

Wilderness species such as grizzly bear, wolf, car-

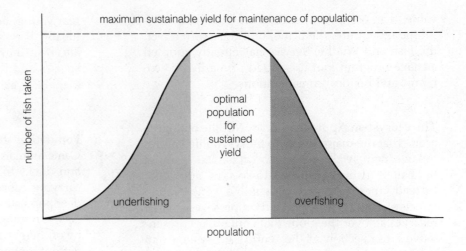

Figure 11-5 Relation between sustained yield and number of individuals of a species of fish harvested.

maximum sustainable yield for maintenance of population

number of fish taken

optimal population for sustained yield

underfishing

overfishing

population

ibou, and bighorn sheep, and prairie chicken flourish only in relatively undisturbed climax vegetational communities such as large areas of mature forest, tundra, and undisturbed grasslands and deserts. Because these species are highly sensitive to human disturbance, their survival depends to a large degree on the establishment of relatively large state and national wilderness areas and wildlife refuges. *Late-successional species* such as wild turkey, marten, Hammond's flycatcher, and gray squirrel require mature forest habitats to produce the food and cover on which they depend. This requires the establishment and protection of moderately sized mature forest refuges.

Midsuccessional species such as elk, moose, deer, ruffled grouse, and snowshoe hare are found around abandoned croplands and partially open areas created by logging, burning, and grazing. Populations of midsuccessional species will decline unless wildlife managers periodically remove vegetation to maintain such areas at this stage of succession. Approaches include periodic timber cutting (Section 10-5), prescribed burning (Section 10-5), applying herbicides (Section 9-9), and clearing for roads, firebreaks, gas pipelines, and electrical transmission lines. In general, logging is more effective when some standing dead trees, called *snags*, and some logs and debris are left as refuges for wildlife. At least 85 species of North American birds and mammals—flying squirrels, for example—use or excavate holes in snags for nests.

Early-successional species such as rabbit, quail, and dove find food and cover in the weedy pioneer plants that invade an area that has been cleared of vegetation for human activities and then abandoned.

Migratory waterfowl such as ducks, geese, and swans require some special management approaches. Many of these species nest in Canada during the summer and migrate to the United States and Central America along generally fixed routes called *flyways* during the fall hunting season. Thus, it is necessary to have international agreements to prevent destruction of the migrants' winter and summer habitats and to prevent overhunting. Waterfowl habitat can be improved by a number of methods including **(1)** periodically draining ponds to retard aquatic succession, **(2)** creating channels and openings in dense marsh vegetation to allow birds to feed and move about, **(3)** constructing artificial ponds, islands, and nesting sites, and **(4)** establishing protected waterfowl refuges. In 1934 Congress passed the Migratory Bird Hunting Stamp Act, which authorized the sale of duck stamps to provide funds for the acquisition, maintenance, and development of waterfowl refuges.

11-6 Fisheries Management

Maximum Sustained Yield Like other forms of wildlife, desired species of freshwater and marine fish are renewable resources if their populations are controlled by natural factors and the annual harvest leaves enough breeding stock to repopulate the species for the next year. Ideally, an annual *maximum-sustained-yield* figure should be established for each species to be taken (Figure 11-5). *Underfishing* occurs when fewer fish are taken than the ecosystem can provide. In this case natural mortality factors rather than fishing for food or sport control the population size of the species. *Overfishing* occurs when so many fish, especially immature individuals, are taken that there is not enough breeding stock left for adequate annual renewal. In this case, the population begins a decline, and if overfishing continues, the species may become extinct.

Freshwater Fisheries Management The goals of freshwater fish management are to encourage the growth of populations of desirable sport fish species and to reduce or eliminate populations of less desirable species. The fisheries biologist must ensure that the desired species of fish has adequate food, cover, and spawning grounds, and lives in water of adequate quality. To escape predators, fish require cover such as stumps, rocks, logs, and beds of weeds. They also require a spawning ground, such as a coastal estuary, a gravel bed in a stream, or a sandy area in a lake.

Some species of game fish can easily be killed by toxic water pollutants, depletion of oxygen by organic pollutants, and changes in temperature by the discharge of heated water from power plants (Section 18-3). Tolerance levels for various water pollutants and temperature, however, vary considerably with different species. Poor watershed management can result in excess runoff of silt and pesticides into aquatic ecosystems. Pesticides can cause direct kills of some fish species. They can also build up to very high levels in fish that feed at high trophic levels (Figure 5-6) and make them unsalable and inedible. Excessive silt, oil, and other water-insoluble wastes can cover spawning grounds, clog the gills of young fish, and destroy bottom-dwelling sources of food for some species.

Techniques for management of freshwater fish species include (1) enacting protective laws, (2) providing adequate natural and artificial habitats, (3) controlling predator species and diseases, (4) restocking depleted areas with fish from hatcheries, and (5) maintaining migration routes for *anadromous species*, which migrate from fresh water to saltwater and back again. As with other wildlife species, state and federal laws can be used to regulate the timing and length of the fishing season for various species, to determine the minimum fish size that can be taken, to establish catch quotas, and to require that commercial fish nets have large enough mesh size to ensure that young fish are not harvested.

Providing and protecting natural or artificial habitats for game fish species is crucial for their survival and reproduction. Hiding places must be provided, and buildup of debris and excessive growth of aquatic plants must be controlled to prevent oxygen depletion. Special attention must be paid to protecting spawning grounds from pollution, siltation, and predation. The habitats of some species can be improved by placing small check dams to control the rate of water flow. Artificial habitats such as fish ponds and new lakes formed by large dams can be created. Attention must also be paid to factors such as water temperature. For example, trout generally need ponds in which the surface water temperature never exceeds 18°C (65°F). Warmer water can be used for species such as bass, catfish, and bluegill. Fish ponds and other habitats should also be harvested regularly to provide the maximum sustained yield.

Fisheries biologists also try to control or eliminate undesirable species that prey on game fish species. For example, the control of the sea lamprey that preyed on sport fish species in the Great Lakes was discussed in Section 11-3. The fungi, algae, parasitic protozoa, leeches, roundworms, tapeworms, bacteria, and viruses that attack fish can be controlled by habitat improvement, breeding genetically resistant varieties, and using antibiotics and disinfectants.

Using hatcheries to restock ponds, lakes, and streams with various species of fish is required to maintain populations of trout and salmon at reasonably high levels. For this reason, the Fish and Wildlife Service and several states maintain a number of salmon and trout hatcheries. In the West, salmon hatch in high mountain streams in the Pacific region through Alaska. They make their way downstream and remain in the open ocean for 3 to 4 years. Then the adults, apparently using their sense of smell, attempt to return to the streams in which they hatched, to spawn. State and federal wildlife agencies attempt to provide unobstructed ways for salmon to make this journey, but dam construction and pollution reduce the number able to return to their spawning area. To maintain the salmon population, the Fish and Wildlife Service releases young salmon raised in hatcheries to various rivers in eastern and western states.

Marine Fisheries Management The commercial hunting and harvesting of fish from the ocean is an important source of food and protein for much of the world's population (Section 9-6). The annual world fish catch is worth almost $20 billion a year, with Japan and the Soviet Union being the two major fishing nations. Over 90 percent of the catch is fin fish such as anchovies, which live in the upper levels of the ocean, and cod, hake, haddock, flounder, sole, mullet, sea perch, and others found on or near the ocean bottom. The remaining 10 percent, which are not fish at all, consists of whales, crustaceans, and mollusks.

The history of the world's commercial fishing and whaling industry is an excellent example of the *tragedy of the commons*—the abuse and overuse of a common resource such as ocean fish and mammals not owned by anyone and available for use by anyone. Such depletion of a resource occurs through the ignorance and greed of individuals, industries, or nations as they attempt to get all of a resource they can in as short a time as possible with little concern for future supplies. Otherwise, it is argued that some other group or nation will exploit these commonly owned resources.

As a result, many species of commercially valuable fish and whales found in international waters and in the waters off of coastal nations have been overfished (Figure 11-5) to the point of *commercial extinction*; that is, they are so rare that it no longer pays to hunt them. For example, the catch of cod, halibut, herring, haddock, and other commercially preferred species in the northwest Atlantic Ocean, has been declining for over a decade. Some species, such as the blue whale, have also been driven almost to the point of biological extinction. Another threat to commercially important fish species and the other species on which they depend for food and other services is pollution of estuaries and the ocean by toxic chemicals, radioactive wastes, oil, and excess heat (Section 18-5).

Techniques used to manage marine fisheries in the United States include (1) the introduction of food and game fish species such as the striped bass along the Pacific and Atlantic coasts, (2) the construction of artificial reefs from boulders, building rubble, and automobile tires to attract desirable species, and (3) the extension by law of the 19 kilometer (12-mile) offshore fishing zone to 322 kilometers (200 miles), where foreign fishing vessels without government permission are banned.

Whaling Industry Whales, ranging in size from the 0.9-meter (3-foot) porpoise to the giant 15- to 30-meter (50- to 100-foot) blue whale, can be divided into two major groups, *toothed whales* and *baleen whales* (Figure 11-6, page 210). Toothed whales, such as the porpoise, sperm whale, and killer whale, feed mostly on squid, fish, octopuses, and other marine animals. Baleen whales, such as the blue, gray, humpback, and finback, have several hundred horny plates in their jaws that filter plankton, krill, and other small marine organisms from seawater.

In 1900 an estimated 4.4 million whales swam the ocean. Today only about 1.1 million remain, with sperm, minke, and sei whales making up 90 percent of the total. The pattern of the whaling industry has been to hunt one species until it becomes too scarce to be of commercial value and then turn to another species. Today only the sperm, minke, and sei of the 11 major species of whales once hunted by the whaling industry, remain unendangered, and their days may be numbered.

After World War II the 17 major whaling nations established the International Whaling Commission (IWC). Today 39 whaling and nonwhaling nations belong to the commission. The goal of the IWC has been to regulate the annual harvest by setting annual quotas for hunted species of whales, to ensure a sustainable supply of all commercially important species. Annual quotas for all species have been reduced from 45,000 in 1972 to only 7,000 in 1983. Most of these reductions, however, came only after species had already been hunted to commercial extinction.

The United States and a number of other nations in the IWC have repeatedly called for a ban on all commercial whaling. Environmentalist groups such as the Greenpeace movement have used bold commandolike tactics to embarrass whaling nations, stop pirate whalers who ignore the quotas, and gain worldwide publicity and support for protecting whales. In 1982 the IWC voted to end all commercial whaling by the end of 1985, with a gradual phasedown of the catch quota until that date. But Japan, the Soviet Union, and Norway, the three major whaling nations, filed formal protests against the ban. According to IWC rules, such protests free the objecting nation from any obligation to comply with the ruling.

A Case Study: The Near Extinction of the Blue Whale An estimated 200,000 blue whales may once have roamed the Antarctic waters. These whales, the world's largest animals, spend about 8 months of the year in the Antarctic region, where the tiny, shrimplike krill they filter from seawater and then consume are abundant. Then they migrate to warmer waters, where their young are born. Unfortunately, this graceful, playful, gentle species has been hunted to near extinction for its oil, meat, and bone. By 1930 the annual catch of blue whales reached a peak of almost 30,000. Since then overexploitation has caused the annual catch to drop sharply until 1964, when it reached nearly zero. Probably only a few hundred to a few thousand blue whales remain— perhaps too few for the species to recover.

This sharp decline can be attributed to a ruthless, greedy whaling industry as well as to three natural characteristics of the blue whale (Table 11-2). First, they are large and thus easy to spot. Second, they can be caught in large numbers because they tend to congregate in the Antarctic feeding grounds. Third, they multiply very slowly, taking up to 25 years to mature sexually and having one offspring every 2 to 5 years. Once the total population is reduced below a certain level, mates may no longer be able to find one another, and natural death rates may exceed natural birth rates until extinction occurs. Within the next few decades, blue whales could pass from endangered to extinct, even though they are protected by law as an endangered species.

Love the animals, love the plants, love everything. If you love everything, you will perceive the divine mystery in things. Once you perceive it, you will begin to comprehend it better every day. And you will come at last to love the whole world with an all-embracing love.

Feodor Dostoevsky, The Brothers Karamazov

Discussion Topics

1. Discuss your gut-level reaction to the statement: "Who cares that the passenger pigeon is extinct and the buffalo, the blue whale, the whooping crane, the bald eagle, the grizzly bear, and a number of other species are nearly extinct. They are important only to a bunch of bird watchers, Sierra Clubbers, and other ecofreaks." Be honest about your reaction, and try to organize arguments for your position.

2. Why should an urban dweller be concerned about preservation of wildlife and wildlife habitat?

3. Make a log of your own consumption for a single day and relate it to the increased demand for destroying wildlife and wildlife habitats in the United States and throughout the world.

4. Criticize the idea that since 70 to 98 percent of the species that have existed on earth have become extinct by natural selection, we should not be concerned about the several hundred animal species and thousands of plant species that have become extinct primarily because of human activities.

5. Some argue that all species have an inherent right to exist and should at least be preserved in a natural habitat somewhere on earth. Do you agree or disagree with this position? Why?

6. Do the species listed below have an inherent right to exist? Why or why not?
   a. Anopheles mosquitoes, which transmit malaria.
   b. Tigers that roam the jungle along the Indian-Nepalese border and killed at least 105 persons between 1978 and 1983.
   c. Bacteria that cause smallpox or other infectious diseases.
   d. Rats that compete with humans for many food sources.

7. Use Table 11-2 to predict a species that may soon be endangered. What, if anything, is being done for this species? What pressures is it being subjected to? Try to work up a plan for protecting it.

8. Give the pros and cons of sport hunting. Find out how much revenue your state fish and game department receives each year from taxes and from the sale of fishing and hunting licenses, and find out how this money is used.

9. The chimpanzee is an endangered species with perhaps no more than 50,000 individuals remaining in the wild. In 1978 an American pharmaceutical company requested that the Fish and Wildlife Service allow it to import 125 young chimpanzees to be used in testing a vaccine against hepatitis B. The company argued that the animals would be used for one low-risk test each and then transferred to a captive breeding colony, that the chimp's habitat was being destroyed, such that their best hope lay in captivity, and that drug companies in other nations with fewer restrictions on endangered species would end up using chimps and developing the vaccine anyway. Primatologists opposed this request on many grounds: that the vaccine was being developed for a disease that is rarely fatal, that nonendangered animals could be found to test the vaccine, that the endangered species would be further imperiled because about 500 chimps would die in the process of delivering 125 healthy ones and 125 others would die because the standard method of capture is to shoot a mother and take the child, and that efforts are being made to decrease habitat destruction. Moreover, they said, whether other nations approve killing members of an endangered species should be irrelevant in justifying such actions by the United States. Would you approve or deny this request? Defend your choice.

10. On balance, do the benefits of the following examples of wildlife management outweigh their disadvantages? Explain each answer and give specific reasons: (a) killing lampreys with chemicals, (b) introducing the grass carp to America, (c) introducing major food crops to America, and (d) introducing the water hyacinth to America.

11. Should a ban be placed on the importation of all new plant and animal species into the United States for use as pets, observation in zoos, scientific and medical research, and use as predators or parasites of pests already here? Develop guidelines and criteria that should be met before any new species is introduced.

Figure 11-6 Relative sizes of major species of whale.

All species on this chart are to scale

Killer whale

White-sided dolphin

Pilot whale

Bottlenosed dolphin

Gray whale

Fin whale

Right whale

Sei whale

False killer whale

Cuvier's beaked whale

Baird's beaked whale

Sperm whale

Pygmy sperm whale

| 10 | 20 | 30 | 40 | 50 | 60 | 70 | 80 | 90 | 100 feet |
| 5 | | 10 | | 15 | | 20 | | 25 | 30 meters |

12

Urban Land Use and Land-Use Planning

Modern cities are centers of employment, education, and culture. But they are also centers of poverty, delinquency, crime, prostitution, alcoholism, and drug abuse. As a rule, cities offer less space, less daylight, less fresh air, less greenery, and more noise.

Georg Borgstrom

12-1 Urbanization and Urban Growth

The World Situation *Urbanization* is the percentage of the population living in cities and towns and *urban growth* is the process of increasing this percentage. At the beginning of this century less than 3 percent of the world's population lived in **urban areas**—places with a population of more than 20,000 people. By 1984, 40 percent of the world's population lived in urban areas. The United Nations estimates that if present trends continue, by the close of this century at least 50 percent of the people in the world will be urban dwellers, half of them unemployed or underemployed. Accommodating these new urban dwellers will be a monumental task.

Table 12-1 shows how the MDCs and LDCs dif-

Enrichment Studies 2, 5, 7, 10, 12, and 13 are related to this chapter.

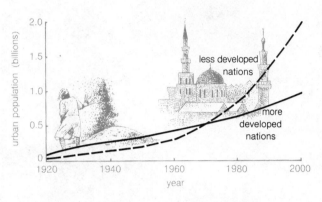

Figure 12-1 Actual and projected urban population growth in more developed and less developed nations between 1920 and 2000. (Source: United Nations.)

fer in the present and projected percentage of total population living in urban areas, and in urban population size. The rate of urban population growth in LDCs surpassed that in MDCs around 1970 and is expected to increase more rapidly (Figure 12-1), because the LDCs are simultaneously experiencing high population growth *and* rapid migration of people into urban areas. Already at least one-third of the urban dwellers in LDCs live in slums and shantytowns with inadequate drinking water, sanitation, food, health care, housing, schools, and jobs. The population of many of these overburdened slums is doubling every 5 to 7 years.

Unprecedented urban growth in MDCs and LDCs has given rise to a new concept—that of the

Table 12-1 Degree of Urbanization and Urban Population for MDCs and LDCs in 1984 and 2000 (projected)

Category	1984		2000	
	Degree of Urbanization (% of total population)	Urban Population (billions)	Degree of Urbanization (% of total population)	Urban Population (billions)
World	40	1.9	50	3.1
MDCs	71	0.8	80	1.1
LDCs	32	1.2	41	2.0

Source: United Nations

"supercity," or urban area with a population of more than 10 million people. In 1980 there were 10 supercities, four of them located in MDCs (Table 12-2). By 2000, the United Nations projects that there will be 25 supercities. Most will be located in LDCs (Table 12-2), and four of them are projected to have over 22 million people.

The U.S. Situation According to latest U.S. Census Bureau definitions, Americans live in areas of three types: **(1)** *rural areas*, places with a population less than 2,500, **(2)** *urban areas* or *standard metropolitan statistical areas (SMSAs)*, consisting of a central city and surrounding suburbs containing 50,000 or more residents and with an average population density of at least 1,000 per square mile, and **(3)** *other urban places*, small cities and towns not associated with an SMSA and with a population between 2,500 and 50,000. Sometimes rural areas and other urban places are lumped together and called *nonmetropolitan areas*.

Since 1800 there have been four major population shifts in the United States: **(1)** *the rural-to-urban shift* between 1800 and the present, **(2)** *the central city-to suburbs shift* between 1950 and the present, **(3)** *the metropolitan-to-nonmetropolitan shift* between 1970 and the present, and **(4)** the *shift from northeastern and midwestern states to southern and western states* between 1970 and the present.

The most significant of these shifts is the *rural-to-urban shift* (Figure 12-2). It was caused by industrialization, which created new jobs in cities and led to a loss of agricultural jobs in rural areas (Figure

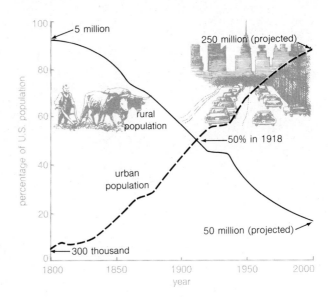

Figure 12-2 Actual and projected percentages of the rural and urban populations. in the United States between 1800 and 2000. (Source: U.S. Bureau of the Census.)

9-5). In 1800 only 5 percent of the U.S. population lived in cities and towns larger than 2,500. By 1984, 74 percent of all Americans were urban dwellers. This rural-to-urban shift is expected to continue and the Census Bureau projects that 80 to 90 percent of all Americans will live in urban areas or other urban places by 2000 (Figure 12-2).

Since 1950 many urban areas have spread outward and merged physically with neighboring cities and suburbs to form a large **urban region** or

Table 12-2 The 10 Largest Urban Areas in the World in 1983 and 2000 (projected)

1983		2000	
Urban Area	Population (millions)	City	Population (millions)
Tokyo–Yokohama	21.1	Mexico City	27.6
New York–northeast New Jersey	18.1	Shanghai	25.9
Mexico City	17.0	Tokyo–Yokohama	23.8
Shanghai	16.5	Peking	22.8
São Paulo	14.0	São Paulo	21.5
Peking	13.5	New York–northeast New Jersey	19.5
Los Angeles-Long Beach	11.6	Bombay	16.3
Rio de Janeiro	10.7	Calcutta	15.9
Greater Buenos Aires	10.5	Jarkarta	14.3
London	9.9	Rio de Janerio	14.2

Source: United Nations

Figure 12-3 Urban regions in the United States. (Source: U.S. Bureau of the Census.)

c Southern California		f Northern California	
1980 population	12,647,607	1980 population	7,221,281
change in 1970–80	16.2%	change in 1970–80	16.0%
share of U.S. population	5.6%	share of U.S. population	3.2%

MN

ME

WI

MI

NY

VT

NH

Twin Cities

St. Paul

Minneapolis

Albany

MA

a

Boston

IA

Upstate New York

Rochester

Buffalo

CT

RI

New York City

NJ

a

Milwaukee

b

Detroit

PA

IL

b

Cleveland

a

Chicago

IN

OH

Toledo

e

Pittsburgh

Philadelphia

a

MO

b

Columbus

e

MD

Baltimore

Indianapolis

Southern

Ohio

WV

Washington, D.C.

a

DE

Cincinnati

Central Indiana

VA

Topeka

Kansas City

St. Louis

Louisville

Richmond

Missouri-Kansas

Valley

KY

Bluegrass

Southern

Virginia

Norfolk

TN

NC

g

Charlotte

Tulsa

AR

Nashville

Greenville

SC

Oklahoma City

MS

AL

GA

Soonerland

g

Atlanta

Augusta

Charleston

Birmingham

Coastal

Dalworth

Central

Plain

Fort Worth

Dallas

LA

Alabama

Central Gulf Coast

FL

Jacksonville

Centex

Texas

Mobile

d

Austin

Gulf Coast

New

Orleans

Orlando

San

Houston

d

Tampa

Antonio

d

d

Miami

a Boswash		**b Lower Great Lakes**		**d Florida Peninsula**	
1980 population	41,786,061	1980 population	20,827,980	1980 population	8,290,959
change in 1970–80	0.2%	change in 1970–80	2.8%	change in 1970–80	44.7%
share of U.S. population	18.4%	share of U.S. population	9.2%	share of U.S. population	3.7%

e Cleveburgh		**g Piedmont**	
1980 population	8,141,391	1980 population	6,359,479
change in 1970–80	–2.7%	change in 1970–80	20.4%
share of U.S. population	3.6%	share of U.S. population	2.8%

megalopolis containing at least 1 million people. Figure 12-3 identifies the nation's 28 largest urban regions, where more than two out of three Americans live, and provides details on the seven largest ones.

Between 1950 and the present, large numbers of middle- and upper-class citizens moved from the central city to the suburbs within most SMSAs in what is known as the *central city-to-suburbs shift*. As a result, today more Americans—almost one out of three—live in the suburbs than in central cities, other urban areas, or rural areas. In addition, approximately two out of every three metropolitan manufacturing jobs are now located in the suburbs. Major factors causing this shift include **(1)** rising automobile ownership and improved highway systems between the suburbs and central cities, **(2)** the GI housing bill enacted after World War II, which subsidized single-family dwellings—mostly in the suburbs—for middle-class Americans, **(3)** the rapidly expanding economy of the 1950s and 1960s, which allowed people to buy homes outside the central city, **(4)** dissatisfaction with high living costs, crime, inferior schools, pollution and congestion, and other deteriorating conditions in central cities, **(5)** the desire of many Americans to live in a small town or suburban setting, and **(6)** the steady movement of jobs from central cities to the suburbs.

The 1980 census revealed that between 1970 and 1980 a *metropolitan-to-nonmetropolitan shift* was taking place in all regions. During this decade the number of people living in both metropolitan areas (SMSAs) and nonmetropolitan areas (rural areas and other urban areas) increased. However, for the first time since the census was begun in 1790, nonmetropolitan areas had greater rates of growth than SMSAs. The apparent reasons for this shift, which continues during the 1980s, include **(1)** disenchantment with deteriorating conditions and high living costs in many SMSAs, especially older ones in the East and Midwest, **(2)** more jobs in rural areas and small cities, and **(3)** advanced communications technology, the interstate highway system, lower taxes, and room to expand, which make it easier and usually financially advantageous for business and families to locate outside metropolitan areas.

This shift does not mean that the American population is moving away from cities as such, but away from some cities—especially larger ones—in favor of other smaller towns and cities. Indeed, if this shift continues as expected, many small towns and cities and rural areas will grow enough to become urban areas, often against the wishes of the majority of their residents. The influx of people to rural counties and small towns and cities has increased the stress on many overburdened local governments, hindering their ability to provide

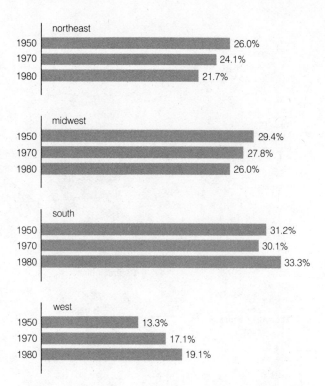

Figure 12-4 Percentage of total U.S. population by region: 1950, 1970, 1980. (Source: U.S. Bureau of the Census.)

schools, houses, sewage disposal, and other services. An increasing number of small towns and rural areas have been so alarmed by this "rural urbanization" that they have tried to discourage or halt further growth.

In 1980, for the first time, the population of the South and West exceeded that of the Northeast and Midwest (Figure 12-4) with particularly high population growth in the Sun Belt states of California, Texas, and Florida. This more recent *shift from northeastern and midwestern states to both southern and western states* has been attributed to several factors: **(1)** the decline of steel, automobile, and other traditional industries in the Northeast and Midwest as a result of the ongoing switch from an industry-based manufacturing society to one based primarily on the production and distribution of information, **(2)** the switch from a national economy to a global economy in which other nations with cheap labor and new, highly automated factories can produce manufactured goods more cheaply than the United States, thus causing a sharp decline in the work force in the aging steel mills, auto plants, and other heavy industries concentrated in the Northeast and Midwest, **(3)** the creation during the 1970s of almost twice as many new service and information-related jobs in the South and West as in the Northeast and Midwest, **(4)** the rise of energy industries in the

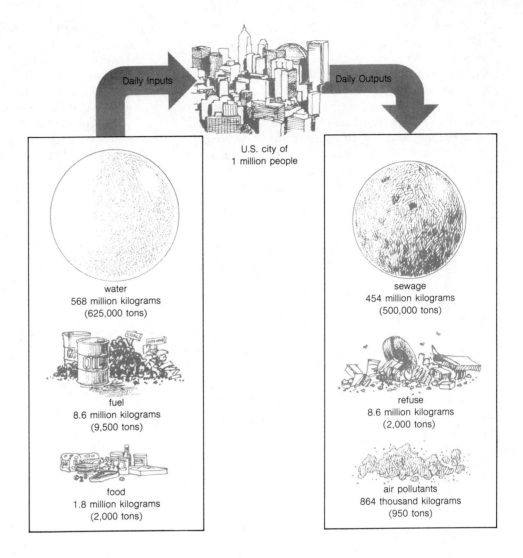

Figure 12-5 Typical daily inputs and outputs for a U.S. city of 1 million people.

Daily Inputs

Daily Outputs

U.S. city of
1 million people

water
568 million kilograms
(625,000 tons)

fuel
8.6 million kilograms
(9,500 tons)

food
1.8 million kilograms
(2,000 tons)

sewage
454 million kilograms
(500,000 tons)

refuse
8.6 million kilograms
(2,000 tons)

air pollutants
864 thousand kilograms
(950 tons)

South and West, especially since the 1973 oil embargo, **(5)** the decentralization of society, with people moving from densely populated large cities in the Northeast and Midwest to more spread-out large and small cities in the South and West, and **(6)** the more favorable climate of Sun Belt states compared to that of Snow Belt states. This shift in population and economic and political power from northeastern and midwestern states to both southern and western states is expected to continue between 1980 and 2000.

12-2 Urban Systems and Natural Ecosystems

Is an Urban System an Ecosystem? Some ecologists and urban experts treat cities and urban regions as ecosystems. Others argue that an urban system has only some characteristics of a natural ecosystem. In Section 3-l an ecosystem was defined as a community of plants and animals interacting with one another and with their environment. Technically, a city meets the requirements of this defini-

tion, but there are important differences between natural ecosystems and artificial urban ecosystems.

Unlike natural ecosystems, cities do not have enough producers (green plants) to support their inhabitants. Cities may have some trees, lawns, and parks, but these are not major sources of food. As one observer remarked, "Cities are places where they cut down the trees and then name the streets after them." This scarcity of vegetation is unfortunate, because urban plants, grasses, and trees absorb air pollutants, give off oxygen, help cool the air as water is evaporated from their leaves, muffle noise, and satisfy important psychological needs of city dwellers.

Cities also lack animals or plants that can be used as food for humans. Thus, urban systems survive only by importing food from external plant-growing ecosystems located throughout the world. Cities also obtain fresh air, water, minerals, and energy resources from outside ecosystems. Instead of being recycled, their solid, liquid, and gaseous wastes are discharged to ecosystems mostly outside their boundaries (Figure 12-5).

At best, cities can be classified as immature ecosystems that depend on other ecosystems for their survival. Urban systems can be classified as self-sustaining ecosystems only if their boundaries are expanded to include (1) the farmlands, forests, mines, watersheds, and other areas throughout the world that provide input materials, and (2) the air, rivers, oceans, and soil that absorb their massive outputs of wastes. Since the oil embargo of 1973, however, some cities have attempted to become more self-sufficient in providing more of their own matter and energy resources.

Urban Niches and Spatial Structure By analogy, we can apply the ecosystem characteristics of niche (Section 4-4) and spatial structure to urban systems. In a natural ecosystem we usually find many species, each occupying a different role or niche. By contrast, urban systems have one major species whose individuals occupy many different niches.

Like natural ecosystems, cities have recognizable spatial and physical structures. Three classic models of city spatial structures are the concentric circle model, the sector model, and the multiple nuclei model (Figure l2-6). A city resembling the *concentric circle model* develops outward from its central business district (CBD) in a series of rings (Figure 12-6, top). Typically, industries and businesses in the center zone are surrounded by circular zones of housing that normally represent more affluent areas as one moves outward into the suburbs. A city resembling the *sector model* is a system of pie-shaped wedges, or ribbons, formed when high-, intermediate-, and low-rent commercial, industrial, and housing districts push out from the center along major transportation routes (Figure 12-6, middle). In the *multiple nuclei model*, a large city develops around a number of independent centers, or nuclei, rather than a single center (Figure 12-6, bottom). Although no city perfectly matches any of them, these simplified models can be used to identify key characteristics. If you fly over, live in, or visit a city, see which—if any—of these models best describes its spatial form.

Urban Economic and Social Succession Undisturbed natural ecosystems tend to undergo ecological succession and become more biologically mature and diverse (Section 5-1). By analogy, urban development can be described as *economic and social succession*. A city, like a biological community undergoing secondary succession (Section 5-l), begins as an immature pioneer settlement when land is cleared. The early stages of city development are characterized by high productivity to build the necessary structures and products, few services, inefficient use of matter and energy resources, little community organization, and a rapid spread outward of small structures.

As an urban area continues to spread, its services—especially in the central city—may begin to break down. Let's look at one way this happens. In the early stages of urban growth, housing, industry, and employment increase rapidly. As the original central city housing deteriorates, many middle- and high-income residents leave and build homes beyond the city core. The resulting loss of business means that many low-income residents left in the central city are unable to find work. Rising unemployment generates the need for welfare, public housing, and other expenditures.

As middle- and upper-income residents leave, property values in the central city decline. These lower property values mean lower tax revenues because about 87 percent of the operating revenue for local governments is derived from property taxes. Because there are no new tax revenues to absorb the added financial load, the city government typically raises business and private property taxes and cuts back services and maintenance—causing more businesses and individuals to flee to the suburbs.

When more people move to the suburbs, freeways and mass transit systems are built to accommodate commuters—making it easier for more people to live in the suburbs. Freeways and mass transit systems are often built through poor neighborhoods, which usually constitute the cheapest route, because residents do not have enough economic and political power to block such projects. As a result, the poor lose homes and local businesses and endure increased air pollution, noise, and other environmental insults. For example, each year about 51,000 mostly low-income Americans are displaced from their urban homes to make way for freeways and highways that most of them don't use.

As more freeways to the suburbs are built, transit systems within the central city usually deteriorate. This means that low- and middle-income workers find it more difficult to get to and from work. This accelerating cycle of more unemployment and more poverty breeds despair. In turn, this can lead to an increase in drug use, crime, and other forms of social disruption. These conditions increase the fear and tension for the poor, the elderly, and the handicapped who remain in the central cities. This model of urban growth and decay is typical for cities in MDCs. By contrast, in many LDCs, the middle class and the affluent live in central cities, while the poor live in surrounding slums.

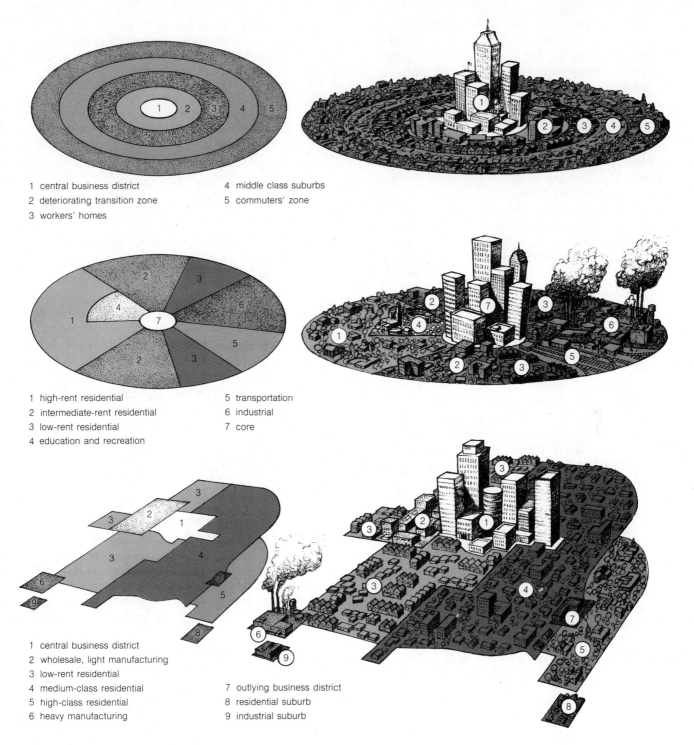

1 central business district
2 deteriorating transition zone
3 workers' homes
4 middle class suburbs
5 commuters' zone

1 high-rent residential
2 intermediate-rent residential
3 low-rent residential
4 education and recreation
5 transportation
6 industrial
7 core

1 central business district
2 wholesale, light manufacturing
3 low-rent residential
4 medium-class residential
5 high-class residential
6 heavy manufacturing
7 outlying business district
8 residential suburb
9 industrial suburb

Figure 12-6 Some models of urban spatial structure. (Modified with permission from Harm J. deBlij, *Human Geography*, 1977, New York: John Wiley.)

12-3 The Urban Environment: Benefits and Stresses

Benefits of Cities Throughout history, people have flooded into cities to find jobs. Those who get good jobs and do well financially often are enthusiastic about living in cities, which provide a variety of goods and services and an exciting diversity of social and cultural activities. In addition, urban social and cultural activities enrich the lives of people who live far from city boundaries.

Many European cities and some American cities are beautiful aesthetically, culturally, and socially.

Their central cities and other centers of population and economic activity are full of life, with ever-changing patterns and moods. Their parks, museums, restaurants, theatres, and businesses bustle with activity. As people live, work, and play in such cities, they can by chance meet new and interesting people of all ages, in all walks of life, and from all over the world.

Urban Problems and Stresses in the United States Not all cities are pleasant places to live. People in many medium-sized to large cities are increasingly subjected to problems related to crowding, such as traffic snarls, housing shortages and high rents, lack of parking spaces, increased fares and crowding on deteriorating and inefficient public transportation systems, loud music in public, crime, ethnic tensions, air and water pollution, and long lines at grocery stores, banks, movies, and restaurants.

According to surveys, an increasing number of residents in many central cities feel isolated, powerless, and entrapped. They are afraid to go out at night, and they surround themselves with locks, alarm systems, and other security precautions. Older people are particularly susceptible to these and other strains of urban life. For many young people, street life and peer group pressure in an urban ghetto tend to reinforce ideas that hard work and traditional employment have few rewards, that crime does indeed pay, and that one who is not part of the predominant society has no obligation to it.

Many low- and middle-income people living in decaying central cities regard attempts to control pollution as largely irrelevant to their most pressing needs: jobs, housing, health care, and education. Although pollution control benefits everyone, it is even more important for the health of the urban poor than for other urban dwellers and those dwelling in rural areas. Studies done in over 114 cities showed that the urban poor have higher rates of illness and death from diseases associated with air pollution (Chapter 19) than persons living in higher-income neighborhoods.

Lead poisoning also occurs more often among city ghetto residents, particularly children (Enrichment Study 12). This is because so many of the poor live near freeways where the air has a higher lead content and because many older houses still have walls and windows painted with cracking and peeling lead-based paint. In addition, low- and middle-income workers living in the cities have little choice but to take on jobs in the remaining factories and sweatshops, where they are often exposed to serious noise and health hazards, leading to loss of hearing, black lung, brown lung, and cancer of several forms (Enrichment Study 7).

The National Advisory Commission on Civil Disorders summarized other environmental and social problems found in low-income urban areas:

1. Crowding
2. Poor medical services
3. Inadequate sanitation, garbage removal, street cleaning, snow removal, and other services
4. Infestation by rodents and other pests
5. Little or no public transportation
6. Uprooting of homes and community structure by freeway construction
7. High noise levels (Enrichment Study 10)
8. Higher cost for heating because of poorly insulated homes and buildings

Urban Problems in Less Developed Countries Uncontrolled population growth and diminishing job opportunties in overpopulated rural areas in LDCs force people to migrate from the countryside into urban areas. There, too, jobs are seldom available. For this rapidly growing number of migrants, the city becomes a poverty trap, not an oasis of economic opportunity and cultural diversity. The urban poor are forced to live on the streets or crowd into the *callampas* (mushroom cities) of Chile, the *favelas* of Brazil, the *gourbivilles* of Tunisia, the *barriadas* of Peru, and the *gecekindos* (meaning "built between dusk and dawn") of Turkey.

The names of these human anthills vary. But their inhabitants all face poverty—grubbing for food and fuel, minimal housing, open sewers, untreated drinking water from filthy sources, and little access to schools and hospitals. Ironically, expanded services usually do little to improve conditions, since they attract more of the rural poor to the city.

In spite of joblessness and squalor, shantytown residents cling to life with resourcefulness, tenacity, and hope. Most of them are convinced that the city offers, possibly for themselves and certainly for their children, the only chance of a better life. On balance, most tend to have more opportunities and are often better off than the rural poor they left behind. They also tend to have fewer children, since they are more readily reached by family planning and population control programs (Section 7-3). In the long run, this helps prevent population growth from swamping economic growth.

12-4 Urban Transportation

Transportation Options Transportation systems and options within and between urban areas are a

Table 12-3 Major Forms of Urban Transportation

Type	Advantages	Disadvantages
Individual Transit		
Automobile and taxi	Allows freedom of movement (door-to-door service) Convenient Usually not crowded Can carry one or several people	Requires much land (highways, parking areas, etc.) Wastes energy and matter resources Pollutes air Promotes urban sprawl Increasingly expensive to buy and operate or to hire
Motorcycle and moped	Allows freedom of movement Convenient Less expensive to buy and operate than car Uses and wastes less matter and energy resources than car Requires relatively little land Pollutes less than car	Rider not sheltered from weather, noise, and air pollution Carries only one or two persons Less protection from injury
Bicycle	Allows freedom of movement Convenient As fast as car in urban trips less than 8 km (5 mi) Very inexpensive to buy and operate Provides exercise Conserves energy and matter resources Requires little land Nonpolluting	Does not shelter rider from weather, noise, and air pollution Carries only one or two persons Provides less protection from injury Slow for trips greater than 8 km (5 mi)
Walking or running	Allows freedom of movement Convenient for short trips Free Provides exercise Conserves energy and matter resources Requires very little land Nonpolluting	Slow and difficult for long trips Does not protect from weather, noise, and air pollution
Mass Transit		
Railroad and subway (heavy rail systems)	Handles large number of passengers Rapid once boarded and if on time Safer than car Fairly inexpensive for rider Uses fewer matter and energy resources than car Requires much less land than car Pollutes less than car	Very expensive to build and operate Economically feasible only along heavily populated routes Lacks door-to-door service Requires fixed routes Can be crowded and noisy
Trolley and streetcar (light rail systems)	Handles large number of passengers Fairly rapid once boarded and if on time Safer than car Fairly inexpensive for rider Uses fewer energy and matter resources than car Requires less land than car Pollutes relatively little if electric Cheaper to build and operate than railroad and subway	Expensive to build and operate Economically feasible only along heavily populated routes Lacks door-to-door service Requires fixed routes Can be crowded and noisy
Bus	Handles large number of passengers Has more flexible routes than railroad and trolley Safer than car Fairly inexpensive for rider Uses fewer energy and matter resources than car Requires less land than car Normally cheaper to build and operate than railroads	Fairly expensive to build and operate Lacks door-to-door service Fairly fixed routes Often not on time Can be crowded and noisy Pollutes air
Paratransit		
Carpools and vanpools	Carries small group of people Saves money Wastes fewer energy and matter resources than car Provides social interaction	Fairly inconvenient Promotes urban sprawl Requires much land Pollutes air Wastes matter and energy resources

Table 12-3 Major Forms of Urban Transportation *(continued)*

Type	Advantages	Disadvantages
Dial-a-ride (minibuses, vans, jitneys, and shared taxicab systems)	Handles small to moderate number of passengers Safer than car Moderately inexpensive for rider Usually provides door-to-door service Uses fewer energy and matter resources than car Requires less land than car Cheaper to build and operate than railroad Very useful for the poor, young, elderly, and handicapped	Fairly expensive to operate Can require long waits Can be crowded and noisy Pollutes air

major factor determining the spatial pattern, degree of sprawl, and rate of economic growth of an urban area. People in urban areas move from one place to another by three major types of transportation: **(1)** *individual transit* (private automobile, taxi, motorcycle, moped, bicycle, and walking), **(2)** *mass transit* (railroad, subway, trolley, and bus), and **(3)** *paratransit* (carpools, vanpools, jitneys or van taxis traveling along fixed routes, and dial-a-ride systems). Each type has certain advantages and disadvantages, as summarized in Table 12-3. Any successful urban transportation system requires a mix of individual, mass transit, and paratransit methods designed to suit a particular urban area.

The Automobile and Decentralized Cities Before the automobile was invented, cities tended to be compact. By necessity most urban dwellers lived within easy walking distance of their jobs, the stores where they shopped, and the schools their children attended. Stores and offices often had living quarters above. This compactness was convenient and fostered a close identification with one's neighborhood and neighbors. But it also meant that prices were high and merchandise limited in the small neighborhood shops where people did most of their shopping. Also housing near factories was almost always dirty, crowded, and noisy.

After 1870 these limitations on individual freedom were improved somewhat by the development of fixed-rail urban transit, first in the form of horse-drawn trolleys and streetcars and later in the form of steam- or electricity-driven trolleys, streetcars, and commuter trains. But people and goods still had to go where the rails led, when the transit company was ready to take them.

The introduction of the automobile in the early 1900s and particularly the lowering of the cost per vehicle through mass production in the 1920s began changing all this. By providing almost unlimited mobility, automobiles and the highways that followed have been a major factor in the *urban sprawl* that characterizes the highly decentralized cities of the United States today. Because the automobile has allowed a mass exodus from the central city to the suburbs and surrounding areas, downtown shopping and business areas in most central cities have deteriorated. They have been replaced with a hodgepodge of widely dispersed shopping centers, housing developments, and tangled highway networks whose locations have been determined largely by where developers could buy land instead of being based on a land-use plan for orderly development.

Between 1945 and 1970 states and localities tried to reduce auto congestion by constructing thousands of miles of roads, but this has encouraged more automobiles and travel, causing congestion that decreases the average automobile speed. In 1907 the average speed of horse-drawn vehicles through Manhattan was measured at 18.5 kilometers per hour (11.5 miles per hour). Today, crosstown Manhattan traffic, in cars and trucks with the potential power of 200 to 300 horses, creeps along at an average of 8.4 kilometers per hour (5.2 miles per hour).

After a long battle by environmentalists, the Federal Aid Highway Acts of 1973 and 1976 allowed some money from the Highway Trust Fund to be used for mass transit systems. Policy makers hoped this increased focus on mass transit would get more people out of their cars to save oil and to help relieve urban traffic congestion. But the building of mass transit systems has been discouraged because the federal government puts up 90 percent of the cost of highway projects and only 80 percent of the cost of other transportation projects.

In 1983 there were approximately 450 million motor vehicles in the world, with 700 million projected by the end of the century—one for every eight people. With only 5 percent of the world's population, the United States had 36 percent (164 million) of the world's motor vehicles in 1983. In the United States the car is now used for about 98 percent of all urban transportation and 85 percent of all travel between cities. Today 84 percent of all working Americans go to and from work every day by car. Another 5.5 percent walk or bicycle to work and only 6.3 percent take mass transit. No wonder

British author J. B. Priestly remarked, "In America, the cars have become the people."

Advantages and Disadvantages of the Automobile

The automobile provides many advantages. Above all it offers those who drive privacy, security, and unparalleled freedom to go where they want to go, when they want to go there. In addition, much of the U.S. economy is built around the automobile. One out of every five dollars spent and one out of every six nonfarm jobs is connected directly or indirectly to the automotive or related industries such as oil, steel, rubber, plastics, and highway construction. This industrial complex accounts for 20 percent of the annual gross national product (GNP) and provides about 18 percent of all federal taxes.

In spite of their advantages, cars and trucks have harmful effects on human lives and on air, water, and land natural resources. By fostering urban sprawl, they have been a key factor in the decline of mass transit systems in the central cities, where up to 60 percent of the people do not own a car. Without cars and adequate public transportation, almost 100 million poor, young, elderly, and handicapped Americans have very little freedom of travel.

The world's 450 million cars and trucks also kill an average of 170,000 people, maim 500,000, and injure 10 million each year. In the United States about 25 million motor vehicle accidents each year kill about 50,000 people and injure about 5 million, at a cost of about $60 billion annually in lost income, insurance, and administrative and legal expenses. This is equivalent to a death every 10 minutes and a disabling injury every 16 seconds of every day. Since the automobile was introduced, almost 2 million Americans have been killed on the highways—about twice the number killed in all U.S. wars.

Motor vehicles also use vast amounts of mineral and energy resources, including 56 percent of the petroleum, 74 percent of the rubber, 62 percent of the lead, 15 percent of the steel, and about 12 percent of the aluminum used each year in the United States. Freight and passenger transportation accounts for about 34 percent of all energy used each year in the United States—a major factor in U.S dependence on other nations for much of its oil supply (Section 14-2). But cars and trucks are so inefficient (Sections 2-3 and 14-4) that they waste 90 percent of the energy available in gasoline. Automobiles also produce about 60 percent (by weight) of all air pollution—85 percent in many cities— (Chapter 19) and about 85 percent of all urban noise.

Large areas of land are also utilized by motor vehicles. Roads and parking spaces take up 65 percent of the the total land area in Los Angeles, over half of Dallas (see photo on page 3) and over one-third of New York City and the nation's capital. Highways cover a total land area in the United States about equal to the areas of Vermont, New Hampshire, Connecticut, Massachusetts, and Rhode Island combined.

Three basic methods have been proposed for reducing the problems created by the automobile: (1) encouraging the use of bicycles and develop urban mass-transit and paratransit systems, (2) discouraging automobile use, and (3) reducing pollution and energy and matter waste in automobiles. Let's look at these options.

Bicycles The leg-powered bicycle won't replace cars in urban areas, but its use could be greatly increased. With more bike paths and lanes and secure bike parking (to prevent theft), the Department of Transportation hopes that the number of bike commuters in the United States will increase from about 470,000 in 1975 to 2.5 million by 1985, saving as many as 77,000 barrels of oil a day. Indeed, between 1969 and 1984, more bicycles than cars were sold in the United States and West Germany. The bicycle, using no fossil fuels and requiring few resources to produce, is very useful for the trips under 8 kilometers (5 miles) that make up about 43 percent of all urban travel. In traffic, cars and bicycles move at about the same average speed.

The ability to use bikes in cities varies with the terrain. Manhattan's compactness and comparatively flat terrain make it useful—but dangerous— for bicyclists. Los Angeles is flat, but its sheer distances tend to rule out anything but neighborhood cycling. San Francisco's hills discourage cycling for most people. Eugene, Oregon, encourages bicyclists and, helpfully, Oregon allocates 1 percent of its highway funds for the building of bicycle paths and lanes.

Davis, California, a city of 38,000 with a favorable climate and flat terrain, has set an example for the rest of the United States. Its 28,000 bicycles account for about one-fourth of all travel within the city. City employees are provided with bikes to get around, older residents drive large tricycles, and people haul groceries in trailer buggies attached to the rear of their bikes. There are 64 kilometers (40 miles) of bicycle lanes and paths, and some streets are closed to automobiles.

Mass Transit The number of riders on all forms of mass transit (buses, subways, and trolleys) declined from about 19.5 billion passengers in 1950 to about 6.7 billion passengers in 1973 before the oil embargo. Even with higher gasoline prices and federal subsidies for mass transit since 1973, ridership had climbed back to only about 8 billion by

1983. Fares that used to cover most operating costs of mass transit systems now cover only about 45 percent of such costs, with the difference made up by local, state, and federal subsidies.

Some critics blame financial losses on powerful transit labor unions. Labor costs now account for 70 to 80 percent of transit operating expenses. In Boston the average transit worker earns $33,000 a year in wages and benefits, and the transit system employs 200 "doorguards" just to make sure automatic doors open and close. Other transit critics say inept management is at least as much a problem as transit labor unions. They point out that artificially low fares and dependence on government to cover losses encourage inefficient management.

Some analysts see the building of new *fixed-rail rapid transit systems* and improving existing systems as a key to urban transportation problems in most large cities. Others argue that such technological solutions are extremely expensive and do not serve many people in today's spread-out cities. They are primarily useful where many people live along a narrow corridor, and even then their high construction and operating costs may outweigh their benefits. Some contend that subway cars and large buses use less energy than cars, but this argument is being challenged. With low average daily loads (typically only 25 percent occupancy), trains, trolleys, and buses use about the same amount of energy per passenger as private automobiles. There is much talk about building high-speed trains, but Japan's trains that whiz along at 193 kilometers per hour (120 miles per hour) consume much energy because of wind resistance, produce vibrations that have cracked buildings, and are extremely noisy. In addition, Japan's national railway system had an accumulated deficit of $37 billion by 1983. A 1984 Office of Technology Assessment study warned that high-speed trains being considered to link several U.S. cities will not be able to attract enough riders to make a profit.

Older subway and commuter train systems in many cities have been plagued with deteriorating equipment and tracks and massive financial losses. An estimated $60 billion is needed between 1983 and 1993 to repair existing mass transit systems. New York City's aging mass transit system—the largest in the nation—needs $14 billion worth of repairs and improvements. One-fourth of its subway cars are normally out of service at any one time, mostly because management didn't order spare parts or because the parts aren't made any more.

The current era of new fixed-rail mass transit projects began with the opening in 1972 of San Francisco's computer-controlled Bay Area Rapid Transit (BART) system. Later Washington D.C., Atlanta, and Baltimore partially completed subway systems, and others are planned or being built for Miami, Dallas, and Los Angeles. The $1.7 billion BART system was supposed to be a model for future rapid mass transit systems. However, since its opening it has suffered from breakdowns, fires, brake problems, computers that failed in the rain, massive financial losses, and too few riders. Part of the problem may be that BART is too rapid, with stations widely spaced so that trains can run at high speeds. Since many passengers would have to take a bus or car to the nearest BART station, they don't bother to use it at all. A whole fleet of new buses that would carry all BART's passengers would have cost only 2.5 percent of BART's original cost.

The partially completed METRO system of Washington, D.C., is better planned than BART and has the advantage of serving a concentrated urban area. But this Rolls Royce of the mass transit systems cost $71.3 million a mile compared to $22.5 million a mile for BART, was built entirely at federal expense, and in 1983 had an operating deficit of $61 million, which is expected to double by 1986.

Other cities such as Buffalo, San Diego, and Portland, Oregon, have built or are building light rail trolley systems—modernized versions of the streetcar systems torn up in the nation's major cities in the 1940s. By upgrading an existing railroad bed, San Diego has built its "Tijuana Trolley" system running between downtown San Diego and the Mexican border at a cost per mile almost one-fourth that of BART and one-fifteenth that of METRO. The trolley system, which opened in 1981, was funded by the state gasoline tax and a local sales tax; it was completed on time and $500,000 under budget. The Tijuana Trolley carries an average of 11,000 riders a day, and their fares pay 88 percent of the system's operating costs. Costs are kept low by cutting out red tape, having a nonunion transit work force (possible because no federal funds were involved), and collecting fares on the honor system.

Buses are even cheaper and more flexible than trolleys. They can be routed to almost any area in widely dispersed cities. To attract more riders and to help buses avoid traffic congestion, more than 50 urban areas in the United States and 30 European cities have express bus lanes. In Los Angeles the use of such lanes tripled bus ridership and increased carpool riders by 65 percent. The project was abandoned, however, after protests by car commuters, outraged at being restricted to lanes more jammed than ever. Despite increases in ridership since 1975, buses in Los Angeles are used by less than 2 percent of the population. Other cities have cut fares to attract riders.

Bus systems also require less capital and have lower operating costs than most light and heavy rail mass transit systems. But by offering low fares to attract enough riders, they usually lose money. To make up for losses, bus companies tend to cut service and maintenance. Almost half of the city buses in Houston are idled by breakdowns, with riders often waiting an hour for service. Philadelphia's aging fleet of buses averages about 10 accidents a day, often because of bad brakes and because, according to a survey, 35 percent of bus repairs are done improperly.

Paratransit Most analysts argue that buses, vans, and cars that can go anywhere are the only practical solution to the transportation problems of today's dispersed urban areas. Because full-sized buses are cost effective only when full, they are being supplemented by carpools, vanpools, jitneys, and dial-a-ride systems. These paratransit methods attempt to combine the advantages of the door-to-door service of a private automobile or taxi with the economy of a 10-passenger van or minibus.

States and private companies have set up vanpools in many areas to get employees to and from work. Seattle increased the number of ride pools, carpools and vanpools significantly by providing free downtown parking for users. Dial-a-ride systems are in operation in an increasing number of American cities. Passengers call for a van, minibus, or tax-subsidized taxi that comes by to pick them up at the doorstep, usually in about 20 to 50 minutes. Efficiency can be increased by the use of two-way radios and routing by a central computer. These systems are fairly expensive to operate. But compared with most large-scale mass transit systems, they are a bargain, and each vehicle is usually filled with passengers. They are one of the best ways to provide transportation for the poor, the young, the elderly, and the handicapped.

One cheaper and simpler approach to the dial-a-ride concept is tax-subsidized taxi fares. In El Cajon and La Mesa, California, the local cab company offers fairly cheap, citywide dial-a-ride services, with city taxes paying the company a given amount for each trip. In Phoenix, Arizona, the transit authority pays a subsidy to a local cab company to provide rides on Sunday, when the bus system is shut down because of low ridership. Phoenix transit officials say this saves them $300,000 to $500,000 a year.

In cities such as Mexico City, Caracas, and Cairo, large fleets of *jitneys*—small vans or minibuses that travel relatively fixed routes but stop on demand—carry millions of passengers each day. After laws banning jitney service were repealed in 1979, privately owned jitney service has flourished in San Diego, San Francisco, and Los Angeles and may spread to other cities. Analysts argue that deregulation of taxi fares and public transport fares would

greatly increase the number of private individuals and companies operating jitneys in most major cities.

Discouraging Automobile Use Proposed means of reducing automobile use in cities include: **(1)** refusing to build new highways into and out of the city, **(2)** raising the price of gasoline significantly by adding higher federal and state taxes (as has been done in most European nations, where gasoline costs $2 to almost $4 a gallon), **(3)** setting aside express lanes for buses, streetcars, bicycles, and carpools during peak traffic hours (as in London, Paris, and Washington, D.C.), **(4)** charging higher road and bridge tolls during peak hours, **(5)** eliminating or reducing road and bridge tolls for cars with three or more passengers, **(6)** taxing parking lots, **(7)** eliminating some downtown parking lots, **(8)** charging automobile commuters high taxes or fees, and **(9)** prohibiting cars on some streets or in entire areas (as in many European cities). However in the United States, most elected officials are unwilling to risk the wrath of commuters and voters by imposing such coercive measures.

Improving the Automobile In spite of attempts to increase the use of mass transit and paratransit systems, the private automobile will likely remain the primary means of transportation in widely dispersed urban areas. Thus in recent years, increasing emphasis has been placed on reducing energy and matter wastes and pollution caused by automobiles. Methods include: **(1)** modifying internal combustion engines so that they burn less fuel and produce less pollution (Section 19-7), **(2)** shifting to more energy-efficient engines that yield less pollution (Section 19-7), and **(3)** reducing car weight by using more plastics and lightweight metals. Renault plans to have a vehicle on the market by 1985 that will get 34 kilometers per liter (80 miles per gallon) on the highway, and Volkswagen and several Japanese automakers have been testing similar highly fuel-efficient cars.

12-5 Urban and Nonurban Land-Use Planning and Control

Methods of Land-Use Planning Land-use planning involves deciding the best use for each parcel of land in an area and mapping out suitable locations for houses, industries, businesses, open space, roads, water lines, sewer lines, hospitals, schools, waste treatment plants, and so on. The first step in the development of a comprehensive land-use plan is to gather geological, biological, and sociological data on the state and use of each parcel of land. These data are used to make projections about how humans may need to use the land in the future; and this information is evaluated to determine the best present and future use for each parcel of land. Four major methods are used to make projections and develop a land-use plan: **(1)** extrapolation of existing trends, **(2)** reaction to crisis, **(3)** systems analysis and modeling, and **(4)** ecological planning.

Planning by extrapolating or projecting existing trends into the future is the most widely used approach but one of the least effective. For a 1- or 2-year period this method is normally useful, but for longer terms it can be disastrous because of inability to predict accurately new trends and events (Enrichment Study 2). Another widely used and usually ineffective approach is to wait to until problems reach the crisis stage before developing a plan of action.

Systems analysis and modeling simulates cities and land areas. Data are collected, goals are set, mathemathical models are constructed based on different assumptions, and a computer is programmed to project and compare these models. If goals are agreed on, such models can provide planners with a useful tool for evaluating alternative land-use plans. However, a computer model, like any model, is no better than the data and assumptions on which it is based.

In recent years new ecological approaches to land-use planning have been developed by planners such as Ian L. McHarg (see *Design with Nature*, 1969). Although based on classifying land according to its capability, as shown earlier in Figure 8-12, this approach goes much further. McHarg's basic theme is that to use land wisely, we should work with—not against—nature. This means that **(1)** top-quality farmland should be preserved; **(2)** building and farming should not occur on hillsides subject to erosion or on valuable wetlands and flood plains; **(3)** building near surface waters should be regulated to keep water levels constant and to reduce pollution; **(4)** land use over underground water aquifers should be strictly regulated; **(5)** mature woodlands and forests, which act as watersheds to provide water, reduce the likelihood of floods, and absorb noise and air pollution, should be saved; and **(6)** social needs and public participation should be part of all planning.

In its ideal form, ecological land-use planning by McHarg and others consists of six steps.

1. *Making an environmental and social inventory*: A comprehensive geological, ecological, and social survey of the land is made. This includes an analysis of **(a)** geological variables, such as slopes, soil types and limitations, and aquifer and other hydrological data, **(b)** ecological variables, such as forest types and quality, ecological value, wildlife habitats, stream quality, estuaries, and historical or unique sites, and **(c)** social and economic variables, such as recreation areas, urban development, social pathology (rates of homicide, suicide, robbery, and drug addiction), physical pathology (rates of tuberculosis, diabetes, emphysema, and heart disease), pollution, ethnic distribution, illiteracy, overcrowding, housing quality, and industrial plant quality.

2. *Determination of goals and their relative importance*: Experts, public officials, and the general public decide on goals and weigh each goal. This is one of the most important and difficult planning steps, in which ethical land-use conflicts (Section 10-1) are resolved.

3. *Production of individual and composite maps*: Data for each variable obtained from step 1 are plotted on separate transparency maps. The transparencies are superimposed on one another or combined by computer to give three composite maps—one each for geological variables, ecological variables, and social and economic variables. Each map shows how the variables interact. Computers and systems analysis models can be used to plot these composite density maps and to weight each value numerically according to decisions made in step 2. Computer modeling can also be used to update maps and to make alternative composites based on different goals and weighting factors.

4. *Development of a comprehensive plan*: The three composite maps are combined to form a master composite, which shows the suitability of various areas for different types of use. In some cases a computer-generated series of master composites shows the effects of weighting key variables in different ways. Using this technique, it often becomes clear how certain areas of land should or should not be used. For example, land near an existing population center, that has poor soil but good road access would be a logical place for a high-density development.

5. *Evaluation of the comprehensive plan*: The comprehensive plan (or series of alternative comprehensive plans) is evaluated by experts, public officials, and the general public, and a final comprehensive plan is drawn up and approved.

6. *Implementation of the comprehensive plan*: The plan is set in motion and monitored by the

appropriate governmental, legal, environmental, and social agencies.

The goal of ecological planning is to help planners and citizens strike a balance among the four major types of ecosystems: **(1)** *unmanaged natural ecosystems* (wilderness, including deserts and mountains), **(2)** *managed multiple-use ecosystems* (parks, estuaries, and some managed forests), **(3)** *managed productive ecosystems* (farms, cattle ranches, other managed forests, and surface mines), and **(4)** *managed urban ecosystems* (cities and towns). Still in its infancy, this approach has been applied with partial success to many areas.

Problems associated with ecological land-use planning include **(1)** difficulties in getting reliable scientific, economic, and social data, **(2)** difficulty of weighting the aesthetic and ecological factors, **(3)** lack of effective means for implementing land-use plans, and **(4)** political conflicts between those with differing ethical views on how land should be used.

Examples of Land-Use Planning   In ecological or any other form of land-use planning, decisions to grant permits for residential, commercial, industrial, or other use of land are normally made by the nation's 10,000 separate city and county governments. Relatively few of these local governments have the money, staff, and information needed to do comprehensive land-use planning. This major problem has resulted in a hodgepodge of attempts to limit or promote growth, based primarily on the extrapolation and reaction to crisis methods of land-use planning. The artificial political boundaries of cities, towns, and counties bear little relation to the natural airsheds, watersheds, and ecosystems in each region. As a result, land-use planning and control in one area may be undercut by lack of planning or by planning with opposite goals in surrounding areas. For example, the Greater New York area has 1,476 governmental jurisdictions, each making decisions about land use that affect other jurisdictions.

Many states have set up advisory councils of government (COGs) to draw up and coordinate integrated land-use plans for an entire region. But such councils often lack expertise, funds, and the authority to implement decisions. The Nature Conservancy has helped 21 states make ecological inventories of their respective natural communities and the plant and animal life they contain. Such information can be useful in developing comprehensive land-use policies at the state, regional, and local levels.

Hawaii, Massachusetts, Connecticut, New York, New Jersey, Washington, Vermont, Florida, California, Pennsylvania, and Oregon have attempted to develop and in some cases have implemented laws for land-use planning and control. Japan is the only country with comprehensive planning and zoning — the entire nation is divided into five major land-use zones (urban, agricultural, parks, nature reserves, and forests). During the 1960s Belgium, West Germany, France, and the Netherlands passed laws establishing guidelines for land use but left the actual planning to localities. Canada has also developed a fairly comprehensive land-use planning program.

Preserving Urban Open Space   Most planners are concerned with preserving open space within and around urban areas. **Urban open space** is any large, medium-sized, or small area of land or water in or near an urban area that can be used for recreational, aesthetic, or ecological functions. To some people urban open space means large areas of woods, wildlife sanctuaries, and other natural areas that should be preserved near or within urban areas. Such spaces provide habitats for wildlife, help reduce noise and air and water pollution, provide quiet and beautiful places where urban dwellers can experience natural diversity, and can help block harmful patterns of urban growth and development.

To others urban open space means *moderate-sized* areas set aside within urban areas for picnics, boating, swimming, playgrounds, zoos, and other forms of recreation. To other individuals it means *small* spaces such as abandoned lots, dried-up creek beds, abandoned road beds, and other strips and patches of unused urban land that can be revitalized for use as vest-pocket parks and playgrounds, bicycle and jogging trails, and other recreational or aesthetic uses.

One of the most ambitious efforts at preserving *large* open spaces to reduce urban sprawl is the 10- to 16-kilometer (6- to 10-mile) wide greenbelt around London. This example of long-range planning, begun in 1931, has preserved some land-use choices that most cities squandered long ago. But it has failed to halt urban growth; the suburbs have jumped the belt. The large belt also has been criticized as not being available to people, and there is continuing pressure to develop some of the space. As open space expert William Whyte (see *The Social Life of Small Urban Spaces*, 1980) points out, "Open space has to have a positive function. It will not remain open if it does not. People must be able to do things

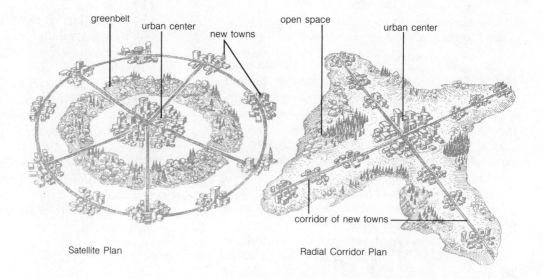

Figure 12-7 Two plans for preserving large blocks of urban open space.

greenbelt   urban center   new towns   open space   urban center

Satellite Plan   Radial Corridor Plan

corridor of new towns

on it or with it—at the very least to be able to look at it."

Another way to preserve large open spaces near an urban area is to build a series of *new towns* beyond the central urban area, as shown in Figure 12-7. Among the possibilities are the *satellite plan*, where a ring of new towns connected by a beltway is built beyond a greenbelt and the *radial corridor plan*, where new towns are built along corridors separated by wedges of open space. New towns are discussed in Section 12-6.

Some cities have had the foresight to preserve open space in moderate-sized to large *municipal parks*. Central Park in New York City and Golden Gate Park in San Francisco are two famous examples. Even though Central Park is now crisscrossed by six-lane roads and is crime infested at night, it is heavily used. Cities with large municipal parks must continually resist efforts to build freeways through them. Unfortunately, cities that did not plan for such parks early in their development have little or no chance of getting them now.

Since World War II the typical pattern of a suburban housing development in the United States has been to bulldoze a patch of woods or farmland and build rows of houses, with each house having a standardized lot (Figure 12-8). In recent years a new pattern, known as *cluster development* or *planned unit development* (PUD), has been used with increasing success to preserve moderate-sized blocks of open space. Houses, townhouses, condominiums, and garden apartments are built on a relatively small portion of land, with the rest of the area left as open space, either in its natural state or for recreation areas (Figure 12-9).

The most overlooked and probably most important open spaces are the small strips and odd-shaped patches of unused land that dot urban areas.

Figure 12-8 A suburban housing development tract developed in the usual way.

The Illinois Prairie Path is a walkway and bridle path running from downtown Chicago to its western suburbs along an abandoned trolley line. Other cities have converted abandoned railroad beds into bicycle, hiking, and jogging paths. In Santa Barbara, California, dry creek beds have been developed as bicycle paths and walkways. San Antonio, Texas, has revitalized much of its downtown area by developing shops, restaurants, and other businesses along the San Antonio River, which runs through a 21-block area of the city.

Within cities, abandoned lots can be developed as small plazas and vest-pocket parks such as Paley Park in midtown Manhattan—a refreshing refuge for about 3,000 people each day. Research by William H. Whyte, director of the Street Life Project in New York City, has shown that the most widely used small urban plazas and miniparks are located

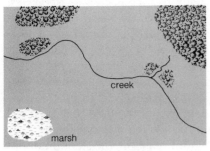

Undeveloped Land

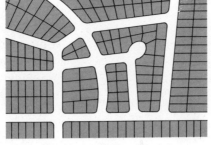

Typical Housing Development

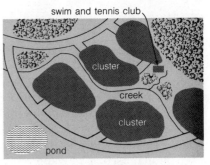

Cluster Housing Development

Figure 12-9 Tract and cluster development forms on the same land area.

just a few steps from busy streets so that people can easily see and enter them. They also tend to have **(1)** ledges deep enough for sitting on both sides near the street, and steps, benches, and a variety of other sitting places within, **(2)** building or other walls on three sides to provide protection from the wind and give a feeling of comfort and safety, **(3)** patches of trees planted close together and near sitting ledges and benches, for a pleasing combination of shade and sunlight, **(4)** sculpture or occasional art exhibits to draw people in and provide something to talk about, **(5)** places for food vendors, a snackbar or sidewalk cafe, picnic and game tables, and street musicians and entertainers, and **(6)** water, in the form of waterfalls, waterwalls, fountains, or brooks, to provide "white sound" to mask street noises and nearby conversations.

Abandoned lots cluttered with old car hulks, tires, and piles of dirt and rocks can be cleaned up slightly and used as "adventure playgrounds," which are usually jampacked with children. These places look dangerous to parents, but studies have shown that fewer accidents occur there than in the more expensive traditional playgrounds, neatly laid out with swings, slides, and steel climbing bars.

Methods of Land-Use Control Unless it can be effectively implemented, a land-use plan merely gathers dust. Major methods for controlling land use include: **(1)** direct purchase of land by a public agency or by private interests to ensure that it is used for the prescribed purposes, **(2)** zoning land so it can be used only in certain ways, **(3)** giving tax breaks to landowners who agree to use land only for given purposes such as agriculture or open space, **(4)** purchase of land development rights by public agencies that restrict the way the land can be used, **(5)** assigning a limited number of transferrable development rights to a given area of land, **(6)** controlling population growth and land development by limiting building permits, sewer hookups, roads, and other services, and **(7)** using envi-

ronmental impact statements (EISs) to stop or delay harmful projects by forcing consideration of adverse impacts and alternatives to all federal land-use projects, as discussed in Section 21-2.

The surest way to protect land from development or other potentially harmful uses is to arrange that the land must be purchased by a government conservation agency or private foundation, corporation, or individual. Purchase of land by a local, state, or federal agency, however, has several drawbacks. It is costly, it removes land from the tax base, and it requires public funds to buy and maintain. Moreover, owners often inflate the price if they learn that a government agency is a prospective buyer. Experience in Sweden and other countries shows that to avoid inflated prices, the government must purchase the land 20 to 30 years before it is to be used, leased, or sold for controlled development. An additional drawback is that governments usually move too slowly to buy up areas threatened by immediate development.

Private organizations such as the Nature Conservancy and the Audubon Society have performed a valuable public service by buying and protecting land, often until government or other private purchase funds are available. Today over 500 private land trusts have bought and protected close to 3 million acres of rare, beautiful, and threatened areas of land—an area equivalent in size to the state of Connecticut.

The first comprehensive zoning law was established in 1916 by New York City to limit the size of new skyscrapers that were casting shadows on nearby streets. Today most city and county governments have zoning or planning boards that classify the various areas of land under their jurisdiction in such major use categories as industrial, commercial (stores and offices), multifamily residential, single-family residential, recreational, and agricultural. One widely used zoning technique is to require developers to use large lots for each house in single-family residential areas. This practice prevents high-density development but in most cases also excludes residents who cannot afford to buy and build on large lots.

Developers can also be required to set aside a certain fraction of the land they wish to develop as open space or to provide other facilities. Floodplain zoning has also been used in a number of communities to exclude permanent buildings from low-lying areas near rivers and streams that are periodically flooded. Often such areas are set aside for recreational uses or as wildlife preserves.

Local zoning boards, however, are vulnerable to political and economic pressures from developers. Often such boards contain realtors, developers, or local business people who can profit directly or indirectly from having parcels of land zoned or rezoned. Most local governments also lack funds to hire professional planners. As a result, land is usually zoned for its current use with little or no efforts to develop a long-range land-use plan on which to base zoning decisions. In spite of its disadvantages, zoning can be an effective land-use control if based on comprehensive ecological land-use planning, strictly enforced, and supported by the public.

Zoning can be more effective when coupled with taxation policies that discourage harmful forms of development such as conversion of prime agricultural land to urban housing and business areas. In some states land is taxed on the basis of its highest *potential* use, which is usually high-density urban development. Faced with high tax bills, owners of agricultural land and undeveloped forest and other lands are often forced to sell their land or develop it. To relieve this pressure for development, about half the states now base property taxes on *current use* of land rather than on its *highest potential use*. Some states also require that a certain number of years of back taxes must be paid at a higher rate if and when agricultural land is developed for urban use.

In another method of land-use control, landowners donate or sell to state or local governments, often in return for lower property taxes, their rights to develop the land in certain ways. This approach ensures that the land will continue to be used only for specified purposes—such as farmland. Present and all future owners keep and use the land, but not for urban development. The purchase of development rights by a public agency normally costs less than direct purchase, does not remove the land completely from the tax base, and imposes no maintenance costs on the community. Sometimes, however, the cost of purchasing development rights for land most in need of protection almost equals that of direct purchase.

In another relatively new and promising approach, a zoning board or other public agency assigns a limited number of *transferrable development rights* for a given area of land, based on a comprehensive plan showing permissible areas of low-, medium-, and high-density development. Initially, each landowner is assigned the same number of development rights for each acre owned. Landowners can sell or transfer their development rights, which means that parts of the land may be developed while other parts remain undeveloped.

Since 1970 hundreds of U.S. communities, especially those near large urban areas, have attempted to stop or slow local population growth and land development. Some have tried to accomplish this form of land-use control by passing laws that establish population limits or prohibit further development. Such schemes, however, are often thinly veiled ways to exclude minority and low-income individuals. Furthermore, such laws are usually overturned by courts on the grounds that they deny the constitutional right of individual landowners to use their land in a reasonable manner.

The more common approach is to slow growth by temporarily controlling the nature, location, and timing of future growth. Typically this phased development approach is implemented by controlling the number of new housing permits, sewer hookups, roads, or other public services. In general, the courts have upheld a community's efforts to slow its rate of growth provided the plan is temporary and makes a specific provision for minority and low-income housing.

12-6 Coping with Urban Problems

Approaches to Urban Problems Trying to solve or mitigate the problems of the cities is difficult, complex, and costly. The major approaches for dealing with urban problems include (1) repairing the damage done to the physical plant of older cities to preserve and strengthen what is already there and to prevent further decay, (2) revitalizing existing cities economically and socially, and (3) designing and building new more ecologically sound and self-reliant cities and towns. Let's look at how these three approaches are being used. Although emphasis is on the United States, the principles involved can be applied to most cities throughout the world.

Repairing Existing Cities Like everything else, cities are subject to physical decay. As they age, they must use more and more of their matter, energy, and money resources for the repair, maintenance, or replacement of old facilities and for preventive maintenance on new ones. As philosopher-longshoreman Eric Hoffer observed, "History shows that the level achieved by a civilization can be measured by the degree to which it performs maintenance."

America's older cities have massive maintenance and repair problems—most of them aggravated by neglect. Most of the sewers of New Orleans, some of which were purchased secondhand from Philadelphia in 1896, need replacement. When it rains in Chicago, sewers back up into basements of about one-fourth of the homes. An estimated 46 percent of Boston's water supply and 25 percent of that in Pittsburgh is lost through leaky pipes. Two massive tunnels bringing fresh water into New York City are crumbling. One out of every five bridges in the country and two out of every five in urban areas are structurally deficient and considered safe for cars and light trucks only.

The maintenance and repair of existing U.S. bridges, roads, mass transit systems, water supply systems, sewers, and sewage treatment plants could cost a staggering $1.2 trillion or more between 1984 and 2000, according to a 1984 study for Congress's Joint Economic Committee. These massive repair and maintenance bills are coming due at a time when the federal government, to help hold down record budget deficits, is cutting back funds available for building and maintaining public works.

The ability of cities to generate their own funds and decide how to solve their own problems has declined considerably while their responsibilities and budgets have increased. Today most cities receive more money from state legislatures and the federal government than from their own tax revenues. Much of this aid must be spent in ways determined by federal and state bureaucracies far removed from local problems. To make matters worse, cities have to rely on increasingly unpopular property taxes for about 87 percent of their tax revenues. Rather than pay higher taxes and user fees, residents of some cities choose to settle for lower levels of service. They learn to live with potholes, periodic water shortages, and less public transit.

Revitalizing Existing Cities   Other planners have concentrated on revitalizing the economic and social life of existing cities. Billions of dollars are spent in decaying downtown areas to build new civic centers, museums, office buildings, parking garages, and high-rise luxury hotel and shopping center complexes. Such projects have done much to revive the economy of cities such as Baltimore and can indirectly benefit the poor by providing additional tax revenues. But they are of little direct benefit to the poor because they mainly provide white-collar jobs for suburbanites and shopping and cultural facilities for suburban families and tourists.

In most major cities many older neighborhoods are being revitalized by middle- and high-income residents who buy rundown houses at low prices and renovate them. This trend benefits the city economically by increasing property values and slowing the flight to the suburbs, but it can also displace low-income residents. Therefore, a number of cities have set up *urban homesteading programs* to help middle- and low-income individuals improve and live in abandoned housing. Old houses and apartment buildings, abandoned or acquired by a city because of failure to pay taxes, are resold to individuals or to cooperatives of low-income renters, typically for $1 to $100. The new owners must agree to renovate the buildings and live in them for at least 3 years. In some cases, the city also provides low-interest, long-term loans, which in effect become mortgages on the property. This approach has been particularly successful in Wilmington, Delaware and in Baltimore.

Most urban renewal projects are approved and designed by planners, architects, bureaucrats, and other professionals with very little, if any, input from the people whose problems and needs such projects are supposed to solve. For example, a number of cities have tried to improve slums by tearing down blocks of slum dwellings and replacing them with high-rise public housing projects. Some of these projects have been successful, but today there is general agreement that many have destroyed more than was rebuilt. Studies have shown that they disrupt families, destroy protective neighborhood social structures, and eliminate many essential neighborhood stores. In addition, the new rents are often too high.

By 1984 nearly a quarter of the country's federally financed public housing authorities were losing money, primarily because of local mismangement, tenant abuse of property, and shoddy or nonexistent maintenance has left many of the units so dilapidated that they can no longer be rented. Operating subsidies provided by the Department of Housing and Urban development (HUD) for the nation's 1.2 million public housing units ballooned from $28 million in 1970 to a projected $4.4 billion in 1984.

The outlook for abandoned high-rise, low-income public housing developments, however, is not totally bleak. Some have been converted to schools and commercial buildings. In Jersey City, New Jersey, a rundown high-rise project with a high crime rate was turned around by a tenant committee. The tenants themselves replaced broken windows with unbreakable plastic glass, installed indoor and outdoor unbreakable lights, repaired broken elevators and rubbish chutes, repainted the building, and planted grass and flowers. They also found building managerial and service jobs for some of the tenants.

Some analysts call for increased federal aid to help revitalize the cities. Others argue that such federal aid is often wasted and is controlled by distant bureaucrats who have little knowledge of the needs of local people. Instead, they propose that private companies be encouraged to carry out urban redevelopment by reducing regulatory requirements and providing tax credits for investment. Another important incentive is the granting of tax reductions to employers who create new jobs, hiring the unemployed or disadvantaged in *free enterprise zones* in economically depressed urban neighborhoods.

In addition, special emphasis should be placed on helping create small businesses in such zones— a study of 5.5 million businesses throughout the United States revealed that two-thirds of all *new* jobs are created by small companies employing 20 or fewer people. Proponents of this approach point to the example set by Control Data Corporation (CDC), a Minneapolis-based computer firm guided by William C. Morris, which since 1968 has shown that a business can be run profitably in inner-city poverty areas. CDC has successfully built factories, created jobs, set up career counseling and job training programs, provided day care centers for working mothers, and stimulated renewal in blighted urban areas in Minneapolis, St. Paul, San Antonio, Baltimore, Toledo, and Washington, D.C.—all without federal aid.

Building New Cities and Towns In l898 English planner Ebenezer Howard urged that new towns be built to lure Londoners from the city. Since then Great Britain has built 16 new towns and is building 15 more. New towns have also been built in Singapore, Hong Kong, Finland, Sweden, France, the Netherlands, Venezuela, Brazil, and the United States. There are three types: **(1)** *satellite towns,* located relatively close to an existing large city (Figure 12-7), **(2)** *freestanding new towns,* located far from a major city, and **(3)** *"in-town"* new towns, located in existing urban areas. Typically, such towns are conceived for populations of 20,000 to 100,000 people.

The most widely acclaimed new town is Tapiola, Finland, located not far from Helsinki. Designed in 1952, it is being built gradually in seven sections with an ultimate projected population of 80,000. Today many of its more than 30,000 residents work in Helsinki, but the long-range goal is industrial and commercial independence for the town. Tapi-

ola is divided into several villages separated by greenbelts. Each village has its own architect, selected by competition, and consists of several neighborhoods clustered around a shopping and cultural center. Each neighborhood has a social center and contains a mix of high-rise apartments and single-family houses. Finland has drawn up plans for building six more new towns around Helsinki.

Unfortunately new towns rarely succeed without massive government financial support, and some don't succeed even then, primarily because of poor planning and management. Private developers must put up large amounts of money to buy the land and install facilities and must pay heavy taxes and interest charges for decades before any profit is made. In the United States two privately developed new towns—Columbia, Maryland, and Reston, Virginia—have been in constant financial difficulty since they were started almost two decades ago, although their situations are gradually improving.

Probably the most notable and successful example is Columbia, located between Baltimore and Washington, D.C., and designed and built by James Rouse. This new town has five self-sufficient village centers, each made up of three or four neighborhoods. Almost one-third of its area consists of parklands, streams, and other forms of open space. It now has a population of nearly 60,000, a highly regarded school system, branches of four colleges, one hospital, and almost 30,000 jobs. One of its aims was to show that different races can live and work together. About 20 percent of its population is black, and 18 of its 134 businesses are black owned, some with aid from the Rouse Company, which developed the town. Columbia was also supposed to provide some housing within the financial capabilities of low-income groups, but free market forces have driven the cost of such units beyond the reach of people with modest incomes.

In 1971 HUD provided more than $300 million in federally guaranteed loans for developers to build 13 new towns. By 1980, however, HUD had to take title to 9 of these towns, which went bankrupt, and won't provide money for more new towns.

Planners such as George B. Dantzig and Thomas L. Saaty (*Compact City: A Plan for a Liveable Environment,* 1973), Percival Goodman (*The Double E,* 1977), and David Morris (*Energy and the Transformation of Urban America,* 1982) have proposed guidelines and models for building compact towns and cities that waste less matter and energy resources and are more self-reliant than conventional municipalities. Such self-sufficient cities would be surrounded by farms, greenbelts, and community gardens. Homes and marketplaces would be close together, and most local transportation would be by bus, bicycle, and foot.

Buildings would be cooled and heated by sun and wind and wastes would be recycled. Food would be grown locally, and huge factories would be scarce.

Some cities have also begun efforts to become more self-sufficient for some of their matter and energy resources. Erie, Pennsylvania, for example, drilled two producing oil wells between 1978 and 1980; Youngstown, Ohio, is leasing subsoil mineral rights to private companies and taking a portion of the profits; and Palo Alto, California, has rezoned almost 5,000 acres within the city as open space to be used primarily for agricultural purposes. Fort Collins, Colorado, runs much of its city transportation system on methane gas generated from its sewage plant and uses nutrient-rich sludge from the sewage plant to fertilize 600 acres of city-owned land to grow corn, which might be converted to alcohol to fuel more city cars. St. Paul, Minnesota, is planning to build the nation's first system that will heat all major downtown buildings with "waste heat" now being dumped into the Mississippi River by an electric utility.

Planners such as R. Buckminster Fuller, C. A. Doxiadis, and Paolo Soleri have developed visionary schemes for building new cities. The late Buckminster Fuller envisioned using technology to control nature by building cities of a million people each inside gigantic, climate-controlled geodesic domes that could be located in inhospitable areas, such as oceans, polar regions, and deserts. Critics, however, argue that Fuller's designs pay too little attention to the ecological relationships within cities and those between cities and the rest of the ecosphere. They also point to Fuller's assumption that advances in technology would give us infinite supplies of water, food, energy, and mineral resources and would allow the elimination of wastes produced by resource use without serious ecological disruption.

C. A. Doxiadis has developed a land-use plan in which a network of cities comprising a single supercity would accommodate 20 billion to 30 billion people on only 2.5 percent of the world's land. Paolo Soleri has concentrated on the design of smaller cities that combine architecture and ecology in what he calls "archology." Without public funding, he is building Arcosanti in an Arizona desert with a crew of about 100, mostly college-educated volunteers. Arcosanti is designed to be a self-sufficient city for 5,000 people. If completed as envisioned, this 15-acre city will contain shopping centers, open space (including parks), and a 25-story complex of apartments and light industries, all housed under an enormous glass roof. A number of greenhouses attached to the city's southern exposure will supply solar heat and food for a primarily vegetarian diet. Most of the city structure is to be made of concrete,

which will store solar heat, releasing it when the surrounding air cools. No cars, prisons, or cemeteries will be permitted. By 1983, after 13 years of work, the city was only about 2 percent finished, and it may take 20 to 200 years to complete.

The city is not an ecological monstrosity. It is rather the place where both the problems and the opportunities of modern technological civilization are most potent and visible.

Peter Self

Discussion Topics

1. Explain how the MDCs can be more urbanized although LDCs have higher rates of urban growth.

2. Discuss the positive and negative effects of the central city-to-suburb shift and the metropolitan-to-nonmetropolitan shift in the United States on (a) the problems of central cities, and (b) the problems of land use. Should these two shifts be encouraged or discouraged?

3. List the advantages and disadvantages of living in (a) the central area of a large city, (b) suburbia, (c) a small town in a rural area, (d) a small town near a large city, and (e) in a rural area. Which would you prefer to live in? Why?

4. Give advantages and disadvantages of emphasizing rural rather than urban development in LDCs. Why do most LDCs emphasize urban development, even though most of their population still lives in rural areas?

5. Explain why a city is really a global ecosystem. Are most city dwellers aware of this? How would you make them aware?

6. Describe how urban systems and natural ecosystems are similar and how they differ.

7. What life-support resources in your community are the most vulnerable to interruption or destruction? What alternate or backup resources, if any, exist?

8. Explain how each of the following common practices could hasten the decay of a city: (a) raising taxes, (b) building freeways and mass transit systems to the suburbs, and (c) replacing slums with low-cost housing projects. Suggest alternative policies in each case.

9. Massive traffic jams hinder you from getting to and from work each day. Government officials say that

the only way to relieve congestion is to build a highway through the middle of a beautiful urban park. As a taxpayer, would you support this construction? Why or why not? What would you suggest to relieve the situation?

10. Examine your own dependence on the automobile. What conditions, if any, would encourage you to rely less on the automobile? Would you regularly ride to school or work in a carpool? Why or why not?

11. What types of mass transit and paratransit system are available where you live? What systems were available 20 years ago?

12. Debate the pros and cons of (a) charging commuters who drive to work alone very high commuting taxes and parking fees, and (b) setting aside express lanes on freeways for buses and carpool vehicles.

13. Debate the idea that private landowners have the right to do anything they want with their land.

14. Evaluate land use and land-use planning by your college or university.

15. Make a class survey and draw a map identifying good and poor uses of small, medium-sized, and large open spaces in your area.

13

Nonrenewable Mineral Resources

The extensive use of nonrenewable metallic and nonmetallic minerals like copper, lead, mercury, zinc, sand, and stone (Figure 1-3) and nonrenewable mineral fuels such as coal, oil, natural gas, and uranium is the basis for the high standards of living enjoyed by most people in industrialized nations. They provide the materials for building and powering transportation and communication networks and for homes, factories, office buildings, dams, roads, and other engineering works; for heating,

Enrichment Studies 2, 11, 12, and 13 are related to this chapter.

cooling, and lighting systems; for labor-saving industrial and agricultural machines; and most medicines, fertilizers, insecticides, paints, ceramics, and other materials. This chapter discusses nonfuel mineral resources; the next three consider energy resources.

13-1 Abundance and Formation of Mineral Resources

Mineral Resource Abundance Figure 13-1 shows the relative percent abundances of the elements in the earth's crust (to a depth of 16 kilometers, or 10 miles) and in seawater. Notice that only 10 elements make up 99.3 percent of the earth's crust. Most of the remaining elements are found only in trace amounts. For example, the average abundance of copper in the earth's crust is 0.007 percent.

Although elements like copper comprise a tiny portion of the earth's crust, compounds of copper and many other trace elements are concentrated in

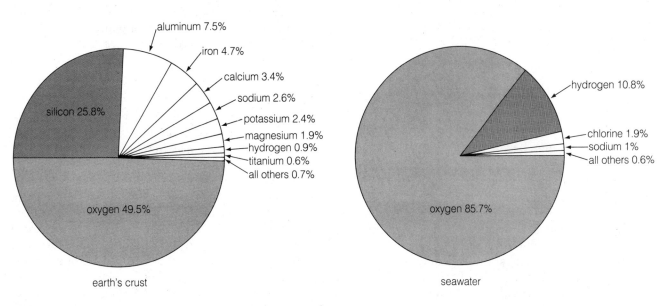

Figure 13-1 Percent by weight of elements in the earth's crust and seawater.

certain *mineral deposits* found at various places in the earth's crust. Any natural occurrence of an element, normally in compound form, is called a **mineral deposit**. Any mineral deposit with a high enough concentration of an element to permit it to be mined and sold at a profit is called an **ore**. *High-grade ores* contain relatively large concentrations and *low-grade ores* relatively low concentrations of the desired element.

Formation and Distribution of Mineral Resources
Copper and other elements are more concentrated at some locations than at others as a result of various geological and chemical processes taking place during the earth's geologic history. In general, minerals become concentrated in ores in five major ways: **(1)** separation and leaching of minerals when hot molten magma breaks through portions of the earth's crust and then cools as the slowly moving tectonic plates on which the continents float either collide or move apart, **(2)** deposition of dissolved minerals from hot, watery solutions like brine, which can move through cracks and fractures in the earth's crust and experience sudden changes in temperature and pressure, **(3)** deposition when water is evaporated from seawater or salty lake water (brine), **(4)** dissolving and removal of a mineral from one place and deposition in another or dissolving of chemicals not classified as minerals, leaving behind a deposit of a valuable mineral, and **(5)** mechanical concentration of *placer deposits* in flowing water, as when gold particles freed from rocks are carried downstream and concentrated in low points or pockets in the bed of the stream.

13-2 Location, Mining, and Processing of Mineral Resources

Locating Ore Deposits Ore deposits are located from geological knowledge about crustal movements and ore formation, along with uses of various instruments and measurements and luck. Seismic devices that set off small artificial earthquakes can enable a geologist to learn much about the subterranean rock structure of an area. Rock croppings or mounds that contain ores of certain types can be detected using photographs made from airplanes or satellites. Gravimeters and magnetometers can also be used to detect certain ore deposits from aircraft and satellites. Information about the minerals in an area can also be obtained by chemical analysis of the through-flowing waters.

Metallurgical Processes A typical metallurgical process involves the following steps:

mining→purification and concentration of the ore →chemical reduction of the ore to the free metal → refining and purification of the metal→ alloying (melting and mixing the metal with other metals) → finishing the metal or alloy

Once an ore deposit has been located, it must be extracted, normally by *surface mining* or *subsurface mining*, described later in this section. After a metal ore has been mined, physical processes such as crushing and washing are used to remove impurities and obtain the ore in concentrated form. The ore compound must then undergo a chemical reaction to obtain the free metal. For example, aluminum is found in bauxite ore in the form of aluminum oxide (Al_2O_3). Electrical current is passed through molten aluminum oxide to convert it to aluminum metal and oxygen gas ($2Al_2O_3 \rightarrow 4Al + 3O_2$). Iron ore in the form of iron oxide (Fe_2O_3) is converted to iron by reaction with carbon monoxide gas ($Fe_2O_3 + 3CO \rightarrow 2Fe + 3CO_2$). Copper ore in the form of copper sulfide (Cu_2S) can be converted to copper metal by heating the ore to high temperatures in air in a copper smelter ($Cu_2S + O_2 \rightarrow 2Cu + SO_2$). This process also produces sulfur dioxide gas (SO_2), a dangerous and highly corrosive air pollutant (Chapter 19).

Next the free metal is refined and purified. Then in many cases it is melted and mixed in molten solution with one or more other metals or other elements to form *alloys* with desired properties. Dental amalgam used to fill teeth, for example, is an alloy containing silver mixed with smaller amounts of lead, copper, and mercury; stainless steel is an alloy of iron mixed with smaller amounts of chromium, nickel, and carbon. Often the metal or alloy is finished by heating, polishing, or other methods, to obtain a surface with desired characteristics, such as hardness or corrosion resistance.

Subsurface Mining When a metal ore, or a fuel deposit such as coal, lies so deep in the ground that it is too expensive to remove the covering soil and rock (called *overburden*), it must be extracted by **subsurface mining.** This is usually done by digging a vertical shaft deep into the ground, blasting tunnels and rooms to get to the deposit, and hauling the ore to the surface. Underground mines occasionally collapse, trapping miners. Most cases of mine collapse, however, occur in the more than 90,000 abandoned coal mines in the United States. Such collapses can be prevented by injecting a mud slurry into abandoned tunnels and rooms and then

National Coal Association. Photo by Bucyrus-Erie Company

Figure 13-2 A giant shovel used for strip mining coal. The cars behind the shovel look like toys.

letting the water drain away, but this is not often done.

Underground deposits of certain soluble minerals, such as salt, can be removed by *subsurface solution mining*. In this technique, hot water is pumped down an injection well to the deposit, where it dissolves the soluble minerals. The resulting solution is pumped back to the surface and the salt or other mineral is recovered by evaporation of water. This type of mining carries the potential for contaminating groundwater reservoirs.

Surface Mining The trend in recent years has been away from subsurface mining and toward surface mining. About 90 percent of the rock and mineral resources used in the United States and more than 63 percent of the nation's coal output (compared to only 9 percent in 1940) are extracted by **surface mining.** In surface mining the overburden of topsoil, subsoil, rock, and other strata is taken away so that underlying mineral deposits can be removed with large power shovels. You can get some idea of this equipment by imagining a shovel 32 stories high, with a boom as long as a football field, capable of gouging out 152 cubic meters (200 cubic yards) of land every 55 seconds and dropping this 295,000-kilogram (325-ton) load the equivalent of a city block away. This is a description of Big Muskie, a $25 million power shovel used for surface mining coal in the United States (Figure 13-2).

An estimated 52,000 square kilometers (13 million acres) of land in the United States has been disrupted by surface mining of all types. The mining of metals accounted for about 14 percent of this disturbed land, with the remaining 86 percent divided evenly between coal and nonmetals (mostly sand and gravel). So far only about 64 percent of the land area disturbed by coal mining, 26 percent by nonmetals, and 8 percent by metals has been reclaimed. It is projected that by the year 2000 an additional 60,000 square kilometers (15 million acres) will have been disrupted by surface mining.

There are several types of surface mining: **(1)** *open pit mining,* **(2)** *dredging,* **(3)** *area strip mining,* and **(4)** *contour strip mining. Open pit mining* is used primarily for the extraction of stone, sand, gravel, iron, and copper. Sand and gravel are removed from small pits in many parts of the country. Rocks such as limestone, granite, and marble are taken from larger pits called *quarries.* In the Mesabi Range near Lake Superior and in some western states, ores of copper (see photo on p. 119) and iron are removed from huge open pit mines dug to considerable depths. Deposits of sand and gravel found in stream and ocean beds are removed by *dredging,* performed with draglines and chain buckets.

There are two basic types of strip mining: area and contour. In *area strip mining,* which is carried out on flat or rolling terrain, the overburden is stripped away to form a series of parallel trenches

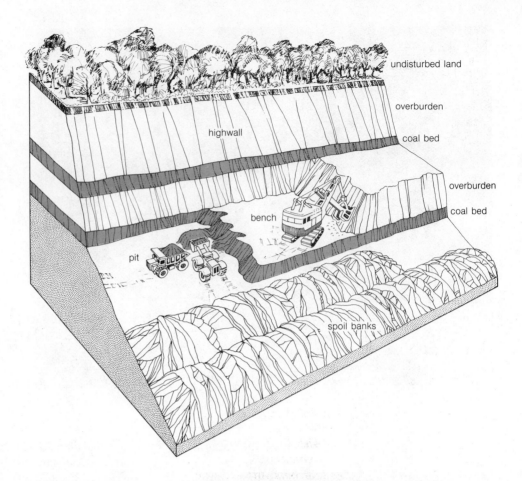

Figure 13-3 How area strip mining of coal works. Bulldozers and power shovels clear away trees, brush, and overburden. Explosive charges loosen the coal deposits, and power shovels or auger drills load the coal onto trucks in the pit area. Strip mining exposes cross sections of the earth's crust (the highwalls), and the overburden from the trench being mined is placed in an adjacent trench, which has already been mined.

(Figure 13-3). Overburden taken from one trench is placed in an adjacent one, leaving a wavy terrain. This technique is used primarily for mining gypsum, for coal in many western and midwestern states (Section 15-4), and phosphate rock—especially in Florida, North Carolina, and Idaho. In *contour strip mining*, used in hilly or mountainous terrain, a series of shelves, or terraces, is cut into the side of a mountain. The overburden from each new terrace is dumped onto the one below. Contour strip mining is used primarily for extracting coal in the mountainous Appalachian region.

Reclamation of surface-mined land includes revegetation of the disturbed land and control of erosion and runoff of acids and other chemicals leached out of mine wastes or spoils. Temporary sediment basins, terraces, diversion dams, and other techniques can be used to help prevent erosion and acid runoff while mining takes place. After mining activities have ceased, steep slopes are graded and the topsoil is replaced. Recent research has shown that surface-mined land will return to its natural state faster if the topsoil removed during the operation is replaced as soon as the mining is complete, instead of being stored for up to 2 years as many companies now do.

The final step in reclamation is the establish-

ment of cultivated crops, perennial vegetation, ponds, or lakes over the entire area. Sometimes temporary vegetation is used to reduce soil and wind erosion until perennial vegetation can be established. The productivity of disturbed soil can be improved by adding a layer of nutrient-rich topsoil, or lime, if the soil is acidic, and artificial or natural fertilizers (Section 8-6). Reclamation of surface-mined land in the arid and semiarid regions, which contain 90 percent of the nation's low-sulfur coal, is difficult. Problems include fewer plant species adapted to such conditions, lack of water to establish new vegetation, and soils that are often too acidic and contain minerals such as selenium, which are toxic to livestock.

Environmental Impact of Resource Use The mining, processing, and use of any energy or nonfuel mineral resource causes some form of land disturbance along with air and water pollution (Figure 13-4). Most land disturbed by mining can be reclaimed to some degree, and some forms of air and water pollution can be controlled (Chapters 18 and 19). But these efforts are expensive and also require energy, which in being produced and used also produces pollution (Chapter 14).

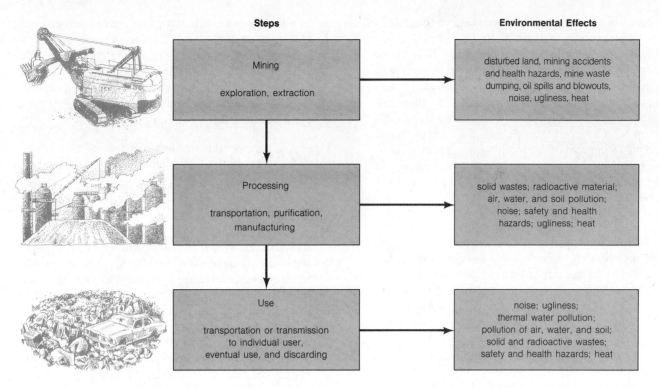

Steps	Environmental Effects
Mining exploration, extraction	disturbed land, mining accidents and health hazards, mine waste dumping, oil spills and blowouts, noise, ugliness, heat
Processing transportation, purification, manufacturing	solid wastes; radioactive material; air, water, and soil pollution; noise; safety and health hazards; ugliness; heat
Use transportation or transmission to individual user, eventual use, and discarding	noise; ugliness; thermal water pollution; pollution of air, water, and soil; solid and radioactive wastes; safety and health hazards; heat

Figure 13-4 Some environmental effects of resource use.

For each unit of mineral produced, subsurface mining disturbs less than one-tenth as much land as surface mining. It also generally produces less waste material than surface mining. But rainwater seeping through surface wastes or spoils and through abandoned mines—especially coal mines rich in sulfur compounds—causes chemical reactions that produce sulfuric acid. This acid can run off into nearby rivers and streams, contaminating water supplies and killing aquatic life. Although subsurface mining normally causes less environmental disruption than surface mining, it is usually more dangerous and more expensive than surface mining.

Large surface mining operations disturb land by directly removing material from one place and depositing it in another. Strip mining is usually the most destructive surface mining method, primarily because it disrupts such a large surface area. Environmental problems associated with surface mining include **(1)** disposal of mine spoils, **(2)** water pollution of nearby rivers and streams from runoff of sediment, acids, and toxic metals from mine spoils, **(3)** pollution of groundwater from leaching of toxic materials from mine spoils, **(4)** air pollution from dust, and **(5)** land disruption. Almost 18,000 kilometers (11,000) miles of U.S. waterways have been polluted by runoff of sulfuric acid from coal wastes left by both subsurface and surface mining. Surface mining, largely for coal, now consumes about

200,000 acres of farmland a year, especially in the Midwest. Federal and state laws now regulate the strip mining of coal and require that the disturbed land be reclaimed, as discussed in Section 15-4. But few laws exist for the regulation of strip mining of other minerals.

The processing and the refining of ores produce large quantities of waste materials that pollute the air and water (Chapters 18 and 19). People who work in some metal processing industries or live near plants with inadequate safeguards have an increased risk of getting some forms of cancer. For example, the lung cancer death rate for arsenic smelter workers is almost three times the expected rate and that for cadmium smelter workers is more than twice the expected rate. Lead smelter workers have higher incidences of lung and stomach cancer (see Enrichment Study 12).

13-3 Population, Technology, and Resources

Resource Use in the World and in the United States *In attaining their standard of living, Americans have used more nonfuel minerals and fossil fuels during the past 40 years than all the peoples of the world have used throughout human history. Between 1980 and 2000, the world's people are projected to use three to four times as much matter resources as in all of human* history. As a result, some analysts believe that future economic growth may be limited by shortages of some nonrenewable metal resources, while others believe that supplies are essentially infinite or that substitutes for scarce metals can be found. Others argue that even if supplies are sufficient they will continue to be used primarily for economic growth in the MDCs. Even though the LDCs are expected to have 78 percent of the world's population in 2000, their projected use of the world's resources is only 23 percent—slightly more than the 20 percent they currently use.

Relations Among Resources, People, Technology, and Economics Recall from Section 1-3 that a material such as copper or sand becomes a *natural resource* because of human ingenuity in finding, extracting, processing, and converting it to a useful state. Many of the mineral deposits mined today were not considered to be resources in 1900 because they were too low in grade, relatively inaccessible, or too expensive to recover. Even though resources are created by human ingenuity, the earth's recoverable mineral deposits are not inexhaustible. Several minerals such as silver and mercury are becoming scarce, and affordable supplies of others may not be available within the next few decades.

Estimating how much of a particular mineral resource exists on earth and how long its supply might last is a complex and controversial process. The term **resources** (or *total resources*) refers to the total amount of a particular material that exists on earth. A simple equation expresses the relationship between resources and people and gives the average amount of a particular resource potentially available per person in the world (AAP).

$$\text{AAP} = \begin{array}{l} \text{average amount of a resource} \\ \text{potentially available per person} \end{array}$$
$$= \frac{\text{resources}}{\text{population}} \qquad (13\text{-}1)$$

With finite supplies and an increasing population, the AAP decreases. According to this equation, population control (Chapter 7) is essential if the average standard of living based on AAP is to remain at the present level, or to increase.

The situation, however, is not so simple. It is difficult to estimate the total available amount of a particular resource because the entire world has not been explored for each resource. Even if most deposits of a particular resource were identified, much of the total supply might never be mined because it occurs in such low concentrations that it would cost more to get than it would ever be worth. As a result, most estimates of the available supply

of a resource are actually of resource *reserves*—not resources or total supply. The term **reserves** (or *economic resources*) refers to the estimated amount of a particular material in known locations that can be extracted profitably at present prices, using current mining technology. Thus, a more widely used equation for estimating AAP is:

$$\text{AAP} = \begin{array}{l} \text{average amount of a resource} \\ \text{potentially available per person} \end{array}$$
$$= \frac{\text{reserves}}{\text{population}} \qquad (13\text{-}2)$$

The estimation of available supplies of a resource, however, is more complex than this simple equation indicates. The U.S. Geological Survey, for instance, classifies resources according to the relative certainty of their existence and the economic feasibility of mining and processing them according to the scheme shown in Figure 13-5. Resources are first broadly classified as either identified or undiscovered. **Identified resources** are specific bodies of mineral-bearing rock whose existence and location are known. This category is subdivided into *reserves* (or economic resources) and *subeconomic resources*, identified resources that cannot be recovered profitably with present prices and technology. Estimates of reserves and subeconomic resources are based on analyses of rock samples and on geological projections. Since the certainty of these measurements and projections varies, the categories are subdivided further into *measured* (or *proven*), *indicated* (or *probable*), and *inferred* (or *possible*) (Figure 13-5).

Undiscovered resources are those believed to exist although their specific location, quality, and amount are unknown. They are described as either hypothetical resources or speculative resources. **Hypothetical resources** are deposits that reasonably can be expected to exist in areas where deposits have been found in the past. **Speculative resources** are deposits thought to be in areas that have not been examined and tested for resources. If actual discoveries are made, hypothetical and speculative resources may then be reclassified as reserves (economic resources) or subeconomic resources. Published estimates, which often do not specify the category being used, usually refer to reserves.

Equation 13-2 gives a fairly accurate estimate of the present AAP for a particular resource. The actual supply available in the future is normally higher, however, because reserves increase by discoveries of new supplies, and by improved technology and price increases due to shortages, which permit profitable mining of low-grade deposits initially classified as subeconomic resources. The life of most nonrenewable mineral resources also can be in-

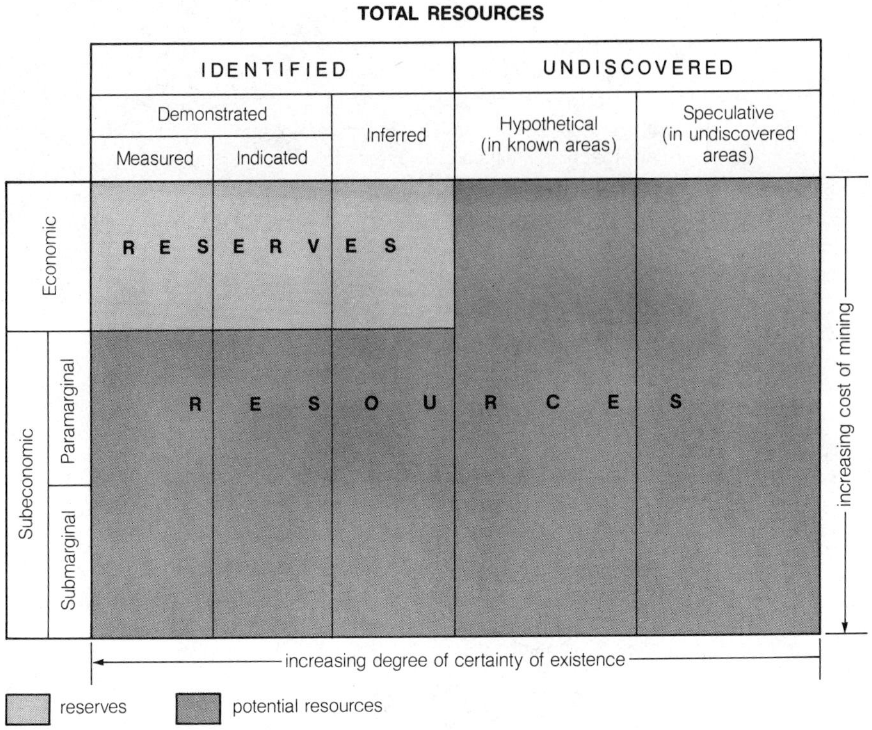

IDENTIFIED			UNDISCOVERED	
Demonstrated		Inferred	Hypothetical (in known areas)	Speculative (in undiscovered areas)
Measured	Indicated			

Figure 13-5 Classification of nonfuel and fuel mineral resources. (Source: U.S. Geological Survey.)

increasing cost of mining

Economic — R E S E R V E S

Subeconomic — Paramarginal / Submarginal — R E S O U R C E S

increasing degree of certainty of existence

reserves   potential resources

creased by recycling and reuse, by designing products to last longer, and by using substitutes—all stimulated by rising prices due to shortages. From this discussion you can see why there are so many conflicting estimates of the potential supply of a resource.

13-4 Are We Running Out of Mineral Resources?

An Environmental Controversy: Optimists Versus Pessimists In Section 1-5 you learned that there is much controversy over the potentially available future supplies of metals and other nonfuel mineral resources. One group, called *cornucopians* (or "technological optimists" by their opponents), holds that we will never run out of needed metallic and nonmetallic minerals. Their position is based on the *economic* idea that reserves of a resource increase indefinitely: scarcity causes prices to rise, which enables lower-grade deposits to be mined and stimulates the search for new deposits and substitutes. This group also believes that new technology can always be developed to mine lower-grade deposits and that substitutes can be found for essentially any mineral resource.

The opposing group, called *neo-Malthusians* (or "gloom-and-doom pessimists" by their opponents), believes that affordable supplies of metals and minerals are finite, that there will be shortages

of some key materials within the next few decades, and that the environmental effects from using resources at high rates will probably limit resource use in the future even if supplies are adequate. They emphasize not only discovery of new resources but also recycling, reuse, conservation, reducing average per capita consumption, and slowing population growth. The major views of these opposing schools of thought are summarized in Table 13-1. Let's look at the major parts of this controversy in more detail.

Economics and Resource Supply According to standard economic theory, a competitive free market controls supply and demand of all goods and services. If a resource becomes scarce, prices rise; if there is a glut, they fall. Some economists have pointed out that there are several reasons for the frequent failure of this idea to apply to the supply and demand for nonfuel mineral resources.

First, instead of an open, competitive market, both industry and government in the United States (and in many other industrial nations) have gained increasing control over supply, demand, and prices of raw materials and products. *Second*, the costs of nonfuel mineral resources account for only a small percentage of the total costs of goods and services in the United States. Thus, increased demand for cars or dishwashers has little effect on the prices of nonfuel mineral raw materials used to make these

Table 13-1 Views on Future Availability of Mineral Resources

Optimistic (Cornucopian)	Pessimistic (Neo-Malthusian)
Reserves can be increased indefinitely, as in the past; we are still far from the limits to growth.	Reserves cannot be increased indefinitely on a finite earth, and there are increasing signs that we are approaching limits to growth (see Enrichment Study 2).
Scarcity causes price rises that lead to an increased supply of key raw materials.	We can't get a resource out of the ground if it isn't there. In addition, the cost of raw materials makes up such a small part of the total cost of consumer goods that the market prices of goods do not effectively control the supply an demand of most raw materials.
Price rises will stimulate new discoveries.	Continuing large-scale discoveries of most key resources are unlikely, and the costs of mineral exploration and environmental cleanup are increasing enormously and are expected to cost from $100 billion to $1 trillion between 1980 and 1990.
The oceans contain vast, untapped supplies of key resources.	With only a few exceptions, the resources in the ocean are so dispersed or inaccessible that they will cost more to get than they are worth.
Price rises will stimulate the development of new, more efficient mining technology.	There is a limit to the efficiency of any process, and new technologies (such as nuclear explosions) needed to mine low-grade deposits can cause serious environmental disruption. Also, since technological improvements in mining generally cannot be protected by patents, individual companies have little incentive to develop them.
Human ingenuity and technology will find substitutes for scarce resources.	Substitutes for some key resources will not be found. Some substitutes will be unprofitable because getting them requires too much energy, and other substitutes will cause unacceptable environmental disruption.
Price rises will stimulate recycling and reuse.	Greatly increased recycling and reuse are very important but are limited by the availability of energy. Because some materials have been so widely dispersed, it costs more money to recycle them than to mine concentrated virgin deposits.
Price rises and inexhaustible supplies of cheap energy will make it profitable to mine lower and lower grades of key minerals.	Energy supplies are neither inexhaustible nor cheap (Chapter 14). Rising energy prices will limit the future mining of low-grade ores. The idea that lower grades of minerals can be mined is also based on a naive and incorrect view of how minerals are found in the earth's crust. Whereas iron, copper, and aluminum are widely distributed and found in deposits that range almost continuously from high grade to low grade, most minerals occur only in a few high-grade or a few low-grade deposits. Once these deposits have been mined, it is not profitable or environmentally acceptable to mine massive quantities of average rock to extract very small amounts of the desired mineral.
Environmental effects from increased mining and resource use either are exaggerated or can be controlled.	Many environmental effects from resource use are very serious and can limit resource use even if supplies are available. Many effects can be controlled, but in some cases the resulting cost increase will make it unprofitable to increase use rates.
World population will level off in the next few decades, reducing demand for resources.	It is unlikely that world population will level off in time to prevent serious shortages of key resources (Chapter 7). In any event, rising affluence will increase demands for resources.

items. This occurs primarily because the average per capita cost of raw materials in the United States stayed about the same, or declined between 1900 and 1975, even though costs (in constant dollars) of products rose during this period. These artificially low prices of raw materials have been due to market control by the MDCs, low-cost mining leases, and exclusion of many of the environmental costs of mining from the price of minerals. Since 1975, however, the prices of raw materials have risen somewhat as the costs of mining and environmental protection have increased and some long-term, low-cost mining leases have expired.

Third, the supply of a nonrenewable mineral resource is not infinite. Indeed, several analysts have argued that failure to recognize this is the fatal flaw in the cornucopian position of economist Julian

Simon (see *The Ultimate Resource,* 1981). They point out that Simon bases most of his key arguments on the idea that all resource supplies are infinite because anything that is infinitely divisible is infinite in quantity. This is equivalent to saying that since you can theoretically divide the money in your bank account into an infinite number of fractions of a cent, you have an infinite amount of money. Other cornucopians agree that supplies of nonrenewable resources are finite but insist that the only relevant issue is when economically affordable supplies of such resources might become too scarce for widespread use: in this generation, in 100 years, or in 10,000 years? They do not think that these limits to resource use will be reached in the foreseeable future because of improvements in mining technology and rising prices that will make mining of low-grade

Continental Shelf **Continental Slope** **Ocean Basin**

Figure 13-6 Location of oceanic mineral resources.

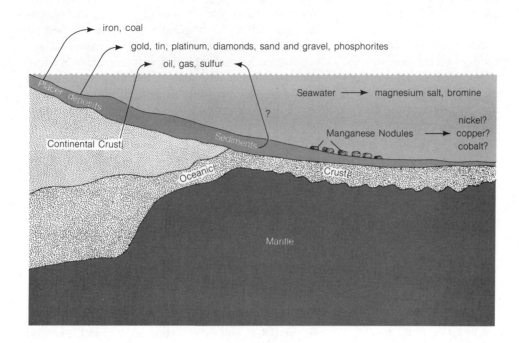

ores feasible and because substitutes will be found for resources in critical supply.

Fourth, resource supplies may be limited in the future because mining and processing require too much expensive energy. Between 1950 and 1980, U.S. mineral production rose 50 percent, but the energy needed to find, extract, and process these materials increased 600 percent. *Fifth*, there may not be enough investment capital available for continued expansion of mining activities.

New Discoveries There is little doubt that geological exploration—guided by better knowledge about the earth—will extend present reserves of most minerals. Remote-sensing cameras in orbiting satellites (such as Landsat) are now used to scan the globe for land, forest, mineral, energy, and water resources. According to geologists, some rich new deposits will probably be found in unexplored areas in LDCs; but in the MDCs and in many LDCs, most of the easily accessible high-grade deposits have already been discovered. Remaining deposits are harder and more expensive to find and mine and are usually less concentrated. Exploration for new resources requires a large capital investment and is a risky financial venture.

Typically, if geologic theory identifies 10,000 sites where a deposit of a particular resource might be found, only 1,000 sites are worth costly exploration; only 100 warrant even more costly drilling, trenching, or tunneling; and only one is likely to be a

producing mine. Even if large new supplies are found, no mineral supply can stand up to continued exponential growth in its use. For example, a 1-billion-year supply of a resource would be exhausted in only 584 years if the level at which it was used increased at 3 percent a year.

What about the oceans? Do they contain vast supplies of mineral and energy resources? As shown in Figure 13-6, potential resources of the ocean are found in three areas **(1)** seawater, **(2)** sediments and deposits on the shallow continental shelf and slope, and **(3)** sediments and nodules on the deep ocean floor.

The huge quantity of seawater appears to be an inexhaustible source of minerals, but most of the 90 chemical elements found there occur in such low concentrations that it takes more energy and money to recover them than they are presently worth. For example, to get a mere 0.003 percent of the annual U.S. consumption of zinc from the ocean would require processing a volume of seawater equivalent to the combined annual flows of the Delaware and Hudson rivers. Only magnesium, bromine, and common table salt (sodium chloride) are abundant enough to be extracted profitably from seawater at present prices with current technology.

Offshore deposits and sediments in shallow waters are already important sources of oil, natural gas, sand, gravel, and 10 other minerals. These resources are limited less by supply or mining technology than by increasingly higher costs of the energy needed to find and remove them, the ecological side effects of oil leaks and spills (Section 18-5), and the potentially serious effects of extensive dredging and mining on food resources of the sea (Section 9-6).

Mineral-containing nodules, discovered in 1872, are believed to be unevenly distributed on the deep ocean floor. These potato-sized rocks contain mostly manganese and iron, with small amounts of copper, nickel, cobalt, molybdenum, and vanadium. These nodules may be valuable, not so much for their manganese (used in making steel) but for their copper (electrical wiring), nickel, and cobalt (both used in steel alloys).

Six major consortia of private companies from several nations have pooled their resources to share the risks of locating deposits and developing a mining technology to extract these nodules. These companies have found nodules in every ocean, but particularly rich beds are in the deep central Pacific Ocean between Hawaii and the North American mainland. They have also developed and successfully used two small prototype systems—a suction dredge and a continuous bucket line—to remove nodules from the deep ocean bed.

Environmentalists recognize that seabed mining would probably cause less harm than mining on land. They are concerned, however, that vacuuming nodules off the seabed and stirring up deep ocean sediments could destroy seafloor organisms, have unknown effects on poorly understood deep-sea food webs, and pollute surface waters by discharge of sediments from mining ships and rigs.

Because of economic and political uncertainties, however, it is unclear whether these resources will be mined in the near future. There is no guarantee that metal prices will be high enough for the consortia to profit on such a large and risky investment, especially since ample and much cheaper supplies of the metals involved are expected to be available for many decades.

An even greater threat is posed by international legal and political squabbles over ownership of these resources. Since 1968, 160 nations have been working to develop the UN-sponsored Law of the Sea Treaty to govern ocean pollution and exploitation of mineral and living ocean resources in international waters. In 1982, 130 UN member nations approved a final draft of this treaty. But four nations, the United States, Turkey, Venezeula, and Israel voted against approval, and 17 other nations abstained. The only major industrial nations voting for the treaty were France and Japan.

The treaty will take effect as a form of international law when it has been ratified by at least 60 nations. This treaty (1) acknowledges that coastal nations have jurisdiction over mineral resources for a distance up to 320 kilometers (200 miles) beyond their continental shelves, (2) guarantees rights for submarines to pass through territorial seas and international straits, (3) would provide a $1 billion loan from MDCs to establish an International Seabed Authority, which would control licenses and set production levels for mining in international waters and establish a UN seabed mining company, (4) would require privately owned mining companies to sell their technology to the UN mining company, pay fees up to $1 million a year, and be subject to UN production controls and to a UN-levied taxation rate of up to 70 percent of income, (5) would require the distribution of taxes collected to the LDCs, and (6) could be altered 20 years after it goes into effect without approval of the U.S. Senate or ratifying bodies of other participating nations.

Jacques Cousteau, an early supporter of the treaty, has reversed his stand stating that ". . . the Law of the Sea Treaty's sole effect will be that of discouraging useful initiatives and institutionalizing unruly abuses." In 1983, the United States refused to sign the treaty, citing objections especially to provisions 3, 4, 5, and 6 listed above. Whether the United States and other industrialized nations not ratifying the treaty can legally carry out seabed mining operations in international waters is uncertain. Private mining companies and the lending institutions providing them with capital would have to have guaranteed legal access to undersea mining sites for at least 20 years before risking billions of dollars. Because of these legal uncertainties, research and development by the private ocean-mining consortia had come to a virtual halt by 1984.

Improved Mining Technology and Mining Low-Grade Deposits There is no question that advances in mining technology during the past few decades have allowed the mining of low-grade deposits without significant cost increases. For example, the grade for minable copper ore has been reduced by a factor of 10 since 1900.

Despite such successes, eventually we run into geological, energy, and environmental restrictions. Only six metals are found in large amounts in the earth's crust: iron, aluminum, magnesium, manganese, chromium, and titanium, in deposits ranging from high grade to low grade. Other important metals, such as copper, tin, lead, zinc, uranium, nickel, tungsten, and mercury, are relatively scarce. Because of the second law of energy (Section 2-3), remaining deposits have eventually come to have such low metal concentrations that the costs of digging, transporting, crushing, and processing, and hauling away the waste rock, discourage mining.

A fundamental assumption of the cornucopian view is an inexhaustible source of cheap energy—

something most energy experts believe is highly unlikely. If energy prices continue to rise, the cost of energy could become a limiting factor in finding, mining, and processing nonfuel mineral resources. Available supplies of water may also limit the supply of some mineral resources because large amounts are needed to extract and process most minerals. Many areas with major mineral deposits are poorly supplied with water (Enrichment Study 11).

Substitution   Cornucopians insist that if supplies of minerals run out, technology will find substitutes. They argue that either plastics, high-strength glass fibers made mostly from silicon (the second most abundant element in the earth's crust), or four of the most abundant metals in the earth's crust (aluminum, iron, magnesium, and titanium) can be substituted for most scarce metals. For example, in automobiles, plastics are increasingly substituted for copper, lead, tin, and zinc. Aluminum and titanium are also replacing steel in cars and for some other purposes. In 1981 a Japanese company showed off a prototype car engine made of steel and ceramic parts. Glass fibers are beginning to replace copper wires in telephone cables. They weigh less, can transmit more information and electrical signals, and cost half as much as copper wire. Even if substitutes are not found, cornucopians argue that no material is so vital that its exhaustion would be catastrophic.

Finding substitutes for scarce resources is extremely important, but there are problems to be solved. *First*, failure to find a substitute could cause serious economic hardships during the adjustment period that would occur when a key material ceased to be available. *Second*, finding possible substitutes and phasing them into complex manufacturing processes requires costly development programs and long lead times.

Third, some materials have unique properties such that adequate substitutes cannot be found. For example, helium remains a liquid at a lower temperature than any gas or liquid. For low-temperature cooling in electrical superconductors and for generating and transmitting energy, helium has no known substitute. A National Academy of Sciences report pointed out that substitutes for chromium (in stainless steel), platinum (as an industrial catalyst), gold (for electrical contacts), cobalt (in magnets and steel alloys), silver (for photography), and manganese (for making bubble-free steel) probably will be inferior.

Fourth, some proposed substitutes, such as cadmium and silver for mercury in batteries, are also scarce. *Fifth*, some future technologies may themselves depend on scarce resources that have no known substitutes. Conventional nuclear fis-

sion energy may eventually be limited by shortages of affordable uranium (Section 15-5). Replacing these reactors with breeder reactors that synthesize their own plutonium fuel is jeopardized by environmental concerns, high costs, and by the potential use of plutonium as a component of atomic bombs (Section 15-6). Nuclear fusion reactors, if ever developed, would put heavy demands on scarce beryllium, niobium, lead, helium, and chromium (Section 15-6). And the development of efficient solar photovoltaic cells that produce electricity from sunlight (Section 16-1) may require large amounts of scarce gallium.

Recycling   Poor people in LDCs have long recognized the need to recycle or reuse almost everything—discarded glass, paper, plastic, rags, tin, and bones. In the MDCs both cornucopians and neo-Malthusians agree on the importance of recycling nonrenewable mineral resources. This practice decreases the need for virgin resources, usually saves energy, causes less pollution and land disruption, and cuts waste disposal costs by reducing the volume of solid wastes, thus relieving the pressure on overflowing landfills. Despite these advantages only about one-fourth of the world's paper, aluminum, and steel is recovered for recycling.

World steel production alone requires as much energy each year as that in the oil extracted annually by Saudi Arabia. Using scrap iron to produce steel conserves virgin iron ore and coal; it requires 65 percent less energy, 40 percent less water, 97 percent fewer raw materials; and it cuts air pollution by 90 percent and water pollution by 76 percent, compared to using virgin ore to make steel.

Recycling half of the paper used each year in the United States would save about 150 million trees and conserve enough energy to provide residential electricity for about 10 million people (see Enrichment Study 13). Failure to recycle a single copy of a weekday edition of a typical major newpaper is equivalent to throwing away half a glass of gasoline. If returnable bottles replaced the 80 billion throwaway beverage cans now produced annually, enough energy would be saved to provide electricity for another 13 million people. Recycling aluminum reduces air pollution associated with its production by 95 percent and requires 92 percent less energy then mining and procesing virgin aluminum ore.

In recent years, Americans have been reminded that "Waste is a resource out of place," "Urban waste is urban ore," "Trash is cash," "Landfills are urban mines," and "Trash cans are really resource containers," and have been urged to shift from a high-waste society (Figure 2-4) to a low-waste society based on recycling and resource conservation (Figure 2-5). Although surveys indicate that 75 percent of all Americans favor more recycling, only about 10 percent of the waste in the United States is now recycled—compared to 40 to 60 percent in Japan and many European countries.

Environmentalist Dennis Hayes (see *Repairs, Reuse, Recycling—First Steps Toward a Sustainable Society*, 1978) estimates that with proper economic and political incentives about two-thirds of the material resources used in the United States each year could be recycled without significant changes in life-styles. For example, though an estimated 80 percent of the aluminum produced each year could be recycled, only about 32 percent is recycled in the United States and 10 percent in the Soviet Union—the two largest aluminum producers. In contrast, the aluminum recycling rate in the Netherlands and Italy is about 42 percent. According to Hayes and other analysts, recycling even 25 percent of U.S. urban solid wastes will not occur as long as government subsidies, depletion allowances, and other economic and political factors favor the use of virgin resources over recycled resources.

There is disagreement over whether most resources should be recycled by a *centralized, high-technology approach* or by a *decentralized, low-technology approach*. In the high-technology approach, large, centralized resource recovery plants ideally would shred and automatically separate mixed urban wastes to recover glass, iron, aluminum, and other valuable materials, which would be sold to manufacturing industries for recycling. The remaining paper, plastics, and other combustible wastes would be incinerated to produce steam, hot water, or electricity, which could be used in municipal facilities or sold to nearby buildings and manufacturing plants. The incinerator residue, including particulates removed to prevent air pollution, could be used as landfill to reclaim damaged land or processed into cinder blocks, bricks, or other building materials.

In the 1970s several dozen large and medium-sized U.S. cities that were running out of sites for sanitary landfills began building large-scale resource recovery plants. They were aided by passage of the Resource Recovery and Conservation Act of 1976, which provided some funds to build demonstration plants and to help state, regional, and local agencies to develop programs for resource recovery and conservation. By 1983, over 34 of these plants had been built and 20 others were under construction. Although a few of these plants separate and recover some iron, aluminum, and glass for recycling, most are sophisticated incinerators used to produce energy by burning trash. By 1977 Denmark was using incinerator plants to convert 60 percent of its burnable wastes to energy, Switzerland 40 percent, and the Netherlands and Sweden each 30 percent.

Unlike their European counterparts, most resource recovery plants in the United States have been a bitter disappointment. They have been expensive to build ($50 million to $500 million per plant) and have suffered from delays, breakdowns, high operating and maintenance costs, lack of enough waste each day to make them economical to operate, and continuing financial losses. Even though 55 percent of the cost of these facilities was subsidized by federal funds, several have gone bankrupt and have been abandoned. One notable exception is a steam-producing plant in Saugus, Massachusetts, which has a steady and reliable supply of refuse and was built using tried-and-true European technology. Even so it took the plant 4 years to make a profit—the only U.S. resource recovery operating in the black by 1983. Some cities talk about a new wave of resource recovery plants based on the Saugus model. Such efforts, however, may be hindered by drastic cutbacks in federal funds since 1982 and by vigorous objections by citizens to having landfills or resource recovery plants nearby.

Most waste materials recovered in the United States are recycled in a *low-technology approach* involving source separation. In this, simpler, small-scale approach, homes and businesses place waste materials such as glass, paper, metals, and food scraps into separate containers. Compartmentalized city collection trucks, private haulers, or voluntary recycling organizations pick up the segregated wastes, clean them up if necessary, and sell them to scrap dealers, compost (organic garbage) plants, and manufacturers. Studies have shown that this source separation takes only 16 minutes a week for the average American family.

By 1983 more than 250 U.S. cities had curbside pickup of separated wastes. There were also more than 3,000 municipal or community-based recycling centers operating in the United States, together converting 12 million tons of trash into over $360 million each year. Wilton, New Hampshire, is now recycling 50 percent of its total waste and is composting another 30 percent, and Davis, California, is recycling 50 percent of its household waste using this approach. New Jersey has embarked on a statewide recycling program, partially financed by surcharges for using the state's dumps, aimed at recycling 25 percent of all residential refuse by 1986.

If 75 percent of all municipal waste were burned for energy recovery, this would provide only 1 percent of the nation's annual energy use. By contrast, a comprehensive low-technology recycling program could save 5 percent of the annual U.S. energy use—more than the energy generated by all U.S. nuclear power plants—at perhaps one-hundredth of the capital and operating costs.

Mixing wastes and sending them off to landfills or resource recovery plants also hinders the recycling of paper (Enrichment Study 13) and encourages the use of throwaway cans and bottles. Indeed, proponents of large-scale resource recovery plants in the United States have opposed federal and state laws to ban or discourage the use of nonreturnable cans and bottles and to encourage the recycling of paper, because removal of these materials from mixed urban refuse could make such plants unprofitable.

Several technological, economic, and political factors hinder both high- and low-technology recycling in the United States by causing an uncertain demand and wildly fluctuating prices for recycled materials. *First*, the abundance of cheap raw materials in the past has favored the development of manufacturing processes that use only virgin resources. For example, in 1983 less than 10 percent of all steel made in the United States was produced from recycled iron. In contrast, Japanese and West German steel plants, built after World War II, employ the electric furnace process, which can use large amounts of scrap iron.

Second, subsidies in the form of tax breaks and depletion allowances are given to primary mining and energy resource industries, to encourage them to find and get resources out of the ground as fast as possible. Subsidies, now amounting to $375 million each year for nonfuel mineral production in the United States were useful for fostering industrial development in the nineteenth century. But some analysts believe that it is now time to gradually switch these economic incentives from primary mining resource industries to recycling industries that recover and reuse resources from wastes.

Third, in most cases the cost of recycled materials in the United States is equal to or higher than that of virgin materials. This is attributed to several factors, including (1) the tax advantages just mentioned, (2) the railroad and trucking rates, which have often been 50 to 100 percent higher for scrap materials than for virgin materials (especially glass and paper), (3) the lack of large and steady markets for recycled materials from mixed wastes, (4) the high labor costs involved in recovering materials from mixed wastes, and (5) the failure to include the cost of disposal in the price of a product. *Fourth*, many modern products are such complex mixtures of materials that it is too expensive, and too energy consuming, to separate the materials for recycling.

Fifth, the second law of energy (Section 2-3) sets a physical limit on recycling. All recycling takes energy, which cannot be recycled. Remelting scrap wastes *usually* requires less energy than extracting and processing most virgin materials. However, the total energy needed for the entire process of collecting, transporting, and remelting widely scattered scrap materials sometimes exceeds that used for extracting and processing virgin materials. For example, consider people who drive around in their cars collecting bottles, cans, and newspapers, and later taking them to recycling centers. This probably wastes more energy in the form of gasoline, produces more pollution, and depletes more resources than extracting and processing the equivalent quantity of virgin materials.

Reuse and Resource Conservation *Recycling* is the collecting, reprocessing, and refabricating of a resource, whereas *reuse* involves the same product, employed over and over again in its original form. For glass bottles, reuse makes more ecological sense than recycling because it takes three times more energy to crush and remelt a glass bottle than it does to refill it. Thus, it makes more sense to ban nonreturnable glass bottles and use returnable bottles instead.

Today almost 80 percent of all U.S. beer and soft drink containers are nonreturnable, throwaway bottles and cans. A major force behind this shift has apparently been the attempt of larger can and bottle manufacturers to expand their markets by forcing smaller bottlers and brewers out of business. With refillable deposit bottles, the market area is determined by how far delivery trucks from local breweries and bottling plants can carry filled bottles and return with empties. Using lightweight throwaway containers, large companies can ship their products anywhere in the country, invading the territories once dominated by local breweries and soft drink companies, many of which then go out of business.

According to the Worldwatch Institute, throwing away an aluminum beverage container wastes as much energy as pouring out such a can half-filled with gasoline. At least one-fourth of all U.S. aluminum production goes into packaging, half of which is for beverage containers. Though it is encouraging that about 54 percent of the aluminum beverage cans made and used in the United States are recycled at over 2,500 recycling centers set up by the aluminum industry, this percentage could be increased to at least 90 percent by (1) *banning nonreturnable beverage containers*, as has been done in Denmark, and requiring that all beverages be supplied in standardized bottle sizes refillable by any bottler, or (2) discouraging the use of throwaways by *requiring a deposit on each nonreturnable beverage bottle and can*. By 1983, this second approach had been adopted in Sweden, Norway, the Netherlands, several provinces in Canada, and in nine states in the United States: Oregon (in 1972), Vermont (in 1973), Maine (in 1978), Michigan (in 1979), Iowa (in 1979), Connecticut (in 1980), Delaware (in 1982), Massachusetts (in 1983), and New York (in 1983).

Efforts have been made since 1975 to pass a national beverage container deposit bill. By mid-1984, however, the beverage container industry had prevented such a bill from being passed, even though surveys show that 73 percent of the Americans polled would support such legislation. Environmental Protection Agency and the General Accounting Office studies estimate that a national container deposit law would **(1)** reduce roadside beverage container litter by 60 to 70 percent, **(2)** reduce urban solid waste by 1 percent and thus save $25 million to $50 million a year in waste disposal costs, **(3)** reduce the use of bauxite ore to make aluminum by 53 to 74 percent and the use of iron ore by 45 to 83 percent, **(4)** reduce air, water, and solid waste pollution from the beverage industry by 44 to 86 percent, **(5)** save energy equivalent to that needed to provide the annual electrical needs for 2 million to 7.7 million homes, **(6)** produce a net increase of 80,000 to 100,000 jobs,* and **(7)** save consumers at least $1 billion annually.

The approach, favored by steel, aluminum, and glass companies, and others involved in the sale of beverage containers, is to enact *litter recycling laws.* This type of law levies a tax on industries whose products pose a potential threat as litter or landfill clutter. Revenues from the tax are used to establish and maintain statewide recycling centers. By 1983, at least eight states had this type of law: Washington, Virginia, Ohio, Nebraska, Louisiana, California, Arkansas, and Tennessee.

In addition to increased recycling and reuse, environmentalists also call for increased *resource conservation,* especially in MDCs. They point to unnecessary waste of matter and energy resources. An example of unnecessary waste is overpackaging. Product packaging in the United States consumes 65 percent of all paper, 15 percent of all wood, and 3 percent of all energy used. This amounts to an annual average of 281 kilograms (618 pounds) of packaging for each American. Some grocery store items have containers that cost five times as much as the food that's in them. How often do you find a product that has unnecessary packaging or a grocery item that has two or three layers of packaging?

Reducing paper packaging saves not only trees but energy. For example, halving paper packaging in the United States would save the energy equivalent of residential electricity for 20 million people.

Many environmentalists argue that the present one-way flow of matter resources from raw materials to wasted solids (Figure 2-4) found in most industrial societies should be replaced with a sustainable earth or low-waste system (Figure 2-5) that reduces matter and energy consumption. Table 13-2 compares the present throwaway resource system used in the United States, a resource recovery and recycling system, and a sustainable earth or low-waste resource system.

13-5 Key Resources: The World Situation

Depletion Curves and Depletion Rate Estimates How can the life of a nonrenewable resource be estimated accurately? Projection of the *depletion time* of a resource is based on two major sets of assumptions: **(1)** the actual or potential available supply at existing (or future) acceptable prices and with existing (or improved) technology (Figure 13-5), and **(2)** the annual rate at which the resource is used. Obviously, differing assumptions yield different answers. It is almost certain that no resource will be completely exhausted. Instead, its use is normally limited by the prohibitively high cost of mining less accessible and lower-grade deposits. For this reason, **depletion time** is defined as the period required to use a certain fraction—usually 80 percent—of the known reserves or estimated total supply (Figure 13-5) of a resource, according to various assumed rates of use.

One estimate, the **static reserve index,** projects the number of years until the known world reserves of a resource will be 80 percent depleted at the present annual rate of consumption. Because of increases in population and resource use, it is often more realistic to project the number of years until the known reserves of a resource will be 80 percent depleted if its consumption rate increases annually by a given percentage—typically 2 or 3 percent. Such an estimate is known as the **exponential reserve index.**

A series of projections of different depletion times in the form of *depletion curves* can be obtained by combining the static reserve index or exponential reserve index with additional assumptions about how the resource might be used. A typical set of depletion curves for a hypothetical nonrenewable resource is shown in Figure 13-7. For example, one

---

*There would be a decrease in the number of jobs in the throwaway container manufacturing and supply industries. However, a larger number of jobs would be created in the returnable container filling, distribution, and refilling industries.

Table 13-2 Three Systems for Handling Discarded Materials

Item	For a Throwaway System	For a Resource Recovery and Recycling System	For a Sustainable Earth Resource System
Glass bottles	Dump or bury	Grind and remelt; remanufacture; convert to building materials	Ban all nonreturnable bottles and reuse (not remelt and recycle) bottles
Bimetallic "tin" cans	Dump or bury	Sort, remelt	Limit or ban production; use returnable bottles
Aluminum cans	Dump or bury	Sort, remelt	Limit or ban production; use returnable bottles
Cars	Dump	Sort, remelt	Sort, remelt; tax cars lasting less than 15 years, weighing more than 818 kilograms (1,800 pounds), and getting less than 13 kilometers per liter (30 miles per gallon)
Metal objects	Dump or bury	Sort, remelt	Sort, remelt; tax items lasting less than 10 years
Tires	Dump, burn, or bury	Grind and revulcanize or use in road construction; incinerate to generate heat and electricity	Recap usable tires; tax all tires not usable for at least 64,400 kilometers (40,000 miles)
Paper	Dump, burn, or bury	Incinerate to generate heat	Compost or recycle; tax all throwaway items; eliminate overpackaging
Plastics	Dump, burn, or bury	Incinerate to generate heat or electricity	Limit production; use returnable glass bottles instead of plastic containers; tax throwaway items and packaging
Garden wastes	Dump, burn, or bury	Incinerate to generate heat or electricity	Compost; return to soil as fertilizer; use as animal feed

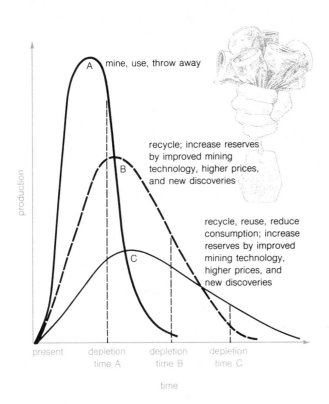

Figure 13-7 Depletion curves for a nonrenewable resource, based on different sets of assumptions, showing when 80 percent depletion occurs (dashed lines).

estimate of depletion time might be based on assuming that the resource is not recycled or reused and that there will be no increase in its estimated reserves, as shown by curve A. A longer depletion time estimate can be obtained by assuming that recycling will *extend* the life of existing reserves and that improved mining technology, price rises, and new discoveries will *expand* existing reserves by some factor, say, 2, as shown in curve B. Curve C projects an even longer depletion time by assuming that reserves will be expanded by an even larger factor by new discoveries and through recycling, reuse, and reduced consumption. Of course, finding a substitute for a resource cancels all these curves, and requires a new set of depletion curves for the new resource.

Figure 13-8 shows estimated times for 80 percent depletion of the world reserves for 16 important minerals based on two sets of assumptions. The second more optimistic set of assumptions shows that even if reserves are increased fivefold, the world could run short of tin, tungsten, copper, lead, zinc, silver, mercury, and gold between 2000 and 2040, and could be low on molybdenum, manganese, aluminum, platinum, and nickel between 2060 and 2090.

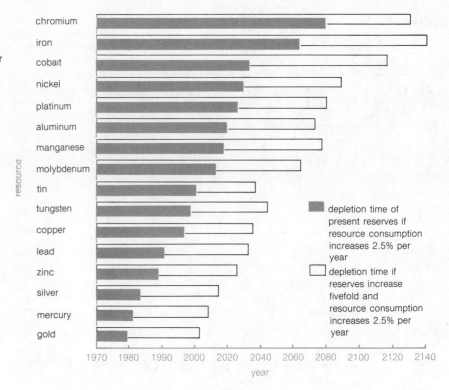

Figure 13-8 Projected times for 80 percent depletion of world reserves of 16 key metal resources based on two sets of assumptions. Note that the time scale changes after the year 2000.

Resources listed (top to bottom): chromium, iron, cobalt, nickel, platinum, aluminum, manganese, molybdenum, tin, tungsten, copper, lead, zinc, silver, mercury, gold

Legend:
- depletion time of present reserves if resource consumption increases 2.5% per year
- depletion time if reserves increase fivefold and resource consumption increases 2.5% per year

x-axis (year): 1970 1980 1990 2000 2020 2040 2060 2080 2100 2120 2140

Figures 13-7 and 13-8 show why there is so much controversy between cornucopians and neo-Malthusians (Table 13-1). One can get opimistic or pessimistic projections of the depletion time of a particular resource by making different sets of assumptions (see Enrichment Study 2). The following guidelines can be used to evaluate different estimates of resource depletion times like those shown in Figure 13-8:

1. Remember that all the curves and estimated depletion times are projections of what *could* happen based on a different set of assumptions, not necessarily what *will* happen.

2. Find out what specific assumptions were used to make each projection.

3. Evaluate the assumptions (and, where possible, the data on which they are based) to see which set seems to be the most reasonable.

Rich Nations Versus Poor Nations: A New International Economic Order Some have charged the industrialized nations with exploiting LDCs by controlling international trade so that the LDCs are forced to sell their resources at a price far below their value. In effect, the MDCs are accused of stripping the world of its fossil fuel and other nonrenewable mineral resources without sufficient regard for the future resource needs of the LDCs.

To help correct this imbalance the LDCs have called for a *new international economic order*—a proposal designed to shift more of the world's wealth from the MDCs to the LDCs. This idea was summarized by Carlos Perez, president of Venezuela:

We aren't out to destroy the values or prosperity of the industrialized countries. What we want is for them to accept a new relationship in which our raw materials and our labor are given their proper value, which in turn will give us the opportunity to develop our economies.

This plan includes **(1)** a substantial increase in aid from industrialized nations to LDCs, with special emphasis on the extension of new credit at favorable terms, **(2)** removal of trade barriers that restrict LDCs from selling some of their products to MDCs, **(3)** increasing the prices of raw materials exported from LDCs to MDCs, **(4)** providing LDCs with a greater say in the running of international lending institutions, such as the World Bank and the International Monetary Fund, and **(5)** relieving the LDCs from some of their massive debt to the MDCs and private banks.

How valid are these charges of resource exploitation of the LDCs by the MDCs? The truth may lie somewhere between gross exploitation and useful aid. Some analysts argue that when MDCs buy raw materials from LDCs, they provide funds that the LDCs need for their own economic development. Critics of this view counter that if the LDCs continue to sell off their resources at low prices to MDCs to get money for economic development, they may not have enough of these resources left to sustain their own development in the future.

Some analysts also argue that the data show that the MDCs are not paying a just price for many resources. For example, average per capita GNP in the United States has been rising steadily, equaling about $13,160 in 1984. But the average per capita cost of raw materials in the United States is less than $150, a price only slightly higher than at the beginning of the century. Between 1945 and 1977 the United States gave to LDCs about $4 billion in economic aid, $63 billion in loans through international agencies, $3.2 billion in trade concessions, and a great deal of advice and technical help. But Thomas Ehrlich, former president of the International Development Corporation Agency, which coordinates U.S. foreign aid, has pointed out that this aid has been mostly for economic and political rather than for humanitarian reasons and has amounted to only a token in comparison to the profits from sales of products made from raw materials bought cheaply from LDCs.

Other analysts point out that the charges of exploitation overlook the fact that with a few important exceptions, most of the world's nonfuel mineral resource supplies are found in the MDCs. Five MDCs—the Soviet Union, the United States, Canada, Australia, and South Africa—supply the world with most of the 20 minerals that make up 98 percent of the total value of all minerals consumed in the world. The major exceptions include copper in South America and Africa, tin and tungsten in Southeast Asia, aluminum ore (bauxite) in the Caribbean, and cobalt in Zaire. Others argue that the government leaders and rich elites in most LDCs are really exploiting their own people. They contend that much of the aid given or loaned to LDCs ends up in the pockets of leaders and the rich instead of reaching the poor.

13-6 Key Resources: The U.S. Situation

Increasing U.S. Dependence on Imports The United States is more self-sufficient in key metals and other nonfuel minerals than any other nation except the Soviet Union. Nevertheless, high consumption rates and cheaper resource supplies in other countries have prompted the United States to import more minerals from resource-rich nations like the Soviet Union, the People's Republic of China, Canada, and several African and South American nations.

Table 13-3 U.S. Import Dependence for Selected Key Nonfuel Minerals in 1982

Mineral	Percentage Imported	Rank of Major Suppliers
Niobium	100	Brazil, Canada, Thailand
Manganese	98	South Africa, Gabon, Brazil, France
Tantalum	91	Thailand, Canada, Malaysia, Brazil
Cobalt	91	Zaire, Belgium-Luxembourg, Zambia, Finland
Chromium	90	South Africa, Philippines, Soviet Union, Turkey
Platinum	85	South Africa, Soviet Union, United Kingdom
Nickel	72	Canada, Norway, Botswana, Australia

Source: U.S. Bureau of Mines.

Currently the United States stockpiles 93 materials, 80 of them nonfuel minerals, considered to be vital to domestic industry. Strategic stockpiles of these materials are supposed to be large enough to last through a 3-year war, but most supplies are well below this level. Of the 42 most critical nonfuel minerals, the United States was dependent on foreign sources for more than 50 percent of 24 of them by 1982—compared to only 43 percent dependence on imported oil. This included heavy import dependence for chromium, cobalt, manganese, nickel, niobium, platinum, and tantalum, which are particularly important to defense and energy programs, as shown in Table 13-3. Even heavier dependence on imports for these 24 vital nonfuel minerals and others is projected by 2000. Japan and many western European nations are even more dependent on imports of vital nonfuel minerals.

Is Import Dependence Good or Bad? Some argue that U.S. dependence on other countries for key resources threatens economic security (if prices increase sharply) and military security (if supplies of vital resources are cut off or severely restricted). Any nation importing a large fraction of its supply of a particular mineral resource would be vulnerable under the following conditions: (1) when most of the world's supply of a resource is held by one country, as is the case with tungsten (China), mercury (Spain), and palladium (Soviet Union), (2) when a group of nations holding most of the world's supply of a resource band together to form an OPEC-style cartel to control supplies and raise prices, and (3) when substitute materials are not readily available, as for chromium, platinum, and manganese. Threats to world peace could also occur in such situations because of conflicts between MDCs competing for scarce supplies.

Mineral experts point out, however, that large percentages of many nonfuel minerals are imported because they are cheaper to extract from the higher-grade ores found in other nations than from more plentiful lower-grade domestic reserves. According to the Bureau of Mines and the Geological Survey, the United States has adequate domestic reserves of most key minerals—except chromium, cobalt, platinum, tin, gold, and palladium—for at least the next several decades. However, the Geological Survey estimates that present reserves for most key minerals will not satisfy U.S. needs for more than 100 years without increased recycling, conservation, and a search for substitutes.

Hans Landsberg, a minerals expert with Resources for the Future, believes that the formation of cartels for nonfuel mineral resources is unlikely. He points out that stable countries such as Canada, Australia, and possibly Mexico, which are major exporters of strategic minerals, are not likely to form cartels. In addition, less stable nations of Central and South Africa are too poor to do without the income from minerals exports. Landsberg and others also point out that, unlike oil, which is consumed directly, raw materials contribute such a small percentage to the cost of finished products that increases in their prices have relatively small effects. Other analysts argue that mutual import dependence of nations is a stabilizing force for world peace, since conflicts are likely to be dealt with by negotiation rather than by military action.

Are Environmentalists Hindering Mineral Exploration? Mining company officials contend that pressures from environmentalists to preserve valuable wilderness, parks, and forest areas (Chapter 10) prevent some areas from being fully explored and mined. Using older figures, the Secretary of the Interior declared in 1981 that mining had been prohibited on about 70 percent of public lands and proposed increasing the amount of exploration and mining on these lands to provide enough strategic materials in the future (Section 10-2). More recent studies by the General Accounting Office, however, indicate that only about 25 percent of public lands—mostly military reservations, parks, and public power facilities—have been withdrawn from mineral production. New leases for mining in wilderness areas have been prohibited since 1983, but

these areas had been open for both mineral exploration and development for 80 years previously. Environmentalists also point out that wilderness areas with significant mineral potential were excluded by Congress from protection when the areas were designated and that Congress has the power to open up wilderness areas for mining in cases of national emergency.

Mining interests also contend that environmental and safety regulations have increased the cost of mining and processing of mineral resources and call for a relaxation of these regulations. For example, between 1970 and 1980 eight zinc smelting plants in the United States were shut down because the owners couldn't afford to comply with new strict environmental regulations. As a result, U.S. imports of zinc rose from 25 to 62 percent during this period. Copper mined domestically is more expensive because its price includes the cost of environmental protection, whereas imported copper seldom does. Environmentalists contend, however, that the major factors in increased mining costs are depletion of many high-grade domestic ore deposits, inflation, and higher energy costs.

Suggestions for a U.S. Minerals Policy It has been suggested that any plan to provide sufficient non-fuel mineral resources for future economic growth and development should involve a mixture of the following approaches: (1) development of a major program to find new deposits, improve the efficiency of mineral extraction from ores, and find substitutes for scarce materials, (2) improvement of mining technology, (3) greatly increased resource recovery, recycling, reuse, and resource conservation (Table 13-2), (4) control of population growth (Chapter 7), (5) maintenance of sufficient stockpiles of vital materials, and (6) establishment of world trade agreements to see that resource-endowed nations receive fair prices for their raw materials.

Environmentalists urge that to increase the efficiency of use of nonfuel mineral resources, much more attention be paid to approach number 3. Here the challenge is to learn how to have satisfying, rewarding, and healthy lives while using and wasting less of our irreplaceable nonrenewable resource capital.

Solid wastes are only raw materials we're too stupid to use.

Arthur C. Clarke

Discussion Topics

1. Why should an urban dweller be concerned about the environmental impact from increasing surface mining of land for mineral resources?

2. Make a log of your own consumption for a single day and relate it to the increased demand for subsurface and surface mining of coal and nonfuel mineral resources.

3. Give some limitations on the use of Equations 13-1 and 13-2 for describing the relations between population size and resource supplies.

4. Debate the following resolution: The United States uses too many of the world's resources, relative to its population size, and should cut back on consumption.

5. Summarize the neo-Malthusian and the cornucopian views on the availability of resources. Which, if either, of these schools of thought do you support? Why?

6. Debate each of the following propositions.
   a. The competitive free market will control the supply and demand of mineral resources.
   b. New discoveries will provide all the raw materials we need.
   c. The ocean will provide all the mineral resources we need.
   d. We will not run out of key mineral resources because we can always mine lower-grade deposits.
   e. When a mineral resource becomes scarce, we can always find a substitute.
   f. When a nonrenewable resource becomes scarce, all we have to do is recycle it.

7. Use the second law of energy (thermodynamics) to show why the following options are not profitable.
   a. Extracting most minerals dissolved in seawater
   b. Recycling minerals that are widely dispersed
   c. Mining increasingly low-grade deposits of minerals
   d. Using solar energy to mine minerals
   e. Continuing to mine, use, and recycle minerals at increasing rates

8. Debate the pros and cons of the following proposals:
   a. Eliminate all tax breaks and depletion allowances for mining industries to reduce use and waste of minerals.
   b. Provide tax breaks and incentives for reycling industries and for all manufacturers who use recycled materials.
   c. Ban nonreturnable bottles.
   d. Pass a national law requiring deposits on all beverage containers.
   e. Add a disposal tax to all items that last less than 10 years.
   f. Standardize package and bottle sizes for each item of comparable products.
   g. Require standardized, easily replaceable parts for products.
   h. Require homeowners, businesses, and industries to separate wastes to facilitate recycling.
   i. Label all products to show the amount and type of recycled materials.
   j. Require local, state, and federal agencies to buy materials composed of the highest feasible percentage of recycled materials.

9. Compare the throwaway, recycling, and sustainable earth (or low-waste) approaches to waste disposal and resource recovery and conservation for (a) glass bottles, (b) "tin" cans, (c) aluminum cans, (d) plastics, and (e) leaves, grass, and food wastes (see Table 13-2).

10. Why is there so little recycling in the United States? How would you change this?

11. List the major advantages and disadvantages of the high-technology (resource recovery and incineration plant) and the low-technology (source separation) approaches to recycling. Which approach do you favor? Why?

12. Investigate to determine whether (a) your college and your city have recycling programs, (b) your college and your local government require that a certain fraction of all paper purchases contain recycled fiber, (c) teachers in your college and in local schools expect everyone to write on both sides of paper, (d) your college sells soft drinks in throwaway cans or bottles, (e) your state has or is contemplating a law requiring deposits on all beverage containers.

13. Why is it is difficult to get accurate estimates of mineral resource supplies? Be sure to distinguish among reserves, subeconomic resources, hypothetical resources, speculative resources, and depletion curves based on static reserve indexes and exponential reserve indexes.

14. What is the difference between a prediction and a projection? Discuss the limitations of the projections of world resource supplies shown in Figure 13-8. Which, if either, of these projections do you believe may turn out to be more accurate? Why?

15. Study Figure 13-8 to determine which key metals might be in short supply during your expected lifetime. How might such shortages affect your expected life-style?

16. Is the increasing U.S. dependence on foreign imports for critical resources a desirable trend in relation to world peace? Why or why not?

14

Energy Resources: Types, Use, and Concepts

How quickly we can poison the earth's lovely surface—but how wondrously it responds to the educated caress of conservation.

Donald E. Carr

The amounts and types of *useful* energy available shape not only individual life-styles but also national and world economic systems. This chapter examines types of energy resources and global and U.S. energy use. It also shows how the two energy laws (Chapter 2) can help us evaluate present and future energy alternatives. The next two chapters discuss the advantages and disadvantages of each major energy alternative.

14-1 Types of Energy Resources

Primary Energy Resources The *direct* input of essentially inexhaustible *solar energy* alone provides 99 percent of the thermal energy used to heat the earth and all buildings free of charge (Figure 14-1). Were it not for this *direct* input of radiant energy from the sun (Figure 3-2), the average temperature outside would be $-240°C$ ($-400°F$).

Human ingenuity developed a number of renewable and nonrenewable **primary energy resources** to supplement this direct input of solar energy and to provide the remaining 1 percent of the energy we use on earth. These primary energy resources can be classified as either *renewable* (permanent) or *nonrenewable* (temporary) (Figure 14-1 and Table 14-1).

The *energy flow or "spaghetti" chart* in Figure 14-1 also shows that the world's sources of primary energy can be converted by human ingenuity into electrical, chemical, thermal (heat), or mechanical energy to provide: **(1)** *low-temperature heat* [less than $140°C$ ($284°F$)] for heating water and homes and

Enrichment Studies 1, 2, 5, 7, and 11 are related to this chapter.

buildings (space heating), **(2)** *high-temperature heat* (up to several thousand degrees) for *industrial processes,* **(3)** *high-temperature heat* used for *electrical energy,* when the heat produced by burning a fossil fuel—usually coal—in a boiler or by controlled nuclear fission in a nuclear reactor powers the blades of a turbine, which rotate a shaft in a generator to produce a flow of electrons in a wire or other conductor, **(4)** *mechanical energy for propelling vehicles,* obtained when the chemical energy stored in natural gas or liquid fuels is converted by combustion to high-temperature thermal energy, which is then converted to mechanical energy, **(5)** *material items* made from wood, natural fibers, and other forms of *renewable biomass,* and **(6)** *material items* such as plastics, synthetic fibers, pesticides, and many medicines made from *petrochemicals* obtained mostly from natural gas and crude oil.

Nonrenewable and Renewable Primary Energy Resources The outer limit on the supply and use of each of the *nonrenewable* primary energy resources shown in Table 14-1 is the *quantity* of useful energy available—the total amount of energy that can be found, converted to useful forms, and used at an affordable cost and with acceptable environmental impacts (Figure 13-4). Once depleted, these resources are gone forever.

Most people think of solar energy in terms of direct heat from the sun. But broadly defined, **renewable solar energy** includes not only *direct* radiant energy from the sun but also a variety of *indirect* forms of solar energy (Table 14-1). The major factor limiting the direct use of *renewable* primary energy resources based on the essentially limitless supply of energy from the sun is *flux*—the amount of direct sunlight or indirect solar energy in the form of wind or water flowing into a given area of the earth during each unit of time compared to the rate at which it is being used. For most uses, direct solar energy and indirect solar energy must be stored as thermal, electrical, chemical, or other form of energy for use when the sun isn't shining, the wind isn't blowing, or water flows have been reduced.

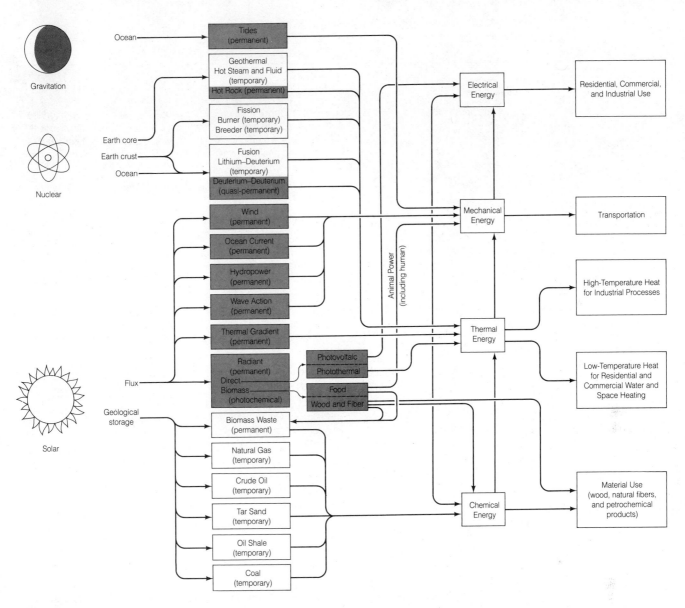

Figure 14-1 Energy flow or "spaghetti" chart showing the earth's major renewable or permanent (shaded) and nonrenewable or temporary (unshaded) sources of energy and how they can be converted into chemical, thermal, mechanical, and electrical energy. (Adapted from Office of Energy Research and Planning, State of Oregon.)

Humans have developed two major ways to collect some of the world's *direct* input of renewable solar energy and use it as primary energy to provide from 50 percent to all of the space heating and hot water in homes and commercial buildings: *passive and active solar energy systems*. A typical solar-heated house has several major components: **(1)** a *solar heat collector*, oriented to face the sun, consisting of double- or triple-paned windows in a *passive system* and a specially designed solar collector* normally mounted on the roof in an *active system*, **(2)** a heavily insulated, airtight house for either system to help retain as much of the captured heat as possible, often with movable insulated shutters or curtains covering windows to reduce heat loss at night during cold weather or excessive heat gain during the day in hot weather, **(3)** a heat storage system typically consisting of concrete, brick, or stone walls, or barrels or columns of water (in a passive system) or insulated tanks of water or crushed stone (in an active system) to store captured heat for slow release at night or during cloudy days, **(4)** a heat circulating system consisting, in a passive system, of an open design that in cold weather allows heat to flow throughout the house by convection and, in an active system, the use of thermostatically controlled pumps

*A typical *active solar collector* consists of a coil of copper pipe attached to a blackened metal base and covered with a transparent layer of glass or plastic. Radiant energy from the sun passes through the glass cover, is absorbed by the blackened surface, and transferred as heat to water, an antifreeze solution, or air pumped through the copper pipe (Section 16-1).

Table 14-1 Nonrenewable and Renewable Primary Energy Resources

Type	Description
Nonrenewable	
Conventional fossil fuels	Underground deposits of crude oil, natural gas, and coal representing the storage of solar energy as chemical energy in geological deposits believed to be formed over millions of years from the decay of dead vegetation and animals under high temperatures and pressures in the earth's crust
Derived fossil fuels	Liquid fuels such as gasoline, diesel fuel, and heating oil obtained by distilling and processing crude oil
Derived synfuels	Synthetic crude oil and synthetic natural gas produced by the liquefaction or gasification of solid coal
Unconventional heavy oils	Underground deposits with an asphaltlike consistency that can be extracted from conventional crude oil deposits by enhanced recovery methods, oil shale rock, and tar sands, which can then be upgraded to crude oil and converted to derived fossil fuels
Unconventional natural gas	Deep underground deposits found in tight sands, Devonian shale rock, and coal seams, and dissolved in deep underground deposits of saltwater at very high temperatures and pressures (geopressurized zones)
Conventional nuclear fission (natural fuel)	High-temperature heat released when the tiny centers or nuclei of certain types of uranium atoms found in the earth's crust are split apart by atomic particles called neutrons
Breeder nuclear fission (derived fuel)	Extending the world's uranium supplies by converting a certain nonfissionable type of uranium atom into a type of fissionable plutonium atom not found in nature
Nuclear fusion	High-temperature heat released when temperatures of 100 billion degrees or more are used to fuse together the nuclei of certain types of hydrogen atoms found in water or produced from lithium in the earth's crust to form nuclei of heavier atoms
Trapped geothermal deposits	Low-temperature heat deposited in underground zones of dry steam, hot water, or a mixture of dry steam and hot water primarily from heat released by radioactive substances found in the *mantle* of partially molten rock beneath the earth's crust and the molten rock, called *magma*, located underneath this mantle in the earth's core
Derived hydrogen gas (H_2)	A gaseous fuel produced by using heat or electricity produced by a nonrenewable energy resource to decompose water ($2H_2O$ + energy $\rightarrow$ $2H_2$ + O_2), with the H_2 gas then burned in air or oxygen to produce energy ($2H_2$ + $O_2 \rightarrow 2H_2O$ + energy)
Renewable	
Tidal energy	Mechanical energy extracted from the abnormally high rise and fall of the tides twice a day in certain parts of the world
Flow-regulated geothermal energy	Medium- to high-temperature heat released by radioactive elements that flows slowly into deep underground deposits of hot dry rocks, partially molten rock (mantle), and molten rock (magma)
Direct solar energy	Radiant energy from the sun that can be used to provide low-temperature heat and hot water for residential and commercial buildings, concentrated to provide high-temperature heat for industrial processes and conversion to electricity, and converted by solar photovoltaic cells directly into electrical energy
Indirect solar energy	Solar energy stored in biomass (trees and other plants), direct and indirect biomass wastes (such as dung, crop wastes, and paper), winds, falling or flowing water (hydro), ocean currents, wave action, and temperature differences (thermal gradients) between the surface and bottom water in tropical oceans, shallow saltwater seas such as the Dead Sea in Israel, and artificially produced saltwater solar ponds
Derived biogas	A form of natural gas produced by the decomposition of biomass wastes

Table 14-1 Nonrenewable and Renewable Primary Energy Resources (*continued*)

Type	Description
Derived liquid biofuels	Liquids such as ethyl alcohol and methyl alcohol produced by fermentation and anaerobic decomposition of various types of biomass and biomass waste and pyrolysis oil produced by thermal decomposition of biomass and biomass wastes
Derived hydrogen gas (H_2)	A gaseous fuel produced by using direct sunlight to decompose water
Improving energy efficiency (energy conservation)	Conserving energy by getting more useful energy out of the primary energy we use

and fans to circulate heat by conduction, **(5)** an air-to-air heat exchanger to provide fresh air without significant heat loss or gain, to prevent buildup of excessive moisture and indoor air pollutants in an airtight passive or active solar home, **(6)** a batch passive solar water heater (one or more metal tanks painted black, placed in an insulated box, and covered with glass or plastic) or additional active solar collectors to provide hot water, and **(7)** when necessary a small backup energy-efficient conventional heating system or wood stove and a conventional well-insulated tank water heater or a tankless instant water heater that operates only as needed.

Because it is thermostatically controlled, an active solar heating system can give more even heating with less involvement by homeowners (in opening doors and windows) than a passive system. However, active systems are more expensive than passive systems and require pumps, motors, fans, and collectors that need periodic repair and maintenance like conventional heating systems. Both these systems are described more fully in Section 16-1.

Worldwide by early 1984 there were at least 4.5 million homes receiving all or part of their heat and hot water by passive or active solar systems: 3 million homes and buildings in Japan, 1 million in the United States (up from only 9,000 in 1977), 450,000 in Israel, and 35,000 in France. The number of solar homes is rising rapidly.

Energy Conservation: Improving Energy Efficiency
Energy efficiency is the amount of useful energy produced by a source compared to the energy needed to obtain this amount of useful energy. Thus, improving energy efficiency means getting more useful energy out of the primary energy we use. It means having an efficient space heating system and a well-insulated, airtight house, not enduring a cold house. For car owners, it means driving a car that typically runs an average of at least 17 kilometers per liter of gasoline (40 miles per gallon), not giving up a car altogether. Major ways to improve energy efficiency are listed in Table 14-2.

Energy conservation is usually classified as a *renewable* primary energy resource because using any primary energy resource more efficiently makes more useful energy available. For example, the largest and cheapest single source of new energy for the United States is the 43 percent of the primary energy input that is wasted. Between 1979 and 1983 energy conservation in the United States saved 100 times more energy than was obtained from finding new supplies of oil, natural gas, coal, and uranium and from phasing in new nuclear power plants.

Despite these important improvements in energy efficiency, there is a long way to go: Most cars on American roads still get relatively poor gas mileage; most existing houses and buildings are still underinsulated and leaky; and most new buildings do not take advantage of available energy-efficient construction techniques. For instance, building a **superinsulated house** is the cheapest and most effective way to improve the efficiency of home energy use, especially in cold climates. Such a house contains massive amounts of insulation, is extremely airtight, uses double- or triple-paned windows with movable insulating shutters for passive solar heating, has few if any windows on the sides not facing the sun to prevent heat loss, uses active or passive solar collectors to heat water, and has an air-to-air heat exchanger to prevent buildup of excessive moisture and indoor air pollutants.

A well-designed superinsulated house can get *all* its space heating and hot water without a conventional backup system, typically from a combination of **(1)** passive solar gain (about 59 percent), **(2)** waste heat from appliances (about 34 percent), and **(3)** the body heat of the occupants (about 8 percent) even in Saskatchewan, Canada, where winter temperatures may average −40°C (−40°F). Such houses retain most of this heat input for at least 100 hours, and inside temperatures would probably never fall below 10°C (50°F) even in extremely cold weather. By the end of 1983 there were over 5,000 superinsulated houses in Canada (3,000 in the province of Saskatchewan) and at least 5,000 in the United States. The number of such houses is growing rapidly as consumers, architects, and builders become familiar with their advantages and construction techniques.

Table 14-2 Majors Ways to Improve Energy Efficiency

Method	Examples
Tightening existing buildings	Insulating; caulking; weatherstripping; adding storm windows and doors; having "house doctors" make energy audits
Retrofitting existing buildings	Passive solar heating by adding south-facing windows, solar greenhouses or sun rooms, solar window box heaters, and batch hot water heaters; active solar heating by adding rooftop collectors for space heating and providing hot water
New buildings	Building superinsulated, passive solar, earth-sheltered, or active solar homes and buildings
Efficient appliances	Purchasing new high-efficiency appliances such as furnaces, refrigerators, stoves, washers, freezers, dryers, air conditioners, heat pumps, and lighting
Efficient transportation	Shifting to vehicles with high fuel efficiency; improving driving habits to reduce gasoline use; using mass transit; walking or riding bicycles where possible; shipping more freight by rail, water, and pipeline rather than by truck or airplane
Computerization and substituting low-energy communication systems for high-energy transportation	Using computerized monitors and controls to improve automobile fuel efficiency and home and factory heating, cooling, and lighting systems; using industrial robots and computerized communications systems to reduce business commuting, meetings, and other forms of travel and to save money and time through video conferencing, electronic mail, and allowing many employees to work at home (the electronic cottage concept)
Retooling of factories	Switching to more energy-efficient manufacturing processes, materials, and electric motors
Industrial heat recovery and cogeneration	Recovering waste heat for use in heating water and space heating; using high-temperature waste heat to generate electricity (cogeneration)
Matter recycling	Recycling steel, aluminum, paper, and other forms of matter to reduce use of more energy-intensive virgin matter resources (Section 13-3).
Urban planning	Building efficient mass transit and paratransit systems and bike paths (Section 12-4); building more compact and self-sufficient towns and cities (Section 12-6); developing municipally or neighborhood-owned district heating systems based on locally available renewable energy resources; altering building codes, using zoning ordinances, and providing tax breaks to require or encourage more insulation and minimum energy-efficiency standards for new houses and buildings, energy audits of all buildings, active and passive solar heating of buildings and hot water, and high-density housing developments; providing tax breaks and free or low-cost loans for improving the energy efficiency of housing occupied by low-income individuals

Present Global Primary Energy Resources Figure 14-2 shows that by 1983 about 82 percent of the primary energy used throughout the world was provided by the burning of three *nonrenewable* fossil fuels—oil (36 percent), coal (27 percent), and natural gas (17 percent)—and by the nuclear fission of *nonrenewable* uranium atoms to produce electricity (2 percent). The remaining 18 percent of the world's primary energy was provided by burning *renewable biomass energy sources* such as wood, dung, and crop residues (13 percent) and by using *renewable* falling water (hydropower) to produce electricity (5 percent).

Hard Versus Soft Paths to a New Energy Era Because the supply of nonrenewable conventional crude oil is being depleted rapidly, most analysts argue that a transition to dependence on other primary energy resources will be necessary over the next 50 years. There is considerable disagreement over the most desirable and affordable intermediate- and long-term energy strategy for making this transition in the world and in individual nations.

Two approaches for providing projected primary energy needs and services in the future are the *hard path* and the *soft path* (Table 14-3). Propo-

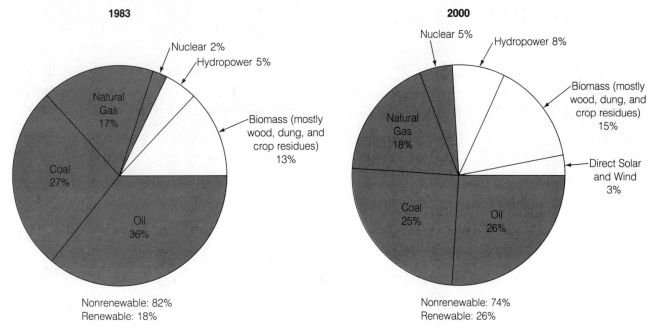

1983

Nuclear 2%
Hydropower 5%

Natural Gas 17%

Coal 27%

Oil 36%

Biomass (mostly wood, dung, and crop residues) 13%

Nonrenewable: 82%
Renewable: 18%

2000

Nuclear 5%
Hydropower 8%

Natural Gas 18%

Coal 25%

Oil 26%

Biomass (mostly wood, dung, and crop residues) 15%

Direct Solar and Wind 3%

Nonrenewable: 74%
Renewable: 26%

Figure 14-2 World consumption of primary nonrenewable (shaded) and renewable (nonshaded) energy by source in 1983 with projections for 1990 and 2000, excluding sunlight incorporated into food crops and used to heat the earth. If direct solar energy input were included, the supplemental primary energy sources shown would make up only about 1 percent of annual world energy use. (Sources: U.S. Department of Energy and Worldwatch Institute.)

nents of the *hard-path energy strategy* emphasize using human ingenuity and tax breaks and other forms of government (taxpayer) subsidies for energy companies to increase supplies of nonrenewable petroleum (conventional and heavy oils), natural gas (conventional and unconventional), coal, and uranium. Emphasis is also placed on providing an increasing amount of electricity for future primary energy needs by building a number of huge, complex, centralized coal-burning and nuclear fission electric power plants between 1985 and 2020. After 2020 there would be a shift from conventional nuclear fission to breeder nuclear fission power plants, which could synthesize some of their nuclear fuel and thus prolong uranium supplies for at least 1,000 years. After 2050 there would be a gradual shift to almost complete dependence on centralized nuclear fusion electric power plants, if this energy alternative should ever prove to be technologically, economically, and environmentally acceptable (Section 15-6). The political and economic power concentrated in the large energy companies is presently being used to persuade the United States to follow the hard path, with most annual federal energy research and development expenditures being devoted to this path (Section 16-8).

Proponents of the *soft-path energy strategy*, such as physicist and energy expert Amory Lovins (see his end-of-chapter Guest Editorial), recognize that people do not want kilowatt-hours, kilocalories, or barrels of oil. Instead they want the services that energy provides, such as comfortably heated and cooled homes and buildings, reliable transportation, and manufactured goods—all as cheaply as possible. Lovins and others argue that the most energy-efficient, quickest, and cheapest way to meet projected energy services is through a combination of **(1)** improving energy efficiency (Table 14-2), **(2)** decreasing the use of nonrenewable oil, coal, and natural gas, **(3)** phasing out nuclear power because it is uneconomic, unsafe, and unnecessary (Sections 15-4 and 15-5), and **(4)** increasing the use of a mix of *renewable* direct and indirect solar energy resources (Chapter 16).

With the soft path, most *space heating and hot water* for houses and commercial buildings would be provided by a combination of passive and active solar systems, superinsulation, efficient natural gas furnaces, and efficient wood stoves equipped with catalytic converters to reduce air pollution. *Electricity* would be provided by a combination of existing coal-fired plants equipped with the latest air pollution control equipment, cogeneration at industrial plants, large farms of wind turbines, recommissioning abandoned small hydroelectric power plants, and solar photovoltaic cells. *High-tempera-*

Table 14-3 Comparison of Hard- and Soft-Path Energy Resource Strategies

Hard Path: Supplies of nonrenewable fossil fuels and uranium are unlimited because of human ingenuity	Soft Path: Supplies of nonrenewable fossil fuels are limited; some, such as oil, are being depleted rapidly
Increase the supply of fossil fuels and uranium primarily through investment in exploration and recovery of conventional and nonconventional fossil fuels.	Decrease the demand for fossil fuels and uranium and increase the supply of primary energy especially through investment in improvements in energy efficiency (i.e., do more with the energy we have).
Emphasize the increased use of nonrenewable fossil fuels and uranium.	Decrease dependence on fossil fuels and uranium and emphasize the increased use of a mix of renewable energy resources based on locally available direct and indirect solar energy resources to supplement the primary energy made available through using energy more efficiently.
Provide an increasing amount of primary energy in the form of electricity by greatly increasing the number of large, centralized coal-burning and conventional nuclear fission power plants. If possible, gradually replace these with large breeder nuclear fission and nuclear fusion power plants.	Use electricity only for essential purposes, since it is an extremely wasteful way to produce energy. Decrease dependence on large, centralized power plants of any type through increased energy efficiency and use of a variety of small to intermediate-sized, decentralized energy production facilities using renewable direct and indirect solar energy. Coal might be used slightly more between today and 2000 as a transition fuel, but only with adequate pollution controls and land reclamation and only if increases in energy efficiency are not adequate to meet essential electrical energy needs. For economic and safety reasons, conventional nuclear fission power plants would be gradually phased out in most parts of the nation beginning in 1990. Breeder fission and nuclear fusion reactors would not be developed.

ture heat for industrial processes would be provided by boilers fired by natural gas, forestry wastes, and municipal wastes. Each boiler would be equipped with air pollution control equipment and waste heat would be used to produce electricity (cogeneration).

Fuel for transportation would be provided by gasoline, biofuels such as alcohols and pyrolysis oils (Table 14-1) derived from forestry and farm wastes and from energy crops grown on otherwise unproductive land, and possibly renewable derived hydrogen gas if efficient and affordable ways of decomposing water with sunlight are developed in the future (Sections 16-5 and 16-6). Because they are too costly, energy inefficient, and environmentally harmful compared to other alternatives, little, if any, emphasis would be placed on using *solar hard technologies* such as biomass plantations of fuel crops grown on land that could be used for food crops, and electricity produced by large solar-powered satellites (Enrichment Study 4), solar power plants (power towers, Section 16-1), ocean thermal gradient power plants (Section 16-3), and large hydroelectric plants (Section 16-2).

Amory Lovins argues that by 2000, using the soft-path approach, the United States would (1) cut energy waste in half and provide the same or higher average standard of living, (2) extend the reserves of conventional fossil fuels several decades, because doubling the efficiency of use of a primary energy resource such as oil has the same effect as doubling oil reserves, (3) eliminate or sharply reduce the need for imported oil and natural gas, (4) eliminate or sharply reduce the need to build additional electric power plants of any type, as well as allow the phaseout of existing nuclear power plants, (5) buy time to phase in a diverse and flexible array of decentralized, renewable primary energy resources depending on local availability of direct sunlight, wind, biomass resources, and falling and flowing water, (6) decrease the overall environmental impacts of primary energy use, (7) be cheaper and quicker to implement than the hard path because direct and indirect solar technologies and ways to improve energy efficiency are already available at affordable prices, require no major technological breakthroughs such as nuclear fusion, and generally can be installed in days, weeks, or months rather than the 7 to 15 years it takes to build a coal-fired or nuclear power plant, and (8) give individuals and communities more control over how they wish to provide desired energy services based on locally available renewable resources.

Lovins and other energy experts (see, for example, Wilson Clark and Jake Page, *Energy, Vulnerability, and War: Alternatives for America*, 1981) also argue that the trend toward large, centralized electric power plants and other energy facilities threatens national security by making the entire U.S. energy system vulnerable to a limited nuclear strike. For example, the detonation of a single, well-placed 1-megaton nuclear bomb at about 500 kilometers (310 miles) above the United States could release an *electromagnetic pulse* (EMP)—a microsecond burst of electromagnetic energy—100 times more powerful than a lightning bolt. Such a high-altitude detonation might not kill anyone directly, but its EMP could overload and burn out every unprotected electronic circuit in the United States, including radios and television sets, computers and computer-controlled equipment, vehicle engines, and all telephone and electronic communications systems. These effects could knock out electronic control facilities at all power plants and disable the computers controlling the flow of fuels through pipelines, thus causing failure of the national electric power grid. Electronic equipment can be protected from an EMP. But such protection is costly and is being installed gradually, only for vital military electronic control, communications, and weapons systems.

Lovins and Wilson argue that the United States can strengthen its national security and reduce vulnerability to both cutoffs of imported oil and destruction of electronic control and communications equipment from an EMP or other forms of nuclear attack (Enrichment Study 3) by greatly increasing the use of more dispersed, decentralized, small-scale renewable energy resources.

An increasing number of individuals and communities in the United States are shifting to the soft path. But Lovins contends that a more rapid spread of this approach is being hindered by government (taxpayer) subsidies of the hard-path approach (Section 16-8), outdated building codes that discourage energy conservation and sometimes require unnecessary backup conventional heating systems, inadequate access to capital for development of solar energy resources, and the false belief that it will be a long time before solar energy can provide a significant fraction of primary energy. In 1983, for example, about 18 percent of all primary energy used in the world and 8.5 percent of that used in the United States came from renewable solar energy resources—mostly biomass (wood, dung, and crop residues) and hydropower (Figures 14-2 and 14-3). It is projected that by 2000 direct and indirect renewable solar energy can provide 26 percent of the world's and U.S. primary energy (Figures 14-2 and 14-3). Several energy analysts go further and

project that with a massive development program, direct and indirect solar energy could provide 30 to 40 percent of the world's primary energy by 2000 and 75 percent by 2025.

14-2 Brief History of Energy Use

Energy Use from Primitive to Modern Times Cultural history (Enrichment Study 1) has been based on using human ingenuity to increase the average amount of primary energy used per person (Figure 14-4). Average daily energy use per person increased from about 2,000 kilocalories from food energy for early hunter-gatherers, who had not discovered how to burn wood for heat and cooking, to 12,000 kilocalories by early farmers, who burned wood for cooking and heating and used the muscle power of domesticated animals to help them raise grains and vegetables.

During the industrial revolution in the 1800s, heat from the burning of *wood*—a potentially renewable resource—was used to run machines and locomotives, to convert ores into metals (Section 13-1), and to fuse sand into glass. By 1850 the direct and indirect average per capita fuel consumption in industrializing nations like Great Britain and the United States had risen to about 60,000 kilocalories per day, with wood providing 91 percent of all the primary energy used in the United States (Figure 14-3). Virgin forests were being cut down at an alarming rate, and many feared that shortages of wood would halt the industrial revolution.

Then people discovered that nonrenewable *coal* could be mined from the earth's crust and substituted for wood. By 1900 coal had replaced wood as the major primary energy source in industrializing European nations and in the United States. In 1869 the first oil well was drilled. This event, coupled with later discoveries of how to distill or refine crude oil into gasoline, fuel oil, and diesel fuel eventually led to a dramatic change in worldwide primary energy consumption patterns. It was also discovered that the deposits of natural gas found with most oil deposits could be burned as a fuel.

By 1950 *crude oil* had become the major primary energy source and *natural gas* the third largest source of primary energy in the United States. Note from Figure 14-3 that between 1850 and 1950 the United States switched from being 91 percent dependent on *renewable* wood to being 96 percent dependent on *nonrenewable* oil, coal, and natural gas. Use of oil and natural gas increased sharply in the industrialized nations until by 1983 they provided 53 percent of the world's primary energy (Figure 14-2) and 67

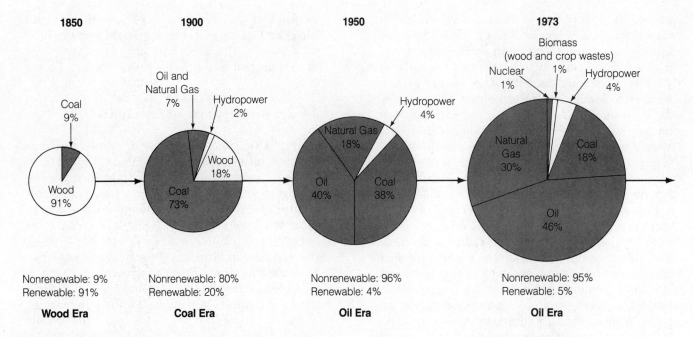

1850

Coal
9%

Wood
91%

Nonrenewable: 9%
Renewable: 91%

Wood Era

1900

Oil and
Natural Gas
7%

Hydropower
2%

Wood
18%

Coal
73%

Nonrenewable: 80%
Renewable: 20%

Coal Era

1950

Hydropower
4%

Natural Gas
18%

Oil
40%

Coal
38%

Nonrenewable: 96%
Renewable: 4%

Oil Era

1973

Biomass
(wood and crop wastes)
1%

Nuclear
1%

Hydropower
4%

Natural
Gas
30%

Coal
18%

Oil
46%

Nonrenewable: 95%
Renewable: 5%

Oil Era

Figure 14-3 Changes in consumption of primary nonrenewable (shaded) and renewable (unshaded) energy resources in the United States between 1850 and 1983 with a projection for 2000. Relative circle size indicates the total amount of energy used. (Sources: U.S. Department of Energy; National Audubon Society for year 2000 projection.)

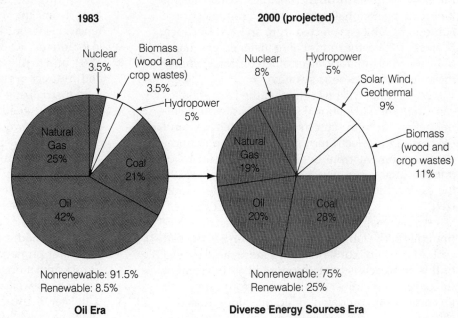

1983

Nuclear
3.5%

Biomass
(wood and
crop wastes)
3.5%

Hydropower
5%

Natural
Gas
25%

Coal
21%

Oil
42%

Nonrenewable: 91.5%
Renewable: 8.5%

Oil Era

2000 (projected)

Nuclear
8%

Hydropower
5%

Solar, Wind,
Geothermal
9%

Biomass
(wood and
crop wastes)
11%

Natural
Gas
19%

Oil
20%

Coal
28%

Nonrenewable: 75%
Renewable: 25%

Diverse Energy Sources Era

percent of the primary energy used in the United States (Figure 14-3).

Primarily because of the increased availability of relatively inexpensive oil and natural gas, world primary energy consumption more than tripled between 1950 and 1983 , and average annual energy consumption per person doubled. As a result, by 1983 each person in most industrial nations used directly and indirectly an average of about 125,000 kilocalories a day—almost 63 times the average per capita energy use at the primitive survival level (Figure 14-4). By 1983 each American directly and indirectly used an average of 230,000 kilocalories of energy per day—115 times the survival level. In 1984, 236 million Americans used more energy for

air conditioning alone than 1.03 billion Chinese used for all purposes!

Most of the increase in primary energy consumption per person since 1900 has taken place in the MDCs, and the gap in average per capita primary energy use between the MDCs and LDCs has widened (Figure 14-5). In 1983, with about 5 percent of the world's population, the United States accounted for about 25 percent of the world's primary energy consumption. India, with about 15 percent of the world's population, consumed only about 1.5 percent of the world's primary energy. In rural India bullock-drawn carts, bicycles, and coal-powered trains still carry the bulk of passengers and freight.

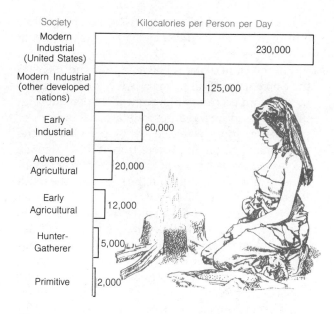

Figure 14-4 Average daily per capita energy use at various stages of human cultural evolution.

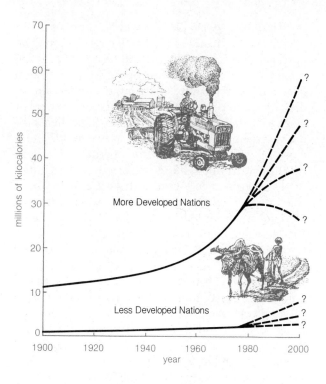

Figure 14-5 Average per capita annual primary energy consumption in the MDCs and LDCs between 1900 and 1983 and projections (dotted lines) to 2000. (Sources: U.S. Department of Energy and International Energy Agency.)

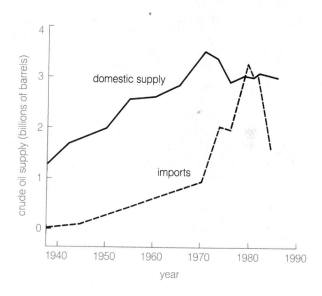

Figure 14-6 Annual domestic extraction and imports of crude oil in the United States, 1940-1983. (Source: U.S. Bureau of Commerce.)

The 1973 OPEC Oil Embargo and 1979 Iranian Oil Cutoff Since 1940 the depletion of many low-cost domestic oil deposits has made it cheaper for the United States to import much of its oil (Figure 14-6). By 1973, about 48 percent of this imported oil came from the 13 nations in the Organization of Petroleum Exporting Countries (OPEC), which together accounted for 56 percent of the world's oil production and about 84 percent of all oil exports. OPEC's 13 member countries are located in the Middle East (Iran, Iraq, Kuwait, Qatar, Saudi Arabia, and the United Arab Emirates), in sub-Saharan Africa (Gabon and Nigeria), in South America (Ecuador and Venezuela), in North Africa (Algeria and Libya), and in Asia (Indonesia).

OPEC was founded in 1960 by Venezuelan Juan Perez Alfonso, a multimillionaire who lived a simple life in the suburbs of Caracas, rode a bicycle instead of driving a car, read by candlelight, and reportedly asked all visitors to leave by nightfall so that he did not have to waste electricity. He viewed the organization as a means of reducing the wasteful use of oil and slowing down the rapid rate at which the world's oil reserves were being depleted.

On October 18, 1973, the Arab members of OPEC reduced oil exports to Western industrial nations and prohibited all shipments of their oil to the United States because of its support of Israel in the 18-day war waged by Egypt and Syria against Israel. The embargo lasted until March 1974 and caused a fivefold increase in the average world price of crude oil (from $2.70 to almost $10 a barrel) that helped lead to double-digit inflation, high interest rates, and a global economic recession. Americans accustomed

to cheap and plentiful fuel had to wait for hours to buy gasoline, and thermostats in homes and offices were turned down. Despite the sharp price increase, however, the percentage of U.S. oil imports obtained from OPEC nations increased from 48 to 67 percent between 1973 and 1978.

Then in 1979 available world oil supplies again decreased as a result of the Iranian revolution. The average world price of crude oil rose to nearly $34 a barrel by 1982 before dropping to about $29 a barrel by early 1984. By 1980 a large number of middle-class Americans heating their homes with oil or electricity had monthly bills higher than their rent or mortgage payments. Thus, between 1973 and early 1984, the price of a barrel of crude oil bought on the world market and imported in the United States increased *974 percent* (from $2.70 to about $29) or *517 percent* adjusted for inflation in constant 1975 dollars (from $3.53 to about $21.77). This meant that between 1973 and early 1984 OPEC had engineered history's largest international transfer of wealth and power from oil-importing to oil-exporting nations. In 1980, for instance, the United States paid an average of $9.4 million *each hour* for imported oil, and each American paid an average of $363 to oil-exporting nations. A few oil-exporting MDCs—Norway, the United Kingdom, and the Soviet Union—benefited from higher oil prices, but Mexico and the OPEC nations gained the most.

Other MDCs such as Japan and most western European nations are even more dependent on imported oil because they have little or no domestic supplies. For example, Japan relied on imported oil for 70 percent of its total primary energy needs in 1983 (down from 80 percent in 1973), with 63 percent of its oil coming from OPEC nations in the Persian Gulf. To reduce the use and waste of gasoline and heating oil and to decrease dependence on oil imports, Japan and most oil-importing European nations tax gasoline at the retail level and in some cases add a tariff to each barrel of imported oil. As a result, the average price of gasoline in Japan and most European nations was about 79 cents a liter ($3 a gallon) in 1984.

In the United States federal and state gasoline taxes are still low and tariffs are not placed on imported oil. As a result, the average price of gasoline in the U.S. in 1983 was about 32 cents a liter ($1.20 a gallon)—not much higher than it was in 1972 when adjusted for inflation. This sharp difference in the prices of gasoline in the United States and many other nations helps explain why **(1)** most new cars and trucks used in Japan and Europe and those imported from these nations into the United States get much better gasoline mileage than most similar new U.S.-made vehicles, and **(2)** in the 1980s many Americans are still purchasing new vehicles with relatively poor gas mileage.

The Soviet Union, the world's leading oil-producing nation, was the only major industrialized nation not reducing its annual consumption of oil between 1973 and 1983. This worldwide drop in oil consumption resulted primarily from a combination of substituting energy from other sources, improving energy efficiency (Table 14-2), and economic recession.

In the United States between 1973 and 1983: **(1)** the percentage of all primary energy use supplied by oil dropped from 46 percent to 42 percent (Figure 14-3) and average per capita consumption of primary energy decreased by 14 percent; **(2)** the percentage of oil imported from OPEC nations decreased from 48 percent to about 30 percent, with Saudi Arabia dropping from the second to the tenth largest supplier of oil imports, and Mexico—itself an oil importer in 1973—being the principal U.S. supplier of imported oil in 1983, followed by Canada and Venezuela; and **(3)** the gas and electric utilities that produce or distribute about 40 percent of the nation's primary energy stopped encouraging householders to use more energy and began offering free or low-cost energy audits and loans for reducing home energy use.

This decade of significant progress notwithstanding, domestic extraction of crude oil remained about the same (Figure 14-6) and domestic extraction of natural gas declined by 18 percent, despite greatly increased exploration and drilling efforts; moreover, most American buildings were still underinsulated and leaky, and average fuel consumption for the entire U.S. car fleet increased only from 5.6 to 7 kilometers per liter (13 to 16 miles per gallon) because of the large number of gas-guzzlers still on the road.

By early 1984 energy conservation and several years of worldwide economic recession had led to a temporary oil glut, with the average price of crude oil falling from $34 to $29 a barrel between 1982 and early 1984. As long as supply exceeds demand, some observers predict a further drop, to $20 to $25 a barrel. Such a drop in oil prices would stimulate economic growth in oil-importing countries such as the United States but would discourage the search for new oil and undermine improvements in energy efficiency and development of other energy alternatives.

Most analysts agree that the so-called oil glut of the early 1980s is only temporary and could disappear at any time because **(1)** a war or other crisis such as the collapse of Saudi Arabia's monarchy, the Iran-Iraq conflict that led to sinking of oil tankers in 1984, or a takeover of Mexico's oilfields by Central American guerrillas could cause a sudden cutoff of oil supplies; **(2)** the time when the world demand for oil exceeds the rate at which it can be produced, presently projected between 1990 and 2005, could occur sooner because lower oil prices in the 1980s may increase the use and waste of oil and decrease the search for new oil; or **(3)** the OPEC nations might agree to pump less oil each year to

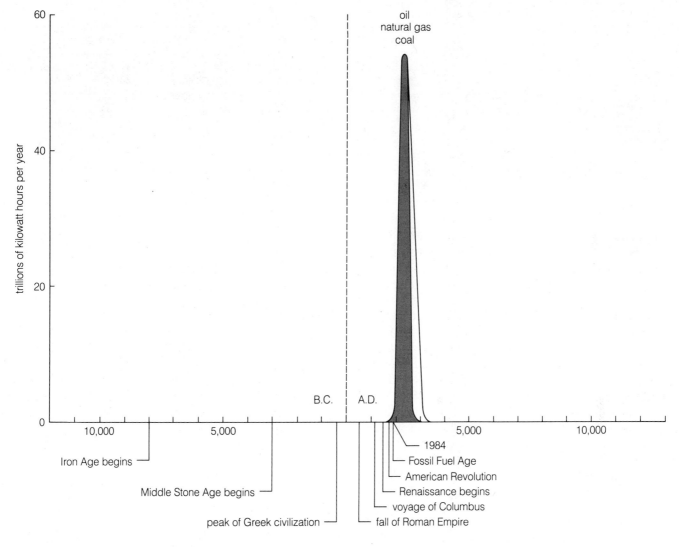

Figure 14-7 The fossil fuel age. Present dependence on nonrenewable oil, natural gas, and coal for 84 percent of the world's primary energy represents a temporary and relatively brief period in human history.

maintain or raise their price (although some consider this unlikely because OPEC's share of the world's oil production fell from 56 percent in 1973 to 30 percent in 1983).

The Congressional Research Service and the International Energy Agency warn that another oil embargo or cutoff of oil supplies because of a Mideast war or revolution in Mexico could cause oil prices to reach $50 to $98 a barrel, reduce the U.S. GNP by as much as 29 percent, cut jobs by as much as 28 percent, and increase the chances of war.

14-3 How Long Can the Fossil Fuel Era Last?

The Fossil Fuel Era The era we now live in is a unique and temporary period in human history

(Figure 14-7). No one knows when affordable supplies of oil, natural gas, and coal may run out. However, projections can be based on the estimated supply of a resource and assumptions about the rate at which it will be depleted (Section 13-3).

When you read about the estimated lifetime of a nonrenewable resource such as crude oil, it is important to note the assumed annual rate of depletion and whether this represents the depletion of reserves, identified resources, or a combination of identified and estimated unidentified resources (Figure 13-6).

Supplies of many nonrenewable mineral resources such as copper and aluminum can be extended by recycling and reuse. Nonrenewable fossil fuels, however, cannot be recycled or reused as a result of the first and second laws of thermodynamics (Sections 2-2 and 2-3). Once burned, the high-quality energy they contain is gone forever.

Table 14-4 Depletion of the World's Oil Resources

Resource	Estimated Supply in 1983 (billions of barrels)	Annual Rate of Depletion in 1983 (billions of barrels)	Years to 80% Depletion at		
			1983 Rate	2% Annual Increase	4% Annual Increase
Proven reserves	670	18	30	23	20
Ultimately recoverable reserves (identified plus unidentified resources)	2,100	18	93	53	39

Sources: American Petroleum Institute and U.S. Department of Energy.

Supplies of Conventional and Unconventional Crude Oil Until the 1973 and 1979 oil supply disruptions, most nations, rich and poor, assumed that an ample and relatively cheap supply of crude oil would always be available to fuel economic growth and more energy-intensive life-styles. Although these disruptions were temporary and did not represent a true shortage of crude oil, the world's supplies of nonrenewable fossil fuels are finite. Experts disagree, however, over how long the identified and unidentified fossil fuel resources will last.

Cornucopians like Julian Simon and the late Herman Kahn have said that we will have an abundant supply of crude oil, arguing that higher prices for crude oil will stimulate the location and extraction of unidentified crude oil resources, as well as the extraction and upgrading of heavy oils from oil shale and tar sands and from oil too thick to pump out of existing oil wells (Section 15-2).

Other analysts, however, point out that people who hold the cornucopian beliefs just mentioned do not understand the arithmetic and consequences of exponential growth in the use of a resource (Section 1-2). Table 14-4 shows the depletion rate of the world's crude oil resources assuming various annual rates of depletion. Note that the world's known *reserves* of crude oil will be 80 percent depleted in 30 years (by 2013) if annual oil consumption remains at the 1983 rate and in 23 years (by 2006) if the annual depletion rate increases by a modest 2 percent because of world economic growth, a drop in oil prices, or both. The ultimately recoverable supplies of crude oil based on undiscovered deposits is estimated to be over three times today's proven reserves (Table 14-4). Even if *all* these estimated supplies of crude oil are discovered and developed—which many experts consider unlikely—and sold at a price many times the early 1984 price of $29 a barrel, this ultimately recoverable supply would be 80 percent depleted in 93 years (by 2076) at 1983 usage rates and in 53 years (by 2037) if the rate of oil usage increases by a modest 2 percent a year (Table 14-4).

The world's four largest producers of crude oil are the Soviet Union, Saudi Arabia, the United States, and Mexico. Assuming that the 1983 rate of crude oil consumption is maintained:

1. Saudi Arabia, with the world's largest known crude oil reserves, could supply the world's total crude oil needs for only 10 years if it were the world's only source.

2. Mexico, which has the world's second largest crude oil reserves could supply the world's total crude oil needs for only about 3 years.

3. The estimated crude oil reserves under Alaska's north slope—the largest deposit ever found in the United States—used by itself, would meet world demand for only 6 months and U.S. demand for 2 to 4 years.

4. If drilling off the east coast of the United States meets the most optimistic estimates, these potential crude oil reserves could satisfy world crude oil needs for 1 week and U.S. needs for less than 3 months.

5. The recently developed North Sea crude oil reserves would meet world crude oil demands for only about 1.5 years.

Thus, anyone who tells us that new discoveries will solve world crude oil supply problems is saying that we need to discover the equivalent of a new Saudi Arabia deposit *every 10 years* just to maintain the world's 1983 level of oil use. If, as some energy analysts project, oil use rates rise above 1983 levels, the world's identified and unidentified crude oil resources would be depleted much faster.

To many analysts the messages of Table 14-4 and Figure 14-6 are clear: Use crude oil only for essential purposes; look for more crude oil to buy a little time; use less crude oil and other types of energy by improving energy efficiency and reducing energy waste; and begin a program to shift to other renewable energy alternatives over the next 50 years.

Large supplies of heavy oil that can be upgraded

to crude oil are potentially available from oil shale and tar sands and could extend world supplies of crude oil for at least 100 years. However, extracting these heavy oils is expensive and environmentally harmful (Section 15-2). With the additional processing costs of purification and upgrading, these heavy oils may always cost 1.5 to 2 times more than conventional crude oil unless their price is heavily subsidized by the government—or, more accurately, by taxpayers.

Conventional and Unconventional Natural Gas
Supplies of conventional natural gas are projected to last somewhat longer than those of crude oil, but are also limited. The world's identified reserves of natural gas will last about 50 years (to 2033) at 1983 usage rates and 35 years (to 2018) if annual usage increases by 2 percent a year. The world's estimated ultimately recoverable supply of natural gas that may be found and recovered at much higher prices would last about 200 years (to 2183) at 1983 usage rates and 80 years (to 2063) if annual usage increases by 2 percent a year.

Some energy analysts believe that large additional supplies of natural gas may be obtained from unconventional sources such as tight sands and geopressurized zones (Section 15-3). Other ana-

lysts, however, believe that these sources will prove to be disappointing because drilling and extracting from such deep underground sources may take more energy and money than the resulting gas would be worth.

Coal Based on known reserves, coal is the most abundant conventional fossil fuel in the world and the United States. The Soviet Union has an estimated 56 percent of the world's coal reserves, the United States about 19 percent, and China about 8 percent. Identified world reserves of coal should last for about 276 years (to 2259) at 1983 usage rates and 86 years (to 2069) if annual usage increases by 2 percent a year. The world's estimated ultimately recoverable supply of coal that may be found and recovered at much higher prices would last about 900 years at the 1983 usage rate and 149 years if annual usage increases by 2 percent a year.

Coal is not only more plentiful, it is also cheaper to use for producing electricity than oil, natural gas, and nuclear energy even if coal-burning power plants are equipped with the latest and most effective air pollution control equipment. It is projected to remain cheaper well into the next century. For these reasons, some energy analysts suggest that the use of coal be increased to help the world make the tran-

---

Present and Projected Global Energy Crises

Today's Food and Firewood Energy Distribution Crisis

At least one-fourth of the people in less developed nations do not have an adequate daily intake of food or protein energy (Sections 9-1 and 9-2), and the 90 percent of the people in LDCs for whom firewood is the main fuel are having more and more trouble getting enough of it (Section 10-6).

Today's Energy Policy Crisis

There is an urgent need to develop and carry out a carefully integrated set of short-, intermediate-, and long-term energy plans over the next 50 years. These plans will allow the replacement of dwindling supplies of crude oil and perhaps natural gas and uranium with a new mix of affordable and environmentally acceptable energy sources based on improving energy efficiency and increased use of nuclear energy (the hard path), renewable energy alternatives (the soft path), or some mix of these two approaches.

The Oil Energy Shortage Crisis of 1990 to 2020

It is projected that if world oil use continues at 1983 or slightly higher levels, the world demand for crude oil will probably exceed the rate at which it can be supplied some time between 1990 and 2020. If this happens, crude oil prices will rise catastrophically, triggering a global economic depression and intensifying international tensions as industrialized nations compete for available supplies.

The Energy Shortage Crisis of 2020 to 2060

Affordable supplies of crude oil and possibly natural gas will probably begin running out between 2020 and 2060. During this period the world faces massive economic disruption, probably coupled with a major population decline (Section 7-1 and Enrichment Study 2), unless it has significantly improved the efficiency of use of primary energy resources and shifted to a mix of affordable and environmentally acceptable energy resources to replace dependence on crude oil.

Table 14-5 Energy Quality of Different Forms of Energy

	Energy Quality	
Form of Energy	Relative Value	Average Energy Content (kilocalories per kilogram)
Electricity	Very high	
Very high-temperature heat (greater than 2,500°C)	Very high	
Nuclear fission (uranium)	Very high	139,000,000*
Nuclear fusion (deuterium)	Very high	24,000,000†
Concentrated sunlight	Very high	
Concentrated wind (high-velocity flow)	Very high	
High-temperature heat (1,000°–2,500°C)	High	
Hydrogen gas (as a fuel)	High	30,000
Natural gas (mostly methane)	High	13,000
SNG (synthetic natural gas made from coal)	High	13,000
Gasoline (refined crude oil)	High	10,500
Crude oil	High	10,300
LNG (liquefied natural gas)	High	10,300
Coal (bituminous and anthracite)	High	7,000
Synthetic oil (made from coal)	High	8,900
Sunlight (normal)	High	
Concentrated geothermal	Moderate	
Water (high-velocity flow)	Moderate	
Moderate-temperature heat (100°–1,000°C)	Moderate	
Dung	Moderate	4,000
Wood and crop wastes	Moderate	3,300
Assorted garbage and trash	Moderate	2,900
Oil shale	Moderate	1,100
Tar sands	Moderate	1,100
Peat	Moderate	950
Dispersed geothermal	Low	
Low-temperature heat (air temperature of 100°C or lower)	Low	

*Per kilogram of uranium metal containing 0.72% fissionable uranium-235.
†Per kilogram of hydrogen containing 0.015% deuterium.

sition from dependence on oil and natural gas to dependence on energy conservation and a mix of renewable energy resources over the next 50 years (Section 15-4).

Present and Projected Global Energy Crises
Based on projections of world energy use and estimated crude oil supplies, some energy experts have distinguished between four closely related, present and projected global energy crises (see box). Here the term **energy crisis** refers to a temporary or permanent shortage, a catastrophic price rise for one or more forms of widely used useful energy, or a situation in which energy use is so great that the resulting pollution and environmental disruption threatens human health and welfare, along with the diversity and sustainability of the ecosphere at a national, regional, or global level. Most people equate "crisis" with "disaster," but it should be emphasized that a *crisis* is a turning point—an opportunity for change.

With this historical background in energy use, we are ready to look at some energy concepts that can help us evaluate present and future energy alternatives.

14-4 Energy Concepts: Energy Quality, Energy Efficiency, and Net Useful Energy

Energy Quality and Flow Rates According to the second law of energy (Section 2-3), whenever we use any form of energy, it is automatically degraded to a lower-quality or less useful form of energy—usually low-temperature heat that flows into the environment. Thus, *a major factor determining the usefulness of an energy resource is its quality, not its quantity.*

Different forms of energy vary in their quality (Table 14-5). High-quality energy, like that in electricity, oil, gasoline, sunlight, wind, uranium, and high-temperature heat, is concentrated. By contrast, low-quality energy, like low-temperature heat, is dispersed, or dilute. For example, there is more low-temperature heat in the Atlantic Ocean than in all the oil in Saudi Arabia. But this heat stored in the ocean is so widely dispersed that we can't do much with it.

High-quality incoming ultraviolet, visible, and near infrared radiation from the sun is degraded into low-quality far infrared radiation (Figure 3-2). Sunlight does not melt metals or char our clothes because only a relatively small amount of this high-quality energy reaches each square meter of the earth's surface per minute or hour during daylight hours—even though the total amount of solar energy reaching the entire earth is enormous. Wind energy also has a high energy quality, but to perform large amounts of useful work it must flow into a given area at a fairly high rate. Thus, *the overall usefulness of a given renewable energy source (direct sunlight, flowing water, or wind) is determined both by its energy quality and by its flow rate (flux)—the amount of high-quality energy reaching a given area of the earth per minute or hour.*

Unfortunately, many of the highest forms of energy quality, such as high-temperature heat, electricity, gasoline, hydrogen gas, and concentrated sunlight do not occur naturally. We must use other forms of high-quality energy like fossil, wood, or nuclear fuels to produce them, to concentrate them, or to upgrade their quality.

Matching Energy Quality to End Uses In terms of the laws of thermodynamics, it is wasteful to use high-quality energy to perform a task that could be accomplished with low- or moderate-quality energy. Thus, *an important way to reduce energy waste is to supply energy only in the quality needed for the task at hand, using the cheapest possible approach*, as discussed in more detail by Amory Lovins in the end-of-chapter Guest Editorial.

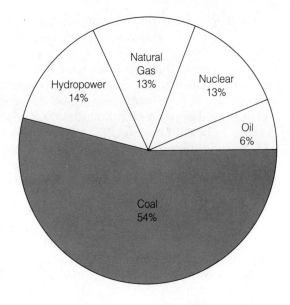

Figure 14-8 Production of electricity in the United States by source in 1983. (Source: U.S. Department of Energy.)

From a thermodynamic standpoint, for example, using high-quality electrical energy to heat a home to 20°C (68°F) or to provide hot water at 60°C (140°F) wastes large quantities of high-quality energy. First, at a power plant, high-quality energy from a fossil fuel or nuclear fuel is converted to high-quality heat energy at several thousand degrees with an automatic loss of some of the heat to the local environment, as required by the second energy law. The remaining high-quality heat is used to convert water to steam and to spin turbines to produce high-quality electrical energy, with a further loss of heat to the environment. More degraded energy or heat is lost when electricity is transmitted to a home. There the high-quality electrical energy is converted to relatively low-quality heat energy to heat the home or to provide hot water. According to Amory Lovins, using electricity to heat a house or provide hot water, "is like using a chain saw to cut butter."

In 1983, electrical energy provided about 33 percent of all primary energy used in the United States, with coal-burning power plants producing more of this electricity than all other types of power plant combined (Figure 14-8). But according to Lovins, the essential uses for electricity in the U.S. amount to only about 8 percent of annual primary energy needs, mostly for running lights and motors, refining copper, and producing glass, iron, and steel by certain methods. This means that the United States already has more than enough power plants to produce electricity to meet all essential needs until 2005—perhaps until 2025. Critics of this idea point out that even though electricity is wasteful of energy when used for certain purposes, people use it to heat their homes, provide hot water, and for various nonessential industrial purposes because it is convenient.

From a temperature-matching standpoint, a typical home furnace or hot water heater also wastes large amounts of high-quality energy by burning the oil or natural gas at about 2,000 to 3,000°C (3,632 to 5,432°F) to heat a house to 20°C (68°F) or water to 60°C (140°F). Physicist and energy expert Alvin Weinberg argues that because of energy waste from flue losses, pilot lights, and improper burning due to inadequate maintenance, using a furnace that burns oil or natural gas may be about as inefficient as using electric resistance heating. In addition, the sensitive room-to-room control possible with electric resistance heating wastes less energy than the whole-house control with a typical home furnace system.

However, from a thermodynamic standpoint, both approaches are wasteful ways to heat a house or provide hot water. It is much less wasteful of energy to extract heat from the air (active or passive solar) or from groundwater and use energy-efficient heat pumps to raise the temperature slightly to provide space heating or hot water.

First-Law Energy Efficiency *Another way to cut energy waste and save money—at least in the long run—is to use an energy-conversion device such as a light, home heating system, refrigerator, or automobile engine of maximum energy efficiency.* There are two types of energy efficiency, one based on the first energy law (Section 2-2), and the other on the second energy law (Section 2-3).

The first-law energy efficiency is the ratio of the useful energy (or work) output to the total energy (or work) input for an energy-conversion device or process. Normally this energy ratio is multiplied by 100 so that the efficiency can be expressed as a percentage:

$$\begin{array}{c} \text{first-law} \\ \text{energy} \\ \text{efficiency} \\ (\%) \end{array} = \frac{\begin{array}{c}\text{useful energy} \\ \text{(or work) output}\end{array}}{\begin{array}{c}\text{total energy} \\ \text{(or work) input}\end{array}} \times 100$$

Table 14-6 lists the first-law energy efficiencies for several commonly used devices. When energy was cheap, industrialized nations freely used inefficient but relatively inexpensive devices such as incandescent light bulbs. Light bulbs use about 20 percent of America's electricity—about twice the electrical output of the nation's 83 nuclear power plants. Yet, the incandescent light bulb, which is really a heat bulb, used for 95 percent of all home lighting in the United States, has a first-law energy

Table 14-6 Some Typical First-Law Energy Efficiencies

Device	First-Law Energy Efficiency (%)	Waste Heat (%)
Lighting		
Fluorescent light	22	78
Incandescent bulb	5	95
Automobile Engine		
Gas turbine	44	56
Diesel	35	65
Internal combustion	30	70
Electric Power Plant		
Coal	38	62
Natural gas	38	62
Oil	31	69
Nuclear	31	69
Home Heating		
Well-designed passive solar (film-coated glass)	90	10
Well-designed active solar collector	90	10
High-efficiency gas furnace	90	10
Typical gas furnace	75	25
High-efficiency wood stove	65	35
Typical oil furnace	63	37
Typical wood stove	40	60

efficiency of only 5 percent. This means that 95 of every 100 kilocalories of electrical energy supplied to the bulb is immediately degraded to low-quality heat, and only 5 kilocalories is converted to light.

Large amounts of energy could be saved by switching to fluorescent light bulbs with a first-law energy efficiency four times that of the incandescent bulb (Table 14-6). New fluorescent light bulbs that look like the screw-in incandescent bulbs are much more expensive than incandescent bulbs of the same wattage, but the new bulbs last 10 years or more compared with about 6 months for incandescent bulbs. This extended life plus its use of 70 percent less electricity than the incandescent bulb means that the fluorescent bulb will be cheaper to buy and run over a 10-year period. Costs should fall with mass production and increased use of these bulbs.

The first-law efficiencies in Table 14-7 do not give the whole picture. The overall first-law effi-

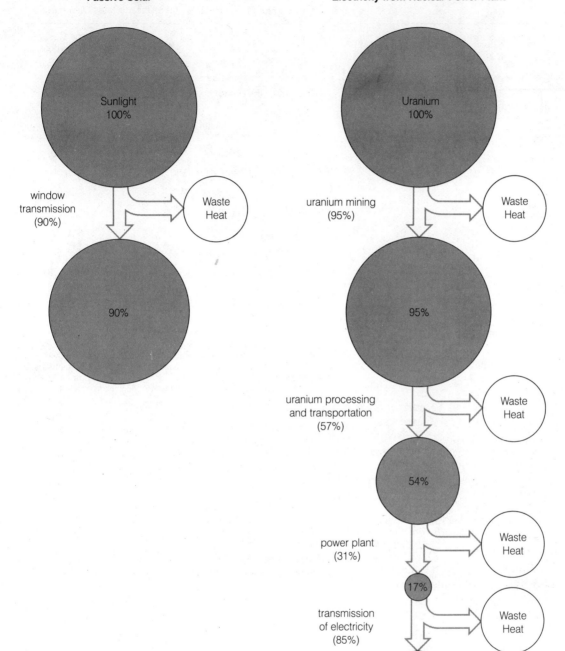

Figure 14-9 Comparison of net first-law energy efficiency for two types of space heating system. The cumulative net efficiency for each step is obtained by multiplying the percentage shown inside each circle by the first-law energy efficiency shown in parentheses for each step.

ciency of a home heating system, for example, is not determined solely by the first-law efficiency of the furnace. Instead it is necessary to determine the *net first-law energy efficiency* of the entire energy delivery system by finding the first-law efficiency

for each of the energy-conversion steps in the system, including extracting the fuel, purifying and upgrading it to a useful form, transporting it, and finally using it. Figure 14-9 shows how net first-law energy efficiencies are determined by comparing

Table 14-7 Net First-Law Energy Efficiency for Various Space Heating Systems

Space Heating System	Net First-Law Energy Efficiency (%)
Superinsulated house (100% of heat)	98
Passive solar (100% of heat)	90
Passive solar (50% of heat) plus high-efficiency natural gas furnace (50% of heat)	87
Natural gas with high-efficiency furnace	84
Electric resistance heating (electricity from hydroelectric power plant	82
Natural gas with typical furnace	70
Passive solar (50% of heat) plus high-efficiency wood stove (50% of heat)	65
Oil furnace	53
Electric heat pump (electricity from coal-fired power plant)	50
High-efficiency wood stove	39
Active solar	35
Electric heat pump (electricity from nuclear plant)	30
Typical wood stove	26
Electric resistance heating (electricity from coal-fired power plant)	25
Electric resistance heating (electricity from nuclear plant)	14

Table 14-8 Comparison of Average Cost of Unit of Energy Provided for Space Heating in the United States During 1983

Space Heating System	Average Cost per 250,000 kilocalories (1 million Btu)
Electricity (resistance heating)	$22.86
Kerosene	$11.10
Electric heat pump	$11.00
Active solar new house*	$10.00
Wood (50% efficient stove, $90 a cord)	$ 9.00
Fuel oil	$ 8.80
Propane (LP)	$ 8.65
Natural gas	$ 6.27
Passive solar new house*	$ 5.50
Improving energy efficiency (existing houses)*	$3–$5.50
Superinsulated new house (100% of heat)*	$0–$1.20

Sources: Federal Trade Commission, U.S. Department of Energy, U.S. Office of Technology Assessment, and Worldwatch Institute.
*Average lifetime cost is lower because fuel (solar energy) is free after initial investment has been recovered through fuel savings. Federal and state tax credits also reduce the cost of the initial investment.

Table 14-9 Net First-Law Energy for Various Hot Water Heating Systems

Hot Water Heating System	Net First-Law Energy Efficiency (%)
Natural gas (tankless instant heater)	75
Passive solar (efficient batch heater for 50% plus instant natural gas heater, 50%)	65
Natural gas (conventional tank heater)	60
Active solar tank (50%) plus instant gas heater (50%)	58
Passive solar efficient batch tank heater (100%)	45
Active solar tank heater (100%)	30
Electric tank heater (electricity from coal-fired plant)	24
Electric tank heater (electricity from nuclear plant)	13

net first-law energy efficiencies for two types of space heating systems.

Table 14-7 lists the net first-law energy efficiencies for a variety of commonly used space heating systems, and Table 14-8 gives the 1983 average price per 250,000 kilocalories (1 million Btu) for space heating with various fuels in the United States. Such analysis reveals that superinsulation and a passive solar system are the two most efficient and cheapest space heating systems for a new house. For an existing house, the most efficient and cheapest approach is to heavily insulate the house, make it airtight, and use one of the new high-efficiency natural gas furnaces, electric resistance heating (if you live in one of the few areas where *all* the electricity is produced at a hydroelectric power plant), or an efficient solar-assisted heat pump.

Other energy-efficient ways for space heating parts of an existing house are to add **(1)** simple passive solar window box heaters, which cost about $60 and can be built by most individuals in a few hours, or **(2)** solariums or solar greenhouses, which can serve as comfortable living rooms or be used to grow flowers and vegetables throughout the year on the side of the house facing the sun. The least efficient way and most expensive way to heat a house is to use the electricity produced by a nuclear power plant for electric resistance heating (Tables 14-7 and 14-8).

Table 14-9 gives a similar analysis for heating

Table 14-10 Net First-Law Energy Efficiency for Automobiles with Various Engine Systems

Engine System	Net First-Law Energy Efficiency (%)
Electric Car with Electricity Produced by	
Hydro	25
Coal	9
Nuclear	5
Combustion Engines	
Gas turbine	12
Diesel	9
Gasoline (conventional internal combustion)	8
Natural gas	8
Steam (Rankine external combustion)	8

water for washing and bathing. In terms of the first energy law, the least efficient way to provide hot water in a home is to use electricity produced by a nuclear power plant, and the most efficient method is to use a natural or LP gas-fired *tankless instant hot water heater* that comes on only when the hot water faucet is turned on and heats the water instantly as it flows through a small burner chamber. This is in sharp contrast to conventional natural gas and electric resistance heaters that keep a large tank of water hot all day and night whether you need it or not. Tankless, instant hot water heaters are widely used in many parts of Europe and are slowly beginning to be used in the United States.* A well-insulated conventional natural gas water heater is also fairly efficient.

Table 14-10 lists net first-law energy efficiencies for several automobile engine systems. Note that the net first-law energy efficiency for a car powered with a conventional internal combustion engine is only about 8 percent. In other words, about 92 percent of the energy in crude oil has been wasted by the time it has been converted to gasoline and used to move a car. Most other combustion engines and electric cars with their batteries recharged by electricity produced in a coal-burning power plant have about the same net first-law efficiency as cars with conventional internal combustion engines.

An electric engine with batteries recharged by electricity from a hydroelectric power plant has a net first-law efficiency of 25 percent—almost 3 times that of a gasoline-burning internal combustion engine. But this system cannot be widely used in the United States because most of the nation's major hydroelectric dam sites have already been used (Section 16-2). In addition, present electric-powered cars are expensive (average price: $15,000) and cruise efficiently at no more than 72 kilometers per hour (45 miles per hour). Furthermore, their batteries must be recharged about every 96 kilometers (60 miles) and replaced every 48,300 kilometers (30,000 miles) at a cost of several thousand dollars—although scientists are trying to develop affordable, longer-lasting batteries. The second most efficient system is a car with a gas turbine engine. American, Japanese, and several European car makers have prototype gas turbine engines, but they need more development and may turn out to be quite expensive even when mass produced.

Second-Law Energy Efficiency First-law energy efficiency does not distinguish between the automatic losses imposed by the second energy law and those that result from using imperfect, unnecessarily wasteful energy-conversion devices. To get a more complete picture of energy loss and waste, we can use **second-law energy efficiency.** This is the ratio of the minimum amount of useful energy needed to perform a task in the most efficient way that is theoretically possible (whether we know how to do it or not) to the actual amount used to perform the task.

$$\text{second-law energy efficiency (\%)} = \frac{\text{minimum amount of useful energy needed to perform a task}}{\text{actual amount of useful energy used to perform a task}} \times 100$$

This ratio shows how far the performance of an energy device or system falls short of what is theoretically possible according to the second energy law.

Table 14-11 lists estimated second-law energy efficiencies for various energy systems in the United States and Figure 14-10 shows the overall second-law energy efficiency for all primary energy used in the United States during 1983. In terms of second-law energy efficiency about 84 percent of all primary energy used each year in the United States is wasted. About 41 percent of this waste is unavoidable and occurs as a result of the second energy law. But at least 43 percent of the primary energy wasted in the United States could be recovered by **(1)** using available, more energy-efficient devices

---

*Two examples of instant hot water heaters are the German-made *Junkers* models available from Appropriate Energy Systems, P.O. Box 867, Point Reyes, CA 94956 and *Paloma* models available from Real Goods Trading Co., 308C East Perkins, Ukiah, CA 95482.

Table 14-11 Estimated Second-Law Energy Efficiencies for U.S. Energy Systems

Energy System	Second-Law Energy Efficiency (%)
Space heating	
Heat pump	9
Furnace	5–6
Electric resistance	2.5
Water heating	
Gas	3
Electric	1.5
Air conditioning	4.5
Refrigeration	4
Automobile	8–10
Power plants	33
Steel production	23
Aluminum production	13
Oil refining	9
All systems	10–15*

*Other estimates put this much lower (3–5%).

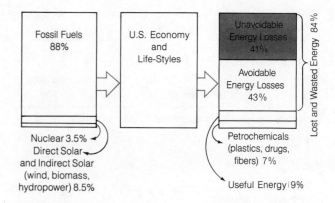

Figure 14-10 Flow and conversion of primary energy to useful energy in the United States based on overall second-law energy efficiency.

and systems (Tables 14-7, 14-9, and 14-10), **(2)** using well-known conservation techniques, such as insulation, natural ventilation, lower and more comfortable lighting levels, and buildings aligned to take advantage of sunlight and wind (Table 14-2), and **(3)** developing affordable new energy devices such as space heating systems that heat only the occupants of a building rather than the entire inside space, and plastic light pipes and light-emitting diodes that convert 10 to 20 times more of the input of electrical energy to visible light than incandescent or fluorescent bulbs.

Lifetime Versus Initial Costs of Energy Systems A well-designed, passive solar home or commercial building should have lower construction and operating costs than a conventionally built structure of similar size. But the initial costs of active solar heating systems and highly energy-efficient natural gas furnaces, appliances, and automobile engines are sometimes greater than for conventional and less efficient systems. Over their lifetimes, however, most energy-efficient devices save both energy and money. Thus, *it is the lifetime (or life-cycle) cost—not the initial cost—that determines whether an energy-conversion device is a bargain*:

lifetime cost = initial cost + lifetime operating cost

Using Waste Heat Because of the second energy law, high-quality energy cannot be recycled and is eventually degraded to low-temperature heat that flows into the environment. However, the rate at which waste heat flows into the environment can be slowed. An uninsulated and leaky house, for instance, loses heat in cold weather almost as fast as it is produced. By contrast, a well-insulated and airtight house can retain most of its heat for 5 to 10 hours, and a well-designed superinsulated house can retain most its heat input for up to 4 days.

In some office buildings, waste heat from lights, computers, and other machines is collected and distributed to reduce heating bills during cold weather, or exhausted in hot weather to reduce cooling bills. Waste heat from industrial plants and electrical power plants can be distributed through insulated pipes and used as a *district heating system* to provide space heating for nearby buildings and homes, greenhouses, or aquaculture ponds.

Waste heat from coal-fired industrial boilers can also be cogenerated to produce electricity at about half the cost of buying it from a utility company. This electricity can then be used by the plant or sold to the local power company for general use. Cogeneration is widely used in industrial plants throughout Europe. In 1920, 22 percent of the electricity used in the United States was produced by cogeneration at industrial sites. By 1983, however, this percentage was only about 5 percent, primarily because most utility companies charge high backup rates when a cogenerating system is out of operation and pay low prices for cogenerated electricity. If all large industrial boilers in the United States used cogeneration, they could produce electricity equivalent to that from 30 to 200 nuclear or coal-fired power plants (depending on the technology used), at about half the cost. This could reduce the average price of electricity and essentially eliminate the need to build any new large electric power plants in the United States, probably at least through 2020.

Net Useful Energy: It Takes Energy to Get Energy   The two energy laws tell us that the only energy that really counts is *net* useful energy—not the *gross* or *total* energy obtainable from a given quantity of an energy resource. **Net useful energy** can be defined as the total energy produced during the lifetime of an entire energy system minus the energy used, lost, and wasted in making this energy available.

net useful energy = total energy produced during the lifetime of an entire energy system

− energy used, lost, and wasted in making this energy available

For convenience in comparing different energy systems, **net useful energy** can also be expressed as the ratio of these two factors:

$$\text{net useful energy} = \frac{\text{total energy produced during the lifetime of an entire energy system}}{\text{energy used, lost, and wasted in making this energy available}}$$

The higher this ratio, the greater the net useful energy yield. When this ratio is less than 1, there is a net energy loss over the lifetime of the system.

Net useful energy is like net profit. If you have a business with a total income of $100,000 with annual operating costs of $90,000, then your net profit is only $10,000 a year. With operating expenses of $110,000 a year, you would have a net loss of $10,000 a year. If you had $200,000 in savings, you could use this capital to subsidize your losses. In 20 years, however, you would go bankrupt and have no capital to keep your business afloat.

Table 14-12 lists the estimated net useful energy ratios for various energy alternatives that can be used to provide space heating, high-temperature heat for industrial processes, and gaseous or liquid fuels for propelling vehicles. Although refined crude oil burned as fuel oil for space heating or as gasoline in vehicles has a fairly high net useful energy, these yields should decline in the future. Crude oil deposits in the Middle East are very accessible and thus have high net useful energy yields and low costs. Some new high net energy yield deposits of fossil fuels like those in the Middle East may be found in relatively unexplored parts of the world. But in most MDCs it is reasonable to assume that most new large high net energy yield deposits will have lower net useful energy yields. For example, only 19 large oil fields (10 million barrels or more)

Table 14-12   Net Useful Energy Ratios for Various Energy Systems

System	Net Useful Energy Ratio
Space Heating	
Passive solar	5.8
Natural gas	4.9
Oil	4.5
Active solar	1.9
Coal gasification	1.5
Electric resistance heating (coal-fired plant)	0.40
Electric resistance heating (natural-gas-fired plant)	0.35
Electric resistance heating (nuclear plant)	0.25
High-Temperature Industrial Heat	
Surface-mined coal	28.2
Underground-mined coal	25.8
Natural gas	4.9
Oil	4.7
Coal gasification	1.5
Direct solar (highly concentrated by mirrors, heliostats, or other devices)	0.9
Transportation	
Natural gas	4.9
Gasoline (refined crude oil)	4.1
Biofuel (ethyl alcohol)	1.9
Coal liquefaction	1.4
Oil shale	1.2

Sources: Colorado Energy Research Institute, *Net Energy Analysis: An Energy Balance Study of Fossil Fuel Resources*, 1976; and Howard T. Odum and Elisabeth C. Odum, *Energy Basis for Man and Nature*, 3rd ed., 1981.

have been found in the United States during the past 100 years despite intensive exploration.

To find new oil and natural gas, energy companies now must drill deeper into the earth, tap dilute deposits, and extract deposits in remote and hostile areas like the Arctic—far from where the energy is to be used. This means that more money, and more of the world's high-quality fossil fuel energy sources are being used to find, deliver, and process new fossil fuel deposits with lower net useful energy yields. In 1983, about one-fourth of the primary energy consumption in the United States was used to mine, extract, concentrate, and transport fuels. By year 2000 the Department of Energy projects that as much as two-thirds of the primary energy consumption could be used to provide

Americans with useful energy. This means that there will be less useful energy available from identified reserves and unidentified deposits of nonrenewable energy sources like oil, natural gas, and coal than present estimates indicate (Section 14-3).

Limitations of Thermodynamic Analysis of Energy Alternatives The crude net useful energy estimates in Table 14-12 are not the final word. Some have been disputed because of the complexity of such calculations and because all energy inputs in some systems are still not known. Moreover, a consistent set of guidelines has not always been used to determine what energy inputs are to be included or omitted, and there has been disagreement over estimates of some of the energy inputs. As net useful energy analysis improves in coming years, many of these difficulties should be resolved.

Despite their usefulness in evaluating energy alternatives, first- and second-law energy efficiencies and net useful energy analysis may not always match up with what people and governments consider to be the most efficient social use of an energy resource. For example, homeowners may find electric space heating so convenient and maintenance free (at least at the home site) that they will exert political pressure to maintain artificially low prices for electricity and have the losses made up by government subsidies paid for by all taxpayers.

Another factor not included in such analyses is the *time* individuals are willing to spend to save money and improve energy efficiency. For example,

a wood burning stove takes more time to load, adjust, check periodically, and clean out than merely moving the dial on a home furnace thermostat. Even more time is required by those who cut and haul their own supply of wood. Similarly, an owner of a typical passive solar energy system must take more time to **(1)** close insulated shades at night to prevent excessive heat loss and open them early in the morning to capture the sun's heat, **(2)** close insulated shades, open doors, or open windows throughout the day to prevent excessive heating, and **(3)** keep windows clean to ensure maximum solar gain. Individuals who get their electricity from panels of solar photovoltaic cells on the roof must also be willing to invest some time to periodically check battery water and levels of electricity stored in batteries and to be sure that the panels of solar cells are clean enough to maximize solar input.

Thermodynamics, Economics, and Conserving Energy: A Summary The box below presents five guidelines, based on the two laws of energy and common-sense economics, that can be used to evaluate energy alternatives, reduce energy waste, and save money in the long run.

In the next two chapters we will use these energy concepts to evaluate the various energy alternatives for the world and for the United States.

A country that runs on energy cannot afford to waste it.

Bruce Hannon

Guidelines For Evaluating Energy Options and Conserving Energy

1. Try to supply energy only in the quality needed for the task at hand, using the cheapest possible source. Where feasible economically, match the temperature of the energy-producing process with the temperature needed by energy users and, ideally, use high-quality electrical energy only when it is the best way to perform a task (see Guest Editorial).

2. In buying any energy-conversion device such as a car, heating system, or household appliance, purchase the most energy-efficient model available and use the *lifetime* cost—not the *initial* cost—to determine whether it is affordable.

3. Use devices such as insulation and caulking, and cogeneration of steam and electricity to capture and use some of the waste heat

produced in energy systems before allowing it to flow into the atmosphere.

4. Improve energy efficiency by having houses and buildings well insulated or superinsulated, airtight but well ventilated, and where possible, designed to gain much of their heat from the waste heat given off by appliances and occupants (*superinsulated houses*), most or all of their heat from the sun (*passive solar heating*), and most of their cooling by a combination of wind flow, natural shading (deciduous trees), and window awnings or overhangs to block out the summer sun (*passive cooling*).

5. In evaluating any energy option, consider the net useful energy it delivers—not just total energy available—along with its lifetime cost.

Guest Editorial: Technology Is the Answer (But What Was the Question?)

Amory B. Lovins

Physicist and energy consultant Amory B. Lovins is one of the world's leading experts on energy strategy. He was based in England from 1967 to 1981, and since 1981 he has worked for Friends of the Earth, (FOE), a U.S. nonprofit environmental conservation lobbying group. In 1979 he became vice-president of the FOE Foundation. He has served as a consultant to several United Nations agencies, the Organization for Economic Cooperation and Development, the MIT Workshop on Alternative Energy Strategies, the Science Council of Canada, the U.S. Department of Energy (joining its Energy Research Advisory Board in 1980), the Congressional Office of Technology Assessment, the U.S. Solar Energy Research Institute, Resources for the Future, the governments of California, Montana, Alaska, and Lower Saxony, and other organizations in several countries. He is active in energy affairs in about 15 countries, and has published 9 books (including the important and widely discussed Soft Energy Paths, *New York: Harper Colophon, 1979, and the nontechnical version of this work with coauthor L. Hunter Lovins,* Energy Unbound: Your Invitation to Energy Abundance, *San Francisco: Friends of the Earth, 1984), and many technical papers.*

The answers you get depend on the questions you ask. But sometimes it seems so important to resolve a crisis that we forget to ask what problem we're trying to solve.

It is fashionable to suppose that we're running out of energy, and that the solution is obviously to get lots more of it. But asking how to get more energy begs the question of how much we need. That depends not on how much we used in the past but on what we want to do in the future and how much energy it will take to do those things. How much energy it takes to make steel, run a sewing machine, or keep you comfortable in your house depends on how cleverly we use energy; and the more it costs, the smarter we seem to get. It is

now cheaper, for example, to double the efficiency of most industrial electric motors than to get more electricity to run the old ones. (Just this one saving can more than replace the entire U.S. nuclear power program.) We know how to make lights five times as efficient as those presently in use, and how to make household appliances that give us the same work as now, using one-fifth as much energy (saving money in the process). The Volkswagen Corporation has made a good-sized, safe car averaging about 34 to 42 kilometers per liter (80 to 100 miles per gallon). We know today how to make new buildings and many old ones, so heat-tight (but still well ventilated) that they need essentially no energy to maintain comfort year-round, even in severe climates. These energy-saving measures are uniformly cheaper than going out and getting more energy. Detailed studies in over a dozen countries have shown that supplying energy services in the cheapest way—by wringing more work from the energy we already have—would let us increase our standard of living while using several times less total energy (and electricity) than we do now.

But the old view of the energy problem embodied a worse mistake than forgetting to ask how much energy we needed: It sought more energy, in any form, from any source, at any price—as if all kinds of energy were alike. This is like saying, "All kinds of food are alike; we're running short of potatoes and turnips and cheese, but that's OK, we can substitute sirloin steak and oysters Rockefeller." Some of us have to be more discriminating than that. Just as there are different kinds of food, so there are many different forms of energy whose different prices and qualities suit them to different uses. There is, after all, no *demand for energy* as such; nobody wants raw kilowatt-hours or barrels of sticky black goo. People instead want energy *services:* comfort, light, mobility, ability to bake bread, ability to make cement. We ought therefore to start at that end of the energy problem: to ask, "What are the many different tasks we want energy for, and what is the amount, type, and source of energy that will do each task *in the cheapest way?*"

Electricity is a particularly special, high-quality, expensive form of energy. An average kilowatt-hour delivered in the United States in early 1984 was priced at about 7 cents, equivalent to buying the heat content of oil costing $112 per barrel (70 cents per liter)—almost four times the early 1984 OPEC price. A power station ordered in 1984 and completed in 1994 will deliver electricity costing, in 1984 dollars, at least 10 cents per kilowatt-hour, equivalent on a heat basis to buying oil at about $160 per barrel.

Such costly energy might be worthwhile if it could be used for the premium tasks that require it, such as lights, motors, electronics, and smelters. But those special uses, only 8 percent of all delivered U.S. energy needs, are already met twice over by today's power stations. Two-fifths of our electricity is already spilling over into uneconomic, low-grade uses such as water-heating, space heating, and air conditioning. Yet no matter how efficiently we use electricity (even with heat pumps), we can never get our money's worth on these applications. Electricity is far too expensive to be worthwhile for the 58 percent of the delivered energy that is needed in the form of heat in the United States, and for the 34 percent needed to run nonrail vehicles. But these tasks are all that additional electricity could be used for without wasting energy and money, because today's power stations already supply the real electric needs twice over.

Thus, *supplying more electricity is irrelevant to the energy problem that we have.* Even though electricity accounts for two-thirds of the federal energy research and development budget and for about half of national energy investment, it is the wrong kind of energy to meet our needs economically. Arguing about what kind of new power station to build—coal, nuclear, solar—is like shopping for the best buy in Chippendales to burn in your stove. *It is the wrong question.*

Indeed, *any* kind of new power station is so uneconomical that if you have just built one, you will save the country money by writing it off and never operating it. Why? Because its additional electricity can be used only for low-temperature heating and cooling (the premium, "electricity-specific" uses being already filled up); but to do low-temperature heating and cooling, it is worth paying only what it costs to do the job in the cheapest way. That means weatherstripping, insulation, heat exchangers, greenhouses, window shades and shutters and overhangs, trees, and so on. These measures generally cost about half a penny per kilowatt-hour, whereas the running costs *alone* for a new nuclear plant will be nearly 2 cents per kilowatt-hour, so it is cheaper not to run it. In fact, under our crazy U.S tax laws, the extra saving from not having to pay the plant's future subsidies is probably so big that society can also recover the capital cost of having built the plant!

If we want more electricity, we should get it from the cheapest sources first. In approximate order of increasing price, these include:

1. Eliminating pure waste of electricity, such as lighting empty offices at headache level. Each kilowatt-hour saved can be resold without having to generate it anew.

2. Displacing with good architecture, and with passive and some active solar techniques, the electricity now used for water heating and space heating and cooling. Some U.S. utilities now give zero-interest weatherization loans, which you need not start repaying for 10 years or until you sell your house—because it saves them millions of dollars to get electricity that way compared with building new power plants.

3. Making lights, motors, appliances, smelters, and the like cost-effectively efficient.

Just these three measures can quadruple U.S. electrical efficiency, making it possible to run today's economy, with no changes in life-styles, using no thermal power plants, whether old or new, and whether fueled with oil, gas, coal, or uranium. We would need only the present hydroelectric capacity, readily available small-scale hydroelectric projects, and a modest amount of wind power. But if we still wanted more electricity, the next cheapest sources would include:

4. Industrial cogeneration, combined-heat-and-power plants, low-temperature heat engines run by industrial waste heat or by solar ponds, filling empty turbine bays in existing big dams, modern wind machines or small-scale hydroelectric turbines in good sites, and perhaps even some recent developments in solar cells with waste heat recovery.

It is only after we had clearly exhausted all these cheaper opportunities that we would even consider:

5. Building a new central power station of any kind—the slowest and costliest known way to get more electricity (or to save oil).

To emphasize the importance of starting with energy *end uses* rather than energy *sources*, consider a sad little story from France, involving a "spaghetti chart" (or energy flow chart)—a device energy planners often use to show how energy flows from primary sources via conversion processes to final forms and uses. (An example is shown in Figure 14-1.) In the mid-1970s the energy conservation planners in the French government started, wisely, on the right-hand side of the spaghetti chart. They found that their biggest single need for energy was to heat buildings, and that even with good heat pumps, electricity would be the most uneconomic way to do this. So they had a fight with their nationalized utility; they won; and electric heating was supposed to be discouraged or even phased out because it was so wasteful of money and fuel.

But meanwhile, down the street, the energy supply planners (who were far more numerous and influential in the French government) were starting on the left-hand side of the spaghetti chart. They said: "Look at all that nasty imported oil coming into our country! We must replace that oil. Oil is energy. . . . We need some other source of energy. Voilà! Reactors can give us energy; we'll build nuclear reactors all over the country." But they paid little attention to what would happen to that extra energy, and no attention to relative prices.

Thus, the two sides of the French energy establishment went on with their respective solutions to two different, indeed contradictory, French energy problems: *more energy of any kind*, versus *the right kind to do each task cheapest*. It was only in 1979 that these conflicting perceptions collided. The supply planners suddenly realized that the only way they would be able to sell all that nuclear electricity would be for electric heating, which they had just agreed not to do.

Every industrial nation is in this embarrassing

position (especially if we include in "heating" air conditioning, which just means heating the outdoors instead of the indoors). Which end of the spaghetti chart we start on, or *what we think the energy problem is*, is not an academic abstraction: It *determines what we buy*. It is the most fundamental source of disagreement about energy policy. People starting on the left side of the spaghetti chart think the problem boils down to whether to build coal or nuclear power stations (or both), while people starting on the right realize that *no* kind of new power station can be an economic way to meet the needs for low- and high-temperature heat and for vehicular liquid fuels that are 92 percent of our energy problem.

So if we want to provide our energy services at a price we can afford, let's get straight what question our technologies are supposed to provide the answer to. Before we argue about the meatballs, let's untangle the strands of spaghetti, see where they're supposed to lead, and find out what we really need the energy *for*!

Guest Editorial Discussion

1. List the energy services you would like to have, and note which of these must be furnished by electricity.

2. The author argues that building more nuclear, coal, or other electrical power plants to supply electricity for the United States is unnecessary and wasteful. Summarize the reasons for this conclusion and give your reasons for agreeing or disagreeing with this viewpoint.

3. Do you agree or disagree that increasing the supply of energy for the United States, instead of concentrating on improving energy efficiency, is the wrong answer to U.S. energy problems? Why?

Discussion Topics

1. Try to trace your own direct and indirect energy consumption each day to see why it probably averages 230,000 kilocalories per day (Figure 14-4).

2. Why has the United States in recent years shifted from coal to natural gas and oil, even though coal is the nation's most abundant fossil fuel?

3. Explain why improving energy efficiency should form the basis of any individual, corporate, or national energy plan. Does it form a significant portion of your personal energy plan or life-style? Why or why not? Is it a significant factor in the national energy policy? Why?

4. List the following forms of energy in order of increasing energy quality: heat from nuclear fission, normal sunlight, oil shale, air at 500°C (932°F).

5. Give three examples of the use of high-quality energy for tasks requiring low-quality energy.

6. Distinguish among first-law energy efficiency, second-law energy efficiency, and net useful energy, and give an example of each. Explain how net useful energy is related to dollar flow and inflation.

7. Explain how using a gas-powered chain saw to cut wood for burning in a wood stove could use more energy than that available from burning the wood. Consider materials used to make the chain saw, its fuel, and periodic repair.

8. You are about to build a house. What energy supply (oil, gas, coal, or other) would you use for space heating, cooking food, refrigerating food, and heating hot water? Consider long-term economic and environmental impact factors.

15

Nonrenewable Energy Resources: Overall Evaluation

In retrospect, the world may be heavily indebted to OPEC for having raised the price of oil.

Lester R. Brown

15-1 Evaluating Energy Resources

Questions to Ask In trying to determine which mix of energy alternatives might provide primary energy for the future, we must think and plan in three time frames that cover the 50-year period normally needed to develop and phase in new energy sources: the *short term* (1985 to 1995), the *intermediate term* (1995 to 2005), and the *long term* (2005 to 2035).

The first step is to decide how much of what kinds of primary energy such as low-temperature heat, high-temperature heat, electricity, and liquid fuels for transportation are needed. Then we project the mix of energy alternatives—including improving energy efficiency—that can provide the necessary energy services at the lowest lifetime cost and with acceptable environmental impacts. This means that for each energy alternative, we need to know **(1)** total estimated supply available in each time frame, **(2)** estimated net useful energy yield, **(3)** projected costs for development and lifetime use, and **(4)** potential environmental impacts.

Since the 1973 oil embargo there have been major efforts to gather such information to help nations develop a long-term energy strategy. Projections about the future are always controversial. Yet, despite difficulties in weighting and ascertaining the reliability of data, nations and individuals must try to evaluate the information available and use it to implement short-, intermediate-, and long-term energy plans, to be updated and revised as new information becomes available.

Enrichment Studies 3, 5, and 11 are related to this chapter.

Environmental Impact of Energy Alternatives Using any form of energy or nonrenewable metal or mineral resource has harmful impacts on the environment (Figure 13-5). The faster the rate of energy use or flow, the greater the impact. This is why energy use is directly or indirectly responsible for most land disruption (Chapter 10 and Section 12-4), water pollution (Chapter 18), and air pollution (Chapter 19 and Enrichment Study 5). For example, nearly 80 percent of all U.S. air pollution is caused by fuel combustion in cars, furnaces, industries, and power plants.

Choosing any energy option or mix of options involves making choices and trade-offs between several potential environmental impacts. The problem is to choose an option that provides the least environmental damage at an acceptable price, assuming that all other factors are equal. This chapter describes and evaluates the major nonrenewable energy alternatives for the world and the United States. The next chapter consists of an evaluation of renewable energy alternatives and attempts to develop an energy strategy for the United States.

15-2 Conventional and Unconventional Oil

Conventional Crude Oil **Crude oil** or **petroleum,** is a gooey, dark greenish-brown, foul-smelling liquid; hydrocarbon compounds make up about 90 to 95 percent of its weight, and about 5 percent by weight is in the form of oxygen, sulfur, and nitrogen compounds. Typically, deposits of crude oil and natural gas are trapped together deep underground, beneath a dome of sedimentary rock such as sandstone and shale, with the natural gas lying above the crude oil.

Figure 15-1 shows the locations of the major petroleum and natural gas fields in the United States. Note that most are in Texas, Louisiana, and Oklahoma and in the outer continental shelf of the Pacific, Atlantic, Gulf, and Alaskan coasts. The federal government leases areas of the outer continental shelf by selling to private companies the rights to explore,

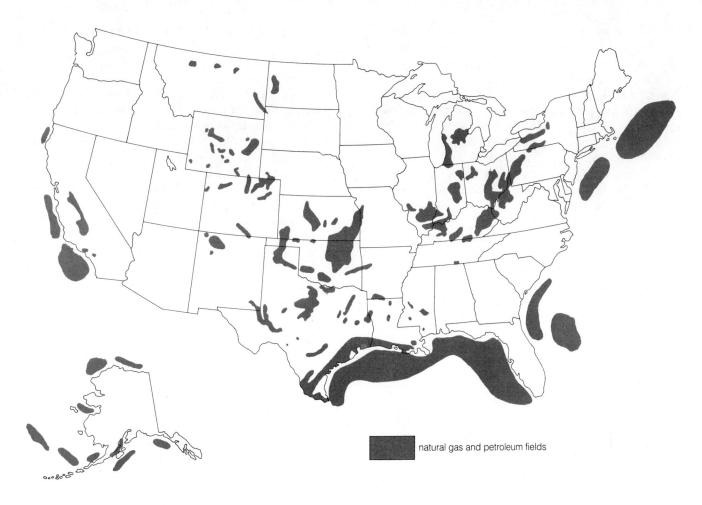

natural gas and petroleum fields

Figure 15-1 Major deposits of natural gas and petroleum in the United States. (Source: Council on Environmental Quality.)

develop, and produce crude oil and natural gas. If fuel deposits are found, the buyer of the lease pays the government a royalty based on the amount produced.

Typically, crude oil is dispersed throughout the pores and cracks of an underground sandstone rock formation, much like a sponge filled with water. In some wells—called gushers—there is enough pressure from water and natural gas under the dome of rock to force some of this crude oil to the surface when the well is drilled—a process known as *primary recovery*. However, such oil wells are relatively rare.

Since oil floats on water, water is injected to force out some of the remaining crude oil when the initial pressure of a gusher has been released or when the well has too little pressure for primary recovery, This technique is known as *secondary recovery*. Typically the combination of primary and secondary recovery removes only about one-third of the crude oil in a well. This means that two barrels of *heavy oil* with the consistency of asphalt is

left in a typical well for each barrel removed by primary and secondary recovery.

As oil prices rise, it may become economical to remove about 10 percent of the heavy oil remaining in a petroleum deposit by *enhanced oil recovery* (EOR) processes such as **(1)** forcing steam into the well to soften the heavy oil so it can be pumped to the surface, **(2)** igniting some of the heavy oil to decrease the viscosity of the surrounding oil so that it can be pumped to the surface, and **(3)** injecting a chemical such as alcohol into the well to dissolve the oil, pumping the mixture to the surface, and extracting the heavy oil. However, these processes are expensive and take energy equivalent to that in one barrel of oil to pump each three barrels to the surface, thus reducing the net useful energy yield. Additional energy is needed to increase the flow rate and remove impurities such as sulfur and nitrogen before the heavy oil can be sent via pipeline to an oil refinery. Recoverable heavy oil from known U.S. crude oil reserves could supply U.S. oil needs for only about 7 years at 1983 usage rates.

Crude oil extracted by primary or secondary recovery is *refined* in gigantic distillation columns to separate it into various components, which boil at different temperatures (Figure 15-2). Some of the chemicals extracted from crude oil and natural gas are sent to petrochemical plants for use as raw materials in the manufacture of most industrial chemicals, fertilizers, pesticides, plastics, synthetic fibers, and medicines. About 3 percent of all the fossil fuels used in the world and 7 percent of those used in the United States are used to produce these *petrochemicals*. From Figure 15-2 you can see why most product prices rise when crude oil and natural gas prices rise. Most of these chemicals can also be produced from coal or the fermentation of plants (biomass), but such a transformation of the entire chemical industry in an industrialized nation would be an expensive, decades-long process. Presently only Brazil plans to ferment biomass to produce most of its petrochemicals.

Conventional Crude Oil

Advantages

1. Versatile. Can be transported easily within and between nations and burned to propel vehicles, provide low-temperature heating of water and buildings, and high-temperature heat for industrial processes and production of electricity, although rising oil prices have sharply reduced this use.

2. High net useful energy yield (Table 14-10).

3. Technology well developed.

4. Does not produce radioactive materials or materials that can be used to produce nuclear weapons.

Disadvantages

1. Affordable supplies may be depleted within 40 to 80 years (Section 14-3).

2. Net useful energy yield will decline and prices will rise as more accessible deposits are depleted (Section 14-4).

3. Air pollution: releases sulfur oxides, nitrogen oxides, and hydrocarbons when burned without adequate pollution control devices (Chapter 19); releases carbon dioxide when burned, which could alter global climate and food-growing regions, and gradually raise sea levels (Enrichment Study 5).

4. Water pollution: oil spills from offshore well blowouts, tanker accidents, and pipeline ruptures (Section 18-5); thermal water pollution if burned to generate electricity (Section 18-3); contamination of underground water by brine solution reinjected into wells (Section 18-4).

5. Land disruption: subsidence (caving in over wells).

6. Possible large-scale disasters: water and estuary pollution from large-scale tanker accidents and offshore well blowouts; massive spills on land from pipeline blowouts; refinery fires.

Heavy Oils from Oil Shale and Tar Sands Oil shale is a marlstone sedimentary rock consisting mostly of mud and clay mixed with limestone. These deposits also contain varying amounts of a rubbery, solid organic material called **kerogen,** a mixture of heavy hydrocarbon compounds with a high content of sulfur, nitrogen, oxygen, and other impurities. Typically the shale rock is removed by mining, crushed, and heated to about 460°C (900°F) in a container called a *retort* to vaporize the solid kerogen. The vapor from this distillation process is then condensed to yield a slow-flowing, dark brown *heavy oil* called **shale oil.** It must be upgraded by increasing its flow rate and hydrogen content and by removing impurities such as sulfur, nitrogen, and metal compounds before it can be piped to an oil refinery.

The world's largest known deposits of oil shale are in the United States, with significant amounts also in Canada, China, and the Soviet Union. At least 80 percent of the rich deposits in the United States are on federal lands in Colorado, Utah, and Wyoming, which contain other energy resources (Enrichment Study 11). It is estimated that the potentially recoverable heavy oil from oil shale in the United States could supply the nation with crude oil for 44 years if consumption remains at 1983 levels, and for 32 years if annual crude oil consumption rises by a modest 2 percent a year.

However, the estimated cost of making this oil available was about $55 a barrel in early 1984—almost twice the average world price of conventional crude oil. It takes the energy equivalent of about one barrel of conventional crude oil and two to six barrels of water that end up contaminated to produce one barrel of shale oil. This means that shale oil may always be 1.5 to 2 times more costly than conventional crude oil unless the price is heavily subsidized. This also results in a low net useful-energy yield compared to conventional crude oil (Table 14-12). Other problems that may limit shale oil production are listed in the summary table.

One way to avoid some of these problems is to remove the shale oil in place (*in situ*) by breaking up the rock with hydraulic pressure or liquid explosives, retorting and distilling the rock, still underground, and pumping up the shale oil. By 1984, no oil shale extraction and processing technology had reached the commercial stage. In addition, most pilot-plant projects of major oil companies in the United States have been abandoned; both surface mining and *in situ* methods proved to be too expensive even with large government subsidies.

Tar sands (or oil sands) are swamplike deposits of a mixture of fine clay, sand, water, and variable amounts of a black, high-sulfur, tarlike heavy oil known as **bitumen.** Typically, the tar sand is removed

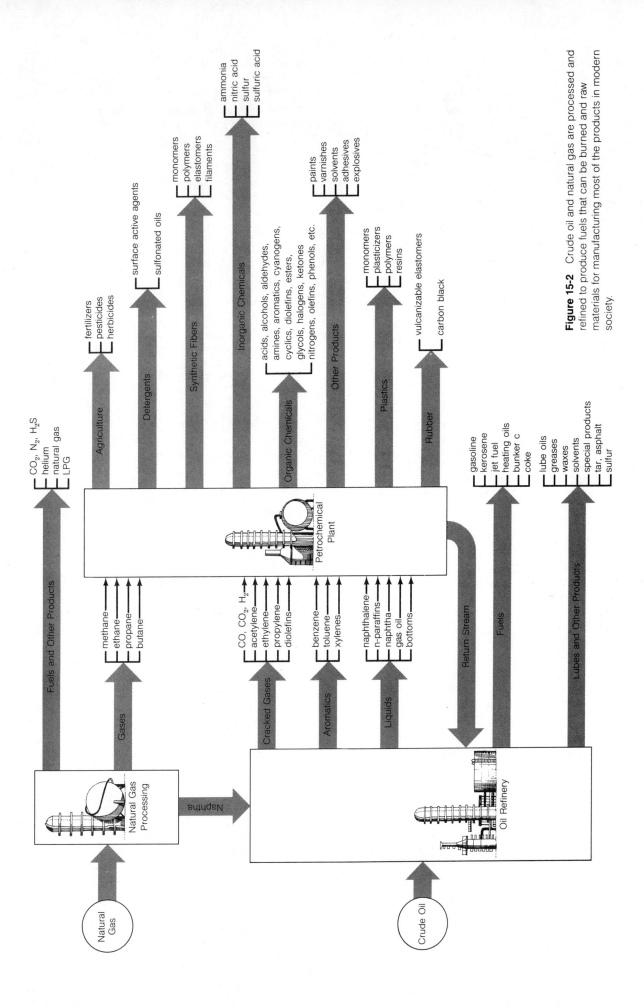

Figure 15-2 Crude oil and natural gas are processed and refined to produce fuels that can be burned and raw materials for manufacturing most of the products in modern society.

Heavy Oils from Oil Shale and Tar Sands

Advantages

1. Large supplies, if they can be developed at an affordable cost.

2. Versatile (see conventional oil summary).

3. Does not produce radioactive materials or materials that can be used to produce nuclear weapons.

Disadvantages

1. Technology not fully developed.

2. High cost except for Athabascan tar sands.

3. Relatively low net useful oil energy yield (Table 14-12).

4. Requires large amounts of water for processing (Enrichment Study 11).

5. Air pollution: releases sulfur oxides, hydrogen sulfide, nitrogen oxides, particulate matter, possibly cancer-causing substances (oil shale), and hydrocarbons during processing and when burned without adequate pollution control devices (Chapter 19); releases carbon dioxide when processed and burned, which could alter global climate and food growing regions, and gradually raise sea levels (Enrichment Study 5).

6. Water pollution: possible contamination of nearby surface water with dissolved solids (salinity), possible cancer-causing substances (oil shale), and toxic metal compounds from processed shale rock and tar sands; possible contamination of groundwater if processed underground (Section 18-4); thermal water pollution if burned to produce electricity (Section 18-3).

7. Land disruption: processed shale rock, which breaks up and expands when heated (somewhat like popcorn), and tar sands must be disposed of, normally on land; subsidence.

8. Possible large-scale disasters: depletion and contamination of water supplies in arid regions; massive oil spills from pipeline breaks (Section 18-5)

Conventional Natural Gas

Advantages

1. Versatile (see conventional oil summary), but cannot be transported easily between areas separated by water.

2. Easy to process and transport in pipelines within nations.

3. Burns hotter than other fossil fuels.

4. High net useful energy yield, (Table 14-12), but is reduced by about one-fourth when converted to liquefied natural gas (LNG).

5. Technology well developed.

6. Does not produce radioactive materials or materials that can be used to produce nuclear weapons.

7. Cleanest-burning fossil fuel.

Disadvantages

1. Expensive and dangerous to transport as volatile and unstable LNG between areas separated by water. An accidental explosion of the LNG in a tanker could create a massive fireball that would burn everything within its volume, and its radiant energy would start fires and cause third-degree burns 1.6 to 3.2 kilometers away.

2. Affordable supplies in the world may be depleted within 40 to 100 years (Section 14-3).

3. Net useful energy yield will decline and prices will rise as more accessible deposits are depleted (Section 14-4).

4. Air pollution: produces small amounts of nitrogen oxides when burned; produces carbon dioxide when burned, which could alter global climate and food growing regions, and gradually raise sea levels (Enrichment Study 5).

5. Water pollution: thermal water pollution if burned to produce electricity (Section 18-3).

6. Land disruption: subsidence.

7. Possible large-scale disasters: LNG tanker explosion; pipeline explosion.

---

by surface mining and heated with steam at high pressure to make the bitumen fluid enough to float to the top. Like heavy oil from oil shale, the bitumen must be purified and upgraded to synthetic fuel oil before being refined. So far it is not technically or economically feasible to remove deeper deposits by underground mining or by extracting the bitumen *in situ*.

The world's largest known deposits of tar sands lie in a cold, desolate area along the Athabasca River in northern Alberta, Canada. Other fairly large deposits are in Venezuela, Colombia, and the Soviet Union. There are smaller deposits in the United States, with 70 percent of these located in Utah (Enrichment Study 11). For several years two experimental plants have been supplying about 10 percent of Canada's annual oil demand by extracting and processing heavy oil from Athabasca tar sands at a cost of about $25 to $30 a barrel—equivalent to

the average world price for conventional crude oil in early 1984. However, using the same process to produce heavy oil from U.S. deposits of tar sands is estimated to cost as much as $45 a barrel. Recoverable deposits of heavy oil from Canadian tar sands could supply that nation's oil needs for about 36 years at 1983 consumption rates. Because domestic reserves of conventional crude oil may be depleted by 1992, Canada hopes to obtain a significant fraction of its crude oil needs from tar sands by 1990.

Large-scale production of synthetic crude oil from tar sands, however, is beset with problems. The net useful energy yield is low. It takes the energy equivalent of one barrel of conventional oil to produce the steam and electricity needed to liquefy and remove three barrels of heavy oil. More energy is needed to remove sulfur impurities and to upgrade the bitumen to synthetic crude oil before it can be

Figure 15-3 Route of the Alcan pipeline, which should soon begin supplying natural gas to the Midwest and the West Coast.

Legend:
— completed
— not completed

sent to an oil refinery. Tar sands are also so abrasive that the teeth of gigantic bucket-wheel excavators half a city block long and as high as a 10-story building are worn out every 4 to 8 hours. In addition, the gooey sands stick to almost everything, clog extraction equipment and vehicles, and slowly dissolve natural rubber in tires, conveyor belts, and machinery parts. Strip mining the tar sands produces even more waste per unit of heavy oil than is produced in mining oil shale. Other problems associated with the production of heavy oil from tar sands are given in the summary table on p. 284.

15-3 Conventional and Unconventional Natural Gas

Conventional Natural Gas Natural gas consists of 50 to 90 percent methane (CH_4) and small amounts of other more complex hydrocarbon compounds such as propane (C_3H_8) and butane (C_4H_{10}). It is found lying above underground deposits of crude oil and by itself in other underground deposits. When a natural gas deposit is tapped, propane and butane gases are liquefied and removed as *LPG (liquefied petroleum gas)* before the remaining gas (mostly methane) is dried, cleaned of hydrogen sulfide and

other impurities, and pumped into pressurized pipelines for distribution. LPG is stored in pressurized tanks for use in mostly rural areas not served by natural gas pipelines.

At the 1983 usage rate, the world's known reserves of natural gas will last until around 2033 and those in the United States until 1993. America's largest known deposits of natural gas lie in Alaska's Prudhoe Bay, thousands of kilometers from natural gas consumers in the lower 48 states. If made available, the natural gas under Alaska's North Slope could supply U.S. needs for about 25 years at 1983 natural gas consumption rates. Geologists estimate that up to eight times as much natural gas awaits discovery in the North Slope area.

In 1977 the U.S Congress and the Canadian government approved construction of a pipeline to bring this natural gas to San Francisco and Chicago (Figure 15-3). At a cost that could exceed $43 billion, this 7,725-kilometer (4,800-mile) pipeline will be the most expensive privately financed construction project in history, exceeding by far the $9 billion spent on the 1,270-kilometer (790-mile) Alaskan oil pipeline built during the 1970s (Figure 15-3). If everything goes as planned, this pipeline could begin delivering natural gas to the United States by 1986.

See the summary table on p. 284.

Figure 15-4 Stages in formation of different types of coal over millions of years.

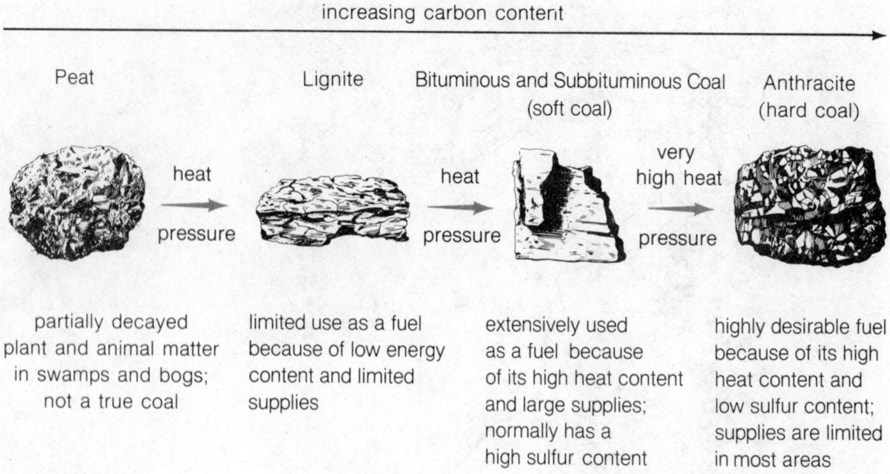

increasing carbon content →

| Peat | | Lignite | | Bituminous and Subbituminous Coal (soft coal) | | Anthracite (hard coal) |

heat / pressure →   heat / pressure →   very high heat / pressure →

partially decayed plant and animal matter in swamps and bogs; not a true coal

limited use as a fuel because of low energy content and limited supplies

extensively used as a fuel because of its high heat content and large supplies; normally has a high sulfur content

highly desirable fuel because of its high heat content and low sulfur content; supplies are limited in most areas

Unconventional Natural Gas As conventional natural gas prices rise, some analysts believe that it may become economical to drill *deep* into the earth and extract and process *unconventional natural gas* from **(1)** concrete-hard deep geologic formations of *tight sands*, **(2)** *geopressurized zones* containing deposits of hot water under such high pressure that large quantities of natural gas are dissolved in the water, **(3)** *coal seams*, and **(4)** deposits of *Devonian shale rock*.

Unconventional Natural Gas

Advantages

1. Versatile (see conventional oil summary), but cannot be transported easily between areas separated by water.
2. Easy to process and transport in pipelines within nations.
3. Burns hotter than other fossil fuels.
4. Does not produce radioactive materials or materials that can be used to produce nuclear weapons.
5. Clean-burning fuel.
6. Large supplies of gas can be extracted at affordable price.
7. Moderate net useful energy yield.

Disadvantages

1. Expensive and dangerous to transport between areas separated by water as volatile, unstable *liquefied natural gas* (LNG).
2. Cost probably fairly high because of deep drilling and processing.
3. Deep-drilling technology not fully developed.
4. Air pollution: produces small amounts of nitrogen oxides when burned; produces carbon dioxide when burned, which could alter global climate and food growing regions, and gradually raise sea levels (Enrichment Study 5).
5. Water pollution: thermal water pollution if burned to produce electricity (Section 18-3).
6. Land disruption: subsidence.
7. Possible large-scale disasters: LNG tanker explosion; pipeline explosion.

Experts agree that there are large deposits of unconventional natural gas but disagree over whether, in practice, the gas can be recovered at affordable prices. If a reasonable amount of this natural gas can be recovered, world supplies of natural gas would be extended for anywhere from several hundred to a thousand years, allowing natural gas to become the most widely used fuel for space heating, industrial processes, producing electricity, and transportation. However, such an increase in the annual usage rate of unconventional natural gas could deplete these supplies within a century or two. The summary table at left lists the advantages and disadvantages.

15-4 Coal

Mining Conventional Coal Coal is the most abundant conventional fossil fuel in the world (Section 14-3) and in the United States. However, three major properties limit its use: It's dangerous to mine, expensive to move and dirty to burn. **Coal** is a solid containing 55 to 90 percent carbon and small amounts of hydrogen, nitrogen, and sulfur compounds. It is formed from fossil remains over millions of years in several stages, with each type of coal representing an increase in carbon content and fuel quality (Figure 15-4). Anthracite releases the largest quantity of heat per unit of weight burned, followed by bituminous coal. Anthracite, however, is not as common as the other types of coal and is usually more expensive. Though they have less heat content, lignite and subbituminous coal normally have the lowest sulfur content and thus produce less air pollution from sulfur dioxide per unit of weight burned than anthracite and bituminous coal.

Some deposits of coal are found deep underground and must be removed by *underground or deep-shaft mining* (Section 13-2). Once an underground mine has been abandoned, surface water entering the mine washes acidic impurities (iron pyrites) from the remaining coal into nearby streams, damaging aquatic plant and animal life. Such acid mine drainage can be controlled by filling sinkholes and rerouting gulleys to prevent surface water from entering abandoned mines or by treating acidic water draining from mines with crushed limestone to neutralize the acidity. When an abandoned mine shafts collapses, a depression in the surface of the earth above the mine, known as *subsidence*, often occurs.

Underground mining is expensive and dangerous because of injuries and deaths from cave-ins and explosions—a single spark can ignite underground air laden with coal dust or methane gas. Between 1900 and 1983 underground mining in the United States killed more than 100,000 miners, permanently disabled at least 1 million miners, and caused at least 250,000 retired miners to spend their last years gasping for breath from black lung disease.

Existing U.S. mine safety laws require ventilating systems and protective masks to reduce the quantity of coal dust reaching worker's lungs. However, worker safety could be improved significantly by stricter enforcement of these laws and enactment of tougher new laws requiring a higher level of ventilation and improved control and removal of explosive methane gas and coal dust, and methane detection equipment for all mine shafts.

When the overburden or amount of material on top of a vein of coal is less than 100 meters (328 feet) thick, it can be removed by various types of *surface mining*, described in Section 13-2. This type of mining removes at least 90 percent of the coal in a deposit, costs less per ton of coal removed than underground mining (including the cost of restoring most types of disturbed land), and is less hazardous for miners than underground mining. Without adequate land reclamation, however, surface mining can have a devastating impact on land and also on water supplies and wildlife. By 1983 surface mining accounted for about 62 percent of the coal extracted in the United States and was increasing dramatically in the western half of the United States. Arguments for and against the surface mining of coal are summarized in Table 15-1.

To help control the surface mining of coal in the United States, the Surface Mining Control and Reclamation Act of 1977 was enacted. These are its major features.

1. Mine operators must prove that they can reclaim the land before they are granted a mining permit.

2. Land must be restored so that it can be used for the same purposes as served before

mining. Restoration includes filling holes, contouring the land to its original shape, preserving soil, removing wastes, and replanting vegetation.

3. Surface mining is banned on some prime agricultural lands in the West, and farmers and ranchers can veto mining under their lands, even though they do not own the mineral rights.

4. Mining companies must minimize the effects of their activities on local watersheds and water quality by using the best available technology, and they must prevent acid from entering local streams and groundwater.

5. A $4.1 billion fund is provided for restoring surface-mined land not reclaimed before 1977. The fund is financed by a fee of 35 cents per ton of surface-mined coal and 15 cents per ton of underground-mined coal; the fees will be collected until 1993. This fund is administered by the Office of Surface Mining Reclamation and Enforcement in the Department of the Interior.

6. Responsibility for enforcement of the law is delegated to the states, with enforcement by the Department of the Interior where the states fail to act and on federally owned lands.

If strictly interpreted and enforced and adequately funded, this law could go a long way in protecting valuable ecosystems. Since the law was passed, however, there has been growing pressures from the coal industry (much of which is owned by the major oil companies) to have it weakened or declared unconstitutional. The Reagan administration in the early 1980s withdrew federal regulations designed to protect prime farmland from surface mining and cut inspection and enforcement staff by 70 percent. Environmentalists argued that the federal government was not fulfilling its responsibility to enforce the 1977 act when states failed to act—the major reason for passing the act in the first place—and was not adequately enforcing surface mining regulations on federally owned lands. To cite only one example, in 1983 Utah state officials were carrying out fewer than half the inspections required by law.

Uses of Coal   In 1983 coal was used to provide 27 percent of the primary energy used in the world and 21 percent of that used in the United States. Coal is not as versatile as oil and natural gas and cannot be burned conveniently to propel cars and trucks. About 60 percent of the coal extracted in the world and 70 percent of that in the United States is burned in boilers to produce steam used to gener-

Table 15-1 The Surface Mining of Coal Controversy

Arguments in Favor	Arguments Against
The maximum amount of strip mining of coal projected by 2000 would disturb only about 0.2% of the total land area of the United States.	Comparing the total amount of strip-mined area to the total land area of the United States is misleading. Strip mining affects the people, land, and wildlife of large sections of the country very intensely.
Strip mining produces short-term environmental damage that can be repaired with available technology. Surface mining and reclamation often improve the land.	Surface mining destroys land, forests, soil, and water. It scars the landscape, disrupts wildlife habitats and recreational areas, can cause landslides and soil erosion, and may pollute nearby rivers and streams with silt and acid runoff. Some land can be reclaimed; but without strictly enforced regulations, the coal companies do not restore it. In addition, reclamation costs are very high, ranging from $741,000 to $2,471,000 per square kilometer ($3,000 to $10,000 per acre).
Strip mining is the cheapest and best way to produce coal and meet growing energy demands. A ban or severe restriction would disrupt energy supplies and damage the economy by raising the price of coal.	The nation's energy needs could be met by greater development of underground coal reserves, which are 8 times more plentiful than surface coal reserves. Strip mining is cheaper than underground mining only because coal companies are not paying the environmental and social costs of their ecological disruption of land and water resources.
Coal companies cannot convert to deep mining quickly enough to replace the surface coal that is now used for electric power generation.	More than 1,500 deep mines have been closed since 1969; many still contain coal that could replace the supplies lost due to restriction of strip mining.
It takes 5 years to bring an underground mine to full production.	With more efficient technology and management, new underground mines could start production within 18 months.
Surface mining recovers nearly 100% of the coal, compared with 55% for underground mining. New technology that permits a higher recovery of underground coal cannot be used in all mines.	Recovery in most deep mines coud be increased significantly by using new mining technology.
Underground miners who have been laid off are too old to return to the mines, and their skills are outdated because of new technology.	Underground mining requires 20 times more workers than strip mining. Enough miners can be trained to greatly increase the amount of underground mining, reducing unemployment and helping the economy.
Surface mining is safer than underground mining by a ratio of 1.5 to 1.	Although underground mining is one of the most hazardous occupations, it can be made as safe as surface mining by enacting and enforcing more stringent safety standards. The injury rate in the safest mines is lower than injury rates for real estate, higher education, and the wholesale and retail trade. Black lung disease could be almost eliminated if existing dust-level regulations were enforced.

ate electrical power—providing about 85 percent of the electricity used in the world and 54 percent of that used in the United States.

Most of the remaining 40 percent of the coal extracted each year is either burned in boilers to produce steam used in various manufacturing processes or changed to *coke* (a hard mass of almost pure carbon) for use in converting iron ore to iron and steel. One of the major by-products of the process is *coal tar*, which is used for roofing and road surfacing and in various drugs and dyes.

Air Pollution from Burning Coal Without effective air pollution control devices, emissions of sulfur dioxide, particulate matter, cancer-causing substances, and small amounts of radioactive substances

from all U.S. coal-fired electric power plants cause an estimated 10,000 premature deaths, over 100,000 cases of respiratory disease, and several billion dollars in property damage each year to aquatic life, trees, crops, metals, stone, and cement (Sections 19-3 and 19-4). Coal, however, need not be such a dirty fuel to burn. Air pollution emissions from coal-burning power and industrial plants can be sharply reduced by using various pollution control devices (Section 19-5) required by federal law on all U.S. coal-fired plants built since 1978. Because older coal-fired plants are not required to meet the same air pollution control standards as new ones, it is estimated that average air pollution control on all coal-burning plants in the United States is only about 50 percent effective, leading to about 5,000 premature deaths a year.

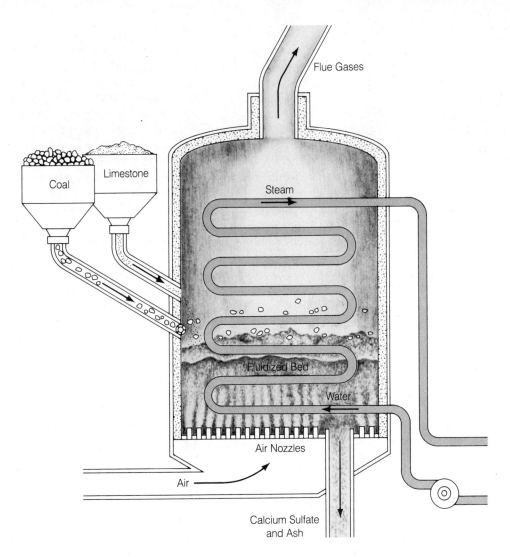

Flue Gases

Coal

Limestone

Steam

Fluidized Bed

Water

Air Nozzles

Air

Calcium Sulfate
and Ash

Figure 15-5 Fluidized-bed combustion of coal.

Requiring all U.S. coal-burning plants to have the latest air pollution control devices to remove 95 percent of sulfur dioxide as well as other harmful emissions would reduce the risks from burning coal to about 500 deaths per year for all U.S. coal-burning power plants. But requiring this level of control for *all* harmful air pollutants—not just sulfur dioxide—would probably make it much more expensive to produce electricity in a coal-fired plant than in a nuclear plant with the same output.

Burning Coal More Cleanly and Efficiently One way to burn coal more efficiently, cleanly, and cheaply is to use *fluidized-bed combustion* (FBC). In FBC a stream of hot air is blown into a boiler from below to suspend a mixture of sand, powdered coal, and crushed limestone. The upward flow of air constantly churns and tumbles this powdered mixture so that it resembles a boiling liquid with the consistency of thin oatmeal—hence the name (Figure 15-5). When the mixture is heated red hot to about 480°C (900°F) the powdered coal is burned

very efficiently and the limestone ($CaCO_3$) is converted to calcium oxide (CaO), which reacts with the sulfur dioxide released from the coal to form dry, solid calcium sulfate ($CaSO_4$) or gypsum. This process removes from 90 to 98 percent of the sulfur dioxide gas produced during combustion.

Successful FBC pilot plants have been developed in the United States, Great Britain, Sweden, Finland, China, the Soviet Union, and West Germany. Over 2,000 FBC units are supplying electricity and heat to villages in China. In the United States, one small-scale commercial FBC power plant at La Crosse, Wisconsin, has been running smoothly since 1981, and larger plants are being built. A British firm has developed several fully automated prototype FBC units, smaller than a family freezer, that can be used to provide space and water heating in homes.

It is expected that by the 1990s full-scale FBC boilers will be replacing conventional coal boilers fitted with scrubbers because FBC boilers **(1)** are projected to have lower construction and operating

Conventional Coal

Advantages

1. Technology well developed.

2. Large world supplies that should last from about 100 to 900 years, depending on discovery of unidentified resources and rate of use (Section 14-3).

3. High net useful energy yield for producing high-temperature heat for industrial processes and generation of electricity (Table 14-10).

4. Cheapest way to produce high-temperature heat and electricity in nations with adequate coal supplies.

5. May be burned in the future more efficiently and cleanly by fluidized-bed combustion (FBC) and perhaps by magnetohydrodynamic (MHD) generation.

6. Does not produce materials that can be used to produce nuclear weapons.

Disadvantages

1. Not versatile. Not useful for transportation unless affordable and acceptable electric cars can be developed. Considered too dirty to burn for cooking and space heating in most MDCs.

2. Messy to store.

3. Expensive to transport.

4. Requires large amounts of water for processing and cooling of power plants.

5. Dangerous to mine, especially in underground mines, in the absence of strictly enforced safety regulations.

6. Air pollution: releases sulfur oxides, particulate matter, nitrogen oxides, toxic metal compounds, radioactive substances, and cancer-causing substances when burned without adequate pollution control devices (Chapter 19); produces more carbon dioxide per weight burned than oil or natural gas, which could accelerate possible global climate change (Enrichment Study 5).

7. Water pollution: acid mine drainage pollutes nearby streams and waterways; acid deposition (Section 19-4); dissolved solids from washing coal; thermal water pollution from burning to produce electricity (Section 18-3).

8. Land disruption: surface mining disrupts large amounts of land without adequate controls and land reclamation; subsidence; slag disposal.

9. Possible large-scale disasters: mine accidents; landslides; sudden subsidence; depletion and contamination of water resources in arid regions.

costs, **(2)** can burn a variety of low-grade fuels including rice hulls, heavy oils, wood and wood wastes, urban and industrial trash, sewage sludge, and high-sulfur coal, **(3)** can be retrofitted to a conventional boiler, **(4)** are simpler, more reliable, and use less water than scrubbers for sulfur dioxide removal, **(5)** produce fewer nitrogen oxides than conventional coal boilers because the coal is burned at a lower temperature, and **(6)** have a useful by-product, namely solid calcium sulfate, which can be removed and sold as a road subbase, or for cement, soil conditioner, or other uses.

Another approach to burning coal more efficiently and cleanly is *magnetohydrodynamic (MHD) generation*. In **MHD generation,** crushed coal is mixed with a chemical such as limestone and burned at very high temperatures [above 2,500°C (4,500°F)] to produce a hot stream of ionized gases (plasma) that is forced down a pipe and through a magnetic field. This yields electricity directly, eliminating the turbine step entirely. At least 95 percent of the sulfur dioxide released when the coal is burned is removed in the form of calcium sulfate, but emissions of nitrogen oxides are higher than those in conventional coal-burning power plants because of higher combustion temperatures. MHD generation, however, is considered by many to be an engineer's nightmare and after 25 years of research in the United States, the Soviet Union, and Japan only a few pilot plants are in operation.

U.S. Coal Supplies The United States has enough identified coal reserves that can be mined economically using existing technology to last about 300 years at 1983 usage rates. However, the rapid rise in oil prices between 1973 and 1980 and the extremely high cost of new nuclear power plants (Section 15-5) have caused utilities to shift back to using coal. As a result, since 1979 coal usage in the United States has been increasing by about 6 percent a year. If coal usage in the United States continues to increase at this rate, proven U.S. reserves would be depleted around 2032. Unidentified U.S. coal resources could extend these supplies at such high use rates for perhaps 100 years at a much higher average cost.

Figure 15-6 maps the major coal fields in the United States, located primarily in 17 states. Note that there is relatively little anthracite, the most desirable form of coal. About 45 percent of U.S. coal reserves—containing mostly high-sulfur, bituminous coal with a relatively high heat content—are found east of the Mississippi River in the Appalachian region, particularly in Kentucky, West Virginia, Pennsylvania, Ohio, and Illinois. Most of this coal must be removed by underground mining and has such a high sulfur content (typically 2 to 3.5 percent) that it cannot be burned without using scrubbers or other devices to reduce emissions. For these reasons, the percentage of all U.S. coal extracted from fields east of the Mississipi River fell from about 93 percent to 66 percent between 1970 and 1984.

About 55 percent of U.S. coal reserves and three-fourths of the nation's surface-minable coal are found west of the Mississippi River, primarily in North Dakota, South Dakota, Montana, Wyoming, Colorado, New Mexico, Arizona, and Alaska. Most of these deposits consist of low-sulfur (typically 0.6

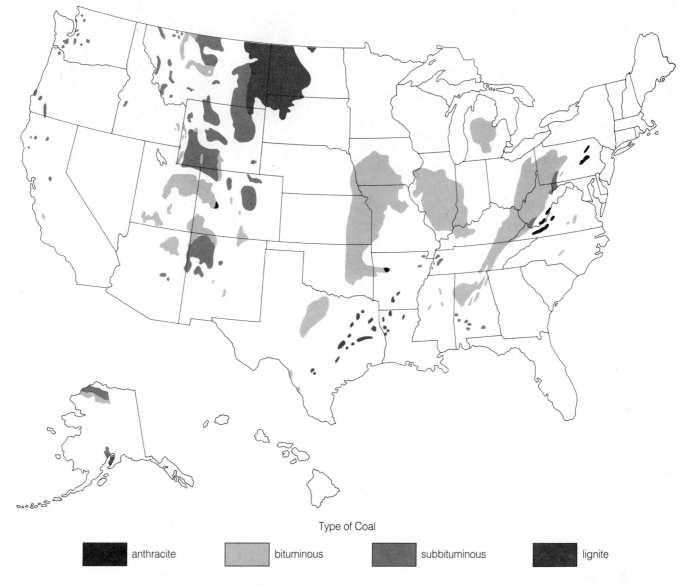

Type of Coal

anthracite   bituminous   subbituminous   lignite

Figure 15-6 Major coal fields in the United States. (Source: Council on Environmental Quality.)

percent), subbituminous, and lignite coals with relatively low heating values (Figure 15-4), which can be surface mined more safely than the underground deposits of bituminous coal found east of the Mississippi. This helps explain why surface mining of western coal deposits now accounts for 34 percent of the coal mined in the United States.

However, the heaviest concentration of coal-burning industrial and electric power plants is located east of the Mississippi River—far from these western coal deposits. When long-distance transportation costs are added, the average cost of coal surface mined in the West and delivered by rail to the East is comparable to that of producing coal by expensive underground mining in the East and delivering it over shorter distances. Slurry pipelines are cheaper than rail for transporting western coal over long distances. However, this method of transpor-

tation, along with reclamation of land disturbed by surface mining, is limited by a lack of water in most of the West (Section 17-2 and Enrichment Study 11). Because about 70 percent of western coal reserves are under federally owned lands, development of these resources will depend primarily on the actions of government agencies and, to a lesser degree, on those of private groups including American Indian tribes holding the remaining western coal reserves and water rights.

See the summary table on the opposite page.

Synfuels from Coal Gasification and Liquefaction
Coal gasification involves converting coal to a gas that can be burned more cleanly as a fuel and is easier and cheaper to transport through a pipeline. In one process coal is converted to coke, which is heated with steam to produce a gaseous mixture of

Synfuels from Coal Gasification and Coal Liquefaction

Advantages

1. Versatile (see conventional oil and natural gas summaries).

2. Does not produce materials that can be used to produce nuclear weapons.

3. Cleaner burning than coal.

4. Technology fairly well developed, especially for coal gasification.

Disadvantages

1. Accelerates depletion of world coal supplies because 30 to 40 percent of the energy content of the coal is lost in the conversion process.

2. Low net useful energy yield (Table 14-12).

3. High costs.

4. SNG is as difficult and expensive to transport across oceans as LNG (see conventional natural gas summary).

5. Requires large amounts of water for processing.

6. Air pollution: similar to coal but somewhat less; without adequate pollution control, conversion processes produce hydrogen sulfide, organic sulfur compounds, carbon monoxide, and several compounds that might cause cancer; when processed and burned, produces larger amounts of carbon dioxide per unit of weight than coal, natural gas, or oil and could accelerate global climate change (Enrichment Study 5).

7. Water pollution: same as coal plus increased pollution from dissolved hydrogen sulfide gas, ammonia, cyanides, phenols, benzene, oils, and tars.

8. Land disruption: same as coal but greater disruption from surface mining because of increased used of coal per unit of energy produced; increased solid wastes such as toxic metal compounds and organic compounds produced during the conversion processes.

9. Possible large-scale disasters: same as for coal, conventional natural gas, and conventional oil.

carbon monoxide (CO) and hydrogen (H_2) with a relatively low heating value: H_2O (steam) + C (carbon in coke) $\rightarrow$ CO + H_2. Because of its low heat content, this gas is not worth transporting by pipeline and is normally used only for heating or producing electricity by industries that produce it. A second and more useful process converts coal to synthetic natural gas (SNG), which has a high heating value and can be transported by pipeline.

Coal liquefaction involves converting coal to a liquid hydrocarbon fuel such as methanol or synthetic gasoline. In South Africa a commercial plant has been converting SNG made from coal to gasoline and other motor fuels for over 25 years.

Although converting solid coal to more versatile and cleaner-burning synthetic gaseous or liquid *synfuels* is technically possible, it is much more expensive to build a synfuels plant than an equivalent coal-fired power plant fully equipped with air

pollution control devices. Other problems are given in the summary table. Most of these problems (except CO_2 emissions and low net energy yields) could be avoided or reduced by the underground gasification of coal. The Soviet Union has several underground gasification plants that fuel electric power plants, and the United States has several pilot plants.

The major factor holding back the large-scale production of synfuels in the United States is high cost compared to conventional oil and natural gas. In 1980 Congesss set up the U.S. Synthetic Fuels Corporation to provide up to $88 billion in grants to oil companies to promote development of a synfuels industry. By 1984, however, oil companies found it too expensive to initiate or to continue most of these synfuel projects, even with government subsidies. It was estimated that in 1984 synfuels produced from coal would be equivalent to buying oil at $35 to $45 a barrel with government subsidies (compared to a world oil price of $29 a barrel) and equivalent to buying oil at $90 a barrel without government subsidies. Until oil and natural gas prices rise significantly, most analysts expect synfuels to play only a minor role in primary energy production until after 2000.

The table opposite summarizes the advantages and disadvantages of synfuels.

15-5 Conventional Nuclear Fission

Nuclear Power: A Fading Dream The debate among scientists and engineers over whether nuclear power should be a major energy alternative for producing electricity is intense. Physicist and nuclear power expert Bernard L. Cohen contends that "Nuclear power is perceived to be *thousands of times* more dangerous than it is. . . . I am personally convinced that citizens of the distant future will look upon it as one of God's greatest gifts to humanity." Phil Bray, head of General Electric's nuclear reactor division in San Jose, California, says, "I could take a reactor, lose every pump, break every valve, blow every electrical unit, melt the core, and eventually bust the containment building, and we still think no one beyond the site boundary would be hurt." Although nuclear expert and strong advocate of nuclear power Alvin M. Weinberg believes that nuclear power can be safe, he emphasizes that the widespread use of nuclear power is the greatest single long-term risk ever taken by humankind, one that should be accepted only after intensive public education and debate. In his words, "We nuclear people have made a Faustian compact [a compact with the devil] with society; we offer . . . an inexhaustible energy source . . . tainted with potential side effects that if not controlled, could spell disaster."

On the other hand, according to Nobel Prize-winning physicist Hannes Alfvén:

Nuclear fission energy is safe only if a number of critical devices work as they should, if a number of people in key positions follow all their instructions, if there is no sabotage, no hijacking of the transport, if no reactor fuel processing plant or repository anywhere in the world is situated in a region of riots or guerrilla activity, and no revolution or war—even a "conventional one"—takes place in these regions. . . . No acts of God can be permitted.

And upon his retirement in 1982, Admiral Hyman G. Rickover, father of the U.S. nuclear submarine program and its director for over 40 years, told members of Congress "The most important thing we could do is have an international meeting where we first outlaw nuclear weapons, then nuclear reactors."

Regardless of one's view on nuclear power, its widespread use in the United States and in many other nations appears to be a rapidly fading dream. Originally nuclear power was heralded as a clean, cheap, safe, and already developed source of energy that with 1,800 projected plants could provide as much as 21 percent of the world's primary energy and one-fourth of that in the United States by the year 2000. However, by the end of 1983 after over 30 years of development, 300 commercial nuclear reactors in 25 countries were providing only 9 percent of the world's electricity—amounting to 2 percent of the world's primary energy (Figure 14-2). Another 210 reactors were either under construction or planned, although some of these may never be completed. The largest number of commercial reactors is in the United States (83), followed by the Soviet Union (40), France (34), Great Britain (32), and Japan (25).

Since 1975 the projected use of nuclear power for producing electricity throughout the world has decreased sharply because of (1) concerns over the safety of nuclear power plants, especially after the much publicized accident in 1979 at the Three Mile Island nuclear plant in Pennsylvania, (2) the need to find safe and politically acceptable methods for storing high-level radioactive wastes for hundreds to thousands of years, (3) concern that nuclear fuel will be diverted from civilian reactors by governments and upgraded to make nuclear fission bombs, (4) decreased demand for electricity in most industrialized nations, (5) much higher than projected construction and operating costs (a typical new U.S. nuclear reactor costs from 2 to 10 times the original estimate, and costs are rising sharply everywhere), and (6) increasing reluctance of lending institutions to provide large amounts of capital to public utility companies to develop an energy alternative that is not considered to be economic compared to others.

Before looking at these major problems in more detail, we need to know something about radiation, nuclear fission, and how a nuclear power plant operates.

Atomic Theory and Isotopes Recall from Section 3-4 that an *atom* consists of an extremely small dense center, called the nucleus, and one or more negatively charged *electrons (e)* whizzing around the nucleus. According to a crude model, the nucleus of all atoms (except one form of hydrogen) contains a mixture of one or more uncharged particles called *neutrons (n)* and positively charged particles called *protons (p)*, each with a relative mass of 1. The number of protons plus the number of neutrons gives the **mass number**—a measure of the atom's mass because the electrons outside the nucleus have such a low mass that they contribute very little to the overall mass of the atom.

Uncharged atoms of the same element all have the the same number of negatively charged electrons outside their nuclei and the same number of positively charged protons inside. For example, the lightest element, hydrogen (H), has one positively charged proton in its nucleus and one negatively charged electron outside. A much heavier element, uranium (U), has 92 protons and 92 electrons.

Atoms of the same element, however, may have different numbers of uncharged neutrons in their nuclei, and thus different mass numbers. These different forms of a particular element with different mass numbers are called **isotopes.** Isotopes of the same element are identified by appending the mass number to the name or symbol of the element: hydrogen-1, H-1; hydrogen-2 (common name, deuterium), H-2; and hydrogen-3 (common name, tritium), H-3. Each of the 92 elements found in nature consists of a mixture of its isotopes, each with a certain percentage abundance. Table 15-2 shows the three naturally occurring isotopes of hydrogen (H) and uranium (U). Note that 99.985 percent of the hydrogen found in nature is in the form of hydrogen-1 and 99.3 percent of the uranium is found as uranium-238.

Radioactive Isotopes The nuclei of isotopes of a particular element are either *stable (nonradioactive)* or *unstable (radioactive).* For example, the hydrogen-1 and hydrogen-2 (deuterium) isotopes of hydrogen are nonradioactive (stable) and the hydrogen-3 (tritium) isotope is radioactive (unstable). A **radioisotope** is an isotope whose nuclei spontaneously emit particles, high-energy electromagnetic radiation, or both, at a certain rate to form a different nonradioactive or radioactive isotope.

Radiation is the propagation of energy through matter and space in the form of fast-moving particles (particulate radiation) or waves (electro-

Table 15-2 Isotopes of Hydrogen and Uranium

Isotope	Natural Abundance (%)	Number of Electrons, e	Number of Protons, p	Number of Neutrons, n	Mass Number, $n + p$
Hydrogen					
Hydrogen-1	99.985	1	1	0	1
Hydrogen-2 (deuterium or D)	0.015	1	1	1	2
Hydrogen-3 (tritium or T)	Negligible	1	1	2	3
Uranium					
Uranium-233	Negligible	92	92	141	233
Uranium-235	0.7	92	92	143	235
Uranium-238	99.3	92	92	146	238

magnetic radiation). Ordinary light is a form of low-energy electromagnetic radiation (Figure 3-2). **Ionizing radiation** is high-energy radiation that can dislodge one or more electrons from atoms it hits to form highly reactive charged particles, called *ions*. The most common types of particulate ionizing radiation are high-speed **alpha particles** (positively charged helium nuclei, each with two protons and two neutrons) and **beta particles** (negatively charged electrons) emitted by the nuclei of unstable isotopes and *neutrons* emitted when an isotope is split apart by nuclear fission. The most common forms of electromagnetic ionizing radiation are high-energy **gamma rays,** from the nucleus of an unstable isotope, and high-energy **X rays** given off when some of the electrons outside the nucleus of an atom release energy after exposure to a high-energy source such as an electrical current. Nuclei of unstable hydrogen-3 spontaneously emit beta particles, and nuclei of unstable uranium-235 and uranium-238 spontaneously emit both alpha particles and gamma rays.

The rate at which a particular radioactive isotope spontaneously emits one or more forms of radiation is usually expressed in terms of its **half-life**: the length of time it takes for half the nuclei in a sample to decay by emitting one or more types of radiation and, in the process, to change into another nonradioactive or radioactive isotope. Each radioisotope has a unique, characteristic half-life. For example, tritium has a half-life of 12.5 years and uranium-238 a half-life of 4.5 billion years. Thus, half of a given sample of tritium is still radioactive after 12.5 years and one-fourth is still radioactive after two half-lives, or 25 years. Similarly, one-half of a given sample of uranium-238 is still radioactive after 4.5 billion years and one-fourth after 9 billion years.

Effects of Radiation on the Human Body
Scientists agree that exposure to any type or amount of ionizing radiation has the potential to damage cellular tissue in the human body. The two major types of cellular damage are *genetic damage*, which alters genes and chromosomes and may show up as a genetic defect in immediate offspring or several generations later, and *nongenetic (somatic) damage*, which can cause harm during the victim's lifetime. Examples of nongenetic damage include burns, some types of leukemia, miscarriages and cataracts, and bone, thyroid, breast, and lung cancer.

The danger from exposure varies with the type, energy, and half-life of ionizing radiation, the quantity of ionizing radiation (dose) received by body tissues of various types, and age. High-energy gamma rays and X rays and high-speed neutrons are so penetrating that they pass through the body easily and inflict damage. They can be stopped only by several inches of lead or about 30 centimeters (1 foot) of concrete. Neither alpha nor beta particles can penetrate the skin. But once radioisotopes emitting these particles have been inhaled into the lungs or ingested into the body, their emissions can cause considerable damage to vulnerable cellular tissue.

Tissues with cells that divide and reproduce rapidly are normally the most sensitive. Most easily damaged are bone marrow (where blood cells are made), the spleen, the digestive tract (whose lining must be constantly renewed), the reproductive organs, and the lymph glands. The fast-growing tissues of a developing embryo are extremely sensitive, and pregnant women should avoid all unnecessary exposure to X rays and radioactivity. Studies have shown that people under 35 have four

Table 15-3 Effects on People of Exposure to High Radiation Doses

Dose (rems)*	Effect
100,000	Death in minutes
10,000	Death in hours
1,000	Death in days
700	Death for 90% within months
200	Death for 10% within months
100	No short-term deaths, but chances of cancer and other life-shortening diseases greatly increased. Permanent sterility in females; 2–3 year sterility in males.

*The rem is a radiation dose unit that measures damaging effect in mammals.

times the risk of radiation-caused cancer as those over 50. Women are particularly vulnerable between ages 20 and 30.

Two related units used to measure the dose or amount of radiation the body absorbs over time are the *rem* and the *millirem* (mrem), which is one-thousandth of a rem (1 rem = 1,000 mrem; or 1 mrem = 0.001 rem). A single dosage of 10,000 mrem (10 rems) or less is generally referred to as *low-level radiation* and a single dosage of 100,000 mrem (100 rems) or more is considered to be *high-level radiation*. Exposure to high levels of ionizing radiation such as that released from the detonation of a nuclear bomb or warhead can be fatal (Table 15-3).

Exposure to Ionizing Radiation Regardless of the risks, it is impossible to avoid all exposure to ionizing radiation. Each of us is exposed to a certain amount of *natural or background radiation* (Table 15-4) mostly from **(1)** cosmic rays entering the earth's atmosphere from outer space; **(2)** naturally radioactive isotopes found in the soil and in bricks, stone, and concrete, and **(3)** radioactivity from natural sources that finds its way into our air, water, and food.

Your exposure to background ionizing radiation varies considerably with factors such as elevation (at high altitudes there is less overlying air to shield you from cosmic rays), soil type, water supply, occupation, and the type of building you live and work in. Table 15-4 shows that the average American receives about 130 mrem per year from background sources and an additional 100 mrem from human-related activities. You can use Table 15-4 to estimate your own average total exposure to ionizing radiation each year and compare it with aver-

age annual exposure per person in the United States of 230 mrem.

How Dangerous Is Ionizing Radiation? Nothing in life is free from risk. The chances we are willing to take depend on how grave we perceive the risks to be compared to the possible benefits. Every second of your life you are struck by an average of about 27,000 radioactive particles or pulses of high-energy electromagnetic radiation from a combination of sources. Each of these hits can cause a fatal cancer during your lifetime or a genetic defect in your offspring. We're not all dying of radiation-induced cancer, however, because the probability of a single radioactive particle or high-energy electromagnetic wave causing a fatal cancer is very low—about one chance in 50 quadrillion (50,000,000,000,000,000). The NAS committee on the effects of ionizing radiation and several other radiation experts such as Bernard L. Cohen (see *Before It's Too Late: A Scientist's Case for Nuclear Power*, 1983) estimate that an average annual exposure of about 200 mrem of ionizing radiation per person in the United States over an average lifetime causes about 1 percent of all fatal cancers and about 5 to 6 percent of all normally encountered genetic defects.

Our largest average exposure to ionizing radiation each year comes from dental and medical X rays and diagnostic tests involving the the injection or ingestion of radioactive isotopes. These important tools save many thousands of lives each year and prevent human misery. But some observers contend that many of these X rays and diagnostic tests are taken primarily to protect doctors and hospitals from liability suits. They suggest that if your doctor or dentist proposes an X ray or diagnostic test involving radioisotopes, ask why it is necessary, how it will help find out what is wrong and influence possible treatment, and what alternative tests are available with less risk.

The smallest average exposure to ionizing radiation in the United States comes from nuclear power plants and other nuclear facilities—assuming that they are operating normally. According to the NAS radiation panel and UN Scientific Committee on Effects of Atomic Radiation, exposure to 1 mrem of ionizing radiation—10 times the average from normally operating nuclear power plants and other nuclear facilities—increases the risk that an individual will die from cancer by about one chance in 8 million. Cohen has calculated that this risk corresponds to a 1.2 minute reduction in life expectancy and is equivalent to the risk from taking about 3 puffs on a cigarette (each cigarette reduces life expectancy by about 10 minutes) or an overweight person eating 10 extra calories by taking a small bite from a piece of buttered bread. Similarly, the risk

Table 15-4 Estimating Your Average Annual Radiation Dose from Background Radiation and Human Activities

Source of Radiation	Approximate Annual Dose (millirems)
Natural or Background Radiation	
Cosmic rays from space	
At sea level (average)	40
Add 1 mrem for each 30.5 m (100 ft) you live above sea level	_____
Radioactive minerals in rocks and soil: ranges from about 30 to 200 mrem depending on location	55 (U.S. average)
Radioactivity in the human body from air, water, and food: ranges from about 20 to 400 mrem depending on location and water supply	25 (U.S. average)
Radiation from Human Activities	
Medical and dental X rays and tests; to find your total, add 22 mrem for each chest X ray, 500 mrem for each X ray of the lower gastrointestinal tract, 910 mrem for each whole-mouth dental X ray film, 1,500 mrem for each breast mammogram, 8,000 mrem for a barium enema, and 5 million mrem for radiation treatment of a cancer	80 (U.S. average)
Living or working in a stone or brick structure; add 40 mrem for living and an additional 40 mrem for working in such a structure	_____
Smoking a pack of cigarettes a day: add 40 mrem	_____
Nuclear weapons fallout	4 (U.S. average)
Air travel: add 2 mrem a year for each 2,400 km (1,500 mi) flown	_____
TV or computer screens: add 4 mrem per year for each 2 hr of viewing a day	_____
Occupational exposure: varies with 100,000 mrem per year for uranium ore miner, 600 to 800 mrem for nuclear power plant personnel, 300 to 350 mrem for medical X ray technicians, 50 to 125 mrem for dental X ray technicians, and 140 mrem for jet plane crews	0.8 (U.S. average)
Living next door to a normally operating nuclear power plant (boiling water reactor, add 76 mrem; pressurized water reactor, add 4 mrem)	_____
Living within 8 km (5 mi) of a normally operating nuclear power plant: add 0.6 mrem	_____
Normal operation of nuclear power plants, nuclear fuel processing, and nuclear research facilities	0.10 (U.S. average)
Miscellaneous: luminous watch dials, smoke detectors, industrial wastes, etc.	2 (U.S. average)
Your annual total	= _____ mrem

Average annual exposure per person in the United States = 230 mrem (with 130 mrem from background radiation and 100 mrem from human activities)

Figure 15-7 Nuclear fission of a uranium-235 nucleus.

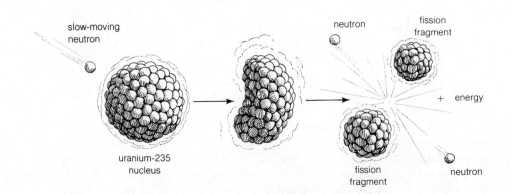

slow-moving neutron

uranium-235 nucleus

neutron

fission fragment

+ energy

fission fragment

neutron

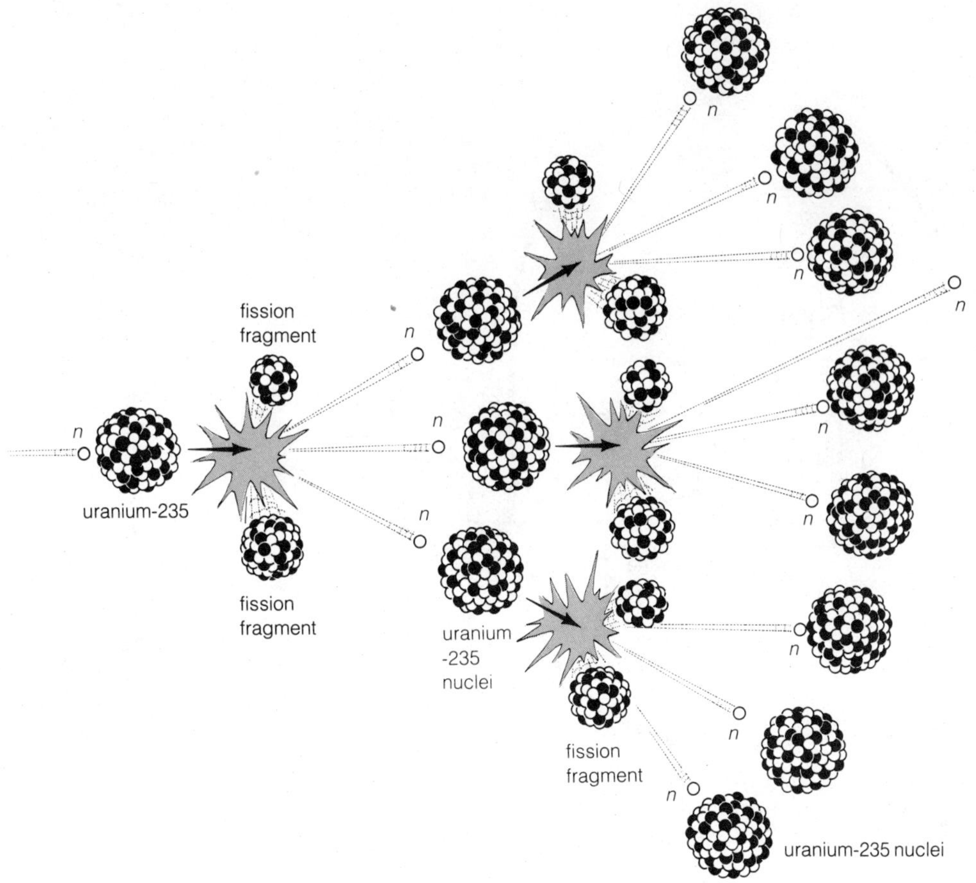

Figure 15-8 A nuclear chain reaction initiated by one neutron fissioning one uranium-235 nucleus.

fission fragment

uranium-235

fission fragment

uranium-235 nuclei

fission fragment

uranium-235 nuclei

of having a genetically defective child because of exposure to 1 mrem of ionizing radiation received before conception is estimated to be about one chance in 40 million—about 140 times lower than the estimated genetic risk from drinking 29 milliliters (1 fluid ounce) of alcohol and 2.4 times that from drinking one cup of coffee.

However, radiation experts such as John W. Gofman, E. J. Sternglass, and Helen Caldicott disagree with these conclusions. They cite some animal studies and recently revised estimates of the effects of low-level radiation on survivors of Hiroshima and Nagasaki that indicate that the risks of harm increases with exposure to some types of low-level ionizing radiation. Nuclear power critics also contend that the real danger from nuclear power is not from small, routine emissions of radioactivity but from the extremely small but real possibility of accidents that could result in the emission of large quantities of high-level radiation. With this background in atomic theory and ionizing radiation, let's see how a conventional nuclear fission power plant works.

Nuclear Fission Reactors The potential energy locked in the nuclei of atoms of certain elements can be released and converted mostly to high-temperature heat by *nuclear fission*. In **nuclear fission** the nucleus of a heavy isotope such as uranium-235 (Table 15-2) found in uranium ore mined from the earth's crust is split or fissioned apart by a slow- or fast-moving neutron into two lighter nuclei called *fission fragments* (Figure 15-7). Fissions of uranium-235 nuclei can produce any of over 450 different fission fragments or isotopes, most of them *radioactive*. During fission some of the mass of each uranium-235 nucleus is converted into energy. Each fission also produces two or three neutrons that can be used to fission many additional uranium-235 nuclei if enough are present to provide the *critical mass* needed for efficient capture of the neutrons. These multiple fissions taking place within the critical mass represent a *chain reaction* that releases an enormous amount of energy (Figure 15-8). The uranium extracted from uranium ore contains about 99.3 percent *nonfissionable* uranium-238 and only 0.7 percent *fissionable* uranium-235 (Table 15-2). The

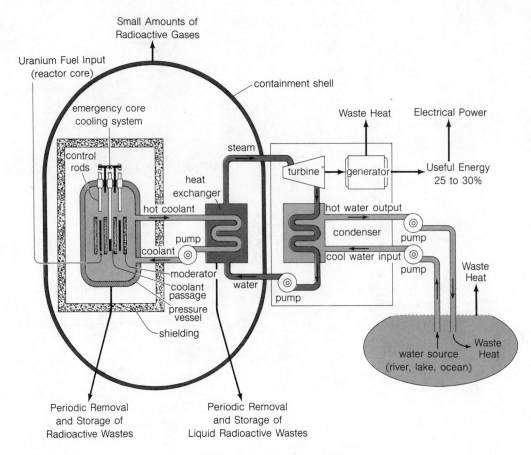

Figure 15-9 A nuclear power plant with a pressurized water reactor.

concentration of fissionable uranium-235 must be increased from about 0.7 percent to about 3 percent by removing some of the uranium-238 at a fuel enrichment plant before it can be used as a fuel in a conventional nuclear fission power plant.

In an *atomic or nuclear fission bomb,* a massive amount of energy is released in a fraction of a second in an *uncontrolled* nuclear fission chain reaction. This is normally done by using an explosive charge to suddenly push a mass of fissionable fuel together from all sides to attain the critical mass needed to capture enough neutrons for a massive chain reaction to take place almost instantly. Scientists also have learned how to carry out a *controlled,* nuclear fission chain reaction in a *nuclear reactor* so that, on the average, *one* of each two or three neutrons released is used to split another nucleus (Figure 15-8). Each nuclear plant may have one or more reactors depending on its overall capacity.

Most nuclear reactors in the United States and throughout the world are *light-water reactors (LWR).* There are two types of LWRs: the *boiling-water reactor (BWR)* and the *pressurized-water reactor (PWR).* About 70 percent of the LWRs in the United States and the world are PWRs, as shown in Figure 15-9. However, BWRs and PWRs are similar. Each con-

sists of **(1)** a *core* containing the fuel and the devices that control the rate at which the self-sustaining chain reaction takes place, **(2)** a *heat-exchange system,* which cools the reactor and transfers the heat produced in the core to a system that produces steam, **(3)** a *turbine-generator system* in which steam spins the blades of a turbine, which runs an electrical generator to produce electricity, and **(4)** a *shielding and containment system* that protects workers from the intense radiation produced inside the reactor core and prevents radiation leakages into the environment.

In both types of LWR the core consists of several hundred *fuel assemblies,* each of which contains several hundred long, thin *fuel rods* made of a zirconium alloy and packed with eraser-sized pellets of uranium oxide (UO_2) fuel containing about 3 percent fissionable uranium-235 and 97 percent nonfissionable uranium-238. The uranium-235 fuel in *each* of the fuel rods in a typical reactor can produce energy equal to that from about three railroad cars of coal. Interspersed between the fuel assemblies are *control rods* made of materials that capture neutrons (Figure 15-9). These rods are moved in and out of the reactor to regulate the rate of fission and thus the amount of power the reactor produces. To stop the fission process (because of an accident, to make repairs, or to remove spent fuel), all the control rods must be inserted.

Both types of LWR have water as a *moderator*, circulating between the fuel rods and between fuel assemblies to slow the neutrons emitted by the fission process and to increase their chances of hitting other fuel atoms to continue the chain reaction.* The water also cools the fuel rods to prevent them and other core materials from melting, and it carries the heat produced by the fission chain reaction out of the core and into the heat exchanger.

Each LWR requires an enormous volume of cooling water. The heat removed by this water must either be transferred to the air by using massive cooling towers (Figure 18-4) or returned to bodies of water, where it can cause thermal water pollution (Section 18-3). Fossil-fuel-burning power plants also require cooling water and can cause thermal water pollution. However, such plants release less heat because they have a higher first-law energy efficiency (40 percent versus 25 to 30 percent efficiency of a LWR).

The Nuclear Fuel Cycle The nuclear power plant with one or more reactors is only one part of the *nuclear fuel cycle* (Figure 15-10) necessary for using nuclear energy to produce electricity. *In evaluating the safety and economics of nuclear power, it is necessary to look at this entire cycle—not just the nuclear plant itself.*

The fuel cycle for an LWR begins with the mining and milling of uranium ore. In mills located near the mines, the ore is crushed, ground, and chemically concentrated into *yellowcake*, which contains 70 to 90 percent uranium oxide (U_3O_8) with about 99.3 percent of the uranium in the form of uranium-238 and 0.7 percent as uranium-235.

The most serious health threat from this phase of the nuclear fuel cycle is the inhalation of radioactive radon-222 gas produced by the decay of uranium-238. Miners in poorly ventilated uranium mines were exposed to dangerous levels of radon and had an average death rate from lung cancer 6 times the normal rate. Since 1970 mine ventilation has been drastically increased and has reduced average radon levels about twenty-fold.

The uranium mining and milling process also produces debris or *tailings*, which emit radioactive

radon-222 gas. Until 1978, these tailings were normally left piled on the ground or suspended in water and pumped into holding ponds, which eventually dried out. In 1970 it was discovered that 3,000 private homes and other buildings in Grand Junction, Colorado had been built in the 1950s on top of tailings used as landfill and in some cases were built from materials containing tailings. A federal project is now under way to dig up, replace, and seal the foundations and other parts of these buildings. Bernard Cohen estimates that the radon gas released from uncovered uranium tailings used to provide a one-year fuel supply for a 1,000 megawatt nuclear reactor causes an estimated 0.003 fatality per year or 3 deaths every 1,000 years—compared to an estimated 11 deaths a year from the radon impurities released when coal is burned to supply a 1,000-megawatt coal-fired plant. The 1978 Uranium Mill Tailings Radiation Control Act requires that these tailings be covered up so that this already small risk is reduced 200-fold (to about 0.000015 death per year, or 1.5 deaths every 100,000 years for each 1,000-megawatt nuclear reactor).

Yellowcake is shipped to a plant that converts it to gaseous uranium hexafluoride (UF_6). This gas is sent to a government-owned gaseous diffusion enrichment plant, where the concentration of uranium-235 in the hexafluoride form is increased from 0.7 percent to about 3 percent for use as fuel in an LWR. The enriched uranium hexfluoride goes to a fuel fabrication plant where it is converted to uranium dioxide (UO_2), encapsulated in pellets about the size of an eraser, placed in zirconium alloy fuel tubes about 3 meters (10 feet) long, and put together in bundles or fuel assemblies for shipping to commercial power plants.

After about 3 years of operation, the fission efficiency of fuel rods is decreased because the amount of uranium-235 fuel in each unit decreases from about 3 percent to 1 percent and radioactive fission fragments build up inside the rod. Thus each year about one-third of the fuel assemblies in the reactor core are removed and replaced. Each spent fuel rod contains about 1 percent fissionable plutonium-239 produced when neutrons bombard some of the nonfissionable uranium-238 orginally making up about 97 percent of the fuel in each rod.

Spent fuel assemblies in a reactor are removed from the reactor and submerged in cooling water in on-site storage pools. Once the spent fuel has cooled and has lost some of its radioactivity, it can be moved to other storage pools away from the reactor (AFR storage) or sent to a permanent nuclear waste repository. The United States and several other countries are planning to bury these highly radioactive wastes in mines carved out of deep underground formations of certain types of rock, with

---

*A non-LWR reactor such as the *Canadian deuterium uranium (CANDU) reactor,* in commercial operation in Canada and in several other countries, uses heavy water (in which the hydrogen atoms are hydrogen-2 instead of hydrogen-1) as a moderator and heat transfer medium. Another non-LWR reactor, known as the *high-temperature gas-cooled reactor (HTGR),* uses graphite as a moderator and helium gas to transfer heat out of the core.

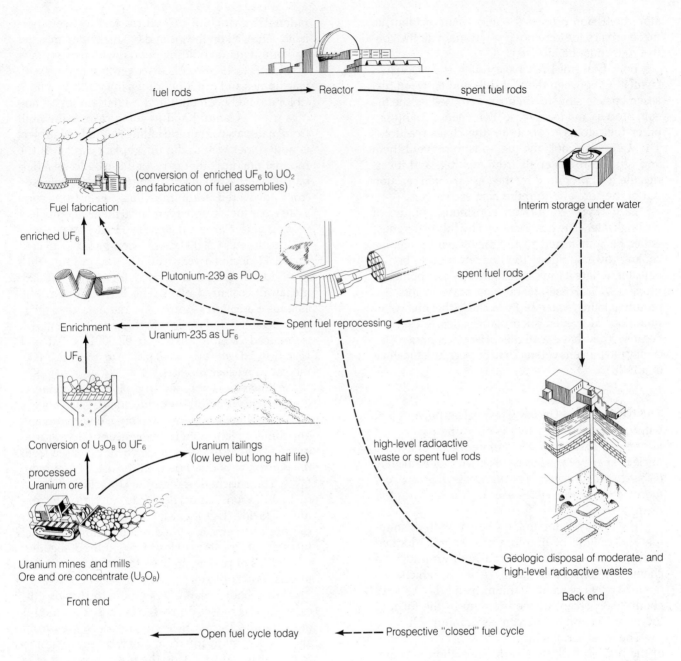

fuel rods → Reactor → spent fuel rods

(conversion of enriched UF_6 to UO_2 and fabrication of fuel assemblies)

Fuel fabrication

Interim storage under water

enriched UF_6

Plutonium-239 as PuO_2

spent fuel rods

Enrichment ← Uranium-235 as UF_6 ← Spent fuel reprocessing

UF_6

Conversion of U_3O_8 to UF_6

Uranium tailings (low level but long half life)

processed Uranium ore

high-level radioactive waste or spent fuel rods

Uranium mines and mills
Ore and ore concentrate (U_3O_8)

Geologic disposal of moderate- and high-level radioactive wastes

Front end

Back end

←——— Open fuel cycle today   ←- - - - Prospective "closed" fuel cycle

Figure 15-10 The nuclear fuel cycle.

the first commercial repository to be available in the United States around 2000, if everything goes as planned.

Instead of being placed in a nuclear waste repository, the radioactive spent fuel can be sealed in heavily shielded, crash-proof casks and transported by truck or train to a fuel-reprocessing plant. There the plutonium and uranium extraction process (PUREX), developed during World War II, can be used to separate the remaining fissionable uranium-235 and the fissionable plutonium-239 produced in the reactor by **(1)** chopping the fuel rods into fragments, **(2)** dissolving the fragments in nitric acid, and **(3)** using a solvent to extract uranium-235

and plutonium-239 from the solution. The plutonium-239 is recovered as plutonium oxide (PuO_2) and sent to a fuel fabrication plant for use as a fuel in a conventional nuclear reactor or a breeder nuclear reactor (Section 15-6). The recovered uranium-235 is converted to the hexafluoride, and sent to an enrichment plant for reuse in the cycle. Fuel reprocessing produces large quantities of solid, liquid, and gaseous low- and high-level radioactive wastes that must be stored safely until they have decayed to safe levels.

The United States has delayed the development of commercial nuclear-fuel-reprocessing plants because such facilities would be handling and shipping nuclear fuel in a form that could be used to make nuclear weapons and because of technical difficulties and high construction and operating costs. By 1984 there was uncertainty over when or if a commercial fuel-reprocessing plant constructed at Barnwell, South Carolina, would be licensed to operate. Great Britain has a large fuel-reprocessing plant under construction, France has two small plants in operation, and Germany has one such plant in operation.

Nuclear Reactor Safety Fission converts some fuel to radioactive fission fragments, and under intense neutron bombardment the metals in the fuels rods and other metal parts in the core are converted to radioactive isotopes. Because these radioactive fission products also produce lots of heat, they continue to heat the fuel even after the reactor has been shut down. Thus, water must be circulated through the core to prevent a *meltdown* of the fuel rods and the reactor core. An *emergency core cooling system (ECCS)* serves as a backup to flood the core automatically with water to prevent meltdown of the reactor core.

A light-water reactor cannot blow up like an atomic bomb because neither the fissionable uranium-235 nor the fissionable plutonium-239 produced in the reactor when neutrons bombard nonfissionable uranium-238 is present in sufficient concentration or in the proper geometry to create a runaway chain reaction. However, a reactor core might lose its cooling water through a break in one of the pipes that conduct cooling water and steam to and from the reactor core (Figure 15-9). If the ECCS also failed, *such a loss-of-coolant accident (LOCA)* would cause the reactor core to overheat, eventually melt down, melt through its thick concrete slab, and melt itself into the earth. Depending on the geological characteristics of the underlying strata, it might sink 6 to 30 meters (20 to 100 feet) and gradually dissipate its heat, or it might burn itself deeply into the earth's crust and contaminate groundwater with radioactive materials.

Another possibility is that a powerful gas or steam explosion inside the reactor containment vessel could split the vessel open and release its highly radioactive contents directly to the atmosphere. This cloud of radioactive materials which would be at the mercy of the winds and weather, could kill and injure many thousands of people and contaminate large areas for hundreds to thousands of years. Because of these very remote but real possibilities for serious accidents, nuclear fission is considered by most analysts to be *potentially* the most hazardous of all energy alternatives.

Advocates of nuclear power, however, argue that a catastrophic nuclear accident is so unlikely that nuclear power is worth the risk compared to the benefits it provides and the even greater hazards from burning coal. They point out that a meltdown and release of radioactivity to the environment would require the almost simultaneous failure of a series of safety systems designed to prevent this from happening, as summarized in the box on page 302.

The Atomic Energy Commission (AEC), established in 1946, commissioned several studies to assess the probability of a serious nuclear accident and to project the resulting deaths, injuries, and property losses. Documents obtained under the Freedom of Information Act reveal that between 1955 and 1975, the AEC made little of this information on nuclear safety available to the public. This is not surprising, because the AEC had the dual and often conflicting roles of promoting and regulating nuclear power. In 1975 the AEC was dissolved; its research role was assigned to the Energy Research and Development Administration (ERDA), now part of the Department of Energy, and its regulatory role was assigned to the Nuclear Regulatory Commission (NRC).

One of the most extensive reactor safety studies was WASH-1400, or the Rasmussen report, published in 1975. According to this study **(1)** a meltdown is highly unlikely; **(2)** in 98 out of 100 cases the safety and containment systems would prevent any radioactivity from reaching the environment and no public fatalities would occur; **(3)** in the estimated 2 out of every 100 cases where the containment system did not hold, the average meltdown would cause between 400 and 5,000 fatalities and an average of $100 million (1975 dollars) in property damages; and **(4)** in the worst possible accident, which is so unlikely that its probability of occurrence is only once during every billion years of reactor operation, there would be an estimated 825 to 13,200 immediate deaths and 7,500 to 180,000 later deaths from cancer (a mean of 50,000 total deaths), 12,375 to 198,000 illnesses, 4,750 to 171,000 delayed genetic effects, contamination with radioactive materials of a 9,000-square-kilometer (3,500-square-mile) area (almost equivalent to the size of Connecticut), and property damage ranging from $2.8 billion to $28 billion (a mean of $15 billion).

The Rasmussen report, however, was criticized by a number of prominent scientists and nuclear safety experts, and in January 1979 the NRC withdrew its endorsement of this document, stating that it no longer considered the risk estimates to be reliable. A 1983 study performed for the NRC by the Sandia National Laboratories, in Albuquerque, New Mexico, estimated that an extremely improbable worst possible nuclear accident, which has only a

Factors Contributing to Nuclear Plant Safety

1. The uranium fuel pellets are clad in a metal, such as an alloy of zirconium, that can withstand temperatures up to 980°C (1800°F) to confine most of the fission products.

2. The reactor vessel has steel walls about 20 centimeters (8 inches) thick that can withstand high internal pressures. It is surrounded by concrete and steel shields several feet thick, which absorb neutrons and radiation emitted from the reactor core.

3. A sophisticated backup system automatically inserts control rods into the core to stop fission if certain emergency conditions occur.

4. Even if a meltdown, pipe leak, or internal explosion occurs, there is little likelihood of radioactive materials reaching the environment because the shielded reactor vessel and, for PWRs, the closed reactor coolant system loop, is set inside a containment building constructed of concrete walls about 0.9 meter (3 feet) thick, and heavily reinforced by a network of steel rods the diameter of a soft drink can. Containment buildings are designed to withstand high internal pressures up to seven times normal atmospheric pressure, which can contain a temporary LOCA but not the meltdown of a complete reactor core. Externally the containment building is designed to withstand tornadoes, direct collisions from light aircraft, artillery shells, and earthquakes.

5. Large filter systems (somewhat like giant vacuum cleaners) and chemical sprayers inside the containment building remove radioactive dust from the air and further reduce the chances of radioactivity reaching the environment. Several water spray and fan systems also operate inside the containment building to condense steam released from a reactor vessel rupture and to prevent the pressure of superheated steam from rising until it exceeds the holding power of the containment building walls.

6. If a coolant water pipeline breaks, the ECCS is designed to flood the reactor core with cooling water within one minute. To guard against failure of electric power needed to drive the pumps in the ECCS, two separate power lines are brought into the plant and these are backed up by several diesel generators, any one of which can provide the necessary electricity. Several tests conducted since 1973, as well as the 1979 accident at the Three Mile Island nuclear plant in Pennsylvania, have demonstrated that the ECCS system works.

7. During plant construction welds are subjected to X-ray inspection. When the plant goes into operation, an automatic system detects pipe leaks, and pipes and other metal parts are also checked periodically by visual and ultrasonic inspections for signs of leaks or corrosion cracking. All other safety systems are also inspected frequently.

8. Each major safety system has an automatic backup system, such as the ECCS, to replace it in the event of a failure. Although this elaborate strategy (known as *defense in depth*) is not infallible, it is designed to prevent serious accidents by assuming that all sorts of things will go wrong—pipes will break, motors and alarm indicators will fail, valves will stick, operators will push the wrong buttons and make judgment errors, and so on.

0.00002 percent chance of taking place before the year 2000, could cause as many as 100,000 deaths within a year and up to $300 billion in property damage—considerably higher than estimates in the Rasmussen study. The probability of such an event happening is about equal to that of a major dam collapsing. The Sandia study, however, did not involve a comprehensive evaluation of safety conditions for the entire nuclear fuel cycle. Thus, after over 25 years of studies, we have no authoritative evaluation of nuclear reactor safety and of the safety of the entire nuclear fuel cycle.

Nuclear power expert Alvin M. Weinberg and the Office of Technology Assessment are looking into ways to improve reactor safety in existing LWRs and to develop other safer reactor designs, including a new LWR Swedish design called PIUS, for *Process-Inherent Ultimately Safe Reactor*. The PIUS is designed to prevent the core from overheating under any foreseeable circumstance by placing the reactor core at the bottom of a huge pressure vessel with reinforced concrete walls 6 meters (20 feet) thick and two steel liners to prevent leaks. The pressure vessel is to be filled with water containing high concentrations of boron, which absorbs neutrons and is available at all times to flow into the core and shut the reactor down. However, utilities find present LWRs too expensive to build, and it is doubtful that they would be willing to switch to new and probably even more expensive reactor types—a move that would also leave them with older, less safe reactors that cost hundreds of billions of dollars.

In 1979 a highly improbable series of mechanical failures and human operator errors caused a partial meltdown of the core and release of small amounts of radiation from one of the reactors at the Three Mile Island (TMI) nuclear plant in Pennsylvania. In this accident, described as the worst in the history of commercial nuclear power, no lives were lost. Furthermore, according to the presidential commission that investigated the accident, there will be few if any, long-term health effects from the accident. Many nearby residents, however, are not convinced and bear increased anxiety about their health and the long-term health of their children and about the devaluation of their property.

The cleanup of the damaged TMI reactor, which will probably cost at least $1 billion (more than the $700 million cost of building the reactor), threatens the utility with bankruptcy and may not be completed until 1988 or later. Furthermore, confusing and misleading statements about the seriousness of the accident by Metropolitan Edison power plant officials and NRC officials eroded public confidence in the safety of nuclear power and the ability and desire of nuclear officials to provide the public with accurate information about the potential or actual dangers of nuclear power.

In response to the TMI accident, the nuclear industry and utilities moved to upgrade reactor safety by (1) establishing a Nuclear Safety Analysis Center (NSAC) to study safety problems, devise solutions, and distribute this information to utility companies, (2) setting up the Institute of Nuclear Power Operations (INPO), charged with establishing better management and operator training and standards, (3) installing two telephone hotlines to link each reactor in the country to the NRC's emergency response center, and (4) financing a $40 million ad campaign launched in 1983 by the Committee for Energy Awareness to improve the nuclear industry's image and resell nuclear power to the American public.

Nuclear critics, however, attribute the absence of catastrophe at Three Mile Island partially to luck, and further argue that coal (except for the potential danger of climate change from carbon dioxide emis-

sions) can be made acceptably safe or that energy conservation and a mix of renewable energy resources (Chapter 16) can reduce dependence on both coal and nuclear power for producing electricity. They also charge the nuclear industry and the NRC with making only cosmetic design and operational changes rather than dealing with the serious safety problems raised by the TMI accident.

The need for better safety control and emergency planning was underscored by an accident in February 1983 at the Salem I reactor in New Jersey. While the reactor was operating at low power, the SCRAM system, which is supposed to shut down the reactor in case of trouble, failed because of poor maintenance of electrical motors and circuit breaker switches. This failure went unnoticed because an inexperienced operator wiped out an electronic display that would have revealed the problem. The reactor, 30 seconds away from a partial or complete meltdown, had to be shut down manually. Had the Salem reactor been running at full power, emergency evacuation measures might have been necessary for the safety of the 890,000 people living within a 50-kilometer (30-mile) radius of the plant.

Another inherent safety problem in the 47 PWRs in operation in the United States is that intense neutron bombardment gradually embrittles the steel walls and welds of the reactor pressure vessel. In acknowledgment of this circumstance, reactors are licensed to operate only 30 to 40 years. Recent data, however, suggest that the rate of embrittlement, especially in welded PWR vessels built before 1971, may be greater than originally anticipated and that some of these older reactors could become unsafe after as few as 12 years of operation. Some engineers fear that older embrittled PWR vessels might crack when suddenly cooled with cold water while the core remains highly pressurized. This condition, known as *pressurized thermal shock (PTS)*, could occur while a reactor is being turned on or shut down, and especially during an emergency shutdown requiring use of the ECCS. PTS would lead to a loss of coolant and a core meltdown because the ECCS is not designed to prevent core melting if the reactor vessel is ruptured.

The nuclear industry and the NRC maintain that such an accident due to embrittlement is not likely and that no reactor is currently in danger of cracking under *normal* circumstances. However, in 1982 Demetrios Basdekas, a reactor safety engineer with the NRC, reported that:

There is a high, increasing likelihood that someday soon, the steel vessel that houses the radioactive core at any of a dozen or more nuclear power plants around the United States is going to crack like a piece of glass . . . and the best safety systems in the world would not be effective.

The result will be a core meltdown which will injure many people, destroy the plant, and probably destroy the nuclear industry with it.

In 1983, the NRC reported that because of potential embrittlement problems, at least 11 older PWR plants will need "hardware and procedural modifications" within the next 5 years to prevent rupture of their reactor walls.

Nuclear Accident Insurance Liability Because refusal by the insurance companies to fully insure against large-scale damages from a nuclear reactor accident would have grounded the fledgling nuclear industry, Congress in 1957 passed the Price-Anderson Act. Under this act, liability claims paid out as a result of a nuclear accident cannot exceed $560 million—a small sum in the event of a major nuclear accident. Individuals cannot sue for damages in court beyond the Price-Anderson ceiling; and home-owner insurance policies have a waiver excluding damage from a nuclear power plant accident.

In 1983 the NRC suggested that damages to the public might be hundreds of times higher than the $560 million limit and asked Congress to increase the possible damage liability through a pool paid into by utilities at a rate of $10 million per reactor, per accident, per year, until all damages had been paid off. If approved by Congress, this measure would make about $830 million available annually for the 82 nuclear reactors operating in 1983. Even a relatively small major accident could take the pool a lifetime to pay off, however, and critics want all liability limits removed. Nuclear expert Weinberg has called for utilities to show that they really believe in the low-risk figures they quote to the public by insuring each reactor for damage up to $1 billion with their own funds, with the government assuming responsibility for losses greater than $1 billion, as it now does in the case of floods and natural disasters.

Disposal and Storage of Radioactive Wastes Each part of the nuclear fuel cycle produces a mixture of solid, liquid, and gaseous radioactive wastes that must be stored until their radioactivity is no longer harmful. The largest amount of high-level radioactive wastes are produced at nuclear power plants and at reprocessing plants. In addition, large amounts of high-level radioactive wastes are produced by nuclear weapons facilities, and large quantities of low-level wastes are produced by defense facilities, nuclear power plants, hospitals, and at government and university nuclear research laboratories.

Iodine-131 with a half-life of 8 days, cesium-137 with a half-life of 27 years, and strontium-90 with

a half-life of 28 years are particularly dangerous. Unlike most radioisotopes, they can become biologically magnified in food chains and webs (Figure 5-6) if released to the environment as a result of an accident or faulty storage at a waste depository. Iodine-131 does not need to be stored for a long time before it decays to a safe level. But high-level radioactive wastes containing cesium-137 and strontium-90 must be stored safely for about 280 to 560 years (10 to 20 times their half-life). If reprocessing plants are not developed in the United States, spent fuel assemblies containing radioactive plutonium-239 will have to be stored permanently. Plutonium-239 emits beta particles and gamma rays and has a half-life of 24,400 years and thus would have to be stored safely for at least 244,000 years. Although not biologically magnified in food webs and not intensely radioactive, plutonium-239 can cause lung cancer if only a few particles, each smaller than a speck of dust, are inhaled.

Three methods are used to dispose of or store radioactive wastes: dilution and dispersion, delay and decay, and concentration and containment. In *dilution and dispersion*, low-level wastes are released into the air, water, or ground to be diluted to presumably safe levels. Nondefense low-level wastes from U.S. nuclear plants, hospitals, and nuclear research laboratories are being stored at six commercial sites, three of which no longer accept any additional waste. In 1980 Congress passed a law that by 1986 may prevent many states from using the nation's three remaining commercial low-level nuclear waste dump sites. States are trying to establish a series of new regional dump sites.

Delay and decay involves storing medium- to high-level radioactive wastes, such as iodine-131, with relatively short half-lives, as liquids or slurries in double-shell tanks. After 10 to 20 times their half-lives, they normally decay to relatively harmless levels, at which time they can be diluted and dispersed to the environment.

Concentration and containment is used for high-level radioactive wastes with long half-lives. These materials must be stored for tens, hundreds, thousands, or even millions of years, depending on their composition. They are not only extremely radioactive but also thermally hot. By the year 2000, it is projected that there will be enough accumulated high-level radioactive wastes produced by U.S. nuclear weapons facilities and nuclear power plants to construct a four-lane highway 30 centimeters (1 foot) deep from coast to coast. Presently highly radioactive spent fuel assemblies from U.S. nuclear power plants were being stored temporarily in deep pools of water at nuclear plant sites, pending the development of a method for long-term storage or disposal.

Table 15-5 Proposed Methods for Long-Term Storage or Disposal of Nuclear Wastes

Proposal	Possible Problems
Surround wastes with concrete or several layers of metal and store in surface warehouses or underground tunnels with careful monitoring until a better solution is found.	Concrete or metal liners might deteriorate; above-ground warehouses may be difficult to guard against sabotage; states may not want the storage sites or the transshipment of wastes; the government might not provide enough funds to investigate more permanent storage methods.
Solidify wastes, encapsulate them in glass or ceramic, place in metal containers, and bury the containers deep underground in earthquake- and flood-proof geological formations, such as dug-out salt or granite deposits.	Occurrence of natural disasters cannot be predicted; heat from radioactive decay might crack glass containers, fracture salt or granite formations so that groundwater could enter the depository, or release from water-containing minerals water that could leach radioactive materials into groundwater supplies; transportation of deadly radioactive wastes to depository sites could be dangerous; wastes might be difficult to retrieve if project fails.
Use rockets or a space shuttle to shoot the wastes into the sun or into space.	Costs would be very high, and a launch accident coud disperse deadly radioactive wastes over a wide area. The project may not be technically feasible.
Bury wastes in an underground hole created by a nuclear bomb so that the wastes eventually melt and fuse with surrounding rock into a glassy ball.	Effects unknown and unpredictable; if project fails, wastes cannot be retrieved and could contaminate groundwater supplies.
Bury wastes under Antarctic ice sheets or Greenland ice caps.	Long-term stability of ice sheets is unknown; knowledge about thermal, chemical, and physical properties of large ice sheets is lacking; retrieval could be difficult or impossible if project fails.
Encase wastes in well-designed containers and drop them into the ocean in isolated areas.	No one knows how to design a container that will last long enough; oceans and marine life could become seriously contaminated if containers leak; small currents near the ocean bottom could move the wastes to less isolated sites over hundreds to thousands of years.
Enclose wastes in well-designed containers and drop them into deep ocean bottom sediments that are descending deeper into the earth.	Long-term stability and motion of these sediments are unknown; containers might leak and contaminate the ocean before they are carried downward; containers might migrate back to the ocean or be spewed out somewhere else by volcanic activity; wastes probably could not be retrieved if project fails.
Change harmful isotopes into harmless ones by using high-level neutron bombardment, lasers, or nuclear fusion.	Technological feasibility has not been established; costs would be extremely high; process would create new toxic materials also needing disposal; main effect would be to spread long-lived radioactive isotopes into more dilute radioactive wastes, not to eliminate them.

High-level liquid wastes from nuclear weapons production (equal in volume to about 200 Olympic-sized swimming pools) and from nuclear power plants are also awaiting permanent storage. Presently they are stored in underground tanks in government facilities in Idaho, South Carolina, and Washington State. These tanks must be carefully guarded and continuously monitored to prevent corrosion and leaks. Underground storage tanks built between 1943 and 1965 were single-shell tanks, consisting of a corrosion-prone carbon steel liner surrounded by reinforced concrete and covered by a dome. More than 1.7 million liters (450,000 gallons) of highly radioactive wastes has already leaked from 20 of these older single-shell tanks at the Richland, Washington, storage site. However, a study by the NAS concluded that because of the isolation of the site, the leaks have not caused any significant radiation hazard to public health and would take nearly 1 million years to reach the nearest river. Storage tanks constructed after 1968 have a *double shell*; thus if the inner wall corrodes, the liquid will spill into the space between the two walls, where it can be detected in time to be pumped into another tank. These tanks have developed no leaks so far.

Table 15-5 lists the major methods proposed for long-term storage or disposal of high-level radioactive waste. Technically, the safe disposal of high-level radioactive wastes is believed to be possible. But after 30 years of research and debate there is still no widely agreed upon scientific and political solution to this problem. One proposed method is to concentrate the waste, convert it to a dry solid, fuse it with glass or a ceramic material, seal it in a metal canister, and bury it permanently in deep underground salt, crystalline granite, basalt, or tuff rock formations, which have beeen stable for millions of years and are expected to remain so for millions of years more.

But some geologists and other scientists question this approach, arguing that extensive drilling and tunneling can destabilize such rock structures and that present geological knowledge is not sufficient to predict the paths of subterranean water flows that could contaminate groundwater drinking supplies with radioactive wastes. These analysts believe that radioactive wastes should be stored in retrievable form in above- or below-ground facilities until further research establishes the safety of proposed geological storage sites.

Nuclear physicist Bernard Cohen, however, points out that once high-level nuclear wastes have been solidified, encased in glass or a ceramic material, and enclosed in a metal canister, they pose no significant health risks even if there is an accident. He estimates that underground storage of high-level radioactive wastes from 1,000 nuclear plants would be expected to cause only 1 death over a 500-year period. Some scientists, however, argue that such average estimates for the entire United States significantly underestimate the risk for people located near nuclear waste repositories and along shipping routes to such sites.

Regardless of the storage method, most citizens strongly oppose the location of a nuclear waste disposal facility anywhere near them. By 1983 at least 22 states had enacted laws banning radioactive waste disposal within their borders, and 7 states had laws prohibiting construction of any new nuclear power plants until the government demonstrates a safe method for long-term nuclear waste disposal. In addition, 15 states and over 200 local communities had by 1983 enacted laws banning or regulating shipments of nuclear material.

To avoid such political difficulties, some scientists favor dumping wastes into deep bottom sediments of the ocean. They argue that this method may be technically and environmentally feasible, could cost about one-tenth what land storage costs, and would be especially useful for long-lived, gaseous radioisotopes of iodine, carbon, hydrogen (tritium), and krypton, which are difficult to contain and store on land. Other analysts, however, have pointed out some possible problems with this method, as summarized in Table 15-5.

In 1983 the Department of Energy (DOE) began building the first major geologic repository in the United States, to be used only for storage of high-level radioactive wastes produced by the nuclear weapons program. This $1 billion Waste Isolation Pilot-Plant Project (WIPP) is being built in a bedded salt formation deep under federal land about 40 kilometers (25 miles) east of Carlsbad, New Mexico.

In 1982 Congress passed the Nuclear Waste Policy Act (NWPA), which (1) established a timetable for the DOE to choose a site and build the nation's first deep underground repository for long-term storage of high-level radioactive wastes from commercial nuclear reactors by 2000, (2) calls for DOE to design and find a site for a monitored retrievable storage (MRS) facility for temporary storage of high-level nuclear waste as a backup for the permanent repository, (3) establishes an interim storage program to ease the backlog of spent nuclear fuel at power plants, (4) permits states and American Indian tribes to turn down repository locations in their jurisdictions unless overridden by simple majorities in both houses of Congress, and (5) provides financing for the estimated $40 billion needed for the project between 1983 and 2020 from a one-time fee amounting to $2 billion for nuclear fuel used by utilities before April 1983 and a federal fee per kilowatt-hour of electricity generated since April 1983.

Marvin Resnikoff has argued that (1) present casks for shipping high-level nuclear wastes to repositories are outmoded and quite vulnerable to serious accidents; (2) nuclear waste truck drivers are inadequately trained; (3) communities along nuclear waste transportation routes are poorly prepared for emergency situations; (4) accident consequences are underestimated by the NRC; and (5) accident insurance is inadequate. The NRC, however, contends that the present shipping casks have been used to carry spent fuel all over the country for more than 35 years and have been in accidents without any release of radioactivity. The original design was tested by being crashed into solid walls at 130 kilometers per hour (80 miles per hour), hit by locomotives traveling at similar speeds, engulfed in gasoline fires for 30 minutes, and submerged in water for 8 hours without ever releasing any of its radioactive contents. The NRC also points out that even if the casks somehow rupture, their radioactive wastes are in solid form, hence couldn't leak out like a liquid or gas and contaminate a large area.

Decommissioning Nuclear Power Plants After 30 to 40 years of neutron bombardment, the carbon steel reactor vessel becomes too brittle to use and the miles of cooling water pipes become too corroded for safe use. Since the high levels of radiation in the reactor vessel make repairs unthinkable, the plant must be shut down in a safe condition. This *decommissioning* process is the final step of the nuclear fuel cycle.

Scientists have proposed three ways for decommissioning a nuclear power reactor: (1) *mothballing* by removing spent uranium fuel assemblies, draining all slightly radioactive water from its cooling pipes, setting up a 24-hour security guard system to prevent public access for at least 100 years and perhaps 1,000 years, and doing periodic radiological surveys and maintenance; (2) *entombment*, or sealing the entire reactor with reinforced concrete after radioactive fuel assemblies, liquid radioactive waste, and surface contamination have been removed to the greatest extent possible; and (3) *dismantlement*, the removal of all radioactive materials, which are stored in a radioactive waste disposal facility.

Dismantlement seems to be the most likely method. Present official cost estimates run to at least $100 million per reactor, but economist Duane Chapman estimates that full dismantlement could cost as much as $1 billion per reactor. By the year 2000, at least 12 presently operating commercial reactors may be candidates for decommissioning. The NRC will have to decide soon whether to require a prepayment, funding reserve, or insurance scheme to ensure that decommissioning funds will be available even if the utility that built the reactor in question has gone bankrupt.

Proliferation of Nuclear Weapons   Since the late 1950s the United States has been giving away and selling various forms of nuclear technology to other countries, and by 1984 at least 14 other countries* had entered the international market as sellers. Although intended for peaceful uses, the information, components, and materials used in the nuclear fuel cycle could be used to make nuclear weapons.

Nuclear weapons can be made from any one of three major fissionable isotopes: highly enriched uranium (HEU) containing 50 to 93 percent uranium-235, relatively pure plutonium-239 (ideally about 94 percent plutonium-239 and 6 percent plutonium-240), and relatively pure uranium-233. Between 4 and 9 kilograms (9 to 20 pounds) of plutonium-239 or uranium-233 (about the size of an orange) and 11 to 25 kilograms (24 to 55 pounds) of uranium-235 are needed to make a small atomic bomb capable of blowing up a large building or a city block and contaminating a much larger area with radioactive materials for centuries. Unfortunately, the basic principles of building an atomic bomb are well known: Obtain a large enough mass of fissionable material (uranium-235, plutonium-239, or uranium-233) and force it together long enough

to achieve the critical mass. There is relatively little doubt that a small group of trained people could make a nuclear bomb if they had enough fissionable bomb-grade material.

Highly enriched uranium-235 could be (1) stolen from a military weapons facility or from shipments to or from such a place, (2) obtained directly by gift or purchase for use in some of the over 150 research and test reactors operating in about 30 countries,* or (3) manufactured, by concentrating the 3 percent uranium-235 fuel used in a commercial reactor by means of the complex and expensive isotope separation and enrichment process now in commercial operation in nine nations or by one of the simpler and cheaper technologies for isotope separation presently being developed.

Plutonium-239 could be (1) stolen from a military weapons facility or from concentrated, bomb-grade plutonium fuel being shipped to breeder nuclear fission plants (Section 15-6), (2) diverted by nations or stolen from commercial fuel reprocessing plants, (3) made in a research reactor or specially designed plutonium production reactor (either of which could be built in a few years for perhaps $15 million to $30 million dollars, by bombarding uranium-238 with neutrons), or (4) made in a commercial reactor, in a similar manner.

Bomb-grade plutonium-239, which is heavily guarded, could be stolen from nuclear weapons facilities, especially by people working there, or from shipments of weapons-grade plutonium and nuclear fuel. Each year about 3 percent of the approximately 126,000 people working with U.S. nuclear weapons are relieved of duty because of drug use, mental instability, or other security risks. By 1978 at least 320 kilograms (700 pounds) of plutonium-239 was missing from commercial and government-operated reactors and storage sites in the United States—enough to make 32 to 70 atomic bombs (each capable of blowing up a city block). No one knows whether this missing plutonium was stolen or whether it represents sloppy measuring techniques and bookkeeping.

Some have pointed out that those who steal plutonium need not bother to make atomic bombs. They could simply use a conventional explosive charge to dispense the stolen plutonium into the atmosphere from atop any tall building. Dispersed in this manner, 2.2 kilograms (1 pound) of plutonium oxide powder could theoretically contaminate

---

*The Soviet Union, Czechoslovakia, East Germany, Poland, Great Britain, France, West Germany, the Netherlands, Belgium, Sweden, Switzerland, Italy, Canada, and Japan.

*The United States alone has given away at least 26 HEU-fueled research reactors to Argentina, Brazil, Iran, Israel, South Korea, Pakistan, Spain, and Taiwan and has supplied enough HEU for many bombs to France, West Germany, Italy, Japan, and South Africa. In addition, France and West Germany have sold such reactors to other countries.

7.7 square kilometers (3 square miles) with radioactivity, which could cause lung cancer for 100,000 years among those who inhaled contaminated air. Physicist Bernard Cohen, however, points out that it is rather difficult to disperse plutonium oxide in the air as a breathable dust because individual particles tend to stick together and form lumps too large to be inhaled into the lungs. He argues that terrorists have many easier ways to kill large numbers of people, such as releasing poison gas into the ventilation system of a large building, blasting open a large dam, or poisoning a city's water or produce supply.

By mid-1984 no country had been detected using commercial nuclear power plants to make nuclear weapons, but at least two countries had used research reactors and related civilian nuclear facilities to produce or attempt to produce nuclear weapons material. India made and tested its first nuclear device by using plutonium produced in a research reactor and recovered in a pilot reprocessing plant. In 1981 Israel bombed a research reactor Iraq had bought from France because Israel believed that Iraq planned to use the reactor to produce plutonium for nuclear weapons.

In 1968 the Treaty on Nonproliferation of Nuclear Weapons (NPT) was signed. The nuclear nations—then, the United States, France, Great Britain, China, and the Soviet Union—agreed to reduce their nuclear arsenals (which has not happened) and to assist non-nuclear nations with civilian nuclear power programs if these nations agreed not to use the information and technolgy to develop nuclear weapons and placed all their civilian nuclear power activities under a system of safeguards administered by the UN-sponsored International Atomic Energy Agency (IAEA). Eventually, about 114 nations signed the agreement, but 50 did not—including France, China, India, Pakistan, Argentina, Brazil, Israel, and South Africa. By mid-1984 six nations had built and tested nuclear devices, and nine others were believed capable of building nuclear bombs. An additional 16 countries could be capable of building such bombs by 1991 or sooner.

The NPT requires participating nations to submit their designs to the IAEA upon request, to maintain an accurate accounting of nuclear material open to IAEA inspection, and to allow inspection by IAEA officials of all civilian nuclear facilities to verify that they are being used for peaceful uses only. But the IAEA has no enforcement power if a diversion of bomb-grade material is detected, and any member nation can withdraw from the treaty and escape scrutiny with 90 days notice—though none had done so by mid-1984. IAEA critics point out that on-site inspections are made only every few months, even though a country could divert plutonium from a civilian nuclear facility and fabricate it into a nuclear weapon within a week.

One suggestion for reducing diversion of plutonium fuel from the nuclear fuel cycle is to contaminate it with other substances that render it dangerous to handle and unfit as weapons material. But so far no acceptable spiking agent has emerged that could not be removed by reprocessing or isotope separation. It has also been suggested that the NPT be strengthened by inducing more nations to ratify the treaty, increasing IAEA funds for inspection, and adding sanctions to be imposed on violators.

Some argue that trying to stop nuclear proliferation by reducing the spread of nuclear technology is hopeless because the genie is out of the bottle. Although nuclear technolgy is spreading, others point out that this does not relieve nuclear nations from the responsibility of keeping its rate of spread as low as possible, especially by slowing the transfer of isotope separation, research reactors, fuel reprocessing, and breeder fission reactors throughout the world. They argue that time is a precious commodity in the nuclear age, to be used by politicians and ordinary citizen groups to reduce international tensions that could lead to nuclear war, perhaps to find ways of reducing the world's nuclear arsenal, and to develop less potentially dangerous energy alternatives.

Soaring Costs: The Achilles Heel of Nuclear Power Regardless of how one feels about nuclear power, the major factor slowly shutting down the world's nuclear industries is economics. Only where nuclear power is pushed, controlled, and heavily subsidized by a strong central government is development now proceeding even close to the rate projected just a decade ago.

The largest cutback in nuclear power has taken place in the United States. By 1984, after 34 years of development and a $154 billion investment, including $43 billion in government (taxpayer) subsidies, it appeared that nuclear power might be both uneconomical and unnecessary to meet future U.S. energy needs. Even with such massive subsidies, the 82 nuclear power reactors in operation in the United States at the end of 1983 produced only 13 percent of the nation's electricity and 3.5 percent of the nation's primary energy—about equal to that provided by wood and crop wastes without any significant government subsidies.

Utility companies originally began ordering nuclear power plants in the late 1950s for three major reasons: (1) the AEC and builders of nuclear reactors projected that nuclear power would produce electricity at such a low cost that it would be too cheap to meter; **(2)** the nuclear industry projected that the reactors would have an 80 percent *capacity factor*—a measure of the time a reactor is able to produce electricity at its full power potential; and **(3)** the first round of commercial reactors was built with the government paying approximately one-fourth of the cost, using the Price-Anderson Act to protect the nuclear industry and utilities from significant accident liability, and at a fixed cost with no cost overruns allowed. It was an offer utilities could not resist.

It has since become clear that nuclear power is a very expensive way to produce electricity. Construction cost overruns have risen sharply, largely because of delays from mismanagement, legal suits, government redtape, and new and more stringent safety requirements (especially since the TMI accident). This has increased the average construction time for a U.S. reactor from 7 years in 1971 to 12 years in 1983, compared to an average construction time of 6 years in France and 7 years in Japan. Construction costs have been increasing so rapidly that some U.S. utilities are faced with bankruptcy. For example, in 1983 the Washington Public Power Supply System (WPPSS) was unable to pay the interest on $2.25 billion it had borrowed to finance the construction of two cancelled nuclear reactors and admitted in court that it had no realistic hope of ever repaying any of the borrowed money, This largest bond default in American history left banks, insurance companies, and individual investors (including many elderly persons who had been depending on the securities for retirement income), with the massive financial loss.

Operation and maintenance costs, once expected to be negligible, rose during the 1970s at an average annual rate of 18 percent—far above the inflation rate. Furthermore, commercial nuclear power plants in the United States have operated far below the projected 80 percent capacity factor level because of frequent breakdowns, lengthy maintenance operations, and the need to comply with federal safety standards. Studies by nuclear economics expert Charles Komanoff (See *Power Plant Cost Escalation*, 1981) have shown that the average capacity factor for all operating U.S. nuclear reactors was 56 percent in 1982 and 59 percent for all years through 1982, with the newer and larger reactors (over 800 megawatts) having an even lower average of only 51 percent. Coal-fired plants performed only slightly better, but with their lower construction costs today they can produce electricity more cheaply in nations with ample supplies of coal (Table 15-6).

The nuclear industry disputes these figures, saying that they overestimate the cost of nuclear power and underestimate the cost of coal. After

Table 15-6 Estimated Cost of Electricity Including Construction, Fuel, and Operation from New Power Plants in the United States in 1983, with Projections for 1990

| Energy Source | Cost (cents per kilowatt-hour) | |
	1983	1990 (projected)
Improved energy efficiency (to reduce quantity of electricity needed)	1–2	3–5
Cogeneration	4–6	4–6
Coal	5–7	8–10
Small hydropower	8–10	10–12
Biomass	8–15	7–10
Nuclear	10–12	14–16
Wind power	15–20	6–10
Solar photovoltaic cells	50–100	10–20

Sources: Charles Komanoff and Worldwatch Institute, January 1984.

making detailed analyses of nuclear cost estimates, Komanoff concluded that the industry has underestimated the cost of nuclear power and overestimated the cost of coal.

Primarily because of declining demand for electricity and rapidly rising costs for building and operating new nuclear power plants in the United States, no new nuclear power reactors were ordered by utility companies between 1978 and mid-1984. In addition, by mid-1984 orders for 90 nuclear plants—repesenting all new plants ordered since 1974—had been canceled. A number of financial analysts and energy experts project that at least half of the 45 reactors ordered before 1974 and still under construction in early 1984 may also be canceled to prevent financial strain or bankruptcy of utility companies. The financial community became quite skeptical about financing new U.S. nuclear power plants after the TMI accident showed that they could lose $1 billion or more in equipment in an hour, even without any serious health effects for the public.

In addition, consumer protests are expected to increase because of **(1)** the sharp rise in electricity rates in areas getting a significant fraction of their electricity from costly new nuclear reactors beginning operation between 1984 and 1990, and **(2)** attempts by utility companies to have consumers pay for plants under construction and for losses from cancellation of partially completed nuclear reactors. With average electricity rates more than tripling between 1973 and 1983, state utility commissions have been caught between the desires to keep electricity affordable and at the same time to allow utilities, overextended with nuclear plants, enough revenue to preserve their financial health.

A 1984 report by Office of Technology Assessment concluded that nuclear power in the United States is not likely to be expanded in this century beyond the reactors already under construction because of the increased financial risks to utilities. Nuclear industry officials believe that this bleak outlook for the future of nuclear power in the United States could change if **(1)** electricity demand were to rise sharply in the 1980s and 1990s, **(2)** the costs and time needed to build a nuclear plant were cut significantly by standardizing design and by reducing the paperwork and tests needed to obtain government approval for operating a plant (e.g., cutting the average construction time from 12 to 6 years would almost halve construction costs), and **(3)** public confidence in the safety of nuclear power were restored.

Since 1982 President Reagan vowed to speed up the licensing of new plants, lift the ban on reprocessing spent uranium fuel in the United States, promote the controversial breeder reactor (Section 15-6), promote export sales of nuclear technology to other nations, and find a solution to the nuclear waste disposal problem. By mid-1984, except for nuclear waste disposal, Congress had failed to agree to such changes in U.S. nuclear power policy.

The rate of growth of nuclear power in most other nations has also decreased since the mid-1970s, with nuclear power projected to supply only about 15 to 20 percent of the world's electricity and about 5 percent of the world's primary energy by 2000 (Figure 14-2). Most governments with major nuclear power programs—especially Japan, France, Great Britain, and the Soviet Union—remain strongly committed to using nuclear power to produce a significant amount of their electricity by 2000. But public opposition to nuclear power is growing in these nations (except the Soviet Union) and others, costs have been much higher than projected, and plans have been scaled back sharply.

A 1980 national referendum in Sweden, which now gets 15 percent of its electricity from nuclear power, banned the construction of new nuclear plants and called for replacing nuclear power with a mix of renewable energy alternatives by 2010. The Soviet Union, with 40 operating reactors providing 6 percent of its electricity in 1983, planned to increase its nuclear power generating capacity significantly by constructing Atommash, a gigantic facility 9.6 kilometers (6 miles) long, to build 8 reactors a year, to be towed by barge to construction sites in Russia and eastern Europe. By 1983, however, this ambitious plan had been delayed for at least a decade and perhaps indefinitely by inept management, higher than projected costs, and the collapse of the

walls and foundation of the partially completed facility.

Japan, which has no coal or oil, has an aggressive nuclear power program with 25 operating reactors supplying 16 percent of the country's electricity in 1983, and another 13 under construction. Japan is the world's leader in new reactor technology and has ambitious plans to provide half its electricity by nuclear power by 2000. But cost overruns and frequent shutdowns for repairs are causing concern, and political opposition is growing as more and more communities in this small nation are affected by new plant construction. Public confidence in the government-run nuclear industry was eroded in 1981 when it was learned that a utility company had deliberately covered up a spill of radioactive water into a remote fishing area.

France has the world's most ambitious and cost-efficient plan for using nuclear energy and builds its reactors in less than 6 years, using standardized government-developed designs. By the end of 1983 it had 30 operating nuclear reactors providing 40 percent of its electricity and 28 more under construction with the goal of generating 75 percent of its electricity in this way by 1990. However, a 1984 report showed over the next 20 to 30 years building coal-fired plants in France would be 35 to 60 percent cheaper than building new nuclear plants. Critics also charge that France's nuclear program survives largely through taxpayer subsidies and increasing the national debt rather than through open-market economic competition with coal and other nonrenewable energy alternatives. Because of this debt and a glut of electricity, France reduced its orders for new reactors from six to two per year in 1984 and 1985. The French Planning Ministry concluded that the only reason for not halting all orders for new reactors until at least 1987 was to preserve jobs at its goverment-run reactor manufacturing company. See the summary table opposite.

15-6 Breeder Nuclear Fission

Breeder Reactors At present use rates the world's supply of uranium should last for at least 100 years. However, some scientists believe that if there is a sharp rise in the use of nuclear fission to produce electricity after the year 2000, *breeder nuclear fission reactors* can be developed to avoid rapid depletion of the world's supply of uranium fuel. A breeder reactor produces within itself new fissionable fuel in the form of plutonium-239 from nonfissionable uranium-238, an isotope that is in plentiful supply.

The fuel in a breeder fission reactor consists of a mixture of uranium-238 and an initial charge of

Conventional Nuclear Fission Energy

Advantages

1. Technology is well developed.
2. Cannot blow up like an atomic bomb.
3. Produces no carbon dioxide.
4. Because of multiple safety systems, a catastrophic accident releasing deadly radioactive material into the environment is extremely unlikely.
5. Air pollution: low under normal operation of the nuclear fuel cycle. Does not release air pollutants such as particulate matter and sulfur and nitrogen oxides like coal-fired plants. A normally operating PWR (but not BWR) releases less radioactivity than a comparable coal-fired plant, but the entire fuel cycle for a nuclear plant releases more radioactivity (especially krypton-85) than a comparable coal-fired plant.
6. Water pollution: low environmental impact on water if entire fuel cycle operates normally.
7. Land disruption: moderate environmental impact on land primarily from open pit and underground mining and storage of radioactive wastes, if entire fuel cycle operates normally.
8. Could become more versatile if affordable and acceptable electric cars are developed.

Disadvantages

1. High and rapidly rising construction and operating costs, even with with massive government subsidies.
2. Affordable supplies of uranium may be depleted within 50 to 200 years, depending on rate of development of nuclear power.
3. Not versatile. Can be used only to produce electricity and pressurized high-temperature steam.
4. Low net useful energy yield (Table 14-12).
5. Requires large quantities of water for cooling (Section 18-3).
6. A presumably safe method for storing radioactive wastes for hundreds to thousands of years will not be available until at least 2000.
7. Commits future generations to task of safely storing radioactive wastes for hundreds to thousands of years even if nuclear fission power is abandoned.
8. Spreads knowledge and materials that could be used to make nuclear weapons.
9. Possible large-scale disasters: although extremely unlikely, a combination of mechanical and human errors, sabotage, or shipping accidents could result in release of deadly radioactive material into the environment.

Breeder Nuclear Fission Reactors

Advantages

1. Extends affordable supplies of uranium for 1,000 to several thousand years.
2. Cannot blow up like an atomic bomb, although a small explosion equivalent to that from several hundred pounds of TNT can occur if all safety systems fail.
3. Produces no carbon dioxide.
4. Because of multiple safety backup systems, a catastrophic accident that releases deadly radioactive material into the environment is extremely unlikely.
5. Air pollution: low under normal operation of the nuclear fuel cycle. Does not release air pollutants such as particulate matter and sulfur and nitrogen oxides, like coal-fired plants.
6. Water pollution: low environmental impact if entire fuel cycle operates normally.
7. Land disruption: moderate environmental impact primarily from open pit and underground mining and storage of radioactive wastes, if entire fuel cycle operates normally.
8. Could become more versatile if affordable and acceptable electric cars are developed.

Disadvantages

1. High construction costs, estimated to be two to three times as high as comparable conventional fission reactors already being canceled because of excessive costs.
2. Technology is not fully developed.
3. Not versatile. Can be used only to produce electricity and pressurized steam.
4. Net useful energy yield unknown. Estimated to be higher than conventional nuclear fission but still low to moderate.
5. Greater risk of proliferation of nuclear weapons throughout the world than conventional nuclear fission.
6. Requires large quantities of water for cooling (Section 18-3).
7. A presumably safe method for storing radioactive wastes for hundreds to thousands of years will not be available until at least 2000.
8. Commits future generations to task of safely storing radioactive wastes for hundreds to thousands of years even if nuclear power is abandoned.
9. Spreads knowledge and materials that could be used to make nuclear weapons.
10. Possible large-scale disasters: although extremely unlikely, a combination of mechanical and human errors, sabotage, or shipping accidents could result in release of deadly radioactive material into the environment.

---

fissionable plutonium-239, made by the bombardment of uranium-238 with neutrons inside a conventional fission reactor. Radioactive waste from the conventional reactor is taken to a fuel-reprocessing plant, where the plutonium-239 is separated and purified for use as fuel in a breeder reactor. In the breeder reactor *fast neutrons* are used to fission the nuclei of plutonium-239 and convert the *nonfissionable* uranium-238 into *fissionable* plutonium-239. These devices are often called *fast breeder reactors* (FBR).

Once provided with an initial amount of plutonium-239, a breeder fission reactor should have bred enough fissionable plutonium-239 fuel to start up another breeder reactor after 30 to 50 years. This could increase the present 50- to 200-year estimated lifetime of the world's affordable uranium supplies for at least 1,000 years and perhaps several thousand years.

Because water slows neutrons, liquid sodium metal is normally used as a coolant to ensure sufficient fast neutrons for efficient fissioning and breeding. Such a reactor, known as a *liquid metal fast breeder reactor* (LMFBR), looks something like the reactor in Figure 15-9, except that its core contains a different fuel mixture and its two heat-

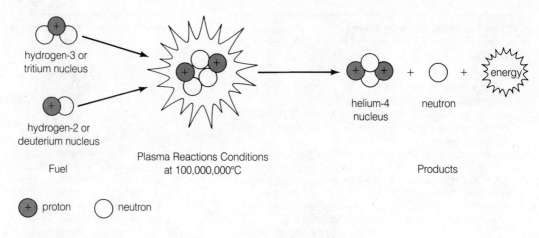

hydrogen-3 or
tritium nucleus

hydrogen-2 or
deuterium nucleus

Fuel

Plasma Reactions Conditions
at 100,000,000°C

helium-4
nucleus

neutron

energy

Products

+ proton   neutron

Figure 15-11 The deuterium-tritium (D-T) nuclear fusion reaction.

exchanger loops contain liquid sodium instead of water. Under normal operation a breeder reactor is considered to be much safer than a conventional LWR. But in the unlikely event that all its safety systems failed and the reactor lost its sodium coolant, there would be a runaway fission chain reaction, and perhaps a small nuclear explosion with the force of several hundred pounds of TNT. Such an explosion could blast open the containment building, releasing a cloud of highly radioactive gases and particulate matter. A more common problem that could lead to temporary shutdowns, but poses no significant health hazards, involves the leakage of molten sodium, which ignites on exposure to air and reacts violently with water.

Since 1966 several small-scale experimental breeder reactors have been built in the United States, Great Britain, the Soviet Union, and West Germany. Intermediate-scale demonstration breeder reactors with about one-third to one-half the output of a typical commercial nuclear plant have been in operation in Great Britain since 1975 and in France and the Soviet Union since 1977. Since 1977 France has been building Superphénix 5, a full-sized commercial breeder reactor scheduled to begin operation in 1985. Tentative plans to build full-sized commercial breeders in West Germany, the Soviet Union, and the United Kingdom may be canceled because of the excessive cost of Superphénix (three times the original estimate) and because some studies indicate that breeders will not be competitive economically with conventional fission reactors for at least 50 years.

In 1983, after 13 years of political and scientific debate and a government expenditure of $1.7 billion merely for planning, the proposed Clinch River intermediate demonstration breeder reactor in Tennessee was canceled because **(1)** it would cost from $3.6 to $8.5 billion (5 to 12 times the original estimate); **(2)** its design was already outdated by other demonstration breeders; **(3)** numerous studies have shown that the United States will not need breeder reactors until at least 2025, given the slowdown in the building of conventional nuclear fission reactors; **(4)** energy conservation and various renewable energy alternatives can be developed faster and cheaper; and **(5)** fear over the worldwide proliferation of nuclear weapons.

A summary table is given on p. 311.

15-7 Nuclear Fusion

Controlled Nuclear Fusion In the distant future—probably no sooner than 2050, if ever—scientists in the United States, the Soviet Union, Japan, and a consortium of European nations hope to use *controlled nuclear fusion* to provide an essentially inexhaustible source of energy for producing electricity. **Nuclear fusion** takes place in the sun and other stars. At temperatures of 100 million degrees or more, nuclei of light atoms such as hydrogen are forced together until they fuse to form a heavier nucleus, and in the process, convert some of their mass into energy. Once initiated, nuclear fusion releases 4 times as much energy per gram as the fission of uranium-235 nuclei and about 10 million times as much per gram as the combustion of fossil fuel.

Theoretically, at least 100 different nuclear fusion reactions are possible. Presently, however, only the *D-T fusion reaction* is being studied seriously because it has the lowest ignition temperature of about 100 million degrees. In the *D-T fusion reaction*, a hydrogen-2 or deuterium (D) nucleus and hydrogen-3 or tritium (T) nucleus are fused together to form a larger helium nucleus, a neutron, and energy (Figure 15-11). The temperature required to initiate this fusion reaction is about five times hotter than the temperature of the sun's core. A pinhead of D-T fuel at this temperature would give off enough heat to boil water 10,000 miles away!

Deuterium is found in about 150 out of every million molecules of water (150 ppm) and can be separated from ordinary hydrogen atoms fairly easily. Thus, the world's oceans provide an almost inexhaustible supply of this isotope. Although there is no significant natural source of tritium, an extremely small quantity can be extracted from seawater. This can be used as an initial charge in a fusion reactor, with the neutrons emitted in D-T fusion reactions used to bombard a surrounding blanket of lithium to breed additional tritium fuel. The scarcity of lithium will eventually limit the use of D-T fusion, but the earth's estimated supply should last for 1,000 to several thousand years, depending on rate of use.

Another possibility is the D-D fusion reaction, in which the nuclei of two deuterium (D) atoms would be fused together to form a helium nucleus. But this reaction requires an ignition temperature about 10 times higher than that for D-T fusion and is not being pursued at this time. If controlled D-D nuclear fusion were developed, the deuterium in the ocean could supply the world with primary energy at many times present consumption rates for 100 billion years—about 10 times the estimated age of the universe. Although D-D fusion represents a potentially *renewable* source of energy, few scientists expect it to become a major source of energy until 2100, if ever.

Achieving Controlled Nuclear Fusion *Uncontrolled nuclear fusion* of deuterium and tritium produced from lithium is presently used in *hydrogen* or *thermonuclear bombs*; the high temperature needed to initiate nuclear fusion is produced by a nuclear fission explosion. The first test explosion of a thermonuclear bomb was carried out by the United States in 1952. However, *controlled nuclear fusion* by the D-T reaction to produce thermal energy that can be converted into electricity is still at the laboratory stage despite almost 35 years of research, costing about $4 billion in the United States alone.

The first step in bringing about a self-sustaining controlled nuclear fusion reaction is to heat the D-T fuel to about 100 million degrees so that the positively charged fuel nuclei are moving fast enough to overcome their mutual electrical repulsion when they collide. Heating deuterium and hydrogen atoms to such a high temperature creates a gaslike *plasma* in which the deuterium and tritium atoms are so energetic—so hot—that the nuclei lose their electrons. The next step is to find a way to hold and squeeze the plasma together long enough and at a high enough density to ensure that sufficient num-

bers of positively charged nuclei of the D-T fuel atoms collide and fuse. No physical walls can be used to confine the hot plasma, not only because any known material would be vaporized but also because the walls would contaminate the fuel and instantly cool it below its ignition temperature.

So far the most promising approach is *magnetic confinement*, in which powerful electromagnetic fields confine and force the atomic nuclei in the plasma together within a vacuum—a sort of invisible electromagnetic "bottle." The plasma and vacuum region is surrounded by a wall made of a metal alloy that retains its strength at very high temperatures. A blanket of rapidly circulating liquid lithium would probably be used to remove heat and prevent the metal wall from melting, and to breed tritium fuel. The molten liquid coolant would be piped out of the reactor and used to produce steam, which would be used to generate electricity. Outside the blanket, powerful electromagnets, cooled by liquid helium to about $-272°C$ ($-458°F$) to make them superconducting and to reduce their energy requirements, would provide the magnetic fields needed to confine the plasma.

Research so far has concentrated on finding a geometric shape for the confined plasma that minimizes plasma leakage so that effective fusion of the fuel nuclei can take place. One promising magnetic confinement approach is to use electromagnetic fields to squeeze the plasma into the shape of a large toroid or doughnut (Figure 15-12). Such a reactor is known as a *tokamak* (after the Russian words for "toroidal magnetic chamber"), a design pioneered by Soviet physicists, including Andrei Sakharov.

By mid-1984, none of the several test reactors throughout the world had been able to reach the *break-even point*, where the energy pumped into the reactor equals the energy it produces—much less produce net useful energy. Scientists hope to achieve the energy break-even point by 1986 using the recently completed $314 million tokamak fusion test reactor (TFTR) at the Plasma Physics Laboratory at Princeton University. If this point is reached in the laboratory, the next, even more difficult step will be to achieve the *burning point*, or true ignition, where the D-T nuclear fusion reaction becomes self-sustaining and releases more energy than is put in. Even if this occurs, several prominent fusion research scientists believe that tokamaks may be too huge, cumbersome, and expensive to be scaled up to make an economically feasible commercial-sized nuclear fusion reactor.

Scientists at the Lawrence Livermore National Laboratory in California are building a competing experimental reactor, the Mirror Fusion Test Facility. In this approach, electromagnetic fields are used to

Figure 15-12 The magnetic confinement approach to nuclear fusion in a Tokamak reactor.

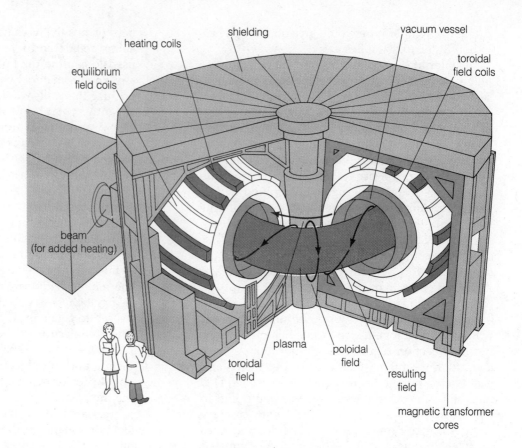

compress the plasma into a long, pipelike shape; at each end, opposing magnetic fields known as tandem mirrors, deflect and prevent the plasma from leaking out.

A second approach to nuclear fusion is *inertial containment*. Dozens of high-powered laser beams, electron beams, or beams of light atoms (such as carbon or oxygen) are used to bombard and implode pinhead-sized pellets containing deuterium and tritium fuel, which are dropped into the center of the reactor as needed. Ideally, the impact would drive the contents of the pellet inward, creating an intensely hot, dense core where fusion can take place. By 1984 it appeared that lasers with enough power to get a net useful energy yield could not be developed, and government funds for developing this approach in the United States had been significantly decreased.

Building a Commercial Nuclear Fusion Reactor
Assuming that the burning point can be reached, the next step is to build a small demonstration fusion reactor and then scale it up to commercial size. This task is considered to be one of the most difficult engineering problems ever undertaken. For example, the electromagnets, cooled to practically the lowest possible temperature on earth, would be located only a few meters from the plasma, at the

highest temperature produced on earth. Protecting the extremely sensitive electromagnets from heat and radiation damage would be somewhat like trying to preserve an ice cube next to a blazing fire, only much harder. Moreover helium, which would be used to cool the magnets, is a very rare element, and supply problems might limit the long-term use of nuclear fusion unless the United States and other nations established a helium conservation program.

Another engineering problem would be posed by the necessity of maintaining the interior section of the reactor containing the plasma at a near-perfect vacuum. More mind-boggling still, the inner walls of the reactor surrounding the lithium blanket must resist constant baths of highly reactive liquid lithium at 1,000°C and steady bombardment by fast-moving neutrons released when deuterium and tritium fuse. Since neutron bombardment eventually destroys or alters the composition of presently known materials, reactor walls would have to be replaced about every 5 years, at such enormous cost that some scientists doubt whether fusion will ever be economically feasible. Scientists hope to overcome some of these problems by developing special new alloys, but some of the elements to make these new alloys may be unaffordably scarce.

There are other problems. The neutron bombardment of the walls and other structural materials near the reactor core would convert many of

Advantages

1. D-T reaction could provide electrical energy for 1,000 to several thousand years. D-D reaction, if ever developed, would be an essentially infinite source of electrical energy.
2. Cannot blow up like an atomic bomb.
3. Produces no carbon dioxide.
4. Because of multiple safety backup systems, a catastrophic accident that releases deadly radioactive material into the environment is extremely unlikely.
5. Produces smaller amount of radioactive waste than conventional and breeder fission reactor of comparable size.
6. Air pollution: low under normal operation of the nuclear fuel cycle. Does not release air pollutants such as particulate matter and sulfur and nitrogen oxides, like coal-fired plants.
7. Water pollution: low environmental impact under normal operation.
8. Land disruption: low environmental impact under normal operation.
9. Could become more versatile if affordable and acceptable electric cars are developed.

Disadvantages

1. Estimated costs very high: two to four times that for a comparable breeder fission reactor and four to eight times that for a comparable conventional fission reactor.
2. Technology is in very early stages of development and may never be developed fully.
3. Would not supply large amounts of energy for 75 to 100 years, if ever.
4. Not versatile. Can be used only to produce electricity and pressurized steam.
5. Net useful energy yield unknown—probably low to moderate.
6. Chance of numerous small accidents higher than that for conventional and breeder fission reactors.
7. Radioactive wastes are produced that must be stored safely for 100 to several thousand years, depending on materials used to build reactor.
8. Commits future generations to task of safely storing radioactive wastes for 100 to 1,000 years even if nuclear fusion is abandoned.
9. Use may be limited by available supplies of helium (for cooling magnets) and vanadium or other alloying metals needed for reactor walls.
10. Requires very large amounts of cooling water.
11. Will release radioactive tritium unless control methods can be developed.
12. Produces tritium, which can be used to make hydrogen bombs, and produces neutrons, which can be used to breed materials for making atomic bombs.
13. Possible large-scale disasters: although even more unlikely than for conventional and breeder reactors, a combination of mechanical and human errors, sabotage, or shipping accidents could result in release of deadly radioactive material into the environment.

the chemical elements into radioactive materials. As a result, repairs would have to be made by automatic devices, still to be developed, since no human worker could withstand the radiation. There is also concern over the high-level magnetic and electrical fields near the reactor, which might be hazardous to power plant employees.

The estimated cost for a commercial fusion reactor based on presently known approaches is two to four times that for a comparable breeder fission reactor and four to eight times that for a comparable conventional fission reactor. Other disadvantages of nuclear fusion are given in the summary table opposite.

U.S. Timetable for Fusion The Magnetic Fusion Energy Engineering Act of 1980 established a national goal of demonstrating the engineering feasibility of magnetic fusion in the early 1990s and building a workable fusion demonstration reactor by 2000. The DOE was authorized to spend up to $20 billion between 1980 and 2000 in pursuit of this goal. By 1984, however, this ambitious schedule was not being met.

If everything goes as planned—which may be one of the biggest ifs in scientific and engineering history—the break-even point might be reached in a laboratory test reactor in the United States by 1986, engineering feasibility established perhaps somewhere between 1995 and 2005, and the first U.S. commercial reactor completed sometime between 2010 and 2025. If this happens, then between 2050 and 2150 nuclear fusion might produce as much as 18 percent of U.S. annual primary energy needs.

15-8 Geothermal Energy

Nonrenewable Geothermal Energy The decay of radioactive elements deep within the earth generates heat that slowly flows into buried rock formations. Under intense pressure and lava flow from the molten interior of the earth, some of the earth's geothermal energy escapes through hot springs, geysers, and volcanoes, and some is transferred over thousands to millions of years to normally *nonrenewable* deposits of dry steam, wet steam (a mixture of steam and water droplets), and hot water lying relatively close to the earth's surface.

Geothermal wells can be drilled like oil and natural gas wells to bring this dry steam, wet steam, or hot water to the earth's surface. Although not yet a major component of the world's primary energy budget (Figure 14-2), by 1983 about 20 countries were tapping such deposits of geothermal energy to produce electricity, provide low- to moderate-temperature heat for some industrial processes, to heat water in homes and businesses, and to provide space heating. Although such sources are nonre-

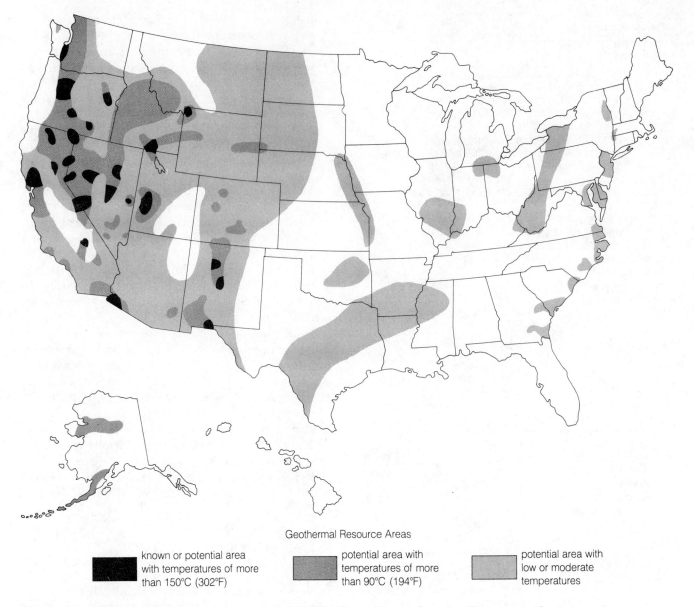

Geothermal Resource Areas

| known or potential area with temperatures of more than 150°C (302°F) | potential area with temperatures of more than 90°C (194°F) | potential area with low or moderate temperatures |

Figure 15-13 Major deposits of geothermal resources in the United States. (Source: Council on Environmental Quality.)

newable, they are projected to last for 100 to 200 years in most places. Figure 15-13 shows that most of the accessible and fairly hot geothermal deposits in the United States lie in the western states.

Dry steam deposits are the preferred geothermal resource, but they are also the rarest. Only dry steam wells can be tapped easily and economically at present. This is done by drilling a hole into the reservoir, releasing the superheated steam through a pipe, filtering out solid material, and piping the steam directly to a turbine to generate electricity.

A large natural dry steam well near Larderello, Italy, has been producing electricity since 1904 and is a major source of power for Italy's electric railroads. Two other major dry steam sites are in Japan (Matsukawa) and the Geysers steam field, located

about 145 kilometers (90 miles) north of San Francisco. The Geysers field has been producing electricity since 1960 more cheaply than fossil fuel and nuclear plants. By 1983 it was supplying 2 percent of California's electricity, enough to satisfy the electrical needs of more than a million people, and may supply 25 percent of California's electricity by 1990.

Underground *wet steam deposits* are more common but are harder and more expensive to convert to electricity. These deposits contain water under such high pressure that its temperature is unusually high (180 to 370°C), unlike water under normal atmospheric pressure, which cannot exceed the boiling point [100°C (212°F)] without being converted to steam. When a geothermal well is drilled to bring this superheated water to the surface, about

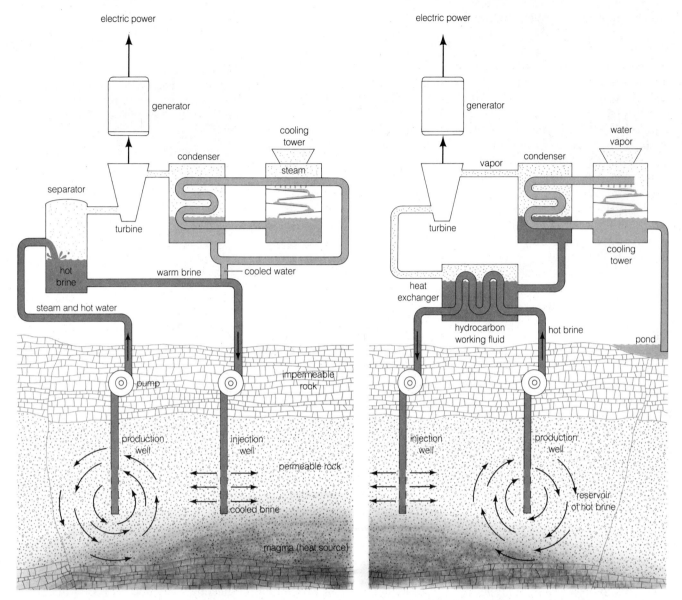

Figure 15-14 . Direct flash (left) and binary cycle (right) methods for extracting and using geothermal energy to produce electricity.

10 to 20 percent of the flow flashes into steam because of the decrease in pressure. A centrifugal separator is then used to separate the steam from this mixture of steam and water droplets, and the steam spins a turbine to produce electricity (Figure 15-14). The remaining hot water, which is often high in dissolved salts, and the condensed steam, are usually reinjected into the earth to prevent buildup of dissolved salts in nearby bodies of water and to reduce subsidence of the ground above the geothermal wells. The largest geothermal electric power plant in the world based on wet steam wells is in Wairakei, New Zealand.

Other wet steam power plants are in operation in Mexico, Japan, and the Soviet Union. Between 1980 and 1984 three demonstration wet steam power plants were built in the United States: two in the Salton Sea area of southern California's Imperial Valley district, and the third at Valles Caldera, New Mexico. Although these plants are producing electricity, drilling problems and corrosion from the salty water have reduced yields, with the energy produced equivalent to that from oil at $40 a barrel.

The third type of nonrenewable geothermal deposit contains *hot water* only, and examples are even more common than dry steam and wet steam deposits. Almost all the homes, buildings, and food-producing greenhouses in Reykjavik, Iceland, with a population of about 85,000, are heated by hot water drawn from deep geothermal deposits under the city. In the United States, hot water deposits in over 180 locations have been used to heat homes in Boise,

Idaho, and Klamath Falls, Oregon, and to dry crops and heat farm buildings in South Dakota. If oil prices continue to rise, one expert estimated that just the hot water geothermal resources below southern California's Imperial Valley could produce enough electrical energy to meet the needs of the American Southwest for at least 200 years.

The hot brine water pumped up from such wells can also be used to produce electricity in a *binary cycle system* (Figure 15-14). The hot brine flows through a heat exchanger containing a working fluid (such as isobutane or a Freon), which boils at a lower temperature than water. This converts the working fluid to a vapor that is used to spin a turbine. The working fluid vapor passes through a second heat exchanger, where it is condensed and returned to the first heat exchanger for reuse. The brine is pumped back into the earth to be reheated for future generations.

A demonstration binary cycle went into operation in 1984 in the Imperial Valley at Herber, California. The main problem is that the brine corrodes metal parts and clogs pipes. In another method, now being tested, a heat exchanger containing the working fluid is immersed in the underground well. The heat from the hot water vaporizes the liquid, which is brought to the surface to spin the turbine. Not only does this approach avoid corrosion and wastewater problems, but it leaves the water and steam in the well for continual reheating rather than depleting the resource.

A fourth potential source of geothermal energy consists of *geopressurized zones*, high-temperature, high-pressure reservoirs of water (often saturated with natural gas because of the high pressure), trapped deep beneath beds of shale or clay, usually far beneath ocean beds. If tapped, they could yield three types of energy: electrical (from high-temperature water), mechanical or hydraulic (from the high pressure), and chemical (from the natural gas). These resources could be tapped by very deep (and expensive) drilling, but the extremely high pressures create some technical problems. At present, this potential geothermal resource is in the early, exploratory phase.

Potentially harmful environmental effects from geothermal energy vary widely from site to site and with the type of geothermal resources being used. But most experts consider these effects, listed in the summary table, to be less than or at worst about equal to those from fossil fuel and nuclear power plants. If developed, known geothermal reserves could supply about 5 to 6 percent of 1983 electrical demands. According to DOE estimates, undiscovered geothermal resources contain about 10 times as much heat as known reserves.

Nonrenewable Geothermal Energy

Advantages

1. Technology well developed and relatively simple.
2. Large 100- to 200-year supply for areas near deposits.
3. Moderate cost.
4. Moderate net useful energy yield for large and easily accessible deposits.
5. Does not produce carbon dioxide.
6. Does not produce materials that can be used to produce nuclear weapons.
7. Land disturbance: low to moderate impact from subsidence, which can be decreased by reinjection of wastewater.

Disadvantages

1. Low overall supply of easily accessible deposits.
2. Cannot be used to power vehicles unless affordable and acceptable electric cars can be developed.
3. Requires larger amounts of cooling water than nuclear and coal-burning power plants.
4. Air pollution: moderate to high potential impact from hydrogen sulfide, ammonia, radioactive materials, noise, odor, and local climate change.
5. Water pollution: moderate to high potential impact from dissolved solids (salinity); runoff of toxic compounds of boron, mercury, and other toxic elements; and excess heat.
6. Possible large-scale disasters: depletion and contamination of water resources in arid regions.

Renewable Geothermal Energy   Three potentially *renewable* geothermal energy sources are (1) deposits of *molten rock (magma)* at temperatures around 1000°C (1832°F) found in some places not far below the earth's surface, (2) *dry hot rock* zones, where magma has penetrated into the earth's crust and is heating subsurface rock to high temperatures, and (3) low-to-moderate temperature *warm rock deposits* useful for pre-heating water and for geothermal heat pumps for space heating and air conditioning.

The U.S. Geological Survey estimates that bodies of *molten rock* located no more than 9.6 kilometers (6 miles) below the earth's surface in the continental United States could supply 800 to 8,000 times the primary energy that the nation consumes each year. But extracting energy from magma is complicated and expensive. In 1981 researchers from the Sandia National Laboratory demonstrated that it is possible to drill through magma and keep the hole open for extraction of geothermal energy. In 1984 the DOE was funding additional research to determine the technological feasibility of extracting heat from magma at an affordable price.

Dry and warm hot rock deposits lying deep underground are potentially the largest and most widely distributed geothermal resource in the United States and in most countries, but they tend to be expensive to locate, tap, and use. By 1984 researchers in the United States and Great Britain had drilled several test wells and successfully extracted heat, and a demonstration plant was being built in New Mexico. However, before this approach can be developed on a commercial scale, several technical problems must be solved and the economics of the process must be evaluated.

Renewable Geothermal Energy

Advantages

1. Moderate to large overall supply and essentially infinite supply in magma areas fairly close to the surface.
2. See items 5, 6, and 7 for nonrenewable geothermal energy.

Disadvantages

1. Location, deep drilling, and extraction technology not fully developed.
2. Net useful energy yield unknown, but probably fairly low.
3. Costs unknown but may be fairly high.
4. See items 2, 3, 4, 5, and 6 for nonrenewable geothermal energy.

Summary of Nonrenewable Energy Resources Oil and natural gas have advantages that explain why they are so widely used. But oil supplies are dwindling rapidly, and there is uncertainty over how much affordable natural gas will be available in the future. Affordable coal is plentiful but is not as versatile as oil and in the absence of effective control of mining activities and air pollution emissions, has a significant environmental impact. Conventional and breeder nuclear fission are proving to be uneconomic. Nuclear fusion will not provide any significant amount of energy before 2050, and the technology is so complex and expensive that it may never be developed. Geothermal energy has limited potential worldwide over the next 20 to 30 years, but may eventually make a significant contribution.

The United States, the country that led the world into the age of nuclear power, may well lead it out.

Lester R. Brown

Discussion Topics

1. Contrast large-scale coal-burning, conventional fission, breeder fission, and geothermal power plants: how they work, their environmental impact, and their technological and economic problems.
2. Why is surface-mined coal gradually replacing coal from deep mines? Do you believe that this is a

desirable or undesirable trend? Why? What are the alternatives?

3. Should present U.S. surface mining laws be strengthened or weakened? Defend your choice.
4. Coal-fired power plants in the United States cause at least 5,000 deaths a year, primarily from atmospheric emissions of sulfur oxides and particulate matter. These plants also cause extensive damage to many buildings and to some forests and aquatic systems. Should air pollution emission standards for all coal-burning plants be tightened significantly even if this raises the price of electricity sharply and makes it cheaper to produce electricity by using conventional nuclear fission?
5. Criticize the following statements:
   a. A conventional nuclear fission plant can blow up like an atomic bomb.
   b. A nuclear fusion plant can blow up like a hydrogen bomb.
6. Why are there no fuel-reprocessing plants in the United States? Should the United States build such plants? Should it rely on underground repositories for storage of spent nuclear fuel? Why or why not?
7. What method should be used for the long-term storage of high-level nuclear wastes? Defend your choice.
8. Do you favor a U.S. energy strategy based on greatly increased use of coal-burning plants to produce electricity between 1985 and 2020? Why or why not?
9. Do you favor a U.S. energy strategy based on greatly increased use of conventional nuclear fission reactors to produce electricity between 1985 and 2020? Why or why not?
10. Do you favor a U.S. energy strategy based on the widespread use of breeder reactors between 2000 and 2040? Why or why not? What are the alternatives?
11. Explain why you agree or disagree with each of the following proposals.
    a. The licensing time of new nuclear power plants in the United States should be halved (from an average of 12 years to 6 years) so these facilities can be built more economically and can compete more effectively with coal and other renewable energy alternatives.
    b. A crash program for developing the nuclear breeder fission reactor should be developed and funded by the federal government to conserve uranium resources and eventually to keep the United States from being dependent on other nations for uranium supplies.
    c. To help stimulate the economy and preserve the U.S. nuclear industry, the United States should promote export sales of nuclear technology.

16

Renewable Energy Resources: Overall Evaluation

Throughout most of human history, people have relied on renewable resources—sun, wind, water, and land. They got by well enough, and so could we.

Warren Johnson

16-1 Direct Solar Energy for Producing Heat and Electricity

Direct Solar Energy for Low-Temperature Heating of Water and Buildings Passive solar systems are the simplest, cheapest, most maintenance-free, and least environmentally harmful energy systems for providing hot water and space heating (Tables 14-5, 14-6, and 14-7). This economic advantage will increase as fossil fuel and electricity prices rise. Passive and active solar systems can provide from 50 percent to all of the space heating and hot water needs of well-designed, heavily insulated, airtight homes and buildings equipped with air-to-air heat exchangers to prevent buildup of indoor air pollutants (Section 14-1). Furthermore, with proper design for each type of climate, passive or actively heated solar homes can be built almost anywhere in the United States (Figure 16-1).

Using active or passive solar collectors to heat water is the simplest task (Figure 16-2). Depending on the yearly amount of sun available, solar water heaters can provide 30 to 100 percent of the hot water needs of a typical home, business, school, or hospital. Solar water heaters can compete with natural gas, oil, or electric water heaters almost anywhere that price controls on natural gas and electricity are not in effect. Already several million solar water heaters are used in Japan, Israel, Spain, Australia, and the United States. As energy prices rise, small rooftop solar collectors for heating water will be a common sight throughout the world.

As discussed in Section 14-1, *passive solar heating systems* rely on natural energy flows and on

Direct Solar Energy for Low-Temperature Heating

Advantages

1. Energy supply free and readily available on sunny days.

2. Technology is well developed, fairly simple, and quickly installed. Many homeowners can cut costs by building and/or installing the devices themselves.

3. Passive solar is cheapest way to provide space heating almost anywhere on a lifetime-cost basis. Active solar systems for hot water and space heating are cost competitive on a lifetime-cost basis in most areas.

4. Moderate to high net useful energy yield.

5. Does not add carbon dioxide to the atmosphere.

6. Does not produce radioactive materials or materials that can be used to make nuclear weapons.

7. Air pollution, water pollution, and land disturbance: low, primarily from pollutants released during manufacture of materials used in construction of collectors and heat storage systems. Material use is much lower than in the construction of large-scale fossil fuel and nuclear power plants.

8. Possible large-scale disasters: none, although occasional home fires can result if the heat-transfer fluid in active solar collectors stops circulating and temperatures become high enough to cause wood in roof rafters to ignite.

Disadvantages

1. Energy supply not available at night and cloudy days; thus except in superinsulated houses, thermal storage systems or conventional backup systems are necessary.

2. Usefulness depends on relative availability of solar energy and on how well insulated and airtight the building is.

3. Active systems using liquids for heat transfer can develop leaks and cause serious water damage to buildings.

4. Some people consider solar collectors ugly.

5. Requires laws to guarantee that others cannot build structures that block a user's access to sunlight.

6. Initial costs often considerably higher than for conventional systems.

Enrichment Studies 4 and 11 are related to this chapter.

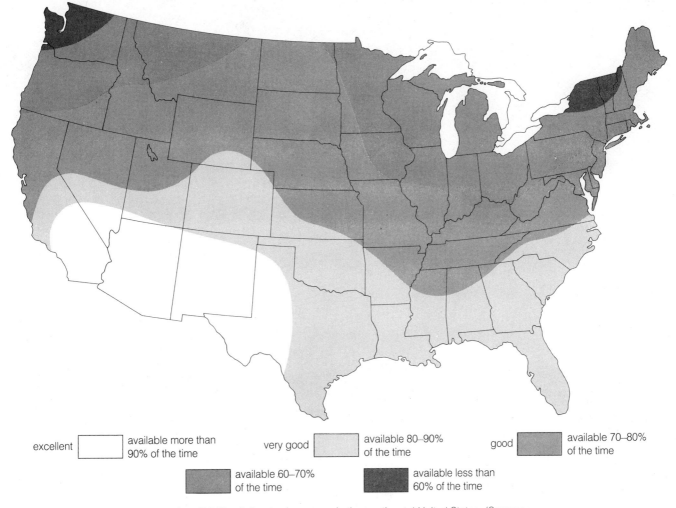

excellent	available more than 90% of the time	very good	available 80–90% of the time	good	available 70–80% of the time

	available 60–70% of the time		available less than 60% of the time

Figure 16-1 Estimated year-round availability of direct solar energy in the continental United States. (Sources: U.S. Department of Energy and the National Wildlife Foundation.)

building design and composition to capture and store the sun's energy rather than on an array of fans, pumps, and special collectors. The major features of a typical passively heated and passively cooled house are shown in Figure 16-3 (pp. 324–325). Unless the house is superinsulated (Section 14-1), a large *thermal mass* is necessary: stone, concrete, adobe, or brick walls and floors, glass columns or black-painted barrels filled with water, or panels or cabinets containing chemicals that store and release heat through phase changes. The thermal mass stores the heat and slowly radiates it into the house at night or on a cloudy day, and helps reduce temperature fluctuations year round. Advanced glazing on window glass or easily movable insulating panels can cover the windows at night during cold weather to retard loss of heat stored in the walls and floors. During hot weather the panels can be closed during the day and opened at night.

Other approaches to passive solar heating include (1) attaching a greenhouse to serve as a solar collector, to grow food and ornamental plants or to serve as a sun room (Figure 16-3), (2) reducing temperature variations by storing the solar energy in special heat-storage walls, called Trombe walls* (Figure 16-3), and (3) storing heat in a roof pond exposed to the sun during the day and covered with an insulated panel at night (and vice versa during the summer).

Another increasingly popular option is to build a passively heated and cooled *earth-sheltered* (underground) house (Figure 16-3) or commercial build-

---

*Named after its designer, Felix Trombe, a Trombe wall is a thermal storage wall placed several centimeters inside a large expanse of glass or plastic on the side of a building facing the sun. The wall is either constructed of masonry or filled with water, usually in tall cylindrical columns, and is painted a dark color to absorb heat from the sun. It provides thermal mass, and at night or on cloudy days, it radiates into the house heat collected during sunny periods.

Figure 16-2 Active and passive solar hot water heaters.

Figure 16-2 Active and passive solar hot water heaters.

Active Solar Hot Water Heating System

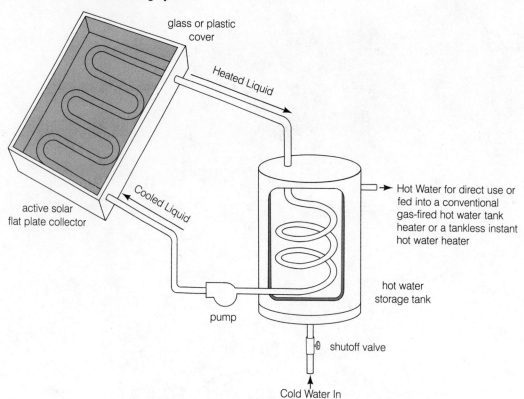

Passive Solar Hot Water Heating System

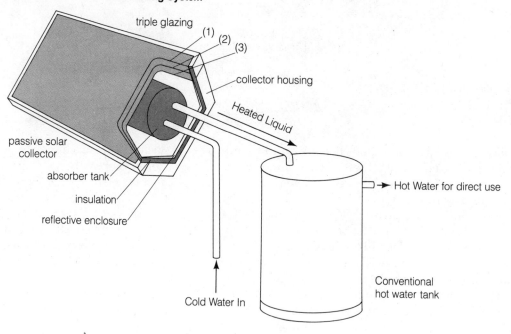

ing. By having the only exposed wall facing the sun and using windows or an attached solar greenhouse or sun room to capture solar energy, such structures can provide from 50 to 100 percent of the heating and cooling needs of the building. Typically, they cost about 10 to 20 percent more to build initially than a comparable above-ground structure, primarily because of the large amount of concrete needed to carry the heavy load and pressure from the earth. But on a lifetime-cost basis, they should be cheaper than a conventional above-ground house because of reduced heating and cooling requirements, elimination of exterior maintenance and painting (and interior maintenance if interior walls and floors are built of natural materials), and reduced fire insurance rates. They also provide more privacy, quietness, and security from break-ins, fires, hurricanes, tornadoes, earthquakes, storms, and nuclear attack than conventional above-ground buildings.

Living in an earth-sheltered building is not like living in a cave. The interior can look like that of any ordinary home, the solar-collecting windows or attached greenhouse, sunken atrium, and skylights can provide more daylight than is found in most conventional dwellings. By mid-1984, at least 4,000 earth-sheltered structures had been built or were under construction in the United States.

During hot weather passive solar cooling can be provided by using (1) heavy insulation, (2) deciduous trees and window overhangs or shades on the side facing the sun to block the high summer sun (Figure 18-3), (3) evaporative coolers in fairly dry climates, to remove heat when sunlight evaporates water, (4) earth pipes, buried 3 to 6 meters (10 to 20 feet) underground where the temperature remains around 13°C (55°F) all year long, to bring in cool and partially dehumidified air, and (5) a well-designed ventilation system to take advantage of breezes and to keep air moving continuously. According to some experts, the use of passive solar cooling and natural ventilation should make it possible to construct all but the largest buildings without air conditioning in most parts of the world.

Passive solar heating coupled with improving energy efficiency is also the best and cheapest way to retrofit existing buildings. This is very important, since even if all the homes and commercial structures built between 1980 and 2000 were solar buildings, they would make up only about one-third of the homes and buildings in the United States by the year 2000. Once an existing building has been made energy efficient, however, a passive solar greenhouse or sun space can be attached to the side facing the sun without replacing the existing wall. Vents can be cut in the existing wall, and a fan can be used to circulate the captured heat into the house. Such a greenhouse can be built at a low cost by a homeowner or can be bought in prefabricated form for about $2,000 to $3,000. Two other retrofit possibilities include creating a Trombe wall by adding glazing (glass or plastic) a few centimeters outside an existing masonry wall and adding simple window-box solar collectors, which can be built in a few hours for about $75 each, to all windows facing the sun.

In a typical *active solar heating system*, flat-plate solar collectors, evacuated tubes, or other even more efficient concentrators are mounted on the roof and angled to capture the sun's rays. A flat-plate collector typically consists of a shallow, rectangular box with a glass or other transparent lid and a dark bottom that absorbs solar radiation and converts it to heat. Then air or water (with antifreeze added in cold climates) is pumped through coils in the collector to transfer the trapped heat into the building's radiators and ducts. The heat may also be stored in a large bed of rocks or in an insulated hot water tank for release at night or in cloudy weather.

Active collector designs differ widely in cost, efficiency, and durability. Evacuated tube collectors, which can be twice as efficient and half as costly as flat-plate collectors, resemble fluorescent light bulbs and consist of blackened air-filled glass tubes enclosed in an outer tube from which the air has been evacuated. The vacuum operates as a perfect insulator, so the cold weather and high winds that reduce the efficiency of flat-plate collectors do not affect the tubes. Freezing is not a problem because air is used as the heat-transfer medium. These tubes can be mass produced in a highly automated factory, but they are fragile and easily broken.

Although the solar energy fuel is free, active solar heating systems require more materials to build the collectors, pipes, and storage systems than passive systems and thus have a lower net useful energy yield. They are also more expensive both initially and on a lifetime basis because they require more maintenance and because eventually collectors deteriorate and must be replaced. An active solar heating system for a moderate-sized American home costs from $5,000 to $12,000 in 1984. These costs, however, can be cut considerably by building a highly energy-efficient house (which cuts the solar system size five- to tenfold) and by having the collectors assembled at the building site instead of buying packaged collectors (cuts collector cost by a factor of 2 to 3). Active solar heating systems are economically feasible in much of the United States, however, when both lifetime costs and tax credits for installation (up to 70 percent of the cost) are considered.

To overcome the initial cost barrier several firms have begun leasing solar systems or selling the solar output to businesses and other clients. An Israeli firm has several 20-year multibillion dollar contracts to provide steam produced by highly efficient solar collectors for textile manufacturers in North Carolina and Georgia. A laundromat will save an estimated $165,000 in energy costs in 7 years by leasing solar collectors from a small southern California firm. The Tennessee Valley Authority (TVA) and several other U.S. utility companies provide low-interest loans and cash rebates to customers purchasing solar water and space heating systems,

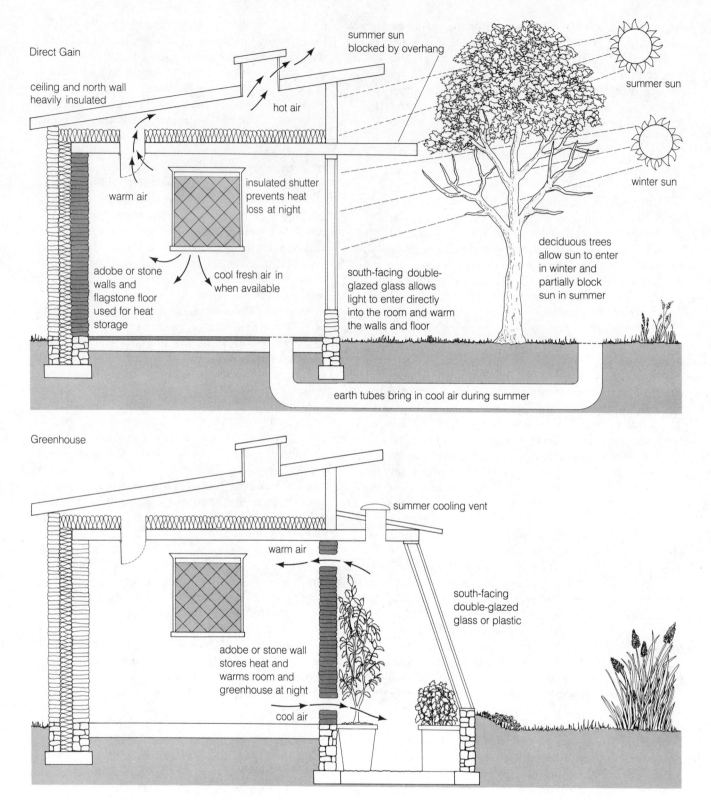

Direct Gain

ceiling and north wall heavily insulated

summer sun blocked by overhang

hot air

warm air

insulated shutter prevents heat loss at night

summer sun

winter sun

deciduous trees allow sun to enter in winter and partially block sun in summer

adobe or stone walls and flagstone floor used for heat storage

cool fresh air in when available

south-facing double-glazed glass allows light to enter directly into the room and warm the walls and floor

earth tubes bring in cool air during summer

Greenhouse

summer cooling vent

warm air

south-facing double-glazed glass or plastic

adobe or stone wall stores heat and warms room and greenhouse at night

cool air

Figure 16-3 Examples of passive solar design.

saving these companies hundreds of millions of dollars in power plant construction costs.

Active solar systems can also be used to provide air conditioning, which uses 20 percent of all primary energy expended to heat and cool buildings in the United States and half the electricity produced in some tropical LDCs. In 1983 an ice pond was used to cool the Prudential Life Insur-

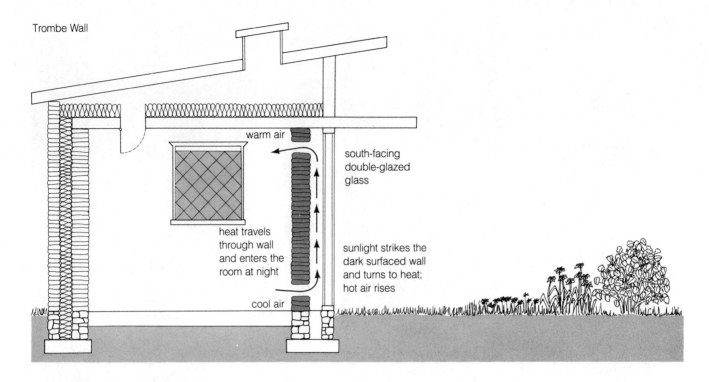

Trombe Wall

warm air

south-facing
double-glazed
glass

heat travels
through wall
and enters the
room at night

sunlight strikes the
dark surfaced wall
and turns to heat;
hot air rises

cool air

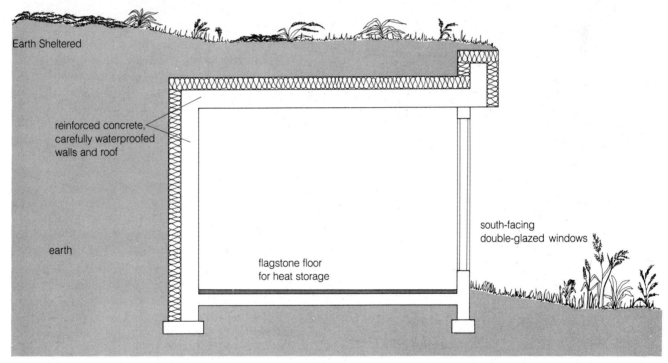

Earth Sheltered

reinforced concrete,
carefully waterproofed
walls and roof

earth

south-facing
double-glazed windows

flagstone floor
for heat storage

ance Company's large, energy-efficient office complex in Princeton, New Jersey, with a savings of at least $12,000 a year in electricity costs for conventional air conditioning. In the winter a snow maker, like those used by ski resorts, is used to build a large mountain of slush, which is stored in a pond-like basin under an insulated dome. As the slush slowly melts during the summer, the cold water is

pumped through the building's air conditioning system. See the summary table on p. 320.

Direct Solar Energy for Producing High-Temperature Heat You can use a magnifying glass to focus sunlight on a small area to produce temperatures high enough to ignite paper or wood chips. In ancient times the Greeks and the Chinese are

Figure 16-4 Solar I power tower used to generate electricity in the Mojave Desert near Barstow, California.

Direct Solar Energy for Producing High-Temperature Heat

Advantages

1. Energy supply free and readily available on sunny days.

2. Does not add carbon dioxide to the atmosphere.

3. Does not produce radioactive materials or materials that can be used to make nuclear weapons.

4. Operating costs probably low.

5. Air pollution and water pollution: fairly low to moderate, primarily from pollutants released during manufacture of the large amounts of materials used in construction of collectors, focusing heliostat mirrors, plumbing, and heat storage systems.

6. Possible large-scale disasters: depletion of water resources in arid regions with ample sunlight.

Disadvantages

1. Supply not available at night, necessitating the use of thermal storage systems or conventional backup systems.

2. Usefulness depends on availability of ample sunlight (usually in desert areas).

3. Commercial-scale technology still being developed.

4. Net useful energy expected to be moderate at best, and may be low.

5. Moderate to high construction costs.

6. Not versatile. Can be used only to produce electricity or high-temperature heat for industrial use.

7. Land disruption: moderate, from fairly large area required (Figure 16-4); could disrupt ecosystems if used in the desert on a large scale.

---

believed to have lit temple fires by means of parabolic mirrors. A modern system for concentrating direct solar energy to produce high-temperature heat for direct use or to produce electricity is called a **solar furnace** or a **power tower**.

The world's largest solar furnace, known as the Odeillo Furnace, has been in operation high in the Pyrenees Mountains in southern France since 1970. It contains a gigantic fixed parabolic mirror made up of 9,000 smaller mirrors. Facing it are 63 electronically controlled mirrors or *heliostats* (named after the Greek god of the sun, Helios) that swivel to follow the path of the sun throughout the day. The heliostats beam the sun's rays to specific parts of the fixed parabolic mirror, which focus the rays on a structure in front of the mirror to produce temperatures as high as 2,000°C (5,000°F)—hot enough to melt metals and sand! This solar furnace serves in the manufacture of pure metals and other substances, with the excess heat used to produce steam for spinning a turbine to generate electricity. The electricity not used at the plant is fed into the public utility grid. The cost of such an installation is very high, but unlike coal-fired and nuclear power plants it produces negligible pollution and no radioactive materials. Other smaller units are being tested in France, Italy, Spain, and Japan.

Two government-financed experimental solar power towers have been built in the United States to produce electricity, one in the Mojave Desert near Barstow, California, and the other in the desert near Albuquerque, New Mexico. At the Barstow plant, known as Solar I, 1,818 computer-controlled heliostats track the sun and focus its rays on a central receiver perched atop a 20-story tower and containing a boiler (Figure 16-4). The high-temperature heat is used to produce steam, which can be used to produce up to 10 megawatts of electricity. The next step may involve building a larger (100-megawatt)

Advantages	Disadvantages
1. Solar cells are reliable and quiet; they have no moving parts, need little maintenance (occasional washing to prevent dirt from blocking the sun's rays), and should last for 20 to 30 years if encased in glass or plastic. Most are made from silicon, the second most abundant element in the earth's crust.	1. Affordable commercial technology still being developed but is expected to be available within a few years.
2. Energy supply is free and readily available on sunny days.	2. Fuel supply not available at night and on overcast days, so storage and/or backup must be provided.
3. Does not add carbon dioxide to the atmosphere.	3. Initial construction and equipment costs are high. Operating costs are also high, but are expected to become competitive by mid-1990s.
4. Does not produce radioactive materials or materials that can be used to make nuclear weapons.	4. Moderate to low net useful energy yield.
5. If costs per kilowatt-hour drop as projected by the mid-1990s, lifetime costs should be lower than for electricity produced by conventional electric power plants.	5. Use may be limited eventually by supplies of expensive or rare elements such as gallium and cadmium used to produce some type of cells.
6. May allow individuals to disconnect from electric utility company or use power from utility only as a backup.	6. Use to produce electricity in large, centralized power plants depends on availability of ample sunlight, usually in desert areas.
7. Widespread use could eliminate need to build new coal-burning or nuclear electric power plants.	7. Widespread use could cause economic disruption from bankruptcy of utilities with unneeded large-scale power plants.
8. Fairly versatile: can be used to produce electricity on a small scale or large scale. Could be used to run vehicles if affordable technology developed to produce hydrogen gas from electricity generated by solar cells.	8. Cannot be used to power vehicles unless acceptable and affordable hydrogen-powered or electric cars are developed.
9. Air pollution: low, mostly from manufacture of cell materials; this requires burning only 1 to 3 percent as much coal as is needed to produce the same amount of electricity in a coal-fired power plant.	9. Water pollution: moderate without stringent controls because solar cell manufacture produces fairly large amounts of hazardous chemicals such as hydrofluoric acid and toxic compounds of arsenic, cadmium, tellurium, and selenium. (Enrichment Study 13).
10. Land disturbance: very low for roof-mounted systems; moderate for large-scale power plants, which could disrupt desert ecosystems if widely used.	10. Possible large-scale disasters: depletion of water supplies in arid regions with numerous big power plants; contamination of surface and groundwater supplies from accidents or inadequate control of toxic chemicals produced during manufacture of solar cells.

power tower plant. However, building and maintaining the complex of solar collectors, focusing mirrors, plumbing, and other materials reduces the net useful energy yield so much that such systems are projected to have low to moderate net useful energy yields. It remains to be seen whether they can produce electricity at costs competitive with hydro, wind, coal-burning, and conventional nuclear power plants. See the summary table on p. 326.

Using Photovoltaic Cells to Produce Electricity from Direct Solar Energy The earth's direct input of solar energy can be converted by **photovoltaic cells,** commonly called *solar cells,* directly into *electrical energy* in one simple, nonpolluting step. Expensive solar cells are already used to power satellites orbiting the earth (Enrichment Study 4) and to provide electricity for at least 12,000 homes worldwide (6,000 in the United States), located mostly in isolated areas where power companies charge a great deal to run electrical lines to individual dwellings.

A photovoltaic cell is based on the use of *semiconductors*—materials that conduct electricity—but only slightly. Each cell is made of two layers of semiconductor material containing highly purified silicon, separated by junctions. Light energy striking the silicon atoms knocks electrons free, producing a direct electric current (DC) with a voltage of about 0.45 volt for a typical cell as the electrons flow across the junctions between the two semiconductor layers (Figure 16-5). Because the voltage and current produced by a single cell are very small, many cells are wired together in a solar panel (Figure 16-5) to provide a generating capacity of 30 to about 100 watts. A number of these panels wired together can be mounted on a roof facing the sun (Figure 16-5), to produce electricity for a home or building. The resulting current can be used to power electric lights and most common appliances, which can be purchased to run on DC (like those found in recreational vehicles) or converted to alternating current (AC) by an inverter to power conventional lights and appliances.

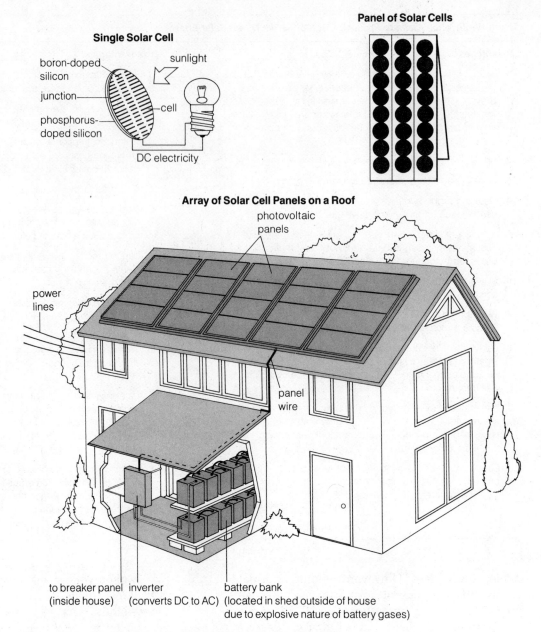

Single Solar Cell

boron-doped silicon

junction

phosphorus-doped silicon

sunlight

cell

DC electricity

Panel of Solar Cells

Array of Solar Cell Panels on a Roof

photovoltaic panels

power lines

panel wire

to breaker panel (inside house)

inverter (converts DC to AC)

battery bank (located in shed outside of house due to explosive nature of battery gases)

Figure 16-5 Use of photovoltaic or solar cells to provide electricity.

Companies are also developing designs in which solar cells can be built into the roof during construction, as well as a photovoltaic shingle that can be used as a roofing material. Solar electric systems can be installed in just a few hours in a properly designed and oriented house. Some of the electrical energy can be stored for use at night and on cloudy days in fairly long-lasting, rechargeable batteries (like those in boats and golf carts) or used to decompose water to produce hydrogen gas (H_2), which can be stored in a pressurized tank and burned in fuel cells (Section 16-6).

Several experimental photovoltaic electric power plants are also being built that use large banks of solar cells to track the sun. A government-financed 240-kilowatt solar-powered plant has been providing electricity for an airport near Phoenix, Arizona, since 1982. A similar system, financed jointly by the Saudi Arabian and U.S. governments, has been providing electricity for three Saudi villages since 1982. In 1983 a larger 1-megawatt photovoltaic electric power plant went into operation near Hesperia, California, and a 100-megawatt photovoltaic power plant near Sacramento is scheduled for completion in 1994 at an estimated cost of $250 million. At least a dozen similar projects are expected to be built in the next few years, mostly in the western United States and southern Europe where ample sunlight is available.

With about 60 percent of the world's population having no access to utility power grids, the worldwide market is expected to reach $10 billion by 2000, increasing even more rapidly thereafter. The key to such expansion in this industry lies in cost reduction. Some observers believe that solar cells will never become competitive with producing electricity by conventional means when the total costs of the system are included. But the U.S. Department of Energy and solar cell researchers and manufacturers in the United States and Japan project that solar cells should be a competitive electricity source almost everywhere by the mid-1990s through a combination of (1) raising the average efficiency of single-crystal silicon cells from 10 to 15 percent, (2) making cells directly from liquefied silicon (energy efficiency of 10 to 11 percent), (3) mass producing long rolls of cells made by spraying extremely thin films of amorphous (noncrystalline) silicon on thin stainless steel sheets (energy efficiency of about 8 percent*), (4) mass producing polycrystalline silicon cells (energy efficiency as high as 18 percent), (5) using concentrator systems to increase the amount of solar energy striking a solar cell 10 to 1,000 times, and (6) developing a new generation of nonsilicon solar cells from materials such as cadmium sulfide, gallium arsenide, and copper alloys (energy conversion efficiencies perhaps as high as 30 percent). Extensive use of the more efficient nonsilicon cells, however, might eventually be limited by the relative scarcity of cadmium and gallium.

Still another possibility is the development of *photoelectrochemical solar cells*, in which light falling on silicon or other electrodes immersed in a chemical solution can produce electricity. This energy can be "stored" by producing hydrogen gas from the decomposition of water (Section 16-6). By early 1984 such wet solar cells had been developed at the laboratory stage with efficiencies as high as 14 percent.

Once solar cells can produce electric power at a competitive price, they are likely to be introduced gradually over a 20-year period. Within a few years they should be in widespread use for water pumping and other electrical needs in rural villages in LDCs not attached to electrical grid systems. In the 1990s a number of centralized photovoltaic power stations could begin producing electricity at prices competitive with conventional systems in MDCs. Because of the large initial investment, solar cell installations in MDCs are then likely to be used to

provide much of the electricity for wealthy homeowners and commercial buildings. If prices continue to fall as projected, by 2000 or sooner solar power should be able to provide at least 25 percent of the electrical needs of a large, properly oriented all-electric new house, all the electricity for smaller, energy-efficient new houses, and 25 to 75 percent of the electricity in many existing homes. Most homeowners will probably use electricity from utilities as a backup.

Advocates of the hard-path energy strategy (Table 14-3) favor using solar cells primarily to produce electricity in large, centralized power plants and commercial installations. This appproach is being pushed by oil companies, which own most solar cell companies, and by utilities, which would be bankrupted if so many people began producing their own power that coal and nuclear power plants with net assets of over $300 billion no longer produced revenue. Some scientists have also proposed another hard-path approach: a series of satellites powered by millions of solar cells to collect direct solar energy in space, convert it to microwave radiation, and beam the radiation back to earth for collection and conversion to electricity at giant microwave antenna farms. This futuristic scheme is not presently technologically or economically feasible (Enrichment Study 4). Advocates of the soft-path energy strategy (Table 14-3) favor the widespread use of solar cells by individual homeowners and small community co-ops to free them from dependence on large, centralized power plants and powerful oil and utility companies.*

If all the projected uses of solar cells in hard- and soft-energy technologies take place, they could be providing 20 to 30 percent of the world's electricity by 2050. Given widespread use, no new large-scale power plants of any type would have to be built, and many existing plants, nuclear and other, could be phased out. See the summary table on p. 327.

16-2 Indirect Solar Energy from Falling Water and Ocean Waves

Hydroelectric Power Humans have used falling water as a source of energy for centuries. Water evaporated from bodies of water, land, and plants by energy from the sun returns to the earth as precipitation in the hydrologic cycle (Figure 4-12). As this water flows toward lower elevations, its grav-

---

*Until their efficiency can be improved, these cells are being used primarily in inexpensive pocket calculators and other low-power devices.

*Two of the increasing number of small companies that provide consultant advice and sell the components needed for photovoltaic systems are the Real Goods Trading Company, 308C East Perkins, Ukiah, CA 95482 (catalog $3.50 in 1984), and Alternative Energy Engineering, Box 339, Briceland Road, Redway, CA 95560.

itational potential energy—an indirect or stored form of solar energy—is converted into the kinetic energy of flowing streams and rivers. This kinetic energy can turn waterwheels, which can grind grain, drive machinery, or spin turbines to produce electricity.

To produce hydroelectricity (*hydropower*), a dam is built across a stream or river to create a storage reservoir providing a year-round supply of water. Most storage reservoirs can also be used for recreational activities such as boating and fishing. Water from the reservoir is allowed to flow at controlled rates to spin turbines as it falls to the river below the dam. Although the energy contained in falling and flowing water is theoretically a renewable resource (Table 14-1), all hydroelectric power dams have finite lives, typically ranging from 30 to 300 years, because their reservoirs eventually fill with silt.

Falling water can also be used in *pumped storage systems* to provide supplemental power during times of peak electrical demand. Pumps are used to transfer water from a lake or reservoir to one or more specially built pumped-storage reservoir at a higher elevation—usually on a mountain. When a power company temporarily needs more electricity than can be provided by its conventional hydro, coal-fired, or nuclear plants, water in the upper reservoir(s) is released and passed through turbines to generate electricity as it returns to the lower reservoir. Such a system, however, is costly and has a low net useful energy yield because of the electricity needed to pump water up to the high reservoir. Utility companies are finding that peak power demands can be met at much lower cost by loaning their customers money for making improvements that will conserve electricity at low or zero interest rates.

In 1983 hydropower supplied about one-fourth of the world's electricity—twice that from nuclear power—and about 5 percent of the world's total primary energy (Figure 14-2). Among renewable energy resources, only wood presently makes a larger contribution. The United States leads the world in the production of hydroelectric power, although other industrialized nations including the Soviet Union, Canada, Japan, France, Norway, Switzerland, and Austria generate large amounts of electricity from falling water. Norway, for example, uses hydropower to provide 99 percent of its electricity and 50 percent of all its primary energy. By tapping the headwaters of Alpine rivers, Switzerland produces most of its electricity and even sells some to neighboring France and Italy. The United Nations estimates that 44 percent of the much smaller amount of electricity used in the LDCs comes from hydropower.

The potential for increased development of hydropower varies throughout the world. The smallest potential is in Europe, where 59 percent of the estimated hydropower potential has been developed, and in North America (especially the United States), with 36 percent of its potential exploited. In these areas most of the best major hydroelectric sites have already been developed. By contrast, the LDCs, with close to half the world's hydroelectric potential, have developed only about 9 percent of this resource.

The Worldwatch Institute estimates that projects already being constructed or in the planning stages will double the output of electricity from hydropower between 1980 and 2000. By 2000 this could provide an estimated 8 percent of the world's primary energy (Figure 14-2) and perhaps 40 to 50 percent of its electricity, depending on demand. China, with one-tenth of the world's hydropower potential, will probably become the world's largest producer of hydroelectricity. Work has begun at a site on the Yangtze River that will probably be the world's biggest dam, capable of producing electricity equal to that from 25 large 1,000-megawatt nuclear or coal-fired power plants. This project, however, will force 2 million people to leave their homes. American, Canadian, and Soviet planners have even more grandiose visions of damming and reversing the flow of giant rivers such as the Yukon, MacKenzie, Ob, and Lena, which now flow into the Arctic, to provide freshwater supplies and electricity (Section 17-4).

Environmental impact and displacement of people can be reduced sharply by developing small-scale hydroelectric plants on small rivers near villages and other populated areas, as has been done throughout much of China and to some extent in Nepal, Peru, and several African nations. Unfortunately, such small-scale hydroelectric development projects have received little support from international aid programs and international lending agencies and banks.

Major lending institutions tend to favor development of large-scale, politically visible, showcase projects because **(1)** much of the loaned money is used to purchase engineering and construction services, generators, turbines, and other equipment from corporations in MDCs, and **(2)** such projects can generate a steady, predictable flow of income by selling power to energy-intensive factories owned by multinational corporations. However, the energy-intensive industries that locate near large dams seldom provide many jobs for unskilled local residents, and the power generated is often transmitted to distant cities, leaving most villages along the way without any electricity.

In the United States hydroelectric capacity more than doubled between 1950 and 1983 and in 1983 provided about 13 percent of the electricity and about

Hydropower: Producing Electricity from Falling Water

Advantages

1. Technology well developed.

2. Large untapped potential in many LDCs; but many sites are in remote locations, far from point of use.

3. High energy-conversion efficiency (75 to 90 percent) and moderate to high net useful energy yield for conventional hydropower systems.

4. Long life (typically 30 to 300 years) before reservoirs fill with silt.

5. Free fuel (running water).

6. Fairly low operating and maintenance costs.

7. Does not add carbon dioxide to the atmosphere.

8. Does not produce radioactive materials or materials that can be used to make nuclear weapons.

9. Reservoirs (except those for pumped storage systems) typically behind dams can be used for boating and fishing.

10. Can provide a regulated flow of irrigation water for crops below the dam.

11. Flood control in areas below dam.

12. Electrification of rural villages in LDCs.

13. Hydropower production in the United States could be increased at a moderate cost and with low environmental impact by putting thousands of abandoned small- to medium-sized dams and plants back into service and by increasing the capacity and improving the efficiency of many existing large hydroelectric power plants.

14. Air pollution: low, with essentially no emissions of health-threatening air pollutants during operation; air pollution during construction comparable to that from a coal-fired or nuclear power plant of similar size.

Disadvantages

1. High construction costs.

2. Not versatile. Can be used to produce electricity and grind grain.

3. Low net useful energy yield for pumped-storage systems.

4. Most suitable rivers for large-scale hydropower projects in the United States and Europe have already been developed or are protected from development for environmental reasons.

5. Disruption of the lives of people who live behind potential dam sites.

6. Barrier to upstream fish migration for some species and decline of fishing industries below the dam.

7. Increased dependence of LDCs on MDCs from borrowing the money to finance expensive hydropower projects.

8. Increased waterborne diseases among people living and working in irrigated land below the dam (Enrichment Study 7).

9. Water pollution: moderate, potential for greatly increased soil erosion and sediment pollution near reservoir above the dam without careful planning and proper controls.

10. Land disruption: high, due to flooding of large areas of farmland, wildlife habitats, mineral deposits, timber areas, and historical and archaeological sites above the dam and alteration of ecosystems below the dam.

11. Possible large-scale disasters: although highly unlikely, rupture of a large dam accidentally or by sabotage could kill several hundred thousand people living below the dam and cause massive property losses.

---

5 percent of the total primary energy used (Figure 14-3). Most large-scale U.S. hydroelectric projects are concentrated in the Southeast and the Northwest in areas with ample rainfall and high elevations. Because most of the sites suitable for large-scale dams in the United States either have been used or are located on rivers protected from development by the Wild and Scenic Rivers Act of 1968 (Section 10-3), hydroelectric power is projected to supply about 5 percent of the nation's primary energy in 2000—the same percentage as in 1983 (Figure 14-3).

In many locales, however, the fraction of electricity supplied by hydropower is being increased by putting some of the nation's 50,000 abandoned small- and medium-sized hydroelectric dams and power plants back into service. According to a study by the Corps of Engineers, over 5,100 of these abandoned dams could be put to use, supplying electricity equal to that from 6 to 24 large 1,000-megawatt nuclear or coal-fired power plants. The environmental impact from rehabilitating these existing dams is often small and does not require any new technology. Once rebuilt, such units have a long life, need minimal operating crews, and require little maintenance.

Between 1976 and 1983 there were about 4,500 applications to the Federal Energy Regulatory Commission for permits to produce power from small hydroelectric sites in the United States. Most of the applications have been made by private individuals and small companies, which can make a considerable profit (averaging about 20 to 40 percent annually) by (1) receiving large tax benefits and reduced regulatory burdens from the federal government and (2) selling surplus electricity to utility companies. However, there has been growing opposition by local residents and environmentalists, who feel that some small-scale hydro projects are environmentally harmful.

Another way to increase the use of hydropower in the United States at a relatively low cost and low environmental impact is to upgrade the power-generating capacity of many existing dams by adding new or more efficient generators and in some cases slightly increasing reservoir size. Such upgrading could supply electricity equivalent to that from 46 large 1,000-megawatt coal-fired or nuclear power plants. However, since the federal government owns most of these dams, developing this potential would require the government to provide the funds or allow the dams to be developed by private firms.

The advantages and disadvantages of hydropower are summarized in the table on p. 331.

Indirect Renewable Solar Energy from Ocean Waves Wave energy is derived from wind energy, which in turn is derived from direct solar energy. Capturing this energy has been a dream since at least 1799, when two Frenchmen patented a wave power device. Today research is under way, especially in Japan, Norway, France, and Great Britain,

---

Indirect Solar Energy from Ocean Waves

Advantages

1. Source of energy is free.

2. Does not add carbon dioxide to the atmosphere.

3. Does not produce radioactive materials or materials that can be used to make nuclear weapons.

4. Air pollution: very low, with essentially no pollutants emitted during operation.

5. Land disruption: very low, since plants would be floating on the ocean with only electrical transmission lines located on land.

6. Possible large-scale disasters: none.

Disadvantages

1. Available only near coastal areas with waves of sufficient height.

2. Electrical output varies because of differences in wave height at different times.

3. High construction and operating costs.

4. Technology in early state of development.

5. Low net useful energy yield.

6. Output disrupted and equipment damaged or destroyed by saltwater corrosion and severe storms.

7. Not versatile. Used primarily to produce electricity.

8. Widespread use could interfere with ocean shipping.

9. Water pollution: moderate, large-scale use could disrupt ocean aquatic life, and chemicals used for cleaning and prevention of buildup of algae and barnacles could contaminate the water.

---

to harness the mechanical energy of wave motion and convert it into electricity or perhaps hydrogen gas fuel (Section 16-6).

Most wave power devices presently being tested involve using submerged-tubes or floating buoys having pneumatic systems that use the mechanical energy from the up-and-down motion created by passing waves to compress air or hydraulic fluids. This extracted mechanical energy can then spin a turbine to produce electricity. Another system being tested in Norway involves concentrating wave energy with a "wave lens," for more ready conversion to mechanical energy by a pneumatic system. The lens consists of a submerged cylinder that changes the direction of a series of waves so that they meet at a focal point.

So far none of these experiments has led to the production of electricity at an affordable price. But some scientists believe that with sufficient research and development, wave power could supply electricity cleanly and safely at a competitive price during the 1990s. Other scientists, however, doubt that wave power will ever be a significant source of primary energy because of the disadvantages listed in the summary table at left.

16-3 Indirect Solar Energy from Thermal Gradients in Oceans and Solar Ponds

Ocean Thermal Gradients The world's oceans collect and store solar energy. This results in **thermal gradients**—the temperature differences between sun-warmed, surface waters and cold, ocean depths where the sun's rays do not penetrate. In tropical areas where the surface water is at least 27°C (80°F), the temperature difference between surface water and deep water 0.8 kilometer (0.5 mile) below is large enough to permit the extraction of sufficient heat to produce electricity using a large floating *ocean thermal energy conversion (OTEC)* power plant (Figure 16-6). Some 62 nations, mostly LDCs, have national or territorial waters capable of supporting an OTEC plant. For the United States, favorable sites include portions of the Gulf of Mexico and offshore areas near southern California and the islands of Puerto Rico, Hawaii, and Guam.

A full-scale OTEC plant would be a gigantic floating platform with massive pipes 30 meters (100 feet) in diameter reaching down as far as 900 meters (3,000 feet) to the ocean bottom. In a typical plant, warm surface water would be pumped though a large heat exchanger and used to convert a low-boiling fluid such as ammonia, Freon, or propane to a vapor (Figure 16-6). As the vapor expanded, it would cause a turbine to turn, generating electricity. The vapor would pass through another heat

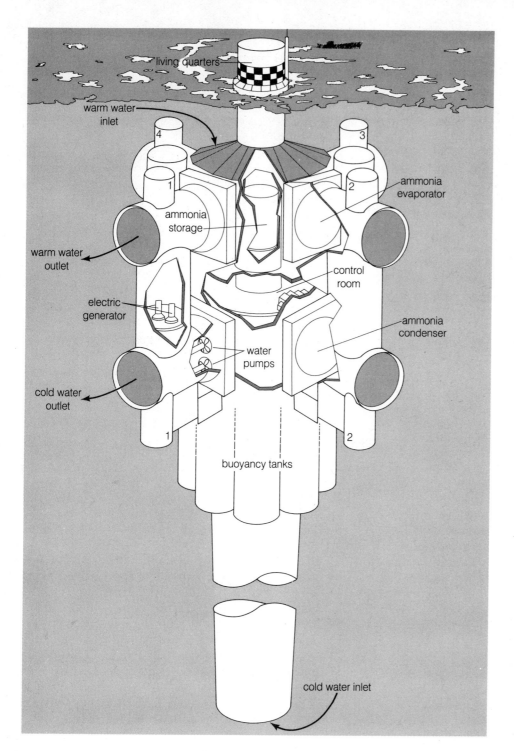

Figure 16-6 Possible design of a large-scale ocean thermal electric plant (OTEC) for generating electricity from the temperature gradient in a tropical ocean.

living quarters

warm water inlet

4

3

1

2

ammonia evaporator

ammonia storage

warm water outlet

control room

electric generator

ammonia condenser

water pumps

cold water outlet

1

2

buoyancy tanks

cold water inlet

exchanger, to be cooled by cold water pumped from the ocean's depths and recondensed to the liquid state. Then the liquid would be pumped back to the first heat exchanger for the entire cycle to begin again. The pumps in a moderate-sized 250-megawatt plant would have to be capable of pumping water *each second* greater than the average flow rate of the Mississippi River. A large cable might transmit the electricity to shore, or the plant could use its electricity to desalinate ocean water and extract

minerals and chemicals from the sea or to electrolyze water to produce hydrogen gas, which could be piped or transported to shore for use as a fuel (Section 16-6).

Advocates of this approach believe that with enough research and development funding, large-scale OTEC plants could be built within 5 to 10 years, to produce electricity equivalent to that from 10 large 1,000-megawatt coal-fired or nuclear power plants by the year 2000. Congress passed legislation

Advantages

1. Source of energy is free.

2. Does not require costly energy storage and backup system.

3. Essentially infinite supply at favorable sites.

4. Does not produce radioactive materials or materials that can be used to make nuclear weapons.

5. Nutrients brought up when water is pumped from the ocean bottom might nourish schools of fish and shellfish.

6. Air pollution: low, with essentially no pollutants emitted during normal operation.

7. Land disruption: very low, since plants would be floating on the ocean with only electrical transmission lines located on land.

8. Possible large-scale disasters; collision hazard for ocean vessels.

Disadvantages

1. Technology for large-scale plants and ways to transmit electricity to shore in rough seas still in early stages of development.

2. Construction costs two to three times those of comparable coal-fired plants; high operating and maintenance costs, primarily from seawater corrosion of metal parts and fouling of the heat exchangers by algae and barnacles (which must be scraped off once a week).

3. Low net useful energy yield for the entire system because of a low energy-conversion efficiency (2 to 3 percent), energy losses during transmission of electricity to the shore, and use of one-third of the energy produced by the plant to pump enormous amounts of water through the plant.

4. Only available in certain tropical ocean sites; most good sites located far offshore and far from population centers where electricity is needed.

5. Damage from tropical cyclones (hurricanes and typhoons) that periodically sweep tropical seas.

6. Possible climate alteration from withdrawal of large amounts of heat from tropical waters and warm-water currents such as the Gulf Stream, and the release of dissolved carbon dioxide gas into the atmosphere when large volumes of deep ocean water are pumped to the surface (Enrichment Study 5).

7. Not versatile: useful primarily for producing electricity.

8. Entrapment and killing of marine organisms in cold-water intake.

9. Potentially harmful changes in the ecology of ocean areas near plants.

10. Water pollution: moderate, from release of antifouling chemicals and working fluids and possible disruption of local ocean ecosystems from large-scale pumping of water from the ocean bottom to the surface and back.

---

in 1980 setting up $2 billion in loan guarantees to underwrite the development of commercial OTEC plants by 2000. Despite large research expenditures by the United States and Japan and the enthusiasm of OTEC experts, many energy analysts believe that large-scale extraction of energy from ocean thermal gradients may never compete economically with other energy alternatives because of the problems listed in the summary table above.

Solar Ponds The thermal gradient between the surface and bottom waters in relatively shallow salt-water seas such as the Dead Sea, and shallow salt-water solar ponds constructed inland, can be used to generate electricity. A **solar pond** is a highly efficient collector of solar energy consisting of at least 0.5 hectare (1 acre) of relatively shallow water [typically about 4.6 to 6 meters (15 to 20 feet) deep] with a layer of saline water on the bottom and a less saline layer on top. When the sun shines on a body of fresh water, heat absorbed by the deep layers on the bottom rises to the surface, where it quickly dissipates. In a solar pond, however, the higher-salinity lower layer has a higher density or mass per unit volume, hence does not rise to the surface when heated. As a result, heat accumulates in the bottom layer. In the Dead Sea, there is a 50°C (90°F)

difference between the lower and upper layers, with the temperature of the bottom layer varying from 80 to 95°C (180 to 210°F).

The solar energy so stored can be used to produce electricity using the same approach as in tapping the thermal gradient in the ocean (OTEC). In this case, however, the hot brine solution at the bottom of the sea or pond is pumped to the surface and used to vaporize a low-boiling working liquid such as ammonia or Freon. As in an OTEC plant, the vapor spins a turbine to generate electricity and is recondensed to the liquid state by passage through a heat exchanger cooled with the colder upper layer of the pond. An experimental solar pond power plant on the Israeli side of the Dead Sea has been operating successfully for several years. By 2000, Israel plans to build a cluster of plants around the Dead Sea to provide most of the electricity it needs for air conditioning and desalinating water.

Artificial solar ponds probably can be built near most desert areas in parts of Africa and the United States by using a dried lake bed or by digging out an area of 0.5 hectare (1 acre) or more, lining the sides with a black plastic or other material to absorb heat and raise the temperature of the water, adding lots of salt, and providing a turbine generator and electric transmission lines. Several small research

Indirect Solar Energy from Solar Ponds

Advantages

1. See items 1, 2, 3, 4, 6, and 8 for ocean thermal gradients.

2. Moderate net useful energy yield.

3. Moderate construction and operating costs.

4. Fairly low maintenance (e.g. plastic liner repair; replacement and periodic injections of brine at the bottom and fresh water at the top of the pond).

5. Stores heat for longer periods than the open ocean.

6. Unlikely to be battered by typhoons and hurricanes, like OTEC plants.

Disadvantages

1. Primarily feasible only near desert areas with ample sunlight.

2. Technology for large-scale projects still being developed.

3. Not versatile. Useful primarily for producing electricity.

4. Corrosion of pipes and heat exchangers by salty water.

5. Leaching of metals and salts from unlined dry seabeds by the concentrated salt solution, which turns the gradient dark and prevents sunlight from reaching the bottom of the pond.

6. Water pollution: moderate; breaks in plastic liners could allow concentrated saline solution to leak out, killing plants and contaminating groundwater supplies.

7. Land disruption: moderate to fairly high; fairly large areas of land would be disrupted, harming desert ecosystems.

solar ponds have been built in the United States. A slightly larger $100 million experimental 12-megawatt solar pond, being built in a dry lake bed in San Bernadino County about 280 kilometers (175 miles) east of Los Angeles, should go into operation in 1985. Solar pond enthusiasts project that with adequate research and development support, they could supply 3 to 4 percent of the nation's primary energy needs by the year 2000, twice the amount projected for wind power, if the problems listed in the summary table above can be overcome.

16-4 Indirect Solar Energy from Wind

Brief History of Wind Use Wind energy is produced by the unequal heating of the earth's surface and atmosphere by about 2 percent of the solar energy reaching the earth. Wind is then given characteristic flow patterns by the earth's rotation (Figure 3-3). Prevailing winds have been used for centuries to propel ships, grind grain, pump water, and produce electricity (by windmill).

In the early 1900s nearly 6 million multivaned windmills pumped water and generated electricity in rural areas throughout the United States. By the 1940s cheap hydropower, fossil fuels, and rural electrification distribution systems replaced many windmills, but worldwide there are about 1 million mechanical wind pumps in use, mostly providing water for livestock in Argentina, Australia, and the United States. In the 1950s the promise of cheap nuclear power (Section 15-5) caused the United States to abandon the development of wind turbines to produce electricity—a trend that is presently being reversed at a rapid pace.

Wind Power Today Today's wind machines range from simple water-pumping devices made of cloth and wood to large wind turbines with blade spans up to 100 meters (328 feet). With blades of wood, metal, or fiber glass, these modern wind turbines are stronger and lighter than older models.

In countries such as the United States modern wind turbines are being used by individual homeowners to provide most, if not all, of their electricity and by small private companies and utilities in *wind farms* consisting of clusters of up to several hundred wind turbines connected to an electric grid to generate power commercially. To develop a wind farm, a private company (1) goes wind prospecting for appropriate sites, (2) does wind studies, (3) arranges to buy or lease the land, (4) negotiates with utilities to get a fair price for the electricity to be produced, (5) lines up investors, who will receive tax credits as well as a share of any profits from the sale of the electricity, (6) erects the wind machines (usually within 2 to 3 years), and (7) begins producing electricity.

Other countries conducting wind power research and projected to make increasing use of wind energy include Denmark, Canada, Argentina, Great Britain, the Netherlands, Sweden, West Germany, Australia, and the Soviet Union (with 5,000 wind turbines in operation by the end of 1983). A "sun city" powered with wind and direct solar energy is being built in the Soviet Union and will house more than 300 scientists.

Suitable sites for using larger and more efficient wind turbines to capture energy from the wind must have fairly steady and moderate winds—neither weak (which produces too little useful energy) nor strong (which could damage the rotors). The minimum average annual wind speed normally practical for a small home wind system is about 16 to 19 kilometers (10 to 12 miles) per hour. Larger wind turbines are designed to operate at wind speeds between 17 and 58 kilometers (10 to 35 miles) per hour.

Wind Power

Advantages

1. Wind is an almost unlimited, free, and safe source of energy that can be tapped almost continuously at favorable sites.

2. Technology is fairly well developed and improving rapidly.

3. Modern wind turbines are about 20 to 30 percent efficient (high compared with most other energy-conversion technologies) and have a moderate net useful energy yield for the entire system. Most wind turbines generate as much energy as is needed for their manufacture in less than 5 years—much quicker than most nonrenewable technologies and most other renewable solar technologies.

4. Wind turbines have low material requirements and can be put into use much quicker than large-scale coal-fired, hydroelectric, and nuclear power plants.

5. Homeowners or small communities and companies with wind generators in the United States can buy electricity from the utilities when the wind dies down and can automatically deliver and sell excess electricity to utilities when the wind comes up, under provisions of PURPA.

6. Does not add carbon dioxide to the atmosphere.

7. Does not produce radioactive materials or materials that can be used to make nuclear weapons.

8. Air and water pollution: low; the manufacture and use of wind systems produces less air and water pollution than other renewable and nonrenewable energy alternatives.

9. Possible large-scale disasters: none, as long as wind farms are located far enough from heavily populated areas to prevent injuries from occasional blade loss.

Disadvantages

1. Can be used only in areas with sufficient winds.

2. Requires backup electricity from utility company or fairly expensive energy storage system (batteries, pumped-water storage, hydrogen production, or a spinning flywheel) when wind dies down.

3. Possible visual pollution similar to that from today's large electrical transmission lines (from farms of large turbines, towers, and transmission lines dotting the landscape), especially in wind-rich scenic areas.

4. Without proper design, low-frequency noise pollution, inaudible vibrations, and possible interference with local television reception and microwave communications.

5. Widespread use of wind farms might cause interference with migratory-bird flight patterns.

6. Possible blade loss will limit their use in densely populated areas.

7. Initial costs moderate to high and operating costs still fairly high, but technological improvements and mass production should give wind farms an economic advantage over coal-fired and nuclear power plants in the United States and many other parts of the world by the 1990s (Table 15-6).

8. Not versatile: used primarily for producing electricity and moving sailing vessels.

9. Land disturbance: moderate; a wind farm producing the same amount of electricity as a 1,000-megawatt conventional power plant requires at least 500 large wind turbines typically occupying about 82 square kilometers (32 square miles). However, estimates by the Worldwatch Institute indicate that wind-rich countries should be able to get up to half their electricity from wind machines occupying no more than 1 percent of their land area.

Figure 16-7 shows the general feasibility for using wind energy in the continental United States, excluding Alaska and Hawaii, which contain some of the world's best wind areas. There are many locally favorable exceptions to this generalized map, including hilltops that do not have air turbulence, mountain passes, some coastal areas, lakeside sites, and unobstructed areas on flat, windy plains. A 1980 study by the Solar Energy Research Institute (SERI) indicated that 3.8 million homes and hundreds of thousands of farms in the United States are located in areas having sufficient wind speeds to make use of small wind generators.

Small 3- to 5-kilowatt wind turbines costing from $5,000 to $20,000 completely installed, but with no power storage system, could be the first energy technology that allows a significant number of individuals in favorable wind areas to generate all their own power at an affordable cost. This fairly high initial cost can be reduced by the 40 to 70 percent tax credits now available from the federal government and in some states. Further savings can be

obtained by using reconditioned wind turbines. One do-it-yourself system using wooden propellers and a car alternator salvaged from a junkyard cost only $75 to build, excluding the homeowner's labor.

Additional savings can be made by selling surplus electricity to the local power company and using the electricity produced at night (when home needs are low) to recharge the batteries in an electric car. The Public Utilities Regulatory Policies Act (PURPA) of 1978 requires electric utilities to buy excess electricity from customers who develop wind, hydro, geothermal, solar, biomass, cogeneration, and other small-scale power producing systems at a fair price (i.e., equal to what the utility saves by not having to produce the electricity). The economic break-even point for wind power will drop sharply as electricity prices rise and projected technological improvements and mass production reduce the initial costs of wind systems.

After a slow start, *wind energy* is turning out to be one of the energy success stories of the 1980s in the United States. Its momentum has been slowed,

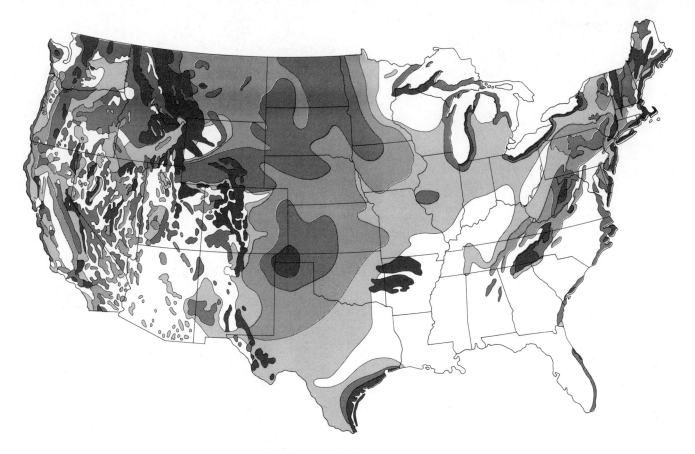

Figure 16-7 General areas of greatest wind energy potential in the United States (excluding Alaska and Hawaii, which contain some of the world's best wind areas). The darker the shading, the more wind power available. There are numerous local exceptions to the general information shown on this map. (Source: U.S. Department of Energy.)

however, by a drastic cut in federal wind energy research and development funds between 1980 and 1984. Blessed with windy mountain passes and other favorable sites, and aided by federal tax incentives and state tax credits for wind farm investors, California had at least 65 wind farms using 5,000 wind turbines by mid-1984 (enough to meet the electrical needs of about 40,000 households) and expects to get 8 percent of its electricity from wind power by 2000. By mid-1984 wind farms had been built or were under construction in Vermont, New Hampshire, Montana, Oregon, and Hawaii, and over 175 U.S. utility companies had wind energy programs.

Improved, mass-produced wind machines are projected to be able to produce electricity in the 1990s cheaper than coal and nuclear power plants in the United States and many other parts of the world (Table 15-6). Wind turbine manufacturers argue that mass production could begin now, given a guarantee of enough government orders to reduce the financial risks to investors.

Other observers believe that building large-scale wind systems to produce large quantities of elec-

tricity is not the way to go, since excess electricity is already being produced. Some of these analysts think that developing sophisticated moderate-sized 10- to 50-kilowatt wind turbines to be shared by a small community or group of homeowners makes more economic sense. Small- and intermediate-sized wind turbines are easier to mass produce, and their small rotors are less vulnerable to the stress and metal fatigue that make large wind turbines expensive to build and maintain. In addition, small windmills can produce more power in light winds than large ones, hence can operate a greater percentage of the time. They are also easier to locate close to the ultimate users (thus reducing electricity transmission costs) and they allow greater decentralization of ownership and control, as favored by advocates of the soft energy path (Section 14-1).

Wind Power in the Future The Worldwatch Institute estimates that a combination of wind farms and smaller wind machines used by individual homeowners, farmers, and businesses and occupying 0.5 percent of the world's land *could* provide 20 to 30

Figure 16-8 Major types of biomass fuel.

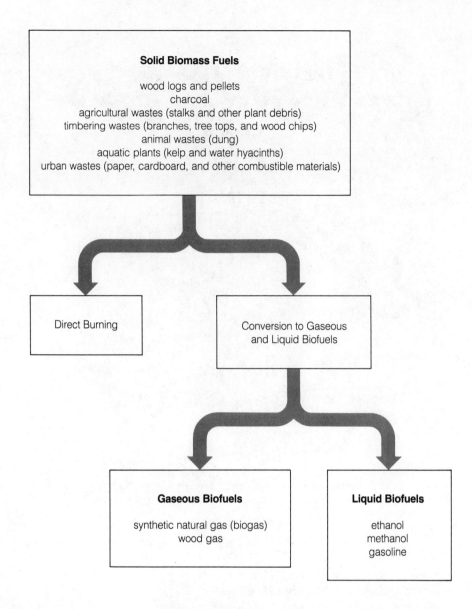

---

percent of the electricity needs of many countries and about 12 percent of the world's electricity. Wind experts estimate that with a vigorous development program, wind energy could provide 13 to 19 percent of the projected demand for electricity in the United States by 2000.

Wind power expert William E. Heronemus suggests that a band of about 300,000 to 1 million giant wind turbines in the high-wind belt from Texas to the Dakotas could provide half the annual electrical needs of the United States. For the heavily populated eastern seaboard, these huge wind turbines could float on offshore platforms, with the electricity produced either transmitted to shore or used to produce hydrogen gas from the electrolysis of seawater, which could be transported to shore in special tankers or perhaps by pipeline for use as fuel for homes, factories, and cars. Heronemus believes that enough hydrogen could be produced to supply all the heating needs of the industrial Northeast. A

1980 study by the National Swedish Board for Energy Source Development concluded that offshore wind turbines are both technically and economically feasible. Such widespread use of wind power is possible only with massive private and government-funded research and development programs that will lead to the mass production of highly reliable wind machines and ensure the social, economic, and environmental acceptability of wind power.

See the summary table on p. 336.

16-5 Indirect Solar Energy from Biomass

Biomass Fuel *Biomass fuel* is organic matter that can be burned directly as fuel or converted to a more convenient gaseous or liquid form known as *biofuel* by processes such as fermentation and pyrolysis (heating in the absence of air) (Figure 16-8). In 1983 energy from biomass, mostly from the direct

Indirect Solar Energy from Wood, Crop Wastes, Timbering Wastes, and Animal Wastes

Advantages

1. Versatile. Can be tapped as needed either by direct burning or by conversion to gas or liquid biofuels that can be used for producing heat and electricity or to power vehicles.

2. When collected and burned directly and efficiently near its source, biomass has a moderate to high net useful energy yield. Yields are low for some forms of biomass such as aquatic plants (which must be dried), urban wastes, and some crop wastes when the biomass must be collected in areas of sparse plant growth and then transported long distances for use.

3. As long as trees and plants, which use carbon dioxide in photosynthesis, are not cut faster than they grow back, burning biomass and biofuels will not add to the net amount of carbon dioxide in the atmosphere.

4. Technology is well developed.

5. Moderate costs, but may be high for aquatic plants and urban waste.

6. Unlimited supply in areas with adequate forests and replanting programs. Moderate to large supplies of urban wastes in heavily populated areas without large-scale recycling programs (Section 13-3).

7. Does not produce radioactive materials or materials that can be used to make nuclear weapons.

8. Burning urban wastes decreases need for solid waste disposal (Enrichment Study 13).

9. Possible large-scale disasters: none.

Disadvantages

1. Without adequate reforestation, large-scale use of wood for fuel causes deforestation, soil erosion, siltation, flooding, and loss of wildlife habitat.

2. Because wood has a much lower energy content per unit of weight than coal, oil, or natural gas, large quantities must be burned to get the amount of energy provided by a much smaller quantity of fossil fuel. Wood also contains a lot of water that must be removed by drying, often by burning fossil fuels.

3. Wood-burning stoves increase the chances of home fires.

4. Whole-tree removal and removal of forest, crop, and animal wastes for burning or conversion to biofuels could hinder recycling, deplete the soil of valuable plant nutrients, and cause increased soil erosion.

5. Burning urban wastes hinders recycling of paper and other recyclable materials.

6. Widespread use of energy plantations could lead to competition with food crops for prime farmland, possibly raising food prices.

7. Air pollution: moderate, because without adequate air pollution control, wood burning and the burning of urban wastes can create public health problems from the soot, small particles, and cancer-causing substances emitted into the air. However, because biomass and biofuels are low in sulfur, they cause less air pollution from sulfur dioxide than the burning of coal and oil.

8. Water pollution: moderate to high, because unless done with great care, intensive tree farming could pollute water with sediments from soil erosion and runoff of fertilizers and pesticides.

9. Land disturbance: moderate to high, because of deforestation if adequate replanting not ensured, and large land requirements for energy plantations.

---

burning of wood and animal wastes to heat buildings and cook food, supplied about 11 percent of the world's primary energy; by 2000 biomass (including biofuels) is expected to provide 15 percent of the world's primary energy (Figure 14-2).

In the United States biomass provided 91 percent of all primary energy from wood burning in 1850, but only 3.5 percent in 1983—about the same as that from nuclear power (Figure 14-3). By 2000 biomass (including biofuels) is expected to exceed the energy produced by nuclear power, providing about 11 percent of the nation's primary energy.

Wood, Crop Wastes, Timbering Wastes, and Animal Wastes   Today wood is the most widely used renewable energy source, being the primary source of energy for cooking and heating for about 42 percent of the world's population and for 80 percent of

all people in LDCs. The heavy use of wood in LDCs results primarily because only about only one village out of seven in LDCs has electricity, and most of the poor have been unable to afford fossil fuels since the oil price rises of the 1970s. However, in many LDCs there are shortages of firewood because of deforestation (Section 10-6). According to UN estimates, by 1981 more than 100 million people were not able to get enough firewood to meet minimum needs, and another 1 billion people had insufficient firewood. By the year 2000, the United Nations projects that over 2 billion people will live in areas with inadequate firewood supplies.

In MDCs with adequate forest reserves, the use of wood for heating homes and for producing heat and steam in industrial boilers is increasing rapidly because of price rises in heating oil and electricity. The use of wood in U.S. industries has been rising for decades and accounted for 60 percent of wood energy consumption in 1982, with homes and small businesses burning the rest.

The U.S. pulp and paper industry obtains over half its energy needs by burning pellets made from bark, branches, roots, and diseased trees left over from timber and pulp operations. The wood products industry now gets about 70 percent of its energy from burning wood wastes. Some of these companies are supplying nearby industries and communities with cogenerated power produced from wood burning. A few utilities in heavily forested states such as Vermont have begun retrofitting coal-fired power plants to burn wood pellets. By 1990 at least 25 U.S. utility plants are expected to be burning wood.

By 1983 one out of every five U.S. households was heated entirely (4.6 million households) or partially (10 million households) with wood, and the number is increasing by about 1 million a year. Fireplaces, which are typically only 10 percent efficient, can remove more heat from a home than they add because unless the room with the fireplace is carefully sealed off from the rest of the house, as the heat goes up the chimney, it will drain heated air out of the house. A well-designed, airtight wood stove, costing about $600 to $1,000 ($800 to $2,000 installed) typically has a first-law energy conversion efficiency of about 50 to 65 percent and distributes most of the heat into the room. Efficiencies of 90 percent have been reported for massive "Finnish" or "Russian" brick wood stoves, built with a convoluted series of baffles that delay the exhaust of the hot gases and allow the large brick thermal mass to absorb the heat and radiate most of it into the house.

Compared to electric heating or an oil-burning furnace, a wood stove in a well-forested area can save a household hundreds of dollars a year in fuel bills (more if the family cuts and hauls their own firewood). In urban areas, where wood must be hauled long distances, many residents pay as much, if not more, for wood as for oil and electricity.

This increase in wood burning, however, can cause some problems, including increased outdoor and indoor air pollution and, without proper controls, excessive deforestation in some areas. Wood burning by industries and utilities causes relatively little air pollution because most large commercial wood boilers come equipped with pollution control systems. Small wood stoves, however, can add significant quantities of pollutants to the atmosphere unless equipped with a $100 catalytic combuster, which burns off most polluting gases and also increases the energy-conversion efficiency of most stoves by 15 to 25 percent. By 1984 Oregon, Colorado, and Montana had passed laws regulating wood

stove emissions, and at least twenty other states were considering such laws. In London and in South Korean cities wood fires have been banned to reduce air pollution. Some observers argue that catalytic combusters should be required on all new and old wood burning stoves to reduce the health hazard.

In agricultural areas, *crop residues* (the inedible, unharvested portions of food crops) and *animal manure* can be collected and burned or converted to biofuels. Hawaii, which plans to produce 90 percent of its electricity from renewable energy by 2005, was burning enough bagasse (the brownish fibrous residue from sugarcane) in 1983 to produce almost 8 percent of its electricity. In most areas, however, plant residues are widely dispersed and require large amounts of energy to collect, dry, and transport—unless collected along with harvested crops. In addition, ecologists argue that it makes more sense to use these valuable nutrients to feed livestock, retard erosion, and fertilize the soil.

There is also greatly increased interest in burning *urban wastes* as a source of energy (Section 13-3), but some observers believe that it may be more sound ecologically to compost or recycle these organic wastes (Table 13-2).

Another approach is to establish large *energy plantations* or *farms,* covering areas of 130 to 260 square kilometers (50 to 100 square miles), where trees, grasses, or other crops would be grown and harvested by automated methods for use as biomass fuel. The biomass would be directly burned, converted to biofuels, or converted to plastics, rubber, and other products of petroleum and natural gas. Ideal energy crops would be fast-growing, high-yield perennials that reproduce themselves from cuttings, since seeding requires costly collection and sowing. Grasses would be harvested every few weeks. Trees, planted close together like crops, would be harvested by clearcutting (Section 10-5) every 3 to 5 years on a rotating schedule. However, without careful planning and land-use controls, the energy plantation approach can deplete soil nutrients more rapidly than traditional silviculture, reduce habitats for many plants and animals found in natural forests, require increased use of herbicides and pesticides, and in some cases compete with food crops for prime farmland.

Another suggestion is to plant *petroleum plantations* of plants such as some of the 2,000 varieties of plants of the genus *Euphorbia,* which store energy in hydrocarbon compounds (like those found in oil) rather than carbohydrates. After harvesting, the oil-like material would be extracted (much like crushing grapes to make wine) and refined to produce gasoline, and the unused woody plant residues converted to alcohol fuel. Such plants could be grown on semiarid, currently unproductive land.

The recent discovery of the properties of another tree, the copaiba (*Copaifera langdorfii*), might eliminate the refining step, since every 6 months the copaiba produces oil that can be used directly to power a diesel engine. Planting a land area the size of Arizona with *Euphorbia* or copaiba plants could produce all the gasoline needed by the United States. The economic feasibility and net useful energy yield of this approach, however, have not been determined, and large-scale plantations may be out of the question because of insufficient water.

Another category of potential biomass resources is the large-scale growth and harvesting of *aquatic plants* such as algae, water hyacinths, and kelp seaweed. Collecting, drying, and processing these plants, however, might require so much energy (and money) that net useful energy yields would be too low and costs too high. Also, large-scale harvesting might disrupt ocean and freshwater ecosystems.

See the summary table on p. 339.

Biofuels Plants, organic wastes, and other forms of solid biomass can be converted by bacteria and various chemical processes into gaseous and liquid biofuels such as *biogas* (a gaseous mixture of methane and carbon dioxide), liquid methanol (methyl alcohol or wood alcohol), and liquid ethanol (ethyl alcohol or grain alcohol), and other liquid fuels.

In China millions of biogas digesters convert organic plant and animal wastes into fuel for heating and cooking. After the biogas has been removed, the remaining solid residue can be used as fertilizer on food crops or, if contaminated, on nonedible crops such as trees. When they work, biogas digesters are highly efficient. However, they are somewhat slow and are vulnerable to low temperatures, acidity imbalances, and contamination by heavy metals, synthetic detergents, and other industrial effluents. Because of these problems, few MDCs use anaerobic digestion on a large scale, and their use in LDCs is declining.

Anaerobic digestion also occurs spontaneously in the estimated 20,000 landfill sites around the United States. Los Angeles has tapped into this source to heat some 3,500 homes. In 1976 Calorific Recovery by Anaerobic Processes, Inc.—CRAP for short—began providing Chicagoans with methane made from cattle manure collected from animal feedlots. Converting to methane all the manure that U.S. livestock produce each year could provide nearly 5 percent of the nation's total natural gas consumption at 1983 levels. But collecting and transporting the manure for long distances would require a large energy input. Recycling the manure to the land to replace artificial fertilizer, which requires large amounts of natural gas to produce, would probably save more natural gas.

Biofuels

Advantages

1. Technology fairly well developed.
2. Versatile. Can be used for space heating, cooking, and for powering vehicles.
3. Biogas and methanol can be produced from many different types of biomass, and ethanol can be produced from many food crops.
4. Ethanol and methanol could replace gasoline as world petroleum supplies decline.
5. Alcohols are fairly easy to transport within and between nations.
6. Moderate costs for ethanol and high costs for methanol, but new and more energy-efficient production methods may bring costs down. Biogas generators are cheap and easy to build, but maintenance costs are high.
7. Conventional engines can run on gasohol and can be converted fairly easily to run on pure ethanol or methanol.
8. Does not lead to a net increase in carbon dioxide in the atmosphere if trees and crops are replanted as fast as they are harvested, converted to biofuels, and burned.
9. Does not produce radioactive materials or materials that can be used to make nuclear weapons.
10. Air pollution: fairly low, but burning ethanol and methanol produces acetaldehyde, which without adequate pollution control can harm vegetation and can irritate the skin and eyes and damage the lungs at high concentrations.
11. Possible large-scale disasters: none.

Disadvantages

1. Biogas generators often don't work and can be contaminated easily.
2. Ethanol and methanol have significantly lower energy values than an equivalent amount of gasoline.
3. Large-scale use of ethanol fuel may decrease food production because corn and other crops would be more valuable when grown for conversion to ethanol than for food.
4. Low to moderate net useful energy yield for alcohol production, depending on fuel used and energy-efficiency of the process used. Fairly low net useful energy yield for biogas generators because of frequent breakdowns.
5. Converting manure to biogas prevents recycling of manure to the land as fertilizer.
6. Methanol is very corrosive.
7. Water pollution: moderate; in the absence of adequate waste treatment, large amounts of toxic swill produced by distilling ethanol could pollute nearby bodies of water.
8. Land disturbance: high, with large-scale production of methanol from wood depleting forests and increasing soil erosion and large-scale production of ethanol requiring a large land area and increasing soil erosion if grains are grown on marginal cropland.

One of the major and most urgent energy problems facing the world today is to find a liquid fuel substitute for gasoline and diesel fuel. Some analysts see the biofuels, methanol and ethanol, as the answer to this problem, since both alcohols can be burned directly as fuel without requiring lead compounds or other additives to boost octane ratings. Pure ethanol is being burned in specially adapted conventional engines in Brazil, and methanol has long been used as a racing fuel. By 1983 Brazil was obtaining one-fourth of its motor fuel from ethyl alcohol produced by fermentation of sugarcane and cassava and plans to use ethyl alcohol to produce some of the industrial chemicals now produced as petrochemicals.

However, the burning of pure methanol and ethanol produces acetaldehyde, which smells bad, harms vegetation, and at high concentrations can irritate the skin and eyes and damage the lungs. These harmful emissions could be eliminated by better design or by equipping cars with pollution-control devices. In addition, methanol is highly corrosive and distilling ethanol produces large volumes of a toxic waste material known as "swill," which if allowed to flow into waterways would kill algae, fish, and plants.

In addition, gasoline can be mixed with 10 to 20 percent by volume ethanol to make *gasohol*, a form of unleaded gasoline that burns in conventional gasoline engines. A mixture of diesel fuel with 15 to 20 percent by volume methanol, called *diesohol*, is also being tested and probably will lower the emissions of nitrogen oxide pollutants that are a drawback of regular diesel fuel.

There is concern, however, that Brazil's ambitious alcohol fuels program will drive up food prices and increase malnutrition among the poor by making it more profitable to plant land devoted to growing rice, wheat, and pasture for livestock with sugarcane for alcohol production. In addition, Brazil will have to invest heavily in waste treatment facilities to avoid severe water pollution from toxic swill.

The United States is the world's second largest ethanol fuel producer, mostly from grain and from sugarcane in Hawaii. By 1983 gasohol accounted for 4 percent of the nation's gasoline sales, and it is now sold in many stations as a form of unleaded gasoline, not labeled as gasohol. Presently gasohol is competitive with unleaded gasoline because it is exempt from the federal gasoline tax and from varying amounts of state gasoline taxes in at least 35 states. New energy-efficient distilleries are reducing the costs of producing ethanol, and soon this fuel may be able to compete with unleaded gasoline without tax breaks.

Some observers have argued that if large areas of U.S. cropland are used to produce corn or other grains for conversion to ethanol, the United States may not have an exportable surplus of grain to help feed the world's growing population and to help counter American trade deficits from importing oil. This problem would be greatly reduced if grain-producing nations fed more of their cattle and other grass-eating livestock on rangeland or perhaps on the grain residues produced in alcohol distilleries (if these residues are enriched by yeast proteins) instead of grain .

The net useful energy yield for producing ethanol for use as a fuel is moderate to low or can even be negative, depending on how it is produced. If the alcohol is produced in an oil-fueled distillery, there is no net useful energy gain. However there is a low net useful energy yield if the distillery is powered by coal, wood, or solar energy, and replacing older distilleries with new more energy-efficient ones would increase the net useful energy yield somewhat.

Wood, wood wastes, other woody crop residues, sewage sludge, garbage, and coal (Section 15-4) can be gasified and converted to *methanol*. Recently chemists have reported that carbon dioxide, a waste product of fossil fuel combustion, can be converted efficiently to methanol in an experimental process that may ultimately be made to work with solar energy instead of electricity. In destructive distillation, wood is heated in the presence of little air to form charcoal, carbon dioxide, and hydrogen gas. When subjected to high pressures in the presence of catalysts (chemicals that speed up particular chemical reactions), these gases combine to form methanol.

So far methanol has had little use as a fuel for conventional vehicles because it blends poorly with gasoline and corrodes rubber, plastic, and some metal parts in conventional internal combustion engines. However, automotive engineers point out that mass-produced engines redesigned to burn methanol should cost no more than gasoline engines, and road tests in West Germany, the United States, and Brazil have shown that methanol-powered engines perform at least as well as their gasoline-powered counterparts. California is presently testing over 500 factory-built cars designed to run on pure methanol and is offering a $1,000 tax credit to citizens who convert their cars to run on pure methanol. Unless more efficient production methods can be developed, the use of pure methanol as a fuel will not be economically feasible until gasoline prices reach about $0.79 to $1.06 per liter ($3 to $4 a gallon)—already a reality in many European nations where gasoline taxes are high to encourage conservation.

Advantages

1. Technology fairly well developed.
2. Source of energy (tides) is free.
3. Fairly low operating costs.
4. Does not add carbon dioxide to the atmosphere.
5. Moderate net useful energy yield.
6. Does not produce radioactive materials or materials that can be used to produce nuclear weapons.
7. Air pollution: very low, with no emissions produced during operation.
8. Land disturbance: low, because the plant is located on water.
9. Possible large-scale disasters: none.

Disadvantages

1. Few suitable sites.
2. High construction cost.
3. Subject to seawater corrosion and storm damage.
4. Plants often located far from point of use, thus requiring costly electric transmission lines.
5. Produces power only periodically, and the time of day that power is generated varies daily with changes in times for high and low tides. Because of this intermittent operation, the plant must be coupled with other power plants to meet electricity demands, or an expensive pumped-storage system must be used.
6. Not versatile. Can be used only to produce electricity.
7. Large-scale use could gradually slow the rotation of the earth on its axis.
8. Water pollution: moderate, with possible damage to ecology of bays and estuaries by alteration of water flows and increasing average tidal height in the bays.

Oil companies with large coal holdings are interested in using methanol as a fuel because it can be produced from coal as well as biomass—thus giving these diversified companies an added share of the total energy market. Because it can be produced readily from a variety of food crops such as corn, sugarcane, sugar beets, and cassava, farmers favor using ethanol as a fuel.

16-6 Tidal Power and Hydrogen Fuel

Tidal Power In a few places in the world, *gravitational attraction* between the moon and the rotating earth, and to a lesser extent between the sun and the rotating earth, causes a rise and fall of tides large enough to constitute a source of *renewable (tidal) energy.* Twice a day high tides cause large volumes of water to flow inland, and twice a day low tides

French Engineering Bureau, Washington, D.C.

Figure 16-9 Tidal power electric plant across the estuary of the Rance River in France.

cause these large volumes of water to flow back into the sea. The largest tidal fluctuation in the world—16 meters (52 feet)—is found along the Bay of Fundy in Canada. If the opening to such bodies of water is narrow enough to be obstructed by a dam with gates that can be opened and closed, the energy in the tidal flow can be used to spin turbines to produce electricity.

However, only about two dozen places in the world have enough change in water height between tides to produce electricity at an affordable cost. Since 1968 a small 250-megawatt commercial tidal power station has been in operation in France on the Rance River with tides up to 13.5 meters (44 feet), and another commercial station is in operation in the Soviet Union. Sluice gates on a dam built across the estuary of the Rance River (Figure 16-9) are kept closed until the head of water on the seaward side of the dam exceeds that on the inland side. The gates are opened, to allow water to flow into the river through turbines that generate electricity, and then closed. When the head of the water trapped inland is higher than that on the seaward side, the gates are reopened to allow the water to flow through turbines back into the sea as the tide recedes, again generating electricity. Since there are two high tides and two low tides a day, this process can produce electricity during four periods each day. Although operating costs are fairly low, the Rance

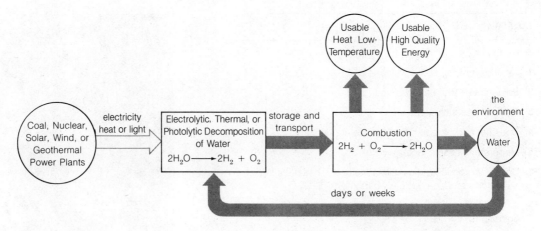

Figure 16-10 The hydrogen energy cycle has a number of advantages over the present fossil fuel energy system. But since hydrogen gas doesn't occur in nature, it must be produced by using electricity, heat, or perhaps solar energy to decompose water—thus reducing the net useful energy yield and increasing the cost of hydrogen fuel.

River project cost about 2.5 times more than a conventional hydroelectric power plant station with the same output built further up the Rance River. Other problems are listed in the summary table on page 343.

Another successful experimental tidal plant has been in operation since 1968 in the Russian Arctic, east of Murmansk. In China 128 small tidal power units have been built along the coast in recent years to supply local populations with electricity. Two possible locations for tidal power stations in the United States are the Cook Inlet in Alaska and Passamaquoddy Bay in Maine. However, government studies concluded that at 1983 electricity prices tidal power projects at these two locations would not be economical. By early 1983, Canada had completed a small-scale tidal demonstration project on the Bay of Fundy. If this project is successful, a number of large-scale commercial tidal power stations may eventually be built.

Hydrogen Gas as a Fuel Some scientists have suggested the use of *hydrogen gas (H₂)* to fuel cars and heat homes and buildings when oil and natural gas run out. Although hydrogen gas does not occur in significant quantities in nature, it can be derived—that is, produced by chemical processes from nonrenewable coal or by using heat, electricity, or perhaps sunlight to decompose water (Figure 16-10). Seawater could be used to provide an almost infinite supply of hydrogen gas, in sharp contrast to fossil fuels.

Although hydrogen gas is highly explosive, most analysts believe we could learn how to handle it safely, as we have learned to manage gasoline and natural gas. Hydrogen gas could be transported by pipeline to households, industries, and the fueling stations that would replace today's gas stations. If affordable solar photovoltaic cells are developed, individual homeowners could produce their own hydrogen for motor fuel and for cooking, space heating, and water heating.

Hydrogen gas can be burned cleanly by reaction with oxygen gas to produce water. This reaction could take place in a power plant, a specially designed automobile engine, or in a *fuel cell* that converts the chemical energy produced by the reaction into direct current electricity. Burning in pure oxygen yields no emissions of air pollutants. However, burning in atmospheric oxygen results in small amounts of nitrogen oxides formed as by-products, as occurs when fossil fuels are burned.

The major catch to the widespread use of hydrogen as a clean source of energy is that it is not found as H₂ in nature and may take more energy to produce the fuel than we would obtain by burning it. Thus, a large-scale hydrogen energy system is feasible only if an essentially renewable or limitless high-quality energy source such as nuclear fusion, direct solar energy, or wind energy can be used to produce the hydrogen at an affordable price and with acceptable environmental impacts.

Scientists are trying to develop *photoelectrochemical cells* in which light or solar energy can split water molecules into hydrogen and oxygen gases with reasonable efficiency. By 1984 some solar energy water-splitting reactions carried out in the laboratory had reached conversion efficiencies of 8 to 16 percent. But widespread use of these systems would be limited because they call for platinum electrodes or electrodes coated with compounds of other expensive and rare elements such as ruthenium and rhodium. One experimental cell uses electrodes made of cheap and readily available iron oxide (rust), but so far its energy-conversion efficiency is only 1 percent. Even if affordable materials are used and

Advantages

1. Essentially limitless supply from decomposition of water.

2. Technology for burning gaseous hydrogen fairly well developed.

3. Versatile. Can replace oil and gasoline and can be used for space heating, producing electricity, or propelling vehicles.

4. Burns cleanly.

5. Fairly easy to transport over land.

6. Does not add carbon dioxide to the atmosphere if direct or indirect solar energy or nuclear power is used in the decomposition of water.

7. Does not produce radioactive wastes or materials that could be used to produce nuclear weapons if direct or indirect solar energy is used in the decomposition of water.

8. Air and water pollution, land disruption, and the possibility of large-scale disasters could be low if direct or indirect solar energy is used in the decomposition of water.

Disadvantages

1. Does not exist in significant amounts in nature.

2. Energy must be used to decompose water to produce hydrogen fuel.

3. Low to moderate net useful energy yield, depending on source of energy used to decompose water.

4. Costs probably high, but will vary depending on source of energy used to decompose water.

5. Technology for fairly efficient decomposition of water by sunlight still at laboratory stage and probably will not be available for commercial use until after 2000, if then.

6. Difficult, expensive, and dangerous to transport over water.

7. Produces radioactive wastes and materials that could be used to make nuclear weapons if water is decomposed by electricity produced by nuclear power.

8. Adds carbon dioxide to the atmosphere if electricity from coal-burning or other fossil-fuel-burning power plants is used to decompose water.

9. Air and water pollution, land disruption, and the possibility of large-scale disasters could be high if coal-fired or nuclear power plants are used in the decomposition of water.

Advantages

1. Many savings can be implemented fairly quickly.

2. Technology fairly simple and well developed.

3. Essentially unlimited source for providing energy by reducing unnecessary waste of energy obtained from any source.

4. High net useful energy yield.

5. Saves money. Many initial costs are paid back by energy savings within one to several years.

6. Reduces environmental impact of all other energy resources by reducing use and waste of energy.

7. Extends supplies of petroleum, natural gas, coal, and other nonrenewable energy resources.

8. Reduces dependence on imported oil and other imported energy resources.

9. Greatly reduces or eliminates the need for any new coal-fired and nuclear power plants.

10. Reduces international competition for oil, hence diminishes the chances of conventional and nuclear wars (Enrichment Study 3).

11. Adds no carbon dioxide to the atmosphere.

12. Produces no radioactive wastes or materials that can be used to make nuclear weapons; reduces the need for nuclear energy.

13. Buys time and frees capital for developing and phasing in new energy alternatives.

14. Provides jobs and promotes economic growth.

Disadvantages

1. Requires individuals to consider more complex but realistic lifetime costs for energy systems and devices rather than just initial costs.

2. Replacing most existing energy-inefficient houses, buildings, and industries with new energy-efficient units would take 30 to 50 years, and improving the average efficiency of the automobile fleet and building mass transit systems would take about 10 years.

3. While lifetime costs may be relatively low, initial costs for some equipment may be high to very high.

4. Some measures require individuals to alter their lifestyles, which may be judged inconvenient or impractical.

reasonable efficiencies are obtained, it may be difficult and expensive to develop large-scale commercial cells. According to the most optimistic projections, affordable commercial cells for using solar energy to produce hydrogen will not be available until after 2000.

16-7 Energy Conservation: Improving Energy Efficiency

A number of studies have shown that improvements in energy efficiency such as those summarized earlier in Table 14-1 could cut 1984 U.S. average per capita primary energy use by 50 percent and perhaps *ultimately* by 90 percent without decreasing the quality of life. American buildings typically consume about 50 to 90 percent more energy than they would if oriented, designed, insulated, and lighted to use energy more efficiently.

A monument to energy waste is the 110-story World Trade Center in Manhattan, which uses as much electricity as a city of 100,000 persons. Not a single window in its walls of glass can be opened to take advantage of natural warming and cooling; its heating and cooling systems work around the clock, even when no one is in the building. This is in contrast to Atlanta's 24-story Georgia Power Company building, which uses 60 percent less energy than conventional office buildings. Energy-saving features include (1) innovative design (each floor extends over the one below to allow heating by the low winter sun while blocking out the higher summer sun to reduce air conditioning costs), (2) a computer programmed to turn off all lights at 6 P.M. unless instructed otherwise, (3) efficient lights to focus on desks rather than illuminating entire rooms, and (4) an adjoining three-story building where employees can work at unusual hours, thereby saving energy that would be necessary to service the larger building.

To encourage greater energy conservation in buildings, several energy analysts have suggested a law that makes it impossible to sell a house that has not undergone an energy audit by a certified inspector and been weatherproofed up to certain minimum standards (and inspected to be sure the job has been done correctly). A program similar to this went into effect in Portland, Oregon, in 1984. It has also been suggested that federal and state governments maintain and extend tax credits for homeowners and businesses who use energy-conserving devices, materials, and construction (including passively heated or cooled above- or below-ground buildings and superinsulated buildings).

Some improvements in energy efficiency, such as adding insulation, making existing houses more airtight, buying a more energy-efficient car, and making minor changes in industrial processes to save energy, can be accomplished very quickly. However, improving overall energy efficiency by building new superinsulated and passive and active solar houses and buildings takes longer. Cars are available now that easily average 17 kilometers per liter of gasoline (40 miles per gallon) and Volkswagen, British Leyland, and several Japanese companies are testing cars that average 34 kilometers per liter (80 miles per gallon). But most people can't afford to buy new cars, many new car buyers select relatively inefficient models, and the present U.S. fleet contains many older gas-guzzling cars.

New energy-efficient processes can be used in the chemicals, petroleum refining, iron and steel, farming, food processing, paper, cement, and aluminum industries, which account for about two-thirds of all energy used by U.S. industry. However, such *reindustrialization* will be expensive and will take 20 to 30 years once the commitment has been made. Some argue that it would be better to

use U.S. financial, material, and energy resources to develop new high-technology industries of the future (computers, solar photovoltaic cells, robots, materials recycling, pollution control, genetic engineering, etc.), rather than trying to revitalize older industries, whose products can be made cheaper elsewhere in more modern factories.

Japan and most industrialized Western European nations with standards of living equal to or greater than that in the United States use only one-third to two-thirds as much energy per person. This is due to a combination of factors including greater emphasis on energy conservation and fewer passenger miles traveled per person (made possible because of more compact cities), as shown in Table 16-1. However, national energy use patterns vary, and approaches that save energy in one nation can't always be used in other countries. Table 16-2 lists some ways you can save energy.

Improving energy efficiency is also the cheapest energy alternative for individuals, industries, and nations. Because one barrel of oil is saved for every $10 to $15 spent on energy conservation, this approach is equivalent to buying oil at $10 to $15 a barrel compared to the $29 average world price of oil in 1983. Energy conservation also provides jobs and stimulates economic growth. Improving energy efficiency was a $10 billion business in the United States in 1984 (an increase of 9,000 percent over 1974), and is projected to gross $50 billion a year by 1990. The advantages and disadvantages are summarized in the table on p. 345.

16-8 Developing an Energy Strategy for the United States

Overall Evaluation of U.S. Energy Alternatives Table 16-3 on pp. 350–351 evaluates energy alternatives for the United States. Study this table carefully. It represents a summary of many thousands of pages of information in articles, reports, and books about energy alternatives. This table is not the final word in U.S. energy options, but it does provide a useful framework for making decisions based on presently available information. Energy experts will continue to argue over these and other futuristic projections, and new data may affect some of the information in the table.

General Conclusions Four major conclusions can be drawn from the detailed analysis of each major energy alternative for the world given in this chapter and the preceding one and for U.S. energy alternatives as summarized in Table 16-3:

Table 16-1 Energy Use in the United States and Sweden

United States	Sweden
Average per capita energy use is 230,00 kcal/day.	Average per capita energy use is 150,000 kcal/day
Average gross national product per person in 1984 was $14,040	Average gross national product in 1984 was $13,160.
Energy use for transportation is high because the nation is large, cities are dispersed, mass transit is not widely used, and the average car gets relatively low gas mileage.	Energy use for transportation is one-fourth that in the United States because the country is smaller, cities are compact, mass transit is efficient and widely used. Many Swedes walk and use bicycles for short trips, and the average car gets better gas mileage.
Energy waste is encouraged by low taxes on gasoline and low tariffs on oil imports.	Energy conservation is encouraged by high taxes on gasoline and high tariffs ($10 per barrel) on oil imports
Mass transit within cities is inefficient and is not available to many suburbs (Section 12-4). Intercity rail service has been cut sharply and is not available to most areas.	Mass transit within cities is highly efficient and the intercity system provides rapid and direct service to most areas.
Large amounts of energy are used to produce a given amount of steel, copper, oil, cement, paper, and most chemicals because most aging American industries still use older, less energy-efficient technologies.	Less energy is used to produce the same quantity of steel, copper, oil, cement, paper, and most chemicals because most Swedish industries use newer, more energy-efficient technology
Building codes in most areas do not require adequate insulation.	Building codes require adequate insulation.
Low priority is given to energy conservation in granting housing loans.	High priority is given to energy conservation in granting housing loans.
Cities are not required to develop a government-approved energy plan.	Cities are required to develop a government-approved energy plan.
Municipally-owned district heating systems do not exist.	Municipally owned district heating systems provide heat for 30 percent of the population.
Kitchen stoves are used for cooking only.	Often a coil of pipe passing through the oven carries stove-heated water to the kitchen sink and to a bathroom.
Water is kept hot 24 hours a day in 150- to 225-liter (40- to 60-gallon) tanks.	Hot water is often supplied only when needed by use of tankless demand hot water heaters.
Large frost-free refrigerators use about 1,700 kW-hr of electricity per year.	Smaller nonfrost-free refrigerators use about 550 kW-hr of electricity per year.
The government has no long-range energy plan, government expenditures for energy conservation and development of renewable energy sources have been sharply reduced, and nuclear power receives most of the federal energy funds (Table 16-5).	By 2005 the government plans to use one-third to one-fourth as much energy as in 1982 through energy conservation and to eliminate dependence on imported oil, phase out nuclear power, and increase dependence on renewable energy (from 20 percent in 1982) to 70 percent.

1. The best short-, intermediate-, and long-term alternative for the United States and other nations is to reduce unnecessary energy waste by improving the efficiency of energy use.

2. Total systems for future energy alternatives in the world and in the United States will probably have low to moderate net useful energy yields and moderate to high development costs. Since there may not be enough capital available to develop all alternative energy systems, projects must be carefully chosen so that capital will not be depleted on systems that yield too little net useful energy or prove to be unacceptable economically or environmentally.

3. Instead of depending primarily on one nonrenewable energy resource like oil, the world and the United States will probably shift

Table 16-2 Ways You Can Save Energy

Home Heating

1. Have the local power company or a qualified energy auditor inspect your home (sometimes free but usually costs $10 to $20) to determine the best ways to improve energy efficiency (15 to 50% savings, depending on what is done).

2. Turn thermostat down to 18°C (65°F) during the day and 13°C (55°F) at night, use a humidifier to provide comfort at lower temperatures, wear sweaters or insulated underwear indoors, and use sleeping bags or extra nonelectric blankets at night [saves 1.6%/°C (3%/°F)].

3. Close off and do not heat closets and unused rooms (variable savings).

4. Add extra insulation in ceilings, walls, and floors, and insulate heating ducts (20 to 50% savings).

5. Caulk and weatherstrip leaky windows, doors, and electric receptacles (10 to 30% savings).

6. Cover windows with insulated draperies, quilts, or shutters at night and during cloudy days; open the covers for windows exposed to the sun during the day, and keep the windows clean to ensure maximum solar gain (5 to 25% savings).

7. Have furnace cleaned and tuned at least once a year, clean furnace air intake filters at least every 2 weeks and replace as needed, and clean thermostat once a year to remove dust (10 to 20% savings).

8. Do not use a conventional fireplace for heating unless the doors and heating ducts in the room where it is located are covered and a window closest to the fireplace is cracked about 1 cm (0.5 in.) to reduce overall loss of heat from the house (10 to 20% savings).

9. Add storm windows and doors or double-airlock entry doors (10 to 15% savings).

10. When fireplace is not in use, cover opening with a glass screen or insulated cover and close dampers (8% savings).

11. Do not block heating duct outlets with drapes, furniture, or other items (variable savings).

12. Use kitchen and bathroom exhaust fans only when absolutely necessary, since they remove house heat (variable savings).

13. After taking a bath or washing dishes, let the hot water stand in the tub or sink until it cools to room temperature so that heat is added to house rather than going down the drain.

Home Cooling (variable savings)

1. Add extra insulation and make house airtight (see items 4 and 5 for home heating).

2. Use natural breezes as much as possible by opening windows and doors.

3. Shade windows from direct sunlight by using awnings, overhangs, leaf-shedding (deciduous) trees, vines, or insulated drapes or shutters with light colors to reflect sunlight.

4. Use a manual or automatic clock to raise minimum temperature for an air-conditioned house to 26°C (78°F) during the day and a few degrees higher at night, and wear light clothing indoors.

5. Close insulated drapes, quilts, or shutters on the sunny side of the house during the day and open them at night.

6. Use energy-efficient ceiling fans, small room fans, or whole-house window or attic fans to eliminate or reduce the need for air conditioning.

7. Open windows at night to bring in cooler night air, close them during hot days, keep closet doors closed, and close off rooms on the nonsunny side of the house during the day to keep them several degrees cooler.

8. Close off doors and air conditioning ducts to unused rooms.

9. In warm climates use light-colored roofing and outside paint to reflect incoming solar radiation.

10. During baths or showers, close bathroom doors and use exhaust fan or open bathroom window to prevent transfer of heat and humid air to rest of house.

11. Try to schedule heat- and moisture-producing activities such as bathing, mopping, ironing, and washing and drying clothes for the coolest part of the day; cover pans when cooking.

12. Turn off pilot light on gas stove (saves $20 a year).

13. To reduce heat load and electricity, use lower lighting levels, turn off lights, television sets, and other appliances as much as possible, switch to more efficient screw-in fluorescent light bulbs, use low-wattage (4 or 7 watt) night lights to light hallways, bathrooms, and other rooms when brighter lighting is not needed, and use dimmer switches and lights focused on desks and other areas to provide lighting only as needed.

Hot Water (savings variable)

1. Insulate hot water pipes and hot water heater (saves at least $60 a year).

2. Repair all leaky faucets—especially those providing hot water.

3. Install aerators on all sink faucets and flow restrictors on showerheads to reduce overall water use and hot water use.

4. Wash dishes no more than once a day in a double sink or two pans (one for washing and one for rinsing), without running water except to fill the sinks or pans; or use a dishwasher only with a full load and disconnect drying cycle to let dishes air dry.

5. Machine-wash clothes in cold or warm water using only a full load, or adjust water level for small loads. Hang clothes on outside line during summer instead of using dryer.

6. Adjust the thermostat on hot water heater to 49°C (120°F) (15% savings) or no higher than 60°C (140°F) if you have an automatic dishwasher.

7. Once or twice a year remove sediment (which reduces efficiency) by hooking up a hose to drain pipe on hot water tank.

8. Turn off hot water heater when house will be empty for a few days.

9. Take 3- to 5-minute showers instead of baths. After getting wet, turn off water, soap down, and then turn water on again for rinsing.

Table 16-2 Ways You Can Save Energy *(continued)*

10. Do not let water run while bathing, shaving, brushing teeth, or washing dishes.

11. When purchasing a new hot water heater try to buy a tankless instant gas-fired heater or an active or passive solar water heater.

12. See if your utility company provides a lower rate allowing them to install a meter with a timer that cuts off your hot water heater for a few hours a day when the utility's electric load is highest.

Appliances

1. When purchasing a new stove, refrigerator, air conditioner, dishwasher, furnace, hot water heater, or other appliance, buy the most energy-efficient model available to save energy and money on a lifetime-cost basis.

2. When possible, use a microwave oven instead of a conventional oven, especially during the summer.

3. Choose the smallest refrigerator or freezer that will meet your needs and keep it full but not overfull. Select a chest freezer rather than an upright model to prevent unnecessary loss of cool air when the door is opened.

4. Keep the condenser coils at the back of refrigerators and freezers clean and unobstructed to improve cooling efficiency.

5. If possible, do not locate a refrigerator or freezer near a stove or other source of heat.

6. Thaw frozen foods before cooking.

7. Don't place hot foods in the refrigerator.

Transportation

1. Walk or use a bicycle or moped as much as possible, especially for trips less than 8 kilometers (5 miles) (80 to 100% savings).

2. Use a carpool, mass transit, or paratransit as much as possible (50% or more savings).

3. Plan carefully to eliminate unnecessary trips (up to 50% savings).

4. Purchase the most energy-efficient vehicle available (30 to 70% savings).

5. Keep engine well tuned, and clean or replace air filter regularly (20 to 50% savings).

6. Obey speed limits (20% or more savings).

7. Drive smoothly (no jerks, fast starts, or excessive braking), and turn off engine if car must be idled longer than a minute (15 to 20% savings).

8. Purchase car without air conditioner or use air conditioning sparingly (9 to 20 percent savings).

9. Keep tires inflated to proper pressure (2 to 5% savings).

---

to much greater dependence on improving energy efficiency and a mix of renewable energy sources over the 50 years it typically takes to develop and phase in new energy resources (Figures 14-2 and 14-3). To provide flexibility and to reduce chances of shortages, each major energy alternative in the future may provide 10 to 20 percent of the world's or a nation's primary energy.

4. As improvements in energy efficiency are made and dependence on renewable primary energy resources is increased, primary energy production will become more localized and variable, depending on local climatic conditions and availability of renewable energy resources.

Economic Incentives and Disincentives   Cost is the major factor in determining which primary energy resources are widely used by consumers. Governments can **(1)** use price controls on domestically produced supplies of nonrenewable energy resources such as crude oil and natural gas and provide tax write-offs, research and development grants, and other forms of subsidies to encourage use of a primary energy resource by keeping prices artificially low; **(2)** add taxes and remove government subsidies to discourage use of a primary energy

resource by keeping prices artificially high; and **(3)** remove all price controls, taxes, and subsidies and allow each energy alternative to compete in a free market.

Each of these approaches has certain advantages and disadvantages, as summarized in Table 16-4. Clearly effective short-, intermediate-, and long-term energy strategies for a particular nation will involve a carefully balanced mixture of these approaches.

Attempts to Develop a Short-Term U.S. Energy Plan   After the 1973 oil embargo, Congress was prodded to pass a number of laws, including the Energy Reorganization Act of 1974, the Federal Nonnuclear Energy Research and Development Act of 1974, the Energy Policy and Conservation Act of 1976, the Energy Conservation and Production Act of 1976, the National Energy Act of 1978 (amended in 1980), and the Public Utility Regulatory Policies Act of 1978 (PURPA). The box on page 353 summarizes some of the major features of these acts.

Despite the important changes that have occurred, most energy experts agree that these laws do not represent a comprehensive short-, intermediate-, or long-term energy strategy for the United States.

In 1981, President Reagan proposed to increase

Table 16-3 Evaluation of Energy Alternatives for the United States (shading indicates favorable conditions)

Energy Resource	Estimated Availability*			Estimated Net Useful Energy of Entire System†	Projected Cost of Entire System	Actual or Potential Environmental Impact of Entire System‡
	Short Term (1985–1995)	Intermediate Term (1995–2005)	Long Term (2005–2035)			
Nonrenewable Resources						
Fossil fuels						
Petroleum	High (with imports)	Moderate (with imports)	Low	High but decreasing§	High for new domestic supplies	Moderate
Natural gas	High (with imports)	Moderate (with imports)	Low	High but decreasing§	High for new domestic supplies	Low
Coal	High‖	High‖	High‖	High but decreasing§	Moderate but increasing	Very high‖
Oil Shale	Low	Low to moderate	Low to moderate	Low to moderate	Very high	High
Tar sands	Low	Fair? (imports only)	Poor to fair (imports only)	Low	Very high	Moderate to high
Biomass (urban wastes for incineration)	Low	Low	Low	Low to moderate	High	Moderate to high
Synthetic natural gas (SNG) from coal	Low	Low to moderate	Low to moderate	Low to moderate	High	High (increases use of coal)
Synthetic oil and alcohols from coal and organic wastes	Low	Low	Low	Low to moderate	High	High (increases use of coal)
Nuclear energy						
Conventional fission (uranium)	Low to moderate	Low to moderate	Low to moderate	Low to moderate	Very high	Very high
Breeder fission (uranium and thorium)	None	None to low (if developed)	Moderate	Unknown, but probably moderate	Very high	Very high
Fusion (deuterium and tritium)	None	None	None to low (if developed)	Unknown	Very high	Unknown (probably moderate)
Geothermal energy (trapped pockets)	Poor	Poor	Poor	Low to moderate	Moderate to high	Moderate to high
Renewable Resources						
Conservation (improving energy efficiency)	High	High	High	Very high	Low	Decreases impact of other sources
Water power (hydroelectricity)						
New large-scale dams and plants	Low	Low	Very low	Moderate to high	Moderate to very high	Low to moderate
Reopening abandoned small-scale plants	Moderate	Moderate	Low	Moderate to high	Moderate	Low

Table 16-3 Evaluation of Energy Alternatives for the United States *(continued)*

Energy Resource	Estimated Availability*			Estimated Net Useful Energy of Entire System[†]	Projected Cost of Entire System	Actual or Potential Environmental Impact of Entire System[‡]
	Short Term (1985–1995)	Intermediate Term (1995–2005)	Long Term (2005–2035)			
Tidal energy	None	Very low	Very low	Unknown (moderate)	High	Low to moderate
Ocean thermal gradients	None	Low	Low to moderate (if developed)	Unknown (probably low to moderate	Probably high	Unknown (probably moderate)
Solar energy						
Low-temperature heating (for homes and water)	Moderate	Moderate to high	High	Moderate to high	Moderate to high	Low
High-temperature heating	Low	Moderate	Moderate to high	Moderate	Very high initially (but probably declining fairly rapidly)	Low to moderate
Photovoltaic production of electricity	Low to moderate	Moderate	High	Moderate	High initially but declining fairly rapidly	Low
Wind energy						
Home and neighborhood turbines	Low	Moderate	Moderate to high	Moderate	Moderate to high	Low
Large-scale power plants	None	Very low	Probably low	Low	High	Low to moderate?
Geothermal energy (low heat flow)	Very low	Very low	Low to moderate	Low	High	Moderate to high
Biomass (burning of wood, crop, food, and animal wastes)	Moderate	Moderate	Moderate to high	Moderate	Moderate	Moderate to high
Biofuels (alcohols and natural gas from plants and organic wastes)	Low to moderate?	Moderate	Moderate to high	Low to moderate	Moderate to high	Moderate to high
Hydrogen gas (from coal or water)	None	Low	Moderate[#]	Unknown (probably low to moderate)[#]	Unknown (probably high)[#]	Variable[#]

*Overall availability based on supply and technological, net useful energy, economic, and environmental impact feasibility.
[†]Rough estimates only. Better and less conflicting estimates will be available when standard guidelines for net energy analysis are adopted by all investigators.
[‡]See summaries for each alternative in Chapters 15 and 16 for details.
[§]As accessible high-grade deposits are depleted, more and more energy and money must be used to find, develop, upgrade, and deliver remote and low-grade deposits.
[‖]Coal's very high environmental impact can be reduced to an acceptable level, however, by methods that are technically and economically feasible today.
[#]Depends on whether an essentially infinite source of heat or electrical energy (such as fusion, breeder fission, wind, or the sun) is available to produce hydrogen gas from coal or water. Net useful energy, costs, and environmental impact will depend on source of heat or electricity. A breakthrough in using sunlight to break down water directly (photolysis) could occur at any time, yielding dramatic advantages.

Table 16-4 Evaluation of Economic Approaches to Encouraging and Discouraging Use and Development of Energy Resource Alternatives

Advantages	Disadvantages
Price Controls and Subsidies	
1. Protects consumers, espcially the poor, from sharp price increases.	1. Hides real price of an energy resource from consumers.
2. Encourages use of a resource with large domestic supplies (such as coal in the United States).	2. Encourages depletion of a resource in relatively short time (such as crude oil and natural gas in the United States).
3. Can encourage the development and use of a new energy alternative if applied exclusively or with greater emphasis on that alternative.	3. Can discourage improvements in energy efficiency and development of new energy alternatives.
	4. By decreasing profits, discourages energy companies from looking for new domestic supplies of nonrenewable energy resources such as crude oil and natural gas.
	5. Since not all companies and individuals can afford to make a capital investment to qualify for the subsidy, those without adequate cash flow are discriminated against.
Adding Taxes to Energy Prices	
1. Encourages improvements in energy efficiency by making energy prices higher.	1. Increases consumer energy prices, especially for the poor,* unless tax revenues are used to help the poor reduce energy expenditures and to provide a minimum lifeline amount of electricity and heating fuel at a low rate.
2. Discourages use of an energy resource that is or will be in short supply or has a high environmental impact.	2. Can increase inflation and discourage economic growth unless tax revenues are recycled in a way that stimulates desirable and labor-intensive forms of economic growth, such as energy conservation (as opposed to national defense, which creates far fewer jobs per dollar spent).
3. Taxes on imported oil and other imported energy resources discourage dependence on imports and encourage use of other energy alternatives.	
4. Taxes collected can be used to aid the poor in obtaining a basic supply of energy and as subsidies to encourage improvements in energy efficiency (Table 14-2) and development of new energy alternatives.	
Free Market Competition	
1. Ideally, allows energy resources to be supplied at the lowest prices for consumers.	1. Despite much talk, a free market does not exist because of numerous direct and indirect government subsidies and monopolistic control of prices by a few companies with a large share of the market.
2. Discourages dependence on resources presently in short supply or with low net useful energy yields and high costs.	2. Marketplace does not deal well with the future because future value is heavily discounted. Thus its emphasis on today's prices greatly reduces chances for the long-term development of new energy alternatives without government research and development and tax write-off subsidies.
3. Ideally, allows consumers to know present true prices of each energy alternative.	3. Emphasis on present rather than future prices can encourage rapid depletion of resources that should be conserved, such as crude oil.

*In the United States the poor (with annual disposable incomes under $5,000) must devote nearly 20 percent of this amount to the direct purchase of energy, while Americans with incomes of $35,000 or more spend less than 5 percent on energy.

the total energy supply of conventional fossil fuels and increase dependence on nuclear power for producing electricity, while decreasing federal support for improvements in energy efficiency and devel-

opment of renewable energy alternatives. In this hard-path approach, domestic supplies of nonrenewable oil and natural gas would be increased by removing all government price controls, opening

Major Features of U.S. Energy Policy Laws Passed Between 1974 and 1980

1. Established the Department of Energy (DOE) to oversee national energy policy and government-supported energy research and development.

2. Increased federal budget allocations for energy research and development.

3. Established a national speed limit of 88 kilometers (55 miles) per hour.

4. Required new fleets of automobiles to get an average of 8.5 kilometers per liter (20 miles per gallon) by 1980 and 12 kilometers per liter (27.5 miles per gallon) by 1985.

5. Deregulated the price of domestically produced crude oil by 1983, thus allowing it to rise to the average world price ($29 a barrel by early 1984).

6. Taxed windfall profits for oil companies resulting from price deregulation of domestic oil, with the revenues going **(a)** to an Energy Security Fund to set up and finance the U.S. Synthetic Fuels Corporation to subsidize energy companies in the production of fuels from coal, oil shale, and other sources; **(b)** to help low-income families with fuel bills; and **(c)** to stimulate the development of energy-efficient mass transit systems and upgrade existing systems (Section 12-4).

7. Established a goal of having a 10-month strategic oil reserve by 1985. (By mid-1984 only a 3-month supply was available.)

8. Banned the burning of oil and natural gas to generate electricity after 1990 except in special cases.

9. Gradually deregulated the price of natural gas produced in the United States with full deregulation planned by 1986. (Repeal by Congress is possible because of consumer opposition.)

10. Established a goal of increasing the use of coal to 25 percent of U.S. primary energy use by 1985—a goal that will probably not be met.

11. Required labels for all major appliances, indicating energy efficiency or average annual operating cost.

12. Required the DOE to establish federal energy-efficiency standards for major home appliances. (Most of these were canceled by administrative order in early 1984.)

13. Provided tax credits for homeowners and businesses installing insulation, solar heating, and energy-saving equipment.

14. Provided tax incentives to encourage businesses to develop energy alternatives, such as solar, wind, and geothermal power.

15. Authorized a $35 million fund to provide low-interest loans to homeowners and businesses to install solar energy equipment (by mid-1984, most of these funds had not been made available).

16. Required utilities to buy surplus electric power from industries or private individuals producing their own power from waste heat (cogeneration) and from other sources such as windpower and small hydroelectric plants. (By mid-1984 full implementation was being stalled by lawsuits, and some utilities were levying large hookup charges and offering low buy-back prices.)

17. Shelved indefinitely plans to build a nuclear breeder demonstration reactor.

---

more publicly owned lands for energy development (Section 10-2), reducing environmental protection controls if they hinder energy development, and reducing local and state participation in determining land and offshore areas to be leased for energy development.

The proposed plan was based on a stated philosophy of letting free market competition (Table 16-4) determine which energy alternatives are used. In practice, however, already large federal subsidies for developing nuclear fission and nuclear fusion (which amounted to $42 billion between 1950 and 1984) would be increased, even though the marketplace has shown these alternatives to be economically unsound (Section 15-5).

The Reagan administration plan also proposed essentially eliminating federal support for increasing energy efficiency and development of renewable energy resources, along with sharp cutbacks in energy-assistance programs for the poor, who are

Table 16-5 Proposed 1985 Federal Expenditures for Energy Research and Development

Program	Expenditure (millions of dollars)	Percentage of Total Energy Budget	Approximate Military Expenditure Equivalent
Nuclear energy	1,101	35	One missile-carrying submarine
Fission	(618)	(20)	Six long-range bombers
Fusion	(483)	(15)	Five long-range bombers
High-energy physics*	561	18	Four destroyers
Basic energy sciences	420	14	Three destroyers
Fossil fuels	273	9	Two destroyers
Environmental research	228	7	Two long-range bombers and two jet fighter planes
Solar energy (direct and indirect)	191	6	One MX missile and one jet fighter plane
Nuclear physics*	183	6	Two long-range bombers
Conservation	148	5	One destroyer
Total	3,105	100	Three missile-carrying submarines

*Because these expenditures are spread over several categories, the actual fraction of the budget devoted to nuclear fission and nuclear fusion approaches at least 60% of the total.

hardest hit by rising energy prices. Congress refused to accept all the proposed cuts in energy conservation and renewable energy resources and in 1983 made a $200 million a year cut in proposed expenditures for nuclear fission energy by eliminating support for the Clinch River demonstration breeder fission reactor.

As Table 16-5 reveals, *the total government energy research and development expenditure approved by Congress for 1984 was no more than the amount spent on building three missile-carrying submarines.* Table 16-5 also reveals that nuclear energy still makes up the largest fraction of the total energy budget, despite the belief of most financial experts and utility company executives that nuclear power is an uneconomic energy option, even with massive government subsidies (Section 15-5). Much of the remaining support for renewable energy alternatives is devoted to such hard-path methods of electricity production as solar power towers and ocean thermal electric conversion plants. As a result, about two-thirds of the entire energy budget in 1984 was used to develop ways of generating electricity—a type of energy that

some energy experts believe may already be oversupplied in the United States.

Horizontal Integration of Large Energy Companies Major oil companies—which are now more accurately called energy companies—have gained increasing control over most major energy alternatives for the United States. Government records show that by 1983 the large oil companies owned (1) at least 70 percent of U.S. natural gas reserves, (2) 70 percent of uranium production and reserves, (3) nearly half the nation's privately held coal reserves, one-third of the coal mined each year, and 9 of the top 15 coal-mining companies, (4) leases for much of the rich oil shale and geothermal energy reserves on federal lands (Enrichment Study 11), and (5) 5 of the 10 largest solar photovoltaic companies, 8 of the 25 largest companies making active solar collectors, and a significant percentage of solar energy patents.

The oil companies argue that (1) because oil is in the long run a declining business, it makes economic sense for them to invest in other alternatives; **(2)** they have the capital needed to stimulate development of other energy alternatives at a time when government support is decreasing; and **(3)** there is no law preventing them from diversifying their economic interests.

However, some analysts fear that such *horizontal integration* will allow the big energy companies too much control over the price and rate of development of most major energy alternatives. Some observers have suggested that Congress pass legislation prohibiting or carefully regulating such horizontal integration of energy alternatives by large energy companies.

Developing an Intermediate- and Long-Term Energy Strategy So far, most government policies and expenditures have emphasized development of the hard path. In 1981 the National Audubon Society proposed an intermediate national energy strategy that represents a mix of the hard and soft energy paths without sacrificing the nation's economic growth or requiring major changes in life-style. With this plan **(1)** improvements in energy efficiency would be used to keep the total amount of energy used by all Americans in 2000 about equal to the amount used in 1982; **(2)** dependence on imported oil would be reduced from 15 percent of all energy used and 35 percent of all oil used in 1982 to only 3.8 and 19 percent, respectively, in 2000; **(3)** the share of primary energy obtained from renewable energy sources would be increased from 8.5 percent in 1982 to 25 percent in 2000 (Figure 14-3); and **(4)** nuclear and coal-fired power plants under construction in 1980 would be completed, but no new nuclear power plants would be built and a few new coal-fired power plants would be built, if needed.

This strategy would require investments of $675 billion (roughly $150 per capita per year) in energy conservation and $570 billion (about $130 per capita per year) on development of renewable energy resources between 1980 and 2000. According to the Audubon Society, this $1.2 trillion investment over 20 years is much smaller than that necessary to produce the equivalent amount of energy from new oil and gas supplies, synthetic fuels, and new coal-fired and nuclear power plants.

While politicians, energy company executives, and environmentalists argue over which path to follow, an increasing number of citizens have chosen the soft path, taking energy matters into their own hands. They are insulating, caulking, and making other improvements to conserve energy and save money, building new passively heated and cooled solar homes, adding passive solar heating to existing homes, and growing more of their own food. Between 1979 and 1983 these common-sense actions by individuals and businesses provided the United States with over 150 times more energy than new supplies of energy obtained from finding more nonrenewable supplies of coal, oil, and natural gas, and from new nuclear power plants.

Similarly, local governments in a growing number of cities, including Portland, Oregon; Seattle, Washington; San Diego, Los Angeles, and Davis, California; St. Paul, Minnesota; and Wichita, Kansas, are developing their own successful programs to improve energy efficiency. They are showing that local initiative is a faster and cheaper way to improve energy efficiency and to develop their own direct and indirect solar energy resources than waiting for action at the federal and state levels.

Some analysts believe that making a relatively smooth transition to a new sustainable earth energy era over the next 50 years is one of the most important, complex, and difficult problems facing the world and the United States. They argue that we have enough time to change to a new sustainable earth energy era, but only if we begin now.

In the long run, humanity has no choice but to rely on renewable energy. No matter how abundant they seem today, eventually coal and uranium will run out. The choice before us is practical: We simply cannot afford to make more than one energy transition within the next generation.

Daniel Deudney and Christopher Flavin

Discussion Topics

1. How is the sun's energy responsible for wind energy, biomass energy, and hydroelectric energy?

2. Explain how the use of nonfuel mineral resources (Chapter 13) and food production (Chapter 9) depend on the availability of energy resources.

3. Give your reasons for agreeing or disagreeing with the following propositions, which have been suggested by various analysts.

   a. To solve present and future U.S. energy problems, all we need to do is find more domestic supplies of oil and natural gas (the basic idea of the Reagan energy plan).

   b. Tidal energy is a clean, untapped source that can solve the world's major energy problems.

   c. To conserve finite and dwindling supplies of oil and natural gas, the United States should shift back to coal, easing air pollution and surface-mining regulations to make this possible.

d. The energy crisis of the early 1970s was staged by the major U.S. oil companies to drive prices up, increase profits, and eliminate competition from independent gas stations.

e. To conserve finite and dwindling supplies of oil and natural gas and to decrease reliance on imports, the United States should greatly increase its use of nuclear power as soon as possible.

f. The price of electricity and domestically produced fossil fuels in the United States should be deregulated and allowed to increase significantly, to promote energy conservation and to reduce environmental impacts of energy use. Such price increases, however, should be coupled with tax rebates or other devices to ensure that poor and lower-middle-income citizens do not bear the brunt of the higher prices.

g. The United States should not worry about foreign oil imports because they improve international relationships and prevent the nation from depleting its own supplies of oil and natural gas.

h. The United States should cut average per capita energy use by at least 50 percent between 1985 and 2000.

i. The United States should declare an official moratorium on the building and licensing of new nuclear power plants until there is greater assurance of their safety and of the feasibility of safe transportation and long-term storage of nuclear wastes.

j. Between 1990 and 2020 the United States should phase out all use of nuclear power to generate electricity.

k. A mandatory energy conservation program should form the basis of any energy policy for the United States.

l. No oil company or other large company should be allowed to own interest in more than one energy alternative.

m. To help protect consumers from rising prices, a National Energy Company, supported by taxes, should be established to develop and control about one-fourth to one-third of federally owned energy resources (Enrichment Study 11), in competition with major private energy companies.

n. A National Energy Company should be created, but instead of competing directly with private energy companies, its mission should be to develop a 2-year reserve supply of oil and to evaluate how and which energy resources on federally owned lands should be developed.

o. To solve world and U.S. energy supply problems, we need to begin recycling energy.

p. Federal subsidies for all hard- and soft-energy alternatives should be eliminated so that all choices can be evaluated in an open, competitive marketplace.

q. All government tax breaks and other subsidies for conventional fuels (oil, natural gas, coal), synthetic natural gas and oil, and nuclear power should be removed, and limited subsidies granted for the development of energy conservation, and solar, wind, and biomass energy alternatives.

r. Large solar electric power plants shouldn't be developed because they will occupy 10 percent of the desert area in the United States.

s. Development of solar and wind energy should be left up to private enterprise, without help from the federal government.

t. To save energy, emphasis should be placed on building a network of sophisticated mass transit systems in all major urban areas.

u. Requiring all new homes to be heavily insulated and oriented to take advantage of sunlight and prevailing winds is unacceptable because it violates the rights of homeowners to do as they please with their homes.

v. Hydroelectric power can solve America's energy problems.

x. We can solve present and future U.S. energy problems by converting agricultural, timbering, animal, and urban wastes to biofuels.

y. We can solve present and future U.S. energy problems by building a network of large-scale solar electric power plants.

4. List 20 ways in which you unnecessarily waste energy each day, and try to order them according to the amount of energy wasted. Draw up a plan showing how you could eliminate or reduce each type of waste. Which ones are the most difficult to reduce? Why?

5. Make an energy use study of your campus or school, and use the findings to develop an energy conservation program.

6. What are some of the major political roadblocks to the transition to a world depending primarily on renewable direct and indirect solar energy for most of its energy needs?

7. What might be some of the consequences for your life and life-style if such a transition to solar energy is not made?

8. Can you think of any disadvantages of making the transition to a world heavily dependent on renewable, solar-derived energy resources?

17

Water Resources

If there is magic on this planet, it is in water.
Loren Eisley

17-1 Importance and Properties of Water

A Vital Resource Water is our most abundant substance, covering about 71 percent of the earth's surface. Indeed, life is mostly water, making up about 50 to 97 percent of the weight of all plant and animal life and about 70 percent of your body. Nothing can live without water. You might survive a month without food, but only a few days without a daily intake of about 2.1 liters (2 quarts) of water.

Water is necessary to grow plants and trees through the process of photosynthesis (Section 4-3); to dissolve and transport nutrients from the soil into and through plants and animals to keep them alive; to process metal, mineral, and energy resources; to manufacture most things; and to dissolve and dilute the wastes of an urbanizing, industrializing, growing world population. It is also a major factor in determining world climate and weather patterns (Section 3-6).

Unusual Physical Properties Much of water's usefulness results from its unique physical properties.

1. *Liquid water has a high boiling point (100°C or 212°F) and solid water or ice has a high melting point (0°C or 32°F).* Otherwise, water at normal temperatures would be a gas rather than a liquid. There would be no oceans, lakes, rivers, plants, or animals.

2. *Liquid water has a very high heat of vaporization (540 calories per gram).* Because water

molecules have strong forces of attraction for one another, it takes 540 calories to evaporate one gram of water—about seven times the energy needed to vaporize one gram of gasoline. Similarly, when a gram of water vapor condenses back to the liquid state, 540 calories is given off. This storage of energy when water is evaporated by solar energy from oceans and other bodies of water, and its release when the water vapor in the atmosphere condenses and falls back to the earth as precipitation, is a major factor in distributing heat from the sun throughout the world. Water's high heat of vaporization is also important in regulating the temperature of your body. Each gram of water evaporated from your skin removes 540 calories (of heat) from your body.

3. *Liquid water has an extremely high heat capacity, or ability to store heat.* For example, water absorbs five times as much heat per gram as rock for a given change in temperature. As a result, water heats and cools more slowly than most other substances. This property prevents extreme climatic temperature changes, helps protect living organisms from the shock of abrupt temperature changes, and makes water effective in removing heat from power plants and other industrial processes.

4. *Liquid water is a superior solvent.* The ability of water to dissolve a great variety of substances enables it to carry nutrients throughout the tissues and organs of plants and animals, to be a good cleanser, and to remove and dilute water-soluble wastes. Because water dissolves so many things, it is also easily polluted.

5. *Liquid water has a very low viscocity, or resistance to flow.* As a result, it flows easily and quickly downhill and is easy to pump.

6. *Liquid water has an extremely high surface tension and an even higher wetting ability.* Together, these properties are responsible for capillarity—the ability of water to be drawn upward from tiny pores in the soil into thin, hollow filaments or capillaries, as in the stems of plants.

Enrichment Studies 7, 11, 13, and 14 are related to this chapter.

7. *Liquid water is the only common substance that expands rather than contracts when it freezes.* Thus, ice floats on water and bodies of water freeze from the top down instead of from the bottom up. Without this property most aquatic life as we know it would not exist, and the earth's surface would be permanently covered with ice. Because water expands on freezing, it also breaks pipes, cracks engine blocks (which is why antifreeze is used in cars), and cracks streets, soil, and rocks.

Some Important Questions With increasing demands for water and with world population increasing by 221,000 each day in 1984, is the world in danger of running out of usable water? What are the present and future water situations in the United States? How can we manage the world's fixed supply of water to get enough of it in the right place, at the right time, and with the right quality? This chapter will deal with these questions of water supply, while the next discusses water pollution.

17-2 Worldwide Supply, Renewal, Distribution, and Use

World Water Resources The world's fixed supply of water in all forms (vapor, liquid, and ice) is enormous. If it could be distributed equally, there would be enough to provide every man, woman, and child on earth with 292 trillion liters (77 trillion gallons). *However, about 99.997 percent of the world's water supply is not readily available for human use (Table 17-1) and the 0.003 percent that is available is unevenly distributed.*

To understand why only 0.003 percent of all water is available as fresh water for human use, imagine that the total planetary water supply is 38 liters (10 gallons). After we take out the ocean water that is too salty for drinking, for growing crops, and for most industrial purposes, about 1.1 liters (4.5 cups) remains. Of this, about 0.83 liter (3.5 cups) lies too far under the earth's surface or is tied up in glaciers, in ice caps, in the atmosphere, and in the soil as "bound water," unavailable for use by plants or for extraction by wells. This leaves only about 0.27 liter (1 cup). When we take out the water that is polluted, relatively inaccessible, and too expensive to get, the remaining supply of usable fresh water is only about 0.001 liter (10 drops).

The Hydrologic Cycle Even this tiny fraction of usable fresh water amounts to about an average of 879,000 liters (232,000 gallons) for each person on earth. Furthermore, this supply is continually pur-

Table 17-1 World's Water Resources and Their Average Rates of Renewal

Location	Percentage of World Supply	Average Rate of Renewal
Oceans	97.134	3,100 years (37,000 years for deep ocean water)
Atmosphere	0.001	9 to 12 days
On land		
Ice caps	2.225	16,000 years
Glaciers	0.015	16,000 years
Saline lakes	0.007	10 to 100 years (depending on depth)
Freshwater lakes	0.009	10 to 100 years (depending on depth)
Rivers	0.0001	12 to 20 days
In land		
Soil moisture	0.003	280 days
Groundwater		
To a depth of 1,000 meters (1.6 miles)	0.303	300 years
1,000 to 2,000 meters (1.6 to 3.2 miles)	0.303	4,600 years
Total	100.000	

ified in the natural *hydrologic (water) cycle* (Figure 4-12) at a rate 36,000 times faster than we can drink it—as long as we don't pollute it faster than it is replenished. Although all the world's water is recycled eventually by the hydrologic cycle, parts of the supply are renewed at different average rates ranging from 9 days to 37,000 years (Table 17-1). Only the water in the atmosphere, the rivers, and the soil is recycled at relatively rapid rates. Water also cycles through living organisms. For example, the water making up 70 percent of your body is replenished several times each year.

The water we use comes from two sources: surface water and groundwater. **Surface water** flows in streams and rivers and is stored in natural lakes, in wetlands, and in reservoirs constructed by humans. Surface water entering rivers and freshwater lakes is called **runoff**. This source of water is renewed fairly rapidly (12 to 20 days) in areas with average precipitation (Table 17-1).

Water that sinks into the soil where it may be stored for long times in slow flowing and slowly renewed (hundreds to thousands of years) underground reservoirs, called **groundwater,** makes up about 95 percent of the world's supply of fresh water. Groundwater constitutes more than 3,000 times the

Figure 17-1 The groundwater system.

precipitation

recharge

percolation

percolation

well

artesian well

water table

Impervious Stratum

Zone of Saturation

Aquifer

volume of fresh water found in all the world's rivers at any given time and 33 times the volume found in all the world's rivers and freshwater lakes (Table 17-1).

The flow of surface water on land in a country or region is divided into natural drainage patterns called watersheds. A **watershed** or **drainage basin** is simply an area of land; all precipitation falling anywhere in a given watershed that is not evaporated, stored, or transported out of the area by groundwater flows will run off in the same rivers and streams. The amount of surface water runoff in different watersheds varies considerably because of different climate patterns (Section 3-6), rock and soil types (Section 8-4), and land use patterns (Section 12-5).

Figure 17-1 shows the basic features of the groundwater system. Some of the rainwater falling on land slowly percolates through the soil until it reaches a layer, or stratum, of rock that the water cannot penetrate (Figure 17-1). Water builds up in the overlying sand and rock above this impervious rock layer and fills all the openings and cracks. The soil and rock become saturated up to a certain level, called the **water table** (Figure 17-1); above the water

table line, the soil is relatively dry. In swamps and areas with high rainfall, the water table may lie at or near the land surface, while in dry areas it may be hundreds to thousands of meters below ground or not exist.

Water below the water table slowly flows toward the sea in **aquifers** (Latin for "water bearing"). These permeable underground layers of gravel, sand, or porous rock conduct water slowly from mountain areas with heavy rainfall and snowfall toward the oceans. The rate of flow toward the oceans is determined by the difference in the elevation of the aquifer and sea level and by the permeability of the intervening sediment or rock. *Unconfined aquifers* are found above the first impervious rock layer; *confined aquifers* are between two impervious rock layers.

The difference in water height from one place to another in an aquifer generates hydraulic pressure at the lower point. To get fresh water, a well is drilled below the water table. If a well reaches into a confined aquifer, the hydraulic pressure may be so great that the water flows freely out of the well without pumping. Such wells are called artesian wells (Figure 17-1). Most aquifers represent rela-

Table 17-2 Average U.S. Water Use in 1983

Use or Product	Average Amount Withdrawn		Use or Product	Average Amount Withdrawn	
	Liters	Gallons		Liters	Gallons
Total Use	7,402	1,953			
Home Use			454 grams (1 pound) of corn	645	170
Total per person (per day)	341	90	454 grams (1 pound) of sugar from sugarbeets	872	230
Drinking water (per day)	2	0.5	454 grams (1 pound) of rice	2,122	560
Shaving, water running (per minute)	8	2	454 grams (1 pound) of grain-fed beef	3,032	800
Shower (per minute)	19	5	454 grams (1 pound) of cotton	7,732	2,040
Toilet (per flush)	23	6	**Industrial and Commercial**		
Cooking (per day)	30	8	Total per person (per day)	4,518	1,192
Washing dishes, water running (per meal)	38	10	Cooling water for electric power plants per person (per day)	3,707	978
Watering lawn or garden (per minute)	38	10	Industrial mining and manufacturing per person (per day)	695	183
Automatic dishwasher (per load)	60	16	Refine 3.8 liters (1 gallon) of gasoline from crude oil	38	10
Bath	135	36	454 grams (1 pound) of steel	133	35
Washing machine (per load)	230	60	Refine 3.8 liters (1 gallon) of synthetic fuel from coal	1,000	265
Leaky toilet (per day)	90–455	24–120	One Sunday newspaper	1,060	280
Leaky faucet (per day)	180–910	48–240	454 grams (1 pound) of synthetic rubber	1,140	300
Agricultural Use (irrigation)			454 grams (1 pound) of aluminum	3,790	1,000
Total per person (per day)	2,543	671	One automobile	379,000	100,000
One egg	150	40			
454 grams (1 pound) flour	284	75			
Orange	380	100			
Glass of milk	380	100			
Loaf of bread	570	150			

Source: U.S. Geological Survey, *Estimated Use of Water in the United States in 1980*, 1984.

tively fixed deposits of water accumulated over thousands to millions of years that are normally recharged by precipitation quite slowly. Because of their location deep under the ground, it is difficult—if not impossible—to clean up an aquifer once it has been polluted.

Water Use in the United States   Of the total water withdrawn each year in the United States, only about 8 percent is used for *domestic* purposes (cooking, drinking, washing, watering lawns and gardens, and flushing away wastes). Because most Americans live in urban areas, about 86 percent of this water passes through public water facilities, and the remaining 14 percent is obtained mostly in untreated form from private wells. In 1983 each American used an average of 341 liters (90 gallons) a day for domestic purposes (Table 17-2)—about 3 times the per capita average for the world as a whole, and 15 to 20 times that of most LDCs. But average daily domestic use per person is two to five times higher in some cities.

The remaining 92 percent of all water withdrawn is used for *irrigation* to produce food (33 percent), by *industries and businesses* (10 percent), and for *cooling electric power plants* (49 percent). These uses and others like those shown in Table 17-2 meant that in 1983 an additional average of 7,061 liters (1,863 gallons) of water was withdrawn from rivers, lakes, and underground aquifers each day to provide each American with food, energy, and manufactured goods and to run stores and offices. *Thus, in 1983 an average of 7,402 liters (1,953 gallons) of water per day per person was withdrawn from rivers, lakes, and underground aquifers.*

In the United States about 88 percent of the water withdrawn from runoff and groundwater sources each year is returned to rivers and lakes.

Much of this comes from electric power plants, which withdraw 49 percent of all water and return all but about 2 percent. Most water withdrawn by U.S. industries is recycled and reused within the plants an average of 2.2 times before it is discharged. Much of the water returned to rivers and lakes, however, is degraded by pollution. In 1979 the U.S. Water Resources Council listed only two states—Kansas and Montana—as having no serious occurrences of surface water pollution and only 8 states as having no serious occurrences of groundwater pollution.

17-3 Water Supply Problems

The World Situation Although the average world water supply seems to be sufficient, many areas of the world, including many parts of the United States, are experiencing serious water resource problems. Indeed, a number of experts agree with Gerald D. Seinwill, former acting director of the U.S. Water Resources Council who considers *the availability of adequate water resources to be the most serious long-range problem confronting the world and the United States.* At least 80 countries, accounting for nearly 40 percent of the world's population, now experience serious droughts. Water shortages vary but are particularly acute in parts of Europe (especially Spain, southern Italy, and Greece), parts of Latin America (especially Panama, northern Mexico, central Chile, Brazil, and the Peruvian coast), mid- and southern Africa, eastern Australia and New Zealand, Asia (especially all Arab states except Syria, and most of Iran, Pakistan, Turkey, western India, Taiwan, Japan, and Korea), and the southwestern United States.

By the year 2000 the situation is expected to get much worse because of increasing population and water use and because much of the world's water is located in the wrong place, available at the wrong time of the year, or of poor quality. According to UN projections, most of the Soviet Union except Siberia, most of Europe, almost half the United States, most of India, the central Thailand plains, Tasmania, the islands east of Java, the larger Caribbean islands, Mexico, and parts of Brazil and Argentina will be short of water by the year 2000. This will lead to increasing conflicts within countries and between countries because about one-third of the major world river basins are shared by three or more countries.

Although water scarcity, droughts, and flooding are serious in some regions, drinking impure water is the major hazard to humans throughout much of the world. In its 1975 survey, the World Health Organization (WHO) found that *almost 2 out*

Figure 17-2 Four out of five of the world's rural people and one out of five city dwellers don't have ready access to uncontaminated water. These two in Lima, Peru, are bailing their drinking water from a puddle because the nearby public pump is inadequate.

of 3 people living in LDCs did not have water safe enough to drink and also lacked access to suitable waste disposal systems. In rural areas in LDCs the situation was even worse, with 4 out of 5 people not having access to reliable, safe drinking water supplies and 9 out of 10 lacking adequate sanitation facilities. WHO estimates that 25 million people die every year from cholera, dysentery, diarrhea, and other waterborne diseases caused by unclean or inadequate water—an average of 68,500 deaths each day (Enrichment Study 7).

Scarcity of pure drinking water in many LDCs means that every day women and children carry heavy cans or jugs long distances to get untreated, often polluted water from a river or community pump (Figure 17-2). The daily round-trip distance may be 24 kilometers (15 miles).

To help correct this situation, the UN General Assembly declared the 1980s as the International Drinking Water Supply and Sanitation Decade, with the goal of bringing clean water and adequate sanitation to all people by 1990. To achieve this goal will require at least $300 billion (in 1978 dollars), assuming use of cheaper, appropriate technology like using public standpipes instead of home hookups. This is an average expenditure of $80 million per day between 1980 and 1990. This may seem like a lot of money. However, the world spends an average of $240 million dollars a day on cigarettes.

Water problems often differ between MDCs and LDCs. LDCs may or may not have enough water, but they rarely have the money needed to develop water storage and distribution systems. People must settle where the water is. In MDCs people tend to live where the climate is favorable and then bring

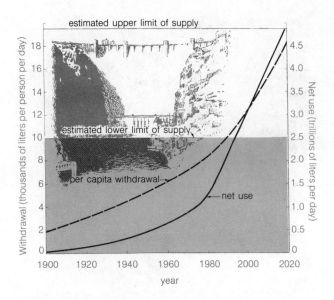

Figure 17-3 The J-shaped curves of present and projected average per capita withdrawal and net water use in the United States. (Source: U.S. Water Resources Council, 1979.)

in water through sophisticated systems. As Raymond Dasmann put it, "Today people in affluent nations often settle in a desert and demand that water be brought to them, or they settle on a floodplain and demand that water be kept away."

The U.S. Situation Although the United States has plenty of fresh water, much of its annual runoff is not in the right place, at the right time, or of high enough quality. In addition, water use has been increasing rapidly since 1900 and is expected to increase even more between 1984 and 2020 (Figure 17-3). Between 1900 and 1980 U.S. population increased by 320 percent and water use by about 1,250 percent. Increasingly, Americans are learning the hard way what Benjamin Franklin told us in 1746: "When the well is dry, we learn the worth of water." In 1979 the U.S. Water Resources Council projected that by the year 2000 only 3 of the 21 federally designated water regions—New England, the Ohio basin, and the South Atlantic-Gulf area—will have ample water supplies. (Figure 17-4)

In the eastern half of the United States the major problem is not a shortage of water, but inability to supply enough water to some urban concentrations of population and industry, coupled with increasing pollution of rivers, lakes, and groundwater by industries and cities (Chapter 18). Some water problems and controversies in the eastern half of the country are:

• Water-rich states in the upper Midwest and Canada are organizing to head off attempts by

arid western states to tap water from the Great Lakes, the largest body of fresh water on earth. As water becomes more scarce in Sun Belt states, people and industry may have to move back to the Water Belt.

• Nearly 300 families around Fonda Lake in southeastern Michigan have had to use bottled water since 1978 because 800 groundwater sites either have been contaminated or are suspected of contamination by road salt stored by the State Highway Department.

• Long Island's 3 million residents must draw all their water from an underground aquifer that is becoming severely contaminated by industrial wastes, leaking septic tanks, and salty ocean water that is drawn into the aquifer as more fresh water is withdrawn.

• New York City and other eastern cities compete with western cities and states for limited federal funds to replace old water delivery systems. New York City officials hope that one of the two huge tunnels built in 1917 and 1937, which bring water into the city from aqueducts connected to 1,000 different streams and 27 artificial lakes throughout the state, will not fail before a third $3.5 billion tunnel can be completed around 2000. Failure of just one tunnel would make fire fighting difficult, shut down many businesses, and leave many New Yorkers without adequate water. These aging tunnels (which can't be shut down for inspection or repair) and the city's maze of water pipes already leak an estimated 380 million liters (100 million gallons) of water a day.

• Water is being pumped from underground Florida aquifers so rapidly to meet the needs of a mushrooming population that water tables are falling and the ground around Orlando is collapsing upon itself to create huge sinkholes.

The major problem in many of the areas in the western half of the country is a shortage of runoff due to low average precipitation and rapidly declining water tables in many areas as farmers and cities deplete groundwater aquifers faster than they are recharged. Present water shortages could get much worse if more industries and people move in (Figure 12-3) and if more of this region's precious water is used to mine coal and oil shale and to tap geothermal energy resources found there (Enrichment Study 11). Some typical western-half water problems and controversies are:

• A fight for water has been raging for decades between residents of arid, fast-growing southern California and those in the water-rich northern end of the state. Northern California receives more than two-thirds of the state's

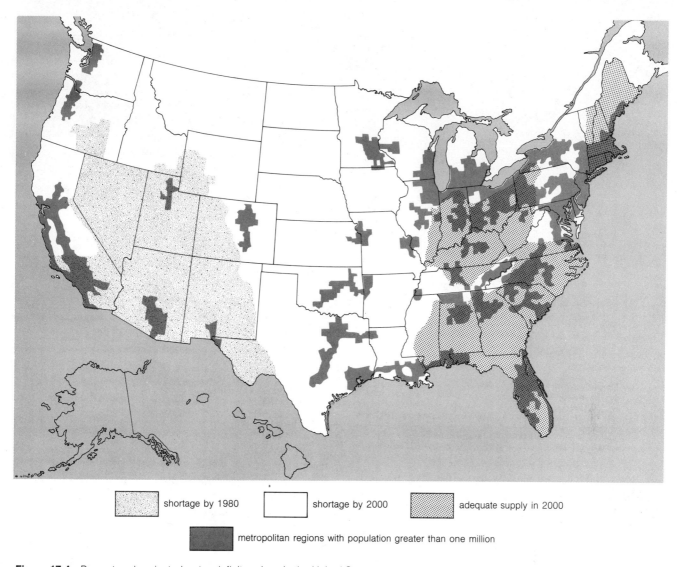

	shortage by 1980		shortage by 2000		adequate supply in 2000

	metropolitan regions with population greater than one million

Figure 17-4 Present and projected water-deficit regions in the United States compared with present metropolitan regions with populations greater than 1 million. By the year 2000, only 3 of the 21 water regions are expected to have ample water supplies. (Source: U.S. Water Resources Council, 1979.)

rainfall, but about half of the state's population lives in the Los Angeles basin, which receives enough rain to support only a little over 100,000 people. The latest battle is over the proposed $5 billion to $23 billion Peripheral Canal to carry water south from the Sacramento River to Los Angeles. Opponents call this a costly boondoggle that would degrade the Sacramento River, threaten fishing, and inhibit the flushing action that helps cleanse the San Francisco Bay of pollutants. Proponents say that the proposed canal could offset a crippling drought that could bring economic ruin to much of southern California. In 1982 voters rejected the project by a 3-to-2 margin, but the issue is far from dead.

- Planned price increases for water will force most Arizona farmers to sell their land for other uses by 2006.

- Arkansas and Louisiana are fighting efforts by Texas to import water from the Mississippi River to arid, western Texas to replace supplies now being drawn from the underground Ogallala aquifer, which is being depleted rapidly.

- Tribes of Native American Indians in Wyoming, Montana, and other states have filed over 50 lawsuits claiming rights to vast amounts of water in every major western water-user system based on a Supreme Court ruling that treaties and executive orders dating from the late 1800s entitle Native American Indians to enough water to irrigate their reservations.

Table 17-3 Major Methods for Managing Water Resources

Input (increase supply in selected areas)	Output (reduce degradation and loss of existing supplies)	Throughput (reduce waste and per capita use)
Build dams to create lake reservoirs	Decrease evaporation losses in irrigation	Reduce overall population growth and growth in areas with water problems (arid regions and floodplains)
Divert water from one region to another	Use better drainage for irrigated agriculture to minimize salt buildup in soils	
Tap and artificially recharge more groundwater	Purify polluted water for reuse (Chapter 18)	Redesign mining, industrial, and other processes to use less water
Desalt seawater and brackish water		Reduce water waste
Tow freshwater icebergs from the Antarctic to water-short regions		Decrease the average per capita use of water
Control the weather to provide more desirable precipitation patterns		
Control pollution by preventing or limiting the addition of harmful chemicals (Chapter 18)		Increase the price of water to encourage conservation
Encourage people to move to areas with adequate water		

If present trends continue, most sections of the country are expected to face some form of water shortage by the turn of the century. As a result, you might find Figure 17-5 useful in helping you decide where to live in the coming decades.

Methods for Managing Water Resources Although we can't increase the earth's supply of water, we can manage what we have more effectively. The major methods for managing water resources are summarized in Table 17-3. Some water resource experts favor a "hard path," trying to increase water supplies in an area by building large-scale dams, reservoirs, and canals to transfer water from one water basin to another. Others favor a "soft path," emphasizing voluntary and compulsory water conservation programs coupled with price increases to reflect the true costs of using water for irrigation and for industrial, commercial, and domestic purposes. Others argue that any effective plan for water management must use a combination of all the approaches shown in Table 17-3. In the remainder of this chapter we will look at some advantages and drawbacks of the major methods for managing water resources.

17-4 Building Dams and Water Diversion Projects

Dams and Channelization Ever since people began to irrigate cropland and to live in cities, they have built dams, reservoirs, aqueducts, and pipes to store and carry water. When a river is dammed, a reservoir or lake forms behind the dam for temporary storage of water. A dam that captures high spring water flows resulting from heavy rainfall and melting snow in mountains above the barrier can release this water as needed to areas below. The major advantages and disadvantages of dams are given in Table 17-4.

Ideally, the decision to build a dam should involve a careful analysis of potential benefits and drawbacks. However, many dams are built for political reasons, even when analysis shows that cheaper, less harmful, and better alternatives are available. U.S. senators and representatives, for example, want visible evidence of their power to funnel federal money into their state or district. For years environmentalists have opposed completion of a number of big dams and water diversion projects, which they contend would cause more harm than benefits and represent a waste of billions of dollars of taxpayers' money.

Another engineering technique used to control floods and soil erosion, drain wetlands, and improve navigation is **channelization** of streams. It consists of straightening, deepening, widening, clearing, or lining existing stream channels. Many U.S. streams have been channelized by the Army Corps of Engineers and more are planned for the future. Because of political considerations and the expense involved, most streams are only partially channelized. While this can lead to better flood control in the channelized upstream area, the greater water flow in the area usually increases the amount of flooding, sediment deposits, and bank erosion in downstream areas. The drainage of wetlands as a result of channelization eliminates the habitats of certain fish and

Table 17-4 Major Advantages and Disadvantages of Using Dams

Advantages	Disadvantages
Reduces the danger of flooding in areas below the dam.	Large acreages of land behind the dam are permanently flooded to form the reservoir. This displaces people and destroys scenic natural areas and wildlife habitats. Abnormally high rains can cause a dam reservoir to overflow its spillways and flood areas below the dam. Because of the mistaken belief that dams protect them from all floods, people build cities and grow crops on floodplains* below dams. Many experts contend that flood control and reduction of flood losses are better accomplished by reforestation, erosion control (Section 8-6), upstream watershed management, and land-use zoning that prohibits or limits human settlements and farming on floodplains.
Increases local water and food supplies by providing a controllable and reliable flow of water for irrigating areas below the dam.	Often decreases the available water supply because water that would normally flow in a river evaporates from the reservoir's surface or seeps into the ground. This evaporation also increases the salinity of the remaining water, decreasing its usefulness for irrigation. Sometimes does not increase food supplies for local residents in LDCs because the irrigation water is used by large landowners to grow cash crops for export.
Creates a large water reservoir that can be used for water recreation.	In the opinion of some, replaces more-desirable forms of water recreation (white water canoeing and stream fishing) with less-desirable forms (motor and sail boating and lake fishing).
Produces relatively cheap hydroelectric power (Section 16-2) for local and regional residents.	In LDCs the hydroelectric power is sometimes sold to foreign industries rather than being used by local and regional residents. For example, the giant Volta Dam in Ghana is used primarily to supply power to the Kaiser Aluminum Corporation at 5 percent of the average world price for hydroelectric power.
Large dams are safe because none have failed.	Most of the world's large dams are less than 20 years old. The older dams get, however, the higher the risk of failure. Comprehensive risk analyses, like those done for nuclear plants (Section 15-5), are rarely done for large dams. Failure of a large dam could easily kill as many as 200,000 people and cause billions of dollars in damages. Failure of the intermediate-sized Teton Dam killed 14 people and caused $1 billion in damages, and the failure of a small dam above Johnstown, Pennsylvania, killed thousands of people.
	Interrupts the natural flow of a river below the dam, which disrupts fish migration and alters the water's oxygen content (Section 18-3).

*Flood plains—areas vulnerable to periodic flooding—are normally classified as 18-year, 25-year, 50-year, or 100-year flood plains, according to the average interval between major floods. As a result, people mistakenly believe that floods occur only every 18, 25, 50, or 100 years. But this is merely a statistical average; major floods could occur three times in a month or annually for five consecutive years.

wetland plant and animal species. To many people the conversion of a winding stream to a straight, open ditch seriously degrades the aesthetic value of a natural area. Thus, the benefit from an increase in partially protected floodplain area upstream must be weighed against the downstream costs from increased flooding, loss of aquatic plant and animal life, increased bridge repair due to bank erosion, and loss of farmland due to increased erosion.

Water Diversion Projects Water diversion projects usually involve building huge canal systems to transport water from one river basin to another. A grandiose but presently abandoned water diver-

sion scheme was the North American Water and Power Alliance (NAWAPA) proposal to make all major rivers in Alaska and northwest Canada run backward by building massive dams on most north-flowing rivers above the 55th parallel. Some of the world's most beautiful valleys would be flooded to create gigantic reservoirs, 15 of them larger than Lake Mead, North America's largest artificial lake. Water would then be pumped uphill through gigantic pipelines to 7 provinces in Canada, 33 U.S. states, and 3 states in Mexico. The economic, hydrologic, ecological, and political problems—to say nothing of possible effects on climate—of a project this size would be profound throughout its 30- to 50-year

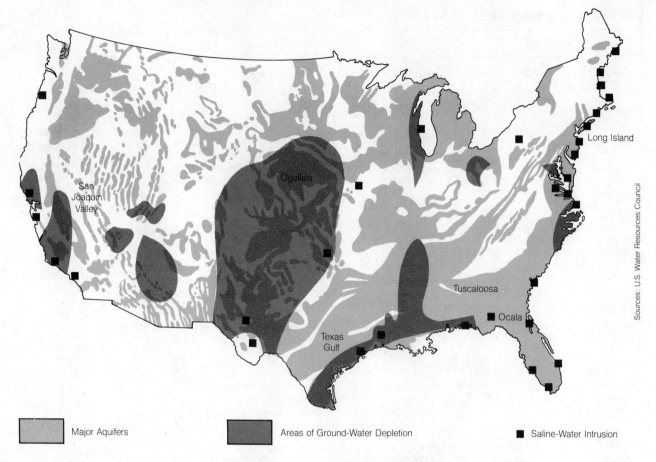

San
Joaquin
Valley

Ogallala

Long Island

Tuscaloosa

Ocala

Texas
Gulf

Sources: U.S. Water Resources Council

Major Aquifers   Areas of Ground-Water Depletion   ■ Saline-Water Intrusion

Figure 17-5 Major underground aquifers containing 95 percent of all fresh water in the United States are being depleted in many areas and contaminated elsewhere through pollution and saltwater intrusion. (Source: U.S. Water Resources Council, 1979.)

construction period and thereafter. The estimated cost in 1969 (before energy prices rose dramatically) was $200 billion.

Another scheme, called the Grand Canal concept, has been proposed recently to solve many of the water supply problems for Canada and the United States. Much of the freshwater runoff now flowing into the Arctic Ocean from the James River Bay in eastern Canada would be recycled (not diverted) to form a new, dike-enclosed freshwater lake within the James Bay. From there it would flow by way of rivers into the Great Lakes to reduce the need to flood lands to provide reservoirs. Then, open channels and pumping stations would be used to distribute the water to the major rivers flowing into the Canadian prairies and most of the United States.

The Army Corps of Engineers has also proposed building four separate canals to divert water from the Missouri River and other tributaries of the Mississippi River to the High Plains states now served by the disappearing Ogallala aquifer (Figure 17-5). The cost of each canal ranges from $13.4 billion to $40 billion, excluding distribution canals,

which could easily double the amount. Nearly one-fourth of the water would be lost through evaporation, spillage, and seepage. Furthermore, the cost of pumping the water through the canals would be at least 10 times what farmers in the area now pay for water.

In the 1990s the Soviet Union plans to begin work on a massive water diversion project. On paper, the Soviet Union has plenty of fresh water—about 12 percent of the world's total. The trouble is that most of it is in the sparsely populated northern and eastern regions. To correct this situation, the government plans to build 25 large dams to block the flow of at least a dozen north-flowing rivers and pump this water back over mountains to the south. The project is expected to take 50 years and to cost at least $100 billion. Such an expenditure would put an enormous drain on the Soviet economy and might cost more than its estimated economic benefits. It would flood an area larger than western Europe, displacing tens of thousands of people.

It could also have potentially serious ecological and climatic effects not only in the Soviet Union, but as far off as North America. Since these rivers now flow into the Arctic Ocean, reversing their flow would diminish freshwater flows into the Arctic Ocean and increase its salinity. Some climatologists believe that this increased salinity would lower the freezing point of the Arctic Ocean and cause the ice cap to melt, possibly starting a global warming trend (Enrichment Study 5). Other scientists project the opposite effect: that is, global cooling, because a reduced flow of warm fresh water into the Arctic Ocean could cause an increase in the amount of polar ice.

Irrigation Problems: Salinity and Waterlogging Like past civilizations, we are learning that building dams and diverting surface water from rivers and streams to irrigate land without providing adequate underground drainage eventually destroys the cropland because of salinity and waterlogging. As irrigation water flows over and through the ground, it dissolves salts, causing **salinity.** This saline water is again spread over the soil for irrigation and more salts are left behind when much of the water is lost to the atmosphere by evaporation and transpiration. Unless these salts are somehow flushed or drained from the soil, their buildup kills crops, decreases yields, forces changes to less profitable crops, promotes excessive water use, and increases capital and operating costs (Figure 8-7).

Flushing the salts out, however, increases the salinity of rivers used for irrigation by those further downstream. For example, the salinity of the Colorado River increases twentyfold as it passes through irrigated cropland between Grand Lake in north central Colorado and the Imperial Dam in southwest Arizona. A problem that often accompanies soil salinity is **waterlogging.** Irrigation water percolating down and accumulating underground can gradually raise the water table close to the surface. Too much water around plant roots inhibits growth.

Salinity and waterlogging are decreasing the productivity of at least one-third and perhaps as much as 80 percent of all irrigated lands throughout the world, especially in hot, dry climates where evaporation is rapid. Once fertile areas of southern Iraq and Pakistan now glisten with salt—looking like fields of freshly fallen snow. Salt buildup is a potential hazard on half of all irrigated land in the 17 western U.S. states, already reducing crop production in many areas (Figure 8-7). One costly solution is to take the land out of production for 2 to 5 years, use large quantities of water to flush out the salts, and then install perforated drainage pipes underground. However, such drainage schemes only slow the destruction of fertile soil by salinity; they do not stop the process.

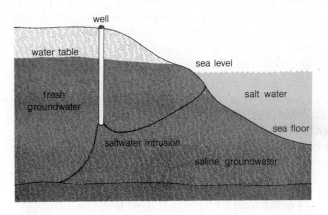

Figure 17-6 Saltwater intrusion along a coastal region. As the water table is lowered, the interface between fresh and saline groundwater moves inland.

17-5 Groundwater Use, Desalination, Towing Icebergs, and Controlling the Weather

Use of Groundwater About half of all U.S. drinking water (96 percent in rural areas and 20 percent in urban areas), 40 percent of the water used for irrigation, and 25 percent of water used for all purposes is withdrawn from underground aquifers. Twenty large cities depend solely on groundwater for their public water supply, and 12 states use groundwater for more than half their public supplies.

One solution to water supply problems is heavier reliance on groundwater. While more groundwater can be used, there are several problems: **(1)** *aquifer depletion* when groundwater is withdrawn faster than it is recharged by precipitation, **(2)** *subsidence* or sinking of the ground as groundwater is withdrawn, **(3)** *saltwater intrusion* into freshwater aquifers in coastal areas as groundwater is withdrawn faster than it is being recharged (Figure 17-6), and **(4)** groundwater contamination from human activities (Section 18-4).

Groundwater depletion is serious in some areas—especially along the Texas Gulf Coast and in parts of the great Ogallala aquifer—stretching across the important farming belt from northern Texas through parts of Oklahoma, New Mexico, Kansas, Colorado, Nebraska, Wyoming, and South Dakota (Figure 17-5). This California-sized aquifer, which contains about as much water as Lake Michigan, was formed about 3 million years ago by receding waters of the Ice Age.

Today, farmers withdraw so much water from this aquifer that the annual overdraft (the amount of water not replenished) is nearly equal to the annual flow of the Colorado River. As a result, the already low water tables in much of the region are falling rapidly and stream and underground spring flows are diminishing. Experts project that at its present rate of depletion, most of this aquifer could be run dry within 40 years and much sooner in areas where it is only a few meters thick. Long before this happens, however, area farmers will be forced to abandon irrigated farming. Already the amount of irrigated land is declining in five of the seven states using this aquifer because of the high cost of energy to operate pumps and the rising cost of pumping water from a depth in some places of 1,825 meters (6,000 feet). Other areas with falling water tables from excessive withdrawal of groundwater include California's San Joaquin Valley, Houston, southern California, and Savannah, Georgia.

One partial solution is to recharge groundwater artificially. Deep groundwater can be pumped up and spread out over the ground to recharge shallow groundwater aquifers. But this can deplete deep groundwater deposits; also, because deep groundwater is often very salty, it can contaminate shallow deposits. Another approach is to use irrigation water, wastewater, and cooling water from industries and power plants to recharge aquifers. But much of this water is lost by evaporation, and in many cases it is better and cheaper to reuse this cooling water in industries and power plants.

Another problem is *groundwater contamination* from large animal feedlots (Enrichment Study 14), landfills, septic tanks, land disposal of waste waters, mining, oil and natural gas production, agricultural chemicals, underground injection wells, and other sources (Section 18-4). Once contaminated, groundwater may remain unusable for hundreds to thousands of years. So far an estimated 1 percent of the nation's vast groundwater supply is polluted. However, numerous contaminated drinking water wells have been shut down in industrial sections of New York (especially Long Island), New Jersey, Massachusetts, Tennessee, Florida, and several other states. A 1980 report by the Environmental Protection Agency indicated that groundwater depletion and contamination will be one of the nation's most serious environmental problems of the 1980s.

Sometimes polluted aquifers can be cleaned up or water removed from them can be treated before use, but both these solutions are very costly. To keep this problem from getting out of hand, numerous water resource and pollution experts have urged the passage and enforcement of laws to protect underground water supplies (Section 18-9).

Desalination The process of removing dissolved salts from water that is too salty for irrigation or human use is known as **desalination** or desalinization (either term is correct). The two major meth-

ods of desalination are *distillation*, in which energy is used to evaporate fresh water from saltwater to leave the salts behind, and *osmosis*, in which energy is used to force saltwater through membranes with pores too small to permit the salts to pass through. Both these processes require large inputs of energy.

Most people think of desalination in connection with oceans, which make up 97 percent of our total water supply. Actually, **saline water** is any water containing more than 1,000 parts per million (ppm) of dissolved solids of any type. Saline water includes *brackish water* (having 1,000 to 4,000 ppm of dissolved solids), *salted water* (having 4,000 to 18,000 ppm), and *seawater* (having 18,000 to 35,000 ppm). Thus, desalination can be used on the coasts for purifying seawater and inland for purifying brackish water.

In 1981 desalting plants produced only about 0.005 percent of the world's daily water and only 0.4 percent of the water used daily in the United States. Most of these plants are small and serve coastal cities in arid, water-short regions where the price of water obtained by any method is high.

Some people see desalination as a major solution to freshwater shortages, but widespread use leads to two major problems. One is *economic*: Primarily because of its energy requirements, desalinated water is expensive—costing over six times as much per liter or gallon as water from a tap. Even more energy and money is required to pump desalted water uphill and inland from coastal desalting plants. Most experts project that desalted water will never be cheap enough for widespread use in irrigation—the main use of water throughout the world.

The other problem with desalination is *ecological*. Building and using a vast network of desalination plants would release significant amounts of heat and other air pollutants (depending on the energy source). There would also be the problem of disposing of vast mountains of salt. If the salt were returned to the ocean, it would increase the salt concentration near the coasts and threaten food sources located in the estuaries and the continental shelf.

Towing Icebergs A 1990s travel ad for California might begin, "As the sun slowly sinks behind the icebergs off the golden California shore, tourists return to their hotels after a day of swimming and ice skating."

Some scientists feel it may be economically feasible to tow huge Antarctic icebergs to southern California, Australia, Saudi Arabia, Chile, and other dry coastal places. Antarctic icebergs are broad and flat, resembling giant floating table tops or ice islands, and they represent a potential freshwater source equal to five times the world's current domestic use of water, and one-third of the world's consumption for all purposes. They are better suited for towing than Arctic bergs, which have mountainlike, irregular shapes and frequently roll over. It would probably take about a year to tow such a berg to California. This technological feat, however, has a number of problems:

1. No one really knows how to lasso, wrap, and tow such a huge object, how to prevent most of it from melting on its long journey through warm waters, and how to get the fresh water from the slowly melting iceberg to shore. Perhaps after spending $100 million, the only thing left would be an empty towline.

2. No one knows whether the project is economically feasible, but because of increased water demand and dwindling supplies, some economists believe such a project might be attractive by 2000 and should be cheaper and quicker than most large-scale water diversion projects.

3. Towing and anchoring such a large, cold mass in semitropical areas could cause weather disturbances (possibly creating considerable fog and rain) and could have harmful effects on marine life.

4. The scheme is a source of political conflict over who owns the icebergs in the Antarctic.

5. There would be hazards to other ships if chunks of the icebergs under tow were to break off and be abandoned in international shipping lanes.

Controlling the Weather Several countries, particularly the United States, have been experimenting for years with seeding clouds with chemicals to produce rain over dry regions and snow over mountains to increase runoff in such areas. In principle, cloud seeding involves several steps: (1) find a suitable cloud, (2) fly a plane under or over the cloud or use ground-mounted burners to inject it with a powdered chemical (the particles serve as nuclei that cause the small water droplets in the cloud to coalesce and form droplets or ice particles large enough to fall to the earth as precipitation), and (3) open your umbrella. The most effective cloud-seeding chemical is silver iodide in crystal form, but salt crystals, dry ice, and clay particles have also been used.

We know that cloud seeding works. In 1977 clouds were successfully seeded in 23 states covering 7 percent of U.S. land area. But we do not know whether we are increasing total rainfall or merely shifting rain from one area to another.

There are also some problems: (1) Cloud seeding doesn't work in very dry areas, where it is most needed, because there are rarely any rain clouds available; (2) large-scale seeding could change regional or even global weather patterns in undesirable ways (Enrichment Study 5); (3) there could be serious ecological side effects, including the unknown effects of silver iodide on humans and wildlife, changes in snowfall and rainfall, and additional flooding that could destroy or alter wildlife populations, upset food webs, and modify the soil; (4) the likelihood of precipitation can be reduced if the seeding is done improperly; and (5) there are legal disputes over ownership of rights to water in a cloud (for example, during the 1977 drought in the western United States, the attorney general of Idaho accused neighboring Washington state of "cloud rustling" and threatened to file suit in federal court).

17-6 Reducing Evaporation and Water Conservation

Reducing Evaporation To reduce loss of water from reservoirs and lakes by evaporation, the United States, Israel, Chile, Australia, and Italy have experimented with covering lakes and reservoirs with thin films of chemicals or plastic and with polystyrene spheres. But there are some major problems: (1) The coverings are broken by waves, winds, and boats (thus covered lakes can't be used for recreation); (2) there is evidence that such coverings disrupt aquatic life by increasing the water temperature and by preventing essential oxygen in the air from reaching the water; (3) the resulting increase in water temperature may promote rather than decrease evaporation; and (4) the approach is expensive. Much more research is needed before such films can be widely used.

Techniques for reducing evaporation and using irrigation water more efficiently include (1) lining irrigation ditches to reduce seepage losses (although this could decrease the rate of groundwater recharge), (2) applying water less often and in smaller quantities (most farmers use too much) (3) using trickle or drip irrigation in which a network of underground plastic tubes drip irrigation water directly onto the roots of plants rather than flooding entire fields (a method that can double crop yields, reduce growth of weeds, and cut irrigation water use by 50 to 60 percent), (4) shifting to or developing crop varieties that require less water or have a high enough salt tolerance to permit irrigation with saline water, (5) growing more crops in areas with ample water rather than in arid regions that need expensive irrigation, **(6)** reducing irrigation water runoff by using contour cultivation (Figure 8-10) and terracing, and storing precipitation and irrigation runoff for use in farm ponds or small reservoirs, **(7)** reducing evaporation of irrigation water by covering the soil with a mulch, **(8)** making farmers pay for water on the basis of the amount of water used (in some areas farmers pay based on the number of acres farmed and thus have no incentive to cut consumption), **(9)** allocating more water to those who use conservation measures, and **(10)** raising water prices to promote conservation.

Wasting Less Water Increasing the available supply of water for an area is important, but many water resource experts argue that water conservation is a quicker and cheaper way to provide much of the additional water needed in nations that now waste much of their input. The United States (and other nations) can learn a lot about water conservation from Israel. Between 1950 and 1980, Israel decreased the waste of water it receives from 83 to 5 percent by a combination of reducing evaporation, using trickle irrigation, and extensive water conservation.

It is estimated that *at least 30 percent and perhaps 50 percent of the water used in the United States is unnecessarily wasted*. A major reason for this is that artificially low water prices encourage waste. Leaky pipes, water mains, toilets, and faucets alone waste an estimated 20 to 35 percent of the water withdrawn from public supplies before it can be used. In Boston such losses amount to an estimated 50 percent of all water pumped into the city. There is little incentive to reduce leaks and waste in many cities like New York City because instead of having individual water meters, users are charged flat rates.

Complex and antiquated laws protecting water rights also discourage conservation. Riparian rights—a holdover from English common law—allow landowners to withdraw as much water as they need from any stream on or bordering their property. To maintain these rights, users must continue to withdraw water at rates they have established over the years—"Use it or lose it." As a result, cities, big farms, and other big users are reluctant to cut back on wasteful use of water because this would reduce the amount they can withdraw.

Another problem is that the responsibility for water resource management in a metropolitan area is divided among many local governments rather than being managed in terms of an entire water basin. For example, the Chicago metropolitan area has 349 separate water supply systems and 135 waste treatment plants divided among about 2,000 local units of government over a six-county area.

This is in sharp contrast to the regionalized approach to water management used in England and Wales. There the Water Act of 1973 replaced more than 1,600 separate agencies with 10 regional water authorities based not on artificial political boundaries but on watershed boundaries encompassing one or more river basins throughout the nation. Each water authority owns, finances, and manages all water supply and waste treatment facilities in its region, including water pollution control, water-based recreation, land drainage and flood control, inland navigation, and fisheries in inland waters. Each water authority is managed by a group of elected local officials and a smaller number of officials appointed by the national government.

This approach has a number of advantages including **(1)** reducing water waste, improving management efficiency and integrated planning, and saving money by making each water authority responsible for both water supplies and water pollution control and waste treatment, **(2)** allowing each region to develop policies best suited to the unique characteristics of its watershed, **(3)** having water supply and pollution control financed by the people who benefit from them, and **(4)** encouraging development of *dual water systems*, one providing highly purified (potable) water for drinking and cooking, and the other providing less pure (nonpotable) water for industrial, agricultural, and other uses.

Because water makes up only 0.5 percent of industrial costs, it is not surprising that industry uses and wastes vast amounts. The biggest savings in industry result from cleaning up and recycling wastewater and reusing water that has been used for cooling or other nondegrading purposes. About 49 percent of all water withdrawn in the United States is for cooling electrical power plants, so storing this water in holding ponds and reusing it rather than returning it to rivers and lakes would substantially reduce average per capita water withdrawal. Partially degraded water from waste treatment plants and some industries could be used to water parks, grow trees, and recharge groundwater aquifers. Water conservation could also be encouraged by reducing rates during nonpeak hours (night) and seasons (winter).

Much money is spent to make *all* water coming into U.S. homes, buildings, and factories of drinkable quality (potable water). Yet only about 5 percent of the water in homes and 2 percent of that in industry is used for purposes that require potable water. For example, in a home about 40 percent of the water of drinkable quality is used to flush toilets.

Some U.S. homeowners have set up a dual system with the "gray" water not used in toilets collected in a separate system and used to flush toilets and to water lawns and gardens, reducing average domestic water use by more than 50 percent. However, many health codes forbid such systems even though it has been shown that they are safe with proper installation and controls, and that they can greatly reduce public expenditures for providing water resources and waste treatment. A Boulder, Colorado company (PureCycle) has developed a complete home recycling system that sits in a small shed outside the residence. It costs about the same as a septic tank installation and is serviced for a monthly fee about equal to that for using most city water and sewer systems.

Finally, we get down to what individuals can do to conserve water. We don't have to go as far as the Californian who, in the middle of the 1977 drought, stapled a stamp to an envelope to save saliva, or the California couple who said they were going to get a divorce because of "shower temperature incompatibility." But each of us can each save a lot of water by carrying out the following suggestions:

1. *In the bathroom* (65 percent of residential water use): Begin with the toilet, which accounts for about 40 percent of all water used in a home. To reduce the amount of water used per flush, put a plastic container with its top cut off and weighted with a few stones into each toilet tank or buy (for about $10) and insert a toilet dam made of plastic and rubber; bricks also work but tend to disintegrate and gum up the water. If every toilet in the United States had such a container or dam, about 19 million liters (5 million gallons) of water would be saved each day. Flush only when necessary, using the advice found on a bathroom wall in Marin County, California: "If it's yellow, let it mellow; if it's brown, flush it down." Don't use your toilet for a wastebasket or an ashtray. For new houses, install water-saving toilets or where health codes permit, waterless toilets (Figure 18-11). Take short showers rather than baths (which use more water than a 5-minute shower), or fill the bathtub to the minimal water level. Use water-saving shower flow restrictors (which cost less than a dollar and can be installed in a few minutes by almost anyone), and shower by wetting down, turning off the water while you soap up, and then rinsing off. Check for toilet, shower, and sink leaks about once a week and repair them promptly. Don't keep the water running when brushing your teeth, shaving, or washing.

2. *In the laundry room* (15 percent of residential water use): Wash only when you have a full load using the short cycle and filling to the lowest possible water level. When buying a new washer, get one that uses the least amount of water and fills up to different levels for different sized loads. Check for leaks once a week and repair all leaks promptly.

3. *In the kitchen* (10 percent of residential water use for drinking and cooking): Use an automatic dishwasher only when you have a full load, using the short cycle and let the dishes air dry overnight to save energy. When washing dishes by hand don't let the faucet run. Instead use one filled dishpan for washing and another for rinsing. Keep a jug of cold water in the refrigerator rather than running drinkable water from a tap until it gets cold. While waiting for faucet water to get hot, catch the cool water in a pan and use it for cooking or to water plants. Check for sink and dishwasher leaks once a week and repair them promptly. Try not to use a garbage disposal or water-softening system (both are major water users).

4. *Outdoors* (10 percent of residential use but higher in arid areas): If you own a car, wash it less. Wash vehicles using a bucket of soapy water and use the hose only for rinsing. Sweep walks and driveways instead of hosing them off. Water lawns and gardens in the early morning or in the evening, not in the heat of midday or in the wind. Better yet, landscape with native plants instead of grass or plants that need watering. Do your utmost to conserve water in summer and during hot periods, when stream flows are low and demands are great.

The water you save by these and other practices is only a small portion of the total water wasted each year in the United States. But if hundreds of millions of people do the same thing, the impact will be significant. If you and I don't begin, who will? According to William Ashworth (see *Nor Any Drop to Drink*, 1982), our real problem results from our attitutes toward water use.

Born in a water-rich environment, we have never really learned how important water is to us. . . . Where it has been cheap and plentiful, we have ignored it; where it has been rare and precious, we have spent it with shameful and unbecoming haste. . . . Everywhere we have poured filth into it.

William Ashworth

Discussion Topics

1. What physical property (or properties) of water:

   a. Account(s) for the fact that you exist?

   b. Allow(s) lakes to freeze from the top down?

   c. Help(s) protect you from the shock of sudden temperature changes?

   d. Help(s) regulate the climate?

2. Based on the hydrologic cycle (Figure 4-12), trace a route that the water you drink may take from the ocean to your faucet and back to the ocean.

3. Explain why average precipitation is not a measure of the water available for human use.

4. If groundwater is a renewable resource, how can it be "mined" and depleted like a nonrenewable resource?

5. In your community:

   a. What are the major sources of the water supply?

   b. How is water use divided among agricultural, industrial, and domestic uses? Who are the biggest users of water?

   c. What has happened to water prices during the past 20 years?

   d. What water problems are projected for your community?

   e. How is water being wasted in your community and school?

6. Explain how you and I each can use, directly and indirectly, an average of 7,402 liters (1,953 gallons) of water per day. How much of this is wasted?

7. What are the main functions of dams? What problems can they create? Should all proposed dam projects be scrapped? What criteria would you use in determining desirable dam projects?

8. Explain why dams may lead to more flood damage than might occur if they had not been built.

9. Explain how irrigation can increase the salinity of the soil and of rivers from which irrigation water is drawn and returned.

10. How could we prevent or minimize (a) soil salinity from irrigation, and (b) saltwater intrusion in coastal areas?

11. Explain why desalination, although important, will not solve world and U.S. water problems. Using the second law of energy (Section 2-3), explain why desalted water will not be available for widespread use in irrigation.

12. Describe some ecological problems associated with building desalination plants. Should they be built in arid parts of the United States? Why or why not? What are the alternatives?

13. Debate the proposition that all users should pay more for water because its price is too low compared with the increasing costs of providing adequate, usable supplies for the growing U.S. population. What political effects might this have? What effects on the economy? On you? On the poor? On the environment?

PART FIVE

Pollution

Humans of flesh and bone will not be much impressed by the fact that a few of their contemporaries can explore the moon, program their dreams, or use robots as slaves, if the planet Earth has become unfit for everyday life. They will not long continue to be interested in space acrobatics if they have to watch them with their feet deep in garbage and their eyes half-blinded by smog.

René Dubos

18

Water Pollution

18-1 Types and Sources of Water Pollution

What Is Water Pollution? **Water pollution** occurs when some substance or condition (such as heat) so degrades the quality of a body of water that the water fails to meet water quality standards or cannot be used for a specific purpose. Water that is too polluted to drink may be satisfactory for industrial use. Water too polluted for swimming may not be too polluted for fishing. Water too polluted for fishing may still be suitable for sailing or for generating electrical power.

Even though scientists have developed sensitive measuring instruments, determining water quality is difficult. Interacting chemicals in water, many only in trace amounts, are among the 63,000 chemicals used commercially, with 1,000 new ones added each year. Determining the exact form and concentration of these myriad products in various parts of the ecosphere and their effects on humans and other organisms is extremely difficult and expensive.

The difficulty of determining acceptable levels of water quality is increased because different organisms have different ranges of tolerance (Figure 5-5) and different threshold levels for various pollutants (Figure 1-4). To complicate matters even further, while some pollutants either are diluted to harmless levels in water or are broken down to harmless forms by decomposers and natural processes, others (such as DDT, some radioactive materials, and some mercury compounds) are biologically concentrated in various organisms (Figure 5-6).

Enrichment Studies 7, 12, 13, and 14 are related to this chapter.

Major Water Pollutants Following are eight major types of water pollutants.

1. *Oxygen-demanding wastes*: domestic sewage, animal manure, and some industrial wastes. If water systems are overloaded with these wastes, the resulting population explosion of decomposer organisms uses up so much of the dissolved oxygen supply that most fish and other forms of aquatic life cannot survive.

2. *Disease-causing agents*: bacteria, parasites, and viruses (Enrichment Study 7).

3. *Inorganic chemicals and minerals*: acids, salts, and toxic metals (Enrichment Study 12).

4. *Synthetic organic chemicals (SOCs)*: plastics, detergents, industrial wastes, oil, cleaning solvents, septic tank cleaners, and pesticides (Section 9-9).

5. *Plant nutrients*: nitrates and phosphates (Enrichment Study 14).

6. *Sediments*: soil, silt, and other solids from land erosion (Section 8-5).

7. *Radioactive substances* (Section 15-4).

8. *Heat*: from industrial and electric power plant cooling water.

Table 18-1 summarizes the sources, effects, and methods for controlling these water pollutants.

According to the Environmental Protection Agency (EPA), all but a very few of the 246 water basins in the United States are affected by water pollution. In terms of quantity, sediments or water-suspended solids from soil erosion constitute the largest source of water pollution each year in the United States as well as throughout most of the world. Enough topsoil erodes each year in the United States to fill 18 freight trains, each long enough to reach around the world (Section 8-5).

Some wastes are discharged from identifiable locations called **point sources.** They include **(1)** pipes dumping untreated sewage into waterways and oceans from cities and industries, **(2)** sewage treatment plants that remove some but not all pollutants (Section 18-6), **(3)** combined storm and sewer lines

Table 18-1 Major Water Pollutants

Pollutant	Sources	Effects	Control Methods
Oxygen-demanding wastes	Natural runoff from land; human sewage; animal wastes; decaying plant life; industrial wastes (from oil refineries, paper mills, food processing, etc.); urban storm runoff	Decomposition by oxygen-consuming bacteria depletes dissolved oxygen in water; fish die or migrate away; plant life destroyed; foul odors; poisoned livestock	Treat wastewater; minimize agricultural runoff
Disease-causing agents	Domestic sewage; animal wastes	Outbreaks of waterborne diseases, such as typhoid, infectious hepatitis, cholera, and dysentery (Enrichment Study 7); infected livestock	Treat wastewater; minimize agricultural runoff; establish a dual water supply and waste disposal system (Section 16-6)
Inorganic chemicals and minerals			
Acids	Mine drainage; industrial wastes; acid deposition (Section 19-4)	Kills some organisms; increases solubility of some harmful minerals	Seal mines; treat wastewater; reduce atmospheric emissions of sulfur and nitrogen oxides (Chapter 19)
Salts	Natural runoff from land; irrigation; mining; industrial wastes; oil fields; urban storm runoff; deicing of roads with salts	Kills freshwater organisms; causes salinity buildup in soil; makes water unfit for domestic use, irrigation, and many industrial uses	Treat wastewater; reclaim mined land; use drip irrigation; ban brine effluents from oil fields
Lead	Leaded gasoline; pesticides; smelting of lead (see Enrichment Study 12)	Toxic to many organisms, including humans	Ban leaded gasoline and pesticides; treat wastewater
Mercury	Natural evaporation and dissolving; industrial wastes; fungicides	Highly toxic to humans (especially methyl mercury)	Treat wastewater; ban unessential uses (Enrichment Study 12)
Plant nutrients (phosphates and nitrates)	Natural runoff from land; agricultural runoff; mining; domestic sewage; industrial wastes; inadequate wastewater treatment; food-processing industries; phosphates in detergents	Algal blooms and excessive aquatic growth; kills fish and upsets aquatic ecosystems; eutrophication; possibly toxic to infants and livestock (see Enrichment Study 14); foul odors	Advanced treatment of industrial, domestic, and food-processing wastes; recycle sewage and animal wastes to land; minimize soil erosion
Sediments	Natural erosion, poor soil conservation; runoff from agricultural, mining, forestry, and construction activities	Major source of pollution (700 times solid sewage discharge); fills in waterways, harbors, and reservoirs; reduces shellfish and fish populations; reduces ability of water to assimilate oxygen-demanding wastes	More extensive soil conservation practices (Section 8-6)
Radioactive substances	Natural sources (rocks and soils); uranium mining and processing; nuclear power generation; nuclear weapons testing	Cancer; genetic defects (see Section 15-5)	Ban or reduce use of nuclear power plants and weapons testing; more strict control over processing, shipping, and use of nuclear fuels and wastes (see Section 15-5)
Heat	Cooling water from industrial and electric power plants	Decreases solubility of oxygen in water; can kill some fish; increases susceptibility of some aquatic organisms to parasites, disease, and chemical toxins; changes composition of and disrupts aquatic ecosystems	Decrease energy use and waste; return heated water to ponds or canals or transfer waste heat to the air; use to heat homes, buildings, and greenhouses
Organic chemicals			
Oil and grease	Machine and automobile wastes; pipeline breaks; offshore oil well blowouts; natural ocean seepages; tanker spills and cleaning operation	Potential disruption of ecosystems; economic, recreational, and aesthetic damage to coasts, fish, and waterfowl; taste and odor problems	Strictly regulate oil drilling, transportation, and storage; collect and reprocess oil and grease from service stations and industry; develop means to contain and mop up spills

Table 18-1 Major Water Pollutants *(continued)*

Pollutant	Sources	Effects	Control Methods
Pesticides and herbicides	Agriculture; forestry; mosquito control	Toxic or harmful to some fish, shellfish, predatory birds, and mammals; concentrates in human fat; some compounds toxic to humans; possible birth and genetic defects and cancer (see Enrichment Study 7)	Reduce use; ban harmful chemicals; switch to biological and ecological control of insects (Section 9-9)
Plastics	Homes and industries	Kills fish; effects mostly unknown	Ban dumping, encourage recycling of plastics; reduce use in packaging
Detergents (phosphates)	Homes and industries	Encourages growth of algae and aquatic weeds; kills fish and causes foul odors as dissolved oxygen is depleted	Ban use of phosphate detergents in crucial areas; treat wastewater (see Enrichment Study 14)
Chlorine compounds	Water disinfection with chlorine; paper and other industries (bleaching)	Sometimes fatal to plankton and fish; foul tastes and odors; possible cancer in humans	Treat wastewater; use ozone for disinfection and activated charcoal to remove synthetic organic compounds

that are overloaded during storms, **(4)** feedlots, the tightly restricted quarters where large numbers of animals are kept before slaughter, and **(5)** offshore oil well blowouts and oil tanker accidents.

Nonpoint sources are spread out and difficult to identify and control. They yield the diffuse discharge of wastes from **(1)** runoff of sediment from forest fires, construction, farming, and most logging, **(2)** runoff of chemical fertilizers, pesticides, and saline irrigation water from croplands, **(3)** urban storm water runoff, **(4)** drainage of acids, minerals, and sediments from active and abandoned mines, **(5)** atmospheric precipitation and deposition of acids produced mostly by coal-burning electric power and industrial plants, and **(6)** untraceable spills or

dumping of oil from tankers at sea and various hazardous materials from industries (Enrichment Study 13). Nonpoint source pollution is now recognized as a major and growing problem.

18-2 Effects of Water Pollution and Drinking Water Safety

Types of Effects Water pollution and other forms of environmental stress can have a number of harmful effects on individual organisms, populations, and biological communities and ecosystems, as summarized earlier in Table 5-1. Water and air

Table 18-2 Effects of Water Pollution

Pollutant	Residence Time	Area Affected	When Threshold Levels Reached
Class 1: Nuisance and aesthetic insult			
Color (sediments, acid mine drainage)	Variable, usually short	Local, regional	Now in many places
Odor (phenols, sewage eutrophication)	Weeks to decades	Local, regional	Now, especially in slow-moving rivers and shallow lakes near industrial centers
Taste (organic chemicals, algal blooms, sediment)	Days	Local	Now in some places
Class 2: Property damage			
Dissolved salts (corrosion)	Variable	Local	Now in some places
Muddy water (sedimentation)	Variable	Local, regional	Now in many places
Loss of real estate and recreation values (odor, eutrophication)	Variable	Local, regional	Now in many places

Table 18-2 Effects of Water Pollution *(continued)*

Pollutant	Residence Time	Area Affected	When Threshold Levels Reached
Class 3: Damage to plant and animal life			
Nutrients—nitrogen and phosphorus (eutrophication, excessive plant growth)	Decades	Local, regional	Now in shallow lakes and slow-moving rivers near urban, industrial, and agricultural centers
Heat (fish kills)	Days (but variable)	Local	Rarely, but has increased significantly within last 30 years
Acid deposition	Years	Local, regional, global	Now and increasing (Section 19-4)
Some pesticides and other chemicals (fish kills)	Weeks to years	Local, regional	Infrequently, but could increase soon
Class 4: Damage to human health			
Bacteria	Days	Local, regional, global	Common in LDCs; rarely in MDCs, but could occur without careful supervision
Viruses	Days to months	Local, regional, global	Frequently
Nitrates	Continuous	Local, regional, global	Rarely, but may increase over next 30 years in heavily fertilized areas
Some industrial chemicals	Weeks to years; Centuries if deep underground aquifers contaminated	Local, regional	Now in some areas and increasingly over next 30 years
Some pesticides (in food chain)	Days to years	Local, regional, global	Unknown, but levels may increase over next 30 years
Metals (mercury, lead, cadmium, etc.)	Months to years	Local, regional	Now and increasing
Class 5: Human genetic and reproductive damage			
Pesticides	Days to years	Local, regional, global	Unknown, but probably not serious in water supplies
Some industrial chemicals	Weeks to years	Local, regional	Now and increasing
Radioactivity	Days to years	Local, regional, global	Rarely, but may increase over next 30 years as quantity of radioactive wastes from nuclear power plants rises, or in event of nuclear war (Enrichment Study 3)
Class 6: Major ecosystem disruption			
Oil (especially refined)	Months to years	Local, regional, global	Rarely, but increasing over next 30 years
Some organic chemicals	Months to years	Local, regional	Rarely, but increasing over next 30 years
Some pesticides	Months to years	Local, regional, global	Rarely, but increasing over next 30 years
Erosion	Continuous	Local, regional, global	Now and increasing
Nutrients—nitrogen and phosphorus	Decades	Local, regional, global	Occasionally, but increasing over next 30 years
Acid deposition	Years	Local, regional, global	Now and increasing (Section 19-4)
Heat	Variable	Local	Rarely, but increasing significantly over next 30 years

pollution classes can be ranked in order of increasing danger to humans:

Class 1: *Nuisance and aesthetic insult (odor, taste, and ugliness)*

Class 2: *Property damage*

Class 3: *Damage to plant and animal life*

Class 4: *Damage to human health*

Class 5: *Human genetic and reproductive damage*

Class 6: *Major ecosystem disruption*

Table 18-2 summarizes the estimated effects of various types of water pollutants according to these categories.

Table 18-3 Federal Drinking Water Standards for the United States

Contaminant	Maximum Contaminant Level (MCL)	Possible Effects of Exceeding MCL	Contaminant	Maximum Contaminant Level (MCL)	Possible Effects of Exceeding MCL
Microbiological			**Synthetic Organic Chemicals (SOCs)**		
Coliform bacteria	No more than 4 colonies per 100 milliliters, with the arithmetic mean of all samples from a source not to exceed 1 colony per 100 milliliters	Waterborne infectious diseases	Endrin (pesticide)	0.2 ppb	Carcinogenic, toxic
			Lindane (pesticide)	4 ppb	Suspected carcinogen
			Methoxychlor (pesticide)	100 ppb	Toxic
Inorganic Chemicals			Toxaphene (pesticide)	5 ppb	Toxic
Arsenic	50 parts per billion (ppb)*	Carcinogenic, toxic	2,4,-D (herbicide)	100 ppb	Suspected carcinogen
Barium	1,000 ppb	Toxic	2,4,5-T or Silvex (herbicide)	10 ppb	Suspected carcinogen
Cadmium	10 ppb	Carcinogenic, toxic, biologically magnified	Trihalomethanes (e.g., chloroform)	100 ppb	Some are carcinogenic
Chromium	50 ppb	Carcinogenic, toxic, causes ulcers	**Radioactive Substances**		
Fluoride	1,400–2,400 ppb	Causes fluorosis	Naturally occurring:		
Lead	50 ppb	Toxic, biologically magnified	Radium-226 and radium-228	5 picocuries (pCi) per liter[†]	Tissue and genetic damage
Mercury	2 ppb	Toxic	Gross alpha-particle activity	15 pCi per liter	Tissue and genetic damage
Nitrates	10,000 ppb	Toxic, especially in infants	Human sources of beta-particle and proton activity	4 millirems per year[‡]	Tissue and genetic damage
Selenium	10 ppb	Toxic, linked with dental caries			
Silver	50 ppb	Carcinogenic, toxic			

*One part per billion is equivalent to 0.001 milligram per liter.
[†]The picocurie is a standard unit of measurement of the total amount of radioactivity.
[‡]A millirem is 0.001 rem. The rem is a measure of a dose of radioactivity, weighted to reflect potential biological damage to the human body.

Is the Water Safe to Drink?   For much of the world's population in LDCs, the major water pollution problem is drinking water contaminated with bacteria and viruses that cause sickness and death (Enrichment Study 7). By contrast, in the MDCs, purification of drinking water has led to a sharp drop in the incidence of waterborne diseases. Some scientists, however, are concerned about actual and potential contamination of many U.S. drinking water supplies with some of the 63,000 inorganic and organic chemicals in commercial use.

The EPA has set maximum contaminant levels (MCL) for bacteria, certain radioactive substances, and selected inorganic and synthetic organic chemicals (SOCs) in these community and noncommunity drinking water systems (Table 18-3). According to the EPA, 15 percent of the nation's community water systems did not meet one or more existing federal safe drinking water standards (Table 18-3) in 1982.

Wells for millions of individual homes in suburban and rural areas are not required to meet federal safe drinking water standards—primarily because of the expense of testing each well regularly and the political problems associated with verifying individual compliance. For example, testing for all the federally regulated substances shown in Table 18-3 costs about $1,000. Testing for a single substance not covered by the federal standards typically costs from $50 to $200. A study conducted for the EPA by Cornell University scientists in 1982 indicated that 39 million rural area residents—two out of three of all rural Americans—with private wells were drinking water that did not meet one or more federal water quality standards. No detectable levels of radioactivity, pesticides, or herbicides were found.

Some scientists point out that the 17 types of inorganic and organic chemicals presently regulated in public drinking water supplies represent only a small fraction of the 700 *potentially* dangerous chemicals—especially SOCs—found in some public water supplies. Studies by the National Academy of Sciences (NAS) and the National Cancer Institute (NCI) indicate that high levels of over two dozen SOCs found at much lower levels in some drinking water supplies can cause various types of cancer in mice and male rats (Enrichment Study 7).

Some of these SOCs, like the industrial solvents carbon tetrachloride and trichlorethylene (TCE, also used as a septic tank cleaner), are discharged directly into surface water systems or into underground aquifers by septic tank systems. Others, like the toxic termite killer chlordane, can be washed accidentally into surface water systems. Some SOCs may be formed by chemical reactions between substances discharged into bodies of water. For example, evidence accumulated since 1974 indicates that trihalomethane (THM) compounds, like chloroform ($CHCl_3$), may be formed when the chlorine used to kill bacteria in drinking water combines with natural organic matter in untreated water or with other SOCs discharged into some rivers. NAS and NCI studies showed that high doses of chloroform can cause liver cancer, kidney disorders, birth defects, and central nervous system damage in test animals—the same disorders observed in humans accidentally exposed to high levels of chloroform.

For these reasons, and because about 75 percent of the population drinks chlorine-treated water, an EPA drinking water standard for THMs went into effect in 1982. Because of the high costs of removing THMs, this standard had been applied to less than 5 percent of all community systems, but it includes 80 percent of the population served by such systems.

Contaminated wells and concern about possible contamination of public drinking water supplies has led about 1 out of every 20 Americans to drink bottled water at an average cost of about $1 a gallon (3.8 liters). Bottled water is regulated by the FDA based on standards that are required to be equivalent to EPA standards for drinking water (Table 18-3). However, the FDA does little testing of bottled water and generally relies on tests by the bottled water industry. Furthermore, there is no assurance that such water won't contain SOCs and other chemicals not regulated by EPA standards. Most activated charcoal filter units for attachment under home sinks remove THMs and most SOCs if properly maintained. However, they are not effective in removing bacteria, viruses, and toxic metals. Filter units that contain "bacteriocides" only prevent bacteria from building up in the filter—not in the water.*

18-3 Surface Water Pollution: Rivers and Lakes

Some Indicators of Water Quality Freshwater ecosystems can be classified as *lotic or flowing systems*, like rivers and streams, and *lentic or standing systems*, like lakes and ponds. Because of differences in water movement, lotic and lentic systems differ considerably in their ecosystem structure and functions (Chapters 3 and 4) and in their water pollution problems.

Three indicators of water quality in lotic and lentic systems are the concentration of *dissolved oxygen (DO)*, the *biological oxygen demand (BOD)*, and the *fecal coliform bacteria count*. Most animals and plants that live in water need oxygen to carry out the respiration process that keeps them alive. The **dissolved oxygen content,** or DO content, is the amount of oxygen gas (O_2) dissolved in a given quantity of water at a particular temperature and atmospheric pressure. At a typical temperature of 20°C (68°F) and normal atmospheric pressure, the maximum concentration of dissolved oxygen is 9 parts of oxygen per million parts of water (9 ppm or 9 milligrams of O_2 per liter of water).

Bacteria in water use dissolved oxygen to break down organic wastes. The amount of dissolved oxygen required for such bacterial decomposition is determined by measuring the **biological oxygen demand (BOD)** in terms of the parts per million (or milligrams per liter) of dissolved oxygen consumed over 5 days at 20°C (68°F) and normal atmospheric pressure. If a water system is overloaded with oxygen-demanding wastes, bacterial activity can reduce the dissolved oxygen content to levels so low that some species of aquatic organisms die. Water is considered seriously polluted when the BOD causes the dissolved oxygen content to fall below 5 ppm (5 milligrams of dissolved oxygen per liter of water) and gravely polluted if the DO level falls below 4 ppm. According to the U.S. Fish and Wildlife Service, low DO levels cause harmful effects to fish communities in 10 percent of the nation's waters.

A good indicator of drinking and swimming water quality is the number of colonies of **fecal coliform bacteria** present in a 100-milliliter sample

---

*Tests conducted by the EPA on the effectiveness of some of the commercially available filter units are available from the EPA Public Inquiries Center, 401 M St., S.W., Washington, D.C. 20460. *Consumer Reports* also reported evaluations of various units in 1983.

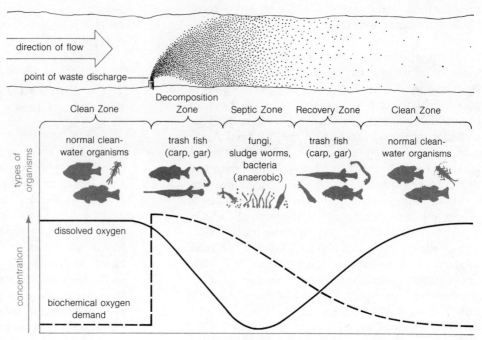

Figure 18-1 Depending on flow rates and the amount of pollutants, rivers recover from oxygen-demanding wastes and heat if given enough time.

of water. Coliform bacteria are intestinal microorganisms found in human and animal wastes. Although most coliform bacteria themselves are not harmful, their presence in water indicates the possible presence of other bacteria from untreated human and animal waste that can cause typhoid fever, cholera, dysentery, viral hepatitis, encephalitis, and other waterborne bacterial diseases (Enrichment Study 7). Usually several samples are taken and water is considered safe to drink by EPA standards when the arithmetic mean of all samples does not exceed 1 coliform bacterial colony per 100 milliliters of water, with no single sample having a count higher than 4 colonies per 100 milliliters. The EPA-recommended level for water safe for swimming is "not more than 200 colonies per 100 milliliters," although some cities and states allow swimming at higher levels. In 1981 about 35 percent of all samples taken from U.S. waters exceeded the EPA fecal coliform bacteria standard for safe swimming.

River Characteristics and Pollution If not overloaded, flowing rivers can dilute many wastes and can renew their supply of dissolved oxygen gas through exposure to the atmosphere. As a result, most rivers recover fairly rapidly from excess heat, oxygen-demanding wastes, and other rapidly degradable pollutants (Figure 18-1)—if not overloaded. Just below the area where large quantities of oxygen-demanding wastes are added, DO levels in the water drop sharply. Further downstream,

however, the DO content returns to its normal level. The depth and width of the *oxygen sag curve*, shown in Figure 18-1, and the time and distance a river takes to recover, depend on a river's volume and flow rate and the volume of incoming oxygen-demanding wastes. Slowly degradable and nondegradable pollutants, however, are not eliminated by dilution and natural breakdown processes in rivers and must be prevented from entering them.

Along many rivers, water for drinking is removed *upstream* from a town, and industrial and sewage wastes are discharged *downstream*. This pattern is repeated thousands of times. Because the rivers normally do not have enough time to recover before receiving the next load of wastes, pollution tends to intensify closer to the ocean. If each town were to withdraw its drinking water downstream rather than upstream, river water quality would improve dramatically!

The Clean Water Act of 1977 requires states to submit water quality reports to Congress. Reports since 1978 reveal that 35 of 37 states reporting have had problems with pollution of rivers by toxic substances—especially mercury, lead, cadmium, and other toxic metal compounds (Enrichment Study 12), pesticides (Section 9-9), and cyanides, phenols, and other hazardous industrial chemicals (Enrichment Study 13). A 1982 report by the United Nations Environmental Program (UNEP) reported that between 1972 and 1982 more U.S. rivers were moderately polluted than in the preceding decade, but fewer rivers were highly polluted.

Perhaps the most spectacular river cleanup has

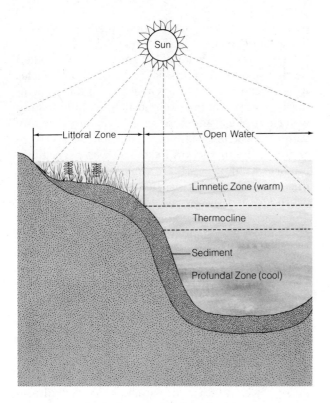

Figure 18-2 The major zones of a lake.

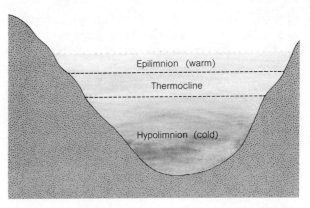

Figure 18-3 Temperature layers in a temperate-zone lake during the summer. A warm layer (epilimnion) floats over a cold layer (hypolimnion); the two layers are separated by a zone of rapid temperature change (thermocline).

occurred in the River Thames. In the 1950s the Thames was little more than a flowing sewer. But after 25 years of effort, $200 million of British taxpayers' money, and millions more spent by industry, the Thames has made a remarkable recovery. By 1978 DO levels had risen almost 30 percent, the river was supporting an increasing population of almost 95 species of fish including pollution-sensitive salmon, commercial fishing was thriving, and many species of waterfowl and wading birds had returned to their former feeding grounds.

Lake Characteristics Because of their low flow rates, the flushing time for lakes is 1 to 100 years, compared to weeks for rivers (Table 17-1). Lakes consist of three distinct zones (Figure 18-2): **(1)** the **littoral zone** near the shore, in which rooted aquatic plants are found, **(2)** the **limnetic zone** (or open water surface layer) through which sunlight can penetrate, which is dominated by tiny floating phytoplankton (which use sunlight to carry out photosynthesis), and free-swimming fish, and **(3)** the **profundal zone** of deep water, which is not penetrated by sunlight and is inhabited by bottom-dwelling aquatic organisms.

Lakes in temperate climate regions tend to have layers of water with different temperatures during the summer and winter. In summer the surface water is heated by the sun, and an upper warm layer called

the **epilimnion** (Greek for "overlake") floats over a denser bottom layer of cold water, the **hypolimnion** ("underlake") (Figure 18-3). These two layers are separated by a fairly thin zone called the **thermocline** (or *metalimnion*), in which the temperature drops sharply. During autumn the entire lake turns over and mixes. In winter the cold layer is on top and the warm layer on the bottom. Turnover normally occurs again in the spring. This movement exposes the bottom layer of a lake to air, enabling it to store dissolved oxygen that can be used by living organisms. Fish kills commonly occur when a lake turns over and oxygen-deficient water moves toward the surface.

A major pollution problem of lakes is contamination with oil, sludge, pesticides, metals, and other toxic substances that can kill fish and destroy bottom life. Lakes, with their low flow rates, are even more susceptible than rivers to biological magnification of persistent and nondegradable chemicals (Figure 5-6).

Cultural Eutrophication of Lakes The process of enrichment of a lake with plant nutrients is called **eutrophication.** A lake with a low supply of plant nutrients is called an **oligotrophic lake** (Greek for "few sources of nutrition"). Such lakes tend to have crystal-clear water, low algae populations and high DO concentrations; they contain fish species like smallmouth bass and lake trout. A lake with a large or excessive supply of plant nutrients like phosphates and nitrates is called a **eutrophic lake** (Greek for "well nourished").

Such lakes tend to have a large blue-green algae population, low DO content, and fish species like bullhead and carp. Most lakes become more eutrophic with time as plant nutrients flow in from surrounding land. Depending on local climate and geologic conditions, the natural eutrophication of a lake typically takes thousands to millions of years.

One of the most widespread pollution problems of lakes—particularly shallow ones near urban or agricultural centers—is the acceleration of this process of *natural eutrophication* from the increased flow of plant nutrients into a lake as a result of human activities. This process, known as **cultural eutrophication,** can produce in a few decades the same effect as natural eutrophication. Cultural eutrophication is caused by excessive addition of phosphates and nitrates from effluents from sewage treatment plants, and runoff of fertilizers and animal wastes, and soil erosion from construction, mining, and poor land use (Figure 5-8).

When a lake is overloaded with phosphate and nitrate plant nutrients, rooted plants like water chestnuts and water hyacinths in the littoral zone and floating phytoplankton like green and blue-green algae in the limnetic zone undergo population explosions (blooms) until they cover much of the lake's surface. Some large algae populations, particularly blue-green algae, make the water taste and smell bad. Large populations of some species of blue-green algae, and of dinoflagellates (red tides) in southern coastal regions, can kill fish.

These blooms contribute oxygen to the upper epilimnion layer during daylight hours through photosynthesis. However, when they die, fall to the bottom, and are decomposed, the decomposing bacteria deplete the lake's lower layer of dissolved oxygen. Trout, whitefish, and many other deep-water species of fish die of oxygen starvation, while species like perch and carp, which need less oxygen and live in the upper layers, thrive. The actual number of fish may even increase, but there will be *fewer kinds* of fish that most humans prefer to catch and eat.

In shallow lakes or in the shore zone in deep lakes, the dead algae can also exhaust dissolved oxygen and kill fish in the surface layer of water. If excess nutrients continue to flow into a lake, the bottom water becomes foul and almost devoid of animals as populations of anaerobic (non-oxygen-requiring) bacteria expand and produce smelly hydrogen sulfide and other chemicals.

A National Eutrophication Survey conducted by the EPA indicated that in 1975 an estimated one-third of the 100,000 medium to large lakes in the United States and about 85 percent of the larger lakes near major population centers were suffering from some degree of cultural eutrophication. The largest and most industrialized lake areas are the Great Lakes, with more than 60 percent of their surface area lying in the United States and the remainder in Canada. Together these interconnected lakes hold about one-fifth of the total surface fresh water of the earth. About one out of every five Americans lives in the Great Lakes basin.

For decades billions of gallons of untreated sewage along with industrial and agricultural wastes were discharged into the Great Lakes, causing cultural eutrophication, killing fish, contaminating water supplies, and forcing the closure of many bathing beaches. Although all five lakes were affected, the impact on Lake Erie was particularly intense. In the 1960s there were persistent rumors that Lake Erie was dying, but in fact much of it was overnourished and too alive with plant life like blue-green algae from cultural eutrophication. Lake Erie's pollution problems are intensified because it is fairly shallow and is located near major population centers. Lake Ontario's small size and shallowness also make it susceptible to cultural eutrophication.

Cultural eutrophication can be controlled either by decreasing nutrient flow into lakes (input approaches) or by cleaning up lakes that are already eutrophic (output approaches), as discussed in more detail in Enrichment Study 14. Although the Great Lakes still receive large inputs of wastes, especially phosphates and toxic chemicals, the rate of cultural eutrophication has been slowed, and even reversed in some areas, by pollution control measures since 1972. For example, between 1975 and 1981, the total point source input from major U.S. industries into Lake Erie was reduced by 61 percent and by an even larger percentage from Canadian industries. As a result, most swimming beaches in Lake Erie that had been shut down for 30 years are again open and crowded with people during the summer. Commercial fishing is also making a comeback.

Thermal Pollution of Rivers and Lakes Almost half of all water withdrawn in the United States each year is for cooling electric power plants, and this use could increase considerably by 2000. About 98 percent of the water withdrawn for cooling is returned to rivers, lakes, and estuaries without incurring significant contamination by chemicals. However, this water contains huge quantities of heat that can have ecological effects on the bodies of water.

Although average temperature increases for the entire body of water may not be large, most of the hot water is discharged near the ecologically vulnerable shoreline where mature fish spawn and young fish spend their first few weeks. One or several power plants may use a given body of water without serious damage, thus giving the misleading impression that others can be built. Then just one more plant can exceed the aquatic system's threshold level (Section 5-2) and cause serious eco-

Table 18-4 Undesirable and Desirable Effects of Heat Added to Water

Undesirable Effects	Desirable Effects
Thermal shock (the sudden death of thermally sensitive aquatic life due to sharp changes in temperature). When a power plant first opens, the sudden injection of hot water can kill some existing species. When the plant shuts down for repairs, the sudden temperature drop could kill the new heat-resistant species that have moved in, especially in winter.	Longer commercial fishing season and increased catches when desirable warm-water species are attracted to heated water areas.
Increased susceptibility of aquatic organisms to parasites, disease, and toxic chemicals.	Reduction in winter ice cover.
Disruption of fish migration patterns.	Increased recreational use because of the warming of very cold bodies of water.
Lowered dissolved oxygen concentrations at a time when the higher water temperature raises organisms' oxygen requirements.	Use of warm water for aquaculture to cultivate catfish, shrimp, lobsters, carp, oysters, and other species eaten by humans.
Fewer eggs and fewer surviving young for thermally sensitive species (Figure 5-5).	Use of heated water to heat buildings and greenhouses, provide hot water, remove snow, desalt ocean and brackish water, and provide low-temperature heat for some industrial processes. These uses, however, require that fossil fuel and nuclear power plants be built near urban areas, increasing the risks from air pollution and accidental releases of radioactivity.
Reduction of diversity of species by elimination of thermally sensitive organisms.	
Shifts in species composition. (This may be beneficial or harmful, depending on the new species that thrive in heated water. Undesirable slime and blue-green algae thrive in heated water.)	
Disruption of food webs by loss of one or several key species, especially plankton, at lower levels of the food webs.	
Delay of spring and fall lake turnover.	
Mutilation or killing of small organisms and fish sucked through power plant intake pumps, pipes, and heat-exchange condensers.	
Fish kills and other ecological damage caused by the chlorine, copper sulfate, or other chemicals used to keep bacteria and other microbes from fouling the water-cooling pipes in power plants.	

logical damage to plant and animal life. A 1983 survey by the Fish and Wildlife Service indicated that high water temperature has harmful effects on fish communities in 26 percent of the nation's waters.

There is controversy over the seriousness of this problem. Some scientists view waste heat as a potential water pollutant that can damage and disrupt aquatic ecosystems, while others talk about using heated water for beneficial purposes and speak of *thermal enrichment* rather than *thermal pollution*, as summarized in Table 18-4. Despite talk about thermal enrichment, most existing and proposed sites for electric power plants prevent the beneficial use of their enormous outputs of hot water. Pumping water for long distances to croplands, aquaculture ponds, and buildings requires energy (and money), and much of the heat is lost in the transport.

Thus, most analysts argue that the best course is to reduce thermal water pollution as much as possible by using one or a combination of the following approaches: **(1)** reducing the need for additional power plants by using and wasting less energy, **(2)** limiting the number of power and industrial plants allowed to discharge heated water into a given body of water, **(3)** minimizing damage by returning heated water away from the fragile shore zone, **(4)** using wet cooling towers (Figure 18-4) to inject waste heat into the atmosphere by spraying heated water up through a draft of air and and allowing it to be cooled by evaporation, **(5)** using dry cooling towers to pump heated water through tubes, with the heat transfered to the atmosphere by conduction, and **(6)** dissipating the heat into the atmosphere by evaporation in shallow cooling ponds or canals by pumping hot water into one end and withdrawing cooler water for reuse from the other end.

The cheapest and easiest method is to withdraw cool water from a nearby body of water and then return the heated water to the same body of water. However, because of strict federal water pollution laws, most new power plants use wet cooling towers. This approach has several disadvantages including a large daily input of cooling water to replace water lost to the atmosphere by evaporation, visual pollution from the gigantic cooling towers (Figure 18-4), high construction costs (about $100 million per tower for a 1,000-megawatt plant) and operating costs, and excessive fog and mist in nearby areas. Dry towers are seldom used because they

Figure 18-4 Cooling towers for the Rancho Seco nuclear power plant near Sacramento, California. Compare the size of the towers with the power plant and automobiles. Each tower is more than 120 meters (400 feet) high and could hold a baseball field in its base.

cost two to four times more to build than wet towers. Cooling ponds and canals are useful where enough affordable land is available (about 1,000 acres for a 1,000-megawatt plant).

18-4 Groundwater Pollution

A Growing Threat One of the major water pollution problems of the 1980s is the growing contamination of underground aquifers that provide drinking water for one out of two Americans and 95 percent of those in rural areas. It also provides 25 percent of the water used for all purposes, including 40 percent of irrigation water. The EPA estimated that by mid-1984 only about 1 percent of the nation's usable groundwater supplies has been polluted. But even this small percentage affects more than 5 million people, and officials are finding that the rate of groundwater contamination is increasing—especially near many of the 75 percent of major

U.S. cities that depend on groundwater for most of their supply.

Between 1978 and 1983 over 2,800 public and private drinking water wells in 20 states were closed because of contamination. Between 1945 and 1980 there were more than 31,000 reported cases of illness caused by contamination of groundwater by viruses, bacteria, or parasites and 57 cases from groundwater contaminated with toxic organic chemicals. In 1983 a New Jersey court awarded over $17 million to 97 Jackson Township families who claimed that toxic waste in a municipal landfill had contaminated their drinking water. A 1984 study by researchers from Harvard University's School of Public Health of 3,000 households in Woburn, Massachusetts, where some residents drank contaminated groundwater from 1963 to 1979, revealed a consistent pattern between contaminated wells and high incidences of childhood leukemia, stillbirths, infant deaths, and certain birth defects (including cleft palate and Down's syndrome), and childhood disorders.

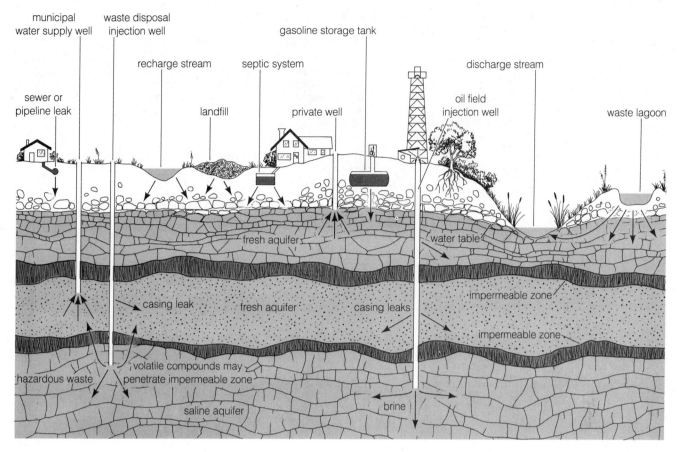

Figure 18-5 Major sources of groundwater contamination.

Sources of Groundwater Contamination Contaminants can leach into groundwater aquifers from many sources (Figure 18-5). These include **(1)** sewer and pipeline leaks, **(2)** accidental chemical or oil spills, **(3)** leaks from the more than 500,000 deep underground injection wells used to dispose of industrial and oil field wastes, **(4)** leaks of about 42 million liters (11 million gallons) of gasoline a year from an estimated 75,000 to 100,000 of the nation's 1.4 million aging underground storage tanks, **(5)** leaks from active and abandoned landfills and toxic waste dumps that are unlined and located above or near aquifers, **(6)** the discharge of 3.8 trillion liters (1 trillion gallons) of sewage and household wastes into the soil each year from the nation's 20 million septic tanks, **(7)** runoff of animal wastes from feedlots (bacteria and nitrates), **(8)** runoff of salts spread on icy roads, **(9)** runoff of fertilizers (nitrates) and pesticides, and **(10)** leaks from at least 26,000 of the 205,000 industrial, mining, municipal, and agricultural surface water impoundments (lagoons, pits, and ponds) used for the storage, treatment, and disposal of liquid wastes, with 95 percent of these impoundments located within 0.4 kilometer (0.25 mile) of drinking water supplies.

Control of Groundwater Pollution Groundwater pollution differs from surface water pollution in several ways. *First*, some bacteria and most suspended solid pollutants are removed as contaminated surface water percolates through the soil into aquifers, but the effectiveness of this process varies with the type of soil, and septic tanks can discharge bacteria and viruses directly into groundwater supplies. *Second*, bacterial degradation of oxygen-demanding wastes reaching aquifers does not occur readily because of a lack of dissolved oxygen in groundwater. *Third*, soil is not effective in filtering out viruses and most synthetic organic chemicals. *Fourth*, the rate of movement of most groundwater is so slow (typically about 30 centimeters or 1 foot a day) that there is relatively little dispersion and dilution of wastes. For example, just 1 gallon of an industrial solvent and septic tank cleaner like TCE can contaminate 76 million liters (20 million gallons) of groundwater to unsafe levels, and 1 gallon of gasoline leaking from an underground storage tank can ruin 2.8 million liters (750,000 gallons) of groundwater for human consumption.

Fifth, it is difficult to monitor pollutants or to predict what happens after they enter groundwater

Table 18-5 Strategies for Protecting Groundwater Quality

Strategy	Advantages	Disadvantages
1. Classifying groundwater according to current or projected uses for drinking water, industry, or agriculture, and establishing pollution control standards for each use	Avoids excessive economic costs that would be needed to have all groundwater conform to the same standards	Difficult and expensive to change the classification and degree of protection in the future
2. Adopting a uniform drinking water quality standard for all groundwater	Administratively simple; avoids unexpected future costs due to reclassification	Imposes greater and perhaps unnecessary costs on all users; requires drinking water standards for all groundwater even though this is not the largest use; difficult to keep groundwater from being degraded below a certain level; unless exempted, aquifers already contaminated would have to be cleaned up at great cost
3. Prevent further degradation regardless of use	Avoids high and unexpected future costs based on mistaken projections about use	Preserves some aquifers at great cost at a higher quality level than necessary for their present and probable future uses; almost impossible to prevent further contamination in recharge areas that have already been developed

because they tend to spread in a plume whose shape and rate of movement depends on the permeability and slope of the aquifer and the rate at which water is pumped from the aquifer by wells. Groundwater may be heavily contaminated in one place and safe for drinking only a few hundred feet away. A well that is pollution free can suddenly become contaminated when it is reached by a plume that may have been spreading for decades. Locating and monitoring groundwater pollution is also expensive—a single test well can cost as much as $10,000. Between 1982 and 1992 groundwater experts estimate that more than 1 million monitoring wells will have to be installed to monitor potential sources of U.S. groundwater contamination.

Sixth, there are only about 3,500 technically trained people in the groundwater field, most of whom are new to the business. *Seventh*, groundwater pollution is essentially irreversible because most aquifers are recharged very slowly. Theoretically, contaminated groundwater can be pumped out of an aquifer and cleaned up. But this process, which costs an estimated $5 million to $10 million for a single aquifer, is usually too expensive. *Eighth*, because of the unique characteristics of groundwater pollution, preventing contamination in the first place appears to be the only effective solution.

Despite the seriousness of this threat to drinking water supplies, by early 1984 there was no sin-

gle federal law designed to protect groundwater supplies. Some aspects of groundwater pollution, however, can be controlled by using parts of existing water pollution control laws (Section 18-7).

By mid-1984 the EPA was still developing a proposed national groundwater strategy. The three basic approaches to preventing groundwater pollution, along with their major advantages and disadvantages, are summarized in Table 18-5, with the EPA expected to propose using the first strategy.

Regardless of the approach used, a number of health and water pollution experts have urged that **(1)** the critical recharge area for each aquifer presently used for drinking water be identified and protected by means of regional, state, and local land-use planning and zoning regulations (Section 12-5), **(2)** the siting of landfills and surface wastewater impoundments above or near vulnerable groundwater aquifers be banned, **(3)** the land disposal of bulk or noncontainerized hazardous wastes be banned or more rigidly controlled, **(4)** operators of all surface impoundments be required to install liners and leachate collection systems, **(5)** injection of hazardous wastes into injection wells located near drinking water aquifers be prohibited, and **(6)** operators of all existing landfills, surface impoundments, and underground storage tanks of gasoline and other hazardous substances be required to monitor each site for leaks.

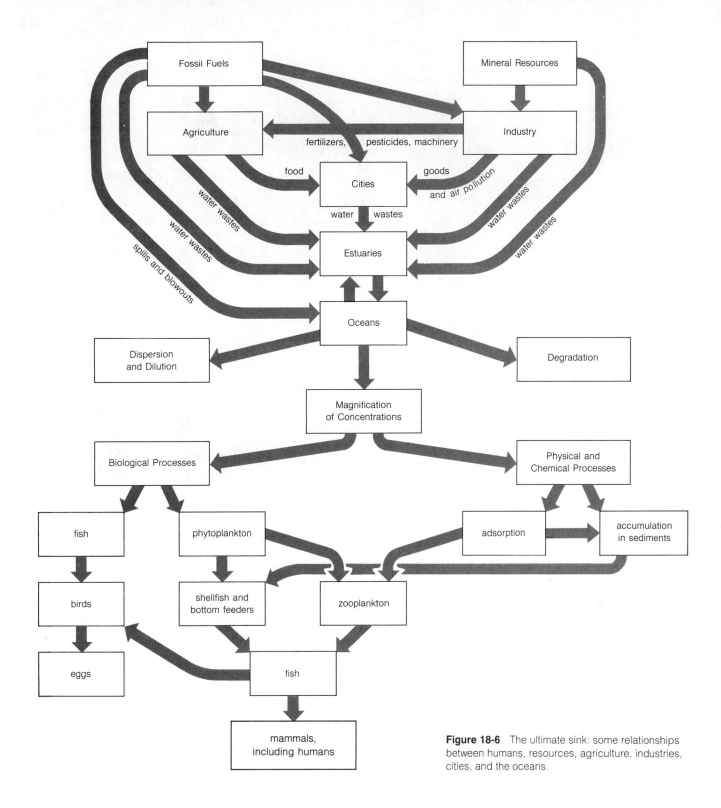

Figure 18-6 The ultimate sink: some relationships between humans, resources, agriculture, industries, cities, and the oceans.

18-5   Ocean and Estuarine Zone Pollution

The Ultimate Sink   The oceans are the ultimate sink for natural and human wastes. Water used and contaminated in homes, factories, and farms flows into rivers, which eventually empty into the ocean (Figure 18-6). In addition, wastes are loaded on barges and dumped directly into the ocean. Although some forms of ocean pollution like DDT and PCBs are global, the major pollution problems of the oceans are around its edges—the estuaries, wetlands, bays, and harbors, and the inland seas like the Baltic and Mediterranean near large cities, industrial centers, and the mouths of polluted rivers.

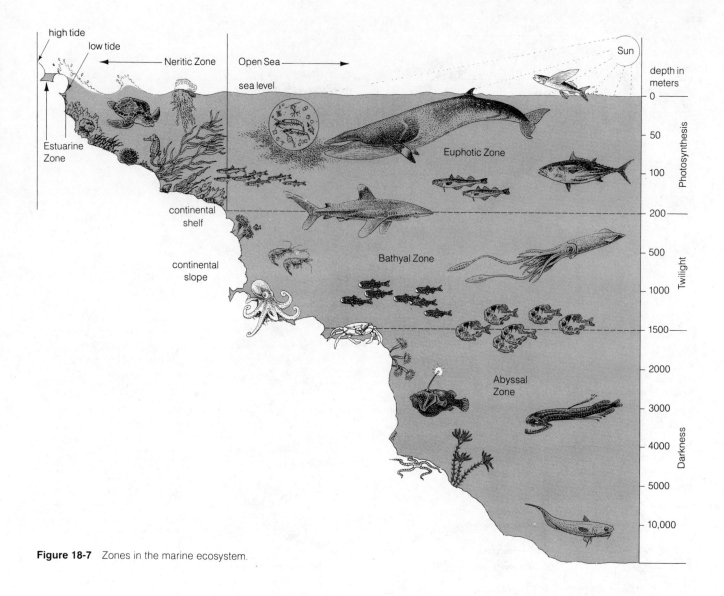

Figure 18-7 Zones in the marine ecosystem.

Reports of the death of the oceans in the late 1960s and 1970s were exaggerated. Fortunately, the vastness of ocean waters and their constant mixing dilute and disperse many types of waste to harmless levels. Other wastes are broken down and recycled by natural chemical cycles (Section 4-3) in ocean ecosystems. Marine life has also proved to be more resilient than some scientists expected.

Although the ocean can dilute and break down large amounts of sewage and some types of industrial waste—especially in its deep-water areas—its capacity to do so has limits. The sheer magnitude of discharges, especially near the coasts, can overload these natural purifying systems. In addition, these natural processes cannot readily degrade many of the plastics, pesticides, and other synthetic chemicals created by human ingenuity. Before focusing on ocean and estuarine pollution, let's look briefly at the ocean as an ecosystem.

The Marine Ecosystem   The ocean can be divided into several zones (Figure 18-7). The **neritic zone** includes the **estuarine zone,** containing estuaries and coastal wetlands, and extends out to the edge of the continental shelf. **Estuaries** are thin, fragile zones along coastlines where freshwater streams and rivers meet and mix with salty oceans. **Coastal wetlands** are normally wet or flooded shallow shelves that extend back from the freshwater–saltwater interface. They consist of a complex maze of marshes, bays, lagoons, tidal flats, and mangrove swamps.

The estuarine zone, representing less than 10 percent of the total ocean area, contains 90 percent of all sea life. Sunlight can penetrate the waters in this shallow zone, allowing photosynthesis to occur among its vast population of phytoplankton, the floating plants that are the grass of the sea. These plants support the zooplankton and bottom-feed-

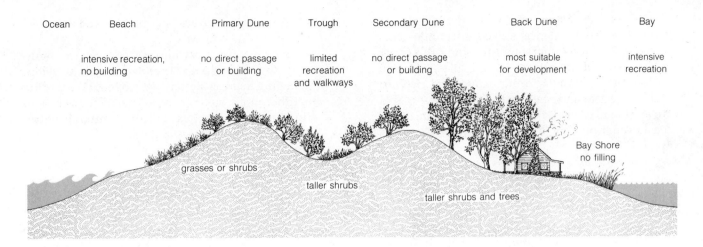

Ocean   Beach   Primary Dune   Trough   Secondary Dune   Back Dune   Bay

intensive recreation, no building   no direct passage or building   limited recreation and walkways   no direct passage or building   most suitable for development   intensive recreation

Bay Shore no filling

grasses or shrubs

taller shrubs

taller shrubs and trees

Figure 18-8 Primary and secondary dunes offer natural protection from flooding. Ideally, construction and development should be allowed only behind the second strip of dunes, with walkways built over the dunes to the beach.

ing invertebrates like shellfish, which in turn support larger fish and add to our food supply. Strings of *barrier islands* are also found in the neritic zone along some coastal areas.

Moving out from the continental shelf, we enter the **open sea** or *oceanic zone*, making up about 90 percent of the total ocean area. Because there are few nutrients in the open sea, it supports relatively little life compared with the neritic zone and is sometimes called a biological desert (Section 9-6).

The open sea is divided into three vertical zones. The layer through which light can penetrate is called the **euphotic zone**; this is the zone in which photosynthesis can occur. Below the euphotic zone is the **bathyal zone**, or *dark open water* zone, in which many of the larger marine organisms like tuna and whales cruise. Finally, we encounter the **abyssal zone** of the ocean, consisting of deep water and the benthos (ocean bottom).

Importance of Estuarine Zones According to the economic land-use ethic (Section 10-1), estuaries and coastal wetlands are desolate, mosquito-infested, worthless lands that should be drained, dredged, filled in, and built on. Nothing could be further from the truth. Because most estuarine zones are at the end of rivers flowing into the ocean, they receive and trap the rich silt and organic matter that rivers wash down from the land. They then hold and use these nutrients to produce an extraordinary bloom of phytoplankton and marsh and sea grasses that are important food sources for a variety of marine life.

An estimated 60 to 80 percent of the commercially valuable species of saltwater fish, mollusks, and shellfish depend on the estuarine zone at some stage of their life for food, spawning grounds, or nurseries for their young. Thus, filling in or dam-

aging the productivity of estuarine zones destroys a major source of protein and affects the livelihood of millions of people involved in the $12 billion a year U.S. commercial and recreational fishing industry. In addition, estuarine zones feed and shelter wading marsh birds (herons, egrets, ibis, and cranes), birds of prey (ospreys, marsh hawks, and bald eagles), and other waterfowl (cormorants, pelicans, grebes, and loons). Also, migratory birds (ducks, geese, and snipes) rest in estuarine zones.

Furthermore, estuarine zones and adjoining sand dunes are two of our most important natural flood control devices, absorbing damaging waves caused by violent storms and serving as a giant sponge to absorb floodwaters before they can reach human coastal habitats on higher ground. Under natural conditions, the area behind most beaches is protected by two sets of sand dunes held together by sea oats and other grasses and shrubs (Figure 18-8). For free and effective flood protection, buildings should be placed behind these primary and secondary dunes, with walkways built over both dunes to the beach. When coastal developments remove these protective dunes or build behind the first set of dunes, minor hurricanes and sea storms can sweep away the cottages, homes, and buildings. Some people call such events "natural" disasters and insist on insurance payments and loans so that they can build again and wait for the next disaster.

If not overloaded, estuaries and coastal wetlands provide another important, free service by removing large amounts of pollutants from coastal waters. It is estimated that 0.004 square kilometer (1 acre) of tidal estuary substitutes for a $75,000 waste treatment plant and is worth a total of $83,000 when sport and fish food production is included.

Stresses on U.S. Estuarine Zones By 1983 almost two out of three Americans lived in counties bordering the nation's shoreline (including the Great Lakes). Nine of the nation's largest cities, about 40 percent of the manufacturing plants, and two out of three nuclear and coal-fired electric power plants are located in coastal counties. Thus, the fate of the coastal environment directly or indirectly affects every U.S. citizen.

Because of these multiple uses and stresses, over 50 percent of the coastal estuaries in the continental United States have been destroyed or damaged, primarily by dredging and filling. Between 1947 and 1967 California lost over two-thirds of its original estuaries. According to a 1983 EPA study, the Chesapeake Bay, the nation's largest estuary, is an ecosystem in decline from pollution by toxic chemicals and excessive inputs of nitrogen and phosphorus plant nutrients, and the region could soon lose its $750 million a year seafood industry. In contrast, the once heavily polluted Delaware Bay was making a comeback by 1984 after three decades of cleanup efforts by federal, state, and local authorities, including improved sewage treatment plants and tougher controls on industrial effluents. Pollution control is made easier because the Delaware Bay flushes itself out in about 100 days, about three to four times faster than the Chesapeake Bay.

Coastal Zone Management Fortunately, about two-thirds of the nation's estuaries and wetlands remain. But trying to protect these lands while still allowing reasonable use is a difficult task because (1) more than 90 percent of the coastline (excluding Alaska) is privately owned; (2) plans for protecting and using one estuarine system may not apply to another; (3) even when an ecologically sound plan exists, there is tremendous pressure to use estuarine areas primarily for economic purposes; and (4) protection plans are hampered because of the conflicting goals of the many different coastal municipalities, counties, and states sharing the use of estuarine zones.

The National Coastal Zone Management Act (NCZMA) of 1972 and 1980 provides federal aid to the 35 coastal states and territories to help them develop voluntary, comprehensive programs for protecting and managing coastlines. Although this law is an important step, it has been hindered by inadequate funding and by the fact that plans drawn up and approved for funding are voluntary. By 1983, 26 of the 35 coastal states had federally approved coastal management plans, and most others were in advanced stages of program development. But many of the voluntary state plans are vague and do not provide sufficient legal authority for adequate protection of coastal lands. Federal budget cuts since 1981 have also sharply reduced the effectiveness of the NCZMA.

Suggestions by various analysts for strengthening the act include: (1) allowing new development only in areas already developed, (2) ensuring that the public has free and unrestricted access to shorelines and beaches, but only through entryways that protect dunes and other natural barriers (Figure 18-8), (3) letting citizens have a voice in deciding how coastal lands will be used, (4) terminating all federal funds provided under the NCZMA if a state fails to meet minimum standards, (5) having the federal government establish a coastal program for states that fail to enact and enforce adequate coastal protection programs, (6) establishing federal or state protection of large areas of coastal areas for recreational public use, as is done in Sweden, and (7) encouraging private foundations to buy and protect the most critical areas until they can be purchased and protected by states or the federal government. In 1983 the Nature Conservancy launched a $50 million, 5-year program to acquire and preserve endangered wetlands.

In 1982 Congress passed the Coastal Barrier Resource Act. Under this law, 195 areas encompassing 1047 kilometers (650 miles) of beach front in various barrier islands will not be eligible to receive federal funds for bridge construction, sewage systems, roads, or low-cost flood insurance.

Ocean Dumping Barges and ships dump sewage sludge, industrial wastes, and dredged material at designated sites near the Atlantic, Gulf, and Pacific coasts. One of the most intensely used shallow-water ocean dumping sites is the New York Bight, 19 kilometers (12 miles) off the New York–New Jersey coast near the mouth of the Hudson River. A 105-square-kilometer (40-square-mile) area of the ocean bottom in the New York Bight is covered with a black toxic sludge, severely altering animal communities living on the sea bottom. Since the 1960s some industrial wastes have also been dumped at a deep ocean site 170 kilometers (105 miles) east of New York City. There scientists have found little degradation of marine life. Because of the greater depth of the water and nearness to Gulf Stream currents, this site apparently has a much greater capacity to dilute and disperse wastes.

By 1975, 54 nations, including all major maritime powers, had agreed to stop dumping high-level radioactive wastes, biological and chemical warfare agents, various kinds of oil, some pesticides, durable plastics, mercury, and cadmium into the ocean. The agreement does not include wastes related to offshore mineral exploration and development of seabed mineral resources (Section 13-4),

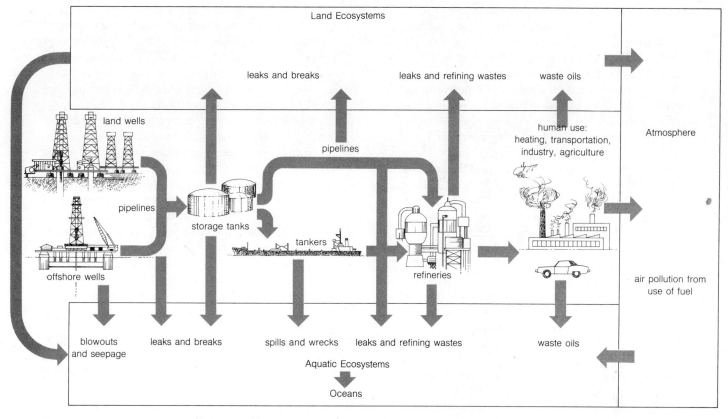

Figure 18-9 Major sources of oil pollution of the hydrosphere, the lithosphere, and the atmosphere.

wastes dumped into rivers and lakes that empty into the oceans, and arsenic, lead, fluorides, cyanides, zinc, and several other toxic substances.

Because of this international ocean dumping agreement and the U.S. Ocean Dumping Act of 1972, the volume of industrial wastes dumped into U.S. ocean waters was cut by almost half between 1972 and 1981. However, the amount of dredged materials, which are not regulated, increased almost fourfold between 1977 and 1983.

A 1977 amendment to the Ocean Dumping Act of 1972 banned all dumping of municipal sludge and industrial wastes into the ocean by 1981. However, this regulation was successfully challenged in court by New York City in 1981 on the grounds that there was evidence that the ocean could assimilate such wastes more effectively, at a lower cost, and with less health risk to humans than burning them in incinerators or dumping them in landfills. In 1982 the EPA allowed six cities in New Jersy to continue dumping such wastes and has been reviewing similar requests for permits from more than 200 other municipalities based on this court decision. Some scientists argue that deep ocean sites near active currents—not shallow dump sites like the New York Bight and the Boston Harbor—may be the safest and cheapest places to dispose of such wastes.

Other scientists argue that while the deep ocean

may be better equipped than land to dilute sewage and some forms of industrial waste to harmless levels, it should not be used for the dumping of slowly degradable or nondegradable pollutants like dioxin, PCBs, some radioactive isotopes and pesticides, mercury compounds, and other persistent substances that can reach human food sources by being biologically magnified in ocean food chains. Unfortunately, many of these materials are mixed in with some types of sludge and industrial waste. Ocean scientists point out that it is difficult—if not almost impossible—to determine the threshold levels (Figure 1-4) at which various ocean pollutants could cause serious harm to marine life and to humans who depend on ocean food sources.

Ocean Oil Pollution Each year over 6 billion kilograms (7 million tons) of oil and petroleum products is added to the oceans (Figure 18-9). According to a 1983 report by the Department of the Interior, about 15 percent of the annual input into U.S. ocean waters comes from natural seeps of crude petroleum from deposits below the ocean bottom. Human activities account for the remaining 85 percent, which is added in the forms of *crude petroleum* (oil as it comes out of the ground) and *refined petroleum* (obtained by distillation and chemical processing of crude petroleum). River and urban runoff, mostly from the disposal of lubricating oil from machines and automobile crankcases, accounts for about 41 percent of the annual input; oil tanker accidents and routine discharges of oil from tankers during loading, unloading, and cleaning, 20 percent; and ruptures or blowouts of offshore oil wells about 0.05 percent.

Tanker accidents and blowouts, however, could become a more important source of ocean pollution in the future, as more oil is drilled and transported to meet world energy demands. On June 3, 1979, a well being drilled in the Caribbean Sea by Pemex, the Mexican national petroleum company, suffered a blowout. Before it was capped 295 days later, it had poured some 531 million liters (140 million gallons) of oil valued at $100 million into the sea. This accident also resulted in costs of $365 million in lawsuits, $21 million for the lost oil rig, and $134 million by the Mexican government and $7 million by the U.S. government for cleanup.

Because even larger supertankers are being built, just one serious tanker accident can release vast quantities of oil. By mid-1984 the largest tanker accident was the breakup of the supertanker *Amoco Cadiz* in 1978. It released more than 254 million liters (67 million gallons) of oil valued at $24 million, polluting 322 kilometers (200 miles) of European coastline. Cleanup costs by the French government amounted to about $95 million, and economic losses in fisheries, oyster farming, tourism, industry, and ocean biota came to another $75 million. In 1984 a U.S. federal district judge ruled that Standard Oil Company of Indiana (Amoco), which operated the tanker, is liable for most of the up to $2 billion in damages caused by the spill. The judge found that Amoco had been negligent "with respect to the design, operation, maintenance, repair, and crew training" of the tanker.

There is considerable dispute, uncertainty, and conflicting evidence concerning the short-term and long-term effects of oil on ocean ecosystems. The effects of oil spills are difficult to predict because they depend on a number of factors, including the type of oil spilled (crude or refined), the amount spilled, the distance of the spill from the shore, the time of year, the weather, the tidal currents, and wave action.

Crude oil and refined oil are collections of hundreds of substances with widely differing properties. The primary cause of immediate kills of a number of aquatic organisms, especially in their larval forms, are low-boiling, aromatic hydrocarbons. Fortunately, most of these toxic chemicals evaporate into the atmosphere within a day or two. Some other chemicals remain on the water surface and form floating, tarlike globs that can be as big as

tennis balls, while other chemicals sink to the ocean bottom. A number of these chemicals are degraded by marine microorganisms, but this natural process is slow (especially in cold Arctic and Antarctic waters), requires a large amount of dissolved oxygen, and tends to be least effective on some of the most toxic petroleum chemicals.

Some marine birds, especially diving birds, die when oil interferes with their normal body processes or destroys the natural insulating properties of their feathers. Some oil components find their way into the fatty tissues of some fish and shellfish, making the fish unfit for human consumption because of their oily taste. Some petroleum chemicals can cause subtle changes in the behavioral patterns of aquatic organisms. For example, lobsters and some fish may lose their abilities to locate food, avoid injury, escape enemies, find a habitat, communicate, migrate, and reproduce. Floating oil slicks can also concentrate oil-soluble compounds like DDT and other pesticides.

There is some evidence that crude oil spills may cause less damage than those of refined oil. Studies of the effects of crude oil spills after the 1969 oil well blowout off the coast near Santa Barbara, California, blowouts in the North Sea during 1977, the 1979 Pemex blowout in the Gulf of Mexico, the 1967 *Torrey Canyon* tanker accident off the shore of England, and the breakup of the *Amoco Cadiz* in 1978 reveal that most forms of marine life recovered nearly completely within 3 years. In contrast, spills of oil—especially refined oil—near shore or in estuarine zones, where sea life is most abundant, have much more damaging and long-lasting effects. For example, damage to estuarine zone species from the spill of refined oil at West Falmouth, Massachusetts, in 1969, was still being detected 10 years later. The major input approaches (used to keep oil from reaching the ocean) and output approaches (to remove or minimize its effects once it gets there) are summarized in Table 18-6.

18-6 Approaches to Water Pollution Control

Methods of Pollution Control Controlling a particular water, air, or land pollutant is not a simple process. It involves a number of scientific, technological, economic, and political factors. Table 18-7 summarizes the major methods of pollution control. Wherever possible, most analysts urge that input, throughput, operation, and substitution pollution control methods be used rather than output control methods, which are normally more expensive and difficult (Table 18-7).

Table 18-6 Approaches to Oil Pollution Control

Input Approaches	Output Approaches
Use and waste less oil per capita (Section 15-1) *and* reduce population growth (Chapter 7).	Use mechanical barriers to prevent oil from reaching the shore, then vacuum oil up or soak it up with straw or pillows filled with chicken feathers. This works well only on calm seas.
Collect used oils and greases from service stations and other sources (possibly by a payment incentive plan) and reprocess them for reuse.	Treat spilled oil chemically (usually with detergents) so that it will disperse, dissolve, or sink. Since this method can kill more marine life than the oil does, it is not favored by ecologists.
Strictly regulate the building, maintenance, and routing of supertankers and superports.	Ship oil in a solid state, much like a gel, so that it can be picked up quickly and easily if an accident occurs.
Use load-on-top (LOT) procedures for loading and emptying all oil tankers (already done on 80 percent of all tankers).	Develop bacterial strains (by genetic recombination) that can degrade compounds in oil faster and more efficiently than natural bacterial strains. Possible ecological side effects of these "superbugs" should be investigated before widespread use.
Build supertankers with double hulls, to reduce chances of a spill and to separate oil cargo from ballast water.	Add oil-soluble ferrofluids (iron-containing material) to the spill, which will enable electromagnets to remove the oil.
Strictly enforce safety and disposal regulations for offshore wells and international agreements prohibiting discharge of oily ballast and cleaning water from tanks.	
Strictly enforce safety and disposal regulations for refineries and industrial plants.	
Strengthen international agreements on oil spills and establish a strong international control authority for the oceans.	

Table 18-7 Approaches to Pollution Control

Input Control	Operation and Substitution Control	Throughput Control	Output Control
Prevent or reduce the amount of pollutant from reaching the atmosphere or a body of water (e.g., use soil conservation techniques to reduce dust blown into the air and sediment washed into aquatic systems).	Alter or replace a process to generate less or none of the pollutant (e.g., develop a car engine or a paper-making process that produces less pollution).	Reduce the rate of throughput; that is, slow down production and consumption (e.g., reduce consumption by price increases, pollution taxes, economic incentives, or, as a last resort, rationing).	Remove the pollutant or dilute it at the emission source (exhaust pipe, smokestack, or sewage line).
Select inputs that contain or produce little if any of the pollutant (e.g., use natural gas, coal gasification, or low-sulfur oil for electric power plants).	Make the process more efficient so that less energy and matter are wasted and less pollution is produced (e.g., convert aluminum ore to aluminum metal with a process requiring less electricity).	Find and promote shifts to substitute products or services that are less harmful (e.g., emphasize mass transit and paratransit rather than cars in cities and use reusable soft drink bottles instead of cans).	Remove the pollutant or lower its concentration (usually harder and more expensive because the pollutant is dispersed—the second energy law again).
Remove the pollutant before using the input (e.g., remove the sulfur from coal and oil).		Stabilize and redistribute population to help reduce total consumption and to prevent pollution buildup.	Convert the pollutant to a less harmful form (e.g., convert very toxic methyl mercury to less harmful inorganic forms of mercury, as discussed in Enrichment Study 12).
Improve the natural ability of an ecosystem to dilute or degrade a pollutant (e.g., add oxygen or air to a river or lake to increase its ability to degrade oxygen-demanding wastes).			Choose the time and place of discharge to minimize damage (e.g., use tall smokestacks to disperse air pollutants at high levels where they may be dispersed more effectively, or stagger work hours to reduce air pollution by motor vehicles). This approach does not reduce the total pollution load, but it can spread it out so that harmful levels may not be exceeded.

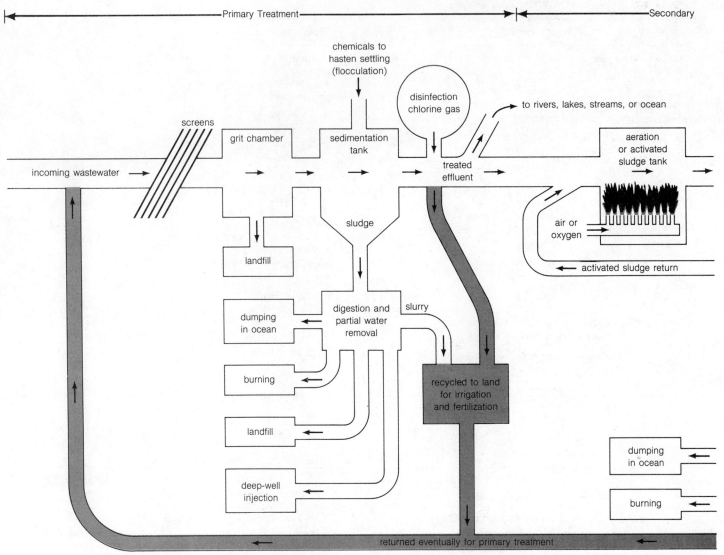

Figure 18-10 Primary, secondary, and tertiary sewage treatment. The shaded areas show the recycling of nutrients to the land, a process that is used little so far.

Because air, water, and soil pollution are interrelated, they should be controlled in an integrated program. Otherwise, we may merely transfer a pollutant from one part of the ecosphere to another and trade one pollution problem for another. Pollution control programs should also be carefully integrated with population, resource use, and land-use control programs.

Because of the complex and mostly unknown effects and interactions of pollutants, we probably will never be able to set exact standards or determine specific pollutant levels that cause certain diseases or ecological effects. However, just because we can't determine allowable pollutant levels perfectly does not mean that we shouldn't establish tentative levels that can be adjusted as we get better information.

As the most obvious and annoying forms of pollution like smoke and foul air and water are elim-

inated, we could be lulled into a false sense of security. Thus, a crucial part of any pollution control program involves educating the general public to realize that some of the more dangerous threats to human health and ecosystems cannot be seen or smelled.

Soil Conservation Because sediment from soil erosion is the single largest source of water pollution, soil conservation is the most important approach for reducing sedimentation in streams and maintaining the fertility of the soil. Methods for reducing soil erosion are discussed in Section 8-6.

Sewage Treatment Two major approaches for dealing with the liquid wastes of civilization are dumping them into the nearest waterway, and puri-

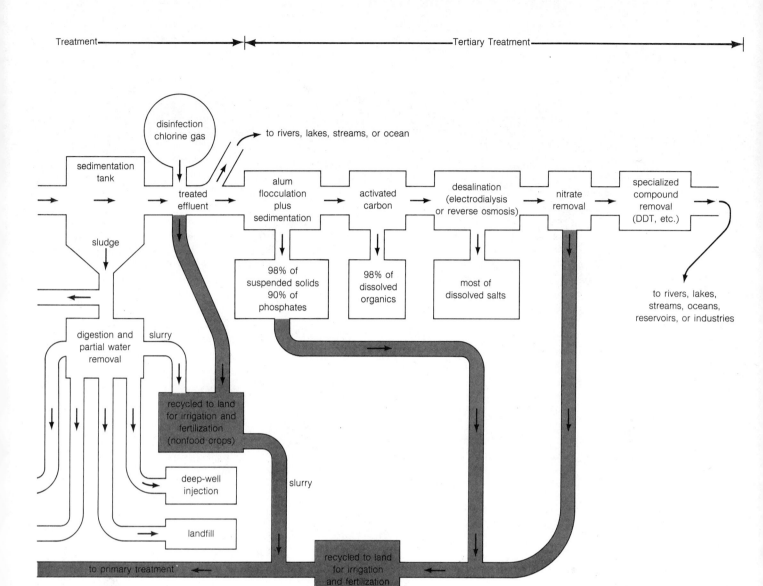

Treatment ——————————————→|←——————————————— Tertiary Treatment ——————————————————→|

disinfection
chlorine gas

to rivers, lakes, streams, or ocean

sedimentation
tank

treated
effluent

alum
flocculation
plus
sedimentation

activated
carbon

desalination
(electrodialysis
or reverse osmosis)

nitrate
removal

specialized
compound
removal
(DDT, etc.)

sludge

98% of
suspended solids
90% of
phosphates

98% of
dissolved
organics

most of
dissolved salts

to rivers, lakes,
streams, oceans,
reservoirs, or industries

digestion and
partial water
removal

slurry

recycled to land
for irrigation and
fertilization
(nonfood crops)

deep-well
injection

slurry

landfill

to primary treatment ←

recycled to land
for irrigation
and fertilization

fying them to varying degrees in septic tanks, lagoons, or sewage treatment plants, which essentially are factories where very clean or relatively clean water is produced by using a combination of physical, chemical, and biological purification processes.

In many LDCs the first approach is used a great deal, causing widespread infection from waterborne diseases. By contrast in MDCs most waterborne wastes from homes, businesses, and factories and from storm runoff flow through a network of sewer pipes to sewage treatment plants. Some areas have separate sewer lines for sewage and storm water runoff. In many areas, however, lines for these two sources are combined because it is cheaper. During almost any rain the total volume of wastewater and storm runoff in such combined systems is too large to be handled completely by the sewage treatment system. When this occurs, some

untreated wastes overflow into rivers and streams.

When sewage reaches a treatment plant, it can undergo various levels of treatment, or purification, depending on the sophistication of the plant and the degree of purity desired. Figure 18-10 and the accompanying box summarize primary, secondary, and tertiary sewage treatment methods. In 1980 the liquid wastes of about 71 percent of the U.S. population and those of 87,000 industries were treated in about 15,000 municipal sewage treatment plants. The wastes of almost two-thirds of these individuals received secondary sewage treatment, 5 percent received some form of tertiary treatment, and the remainder received only primary treatment. The liquid wastes of the 29 percent of the mostly suburban and rural U.S. population not served by sewage treatment plants were either degraded in cesspools and septic tanks or discharged directly into waterways.

Waste Treatment Methods

Primary treatment is a mechanical process that uses screens to filter out debris like sticks, stones, and rags and a sedimentation tank, where suspended solids settle out as **sludge** (Figure 18-10). These two operations remove about 60 percent of the solid material but only one-third of the oxygen-demanding wastes. Chemicals are sometimes added to speed up the settling of suspended solids in a process called *flocculation*.

Secondary treatment is a biological process that uses bacteria to break down wastes. This removes up to 90 percent of the oxygen-demanding wastes by using either **(1)** *trickling filters,* where sewage is degraded by bacteria as it seeps through a bed of stones, or **(2)** an *activated sludge process,* where sewage is aerated with air or pure oxygen to aid bacterial degradation. The water from the trickling filter or aeration basin is then sent to a sedimentation tank, where most suspended solids settle out as sludge. Primary plus secondary treatment still *leaves* 10 to 15 percent of the oxygen-demanding wastes, 10 percent of the suspended solids, 50 percent of the nitrogen (mostly as nitrates), 70 percent of the phosphorus (mostly as phosphates), 30 percent of most toxic metal compounds, 30 percent of most synthetic organic compounds, and essentially all of the long-lived radioactive isotopes and dissolved and persistent organic substances like some pesticides.

Tertiary treatment refers to a series of specialized chemical and physical processes used to reduce the quantity of one or more of the pollutants remaining after primary and secondary treatment. Tertiary treatment is rarely used because many methods are still in the experimental stage and it is expensive (twice as costly to build the plant and up to four times the operating costs of primary plus secondary treatment). Three forms of tertiary treatment used in some places are **(1)** *precipitation,* for removing suspended solids and phosphates, **(2)** *adsorption,* in which activated carbon is used to remove dissolved organic compounds, and **(3)** *electrodialysis* or *reverse osmosis,* for reducing levels of dissolved organic and inorganic substances.

Disinfection is carried on as a part of all three forms of sewage treatment to remove water coloration and to kill disease-carrying bacteria and some (but not all) viruses. Chlorine is the most widely used disinfectant. A newer disinfection method uses ultrasonic energy to break down wastes mechanically, and other disinfectants, such as ozone or chlorine dioxide, to kill bacteria. This approach, however, is more expensive than chlorination. A less costly approach is to wait until the water is filtered, or organic materials have settled, before adding chlorine and then filtering the water with activated charcoal where local supplies are heavily contaminated with trihalomethanes and other synthetic organic chemicals.

Ecological Waste Management and Recycling
Building secondary sewage treatment plants throughout the United States is an important step in water pollution control, especially in reducing oxygen-demanding wastes, suspended solids, and bacterial contamination. But there are problems associated with this engineering approach. When bacteria degrade oxygen-demanding wastes, the resulting effluents are rich in phosphates and nitrates. Allowing these nutrient-rich effluents to flow into lakes and slow-moving rivers can overload these systems, triggering algae blooms and oxygen depletion.

Many scientists argue that instead of overloading aquatic systems with phosphate- and nitrate-rich sewage effluents, these plant nutrients should be returned to the land (forests, parks, and croplands) or to aquaculture ponds as fertilizer. Such a sustainable earth approach to waste management mimics nature by recycling plant nutrient wastes to the land, as shown in the shaded areas of Figure 18-10.

There is concern, however, that this approach could allow bacteria, viruses, toxic metal compounds, and hazardous SOCs to build up in the soil, food crops, and fish and shellfish grown by aquaculture, and to contaminate groundwater aquifers. But others argue that these problems could be controlled by removing certain pollutants, banning the use of highly contaminated liquid wastewater and sewage sludge, and using wastewater and sludge for noncrop purposes on forest lands and surface-mined lands. Liquid effluent from sewage treatment plants is already being used successfully as fertilizer in some cities near farming areas, forest lands, and estuaries. Since this effluent has already been treated, contamination from bacteria, viruses, and toxic metals is not a major problem.

Waterless toilets like the Clivus Multrum (Figure 18-11) and the Carousel use bacteria to break

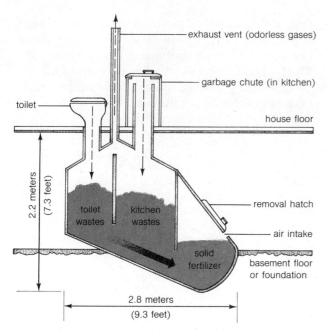

exhaust vent (odorless gases)

garbage chute (in kitchen)

toilet

house floor

2.2 meters (7.3 feet)

toilet wastes

kitchen wastes

removal hatch

air intake

solid fertilizer

basement floor or foundation

2.8 meters (9.3 feet)

Figure 18-11 The Clivus Multrum waterless toilet uses bacteria to break down human and kitchen wastes (food and paper) and form a dry, odorless, solid fertilizer that can be removed every 1 or 2 years.

down human wastes and form a dry, odorless, solid fertilizer that is removed from a chamber about once a year.* These toilets not only save water but also reduce the need for building more expensive sewage treatment plants. If their use was coupled with a dual water supply system (Section 17-6) and a requirement that industries treat and recycle their own wastewater, sewers and municipal waste treatment plants could be phased out in most areas.

At the personal level you should never dispose of products containing harmful chemicals by pouring them down house or street drains or flushing them down the toilet. Examples of products that are harmful to aquatic systems and not usually removed by sewage treatment include **(1)** waste oil drained from automobiles (put it in a container and take to a local service station where it will be turned in for recycling), **(2)** antifreeze (pour it onto a porous surface like gravel away from water supplies), **(3)** pesticides and herbicides, **(4)** paints, lacquers, thin-

*The Clivus Multrum (sold by Clivus Multrum USA, 14a Eliot St., Cambridge, MA 02138) is expensive ($1,500 to $2,000) and takes up a lot of space, but in the long run it should be cheaper than the combined costs of water toilets, septic tanks, water, and monthly sewage treatment fees. Mass use would also bring costs down. Unfortunately, outdated health codes in some parts of the United States still prohibit this safe alternative, which has been used in Sweden since the 1930s. Another waterless toilet, called the Carousel (sold by Enviroscope Corporation, P.O. Box 2933, Newport Beach, CA 92663) has received National Sanitation Foundation approval and costs about $1,000 for the small size and $1,500 for the large size.

ners, brush cleaners, wood preservatives, and turpentine, and **(5)** household cleaners containing organic solvents. Call your local health or water treatment department for information about proper disposal of wastes in categories 3, 4, and 5.

18-7 Water Pollution Control Laws in the United States

Major Laws During the 1970s Congress passed several important pieces of water pollution control legislation: the Federal Water Pollution Control Act of 1972, as amended by the Clean Water Act of 1977; the Safe Drinking Water Act of 1974 (Section 18-2); the Ocean Dumping Act of 1972 (Section 18-5); and the Toxic Substances Control Act of 1976 (Enrichment Study 13).

The Federal Water Pollution Act of 1972 and the Clean Water Act of 1977 These two acts, along with amendments added in 1981, are ambitious, comprehensive, and controversial pieces of environmental legislation. Water pollutants are divided into three categories: **(1)** *toxic* (with the list of such chemicals and the standards for their control to be set by the EPA), **(2)** *nonconventional* (a category that includes some pesticides and metal compounds whose toxicity has yet to be determined), and **(3)** *conventional* (dirt, organic wastes, and sewage).

The two acts, including the 1981 amendments, have the following effects: **(1)** they require the EPA to establish a system of national effluent standards for major water pollutants; **(2)** they require all municipalities to use secondary sewage treatment by 1988; **(3)** they set interim goals of making all U.S. waters safe for fishing and swimming by 1983 and eliminating the discharge of 129 priority toxic pollutants (zero discharge) into U.S. waters by 1985; **(4)** they allow the point source discharge of pollutants into U.S. waterways only with a permit from the EPA or an EPA-approved state agency; **(5)** they require all industries to use the *best practicable technology* (BPT) for control of conventional pollutants by 1984 and nonconventional pollutants by 1987, with the EPA allowed to grant waivers in cases where costs outweigh benefits; **(6)** they require industries to use the BPT for control of 129 priority toxic pollutants by 1984 with no waivers allowed and to use the more stringent *best available technology* (BAT) that is reasonable and affordable to control these pollutants by 1987; and **(7)** they authorized the expenditure of up to $52.5 billion between 1972 and 1986 for federal grants to aid states and localities to construct new secondary sewage plants, upgrade existing ones, or use innovative waste treatment technologies like spraying effluents on land for fertilizer and reclaiming and reusing wastewater.

By 1983, 94 percent of the industries affected had met the goal of using the BPT for control of conventional pollutants. But progress toward achieving BPT control of nonconventional and toxic pollutants by 1984 was far behind schedule. Some 37 states were unable to meet the 1983 goal of fishable and swimmable waters, mainly because of their inability to control nonpoint pollution primarily from agricultural and urban runoff—a type of pollution that by 1983 had received only 1 percent of all federal water pollution funds.

The sewage plant construction program has had numerous problems. By 1983 at least 7,000 waste treatment plants had not met the 1977 goal of secondary sewage treatement. Despite $37 billion in federal grants between 1972 and 1983, only about 4,000 of 19,000 funded projects had been completed by 1983 because of a combination of fraud, overbuilding, bureaucratic and construction delays, and, since 1981, a lack of sufficient funds.

The Clean Water Act of 1977 was due for renewal in 1984. In 1983 the Reagan administration made proposals that would delay industry pollution control deadlines, loosen permit review, and sharply reduce federal grants for sewage plant construction. However environmentalists and many health scientists proposed that the act be strengthened by (1) including goals and standards for preventing groundwater contamination, (2) requiring more stringent monitoring and control of nonpoint sources of water pollution, and (3) requiring the EPA to establish a comprehensive monitoring program for the nation's surface and underground waters, and adequately funding this project. A 1983 Harris poll indicated that by a margin of 94 to 3, Americans want the Clean Water Act kept as is or made even tougher, and 65 percent of those interviewed think that industries should be made to install the BAT, even when it would reduce the number of jobs. By mid-1984 Congress was still debating proposed changes in this important act.

As a result of water pollution laws, the total amount of industrial pollutants entering U.S. waterways was reduced by one-half between 1972 and 1980. Existing laws, if funded and enforced, should lead to greater improvement in the future and could, by 1985, save about $12.3 billion annually in estimated damages from water pollution.

Remaining Major Problems Despite important progress, water pollution is increasing in several major categories where control is more difficult. These include (1) ocean and estuarine zone pollu-

tion, (2) viruses that are hard to destroy by conventional waste treatment, (3) slowly degradable or nondegradable toxic substances (Enrichment Study 13), (4) groundwater contamination, and (5) nonpoint source pollution and cultural eutrophication from land erosion and the runoff of fertilizers and animal wastes (Enrichment Study 14).

The reason we have water pollution is not basically the paper or pulp mills. It is, rather, the social side of humans—our unwillingness to support reform government, to place into office the best qualified candidates, to keep in office the best talent, and to see to it that legislation both evolves from and inspires wise social planning with a human orientation.

Stewart L. Udall

Discussion Topics

1. Quantitatively speaking, what is the largest category of U.S. water pollution? Explain why looking at water pollutants in terms of the annual quantity discharged can be misleading.

2. How would you control (a) nondegradable pollutants, (b) slowly degradable (persistent) pollutants, and (c) rapidly degradable (nonpersistent) pollutants?

3. Give examples of a point pollution source and a nonpoint pollution source in the water and in the air, and explain how you would control pollutants from these sources.

4. What is the source of drinking water in your community? How is it treated? Is chlorination used for disinfection? Are there plans to use activated charcoal or other methods to remove organic contaminants?

5. Explain why "dilution is not always the solution to water pollution," and relate your explanation to the second law of energy (Section 2-3). Cite examples and conditions for which it is and is not the solution.

6. Explain how a river can cleanse itself of oxygen-demanding wastes. Under what conditions can this natural cleansing system fail?

7. Why is water usually tested for coliform bacteria? What is the average annual coliform bacterial count for drinking water in your community? During the past 10 years have any swimming areas in your community been closed because of high coliform counts?

8. Distinguish between natural eutrophication and cultural eutrophication, and explain how eutrophication can deplete dissolved oxygen in the hypolimnion of a lake.

9. Should the injection of wastes into deep underground disposal wells be banned? Under what conditions, if any, should such wells be allowed?

10. Debate the following resolution: We should deliberately dump most of our wastes in the ocean. It is a vast sink for diluting and mixing, and if it becomes polluted, we can get food from other sources. Let the ocean go as a living system so that we can live.

11. Should all dumping of wastes in the ocean be banned? If so, where would you put these wastes? What exceptions, if any, would you permit? Under what circumstances? What types of waste are allowed now? Which of these should be banned? Explain why banning ocean dumping alone will not stop ocean pollution.

12. Explain why aesthetic and economic damage to recreational areas and the killing of seabirds are not necessarily the most serious consequences of oil pollution.

13. Should the United States (or any other coastal nation) ban all offshore oil wells? Why or why not? What might be the consequences of this restriction for the nation? For foreign policy? For security? For your town? For you? What might be the consequences of not doing this?

14. Should we switch from our present engineering approach of sewage treatment to a sustainable earth approach (Figure 18-10)? What are some of the political and economic implications of such a change? What problems would it solve? What problems would it create? What effects might it have on the poor? On you? On the next generation?

19

Air Pollution

Tomorrow morning when you get up take a nice deep breath. It will make you feel rotten.

Citizens for Clean Air, Inc. (New York)

19-1 Types and Sources of Air Pollution

Our Polluted Air Take a deep breath. If the air you just took in was not polluted at least to some degree, you are among a small minority. It makes little difference whether you are in Los Angeles, Denver, Washington, D.C., New York City, Louisville, or Cleveland, in an apartment, or in a rural area.

Since the passage of the Clean Air Act in 1970, the air in most parts of the United States has become measurably cleaner, but there is still a long way to go. The problem is not confined to the United States. Air pollution alerts in heavily populated and industrialized Tokyo have become a way of life, and in Mexico City air pollution on an average day is five to six times greater than maximum safety levels set for U.S. citizens by the EPA. The air pollution capital of the world may be Cubatão, Brazil, a petrochemical center where essentially no birds or insects remain, most trees are blackened stumps, 40 of every 1,000 babies are stillborn, air pollution monitoring machines break down from contamination, and the mayor refuses to live in the city.

Air pollution is normally defined as air that contains one or more chemicals or possesses a physical condition like heat in high enough concentrations to harm humans, other animals, vegetation, or materials. As with all types of pollution, we run into the problem of conflicting views of what constitutes *harm* and what levels of risk we are willing to accept.

Whether chemicals build up to harmful levels in a given area depends on climate, topography, population density, the number and type of industrial activities, and the organisms or materials being affected. Because they contain large concentrations of cars and factories, cities normally have higher air pollution levels than rural areas. However, air pollutants respect no boundaries. Winds can spread air pollutants produced in urban and industrial areas to the countryside and to other downwind urban areas. For example, emissions of pollutants from tall smokestacks in Great Britain and in Europe are believed to be a major cause of acid deposition that is harming trees and aquatic life in Sweden and Norway.

Our Finite Air Supply The earth's atmosphere is primarily a mixture of nitrogen (N_2: 78 percent by volume), oxygen (O_2: 21 percent), argon (Ar: 0.9 percent), carbon dioxide (CO_2: 0.03 percent), and water vapor (H_2O: ranging from near zero up to about 4 percent). Clean air also contains trace amounts of a number of other elements and compounds. Contrary to popular belief, we do not live at the bottom of an infinite sea of air. The *atmosphere*, or gaseous envelope surrounding the earth, consists of several distinct layers (Figure 19-1). About 95 percent of the mass of the air is found in the **troposphere,** extending only 8 to 12 kilometers (5 to 7 miles) above the earth's surface. If the earth were a waxed apple, our vital air supply would be no thicker than the layer of wax.

Most potential air pollutants are added to the troposphere, where they mix vertically and horizontally and often react chemically with each other or with natural components of the atmosphere. For example, the troposphere receives at least 407 million kilograms (448 thousand tons) of *potential* air pollutants *each day* from the United States alone—an average of about 1.7 kilograms (3.7 pounds) per day for each American.

Air Pollution in the Past Air pollution from human activities, of course, is not new. Our ancestors had it in their smoke-filled caves and later in their cities.

Enrichment Studies 2, 3, 5, 7, 10, 11, 12, and 13 are related to this chapter.

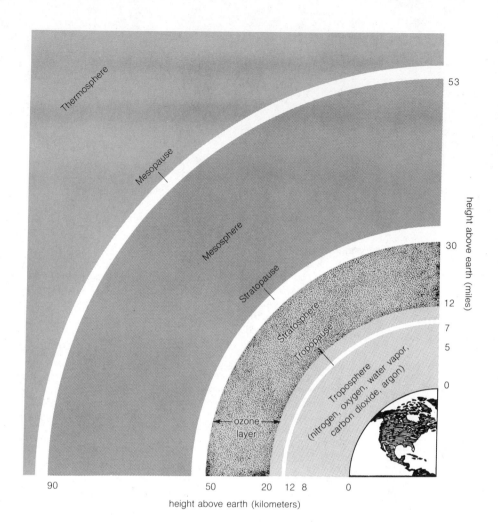

Figure 19-1 Structure of the earth's atmosphere (not drawn to scale). About 95 percent of the air is in the troposphere.

height above earth (miles)

53

30

12

7

5

0

height above earth (kilometers)

90   50   20 12 8   0

In 1273 Edward I of England declared the first known air-quality laws, forbidding the use of high-sulfur coal. Acid deposition was first described in the seventeenth century.

In the early 1800s Shelley wrote, "Hell is a city much like London, a populous and smoky city." In 1911, 1,150 Londoners died from the effects of coal smoke. In his report on the disaster, Dr. Harold Antoine Des Voeux coined the word *smog* for the mixture of smoke and fog that often hung over London. An even more deadly London air pollution incident killed 4,000 people in 1952. Additional air pollution disasters in 1956, 1957, and 1962 killed a total of about 2,500 people. These deadly episodes triggered a massive air pollution control effort that has given London much cleaner air today.

In America the industrial revolution brought air pollution as coal-burning industries and homes filled the air with soot and fumes. In the 1940s the air in industrial centers like Pittsburgh and St. Louis became so thick with smoke that automobile drivers sometimes had to use their headlights at midday. The rapid rise of the automobile, especially since 1940, brought new forms of pollution such as pho-

tochemical smog and lead from the burning of leaded gasoline (Enrichment Study 12).

The first known U.S. air pollution disaster occurred in 1948, when fumes and dust from steel mills and zinc smelters became trapped in a stagnated air mass over Donora, Pennsylvania. Twenty people died and over 6,000 became ill. In 1963 an air pollution disaster in New York City killed about 300 people and injured thousands. The periodic occurrence of serious air pollution episodes during the 1960s in New York, Los Angeles, and other large cities led to efforts to reduce air pollution levels nationwide. As a result, the United States now has one of the strongest air pollution control programs in the world.

Major Types and Sources of Air Pollutants   Table 19-1 lists the major types, sources, effects, and control methods for the chemicals and conditions (heat and noise) from natural and human activities that can build up to harmful levels and become air pollutants. The chemical pollutants listed in Table 19-1 can be classified as either *primary* or *secondary* air pollutants.

Table 19-1 Major Air Pollutants

Pollutant	Major Sources	Effects	Control Methods
Carbon oxides Carbon monoxide (CO)	Forest fires; incomplete combustion of fossil fuels (about two-thirds of total emissions) and other organic matter in cars and furnaces; cigarette smoke	Reduce oxygen-carrying capacity of blood; impair judgment; aggravate heart and respiratory diseases; can cause headaches and fatigue at moderate concentrations; can cause death at prolonged high concentrations	Modify furnaces and automobile engines for more complete combustion; stop smoking
Carbon dioxide (CO_2)	Natural aerobic respiration of living organisms; burning of fossil fuels	Could affect world climate through the greenhouse effect at excessive concentrations (see Enrichment Study 5)	Switch away from use of fossil fuels
Sulfur oxides (SO_2 and SO_3)	Combustion of sulfur-containing coal and oil in homes, industries, and power plants; smelting of sulfur-containing ores; volcanic eruptions	Aggravate respiratory diseases; impair breathing; irritate eyes and respiratory tract; increase mortality; damage plants and reduce growth; probably a cause of acid deposition; corrode metals; deteriorate building stone, paper, nylon, and leather	Use low-sulfur fossil fuels or coal gasification; remove from fuels before use; remove from smokestack exhaust gases; shift to non-fossil-fuel energy sources
Nitrogen oxides (NO and NO_2)	High-temperature fuel combustion in motor vehicles and jet aircraft and industrial and fossil fuel power plants; lightning	Aggravate respiratory disease; increase susceptibility to chronic respiratory infections; can cause acute bronchitis; contribute to heart and lung damage; irritate lungs, eyes, and skin; reduce ability of lungs to cleanse themselves of particulates; probably a cause of acid deposition; decrease atmospheric visibility; take part in formation of photochemical smog; injure respiratory system	Discourage automobile use; shift to mass transit, electric cars, and fuel cells; modify automobiles to reduce combustion temperature; remove from automobile and smokestack exhausts
Hydrocarbons	Incomplete combustion of fossil fuels in automobiles and furnaces; evaporation of industrial solvents and oil spills; tobacco smoke; forest fires; plant decay (about 85% of emissions)	Some injure respiratory system; some cause cancer; take part in formation of photochemical smog; irritate eyes	Modify furnaces and automobile engines for more compete combustion and less evaporation; remove from automobile exhaust; improve handling of solvents and petroleum to reduce spills (Section 18-5) and loss by evaporation
Photochemical oxidants	Sunlight acting on hydrocarbons and nitrogen oxides	Some aggravate respiratory and heart diseases; irritate eyes, throat, and respiratory tract; injure leaves and inhibit plant growth; deteriorate rubber, textiles, and paints	Reduce emissions of nitrogen oxides and hydrocarbons
Particulate matter Dust, soot, and oil	Forest fires, wind erosion, and volcanic eruptions; coal burning; farming, mining, construction, road building, and other land-clearing activities; dust stirred up by automobiles; automobile exhaust; coal-burning electric power and industrial plants	Can cause cancer; aggravate respiratory and heart diseases; causes coughing, irritates throat, and causes chest discomfort; interferes with plant photosynthesis; harms animals; reduces atmospheric visibility; soils and deteriorates buildings and painted surfaces; may affect weather and climate (Enrichment Study 5)	Decrease use of coal; improve land use and soil erosion control; remove from smokestack exhausts; clean streets

Table19-1 Major Air Pollutants *(continued)*

Pollutant	Major Sources	Effects	Control Methods
Asbestos	Asbestos mining; spraying of fireproofing insulation in buildings; deterioration of brake linings	Can cause cancer; hinders breathing; aggravates respiratory and heart diseases; causes fibrosis of lungs	Reduce use; prevent escape into the atmosphere; protect construction workers and miners from inhaling dust
Metals and metal compounds (Enrichment Study 12)	Mining; industrial processes; coal burning; automobile exhaust	Some can cause respiratory diseases, cancer, nervous disorders, and death; toxic to some animals; damaging to plants	Remove from exhaust gases; ban or control input of toxic chemicals (Enrichment Study 13)
Other inorganic compounds Hydrogen fluoride (HF)	Petroleum refining; glass etching; aluminum and fertilizer production	Burns skin and eyes; irritates mucous membranes at high levels; damages plants and animals	Control industrial processes more carefully; remove from smokestack exhausts
Ammonia (NH_3)	Chemical industry; fertilizers; feedlots	Irritates upper respiratory passages; forms particles in atmosphere	Control industrial processes more carefully; remove from smokestack exhausts
Hydrogen sulfide (H_2S)	Chemical industry; petroleum refining; natural decomposition (anaerobic decay); sewage treatment	Has unpleasant odor; causes nausea; irritates eyes and throat; toxic at high levels	Control industrial processes more carefully; remove from smokestack exhausts
Sulfuric acid (H_2SO_4)	Reaction of sulfur trioxide and water vapor in atmosphere; chemical industry	(Same as sulfur oxides)	(Same as sulfur oxides)
Nitric acid (HNO_3)	Reaction of nitrogen dioxide and water vapor in atmosphere; chemical industry	(Same as nitrogen oxides)	(Same as nitrogen oxides)
Pesticides and herbicides	Agriculture; forestry; insect control	Toxic or harmful to some fish, shellfish, predatory birds, and mammals; concentrate in human fat; some may cause birth and genetic defects and cancer (see Section 9-9)	Reduce use; switch to biological and ecological control of insects (see Section 9-9)
Radioactive substances	Natural sources (rocks, soils, cosmic rays); uranium mining; nuclear processing; power generation; nuclear weapons testing; coal burning; nuclear war (Enrichment Study 3)	Cause cancer and genetic defects (Section 15-5); injure leaves; reduce plant growth	Ban or reduce use of nuclear power plants and weapons testing; strictly control processing, shipping, and use of nuclear fuels and wastes; remove from exhausts; reduce burning of coal; use coal gasification
Heat	Use of fossil and nuclear fuels	May affect world climate (see Enrichment Study 5)	Reduce population; reduce energy use
Noise	Automobiles, airplanes, and trains; industry; construction	Causes annoyance; disrupts activities; causes nervous disorders; impairs hearing	Reduce noise levels of automobiles, airplanes, trains, machines, and factories; protect workers and residents from noise by ear cover and better building construction (see Enrichment Study 10)

A **primary air pollutant** is a chemical added *directly* to the air that occurs in a harmful concentration. Examples include sulfur dioxide, two nitrogen oxides (NO and NO_2), carbon monoxide, and some forms of particulate matter like soot and dust.

A **secondary air pollutant** is a harmful chemical formed in the atmosphere through a chemical reaction among air components. For example, sulfur dioxide can react with oxygen gas in the air to form the secondary pollutant sulfur trioxide (SO_3). Then

SO_3 can react with water vapor in air to form sulfuric acid (Section 19-4). Similarly, a mixture of secondary air pollutants like ozone, various aldehydes, and PANs, which can cause the eyes to water and burn like tear gas, are formed in photochemical smog when sunlight brings about a complex series of chemical reactions between hydrocarbons and nitrogen oxides emitted primarily from automobile exhaust (Section 19-6).

Natural decay processes, winds, and volcanic eruptions add to the atmosphere most of the nitrous oxide, carbon monoxide, carbon dioxide, methane, terpenes, radioactive radon and tritium, and particulate matter, and much of the hydrogen sulfide, carbon monoxide, and dust (Table 19-1). However, these natural inputs are usually widely dispersed throughout the world, and except for occasional volcanic eruptions normally don't reach harmful levels. And when they do, as in the case of volcanic eruptions, they are usually taken care of by natural chemical cycles (Section 4-3) and weather patterns (Section 3-6), which also help control levels of potentially dangerous chemicals added to the atmosphere by human activities (Section 5-3).

The primary pollutants produced by human activities, which account for more than 90 percent of the air pollution problems in the United States, are carbon monoxide, sulfur oxides, volatile organic compounds, nitrogen oxides, and particulate matter. Emissions of sulfur dioxide, nitric oxide, and nitrogen dioxide from human activities dwarf natural emissions by a factor of 50 to 100. U.S. power plants and industrial plants alone produce 91 percent of the total weight of sulfur oxide emissions, 82 percent of the particulate matter, 59 percent of the nitrogen oxides, 25 percent of the hydrocarbons, and 17 percent of the carbon monoxide released into the atmosphere each year.

In terms of the *total amount* of primary pollutants emitted each year in the United States, *carbon monoxide* is number one and transportation is its major source. But air pollution experts point out that determinations of air pollutants and their sources should not be based solely on total annual emissions. We should also consider the potential or actual harm to various forms of life, including humans, caused by each type of pollutant. By considering the potentially harmful health effects of the major air primary pollutants, we get a different picture of the relative importance of various air pollutants and their sources, as shown in Table 19-2. On this basis sulfur oxides and particulate matter rank as the top two pollutants, and carbon monoxide drops to last place. In terms of air pollution sources, stationary fuel combustion (primarily at coal-burning power plants) is the most serious, with industry (especially pulp and paper mills, iron and

Table 19-2 Relative Importance of Primary Pollutants and Their Sources in the United States in 1980

	Annual Emissions		Estimated Relative Health Effect	
	Percentage of Total	Rank	Percentage of Total	Rank
Pollutant				
Sulfur oxides	15	2	34	1
Particulate matter	5	5	28	2
Nitrogen oxides	13	4	19	3
Volatile organic compounds	14	3	18	4
Carbon monoxide	53	1	1	5
Total	100		100	
Source				
Stationary fuel combustion	21	2	44	1
Industry	16	3	27	2
Transportation	55	1	24	3
Solid waste disposal	2	5	3	4
Miscellaneous	6	4	2	5
Total	100		100	

steel mills, smelters, petroleum refineries, and chemical plants) and transportation in second and third places, respectively (Table 19-2).

Table 19-1 also summarizes methods for controlling the major forms of air pollution. Unlike water, we can't conveniently get our supply of clean air through pipes. We can control or reject contaminated water and food, but we cannot stop breathing. Thus, the emphasis in air pollution control is on input and throughput approaches to prevent pollutants from entering the air or to reduce their input to keep them from building up to harmful levels. By contrast, control of many water pollutants is based on using an output approach by passing polluted water through water and sewage treatment plants (Section 18-6). More details on pollution control methods for the major primary pollutants are given in Sections 19-5 and 19-6.

National Ambient Air Quality Standards (NAAQS) and the Pollution Standards Index (PSI) The EPA has established primary and secondary *national ambient air quality standards* (NAAQS). Each standard specifies the maximum allowable level for a certain air pollutant averaged over a given period, beyond which harmful health effects may occur (Table 19-3).

Table 19-3 National Ambient Air Quality Standards in 1983

Pollutant	Averaging Time	Primary Standard Levels [micrograms (μg) or milligrams (mg) per cubic meter (m³) and parts per million (ppm)]	Secondary Standard Levels [micrograms (μg) or milligrams (mg) per cubic meter (m³) and parts per million (ppm)]
Particulate matter	Annual (geometric mean) 24 hours*	75 μg/m³ 260 μg/m³	60 μg/m³ 150 μg/m³
Sulfur oxides	Annual (arithmetic mean)	80 μg/m³ (0.03 ppm)	—
	24 hours*	365 μg/m³ (0.14 ppm)	—
	3 hours*		1300 μg/m³ (0.5 ppm)
Carbon monoxides	8 hours*	10,000 μg/m³ (9 ppm)	10,000 μg/m³ (9 ppm)
	1 hour	40 mg/m³* (35 ppm)	40 mg/m³* (35 ppm)
Nitrogen dioxide	Annual (arithmetic mean)	100 μg/m³ (0.05 ppm)	100 μg/m³ (0.05 ppm)
Ozone	1 hour	240 μg/m³ (0.12 ppm)	240 μg/m³ (0.12 ppm)
Hydrocarbons (nonmethane)[†]	3 hours (6 to 9 a.m.)	160 μg/m³ (0.24 ppm)	160 μg/m³ (0.24 ppm)
Lead	3 months	1.5 μg/m³	1.5 μg/m³

Source: Environmental Protection Agency.
*Not to be exceeded more than once a year.
[†]A non-health-related standard used as a guide for ozone control.

Each *primary NAAQS* is designed to include a margin of safety adequate to protect the most sensitive people, such as small children, the elderly, and those with respiratory and other health problems. The U.S. air pollution control laws (Section 19-7) set a deadline for attainment of each primary standard. Although these laws allow no consideration of the costs required to meet the primary standards, there is continuing pressure by industry to allow the use of cost-benefit analysis (Section 20-3) in setting the value for primary standards.

Each *secondary NAAQS* is designed to protect the public against adverse effects of a pollutant not related to human health. These include damage to crops, materials, buildings, wildlife, climate, visibility, and personal comfort. These standards must also be set without consideration of the economic costs of compliance, but there is no deadline for their attainment.

The EPA has developed a relative air *pollution standards index (PSI)*, which can be used to give the public a daily air pollution report and provide warnings when primary NAAQSs are exceeded in a given area (Table 19-4). Note that when the index rises above 100, the air exceeds the national ambient air quality standards and can be harmful. The real test of the U.S. air pollution control program is not the decrease in total emissions, but the decrease in the average number of days each year that NAAQSs are exceeded as measured by the PSI. Between 1974 and 1980 the PSI for 23 major metropolitan areas declined. During this period the average number of days of elevated risk with a PSI of 100 or more in these U.S. cities declined by 39 percent, from 97 to 59 days.

Indoor Air Pollution To escape smog you might go home, close the doors and windows, and breathe in what you believe to be clean air. But a number of scientists have found that the air inside some homes is often more polluted and dangerous than outdoor air on a smoggy day. This is especially true in energy-efficient, relatively airtight houses that do not use an air-to-air heat exchanger to bring in sufficient fresh air, and in the nation's almost 5 million mobile homes. Mobile homes have a smaller volume and lower air-exchange rates than conventional homes, use a larger proportion of plywood and other materials containing volatile organic compounds, and are more likely to use propane (LPG) as a fuel.

Contaminated indoor air is not new. Our cave-dwelling ancestors suffered high levels of soot and other pollutants from open fires in caves without adequate ventilation. Indoor air today is much cleaner than that found decades ago when houses were heated with leaky coal-burning furnaces, but there is still cause for concern.

Table 19-4 U.S. Pollutant Standards Index (PSI)

Air Quality Index Value	Air Quality Level	Health Effect Description	Suggested Actions	Air Pollutant Levels (micrograms per cubic meter)				
				Total Suspended Particulate Matter (24 hours)	Sulfur Oxides (24 hours)	Ozone (1 hour)	Nitrogen Dioxide (1 hour)	Carbon Monoxide (8 hours)
500	Significant harm	Very hazardous	All people should remain indoors, keep windows and doors closed, minimize physical exertion, and avoid traffic.	1,000	2,620	1,200	3,750	57,500
400	Emergency	Hazardous	Elderly people and persons with heart or lung diseases should stay indoors and avoid physical exertion. General population shoud avoid outdoor activity.	875	2,100	1,000	3,000	46,000
300	Warning	Very unhealthful	Elderly people and persons with heart or lung diseases should stay indoors and reduce physical activity.	625	1,600	800	2,260	34,000
200	Alert	Unhealthful	Persons with heart or lung diseases should reduce physical exertion and outdoor activity.	375	800	400	1,130	17,000
100	Primary NAAQS	Moderate	—	260	365 (0.14 ppm)	235 (0.12 ppm)	100* (0.05 ppm)	10,000 (9 ppm)
50	50 percent of Primary NAAQS	Good	—	75*	80*	118	Not reported	5,000
0			—	0	0	0	0	0

Source: Environmental Protection Agency.
*Annual primary NAAQS.

Table 19-5 lists major indoor air pollutants, their sources, and health effects; ways of reducing exposure are also given. Measurements in one relatively airtight, extremely energy-efficient home revealed high levels of formaldehyde throughout the house and indoor radioactivity levels more than 100 times the natural outdoor background level. Measurements in a number of energy-efficient homes revealed radioactivity from radon ranging from 10 to 2,700 times normal background levels. Premature lung cancer deaths from indoor exposure to radon and its decay products are estimated at 5,000 to 20,000 each year in the United States.

19-2 Smog and the Effects of Climate and Topography on Air Pollution

Types of Smog Characteristics of the two major types of smog, *industrial smog* and *photochemical smog*, are summarized in Table 19-6. Although the distinction between photochemical smog and industrial smog is convenient, most cities suffer from both types of air pollution. However, in some cities one type tends to predominate at least for part of the year. For example, industrial smog tends to dominate in London, Chicago, Baltimore, Philadelphia, and Pittsburgh, which usually have long, cold, wet winters and depend heavily on coal and oil for heating, manufacturing, and producing electric power. Burning these fuels releases *particulate matter* and *sulfur oxides*, the major ingredients of *industrial smog*. Details on the formation and control of industrial smog are discussed in Sections 19-4 and 19-5.

Cities in which photochemical smog tends to predominate usually have sunny, warm, dry climates, and their main source of air pollution is the internal combustion engine. Examples include Los Angeles, Denver, Salt Lake City (see opening photo for Part Five, p. 373), Sydney, Mexico City, and Buenos Aires. *Photochemical smog* contains a mix-

Table 19-5 Major Indoor Air Pollutants

Pollutant	Description	Health Effects	Sources in Homes	To Reduce Exposure
Radioactive radon and its more harmful decay products such as polonium-218, lead-214, and bismuth-214	Odorless, colorless, radioactive gases, decay products of radium, which occurs naturally in the earth's crust	Believed responsible for 5 to 20% of all lung cancers; may also cause nasal cancers	Earth and rock beneath home; stone, brick, sand, concrete block used for slab or inside construction; may also enter through the use of well water	Increase ventilation: Open windows and crawlspace vents. Add crawlspace vents. Install air-to-air heat exchanger. Coat cement or stone floors with a sealant and seal cracks, drains, and other openings in floor.
Formaldehyde	Strong-smelling, colorless, water-soluble gas, a component of some insulation and of glues used in making plywood, particle board, and textiles	Nose, throat, and eye irritation, possibly nasal cancer	Various materials, including urea-formaldehyde foam insulation, particle board, plywood, furniture, drapes, and carpet; gas stoves	Don't use formaldehyde materials or use materials that are relatively low in formaldehyde (e.g., low-formaldehyde particle board and exterior-grade plywood, which releases less formaldehyde than interior grades; vent gas stoves (see carbon monoxide)
Asbestos	Fireproof, strong but crumbly mineral fiber, used in a variety of building materials, primarily before the mid-1970's	Skin irritation; lung and abdominal cancer and asbestosis (lung disease), usually after extensive exposure; risk greatly increased for smokers (Enrichment Study 7)	Some wall, ceiling, pipe, and boiler insulation, heat shields, vinyl floor material, patching material, and texture paint	Don't use asbestos materials; take precautions against breathing of asbestos fibers when crumbly asbestos materials are disturbed (e.g., during remodeling); if asbestos-containing materials are in good condition, it is best to leave them alone
Combustion gases Carbon monoxide	Colorless, odorless, tasteless gas from all fuel burning	Lung ailments; impaired vision and brain functioning; fatal in very high concentrations	Unvented kerosene heaters; wood stoves; unvented gas stoves; attached garages	Install air-to-air heat exchanger; increase ventilation (see radon); be sure stoves are properly vented; install exhaust fan above gas stove or use new low NO_2 and CO emitting gas stoves; keep gas appliances properly adjusted; clean chimneys; do not let fires smolder; do not leave car idling in garage; add catalytic oxidizers to wood stoves to convert CO to CO_2
Nitrogen dioxide	Colorless, tasteless gas formed during combustion	Lung damage; lung disease after long exposure	Kerosene heaters; unvented gas stoves	Install exhaust fans above gas stove or use new low NO_2 and CO emitting gas stoves; keep gas appliances properly adjusted; increase ventilation (see radon); install air-to-air heat exchanger

Table 19-5 Major Indoor Air Pollutants *(continued)*

Pollutant	Description	Health Effects	Sources in Homes	To Reduce Exposure
Combustion particles	Tiny smoke particles known as respirable suspended particulates (RSP); also benzo-(α)-pyrene, a tarry, organic particle from incomplete combustion	Lung cancer, emphysema, heart disease, irritation, respiratory infections	Tobacco smoke; wood smoke; unvented gas appliances; kerosene heaters	Avoid smoking tobacco inside or smoke near open window; be sure pipe from wood stove does not leak; vent combustion appliances outdoors; change air filters regularly; use residential air cleaners to control tobacco and wood smoke

Table 19-6 Basic Types of Smog

Characteristic	Industrial Smog	Photochemical Smog
Typical city*	London, Chicago	Mexico City, Los Angeles
Climate	Cool, humid air	Warm, dry air and sunny climate
Chief pollutants	Sulfur oxides, particulates	Ozone, PANs, aldehydes, nitrogen oxides, carbon monoxide
Main sources	Industrial and household burning of oil and coal	Motor vehicle gasoline combustion
Time of worst episodes	Winter months (especially in the early morning)	Summer months (especially around noontime)

*All these cities have both types of smog, but the type listed makes the major contribution.

ture of ozone, PANs, aldehydes like formaldehyde, nitrogen oxides, and carbon monoxide. Details on the formation and control of photochemical smog are discussed in Section 19-6.

Climate, Topography, and Air Pollution The frequency and the severity of smog in a given area depend on climate, topography, heating practices, traffic, and the density of population and industry. Some effects of climate and topography on air pollution are summarized in Table 19-7.

The air near the earth circulates because of the uneven heating of the earth's surface and the rotation of the earth. The combination of these air movements creates specific patterns of prevailing winds that vary throughout the world (Figure 3-9). Because of these mass movements of air, gases and small particles put into the atmosphere are likely to be mixed, diluted, and circulated. Most remain in the troposphere (Figure 19-1) because of gravity.

When our early ancestors lived in small groups throughout the world, the smoke from their fires was effectively diluted and did not pollute other groups in downwind areas. Today, by contrast, pol-

Table 19-7 Effects of Climate and Topography on Air Pollution

Characteristic	Effect
Precipitation	Cleanses the air
Humidity	Dissolves many air pollutants
Sunshine	Initiates formation of photochemical smog, but can reduce industrial smog by decreasing fuel burning for space heating
Wind	Decreases pollution near the source, but can carry it to other areas
Mountains and hills	Hinder dispersion of pollution by reducing winds
Valleys and basins	Trap pollutants

luted air from one heavily populated and industrialized urban area often cannot be diluted to safe levels before it reaches another downwind urban area.

In a localized area, solar radiation warms the earth and adjacent air. Normally this heated air expands and rises, diluting and carrying pollutants into higher layers of the atmosphere. Air from sur-

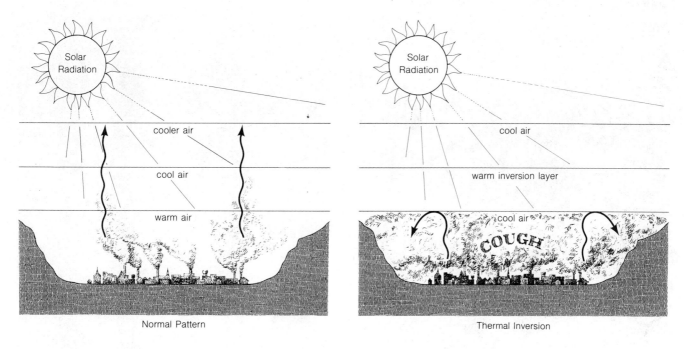

Figure 19-2 Thermal inversion traps pollutants in a layer of cool air that cannot rise to carry the pollutants away.

rounding high-pressure areas moves into the low-pressure area created when the hot air rises (Figure 19-2, left). This continual mixing of the air helps prevent pollutants from reaching dangerous levels.

But under some climatic conditions, often related to topography, a layer of dense cool air is trapped beneath a layer of light, warm air in a particular urban area or valley. This is called a **thermal inversion** or temperature inversion (Figure 19-2, right, and Figure 19-3). In effect, a thermal lid is clamped over the region, and pollutants normally removed by upward air currents slowly accumulate to harmful and even lethal levels. Most air pollution disasters have been caused by prolonged thermal inversions. Such disasters usually happen in fall or winter for two reasons: **(1)** the sun's rays cannot penetrate to create a layer of warm air that would rise from the ground and push away the trapped cold air, and **(2)** the cold weather increases the emissions due to the combustion of fossil fuels for space heating.

In the United States, Atlantic Coast cities have inversions 10 to 35 percent of the time, and Pacific Coast cities 35 to 40 percent of the time. Usually, these inversions last for only a few hours, but occasionally a high-pressure system stalls over an area for several days. Such a high-pressure system over Donora, Pennsylvania, in 1948 allowed pollution to build up to serious levels.

There are several types of thermal inversion. *Subsidence inversions* can occur when a mass of high-pressure air stalls, with the air sinking toward the surface and warming on the way down over the underlying region. These happen over both U.S. coasts but are especially common on the West Coast during the warmer months. *Radiation inversions* are normal at night. After sundown the ground radiates heat into the atmosphere. On a clear night the ground air layer cools quickly and is trapped by the overlying warmer air. Such inversions usually break up when the morning sun heats the ground.

Both types of inversions can happen more often and last longer over a town or city that lies in a valley surrounded by mountains or is near the coast. Put several million people with an almost equal number of automobiles together in a subtropical climate with light winds. Then put mountains on three sides and the ocean on the other and you have Los Angeles, and the ideal recipe for photochemical smog. During the day, when ocean breezes predominate, cool air from the ocean flows into the Los Angeles valley, and after sunset when land breezes predominate, cool air flows from the mountains into the valley. These two processes create almost daily inversions in the Los Angeles basin.

19-3 Effects of Air Pollution

Classification As with water pollution (Section 18-2), we can rank the effects of air pollution in six major classes.

Class 1: *Nuisance and aesthetic insult*: odor; low atmospheric visibility; discoloration of buildings and monuments

New York Daily News, courtesy Environmental Protection Agency

Figure 19-3 Two faces of New York City. The almost clear view photographed on a Saturday afternoon (November 26, 1966). The effect of more cars in the city and a thermal inversion is shown in the right-hand photograph, taken the previous day.

Class 2: *Property damage*: corrosion of metals; accelerated weathering (dissolution) of buildings and monuments; soiling of clothes, buildings, and monuments

Class 3: *Damage to plant and animal life*: leaf spotting and decay; decreased food crop yields; decreased rate of photosynthesis; harmful effects on animal respiratory and central nervous systems

Class 4: *Damage to human health*: oxygen deficiency in the blood; eye irritation; respiratory system irritation and damage; cancer

Class 5: *Human genetic and reproductive damage*: largely unknown at present, but possible

Class 6: *Major ecosystem disruption*: alteration of local and regional climate and perhaps global climate

Let's look more closely at damages from classes 2, 3, and 4 (for a discussion of class 6 effects, see Enrichment Study 5).

Damage to Property, Plants, and Wildlife Marble statues and building materials such as limestone, marble, mortar, and slate are discolored and attacked by sulfuric acid formed from emissions of sulfur oxides and by nitric acid formed from emissions of nitrogen oxides. As a result, some of the world's finest historical monuments are deteriorating rapidly. Atmospheric fallout of soot and grit also soils statues, buildings, cars, and clothing—costing hundreds of millions of dollars each year for cleaning and maintenance.

Sulfuric acid, sulfur dioxide, nitrogen oxides, nitric acid, and some particulates also greatly accelerate the corrosion of metals, especially steel, iron, and zinc. Sulfuric acid and ozone also attack and fade rubber, leather, paper, some fabrics (such as cotton, rayon, and nylon), and paint.

Some forms of air pollution, such as sulfur dioxide, ozone, and PANs, stunt plant growth and damage food crops and trees. Fruits and vegetables grown near big cities are particularly vulnerable. According to a 1982 report by the Office of Technology Assessment (OTA), crop losses from ozone alone amount to about $1 billion a year in California and $1.9 billion to $4.5 billion nationwide.

In the Sudbury area of Ontario, Canada, sulfur dioxide pollution from a complex of nickel smelter plants has essentially destroyed a forest ecosystem

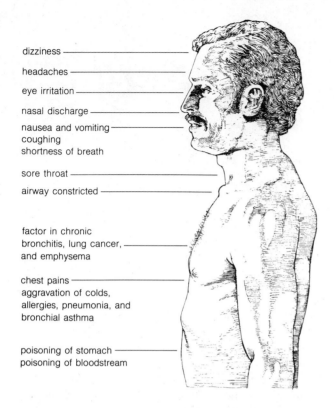

dizziness

headaches

eye irritation

nasal discharge

nausea and vomiting
coughing
shortness of breath

sore throat

airway constricted

factor in chronic
bronchitis, lung cancer,
and emphysema

chest pains
aggravation of colds,
allergies, pneumonia, and
bronchial asthma

poisoning of stomach
poisoning of bloodstream

Figure 19-4 Some possible effects of air pollution on the human body.

for 8 kilometers (5 miles) downwind and has caused tree and plant damage as far as 30 kilometers (19 miles) away. This area is so bleak and lifeless that the U.S. astronauts practiced moonwalking there in the late 1960s. Ozone or a combination of ozone and sulfuric acid have been blamed for damage to various species of trees in two-thirds of the San Bernardino National Forest near Los Angeles, the Shenandoah National Park in Virginia, red spruce trees in high-elevation forests in Vermont, New York, and New Hampshire, and over one-third of all the forests in West Germany.

In addition to humans, other animals are affected by air pollution. For example, excessive exposure to fluoride causes mottled teeth, lameness, and ultimately death in livestock, especially cattle, sheep, and swine.

Damage to Human Health   Air pollution can affect humans in a number of ways (Figure 19-4). After decades of research there is overwhelming statistical evidence that *high levels* of some air pollutants can be fatal and can aggravate and possibly contribute to a number of respiratory diseases (Table 19-1). High levels of air pollution are particularly harmful to the very young, the old, the poor (who often live in highly polluted areas), and those already weakened by heart and lung diseases. According to Harvard professor Richard Wilson and his colleagues (see *Health Effects of Fossil Fuel Burning:*

Assessment and Mitigation, 1981), there is evidence to suggest that air pollution emitted by the burning of fossil fuels in the United States contributes to the premature death of at least 53,000 people each year.

Despite massive statistical evidence that air pollution kills and harms people, it is nearly impossible to establish that a particular pollutant causes a particular disease or death because of **(1)** the number and variety of air pollutants, **(2)** the difficulty in detecting pollutants that may cause harm at extremely low concentrations, **(3)** synergistic interactions of pollutants (Section 5-2), **(4)** the difficulty of isolating single harmful factors when people are exposed to so many potentially harmful chemicals over the years, **(5)** the unreliability of records of disease and death, **(6)** multiple causes and lengthy incubation times of diseases like emphysema, chronic bronchitis, lung cancer, and heart disease (Enrichment Study 7), and **(7)** problems associated with extrapolating test data on laboratory animals to humans.

Largely because of these difficulties, many people are misled when they hear the statement "Science has not proven absolutely that smoking or exposure to a certain level of a particular air pollutant has killed anyone." Like "Cats are not elephants," such a statement is true but meaningless. Science can be used to disprove hypotheses, but it never has proved anything absolutely and never will. Science does not establish absolute truths but only a degree of probability or confidence in the validity of an idea.

To understand the effects of air pollution, look at what happens to the air we inhale into our respiratory system (Figure 19-5). Each breath swirls down the trachea, which divides into two big bronchial tubes that enter the lungs. These tubes divide and subdivide into many small ducts, or bronchiole tubes. At the end of the bronchiole tubes are about 500 million tiny, bubblelike air sacs, called **alveoli,** lying like clusters of tiny grapes inside the lungs. Oxygen in the air passes through the walls of the alveoli and combines with hemoglobin in the blood. At the same time carbon dioxide passes from the blood back through the alveolar walls into the lungs for exhaling.

Carbon monoxide from smoking (Enrichment Study 7) and from automobile exhausts reacts with oxygen-carrying hemoglobin in blood over 200 times more rapidly than the oxygen gas we inhale. The carbon monoxide inhaled during smoking ties up about 5 to 20 percent of the smoker's hemoglobin. This can lead to headaches, fatigue, and impaired judgment; in addition, the heart is forced to pump harder to supply enough oxygen—thus aggravating cardiovascular disease and eventually causing enlargement of the heart. Driver fatigue and im-

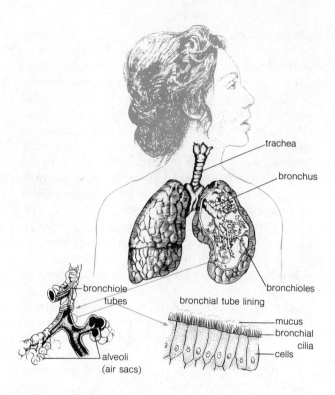

Figure 19-5 The human respiratory system.

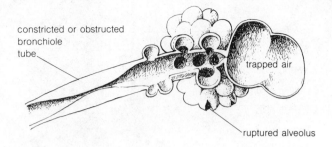

Figure 19-6 Pulmonary emphysema. Constricted or blocked bronchial tubes cause trapped air to enlarge the alveoli so that they lose resilience and sometimes disintegrate. Such damage leads to excessive shortness of breath, susceptibility to respiratory infection, and possible heart strain.

paired judgment from exposure to moderate levels of carbon monoxide during rush hours and in traffic jams is also believed to cause some automobile accidents.

Humans have several defenses against dirty air: **(1)** hairs in the nose filter out large particles; **(2)** small amounts of mucus secreted constantly in the upper respiratory tract wash out or dissolve irritants and trap particles from the air; and **(3)** hundreds of thousands of **cilia,** tiny mucus-coated hairs in the upper respiratory tract, continually wave back and forth to eject mucus and foreign matter. Smoking and exposure to excessive levels of air pollutants like ozone, sulfur dioxide, and nitrogen dioxide and some types of particulate matter apparently destroy, stiffen, or slow the cilia and thus make them less effective. As a result, bacteria and tiny particles can penetrate the alveoli, increasing the chance of respiratory infection and lung cancer. If you smoke or have lived a long time in an urban area, you can assume that your lung tissue is black from deposits of particulate matter. (The lung tissue of a young child is pink.)

If the lungs become irritated, mucus flows more freely to help remove the irritants. A coughing mechanism then expels the dirty air and some of the contaminated mucus. Excessive cigarette smoking and exposure to high levels of pollutants like sulfur dioxide and sulfuric acid can trigger so much mucus flow that air passages become blocked, caus-

ing more coughing. As muscles surrounding the bronchial tubes weaken from prolonged coughing, more mucus accumulates, and breathing becomes progressively more difficult. If this cycle persists, it indicates **chronic bronchitis**—a persistent inflammation of the mucous membranes of the trachea and bronchi. This disease now affects one out of every five American men between the ages of 40 and 60 and has been related to smoking and to living in polluted urban areas.

Bronchial asthma occurs when the bronchial membranes are allergic to certain proteins or to certain types of particulate matter. Asthmatics have recurrent episodes of shortness of breath, prolonged coughing, and difficulty in breathing. These symptoms result from the narrowing of the bronchial passages and excessive mucus secretion, which obstruct the flow of air to the lungs. Most asthma is not caused by air pollution, but air pollutants can trigger attacks in people suffering from this disease.

Pulmonary emphysema, which results when an individual cannot expel most of the air from the alveoli lining the lungs, is usually accompanied by chronic bronchitis. Irritation by cigarette smoke and other forms of air pollution can cause the bronchial tubes to close up. The trapped air may expand and fuse clusters of alveoli together (Figure 19-6). The air sacs then lose their ability to expand and contract and may even tear. As a result, the lungs become enlarged and less efficient. As more alveoli become damaged, the bronchial tubes tend to collapse and breathing gets harder. Walking becomes painful and running impossible. After a period of years breathing efficiency may become so low that the victim dies of suffocation or heart failure.

Pulmonary emphysema affects about 1.5 million Americans (half of them under age 65) and is the fastest-growing cause of death in the United States. This disease is incurable and basically untreatable. It is caused and aggravated by a number of factors, including smoking, air pollution, and heredity. About 25 percent of emphysema cases seem to be due to a hereditary condition characterized by the absence of a protein that is vital in keeping the lungs elastic. Such persons have a very good chance of getting emphysema, especially if they smoke or live or work in a polluted area. A test has been devised to detect this genetic defect. Anyone who smokes or lives in a polluted atmosphere should have this test made.

Lung cancer is the abnormal, runaway growth of cells in the mucous membranes of the bronchial passages. Some air pollutants can cause lung cancer directly, and others can disrupt the action of the cilia. If the cilia and the mucus do not remove carcinogenic pollutants, lung cancer is more likely (see Enrichment Study 7). Although smoking—a form of personal air pollution—is considered the number one cause, lung cancer has also been linked to inhalation of other air pollutants including (1) some radioactive isotopes, such as plutonium-239 (Section 15-5), (2) polynuclear aromatic hydrocarbons (PAHs) such as 3,4-benzopyrene, found in cigarette and other types of smoke, (3) automobile exhaust, and (4) particulate matter—especially particles of asbestos, beryllium, arsenic, chromium, and nickel (Enrichment Studies 7 and 12).

19-4 Industrial Smog Formation and Acid Deposition

The Sulfur Cycle and the Formation of Industrial Smog Sulfur is transformed to different compounds and circulated through the ecosphere in the **sulfur cycle** (Figure 19-7). It enters the atmosphere from natural sources as (1) hydrogen sulfide—which is as poisonous as cyanide and smells like rotten eggs—from anaerobic decay of organic matter in swamps, bogs, and tidal flats and active volcanoes, (2) sulfur dioxide from active volcanoes, and (3) sulfate salts like ammonium sulfate from sea spray. Except for occasional volcanic eruptions, these natural additions of sulfur compounds to the atmosphere are widely dispersed and pose no serious pollution problems.

About one-third of all the sulfur compounds and 99 percent of the sulfur dioxide reaching the atmosphere from all sources comes from these human sources. About two-thirds of the human-related input of sulfur dioxide into the atmosphere results when sulfur-containing coal and oil are burned to produce electric power. The remaining one-third comes from industrial processes such as petroleum refining and the smelting of nonferrous metals with sulfur-containing ores.

When oil or coal is burned, about 97 percent of their sulfur impurities react with oxygen gas in the atmosphere to produce sulfur dioxide gas: $S + O_2 \rightarrow SO_2$. The remaining 3 percent of these impurities react to form sulfur trioxide: $2S + 3O_2 \rightarrow 2SO_3$. If these sulfur oxides are not removed by scrubbers or other devices (Section 19-5), they spew out of chimneys and smokestacks and enter the atmosphere (Figure 19-7). Within several days most of the sulfur dioxide in the atmosphere reacts with oxygen gas: $2SO_2 + O_2 \rightarrow 2SO_3$. The resulting sulfur trioxide reacts almost at once with water vapor in the air or on the ground to form droplets of sulfuric acid: $SO_3 + H_2O \rightarrow H_2SO_4$. This atmospheric mist of sulfuric acid droplets can (1) eat away marble and limestone statues, building stone, and cement, (2) corrode metals, and (3) irritate and damage the lungs.

Some of the sulfuric acid droplets can react with ammonia gas (NH_3) in the atmosphere to form solid particles of ammonium sulfate: $H_2SO_4 + 2NH_3 \rightarrow (NH_4)_2SO_4$. These particles fall to the earth as *dry deposition* or dissolve in rainwater. Small particles of these sulfates by themselves are not harmful to humans and provide plants with an essential nutrient (Figure 19-7). However, droplets of sulfuric acid in the atmosphere can become attached to these particles and inhaled into the lungs. There is some evidence that this combination of sulfuric acid droplets and ammonium sulfate particles can interact synergistically to cause more harm to the lungs than either pollutant acting alone.

Fortunately, in many areas this mist of sulfuric acid droplets and ammonium sulfate particles is washed out of the atmosphere by rain within a few days or weeks. However, if it does not rain and if a prolonged thermal inversion occurs, concentrations of sulfur dioxide, sulfuric acid, and particulate matter in industrial smog can reach deadly levels and can cause air pollution disasters like those that occurred in London, New York City, and Donora, Pennsylvania.

Particles of many different types are found in industrial smog. Unlike most major air pollutants, particulate matter consists of a large number of different chemicals that form particles and droplets of widely varying sizes (Figure 19-8) and with diverse chemical and health effects. *Large particles*, with diameters greater than 10 micrometers (about 0.000039 inch), tend to fall out of the atmosphere within a short time and are not considered to be extremely harmful to humans. Most natural emissions (dust and material from volcanoes) consist of large particles. *Medium-sized particles*, with diameters between 1 and 10 micrometers, tend to remain suspended in the air longer. Many of the particles found in coal dust and in fly ash produced by coal-

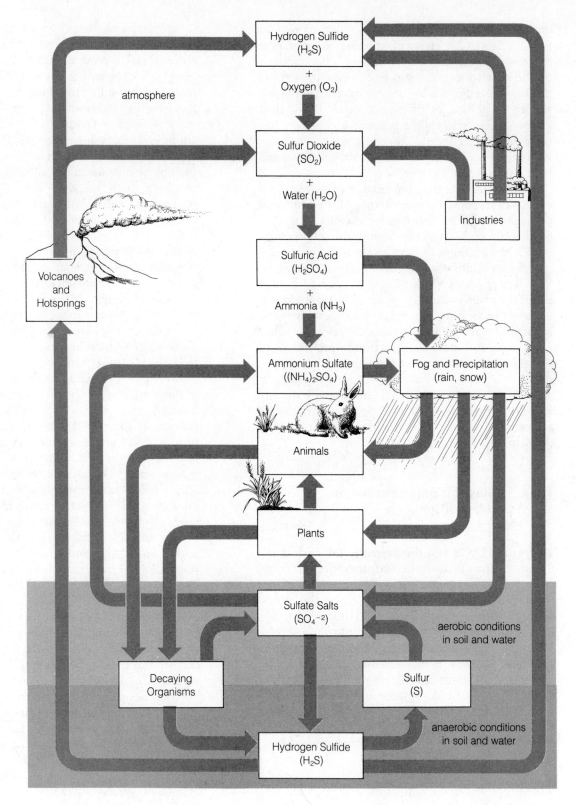

Figure 19-7 The sulfur cycle, showing both natural and human-related additions of sulfur to the atmosphere.

burning electric power and industrial plants fall into this category. Most particles in this size range can be removed by methods discussed in Section 19-5.

The most serious threats to human health are posed by some *fine particles*, with diameters less than 1 micrometer (Figure 19-8). Hazardous types of fine particles remain suspended in the air long enough to be carried all over the world and are small enough to penetrate the natural defenses set up by our lungs. They are also a major factor in

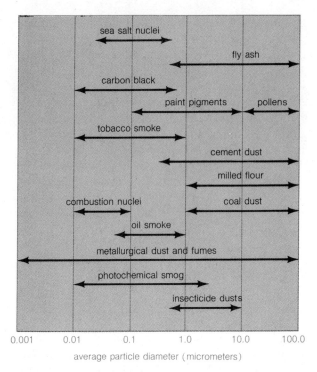

Figure 19-8 Suspended particulate matter is found in a wide variety of types and sizes.

reducing visibility and possibly in altering global weather and climate (Enrichment Study 5). In 1984 the EPA proposed changing the primary and secondary NAAQS (Table 19-3) for particulate matter to regulate only the more hazardous medium-sized to fine particles, 10 micrometers or smaller in diameter.

Acid Deposition Just as emissions of sulfur dioxide from coal-burning power plants, factories, and metal smelters can be converted in the atmosphere to droplets of sulfuric acid and particles of sulfate salts, nitrogen dioxide emissions from cars can be converted in the atmosphere to droplets of nitric acid and particles of nitrate salts like ammonium nitrate. Droplets of sulfuric acid and nitric acid dissolve in rain and snow and fall out of the atmosphere in a process called *wet deposition*. Particles of sulfate and nitrate salts can also be dissolved in rainwater and be removed by wet deposition or simply fall out of the atmosphere as particles in a process called *dry deposition*. The combined dry and wet deposition of these secondary pollutants onto the surface of the earth is known as **acid deposition** (Figure 19-9), commonly and inaccurately referred to as *acid rain* or *acid precipitation*. Acid deposition is a serious and growing problem in many parts of North America, Europe, Scandinavia, and Japan. Using tall smokestacks to inject pollutants above the inversion layer to meet local NAAQS increases acid deposition in areas downwind from the stacks.

Rain and snow become more acidic when they dissolve these atmospheric sulfur and nitrogen compounds. Relative levels of acidity and basicity of water solutions of substances are commonly expressed in terms of **pH.** A water solution with a pH value of 7 is considered *neutral*; one with a pH value below 7 is *acidic*; and one with a pH value above 7 is *basic*, as shown earlier in Figure 8-3. The

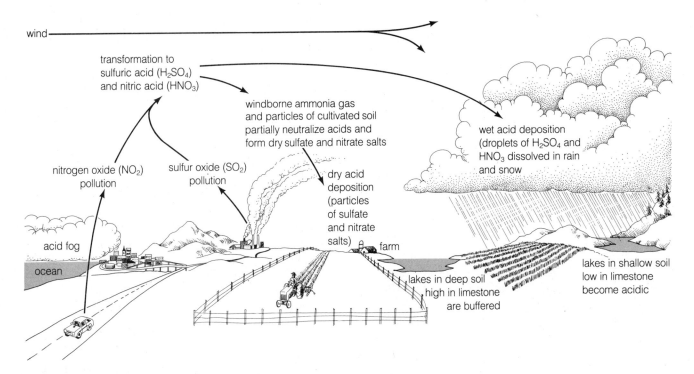

Figure 19-9 Acid deposition and acid fog.

smaller the pH value, the higher the acidity. Also, each whole-number decrease in pH represents a *tenfold increase* in acidity. Thus, a solution with a pH of 3 is 10 times more acidic than one with a pH of 4; 100 times more acidic than one with a pH of 5; and 1,000 times more acidic than one with a pH of 6. Pure distilled water not exposed to the air is neutral (pH = 7).

Normal rainwater, however, is slightly acidic (pH around 5.6) because of the formation of a weak solution of carbonic acid when rainwater dissolves some of the naturally occurring carbon dioxide in the atmosphere. This slight acidity of natural rainfall is beneficial because it helps water dissolve soil minerals for use by plant and animal life. But when the acidity of acid deposition increases beyond this natural level due to human activities, harmful effects occur to trees and aquatic life. Acid deposition has pH values ranging from about 1.9 (some acid fogs in California) to 5.5, with that falling in most of the eastern United States and parts of the West, southeastern Canada, and most of Western Europe having pH values between 4.0 and 5.0.

Thin soils in some areas are especially sensitive to acid deposition because they lack alkaline substances like limestone ($CaCO_3$) or dolomite ($MgCO_3$) that can react with and neutralize the acids. Vulnerable areas include much of New England, southeastern Canada, the Great Smokey Mountains, the lakes of Wisconsin and Minnesota, the Pacific Northwest, and the Colorado Rockies. Acid deposition is also showing up in the South. Most of the soils in the Midwest, where a large part of the sulfur dioxide and nitrogen dioxide emissions is produced, are alkaline enough to prevent serious damage.

According to a 1983 study by the National Academy of Sciences, acid deposition can (1) destroy forms of aquatic life (especially trout and salmon) when large quantities of acidic rain or snow run off into lakes and slow-moving streams; (2) leach toxic nutrients like aluminum salts from the soil (Figure 8-6) and deposit them in lakes and streams, where they can stunt or kill fish and other forms of aquatic life; (3) convert fairly harmless mercury deposits in lake bottom sediments to highly toxic methyl mercury (Enrichment Study 12); (4) kill the microorganisms in the soil responsible for breaking down organic matter and recycling nitrogen and carbon through food webs (Section 4-3); (5) inhibit seed germination, injure leaves of trees and other plants, and break down the waxy coating on leaves that helps prevent damage from diseases and pests; (6) damage trees and reduce timber production when roots take up toxic aluminum and other salts leached out of the soil; (7) leach plant nutrients from the soil; (8) damage and decrease yields of food crops like soybeans, spinach, and alfalfa unless farmers neutralize excessive soil acidity by applying lime or crushed limestone; (9) damage marble and limestone monuments and buildings and corrode exposed metal culverts, roofs, bridges, and expressway support beams that are not adequately painted and maintained; (10) leach toxic metal compounds from soils and water pipes and into drinking water supplies; (11) possibly contribute to the abnormally high incidence of lung cancer in seven coastal counties from South Carolina to Jacksonville, Florida; and (12) possibly play a key role in the premature deaths of 50,000 Americans a year according to a Brookhaven National Laboratory study. Damage to U.S. crops, fish, wildlife, and materials from acid deposition is estimated to be at least $2.4 billion a year.

By 1983, 212 of the 2,200 lakes and ponds in the Adirondack Mountains had a pH of less than 4.5 (500 times more acidic than a normal lake) and were devoid of most forms of life. New York State public health officials advise children and pregnant women not to eat *any* fish caught in the state's lakes because of possible contamination with aluminum and/or mercury leached into the lakes from nearby soil or released from bottom sediments by increased acidity. An estimated 19,000 lakes and 96,000 kilometers (60,000 miles) of streams elsewhere in the East are threatened by acid deposition.

Canada estimates at least 50 percent of its acid deposition comes from the United States and that up to 1,400 of its water bodies have been so seriously affected by acid deposition that they are devoid of fish. Throughout Scandinavia forests are stunted by acid deposition, most of which apparently comes from tall smokestacks in the industrial regions of England and West Germany—and at least 6,000 of Sweden's lakes contain no fish. By 1983, 34 percent of the forests in West Germany had been visibly damaged by a combination of ozone and acid deposition, and increasing forest damage was reported in the United States, especially in the Appalachian range from Maine to Georgia. In 1984, the Organization for Economic Co-Operation and Development (OECD) estimated that acid deposition was causing damages amounting to $50 billion to $66 billion a year in Western Europe.

The coal and automobile industries question the seriousness of acid deposition problems in the United States. They contend that (1) evidence used to show that acidity levels are increasing in intensity and geographic scope is suspect and not based on adequate measurements; (2) the extent of damage from acid deposition is a matter of considerable scientific dispute; (3) there is no reliable evidence linking emissions from specific midwestern power and industrial plants to the alleged increases in the acidity of precipitation in the Northeast and Canada; (4) achieving a 50 percent reduction in sulfur dioxide emissions by installing expensive scrubbers would cause sharp rises in electricity bills; and (5) achieving a 50 percent reduction in sulfur dioxide emissions by switching to low-sulfur western coal, although creating tens of thousands of new jobs in western coal mines, would result in the loss of as many jobs in the Midwest and East. In the early 1980s the Reagan administration used these arguments as reasons for not developing a policy and committing funds for decreasing the damage from acid deposition—despite strong protests by Canadian government officials and many U.S. scientists.

In 1983, however, reports by the NAS and a review panel under the direction of George Keysworth, chief science advisor to the president, provided some definitive answers to these arguments, along with several recommendations. These reports concluded that (1) there is "overwhelming" evidence that emissions from power and industrial plants in the Midwest and Ohio River Valley cause at least two-thirds of the acid deposition in the Northeast; (2) requiring pollution controls on emissions from power plants and industries in the Midwest and in the Ohio River Valley would bring about a corresponding overall reduction in acid deposition (for example, reducing emissions by 50 percent should reduce total acid precipitation by about 50 percent); (3) because of the numerous sources and the complexity of weather patterns, it is essentially impossible to determine that a specific plant in the Midwest is the cause of acid degradation of a spe-

cific lake in the Northeast or Canada; (4) acid deposition would have to be reduced by 50 percent to protect sensitive freshwater ecosystems from damage; and (5) these controls should begin now. Various methods for reducing acid deposition are discussed in Section 19-5.

By mid-1984 the U.S. government had failed to develop a strategy or appropriate funds for decreasing acid deposition. The heart of the controversy over acid deposition involves two issues. Are the effects of acid deposition serious enough to warrant a costly emissions control program? If so, how can the costs for reducing the emissions be equitably divided among the parties involved?

Many analysts doubt that an effective acid deposition control bill will be passed in Congress during a period of budget cuts and concern over the rising national debt. But Richard Ayres, who chairs the National Clean Air Coalition, responds that: "The costs for cleaning up SO_2 emissions aren't trivial. But neither is the damage. A nation that can afford to spend $5 billion a year on video games can afford to spend the same amount to save its lakes and forests."

19-5 Control of Industrial Smog and Acid Deposition

Controlling Emissions of Sulfur Oxides The major methods for controlling emissions of sulfur oxides can be divided into input and output approaches, as summarized in the accompanying box.

Methods for Controlling Sulfur Oxides Emissions

Input Approaches

1. *Reduce population growth and the wasteful use of energy.* Because 50 to 90 percent of the energy used each year in the United States is wasted (Section 14-4), many energy experts argue that reducing waste is the cheapest, easiest, and most effective approach.

2. *Shift from fossil fuels to a mix of other energy sources such as nuclear, solar, wind, hydropower, or geothermal energy (Chapters 15 and 16).* Even if half the electrical power used in the United States is produced by such alternative energy sources by the year 2000, existing and projected coal-burning plants will still emit massive quantities of sulfur

oxides unless other input and output methods are used to reduce these emissions to acceptable levels.

3. *Convert solid coal to a gaseous fuel or a liquid fuel to remove most of its sulfur impurities and to reduce emissions of sulfur oxides from burning solid coal (Section 15-4).* Economic feasibility is still unknown, the net useful energy yield is low, and the solid waste produced must be disposed of safely (Enrichment Study 13).

4. *Shift to low-sulfur coal (containing less than 1 percent sulfur).* Major U.S. supplies of low-sulfur coal are located west of the Mississippi, far from major eastern power plants and industrial centers to which the coal would have to be transported at high

cost and with the use of much energy. In addition, western coal tends to have a lower energy value per unit of weight than high-sulfur eastern coal, and boilers in a number of older power plants could not burn low-sulfur coal without expensive modifications.

5. *Remove sulfur from the fuel before burning.* Existing physical and chemical processes can remove 20 to 40 percent of the sulfur before burning, but can increase fuel costs by 25 to 50 percent depending on the method used and the amount of sulfur removed.

Output Approaches

1. *Require the use of scrubbers to remove sulfur oxides during combustion or from smokestack exhaust gases.* A scrubbing technology that removes as much as 90 percent of the sulfur dioxide from smokestack emissions is *flue-gas desulfurization.* Stack gases pass through a chamber containing a slurry of limestone ($CaCO_3$) and water. The slurry absorbs the sulfur dioxide and converts it to calcium sulfate ($CaSO_4$), which can safely be used as landfill, or to calcium sulfite ($CaSO_3$), a gooey substance that is more difficult to dispose of. Such scrubbers, however, can cost as much as $300 million per plant. In a newer scrubbing technology, limestone injected directly into the furnace of the power plant while the coal is burning combines with sulfur compounds before they are converted to sulfur dioxide to produce calcium sulfate. This process is cheaper (up to about $125 million per plant) than flue-gas desulfurization but removes only about 50 to 60 percent of the sulfur dioxide. A new titanium dioxide (TiO_2) process that can remove as much as 99.7 percent of sulfur dioxide emissions and 99.6 percent of particulate matter emissions is being tested. Since 1980, the EPA has required all new coal-burning power plants to use scrubbers that remove at least 70 percent of the sulfur dioxide from smokestack emissions. However, this standard does not apply to existing coal-burning power plants or to oil-burning plants being converted to burn coal. Each of these older coal-burning plants emits almost seven times as much sulfur dioxide a year as a new plant. Reducing acid deposition by 50

percent probably would require that these older plants be retrofitted with scrubbers. According to the EPA, requiring efficient scrubbers on all plants would increase the consumer's cost of electricity by 15 to 20 percent—far less than the health and materials costs to consumers from uncontrolled emissions. The sludge and fly ash produced each year from the use of scrubbers can be disposed of and represents a far less serious health hazard than emissions of sulfur oxides.

2. *Discharge emissions from smokestacks tall enough to pierce the thermal inversion layer* (Figure 19-2). This widely used approach is strongly favored by industry because it is cheaper than scrubbing stack gases. It is strongly opposed, however, by the EPA and by most environmentalists. This method can decrease emissions of sulfur oxides and particulate matter in areas near the power or industrial plant, but it can lead to increased levels of these pollutants and secondary pollutants making up acid deposition in more distant areas.

3. *Use intermittent emission control.* That is, shut down a plant or switch to low-sulfur fuels during adverse meteorologic conditions, especially during hot, wet months when electricity use is high and acid deposition is apparently heaviest. At other times emissions through tall smokestacks or burning of high-sulfur coal would be allowed. This method is favored by industry but opposed by the EPA and by most environmentalists for the same reasons discussed for output method 2.

4. *Add a tax on each unit of sulfur dioxide emitted, to reduce emissions and to encourage development of more efficient and cost-effective methods of emissions control* (see Section 19-3).

5. *Add lime or ground limestone to soil and acidified lakes to neutralize acidity.* This procedure is favored over the installation of scrubbers by utilities and coal-burning industries. Liming, however, is expensive ($100 to $150 per acre) and must be repeated; and the costs must be borne by individual landowners or by taxpayers through increased state and local taxes. According to environmentalists it is a "Band-aid" approach to acid deposition that does not address the real problem.

Control of Particulate Matter Emissions Major input and output methods for controlling emissions of particulate matter are summarized in the box on page 419.

A combination of most of these methods reduced total particulate matter emissions in the United States by about 60 percent between 1970 and 1982. Despite this significant progress, the total amount of more hazardous fine particles emitted into the atmosphere has increased since 1970 and is expected to increase even more in the future because **(1)** it is extremely difficult and expensive to remove fine particles from smokestacks and automobile exhaust; **(2)** most fine particles are secondary pollutants formed in the atmosphere by the reaction of various chemicals, so that even if effective and affordable methods were developed to remove fine particles from smokestack and automobile exhausts, the situation would not significantly improve; **(3)** there will be more reliance on coal to produce electricity; and **(4)** there are more vehicles than ever on the road. Although automobile emissions account for only about 1 percent of the total mass of atmospheric particles, their impact is more severe because 60 to 80 percent of these are fine particles with diameters less than 2 micrometers.

19-6 Formation and Control of Photochemical Smog: The Automobile Problem

Formation of Photochemical Smog At normal atmospheric temperatures the nitrogen gas (N_2) and oxygen gas (O_2) making up most of the atmosphere do not react with each other. At the high temperatures inside an internal combustion engine or fossil-fuel-burning power plant, however, they react to produce colorless nitric oxide (NO) gas, which is exhausted into the atmosphere: $N_2 + O_2 \rightarrow 2NO$. Once in the atmosphere, nitric oxide reacts with oxygen gas to form nitrogen dioxide, a yellowish-brown gas with a pungent odor: $2NO + O_2 \rightarrow 2NO_2$.

Typically nitrogen dioxide remains in the atmosphere for about 3 days. Just as sulfur dioxide can

Figure 19-10 Four commonly used methods for removing particulates from the exhaust gases of electric power and industrial plants.

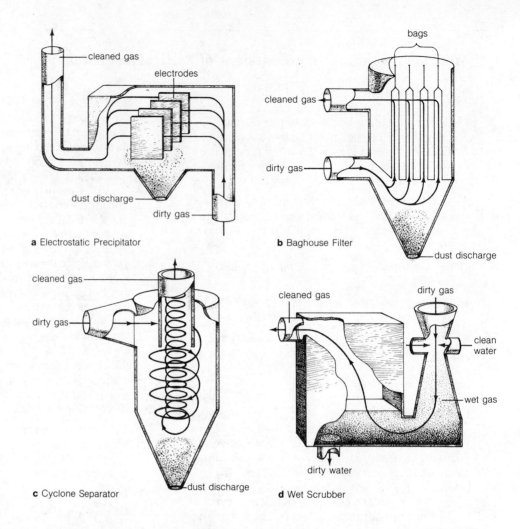

a Electrostatic Precipitator

b Baghouse Filter

c Cyclone Separator

d Wet Scrubber

Figure 19-11 The effectiveness of an electrostatic precipitator in reducing particulates emissions. A stack with the precipitator turned off (left) and with the precipitator operating (right). Although this method can remove up to 99.5 percent of the total mass of particulates in exhaust gases, it does not remove very many of the invisible and more harmful fine particles.

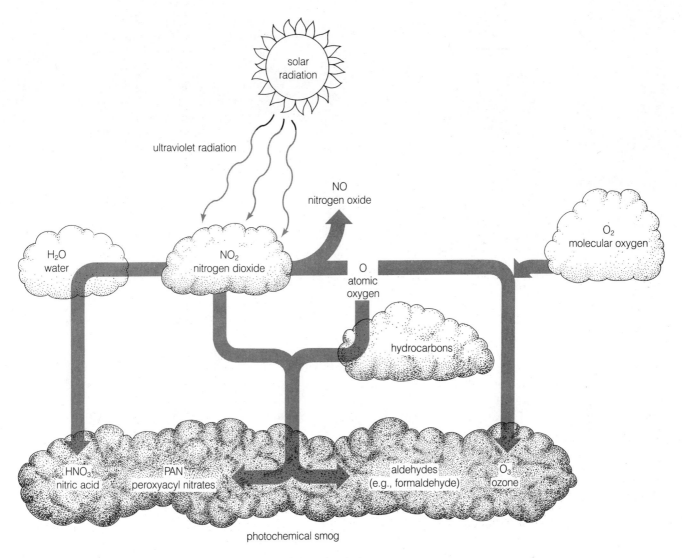

solar
radiation

ultraviolet radiation

NO
nitrogen oxide

O_2
molecular oxygen

H_2O
water

NO_2
nitrogen dioxide

O
atomic
oxygen

hydrocarbons

HNO_3
nitric acid

PAN
peroxyacyl nitrates

aldehydes
(e.g., formaldehyde)

O_3
ozone

photochemical smog

Figure 19-12 Greatly simplified scheme of the formation of photochemical smog.

be converted into sulfuric acid, small amounts of nitrogen dioxide can react with water vapor in the atmosphere to form nitric acid: $3NO_2 + H_2O \rightarrow 2HNO_3 + NO$. Some of this nitric acid is washed out of the atmosphere as another component of acid deposition. Some of the atmospheric nitric acid can also react with ammonia gas in the air to form particles of ammonium nitrate, which eventually fall to the earth's surface or are washed out of the atmosphere by rainfall: $HNO_3 + NH_3 \rightarrow NH_4NO_3$.

Any chemical reaction activated by light is called a **photochemical reaction.** When nitrogen dioxide is exposed to ultraviolet radiation from sunlight, it undergoes a photochemical reaction that converts it to nitric oxide and highly reactive atomic oxygen (O): $NO_2 \rightarrow NO + O$ (Figure 19-12). The atomic oxygen then reacts with O_2 in the atmosphere to produce the photochemical oxidant *ozone* (O_3): $O_2 + O \rightarrow O_3$. Through a complex sequence of reactions, atomic oxygen also reacts with volatile gaseous hydrocarbons (most evaporated into the atmosphere from spilled or partially burned gasoline) to form other photochemical oxidants known as *peroxyacyl nitrates* (PANs). PANs also react with atmospheric hydrocarbons to produce eye-burning *aldehydes* like formaldehyde. Together this complex mixture of secondary pollutants make up what is called **photochemical smog** (Figure 19-12). Mere traces of ozone, PANs, and aldehydes in the air can cause the eyes to burn and water and can damage crops.

Figure 19-13 shows a characteristic pattern of the variation of concentrations of nitric oxide, nitrogen dioxide, and ozone throughout a typical smoggy day in southern California. Early in the morning when commuter traffic begins to build up, atmospheric concentrations of nitric oxide and hydrocarbons start to rise. As some of the NO is

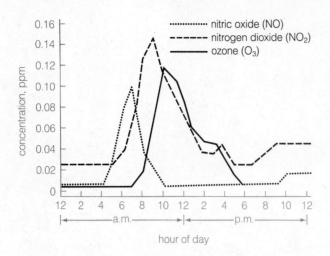

converted to NO_2, its concentration rises. Then under the influence of sunlight, NO_2 concentrations decrease as this gas is converted to O. Highly reactive O atoms combine with O_2 to produce rising levels of O_3, which peak near midday (Figure 19-13).

Methods for Controlling Pollution from Automobiles Controlling emissions from 164 million mobile sources in the United States is more difficult politically and economically than controlling emissions from several thousand stationary sources, explaining in part why emissions of nitrogen dioxide in the United States rose by 12 percent between 1970 and 1980.

The major methods for controlling emissions from mobile sources can be divided into input and output approaches, as summarized in the accompanying box. Table 19-8 compares various methods for controlling emissions from automobiles.

19-7 Air Pollution Control Laws in the United States

Clean Air Act of 1970 By 1970 the automobile industry had made little progress in developing either a clean conventional engine or an alternative engine. Also, emission control systems installed by Detroit usually performed below the level for which they were certified. Dissatisfaction with the automobile industry's progress and rising pressure from those concerned about the effects of air pollution on human health led to the passage of the Clean Air Act of 1970—one of the strongest pieces of environmental legislation passed in the United States.

The goal of the Clean Air Act of 1970 was to have air "safe enough to protect the public's health" by May 31, 1975. To accomplish this goal, the EPA was required to set national ambient air quality standards (NAAQS) for major primary air pollutants (Table 19-3); enforcement was left to the states. For automobiles Congress went even further and

---

Methods for Controlling Emissions from Automobiles and Other Mobile Sources

Input Approaches

1. *Reduce automobile use* by increasing existing taxes on gasoline, horsepower, and car weight, banning cars in downtown areas (Section 12-4), and modifying life-styles and designing cities to require less automobile use (Section 12-5).

2. *Develop mass transit and paratransit systems* (Section 12-4).

3. *Develop less polluting and more energy-efficient engines.* Possibilities include electric, gas turbine, Stirling, and Rankine engines (Table 19-8).

4. *Use a cleaner-burning fuel for the internal comstion engine.* Examples include natural gas, fuel cells, and liquid hydrogen (Table 19-8).

5. *Improve fuel efficiency* by reducing the size, weight, wind resistance, and power of cars and by improving the energy efficiency of transmissions, air conditioning, and other accessories.

6. *Modify the internal combustion engine to lower emissions and improve gas mileage.* Such modifications include carburetor adjustments, fuel injection, and diesel and stratified-charge engines (Table 19-8).

An Output Approach

Control emissions from the internal combustion engine more strictly, for example, by the use of afterburners and catalytic converters (Table 19-8).

Table 19-8 Methods for Controlling Air Pollution from Automobiles

Method	Advantages	Disadvantages
Input Approaches		
Reduced automobile use	Reduces air pollution and use of fossil fuels and other resources (see Table 12-3)	Is inconvenient in absence of mass transit and paratransit; could cause economic disruption and unemployment (see Table 12-3)
Mass transit and paratransit	Reduces air pollution and use of fossil fuels and other resources (see Table 12-3)	Is inconvenient; has high initial cost (see Table 12-3)
New engine designs Electric	Eliminates exhaust emissions; eliminates direct burning of fossil fuels; decreases photochemical smog in urban areas; is quiet; requires little maintenance; is ideal for short trips; has lower fuel costs than gasoline engine; may be used in a hybrid system with electric power for low speeds and short distances and a small combustion engine or fuel cell for highway cruising; new batteries may increase range and cruising speed with less recharging	Could trade one form of pollution for another more harmful one (if daily charging of batteries increases electricity use, thus increasing SO_2 and particulates emissions and radioactive wastes from nuclear power plants); could cause economic depression in oil industry; net energy yield not much higher than that of internal combustion engine; present vehicles are slow, expensive, and inefficient and must be recharged every 80 to 160 kilometers (50 to 100 miles); present batteries must be replaced periodically at costs up to $3,000
Gas turbine	Has low CO and hydrocarbon emissions; runs on most liquid fossil fuels; requires little maintenance; may last longer; vibration-free power; has potentially higher fuel economy per unit of engine weight than conventional engines	Gets poor fuel economy with present designs; operates best at a constant speed; is expensive; depletes fossil fuels; has high nitrogen oxides emissions; breakthrough in ceramic technology needed to permit use of higher combustion temperatures to improve fuel economy
Stirling (external combustion)	Has low emissions; makes few vibrations and little noise; runs on most liquid fossil fuels; has potentially very good fuel economy	Has high cost; is heavy; gets moderate fuel economy with present designs (but should improve); power control is difficult and expensive
Rankine or "steam" (external combustion)	Reduces air pollution; runs on most liquid fossil fuels; should require less service and last longer than conventional engines; has potentially fairly good fuel economy	Is expensive; more research needed before it can be mass produced; has poor fuel economy (but may improve with new designs)
New fuels for internal combustion engines Natural gas	Can burn cleanly with very little pollution (except CO_2)	Supplies are insufficient; range is limited; distribution systems are not in place and each station pump could cost $30,000; could cause economic disruption of oil industry; requires large, strong fuel tank on car
Alcohol (ethanol and methanol)	Could substitute for or be added to gasoline (gasohol) (Section 16-5)	Large land requirements; moderate to high environmental impact from soil erosion; water pollution from runoff of fertilizer and pesticides; competition for cropland to grow grain for fuel may raise prices and reduce food available; net useful energy yield may be low (see Section 16-5)
Fuel cells and hydrogen	Causes no pollution (except heat)	Still being developed; storage and distribution of hydrogen are difficult; requires an economic and environmentally acceptable energy source to produce hydrogen (see Section 16-6)
Improved fuel efficiency	Reduces emissions by burning less gasoline; can be done quickly	Is somewhat costly; is inconvenient for some; may increase emissions of some nontarget pollutants
Modified internal combustion engine Carburetor adjustment	Is easy and quick	Is only a short-term measure; increases emission of other pollutants
Stratified-charge engine	Has low emissions without emission control devices; gets better gas mileage than most conventional engines	Consumes fossil fuels

Table 19-8 Methods for Controlling Air Pollution from Automobiles *(continued)*

Method	Advantages	Disadvantages
Diesel engine	Gets 25% better mileage per gallon than conventional engine; requires little maintenance; has low CO and hydrocarbon emissions; new turbocharged type may sharply reduce emissions; lasts longer and is more efficient than conventional engine; new direct injection diesel engines may improve gas mileage over standard diesels (but increase nitrogen oxides emissions)	Consumes fossil fuel; has higher nitrogen oxides and particulates emissions; is more expensive (but shouldn't be) and noisier than conventional engine; emissions can cause eye irritation and possibly genetic damage; has sluggish performance unless turbocharged
Output Approach		
Emission control	Reduces pollution without major changes in engine design; causes little economic disruption of automobile industry	Consumes fossil fuels; doesn't reduce pollution enough in long run; devices become less effective with use; devices must be adjusted or replaced frequently; catalytic converters may emit toxic metal particles

set standards itself, hoping to force the automobile companies to speed research on emission reduction and alternative engines. The act required a 90 percent reduction in emissions of hydrocarbons and nitrogen oxides from 1970 levels for all 1975 automobiles, and a 90 percent reduction in emissions of nitrogen oxides from 1971 levels for 1976 models. The EPA, however, was empowered to grant 1-year extensions if it found that the technology was not available after the companies had made good-faith efforts to develop it.

Almost immediately the automobile companies requested an extension, claiming that the 90 percent reductions were impossible or so costly that plants would have to shut down. In 1973 the EPA granted Detroit a 1-year delay in meeting the 1975 standards for hydrocarbons and carbon monoxide and the 1976 nitrogen oxides standard. Although Detroit claimed it couldn't develop the technology to meet the 1975 national standards, it met them for cars sold in California. In addition, during 1973 the Honda Motor Company of Japan introduced its stratified-charge internal combustion engine (CVCC), which met the 1975 standards without using any add-on emission control devices. In 1973 Peugeot of France and Mercedes-Benz of West Germany also had diesel-powered cars that met the 1975 standards.

In 1974, in 1975, and in 1976 Detroit was granted additional 1-year extensions, claiming that it couldn't simultaneously reduce emissions and offer the improvements in fuel economy that had become increasingly important in the wake of the 1973 oil embargo. During the same period the Honda CVCC was meeting the standards and getting about 17 kilometers per liter (40 miles per gallon) of gasoline. In 1976 Volkswagen introduced its diesel-powered

Rabbit, which met the 1975 standards and got about 21 kilometers per liter (50 miles per gallon).

In 1977, General Motors announced that it would offer a conventional diesel engine option for some of its models—something Peugeot and Mercedes-Benz had been doing for decades. But diesels emit between 30 and 100 times more particulate matter, mostly as hazardous fine particles, than cars with conventional engines. By 1982 a Volkswagen Rabbit equipped with a new trap oxidizer was able to meet EPA's proposed 1985 standard limiting particulate matter emissions from diesels to 0.2 gram per mile. Nevertheless, in 1984, under pressure from American automobile companies, the EPA delayed this standard until 1987.

There is still another chapter in this story of delaying tactics by Detroit. To meet the federal emissions standards, automobile manufacturers began adding afterburners and catalytic converters to car engines to control emissions. *Afterburners* recirculate exhaust gas into high-temperature chambers to convert carbon monoxide to carbon dioxide and to get more complete combustion of unburned hydrocarbons. Unfortunately, at such high temperatures the nitrogen and oxygen gas used to burn gasoline reacts at a faster rate, causing emission levels of nitrogen oxides to rise. In a *catalytic converter*, engine exhaust is mixed with outside air and passed through a chamber containing two types of catalyst (one for carbon dioxide and one for hydrocarbons). These catalysts speed up the combustion reaction of carbon monoxide and hydrocarbons with oxygen gas.

Detroit claimed that catalytic converters to remove nitrogen oxides couldn't be developed. In 1977, however, Volvo of Sweden introduced a three-way catalyst that reduced nitrogen oxides as well as carbon monoxide and hydrocarbons. The Volvo engine with catalytic converter met the stricter 1978 California standards for carbon monoxide and produced less than half the emissions of hydrocarbons and nitrogen oxides that these "impossible" standards allowed. In addition, by removing nitrogen oxides from the exhaust, Volvo could adjust the spark timing and the fuel-to-air ratio to improve fuel mileage.

Clean Air Act of 1977   After 7 years of pressure from all sides, Congress amended its 1970 legislation by passing the Clean Air Act of 1977. Despite vigorous industry pressure, the principles of the 1970 act were reaffirmed. But the dates set for compliance with standards in the 1970 act were postponed.

The 1977 amendments also established *prevention of significant deterioration (PSD)* regulations, partly to protect parts of the country where the air is cleaner than that required by one or more NAAQSs (Table 19-3), and partly to prevent industries from relocating facilities from exceptionally dirty areas to clean areas. The PSD regulations divided the country into three classes:

Class I: areas that include 158 large national parks and all wilderness areas established before 1977, in which only minimal deterioration of NAAQS levels is allowed

Class II: areas in which moderate deterioration up to 25 percent of NAAQS levels is allowed

Class III: areas in which deterioration up to 50 percent of NAAQS levels is allowed.

Initially all areas not included in Class I were classified as Class II areas, with states having the option to downgrade any or all Class II areas to Class III areas.

The 1977 amendments also allowed the EPA to use *emissions offset, banking,* and *bubble policies* to allow companies to buy, sell, trade, and "bank" permission to pollute up to certain levels in specified areas. These changes were made in response to industry's claim that it can control pollution more effectively and cheaply if regulators simply set overall standards and let the companies decide the best way to meet them.

The EPA *emissions offset policy* permits companies to compensate for emissions from one plant in an area by buying new pollution control equipment for an existing polluting plant, or by buying and closing down an existing plant that is too expensive to clean up.

Another approach is EPA's *banking policy*. When a company makes higher than required reductions in air pollution in an area, it can credit these for use in the future or sell them to another firm wanting to build or modernize in a particular area. Environmentalists warn, however, that some offset and banking transactions do not necessarily result in lower emissions. For example, a company may claim a banking credit for shutting down a plant it had already planned to close for reasons unrelated to pollution. The offset and banking policies have also been criticized because they allow companies to keep competitors from moving into an area by controlling the price and availability of offsets.

Under the *bubble policy*, the EPA permits state authorities to set maximum limits for total air pollution from all types of pollution emitted by a plant instead of for each type of pollutant. This policy treats an entire plant as if it were under a giant dome or bubble. Thus, a company can meet total emission standards by reducing pollution sharply from sources in a plant that are cheap and easy to control, while having higher emissions from point sources that are difficult and expensive to control.

By 1980 over 80 percent of major U.S. stationary air pollution sources had complied with the requirements of the Clean Air acts of 1970 and 1977. Various studies found that primarily as a result of these acts, improved air quality saves an estimated 14,000 lives a year and has saved U.S. citizens $21.4 billion a year in health, cleaning, and other costs, versus $17 billion a year spent on air pollution control—a net benefit of $4.4 billion a year.

Future Changes   In 1981 the Clean Air Act was up for renewal by Congress. However, by mid-1984 Congress, the administration, industry officals, and environmentalists were still arguing over how to amend the Clean Air Act.

Some of the amendments pushed for by industry officials and some state and city officials to weaken the act include **(1)** extending to 1990 the deadline for meeting clean air standards for cities with tough air pollution problems, such as Los Angeles, **(2)** relaxing emission standards for carbon monoxide for cars, **(3)** conducting more research on acid deposition before undertaking a regulatory program, despite the existence of over 3,000 studies, **(4)** setting primary NAAQS to protect the bulk of the population rather than those whose physical condition makes them most vulnerable to air pollution, **(5)** allowing secondary NAAQS to be set by states rather than by the federal government, **(6)** allowing states rather than the EPA to have the primary authority for developing plans to meet federal air pollution standards, **(7)** eliminating specific goals and deadlines for reducing pollution in areas not meeting clean air standards, **(8)** eliminating the EPA's authority to impose fines on businesses not complying with federal pollution standards, and **(9)** repealing the requirement that new coal-fired power plants install stack gas scrubbers to reduce sulfur dioxide emissions 70 to 90 percent.

Most environmentalists opposed all these changes in the Clean Air Act and argued that the act should be strengthened by **(1)** making it illegal to tamper with vehicle emission controls, and enforcing this law with heavy fines, **(2)** setting NAAQS for secondary pollutants like sulfuric acid, nitric acid, and suspended nitrate and sulfate particles to reduce acid deposition, **(3)** requiring scrubbers or other methods on all older coal-burning plants to reduce sulfur dioxide and particulate levels, with the goal of reducing acid deposition by at least 50 percent within 10 years, **(4)** setting primary NAAQS and reducing levels of more dangerous fine particles, **(5)** developing a plan to improve indoor air quality based primarily on modifying building codes and establishing emission and venting standards for gas and wood stoves and unvented kerosene heaters, **(6)** setting primary NAAQS for most of the more than three dozen hazardous primary and secondary air pollutants that have been under review by the EPA for years, and **(7)** increasing fines and maximum jail sentences for violators of federal air pollution standards and increasing the EPA budget and staff for enforcement of existing air and water pollution control laws. It is also suggested that the federal government require annual tests (costing each motorist about $5 to $10) to ensure that vehicular emission control devices are working properly. Such tests are required now by Massachusetts, Rhode Island, Connecticut, and New Jersey. Reports from New Jersey indicate that the emission control system is tampered with in 1 out of every 10 cars tested.

Air pollution can no longer be addressed as simply a local urban problem.
Erik P. Eckholm

Discussion Topics

1. Why is it so difficult to establish an air quality standard for a specific air pollutant? Does this mean that such standards shouldn't be established?

2. Trace your own direct and indirect contribution to air pollution for one day. Try to list pollutants and relative amounts. Don't forget electricity (from all kinds of devices, including hall lights, heating, and air conditioning), and don't forget to trace the air pollution produced back to the power plant, transportation of fuel to the power plant, and the surface mine or oil well.

3. Distinguish between photochemical smog and industrial smog in terms of major pollutants and sources, major human health effects, time when worst episodes occur, and methods of control.

4. Evaluate the pros and cons of the statement "Since we have not proven absolutely that anyone has died or suffered serious disease from nitrogen oxides, automobile manufacturers should not be required to meet the federal air pollution standards."

5. Rising oil and natural gas prices and environmental concerns over nuclear power plants could force the United States to depend more on coal, its most plentiful fossil fuel, for electric power. Comment on this in terms of air pollution. Would you favor a return to coal instead of increased use of nuclear power? Why?

6. How should we deal with the problem of air pollution from fine particulate matter? Why is this one of our more serious pollution problems?

7. Why is controlling air pollution generally a more difficult political problem than controlling water pollution? Give several reasons.

8. Simulate an air pollution hearing at which automobile manufacturers request a 3-year delay in meeting the air pollution standards set for the coming year. Assign three members of the class as members of a decision-making board and other members as the president of an automobile manufacturing company, two lawyers for that company, two government attorneys representing the EPA, the chief engineer for an automobile manufacturer, a public health official, and two citizens (one opposing and one favoring the proposal). Have a class discussion of the implications of the final ruling of the board.

9. Use the literature to determine what changes, if any, have been made since 1984 in the Clean Air Acts of 1970 and 1976. Which changes do you believe strengthened the act? Which ones weakened the act? Explain your position.

PART SIX

Environment and Society

We cannot hope for world peace when 20 percent of the people in the world have 80 percent of the goods.
Father Theodore Hesburgh

There is a need for a revolution in our thinking as basic as the one introduced by Copernicus, who first pointed out that the earth was not the center of the universe.
Lester Pearson

20

Economics and Environment

As important as technology, politics, law, and ethics are to the pollution question, all such approaches are bound to have disappointing results, for they ignore the primary fact that pollution is primarily an economic problem, which must be understood in economic terms.

Larry E. Ruff

20-1 Economic Growth, GNP, and the Quality of Life

The words *economics* and *ecology* come from the same Greek root, *oikos*, meaning "house" or "home." **Ecology** is the study of our earthly home—an analysis of interactions among species and between species and their environment. **Economics** literally means "household management"; today the term refers to the study of principles and customs that affect the production, consumption, growth, and distribution of material wealth for human needs.

In spite of the common origin of these two terms, ecology and economics have scarcely interacted until recently. This interaction has centered on four major questions. **(1)** What types of economic growth are good and what types are harmful? **(2)** What types of economic system are compatible with preserving the environment and the earth's finite resources? **(3)** How can economics be used to protect and improve environmental quality? **(4)** Will the economic costs of environmental protection and improvement be too high relative to the benefits of continuing the present high rate of per capita resource use? This chapter is devoted to a brief discussion of these four questions.

The Economic Growth Debate To most economists, chambers of commerce, and industrialists, economic growth is equated with progress. Only a vigorously growing economy coupled with maximum production and maximum consumption is considered healthy and sound. LDCs are encour-

aged to develop and grow like the MDCs. More economic growth is supposed to increase human well-being, help provide enough jobs, control inflation, help cure poverty, and provide enough funds to clean up the environment, as summarized in Table 20-1.

Since 1970 the goal of ever increasing economic growth has come under attack by a growing chorus of environmentalists, economists, and some industrialists (see Enrichment Study 2). These critics argue that continued economic growth is neither possible nor desirable because of finite resource supplies and the limited ability of the environment to absorb heat and matter wastes, as summarized in Table 20-1. They believe that the harmful consequences of economic growth often outweigh the benefits.

The issue is more complicated than growth-at-any-cost versus no-growth. A number of economists and environmentalists have moved beyond this counterproductive debate. These groups generally agree on the following points.

1. Some forms of economic growth are neither desirable, necessary, nor inevitable. In the words of economist Herman E. Daly, "What we need is growth in things that really count, rather than in things that are merely countable."

2. The major need is to use economic rewards and penalties to redirect growth and eliminate waste. Some things need to grow and some need to decline, because the earth's resources and the ability of the environment to absorb pollution are finite. A detailed study of the American economy by Samuel Bowles and his colleagues (see *Beyond the Wasteland*, 1983) showed that waste in the American economy in 1980 amounted to $1.2 trillion—equivalent to almost 50 percent of the GNP. They argue that eliminating this waste would allow continued economic growth without running into the limits of growth (Enrichment Study 2).

3. We still know relatively little about which types of growth have good effects and which have bad, or about how to measure these effects.

Enrichment Study 2 is related to this chapter.

Table 20-1 Views on Economic Growth

Pro	Con
Economic growth increases human well-being.	Some types of economic growth increase well-being for some, but other types worsen the well-being of others. In spite of decades of worldwide economic growth, the gap between the rich and the poor is growing.
Economic growth promotes full employment and controls inflation.	Recent runaway inflation and growing unemployment in most rich nations despite economic growth cast serious doubt on this idea.
Economic growth is the cure for poverty and makes it easier for the rich nations to help the poor nations. As long as the economic pie is growing, more wealth can "trickle down" to the world's poor.	Even if this hypothesis is valid, most economic growth in the rich countries has not been used to help the poor. The gap between the rich and poor is growing, and most rich nations are giving less and less aid to poor countries. In most cases, this argument is merely a smokescreen to direct attention from the important ethical and political issue of a more just distribution of the world's wealth.
The benefits of economic growth outweigh its harmful effects.	As we approach environmental thresholds, the harmful effects of air, water, heat, and noise pollution, land disruption, traffic jams, and other environmental and social disruptions that result from growing production and consumption begin to outweigh the benefits of economic growth.
Economic growth is necessary to fund environmental cleanup and to pay for higher-priced energy.	It is economically and ecologically unsound to use and waste more matter and energy at ever higher costs. Decreasing the rate of harmful, wasteful growth is a cheaper approach and is the only way to avoid the limits to growth imposed by finite resources and the second law of energy.
Economic growth promotes technological innovation, which can solve the problems of resource depletion and pollution.	Substitutes for some resources will not be found; other approaches, such as mining lower-grade resources, are too expensive. Technology often creates as many problems as it solves. No technological development will overcome the unalterable limits imposed by the second law of energy.

4. If we place monetary costs on the bad effects, the price of any form of economic growth can be made to reflect such costs, and undesirable growth will be discouraged. But putting a price on the value of a human life or storage of nuclear wastes, for example, is difficult and in the case of nuclear wastes the cost is passed on to future generations.

Gross National Product and Gross National Quality The **gross national product** is the market value of all goods and services produced by the economy of a given area (usually a nation) in a given year. To many economists a rising GNP or average per capita GNP indicates improved well-being of a nation's citizens. To many environmentalists and to some economists, however, GNP is a misleading indicator of the quality of life. It does not reveal how well goods and services are meeting human needs or how they are distributed among the people. Some economists have pointed out that the GNP was not meant to be a measure of human well-being, but it is still used that way.

Producing more cigarettes raises the GNP, but it also causes more cancer. This increases medical expenditures, which increases the GNP, but in a negative way. More automobiles cause more accidents, more congestion, and more pollution, causing the GNP to grow, but again by incurring costs of a harmful activity.

Waste in government is also included in the GNP. A 1983 government-sponsored study by a task force of business executives and experts gave detailed suggestion's showing how $100 billion a year could be saved by eliminating government waste. An increasing amount of the annual federal budget, also included in the GNP, goes to pay off the *national debt*—the amount government has to borrow to make up the difference between what it spends and what it takes in from taxes. Many analysts believe that the federal debt is out of control. Between 1940 and 1984 it increased from $43 billion to $1.6 trillion—an average debt of $6,780 for every American man, woman, and child—not including an additional $10 trillion off-the-books debt for obligations such as Social Security and other federal pension plans. This debt is equivalent to half the money in the world. If 1.6 trillion dollar bills were laid end to end, the line would reach to the sun, and back to the planet Mercury. The $170 billion in interest on this debt during 1984 amounted to 17 percent of all federal spending, and resulted in an average interest payment by taxpayers of $19.4 million a minute. Such a large debt crowds other borrowers out of the money market, tends to keep interest rates high, and makes it difficult for the government to meet its obligations and increase expenditures without either raising taxes or further increasing the national debt.

Most economists agree that we need a better

indicator than GNP for determining the quality of life. In theory, we could list and put a price tag on all the "negative" products and services included in the GNP. The total value of these negative factors could be subtracted from the GNP to obtain the **gross national quality,** or **GNQ.**

A number of scholars are attempting to develop definitions and measures of the quality of life based on a concept such as the GNQ. This is a difficult task. For example, how do we put a value on positives such as clean air, clean water, and redwood trees? Should a value be based on the present or the future? Even when we agree on values, it is often hard to put numbers on them. However, analysts argue that the inability to find perfect social indicators should not prevent us from improving the imperfect ones we now use. The Overseas Development Council has devised a Physical Quality of Life Indicator (PQLI) based on three social indicators—life expectancy, infant mortality, and literacy—to be used instead of per capita GNP.

20-2 Dynamic Steady-State and Sustainable Earth Economic Systems

A Dynamic Steady-State Economy It appears that all existing economic systems—including capitalism, socialism, and communism—have the same need to increase economic growth continually by increasing the rate of flow of matter and energy resources through each national economy (Figure 2-4). The resulting rise in pollution is a problem in all industrialized countries.

Economists are also finding that modern economic models cannot be used to predict and control the economy as well as they had hoped. This strongly suggests that the problem is economic theory itself. This was expressed by the editors of *Business Week:* "When all forecasts miss the mark, it suggests that the entire body of economic thinking accumulated during the past 200 years is inadequate to describe and analyze the problems of our times." It has been suggested that instead of tampering with dangerously out-of-date economic models, economists develop a more comprehensive and realistic body of economic theory based on preserving the health of basic biological systems (fisheries, forests, grasslands, and croplands), which form the foundation of the global economic system.

Economists like Herman E. Daly (see *Toward a Steady-State Economy,* 1973 and *Steady-State Economics,* 1977) have proposed that the United States and other MDCs move from the present frontier economy to a *dynamic steady-state economy.* Such an economy would have a constant stock of physical wealth and people, each maintained at some desirable,

chosen level by a low rate of throughput of matter and energy resources. Recall from Section 5-2 that a *dynamic steady state* occurs in an *open system* (like a country or a living organism) when the system's input of matter and energy is balanced by its output of matter and energy (Figure 5-3); in this way the system maintains its stability. Since money is used to regulate the flow of matter (goods) and energy through a society, a dynamic steady-state economy would use monetary rewards and penalties to maintain the desired rate of throughput of matter and energy resources.

There are five important things to remember about a dynamic steady-state economy.

1. *It is a dynamic system.* It is not dull and static.

2. *It is not a "no-growth" system* (a false label used by opponents). The dynamics of the system require that some things grow, some decline, and some remain fairly constant. These dynamic ups and downs help keep the system from destruction or harm by exceeding its limits of tolerance. Some of the things that could grow are art, music, education, athletics, philosophy, aesthetics, religion, cultural and ecological diversity, scientific research, and cooperative rather than competitive human interactions. Areas of business and technology that would be encouraged to grow include pollution control, recycling, intermediate technology, design and production of long-lasting products, medical research, more efficient use of energy, resource recovery, renewable energy resources, resource self-sufficiency, and the psychology and sociology of human behavior and interactions. Industries that couldn't conserve resources and decrease harmful outputs would decline—as they should.

3. *It is not an unnatural, undesirable, or new system.* Since all life represents a dynamic steady state, any linear growth or non-steady-state system is merely temporary and must eventually reach a steady-state level either by slowly leveling off or by a sharp dieback or fallback (Figure 7-2). The main arguments are how close we are to the limits of growth (Enrichment Study 2). Some dynamic steady-state societies with dynamic steady-state economies exist quite happily within modern societies without having changed their life-styles significantly since 1700. Examples include the Amish and Mennonite communities in the United States and the Hutterites in Canada.

4. *It does not necessarily require a fixed level of pollution or resource use.* Many possible combinations of population size and resource use allow a system to exist without exceeding harmful limits. Technological or other changes may make it desirable to grow (or to decline)

to a different level. However, in such cases growth is viewed as a temporary situation needed to move from one steady-state level to another, not as an economic norm.

5. *It is based on greatly increased use of renewable energy resources (sun, wind, water, and biomass) and decreasing the rate at which matter and energy resources are used and wasted, to avoid overloading the ecosphere.*

In a dynamic steady-state economy, *money would be used to reward those who produce goods and services that last the longest and use the least amount of matter and energy resources.* In such a low-waste economic system the throwaway product would become extinct. Instead, products would be durable and recyclable, and consumers would also expect ease of repair, multiple uses, and standardized shapes and sizes. In such a society waste and scrap matter—what we now call secondary materials—would become the primary matter resources, and our natural, untapped matter resources would become our backup supplies—the reverse of our present situation. People would be guided by Malkin's rule: "The more things you own, the more you are owned by things," and Raven's raving: "The best things in life aren't things."

In a dynamic steady-state economic system, most manufacturing would be done on a decentralized, small-scale basis near the point of consumption. This is the opposite of the present system, which uses money and energy to bring raw materials from all over the world to a few, large, centralized, energy-guzzling plants. Then more energy and money are used to ship the resulting products all over the world. When energy and matter resources are cheap, this makes economic—but not ecological—sense. But in the age of resource scarcity that we are in or soon will enter, large, centralized national and international companies may be the first to fall, unless they are artificially and temporarily supported by government aid.

A Sustainable Earth Economy The fourth characteristic of a dynamic steady-state economy is one of its major weaknesses. Since a dynamic steady state could exist in many forms, rich nations could continue to use and waste resources at a fairly high rate and still not aid the LDCs. Moreover, the dynamic steady-state economy can't exist at a world level. A nation is an *open system* through which matter and energy flow, but the world as a whole is a *closed system* sustained by energy flow and matter cycling (Figure 4-1). Instead of reaching a dynamic steady state, a closed system reaches a *dynamic equilibrium state* (Figure 5-3) based on optimal energy flow and matter cycling to keep the system from breaking down or becoming seriously disrupted.

There is confusion over and improper use of the terms "open" and "closed" (state) in many writings. These terms were originally defined in the science of thermodynamics. An *open system*, like a living organism or a nation, is one in which matter and energy are exchanged between the system and its environment. Such a system can reach a *dynamic steady state*. A *closed system*, like a spaceship or the earth, is one in which energy but not matter is exchanged between the system and its environment. This type of system can reach a *dynamic equilibrium state*. Confusion occurs because logic suggests that a system that receives and emits energy does have an element of openness. In thermodynamics, however, a system that does not exchange either matter or energy with its environment is defined as an *isolated system*—not a closed system. Thus, a nation can have a steady-state economy because it is an open system. However, because the world is a closed system, in the long run it can have only a dynamic equilibrium, or sustainable earth economy.

Like the steady state, the equilibrium state is dynamic and not static, is not a no-growth state, and is not unnatural or undesirable. To focus on the earth's life-support system and to shorten the name, I use the term *sustainable earth economy* to signify a dynamic equilibrium economy for the world. Table 20-2 summarizes some of the important differences between our present frontier, throwaway economic system and a sustainable earth economic system.

The transition to a sustainable earth economy will by no means be painless. Critics of this idea argue that **(1)** it could be instituted only by greatly reducing human freedom, and **(2)** it cannot be achieved, even if desirable, because most nations in the world would not agree to such a system and because most people are fundamentally selfish. But to many analysts the alternative of running our present high-waste economy at full speed until environmental disorder and resource depletion overwhelm us is much worse and would lead to an even greater loss of individual freedom.

Herman E. Daly has offered an economic plan for achieving the major goals of a sustainable earth society (which he calls a steady-state society). His suggestions are summarized as follows: **(1)** stabilize population by giving every woman (or couple) a license to have a certain number of children and allowing each woman (or couple) to give away or sell their licenses, an idea originally suggested by economist Kenneth Boulding; **(2)** reduce the throughput of resources by having the government set and auction off depletion quotas for each resource, thus limiting the amount of each resource

Table 20-2 Characteristics of Frontier and Sustainable Earth Economic Systems

Frontier Economic System	Sustainable Earth Economic System
Assumes essentially infinite matter and energy resources.	Assumes finite matter and energy resources (unless solar, wind, or some form of almost unlimted energy can be developed at an affordable economic and environmental cost).
One-way flow of both matter and energy (Figure 2-4).	One-way flow of energy but recycling of matter (Figure 2-5).
Continually increases flow rates of matter and energy through the system (maximizes throughput).	Reduces the flow rate of energy and the flow and cycling rate of matter; throughput is deliberately reduced to reduce waste of matter and energy resources and keep from exceeding the ecosphere's capacity to handle waste heat and matter.
Emphasis on efficiency, quantity of goods, simplication, and cultural and physical homogeneity to maintain short-term stability.	Emphasis on quality of goods and preservation of cultural and physical diversity to attain long-term stability at the expense of some efficiency.
Output control of pollution (consequences of second energy law can be avoided or minimized by cleaning up pollution output).	Input, throughput, and output control (consequences of second energy law can be decreased in the long run by decreasing throughputs of matter and energy and cleaning up pollution output).
Continued growth provides capital for output pollution control and technologicl breakthroughs.	If growth continues, capital must be increasingly devoted to maintenance and repair (because of the second law) instead of being available for technological innovations.
Emphasis on initial cost of goods—buy now, pay more later.	Emphasis on the life cycle costing (LCC) of goods—buy now, pay now.
Assumes that a competitive market system or a centralized controlled economy will respond to undesirable side effects.	Market responds only if quality-of-life indicators help determine the prices of good and services.
Local or national outlook.	Global outlook.

used each year; **(3)** set up a world institution to determine a more just distribution of the world's wealth so that everyone would be guaranteed a fair share of the earth's resources provided they carry out their share of the responsibilities for maintaining an orderly world; and **(4)** not allow anyone to accumulate more than a certain amount of the world's wealth (probably equivalent to a maximum annual income of around $100,000 in today's dollars, with all additional income taxed at 100 percent).*

The fourth goal would allow a fairly broad range of wealth, from a guaranteed minimum to a maximum that should easily satisfy anyone's needs (as opposed to wants, which are often artificially created by advertising). Because each element of this plan complements and interacts with each other element, Daly argues that all four are necessary to make the plan work. Daly, however, does not insist

that this is the only way to achieve a sustainable earth economy and challenges economists to develop other plans for making such a transition.

20-3 Economics and Pollution Control

Internal and External Costs A number of methods can be used to control pollution within existing economic systems as well as in a sustainable earth economic system. To understand these methods, we need to distinguish between what economists call *internal costs* and *external costs*.

In making or using anything there are **internal costs** and benefits (sometimes called *internalities*). For example, the price you pay for a new car reflects the costs of construction and operation of the factory, raw materials and labor, marketing expenses, and shipping, as well as automobile company and dealer profits. There are also side effects not directly associated with the act of production. These **external costs** and benefits (usually called *externalities*) are passed on to someone else.

---

*Such an idea was proposed thousands of years ago by the Greek philosopher Plato. In his book *The Laws*, it is said that no person should be permitted to be four times richer than the poorest person. Herman Daly proposes that the rich be allowed to be ten times richer than the poor.

According to a study by the Organization of Economic Cooperation and Development (OECD), accidents, noise, pollution, and other hidden costs of automobiles to industrialized nations represent about 5 percent of each nation's GNP. For instance, mining and processing the matter and energy used to make a car cause land disruption and air and water pollution. This air pollution may eventually harm you or someone else, but these health side effects are not included in the price of the car. In addition, you have to pay more for water purification because of the additional water pollution—again a cost not included in the car's price. Thus, the true cost of any item or service is its internal cost plus the hidden external costs.

$$\text{True cost} \atop \text{of an item} = \text{interal} \atop \text{(direct)} \atop \text{costs} + \text{external} \atop \text{(indirect)} \atop \text{costs}$$

Because there is no free lunch, external costs are always hidden in the price of any product and must always be paid somewhere, sometime, by someone. Usually they are paid by everyone, not just those wealthy enough to purchase the original goods. In fact, the poor probably pay a disproportionate share of pollution cleanup costs and often end up living or working in high-pollution environments.

Our present economic system makes it profitable to pollute because many of the present and future externalities from producing and using various goods and services are not included in the initial price of the items. Thus, the initial cost of a good or service does not provide the purchaser with accurate information about its true long-term cost. As a way out of this dilemma, economists have proposed *internalizing the externalities,* so that the initial cost of an item or service reflects as closely as possible its true cost.

Approaches to Environmental Improvement   It is easy to suggest that we reduce environmental degradation by internalizing external costs, but how do we accomplish this? The major methods are:

1. *Moral persuasion or preaching:* persuading polluters to refrain voluntarily from polluting as an obligation to society.

2. *Suing for damages:* using the legal system to sue polluters for damages from pollution (Section 21-2).

3. *Prohibition:* establishing and enforcing discharge standards for each pollutant.

4. *Direct regulation:* issuing licenses and permits, and setting up and enforcing compulsory pollution standards.

5. *Payments and incentives:* controlling pollution by paying polluters not to pollute; subsidizing the building of, for example, sewage treatment plants; eliminating or reducing taxes on pollution control equipment; and giving tax credits for investment in control equipment.

6. *Pollution rights:* selling on the open market a limited number of rights to pollute, up to a specified amount in a given place during a particular period.

7. *Pollution charges:* taxing each unit of effluent or emission released during a particular period.

These various methods for environmental control are evaluated in Table 20-3.

No method of pollution control will be fair to everyone. Industries usually favor the subsidy approach (Table 20-3) by which they receive public monies for refraining from doing something—namely, polluting—that they shouldn't be doing in the first place. Because this approach benefits the few at the expense of the many, politicians and environmentalists are beginning to accept the economists' view that the best way to reduce pollution through economic factors is to combine direct regulation and pollution charges. This approach, however, is an output method that operates at the end of the throughput process. As a result, it wastes resources and according to economist Daly is "like letting a two-year-old child loose in a living room full of irreplaceable antiques, and then slapping the tot's hands every time he or she breaks a valuable vase or lamp."

Most economists favor reducing pollution to acceptable levels by requiring that the price of any item or service include both its internal and external costs. In addition, they would emphasize the *life cycle cost*—the total cost of an item or service over its useful life—rather than on its initial cost. Consumers would use a *buy now, pay now* approach so they would know the full cost of an item, rather than the present *buy now, pay more later* approach. Higher prices of environmentally harmful products would discourage their use and would stimulate the technological development of products that use fewer resources and produce less pollution. With this approach of internalizing the external costs, some businesses will flourish, others will level off, and some with high, uncontrollable levels of adverse environmental impact may have to shut down—as they should.

Opponents of adding pollution control costs to prices point out that an inequitable share of such costs would be borne by the poor. In 1983 there were 35 million Americans (15.1 percent of the pop-

Table 20-3 Evaluation of Major Methods for Environmental Improvement

Method	Advantages	Disadvantages
Moral persuasion	1. Educates and sensitizes people. 2. Prepares people for action through other methods.	1. Often produces more guilt and discontent than action. 2. Rewards the socially irresponsible (those who refuse to buy pollution control equipment can make a bigger profit).
Suing for damages (torts)	1. Allows the individual or group to be compensated for damages.	1. Difficult to establish who damaged whom and to what degree. 2. Time-consuming and expensive for both parties. 3. Output approach that does little to prevent damage.
Prohibition	1. Eliminates the damages. 2. May be required for some pollutants, such as toxic metals (Enrichment Study 12) and radioactive materials (Section 15-5). 3. Protects the individual from irresponsible acts by others.	1. Often not economically feasible; due to second energy law, removal of all pollution is prohibitively expensive (Figure 20-1). 2. May not be politically feasible (excessive control may lead to a political backlash that threatens even moderate control). 3. Zero or very low pollution levels are not always necessary (if not overloaded, natural chemical cycles can absorb, degrade, or recycle some types of waste).
Direct regulation	1. Can be used to keep pollution below a threshold level (Section 5-2). 2. Protects the individual from irresponsible acts by others. 3. May be more just than prohibition.	1. Hard to enforce, especially when there are many pollution sources, such as 164 million cars, trucks, and buses. 2. Standards tend to be ones that are enforceable rather than optimal. 3. No incentive for polluter to reduce pollution below the standard. 4. Airsheds and watersheds cross political boundaries, so effective regulation by one governmental unit may be nullified by inaction of another. 5. Polluters can use courts and administrative procedures to delay compliance. 6. Often treats all polluters alike, regardless of amount of pollution contributed. This can discriminate against small polluters and can make the cost of effective pollution control higher than need be.
Payments and incentives	1. Makes it profitable not to pollute and encourages polluter to reduce pollution to lowest possible value. 2. A positive rather than negative approach. 3. Requires fewer enforcement procedures and expenses.	1. May encourage people or industries to pollute so they can qualify for payment.* 2. Pollution costs are still hidden and not internalized in the direct prices of items and services. 3. Drains limited public funds. 4. Taxpayers' money is used to pay individuals and corporations not to do something wrong.
Pollution rights and pollution charges	1. Makes it profitable not to pollute and encourages polluter to reduce pollution to lowest possible value. 2. Generates public revenue instead of draining limited public funds. 3. May reduce political maneuvering to influence or take over regulatory agencies. 4. Biggest polluters will have the greatest incentive to reduce pollution. 5. Administrative and enforcement machinery should be simpler and cheaper.	1. Hard to estimate what to charge for each pollutant. 2. The idea of being able to buy a license to pollute could encourage people to pollute up to a certain level. 3. Increases prices, putting a country's products at a disadvantage in international trade.

*The old joke that farm subsidies send people into the "no-growing business" could apply again if some enter the "no-polluting business" at taxpayer expense.

ulation) living below the poverty level.* However, economists who favor internalizing external costs argue that by paying a higher initial price to avoid the cost of pollution, we reduce later health costs, as well as other costs created by pollution. In addition, because the poor now bear the brunt of environmental pollution (Section 12-3), any scheme that reduces pollution will benefit them more than any other group.

Cost-Benefit and Cost-Effectiveness Analyses To maximize the chance of success at the lowest possible cost, we must combine different approaches for reducing pollution. Two economic tools for making such judgments are *cost-benefit analysis* and *cost-effectiveness analysis*.

In **cost-benefit analysis (CBA)** all nontrivial effects of a proposed action are identified, each effect is categorized as a benefit or as a cost, each cost and benefit is assigned a dollar value for each year, and the costs are compared with the benefits. The idea is to use economics to determine the merits of a particular goal or proposed action. Ideally, a cost-benefit analysis would be made for each of the possible alternatives to determine the least harmful alternative. In practice, however, this is rarely done.

Cost-effectiveness analysis (CEA) involves determining how much it will cost in dollars to achieve a benefit and comparing this amount to the cost of obtaining a higher or lower level of the benefit or using some other alternative. As illustrated in Figure 20-1, a goal of CEA could be to minimize the total costs of pollution control and still reduce harmful environmental effects to a reasonable or acceptable level. Reducing the level of pollution below this level might cost so much that the costs would far outweigh the economic benefits. For example, picking up 90 percent of the bottles and cans thrown away in a large park might be economically feasible, but the labor and energy costs of finding the last 10 percent might be prohibitive. By the same token, not reducing a given pollutant to the optimum level means that the manufacturer is passing on hidden costs to the consumer. Unlike cost-benefit analysis, CEA does not involve an attempt to evaluate the merits of a single goal. Instead, it requires a comparison of alternative actions.

Although sounding simple, neither of these approaches is easy to carry out. Several important questions have to be answered. What risk from a

---

*Two-thirds of the 35 million were white, 58 percent were women, 35 percent were under the age of 16, and 12 percent were age 65 or older.

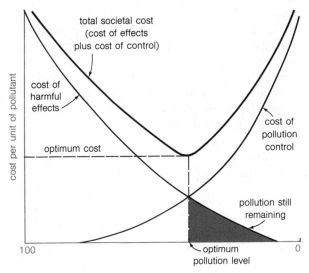

Figure 20-1 Cost-effectiveness analysis involves comparing the costs from the harmful effects of pollution with the cost of pollution control to minimize the total costs of pollution control and still reduce the pollution level to an acceptable level. The shaded area shows that some harmful effects remain, but removing these residual damages would make the costs of pollution control too high.

particular pollutant or environmentally harmful activity are we willing to accept? How much are we willing to pay, individually and collectively, for reducing the risk from pollution to a certain level? The basic problem is that people disagree over what level of risk associated with allowing a certain level of pollution is economically, psychologically, and ethically acceptable. Critics of CBA and CEA argue that estimates of costs and benefits generally come from industries that have an incentive to exaggerate. As a result, the estimates are often ideological documents designed to prove preconceived notions.

An even more serious problem is that many important things cannot be reduced to dollars and cents. Some costs, such as extra laundry bills, house repainting, and ruined crops resulting from air pollution, are fairly easy to estimate. However, it is difficult, if not impossible, to put a price tag on human life, clean air and water, whooping cranes, a clear sky, beautiful scenery, and the ability of natural ecosystems to degrade and recycle our wastes. Economic analysis alone cannot always render such judgments, because they involve political, social, and ethical issues as well. For example, the benefit of electricity from a nuclear power plant over its 30- to 40-year lifetime is fairly easy to calculate. But what are the long-term environmental and social costs of protecting our descendants for thousands of years from the radioactive wastes that the plant produces? Environmentalists contend that in such cases, ethics and common sense—not economic analysis—should be the overriding factors. The absurdity and callousness of the purely economic approach was revealed by an oil company representative who protested clean air standards affecting his firm's operations in Montana: "Some of the people who will die from air pollution are unemployed, and therefore have no economic value."

In the early 1980s the Reagan administration and business interests pushed hard to have all federal regulatory agencies base their regulations and decisions on cost-benefit and cost-effective analysis. This approach, however, received a setback from a 1981 Supreme Court decision stemming from EPA efforts to protect textile workers from inhalation of cotton dust, a cause of brown-lung disease. In this decision, Justice William J. Brennan, Jr., wrote that the health of workers outweighs "all other considerations" and that "Any standard based on a balancing of costs and benefits . . . would be inconsistent with the law."

Do We Have An Obligation to Future Generations? The marketplace usually operates effectively for short-term control but is ineffective in dealing with long-term costs and benefits. In making cost-benefit analyses economists use a **discount factor,** a measure of how much something may be worth in the future compared with what it is worth now. A discount factor less than 1 indicates that something is considered to be worth more now than it will be worth in the future, and a discount factor greater than 1 means that something is expected to be worth more in the future than it is now.

One problem that hinders efforts to control pollution and resource depletion is that in most conventional cost-benefit economic analyses the future is discounted by assuming discount factors less than 1. Reasons for this include (1) uncertainty over the future rate of inflation, which if high enough can reduce future profits in constant dollars below present profits, and (2) fear that innovation or changed consumer preferences may render a product or service obsolete or at least sharply reduce future profits.

On the other hand, there are business entrepreneurs who are willing to take large risks with present capital with the belief or hope that they can make a much larger profit in the future. Although there are exceptions, owners of small businesses tend to be be more innovative and more willing to take financial risks. For example, the personal computer business was started in a backyard garage by two young computer programmers whose bosses wouldn't listen to their ideas. Their innovations and

risk-taking led to the highly profitable Apple Computer Company and made them millionaires within only a few years. A 1977 study by the National Science Foundation showed that small firms produced two dozen times as many industrial innovations per research dollar as the largest firms, and four times as many as medium-sized firms.

In contrast, managers of many large U.S. corporations with a fairly well established market share tend to be concerned with showing short-term profits for their stockholders. They tend to be less innovative and to be less willing to take the risk of plowing present profits into the development of products and services that may be in demand in the future. A number of analysts contend that this is one reason an increasing number of markets once dominated by U.S. businesses are now being taken over by Japanese firms, whose managers are willing to gamble current profits against the possibility of a larger share of the market in the future, hence greatly increased profits.

Environmentalists argue that the external costs associated with a particular product or service should be internalized not only to give consumers a better idea of the risks associated with its use but also because we have an ethical obligation to future generations to leave the environment in as good condition as we found it—if not better. Thus in our economic calculations, the future value of the environment should equal or be greater than its present; that is, we must use discount factors of 1 or higher—rather than less than 1 as is done in most present cost-benefit calculations. But industry representatives contend that despite rhetoric about obligations to future generations, most people—including most environmentalists—place a higher value on what they have today than on what they or their descendants might have in the future. This difference of opinion over our obligation to future generations is a major unsolved problem and source of disagreement between most environmentalists and conventional economists and corporate leaders.

In spite of these difficulties, some important progress has been made in estimating environmental benefits and damages. Sometimes, however, all we can do is make an educated guess and then revise the estimate as new information becomes available.

20-4 Cost of Environmental Improvement

Industrialists often argue that the costs of reducing pollution make their businesses unprofitable, causing them difficulty in raising capital and forcing them to close down plants and lay off employees. Are the estimated costs of environmental protection and improvement in the United States so high that they outweigh the benefits? Have more strict environmental protection standards in the United States caused massive unemployment? Numerous studies have shown that the answer to both these questions is a resounding *no*.

By 1983 U.S. government and industry were spending about $50 billion a year—$220 for every man, woman, and child in the country—to reduce pollution. This amounted to only about 1.6 percent of the GNP for 1983. By 2000 pollution control costs could rise to about 3 percent of the annual GNP— a very small price to pay for a vastly improved environment that would benefit every U.S. citizen. Estimates by the Council on Environmental Quality and the EPA indicate that between 1980 and 1989 industry and government will have to spend about $690 billion (in constant 1982 dollars) for pollution control to meet present federal, state, and local environmental standards. According to EPA figures, industry pays 51 percent of pollution control costs, the government about 13 percent, and consumers 36 percent (mostly for antipollution devices in automobiles).

Of course, all costs of protecting the environment are ultimately paid by consumers through increased taxes and prices. But numerous studies show that failure to control pollution will cost even more in the form of declining health, skyrocketing medical costs, absenteeism, and damage to food crops and other forms of vegetation, farm animals, and wildlife. According to a report prepared for the Council on Environmental Quality by economist Myrick A. Freeman III (see *The Benefits of Air and Water Pollution Control: A Review and Synthesis of Recent Estimates*, 1979), benefits from enforcing existing U.S. pollution control regulations will amount to an estimated $21.4 billion each year by 1985 (with a range of $4.6 billion to $51.2 billion) from air pollution control and $12.3 billion from water pollution control (with a range of $6.6 billion to $24.8 billion).

In addition, pollution control is growing at about 18 percent per year—twice the annual growth rate for all U.S. manufacturing. Pollution control creates many more jobs than it eliminates, and by 1980 it provided employment for 2 million people. A 1982 study by the Conservation Foundation also showed that U.S. environmental laws have not caused industry to move to countries with less strict environmental laws, nor from one state to another.

Pollution control can also save industry money in the long run—as many industries who once fought compliance are finding out. For example, an $8 million pollution control system installed by Great Lakes Paper Company reduced the plant's operating cost by $4 million a year, and paid for itself in only 2 years. The Ciba-Geigy chemical complex in Basel, Switzerland, has eliminated 50 percent of its pollution and saved about $400,000 a year. The Elf Oil Refinery in France has turned its hydrocarbon pollution into usable products with an annual profit of $1.3 million.

The first step is to stop the waste. Perhaps the next might be a greater willingness to share the wealth that has made the waste possible.

Barbara Ward

Discussion Topics

1. Why is a steady-state economy desirable? Compare its advantages and disadvantages.

2. Why does the concept of a steady-state economy— or, more accurately, a sustainable earth economy— force us to face up to the moral issue of the distribution of wealth?

3. Debate the issue that we should establish minimum and maximum limits on personal wealth and income.

4. Debate the proposition that maximizing economic growth is the only way of providing enough money to eliminate poverty and control pollution.

5. If you wanted to develop an index of gross national quality (GNQ), what specific items would you include?

6. Distinguish between a dynamic steady-state economy and a sustainable earth economy, and explain why a dynamic steady state is possible at the national but not the global level.

7. What are the social and environmental costs associated with (a) smoking cigarettes, (b) driving a car, and (c) living or working in an air conditioned building?

8. What good and bad effects would internalizing the external costs of pollution have on the U.S. economy? Do you favor doing this? How might it affect your life-style? The life-style of the poor? If possible, have an economist discuss these problems with your class.

9. Explain how the U.S. economic system makes it profitable to pollute.

10. What obligations, if any, concerning the environment do we have to future generations? Try to list the major beneficial and harmful aspects of the environment that were passed on to you during the past 50 years by the last two generations.

21

Politics and Environment

21-1 Politics and Social Change

Politics is concerned with the distribution of resources in an orderly fashion—*who* gets *what, where, when, how,* and *why.* Since resources such as food, water, and air are provided by natural systems, politics—like economics—rests on an ecological foundation. As resources become scarce, this dependence of politics on ecology is more and more apparent.

Since there is always competition for resources, politicians must always deal with conflicting groups, each asking for resources or for money that will enable them to purchase or control the resources. Because of these conflicts, politics has been called the art of the possible.

For most politicians the "art of the possible" is focused on making their own reelection possible, primarily by not taking stands on controversial or long-range issues and by avoiding change. A favorite strategy of traditional politicians is to say, "I agree with you, but what you are suggesting is not feasible." Such a statement is often a smokescreen used to avoid hard thinking, risk taking, and leadership.

Throughout human history, however, the really important politics has been that of making the seemingly impossible—or the highly improbable—possible. True politics, then, is the art of creating new possibilities for human progress. As George Bernard Shaw put it, "Some see things as they are and say why? I dream of things that never were and say why not?"

Enrichment Studies 2, 3, and 15 are related to this chapter.

But how do we get from the seemingly impossible to the possible? This involves using one or more methods of *social change.* The traditional methods are education and persuasion, legal action (lawsuits), political action to institute new laws or change (mutual coercion mutually agreed on), and revolution.

Education and persuasion are always important in bringing about change, especially in the young. But by themselves these methods do not always work very well. Education can prepare people for change, but it must be coupled with other methods. Similarly, using legal action to bring about change is an important technique but usually is not enough. Revolution is a drastic and often highly destructive approach that should be used only as a last resort. Political action to bring about change is a very useful approach, but traditional politics focuses primarily on short-range planning and action. An increasing number of analysts urge that we go beyond traditional political methods to sustainable earth, or cybernetic, political methods, which couple long-range planning and action with short-term planning and action. This chapter will discuss environmental law and cybernetic politics.

21-2 Environmental Law

A Primer on Law Environmental law is a vital and growing field for lawyers and scientists interested in public service. The pay is low and the hours are long, but the satisfaction is high. In ecopolitics, environmental law plays an important role, particularly as a tool for delaying or preventing abuse of the ecosphere.

In the Anglo-American legal system, one party, the *plaintiff* (an individual, or group of individuals) makes a civil complaint alleging that he or she has been harmed by another party, the *defendant.* If the court decides that harm has occurred, it orders the defendant to pay the plaintiff money to offset the damage. A plaintiff also can request the court to enjoin the defendant from committing a specific wrongful act; that is, the court can be asked to issue an *injunction*.

To use the courts for a civil action the plaintiff must **(1)** allege that an act forbidden by a specific law has been committed, **(2)** file the complaint in the court that has jurisdiction, and **(3)** have standing to pursue a given case in court. Then, of course, the plaintiff must prove that the actions of the accused, for example, a water polluter, caused the damage that was alleged. As in a criminal case, the accused is presumed innocent until proven guilty.

Unfortunately, there are problems with this procedure. *First*, a plaintiff may not have standing to file a suit against a defendant. Standing for damage suits is granted only if it is clear that the harm to an individual plaintiff is distinguishable from that to the general public. For example, you could not sue the Department of the Interior for actions leading to the commercialization of a nearby wilderness area on the grounds that you do not want your taxes used to bring about environmental harm. The harm to you could not be distinguished from that to the general public. However, if the government damaged property you own, you would have standing to sue.

Second, bringing any suit is expensive. Often the defendant in an environmental action is a large corporation or government agency with ample funds for legal and scientific advice. By contrast, the plaintiffs in such cases usually use volunteer legal and scientific talent and rely on donations.

Third, the court (or series of courts if the case is appealed) may take years to reach a decision. During this time the defendant may continue the alleged damage unless the court issues a temporary injunction requiring cessation of the allegedly harmful actions until the case is decided. Furthermore, each new violation requires a new case because a particular decision is not generally binding on future offenders.

Fourth, it is often difficult for the plaintiff to prove that the accused is liable. For example, suppose that one company is charged with bringing harm to individuals by polluting a river. If hundreds of other industries and cities dump wastes into that river, establishing that the defendant company is the culprit will be extremely difficult, requiring extensive, costly scientific testing and research.

Achievements of Environmental Law   Despite these handicaps, proponents of environmental law have accomplished a great deal in a short time. For example, they have formed organizations of public interest lawyers and experts who can raise money and pool talents. In 1965 the handful of lawyers and environmentalists in the field had no victories or proven legal strategies. Conservationist or environmental groups and individuals were not recognized as having standing to sue. Now there are more than 100 public interest law firms and groups specializing partly or totally in environmental and consumer law, and hundreds of other lawyers and scientific experts participate in environmental and consumer law cases as needed.

In 1965, in a landmark case, the Scenic Hudson Preservation Conference, a citizen's group, was given standing to sue the Federal Power Commission over the proposed construction of a hydroelectric power plant at Storm King Mountain. Although the group lost its suit, it won a vital precedent on legal standing.

The next breakthrough came in 1967, when Long Island attorney, Victor J. Yannacone, Jr. (see *Environmental Rights and Remedies*, 1972) filed suit in New York State to stop a county agency from spraying local marshes with DDT. Yannacone and Charles F. Wurster, a professor of biology at the State University of New York at Stony Brook, helped form the Environmental Defense Fund (EDF), a citizen-supported group of lawyers and scientists organized to bring environmental lawsuits. The EDF has brought a number of successful suits on behalf of the general public, including the suit in 1970 that resulted in the banning of DDT in the United States. However, the EDF must decline many important cases because of lack of funds.

Another famous legal environmental controversy raised the question of who speaks for nature in the courts. The question "Do trees have standing?" was raised in the case of *Sierra Club* v. *Norton*. In 1969 the Sierra Club filed suit against the government when the U.S. Forest Service approved a bid by Walt Disney Enterprises, Inc., to develop a $35 million ski resort in the Mineral King Valley recreation area, located in the Sierras of California.

The plaintiff claimed that the proposed development violated federal law governing the preservation of national parks and forests. The Supreme Court refused to hear the case because it concluded that the Sierra Club did not have standing. In his dissenting opinion, Justice William O. Douglas argued that trees and other natural objects should have standing. He referred to the book *Should Trees Have Standing? Toward Legal Rights for Natural Objects* (1974) by law professor Christopher D. Stone, who argued that just as minors and incompetent persons can be represented in court by legal guardians, so should natural objects. Although the case was never tried, the precedent suggested by the Sierra Club was an important factor leading to the abandonment of the proposed project.

In 1982 the Wisconsin Supreme Court ruled in the case *Prah* v. *Maretti* that the plaintiff was entitled to file a nuisance suit against the defendant, a neighbor, who planned to build a two-story house that by blocking access to the sun would have disabled the $18,000 solar heating system that Prah had installed. This contradicted the 150-year-old common law that property owners have no inherent right to sunlight. California, New Mexico, Kansas, Virginia, and Colorado, and numerous local communities have passed laws guaranteeing legal access to solar energy.

Problems to Overcome Although individuals and groups have apparently won the right to sue (on a case-by-case basis) and have won a number of cases, there are still many problems to overcome. Public interest groups have utilized laws that allow *class action suits,* that is actions brought by one group on behalf of a larger number of citizens who allege similar damages but who need not be listed and represented individually.* For example, many people living near an airport may be subjected to harmful, disruptive noise, or a number may become sick or suffer economic loss because of some form of pollution.

In 1973, however, the U.S. Supreme Court restricted federal class action suits by environmentalists and other citizen groups. This ruling requires that each individual claim at least $10,000 in damages to qualify as a member of a class. Although this ruling denies a number of damaged individuals their "day in court," it probably is not disastrous for environmentalists. Class action suits are used mainly to recover damages and have rarely been brought in environmental issues. The real success and importance of environmental and other types of protective legal action is in *preventing damage*— by seeking to enjoin the construction of a jetport, a nuclear power plant, or a superhighway through an urban park, a conservation area, or a poor neighborhood, for example.

Environmental and public interest law is also threatened by lack of money. In 1976 environmental lawyers received a serious setback when the Supreme Court ruled that public interest law groups cannot recover attorney's fees unless Congress has specifically authorized such recovery in the law they have sued to enforce. This could have a disastrous effect on financially struggling public interest lawyers. The costs of research and expert witnesses are high, and these public service organizations exist only because of individual and foundation grants. If you

support their causes, you might consider donating to one or several of these organizations each year.*

Environmental Legislation In recent years a number of important federal laws have been enacted in the United States and are discussed throughout this text, as summarized in Table 21-1. Similar laws, and in some cases even stronger laws, have been passed by most states.

The laws listed in Table 21-1 attempt to provide environmental protection using five major approaches: **(1)** setting pollution level standards or limiting emissions or effluents for various classes of pollutants (e.g., the Federal Water Pollution Control Act of 1972 and the Clean Air acts of 1965, 1970, and 1977), **(2)** screening new substances before they are widely used in order to determine their safety (e.g., the Toxic Substances Control Act of 1976), **(3)** requiring a comprehensive evaluation of the environmental impact of an activity before it is undertaken (e.g., the National Environmental Policy Act of 1969), **(4)** setting aside or protecting various ecosystems, resources, or species from harmful use (e.g., the Wilderness Act of 1964 and the Endangered Species Act of 1973), and **(5)** encouraging resource conservation (e.g., the Resource Conservation and Recovery Act of 1976 and to some extent the National Energy Act of 1978).

The Environmental Protection Agency (EPA), created by administrative reorganization in 1970, has the responsibility for seeing that 31 federal environmental laws are enforced, for administering the Superfund for cleaning up abandoned toxic waste sites (Enrichment Study 13), and for awarding grants for local sewage treatment plants. These laws give the EPA broad powers, including the imposition of jail terms for criminal pollution violations and fines of up to $25,000 a day for polluters, and the power to sue almost any U.S. citizen or company for violation of antipollution laws.

Environmentalists, with backing from many other citizens, have pressured and helped Congress to pass an impressive array of environmental legislation. However, a law is no better than its enforcement. Thus, in the 1980s, environmentalists

---

*Class action suits should not be confused with suits that have many plaintiffs. A group can still still bring a joint suit and share legal costs, as long as all the members of their organizations are represented in court.

*Major public interest law groups include the Environmental Defense Fund, the Sierra Club's Legal Defense Fund, the Center for Law and Social Policy, the National Resources Defense Council, the Center for Science in the Public Interest, the Center for Law in the Public Interest, Public Interest Advocates, Inc., Businessmen and Professional People for the Public Interest, and Ralph Nader's Center for the Study of Responsive Law. Organizations that do not sue but help develop environmental legal concepts are the Environmental Law Institute and the Council for Public Interest Law. Addresses for these organizations are given in Appendix 1.

Table 21-1 Major U.S. Environmental Legislation

Legislation	Text Discussion	Legislation	Text Discussion
General		**Wildlife**	
National Environmental Policy Act of 1969 (NEPA)	Section 21-2	Species Conservation Act of 1966	Section 11-4
Energy		Federal Insecticide, Fungicide, and Rodenticide Control Act of 1972	Section 9-9
National Energy Acts of 1978 and 1980	Section 16-8	Marine Protection, Research, and Sanctuaries Act of 1972	Section 11-6
Water Quality		Endangered Species Act of 1973	Section 11-4
Federal Water Pollution Control Act of 1972	Section 18-7	**Land Use**	
Ocean Dumping Act of 1972	Section 18-5	Multiple Use Sustained Yield Act of 1960	Section 10-2
Safe Drinking Water Act of 1974	Section 18-2	Wilderness Act of 1964	Section 10-3
Toxic Substances Control Act of 1976	Section 18-7 and Enrichment Study 13	Wild and Scenic River Act of 1968	Section 10-3
		National Coastal Zone Management Acts of 1972 and 1980	Section 18-5
Clean Water Act of 1977	Section 18-7	Forest Reserves Management Act of 1974	Section 10-5
Air Quality		Forest Reserves Management Act of 1976	Section 10-5
Clean Air Act of 1965	Section 19-7	National Forest Management Act of 1976	Section 10-5
Clean Air Act of 1970	Section 19-7		
Clean Air Act of 1977	Section 19-7	Surface Mining Control and Reclamation Act of 1977	Section 15-4
Noise Control		Endangered American Wilderness Act of 1978	Section 10-3
Noise Control Act of 1972	Enrichment Study 10		
Quiet Communities Act of 1978	Enrichment Study 10	Alaskan Land-Use Bill of 1980	Section 10-2
Resources and Solid Waste Management			
Solid Waste Disposal Act of 1965	Enrichment Study 13		
Resource Recovery Act of 1970	Enrichment Study 13		
Resource Conservation and Recovery Act of 1976	Enrichment Study 13		

are increasingly turning their attention to seeing that existing laws and regulations are carried out and that such laws are not weakened by amendments favored by special interest groups.

NEPA and Environmental Impact Statements One important environmental law is the National Environmental Policy Act of 1969 (NEPA). This landmark legislation declared that the federal government has a responsibility to restore and maintain environmental quality and established in the Executive Office of the President a three-member Council on Environmental Quality (CEQ). The CEQ determines the condition of the national environment, prepares an annual *Environmental Quality Report*, develops and recommends to the president new environmental policies and programs, appraises and coordinates federal environmental programs and activities, advises the president on environ-

mental problems and solutions, and establishes guidelines for the preparation of environmental impact statements.*

NEPA requires that all federal agencies (except the EPA) file an *environmental impact statement* (EIS) for any proposed legislation or project having a significant effect on environmental quality. Each EIS must **(1)** describe the purpose and need for the proposed action, **(2)** clearly describe the probable environmental impact (positive, negative, direct, and indirect) of the proposed action and of possible alternatives, **(3)** identify any adverse environmental effects that could not be avoided if the proposal were implemented, **(4)** discuss possible alternatives to the proposed action (including not taking the

---

*The importance and influence of the CEQ, however, was sharply reduced in 1981 when President Reagan, who had planned to abolish the council, cut its budget by 70 percent and slashed its staff from 50 to 16.

action), (5) describe relationships between the probable short-term and long-term impacts of the proposal on environmental quality, (6) discuss irreversible and irretrievable commitments of resources that would be involved if the proposal were implemented, (7) discuss objections raised by reviewers of the preliminary draft of the statement, (8) list the names and qualifications of the people primarily responsible for preparing the EIS, and (9) provide references to back up all statements and conclusions. An EIS can be no longer than 150 pages except for projects of unusual scope and complexity, and it must contain a summary not longer than 15 pages.

A draft EIS must be made public for review by the EPA, other appropriate federal, state, and local agencies, and the general public at least 90 days before a proposed action. A final statement, incorporating all comments and objections to the draft statement, must be made public at least 30 days before the proposed action is undertaken.

The EIS process has forced government agencies to think more deeply about the side effects of proposed projects and in many cases to analyze alternatives more carefully. As a result of the EIS process, scores of dams, highways, and airports have been modified or canceled. In addition, by 1983, 32 states had laws or executive orders requiring EISs for state projects. The EIS process has also spread to Australia, Canada, France, Ireland, New Zealand, and Sweden.

Despite its successes, the EIS process in the United States has been criticized. Critics argue that (1) EISs are often prepared to justify a decision that has already been made; (2) an agency can sometimes avoid preparing an EIS by denying that a given project will have a significant environmental impact; (3) an unfavorable EIS does not necessarily mean that the project will be canceled, that a less harmful option will be selected, or that the federal agency has to follow the terms of the EIS; (4) the EIS process has diverted the efforts and limited funds of environmentalists away from questioning and defining agency powers and responsibilities and has focused them on analyzing large numbers of often irrelevant documents; and (5) most EISs do not receive careful scrutiny, since only a few highly controversial projects are important enough to be evaluated.

Environmentalists have suggested that the NEPA should be amended to correct some of these major weaknesses by requiring a federal agency to pick and follow the terms of the least harmful option and by allowing public interest groups to recover attorney's fees when they sue to enforce NEPA or any other environmental law—thus putting public interest law groups on a more equitable footing with federal agencies and large corporations.

21-3 Cybernetic Politics

Characteristics of a Cybernetic Political System
The major characteristics of an effective cybernetic political system based on the principles of cybernetics (Section 5-2) are as follows.

1. *Multiple feedback loops:* Checks and balances with different time lags ensure long-term stability, prevent takeover by a single part of the system, and provide a mechanism for continuing self-renewal and adaptation to change.

2. *Minimum number of feedback loops necessary for stability:* Too many loops block, distort, or overload information flow—causing chaos, overcorrection, undercorrection, and even breakdown rather than gentle and steady oscillation.

3. *Sophisticated methods for short-range, intermediate-range, and long-range forecasting and planning:* Dealing only with the present or the near future often leads to counterintuitive and disastrous long-term behavior (Enrichment Study 2). Short-range goals should always be developed and related by feedback and time lags to intermediate- and long-term goals.

4. *An array of niches (roles) with a balance between specialists and generalists:* Excessive specialization (bureaucracy) leads to waste, inefficiency, obsolete governmental agencies, and inability to develop or act on long-range goals. A government with too many generalists does not have the necessary detailed information and facts.

5. *Accurate information flow (feedback) among all levels of government and between the government and the people:* Proper cybernetic action is possible only with accurate and high-quality information. Capital and labor must be expended to obtain such information. Three major problems are (a) blocked and distorted information flows to decision makers, (b) information overload when more information is received than can be evaluated (an increasingly serious problem in a computer age), and (c) blocked and distorted information flows from government to the people because of excessive government secrecy and media manipulation.

6. *Responsive and responsible decision makers and controllers:* The persons and organizations responsible for making decisions must be willing to bring about change when it is needed. This willingness will depend on their ability as generalists to evaluate conflicting information sources, to get accurate

information, and to relate decisions to short-, intermediate-, and long-term goals.

7. *Flexibility:* It should be possible to change parts of the system as conditions change. Otherwise the people need an orderly mechanism for removing and changing leaders and parts of the political system.

Tactics of Cybernetic Politics Traditional attempts to change the social system tend to be frontal and single purpose—marches, demonstrations, sit-ins, education, persuasion, legislation, and the like. These tactics are very useful for getting media attention, informing others about the need for change, building and maintaining morale, and countering undesirable trends. But they often stop too soon. When the massive inertia of the system makes change appear more superficial than substantial, many political activists decide that it is useless to buck the system and give up.

A political system, however, is a complex and dynamic cybernetic system, and the long-term effect of an action or trend is often the opposite of what would be predicted by short-term linear thinking (see Enrichment Study 2). Thus, it is usually more effective to couple the tactics used in traditional politics with those of cybernetic politics to bring about change. The basic tactics of cybernetic politics are:

1. Use positive synergy (Section 5-2) either to amplify desirable trends or to counteract or delay undesirable trends.

2. Apply political pressure at the right time and place, and long enough to ensure that built-in time delays will amplify efforts until the threshold levels for response have been reached (Section 5-2). True success is not in immediate effects but in the second-, third-, and higher-order effects.

3. If possible, never fight linear battles, where somebody wins and somebody loses (*win-lose games*).

4. Try to find social, scientific, and technological innovations that tunnel through the problem so that everyone wins (*win-win games*).

Let's look more closely at these tactics.

Positive Synergy and Threshold Effects An important tactic of cybernetic politics is to use *positive synergy* to amplify desirable trends. In traditional tactics, 2 plus 2 always equals 4. In cybernetic tactics, 2 plus 2 may be greater than 4 because of positive synergistic interactions, which render the final effect greater than the sum of the individual efforts. This requires cooperation, not competition. For example, if you can lift 50 kilograms (110 pounds) and I can lift 50 kilograms (110 pounds), by working together using positive synergy we can probably lift 150 kilograms (330 pounds) or more.

Positive synergy can be used in two major ways: to amplify a desirable trend, or to counteract, or at least slow down, an undesirable trend. In this way a small group of people can bring about major changes, as discussed in more detail in Enrichment Study 15. For example, in 1970 a small organization called Environmental Action initiated the "Dirty Dozen Campaign"—a program that attempts to defeat in every election year 12 congressional representatives who have consistently opposed sound environmental legislation. Of the 54 persons named to the list between 1970 and 1982 (some were named more than once), 41, or 76 percent, are no longer in Congress, either because they were defeated at the polls or because they decided not to seek re-election. A handful of workers, using the little funding provided by scarce private contributions, instigated this important change—a remarkable example of cybernetic politics in action.

Cybernetic tactics also make use of *lag times* and *threshold effects.* Exerting pressure on a slow-moving, complex political or social system may not seem to have any effect, but if maintained long enough, a threshold level may eventually be reached, thus prompting a major change. Many people push in the right places but give up before built-in delay times have passed.

Win-Win Games and the Tunnel Effect In traditional linear politics, if someone wins, someone else must lose (a *win-lose game*). The hostile or unresponsible majority holds the top of the mountain, and the dissenting minority storms the mountaintop so that they can impose their own views. Then another minority tries to take over, and the win-lose cycle is repeated again and again until everyone loses (a *lose-lose game*). The ultimate lose-lose game is global nuclear war (Enrichment Study 3).

By contrast, a major goal of cybernetic politics is to seek ways in which everyone wins (*win-win games*). This requires a sustainable earth value system emphasizing cooperation, rather than competition (Section 22-2).

One important method for setting up win-win games employs the *tunnel effect.* Think of the problem of bringing about change as getting over a mountain. Laws can be passed that force everyone to go over the mountain (traditional politics), or positive synergy can be used to vault everyone over

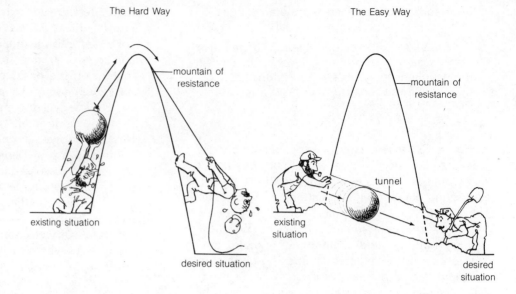

Figure 21-1 The tunnel effect. When an easier path becomes available, change occurs automatically.

The Hard Way

The Easy Way

the mountain (cybernetic politics). But usually the best way is to tunnel through the mountain—to find a social, technological, or scientific innovation that avoids old attitudes and resistance (Figure 21-1); then no one has to struggle over the mountain (*a win-win solution*).

The tunnel effect can be described as a *social catalyst* that lowers the resistance barrier. It is a seed crystal—a social chain reaction that is so obvious and effective that resistance disappears. The social catalyst may be a charismatic leader, like M. K. Gandhi, or persuasive rhetoric as exemplified by Thoreau's essay on civil disobedience. Gandhi skillfully used Thoreau's ideas to develop a nonviolent strategy to win India's independence from Great Britain.

Thoreau's catalytic ideas were also used later by Martin Luther King, Jr., in the civil rights movement in the United States.

A social catalyst may also be a scientific or technological innovation like oral contraceptives and IUDs (Enrichment Study 8), which have revolutionized birth control and made effective population control possible. Another example is the silicon chip, which has revolutionized communication and the processing of information. Other examples of social catalysts are compulsory school attendance, the postage stamp, the credit card, and old-age pensions. Think how much waste and inefficiency in government could be eliminated if there were annual awards like the Nobel Prizes for gov-

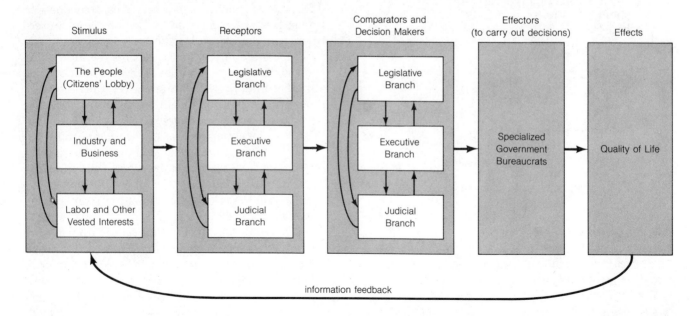

Figure 21-2 A crude cybernetic model of the U.S. political system.

ernment employees who reveal wasteful or corrupt practices.

21-4 Toward a Sustainable Earth Government in the United States

The U.S. Government as a Cybernetic System   The founders of the United States faced an immense problem. What form of government would maximize individual freedom without intruding on the rights of others? They also had to guard against authoritarian takeovers and yet encourage the development of the land and its resources. In other words, the founders wanted to preserve national stability but still allow a range of human choices.

Their solution was a cybernetic marvel, drafted and agreed upon by less than 40 people in only 4 months. In fact, the makers of the U.S. Constitution can be considered the first American cyberneticists. In effect, they preserved stability by creating a diversity of structures all connected by negative feedback loops. The Constitution calls for three major loops and control subsystems—the legislative, executive, and judicial branches—all connected by multiple checks and balances, or negative feedbacks (Figure 21-2).

For the entire system to work, all three branches and the people must cooperate and interact, but checks and balances (corrective feedback mechanisms) are built in to keep one branch from taking over. One result of this system is that problems are dealt with so cautiously and inefficiently and with so much compromise that revolutionary change is discouraged. The government established by the Constitution was not designed for efficiency. Instead it was designed for consensus and accommodation as a key to survival. Thus, by staying as close to the middle of the road as possible, the government *muddles through* crises. Ralph Waldo Emerson once said, "Democracy is a raft which will never sink, but then your feet are always in the water."

The grand design of the Constitution is like a finely balanced watch with gears and springs moving and responding at different *lag times.* For immediate response there is the executive branch. But to avoid hasty changes and to ensure responsiveness to the diversity of national interests, the Congress was created. It, in turn, contains two cybernetic loops: The House of Representatives has the faster response time, because its members are elected every 2 years; the Senate, whose members have 6-year terms, can take a slightly longer view and guard against abuse of power by the executive branch. The counterbalance to the entire system is the Supreme Court, whose members are appointed for life. The functions of the court are to protect the Constitution, to interpret it, and to settle disputes of power between the executive and legislative branches and the states. It tends to move slowly; but in times of crisis court action may come faster than either congressional or executive action.

Cybernetic Flaws of the U.S. Government   The founders of the U.S. system of government were concerned primarily with growth and expanding the frontier. Thus, although they anticipated most of the major cybernetic principles, the system they devised contains a number of defects that can seriously hinder the transition to a sustainable earth society. The major cybernetic weaknesses in the U.S. government system are:

1. Absence of a permanent and effective mechanism for developing and instituting long-range forecasts and plans

2. Disproportionate influence in government by special interest groups

3. Inadequate information flow within Congress and between Congress and the public

4. The bureaucracy bottleneck

5. Failure to ensure the election of sustainable earth leaders (Table 21-2)

Long-Range Planning   Everyone is in favor of long-range planning but nobody in the federal government seems to be doing it. According to Russell W. Peterson, former head of the Council on Environmental Quality, "Nowhere in the Executive Office of the President, or anywhere in government for that matter, does any group exist with the stated responsibility of analyzing global future trends."

This failure to develop and carry out long-range plans may have several causes: **(1)** the difficulty of making long-range projections and the unreliability of those completed, **(2)** the lack of incentive to improve methods of long-range forecasting and to develop and implement long-range plans because the time horizon of almost all government leaders is the next election, the next budget, or the next set of congressional hearings, and **(3)** failure to adopt an ecosphere or sustainable earth world view that considers effective long-range planning as necessary for long-term survival.

Politicians concerned primarily with reelection and wishing to sidestep controversial issues are tempted to put regulatory Band-aids on developing long-term problems and hope they will hold. Eventually, failure to deal with urgent long-range problems can lead to chaos and fear, making the United

Table 21-2 Comparisons of International Frontier Leaders and Sustainable Earth Leaders

International Frontier Leader	Sustainable Earth Leader
International view. Thinks and acts internationally but in terms of national prestige, honor, and power.	Ecosphere view. Thinks in terms of preserving the ecosphere and the world's resources for everyone now and in the future.
Thinks national loyalty is the primary driving force.	Thinks ecosphere loyalty is the only viable approach in the long run.
Thinks and acts in terms of win-lose games and uses sports and battle analogies. ("We won," "Honor is in winning," "This play will win," "Right is right," "Frontiers to conquer," "God is on our side.")	Sees the goal as having everyone in the world win now as well as in the future (win-win games).
Politics of the possible. Avoids really difficult problems or declares them solved. Calls people who talk of the impossible "naive idealists."	Politics of the seemingly impossible or improbable made possible by use of vision, cybernetic politics, and outstanding leadership. Willing to propose solutions for complex and controversial problems.
Simplistic view. Problems are due to a single variable or culprit, and can be solved by enacting a short-term simple cure.	Holistic, cybernetic view. Everything interacts with everything. Problems are complex and ever changing, and require multivariable approaches over long periods of time.
Primarily concerned with his or her role in history.	Primarily concerned with ensuring survival and human dignity for all.
Emphasizes short-term planning. Defends or talks mostly of past accomplishments rather than future goals.	Emphasizes long-term planning, with all short-term planning done in relation to intermediate and long-term goals. Talks of where we must go instead of where he or she has taken us.
Thinks a nation should do whatever can be done technogically to maintain or "win" national prestige, honor, and supremacy.	Thinks a nation should assess all technological solutions to determine possible long-range side effects on the ecosphere and to determine whether the solutions improve human dignity and life quality.
Chooses advisors who say only what he or she wants to hear (information blockage and distortion).	Insists that the best minds project and evaluate major alternatives.
Tries to control the press, which is portrayed as a threat to national security and to individual freedom.	Realizes that a free but accountable press is essential to uncover and prevent information blockage and distortion. Recognizes that politicians have seized or controlled the press in many countries, but the press has not seized power from any government.
Uses secrecy to block information flow to the people.	Operates openly to ensure maximum and accurate information flow to the people.
Believes economic growth is the only way a nation can win or dominate. Sees a steady-state economy as stagnant.	Evaluates growth on the basis of long-term ecosphere goals. A dynamic sustainable earth economy is the only viable long-term goal.
Thinks the problem of social justice will be solved only by economic growth—the "trickle-down" approach.	Believes that in a finite world nearing its limit of resource availability, the problem of social justice must be solved by a more equitable distribution of wealth.
Believes the greatest threat to peace and individual freedom is some outside *-ism* that a nation must overcome.	Thinks the greatest threats to peace and individual freedom are the arms race, overpopulation, overexploitation of finite resources by rich nations, and a world economic system that tends to make the rich richer and the poor poorer.
Talks about peace, poverty, population, and pollution but spends most of the money on armaments so that a nation can act from a position of strength.	Acts to promote peace, eliminate poverty, stabilize population, control pollution, and drastically reduce military expenditures and arms buildup throughout the world.
Thinks the solution to most problems is to buy or build (more missiles, guns, computers, and highways).	Thinks the solution to most problems is to deliberately slow the flow rate of matter and energy in the industrialized nations and to encourage appropriate technologies in LDCs, to meet the people's needs and to foster self-reliance.

States ripe for a demagogic leader who offers simple answers to complex problems. People then might be tempted to surrender freedoms for stability.

Some have suggested that research on the development of effective methods for long-range planning should be a major federal budget priority. It has also been suggested that a national long-range planning board might be created at the executive level or as a separate bureaucratic agency, the Department of Long-Range Planning and Coordination. Congress and the citizenry would need similar boards as checks and balances.

Others have indicated that a better approach might be amending the Constitution to add a fourth branch of government, the planning branch, with members appointed for staggered terms of 15 to 25 years. Ideally, highly respected generalists and sustainable earth thinkers would be appointed to the planning branch of government. This planning branch could form and direct task forces or Councils of Urgent Studies. Such councils would study and make projections of all major national and global problems and direct efforts to find social and technological innovations and tunnel effects for solving short-, intermediate-, and long-range problems. The members of the planning branch would evaluate and integrate what ordinary people think needs to be done with what specialized experts think the people need.

Executive Branch and Election Reform   President Lyndon Johnson once complained, "The only power I've got is nuclear and I can't use that!" As part of the checks-and-balances system, the Constitution provides the president with powers that are largely persuasive rather than coercive. Presidents have complained that their programs for change and improvement are talked to death or gutted by Congress, or, if approved by Congress, either ignored or altered by the federal bureaucracy or overturned by the judicial branch of government.

As a result, it is not surprising that presidents have tried to get Congress to give them more power. In the 1970s, however, events such as the bombing of Cambodia and the Watergate scandals revealed the dangers of too much power in the executive branch of government. As the nation's founders foresaw, this situation can be prevented only by a strong and vigorous Congress and by watchdog activities of citizens, citizen groups, and the press.

Another major problem in the executive branch (and the legislative branch) is undue influence on elections by wealthy and/or special interest groups. This problem plagues all governments and may never be eliminated. But a powerful and active citizens' lobby can help to counterbalance the disproportionate influence of business, industry, labor, and other powerful and well-financed vested interests by providing additional checks and balances. It has also been suggested that federal election campaigns be financed by assessment of all taxpayers, with no other contributions allowed and with spending limits rigidly enforced.

To hold down election costs, some have urged that campaigns (including primaries) for presidential and congressional races be shortened to no more than 6 months. In addition, each candidate meeting certain specific qualifications would be given a fixed number of hours of free television and radio time and a certain amount of free advertising space in the print media (as part of the public service requirements that the media are expected to meet). There would also be a limit on the air time and amount of printed advertising space any candidate could purchase. Because incumbents running for reelection can more easily command and manipulate media attention, new candidates might be given more media time and space. In addition, all major candidates for the presidency would be expected—if not required—to participate in a series of in-depth, televised debates, each focused on one topic. A single moderator would be used to force the candidates to stick to the topic and to address the questions raised.

Congressional Reform   Analysts, including present and former members of Congress, have pointed out several cybernetic problems associated with the legislature. These include **(1)** disproportionate influence by special interests, **(2)** difficulty in getting accurate information, and **(3)** a bloated committee- and subcommittee-structure that often does not reflect the needs of society.

As with presidential elections, disproportionate influence by powerful and well-financed vested interest groups could be diluted by an active citizens' lobby and the public financing of elections, with no outside contributions allowed. Congress is also hindered by misleading and inadequate information flow. Congressional representatives and senators must consider over 25,000 bills per year, many requiring sophisticated knowledge.

Far too often Congress must depend on the president, the bureaucracies, and the industries that it is supposed to monitor and regulate for the "facts." Much of the information that Congress needs is classified as secret by pertinent sources, and the executive branch and industry often hire most of the available experts as employees or consultants. Congress has improved this situation by using the Legislative Reference Service of the Library of Congress, passing the Freedom of Information Act and amendments that help Congress and the public gain access to executive advisory committee reports, and establishing a Congressional Clearinghouse on the Future, the Congressional Office of Technology Assessment, and the Congressional Budget Office.

Until a few years ago seniority determined who chairs the powerful congressional committees. This practice was abolished because some committee leaders abused their power. Today such potential abuses of power have been reduced by having committee chairs named by a caucus of the majority party. Congress has also slightly reduced the number of committees. Unfortunately, it also decreed that each committee have at least four fully staffed subcommittees, greatly increasing the complexity of handling legislation. For example, some energy bills may be dealt with by up to 83 different committees and subcommittees. Many analysts have suggested that the number of subcommittees should be reduced. Such a reform, however, is unlikely because most members of Congress want to be in charge of at least one subcommittee, and the more subcommittees there are, the better their chances.

The Bureaucratic Bottleneck A government bureau is created as a response to a specific problem. In its early pioneer stages a vigorous, small agency with dynamic leadership makes progress. But as it grows, its effectiveness and sense of mission decline. Eventually the agency can become so large, complex, and rigid that it chokes on all the highly specialized rules and regulations it has created. More energy and money are then used to keep the agency operating, while it puts out less useful work and sometimes creates more problems than it solves.

Many government regulations are necessary to protect the environment and consumers from abuse by private industry. However, most observers agree that the number and complexity of government regulations can and should be reduced. In 1980 Americans spent an estimated 1.2 billion hours filling out over 6,000 different kinds of federal forms—producing enough paper each year to lay a strip of paper (0.8 kilometer (0.5 mile in width) from New York to Los Angeles.

Some regulations are unnecessarily complex. Many, however, must be complex and detailed. Government officials know that most industries they are required to regulate have teams of lawyers that will go through laws and regulations to find even the tiniest loophole that will allow these industries to circumvent the intention of the law. Most of the blame for overregulation lies with Congress—not federal regulatory agencies. In a number of cases, Congress writes vague laws and leaves it up to federal agencies and the courts to fill in the details.

Because of bureaucratic overspecialization, government has become an enormous organism composed of separate cells of experts, often remote from the people, unable to see the overall picture, competing rather than cooperating with one another, and incapable of dealing with the multiplicity of interlocking problems that characterizes society today.

Another problem is that each overspecialized bureau becomes more concerned with its own survival than with its mission; some are even taken over by the groups they are supposed to regulate. President Harry S. Truman recognized this latter problem when he said, "You don't set foxes to watching the chickens just because they have a lot of experience in the hen house." For example, a 1981 study by Common Cause showed that 14 of the top 16 officials appointed for the Department of the Interior by the Reagan administration came from the five major industries regulated by Interior—oil and gas, mining, utilities, timber, and grazing.

Often by the time a new agency is fully functioning, events shift public attention to other problems. To justify its existence and its budget, each agency wants a share of such new issues. As a result, responsibility for a given problem may be spread among 20 agencies. Only when the problem becomes a crisis are all the fragments gathered together. Then an umbrella agency, such as the EPA, is created to launch a major offensive that may be a decade or more overdue. Soon institutional rigidity sets in and the cycle repeats.

A number of observers have pointed out that most attempts at bureaucratic reform are ineffective, temporary, or both. The approaches include **(1)** bringing in new chiefs (because a bureau chief rarely lasts longer than 4 years, the agency pretends to change but really continues business as usual), **(2)** establishing interagency committees or task forces to manage conflicts of interest, **(3)** reorganizing and consolidating, **(4)** creating new organizations (good during the first phase if adequately funded), and **(5)** having policy made by White House staff members, who are not subject to public and congressional scrutiny.

New reforms that have been suggested to reduce the size of the bureaucracy and to increase its efficiency include **(1)** exempting half of all annual replacements from turnover (amounting to about 300,000 per year) from civil service protection, **(2)** streamlining the procedures for dismissal, **(3)** overhauling the evaluation and merit raise system, **(4)** empowering the president to appoint more high-level departmental officials (extending this down to level GS-13 civil service employees would allow the president to appoint over 93,000 high-level officials, compared to only 3,000 under the present system), **(5)** providing more effective protection and higher rewards for "whistleblowers" who expose fraud and waste in government, **(6)** giving state and local officials more authority over the spending of federal grants, **(7)** turning more of the federal tax revenues directly back to the states, **(8)** having the states assume full responsibility for some areas, such as education, **(9)** enacting and strictly enforcing sunset laws, under which government agencies and programs are evaluated periodically and eliminated unless they can be shown to be necessary, effective, and efficient.

Electing Sustainable Earth Leaders In criticizing and evaluating leaders we should keep in mind the Spanish verse "Advice pours down from the stadium full,/ But only the matador faces the bull." Instead of merely criticizing, some observers urge that we elect a new breed of sustainable earth leaders, whose primary loyalty is to the ecosphere and to the future of humanity. Table 21-2 compares characteristics of international frontier leaders to those of sustainable earth leaders.

Redefining Politics An increasing number of Americans who are fed up with waiting for government to act are redefining politics. Politics is no longer just a question of what candidate, party, or issues you vote for. Today politics can be as much concerned with how you live your life as with what you think about national security issues or energy policy.

For example, while elected officials argue over a national energy policy, bow to special interests, and spend most of the federal energy budget on centralized nuclear power to provide electricity, a growing number of U.S. citizens are decreasing their personal reliance on such centralized energy sources. Instead of buying oil and natural gas for heating, they are installing heavy insulation and heating their water and homes with energy from the sun. They are also driving fuel-efficient cars or riding bicycles to work. Some get the electricity they need from solar photovoltaic cells mounted on the roof.

In taking these personal steps toward energy self-reliance, these individuals are also acting politically by reducing the need for imported oil and for building more nuclear- or coal-powered power plants to generate electricity. Despite concerns about the safety of nuclear plants and storage of radioactive wastes, a major factor in the cancellation of dozens of U.S. nuclear power plants since 1975 has been the reduction in projected future electricity needs because of energy conservation by individuals and businesses.

By adopting a life-style of voluntary simplicity (doing more with less), individuals are taking political actions to help make the national and global transition to a sustainable earth society. They are learning that buying more products and luxuries doesn't provide security or freedom. Instead it can lead to insecurity because the more things you own,

the more time and money you must spend protecting and repairing them. If enough people voluntarily adopt a simpler life-style, a sustainable earth society will eventually be achieved, with or without government leadership and action.

21-5 Achieving Global Security and Cooperation

The Arms Race Many consider the sharp rise in world military expenditures to be the most dangerous J-shaped curve in the world. In 1982 world military expenditures amounted to $550 billion—an average of about $1.5 billion a day or $1 million a minute—with the United States and the Soviet Union accounting for more than half this amount. The United States alone is expected to spend over $1.6 trillion for military purposes between 1982 and 1987—an amount equivalent to a stack of dollar bills 173,000 kilometers (107,000 miles) high. The $238.6 billion U.S. military budget for 1984 amounts to an average expenditure of half a million dollars a minute. Military spending is also increasing rapidly in the LDCs, which buy 74 percent of their arms from the United States and the Soviet Union.

This situation drains financial, natural, and human resources that could be used for peaceful, constructive purposes. About *half* the world's physical scientists and engineers and one-fourth of all the world's scientists devote their talents and skills to military research and development. By comparison, only 8 percent of are working on energy research and development (with most of these working on nuclear power), 7 percent on health, 5 percent on transportation, and 3 percent on agriculture. Furthermore, in the United States about 50 percent of all annual government research and development expenditures are devoted to military purposes. As President Dwight D. Eisenhower, a former five-star general, put it:

Every gun that is made, every warship launched, every rocket fired, signifies in the final sense, a theft from those who hunger and are not fed, those who are cold and not clothed. This world in arms is not spending money alone. It is spending the sweat of its laborers, the genius of its scientists, the hopes of its children.

Of the three major approaches to maintaining world peace—*deterrence, pacification, and cooperation and sharing*—the superpowers so far have chosen mutual deterrence by continuing the arms race. Many leaders and people believe that more guns, tanks, planes, and bombs equal more security. Although most Americans support a strong defense, they are beginning to ask some important questions: Why is it necessary to spend billions to build more strategic nuclear weapons when the United States could destroy the Soviet Union several times over? Why are 540,000 U.S. troops standing guard throughout the world? Why isn't it possible to have a strong defense without budget increases by eliminating vast areas of wastefulness in military expenditures?

Defenders of the defense budget point out that (1) only about 11 percent of the 1984 budget is earmarked for strategic nuclear weapons; (2) about 42 percent is used to meet payroll, training, and support costs for 3.2 million military and civilian personnel; (3) the defense budget amounts to no more than 8 percent of the nation's GNP and 28 percent of the total federal budget (less than the percentage of the GNP spent on the military during the 1950s and 1960s, and under the 40 to 50 percent of the federal budget spent on the military in many of the years since World War II); and (4) military forces are needed in many parts of the world to help prevent minor clashes from escalating into global nuclear war.

To an increasing number of people throughout the world, however, it is becoming clear that in the long run the arms race leads to mutual insecurity—not mutual security. Arms control treaties are designed primarily to prevent bankruptcy and don't really disarm us, since we already have enough atomic bombs to kill everyone in the world 35 times. As tensions mount and more countries join the "nuclear club," it seems to many that a policy of mutual deterrence through strength is now increasing—not decreasing—the chances of global nuclear war, the ultimate planetary lose-lose game (Enrichment Study 3).

Paths to Global Peace and Cooperation No one knows how to get us out of this global lose-lose game. To a growing number of citizens, however, it is becoming clear that more *community*—not more weapons—equals more security. Recall that in the eighteenth century 13 separate colonies chose to unite and cooperate rather than to perish.

Recognizing that it is too dangerous to leave the fate of the world in the hands of politicians, ordinary citizens are beginning to join together to try to find ways out of the arms race. Their general plan for world peace involves (1) bringing about an attitude change in which people see themselves as members of a global community, bearing their ultimate loyalty to the planet, not to a particular country, (2) learning how to apply the lessons we have learned about using mediation, conciliation, and binding arbitration to bring about nonviolent resolution of conflicts between and within nations by

asking what are the sources of conflict and what is the potential for creative resolution (instead of trying to determine how the other party can be eliminated), (3) using *pacification* to rectify wrongs, calm fears, and provide open information flow and mutual inspection, (4) moving from pacification to cooperation and sharing, as mutual understanding and trust grow between individual citizens in different countries, and (5) establishing the roots of this citizen global pacification, cooperation, and security network at the local level, where all conflicts start, and where they should be handled before they get out of control. This is what it means for individual citizens to think globally and act locally.

Chances of defusing the arms race through actions by ordinary citizens are not high, but are probably better than the chances of avoiding global nuclear war if the arms race and international tensions continue on their present course. For example, Professor J. Kenneth Smail of Kenyon College has suggested a "reciprocal hostage exchange" or "guestage" program to reduce the chances of nuclear war between the United States and the Soviet Union. In this program about 25,000 young Americans would attend Soviet schools and universities located in strategic areas, and 25,000 Soviet youth would attend comparable U.S. schools and universities. These students would be mainly the children of military, political, and industrial leaders, so that generals or politicians who advocated a nuclear strike would in effect be killing their own children. The "guestages" would serve perhaps 2 to 4 years, with some returning home each year and an equal number replacing them. This program should also promote better understanding between the people and leaders of the two superpowers.

Some call for a world government to end the arms race and solve other global problems. Many observers, however, argue that the world is too diverse for a single government—even if it could be instituted without global nuclear war. Furthermore, they point out that variety is not only the spice of life, it is crucial for long-term survival and adaptability of the human race and of other species. A political monoculture, like a vast agricultural monoculture, could easily topple with changing conditions. Thus, preserving biological and cultural diversity should be an important global goal and is probably best achieved by a loose federation of politically autonomous states—like the European Community. A federation of nations would cooperate to prevent nuclear and ecological destruction and to improve the quality of life for everyone.

In effect, we must simultaneously live and act on three cultural levels: a *microculture* of families and local communities based on personal relationships, a *macroculture* of national interests based on common economic and political arrangements, laws, and customs, and a *global culture* based on economic, political, and ethical arrangements in which global loyalty and cooperation are the only viable forms of patriotism.

Indifference is the essence of inhumanity.
George Bernard Shaw

Discussion Topics

1. Do you agree that real politics is the art of making the seemingly impossible possible? Why or why not? On this basis, what have been the major political events of this century, and who was mainly responsible for each?

2. What major trends do you see in society today? Which ones are desirable and which are undesirable? Use various combinations of these trends to construct three scenarios of what the world might be like in 2000. Identify the scenario you favor and outline a program for achieving this alternative future.

3. Do you believe that trees and wildlife should have the legal right to be represented in court? Why or why not? What about rocks? (See Christopher D. Stone, *Should Trees Have Standing? Toward Legal Rights for Natural Objects*, 1974.)

4. In general, why are water pollution laws easier to enforce than air pollution laws?

5. Analyze the civil rights movement and the nuclear freeze movement in terms of using or failing to use cybernetic politics.

6. As a class, analyze the Constitution and the Bill of Rights in terms of cybernetics. Use cybernetics to revise or write a new constitution for the transition to a sustainable earth society.

7. As a class, design a cybernetic constitution for your student government. Why not try to have it passed? Design a strategy for passage based on cybernetic politics.

8. Debate the following resolution: We should create a long-range planning board as a fourth branch of government.

9. Evaluate the past five U.S. presidents in terms of frontier and sustainable earth characteristics (see Table 21-2). Can you identify any existing sustainable earth leaders or people who should be elected because of such potential?

10. Do you believe that all presidential and congressional elections should be funded entirely by taxpayers, with fixed spending limits for each candidate and no donations from other sources allowed? Why or why not?

11. Debate the following resolution: The U.S. military budget should be cut at least by one-third.

12. Debate the following resolution: The only real path to peace calls for the United States to destroy its nuclear weapons.

13. Debate the following resolution: National patriotism is both irrelevant and dangerous. The only viable patriotism is global loyalty.

14. Do you agree or disagree with the "guestage" proposal for helping prevent nuclear war between the United States and the Soviet Union? Why or why not? How could such a proposal be instituted?

22

Environmental Ethics and Hope

Through our scientific and technological genius we have made this world a neighborhood. Now through our moral and spiritual genius we must make it a brotherhood.

Martin Luther King, Jr.

22-1 Hope: The People Are Stirring

A New Dream Faced with the pollution of our water, air, and food, energy problems, land misuse, toxic wastes, species extinction, and potential resource shortages, many of us feel overwhelmed and powerless. Add to these the possibility of massive destruction by nuclear war, and it is no wonder many people ask whether there is any hope.

Despite these problems and dangers, there are grounds for hope—one of the greatest driving forces in life. Present undesirable trends do not necessarily indicate where we are heading. As René Dubos reminds us, "Trend is not destiny." *We can say no!* Nobel Prize-winning chemist Glenn T. Seaborg urges us to look at the present and future with new eyes: "What we are seeking today in all our social upheavals, in all our alarm and anguish over an environmental feedback and, in general, the apparent piling of crisis upon crisis to an intolerable degree, is not a forecast of doom. It is the birth-pangs of a new world view."

The Good News During the short period between 1965 and today, most U.S. citizens became aware of and concerned about the environment. April 22, 1970, was the first Earth Day in the United States, and 20 million people took to the streets to demand better environmental quality. At that time, polls showed that Americans considered reducing pollution to be the second most important problem. A 1984 poll revealed that 70 percent of Americans profess to be even more concerned about the environment than they were in the past and say they are willing to pay for environmental improvement.

Since 1970, over 80 federal laws have been passed to protect the air, water, land, wildlife, and public health, and billions of dollars have been spent on pollution control. Significant progress has been made in reducing air and water pollution as summarized earlier in Section 1-6 and in Chapters 18 and 19.

On the energy front, enormous amounts of energy are still wasted, although important efforts to improve energy efficiency are being made. Some people are driving less; more thermostats have been turned down; more homes have been insulated; and a small but growing number of people are using solar energy to heat their water and homes. But many people conserve energy only when it is required by law or when they clearly see that it saves them money in the short run. Despite higher gasoline prices, carpools and vanpools are not used widely, and the nation lacks extensive and efficient railroad, mass transit and paratransit systems, and bicycle paths to help reduce dependence on automobiles. In polls the favored energy source is solar energy (61 percent) and the least favored is nuclear energy. Most of the federal energy budget, however, is devoted to nuclear energy with little spending on solar energy and conservation. (Table 16-5)

With regard to population, zero population growth in the United States is probably at least 50 years away because of the momentum from the youthful age structure (Section 6-5), but both the birth rate and the total fertility rate have fallen dramatically (Figures 6-4 and 6-5). If these low rates can be maintained, especially through 1987, the United States could have a stable population by 2020, and perhaps as early as 2010 depending primarily on immigration, legal and illegal.

In 1983 some 5 million to 8 million Americans belonged to at least one environmental group (see Appendix 1 for a list of such organizations). While many people sit on the sidelines, talking about how the system can't be changed, these groups are changing it. Environmental causes are not mass movements yet, but the number of dedicated environmental professionals and activists is growing and

---

Enrichment Study 15 is related to this chapter.

nearing the critical mass needed to bring about a gradual change to a sustainable earth society.

Some industrialists still oppose environmental reform, attempt to have environmental laws weakened, and carry out massive ad campaigns depicting environmentalists as elitist, affluent, white, upper-middle-class individuals who want to lock up all the woods and to bankrupt the United States. The public, however, has not been persuaded by such stereotyped images, and poll after poll has shown strong and widespread support for environmental protection throughout the United States.

At the international level, Sweden has set an example. Some of its achievements include (1) reaching zero population growth, (2) instituting national land-use planning and extensive and sophisticated pollution control, (3) protecting large amounts of its shoreline for free public use, (4) having enacted and enforced legislation to protect the health and safety of its workers 20 years before the passage of the (1970) Occupational Safety and Health Act in the United States, (5) using about one-third less energy per capita and having a higher per capita GNP than the United States, (6) providing more than $1 billion (an average of $125 per person) for the installation of energy-saving devices in homes and offices, (7) establishing decentralized district heating systems for about one-fourth of its cities, (8) teaching techniques for energy saving in the schools, (9) planning to phase out nuclear power over the next 25 years and switch to renewable energy resources, (10) having efficient and comfortable mass transit systems extending as far as 40 kilometers (25 miles) from the centers of major cities, (11) encouraging the use of mass transportation through heavy taxes on automobiles based on vehicle weight, and on gasoline, (12) establishing a comprehensive program designed to produce a nonsmoking generation (Enrichment Study 7), (13) alerting the world through its scientific research to a number of environmental dangers and their remedies, (14) developing innovations like pneumatic pipelines for solid waste removal and resource recovery, the Clivus Multrum waterless toilet (Figure 18-11), and a three-way catalytic converter for controlling automobile emissions (Section 19-6), (15) allocating 5 percent of its total budget for environmental programs compared to about 1.5 percent in the United States, and (16) being one of the few affluent nations whose foreign aid to LDCs has increased over the past 15 years. Sweden, like any urbanized country, has serious social and environmental problems, and some have criticized its cradle-to-grave social welfare system. But other nations clearly have many lessons to learn from Sweden's sustainable earth behavior.

Progress in some parts of the world does not mean that things are going well everywhere. We have only begun to recognize our predicament, much less decide on courses of action. But it is amazing how much progress has been made between 1968 and today.

22-2 Environmental Ethics

Attitudes Toward Nature Many analysts argue that ecological concern will be short-lived and ecological action crippled unless we deal with the attitudes and values that have led to environmental degradation. As E. F. Schumacher said, "Environmental deterioration does not stem from science or technology, or from a lack of information, trained people, or money for research. It stems from the life-style of the modern world, which in turn arises from its basic beliefs or its religion."

The attitude of most industrialized nations toward nature can be expressed as eight basic beliefs:

1. Humans are the source of all value (anthropocentrism).

2. Nature exists only for our use.

3. Our primary purpose is to produce and consume material goods. Success is based on material wealth.

4. Matter and energy resources are unlimited because of human ingenuity in making them available.

5. Production and consumption of goods must rise endlessly because we have a right to an ever increasing material standard of living.

6. We need not adapt ourselves to the natural environment because we can remake it to suit our own needs by means of science and technology.

7. A major function of the state is to help individuals and corporations exploit the environment to increase wealth and power. The most important nation-state is the one that can command and use the largest fraction of the world's resources.

8. The ideal person is the self-made individualist who does his or her own thing and hurts no one.

Although we may not accept these statements, most of us act individually, corporately, and politically as if we did—and this is what counts.

How did we get such attitudes toward nature? Historian Lynn White, Jr., among others, traces the Western ecological crisis to the Judeo-Christian acceptance of the biblical directive to "be fruitful and multiply, fill the earth and subdue it, and have dominion over the fish of the sea and over the birds of the air and over every living thing" (Genesis 1:28). Theologians and other scholars have pointed out that this hypothesis treats the Judeo-Christian tradition as a monolithic structure instead of a rich diversity of beliefs operating in many different ways throughout history. They also point out that the Bible calls for stewardship of nature.*

Some have suggested that the answer lies in Eastern religions, which emphasize humans *in* nature rather than humans *against* nature. For example, Taoism and Zen Buddhism include the idea of the harmony and unity of humans with nature, and Buddhism fosters reverence for all living creatures and an appreciation of the beauty of nature. But people guided by these and other non-Western religions have also ruined land through overgrazing, soil erosion, and excessive deforestation. Thus, some scholars argue that it is not one's professed religion or philosophy of life that is to blame, but the failure of humans to put their religious or philosophical beliefs into practice. Others argue that all the world's religions and philosophies contain anthropocentric (human-centered) views that can and usually do lead to environmental degradation.

Sustainable Earth Ethics A number of environmentalists urge that we adopt a sustainable earth or conserver world view based on replacing the eight attitudes toward nature listed earlier with the following ethical guidelines.

1. Humans are not the source of all value.

2. Nature does not exist primarily for human use but for all living species. In the words of Aldo Leopold, each of us is "to be a plain member and citizen of nature."

3. Our primary purposes should be to share and care for all humans and to recognize the right of all species to live without interference or control by humans. Success is based on the degree to which we achieve these goals.

4. Matter and energy resources are finite and must not be wasted. As Arthur Purcell puts it: "A conservation ethic means simply a desire to get the most out of what people use, and a recognition that the wasteful use of precious resources is harmful and detrimental to the quality of everyone's life."

5. Production and consumption of material goods need not increase endlessly—no individual, corporation, or nation has a right to an ever-increasing share of the earth's finite resources. "There is enough for everybody's need but not for anybody's greed" (M. K. Gandhi).

6. As part of nature, humans should work with—not against—nature. In the words of Aldo Leopold, "A thing is right when it tends to preserve the integrity, stability, and beauty of the biotic community. It is wrong when it tends otherwise."

7. Major functions of the state are to supervise long-range planning, to prevent individuals and corporations from exploiting or damaging the environment, and to preserve human freedom and dignity.

8. We can never completely "do our own thing" without exerting some effect now or in the future on other human beings and on other living species. All past, present, and future actions have effects, most of which are unpredictable.

Achieving a Sustainable Earth World View
Achieving a sustainable earth world view is not easy because it goes against many of the things we believe. In general, it involves working our way through the four levels of environmental awareness summarized in the accompanying box.

Shallow and Deep Ecology In 1973 the Norwegian ecophilosopher Arne Naess pointed out two approaches to attempting to solve environmental problems, which he called *"shallow ecology"* and *"deep ecology."* Shallow ecology corresponds roughly to the spaceship earth world view, and *deep ecology* corresponds roughly to the sustainable earth world view. Some of the major differences between these two approaches are summarized in Table 22-1.

Naess believes that if people question what is going on in the world deeply enough, they will emerge with a world view, like that of deep ecology, which can "provide a single motivating force for all the activities and movements aimed at saving the planet from human exploitation and domination." He argues that such a search for meaning reveals that "we need practically nothing of what we are supposed to need for a rich and fulfilling life." Deep ecology, for example, says that instead of having an energy supply crisis, we have a crisis of wasteful energy consumption.

According to Naess, deep ecology gives people the confidence to take stands on complex issues based on intuition about how the natural world works instead of deferring a stand until all the facts

---

*Examples are found in Genesis 2:15; Leviticus 25:2–5; Deuteronomy 8:17, 20:19–20, 22:6; Job 38; Psalms 24:1–6, 65:11–13, 84:3, 148; Isaiah 24:4–6; Malachi 3:11–12; Matthew 6:12, 22–39; Luke 12:16–21, 16:1–2.

Four Levels of Environmental Awareness

First level: Pollution. Discovering the symptoms. At this level, we must point out and try to stop irresponsible acts of pollution by large and small organizations, and resist being duped by slick corporate advertising. But we must at the same time change our own life-styles. We have all been drilling holes in the bottom of the boat. Arguing over who is drilling the biggest hole only diverts us from working together to keep the boat from sinking. The problem of remaining at the pollution level is that individuals and industries see their own impacts as too tiny to matter. Eventually this *tragedy of the commons* can overload our life-support systems. Remaining at the pollution awareness level also leads people to see the crisis as a problem comparable to a "moon shot," and to look for a quick technological solution: Have technology fix us up, send me the bill at the end of the month, but don't ask me to change my way of living.

Second level: Neo-Malthusian overpopulation. Recognizing that the cause of pollution is not just people but their level of consumption and the environmental impact of various types of production (Section 1-5). At this second level the answers seem obvious. We must simultaneously reduce both the number of people in MDCs and LDCs and wasteful consumption of matter and energy resources—especially in the MDCs which, with less than 30 percent of the world's population, account for about 90 percent of environmental pollution worldwide.

Third level: Spaceship earth (shallow ecology). Becoming aware that population and resource use will not be controlled until a reasonable number of leaders and citizens recognize that protecting and preserving the life-support systems that sustain all life must be our primary goal. The goal at this level is to use technology, economics, and conventional politics to control population growth, pollution, and resource

depletion to prevent ecological overload. Some argue that the spaceship earth level is a sophisticated expression of our arrogance toward nature—the idea that through technology we can control nature and create artificial environments to avoid environmental overload. They point out that using this approach eventually will pose a dire threat to individual human freedom because to protect the life-support systems that are necessary in space, a centralized authority (ground control) rigidly controls astronauts' lives. Instead of novelty, spontaneity, joy, and freedom, the spaceship model is based on cultural homogenization, social regimentation, artificiality, monotony, and gadgetry. In addition, it is argued that this approach can cause environmental overload in the long run because it is based on the false idea that we have essentially complete understanding of how nature works. Furthermore, it does not involve seriously questioning the economic, political, social, and ethical foundations of modern industrial society, which some see as major causes of environmental problems.

Fourth level: Sustainable earth (deep ecology). Recognizing that **(1)** everyone and every living species is interconnected; **(2)** the role of humans is not to rule and control nature but to work with nature and selectively control relatively small parts of nature on the basis of ecological understanding; **(3)** since the ecosphere is so complex that its workings can never be fully understood, attempts at excessive control will sooner or later backfire (Section 5-3); **(4)** our major goal should be to preserve the ecological integrity, stability, and diversity of the ecosphere; and **(5)** since all living species by virtue of their existence have an inalienable right to life in their natural environments, the forces of biological evolution, not human technological control, should determine which species live or die.

are in. For example, some experts say nuclear power is unsafe, others say it is safe, and people are bewildered. Naess contends that a deep ecology world view allows people to oppose nuclear power through common sense and intuition based on the ideas that there are other less risky, decentralized energy alternatives that don't make us so dependent on large companies and government agencies and don't pass on the risks of nuclear wastes to future generations. Nuclear physicist Bernard Cohen, however, argues that it is equally unethical for this generation to deplete the world's finite supplies of oil,

coal, natural gas, nonfuel mineral resources, forests, soil, and wildlife.

Those who see the sustainable earth approach as going "back to nature" express the idealized and romanticized view that nature's ways are somehow always kind, beautiful, and gentle. Such people do not know nature's harsh realities, confusing a desire to feel close to nature with living close to nature. A mass return to natural living would also mean death for billions of human beings. Long ago we exceeded the population carrying capacity for a world living at a low technological level. "Back to nature" is an

Table 22-1 Comparison of Shallow and Deep Ecology

Shallow Ecology (Spaceship Earth)	Deep Ecology (Sustainable Earth)
Views humans as separate from nature	Views humans as part of nature
Emphasizes the right of humans to live (anthropocentrism)	Emphasizes the idea that every life form has in principle a right to live; recognizes that we have to kill to eat, but that we have no right to destroy other living things without sufficient reason based on ecological understanding
Concerned with human feelings (anthropocentrism)	Concerned with the feelings of all living things; deep ecologists feel sad when another human or a cat or dog feels sad and grieve when trees and landscapes are destroyed.
Concerned with the wise management of resources for *human* use (anthropocentrism)	Concerned about resources for all living species
Concerned with stabilizing the population—especially in LDCs	Concerned not only with stabilizing the human population worldwide, but also with reducing the size of the human population to a sustainable minimum without revolution or dictatorship
Either accepts by default or positively endorses the ideology of continued economic growth	Replaces this ideology with that of ecological sustainability and preservation of biological and cultural diversity
Bases decisions on cost-benefit analysis	Bases decisions on ethical intuitions about how the natural world really works
Bases decisions on short-term planning and goals	Bases decisions on long-range planning and goals and on ecological intuition when all facts not available
Tries to work within existing political, social, economic, and ethical systems	Questions these systems and looks for better systems based on the way the natural world works

option that is available to only a few in an overcrowded world that has lost its technological and social virginity. Deep ecology does not reject technology. But it does insist that technology be used in just and humane ways to protect—not degrade and destroy—any form of life on earth. A technology should not always be developed and encouraged just because it is possible.

Deep ecology calls for us to distinguish between our wants and our true needs by making our life-styles more harmonious with natural cycles and adopting a philosophy of *voluntary simplicity* based on doing more with less. However, *voluntary simplicity* by those who have more than they really need should not be confused with the *forced simplicity* of the poor who do not have enough to meet their most basic needs for food, clothing, shelter, and good health.

22-3 What Can You Do?

Finally, it comes down to what you and I are willing to do individually and collectively. Begin with yourself.

1. *You can evaluate the way you think the world works and sensitize yourself to the environment.* Stand up, look around, compare what is with what could and should be. Examine your room, your home, your school, your place of work, your street, and your city, state, nation, and the world. What things around you really improve the quality of your life? What are your own environmental bad habits? What is your own world view? Do the assumptions on which it is based represent a valid view of the real world?

2. *You can become ecologically informed.* Give up your frontier, or linear, thinking and immerse yourself in sustainable earth thinking. Don't fall into the "all growth is good" and "technology will save us" traps. Specialize in one particular area of the ecological crisis and pool your specialized knowledge with that of others (networking). Everyone doesn't need to be an ecologist, but you do need to "ecologize" your life-style.

3. *You can choose a simpler life-style by going on an energy and matter resource diet to reduce resource consumption and waste and pollution production.* Do this by distinguishing between your true needs and your wants and using trade-offs. For every high-energy use, high-waste, or highly polluting thing you do (having a child, buying a car, living or working in an air conditioned building), give up a number of other things. Where possible, use low or intermediate technology instead of high-level technology. Such a life-style will be cheaper, and it may add more joy as you learn how to break through the plastic, technological membrane that separates many of us from nature and from one another.

4. *You can become more self-reliant by trying to unhook yourself from dependence on large, centralized systems for your water, energy, food, and livelihood,* as discussed by Geraldine

Watson in her end-of-chapter Guest Editorial. If possible, work for yourself or for a small, locally owned business (the big, centralized, energy-intensive national and multinational corporations will probably be the first to collapse during a major crisis). Learn to use organic, intensive gardening techniques to grow some of your own food. Invest some of your earnings in a year's supply of dehydrated food and vacuum-packed seeds, as a source of food in case of crisis and as a way to beat inflation from rising food prices if no crisis occurs (a win-win situation). Store water or, if possible, have your own well (with a standby hand-operated pump). Accumulate the basic hand tools and other items you would really need to survive on your own. Get as much of your energy as possible from renewable sources such as the sun, wind, water, or biomass (wood).

5. *You can remember that environment begins at home.* Before you start trying to convert others, begin by changing your own living patterns. Move closer to your job, ride a bicycle to the shopping center or to work, refuse to buy drinks in throwaway cans and bottles. If you become an ecological activist, be prepared to have everyone looking for and pointing out your own ecological sins.

6. *You can avoid the four do-nothing traps of technological optimism, gloom-and-doom pessimism, fatalism, and extrapolation to infinity* ("If I can't change the entire world quickly, I won't try to change any of it."). While most people talk about the difficulties of changing the system, others as diverse as Mahatma Gandhi, Rachel Carson, Ralph Nader, and Martin Luther King, Jr., have gone ahead and changed it.

7. *You can become politically involved on local and national levels.* Start or join a local environmental group, and also join national organizations (see the list in Appendix 1). Become the ecosphere citizen of your block or school. Use positive synergy to amplify your efforts. The environment would improve noticeably if each of us made an annual donation to one or more politically active environmental organizations working for causes we believe in. This is a way to hire professional lobbyists, lawyers, and experts to work for us. Better yet, volunteer your services to such organizations. Work to elect sustainable earth leaders and to influence officials once they are elected to public office (Enrichment Study 15).

8. *You can do the little things.* Individual acts of consumption and litter have contributed to the mess. When you are tempted to say "This little bit won't hurt," remember that millions of others are saying the same thing. Picking up a single beer can, joining a carpool, bicycling to work, writing on both sides of a piece of paper, and not buying overpackaged grocery and other products are all very significant acts. Turning off a light when leaving a room or not using more light than is necessary ultimately reduces the need for nuclear and coal-burning electric power plants. Each small act reminds us of ecologically sound practices. Start now with a small, concrete, personal act, and then add more such acts. Little acts can be used to expand our awareness of the need for fundamental changes in our political, economic, and social systems over the next few decades. These acts also help us avoid psychological numbness when we realize the magnitude of the job to be done.

9. *You can work on the big polluters and big problems, primarily through political action.* Individual actions help reduce pollution, give us a sense of involvement, and help us develop a badly needed ecological consciousness. Our awareness must then expand to recognize that large-scale pollution and environmental disruption are caused by industries, governments, and big agriculture. Picking up a beer can is significant, but it does not mean we can allow uncontrolled surface mining of coal in South Dakota. We must think globally and act locally.

10. *You can start a counter-J-shaped curve of awareness and action.* The world is changed by changing the two people next to you. For everything, big or little, that you decide to do, make it your primary goal to convince two others to do the same thing and persuade them in turn to convince two others. Carrying out this doubling process only 28 times would convince everyone in the United States. After 32 doublings everyone in the world would be convinced. But it is not necessary to convince everybody. Most major changes have been brought about by a single individual like Gandhi who convinced a critical mass of people—probably only 5 or 10 percent of the population of a country or of the world—to work actively for a common goal. The national and global environmental movement is nearing this critical mass. Your help and that of others you convince to become activists for the planet may be all that is necessary for success.

11. *Don't make people feel guilty.* If you know people who are overconsuming or carrying out environmentally harmful acts, don't make them feel bad. Instead, find the things that each individual is willing to do to help the environment. There is plenty to do, and no

one can do everything. Use positive rather than negative reinforcement (win-win rather than win-lose games). We need to nurture, reassure, and understand rather than to threaten one another. Keep in mind Norman Cousins's statement: "The first aim of education should not be to prepare young people for careers but to enable them to develop respect for life."

Begin at the individual level and work outward. Join with others and amplify your actions. This is the way the world is changed, as discussed in Geraldine Watson's end-of-chapter Guest Editorial. Envision the world as made up of all kinds of cycles and flows in a beautiful and diverse web of inter-relationships and a kaleidoscope of patterns and rhythms whose very complexity and multitude of potentials remind us that cooperation, honesty, humility, and love must be the guidelines for our behavior toward one another and the earth.

The main ingredients of an environmental ethic are caring about the planet and all of its inhabitants, allowing unselfishness to control the immediate self-interest that harms others, and living each day so as to leave the lightest possible footprints on the planet.

Robert Cahn

Discussion Topics

1. Do you believe that prophecies of ecological doom are useful? Why or why not? Cite examples.

2. Do you agree that "all effective action is fueled by hope"? Cite examples in your own life to support or negate this hypothesis.

3. As a class, list the rationalizations that we typically use to avoid thought, action, and responsibility.

4. Do you agree with the cartoon character Pogo that "We have met the enemy and he [or she] is us"? Why or why not? Criticize this statement from the

---

Guest Editorial: Caring for the Earth and Its Inhabitants

Geraldine Watson is an environmental and social activist who for over 15 years played a major role—along with those she worked with and inspired—in the fight for the establishment of the Big Thicket National Preserve. This diverse array of plant and animal plant communities in southeast Texas was set aside by federal law in 1974 after many years of struggle. Although Geraldine Watson is now somewhat of a local hero, this was not always the case. A pro-Thicket newspaper for which she wrote was firebombed, she was ordered out of the houses of former friends, and her teen-aged sons were often humiliated and insulted. By self-training she has become one of the best field ecologists in the United States, according to the national president and members of the board of directors of the Audubon Society, whom she led on one of her famous tours of the Big Thicket area.

Geraldine Watson is author of Big Thicket Plant Ecology *and works as a naturalist in the Big Thicket National Preserve. She built the house described here completely by herself without the use of power tools. Tragically, it was destroyed by an accidental fire caused by a neighbor burning off brush. She is determined, however, to rebuild.*

For 59 years I have lived in the Big Thicket area of southeast Texas—a land of lush forests, flowing streams, and a pioneer way of life. The cultural systems I have known range from the independent, horse-power family farm to the pure capitalism of the sawmill town, the post–World War II Gulf Coast petrochemical megalopolis, and a university campus. An obsessive curiosity and a conviction that truth lies in all things relating humans, morals, and matter has led me on a lifelong search to find the ideal way for humans—for myself—to live on this earth.

In the naiveté of childhood, adequate necessities—food, clothing, shelter, and someone to take care of me—were sufficient for happiness. Early adulthood was bewildering and traumatic, and I learned what the world ought to be and was not. At middle age, I was appalled at the waste of my early years and how little time I had left to do something about what I saw happening to my world and to my fellow humans.

I saw the by-products of the "good life" pollute and poison the land and water; I saw the beautiful scenes I loved devastated; I saw America squandering its natural resources and refusing to conserve. So I became an activist for the environment.

I watched my government sacrifice morality for political, economic, and military expediency to acquire natural resources, without equal benefit, from less developed nations. So I became an activist for peace, human rights, and international understanding.

I saw the churches of "Christian" America exchanging the simple way of Christ, "Love thy neighbor as thyself," for cold formal ritualism or wild hysteria, and playing the ages-old game of manipulating the minds of the simple for power and profit. So after a cycle of blind faith, agnosticism, atheism, and back to agnosticism, I acquired a reasoning faith and became a teacher of Christ's way.

I saw the dawning of an age of terror as nuclear power plants were built on known earthquake fault zones, a quarter of a million years' worth of radioactive wastes accumulating with no safe storage place, and enough nuclear weapons made to annihilate worlds without end. So I organized an antinuke group.

After my 20 years of fanatic activism, it seems that little has changed. Alienation between humans, and between humans and their God and their natural world, is widening; we are still on the brink of war; and the environment is in even greater peril because we are jostling, shoving, and lining up for the big scramble for the last of the world's nonrenewable fuels and mineral resources.

So I have chosen to walk away.

I have come full circle back to the simple life, to 3 acres of land and a house I designed and built with my own hands, which is independent of the oil and power companies. I still believe that one person, sufficiently motivated and totally oblivious of his or her welfare, can turn the world upside down. But one reaches a time and place for a change in strategy. It is now my intention to prove that anyone, even a 59-year-old woman, can provide personal food, clothing, shelter, and a comfortable and happy life with little help from the self-destructive elements of our society.

My tract of land is located by a small lake with 2 acres of hillside and 1 acre of flat ground in a longleaf pine–bluestem grass habitat. Periodic natural burning maintains a parklike ground cover of native grasses and wildflowers without need for a noisy, gas-consuming lawnmower.

The lakeside habitat was chosen for reasons both practical and aesthetic—an occasional fish to add to a largely vegetarian diet, a source of cool breezes in summer and future wind power, and a source of tranquillity to inspire serenity of spirit.

On the flat ground, I have 4 × 8-foot frames filled with organic matter for intensive gardening. All household wastes are disposed of here. Our mild winters permit year-round gardening, and the frames can be covered in winter for the few freezes. A flock of bantam chicken, which are great foragers, provide eggs for food and manure for the garden; beehives produce honey; dried beans, corn meal, and rice are brought from the town 3 miles distant on my three-wheel carryall bicycle. These staples could be grown if I had sufficient time and ambition. This simple diet is not only economical but healthy. Those who are not dying of stress-related illnesses are dying of too much rich food.

Ninety percent of the clothing we own could be classed as nonessential. Much of our time and money goes into being appropriately attired. Whatever is handy, clean, and does not violate the local laws of decency serves me. In fact, *no* clothing suits me better at times. The freedom and ease with which one can work unhampered by the restraint of sweat-soaked garments is marvelous. I have considered posting a sign: "Warning! Naked woman at work!" to avoid accidentally offending the mores of some chance visitor, but concluded it might attract rather than repel.

My two-and-a-half level, 18 × 20 foot house is on a south slope facing the lake. The entire front of all levels facing south is glass. In winter when the sun is on the south horizon, full sun warms the interior, with much of the heat stored for release at night in the con-crete and stone I have used for the floor and part of the walls; in summer, when the sun is on the north horizon, the glass front is shaded by natural vegetation. The lower underground level is delightfully cool in summer and easy to warm in winter.

There is no conventional furniture—just built-ins—and visitors may carry their pads anywhere they wish to sleep. Water is supplied by an underground reservoir. It operates on the same principle as the springhouse where we kept milk and butter in the early days. The fireplace in the lower room has vents to take heat to the upper levels and serves as a cooking place in winter. For summer cooking there is a stone grill and oven on the terrace. Solar stoves will soon be available, but in the meantime one can pick up enough twigs and fallen limbs about the place for cooking fuel.

Objections most often raised are: "What do you do for a light at night?" and "What on earth do you do for entertainment—for music—with no TV or radio?" I do have a battery-powered tape player, for I love classical music. In addition, there are instruments—drum, tambourine, violin, guitar, flute, and harmonica—so I and anybody else who happens to be in the mood can make any amount and quality of music. Other than these instruments, there are no valuables here to tempt anyone to steal. The door is never locked. People come and go—stay as long as they wish—whether I am home or not.

As for illumination: If I get up in the morning as soon as it is light enough to work, I am quite ready to rest by nightfall. Then I can sit before the fireplace in winter, or practice tai chi chuan in the moonlight on the deck in summer. Or I can play music, or sing, or meditate, or engage in long meaningful conversations with all those interesting people who come to share the love and peace, their own fears and hopes for the world, and to know that, at least in this one place, they need not be afraid.

Guest Editorial Discussion

1. After 20 years of social activism, the author believes that little has changed. Does this mean that what she did, including inspiring other people and helping preserve part of the Big Thicket area, was unimportant? Explain.

2. Do you believe as the author does that "one person sufficiently motivated and totally oblivious of his or her own welfare, can turn the world upside down"? Why or why not? Can you list some individuals who have done this?

3. What is the importance of the author's present strategy "to prove that anyone, even a 59-year-old woman, can provide personal food, clothing, shelter, and a comfortable and happy life with little help from the self-destructive elements of our society"? Is this a way of life you plan to choose? Why or why not?

viewpoint of the poor; from the viewpoint that large corporations and government are the really big polluters.

5. Distinguish carefully between the spaceship earth and sustainable earth world views.

6. What are the useful results of the back-to-nature movement? What are its limitations?

7. Debate the following resolution: The Judeo-Christian tradition of Western civilization is the root of our ecological crisis.

8. Do you agree with the sustainable earth ethics listed in Section 22-2? Why or why not? Can you add others? Which ones do you try to follow?

9. Why is it so important to do the little things? As a class, make a list of all the little things you can do to help protect the environment.

10. What products sold in a typical suburban shopping center are really essential for survival and for a meaningful life?

Epilogue

Where there is no dream, the people perish.
Proverbs 29:18

This book is based on nine deceptively simple theses.

1. The ecological crisis is not only more complex than we think but more complex than we can ever think.

2. In Garrett Hardin's terms, the basic principle of ecology is "that everything and everyone are all interconnected." Truly accepting this and trying to learn how things and people are connected will require a basic change in our patterns of living. But because we can never completely know how everything is connected, we must function in the ecosphere with a sense of humility and creative cooperation rather than blind domination.

3. On earth there are no consumers, only users of materials. We can never really throw anything away, and natural resources are so interdependent that the use or misuse of one will affect others, often in unpredictable ways. This is a threat to a frontier society, but an opportunity for reuse, recycling, and conservation of matter resources in a sustainable earth society.

4. Because of the first law of thermodynamics we can't get anything for nothing, and because of the second law of thermodynamics almost every action we take has some undesirable present or future impact on the environment.

As a result, there can be no completely technological solution to pollution, although technology can help.

5. The earth's resources and matter recycling systems can support only a limited number of people living at a particular average level of affluence; therefore, as the populations of the world and of individual nations increase and as resource supplies decrease, the freedom of individuals to use resources as they wish diminishes.

6. Because we have rounded the bend on the J-shaped curves of increasing population, natural resource use, and pollution, we now have the power to disrupt the earth's life-support systems.

7. Our primary task must be to move from simplistic, linear thinking to circular, cybernetic thinking that is harmonious with the ecological cycles that sustain us; we need to shift to a dynamic, diverse, adaptable, steady-state, sustainable earth society that is in keeping with the fundamental rhythms of life.

8. Informed action based on hope rather than on pessimism, blind technological optimism, or apathy offers humankind its greatest opportunity to come closer to that elusive dream of peace, freedom, brotherhood, sisterhood, good health, and justice for all.

9. It is not too late, if. . . . There is time—probably 50 years—to deal with these complex problems if enough of us really care. It's not up to "them," it's up to "us." Don't wait.

Enrichment Studies

Enrichment Study 1

Human Impact on the Earth

Until about 10,000 years ago people either lived by hunting, fishing, and gathering edible plants, tubers, and roots, or they perished. Today fewer than 1 percent of the earth's inhabitants live by hunting and gathering. The J-shaped curves of increasing population, resource use, and pollution (Chapter 1) are merely symptoms of this fundamental cultural change from humans as hunter-gatherers to humans as shepherds and tillers of the soil to humans in industrial society, as discussed in this enrichment study. These major types of human society are summarized in Figure E1-1 along with the sustainable earth society, which more and more people may change to in the future.

E1-1 Humans in Nature: Hunter-Gatherers

Early humans survived without claws, fangs, or great speed. That they did so, and multiplied, is due to three major cultural adaptations—all the product of intelligence: (1) the use of *tools* for hunting, collecting, and preparing food and making protective clothing, (2) learning to live in an often hostile environment through effective *social organization* and *cooperation* with other human beings, and (3) the use of *language* to increase the efficiency of cooperation and to pass on knowledge of previous survival experiences.

Our early hunter-gatherer ancestors cooperated by living in small bands or tribes, clusters of several families typically consisting of no more than 50 persons. The size of each band was limited by the availability of food. If a group got too large it split up. Sometimes these widely scattered bands had no permanent base, traveling around their territory to find the plants and animals they needed to exist. Hunter-gatherers' material possessions consisted mostly of simple tools such as sharpened

sticks, scrapers, and crude hunting weapons. Much of their knowledge could be described as ecological—how to find water in a barren desert, and how to locate plant and animal species useful as food. Studies of Bushmen, Pygmies, and other hunter-gatherer cultures that exist today have shown the uncertainty of success in hunting wild game; thus often most of the food of primitive people was provided by women who collected plants, fruits, eggs, mollusks, reptiles, and insects.

Many people tend to believe that hunter-gatherers spent most of their time in a "tooth and claw" struggle to stay alive. But research among hunter-gatherer societies in remote parts of the world casts doubt on this idea. These "primitive" people may hunt for a week and then spend a month on vacation. They have no bosses, suffer from less stress and anxiety than most "modern" people, and have a diet richer and more diverse than that of almost everyone else in the world today, rich and poor alike.

Life in early hunter-gatherer societies, however, was harsh. Although malnutrition and starvation were rare, infant mortality was high, primarily from infectious diseases. This factor, coupled with infanticide (killing the young) and geronticide (killing the old) led to an average life expectancy of around 30 years and kept population size in balance with food resources.

With improved weapons such as blade spearheads, members of groups became highly skilled hunters who cooperated to hunt herds of big mammals such as the reindeer and the European bison. They also discovered various methods of mass killing. Fire was frequently used to flush out game from thickets toward hunters lying in wait or to stampede animals over cliffs. Toward the end of the Pleistocene period (several ice ages that occurred between 3 million and 10,000 years ago) about 70 percent of the large North American mammals such as the mammoth, mastodon, and ground sloth

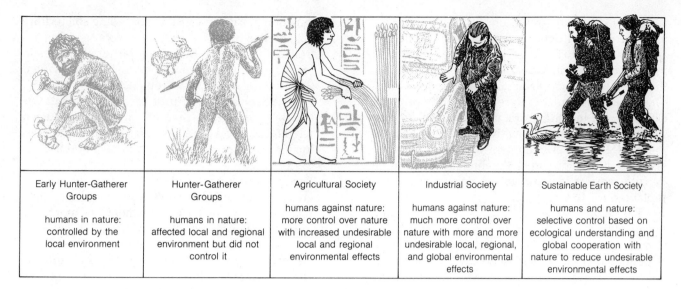

Early Hunter-Gatherer Groups	Hunter-Gatherer Groups	Agricultural Society	Industrial Society	Sustainable Earth Society
humans in nature: controlled by the local environment	humans in nature: affected local and regional environment but did not control it	humans against nature: more control over nature with increased undesirable local and regional environmental effects	humans against nature: much more control over nature with more and more undesirable local, regional, and global environmental effects	humans and nature: selective control based on ecological understanding and global cooperation with nature to reduce undesirable environmental effects

Figure E1-1   Major cultural stages of humanity.

became extinct. Although climatic change was a major cause of these extinctions, some scholars believe that the process was hastened by overhunting.

Hunter-gatherers also learned that after a brush fire plants appeared that were more favorable both for gathering and for attracting grazing wild animals such as deer. Some of the world's major vegetation types, such as the tropical savannas typical of Africa and much of the world's grasslands, are believed to have been created, or at least expanded, by repeated and deliberate burning by hunter-gatherer societies and later by agricultural societies to provide food resources.

With the use of advanced weapons and fire, hunter-gatherer societies made some significant changes in their environment. Because of their small numbers, however, their impact was insignificant on even a regional scale. They were examples of humans *in* nature, who learned to survive by understanding and cooperating with nature.

E1-2 Humans Against Nature: Agricultural Societies

About 10,000 to 12,000 years ago there began one of the most significant changes in human history. People learned how to herd game instead of hunting it, and they invented agriculture to grow selected wild plants close to home instead of having to go out and gather them over a large area. Over several thousand years the importance of hunting and gathering declined as more and more people became shepherds and farmers.

This change may have started with the domestication of dogs found as pets and scavengers around human campsites. Wild sheep were probably domesticated next, and after them, wild goats. Pigs, cattle, and then horses followed. The impact of these early shepherds on the land was often more extensive than that of hunters and gatherers. They burned and cleared forests, replacing them with savannas and grasslands containing annual plants that provided food for their flocks of grazing animals. Some of these grasslands were in turn degraded when too many domesticated animals were allowed to graze in one area or when grazers remained in one place for too long. As a result, grasslands were destroyed and soils were eroded over large areas of the Mediterranean region. Even today these drastic penalties for overgrazing have to be relearned.

The first type of plant cultivation, called *horticulture* ("hoe culture") began when women found that they could quite easily grow some of their favorite food plants by digging a hole with a stick (a primitive hoe) and placing roots and tubers in the ground. People also learned how to plant and grow *seed crops* such as wheat, barley, rice, peas, lentils, corn, and potatoes. We have domesticated very few new major seed crops in the past 2,000 years, although genetically improved strains of these earlier crops have been developed (Section 9–8).

Another method that was developed to grow food plants is called *slash-and-burn* or *shifting* cultivation. It was important in prehistoric and medieval Europe and was used by some of the early colonists in North America. It is still practiced in tropical areas of Africa, South America, and Southeast Asia by an estimated 150 million to 200 million people. A small patch of forest is cleared and the dried vegetation is burned before planting. The ash left after the burning is inorganic fertilizer for the soil. A variety of crops are grown on this forest opening until the plant nutrients in the ash are exhausted—typically after 2 to 5 years. The farmer and his family then move on and clear another patch, leaving the recently used cropland fallow for several years. This allows wild plants to repopulate the original cleared area, making nutrients available again for growing crops. Shifting cultivation works well in the tropical forest environment with its ample sunshine and rain provided the human population density remains low and abandoned areas are not replanted for 10 to 20 years.

True *agriculture* (as opposed to horticulture) began with the invention of the plow, pulled by domesticated animals. At this point people no longer depended on their own muscle power as the prime source of energy for growing food. Later improvements such as irrigation, terracing of hillsides, developing improved strains of crop plants, and using animal manure and commercial fertilizers allowed farmers to harvest more than one crop per year and greatly increased the amount of land under cultivation (Section 9-6).

As people learned to cultivate plants efficiently, they had not only a constant food supply but a regular food *surplus*. This surplus had three important effects: (1) without the threat of starvation, populations began to increase; (2) people cleared more and more land and began to control and shape the surface of the earth to suit their requirements; and (3) urbanization began—villages, towns, and eventually cities slowly formed as people developed specialties other than farming. In hunter-gatherer societies the entire adult population (and sometimes the children) were involved in either hunting or gathering food. In today's less developed nations approximately two-thirds of the adult population is involved in food production. Today in the United States less than 5 percent of the population is involved directly with agriculture, and in some countries in western Europe the figure is less than 2 percent.

Agriculture is the deliberate attempt to alter and control the environment in order to grow food. As farmers grew in numbers and spread out over much of the earth, they created a much greater environmental impact than had hunter-gatherers. Diverse forests and grasslands were replaced with large areas, typically planted with a single food crop such as wheat. Poor management of many of the cleared areas allowed vital topsoil to wash away and pollute streams, rivers, and lakes with silt (Chapters 8 and 18). Land-clearing activities also destroyed and altered the habitats of plant and animal species—endangering their existence and in some cases causing or hastening their extinction (Chapter 11). Irrigation without proper drainage led to the accu-

mulation of salts in topsoil, decreasing soil fertility (Chapters 8 and 17). Pests that were usually controlled naturally by the diverse array of species in forests spread much more rapidly in areas planted with one or only a few crops (Chapters 5 and 9). Pesticides were used to protect food crops, but this led to a new series of problems that threatened wildlife, polluted the air and soil, and in some cases increased the number and size of pest populations (Section 9-9).

The development of agriculture thus brought about a fundamental modification in humanity's relationship with the environment, as more and more people began shifting from hunter-gatherers *in* nature to shepherds, farmers, and urban dwellers *against* nature. But even more fundamental changes were to follow.

E1-3 Humans Against Nature: Industrial Societies

Humans have learned how to find and use more and more energy in their attempts to change and control the environment. Early societies had to rely on the power of their own muscles to survive. Agricultural societies eventually learned to use draft animals and later wind and water power to help them exert more control over the land and their food supplies. During the eighteenth century, however, industrial societies made a gigantic leap in using energy by discovering how to unlock the chemical energy stored in fossil fuels such as coal, oil, and natural gas (Chapters 3, 14, 15, and 16).

The gradual rise of industrial societies, fueled by these new sources of energy, has allowed the creation of many useful products and has raised the standard of living of many people throughout the world. At the same time it has intensified many existing environmental problems and created a series of new ones. By learning to put some of the earth's chemical resources together in new ways, industries have produced metal alloys, plastics, agricultural pesticides and fertilizers, and medicines. But pollution from DDT, lead, mercury, PCBs, solid wastes, radioactive wastes, and a host of other chemicals discussed throughout this book has also increased.

Increased mining to provide industries with raw materials has disrupted more and more of the earth's surface and has threatened plant and animal species. By decreasing the need for most people to engage in agriculture, industrial society has caused massive shifts of population from rural to urban areas—creating a new array of social, political, economic, and environmental problems (Chapter 12).

The benefits of the industrial revolution are great. Very few people would propose that we abandon the technological achievements of the past few hundred years. Increasingly, however, our time, energy, money, and new forms of technology must be used to correct the ill effects of earlier technological advances. We are learning that in many cases the more we try to control nature, the less control we have.

E1-4 Humans and Nature: A Sustainable Earth Society

There are exciting and important indications that we may be ready to move into a new phase of cultural evolution—the transition from an agricultural-industrial society based on humans *against* nature to a sustainable earth society based on humans learning how to cooperate with nature rather than blindly attempting to control it.

Apparently we are all born wanting to get our way about everything. But since there are people besides ourselves on the earth, we soon learn that to survive and get our own way part of the time, we have to cooperate with other human beings. Throughout human existence, human survival has depended on cooperation with other members of the group—in hunting, gathering, and growing food, and in caring for the young. Yet aggression has existed as well, as people try to enforce their own wishes or to express frustration at not getting their way. Indeed, some scholars have argued that humans are innately aggressive and are genetically programmed to kill and make war.

Others, such as anthropologist Richard E. Leakey (see *The Making of Mankind*, 1981), dispute this idea. They point out that **(1)** organized warfare began only a few thousand years ago—too recent an event to have influenced the evolution of human nature over millions of years; **(2)** those who believe that humans are innately aggressive are providing a convenient excuse for violence and organized warfare; **(3)** national leaders who threaten nuclear war are engaged in politics—not aggression; **(4)** soldiers on the battlefields are more like trained sheep than aggressive tigers; and **(5)** cooperation not aggression is the dominant human characteristic (even waging war takes cooperation).

A growing number of people are beginning to see themselves as belonging to a global tribe whose cooperative efforts are necessary for the survival of everyone in an age threatened with destruction. Thus, those who seek to sustain the earth through cooperation are merely renewing and strengthening a fundamental human trait, which has helped keep us from the long list of extinct species.

A continent ages quickly once we come.
Ernest Hemingway

Discussion Topics

1. It is sometimes argued by those wishing to avoid dealing with environmental problems that "Humanity has always been a polluter and despoiler of this planet, so why all the fuss over ecology and pollution? We've survived so far." Identify the kernel of truth in this position and then discuss its serious deficiencies.

2. Imagine that you could assemble representatives from each of the four major phases of cultural change shown in Figure E1-1 to offer an ecology course. Briefly summarize the major ecological lesson that each of the four representatives would give.

3. Humans have been hunter-gatherers for 99 percent of their time on earth. Which traits of this occupation are useful to us today and which are harmful?

4. Debate the following statement: War is inevitable because the human species has inherited the basic characteristic of aggressiveness.

5. Do you believe we should attempt to move to a sustainable earth society over the next few decades? What things in your own life-style promote and what things hinder such a transition?

Enrichment Study 2

The Limits-to-Growth Debate: Projecting Alternative Futures

E2-1 Methods for Projecting Alternative Futures

Types of Models Individuals, businesses, and nations continually make decisions and plans based on generalizations or abstractions about the world known collectively as *models*. In all models certain initial assumptions are made and then used to *project* future events or trends. Obviously, changing the initial assumptions can lead to different conclusions.

There are *mental models, verbal models, mathematical models,* and *computer models*. Most of the models we use every day to make decisions are *mental models*—complex, often unverbalized sets of biases, values, and beliefs about how the world works or should work based on our own experience. Most mental models are eventually expressed in words as *verbal models*. Mental models can include information and intuitive hunches based on experience, motivations, and values and can integrate in creative combinations widely varying types of information from many disciplines. They are also readily available, quick, and cheap. Perhaps without realizing it, you use mental models in deciding whether to wear a raincoat on a certain day, whether to have a baby, or what career to follow.

Mathematical models express the assumptions from mental models in symbolic form, as equations. However, since most people aren't trained to understand mathematical models, their predictions must be translated back into ordinary verbal models. *Computer models* are mathematical models that have been written in computer language so that a computer can be used to calculate or project the conclusions that follow from the assumptions built into the model.

Limitations of Simple Mental Models Unfortunately, our minds can handle only a small number of variables and trends at one time. Thus, intuitive mental models are inadequate to cope with most important world and national changes and prob-lems, which result from many variables and trends that interact in a complex manner in the form of *multiple feedback loops* (Section 5-2).

The problem is complicated even further because of the *time delays* and *synergistic interactions* found in complex systems (Section 5-2). If you do something in a simple system (push a button), the response is usually immediate (the doorbell rings). In a complex system the result of an interaction of some variables and loops might not show up for decades. Furthermore, two variables can interact synergistically so that the net result is greater than the sum of their individual effects.

Using simple linear extrapolation of one or a small number of trends, we devise a solution to a problem only to find that in the long run we have made matters worse, as shown in Table E2-1. It has been suggested that our attempts to make decisions using intuitive linear extrapolation mental models can often be summarized by the equation STS = LTP (short-term solution equals long-term problem). To avoid this danger, we often develop a counterintuitive solution based on a better understanding of complex systems (Table E2-1).

Dynamic Computer Modeling If carefully constructed, computer models can have important advantages over intuitive mental models. *First*, well-designed computer models are rigorous, precise, and logically consistent. They require that all assumptions, terms, weighting factors, data, and other parts of the model be openly listed and described, to develop the mathematical equations. This allows other people to verify the model or to identify points of disagreement so that new, improved models can be developed and tested. By contrast, intuitive mental models are often based on assumptions, biases, and weighting factors that are either hidden or not clearly identified.

Second, computer models attempt to simulate the real world by building in feedback loops and nonlinear relationships between interacting variables. These loops and relationships may be very crude simulations of reality, but they can contain many more variables and more information than any single mental model and can keep track of all

Table E2-1 Intuitive and Counterintuitive Solutions to Problems in Some Complex Systems

Problem	Intuitive Solution	Unexpected Result	Counterintuitive Solution
Bus or airplane company losing money	Raise fares.	Number of passengers decreases; company loses more money than ever.	Lower fares to attract new riders.
City going bankrupt	Raise business and property taxes.	Businesses and homeowners leave city, reducing income from taxes and raising city deficit.	Lower business and property taxes to hold existing businesses and residents and to attract new ones.
People moving to the suburbs	Build freeways into city so people can get to work.	More people move to suburbs, freeways get crowded, taxes rise, businesses flee, jobs get scarcer, and poverty increases.	Instead of freeways between suburbs and city, build good city transportation systems, more people and businesses will stay, raising the tax base, providing more jobs, and combating poverty.
Poor people living in slums	Clear slums and build high-rise, low-income housing.	More poor people move in but can't get jobs, so city has more poor people than before.	Build low-density housing, improve cheap mass transportation within city, and lower tax rate so businesses will stay to provide more jobs for the poor.
Poverty	Establish federal, state, and local government welfare agencies.	More money is spent to run the agencies than is received by the poor.	Allot to any person or family with income below a certain level funds paid out by the Internal Revenue Service to bring them up to the minimum level; entire federal, state, and local welfare bureaucracy would be eliminated, and welfare system would be administered through existing tax agencies based on annual income tax returns.
Waste paper	Establish paper recycling campaign and centers.	Scrap dealers are flooded, so price drops; dealers finally stop buying scrap paper.	Create a large demand for waste paper by having all government agencies buy at least 50% paper products made totally or partially from recycled paper.
Limited supplies of oil and natural gas	Use government regulation to keep prices low for industries and consumers.	Waste is encouraged, finite supplies are depleted more rapidly, prices eventually rise catastrophically but too late to maintain supply, and entire economy is disrupted.	Deregulate prices and add energy taxes so price rises will encourage conservation and help develop other energy sources; use income from energy taxes to develop new sources and to provide relief for the poor.

these variables and their interactions simultaneously. *Third*, well-developed computer models are dynamic and flexible. They can be easily changed, tested, and updated.

In recent years a number of teams have used dynamic computer models to project alternative economic and environmental futures for the world and for various regions. One of the most important and controversial of these world models was developed in 1971 by Jay Forrester. This was refined by Dennis and Donella Meadows and the other members of their interdisciplinary team under the sponsorship of the Club of Rome, an association of about 100 prominent scientists, scholars, and industrialists from 25 nations. The model was data tested for the period 1900–1970, and projections were run to the year 2100. The Forrester-Meadows model was published in popularized form in the book *The Limits to Growth* (see Donella H. Meadows, et al., 1972). The projections of this model were startling; indeed, few books in this century have generated more intense debate. By 1983 more than 3 million copies of this popular and readable book had been printed and translated into 23 different languages.

E2-2 The Forrester-Meadows Global Model

Nature of the Model The Forrester-Meadows model looks at the dynamic interaction of five major variables: population, pollution, natural resources, industrial output per capita, and food per capita. Its developers point out that the model is *extremely crude* in that large multivariable subsystems have been lumped into single systems. For example, all the hundreds of nonrenewable resources, with different and undetermined depletion times are included under a single variable that assumes a supply large enough to last 250 years at 1970 usage rates. Likewise, the pollution variable represents only a "long-lived, globally distributed family of pollutants such as lead, mercury, asbestos, and stable pesticides and radioisotopes."

As with any model, resource supplies, pollution levels, food production, population growth, and industrial growth were estimated from existing knowledge or from educated guesses by experts. Each variable was weighted in the mathematical equations to indicate the intensity of its interaction with other variables. In addition, time-lag variables were introduced to simulate the long delays in feedback processes.* For example, if every couple in the world decided today to have only enough children to replace themselves, it would still take 50 to 70 years for world population to stabilize because there are so many young people in the population (Section 6-5).

The six major assumptions of the Forrester-Meadows model are as follows: **(1)** there is a finite stock of nonrenewable resources, and the lower the supply of such resources, the more capital must be used to obtain them; **(2)** agricultural production depends on a finite amount of land and on the capital investment used to make the land productive; **(3)** the environment has a finite capacity to absorb pollutants produced at exponentially increasing rates; **(4)** the birth rate tends to decrease with a rise in crowding, food intake, pollution, and material standard of living, whereas the death rate decreases with increasing food intake and material standard of living, and increases with increasing pollution and (to a much lesser extent) crowding; **(5)** the material standard of living depends on the level of capital investment (relative to the size of the population) and the productivity of the capital; and **(6)**

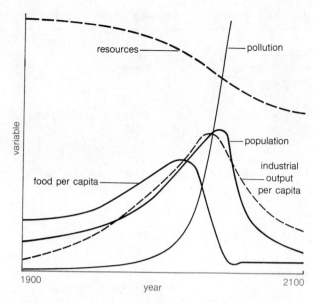

Figure E2-1 Projections of the Forrester-Meadows world model assuming that beginning in 1975, known reserves of resources were doubled and 75 percent of all nonrenewable resources were recycled. At a certain point the soaring pollution curve raises the death rate so that there is a sharp decline in world population. (*These are projections, not predictions.*) (After Meadows et al., *The Limits to Growth*, a Potomac Associates book published by Universe Books, New York, 1972. Used by permission.)

forms of technological change (such as birth control, agricultural yield, and capital productivity) are built into the model, provided there is money to pay for them and assuming that environmental technology (such as resource recycling and pollution control) is also developed.

Projections of the Model One of the nice things about dynamic computer models is that we can play with them by asking various *"What if?"* questions. Let us see what answers the simulated projections of the Forrester-Meadows model give us.

Question 1. *What if*—the population and industrial output continue to expand exponentially at 1970 rates? *Then*—if there are no major changes in the physical, economic, or social relationships that have historically led to these forms of exponential growth, the system will continue to grow exponentially until somewhere around 2020 there will be a global collapse. Nonrenewable resources will be depleted, and there will be a population crash because scarcities of food and medical services will cause death rates to rise. This projection based on present trends, known as the "standard run," was shown in Figure 5-7 and is used as a base for comparing the effects of adopting various policies and strategies to avert such a collapse.

---

*The detailed assumptions, equations, and data underlying the model are found in the technical report (Dennis L. Meadows et al., *The Dynamics of Growth in a Finite World*, 1974) used to back up the more popular presentation of *The Limits to Growth*.

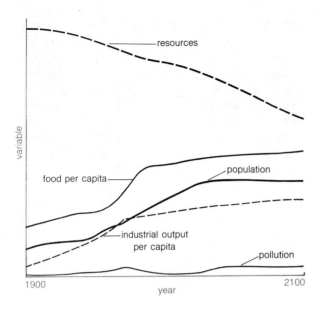

Figure E2-2 Projections of the Forrester-Meadows world model assuming that all the policies listed in question 3 were instituted in 1975. Finally, all variables stabilize. Population rises but then stabilizes, with an average world standard of living higher than today's. (*These are projections, not predictions.*) (After Meadows et al., *The Limits to Growth*, a Potomac Associates book published by Universe Books, New York, 1972. Used by permission.)

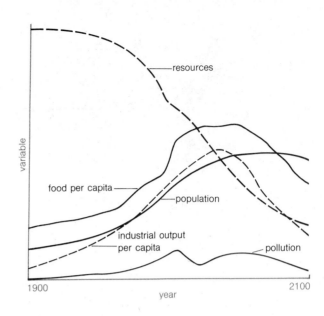

Figure E2-3 Projections of the Forrester-Meadows world model assuming that the policies listed in question 3 are not instituted until the year 2000. Population rises to a much higher level than in Figure E2-2. During the delay in introducing policies, resources are severely depleted, and food and resource shortages begin to reduce population by raising the death rates. (*These are projections, not predictions.*) (After Meadows et al., *The Limits to Growth*, a Potomac Associates book published by Universe Books, New York, 1972. Used by permission.)

Question 2. *What if*—we assume that technological advances will double all nonrenewable resource reserves and allow the recycling of 75 percent of all resources? *Then*—according to the model, pollution will rise so sharply that death rates will rise, leading to a severe population decline (Figure E2-1).

Question 3. *What if*—if beginning in 1975: **(a)** everyone had access to birth control, and couples averaged two children; **(b)** world industrial output per capita were stabilized at 1975 levels; **(c)** resource consumption were reduced to one-fourth of 1970 values per unit of production; **(d)** pollution were reduced to one-fourth of 1970 values per unit of production; **(e)** consumption were shifted from material goods toward services such as education and health; **(f)** capital were directed to food production, soil enrichment, and erosion prevention; and **(g)** the productivity of industrial capital used to develop and build factories and machines were greatly increased. *Then*—population would rise and the standard of living would improve (Figure E2-2).

Question 4. *What if*—we wait until the year 2000 to put the policies of question 3 into effect? *Then*—**(a)** population rise will deplete resources so severely that the population size will eventually drop (Figure E2-3).

E2-3 Evaluating Computer Models

Criticisms of the Forrester-Meadows Model If the Forrester-Meadows model is valid, it challenges the idea that we can continue to have exponentially rising industrial growth and population in a finite world. In other words, sooner or later we must confront the limits to growth on planet earth. The model's developers argue that even though it represents projections—not predictions—it illustrates *that the major variables and problems affecting the world's standard of living cannnot be dealt with separately from one another in the series of simple mental models used by most leaders and governments to develop policies for the future.*

The projections from this model attack some of the fundamental tenets of modern society and project doomsday within 50 years unless we change our ways. Thus, it should not be surprising that there was intense debate over the validity of the model. Many criticisms were anticipated and clearly acknowledged in *The Limits to Growth*. The authors warn us that their model is very crude, uses educated guesses for many important data, oversimplifies by grouping many variables into aggregates, and is a preliminary effort to project current patterns—*not* a prediction of the inevitable. The chal-

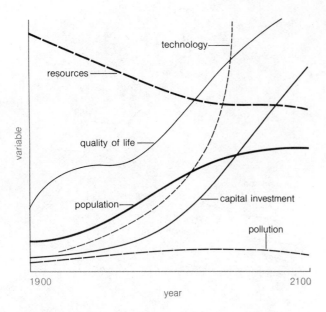

Figure E2-4 A modified version of the Forrester-Meadows model assuming that technology increases exponentially to provide essentially infinite resources, greatly reduced pollution, greatly increased food yields, and perfect birth control for everyone. Population rises, but eventually levels off, resources are not depleted, pollution is kept at low levels, and economic growth and the quality of life keep rising. (*These are projections, not predictions.*) (Modified from Robert Boyd, 1972. "World Dynamics: A Note," *Science*, vol. 177, 516–519.)

lenge is not necessarily for scholars to "believe" in their model but to improve it and to develop other, more sophisticated models.

The major criticism of the model centers on the role of technology in averting catastrophe. The Forrester-Meadows model assumes major technological advances in finding and recycling resources, increasing food productivity, and controlling pollution. But it doesn't assume that technological innovations will increase exponentially on a J-shaped curve and thus solve every problem that might arise. Others, however, believe that technology can grow exponentially. Figure E2-4, for example, shows a modified version of the Forrester-Meadows model using the cornucopian assumption that technological innovations based on human ingenuity *will* grow exponentially. In this case, population rises and then levels off, natural resources are not depleted, pollution levels remain very low, and economic growth and quality of life keep rising.

This result, of course, shouldn't be a surprise. The Forrester-Meadows model was designed to test the implications of different assumptions. Different assumptions should yield different conclusions. The argument in this case is not over the model itself but over which assumptions should be used to give reasonable projections of the future. Neither model can tell us how good our assumptions are.

The Mesarovic-Pestel Model The Forrester-Meadows model is also criticized because it treats the world as a single unit. In reality, the world is divided into rich, poor, and not-so-poor countries and regions, each area having its own economic, food, population, resource, and social problems. To correct this possible defect, the Club of Rome sponsored the development of another computer model that divided the world into 10 fairly homogeneous regions with a submodel for each region. In addition to considering the differences between areas, this approach can aid in developing specific plans for each region. The new model also included assumptions about the amount of economic aid that LDCs might receive from MDCs. The results of this model, issued under the direction of Mihajlo Mesarovic and Eduard Pestel, were presented in popular form in the book *Mankind at the Turning Point* (1974).

The primary conclusions of the Mesarovic-Pestel model are that **(1)** collapses of resource and food supplies and a sharp drop in population are projected before 2050, primarily in the poor regions of the world; **(2)** regional collapses can be prevented only by global cooperation—not confrontation—among the 10 regions, with MDCs using and wasting fewer resources and providing vast amounts of economic aid to the LDCs; **(3)** if any one region fails to cooperate and pursues its own path of rapid population growth or excessive resource use, eventually there will be a collapse in all regions; and **(4)** if the MDCs delay in making massive economic aid available to the LDCs, solutions attempted later will be extremely difficult and expensive.

The Mesarovic-Pestel model did not project that all forms of economic growth must be halted to avoid global collapse, but it did lead its authors to call for less economic growth in the MDCs and more in the LDCs. In general, the conclusions of the Mesarovic-Pestel model at the global level do not differ significantly from those of the Forrester-Meadows model. Indeed, some reviewers found the results of this model even more pessimistic than those of the Forrester-Meadows model.

The Mesarovic-Pestel model has also been criticized for **(1)** incorporating the assumptions of technological optimists, **(2)** being too simplistic politically and economically (by assuming that all the problems of the LDCs can be solved by providing money rather than appropriate technology and technical aid to help them become more self-reliant), **(3)** emphasizing what the MDCs must do rather than what the LDCs must do (such as redistributing land to the poor, and stabilizing population), **(4)** excluding or superficially treating the environmental disruption of the world's fisheries, forests, and air, water, and soil resources, and **(5)** having difficulty determining which of the model's conclusions were already built into the model and which were drawn from it.

Since 1974, this model has been refined and other interdisciplinary groups have developed several other major global models—all described in *Groping in the Dark: The First Decade of Global Modelling*, (Donella Meadows et al., eds., 1982). Despite the wide diversity of these models developed as improvements over the original Forrester-Meadows model, their qualitative projections and conclusions about possible alternative futures for the world if current trends continue are quite similar. *They all conclude that although there must ultimately be real limits to growth, we can change present trends and policies in ways to avert catastrophe and thus supply the basic needs of the world's peoples in the foreseeable future.* One of these more recent models is the *Global 2000 model* developed by the Council on Environmental Quality. Its major conclusions are summarized by Gus Speth in his Guest Editorial at the end of Chapter 1.

Computer Models Are Not Cure-Alls   Despite their usefulness, computer simulation models—no matter how good they become—cannot solve all our problems. They can demonstrate the danger of dealing with only one problem at a time, and they can help us to work with large numbers of interacting variables. But these models cannot choose which assumptions to use or decide which projected alternative solutions are best. Human value judgments enter at every step. Models don't free us from basic ethical and moral questions such as, How much do we really care about the other humans who inhabit the earth and about future generations? and Do we really care about preserving our life-support system, including the other forms of life that share the earth with us? Thus, vigorous debate between cornucopians and neo-Malthusians based on giving different weights to certain assumptions will and should continue so that we can examine these important issues more carefully and critically.

Concern for humanity must always form the chief interest of all technical endeavors in order that the creations of our minds shall be a blessing, not a curse, to humankind. Never forget that in the midst of your diagrams and equations.

Albert Einstein

Discussion Topics

1. Try to add to the examples of unexpected results and counterintuitive solutions shown in Table E2-1.

2. Explain the difference between a projection and a prediction. Why is the Forrester-Meadows model not a prediction?

3. What are some limitations of the Forrester-Meadows and the Mesarovic-Pestel models? What are their major strengths?

4. Debate the following resolution: The Forrester-Meadows, Mesarovic-Pestel, and other global models are useless, misleading gloom-and-doom approaches to the world's problems.

5. Discuss the fallacies of technological optimism (cornucopians) and of technological pessimism (neo-Malthusians). What assumptions underlie the position of each school (see Table 13-1)? Which of these schools of thought, if either, do you support? Why?

Health and Environmental Effects of Nuclear War

The increasingly popular nuclear freeze movement of the 1980s has helped educate a growing number about the dangers of nuclear war. But most people still prefer not to think or even hear about such a horrifying possibility. Somehow we must try and feel the pain and death associated with nuclear war. Listen to the words of a survivor of Hiroshima: "Everything I saw made a deep impression—a park nearby covered with dead bodies waiting to be cremated. . . . Perhaps the most impressive thing I saw was very young girls not only with their clothes torn off but their skin peeled off as well. . . . My immediate thought was that this was like the hell I had always read about."

E3-1 Types and Effects of Nuclear Weapons

Nuclear Fission and Nuclear Fusion Weapons In 1945 the United States dropped a single atomic bomb on Hiroshima and another on Nagasaki: 110,000 people in these two Japanese cities were killed in a flash. By the end of the year another 100,000 had died. Tens of thousands more were severely injured. Even today Japanese citizens continue to die because of leukemia and other ailments traceable to radiation exposure from these two explosions. These figures tell us what a "small" nuclear bomb can do.

Modern nuclear weapons are designed to be dropped as bombs from aircraft or sent to their targets by missiles or artillery shells. There are two major types of nuclear weapon. One is based on *nuclear fission* (Section 15-5) and the other on *nuclear fusion* (Section 15-7). In both types of weapons enormous amounts of energy are released in a fraction of a second in three forms: *heat or thermal radiation* (35 percent of the total energy), *blast and winds* (50 percent of the total energy), and *nuclear radiation* (15 percent, with 5 percent the neutrons and gamma rays released and 10 percent from radioactive fallout).

The *neutron bomb* is a combined nuclear fission–nuclear fusion weapon with the outer blanket of nonfissionable uranium removed. This typically reduces the energy from blast slightly (from 50 to 40 percent), the heat effect from 35 to 25 percent, and indirect radiation from fallout from 10 to 5 percent of the total energy released from detonation of a conventional hydrogen bomb. Without the blanket, the direct radiation effect, primarily from high-speed neutrons, is increased from 5 to 30 percent of the total energy released—killing more people in the vicinity of the blast. The United States plans to install such bombs in some of its short-range nuclear weapons based in Europe. Although the neutron bomb is supposed to be a battlefield weapon, it is still a hydrogen bomb that would cause far greater destruction than any conventional weapon.

The nuclear fission bomb dropped on Hiroshima was a 12.5-kiloton weapon (1 kiloton = 1,000 tons). That is, it released energy equivalent to that from the explosion of 12,500 tons of TNT. The approximately 65,000 nuclear warheads in present-day arsenals (30,000 in the United States and 35,000 in the Soviet Union) range in size from 1 kiloton to 50 megatons (one megaton = 1 million tons)—the latter having an explosive force 4,000 times greater than the Hiroshima weapon. By comparison, all the bombs dropped during the 8.5 years the United States used such weapons in Vietnam were equivalent to 4 megatons or 4 million tons of TNT. A single U.S. Poseidon submarine or a single B-52 bomber carries nuclear fire power equivalent to 720 Hiroshima bombs or equivalent to all the explosives detonated in World War II, and 30 to 40 of these submarines and scores of these bombers are always on patrol. Typical strategic nuclear weapons have yields of about one megaton—80 times the explosive power of the Hiroshima bomb.

Effects from a Nuclear Explosion When a nuclear weapon is detonated, so much energy is released that everything in the immediate vicinity of *ground zero*—the spot directly beneath the point of detonation—is heated to temperatures of tens of millions of degrees. This is high enough to melt any material. The first effect is a silent pulse of *heat or* *thermal radiation* traveling at the speed of light. In a fraction of a second this heat can cause third-degree burns, char the skin of unprotected persons, and blind anyone looking at the explosion up to several miles from ground zero. The initial heat pulse ignites paper and combustible material within several miles from ground zero, as well.

This heat pulse is followed by a gigantic *fireball* expanding outward from ground zero. A few seconds after detonation the fireball cools to several hundred thousand degrees and continues to expand at the speed of sound—about 1,190 kilometers (740 miles) per hour. At this point the superheated and highly radioactive debris blown outward from ground zero catches up with the outer edge of the fireball and moves forward with it as a devastating shock wave called *blast*. This shock wave produces an increase in air pressure, known as *overpressure*, and *winds* with speeds up to 322 kilometers (200 miles) per hour—higher than those from any recorded hurricane. This overpressure crushes wooden, brick, and concrete structures for miles from ground zero. Many people and animals not killed by the heat and falling buildings die when hurled through the air by the hurricane-force winds or when struck by flying debris.

The combination of overpressure and winds creates fires for miles around, from overturned furnaces and stoves, electrical short circuits, and ruptured gas lines and fuel storage tanks. Under certain conditions, these individual fires could combine to form a single *firestorm* that would burn over a large area for days. Violent winds would rush in and feed the flames, producing extremely high temperatures. If a firestorm occurred, many people in underground shelters would be killed by heat, lack of oxygen, and carbon monoxide entering through ventilation systems.

Near ground zero large amounts of *direct radiation* in the form of highly penetrating gamma rays and neutrons are released. Although this intense radiation does not last long, it would kill people and animals not killed by the fireball and blast wave within 1 to 14 days. Additional *indirect radiation* is produced when neutrons from the explosion collide with earth and other matter to produce radioactive debris, which is sucked up into the mushroom cloud. Depending on weather conditions, this radioactive material is carried by winds hundreds and in some cases thousands of miles downwind from the blast. This matter, known as *radioactive fallout*, settles out of the atmosphere and contaminates large areas of land, water, and food supplies. Fallout contains many different types of radioactive material, decaying at different rates (Section 15-5). Thus, areas receiving heavy fallout would remain dangerously contaminated for several weeks. People

in these areas who did not remain in shelters would be exposed to enough radiation to cause acute radiation sickness and death, and those exposed to nonlethal doses could develop cataracts, leukemia, and other forms of cancer years later (Table 15-3). There would also be an increase in the number of stillbirths and deformed births, and genetic defects passed on to future generations.

If a nuclear weapon is exploded on the ground or at an altitude low enough for the fireball to reach the ground, large amounts of fallout are produced. An air burst high in the atmosphere would not produce as large a *local fallout* hazard as a ground burst. Instead, fission products would be carried into the upper atmosphere and dispersed as *global fallout*.

E3-2 Health and Environmental Effects of Global Nuclear War

Increasing Risks of All-Out Nuclear War Some military planners talk of limited nuclear war. Most analysts, however, believe that the chances of a limited nuclear war escalating into an all-out nuclear war are very high. *All-out nuclear war* or *global nuclear war* is usually defined as a massive first strike by either the United States or the Soviet Union against strategic military targets and major economic-industrial centers, followed by a retaliatory strike by the other country. Thousands of high-yield nuclear warheads would be detonated in such an exchange, which could take place within an hour.

The risk of accidental nuclear war increases as the size of the arsenals and the number of people involved with nuclear weapons increase. In the United States about 100,000 carefully screened people are authorized to work with or around nuclear weapons. Between 1975 and 1977, however, 15,067 of these individuals were removed from access to nuclear weapons for a variety of reasons including alcohol and drug abuse, aberrant mental behavior, negligence, and evidence of a contemptuous attitude toward the law. The record of mistakes by the computers that are supposed to warn of a nuclear attack is equally alarming. During an 18-month period the North American Air Defense Command had 151 false alarms. Four resulted in orders to alert B-52 bomber crews and intercontinental ballistic missile units for possible attack. One major false alert, lasting 6 minutes, occurred when a technician mistakenly put a training tape of a Soviet attack on an American military computer.

The risk of nuclear war also increases as the number of countries having nuclear weapons increases. By mid-1984, the United States, the Soviet Union, Great Britain, France, China, and India had built and tested nuclear weapons. Another 10 countries are believed to have the knowledge and materials necessary to build a nuclear bomb, and 16 others could have the bomb by 1990. Between 1990 and 2000, it is estimated that the total of nations capable of building nuclear weapons could increase from 32 to 60—*one out of every three nations in the world* (Section 15-5). Most of the knowledge and materials enabling an increasing number of nations to join the global "nuclear arms club" is the result of the United States, the Soviet Union, France, Italy, and West Germany giving or selling them commercial nuclear power plants and small research nuclear reactors (Section 15-5).

Health Effects   A number of studies of the likely consequences of all-out nuclear war have been made. According to the World Health Organization, an exchange involving about one-third of the U.S. and Soviet nuclear arsenal—about 5,000 megatons— would kill at least 1.1 billion people in the Northern Hemisphere (mostly in the United States, Europe, and the Soviet Union) immediately, with another 1.1 billion so seriously injured and lacking medical care that they would soon die. Since atmospheric circulation patterns would carry radioactive debris over most of the world, at least 1 billion more people in the Southern Hemisphere—not under direct nuclear attack—are likely to die prematurely. Thus, a nuclear war (5,000 megatons) between the superpowers would probably kill from 50 to 75 percent of the world's population.

The U.S. Federal Emergency Management Agency has determined that 65 percent of the U.S. population lives within 32 kilometers (20 miles) of at least one prime military-industrial target, and 95 percent are within 160 kilometers (100 miles) of such targets. Thus, in the United States an estimated 165 million to 200 million people would be killed—almost half the population. Another 60 million would be injured, with 30 million contracting radiation sickness, 20 million experiencing trauma and burns, and 10 million suffering from a combination of trauma, burns, and radiation sickness. An estimated 80 percent of all physicians would be killed and 80 percent of the hospital beds would be destroyed, along with most stores of blood plasma, antibiotics, and other drugs. Most of the injured would have no morphine for pain, no facilities for emergency surgery, and no antibiotics to fight infection.

There would be little food or water that was not contaminated with radiation or with toxic chemicals released into the atmosphere from the destruction and burning of chemical plants and storage tanks. Epidemic diseases long under control—such as cholera, dysentery, typhoid fever, hepatitis, tuberculosis, and plague—could reemerge to threaten all survivors. The severe psychological shock caused by exposure to overwhelming death and destruction would contribute to the deaths of many of those already sick or injured.

Even the estimated third of the population who escaped death and serious injury would face immense hardships and danger. Most would have to stay in shelters under grim conditions for from 1 week to 3 months or more, depending on location, to avoid exposure to dangerous radiation levels. Many shelters would be overcrowded and supplies of food, water, and medicine would be inadequate. Since national electric power and communications systems would be knocked out by the explosions and by the electromagnetic pulses (EMPs) produced during the first few billionths of a second of the attack (Section 15-5), shelters would be dark, damp, cold, and isolated from the outside world. Sick people would vomit frequently; waste disposal systems would be primitive; and diseases such as cholera and dysentery would run rampant—all adding to the panic, stress, and acute psychological shock.

Environmental Effects   Studies published in 1983 and reviewed by more than 100 prominent scientists indicate that survivors emerging from fallout shelters would face a number of short- and long-term survival problems. Within one to two weeks, the massive amounts of dust and soot injected in the lower atmosphere and into the stratosphere would coalesce into a massive dark cloud that would prevent 96 percent of incoming sunlight from reaching most of the Northern Hemisphere, particularly the mid-latitude belt encompassing most of the United States, Canada, Europe, the Soviet Union, and Japan. Incoming sunlight would remain at less than 50 percent of normal for nearly two months. With most of the sunlight blocked, temperatures would drop well below freezing, whatever the season, and remain that way for many weeks. A 5,000-megaton exchange could drop average continental temperatures in the Northern Hemisphere to about $-23°C$ with recovery taking about three months. Even a relatively small nuclear war involving bombs totaling 100 megatons—0.8 percent of the combined nuclear arsenals of the United States and the Soviet Union—would produce sufficient smoke and dust to blacken skies for about six weeks and cool average temperatures in the Northern Hemisphere to $-20°C$ for over two months.

During the resulting "nuclear winter" of darkness and subfreezing temperatures, most livestock, wild mammals, cultivated and uncultivated food supplies, at least in the Northern Hemisphere, would die from the effects of radiation and cold. Food supplies from crops, livestock, wildlife, or fish and other aquatic species would be very scarce for at least a year because photosynthesis by plants on the land and phytoplankton in the sea would cease from lack of sunlight. Thick ice would cover inland surface waters and plagues of insects—the animal life best equipped to survive nuclear war—would damage stored food and spread disease. In addition, huge coastal storms created by land-sea temperature gradients would cause further destruction.

Most crops not destroyed would be contaminated with radioactive fallout particles such as strontium-90, which can be concentrated to higher levels as it passes through food chains and webs. In humans this radioisotope concentrates in the bones, where it can cause leukemia. Radioactive fallout particles such as iodine-131, which can cause thyroid cancer, would contaminate the soil and exposed water systems, also being concentrated to higher levels in the food chain. Radioactive isotopes also tend to concentrate in freshwater fish, and eating contaminated fish would be more dangerous than drinking contaminated water. Humans would only be able to drink groundwater supplies and only then if they had hand-operated pumps or emergency diesel-fueled generators to operate electric pumps.

Countless populations of plant species and animal wildlife would be extinct or contaminated, reducing for years the feasibility of trying to stay alive by hunting and gathering. Large areas of forest and grasslands would be devastated by blast and by fires that would burn out of control for weeks, perhaps months, adding more soot to the atmosphere. The soil—essential to the reestablishment of both plants and animals—on the denuded land would begin to be washed into rivers and eventually, when the rains from winter storms arrived, into the sea. People who went to the shore hoping to subsist on seafood would find most aquatic species surviving the nuclear winter contaminated with radioactivity, silt, and runoff from ruptured tanks of industrial liquids and oil pouring out of damaged offshore rigs. Any farmers in areas where crops could still be grown would be cut off from supplies of seeds, fertilizer, pesticides, and fuel.

The numerous nuclear explosions would cause nitrogen and oxygen in the stratosphere to combine and produce large amounts of nitrogen oxides which would destroy most of the thin and fragile ozone layer that shields the earth from damaging ultra-violet radiation. According to a study by the National Academy of Sciences, all-out nuclear war could cause within a year a 30 to 70 percent reduction of ozone in the Northern Hemisphere and a 20 to 40 percent reduction in the Southern Hemisphere. It would take from 2 to 20 years for the ozone layer to regenerate itself. Meanwhile, the sharp increase in ultraviolet rays reaching the earth's surface would lead to an increase in skin cancers, lethal sunburns, and lethal levels of vitamin D in unprotected people, and blindness and genetic damage (mutations) in many forms of plant and animal life. Levels of nitrogen oxides would also be increased 5 to 50 times in the lower atmosphere—causing large increases in acid deposition (Section 19-4). This would further threaten food crops and many aquatic and land-based life forms.

The partial destruction of the ozone layer and the reduction of sunlight from particulate matter in the atmosphere could also change the climate in unpredictable ways throughout the world. This, along with global fallout and the breakdown in international trade in food, fertilizers, fuel, farm machinery, and technology, could cause waves of famine, disease, severe economic depression, and social unrest in the surviving nations, mostly in the Southern Hemisphere. Although global nuclear war would probably not extinguish the human species, technological society as we know it wouldn't survive. The soils and forests would gradually regenerate themselves after a global nuclear war. But much of humanity would be reduced to small scattered bands of survivors, necessarily returning to a species of hunters, gatherers, and simple farmers (Enrichment Study 1).

The choice is really between two ways of life. One response is to decline to face the peril, and thus to go on piling up the instruments of doom year after year until, by accident or design, they go off. The other response is to recognize the peril, dismantle the weapons, and arrange the political affairs of the earth so that the weapons will not be built again.

Jonathan Schell

Guest Editorial: Nuclear War—The Worst Environmental Threat

Hannes Alfvén

Hannes Alfvén has been professor of applied physics at the University of California, San Diego, since 1967. Before that he was professor of plasma physics at the Royal Institute of Technology in Stockholm, Sweden. He has been science advisor to the Swedish government and member of the Swedish Atomic Energy Commission. In 1970 he received the Nobel Prize in physics. In recent years Hannes Alfvén has used his expert knowledge to warn the world of the grave dangers of nuclear war and nuclear power plants.

The environmentalist movement is now a major factor in the political life of the United States and of the whole world. It started long ago as a protest against the factory around the corner that stinks or fouls the water in the river you used to swim in, or mars the scenic view from your window. Two or three decades ago it was found that in many cases industry had much more serious effects. It made the spring "silent," its waste killed fish and wildlife and was also dangerous to human beings. The processes by which this damage happens are sometimes very complicated and cannot be understood without careful studies of how nature works and how it is affected by industrial wastes.

This introduced a second phase in the environmentalist movement: It was obvious that unless environmentalists acquired at least the same competence in these problems as the industrialists, their fight against industrial pollution was hopeless. This challenge has given rise to the new interdisciplinary field of human ecology, which is introduced in this book.

A third phase in this movement began with the controversy over nuclear energy. The nuclear industry presented nuclear energy as a perfectly clean, cheap, and inexhaustible supply of energy, a wonderful result of the most sophisticated science and technology: no smoke, no dirty water. When some environmentalists objected, they were denounced as ignoramuses. They would understand that nuclear energy was a savior of humanity if only they studied the matter more closely.

The environmentalists followed this advice. Guided by a few very competent biologists, they learned how radioactivity induces cancer and produces genetic damage, and they discovered that the methods to keep the radioactive substances isolated from the air, water, and soil might work in a technological paradise but are unlikely to work in the real world. Now an increasing number of environmentalists have the same knowledge as the nuclear insiders. They can now judge nuclear energy without the unavoidable bias of those who have devoted a lifetime to the development of nuclear power or have invested $100 billion in this development. The result of this spread of knowledge seems to be catastrophic to the nuclear industry: It is increasingly difficult to claim that the radioactive substances are under control; it is increasingly dubious that nuclear energy is cheap; and it is quite clear that there are several other and better ways of solving the energy problem.

The environmentalists have also learned that the most serious objection to nuclear energy is its coupling to nuclear arms. It is now generally admitted that any country—large or small—that can build nuclear reactors will eventually get a nuclear arms capability. The peaceful atom and the militant atom are Siamese twins. This fact has led the environmentalist movement into its fourth phase, which is likely to be the most difficult but also the most important.

Everybody knows that war is more destructive to the environment—and to the human beings living in it—than anything else. Everybody knows that the destruction caused by nuclear arms is enormous compared with that by conventional arms, and that both the United States and the Soviet Union have enough nuclear arms to destroy the whole world. But most people prefer not to think about such horrible things, much less talk about them. They hope that war is something that takes place somewhere else and that it cannot be a threat to *their* environment. But this hope is false and dangerous in the thermonuclear missile age. It is encouraging that in the 1980s large numbers of concerned citizens in the United States and Europe have taken such matters of life and death into their own hands and have created the widely supported nuclear freeze movement. Hopefully, this will encourage more and more environmentalists to lend their support and knowledge to this important global movement.

To protect national security, there are a large number of underground silos in the United States, each containing a missile with a hydrogen bomb warhead. In each of them, four young officers, relieved every morning, are ready round the clock to launch their missiles at the order of the president. Once launched, such a missile will undoubtedly reach its target and will very likely kill a million innocent people. This is a threat to the rest of the world, but not to Americans. However, the Soviets have similar silos, which they claim are necessary for their national security—to deter the United States from blackmailing and killing them. To increase the "security" of the world still more, there are many nuclear submarines and aircraft carrying nuclear arms. Furthermore, when the sales drive of the nuclear industry has spread nuclear power plants to an increasing number of countries, a similar spread of nuclear arms capability will be unavoidable.

Political and military leaders in the United States have attempted to analyze in detail what will happen if a nuclear war breaks out. Considering that no political or military leadership was able to predict how World War I, World War II, or the Vietnam war would develop, we have little reason to suppose that present predictions--which, moreover, are top military secrets—have very much to do with reality. Many people outside the establishment believe that the first few nuclear bombs released will create such political tension that a number of irrational actions will follow, and that after a few hours the result will be nuclear holocaust. It is not certain that the human race would be eliminated, but there would be such destruction of ourselves and our environment that our concern for the stinking factory around the corner, the silent spring, and even the nuclear power plant would seem trivial.

What can the environmentalists do about this? I think the key to the fourth phase of our struggle for a new and better world is the same as in the earlier phases: more knowledge and more concern. We must realize now that our legitimate demand for national security

cannot be satisfied through nuclear armament. Instead, the enormous increase in destruction capability results in a global "insecurity" both for this and for all nations.

As long as the environmentalists were ignorant, there could be no efficient opposition against nuclear energy. As long as the environmentalists know next to nothing about the global destructive power that the political and military leaders of the world have prepared and are perfecting, there will be no popular movement strong enough to avert the approaching catastrophe. But if we all learn about the real situation in the world and act accordingly, there might still be time to stop the "race to oblivion."

Guest Editorial Discussion

1. Have you seriously thought about nuclear war as the world's most serious environmental hazard? Why or why not?

2. Do you think or talk about the possibilities of nuclear war? Why or why not? What causes most people to ignore this subject?

3. What is the connection between the peaceful use of nuclear energy in nuclear power plants and the possible spread of nuclear weapons?

4. Should we ban nuclear power plants in the United States? Why or why not? Should the United States ban export of nuclear power plants and technology to other nations? Why or why not?

Discussion Topics

1. Are you more concerned that the United States will become involved in a limited war like the war in Vietnam or that the United States will become involved in a major war with the Soviet Union? Why?

2. Do you think that a limited war between the United States and the Soviet Union could become an all-out nuclear war? Why or why not?

3. Do you think that your own chances of living through an all-out nuclear war between the United States and the Soviet Union are good, poor, or about 50-50? Why? Compare your answer with those of other members of your class.

4. Someone has remarked that most of the survivors of

a global nuclear war would envy the dead. Do you agree or disagree? Why?

5. Do you believe that the industrialized nations of the world should pledge not to sell or give any additional nuclear power plants or any related forms of nuclear technology to other nations as one way to reduce the risk of nuclear war? Why or why not?

6. There are complex arguments between two opposing groups in the United States, one favoring a freeze on the production of nuclear weapons and the other saying that this would put the nation at a strategic disadvantage and increase the risk of nuclear war. Use the library to research the position of each group and determine your own position. Compare your position with other members of your class and debate this crucial issue.

Enrichment Study 4

Space: High Frontier or Garbage Dump?

E4-1 Space Colonies

Faced with increasing population, pollution, and resource use on earth, some scientists have proposed that space can serve as a "new frontier." Even if we make a garbage dump out of this planet, they argue, we can reduce the effects of overpopulation by shipping people off to space colonies and building other giant solar power satellites to provide us with all the electricity we need. Physicist Gerald K. O'Neill and other scientists have developed detailed plans for putting 1 million people in self-sufficient orbiting space colonies by 2050. Each colony would contain about 10,000 people and would have hills, streams, plants, and wildlife.

Critics of this idea say that it is arrogant to think that we can create and maintain such diverse life-support systems in space for a million people and a variety of plants and other animals when we have yet to understand the complex interactions that maintain life in a small pond or patch of forest.

But let's wave a magic technological wand and assume that starting today we can build a series of livable space colonies. Such colonies would not even put a dent in the world's population problem. After about 70 years and draining the earth of hundreds of trillions of dollars of investment capital, we *might* be able to provide a space habitat for a million people—equal to the world's population increase during the first 4.5 days of the project! Just to stay even with today's world population growth, we would have to ship away about 81 million passengers a year, or 9,250 persons each hour, at incredible cost, use of the world's resources, and damage to the environment. The colonists would have neither security nor freedom. Their lives would depend on the smooth functioning of a complex technological system that probably would at times be governed by Murphy's law (if anything can go wrong, it will) and its corollary (Murphy was an optimist). Furthermore, survival in such a vulnerable habitat would require that each colonist's actions be rigidly controlled by a central authority.

E4-2 Solar-Powered Satellites

Other scientists have proposed that the United States build 60 solar-powered satellites (SPS) in space. Each satellite would use billions of solar photovoltaic cells to convert solar energy into electricity and then convert the electricity to microwaves. The microwaves would be **(1)** beamed to earth and received at giant 225-square-kilometer (55,000-acre) microwave antenna farms, taking up about 1.5 percent of all U.S. land area, **(2)** converted to electricity, and **(3)** fed out over the nation through high-voltage power lines.

Each satellite would be about half the size of Manhattan and would weigh about 51 million kilograms (56,000 tons). Construction of the system would require a trip a day for 30 years by space vehicles with 13 times the cargo capacity of the present space shuttle. To prevent the earth from being drained of vital resources, planners believe that some of the materials for these satellites and O'Neill's space colonies could be mined from the moon and possibly asteroids—rocks ranging in size from a speck of sand to as big as the state of Texas that orbit the sun, mainly between Mars and Jupiter. All this would cost at least $3 trillion and would provide only about 20 percent of projected U.S. electricity demand by the year 2025, at 10 times the price of electricity today.

Such a system would provide electricity 24 hours a day because the satellites' solar cells would be bathed almost continuously in solar energy, which is more intense in space than on the earth's surface. But critics of this scheme point out that the demand for electricity between 1 A.M. and 6 A.M. is not large enough to justify such a large drain of capital, which could be used to develop many other energy alternatives (Chapters 14, 15, and 16).

In 1981 separate evaluations of this proposal by the Office of Technology Assessment, the National Academy of Sciences, and panels of independent scientists recommended against providing funds for building SPSs at this time. These studies concluded that there were probably insurmountable technological, economic, environmental, and political hurdles in building such systems and in providing raw materials from the moon and from asteroids.

E4-3 Existing Satellites: Benefits and Problems

Although planners envision SPSs and space colonies as creating little pollution, the trash we have already discarded on the moon and in space casts doubt on this expectation. *The vastness of space merely encourages the throwaway mentality.* By mid-1984 between 10,000 to 15,000 large objects—satellites that no longer work, empty fuel tanks, and garbage discarded from space missions—were orbiting the earth. Littering space in addition were tens of millions of small metal fragments from the more than 60 satellite and rocket explosions and from killer satellite tests. Objects in low earth orbit circle freely until the slow wear of molecular friction and the force of gravity cause them to reenter the earth's atmosphere at high speeds and in most cases burn up. Since 1957 almost 9,700 such objects have fallen from orbit, including two nuclear-powered Soviet satellites that disintegrated and showered radioactive debris on the earth.

Most of this debris, which is increasing at a rate of about 11 percent a year, is in heavily traveled orbital routes, where it can collide with satellites and spacecraft such as space shuttles. North American Air Defense Command (NORAD) officials warn that space is being so overrun with space debris that detection of incoming missiles is becoming increasingly difficult—thus increasing the risk of nuclear war.

The many satellites now orbiting the earth have a variety of useful functions. These include **(1)** improving global communications (worldwide satellite communications is already a $2 billion-a-year business and is expected to reach $10 billion by 1990), **(2)** providing information for weather forecasting (today's 24-hour forecasts have the same accuracy— 84 percent—as 12-hour forecasts did 15 years ago, and equally accurate 5-day forecasts should be available soon), **(3)** giving advance warnings of hurricanes and typhoons, **(4)** locating and monitoring the growth of crops, forests, grasslands, and fisheries (by 1979, the economic benefits of satellite crop forecasting were about $325 million a year, greatly exceeding the $80 million cost of the program), **(5)** locating deposits of mineral and fossil fuel resources, especially in remote areas, **(6)** monitoring global, regional, and local pollution, and **(7)** helping us understand how the earth's atmosphere, oceans, sunlight, and diverse life forms interact and how they are reacting to the stresses placed on them by human activities.

Many of these peaceful uses of space, however, are not well funded and are overshadowed by emphasis on military uses. By mid-1984 about 81 percent of U.S. and 75 percent of Soviet spending for space programs was for military purposes. If unchecked, these attempts to dominate space militarily could destroy the satellites used for peaceful purposes, divert funds from the peaceful uses of space, and increase the risk of thermonuclear war.

Space exploration has taught us just how rare and precious the earth is.

Daniel Deudney

Discussion Topics

1. Do you believe that large sums of U.S. taxpayer dollars should be used to build large colonies in space? Why or why not?

2. Do you believe that large sums of U.S. taxpayer dollars should be used to build solar-powered satellites to provide the country with electricity? Why or why not?

3. What are the major advantages and disadvantages of calling space the "new frontier"?

4. Explain how space garbage could increase the likelihood of global nuclear war.

5. Do you agree or disagree with the present U.S. and Soviet policies that allocate about three out of every four dollars spent on space activities for military purposes? Why or why not?

Enrichment Study 5

Are We Changing the World's Climate?

E5-1 Possible Effects of Human Activities on Climate

Projecting Future Climate Changes There is a vigorous debate between climatologists over how the overall global climate might change and to what degree human activities might influence these changes. Climate experts have made three general projections about climate change in the next few decades: **(1)** We can't tell what will happen; **(2)** it will get colder because of long-term natural trends in global climate or a combination of natural trends and human activities; and **(3)** it will get warmer over the next century primarily because of human activities that counteract the natural and human-caused cooling trends.

Since these projections cover all the major possibilities, you might wonder why we need experts. However, climate change is a highly complex process, influenced by many factors that interact over short and long periods. Climatologists have developed mathematical models, which are fed into computers to project the effects of changing one climatic factor (such as increasing atmospheric carbon dioxide levels from burning fossil fuels and deforestation) on other climatic factors. Despite these important advances and improved climatic data obtained from satellites, the models are fairly crude.

Why Worry About Climate Change? If the experts can't agree, why should we worry about this issue? Why not wait until the smoke clears and we have a better understanding of climate change? Unfortunately, we can't afford this tempting luxury. Climate change is too important in human affairs to permit the postponement of action until more thorough scientific understanding has been achieved.

Although climatologists disagree on how climate will change and on what the major causes of change are, they generally agree that there probably will be some rather far-reaching changes in climate over the next century. Just a slight rise or fall in the mean global temperature of the atmosphere can trigger effects that could be with us for thousands of years.

Climate and Human Activities Until recently it was assumed that human activities had relatively little effect on global and regional climate compared with volcanic eruptions, sunspots, and other natural phenomena. Now we have evidence that human activities are affecting local climates now, especially in and near urban areas (Section E5-4), and could have major effects on regional and global climate.

From Table E5-1 we see that most human activities tend to warm the lower atmosphere. This is in contrast to the natural trends, which according to past climatic history may lead to cooling. Natural climate trends, however, develop over thousands to hundreds of thousands of years, whereas human activities could trigger climate changes within several decades.

In the remainder of this enrichment study we will look more closely at the possible effects of increasing the amounts of carbon dioxide, particles, and heat in the atmosphere from human activities. The potential effects of Freons on the ozone layer were discussed in Section 5-3.

E5-2 Carbon Dioxide and the Greenhouse Effect: Is the Atmosphere Warming?

The Greenhouse Effect About 70 percent of the incoming radiant energy from the sun passes through the atmosphere and strikes the surface of the earth much like light passing through glass. This incoming radiation is absorbed by the land and water and radiated back toward space as longer-wavelength infrared (IR) radiation, or heat energy (Figure 3-10). But not all this infrared heat makes it back into space. Instead some is absorbed primarily by carbon dioxide (CO_2) gas and water vapor (H_2O) in the atmosphere and reradiated toward the earth's surface to warm the lower atmosphere.

Table E5-1 Climate and Human Activities

Human Activity	Probable Climatic Effect	Present Area of Impact	Estimated Time Before Major Global Impact	Potential for Controlling
Release of carbon dioxide from burning fossil fuels	Warming of lower atmosphere (greenhouse effect) and cooling of upper atmosphere	Regional to global (variable)	25 to 100 years, depending on fossil fuel use	Poor unless fossil fuels are abandoned
Diffusion of chlorofluorohydrocarbons (CFCs) into the stratosphere	Warming of lower atmosphere and cooling of upper atmosphere; reduction of stratospheric ozone, allowing more harmful ultraviolet radiation to reach the earth (Section 5-3)	Regional to global	Major impact within 20 to 30 years	Poor unless worldwide use of CFCs is banned
Land clearing (deforestation, agriculture, overgrazing, irrigation)	Warming or cooling of lower atmosphere because of changes in surface albedo (reflectivity); warming because of CO_2 released from land clearing	Local, regional	Speculative, 20 to 200 years	Fair to poor
Release of particles (aerosols) from industry, burning of fossil fuels, and land clearing and desertification	May cool lower atmosphere by reflecting sunlight over water or heat lower atmosphere by absorbing sunlight over land or ice fields	Local, regional	Unknown	Fair (large particles) to poor (fine particles)
Release of heat from urbanization and burning of fossil and nuclear fuels faster than the heat can be radiated back into space	Direct warming of lower atmosphere	Local, regional	100 to 200 years or never if energy use levels off	Poor unless energy use levels off

This warming effect is sometimes called the **greenhouse effect,** because the atmosphere acts similarly to the glass in a greenhouse or a car window, which allows visible light to enter but hinders the escape of long-wavelength infrared heat.* The mean global atmospheric temperature today is about 10°C (18°F) warmer than it would be without any carbon dioxide or water vapor in the atmosphere. The oceans, as part of the carbon cycle, dissolve within a few years an estimated one-third to one-half of all carbon dioxide injected into the atmosphere. Without this major sink, the average global concentration of carbon dioxide would probably be at least twice its present value and the average global temperature would be considerably higher.

Because of the large amount of water vapor and its relatively rapid rate of cycling, humans can do little to upset the average water concentration in the atmosphere. However, carbon dioxide now makes up only 0.03 percent of the atmosphere. This relatively small average concentration can be increased significantly as the earth's fossil fuels are burned up and as forests are cleared and the wood is burned. When coal, oil, natural gas, wood, or any carbon-containing fuel is burned, carbon dioxide is released into the atmosphere.

Green plants and trees also remove some of the carbon dioxide from the atmosphere through photosynthesis (Section 4-3) during their growing season and return it during winter when fallen leaves decay. This causes annual fluctuations in the average concentration of carbon dioxide in the atmosphere (Figure E5-1). However, if plants and trees throughout the world are cut down and burned faster than they are replanted or faster than they regrow, the amount of carbon dioxide released will be greater than that removed by natural processes.

Increasing Carbon Dioxide Levels Figure E5-1 shows that the average atmospheric concentration of carbon dioxide has been increasing. This increase in atmospheric carbon dioxide since 1850, and especially since 1958, is believed to have resulted primarily from the burning of fossil fuels and from deforestation. Because of lack of information, there is considerable debate over how much carbon dioxide has been added by deforestation in recent years;

---

*Strictly speaking, the term *greenhouse effect* is misleading. A greenhouse, or a closed car on a sunny day, not only traps heat energy but also keeps the warmed air from blowing away and carrying with it the added warmth. Even though technically inexact, the use of this term is widespread.

Figure E5-1 Rising concentration of carbon dioxide as recorded at Mauna Loa Observatory in Hawaii. Annual variations arise because carbon dioxide is removed from the air by plants during the summer growing season and is returned in winter by the decay of fallen leaves.

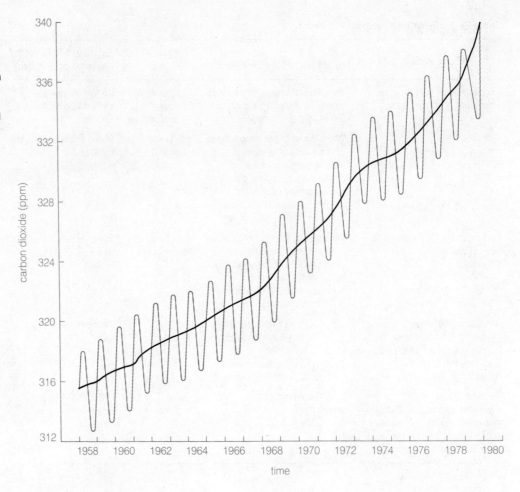

estimates range from 20 percent of the carbon dioxide added from burning fossil fuels to half or more.

Numerous mathematical models have been developed to project how observed changes in average global temperature compare with those based on increases in atmospheric carbon dioxide levels and other factors (Figure E5-2). Scientists have fed such models into computers to project what might happen to average global temperatures based on certain assumptions about the total amount of fossil fuels that might be burned in coming decades and the role of the oceans and plants in removing some of the resulting carbon dioxide from the atmosphere. A recent report by the National Academy of Sciences (see *Changing Climate*, 1983) indicated a general consensus among 70 atmospheric scientists that a doubling of the 1980 atmospheric carbon dioxide levels (Figure E5-1) to 680 ppm would raise the average global temperature of the atmosphere between 1.5 and 4.5°C (2.7 and 8.1°F). Perhaps even more significant, the projected average temperature rise in the North Pole region is projected to be about two to three times larger than the average global increase, with temperature increases as much as 7 to 10°C (13 to 18°F).

Assuming that the use of fossil fuels continues to grow at present rates, that the oceans and plant life remove 50 percent of the total carbon dioxide added to the atmosphere, and that all other factors remain constant, the NAS report projects a 50 percent probability that carbon dioxide levels will double between 2050 and 2100 and a 95 percent probability that they will reach 540 ppm by 2100.

The increase in atmospheric carbon dioxide and the resulting temperature change could occur more rapidly or more slowly than these models predict. For example, scientists still do not know whether the ability of the oceans to remove carbon dioxide will increase or decrease. Some scientists hypothesize that as the lower atmosphere warms, some of the gas now dissolved in the oceans might be released—like the dissolved carbon dioxide released when soda pop or beer warms up. This could accelerate the warming, release even more dissolved carbon dioxide, and intensify the warming effect.

Conversely, the warming of the atmosphere could evaporate more water from the ocean, producing more clouds, which would shield and cool the ocean surface, thus hindering the release of carbon dioxide. But whether clouds tend to warm or

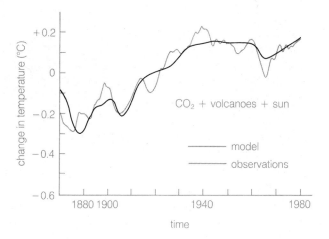

Figure E5-2 Comparison of observed average global temperature changes between 1880 and 1980 and those computed from a mathematical model, including increases in atmospheric carbon dioxide levels, increases in atmospheric particles from volcanic activity, and changes in the energy output of the sun.

cool the earth depends on their altitude; low-level clouds tend to cool the atmosphere, and high-level clouds tend to warm the earth, since water droplets absorb infrared radiation. Scientists are also uncertain about the precise role and projected future importance of other atmospheric components, such as particles released by volcanic eruptions and human activities (Table E5-1) and sulfur dioxide released by the burning of coal and oil (Section 19-4), both of which tend to cool the atmosphere (Section E5-3).

Higher carbon dioxide levels could also increase the rate of photosynthesis, causing plants to grow faster and thus removing more carbon dioxide from the atmosphere. However, even if this hypothesis is valid, such a phenomenon could be overcome by increased cloudiness and deforestation. Atmospheric carbon dioxide levels could also be raised or lowered by unexpected fluctuations in the amount of energy radiated by the sun (solar luminosity).

Possible Effects of Global Warming Why worry about all this? At first thought a slightly warmer climate might seem desirable, resulting in longer growing seasons and possible increases in crop productivity in some parts of the world. The milder winters would also save fuel, although some of these savings would be canceled by increased use of air conditioning during the hotter summers.

Unfortunately along with benefits for some parts of the world there could be serious consequences in other areas. The projected change in average global temperature could modify the distribution of rainfall and snowfall over much of the earth,

reduce the length of crop growing seasons in some parts of the world, and cause some melting of glaciers and ice fields in polar regions, which could cause sea levels to rise.

According to the 1983 NAS study, the most likely threat from global warming over the next 50 to 100 years would be shifts in food-growing regions and capacity during a time when the world's population is expected to at least double. Rainfall and snowfall patterns would shift, and some presently productive cropland would have to be abandoned and replaced with land of unknown quality. Existing irrigation and drainage systems and food storage and transportation systems that cost many billions of dollars would have to be rebuilt to reflect new patterns of precipitation. For example, Canada, the Soviet Union, the northeastern part of the United States and some arid regions like the Sahel area in Africa might get more rain and thus eventually be able to grow more food than they do today. But for several decades there probably would be instability in global food production and distribution because many of the new crop-growing areas would have poor soils and would not be organized to farm, irrigate, store, and distribute large amounts of grain.

The U.S. wheat and corn belt in the Midwest and the irrigated farming areas of California and the Texas Gulf Coast would become much drier. Thus, much of the crop-growing regions in these parts of the United States might be replaced by such northern areas as the Saskatchewan Province in Canada, where the soils are poorer and less productive.

According to the 1983 NAS report, the even greater projected increase in temperature at the earth's poles would cause thermal expansion of warmer ocean water and some melting of the land-based Antarctic ice; hence average sea levels would rise about 0.70 meter (2.3 feet) over the next 100 years.

Eventually most, if not all, of the floating Arctic ice pack would probably melt, thus opening the northwest and northeast passages to ships through most of the year. Since this ice pack is afloat, its melting would not raise the water level in oceans—just as melting a floating ice cube in a glass does not raise the water level. But the absence of polar ice would change ocean currents and trigger unpredictable changes in the climate of the Northern Hemisphere.

Some of the land-based Antarctic glacial ice might melt slowly and cause a rise in average sea levels. Despite stories in the popular press predicting that the world's major coastal cities and floodplains (which produce most of the world's food) will soon be flooded, this melting process, if it occurred, would probably take place over several hundred years. A 1983 EPA report projected a maximum increase in average sea level of 3 meters (10 feet) and a most-probable rise of 2.4 meters (8 feet) by 2100.

What Can Be Done? Suggestions to prevent the problem from reaching crisis levels include **(1)** not shifting to coal, shale oil, or synfuels as a major energy source over the next 50 years and relying more on either nuclear power (Section 15-5) or a combination of energy conservation and increased use of renewable energy resources (Chapter 16), the sun, wind, flowing water, **(2)** using scrubbers to remove carbon dioxide from the stack gases of coal-burning power and industrial plants—a technically feasible but expensive solution, **(3)** planting more trees worldwide to reduce the greenhouse effect by increasing the uptake of carbon dioxide from the atmosphere as well as reducing the harmful effects of deforestation, and **(4)** reducing soil erosion, which releases carbon dioxide (Section 8-6).

Physicist and energy expert Amory Lovins and several of his colleagues (see Lovins et al., *Least Cost Energy: Solving the CO_2 Problem*, 1981) argue that a combination of energy conservation and obtaining much of our energy from the sun, wind, flowing water, and biomass could reduce the projected use of coal by as much as 60 percent by 2050. According to their projections, this would not only avert the major effects of increased atmospheric carbon dioxide levels but would also be a less costly approach than continuing to use fossil fuels.

A 1983 EPA study, however, projected that even a total ban on the burning of fossil fuels in the United States wouldn't have much impact because the country accounts for only about one-fourth of the world's carbon dioxide emissions from human activities. The EPA report also projected that even if a worldwide ban on the burning of coal were indeed instituted in 2000, this would delay the projected doubling of atmospheric carbon dioxide levels by only about 15 years. Such a ban, however, is not considered feasible because of economic hardships on nations highly dependent on coal and because some nations, including Canada and the Soviet Union, stand to benefit from a global warming.

For these reasons, many scientists argue that the best approach is to prepare for the effects of long-term global warming. Suggestions include **(1)** breeding plant strains that need less water and can thrive in water too salty for ordinary crops, **(2)** improving the efficiency of irrigation (Section 17-6), **(3)** erecting levees to protect coastal areas from flooding, as the Dutch have done for hundreds of years, **(4)** using zoning ordinances to prohibit new construction in undeveloped, low-lying areas, and **(5)** storing up several years' supply of food worldwide as insurance against climate change and variability.

E5-3 Particles in the Atmosphere: Is the Atmosphere Cooling?

Dust, soot, and other particles enter the atmosphere from active volcanoes, forest fires, dust storms, sea spray, and other natural sources. Humans also add particles by clearing land for agriculture and urbanization and through smokestack, chimney, and automobile emissions. Unlike carbon dioxide, particles differ markedly in size and chemical makeup (Figure 19-8).

Particles, especially those in the upper atmosphere, can reflect some of the incoming solar radiation back into space, reducing the amount of solar heat reaching the earth's surface and thus tending to cool the atmosphere. For example, large volcanic eruptions, like Tambora in 1815, Krakatoa in 1883, and El Chichón in 1983, generally produce a global climate cooling that lasts for several years.

However, particles from volcanic eruptions and human activities can either raise or lower atmospheric temperature depending on their size, composition, reflective properties, and altitude, and the reflectivity of the earth's surface. Over a dark surface, such as the ocean, particles tend to be net reflectors of incoming sunlight, hence cooling the lower atmosphere. But over much of the land, which is lighter than the oceans, particles can absorb heat energy and radiate some of it back toward the earth, thus warming the lower atmosphere.

Fine particles in the stratosphere cause heating of the air there because the particles absorb light from the sun. In the lower atmosphere near the earth's surface, however, they normally cause a cooling effect primarily because they reflect and radiate some of the incoming radiation back into space. In this case, their effect is opposite that of carbon dioxide, which cools the stratosphere and warms the surface layers of the atmosphere.

Estimates of the human production of atmospheric dust range from 5 to 50 percent of the total annual input. Most emissions of large particles near the earth's surface normally remain in the atmosphere for only a few days before they fall out or are washed out by rain. Although they can affect local weather patterns significantly, these particles are not a major factor in global climate. However, particles that rise in or are injected into the strato-

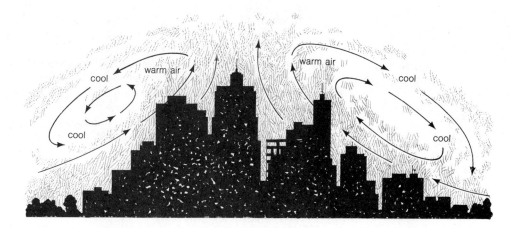

sphere have a residence time of 1 to 5 years and can affect global climate. It is argued that since most particles from human activities end up in the lower atmosphere, their climatic effects are primarily local.

E5-4 Heat: The Ultimate Pollutant

Take a breath, raise your arm, turn on a light, drive a car, or heat or air condition your house or car, and you add heat to the atmosphere. According to the second law of energy (Section 2-3), whenever energy is used, some of it is degraded to infrared heat, which flows into the atmosphere and is eventually radiated back into space (Figure 3-10). If human activities in an area produce energy faster than it can be radiated back into space, the average temperature of the atmosphere in that area will rise—just as an auditorium heats up when it is filled with people, each one giving off heat equivalent to that emitted by a 100-watt light bulb.

This heating effect is already occurring in large cities and urban areas. Anyone who lives or works in a city knows that it is typically warmer there than in nearby suburbs or rural areas. Day in and day out, cities emit vast quantities of heat. Concrete and brick buildings and asphalt pavements absorb heat during the day and release it slowly at night. Tall, closely spaced buildings slow wind velocity near the ground and reduce the rate of heat loss. Water rapidly runs off the paved surfaces in cities, in contrast to rural areas, where water soaks into the soil and then slowly evaporates to cool the surrounding air. Thus, it is not surprising that a dome of heat hovers over a city, creating what is called an *urban heat island* (Figure E5-3). Not only is a city warmer than rural areas, but it typically has lower visibility, more air pollution, less sun, less wind, and lower humidity (Table E5-2).

As urban areas grow and merge into vast urban regions, the heat domes from a number of cities can combine to form *regional heat islands*, which could affect regional climate. The prevailing winds that normally would cleanse the center of the dome would already be polluted, hence air pollution levels under the large regional dome could be raised. In addition, summer heat levels in the center could become intolerable, and the use of millions of air conditioners would add even more heat to the atmosphere and increase the chances of power brownouts and blackouts.

The challenge of responding to the greenhouse effect poses the question of whether human society can respond to any problem beyond the most immediate and potentially catastrophic.

Richard Allen

Table E5-2 Comparison of Urban and Nearby Rural Climates

Variable	Urban Compared with Rural Levels
Temperature	
Annual mean	0.5 to 1.0°C higher
Winter average	1.0 to 2.0°C higher
Visibility	5 to 30% less
Pollutants	
Particles	10 times more
Gases (SO_2, CO_2, CO)	5 to 25 times more
Solar radiation	15 to 20% less
Wind speed	
Annual mean	20 to 30% less
Calms (stagnant air)	5 to 20% more
Relative humidity	
Winter	2% less
Summer	8% less

Discussion Topics

1. Explain why most radiation returning to space has longer wavelengths (lower energy) than incoming solar radiation. Does this mean that less energy flows back than reaches the earth? Explain.

2. Criticize the following statements:
   a. A new ice age could spread across the United States by the year 2050.
   b. Massive global flooding would occur if we melted the floating Arctic ice pack.
   c. Massive global flooding near seacoasts could occur by the year 2050.

3. Explain how particles, depending on their size and location, cause the atmosphere to cool or to heat up.

4. Criticize the statement "We shouldn't worry about the heating of the atmosphere from increased carbon dioxide levels because a warmer climate is more desirable."

5. What effect on climate might each of the following have: (a) oil spills, (b) increased amount of land under cultivation, (c) driving an air conditioned automobile, (d) switching on a light, (e) air conditioning your home or place of work, (f) strip mining, (g) using an electric appliance to dry hair or clothing, (h) switching from coal-fired power plants to nuclear power plants, (i) switching from coal-powered and nuclear power plants to solar energy power plants and solar photovoltaic cells to produce electricity?

6. Are the climate conditions in urban areas shown in Table E5-2 desirable or undesirable in terms of human comfort and energy use during the winter and summer? Explain.

7. Criticize the statement "Human actions will not seriously affect global climate for 100 to 200 years, so we need not be concerned with the problem now."

8. Debate the idea that we should set up a world food bank to store several years' supply of food as insurance against climate change. How would you decide who gets this food in times of need?

Enrichment Study 6

Species Interactions in Ecosystems

In this enrichment study we will look at three major types of species interaction: *interspecific competition, predation, and symbiosis.* These phenomena can affect both the structure (Chapter 3) and the function (Chapter 4) of ecosystems by changing the population size of species and by altering energy flows through food webs.

E6-1 Interspecific Competition

As long as commonly used resources are abundant, different species can share them. However, when one or more of these commonly shared resources is in short supply, these species may end up in competition. When two or more species in the same ecosystem attempt to use the same scarce resources, they are said to be engaging in **interspecific competition.** The scarce resource may be food, water, a place to live, sunlight, or anything needed for survival.

The shorter the supply of the limited shared resources, the greater the competition between the species. The outcome of severe interspecific competition may be **(1)** the extinction or near extinction of one species in the area where competition exists, **(2)** coexistence of the competing species with time through evolutionary changes that reduce or eliminate competition, or **(3)** dominance of one population during one season or year under one set of environmental conditions and dominance of the other population under different conditions.

One competing species may have such an advantage over other species that its population grows and dominates the use of scarce resources by reproducing more young in a given amount of time, obtaining food or defending itself more effectively, or being able to tolerate a greater range of variance in some limiting factor (Section 3-7). For example, if one shade-intolerant tree species in a patch of forest can multiply and grow fast, it can create a dense overhead canopy that prevents other

shade-intolerant species from flourishing on the forest floor.

Populations of some animal species can avoid or reduce competition with more dominant species by moving to another area, switching to a less accessible or less readily digestible food source, or hunting for the same food source at different times of the day. For example, hawks and owls feed on similar types of prey. Competition is reduced, however, because hawks hunt during the day and owls hunt at night.

Without such alternatives, the population size of a less dominant species is reduced. With intensive competition such a population may become extinct or be driven to near extinction in a given area or throughout the world. The grizzly bear requires large expanses of undisturbed wilderness for survival. As humans have cleared large portions of land and engaged in hunting activities, they have competed with the grizzly bear for habitat. Because of habitat loss and hunting, the grizzly bear population in the continental United States has declined to such a low level that it is difficult for mates to find each other. Some evidence suggests that interspecific competition is a more important factor in the extinction of plants than in animals primarily because—unlike most animals—plants have rather similar resource needs and have less flexibility in switching to new food sources.

Over several generations, species may through natural selection evolve new feeding habits or behavior that reduces or eliminates interspecific competition. Ecologist R. H. MacArthur has shown that five species of warbler birds found in Maine spruce forests have evolved feeding habits through natural selection that allow them to coexist with a minimum of competition. Although all five species feed on basically the same type of insect, the hunting activity of each species is confined to a particular part or level of a spruce tree. For example, one kind of warbler hunts insects hidden under spruce needles while another captures insects on top of the needles.

E6-2 Predation

The most obvious form of species interaction is **predation.** It occurs when an organism of one species (the *predator*) captures and feeds on either parts or all of an organism of another species (the *prey*). Predators that dine on plants are *herbivores;* those that dine on animals are *carnivores;* and those that can eat both plants and animals (and other kinds of organism) are *omnivores.*

In most cases a predator species has more than one prey species. Likewise, a single prey species may have several different predators. Eagles, owls, and hawks eat rats, mice, rabbits, and other prey. Mountain lions and wolves eat squirrels, rabbits, deer, and other animals. We usually think of predation in terms of animal-animal interactions, but it can also involve plants. A cow can be classified as a predator when it eats grass (the prey), and carnivorous plants, like the Venus flytrap, catch and digest various insects.

The ability of predators to find and feed on their prey determines the rate at which energy and various types of matter flow from one trophic level to another (Section 4-2). Some predator species have helpful specialized features and behavior patterns. For example, hawks, falcons, and eagles have remarkable eyesight that allows them to spot moving rodents from great heights. Bats have a kind of sonar system that helps them find prey and avoid obstacles. Wolves can take prey much larger than themselves by hunting in packs. Spiders build complex webs to trap insects.

Prey species have developed ways to avoid predators. Species that rely on running, swimming, or flying out of reach of predators usually live in places where there aren't many hiding places. Fast-swimming fish and seals are found in open seas, and fast-running hooved animals such as zebra exist in open areas or savannas. Rabbits run and hide under the cover of vegetation, mice dash into a hole to hide, and lizards hide under rocks.

Some species defend themselves by inflating to a larger size (blowfish), giving off an obnoxious odor (skunk), tasting bad to predators (milkweed bug and monarch butterfly), having a protective shell or covering (turtles and armadillos), having brightly colored tails that break off when seized by an attacker (many lizard species), running in herds (wildebeest), having thorns (roses) and spines (cacti and porcupine), stinging (nettle), and producing chemicals harmful or unpalatable to predators (poison oak and poison ivy). Others have natural camouflage abilities: chameleon lizards can change color,

polar bears blend in with snow, and some cacti look like rocks; the walkingstick looks like something else (a twig), and edible viceroy butterflies resemble bad-tasting monarch butterflies.

The effect of predation on the control of the population size of predator and prey species is hotly debated and poorly understood. Theoretically predator and prey species can regulate each other's population size around some equilibrium value without extreme fluctuations through positive or negative feedback mechanisms (Section 5-2). An increase in the prey population means more food for predators, so then population can also increase. More predators mean that more prey are eaten, and the prey population begins to decrease. Once the prey population has dwindled to a certain level, the predators have a harder time finding enough prey. Some of the predators then die from lack of food. This relieves the pressure on the prey, and their population begins to rise slowly—starting the cycle again. This theoretical model, however, does not apply to all predator-prey populations. In nature things are more complex because most ecosystems have elaborate food webs (Figure 4-5) in which most species are both prey for some species and predators on others.

For small animals, such as insects, predation is one of the major factors limiting population size. For this reason biological control in which the population size of pest species is limited by natural predators is an important alternative to pesticides. The role of large predators in controlling the numbers of prey is not well understood and may vary considerably from one species to another. For example, studies have shown that predation by African lions normally has little effect on the populations of wildebeest unless the latter are confined to a restricted range. However, large predators such as lions do tend to keep prey populations healthy by killing off the weak, diseased, and old members.

Often sport hunting by humans is justified as a means of population control of animals. Lions, wolves, and other natural predators of a species, such as the deer, may be killed off or driven out of an ecosystem. Then human hunters must act as predators to keep the deer population from exploding and destroying much of the vegetation. In other words, once natural predators have been removed, sport hunting by humans may be necessary for population control. But this can cause a serious problem. Human sport hunters usually don't kill the old, sick, and weak animals. Instead, they normally go after the strongest and healthiest ones— the animals most needed for reproduction. Thus, sport hunting can control a population, but the quality of the remaining population can be lowered.

E6-3 Symbiosis

An interaction in which two different species exist in close physical contact, with one living on or in the other so that one or both species benefit from the association is called **symbiosis,** which means "living together." This interaction is an ecological association involving some transfer of energy or other ecological benefit. The three major types of symbiosis are *mutualism, commensalism,* and *parasitism.*

Mutualism is a symbiotic relationship between two different species in which both species benefit from the interaction. Pollination by flowering plants and insects is one of the most common examples of mutualism. Butterflies and bees depend on flowers for food in the form of pollen and nectar. In turn, the flowering plants depend on the bees, butterflies, and other pollinating insects to carry the male reproductive cells contained in their pollen grains to the female flowering parts of other flowers of the same species. Another mutualistic relationship exists in the nitrogen cycle (Figure 4-10) between legume plants (such as peas, clover, beans, and alfalfa) and *Rhizobium* bacteria, which live in nodules on the roots of these plants. Large colonies of bacteria in these nodules "fix," or convert, gaseous nitrogen (N_2) to forms of nitrogen such as nitrate (NO_3^-) and ammonium (NH_4^+) ions that can be used as nutrients by the plant and by the bacteria.

In the second type of symbiosis, called **commensalism,** one species benefits from the association while the other is apparently neither helped nor harmed. For example, in tropical and subtropical forests we find green plants called *epiphytes* (various orchids and bromeliads) living high above the ground on the trunks and branches of trees. With no roots, these so-called air plants are able to use the tree to gain access to sunlight in the relatively dark forest. They also use their own leaves and cupped petals to collect water and minerals that drip down from the tops of trees. Since they take nothing from the tree, the tree is neither harmed nor benefited.

In **parasitism,** the third form of symbiosis, one species (the *parasite*) benefits and the other species (the *host*) is harmed. The parasite usually takes its nourishment from the host, either externally from skin, feathers, hair, or scales (*ecoparasitism*), or internally from the cells, tissues, and other parts of the host (*endoparasitism*). Examples of parasites are leeches (which suck blood from their victims), lice, ticks, fleas, bacteria, protozoans, fungi, and worms such as tapeworms, hookworms, and pinworms. Human diseases caused by parasitic bacteria include typhoid fever, tuberculosis, cholera, syphilis, and gonorrhea (Enrichment Study 7). Diseases such as amoebic dysentery, African sleeping sickness, and malaria are caused by parasitic protozoans. Plants are also plagued by parasites. Parasite fungi cause wheat rust, corn leaf blight, Dutch elm disease, and other destructive plant diseases. By planting large fields of only one species, such as corn, humans make it possible for parasites to wipe out an entire crop. A successful parasite may harm its host, but it does not kill the host. If the host dies, the parasite must find a new host or die.

Like predation, parasitism helps regulate populations. Epidemics can spread rapidly, killing many members of a dense host population. Once the host population has been reduced, the parasites are less likely to find new hosts, and as they die off, the spread of the epidemic is slowed. In this way two species tend to regulate each other's population density.

Parasitism is sometimes classifed as a special type of predation rather than an example of symbiosis. Parasitism, like predation, involves one species feeding on another. But there are significant differences between these two types of species interaction. Parasites are usually smaller than their host, whereas most predators are larger than their prey. Parasites tend to live in, on, or near their host and slowly consume only part of the host. In contrast, predators live apart from their prey and tend to kill and then consume most or all of the prey.

If we love our children, we must love our earth with tender care and pass it on, diverse and beautiful, so that on a warm spring day 10,000 years hence they can feel peace in a sea of grass, can watch a bee visit a flower, can hear a sandpiper call in the sky, and can find joy in being alive.

Hugh H. Iltis

Discussion Topics

1. Explain how predation and competition:
   a. Help control the population size of different species in an ecosystem
   b. Affect energy flow in an ecosystem

2. Discuss the advantages and disadvantages of sport hunting by humans. Do you think sport hunting should be banned? Why or why not? What restrictions would you put on hunting for sport? Why?

3. Explain how parasitism differs from predation.

4. Give an example not discussed in the text of commensalism, parasitism, and predation.

Enrichment Study 7

Environmental Health and Human Disease

E7-1 Types of Disease

Infectious and Noninfectious Diseases We become afflicted with a disease when there is an upset of the complex, delicate balance that normally exists between our bodies and the environment. The upset may result from factors in the physical environment (air, water, food, or sun), the biological environment (bacteria, viruses, plants, and animals, including humans), the social environment (work, leisure, and cultural habits and patterns such as smoking, diet, or excessive drinking), or any combination of these three sources.

Human diseases can be broadly classified as *infectious* and *noninfectious*. An **infectious disease** occurs when we are *host* to disease-causing living organisms called *agents*, such as bacteria, viruses, and parasitic worms. Infectious diseases can be classified according to the method of transmission. **Vector-transmitted infectious diseases** like malaria, schistosomiasis, and African sleeping sickness are carried from one person to another by a living organism (usually an insect), called the *vector*. Some of the major vector-transmitted infectious diseases found in the world today are shown in Table E7-1.

Non-vector-transmitted infectious diseases like the common cold, tuberculosis, cholera, measles, mononucleosis, syphilis, and gonorrhea are transmitted from person to person without an intermediate carrier. This transmission usually takes place by one or a combination of methods: **(1)** close physical contact with infected persons (syphilis, gonorrhea, mononucleosis, and leprosy), **(2)** contact with water, food, soil, or other materials contaminated by fecal material or saliva from infected persons (cholera, typhoid fever, and infectious hepatitis), or **(3)** inhalation of air containing tiny droplets of contaminated fluid expelled when infected persons cough, sneeze, or talk (common cold, influenza, and tuberculosis).

When an infectious disease is carried by many hosts without leading rapidly to many deaths, it is *endemic* to the population. For example, mononucleosis is *endemic* in the U.S. population, and many high school and college students have it unknowingly. An *epidemic* occurs when a sudden, severe outbreak of an infectious disease like influenza affects many people in a population and leads to many deaths. An infectious disease like influenza becomes *pandemic* when it spreads worldwide to infect and kill a large number of people. Because of the exten-

Table E7-1 Major Vector-Transmitted Infectious Diseases

Disease	Infectious Organism	Vector	Estimated Number of People Infected (millions)
Malaria	*Plasmodium* (parasite)	*Anopheles* (mosquito)	500*
Schistosomiasis	*Schistosoma* (trematode worm)	Certain species of freshwater snails	300
Filariasis (elephantiasis and onchocerciasis, or river blindness)	Several species of parasitic worms	Certain species of mosquitoes and blood-sucking flies (elephantiasis); female black flies (onchocerciasis)	250
Trypanosomiasis (African sleeping sickness and Chagas' disease)	*Trypanosoma* (parasites)	Tsetse fly (African sleeping sickness); kissing bugs (Chagas' disease)	100

*150 million new cases each year.

Table E7-2 Comparison of Acute Infectious, Chronic Infectious, and Chronic Noninfectious Diseases

Characteristic	Acute Infectious: Measles, typhoid fever, whooping cough, smallpox	Chronic Infectious: Malaria, schistosomiasis, tuberculosis	Chronic Noninfectious: Cardiovascular disorders, cancer, diabetes, emphysema
Cause	Living organism	Living organism	Usually several, often unknown environmental and/or genetic factors
Transmission	Usually nonvector	Vector and nonvector	Not transmitted directly but some may be transmitted genetically
Time for develoment (latent period)	Short (hours or days)	Long (usually years)	Long (usually years)
Duration	Usually brief (days)	Long (often for life)	Long (often for life)
Effects	Usually temporary or reversible	Usually irreversible	Usually irreversible
Age group	Children and adults	Adults, middle to old age	Adults, middle to old age
Prevalence	High in less developed nations, low in more developed nations	High in less developed nations, low in more developed nations	High, especially in more developed nations where longer life spans allow diseases to develop
Mortality	High in less developed nations, low in more developed nations	High in less developed nations, low in more developed nations	High in more developed nations
Prevention	Sanitation, clean drinking water, vaccination	Sanitation, clean drinking water, vaccination, vector control	Control of environmental factors such as smoking, diet, and exposure to polluted air, water, and food

sive movement of people and food throughout the world, only strict sanitation and public health measures can protect against pandemics from non-vector-transmitted infectious diseases. Vector-transmitted infections can become pandemic only when vector organisms like fleas and bats are transferred throughout the world and can survive under a variety of climates and conditions.

Noninfectious diseases are not relayed by a disease-causing organism, and except for genetic diseases are not transmitted from one person to another. Examples include cardiovascular (heart and blood vessel) disorders, cancers, diabetes, chronic respiratory diseases (bronchitis and emphysema, Section 19-3), allergies (asthma and hay fever), nerve and other degenerative diseases (cerebral palsy and multiple sclerosis), and genetic diseases (hemophilia and sickle cell anemia). Many of these diseases have several, often unknown causes and tend to develop slowly and sometimes progressively over the years. Typically they are caused by **(1)** exposure to certain chemicals (some cancers and emphysema), ultraviolet energy from the sun (some forms of skin cancer), and pollen and other materials found in air, water, and food (asthma and hay fever), **(2)** inherited genetic traits (hemophilia), **(3)** a combination of environmental and genetic factors (emphysema), and **(4)** changes in body chemistry triggered by unknown causes (cerebral palsy and diabetes).

Acute and Chronic Diseases Diseases can also be classified according to their effect and duration. An **acute disease** is an infectious disease like measles or typhoid fever from which the victim either recovers or dies in a relatively short time. A **chronic disease** lasts for a long time (often for life) and may flare up periodically (malaria), become progressively worse (cancer and cardiovascular disorders), or disappear with age (childhood asthma). Chronic diseases may be infectious (malaria, schistosomiasis, leprosy, and tuberculosis) or noninfectious (cardiovascular disorders, cancer, diabetes, emphysema, and hay fever). Table E7-2 summarizes major characteristics of acute infectious diseases, chronic infectious diseases, and chronic noninfectious diseases.

The Social Ecology of Disease By studying Table E7-2 carefully we can see that the prevalence and mortality of the three categories of diseases differ among the MDCs and LDCs. The populations of LDCs tend to have a short average life span, largely because of the complex interactions among poverty, malnutrition, and infectious diseases (Figure 9-4). Poor people in these nations are more likely to come into contact with infectious organisms because of contaminated water and food, crowding, and poor sanitation. According to the World Health Organization, about 80 percent of all infectious disease is caused by unsafe drinking water and inadequate sanitation.

The tropical or equatorial location of most LDCs also increases the chances of infection, because hot, wet climates and the absence of winter enable disease vectors to thrive year round. In addition, poor people—especially infants—tend to be more susceptible to diseases because they are more likely to be weakened by malnutrition. Thus, infectious diseases from which the rich recover—whooping cough, typhoid fever, diphtheria, measles, dysentery, and diarrhea—tend to kill the poor. For example, dehydration from diarrhea kills at least 5 million children a year, mostly in LDCs, and contributes to the malnutrition of many millions more. Most of these deaths from dehydration can be prevented by having children with diarrhea drink enough of a solution made by dissolving a small handful of sucrose (ordinary sugar) and a pinch of salt in a liter of water to match the volume of liquid lost in watery stools. Most poor people don't live long enough to die from chronic noninfectious conditions like heart disease, cancer, or emphysema.

One indicator of the prevalence of infectious diseases in a country is its infant mortality rate. In 1984 the average infant mortality rate in the MDCs was 19 deaths of infants under one year old per 1,000 live births, compared to an average of 94 deaths per 1,000 live births in LDCs. Finland, Denmark, Canada, Hong Kong, Norway, Iceland, France, Japan, Sweden, and several other nations have very low infant mortality rates—from 7 to 10 infants out of every 1,000 born die in their first year of life. In the United States, which in 1984 ranked seventeenth in the world in infant mortality, about 10.9 infants out of every 1,000 live births died in their first year. By contrast, in some African and Asian nations the infant death toll during the first year is 100 to 200 out of every 1,000 live births.

In most MDCs, safe water supplies, public sanitation, adequate nutrition, and immunization have nearly stamped out many infectious diseases. In 1900 the infectious diseases pneumonia, influenza, tuberculosis, and diarrhea were the leading causes of death in the United States. By contrast, the five leading causes of death in the United States today are heart disease, stroke, cancer, accidents (especially automobile accidents),* and pulmonary disease, in that order.

These deaths are largely a result of environment and life-style rather than invasion of the body by an infectious agent. Except for auto accidents,

these deaths result from chronic diseases that take a long time to develop, have multiple causes, and are largely attributable to the area in which we live and work (urban or rural), our work environment, our diet, whether we smoke, and the amount of alcohol we consume.

Even though heart disease, stroke, cancer, and pulmonary disease are among the leading causes of death, the American public is getting healthier both in terms of lower death rates and in terms of a lower incidence of disability due to illness. Average life expectancy for an American born in 1984 is 74 years (77.5 for women and 69.8 for men), compared to 68.2 in 1950 and 47.3 in 1900. Contrary to popular belief, the rise in the average life expectancy in the United States between 1900 and 1950 did not occur primarily as a result of modern medicine. Except for whooping cough, polio, and influenza, the decline in death rates from infectious disease occurred primarily because of improved nutrition and better hygiene and sanitation.

The rise in average life expectancy since 1950 is the result of these factors plus modern medical care—especially the use of antibiotics to treat infections—and preventive health care through changes in life-style. An increasing number of Americans have modified their life-style to prevent illness by not smoking, by using alcohol in moderation or not at all, by getting more exercise, and by getting better nutrition. This, in turn, has created a social environment that supports those who choose to make such changes in life-style. A combination of life-style changes and new treatments led to a 30 percent decline in U.S. deaths from heart disease between 1973 and 1983.

E7-2 Vector-Transmitted Infectious Diseases: Malaria and Schistosomiasis

Malaria People in the United States and in most MDCs tend to view malaria as a disease of the past. But *in the tropical and subtropical regions of the world, malaria is still the single most serious health problem— killing over 1 million people a year and incapacitating many millions.* An estimated 2 billion people—two out of every five people in the world—live in malaria-infested regions.

Malaria's symptoms come and go; they include fever and chills, anemia, an enlarged spleen, severe abdominal pain and headaches, extreme weakness, and greater susceptibility to other diseases. Caused by one of four species of protozoa (one-celled organisms) of the genus *Plasmodium,* the disease is transmitted from person to person by the bite of several species of *Anopheles* mosquito, which act as vectors (Figure E7-1). Malaria can also be transmit-

---

*At least 50 percent of all deaths and injuries from automobile accidents are related to alcohol. A 1983 study of automobile accidents in three states showed that 90 percent of the accidents were alcohol related.

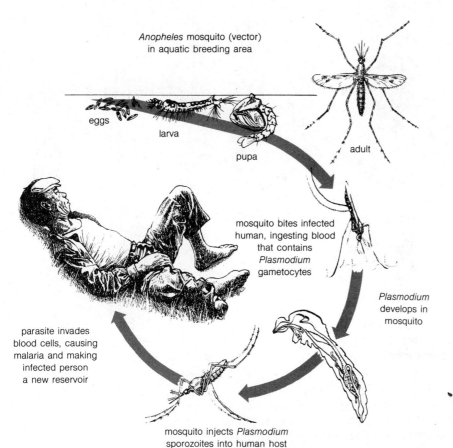

Figure E7-1 The life cycle of malaria.

Anopheles mosquito (vector)
in aquatic breeding area

eggs

larva

pupa

adult

mosquito bites infected
human, ingesting blood
that contains
Plasmodium
gametocytes

Plasmodium
develops in
mosquito

parasite invades
blood cells, causing
malaria and making
infected person
a new reservoir

mosquito injects *Plasmodium*
sporozoites into human host

ted when a person receives the blood of an infected donor and when an infected drug user shares a needle with another user. For this reason heroin is usually "cut" with quinine, an antimalarial drug.

One way to control malaria is to administer antimalarial drugs like chlorquine, which protect people against infection from bites of *Anopheles* mosquitoes. Antimalarial drugs are helpful, but they cannot be used effectively to rid an area of malaria. The cost is too high because people in infected areas would have to take the drugs continuously throughout their lives. In addition, new strains of carrier mosquitoes eventually develop that have genetic resistance to any widely used antimalarial drug (Section 9-9).

Another approach is vector control—trying to get rid of the mosquito carriers by draining swamplands and marshes and by spraying breeding areas with DDT and other pesticides. During the 1950s and 1960s the World Health Organization made great strides in reducing malaria in many areas, eliminating it in 37 countries by widespread spraying of DDT and the use of antimalarial drugs. In India malaria cases were cut from 100 million in 1952 to only 40,000 in 1966, and in Pakistan cases were reduced from 7 million in 1961 to only 9,500 in 1967.

Since 1970, however, malaria has made a dra-

matic comeback in many parts of the world. By 1978 the number of cases in India had risen to 50 million and in Pakistan to 10 million. There are now at least 150 million reported cases of the disease each year, with epidemiologists at the U.S. Centers for Disease Control estimating that the true figure may be close to 800 million new cases a year. In Africa alone the disease kills 1 million children under the age of 5 each year. This tragic resurgence has occurred because of **(1)** increased genetic resistance of mosquito carriers to DDT and other insecticides and to antimalarial drugs, **(2)** rising costs of pesticides and antimalarial drugs (between 1974 and 1975 the price of DDT tripled, primarily because of rising oil prices), **(3)** the spread of irrigation ditches, which provide new mosquito breeding grounds, **(4)** the physical impossibility of reaching and spraying all mosquito-infested areas, and **(5)** reduction of budgets for malaria control due to the belief that the disease had been controlled.

Research is being carried out to develop biological controls for *Anopheles* mosquitoes and to develop antimalaria vaccines, but such approaches are in the early stages of development. The amount of money being devoted to research on malaria and other tropical diseases is shockingly low when we consider that more people suffer and die from these

Environmental Health and Human Disease   **E33**

Figure E7-2 The life cycle of schistosomiasis.

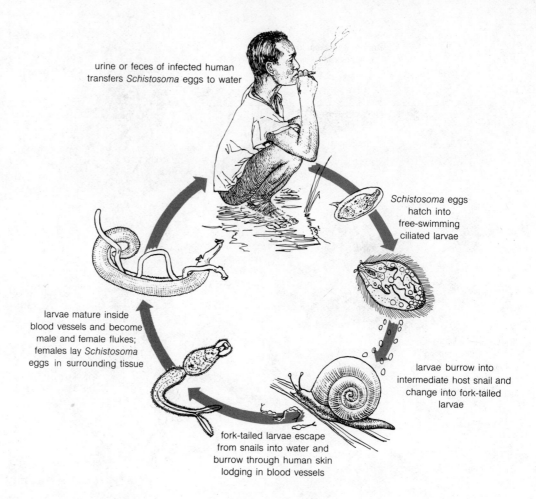

urine or feces of infected human transfers *Schistosoma* eggs to water

Schistosoma eggs hatch into free-swimming ciliated larvae

larvae burrow into intermediate host snail and change into fork-tailed larvae

fork-tailed larvae escape from snails into water and burrow through human skin lodging in blood vessels

larvae mature inside blood vessels and become male and female flukes; females lay *Schistosoma* eggs in surrounding tissue

diseases than all other diseases combined. The World Health Organization estimates that only 3 percent of the money spent each year on biomedical research is spent on tropical diseases.

Schistosomiasis Like malaria, schistosomiasis chronically afflicts hundreds of millions of people (Table E7-1), especially in Africa, South America, the Caribbean, the Middle East, and Asia. Humans are the major hosts, although other hosts include cattle, sheep, goats, cats, dogs, and some wild animals. Schistosomiasis is caused by the trematode worm *Schistosoma*, which is transmitted between human and animal hosts by tiny snails found in freshwater streams, rivers, lakes, and irrigation canals (Figure E7-2). The adult worms lodge in the human host's veins and deposit eggs in surrounding organs and tissues, causing chronic inflammation, swelling, and pain. The urine and feces of newly infected humans can start the entire cycle again.

Victims suffer from cough, fever, enlargement of the spleen and liver, a general wasting away of the body, filling of the abdomen with fluid (which produces the characteristic pot belly), and constant pain; they are more susceptible to other diseases, and are often too weak to work. Although the disease itself is rarely fatal, persons who are severely malnourished or severely infected may die.

In rural areas of Africa and Asia it is difficult for villagers to avoid contact with infested water because they collect it for drinking, cooking, and washing clothes and bathe and swim in it. They are also infected while washing cattle, fishing, planting rice, working in irrigation ditches, and engaging in *wadu*, the ritual washing that devout Muslims perform five times a day before praying. The building of dams such as the Aswan High Dam in India, for hydroelectric power and irrigation, tends to intensify the spread of the disease because the irrigation ditches are ideal breeding places for the snails that transmit the disease. As workers urinate and wade in the ditches, schistosomiasis spreads widely.

Schistosomiasis can be reduced or even eradicated in an area by **(1)** preventing human excreta from reaching the snails through improved sanitation, **(2)** preventing people from swimming or washing in contaminated water, **(3)** protecting people who farm or fish in contaminated waters by the use of boots and protective clothing, **(4)** developing drugs to kill the worms in the body, **(5)** killing the snails with chemical poisons (molluscicides), and (6) using a combination of engineering approaches including draining marshlands where snails breed, increasing the water velocity in irrigation canals to prevent infestation by snails, draining irrigation projects to prevent stagnant pools and seepages, removing aquatic vegetation from irrigation ditches that serve as snail habitats, and keeping irrigation ditches at least 500 meters (1,640 feet) from houses.

In practice, however, schistosomiasis is a very difficult disease to control. The first three approaches are expensive, difficult to put into effect, or both. The fourth approach has had mixed success. Several drugs have been developed that can kill most of the worms in the human body. But so far none works on all people or on all species of the parasite. All are expensive or have serious and occasionally lethal side effects, must be administered continually because they do not prevent reinfestation, and fail after a few years because of drug resistance in the parasite or relaxation of use when the incidence of the disease has fallen off.

So far, the fifth approach has had only limited success because the chemicals are too expensive for the almost continuous use that is required. A few snails that survive by burrowing into the mud, or the influx of snails from outside an area, can rebuild the population to significant levels. In addition, the chemicals can kill fish, poison the water, and have other ecological and health side effects. However, there is some hope. Preliminary results indicate that the dried, ground berries of the endod, used by villagers in Ethiopia as a detergent for washing clothes, may be effective in killing the snails without hurting other animals and plants. Projects in Israel, Japan, China, and the Philippines have shown that the sixth approach can help prevent an increase in the incidence of the disease. However, as long as so little money is spent worldwide on schistosomiasis research, reducing the incidence of this disease in the LDCs is going to be very difficult.

E7-3   Non-Vector-Transmitted Infectious Disease: Cholera

One of the most frightening infectious diseases goes by the name of *cholera*—a term used to describe a collection of infections that result in severe diarrhea and dehydration. The bacteria causing cholera are transmitted from person to person through water and food supplies contaminated with sewage. Within a half-day the infected individual suffers from severe diarrhea and vomiting, which lead to rapid dehydration. Unless the victim is treated with antibiotics to combat the infection and with fluids and salt to counter the effects of dehydration, the blood pressure falls, the skin shrivels up, and severe muscular cramps, coma, and death follow. This sequence of events occurs in 2 to 7 days.

Cholera was once confined to India, but during the nineteenth century, it spread to China, Japan, East Africa, Europe, and North America in a series of six pandemic plagues, each lasting 10 to 20 years and killing thousands. It was not until the middle of the nineteenth century that people learned that contaminated water spread the dreaded disease. After the last great pandemic of 1865 through 1875, cholera was pushed back into its southern Asia homeland as a result of improved sanitation and vaccines. Since 1961, however, cholera has begun to march across continents for a seventh time; today it kills people all over Asia, Africa, and the Middle East. There is fear that an infected traveler may bring this scourge to Latin America, where poor sanitation would allow it to spread rapidly.

Cholera is a major threat to the urban poor who live in crowded, unsanitary conditions and who have no access to vaccines. Even vaccination is not a cure-all, since cholera vaccine gives a 50 percent chance of protection, and that protection lasts for about 6 months. The only effective way to combat cholera—along with a host of other waterborne infectious diseases—is to improve water supplies and sanitation throughout the world, especially in the tropics. Tropical disease experts estimate that chlorinating and filtering water supplies and using fairly simple sanitation measures like pit latrines and simple privies could reduce the incidence of cholera by 60 to 90 percent.

E7-4   Chronic Noninfectious Diseases: Cancer

Nature and Effects of Cancer   Cancer is the name for a group of more than 100 different diseases—one for essentially each of the major cell types in the human body. It is characterized by the uncontrolled or malignant growth of cells in body tissues, leading to the formation of tumors. *Benign tumors* grow slowly, do not spread to other parts of the body, and are enclosed in a fibrous capsule. In contrast, the *malignant tumors* that characterize cancer tend to grow rapidly; they spread to other parts of the body in a process called *metastasis*, and are rarely encapsulated.

Cancer is usually a *latent disease*, having a typical time lag of 15 to 40 years between the initial cause and the appearance of symptoms. The long time lag, along with the number of different types of cancer, makes it extremely difficult to identify

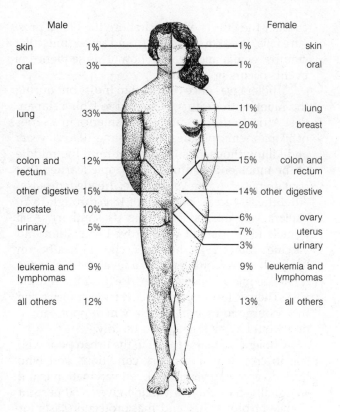

Male			Female
skin	1%	1%	skin
oral	3%	1%	oral
lung	33%	11%	lung
		20%	breast
colon and rectum	12%	15%	colon and rectum
other digestive	15%	14%	other digestive
prostate	10%		
urinary	5%	6%	ovary
		7%	uterus
		3%	urinary
leukemia and lymphomas	9%	9%	leukemia and lymphomas
all others	12%	13%	all others

Figure E7-3 Where fatal cancer strikes; percentages of all U.S. cancer deaths in 1977.

the specific cause or causes of a particular cancer. This time lag also prevents many people from taking simple precautions that would greatly decrease their chances of getting the disease. For instance, it is very difficult for high school students, college students, and other young adults in good health to accept the fact that their smoking, drinking, and eating habits *today* will be major determinants of whether many of them die from cancer during their thirties, forties, or fifties.

Evidence suggests that human cancer is the result of a genetic error or mutation in one or more of the 100,000 genes found in each human cell. This means that cancer is not generally inherited, with mutation of the genes usually occurring after birth. Each gene carries the instructions—or template—for making a single protein used in the body. These instructions are carried in a specific sequence of chemicals called nucleotides, which are linked together like the boxcars of a freight train. A mutation occurs when the sequence of nucleotides in a specific gene is altered by chance or by an environmental agent. Mutated genes can be caused by exposure to an environmental agent like radiation (X-rays, radioactivity, and the sun's ultraviolet rays) or one or more chemicals called **carcinogens,** or in a few cases they can be inherited.

Incidence and Geography of Cancer Cancer affects people of all ages. Although it is mostly a disease of middle and old age because of its long time lag, it is second only to accidents as the leading cause of death in children between the ages of 5 and 14 in the United States. Males and females in the United States have different incidences and death rates from different types of cancer (Figure E7-3). In the United States the incidence of cancer in men begins to increase sharply at 35 and peaks at 65. For women it rises rapidly at age 20 and peaks at age 60.

Lung cancer is the leading cause of cancer deaths in the United States, accounting for one out of four cancer deaths each year. In 1983, lung cancer killed about 83,000 men and 34,000 women, with an estimated 85 percent of these deaths caused by cigarette smoking. Because lung cancer is difficult to detect in its early stages, only about one out of eight victims was saved. People with a nagging cough or hoarseness should see a doctor before it's too late. The best way to avoid lung cancer is prevention—primarily by stopping smoking or never taking up this habit.

The leading cause of cancer in women is breast cancer. In 1983 about 114,000 women were found to have breast cancer and about 37,000 died. Unlike lung cancer, breast cancer can be detected in its early stages. A victim has an 87 percent chance of surviving 5 or more years if the breast cancer is detected before it has spread to other parts of the body. Otherwise, the chances of recovery drop to 47 percent. Monthly self-examination of the breasts for lumps or thickening of the tissue can usually lead to detection of this type of cancer at an early stage. Treatment now rarely involves radical surgery or breast removal.

Many of the 58,000 deaths from bowel or colon-rectum cancer in 1983 could have been prevented if victims had carried out a simple, at-home detection test, the stool slide test, every year after age 50, had a doctor make a proctoscopic examination of the rectum every 3 to 5 years after age 50, and consulted a physician when they experienced any unexplained change in bowel or bladder habits. Similarly, many of the 10,000 deaths of women in 1983 from uterine cancer could have been prevented by regular pelvic examinations by a physician and by use of the Pap test for detection of this form of cancer.

Most cases of skin cancer, except a form known as malignant melanoma, can be cured if detected early enough by regular examination of the skin and by reporting to a physician immediately if a skin sore does not heal quickly, or if a mole or wart begins to increase in size or change in color. Even if cured, however, skin cancers often leave disfiguring scars. Outdoor workers are particularly sus-

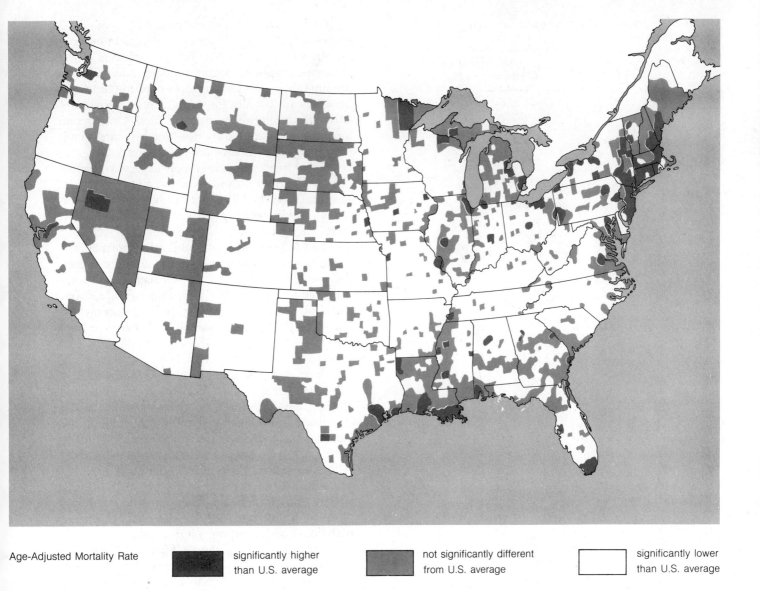

Age-Adjusted Mortality Rate   ■ significantly higher than U.S. average   ▣ not significantly different from U.S. average   □ significantly lower than U.S. average

Figure E7-4   Geographic patterns of cancer mortality rates for all males (at all body sites) in the United States, 1950-1969.

ceptible to cancer on the skin of the face, hands, and arms. White Americans who spend long hours in the sun or under sun lamps (which are even more hazardous than direct exposure to the sun) greatly increase their chances of developing skin cancer and also tend to have wrinkled, dry skin by age 40. Sunbathers can reduce this risk greatly and still get a tan (although more slowly) by using lotions containing sunscreen agents, which block out most of the harmful ultraviolet rays of the sun and sun lamps.

Cancer death rates vary geographically between countries and within countries. The rates for breast cancer and bowel cancer are four to five times higher in the United States than in Japan, whereas stomach cancer rates in Japan are almost seven times higher than in the United States. Figure E7-4 shows how the death rates for cancer vary in white males throughout the United States. Similar patterns have been found for white women and for black men and women. From Figure E7-4 we see that the highest cancer mortality rates are found in large cities and in the heavily industrialized states of the Northeast and Great Lakes regions.

Diagnosis and Treatment   Many people automatically think of death when they hear the word cancer. Oncologists, physicians who specialize in cancer, reckon that any patient who survives for 5 years after treatment and shows no trace of the disease is cured. On this basis, *about 40 to 50 percent of all Americans who get cancer can now be cured because of a combination of early detection and improved use of sur-*

Table E7-3 Chances of Recovering from Cancer in the United States

Type of Cancer	Chance of Survival for 5 Years or More (%)	
	Diagnosed 1960–1963	Diagnosed 1973–1980
Among Adults		
Lining of uterus	73	87
Testis	63	82
Skin (melanoma)	60	79
Breast	63	73
Bladder	53	72
Hodgkin's disease	40	70
Uterine cervix	58	67
Prostate	50	67
Colon	43	50
Kidney	37	50
Rectum	38	48
Ovary	32	37
Leukemia	14	32
Brain	18	22
Stomach	11	15
Lung	8	12
Esophagus	4	4
Pancreas	1	3
Among Children		
Hodgkin's disease	52	84
Wilm's tumor	57	75
Acute lympho-cytic leukemia	4	58
Brain and central nervous system	35	53
Neuroblastoma	25	47
Bone	20	46
Non-Hodgkin's lymphoma	18	46
Acute granulocytic leukemia	3	22

gery, radiation, and drugs (chemotherapy) as treatment (Table E7-3), compared to only a 25 percent cure rate 30 years ago.* Survival rates for many types of cancer now range from 67 to 87 percent (Table E7-3).

*To obtain information from the National Cancer Institute about cancer and to find out where to go for help, call the toll-free number, 1-800-4-CANCER.

Despite this important progress, Table E7-3 shows that there has been little success in increasing the survival rates for victims of cancers of the pancreas, esophagus, lung, stomach, and brain. By the time they are spotted, cancers of the lung and pancreas are usually too far advanced for a cure, although chemotherapy is often tried. Only in one form of lung cancer, known as "oat cell" carcinoma, have drugs shown substantial promise.

Today treatment consists of surgery to remove cancerous growths, and radiation and chemotherapeutic drugs to kill cancer cells. Radiation and today's anticancer drugs are somewhat like shotgun blasts—they kill not only the cancerous cells but also hair follicles, gut cells, and other normal fast-growing cells. This is why extreme fatigue, diarrhea, weight and hair loss, severe nausea and vomiting, reduction in the body's resistance to infection, and destruction of blood platelets are common side effects of the use of radiation and drugs to treat cancer.

Experts are exploring wholly new kinds of treatment that, if successful, should lead to greatly increased survival rates and fewer harmful side effects. One approach is *immunotherapy*, using chemicals and monoclonal antibodies made in the lab by genetic engineering techniques to stimulate the body's own disease defenses to attack cancer cells. Researchers have already identified 50 to 100 proteins like *interferon* that may have antitumor effects, and have located the genes that code for more than a dozen of them. Scientists also have high hopes of developing a series of *monoclonal antibodies* for each type of cancer. Such antibodies are used to carry drugs or radioactive isotopes directly to tumors without harm to healthy tissues. This rifle-shot approach to treatment could eliminate most side effects associated with present chemo- and radiotherapy approaches. In 1982 one of the first patients to be treated with clonal antibodies was cured of a rare type of lymphatic cancer that had spread to his liver, blood, bone marrow, and spleen. Preliminary tests using monoclonal antibodies are also being conducted in patients with colon cancer, breast cancer, and leukemia.

Cancer Risk Factors   Hereditary factors are involved in an estimated 10 to 30 percent of all cancers. Examples of genetically transferable cancer risks include leukemia in mongoloid children (Down's syndrome), breast cancer, ovarian cancer, malignant melanoma, retinoblastoma (a rare form of eye cancer), and lung cancer (although heredity is not nearly as important as smoking).

Environmental factors—including such aspects of life-style as diet and smoking—are believed to contribute to or directly cause the remaining 70 to 90 percent of all cancers. For example, studies have shown that U.S. Mormons, who do not smoke or drink alcohol or anything containing caffeine, have a rate of cancer incidence one-half that of the average U.S. white population. Thus, each of us can greatly reduce the risks of developing cancer by trying to find work in a less hazardous environment, not smoking, drinking in moderation (maximum consumption between two drinks a day and five drinks a week) or not at all, and adhering to a healthy diet.

Cancer and Smoking   There is widespread agreement and overwhelming statistical evidence from more than 30,000 studies that the leading cause of cancer deaths (mostly from lung cancer) is *cigarette smoking*—causing an estimated 30 percent (with a range of 25 to 40 percent) of all cancer deaths in the United States. If Americans stopped smoking this would save about 132,000 lives a year within 20 years at today's cancer death rate.

The effects of smoking on cancer rates can also be increased by synergistic interaction with other factors. For example, more lung cancer is found among cigarette smokers living in a polluted industrial urban environment than among those living in an unpolluted rural environment. Alcohol consumption by itself causes an estimated 3 percent of all cancer deaths in the United States, especially liver cancer. Alcohol and smoking can also interact synergistically. In the United States, for example, moderate smokers who drink heavily are 25 times more likely to develop cancer of the esophagus than smokers who don't drink. Heavy drinkers are two to three times more likely to develop cancer of the mouth and larynx, with smoking multiplying the risk.

A British government study showed that adolescents who smoke more than one cigarette have an 85 percent chance of becoming smokers, indicating along with other data that nicotine is one of the most addictive drugs. Other studies have shown that most teen-agers who smoke more than two cigarettes per day become regular cigarette smokers and that a child is about twice as likely to become a smoker if either parent is one. There is some good news, however. Studies show that about 10 to 15 years after former smokers quit, they have about the same risk of dying from lung cancer as those who never smoked.

Suggestions for reducing the cancer risks from smoking include: **(1)** trying to prevent young people from getting hooked on cigarettes, **(2)** banning all cigarette advertising, or restricting it to simple black-and-white print ads, so that slick presentations can-

not be used to create the impression that smokers are young, attractive, sophisticated, healthy, and sexy, **(3)** passing and enforcing strict laws to protect nonsmokers in public places and encouraging offices and businesses to allow smoking only in designated areas, **(4)** eliminating all financial subsidies to the tobacco industry and offsetting the resulting loss of income and jobs by providing aid and subsidies that would allow farmers to grow more healthful crops, **(5)** specifying for all cigarettes maximum allowable levels of tar, nicotine, and other health-threatening chemicals, and **(6)** increasing research to develop tobacco substitutes and less harmful cigarettes.

Sweden has led the way by putting into effect a 25-year program that hopes to make children born after 1974 the country's first nonsmoking generation. Intensive education on the hazards of smoking will be introduced at all school levels beginning in kindergarten, no one under 16 will be allowed to buy cigarettes, the sale of cigarettes in vending machines will be banned, cigarette prices will be raised gradually, cigarette advertising will be phased out, and all cigarette packs must carry tar and nicotine levels along with 16 different warnings on the specific hazards of smoking.

Cancer and Diet   A second major cause of cancer is improper *diet*, causing an estimated 35 percent (with a range of 10 to 70 percent) of all cancer deaths. However, evidence linking specific dietary habits to specific types of cancer is difficult to obtain and is controversial. The major factors—especially in cancers of the breast, bowel (colon and rectum), liver, kidney, stomach, and prostate—may be fats, fibers, nitrosamines, and nitrites. The incidence of cancers of the colon, rectum, and female breast is about five times higher in Americans than in Japanese, who have low-fat diets. Third-generation children of Japanese immigrants, however, have about the same incidence of these types of cancer as other Americans. A high-fat, high-protein diet may also be a factor in cancers of the breast, prostate, testis, ovary, pancreas, and kidney.

Others have proposed that high incidences of bowel cancer may result from the low fiber content in Western diets, a by-product of the use of highly refined foods. Studies have given conflicting results, however, and the low-fiber hypothesis is still controversial. More recent work indicates that the incidence of bowel cancer is lower in test animals and apparently in individuals whose diet includes daily intakes of cruciferous vegetables. There is also some evidence that the incidence of stomach and bowel cancer may be reduced by adequate amounts of beta-carotene, vitamin C (and perhaps vitamin E), and trace minerals such as selenium and zinc.

High levels of nitrate and nitrite food preservatives (Enrichment Study 9), found in smoked and cured meats and in some brands of beer, may increase the risk of stomach cancer because the body converts them to carcinogenic nitrosoamines, which cause cancer in test animals. This has been implicated in the very high incidence of stomach cancer in Japan, where the diet consists of large amounts of dried, salted, pickled, and smoked fish.

A 1982 study by the National Academy of Sciences recommended that the risk of certain types of cancer like those of the lung, stomach, colon, and esophagus could be significantly reduced by a daily diet that (1) consists of no more than 30 percent saturated and unsaturated fats (compared to the 40 percent fat diet of the average American) by cutting down on fatty meat, whole-milk dairy products, butter, cooking oils, and fats, (2) includes fruits, especially those like oranges and grapefruit that are rich in vitamin C, (3) includes carotene-rich, dark green and deep yellow vegetables and cruciferous vegetables like cabbage, broccoli, cauliflower, and brussels sprouts, (4) includes whole-grain fiber from raw bran (the cheapest source), bran in cereals, and fibers in vegetables and fruits, (5) includes a dietary intake of selenium not exceeding 200 micrograms per day, and (6) includes very little salt-cured, salt-pickled, and smoked foods like sausages, smoked fish and ham, bacon, bologna, salami, corned beef, and hot dogs that contain large amounts of nitrates and nitrites as preservatives.

Cancer and the Workplace   The third major cause of cancer is *occupational exposure* to carcinogens and radiation, causing about 5 percent of cancer deaths according to some health scientists and up to 20 percent according to others. This represents 22,000 to 88,000 deaths each year, depending on the estimate used. Most of these deaths could be prevented by stricter rules and stricter enforcement of existing rules governing exposure of workers to radiation and dangerous chemicals.

The major job risk is exposure to *asbestos,* which has already killed more than 100,000 U.S. workers and will probably kill at least 350,000 additional heavily exposed workers over the next 30 to 35 years through its relationship to cancers of the lung, bowel, stomach, and the linings of the lungs and stomach (mesothelioma).* It also greatly increases the risk

---

*The serious cancer risk from exposure to asbestos is greatly increased by smoking. An asbestos worker who smokes has 11 times the risk of dying from lung cancer as a co-worker who doesn't smoke, and 55 times the risk of a person who neither works with asbestos nor smokes. For this reason, the Johns-Manville Corporation decided in 1977 not to hire smokers to work in their asbestos mines and plants.

of noncancer lung diseases like emphysema and asbestosis.

Asbestos is a major threat to asbestos miners and plant workers, auto mechanics (because of brake linings), steamfitters, carpenters, tile setters, and insulation and construction workers. Asbestos fibers carried home from factories on the clothes and bodies of workers have also caused lung cancer in about one-third of their family members. School children, office workers, and other members of the general public can also be exposed to asbestos used from 1900 to 1980 in U.S. ships, buildings, and schools (primarily as insulation), chemical plants, and other facilities.

Other major job risks include exposure to (1) *vinyl chloride* (3.5 million workers), which increases the risks of a rare liver cancer (hemangiosarcoma), brain cancer, and lung cancer, respectively, 200, 4, and 2 times, (2) *benzene* (2.9 million workers), which increases the risk of leukemia by a factor of 2 to 7, (3) *arsenic* (1.5 million workers), which increases the risk of lung cancer by a factor of 3 to 8, and (4) *coal tar pitch* and *coke oven emissions* (60,000 workers), which increase the risk of cancers of the lung, larynx, skin, and scrotum by a factor of 2 to 6.

Reducing job-related exposure requires strict control of all mining and manufacturing processes involving known or suspected carcinogens. Major methods for controlling exposure to hazardous industrial chemicals include (1) eliminating the chemical, (2) segregating the hazard in a room or building, (3) covering bins, conveyors, and vats containing toxic substances, (4) installing ventilation and exhaust systems that draw workplace pollutants away from workers and replace the exhausted air with fresh air, and (5) rotating workers in and out of hazardous jobs to keep exposure below unsafe levels.

If enforced, the Occupational Safety and Health Act of 1970 and the Toxic Control Substances Act of 1975 (Section 19-7 and Enrichment Study 13) could be important factors in establishing such controls. However, political pressure by industry officials has hindered effective enforcement of these laws. Maximum permissible standards set by the Occupational Safety and Health Administration (OSHA) for many major pollutants in the workplace range from 2 to 100 times higher than those set by the EPA for the general population. Such double standards for protection exist in most other industrialized countries, but occupational standards for most workplace pollutants are much more stringent in the Soviet Union and in many East European countries than in the United States.

Furthermore, according to occupational health expert Samuel Epstein, workers in general are denied knowledge of the types and concentrations of the chemicals they are exposed to and are often not informed whether chemicals have been adequately tested and whether they are toxic or carcinogenic under conditions in the plant. In some cases, research findings that could save the lives of workers have been kept secret or not acted on. For example, studies done several decades ago showed that uranium miners in central Europe were dying of lung cancer with higher than normal frequency and that the risk could be reduced by installing adequate ventilation in uranium mines. But it was not until 1977 that improved ventilation was required in American uranium mines.

Opponents of stricter government control of worker exposure to potentially dangerous chemicals sometimes state that almost anything can cause cancer, so why pick on one particular chemical. Health scientists argue, however, that this is a misleading argument because most chemicals tested don't cause cancer. By 1977 about 700 of the 1,500 chemicals that had been thoroughly tested were found to cause cancer in test animals, and only 26 (18 of them found in the work place) had been directly linked to cancer in humans.

Cancer and Pollution A fourth cause of cancer is *air and water pollution*, estimated to contribute to between 1 and 5 percent of cancer deaths in the United States. This contribution may be more significant, however, for certain individuals, including **(1)** those living in airtight energy-efficient housing without air-to-air heat exchangers (because of higher than normal levels of indoor air pollution— Section 19-1), **(2)** nonsmokers who work or live in an environment that exposes them to cigarette smoke, and **(3)** residents of cities where chlorinated water can interact with industrial organic compounds and bromine to form halomethanes, which have been linked to higher than normal incidences of rectal, bladder, and colon cancer (Section 18-2).

Health and a good state of body are above all gold, and a strong body above infinite wealth.

Ecclesiastes 40:15

Discussion Topics

1. Compare the social ecology of disease patterns in more developed and less developed countries. Why are infectious diseases more common in LDCs? Why do so many infants and young children in LDCs die from measles, diarrhea, and other common childhood diseases?

2. List diseases you or members of your family have had and classify them according to the type of disease and the probable mode of transmission. Which types are likely to be hereditary, making you or your offspring more susceptible to attack?

3. Discuss the life cycle, mode of transmission, effects, possible control, and side effects of control of malaria and schistosomiasis.

4. Should DDT and other pesticides be banned from use in malaria control? Why or why not? (See Section 9-9.)

5. How can cholera be brought under better control? Why are there often outbreaks of cholera in an area struck by an earthquake, flood, or other natural disaster?

6. Analyze the incidence and types of cancer death in the area in which you live. Can you account for the high incidence of certain types of cancer?

7. Give some possible reasons for the death rate from breast cancer in the United States being almost six times higher than in Japan, while the death rate for stomach cancer in Japan is almost seven times higher than in the United States.

8. Analyze your life-style and diet to determine your relative risks of developing some form of cancer before you reach age 55. Which type of cancer are you most likely to get? How could you significantly reduce your chances of getting this cancer?

9. Give your reasons for agreeing or disagreeing with each of the six proposals listed in the text designed to reduce the health hazards of smoking.

Enrichment Study 8

Birth Control Methods Today and Tomorrow

The ideal contraceptive has yet to be found. Indeed, given the diversity of needs of people throughout the world, there will never be a perfect method for everyone. But we can list the desired characteristics of any contraceptive. It should be 100 percent effective, harmless, long lasting, easy to administer, and cheap; its effect should be readily reversible, it should offer protection against sexually transmitted diseases, and it should be acceptable to local populations with respect to cultural, religious, and sexual attitudes.

E8-1 Today's Birth Control Methods

Types and Effectiveness Present methods of birth control can be divided into three basic types:

1. *Biological*
   a. Abstention (no intercourse)
   b. Rhythm method (no intercourse during woman's fertile period)
   c. Coitus interruptus (withdrawal before male's climax)

2. *Mechanical*
   a. Condom (protective sheath that covers penis)
   b. Intrauterine device (IUD) (small plastic or metal device inserted semipermanently into uterus)
   c. Surgical sterilization (tubal ligation and tubal occlusion, which obstruct the tubes that carry eggs in women; vasectomy, which obstructs the tubes that carry sperm in men)

3. *Chemical*
   a. Douche (rinsing vagina with a chemical immediately after intercourse)
   b. Spermicides (sperm-killing foams, jellies, and creams used before intercourse)
   c. Sponge impregnated with spermicide

(inserted into vagina for up to 24 hours where spermicide kills sperm and sponge absorbs sperm and partially blocks cervix)
   d. Diaphragm with spermicide (dome-shaped disk placed over cervical opening before intercourse, with application of spermicide to kill sperm)
   e. Oral contraceptives (the "pill") (hormones to control woman's reproductive cycle, taken as pills)
   f. IUD with slow-release hormone (hormonal control of woman's reproductive cycle)

Table E8-1 summarizes the typical effectiveness of these methods in the United States based on use by couples for one year. Although effectiveness is obviously a major factor, choosing a method for birth control is a highly individual process influenced by possible side effects, cost, inconvenience, and availability, as well as the user's education,[*] motivation, religious views, and age. On a lifetime cost basis per year over a 30-year period, the least expensive mechanical or chemical method of contraception is sterilization and the most expensive is the pill. Various contraceptive methods are suited for different stages of reproductive life or for different life-styles. Sterilization, for example, may be used by couples who have achieved their desired family size, while the IUDs, sponges, and oral contraceptives are more suitable for spacing offspring. Couples with very strong motivation can and do use rhythm and withdrawal methods with reasonable success. However, many others who use these methods or who rely on douches alone are called Mommy and Daddy.

By 1982 about 92 percent of the sexually active U.S. couples capable of having children and between

---

[*]Contraceptive education in LDCs has its special problems. Government birth control workers visiting rural villages in Southeast Asia demonstrated condoms by pulling them over a stick. Returning weeks later, they found that the villagers had faithfully followed their instructions: Each couple had placed a condom over a piece of wood by their sleeping mat.

Table E8-1 Typical Effectiveness of Birth Control Methods Used in the United States

Method	Typical Effectiveness (%)
Extremely Effective	
Abortion	100
Sterilization	
Tubal ligation and tubal occlusion (women)	99.5
Vasectomy (men)	99.5
Highly Effective	
Oral contraceptives	98
IUD with slow-release hormones	98
IUD plus spermicide	98
Diaphragm plus spermicide	98
IUD	
Copper T	97
Older loops	95
Condom (good brand) plus spermicide	95
Effective	
Condom (good brand)	90
Vaginal sponge impregnated with spermicide	85
Spermicide (vaginal foam)	85
Diaphragm alone	81
Moderately Effective	
Rhythm method based on daily temperature readings	76
Spermicide (creams, jellies, suppositories)	75
Relatively Ineffective	
Condom (cheap brand)	70
Withdrawal	70
Rhythm method not based on daily temperature readings	Variable but normally below 60
Unreliable	
Douche	40

the ages of 15 to 44 used some form of birth control. The most popular method was sterilization, relied on by 32 percent of sexually active couples (19 percent of the women and 13 percent of the men) in this age group. This was followed by oral contra-

ceptives (27 percent), condoms (12 percent), IUDs (6 percent), diaphragms (5 percent), spermicides (4 percent), withdrawal (3 percent), rhythm (2 percent), and douche (less than 0.5 percent).

Despite overall widespread contraceptive use, unwanted teen-aged pregnancy remains a major problem in the United States, with 1 million female teen-agers—one out of ten—getting pregnant each year. A 1981 survey showed that about 86 percent of all U.S. teen-agers did not seek any birth control advice before their first sexual encounter because of ignorance, unwillingness, or the unavailability of contraceptive devices. Surveys have shown that teen-agers who have had a sex education course are no more likely to be sexually active than those who have not. However, sexually active young women who have had sex education are less likely to become pregnant than those who have not received such instruction.

Worldwide as well, the most widely used form of birth control by 1982 was sterilization. Between 1970 and 1982, the number of voluntary sterilizations worldwide increased 450 percent, from about 20 million to 110 million (75 million women and 45 million men). Surveys show that more people would choose sterilization if it were more readily available throughout the world. The second most popular form of birth control was oral contraceptives (with approximately 58 million users), followed by IUDs (approximately 52 million users), and condoms (about 37 million users).

From these data we can see that women have assumed the major burden for birth control. This is partly a result of the attitudes of many men and partly because women have more at stake—they are the ones who bear the physical and emotional strain of carrying a child for 9 months, and they face the substantial risk of dying in childbirth. It also happens that scientists have had more difficulty in finding contraceptives to block sperm production or mobility in males than in females, although progress is being made and effective male contraceptives may be available sometime after 1990 (Section E8-2).

Benefits and Risks Table E8-2 summarizes some of the advantages and disadvantages of present birth control methods. The risk of death from usage of oral contraceptives—especially the newer ones low in progesterone—up to age 35 is very low and is significantly lower than the death rate from pregnancy and birth. Indeed, in the United States all major forms of birth control involve considerably less risk than pregnancy except for women over the age of 35 who are pill users and who smoke.

Table E8-2 Comparison of Birth Control Methods

Method	Causes or Technique	Advantages	Disadvantages
Abortion, self-induced or by an unqualified person	Trauma; chemical action on breaking the membranes starts premature labor	Sometimes effective; only alternative to birth where it is illegal	Woman may die of infection or bleed to death; fetus may be damaged
Abortion by a qualified physician			
Vacuum aspiration (during first 12 weeks of pregnancy)	Cervix dilated, embryo and placenta gently sucked out by vacuum pump	100% effective; simple and quick; does not require overnight hospital stay	Possible psychological effects and guilt feelings; does not prevent sexually transmitted disease (STD)
Dilation and curettage (D&C) (during first 12 weeks of pregnancy)	Surgical dilation (widening) of cervix followed by scraping of embryo and placenta from walls of uterus	100% effective; relatively simple 20- to 30-minute procedure	Classed as surgery; normally requires overnight hospital stay; 1 to 2% have complications; possible psychological effects and guilt feelings; does not prevent STD
Intraamniotic injections (after 16 weeks of pregnancy)	Needle inserted through abdominal wall into cavity of uterus; small amount of amniotic fluid withdrawn and replaced with salt solution; induces labor	100% effective	Same as D&C except more serious; slightly higher risk of complications
Sterilization			
Tubal ligation (female)	Fallopian tubes (which carry eggs from ovary to uterus) are cut and tied	99.5% effective; no inherent detrimental effects on sex life; may increase enjoyment of sex by removing fear of pregnancy; low lifetime cost	Surgical procedure; hemorrhage or damage to the bowel occurs in 0.6% of patients; requires 4 to 6 days in hospital (a new, safer technique—laparoscopy—cuts normal hospital stay to 1 day); rarely reversible; moderate to high cost; does not prevent STD
Tubal occlusion	Liquid silicone is pumped through catheter into openings of fallopian tubes, where it hardens to form plug of rubber-band consistency	Can be done in physician's office in one hour; requires only local anesthetic; no detrimental effects on sex life; low lifetime cost	Not reversible now but may eventually be; does not prevent STD
Vasectomy (male)	Very small incision made in scrotum; small section removed from one of the tubes that carry sperm; ends are tied	99.5% effective after sperm counts become zero; simple, safe, 20-minute procedure; no hospitalization needed; no inherent effect on sex life; volume of ejaculate not measurably changed; may increase enjoyment of sex by removing fear of pregnancy; low lifetime cost; may reduce incidence of cervical cancer in female partners	Normally not reversible, but techniques are improving (new microsurgery techniques improve chances of reversing process to about 45%). Tests on monkeys revealed increased risk of atherosclerosis (clogging of blood vessels), but later tests on humans revealed no increased risks of this condition; possible psychological effects; does not prevent STD
Oral contraceptive	Pill containing synthetic female hormones (estrogen and progestin) or just progestin (minipill), taken once a day, keeps ovary from releasing egg	98% effective; separate from intercourse; no loss of sensation; easy to ingest; regulates periods and decreases menstrual cramps; may help prevent cancer of the ovaries and cervix, PID, ectopic pregnancy, and benign breast disease	Possible side effects (nausea, weight gain, headaches, dizziness, tissue swelling, genital irritation), which usually disappear within a few months; should not be used by women suffering from blood-clotting disorders, diabetes, high blood

Method	Cause or Technique	Advantages	Disadvantages
			pressure, liver disease, cystic fibrosis, breast cancer, or obesity; should not be used by heavy smokers, women over 40, or pregnant women; prescription needed; must be taken regularly; periodic medical exam required; does not prevent STD; highest lifetime cost
Intrauterine device (IUD)	Small plastic or plastic and metal device inserted through vagina into uterus; apparently causes minor inflammation of uterine lining, which prevents fertilized egg from implanting on uterine wall	95 to 97% effective; constant protection; separate from intercourse; no loss of sensation; easily and quickly inserted; especially suitable for large-scale programs; moderate lifetime cost	Must be inserted and checked by physician; less likely to be effective during the first few months after insertion; possibility of expulsion (expulsion rate less than 6% with new copper IUDs); possible side effects such as minor pain and bleeding (except for copper IUDs), which usually disappear within a few months; some cases of pelvic infection and puncture of uterus; can cause miscarriages and some complications if user becomes pregnant; not recommended for women who have had recent or repeated gonorrhea, PID, past ectopic pregnancy, heart disease, or diabetes, and those who have multiple sex partners and are under age 25; does not prevent STD (but may in the future)
IUD with slow-release hormone	Unlike pill, which acts throughout the body, hormone stays in uterus to prevent egg release for 12 months; also normal IUD effect	Same as conventional IUD except even more effective (98%); must be replaced once a year in a doctor's office; avoids most side effects of the pill	Same as conventional IUD
Diaphragm plus spermicide	Flexible, hemispherical rubber dome used with spermicidal cream or jelly; inserted by woman into vagina to fit over cervix before intercourse; mechanically blocks sperm from reaching egg and spermicide kills sperm	Highly effective (98%); no side effects; moderate lifetime cost; reduces risk of developing a severe case of PID	May interrupt sexual act (some new foams can be inserted several hours before intercourse); must be inserted correctly; must be fitted and prescribed by physician; requires high motivation; does not prevent STD; not recommended for those allergic to rubber or spermicides
Condom	Thin sheath of rubber or animal skin worn tightly over penis to keep sperm from entering vagina	Effective (90%) with good brand; highly effective (95%) when good brand is used jointly with spermicide; no side effects; used by male; no prescriptions required; prevents STD	May be aesthetically unpleasant; may interrupt sexual act; dulls sensation; can break; demands high motivation; fairly high lifetime cost

Method	Cause or Technique	Advantages	Disadvantages
Vaginal sponge impregnated with spermicide	Sponge that comes impregnated with a spermicide is moistened with water and inserted into vagina. Released over 24 hours, the spermicide kills sperm, which the sponge absorbs while partially blocking cervix	Can be worn for up to 24 hours and used for multiple acts of intercourse; does not interfere with sexual spontaneity; no prescription needed; one size fits all; easy to insert; less messy than foams, creams, and jellies	Moderately effective (85%) but not highly effective; about 4% of users develop allergic reactions including itching, irritation, and rash; must be left in place for at least 6 hours after intercourse; odor if left in for more than 18 hours; some users find it difficult to locate and remove; not recommended for use during menstruation until it can be determined whether device contributes to incidence of toxic shock syndrome; moderately expensive (about $1 per sponge)
Spermicides (foams, creams, jellies, suppositories)	Applicator used to squirt or insert preparations far into vagina before intercourse; kills sperm	Foam 85% effective but creams, jellies, and suppositories only moderately effective (75%); no major side effects; no prescription required; moderate lifetime cost; some types reduce STD in women	Messy; cheap brands relatively ineffective (70%); may interrupt sexual act; uncomfortable for a few users; does not prevent STD for males and only partially for females; risk of getting pregnant while using or shortly after; discontinuance may increase birth defect and miscarriage chances; to be effective, must have intercourse within a half-hour after application; reapplication necessary for additional sex acts; may cause allergic reactions in some women
Rhythm	Intercourse limited to woman's nonfertile period; in calendar method, woman keeps a monthly record of her cycles; in temperature method, temperature taken daily on awakening (a 0.5 to 1.0°F rise occurs just before fertile period)	Temperature method moderately effective (76%); no side effects; no physician needed; only accepted practice for Catholics; no cost except for thermometer	Both methods demand great care and motivation; hard to use; failure rate varies widely but is typically 40% without temperature method; no sex for 11 days out of each 28-day period; cannot be used effectively if woman has irregular menstruation; fear of pregnancy may lessen sexual enjoyment; does not prevent STD
Withdrawal (coitus interruptus)	Male partner withdraws penis from vagina before ejaculation (oldest known contraceptive method)	No cost; better than nothing	Works poorly (30% failure) because some sperm may escape before climax; demands very high motivation and self-control; may limit sexual gratification; does not prevent STD
Douche	Flushing of vagina with spermicide immediately after intercourse to remove or destroy sperm	Slightly better than nothing; low cost	Poor method (60% failure) because sperm enter cervix within 90 seconds after ejaculation; does not prevent STD

E8-2 Possible Birth Control Methods of the Future

Researchers throughout the world are at work trying to develop new and better methods of fertility control. Some of the possibilities for the future are as follows.

1. *Morning-after pill:* The synthetic hormone diethylstilbestrol (DES) will prevent pregnancy if taken for 5 days within 72 hours after intercourse. It was approved in 1975 by the U.S. Food and Drug Administration for use in emergency situations, such as rape. Its use may be limited because of side effects (intense nausea and vomiting) and possible linkage to a rare vaginal cancer in daughters of women who have used it. Research is under way to find safer compounds. One promising approach that could be available by 1990 is the use of vaginal suppositories containing prostaglandin analogue compounds that induce menstruation.

2. *Abortion pills and suppositories:* Prostaglandins that affect hormone actions are being used to abort pregnancies of 12 to 16 weeks' duration. They are not considered as safe as saline injection, and they have side effects, including nausea, vomiting, headache, and sometimes diarrhea. Promising preliminary animal and human tests have been conducted in France on a steroid that can be taken up to several days after intercourse or after a woman has missed her period to guarantee menstruation by blocking the action of progesterone and thus inducing abortion. It could also be taken only 2 to 4 days a month and used as an oral contraceptive. If longer-term tests on humans establish its safety, this drug could be available after 1990.

3. *Long-lasting injections and pills:* Injections of Depo-Provera, a synthetic progestin, provide contraceptive protection for 3 months. It is essentially 100 percent effective in preventing pregnancy, needs to be taken only four times a year, and has been used by 11 million women in 80 countries since 1963. Depo-Provera has been approved by the FDA for the treatment of certain kinds of kidney and uterine cancer. So far, however, the FDA has refused to permit its use as a contraceptive because it has caused breast tumors in beagles and uterine cancers in monkeys. It also can cause weight gain, loss of sex drive, and menstrual irregularities. Supporters of the drug argue that usage in other countries for 20 years has provided no evidence of an increased risk of cancer and that it is as safe as other approved oral contraceptives and IUDs, if not safer. Critics argue, however, that Depo-Provera hasn't been used long enough to tell how risky it is for humans. Preliminary human testing has also begun on a synthetic brain hormone called LHRH (for *luteinizing-hormone-releasing hormone*), which prevents conception by altering the menstrual cycle. It could be taken as a once-a-month injection or in pill form. If tests are successful, LHRH could be available for use by 1995.

4. *Long-lasting hormone implants:* A continuous low dose of progestin can be released into the blood or into the uterus either by a pill in a biodegradable capsule that is implanted under the skin or by a ring that is inserted into the vagina. These implantations would release minute daily doses of only one hormone (not estrogen, which causes most side effects from the pill). The capsule could be removed at any time; but while in place, it would remain effective for 1 to 6 years. Such implants have been widely tested on animals, and human trials are under way. If successful, the method could be available by 1990.

5. *Antipregnancy vaccine:* A vaccine that causes pregnant females to menstruate and thus to wash away a fertilized ovum has been tested on animals with no adverse side effects. Previously sterilized women to whom the vaccine was administered also showed no ill effects. Further tests on fertile women are being carried out, but more work needs to be done to establish reliability and long-term safety.

6. *Male contraceptives:* Earlier male hormone pills tended to reduce sex drive. Recently, however, encouraging results were obtained in human tests using the steroid danazol (which suppresses sperm production) in combination with a monthly injection of a synthetic male hormone, testosterone (to ensure a healthy sex drive). Further testing is needed to establish reliability and long-term effects and to ensure that an egg will not be fertilized by a partially damaged sperm. Human tests have also been made using LHRH, which in large doses shuts down the production of sperm. Unfortunately, this hormone also reduces the sex drive (unless combined with testosterone) and has caused some men to suffer hot flashes like those of menopausal women. Nonhuman animal tests have also been successful on a salve rubbed on the stomach; it contains a combination of testosterone and estradiol (a form of estrogen), which causes the brain to halt sperm production but does not alter the sex drive. Gossypol, extracted from cottonseed oil, has been tested as a male contraceptive in

China since 1978, in Brazil since 1980, and on animals in the United States. But data are still incomplete and some reported side effects include fatigue, temporary paralysis due to reduced levels of potassium in the blood, and continued sterility and low sperm counts in one out of five users 2 years after use was discontinued. Other researchers are trying to develop compounds that will immobilize sperm. Under favorable conditions, a male pill could be on the market by 1990, but probably no sooner than 2000.

7. *Reversible vasectomy:* Microsurgery techniques and implanted valves are being used to increase the possibility of reversing male sterilization, but success is still low (no more than 45 percent).

8. *Influencing brain chemistry:* Research is under way to influence chemicals in the brain that trigger the release of hormones that suppress ovulation in females and sperm formation in males. Preliminary trials in women have not yielded data on long-term effects and reliability.

Some important and promising research is under way, but we should not expect sensational advances. Considerable money (at least $10 million), extensive testing, and much time are required before a new chemical contraceptive can be developed and approved for general use. To make matters worse, there has been a decline in the funding of such research throughout most of the world. As a Ford Foundation study put it, "The future of the human race depends not upon the conquest of cancer but on the control of human reproduction."

The future of the earth is in our hands. How shall we decide?

Pierre Teilhard de Chardin

Discussion Topics

1. What types of contraceptive and abortion counseling and services are available on your campus? Should they be broadened or made more easily available? Interview college officials or have them talk to your class about this problem and their concerns.

2. Debate whether unmarried teen-agers should have free access to birth control counseling and devices without parental permission. Try to get one or more parents who oppose free access to share their concerns with your class.

3. Explain why even the "ideal contraceptive" will not completely solve the world's population problem. Why is there no purely technological solution to the population problem?

4. In the near future couples may be able to choose the sex of their children. What effects might this have on population control in the United States? In most less developed countries? What dangers might arise? Would you use this procedure if it were available? Why or why not?

5. It might be possible, using artificial insemination or genetic alteration, to improve human stock, just as we have bred better strains of plants and livestock. Discuss the pros and cons of doing this. Suppose we could use genetic alteration to breed people who "love" one another in the best sense? Would you favor this? Why or why not?

Enrichment Study 9

The Food Additives Controversy

E9-1 Use of Food Additives in the United States

To the Editor of the [Albany, New York] *Times-Union**:

Give us this day our daily calcium propionate (spoilage retarder), sodium diacetate (mold inhibitor), monoglyceride (emulsifier), potassium bromate (maturing agent), calcium phosphate monobasic (dough conditioner), chloramine T (flour bleach), aluminum potassium sulfate acid (baking powder ingredient), sodium benzoate (preservative), butylated hydroxyanisole (antioxidant), mono-isopropyl citrate (sequestrant); plus synthetic vitamins A and D.

Forgive us, O Lord, for calling this stuff BREAD.

Averill Park   *J. H. Reed*

This letter lists only a few of the 93 different chemicals that may be added to "enriched" bread. A **food additive** is a chemical that is deliberately added to a food to modify its characteristics. Additives may be of natural origin, such as salt and spices, or they may be made synthetically, such as the preservative calcium propionate and the controversial sweetener saccharin.

All food, of course, is just a mixture of chemicals, but today at least 2,800 different chemicals are deliberately added to foods in the United States, and at least another 3,000 are used in food-packaging materials. Each year the average American consumes about 55 kilograms (120 pounds) of sugar, 7 kilograms (15 pounds) of salt, and about 4.5 kilograms (10 pounds) of other food additives.

Table E9-1 summarizes the major classes of food additives. Additives are put in food for at least 45 different reasons: to enhance flavor, color, texture, and appearance; to retard spoilage; to make foods safer for human consumption and easier to prepare; and to improve nutritional value. The most widely used groups of additives—coloring agents, natural and synthetic flavoring agents, and sweet-

eners—have the sole purpose of making food look and taste better. They contribute nothing to food safety, nutrition, or ease of preparation.

Most food additives are probably harmless or at least pose so little risk relative to their benefits, like preventing food spoilage and food poisoning, that we accept their use. However, a handful of once widely used additives like red dyes no. 2 and no. 4 have been banned in the United States because of their potential harm to humans. Most chemicals added to U.S. foods have not been adequately tested for links to cancer, genetic mutations, and birth defects.

The extremes of the controversy over food additives range from "Essentially all food additives are bad" and "We should eat only natural foods" to "There's nothing to worry about because there is no absolute proof that chemical X has ever harmed a human being." As usual, the truth probably lies somewhere between. Some additives are necessary and safe, but others are unnecessary, unsafe, or of doubtful safety. The key questions are: **(1)** What food additives are necessary? **(2)** What food additives are safe? **(3)** How well are consumers protected from unnecessary, unsafe additives?

E9-2 Food Additive Safety: Natural Versus Synthetic Foods

The presence of synthetic chemical additives does not necessarily mean that a food is harmful, and the fact that a food is completely natural is no guarantee that it is safe. A number of natural, or totally unprocessed, foods contain potentially harmful and toxic substances.

Polar bear or halibut liver can cause vitamin A poisoning. Lima beans, sweet potatoes, cassava (yams), sugarcane, cherries, plums, and apricots contain glucosides, which our intestines convert to small amounts of deadly hydrogen cyanide. Eating cabbage, cauliflower, turnips, rutabagas, mustard greens, collard greens, or brussels sprouts can cause goiter in susceptible individuals. Certain amines that can raise blood pressure dramatically are found in

---

*Used by permission of the *Times-Union*, Albany, New York.

Table E9-1 Commonly Used Food Additives and Food Processes

Class	Function	Examples	Foods Typically Treated
Preservatives	To retard spoilage caused by bacterial action and molds (fungi)	Processes: drying, smoking, curing, canning (heating and sealing), freezing, pasteurization, refrigeration	Bread, cheese, cake, jelly, chocolate syrup, fruit, vegetables, meat
		Chemicals: salt, sugar, sodium nitrate, sodium nitrite, calcium and sodium propionate, sorbic acid, potassium sorbate, benzoic acid, sodium benzoate, citric acid, sulfur dioxide	
Antioxidants (oxygen interceptors, or freshness stabilizers)	To retard spoilage of fats (excludes oxygen or slows down the chemical breakdown of fats)	Processes: sealing cans, wrapping, refrigeration Chemicals: lecithin, butylated hydroxyanisole (BHA), butylated hydroxytoluene (BHT), propyl gallate	Cooking oil, shortening, cereal, potato chips, crackers, salted nuts, soup, toaster tarts, artificial whipped topping, artificial orange juice, many other foods
Nutritional supplements	To increase nutritive value of natural food or to replace nutrients lost in food processing*	Vitamins, essential amino acids	Bread and flour (vitamins and amino acids), milk (vitamin D), rice (vitamin B_1), corn meal, cereal
Flavoring agents	To add or enhance flavor	Over 1,700 substances, including saccharin, monosodium glutamate (MSG), essential oils (such as cinnamon, banana, vanilla)	Ice cream, artificial fruit juice, toppings, soft drinks, candy, pickles, salad dressing, spicy meats, low-calorie foods and drinks, most processed heat-and-serve foods
Coloring agents	To add aesthetic or sales appeal, to hide colors that are unappealing or that show lack of freshness	Natural color dyes, synthetic coal tar dyes	Soft drinks, butter, cheese, ice cream, cereal, candy, cake mix, sausage, pudding, many other foods
Acidulants	To provide a tart taste or to mask undesirable aftertastes	Phosphoric acid, citric acid, fumaric acid	Cola and fruit soft drinks, desserts, fruit juice, cheese, salad dressing, gravy, soup
Alkalis	To reduce natural acidity	Sodium carbonate, sodium bicarbonate	Canned peas, wine, olives, coconut cream pie, chocolate eclairs
Emulsifiers	To disperse droplets of one liquid (such as oil) in another liquid (such as water)	Lecithin, propylene glycol, mono- and diglycerides, polysorbates	Ice cream, candy, margarine, icing, nondairy creamer, dessert topping, mayonnaise, salad dressing, shortening
Stabilizers and thickeners	To provide smooth texture and consistency; to prevent separation of components; to provide body	Vegetable gum (gum arabic), sodium carboxymethyl cellulose, seaweed extracts (agar and algin), dextrin, gelatin	Cheese spread, ice cream, sherbet, pie filling, salad dressing, icing, dietetic canned fruit, cake and dessert mixes, syrup, pressurized whipped cream, instant breakfasts, beer, soft drinks, diet drinks
Sequestrants (chelating agents, or metal scavengers)	To tie up traces of metal ions that catalyze oxidation and other spoilage reactions in food; to prevent clouding in soft drinks; to add color, flavor, and texture	EDTA (ethylenediamine-tetraacetic acid), citric acid, sodium phosphate, chlorophyll	Soup, desserts, artificial fruit drinks, salad dressing, canned corn and shrimp, soft drinks, beer, cheese, frozen foods

*Adding small amounts of vitamins to breakfast cereals and other "fortified" and "enriched" foods in America is basically a gimmick used to raise the price. The manufacturer may put vitamins worth about 0.5¢ into 340 grams (12 ounces) of cereal and then add 45 percent to the retail price. Vitamin pills are normally far cheaper sources of vitamins than fortified foods. The best way to get vitamins, however, is through a balanced diet.

bananas, pineapple, various acid cheeses (such as Camembert), and some beers and wines. Although these amines are usually detoxified by the body, people taking tranquilizers can become seriously ill and even die because some tranquilizers inhibit or block the body chemicals that detoxify these compounds. Safrole (a flavoring agent once used in root beer) and one of the components of tarragon oil cause liver tumors in rats. Three chemicals that could cause cancer are formed when parsnips, celery, figs, and parsley are exposed to light. Aflatoxins produced by fungi that are sometimes found on corn and peanuts are extremely toxic to humans and are not legal in U.S. food at levels above 20 parts per billion.

Clams, oysters, cockles, and mussels can concentrate natural and artificial toxins in their flesh. In addition, natural foods can be contaminated with food-poisoning bacteria, such as *Salmonella* and the deadly *Clostridium botulinum*, through improper processing, food storage, or personal hygiene. The botulism toxin from *Clostridium botulinum* is one of the most toxic chemicals known. As little as one ten-millionth of a gram (0.0000001 gram) can kill an adult, and it is estimated that 227 grams (half a pound) would be enough to kill every human being on earth. However, because of modern food processing methods there are only about 10 to 20 cases of botulism annually in the United States.

Not all the news is bad. Natural foods such as citrus fruits and carrots contain natural anticarcinogens. Examples include vitamins C and E, selenium, and carotene, which inhibit or block the action of gene-altering substances that can cause some types of cancer. Many synthetic food additives, such as vitamins, citric acid, and sorbitol, are identical to chemicals found in natural foods. *Whether natural or synthetic, a chemical is a chemical is a chemical, as long as it is pure.* It makes no difference whether you get vitamin C from eating oranges or from taking synthetic vitamin C tablets. It also makes no difference whether you are poisoned by a natural chemical or by a chemical made by humans.

Because there are potentially harmful chemicals in both natural and synthetic foods, the question boils down to whether enough of a chemical is present to cause harmful effects, and whether the effects of a chemical are cumulative. Unfortunately, the answers are not simple because individuals vary widely in susceptibility. Some chemicals are harmful at any levels, while others are harmful only above certain thresholds (Figure 1-4). In addition, a chemical that has been thoroughly tested and found to be harmless by itself may interact synergistically with another chemical to produce a hazard.

Testing a single food additive or drug may take up to 8 years and may cost $200,000 to $1 million. Thus, since it is essentially impossible to test the many thousands of natural and synthetic chemicals for possible synergistic interactions, we must determine whether the *benefits* of using a particular chemical in our food outweigh the *risks*. This involves scientific research, but it also involves economic, political, and ethical judgments that go far beyond science.

E9-3 Consumer Protection: FDA, the GRAS List, and the Delaney Clause

FDA and the GRAS List In the United States the safety of foods and drugs has been monitored by the Food and Drug Administration (FDA) since its establishment by the Pure Food and Drug Act of 1906, which was amended and strengthened by the 1938 Food, Drug, and Cosmetic Act. Yet not until 1958 did federal laws require that the safety of any new food additive be established by the manufacturer and approved by the FDA *before* the additive was put into common use. Today the manufacturer of a new additive must carry out extensive toxicity testing costing upward of a million dollars per item and submit the results to the FDA. The FDA itself does no testing but merely evaluates data submitted by manufacturers.

However, these federal laws did not apply to the hundreds of additives that were already in use before 1958. Instead of making expensive, time-consuming tests on additives, the FDA drew up a list of the food additives in use in 1958 and asked several hundred experts for their professional opinions on the safety of these substances. A few substances were deleted, and in 1959 a list of the remaining 415 substances was published as the "*generally recognized as safe*" or *GRAS* (pronounced "grass") *list*.

Since 1959 further testing has led the FDA to ban several substances that were on the original GRAS list, including cyclamate sweeteners (1969), brominated vegetable oil (1970), and a number of food color dyes, such as red dye no. 2 (1976). The ban on the most widely used artificial food color, red dye no. 2, came 5 years after Soviet scientists reported that it caused cancer in laboratory mice. Between 1969 and 1980 the FDA reviewed all 415 items on the GRAS list: 373 of the additives were considered to be safe as currently used; 19 additives (including caffeine, BHA, and BHT) needed further study; 7 (including salt and 4 modified starches) can be used but only at restricted levels; and 18 were recommended for removal from the GRAS list. By 1982 the FDA had also reviewed all other food additives approved for use since the publication of the original GRAS list.

As a regulatory agency, the FDA is caught in the cross fire between consumer groups and the food industry. It is criticized by consumer groups as being overly friendly to industry and for hiring many of its executives from the food industry—a practice the FDA contends is the only way it can recruit the most experienced food scientists. At the same time, the food industry complains that the FDA sometimes gives in too easily to demands from consumer groups. Both industry and consumer groups have criticized the agency for bureaucratic inefficiency.

Some Controversial Food Additives Three types of allegedly harmful additives are *food color dyes made from coal tar dyes, nitrates and nitrites,* and *sulfites.* Although natural pigments and dyes exist, most artificial food colors are obtained from coal tar dyes. In 1900 about 100 artificial dyes were in use in the United States, but evidence began accumulating that many of them cause cancer in test animals. By 1983 only six coal tar dyes were still approved by the FDA, and critics charge that these had not been tested adequately for safety. Even with this small number, public exposure to coal tar food dyes can be extensive. The FDA estimates that by age 12, 10 percent of all U.S. children have eaten over 454 grams (1 pound) of these dyes. About half the food additives that have been banned by the FDA have been coal tar dye food colorings.

Another controversial group of additives are nitrates and nitrites (mostly as sodium nitrate and sodium nitrite), added to most processed meats to retard spoilage, prevent botulism, enhance flavor, and improve color. Studies have shown that they may form N-nitroso compounds (nitrosoamines), which have been shown to cause cancer of the stomach and esophagus in animals. In 1978 the FDA and the Department of Agriculture created a stir when they proposed the gradual phasing out of these preservatives. Food industry officials and scientists, however, point out that this may not help because humans are exposed to even larger concentrations of nitrosoamines from other sources. For example, a pack of 20 filter cigarettes provides a nitrosoamine intake of about 17 micrograms and a single cigar 11 micrograms, compared to an average dietary intake of about 1.1 micrograms per day.

Nitrates and nitrites continued to be used in 1984 because of opposition to the ban from the food processing industry and because no substitutes had been found that are as effective as nitrates in preventing spoilage of some foods. While the search

for such substitutes goes on, some scientists urge Americans to limit their consumption of bologna, salami, corned beef, hot dogs, bacon, and other cured and smoked meats. Even if nitrates and nitrites turn out to be harmless, these meats are high in sodium, which contributes to cardiovascular disease.

Sulfites are a group of widely used food preservatives that have been linked to acute allergic reactions in some people, especially about 5 percent of those with asthma (amounting to about 450,000 Americans). Sulfites are added to, or applied as a spray or dip to fresh fruits, vegetables, and shellfish by food wholesalers, grocery stores, and restaurants to retard spoilage and to keep the items looking fresh. Sulfites are also used in making beer and wine. People allergic to sulfites develop symptoms that include weakness, severe wheezing, labored breathing, coughing, extreme shortness of breath, blue discoloration of the skin, and loss of consciousness. In 1983 the FDA was planning to declare most sulfites safe. But after protests by consumer and physician groups the FDA recommended that state officials who have the responsibility for regulating food wholesalers, groceries, and restaurants insist that these businesses either cease using the additives or alert consumers to their use of sulfites by signs on grocery bins or notes on menus.

The Delaney Clause One powerful weapon the FDA has is the *Delaney clause.** This 1958 amendment to the food and drug laws prohibits the deliberate use of any food additive that has been shown to cause cancer in animals or humans. The FDA must evaluate the evidence linking an additive to cancer; if the FDA finds a risk, however slight, it must ban the chemical. The amendment is absolute, allowing for no extenuating circumstances or consideration of benefits versus risks. Between 1958 and 1983, the FDA used this amendment to ban only nine chemicals.

Critics say that the Delaney clause is too rigid and is not needed, since the FDA already has the power to ban any chemical it deems unsafe. In general, the food industry would like to see it removed, while some scientists and politicians would like it to be modified to allow a consideration of benefits versus risks. Others point out that it allows chemicals to be banned even if they cause cancer in test animals at doses 10 to 10,000 times greater than the amount a person might be expected to consume.

---

*Named after Representative James J. Delaney of New York, who fought long and hard to have this amendment passed despite great political pressure and heavy lobbying by the food industry.

These critics also argue that cancer tests in animals don't necessarily apply to humans.

Supporters of the Delaney amendment say that since humans can't serve as guinea pigs, animal tests are the next best thing. Such tests don't prove that a chemical will cause cancer in humans, but they can strongly suggest that a risk is present. Moreover, all but two substances known to cause cancer in humans also cause cancer in laboratory animals. Supporters also argue that the high doses of chemicals administered in animal tests are necessary to compensate for the relatively short life spans of test animals and for their relatively fast rates of metabolism and excretion. Tests using low doses not only would be inaccurate but would also require thousands of test animals to demonstrate that an effect was not due to chance. Such tests would be prohibitively expensive. Supporters also favor the rigidity of the law. They argue that a carcinogen should be automatically banned because threshold levels for cancer-causing agents have not yet been established and carcinogens may be nonthreshold agents.

Indeed, instead of revoking the Delaney clause, some scientists feel it should be strengthened and expanded. Some even argue that the clause gives the FDA too much discretion, including the right to reject the validity of well-conducted animal experiments that do show carcinogenicity. These critics cite the FDA's infrequent use of the clause as evidence that the law is too weak. It is also argued that the absence of discretion in deciding whether to invoke the law protects FDA officials from undue pressure from the food industry and politicians. If the FDA had to weigh benefits versus risks, political influence and lobbying by the food industry could delay the banning of a dangerous chemical while it underwent years of study. The long delays and failure to ban other potentially harmful chemicals not covered by the Delaney clause illustrate this problem.

What Can the Consumer Do?   It is almost impossible for a consumer in an affluent nation to avoid all food additives. Indeed, as we have seen, many additives perform important functions, and there is no guarantee that natural foods will always be better and safer. However, to minimize risk, several analysts have suggested we can do the following.

1. Try to eat a balanced daily diet, consuming less sugar, salt, and animal fats and more vegetables, fresh fruits, and whole grains. Foods rich in vitamin C (tomatoes, peppers, and citrus fruits) seem to lower the risk of cancer of the esophagus or the stomach. Vegetables like carrots, spinach, and broccoli are rich in carotene and may reduce the chances of getting cancer of the lung, breast, bladder, and skin.

2. If you drink, consume only moderate amounts of beer, wine, and liquor. According to the National Academy of Sciences, excessive drinking, especially in combination with smoking, can increase the risk of cancer of the upper gastrointestinal and respiratory tracts.

3. Become informed about additives (such as food colorings, nitrates, nitrite, and sulfites) and natural foods that have come under suspicion, and try to avoid them until their safety is established. The National Academy of Sciences suggests that we cut back on salt-cured and smoked foods such as ham, bacon, bologna, and frankfurters to reduce the risks of getting cancer of the esophagus and stomach.

4. Exert political pressure to see that the FDA is adequately funded and staffed and that the FDA and food-manufacturing activities are carefully monitored.

5. Work politically to strengthen existing laws with the following requirements.

    a. All new and presently used additives should be reviewed and tested not only for toxicity and carcinogenic effects but also for their ability to induce birth defects and long-term genetic effects.

    b. All testing of additives should be performed by a third party, independent of the food industry.

    c. All additives, including specific flavors, colors, and sodium content (for people on salt-free diets) should be listed on the label or container of all foods and drugs.

    d. All unnecessary additives should be banned unless extensive testing establishes that they are safe. It is difficult, however, to define what is "unnecessary" and write this definition into an effective and enforceable law. Some have suggested that the only "necessary" additives would be those that enhance the nutritive content of foods or prevent foods from spoilage or contamination by harmful bacteria and molds.

The only certainty is that citizens in the wealthiest countries ingest a few thousand different chemical compounds, most of which have not been adequately tested for links to cancer, genetic mutations, birth defects, and behavioral problems.

Erik P. Eckholm

Discussion Topics

1. **a.** Using Table E9-1 and the label of a food from the grocery store, try to classify the additives listed as necessary and safe, unnecessary but safe, or unnecessary and potentially harmful. Compare evaluations of different common foods by other class members.

   b. Compare brands to see whether there are some that don't contain additives that are controversial, either because of safety or their usefulness.

   c. Evaluate the additives found in baby foods and recommend whether they should be allowed or banned.

2. Explain the fallacies in the following statements:

   a. All synthetic food additives should be banned, and we should all return to safe, nutritious natural foods.

   b. All foods are chemicals, so we shouldn't worry about artificial additives.

   c. Since some natural foods contain harmful chemicals, we should not get so concerned about synthetic food additives.

   d. Food additives are essential and without them we would suffer from malnutrition, food poisoning, and spoiled food.

3. What is the GRAS list? The Delaney clause? Describe weaknesses in both. Do you believe that the Delaney clause should be revoked, left as is, altered to allow an evaluation of risks and benefits, or strengthened and broadened? Give reasons for your position.

Enrichment Study 10

Noise Pollution

E10-1 Sonic Assault

According to the Environmental Protection Agency, about 20 million to 25 million Americans are exposed to noises of sufficient duration and intensity to cause some permanent loss of hearing. Furthermore, this number is rising fast. Industrial workers head the list, with 19 million hearing-damaged people out of a work force of 75 million. Moreover, 5 million children under age 18 have impaired hearing, mostly from listening to loud music from home stereos, portable "jam boxes" held close to the ear, and earphones. According to the EPA nearly half of all Americans are regularly exposed to levels of noise in their neighborhoods and jobs that interfere with communication and sleeping and cause annoyance and dissatisfaction.

E10-2 Noise and Its Effects

Measuring and Ranking Noise Noise is usually defined as "unwanted sound." This is not a precise definition, because one person's favorite music may be another person's earache. Instead we try to talk about noise in ways that can be measured by distinguishing between measured sound power (intensity) and the pressure exerted on our eardrums from sound. The **decibel (db),** named for Alexander Graham Bell, is the unit used to measure both. Sound pressure measurements in decibels can be made using a sound pressure level meter (called a *decibel meter)* that can fit into a coat pocket.

These pressure measurements can be converted to loudness levels by a mathematical equation. Because the loudness scales are logarithmic, a tenfold increase in sound intensity or pressure occurs with each 10 decibel rise in sound pressure. Thus, a rise in sound pressure on the ear from 30 db (quiet rural area) to 60 db (normal restaurant conversation) represents a thousandfold increase in loudness.

The loudness and pressure of a sound, however, are only part of the problem, for sounds also have pitch (frequency). After correcting for the fact that high-pitched sounds annoy us more than low-pitched sounds, we can rank noise sources fairly well according to sound pressure (Table E10-1). The most common sound pressure scale weighted for high-pitched sounds is the A scale, whose units are written "dbA." Hearing loss begins with prolonged exposure (8 hours or more) to 80 to 90 dbA levels of sound pressure. Sound pressure becomes painful at around 120 dbA and can kill at 180 dbA.

Effects of Noise Excessive noise is a form of stress and can cause both physical and psychological damage. Noise effects fall into four general categories: annoyance, disruption of activity, partial or total loss of hearing, and physical or mental deterioration. Continued exposure to high sound levels permanently destroys some of the microscopic hairlike cells (cochlear cells) in the fluid-filled inner ear, which convert sound energy to nerve impulses.

The U.S. Occupational Safety and Health Administration (OSHA) considers the following to be safe time limits for exposure to various sound pressure levels: 90 dbA, 8 hours; 92 dbA, 6 hours; 95 dbA, 4 hours; 100 dbA, 2 hours; 105 dbA, 1 hour; 110 dbA, 30 minutes; 115 dbA, 15 minutes or less; and more than 115 dbA, no exposure at all. By comparing these safety limits with the levels that many people experience (Table E10-1), we can see that more and more Americans are being exposed to potentially damaging sound pressure levels. Sound experts suggest that if you need to raise your voice to be heard above racket, if a noise causes your ears to ring or feel full, or if voices begin to sound as if they're coming from a barrel, the sound level is high enough to cause permanent damage to your ears.

In addition to causing psychic shock, sudden noise automatically constricts blood vessels, dilates pupils, tenses muscles, increases the heartbeat and blood pressure, and causes wincing, holding of

Table E10-1 Effects of Common Sound Pressure Levels

Example	Sound Pressure (dbA)	Effect with Prolonged Exposure
Jet takeoff (25 meters*)	150	Eardrum rupture
Aircraft carrier deck	140	
Armored personnel carrier, jet takeoff (100 meters), earphones at loud level	130	
Thunderclap, textile loom, live rock music, jet takeoff at 61 meters, siren (close range), chain saw	120	Human pain threshold
Steel mill, riveting, automobile horn at 1 meter, jam box stereo held close to ear	110	
Jet takeoff at 305 meters, subway, outboard motor, power lawn mower, motorcycle at 8 meters, farm tractor, printing plant, jackhammer, garbage truck, farm tractor	100	Serious hearing damage (8 hours)
Busy urban street, diesel truck, food blender, cotton spinning machine	90	Hearing damage (8 hours), speech interference
Garbage disposal, clothes washer, average factory, freight train at 15 meters, dishwasher	80	Possible hearing damage
Freeway traffic at 15 meters, vacuum cleaner, noisy office or party	70	Annoying
Conversation in restaurant, average office, background music	60	Intrusive
Quiet suburb (daytime), conversation in living room	50	Quiet
Library, soft background music	40	
Quiet rural area (nighttime)	30	
Whisper, rustling leaves	20	Very quiet
Breathing	10	
	0	Threshold of hearing

*To convert meters to feet, multiply by 3.3.

breath, and stomach spasms. Constriction of the blood vessels can become permanent, increasing blood pressure and contributing to heart disease. Migraine headaches, gastric ulcers, and changes in brain chemistry can also occur. In 1983, data from an 8-year mortality survey involving 200,000 residents living near the Los Angeles International Airport showed a significantly higher than normal incidence of deaths from heart attacks, strokes, suicide, and murder.

Although general urban noise and startling sounds are a serious problem, the noise levels people endure every day at their work are even more serious. Workers who run a high risk of temporary or permanent hearing loss include boilermakers, weavers, riveters, bulldozer and jackhammer operators, taxicab drivers, bus and truck drivers, mechanics, machine shop supervisors, bar and nightclub employees, and performers who use large sound systems to amplify their music.

E10-3 What Can Be Done?

Noise control can be accomplished in three major ways: **(1)** reducing noise at its source, **(2)** substituting less noisy machines and operations, and **(3)** reducing the amount of noise entering the listener's ear. We already know how to produce quieter trucks, motorcycles, and vacuum cleaners. Likewise, houses and buildings can be insulated to reduce sound transfer and at the same time reduce energy waste.

The Soviet Union and many western European and Scandinavian countries are far ahead of the United States in what has been called the "quiet revolution." Europeans have developed quiet jackhammers, pile drivers, and air compressors that do not cost much more than their noisy counterparts. They also muffle construction equipment noise by using small sheds and tents. Some countries use rubberized garbage trucks. Subway systems in Montreal and Mexico City have rubberized wheels to reduce noise. In France, cars have separate city and highway horns. A simple redesign of the tread can decrease the screech of truck tires at no cost to the consumer. The Swiss and the West Germans have established maximum day and night sound pressure levels for various areas, and in 1960 the Soviet Union banned factory sound pressure levels above 85 dbA and residential levels above 30 dbA.

Workers can shield themselves from excessive noise by wearing hearing protectors ranging from wax or plastic plugs to bulky headsets to custom-made plastic inserts with valves that close automatically in response to noise. Noisy factory operations can also be enclosed or partially enclosed. Many countries have noise control specifications for homes and other buildings; noise control for an apartment building adds only about 5 percent to its cost.

At the federal level, Congress passed the Noise

Control Act of 1972. This act gave the EPA broad authority to **(1)** set maximum allowed sound pressure levels for construction equipment, transportation equipment (except aircraft), and all motors, engines, and electrical equipment manufactured after 1972, **(2)** require all manufacturers to label their products according to the amount of noise they produce, **(3)** propose aircraft noise standards for implementation by the Federal Aviation Agency (FAA), **(4)** engage in research, provide technical assistance to communities and states, and disseminate information to the public on noise and noise control, and **(5)** coordinate federal efforts on noise control. By 1983 the EPA had issued noise level regulations for air conditioners, buses, motorcycles, power mowers, some trucks and trains, and some construction equipment. So far, however, enforcement of these regulations has been almost nonexistent because the 1972 law merely fines violators.

OSHA currently sets the standard for overexposure to noise in any work place at 90 db for 8 hours a day—still significantly above the standard of 85 db considered to be the minimum safe level (Table E10-1). Industry officials have opposed lowering the standard to 85 db because implementation would cost them an estimated $20 billion.

A small step in the right direction occurred when Congress passed the Quiet Communities Act of 1978. This law authorizes the EPA to develop programs to help state and local governments combat excessive noise. Since 1978 the EPA has assisted a number of cities and more than half the states in launching noise control programs. By 1982 there were over 1,000 community noise control ordinances, compared to only about 275 in 1972. However, most of these laws have little or no enforcement power behind them.

The EPA has proposed a national plan for noise control. But noise control experts point out that unless Congress strengthens existing noise control laws, allows the EPA to regulate aircraft noise, and increases the amount of money appropriated for noise research, this plan will probably collect dust in bureaucratic files.

Air pollution kills us slowly but silently; noise makes each day a torment.
Robert Alex Baron

Discussion Topics

1. As a class or group project, try to borrow one or more sound pressure decibel meters from the physics or engineering department or from a local stereo or electronic repair shop. Make a community survey of sound pressure levels at several times of day and at several locations; plot the results on a map. Include measurements in a room with a stereo and at an indoor rock concert or nightclub at various distances from the speakers of the sound system. Correlate your findings with those in Table E10-1.

2. Debate the proposition that we have always had noise and we can get used to it.

3. Are there any noise-level regulations in your area? What specifications, if any, for noise control are written into the building codes? Are they adequate? What plans, if any, do local officials have for requiring noise controls on jackhammers, compressors, garbage trucks, garbage cans, and other noisemakers? Are they aware that such devices are readily available?

Enrichment Study 11

Land, Energy, and Water Resources in the Rocky Mountain Region: A Case Study

The major storehouse of undeveloped energy resources in the United States lies in the eight Rocky Mountain states: Arizona, Colorado, Idaho, Montana, Nevada, New Mexico, Utah, and Wyoming. This region is a major battleground over land, energy, and water resources.

E11-1 Energy Resources of the Rocky Mountain Region

The Rocky Mountain region consists of a mix of rolling plains, irrigated farmland, rangelands, forests, arid deserts, some of the nation's most scenic national parks, and lands owned by Native American Indians. It also contains three of the nation's most rapidly growing urban regions (the Phoenix, Denver, and Salt Lake City areas), and is expected to have high population growth rates between 1980 and 2000. Almost half the lands in this region are public lands, owned by the citizens of the United States and managed for them by the federal government.

According to a U.S. Senate study, the region contains about 42 percent of this nation's bituminous and lignite coal, 60 percent of the low-sulfur coal that can be surface mined economically, almost all the rich oil shale deposits, 95 percent of U.S. uranium deposits, vast supplies of geothermal energy, potential sources of natural gas and petroleum, a large, sunny desert area, which could be the site of giant power plants that use solar energy to generate enough electricity to theoretically desalinate water (such as that in Salt Lake) for this water-starved region and to provide about half of all the electricity needed in the United States in the year 2000, a number of the nation's hydroelectric plants, much of the areas with moderate to very high potential for generation of electricity from the wind, and underground salt deposits or other geological formations that might be useful for storing deadly radioactive wastes (Section 15-5). It is estimated that if fully utilized, the energy resources in these eight

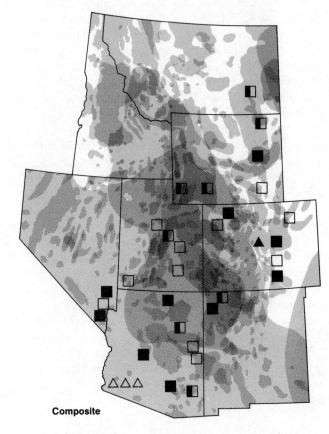

Composite

Figure E11-1 Conflicts between land use, energy resources, and water resources in the eight Rocky Mountain states. Composite map shows areas of most intense overlap and conflict (darkest regions).

states could supply U.S. energy needs for the next 100 years.

As Figure E11-1 shows, the deposits of many of these energy resources either overlap or are located near one another and are found in or near some of the nation's national forests and parks. In addition, some of these energy resources lie under land now used for farming, grazing, timber, and watersheds. About 50 percent of the uranium and 20 percent of the coal reserves lie under lands owned by Native Americans.

Coal

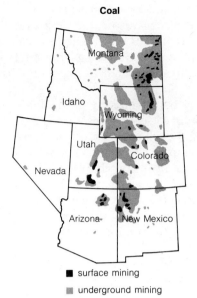

■ surface mining

■ underground mining

Oil and Natural Gas

Oil Shale

Uranium

Geothermal

■ proven reserves

■ likely reserves

Electric Power Plants
(greater than 300 megawatts)

<u>Fossil fuels</u>   <u>Nuclear</u>

■ existing   ▲ existing

◨ expanding   △ under construction

□ proposed

<u>Solar</u>

■ proposed

□ existing

Potential Nuclear Waste Storage

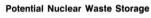

■ major underground salt deposits

National Parks and National Forests

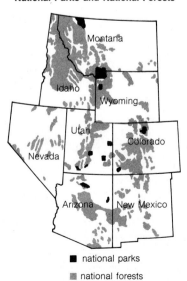

■ national parks

■ national forests

Water Shortages

■ shortages today

□ shortages by 2000

E11-2 Conflicts over Energy Resource Development

The result is an extremely complex conflict over land use—especially over the use and management of the public lands in this region. Farmers and ranchers want enough irrigation water; they don't want land disturbed or water polluted from mining and energy development projects. Many environmentalists and ranchers want to preserve the sparsely populated land from the severe environmental impacts caused by mining and other large-scale energy development projects. Energy companies want to mine the area's rich resources for private profit, to reduce dependence on foreign oil imports, and to provide energy for the future. Some residents of these states welcome the money and jobs that energy development and boom towns bring; others do not want their rural life-style disrupted by rapid population growth.

The federal government, which manages much of the land for the public, is caught in this cross fire of conflicting interests in trying to decide which resources should be developed and when. To complicate matters further, it is proposed that a number of MX missiles be based in this region—the single largest construction project ever proposed for the area. If carried out, this project alone would (1) use vast quantities of nonmineral, energy, and water resources, (2) have major environmental impacts, and (3) lead to rapid population growth during construction. State governments are torn between preserving the environment, encouraging economic growth, and ensuring that developments on federally managed lands do not seriously harm the air, water, and land in nearby areas.

The conflict over the use of land and energy resources is made more intense by water shortages (Figure E11-1), which are expected to get worse by 2000. To extract and process energy resources will require enormous amounts of water. Large quantities are required for cooling in power plants, washing mined coal, gasifying and liquefying coal, forming slurry for transporting coal in pipelines to other parts of the nation, converting oil shale to liquid fuel, and reclaiming surface-mined arid lands. Water needs for coal and synthetic fuel plants could be greatly reduced by treating effluents to remove pollutants and then recycling the water, but this is a costly process.

At present, major emphasis is on increased coal mining to reduce U.S. dependence on oil imports by 1990. Since most of the coal extracted in this region is exported to other heavily populated areas, there is a conflict over whether the coal should be (1) mined and shipped out by rail or slurry pipeline, (2) burned in power plants near mining sites and exported as electricity, or (3) converted to synthetic natural gas in coal gasification plants built near mining sites, and distributed by pipeline to other areas.

Water, then, may be the limiting factor determining which, if any, of the energy resources in the Rocky Mountain region will be extracted on a large scale. With careful planning and management, there may be enough water for considerable extraction of the available fuels, but at the expense of farming, ranching, and forestry. Presently, agriculture uses 90 percent of the region's annual water supply, much of it allegedly inefficiently applied and producing low-value crops.

Some additional water could be supplied by tapping underground aquifers in this region. But some of these aquifers are being depleted faster than they are being recharged by rainfall in this arid region. Furthermore, this amounts to *mining* water needed during drought years, since it took thousands of years to fill these underground aquifers. Depleting this supply for short-term purposes could set up an irreversible conversion of western grasslands to desert if a drought lasts more than a year. Thus, the people of the United States who jointly own much of this land—and especially the people in the Rocky Mountain region who live with the potential benefits and drawbacks of large-scale energy resource development—face some difficult and important questions in this conflict between the use of land, energy, and water resources.

I have a country but no town. . . . Bulldozers cut my lawn.

John Ciardi

Discussion Topics

1. Why are the energy resources in the Rocky Mountain region important to everyone in the United States—not just the inhabitants of the region?

2. Which, if any, of the major energy resources in the Rocky Mountain region located on public lands should be mined first and under what restrictions? Defend your choice. Which resource, if any, should be mined second? If you believe that none of these resources should be mined, what effects (if any) might this have on the United States and on your own expected life-style in 2000?

Enrichment Study 12

Cadmium, Lead, and Mercury in the Environment

E12-1 Hazardous Metallic Elements

From existing evidence, five metallic elements are known hazards to humans (Table E12-1): cadmium, lead, mercury (in the form of methyl mercury), nickel (in the form of nickel carbonyl), and beryllium. The other four elements shown in Table E12-1 either are suspected to be health hazards or are not presently used in sufficient quantities to be of concern to the general public.

In this enrichment study we will examine the effects of cadmium, lead, and mercury. These metals are special threats because they are cumulative poisons, widely used, nondegradable, and sometimes biologically magnified in food chains and webs. Because of their persistence, these metals can accu-

mulate in the body, gradually reaching harmful levels. For example, biological half-life in the human body is about 200 days for cadmium,* 1,460 days (4 years) for lead, and 70 days for mercury.

E12-2 Cadmium

Cadmium is widely used in electroplating metals to prevent corrosion, in plastics and paints, and in nickel-cadmium batteries. It is also a contaminant in phosphate fertilizers.

---

*Whole-body or biological half-life is the time required for half of a given quantity of an element to be excreted from the body. For example, after 200 days, half of a given input of cadmium remains in the body.

Table E12-1   Sources and Health Effects of Some Widely Used Metals

Element	Sources	Health Effects
Class 1: Serious threats now		
Cadmium	Burning of coal; zinc mining; water pipes; tobacco smoke; rubber tires; plastics; superphosphate fertilizers	Heart and artery disease; high blood pressure; bone embrittlement; kidney disease; fibrosis of lungs; possibly cancer
Lead	Automobile exhaust (leaded gasoline); paints (made before 1940)	Brain damage; convulsions; behavioral disorders; death
Mercury (as methyl mercury)	Burning of coal; electrical batteries; many industrial uses	Nerve damage; death
Nickel (as nickel carbonyl)	Diesel oil; burning of coal; tobacco smoke; various chemicals; steel; gasoline additives	Lung cancer
Beryllium	Burning of coal; increasing industrial use (including nuclear power industry and rocket fuel)	Acute and chronic respiratory diseases; lung cancer; beryllosis
Class 2: Potential hazards if levels increase		
Antimony	Industry; typesetting; enamelware	Heart disease; skin disorders
Arsenic	Burning of coal and oil; pesticides; mine tailings	Cumulative poison at high levels; possibly cancer
Selenium	Burning of coal, oil, and sulfur; some paper products	Possibly cancer; possibly tooth decay
Manganese	Metal alloys; smoke suppressant in power plants; possible future gasoline additive	Nerve damage

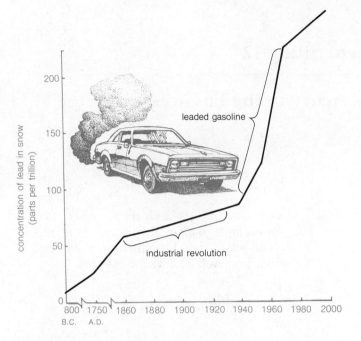

Figure E12-1 Average annual lead content in isolated Greenland glaciers has been increasing since 800 B.C. The data are a series of scattered points, and the curve represents the best average line through these points. In addition, there is considerable seasonal variation in lead levels.

The evidence of cadmium's harmful effects is circumstantial and in some cases contradictory, but concern is growing. Japanese physicians reported in 1955 that *itai-itai byo*, or "ouch-ouch disease," was related to exposure to high levels of cadmium, although some scientists dispute this claim. Ouch-ouch disease causes excruciating pain in the joints and slowly weakens the bones through loss of calcium. Even standing or coughing can break bones, and sufferers may eventually die. Between 1955 and 1968 several hundred cases and at least 100 deaths were reported in northern Japan, mostly among people who ate rice and soybeans grown in fields contaminated by nearby mines and cadmium-using industries.

The real threat to most of us, however, may be exposure to low levels of cadmium obtained from air, water, and diet over long periods. About 4 to 8 percent of the cadmium we eat or drink stays in the body, whereas from 40 to 50 percent of the cadmium we inhale remains. For this reason, tobacco smoke is the major source of cadmium for most people. Pack-a-day smokers carry about twice as much cadmium in their bodies as nonsmokers. People in the same room with smokers are also exposed to cadmium and other dangerous chemicals found in cigarette smoke. Tests on mice indicate that pregnant women probably accumulate cadmium at a rate two to three times higher than other humans.

The second most important source of cadmium is leafy vegetables, which pick it up from agricultural soils polluted primarily from atmospheric fallout of cadmium and commercial fertilizers. Cadmium is also found in small amounts in soft water. Adequate and balanced dietary intake of iron, zinc, calcium, copper, protein, and vitamins D and C can reduce the absorption of cadmium from food and water.

Because of its long biological half-life (200 days), cadmium gradually accumulates in our bodies—primarily in the liver and kidneys. At birth the human body contains only about 1 microgram (one-millionth of a gram) of cadmium, but by age 50 a typical adult has 38,000 times this level. Several studies in test animals and humans have shown that levels of cadmium near or slightly above the average daily intake of 50 to 70 micrograms can lead to high blood pressure (hypertension) and atherosclerosis. Sweden banned most products containing cadmium in 1980.

E12-3 Lead

Lead Is Everywhere   Some lead enters the ecosystem from natural sources, but most comes from human activities. Lead has been used in pottery, batteries, solder, plumbing, cooking vessels, pesticides, and household paints. It is emitted into the atmosphere by lead smelters and by the burning of coal and leaded gasoline.

As a result, lead levels have been increasing throughout the world, even in remote areas. The amount of lead in Greenland ice samples increased 500 percent between 800 B.C. (when humans began mining and using lead) and 1750 (Figure E12-1). Concentrations rose by another 400 percent between 1750 and 1940, when the industrial revolution spawned coal burning (which emits small amounts of lead) and lead smelters (Figure E12-1). An even sharper rise occurred between 1940 and 1967, when many automobiles began burning leaded gasoline, which contains tetraethyl lead as an antiknock additive (Figure E12-1).

The lead concentrations in Figure E12-1 are in parts per trillion and are therefore negligible. But these levels in remote Greenland dramatically illustrate that lead in the environment is widespread and that the level is increasing. Another indication of lead's growing presence is the threefold to fivefold increase in the concentration of lead in the open ocean since 1924, when leaded gasoline was introduced.

Lead is one of the oldest known toxic metals. It may even have hastened the fall of Rome. In the second century B.C., the Roman ruling class suffered widespread sterility, stillbirths, and brain damage—possibly because of lead poisoning from lead wine vessels, cooking pots, and water pipes, which only the rich could afford. Support for this theory comes from the high lead content found in the bones of some ancient Romans.

Many house painters and perhaps some famous artists, such as Goya who licked his paint brush to shape it, probably died of lead poisoning. These deaths resulted from long-term exposure to the lead compounds widely used as paint pigments. Before 1940 lead was used in interior and exterior house paint in the United States. After 1940 lead-based paint was not used for interior painting. Since 1971 the permissible lead content of paint in the United States has been sharply reduced by the Lead Poisoning Prevention Act of 1971.

Sources of Lead In the United States 90 percent of the tiny particles of lead found in the air we inhale comes from the burning of leaded gasoline in cars, and another 5 percent from industrial smelters. As you might suspect, urban air has more lead than rural air, and urban dwellers have more lead in their blood than people living in rural areas.

The National Academy of Sciences estimates that food accounts for 65 to 90 percent of the lead ingested by the average American adult. Airborne lead can enter food when lead particles from vehicle exhausts settle over agricultural and grazing areas, especially those near highways. Some of this is absorbed by the plant, but much of it can be removed by careful washing. Some lead can also be transferred from machinery to foods during the preparation of processed foods. Another significant source of lead in food is the solder used to seal the seams on cans of food. Some manufacturers have reduced the lead content of solder used to seal can seams and others have switched to seamless containers. But to be safe, some scientists have proposed that the FDA ban the use of soldered cans for food. The remaining lead we ingest comes from drinking water contaminated primarily by atmospheric fallout of lead particles. Thus, most of the lead we inhale and ingest comes from particles emitted by vehicles burning leaded gasoline.

Another source of lead for a few people is earthenware pottery with lead glazes. Such pottery is particularly dangerous if used for acidic liquids like orange juice and apple juice, which leach the lead out of the glaze. Lead glazes are no longer used for pottery and china in the United States, but old or foreign-made pieces should be tested for lead content before use.

Children are particularly vulnerable to lead poisoning because they are more likely to ingest things like lead-containing paint chips and dirt and dust containing lead deposited by auto exhaust and industrial emissions, and because their bodies absorb lead more readily than those of adults. Children—mostly from low-income families—living in pre-1940 houses and tenements containing layers of lead-based paint are particularly susceptible. They can also take in lead by inhaling or eating street dust, eating or chewing colored pages from glossy magazines and gift wrapping paper, eating snow or licking icicles contaminated with lead from automobile exhaust, and by exposure to the clothes of members of the household who work with lead. One study showed that an inner-city child can ingest three to four times the recommended 100-microgram daily limit just by licking his or her fingers after playing outdoors.

A 1981 survey by the National Center for Health Statistics revealed that one out of every 25 American preschool children and one out of every five inner-city black preschool children had dangerously high levels of lead in the blood. Most cases of lead poisoning involve children between the ages of 1 and 3 years who have *pica*. This abnormal craving for unnatural foods, including dirt, paper, putty, plastic, and paint chips, may result from a diet deficiency. As a result, about 200 American children die each year from lead poisoning. Another 12,000 to 16,000 children each year are treated for lead poisoning and survive. About 30 percent of those who survive suffer from palsy, partial paralysis, blindness, and mental retardation.

How Serious Is the Threat to Humans? Lead is a cumulative poison. Lead poisoning, for example, is a serious threat to workers in lead smelters and battery plants, and to people who do a lot of soldering. Except in young children and in cases of prolonged exposure at high concentrations, however, most of the lead we inhale or ingest is usually excreted in the urine fast enough to keep the lead content in our blood below a dangerous level.

A small part of our daily lead intake gradually accumulates in our bones, replacing the calcium. Here it is normally insoluble and harmless. But under certain conditions, such as feverish illness, cortisone therapy, and old age, this accumulated lead can be released suddenly into the blood at toxic levels.

Considering the number of cars in the United States, it is not surprising that Americans have the highest average blood levels of lead in the world, although the Japanese may soon take over the number-one spot. These blood levels, though significant, fall 25 to 50 percent below the present threshold for classical lead poisoning. This threshold is constantly being lowered, however. Indeed, some researchers question whether there really is a safe threshold level for lead. Companies making lead additives for gasoline and other lead-using industries note the absence of concrete evidence that airborne lead harms humans. But experiments with animals have indicated that low levels of lead can increase animal death rates at all ages by as much as one-quarter. As a result, a number of prominent scientists have urged that lead additives be banned from gasoline and food cans and that smelting, battery, and other lead-using industries be required to control lead emissions into the air and water.

In 1973 the EPA established a 5-year plan to gradually reduce the average lead content in gasoline by 1978. Because of court challenges and political pressure, however, the final phasedown standard was not met by large gasoline refiners until 1980 and by small refiners until late in 1982. In 1982 the EPA, under pressure from gasoline refiners and the Reagan administration proposed to weaken or rescind the lead phasedown program. But citizens, legislators, and environmental groups protested this proposal and numerous medical and health experts presented such overwhelming evidence about the harmful effects of lead that the EPA reversed itself. For example, researchers at the federal Centers for Disease Control (CDC) were able to link public health impacts directly to reductions in the lead content of gasoline.

Cost-benefit economic analysis by EPA scientists showed that rescinding the lead standard would save industry about $100 million a year, but would cost the government and general public from $140 million to $1.4 billion per year for treating the additional 200,000 to 500,000 children who would develop lead poisoning. As a result, in 1982 the EPA issued new standards allowing no more than 1.1 grams of lead per gallon of gasoline (0.29 gram per liter), with a phaseout of all leaded gasoline by 1990 or perhaps as early as 1988. By 1983 West Germany had a much tighter maximum standard of 0.57 gram of lead per gallon of gasoline (0.15 gram per liter), and Denmark and Great Britain had announced moves to reach this level by 1985 and to phase out the use of leaded gasoline by 1990.

E12-4 Mercury

Natural and Human Sources Get a tooth filled, flip a silent light switch, install an automatic furnace or air conditioner, use fluorescent lights, and you are depending on mercury—a chemical that has been used in various forms for over 27 centuries. It is also used in some paints, floor waxes, and furniture polishes, in antibacterial and antimildew agents, in medicines and in fungicides for seeds, and in making plastics, paper, clothing, and film.

Human input of mercury into the air and water has been increasing, especially because of the burning of coal (which contains mercury as a trace contaminant) and by deliberate and accidental discharges into rivers, streams, and lakes. These inputs, however, are relatively small compared to natural inputs of lead into the environment due to vaporization from the earth's crust and from the vast amounts naturally stored as bottom sediments in the ocean. It is dangerous to consume large amounts of pike, tuna, swordfish, and other large ocean species that contain high levels of mercury. But most, if not all, of this mercury comes from natural sources, and the danger has probably always been present. Although the human input into the ocean is insignificant, some lakes, rivers, bays, and estuaries near mercury-using industries are being threatened.

Mercury and Human Health Suppose you were taking your temperature with a mercury-filled thermometer and you accidentally bit it in half. Would the mercury you swallowed harm you? Elemental mercury is not a dangerous poison unless vaporized and inhaled directly into the lungs. Almost all the mercury you swallowed would pass out of your system in a few days. However, if you spilled some mercury and gradually inhaled its vapor over a fairly long period it could be harmful. While preparing fillings, for example, dentists and dental workers can be exposed to high levels of mercury vapor because of leaky containers, spills, and poor ventilation. A 1983 study showed that 13 percent of the dentists tested had high mercury levels in their body. This condition can cause neurological problems and even death.

The major threat from mercury comes in an extremely toxic organic form known as methyl mercury (CH_3Hg^+). It stays in the body more than 10 times longer than metallic mercury, can attack the central nervous system, kidneys, liver, and brain tissue, and can cause birth defects. The major forms of mercury and the ways they are transformed from one form to another are summarized in Figure E12-2.

Between 1953 and 1960, 52 people died and 150 suffered serious brain and nerve damage from methyl mercury discharged into Minamata Bay, Japan, by a nearby chemical plant. Most of the victims in this seaside village area ate fish contaminated with methyl mercury three times a day. In 1969 a New Mexico farm laborer fed seed grain treated with methyl mercury to his hogs. After he and his family ate this hog meat, three of the children became severely crippled. A fourth child, poisoned in his mother's womb, was born blind and mentally retarded. In Iraq in 1972, a large shipment of seed grain treated with methyl mercury was dis-

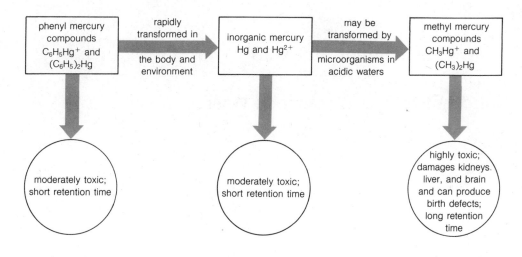

Figure E12-2 Some chemical forms of mercury and how they may be transformed.

tributed to villagers, who fed it to animals and used it to bake bread. It was reported that 459 people died and 6,530 were injured.

An unexpected discovery about mercury occurred in 1969, when two young Swedish scientists, Sören Jensen and Arne Jernelöv, duplicated stream bottom conditions in an aquarium and found that anaerobic (non-oxygen-requiring) bacteria dwelling in bottom mud could convert relatively harmless elemental mercury and inorganic mercury (Hg^{2+}) salts into highly toxic methyl mercury (Figure E12-2). Fortunately, most waters apparently are not acidic enough to enable this transformation. However, we still know far too little about the complex chemistry of mercury in living systems and we may encounter some unexpected changes and effects in the future. In addition, the increases in acidity of many lakes from acid deposition (Section 19-4) may aggravate this problem.

In summary, the danger from mercury is mainly a local problem arising in three special cases: **(1)** when humans eat food contaminated with methyl mercury seed dressings, **(2)** when methyl mercury used or formed in industrial processes enters natural waters, and **(3)** when inorganic mercury or organic phenyl mercury is converted into alkyl mercury compounds by microorganisms found in bottom sediments of acidic waters. A number of scientists have urged that the use of methyl mercury on seed dressings be banned worldwide, along with discharges of mercury and mercury compounds by mercury-using industries. The technology for this control already exists.

The ultimate end . . . is not knowledge, but action. To be half right on time may be more important than to obtain the whole truth too late.

Aristotle

Discussion Topics

1. Since we have always been exposed to background levels of metals from natural sources, the fear of toxic metals is an example of ecohysteria. Criticize this statement.

2. Debate the following resolution: Because of their dangers, we should ban the use of cadmium, lead, mercury, nickel, and beryllium. How would your life be changed if such a ban were instituted?

3. Explain how lead might have been a factor in the downfall of Rome. Could this also happen in the United States? How does the situation in the contemporary United States differ from that in imperial Rome?

4. Criticize the following statements.
   a. Because the average lead level in blood tends to be below the level for classical lead poisoning, there is no serious problem.
   b. Because there is no absolute proof that lead in gasoline has killed any Americans, there is no need to reduce or phase out the use of lead compounds in gasoline.

5. Criticize the following statements.
   a. We are seriously polluting the ocean with mercury.
   b. Because we are not the major source of mercury pollution in the ocean, there is no cause for concern.
   c. We should no longer eat tuna and swordfish.
   d. Since metallic mercury is not highly toxic to humans, we have little to fear.
   e. Mercury poisoning is a global environmental problem.

Enrichment Study 13

Solid Waste and Hazardous Wastes

E13-1 Solid Waste Production in the United States

What Is Solid Waste?   As the gross national product of an affluent nation grows, so does one of its major gross national by-products—garbage, or solid waste. **Solid waste** is any useless, unwanted, or discarded material that is not a liquid or a gas. It is yesterday's newspaper and junk mail, today's dinner table scraps, raked leaves and grass clippings, nonreturnable bottles and cans, worn-out appliances and furniture, abandoned cars, animal manure, crop residues, food-processing wastes, sewage sludge from waste treatment plants (Section 18-6), fly ash from coal-burning electric power plants (Section 19-5), mining and industrial wastes, and an array of other cast-off materials. Although some solid waste that is hazardous to human health must be isolated and stored, most of the things we throw away should be regarded not as solid waste but as *wasted solids*, which we need to reuse or recycle (Section 13-4).

Amount and Sources of Solid Waste   Each American directly or indirectly produces 19,300 kilograms (21 tons) of solid waste each year, or 53 kilogram (115 pounds) a day. Direct per capita production of solid waste amounts to about 0.7 kilogram (1.5 pounds) a day, or 256 kilograms (548 pounds) a year.

As seen from Figure E13-1, most solid waste is produced *indirectly* by agricultural, mining, and industrial activities. Animal, crop, and forest wastes from agricultural activities make up 56 percent of the total, as discussed in Enrichment Study 14. The piles of rock, dirt, sand, and slag left behind from the mining and processing of energy resources and nonfuel mineral resources are the second largest source of solid waste in the United States (Section 13-2).

The total amount of industrial solid waste produced is small compared with solid waste from agricultural and mining activities, with industry

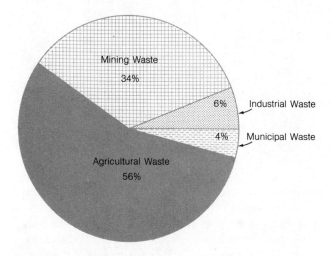

Figure E13-1   Sources of solid waste in the United States in 1982 as a percentage of the total wet weight produced.

accounting for only about 6 percent of the waste produced each year. Much of this is scrap metal, plastics, slag, paper, sludge from sewage treatment plants, and fly ash from electrical power plants. The last two categories, sludge and fly ash, are increasing rapidly because of stricter laws controlling the pollution of water (Sections 18-6 and 18-7) and air (Section 19-7). Fly ash wastes will increase dramatically in coming years if more coal is used to produce electricity (Section 15-4). However, many wastes produced by industry are hazardous to human health even in small amounts and must be stored safely or converted to harmless materials, as discussed in Sections E13-4 and E13-5.

Urban Solid Waste   Most discussions of solid waste emphasize the wastes produced by homes and businesses in or near urban areas, even though this source amounts to only about 4 percent of the total produced each year in the United States (Figure E13-1). There are several reasons for this emphasis. *First*, because this solid waste is concentrated in highly populated areas, it must be removed quickly and efficiently. This is very expensive. In 1983 $6 bil-

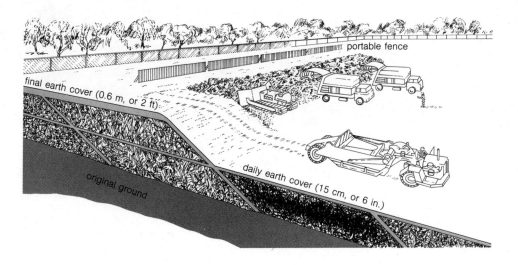

Figure E13-2 A sanitary landfill. Wastes are spread in a thin layer and then compacted with a bulldozer. A scraper (foreground) covers the wastes with a fresh layer of soil at the end of each day. Portable fences are used to catch and hold debris blown by the wind.

lion—mostly as taxes—was spent to collect and dispose of urban solid waste in the United States, with 80 percent of the cost for labor to collect the waste. Between 1975 and 1985, average collection and disposal costs have at least doubled and are continuing to rise as many urban areas run out of places to dispose of their refuse.

Second, urban solid waste typically shows the fastest yearly rate of growth and is expected to almost double between 1978 and 1990. *Third*, present methods for disposal of these wastes are inadequate, as discussed in the next section. *Finally*, we have more information on the amount and composition of this type of waste because most of it (at least two-thirds) is collected.

For these reasons and because solid waste from agricultural (Enrichment Study 14), mining (Sections 13-2 and 15-4), and industrial (Chapters 18 and 19 and Enrichment Study 12) activities are discussed elsewhere in this book, the next two sections of this enrichment study are devoted to possible solutions to the problem of urban solid waste.

E13-2 Disposal of Urban Solid Waste: Dump, Bury, or Burn?

Present Solutions What happens to the trash and garbage that is left on the curb for pickup in the United States? Most citizens and businesses don't care where their trash is disposed of as long as they don't have to smell it, see it, or pay too much to have it taken away. Based on this "out of sight, out of mind" principle, local sanitation departments or privately owned services collect the wastes and dump them on the land, bury them, or burn them. Currently about 82 percent of the collected urban solid waste is deposited in landfills, 8 percent is burned in municipal incinerators, 10 percent is

recycled, and a tiny fraction is composted—that is, organic matter is broken down in the presence of oxygen by aerobic (oxygen-needing) bacteria to produce a humuslike end product, *compost*, which can be used as a soil conditioner.

Table E13-1 lists the major advantages and disadvantages of these methods for solid waste disposal and resource recovery. In the past, the United States dumped some urban solid waste into the ocean. The Environmental Protection Agency banned all ocean dumping of wastes except dredged materials in 1981, but this restriction may soon be lifted for some materials (Section 18-5).

It is important to distinguish four methods for land disposal of solid waste: **(1)** open dumps, **(2)** landfills, **(3)** sanitary landfills, and **(4)** secured landfills. An **open dump** is a land disposal site where solid and liquid wastes are deposited and left uncovered, with little or no regard for control of scavenger, aesthetic, disease, air pollution, and water pollution problems. A **landfill** is a slightly upgraded version of an open dump. This type of land waste disposal site is normally located with little, if any, regard for possible pollution of groundwater and surface water due to runoff and leaching; waste is covered intermittently with a layer of earth. A **sanitary landfill** (Figure E13-2) is a land waste disposal site that is located to minimize water pollution from runoff and leaching; waste is spread in thin layers, compacted, and covered with a fresh layer of soil each day to minimize pests and aesthetic, disease, air pollution, and water pollution problems. A **secured landfill** is a site for the containerized burial and storage of hazardous solid and liquid wastes; the site has restricted access and is continually monitored. The landfill is located above geological strata that should prevent wastes from leaching into groundwater, as discussed further in Section E13-5.

Table E13-1 Comparison of Methods for Solid Waste Disposal and Resource Recovery*

Methods	Advantages	Disadvantages
Littering	Easy	Unsightly; very expensive to clean up,[†] wastes resources
Open dump	Easy to manage; low initial investment and operating costs; can be put into operation in a short period of time; can receive all kinds of wastes.	Unsightly; breeds disease-carrying pests; foul odors; causes air pollution when wastes are burned; can contaminate groundwater and surface water through leaching and runoff; ecologically valuable marshes and wetlands may be erroneously considered "useless" and filled; wastes resources; difficult to site because of public opposition
Sanitary landfill	Easy to manage; relatively low initial investment and operating costs; can be put into operation in a short period of time; if properly designed and operated, can minimize pest, aesthetic, disease, air pollution, and water pollution problems; methane gas produced by waste decomposition can be used as a fuel; can receive all kinds of wastes; can be used to reclaim and enhance the value of submarginal land[§]	Can degenerate into an open dump if not properly designed and managed; requires large amount of land; difficult to site because of citizen opposition and rising land prices[‡]; wastes resources; leaching may cause water pollution; filled land may settle; production of methane gas from decomposing wastes can create a fire or explosion hazard; obtaining adequate cover material may be difficult; hauling waste to distant sites is costly and energy inefficient
Incineration	Removes odors and disease-carrying organic matter; reduces volume of wastes by at least 80%; extends life of landfills; requires little land; can produce some income from salvaged metals and glass and use of waste heat to heat nearby buildings	High initial investment; high operating costs; frequent and costly maintenance and repairs; requires skilled operators; resulting residue and fly ash must be disposed of; causes air pollution unless very costly controls are installed; fine-particle air pollution (Section 19-5) even with pollution control; wastes some resources
Composting	Converts organic waste to soil conditioner that can be sold for use on land; moderate operating costs; most disease-causing bacteria destroyed	Can be used only for organic wastes; wastes must be separated; limited U.S. market for resulting soil conditioner; American solid waste poorly suited for composting because of low organic waste content
Resource recovery plant	High public acceptance; if designed and operated properly; produces little air and water pollution; reduces waste of resources; extends life of landfills; can produce income from salvaged metals, glass, and other materials and from sale of recovered energy for heating nearby buildings; may be easier to site than landfill or conventional incinerator	High initial investment; high operating costs; technology for many operations not fully proven; requires markets for recovered materials or energy produced; costly maintenance and repair; requires skilled operators; can cause air pollution if not properly controlled; profitable only with high volume of waste; discourages low-technology, sustainable earth approach emphasizing reuse and decreased use and waste of resources (Table 13-2)

*The costs for all methods listed vary widely with location, have been rising rapidly and do not include the costs of land, plant construction, and waste collection. Typical collection costs in urban areas range from $50 to $80 per metric ton of waste.
[†]Litter is so widely dispersed that labor and operating costs for collection are extremely high (the second energy law again).
[‡]By 1983 over two-thirds of the cities in the United States had run out of landfill sites.
[§]In Virginia Beach, Virginia, a landfill known as Mount Trashmore is used as an amphitheater; near Chicago, a landfill is used as a ski slope.

The Resource Conservation and Recovery Act of 1976 (RCRA) required that all open dumps be closed or upgraded to landfills by 1983 and banned the creation of new open dumps. Unfortunately, this law does not clearly distinguish between landfills and sanitary landfills. As a result, many of the present sites designated as sanitary landfills are really landfills. Because of their unfavorable location, many of these landfills will cause water pollution problems, especially groundwater contamination (Section 18-4).

By January 1983 the EPA required all new and existing landfills to have (1) a synthetic liner to prevent migration of liquid during the active life of the landfill, (2) a cap of clay or plastic to prevent water from seeping into wastes and leaching toxic substances into nearby surface water and groundwater systems, and (3) a leachate collection system. In addition, all landfills must be monitored and corrected if leaks appear; the disposal of liquids in containers in landfills is not permitted unless the liquid is mixed with an absorbent or is solidified.

Possible Future Methods for Waste Disposal One method for waste disposal that is being tested in several pilot plants is **pyrolysis**—the high-temperature decomposition of waste material in the absence of oxygen. The wastes are converted to oil, organic solids, char, gases such as methane, and inorganic materials. Some of these materials may be resold as fuel to offset the high plant construction costs and the moderately high operating costs. This method, however, uses large amounts of energy to produce the high temperatures needed for waste decomposition, and without expensive controls, pyrolysis plants can cause air pollution problems.

Progress is also being made in developing *biodegradable containers*. The ideal food container is one that is eaten along with its contents, such as an ice cream cone, a taco shell, an apple skin, or a beer bottle made of pretzels. Edible containers could be common within the next 10 years, and some hotels and restaurants are already using nutritious containers that dissolve in water during cooking. Scientists also hope to develop plastics that are readily biodegradable by microorganisms or that decay when exposed to sunlight or rain. We must be cautious, however, about developing packaging that dissolves in water. The resulting chemicals must be carefully tested to be sure that in eliminating some solid waste, we don't create an even worse problem of water pollution. Everything must go somewhere (Section 2-1).

Improving Waste Collection Because collection and hauling account for about 80 to 90 percent of the cost of solid waste disposal, new approaches are being developed to cut human labor costs. One improvement is the modern compaction truck, which uses hydraulic pressure to compress the waste as it is picked up. Even though such trucks can cost $60,000 to $90,000, their increased capacity and lower labor requirements save money. These trash compactors, and home "trashmashers," are ecologically unsound, however. Because they compact mixed trash, it will be difficult and expensive to dig up, separate, and recycle useful resources in the future, if landfills become urban mines. Home garbage disposal units reduce the volume of trash to be collected, but they are also undesirable from an ecological viewpoint. Food and organic wastes are ground up and flushed to a sewage treatment plant and then to water systems, rather than being returned to the soil as compost.

A breakthrough in trash collection is "Son of Godzilla," a truck with a long mechanical arm used to pick up special 300-liter (80-gallon) hard plastic containers set on curbsides. Each truck costs about three to four times more than a conventional truck,

but after a few years a community can save money by using the Son of Godzilla approach. It costs about $70,000 a year to operate this truck, which requires only a driver, compared with about $102,000 a year for a conventional compaction truck with a crew of three. Scottsdale, Arizona, has used this method since 1969, saving at least $375,000 a year; Phoenix, began using this system in 1978.

Even Son of Godzilla can't hold a candle to the pneumatic-type waste collection system used in a number of hospitals, apartment complexes, and housing developments, especially in Sweden. Occupants dump their trash into chutes, and it is sucked through a vacuum-powered pipeline to a central incinerator, for burning. The heat generated is used to melt snow and ice on sidewalks and roads, to generate electricity, and to warm buildings and residences as far as 3.2 kilometers (2 miles) away. Glass and metals can be sorted out for recycling before or after incineration. By 1983 at least 600 pneumatic collection systems were operating in Sweden, England, West Germany, France, the Soviet Union, and other parts of the world. The largest system in the world is at the Disney World complex in Florida.

E13-3 Resource Recovery from Solid Waste

Recycling Paper: A Case Study As discussed in Section 13-3, recycling and reuse can help reduce the use and unnecessary waste of matter and energy resources, and decrease air pollution, water pollution, and solid waste. Thus, a number of observers urge the following national goal: increasing the recycling rate of materials in solid waste from 10 percent to at least 50 percent by a combination of high-technology resource recovery plants, low-technology recycling based on waste separation by consumers, and economic incentives and policies that favor recycling and reuse.

Paper is a widely used material that can be recycled at a much higher rate. Only about 25 percent of the world's waste paper is now recycled; this amount includes 26 percent in the United States, 50 percent in Mexico, 45 percent in Japan, 43 percent in the Netherlands, 35 percent in West Germany, 34 percent in Sweden, and 18 percent in Canada. Mexico, Japan, and the Netherlands have high paper recycling rates primarily because they are sparsely forested. In Sweden, the separation of waste paper from all garbage in homes, shops, and offices has been required by law since 1980. A number of analysts believe that, with sufficient economic incentives and laws, at least half of the world's waste paper could be recycled by the end of the century.

Each American uses directly or indirectly an average of about 275 kilograms (600 pounds) of paper per year—about 8 times the world average and about 40 times that in LDCs. Every Sunday edition of the *New York Times* consumes about 0.60 square kilometer (150 acres) of forest. Almost three-fourths of the U.S. paper production ends up in the trash, with waste paper making up about half the volume of urban solid waste produced each year. During World War II the United States recycled 40 to 45 percent of its waste paper when paper drives and recycling were national priorities.

Recycling a stack of newspapers only 0.9 meter (36 inches) high saves one tree and reduces the harmful environmental effects of clearcutting (Section 10-5). Most trees used to make paper are grown on tree farms especially for this purpose. In addition to saving trees and land, recycling paper saves about 30 to 55 percent of the energy needed to produce paper from virgin pulpwood and can reduce air pollution from pulp mills by about 95 percent. Recycling paper to make high-quality finished products, however, causes more water pollution from the deinking and bleaching of the waste paper than producing such products from virgin pulp. If half the discarded paper were recycled, the United States would save enough energy to provide 10 million people with electrical power each year.

Having individual homes and businesses separate out paper for recycling is an important key to increased recycling. Otherwise the paper becomes so contaminated with other household and municipal trash that waste paper dealers will not buy it. Such source separation is feasible primarily for newspapers from homes, corrugated boxes from commercial and industrial establishments, and printing and writing papers from offices. Slick paper magazines, magazine sections, and advertising supplements, however, cause contamination problems and must not be included. By 1983, over 150 U.S. cities required residences and businesses to separate out newspapers and cardboard for pickup and recycling, and at least 700 American companies and organizations were separating and selling computer cards and high-grade office waste paper for recycling.

Factors hindering waste paper recycling in the United States include **(1)** federal tax subsidies and other financial incentives that make it cheaper to produce paper from trees than from recycling, **(2)** fluctuating prices because of variations in demand, and **(3)** the increased burning of paper in some cities in resource recovery plants to produce energy. Presently the capital gains of producers of virgin timber are taxed at only 30 percent, while the paper recycling industry pays the normal corporate rate of 48 percent. This means that virgin timber pro-

ducers are getting over $100 million a year in tax breaks, to motivate them to grow more pulp trees.

In addition, it is necessary to create a larger and more stable demand for recycled paper to encourage recycling. A requirement at all levels of government that a certain percentage of all paper purchased be made from recycled fibers would help create a fixed demand, which would make it more profitable to recycle paper. The RCRA requires all federal agencies to buy products composed of the highest percentage of recycled materials practicable, but this law has largely been ignored. By contrast, since 1977 Maryland has complied with a similar law and has increased the amount of paper purchased by the state as recycled stock to 25 percent. Presently the U.S. Forest Service helps keep the price of pulp artificially low by leasing large areas of publicly owned softwood forests for cutting by private companies at bargain prices regardless of demand. The U.S. government, which owns half the softwood forests in the country, could boost the incentive for recycling by increasing the price of virgin pulpwood to reflect its true economic value.

Recycled paper is worth about two to three times more than the energy obtained from burning an equal weight of waste paper in a resource recovery plant. Japan, the Netherlands, and several other nations incinerate a large fraction of their wastes for energy recovery, but only after recyclable waste paper has been removed.

You can help by actively supporting legislation to accomplish 50 percent recycling of waste paper in the United States by 1990. You can also start and support recycling drives and centers in your community. Avoid buying and using paper throwaway products, such as paper towels, napkins, plates, cups, and diapers. Bring consumer pressure on manufacturers and store owners by refusing to buy goods that are excessively packaged. When you have a choice between comparable goods, always buy the one that has the least packaging. This will not only reduce environmental pollution and energy use but will save you money. Refuse paper bags and wrapping for small items you purchase, and tell salespersons and store managers why. Take grocery or other bags back to the market and use them again. Carry your lunch in a lunch box rather than a paper sack. Ask the local post office how to stop the flow of junk mail, which wastes paper, time, and energy and results in higher postal rates. Write on both sides of paper, and try to get local colleges and school systems to adopt this practice.

The Low-Waste Society: Going Beyond Disposal and Recycling A number of analysts have urged that a fundamental goal of any national resource and solid waste management program should be to waste fewer resources by a combination of (1) reduced resource use per product (e.g., smaller cars and thinner walled containers), (2) reduced resource use per person (e.g., fewer cars per family), (3) increased product lifetime (e.g., longer lasting cars, tires, and appliances), and (4) increased resource reuse by substituting packaging that can be reused in its original form (e.g., glass bottles, which can be refilled) for throwaway items (e.g., aluminum beverage cans). Some examples of this approach are found in Table 13-2.

E13-4 Types, Sources, and Effects of Hazardous Wastes

What Is Hazardous Waste? Congress has defined **hazardous waste** as discarded solid, liquid, or gaseous material that may pose a substantial threat or potential hazard to human health or the environment when improperly handled. Such materials differ from other forms of solid waste in that they are (1) toxic, (2) so highly reactive when exposed to air, water, or other substances that they can cause explosions and generate toxic fumes, (3) so ignitable that they can undergo spontaneous combustion at relatively low temperatures, (4) so corrosive that they can eat away materials and living tissue, (5) infectious, or (6) radioactive. These wastes, which are growing at a rate of 3 percent a year, include acids, cyanides, and pesticides (Section 9-9); solvents from neighborhood dry cleaners; compounds of lead, mercury, arsenic, and cadmium (Enrichment Study 12); soil contaminated with toxic PCBs and dioxin; infectious wastes from hospitals and research laboratories; improperly treated sewage sludge; obsolete explosives, herbicides, and nerve gas stockpiled and awaiting disposal by the Department of Defense; and low- and high-level radioactive materials.

It is difficult to identify and define toxic and hazardous chemicals because some substances have harmful effects at very low levels of exposure and others only at fairly high exposure levels. Since almost any substance can cause a harmful effect at a high enough level, regulators have great difficulty in classifying individual chemicals as hazardous. Another problem is that a substance normally considered to be fairly harmless may interact synergistically with one or more chemicals in the environment to produce one or more highly toxic substances.

Sources and Volume of Hazardous Wastes In 1983 about 250 billion kilograms (275 million tons) of hazardous wastes were produced in the United States by approximately 750,000 different producers. This amounted to an average of 1,070 kilograms (2,350 pounds) of hazardous waste for each inhabitant of the United States and enough to fill the New Orleans Superdome from floor to ceiling twice a day. Although all states produce hazardous wastes, about 65 percent of the volume is produced, in decreasing order, by Texas, Ohio, Pennsylvania, Louisiana, Michigan, Indiana, Illinois, Tennessee, West Virginia, and California.

The actual amount of hazardous wastes may be much larger because a 1984 study by the National Academy of Sciences revealed that only about 20 percent of the almost 49,000 different chemicals in commercial use have been subjected to extensive toxicity testing, and one-third of these chemicals have never been tested at all for toxicity. The NAS committee found that sufficient data were not available to evaluate any potential health hazards for about 89 percent of the chemicals used commercially, 84 percent of the cosmetics, 81 percent of the food additives, 66 percent of the pesticides, and 64 percent of the drugs.

The proper transportation, disposal, deactivation, or storage of hazardous industrial wastes is a grave environmental problem, which is expected to become more serious in the future. Hazardous waste expert Samuel S. Epstein (see Epstein et al., *Hazardous Waste in America*, 1982) says that hazardous wastes have created "the environmental problem of the century, second only to nuclear war . . . . I've never really been scared until I started working on this issue." On the other hand Edith Efron (see *The Apocalyptics*, 1984), a research associate at the University of Rochester Center for Research in Government Policy and Management, contends that concern over hazardous wastes, pollutants, and other toxic and hazardous materials has little or no scientific foundation.

The EPA estimates that only about 15 percent of the hazardous wastes produced in the United States are disposed of in an environmentally sound manner. About 70 percent are buried in unsafe landfills or unlined lagoons and ponds, and about 15 percent are burned, injected into deep wells, dumped at sea, and illegally dumped (into municipal landfills, rivers, sewer drains, wells, empty lots and fields, old quarries, abandoned mines), or spread along the roadsides by "midnight dumpers." Truckers carrying hazardous liquids often "just drive down the Massachusetts Turnpike and open their spigots," says Paul Keough, EPA deputy administrator in Boston. In Tennessee illegal dumpers have sent freight cars loaded with hazardous wastes to fictitious addresses, C.O.D. Law enforcement officials warn that "midnight dumping" is becoming more frequent as waste generators and haulers try to cut costs. Some officials have also warned that the lure of large profits and generally lax law enforcement has led to increased involvement of organized crime in the hazardous waste disposal industry.

Possible Effects of Hazardous Waste Hazardous wastes can threaten human health from (1) direct exposure of workers in some industries (Enrichment Study 7), transportation accidents, children playing near dump sites or swimming in contaminated streams, (2) long-term or essentially permanent contamination of groundwater from leaching and direct injection wells (Section 18-4), (3) contamination of surface water by runoff from hazardous waste disposal and storage landfills and other areas and overflow of hazardous waste treatment lagoons, (4) biological magnification of some materials in food chains and food webs from improper disposal, and (5) air pollution from open burning or poorly controlled incineration.

When water penetrates buried wastes in landfills it removes various chemicals, producing a polluted liquid leachate that flows out from the dump. Contamination of groundwater when landfills leak or bulldozers disrupt long-forgotten waste sites is probably the most dangerous consequence. An EPA study found that 90 percent of the landfills in the eastern half of the United States were leaking toxic substances into groundwater.

Health effects from exposure to hazardous chemicals can be *acute,* such as skin and eye irritation, disease, dizziness, nausea, blurred vision, tremors, headaches, chemical skin burns, blindness, and death, or *chronic,* such as various types of cancer (Enrichment Study 7), stillbirths, birth defects, sterility, allergies, and heart, liver, and lung damage. Improper management and disposal of hazardous wastes can also cause fish kills, livestock losses, loss of vital habitat for fish and wildlife, soil contamination, cultural eutrophication of lakes (Section 5-3), and depletion of microorganisms that are important in nutrient cycling and nitrogen fixation (Section 4-3).

Transporting hazardous wastes, mostly by truck and train, is another area of increasing concern. The EPA and the Department of Transportation estimate that each year there are about 16,000 transportation incidents involving spills of hazardous materials (not all of them wastes), resulting in about 20 deaths, 600 injuries, and at least $10 million in property damage.

Some Examples A study by the state of California in 1983 revealed that hazardous wastes produced mostly during the manufacture of computer chips were leaking from 36 of the 49 underground storage tanks in one area. These wastes had contaminated surrounding soil, pockets of groundwater, and some private and community water wells in such "Silicon Valley" communities as Santa Clara, Mountain View, Sunnyvale, and San Jose. In 1983 plaintiffs in San Jose filed a multimillion dollar lawsuit against the local plant of the Fairchild Camera and Instrument Corporation, charging the company with negligent contamination of a public well serving 700 residents. There are also suits holding the company responsible for 13 deaths and miscarriages, birth defects, cancers, skin disorders, and blood diseases allegedly resulting from groundwater contamination. In 1984 IBM's large research center in San Jose faced a similar charge of groundwater contamination. A 1980 survey by the California Department of Industrial Relations also found that workers in the microelectronics industry had over three times as many illnesses per 100 workers as those in general manufacturing.

In Bullitt County, Kentucky, an area known as the "Valley of the Drums" contains 100,000 barrels of highly toxic chemicals. All the EPA can do is prevent the chemicals inside the rusting drums from leaking into a nearby stream and periodically check the area for groundwater contamination.

In Elizabeth City, New Jersey, a fire broke out in 1980 at a dump for highly explosive wastes used by the bankrupt Chemical Control Corporation. A serious incident was averted when winds blew the toxic clouds away from heavily populated areas.

In 1983, after finding that the soil in Times Beach, Missouri, a suburb of St. Louis, was contaminated with oil containing dioxin that had been sprayed on dirt roads to control dust, the EPA bought out the entire town at a cost of $36.7 million and had to relocate 300 of its residents. The problem of Times Beach was uncovered when birds and horses exposed to soil sprayed with dioxin-contaminated waste oil began dying. Twenty-six other sites in Missouri are known to be contaminated with dioxin, and 75 more are suspected. Significant levels of dioxin have also been found in some rivers in Michigan, in some fish taken from the Great Lakes, and in flooded basements of homes near the Love Canal in Niagara Falls (Section 5-3).

Technically, the term *dioxin* refers to a family of 75 different organic compounds containing carbon, hydrogen, and chlorine. One form in particular, 2, 3,7,8-tetrachlorodibenzo-paradioxin (2,3,7,8-TCCD, sometimes referred to as TCCD) has been shown to be extremely toxic and to cause cancer and birth defects in animals at very low levels. It also persists in the environment, especially in soil and in the human body, and can apparently be biologically magnified to higher levels in food chains and webs. This dioxin frequently appears as an unavoidable trace contaminant formed as a by-product in the chemical reactions used to make the herbicides Silvex and 2,4,5-T, and Agent Orange (a 50-50 mixture of 2,4-D and 2,4,5-T sprayed to defoliate jungles in South Vietnam between 1962 and 1970). In 1979 the EPA banned certain uses of 2,4,5-T and Silvex. TCCD is also a by-product in the making of chlorophenols, such as the wood preservative pentachlorophenol used to protect telephone poles and railroad crossties, and the antibacterial agent hexachlorophene (which was banned in soaps and deodorants in 1972 after it was shown to cause brain damage in baby monkeys).

TCCD and several other dioxins may also be formed in trace amounts during the high-temperature combustion of various organic compounds in incinerators and other combustion processes. In 1981 the EPA concluded that the quantity of TCCD and other dioxins released into the atmosphere during combustion processes is small and diffuse enough to be relatively harmless, though this finding is disputed by some scientists. The major potential threat comes from larger quantities of TCCD present primarily in industrial dump sites, many of them abandoned.

Although the toxicity of 2,3,7,8-TCCD varies with the test animals exposed, in guinea pigs it is 170,000 times more toxic than cyanide. No one knows the smallest amount of TCCD required to kill or make a person sick, primarily because of lack of reliable data on human exposure and because there is no reliable test to measure TCCD levels in the human body. Workers and others exposed to TCCD in accidents have complained of headaches, weight and hair loss, liver disorders, irritability, insomnia, nerve damage in the arms and legs, loss of sex drive, and chloracne, a severe, painful, and often disfiguring form of acne. Although there have not been enough cases to permit statistical analysis, there is some evidence that humans exposed to chemicals contaminated with TCCD may have a higher than normal incidence of soft-tissue carcinoma, an extremely rare form of cancer that strikes muscles, fat, and nerve cells. Some studies have also suggested that TCCD can cause birth defects, but other studies have failed to confirm this finding. In 1983 the EPA began a 4-year program to identify and clean known and suspected sites believed to contain 80 to 95 percent of the TCCD produced in the United States.

Since 1966 scientists have found widespread contamination from a widely used group of toxic, oily synthetic organic chemicals known as *polychlorinated biphenyls (PCBs)*. PCBs are mixtures of about 70 different but closely related chlorinated hydro-

carbon compounds, made like DDT of carbon, hydrogen, and chlorine. PCBs, which were manufactured in the United States from 1929 to 1979, are still widely used as insulating and cooling fluids in electrical transformers and capacitors. Until 1979 PCBs were also used in the production of plastics, paints, rubber, adhesives, sealants, printing inks, carbonless copy paper, waxes, and pesticide extenders, and for dust control on roads.

There was little concern about PCBs until 1968, when some 1,300 Japanese came down with chloracne and suffered liver and kidney damage after they had eaten rice oil accidentally contaminated with PCBs that had leaked from a heat exchanger. Although precise data are not available, statistical analysis suggests that victims of this accident may suffer from a higher than normal incidence of stomach and liver cancer. Other studies of different occupational groups exposed to PCBs have led to inconsistent and conflicting results, primarily because of the difficulty in determining the amount and types of exposure of individuals to various mixtures of PCBs.

Like DDT, PCBs are insoluble in water, soluble in fats, and very resistant to biological and chemical degradation. Thus, they have the ideal properties for persistence and magnification in food chains and webs. PCBs have been found in Antarctic penguins, in predatory birds at the top of food chains (Figure 5-6), and in the milk of nursing mothers. The EPA estimated that by 1976 at least 98 percent of all Americans had detectable levels of PCBs in their fatty tissues, but that only 8 percent of the population had concentrations above the level (3 ppm) believed to cause any adverse health effects. Two years after most uses of PCBs in the United States had been banned, a nationwide study showed that only 1 percent of the U.S. population had concentrations of PCBs greater than 3 ppm.

As with DDT, the long-term health effects on humans exposed to low levels of PCBs are unknown. But large doses of PCBs have produced liver cancer, kidney damage, weight loss, and reproductive disorders in various laboratory animals. In 1974 the U.S. chemical industry voluntarily stopped producing PCBs for all uses except closed systems such as electrical transformers. In 1979—more than a decade after a similar ban was put into effect in Japan—the EPA banned the production, sale, and use of PCBs in the United States except in sealed systems such as electrical transformers and capacitor systems. But some 341 million kilograms (375,000 tons) of PCBs are still in use, primarily in sealed electrical transformers and capacitors used by electric utility companies. Each year PCBs are released into the environment when some of these transformers and capacitors leak, catch fire, or explode.

Since 1980 the EPA has required that all material containing PCBs be labeled and disposed of only at EPA-approved secured landfills or high-temperature incinerators. In 1983 the EPA issued rules banning the use of PCBs in electrical transformers and other electrical equipment by October 1, 1985, despite protests by manufacturers that the risks from low-level exposure to PCBs had been overstated and that an acceptable substitute was not available. In 1984, however, British researchers developed a substitute for PCBs in electrical equipment.

The EPA estimates that an additional 132 million kilograms (145,000 tons) of PCBs has been disposed of in dumps and landfills, many of them subject to leaking and leaching. It is estimated that an additional 68 million kilograms (75,000 tons) is dispersed throughout the United States, much of it dumped illegally on roadsides and other areas. In 1978 several members of a PCB salvaging firm were convicted of illegally dumping 132,000 liters (35,000) gallons along 336 kilometers (210 miles) of highways in 14 North Carolina counties. These "midnight dumpers" went bankrupt and were sent to jail. The roadside soil contaminated with PCBs was not removed until 1982, primarily because of citizen opposition to proposed locations of a PCB waste disposal dump. After vigorous protests, resulting in 523 arrests, the contaminated soil was dumped in an EPA-approved landfill in rural Warren County, North Carolina. Protesters argued that no landfill was truly secure and that the site was chosen primarily because the county is overwhelmingly black and one of the poorest in the state. The contaminated oil, which could have been disposed of by the original salvaging firm for about $100,000, has cost North Carolina and U.S. taxpayers several million dollars.

E13-5 Control and Management of Hazardous Wastes

Methods for Dealing with Hazardous Wastes The major options for dealing with hazardous wastes include (1) long-term storage in landfills, surface impoundments such as lagoons, underground geologic formations (primarily for radioactive wastes, Section 15-5), and injections into underground wells (Section 18-4), (2) conversion to less hazardous or nonhazardous materials by spreading wastes on the land where they can decompose biologically, incineration on land or at sea using especially designed incinerator ships, thermal decomposition by pyrolysis, and chemical, biological, or physical separation or decomposition processes, and (3) reduction or elimination through modification of industrial processes and recycling and reuse.

Land Disposal of Hazardous Wastes So far the primary method of handling about 70 to 80 percent of the hazardous wastes in the United States has been land disposal—primarily by putting the waste into surface impounds or landfills (secured and unsecured) or injecting them into deep underground wells. This approach is relatively cheap and until recently was not regulated. However, increased regulation, higher land costs, and vigorous opposition by citizens who want hazardous wastes disposed of but not near them have made land disposal a less attractive option.

Since 1976 the RCRA has required that any landfill used for the storage of hazardous wastes be a secure landfill, that operators of such landfills show financial responsibility for up to $10 million in damages due to accidents, and that such landfills be monitored for at least 30 years to minimize the chance of hazardous wastes escaping into the environment. Figure E13-3 shows a typical *secure landfill*. Ideally a secure landfill is sited in thick natural clay deposits, isolated from surface or subsurface water supplies, not expected to be subjected to flooding, earthquakes, or other disruptions, and so located that the transport of leachate to an underground water source is unlikely. In addition, the landfill (1) is sealed in packed clay and has at least one plastic liner about 30 times the thickness of a plastic trash bag to help prevent leakage, (2) has a bottom layer of gravel and perforated pipes to collect the leachate that inevitably seeps down to the bottom of the pit for pumping to the surface for treatment, (3) has drainage ditches to prevent flooding from surface water, (4) has a cover consisting of another plastic liner plus layers of sand, gravel, and clay shaped to divert rainwater, and (5) has a monitoring well system to check for chemicals leaking into groundwater. Various types of hazardous waste in bulk or in drums are placed in the landfill in layers, and each layer is covered with dirt. For even greater security, materials placed in the landfill can be solidified to reduce their volume and encased in cement, asphalt, glass, or organic polymers to decrease the chance of escape into the air or water.

Critics argue that this method does not solve the problem. It only stores and, it is hoped, contains them. In evaluating hazardous waste control methods in 1983, the Office of Technology Assessment stated: "All land disposal methods will eventually fail." The only question is, when? This finding is supported by a National Academy of Sciences report that concluded that land disposal should be the method of last resort. Sooner or later any secure landfill will leak from tears in the plastic liners caused by bulldozers or freezing temperatures, leachate disintegration of the liner, crushing of leachate collection pipes by the weight of the waste, clogging

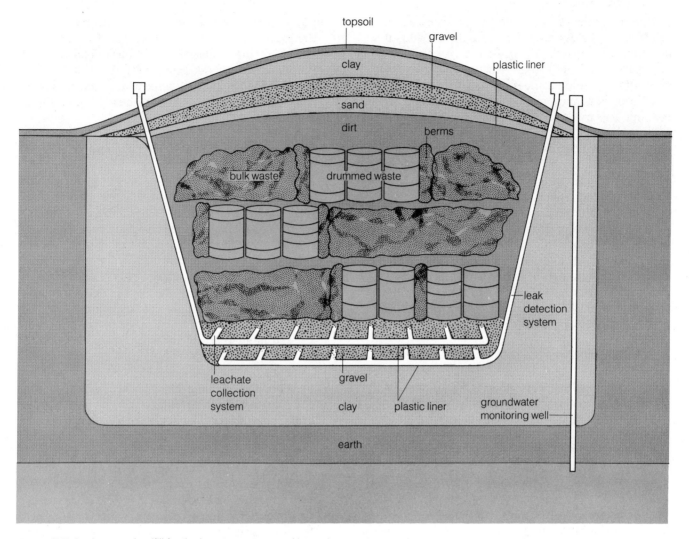

Figure E13-3 A secure landfill for the long-term storage of hazardous wastes.

of the perforations in leachate collection pipes by debris, or disruption of the protective cover by erosion, new construction on the site, or subsidence.

In West Germany 60 percent of the hazardous wastes produced are detoxified rather than being dumped. In Denmark, where 98 percent of the nation's drinking water comes from groundwater, virtually no hazardous wastes are disposed of on land. Sweden, Finland, and the Netherlands are moving rapidly to reduce or ban the land disposal of such wastes.

Because injection of liquid hazardous wastes into underground wells is relatively inexpensive, this approach is widely used in the United States. An estimated 5 percent of all hazardous wastes are currently disposed of this way, and the number of new wells is increasing by 20 percent a year. Deep-well injection is now permitted in only about 20 states, but many other states are under local pressure to allow this form of disposal. However, unless injection wells are located in carefully selected and monitored geologically stable areas, well below groundwater supplies, there is the danger of essentially irreversible groundwater contamination, as discussed in Section 18-4. The disposal of radioactive wastes in deep geologic formations is discussed in Section 15-5.

Conversion to Less Hazardous or Nonhazardous Materials Hazardous organic compounds that contain little or no heavy metal compounds, volatile materials, and persistent organic compounds can be detoxified biologically by landfarming. In *landfarming* wastes are applied onto or beneath surface soil and mixed to expose the contaminated material to oxygen; then microorganisms and nutrients are added as needed to ensure biological decomposition. Care must be taken to prevent soil erosion. This method is particularly useful for sewage, petroleum refinery, and paper mill sludges applied to forestlands and for reclamation of surface-mined land. *Aerobic composting* is more versatile, cheaper, and more widely applicable throughout the United States than landfarming. Other biological treatment and decomposition processes include the use of trickling filters, activated sludge, and aerated lagoons (Section 18-6). There are also experiments with using mutant bacteria produced by genetic manipulation to detoxify specific waste materials. But critics of this approach worry that these "superbugs" may get out of control and destroy other materials before it has a chance to become waste.

Physical processes for detoxifying wastes include (1) neutralization of acidic or alkaline wastes, (2) oxidiation or reduction by chemical reactions into different substances, (3) removal of toxic metals and other compounds by precipitation or absorption (by a chemical such as activated carbon), and (4) selective removal of ions in ion exchangers by passing wastewater over a packed bed of resin. Other approaches being developed and tested include using a microwave plasma process to detoxify wastes and the use of water hyacinths—fast-growing aquatic plants—for treatment of municipal and industrial wastes.

Hazardous wastes can also be decomposed by *incineration* in the presence of oxygen at high temperatures. The Netherlands incinerates about half its hazardous waste, and the EPA estimates that about 60 percent of all U.S. hazardous wastes could be incinerated. Incineration has a number of advantages: (1) it can detoxify complex organic compounds by breaking them down into harmless gases; (2) it is potentially the safest method of disposal for most types of hazardous wastes; (3) it is the most effective method of waste disposal and can destroy at least 99.99 percent of organic waste material such as pesticides, solvents, and PCBs; (4) it greatly reduces the volume of waste (in the form of ash) to be disposed of; (5) large land areas are not required; and (6) the heat produced can be converted to steam and used for electricity or heating nearby buildings.

But there are also some disadvantages: (1) it is the most expensive method (helping explain why only about 3 percent of the hazardous wastes in the United States is burned); (2) the ash left over, whether toxic or nontoxic, must be disposed of; (3)

not all hazardous wastes are combustible; and (4) the gaseous and particulate combustion products emitted by the incinerator can be hazardous to health if not controlled. According to the EPA only about one-third of the industrial hazardous wastes incinerated in the United States are burned in environmentally acceptable facilities.

Because most citizens object to living near incinerators, interest has been growing in incinerating liquid hazardous wastes far from population centers, at sea, in specially designed ships. This approach is about one-third cheaper than on-land incineration and minimizes the dangers to people from an accident. A Dutch company began burning hazardous wastes in 1972 using a cargo ship retrofitted with a furnace. Since 1977, there have been several experimental burns of U.S. hazardous wastes in incinerator ships in the Pacific Ocean and the Gulf of Mexico. Though measurements indicated that the test burns were successful, several scientists contend that the measurements were inadequate and in some cases invalid.

Many environmentalists, however, have opposed the burning of wastes at sea, fearing that chemical spills as a result of accidents from human error, fog, storms, or reefs, or residue from the incomplete destruction of toxic wastes could threaten marine life. In addition, they suspect that some companies would take short-cuts to save money or would cover up accidents at sea, far away from scrutiny. They also point out that at-sea incineration works only for liquid waste and thus is not appropriate for most hazardous wastes generated in the United States. In 1984 the EPA refused to grant permits for test burns of several million pounds of hazardous organic wastes in the Gulf of Mexico until this approach has been evaluated further.

Source Reduction, Recycling, and Reuse Reducing the volume of solid waste can be accomplished by modifying industrial processes to eliminate the production of hazardous wastes, reducing the amount produced, or recycling or reusing the wastes. Epstein and his colleagues (see *Hazardous Waste in America*, 1982) argue that toxic waste outputs "should be regarded as valuable crude resources, to be mined, processed, refined, and recovered." With land disposal costs rising, recycling of hazardous by-products within a plant and between different industries is becoming a more attractive option.

In Europe, waste exchanges or clearinghouses are used to transfer waste produced by one firm to another firm that can use it as raw material. By 1984 European waste exchanges were transferring about 35 percent of the wastes they listed. By 1984 at least 30 regional waste exchanges in the United States were transferring about 10 percent of the listed wastes. Though they currently handle only a tiny fraction of the total volume of hazardous waste, this fraction could be increased.

Federal Legislation and Control of Hazardous Wastes The Toxic Substances Control Act of 1976 and the previously mentioned Resource Conservation and Recovery Act (RCRA) of 1976 require the EPA to identify hazardous wastes, to set standards for their management, and to issue guidelines and provide some financial aid to establish state programs for managing such wastes. The RCRA also requires all firms that store, treat, or dispose of large amounts of hazardous wastes to apply to the EPA for a permit.

Regulations issued by the EPA in 1980 for the handling of hazardous wastes identified certain hazardous chemicals and chemical processes that will require disposal in federally approved secured landfills, if sites can be found, in the face of citizen opposition, for the 50 to 150 such dumps that will be needed by 1990. Other chemicals will be added to the list in the future. Firms producing large amounts of hazardous wastes [more than 1,000 kilograms (2,200 pounds) a month] were required to file an annual report detailing what they did with these materials. In 1982, however, this regulation was suspended by the EPA—an action EPA whistleblower Hugh Kaufman likened to abolishing income tax returns and expecting the IRS to enforce the tax laws.

To reduce illegal dumping, large waste producers must use a "cradle-to-grave" manifest system—that is, they must keep track of hazardous wastes from point of origin to point of disposal. First, a producer of wastes must check the EPA hazardous wastes list. If a waste is classified as hazardous, it must be properly packaged, clearly labeled, and transported only to an authorized disposal site. Both the transporter and the waste disposal site operator are supposed to sign the manifest and return a signed copy to the company that produced the waste. EPA administrators, however, point out that this requirement is almost impossible to enforce because the agency does not have enough personnel to review the paper trails of some 60,000 large hazardous waste generators and 15,000 haulers each year—let alone verify them and prosecute offenders.

Effective July 1982, the EPA required the owners or operators of landfills, impoundments, and land treatment facilities handling hazardous wastes to have accident liability coverage of at least $3 million per incident. Effective January 1983, the EPA required that all new and existing landfills handling hazardous wastes (1) have a synthetic liner to help prevent migration of liquids during the active life

of the landfill, (2) have a leachate collector system, (3) not accept liquids in containers unless the liquid is mixed with an absorbent or is solidified, and (4) have a cap of clay or plastic to help prevent leaching and seepage into buried wastes.

Although these regulations are a step in the right direction, environmentalists point to several serious loopholes and difficulties in the RCRA. These include: (1) the slowness of the EPA to inventory and identify chemicals not presently on the fairly short hazardous wastes list, (2) inadequate sampling and testing procedures for use by waste producers to determine whether their wastes are classified as hazardous under federal guidelines, (3) exclusion from the regulations of hazardous waste mixed with domestic sewage (thus allowing companies to bypass the regulations in a potentially dangerous way by dumping hazardous wastes down sewers), (4) exemption from regulation of recycled or reused hazardous wastes (such as the recycled dioxin-contaminated oil sprayed on roads in Times Beach, Missouri), (5) exemption from the regulations of firms producing less than 1,000 kilograms (2,200 pounds) of hazardous wastes a month,* and (6) no requirement for states to regulate all the hazardous wastes identified by the EPA such that states with weaker programs could be chosen by industry as dumping grounds for certain wastes.

By mid-1984 Congress was still considering amendment to the RCRA that might correct some of these deficiencies. But these amendments were opposed by a number of industries generating hazardous wastes.

Environmentalists and hazardous waste experts have also urged Congress to (1) reduce the production of hazardous wastes and encourage recycling and reuse of such materials by levying a tax or fee on producers for each quantity of such wastes generated, (2) impose a higher fee on the land disposal of high-priority hazardous wastes or ban their disposal on land, as a means of encouraging recycling, reuse, treatment, and destruction technologies, and (3) provide low-interest loans, tax breaks, and other financial incentives for industries to encourage the recycling, reuse, treatment, destruction, and reduced production of hazardous wastes.

In 1980 Congress passed the Comprehensive Environmental Response, Compensation and Liability Act (known as the Superfund program). The Superfund itself consisted of $1.6 billion, to be used by the EPA between 1980 and 1985, to clean up abandoned or inactive hazardous waste dump sites.

---

*These small businesses produce only about 1 percent of the total hazardous wastes produced each year, but this amounts to about 2.5 billion kilograms (2.8 million tons) annually.

The EPA is authorized to collect fines and sue the owners (if they can be found), to recover up to three times the cleanup costs. About 87 percent of these cleanup funds are provided by taxes on certain chemical and petrochemical industries, and the remainder from general federal tax revenues. This legislation also requires states to provide 10 percent of the cleanup costs for sites located on private property and 50 percent of the costs for those in public land. The EPA cannot use any money from the Superfund for cleanup unless the states make their contributions. By mid-1984 only eight states had such cleanup funds in their budgets.

By mid-1984 the EPA had identified 16,300 abandoned waste sites in the United States and estimated that the total could reach 22,000 by 1985. Preliminary evaluation of about 10,000 of these sites had been made by mid-1984, and 546 (many of them used by the Department of Defense) were included on a national priorities list as especially hazardous and eligible for cleanup using federal funds, provided sufficient state funds were made available. New Jersey leads, with 65 priority sites, followed by Michigan (with 46) and Pennsylvania (with 30). Only Alaska, the District of Columbia, Georgia, Hawaii, Nevada, Wisconsin, and the Virgin Islands did not have any sites on the priority list. By mid-1984 the EPA had issued orders for the cleanup of 72 of these uncontrolled or inactive sites, but had cleaned up only six sites, at a cost of $177 million.

By 1981 the EPA was being criticized by environmentalists for being too slow in implementing the new legislation and lax in legal enforcement. A report by the General Accounting Office (see *Hazardous Waste Sites Pose Investigation Evaluation, Scientific, and Legal Problems*, 1981) stated that the EPA was finding it difficult to carry out its mandate to protect human health and the environment from hazardous wastes because (1) new abandoned waste sites were being discovered faster than they could be investigated and evaluated; (2) there was no strong scientific basis for determining risks from various hazardous chemicals; and (3) legal action seeking correction of hazardous waste problems was being pursued at only a few sites. Drastic EPA budget cuts between 1981 and 1983 made it even more difficult to implement the Superfund legislation. In 1983 critics charged the EPA with letting some noncomplying firms off too easily and settling for superficial cleanups. Investigations by Congress in 1983 of Superfund mismanagement and alleged inside deals with some industries generating hazardous wastes led to the firing of the director of the program (who was later convicted of perjury before Congress) and the resignation of the head of the EPA, Anne Gorsuch Burford.

Critics of the Superfund legislation also point

out that $1.6 billion will probably clean up no more than 100 to 300 of the abandoned dump sites—only a fraction of the priority sites the EPA estimates will need cleanup, long-term monitoring, or both. The estimated cost for cleaning up abandoned and inactive hazardous waste sites ranges from $9 billion to $260 billion. A 1983 study by the Office of Technology Assessment concluded that the Superfund program might be ineffective in the long term because wastes are simply moved from one burial site to another, and leakage eventually will occur.

In 1984 Congress was considering expanding the Superfund to $9 billion and also allowing private citizens to file suits in federal courts to recover from owners and operators of hazardous waste dump sites the costs of personal damages and medical expenses incurred as a result of exposure to chemicals from such sites.

Waste is a human concept. In nature nothing is wasted, for everything is part of a continuous cycle. Even the death of a creature provides nutrients that will eventually be reincorporated in the chain of life.

Denis Hayes

Discussion Topics

1. List the advantages and disadvantages of each of the following methods for disposal of solid waste: **(a)** open dumping, **(b)** sanitary landfill, **(c)** incineration, and **(d)** composting.

2. How is solid waste collected and disposed of in your community? Are the land waste disposal sites in the community true sanitary landfills or merely landfills? Does the community have any secured landfill sites for disposal of hazardous wastes?

3. Explain why the solid waste problem in the United States can be viewed primarily as an economic and political problem. What actions or changes would you make to correct this situation?

4. List possible ecological problems with each of the following: **(a)** using home trash compactors, **(b)** having people put their trash in plastic bags, **(c)** developing plastic bottles that dissolve in water, and **(d)** using sink garbage disposal units.

5. Why is there so little recycling and reuse in the United States? How would you correct this?

6. List the advantages and disadvantages of the high-technology (resource recovery plant) and the low-technology (source separation) approaches to recycling. Would you favor requiring all households and businesses to separate recyclable materials? Defend your answer.

7. What is the basic limitation of recycling? What thermodynamic and other alternatives are available (see Section 13-4)?

8. Does your school or city have a paper, can, or glass recycling program? (If not, consider starting one as a class community project.) Must a certain fraction of all paper purchased by your school or local government contain recycled fiber? Why not? Do the teachers in your school expect everyone to write on both sides of paper? Why not start a campaign to have this practice adopted in all local colleges and in the public school system?

9. Give your reasons for agreeing or disagreeing with each of the following proposals for dealing with solid waste in the United States.

   a. Remove all subsidies, preferential transportation charges, depletion allowances, and tax breaks for primary materials industries.

   b. Require deposits on all beverage containers, phasing gradually to a complete ban on all nonreturnable beverage containers.

   c. Give tax breaks on comparable products that use less resources per unit or last longer.

   d. Standardize package sizes for each item and add a tax for excess packaging.

   e. Allow taxpayers to deduct the cost of appliance repairs from their taxable income, to encourage repair rather than disposal.

   f. Require all households and businesses to separate trash into recyclable components.

   g. Require that all products be labeled to show the amount and type of recycled materials.

   h. Require local, state, and federal agencies to buy materials composed of the highest available percentage of recycled materials.

10. Is your state contemplating a law to ban nonreturnable bottles and to require deposits on all beer and beverage containers? If not, why not start a statewide campaign for such legislation?

11. Does your school sell beverages in throwaway cans or bottles? Why not campaign for the use of returnable bottles in school vending machines?

12. Debate the idea that a recycling tax (say $100) be added to the price of all automobiles, as a deposit to be returned when the vehicle is delivered to an official recycling center.

13. Compare the throwaway, recycling, and sustainable earth (or low-waste) approaches to waste disposal and resource recovery and conservation for (a) glass bottles, (b) "tin" cans, (c) aluminum cans, (d) paper, (e) plastics, (f) leaves, grass, and food wastes, and (g) cars (see Table 13-2).

14. Would you oppose the location of a secured landfill for the storage of hazardous wastes on property near your home? If you oppose such a site, what alternatives would you suggest? Would you oppose the location of an incinerator for the decomposition of hazardous wastes near your home? Why or why not?

15. Why is it so difficult to define a hazardous waste?

16. Give your reasons for agreeing or disagreeing with each of the following proposals for dealing with hazardous wastes in the United States.

   a. Burn all liquid hazardous wastes in federally approved at-sea incinerator ships.

   b. Require firms producing small amounts of hazardous wastes per month and all firms recycling and reusing hazardous wastes to be regulated by the EPA.

   c. Require states to regulate all hazardous wastes identified by the EPA.

   d. Reduce the use of hazardous wastes and encourage recycling and reuse of such materials by levying a tax or fee on producers for each quantity of such wastes generated.

   e. Impose a higher fee on the land disposal of high-priority hazardous wastes as a means of encouraging alternative methods of treatment.

   f. Ban high-priority hazardous wastes from land disposal to encourage recycling, reuse, treatment, and destruction technologies.

   g. Provide low-interest loans, tax breaks, and other financial incentives for industries producing hazardous wastes to encourage the recycling, reuse, treatment, destruction, and reduced production of such wastes.

Enrichment Study 14

Controlling Eutrophication and Agricultural Water Pollution

Two related water pollution problems are cultural eutrophication—the overloading of lakes and estuaries with such plant nutrients as nitrates and phosphates (Figure 5-8)—and the runoff of fertilizer and animal wastes from land to nearby lakes and streams. In this enrichment study we will look briefly at these water pollution problems and some possible solutions.

E14-1 Controlling Cultural Eutrophication

Methods for Controlling Cultural Eutrophication There are two basic categories of methods for

controlling cultural eutrophication: *output approaches* (which treat the symptoms) and *input approaches* (which treat the causes), as summarized in the accompanying box.

Figure E14-1 illustrates a comprehensive approach to controlling lake eutrophication, incorporating treatments of both symptoms and causes, as well as preventive medicine to keep healthy lakes from getting sick. Not all the controls would be needed in all areas. Instead, a particular approach or combination of approaches must be carefully chosen for each situation.

The Detergent Controversy Until 1945 soap was used to wash clothes in the United States. But in

Figure E14-1 A comprehensive scheme for reducing nutrient overload in a heavily stressed lake (compare with Figure 5-8).

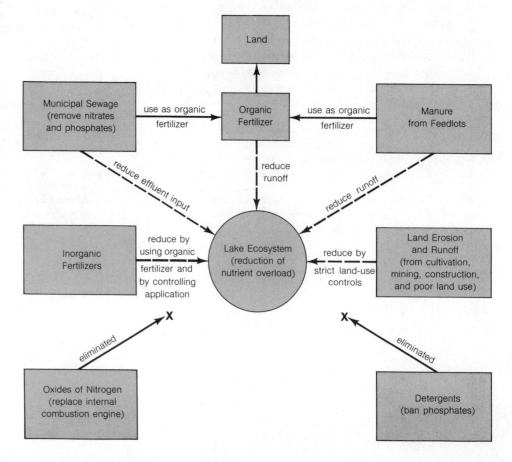

Summary of Methods for Controlling Cultural Eutrophication

Output Approaches

1. Bypass the lake by diverting wastewater to fast-moving streams or to the ocean. This is not possible in most places. Where this approach is possible, it may transfer the problem from a lake to a nearby estuary system.

2. Dredge lake sediments to remove excess nutrient buildup. This is impractical in large, deep lakes and not very effective in shallow lakes. Dredging often reduces local water quality, and the dredged material must go somewhere—usually into the ocean.

3. Remove or harvest excess weeds, debris, and rough fish. Difficult and expensive in large lakes with present technology.

4. Control nuisance plant growth with herbicides and algicides. The direct addition of such toxic substances as well as magnification in the food chain may upset the ecosystem (Section 9-9).

Input Approaches

1. Remove phosphates from sewage treatment plant effluents before they reach the lake. Eliminates most point sources by removing phosphates from industrial and municipal sewage.

2. Ban or set low limits (less than 4 percent) on phosphates in detergents, which would decrease phosphate input by 30 to 70 percent.

3. Conduct research to define the critical nutrients, special problems, characteristics, and control strategy for each major lake, slow-moving river, and estuarine region.

4. Recover valuable phosphate and nitrogen nutrients and recycle them to the land as fertilizers rather than overfertilizing lakes and estuaries. Will require improved technologies for transporting treated sewage to agricultural and forest areas and for preventing toxic metal buildup in the soil (Enrichment Study 12). The basic problem here is economic, not technological, because synthetic fertilizer is so cheap. Some suggest taxing commercial fertilizer to make recycling of natural wastes competitive.

5. Control land use near watershed areas. Ultimately any program to improve water quality must control the use and abuse of the land and emphasize soil conservation (Section 8-6).

6. Use deliberate, carefully controlled enrichment to increase lake or estuarine productivity for cultivating desirable fish and shellfish, and harvest algae as a food for people (aquaculture and mariculture, Section 9-6).

---

areas with hard water (which contains ions of calcium, magnesium, or iron), soap leaves a greasy, grayish film (the soap curd). Around 1945 chemists invented synthetic detergents, which contain chemicals such as sodium tripolyphosphate to prevent the oily film from forming. Manufacturers advertised the new products heavily, and now detergents have almost completely replaced soap for cleaning laundry.

Most laundry detergents sold in the United States in the early 1970s contained about 12 percent phosphorus by weight and accounted for about half of the phosphorus (as phosphates) in domestic wastewater. These phosphates were released into lakes directly or indirectly in the effluents discharged from secondary sewage treatment plants, which do not remove phosphates. By 1983 the average phosphorus content of detergents in the United States had dropped to about 5 percent and accounted

for about 35 percent of the phosphorus in wastewater in regions that did not ban phosphate detergents.

For lakes where phosphorus is the limiting factor, the best approach to minimizing cultural eutrophication is to drastically reduce the input of phosphorus. But there is disagreement over whether this should be done by banning or limiting phosphates in detergents or by removing phosphates from wastewater at sewage treatment plants. To no one's surprise, the detergent industry favors the second plan, and city governments and consumer groups favor the first. Banning or limiting phosphates in detergents is faster and cheaper than upgrading sewage plants and could cut phosphate inputs into lakes where phosphorus is the limiting factor by 30 to 70 percent in a single stroke.

Detergent industry officials, however, contend that in most areas a phosphate ban alone would not eliminate phosphate-related problems because phosphate detergents contribute only a small amount of the phosphorus that finds its way into aquatic systems from natural runoff, human wastes, and fertilizer runoff. They argue that removal of phosphate at sewage treatment plants would eliminate about 50 to 80 percent of the input.

By 1983 Michigan, Wisconsin, Vermont, Indiana, New York, Minnesota, and Canada had banned or limited the amount of phosphate in phosphate-containing detergents, household cleaners, and water conditioners. Bans have also been in effect in Chicago, Miami, Akron, and other cities. The ban of phosphate detergents in Syracuse, New York, caused the phosphate content of Lake Onondaga to drop 57 percent in only a year and a half.

Eliminating phosphates from detergents, however, is not without its problems. The substitute may be worse. For example, a promising substitute, trisodium nitrilotriacetate (NTA), was banned in 1970 by the Surgeon General because of evidence that it might cause urinary tract cancer in rats and mice. But after exhaustive testing, the EPA decided in 1980 that there was no reason to ban the use of NTA in detergents.

Another approach is to return to the use of soap. Approximately 60 percent of the U.S. population lives in areas where soap works well because the water is soft or only slightly hard. People who live in areas with moderate to very hard water (check with local water officials) could use soap with a water softener, such as washing soda.* Clothes will not be quite as bright because modern automatic washers are not designed for soap, even with added water softeners. Even so, soap will work if you are not hooked on having your clothes sparkling white. Maybe someone can design an automatic washer that uses soap.

A Success Story—Lake Washington's Rebirth
What can citizens do to help clean up lakes plagued with cultural eutrophication? A great deal, as shown by the success of Seattle's residents in cleaning up Lake Washington and Puget Sound. In 1952 W. T. Edmondson, a prominent zoologist and pollution expert, began studying pollution in Lake Washington. He found that algal growth had been stimulated by 10 sewage treatment plants built around the lake since 1941. Puget Sound waters were also extensively polluted by large volumes of raw sewage added daily. Both the lake and the sound were unsafe for swimming.

Edmondson's research and James R. Ellis's civic leadership sparked an outstanding pollution cleanup. After several years of careful study, a citizens' committee began to tackle the problem politically. They proposed a single governmental unit that would deal with all the pollution sources in the drainage basin. After extensive lobbying, they persuaded the state legislature to pass a bill in 1957 permitting the formation of METRO, the Municipality of Metropolitan Seattle. In 1958, after 5 years of effort culminating in an intensive 6-week campaign—in which 5,000 men, women, and children rang doorbells, citizen speakers gave over 300 talks, and endorsements were obtained from more than 200 organizations—the voters approved METRO.

More sewers and two big new treatment plants were built to eliminate all sewage discharges into Lake Washington and all raw sewage discharge into Puget Sound. The results were dramatic. Phosphate and nitrate levels in both bodies of water dropped sharply, and the beaches of both are now open.

The Lake Washington success cannot necessarily be repeated in other areas (such as the Great Lakes) for several reasons. First, industrial pollution was not a significant factor in Seattle. Second, surrounding areas were essentially urban or forested rather than agricultural; thus, nutrients were not very concentrated in the runoff. Third, a convenient dumping ground, Puget Sound, was available. Nevertheless, this success story is a dramatic example of what organized, informed, and dedicated action by ordinary citizens can do.

E14-2 Controlling Agricultural Water Pollution

Modern agriculture in the United States is a major polluter of water systems, accounting for 30 to 50 percent of all water pollution. The major factor is the runoff of fertilizer and manure from the land to nearby water systems (Figure E14-2).

The U.S. Fertilizer Runoff Problem During the last several decades the use of inorganic, or synthetic, fertilizer in the world has skyrocketed. It seems logical to suppose that some of this input of nitrogen and phosphorus nutrients is running off from the soil into lakes and streams, and leaching into groundwater.

As with any problem with conflicting and inconclusive information, opposing schools of thought have arisen among environmentalists and

---

*The procedure is as follows. First strip the detergents from your clothes by washing them in hot water containing about 4 tablespoons of washing soda. From then on wash a normal load of clothes with 1 cup of pure soap flakes or powder plus 2 to 4 tablespoons of washing soda, depending on the hardness of the water.

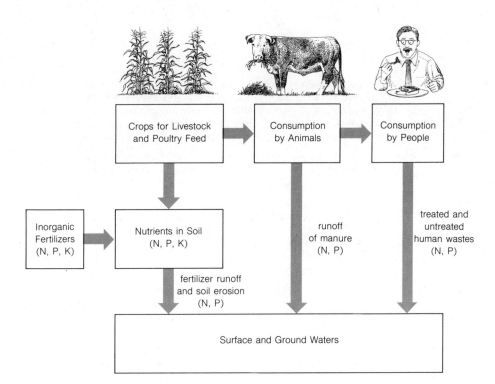

Figure E14-2 Water pollution by commercial fertilizer runoff, feedlot runoff, and human wastes, all of which contain nitrogen (N), phosphorus (P), and/or potassium (K) compounds.

agriculturalists (see Table E14-1). There is probably some truth in both viewpoints. More research, careful evaluation of existing data, and cooperation between agriculturalists and environmentalists may eventually lead to a realistic plan of action.

Some Solutions to the Fertilizer Runoff Problem Scientists have suggested a wide range of solutions for dealing with the fertilizer runoff problem:

1. Improve soil erosion control (Section 8-6).

2. Prohibit spreading of nitrogen or phosphorus fertilizer on frozen soils or on land near surface water supplies that slopes more than 5 percent, unless erosion is controlled.

3. Establish ideal fertilizer amounts for each type of crop and soil, and circulate the information among farmers.

4. Rotate crops and plant nitrogen-fixing legume crops, such as clover and alfalfa, to decrease leaching of nitrates into groundwater.

5. Leave crop residues on soil surfaces to reduce erosion.

6. Use slow-release nitrogen fertilizers.

7. Decrease the amount of phosphorus in fertilizers.

8. Increase research on soil chemistry (especially the movement of nitrogen and phosphate in soil systems), and study ways to remove nitrates from drinking water in home and farm systems.

9. Prohibit or limit fertilizer use in critical areas where it contributes to surface and ground water pollution.

The U.S. Manure Runoff Problem Some consider manure to be one of the major agricultural pollution problems in the United States. In earlier times it was a highly prized fertilizer, and it is still in some countries. Because synthetic fertilizers now cost so little, some feedlot operators can't sell manure, give it away, burn it, or find enough land on which to spread it.

The annual output of animal manure in the United States today is equivalent to the wastes from a human population of 2 billion people—about 10 times the actual U.S. population. At least half these nutrient-rich wastes are recycled by being spread on the land. But in some areas the manure not recycled to the land can be a potential hazard to surface and ground water—not to mention causing problems of odor, dust, and flies.

Twenty years ago animal feedlots were rare in this country, and an average steer roamed and fed on an open range with its waste naturally recycled to the soil. Today at least half the 125 million steers (as well as hogs and poultry) are crowded into land areas holding 1,000 or more animals. Near Greeley, Colorado, almost 100,000 head of cattle are penned on only 1.3 square kilometers (320 acres) of land.

Table E14-1 Summary of the Debate on the Use of Synthetic Fertilizers

Environmental Position	Agriculturalist Position
Fertilizer runoff contributes 30 to 50% of the nitrates in ground and surface waters.	Nitrogen fertilizers undoubtedly contribute nitrates to groundwater systems in some localities, but the data are too scanty and conflicting to make generalizations. Amounts vary considerably with conditions and locations and are usually less than 30 to 50%. Excess nitrates more often come from treated sewage, soil erosion, food processing, and feedlot wastes.
Widespread fertilizer use deteriorates the soil's ability to hold nitrogen.	Nitrogen is naturally lost by erosion, leaching, volatilization, denitrification, and harvesting crops. The purpose of fertilizer is to replace this lost nitrogen. Without its widespread use, soils would be depleted to a much greater extent.
Fertilizer runoff is a major cause of eutrophication.	Although some nitrates in fertilizer can run off, phosphorus (the main cause of eutrophication) is strongly held by soil particles so that relatively little is lost. Municipal and industrial wastes and detergents are the main cause of eutrophication. Fertilizers could contribute in estuarine areas where nitrogen is the limiting agent and where agricultural use of land is heavy.
The situation in Great Britain and the Netherlands differs from that in the United States. These countries have no large lakes, and rivers there are short and fast flowing.	U.S. eutrophication problems due to fertilizer use are not serious. No serious problems have been reported in Great Britain and the Netherlands, where fertilizer use is 3 and 11 times U.S. usage, respectively.
Americans are increasing the danger of being poisoned by excessive nitrate concentrations in public water supplies and wells. If children under 4 months of age are exposed to nitrate levels exceeding the public health limit (10 milligrams of nitrate per liter), they can get sick and even die from methemoglobinemia.	In several surveys less than 1% of public water supplies exceeded the safe limit, but a number of rural wells did, especially in California, Missouri, Illinois, Minnesota, and Wisconsin. Between 1944 and 1972, 41 infants died from methemoglobinemia in the United States (versus 80 in Europe). All cases but one involved poisoning from rural wells, usually from septic tank or feedlot runoff, and most cases occurred between 1945 and 1950.
The fertilizer runoff problem is so serious that we should reduce the use of commercial fertilizer in the United States.	With increasing use and no program for control, fertilizer runoff could become a serious problem in some areas. Control should be based on reducing excess application by farmers, applying at the right time, and reducing use in highly critical watershed or groundwater basin areas. If fertilizer use were banned, food prices could rise considerably, soil fertility would decline sharply, and much additional land would have to be cultivated to feed the U.S. population. Much of this would be marginal land prone to soil erosion, which could add more nitrates than the fertilizer on existing cropland. This could also use up land that should be reserved for recreation and wildlife habitats (Sections 11-4 and 11-5).

State and federal regulations now limit the sites on which feedlots can be built, but some existing operations are located on hillsides so that fluid wastes drain easily into the waterways below. Serious water pollution can occur when rains flush a large amount of waste into nearby streams in a short time. Another important source of excess nitrates in lakes and streams near feedlots may be gaseous ammonia from animal manure decomposing on the feedlot surface.

Solutions to the Manure Problem Scientists have suggested a variety of solutions for dealing with the manure problem.

1. Recycle manure to the land. Unless the use of manure is subsidized by tax incentives or synthetic fertilizers are taxed, this method probably will not be adopted by industrialized agriculture because many feedlots are located near big cities (to cut livestock hauling costs), where land for recycling the manure is not available.

2. Recycle processed manure as livestock feed. This cuts operating costs and returns proteins, vitamins, and other valuable nutrients to the animals. Care must be taken to ensure that contaminants, such as pesticides and toxic metals, do not build up to dangerous levels through recycling and that infectious diseases are not spread.

3. Convert animal manure to low-sulfur, heavy oil that could be used for generating electricity. This process is expensive and normally requires such a large input of energy that the net energy yield is very low or even negative.

4. Require structures around all feedlots that would intercept and divert runoff so that manure does not flow directly into surface water sources.

5. Divert runoff into retention basins from which the water can be pumped for application to cropland or forestland.

Unfortunately, when retention basins are too small or poorly designed, they can overflow into nearby water courses during heavy rains.

6. Set up oxygenation stations (air bubblers) in ponds, lakes, and streams so that they can absorb more manure (an expensive plan).

7. Prohibit the spreading of manure on frozen land or on land located near waterways that slope more than 5 percent.

8. Establish state and federal regulations on the location, operation, and pollution control of feedlots.

9. Use rural land-use zoning (Section 12-5) to set aside areas for feedlots where odors and some water pollution can be tolerated.

10. Dehydrate manure to remove odors, bag it, and sell it to home gardeners.

Today in the United States everybody is downwind or downstream from somebody or something else.

William D. Ruckelshaus

Discussion Topics

1. Explain why building expensive primary and secondary sewage treatment plants (Section 18-6), although necessary, may hasten the deterioration of water quality through cultural eutrophication. What are some solutions to this dilemma?

2. Explain some possible problems and ecological side effects of the following proposed solutions to cultural eutrophication: (a) directing wastewater to the ocean, (b) dredging lake sediments, (c) harvesting excess weeds and fish, (d) using herbicides and algicides to control excessive plant growth, and (e) banning all use of phosphate detergents in the United States.

3. Debate the following statements:

   a. Fertilizer runoff is one of the major causes of cultural eutrophication.

   b. Using fertilizer reduces the ability of the soil to hold nitrogen.

   c. We are in increasing danger of being poisoned by nitrates in our water supplies.

   d. The use of synthetic fertilizers in the United States should be sharply reduced to encourage use of natural fertilizers.

   e. Because Great Britain and the Netherlands, which use 3 to 11 times as much fertilizer per acre as the United States does, are not having any serious eutrophication problems, there is no cause for concern in the United States.

4. Debate the following resolution: Large animal feedlots should be prohibited in the United States.

Enrichment Study 15

How to Influence Elected Officials

E15-1 How to Write Elected Officials

Do you write your congressional representatives and senators opposing or supporting environmental legislation or complimenting them for a particular stand? Writing your elected representatives in the correct way is an extremely important action. You may be thinking, "What can my one letter or one vote do?" But letters supporting or opposing a particular position can slowly accumulate until a threshold is crossed; elected officials are forced to recognize that if they don't vote in a certain way for the people they represent, they are likely not to be reelected.

The best guide for writing to Congress, called *When You Write to Washington*, is issued annually by the League of Women Voters.* The accompanying box lists suggested rules for writing elected officials.

E15-2 Rules for Effective Political Action

Writing letters is essential. But to use positive synergy, citizens need to support national lobbying organizations to counteract the massive lobbying activities of industry and other vested interests. We also need to join or form local ongoing organizations or temporary task forces on particular issues. The basic rules for effective action by political action organizations have been summarized by John W. Gardner, former cabinet official and founder of Common Cause (see *In Common Cause*, 1972).

1. Have a full-time continuing organization.

2. Limit the number of targets and hit them hard.

Most groups dilute their efforts by taking on too many issues.

3. Get professional advisers to provide you with accurate, effective information and arguments.

4. Increase positive synergy by forming alliances with other organizations on a particular issue.

5. Have effective communication that will state your position in an accurate, concise, and moving way.

6. Persuade and use positive reinforcement—don't attack. Confine your remarks to the issue, not to personal attacks on individuals. Try to find allies within the institution, and compliment individuals and organizations when they do something you like. Do your homework and then approach public officials whose support you need privately, without lecturing them or using high pressure tactics. In most cases it is best not to bring something up at a public meeting unless you have the votes lined up ahead of time.

7. Organize for action—not just for study, discussion, or education. Minimize regular meetings, titles, and minutes. Have a group coordinator, a series of task forces with a project leader, press and communications contact, legal and professional advisers, and a *small* group of dedicated workers. A small cadre can accomplish more than a large unwieldy group. Work in small groups but always keep in mind the Abilene paradox: People in groups will tend to act collectively in ways they individually know to be stupid.

8. Don't work exclusively at the national level. Concentrate much of your effort at the state and particularly at the local level.

9. Be honest, accessible, and on good terms with your local press.

---

*This pamphlet, which includes an annual list of all committee members and chairpersons, can be obtained from the League of Women Voters, 1730 M St., N.W., Washington, DC 20005.

The journey of a thousand miles begins with one step.
Lao-tse

Writing Effective Letters

1. Address the letter properly:

   a. The president:

   > The President
   > The White House
   > 1600 Pennsylvania Ave., N.W.
   > Washington, DC 20500

   > Dear Mr. President:

   b. Your senators:

   > The Honorable _____
   > Senate Office Building
   > Washington, DC 20510

   > Dear Senator _____ :

   c. Your representative:

   > The Honorable _____
   > House Office Building
   > Washington, DC 20515

   > Dear Representative _____ :

2. Always concentrate on your own representatives, but also write the chair or members of the committee that is holding hearings on legislation that interests you. Try to write the original committee chair and members, the conference committee members, and the chair and members of the correct appropriations committee.

3. Be brief (a page or less), cover only one subject, and come quickly to the point. Write the letter in your own words and express your own views—don't sign and send a form or mimeographed letter. Make the letter personal, and don't say that you are writing for an organization (the representative should know the official positions of organized bodies).

4. If possible, identify the bill by number (for example, "H.R. 123" or "S. 313") or name, and ask the representative or senator to do something specific (cosponsor, support, or oppose it). You can get a free copy of any bill or committee report by writing to the House Document Room, U.S. House of Representatives, Washington, DC 20515, or the Senate Document Room, U.S. Senate, Washington, DC 20510.

5. Give specific reasons for your position. Try to explain the impact of the legislation on yourself or—better yet—your district or state.

6. If you have expert knowledge, share it. You may give your representative much-needed information.

7. Be courteous and reasonable. Don't be rude, make threats, or berate. Don't pretend that you have vast political influence. Don't begin on a righteous note ("as a citizen and taxpayer . . . ").

8. Don't become a constant penpal. Quality at the right time, rather than quantity, is what counts.

9. Include your name and return address.

10. If you don't have time to write a letter, send a telegram, or make a phone call. Telegrams are particularly useful in the last few days before a vote. You can send a Western Union mailgram with overnight delivery to Congress at a cost of about $3.20 for 50 words or less ($3.75 from Alaska). A Public Opinion Message telegram of 20 words (not counting your name or the recipient's address) can be sent from anywhere in the country for about $3.50. All you have to do is telephone Western Union, which will bill your home phone. A member of Congress (or his or her staff) can also be reached by telephone through the Capitol switchboard: (202) 224-3121. As with letters, be polite, concise, and specific. Introduce yourself as a constituent, and ask to speak to the staff member who works on the issue you are concerned about.

11. Use positive reinforcement. After the vote write your representative a short note of thanks. A general rule here (as well as for life in general) is to give at least two compliments for every criticism.

12. If you are going to Washington, consider visiting your representative to lobby for your position. But go prepared or you risk destroying your credibility and effectiveness. It helps to call or write ahead to ask for an appointment, but you can probably get an appointment (at least with a staff member) by calling after you arrive in Washington. You can also try to make an appointment to talk with your representative when he or she is in the district.

13. Become a contributing member of Common Cause, the Sierra Club, the

League of Women Voters, the Environmental Defense Fund, or other groups (see the list of organizations in Appendix 1), which have full-time professional lobbyists working for you. These organizations exist only by individual support.

14. Remember that getting a bill passed is only the first step. You need to follow up by writing the president to be sure that the bill isn't vetoed or, once the bill has been signed that the money appropriated by Congress is released to be spent as required. Finally, write the federal agency (see addresses in Appendix 1) charged with carrying out the program, asking it to establish effective regulations or to be more active in enforcing the law. It is even more important to monitor and influence action at the state and local levels, where all federal and state laws are either ignored or enforced. As Thomas Jefferson once said, "The execution of laws is more important than the making of them."

Appendix 1

Periodicals, Environmental Organizations, and Government Agencies

Periodicals

The following journals will aid the intelligent citizen in keeping well informed and up to date on environmental problems. Those marked with an asterisk are recommended as basic reading. Subscription prices, which tend to change, are not given.

American Forests, American Forestry Association, 1319 18th St., N.W., Washington, DC 20036. Popular treatment, "seeks to promote an enlightened public appreciation of natural resources."

Audubon, National Audubon Society, 950 Third Ave., New York, NY 10022. Conservationist viewpoint; covers more than birdwatching. Good popularizer of environmental concerns; well-produced, sophisticated graphics.

BioScience, published monthly by the American Institute of Biological Sciences, 1401 Wilson Blvd., Arlington, VA 22209. Official publication of AIBS; gives major coverage to biological aspects of the environment, including population. Style ranges from semipopular to technical. Features and news sections attentive to legislative and governmental issues.

*Bulletin of the Atomic Scientists, 935 East 60th St., Chicago, IL 60637. In recent years has increased coverage of environmental issues, particularly in relation to nuclear power and nuclear testing and fallout.

Catalyst for Environmental/Energy, 274 Madison Ave., New York, NY 10016. High-level, popular treatment; substantial articles on all aspects of environment, including population control. Reviews books and films suited to environmental education.

Ceres, Food and Agricultural Organization of the United Nations (FAO), UNIPUB, Inc., 650 First Avenue, P.O. Box 433, New York, NY 10016. Contains articles on the population-food problem.

*The CoEvolution Quarterly, P.O. Box 428, Sausalito, CA 94965. Covers a wide range of environmental and self-sufficiency topics. Also publishes *The New Whole Earth Catalog* (1980).

*Conservation Foundation Letter, The Conservation Foundation, 1717 Massachusetts Avenue, N.W., Washington, DC 20036. Usually 12 pages long. Good summaries of key issues.

Conservation News, National Wildlife Foundation, 1412 16th St., N.W., Washington, DC 20036. Good coverage of wildlife issues.

Design and Environment, 355 Lexington Ave., New York, NY 10017. Useful for architects, engineers, and city planners.

Earth Shelter Digest, 479 Fort Road, St. Paul, MI 55102. Gives the latest information on earth-sheltered (underground) housing.

*The Ecologist, Ecosystems Ltd., 73 Molesworth St., Wadebridge, Cornway PL27 7DS, United Kingdom. Wide range of articles on environmental issues from an international viewpoint.

Ecology, Ecological Society of America, Dr. Ralph E. Good, Business Manager, Department of Biology, Rutgers University, Camden, NJ 08102. Good source of information on more technical ecology research.

Ecology Law Quarterly, University of California, Boalt Hall School of Law, Berkeley, CA 94720. Good treatment of latest developments in environmental law.

Ekistics, Athens Center of Ekistics, 24 Strat Syndesmou, Athens 136, Greece. Reviews the problems and science of human settlements. Reflects ideas of such planners as Constantine Doxiadis, the late R. Buckminster Fuller, and the late John McHale.

*Environment, Heldref Publications, 4000 Albemarle St., N.W., Washington, DC 20016. Seeks to put environmental information before the public. Excellent in-depth articles on key issues.

Environmental Abstracts, Environment Information Center, Inc., 48 West 38th St., New York, NY 10018. Compilation of environmental abstracts; basic bibliographic tool. Too expensive for individual subscription but should be available in your library.

*Environmental Action, Room 731, 1346 Connecticut Ave., N.W., Washington, DC 20036. Political orientation. Excellent coverage of environmental issues from legal, political, and social action viewpoints.

*The Environmental Professional, Editorial Office, Department of Geography, The University of Iowa, Iowa City, IA 52242. Excellent discussion of major environmental issues.

Environmental Science & Technology, American Chemical Society, 1155 16th St., N.W., Washington, DC 20036. Emphasis on water, air, and solid waste chemistry. Basic reference to keep up to date on technological developments.

EPA Journal, Environmental Protection Agency. Order from U.S. Government Printing Office, Washington, DC 20402. Broad coverage of environmental issues and updates on EPA activities.

Family Planning Perspectives, Planned Parenthood–World Population, Editorial Offices, 666 Fifth Ave., New York, NY 10019. Excellent coverage of population issues and latest information on birth control methods.

*The Futurist, World Future Society, P.O. Box 19285, Twentieth Street Station, Washington, DC 20036. Covers wide range of societal problems, including environmental, population, and food issues. A fascinating and readable journal.

Impact of Science on Society, UNESCO, 317 East 34th St., New York, NY 10016. Essays on the social consequences of science and technology.

Journal of the Air Pollution Control Association, 4400 5th Ave., Pittsburgh, PA 15213. Technical research articles.

Journal of the American Public Health Association, 1015 18th St., N.W., Washington, DC 20036. Some coverage of environmental health issues.

Journal of Environmental Education, Heldref Publications, 4000 Albemarle St., N.W., Suite 504, Washington, DC 20016. Good for teachers.

Journal of Environmental Health, National Environmental Health Association, 1600 Pennsylvania Ave., Denver, CO 80203. Good coverage of technical research.

Journal of the Water Pollution Control Federation, 2626 Pennsylvania Ave., N.W., Washington, DC 20037. Technical research articles.

Journal of Wildlife Management, Wildlife Society, Suite 611, 7101 Wisconsin Ave., N.W., Washington, DC 20014. Good coverage of basic issues and information.

Living Wilderness, The Wilderness Society, 1901 Pennsylvania Ave., N.W., Washington, DC 20006. Strong statement of "wild areas" viewpoint.

*Mother Earth News, P.O. Box 70, Hendersonville, NC 28739. Superb articles on organic farming, alternative energy systems, and alternative life-styles.

National Parks and Conservation Magazine, National Parks and Conservation Association, 1701 18th St., N.W., Washington, DC 20009. Good coverage of parks and wildlife issues.

National Wildlife, National Wildlife Federation, 1412 16th St., N.W., Washington, DC 20036. Good summaries of issues with wildlife emphasis. Action oriented, with a "Washington report."

Natural History, American Museum of Natural History, Central Park West at 79th St., New York, NY 10024. Popular; wide school and library circulation. Regularly concerned with environment.

Nature, 711 National Press Building, Washington, DC 20045. British equivalent to *Science,* enjoys outstanding reputation.

New Scientist, 128 Long Acre, London, WC 2, England. Excellent general science journal with extensive coverage of environmental issues.

*Not Man Apart, Friends of the Earth, 1245 Spear Street, San Francisco, CA 94105. Excellent capsule summaries of information and a few in-depth articles on national and international environmental issues.

Organic Gardening & Farming Magazine, Rodale Press, Inc., 33 E. Minor St., Emmaus, PA 18049. The best guide to organic gardening.

Pollution Abstracts, Data Courier, Inc., 620 S. 5th St., Louisville, KY 40202. Basic bibliographic tool. Too expensive for individual subscription but should be available in your library.

Population and Vital Statistics Report, UN Publications Sales Section, New York, NY 10017. Latest world figures.

*Population Bulletin, Population Reference Bureau, 2213 M St., N.W., Washington, DC 20037. Nontechnical articles on population issues. Highly recommended.

Population Bulletin, UN Publications Sales Section, New York, NY 10017. Statistical summaries. English and French editions.

Rain, 2270 N.W. Irving, Portland, OR 97210. Comprehensive journal of appropriate technology.

Resources, Resources for the Future, Inc., 1755 Massachusetts Ave., N.W., Washington, DC 20036. Free on request; summarizes information and research on natural resources.

*Science, American Association for the Advancement of Science, 1515 Massachusetts Ave., N.W., Washington, DC 20036. A basic resource. Probably the single best source for key environmental articles.

*Science News, Science Service, Inc., 1719 N St., N.W., Washington, DC 20036. Good popular summaries of scientific developments, including environmental topics.

*Scientific American, 415 Madison Ave., New York, NY 10017. Outstanding journal for the intelligent citizen who wants to keep up with science. Many general articles on environment and ecology.

*The Sierra Club Bulletin, 530 Bush St., San Francisco, CA 94108. Excellent coverage of a wide range of environmental problems and of citizen action. Beautiful photographs.

*Technology Review, Room E219-430, Massachusetts Institute of Technology, Cambridge, MA 02139. Not specialized or always technical, but addressed to a sophisticated audience. In recent years has devoted more than half its pages to environmentally related material; also strong on issues of science policy.

UNESCO Courier, UNESCO Publications Center, 317 East 34th St., New York, NY 10016. A magazine for the general reader; frequently attentive to environmental issues.

*Worldwatch Papers, Worldwatch Institute, 1776 Massachusetts Ave., N.W., Washington, DC 20036. A series of reports designed to serve as an early warning system on major environmental problems. Highly recommended.

Environmental Organizations

For a more detailed list of national, state, and local organizations, see *Conservation Directory,* published annually by the National Wildlife Foundation, 1412 16th St., N.W., Washington, DC 20036. For a list of world organizations, see Thaddeus C. Trzyna and Eugene V. Coan, eds., *World Directory of Environmental Organizations,* San Francisco: Sequoia Institute, 1976.

Air Pollution Control Association, P.O. Box 2861, Pittsburgh, PA 15230. Education and air pollution and its control. Publishes *Journal of the Air Pollution Control Association.*

Alliance for Environmental Education, Inc., 1619 Massachusetts Ave., N.W., Washington, DC 20036. Works to further environmental education activities at all levels.

American Forestry Association, 1319 18th St., N.W., Washington, DC 20036. Focuses on forest and soil conservation, although active in air and water pollution concerns. Doesn't lobby directly, but pushes indirectly for preserving and creating parklands. Publishes *American Forests.*

American Institute of Biological Sciences, Inc., 1401 Wilson Blvd., Arlington, VA 22209. Professional organization. Publishes *BioScience.*

American Society for Environmental Education, P.O. Box 800, Hanover, NH 03755. Education of teachers and the public concerning environmental issues. Publishes *Environmental Education Report.*

Association of American Geographers, 1710 16th St., N.W., Washington, DC 20009. Professional association.

Center for Action on Endangered Species, 175 West Main St., Ayer, MA 01432. Develops educational materials, including teaching units, on endangered wildlife.

Center for Environmental Education, Inc., 625 9th St., N.W., Washington, DC 20001. Dedicated to encouraging informed citizen involvement. Also sponsors the Whale Protection Fund.

Center for Renewable Resources, 1001 Connecticut Ave., N.W., Suite 510, Washington, DC 20036. Offers technical assistance to grassroots organizers, conducts policy research, and provides educational materials primarily on solar energy.

Center for Science in the Public Interest, 1755 S St., N.W., Washington, DC 20009. Group of public interest scientists concerned especially with energy, environmental, food, and nutrition issues. Publishes many informative reports.

Center for the Study of Responsive Law, P.O. Box 19367, Washington, DC 20036. A research organization working in the public interest; areas investigated include problems of the environment. Publishes research reports from the Ralph Nader study groups.

Citizens' Clearinghouse for Hazardous Waste, P.O. Box 7097, Arlington, VA 22207. Research, information, and organizing on this issue.

Citizens' Energy Project, 1110 6th St., N.W., Suite 300, Washington, DC 20001. Emphasis on research and education, alternative energy, nuclear power, and appropriate technology.

Clean Water Action Project, 1341 G St., N.W., Suite 204, Washington, DC 20005. National citizen action organization lobbying for strict water pollution control and safe drinking water.

Common Cause, 2030 M St., N.W., Washington, DC 20036. Citizens' lobby with over 100,000 members who work hard on a broad range of political issues including nuclear freeze, arms control, and campaign financing reform.

Congress Watch, 215 Pennsylvania Ave., S.E., Washington, DC 20003. Lobbying group concerned with corporate responsibility, nuclear energy, and campaign financing.

Conservation Foundation, 1717 Massachusetts Ave., N.W., Washington, DC 20036. Active in conservation, analysis of the ecological impact of foreign aid, and conservation education in the schools. Publishes *Conservation Foundation Letter.*

Cousteau Society, 777 Third Avenue, New York, NY 10017. Research and education with emphasis on preservation of the world's oceans.

Critical Mass Energy Project, P.O. Box 1538, Washington, DC 20003. Sponsors national conferences on issues such as nuclear energy, alternative energy sources, and legislative and citizen activities; publishes monthly newspaper promoting safe and efficient energy.

Defenders of Wildlife, 1244 19th St., N.W., Washington, DC 20036. Tries to preserve all forms of wildlife. Research, education, lobbying.

Ducks Unlimited, P.O. Box 66300, Chicago, IL 60666. Has acquired or protected over 2 million acres of vital breeding habitats for migrating waterfowl.

Ecological Society of America, Dr. Paul G. Risser, Secretary, Department of Botany and Microbiology, University of Oklahoma, Norman, OK 73069. Professional society.

Energy Conservation Coalition, 1725 Eye St., N.W., Suite 610, Washington, DC 20036. Education and lobbying.

Environmental Action Foundation, Inc., 724 DuPont Circle Bldg., Washington, DC 20036. Research and education on a broad range of environmental issues.

Environmental Action, Inc., 1346 Connecticut Ave., N.W., Suite 731, Washington, DC 20036. Nonprofit organization that evolved from Earth Day 1970. Lobbies for effective legislation for environmental reform. Publishes *Environmental Action.*

Environmental Defense Fund, Inc., 444 Park Ave. South, New York, NY 10016. A public benefit organization composed of scientists, lawyers, and lay persons; works to link law and science in defense of the environment before courts and regulatory agencies. Other offices at 1525 18th St., N.W., Washington, DC 20036; 2606 Dwight Way, Berkeley, CA 97404.

Environmental Fund, Inc., 1302 18th St., N.W., Washington, DC 20036. Works to educate the public about the need for population control.

Environmental Law Institute, 1346 Connecticut Ave., N.W., Suite 600, Washington, DC 20036. Conducts a wide program of research and education in environmental law.

Environmental Policy Center, 317 Pennsylvania Ave., S.E., Washington, DC 20003. Research, education, and lobbying on a range of environmental issues.

Friends of the Earth, Inc., 1045 Sansome St., San Francisco, CA 94111. Education, lobbying, and litigation on a variety of environmental issues. Its political arm, the League of Conservation Voters, raises funds for congressional candidates having sound environmental records.

Fund for Animals, Inc., 1765 P St., N.W., Washington, DC 20036; 140 W. 57th St., New York, NY 10019. Education, lobbying, and litigation on animal rights, endangered species, and wildlife conservation.

Greenpeace, USA, Inc., 2007 R St., N.W., Washington, DC 20009. Lobbying, organizing, and direct action with emphasis on whales, seals, nuclear energy, and toxic wastes.

INFORM, 381 Park Ave., New York, NY 10016. Research and education with emphasis on energy, environment, and occupational safety and health.

Institute for Local Self-Reliance, 1717 18th St., N.W., Washington, DC 20009. Research and education; promotion of appropriate technology for communities.

International Union for the Conservation of Nature and Natural Resources (IUCN), Ave. du Mont Blanc, CH-1196 Gland, Switzerland (022.64 71 81). Promotes scientifically based action for the conservation of wildlife.

Izaak Walton League of America, 1800 North Kent St., Suite 806, Arlington, VA 22209. Research and education on wildlife conservation, renewable natural resources, and water quality.

John Muir Institute for Environmental Studies, 743 Wilson St., Napa, CA 94558. Research and education on a wide range of environmental issues.

Keep America Beautiful, 99 Park Ave., New York, NY 10016. Education to combat litter as a necessary first step toward solving broader environmental problems and a program to increase knowledge of solid waste disposal techniques. Organization provides assistance, materials, and advice for grass-roots efforts by some 7,000 community groups and 32 statewide affiliates.

League of Conservation Voters, 317 Pennsylvania Ave., S.E., Washington, DC 20003. Political action and national campaign committee working to promote the election of legislators pledging to seek a healthy environment. Publicizes roll call votes on environmental issues. Political arm of Friends of the Earth.

League of Women Voters of the United States, 1730 M St., N.W., Washington, DC 20036. Lobbies for a wide range of environmental issues; local and state leagues work for political responsibility through an informed and active citizenry. Played a central role in bringing water pollution to the public's attention. Research and education by the League of Women Voters Education Fund (same address).

National Audubon Society, 645 Pennsylvania Ave., S.E., Washington, DC 20003; 950 3rd Ave., New York, NY 10022. Research and lobbying on a wide range of environmental issues. Operates 40 wildlife sanctuaries across the country and provides a wide variety of ecology education services. Publishes *Audubon* and *Audubon Field Notes*.

National Parks and Conservation Association, 1701 18th Street, N.W., Washington, DC 20009. Research and education. Urges acquisition and protection of public parklands. Now active in general environmental issues, such as resource management, pesticides, and pollution. Publishes *National Parks and Conservation Magazine*.

National Science Teachers' Association, 1742 Connecticut Ave., N.W., Washington, DC 20009. Educational affiliate of the American Association for the Advancement of Science. Dedicated to improving the teaching of science (including environmental issues) from preschool through college.

National Wildlife Federation, 1412 16th St., N.W., Washington, DC 20036. Research and education. Encourages citizen and governmental action for conservation. Publishes *National Wildlife* and a comprehensive annual conservation directory.

Natural Resources Defense Council, 122 East 42nd St., New York, NY 10017; 1725 Eye St., N.W., Suite 600, Washington, DC 20006. Research, organizing, and litigation on a wide range of environmental issues.

The Nature Conservancy, 1800, N. Kent St., Suite 800, Arlington, VA 22209. Research and preservation of natural areas. Often acquires endangered property and holds it for later resale to public agencies.

New Alchemy Institute, 237 Hatchville Rd., East Falmouth, MA 02536. Research and education with emphasis on self-sufficient agriculture, aquaculture, passive solar energy, wind power, and energy conservation.

Physicians for Social Responsibility, 639 Massachusetts Ave., Cambridge, MA 02139. Research and education on the health effects of nuclear weapons and nuclear war.

Planet/Drum Foundation, P.O. Box 31251, San Francisco, CA 94131. Research and education with emphasis on wise use of land and watersheds.

Population Reference Bureau, 2213 M Street, N.W., Washington, DC 20037. Clearinghouse for data concerning the effects of the worldwide population growth. Publishes *Population Bulletin*.

The Public Citizen, 1346 Connecticut Ave., N.W., Washington, DC 20036. Ralph Nader's political action and lobbying organization.

Public Interest Research Group, P.O. Box 19312, Washington, DC 20036. Organizes research and education in environmental issues.

RAIN, 2270 N.W. Irving, Portland, OR 97210. Research and education on appropriate technology and community and regional self-reliance.

Resources for the Future, 1775 Massachusetts Ave., N.W., Washington, DC 20036. Research and education in the development, conservation, and use of natural resources and on the quality of the environment. Publishes *Resources*.

Scientists' Institute for Public Information, 355 Lexington Ave., New York, NY 10017; 1256 National Press Building, Washington, DC 20045. Utilizes scientists of all disciplines in public information programs dealing with many social issues. Serves as national coordinating body for local scientific information committees.

Sierra Club, 530 Bush St., San Francisco, CA 94108; 330 Pennsylvania Avenue, S.E., Washington, DC 20003. Lobbying and education on a wide range of environmental issues. Provides films, manuals, exhibits, and speakers; publishes books and a monthly bulletin.

Smithsonian Institution, 1000 Jefferson Drive, S.W., Washington, DC 20560. Promotes environmental education through a wide variety of programs.

Soil Conservation Society of America, 7515 N.E. Ankeny Rd., Ankeny, IA 50021. Professional society dedicated to soil and water conservation.

Solar Lobby, 1001 Connecticut Ave., N.W., Suite 510, Washington, DC 20036. Lobbying for solar energy and energy conservation.

Student Conservation Association, Inc., Box 550, Charlestown, NH 03603. Promotes and coordinates work and learning opportunities during summer vacations for students at the high school, college, and graduate levels.

Union of Concerned Scientists, 1346 Connecticut Ave., N.W., Suite 1101, Washington, DC 20036; 1384 Massachusetts Ave., N.W., Cambridge, MA 02238. Lobbying, research, education, and litigation with emphasis on nuclear power safety and arms control.

Water Pollution Control Federation, 2626 Pennsylvania Ave., N.W., Washington, DC 20037. Professional society devoted to research and dissemination of technical information.

The Wilderness Society, 1901 Pennsylvania Ave., N.W., Washington, DC 20006. Research, education, and lobbying with emphasis on wilderness, parks, and public lands. Publishes *Living Wilderness*.

Wildlife Society, Suite 611, 7101 Wisconsin Ave., N.W., Washington, DC 20014. Major concern is wildlife preservation, but its base is broadening.

World Environment Center, Inc., 605 Third Ave., New York, NY 10158. Information and education with emphasis on international environment and development issues.

World Wildlife Fund, 1601 Connecticut Ave., N.W., Washington, DC 20009. Research and education on endangered species and acquisition of wildlife habitats.

Worldwatch Institute, 1776 Massachusetts Ave., N.W., Suite 701, Washington, DC 20036. Research, early warning, and education on major environmental problems. Publishes several very informative and well-researched *Worldwatch Papers* each year on selected environmental issues.

Zero Population Growth, 1346 Connecticut Ave., N.W., Washington, DC 20036. Education and lobbying on population and immigration issues.

Addresses of Federal Agencies

Bureau of Land Management
Interior Building, Room 5660
Washington, DC 20240

Bureau of Mines
2401 E St., N.W.
Washington, DC 20241

Bureau of Outdoor Recreation
Interior Building, Room 4410
Washington, DC 20240

Bureau of Reclamation
Interior Building, Room 7654
Washington, DC 20240

Council on Environmental Quality
722 Jackson Place, N.W.
Washington, DC 20006

Department of Agriculture
14th St. and Jefferson Dr., S.W.
Washington, DC 20250

Department of Commerce
14th St. between Constitution Ave. and E St., N.W.
Washington, DC 20230

Department of Energy
1001 Independence Ave., S.W.
Washington, DC 20545

Department of Health and Human Services
200 Independence Ave., S.W.
Washington, DC 20585

Department of Housing and Urban Development
451 7th St., S.W.
Washington, DC 20410

Department of the Interior
18th and C Sts., N.W.
Washington, DC 20240

Department of Transportation
400 7th St., S.W.
Washington, DC 20590

Environmental Protection Agency
401 M St., S.W.
Washington, DC 20460

Federal Energy Regulatory Commission
825 N. Capitol St., N.E.
Washington, DC 20426

Fish and Wildlife Service
Department of the Interior
18th & C Sts., N.W.
Washington, DC 20240

Food and Drug Administration
Department of Health and Human Services
5600 Fishers Lane
Rockville, MD 20852

Forest Service
P.O. Box 2417
Washington, DC 20013

Geological Survey
Reston, VA 22092

Government Printing Office
Washington, DC 20402

National Academy of Sciences
2101 Constitution Ave., N.W.
Washington, DC 20418

National Center for Appropriate Technology
3040 Continental Dr.
Butte, MT 59701

National Oceanic and Atmospheric Administration
Rockville, MD 20852

National Park Service
Department of the Interior
Washington, DC 20240

National Science Foundation
Washington, DC 20550

National Solar Heating and Cooling Information Center*
P.O. Box 1607
Rockville, MD 20850

National Technical Information Service (NTIS)†
Department of Commerce
5285 Port Royal Rd.
Springfield, VA 22161

Nuclear Regulatory Commission
1717 H St., N.W.
Washington, DC 20555

Occupational Safety and Health Administration
Department of Labor
200 Constitution Ave., N.W.
Washington, DC 20210

Office of Coastal Zone Management
3300 Whitehaven St., N.W.
Washington, DC 20235

Soil Conservation Service
P.O. Box 2890
Washington, DC 20013

Solar Energy Research Institute (SERI)
6536 Cole Blvd.
Golden, CO 80401

Water Resources Council
2120 L St., N.W.
Washington, DC 20423

---

*Call toll free for information on solar energy: (800) 523-2929 anywhere in the United States except Pennsylvania; call (800) 462-4983 in Pennsylvania.

---

†Sells publications of government-sponsored research.

Appendix 2

Unit Conversions

Metric and English Systems of Units

The United States is the only major nation in the world not using an updated version of the *metric system of units*, first developed in France in 1799, for measurements of basic quantities such as length, mass, time, area, volume, temperature, and energy. Instead, most of our measurements are expressed in the *English system of units*. A gradual shift from the English to the metric system is supposed to be taking place in the United States, but it may be delayed indefinitely. The metric system, however, is used by all American scientists and in scientific textbooks.

Conversion factors are used to change measurements to larger or smaller units in the same system of units or to express units from one system in the form of units of another system. To convert from one metric unit to another, we merely multiply or divide by the appropriate multiple of 10. For example, 1 kilogram (kg) = 1,000 grams (g) and 1 centimeter (cm) = 1/100 meter (m) or 0.01 meter (m). The unit abbreviations are shown in parentheses. Thus, if you wanted to know how many kilograms are in 948 grams, you would multiply 948 g by the conversion factor relating kilograms and grams (1 kg = 1,000 g), expressed as the ratio 1 kg/1,000 g:

$$948 \, g \times \frac{1 \, kg}{1,000 \, g} = 0.948 \, kg$$

Any unit conversion factor can be also be written in its inverse form: for example, 1,000 g/1 kg. A conversion factor must be used in the form that cancels out the initial unit (in this case grams) to give the desired units (kilograms). For example, you would get an incorrect answer both numerically and in terms of units in working out the foregoing unit conversion if you multiplied 948 grams by the inverted form of the·conversion factor:

$$948 \, g \times \frac{1,000 \, g}{1 \, kg} = 948,000 \, g^2/kg \quad \textbf{Incorrect}$$

By contrast, the units in the *English system* of measurements, still widely used the United States, are not systematically related. Therefore, the whole system must be memorized, or separate units looked up, before one can be converted to another. For example, 1 pound (lb) = 16 ounces (oz); 1 foot (ft) = 12 inches (in.); and 1 mile (mi) = 5,280 feet (ft). The number of ounces in 25 pounds is found by multiplying 25 lb by the conversion factor relating pounds and ounces (1 lb = 16 oz) so that the *initial unit* (pounds) is canceled out to give the *desired unit* (ounces):

$$25 \, lb \times \frac{16 \, oz}{1 \, lb} = \quad \textbf{400 oz}$$

In this book, essentially all units are given in metric form, usually followed by their equivalent in the English system in parentheses. The conversion factors listed in the remainder of this section can be used to make conversions between the metric and English systems as well as within these systems. For example, to find the number of miles represented by 85 kilometers, you would multiply 85 km by the conversion factor relating kilometers in the metric system to miles in the English system (1 km = 0.621 mi), so that the *initial unit* (kilometers) is canceled out to give the *desired unit* (miles):

$$85 \, km \times \frac{0.621 \, mi}{1 \, km} = \quad \textbf{53 mi}$$

Common Unit Equivalents

Length

Metric
1 kilometer (km) = 1,000 meters (m)
1 meter (m) = 100 centimeters (m)
1 meter (m) = 1,000 millimeters (mm)
1 centimeter (cm) = 0.01 meter (m)
1 millimeter (mm) = 0.001 meter (m)

English
1 foot (ft) = 12 inches (in.)
1 yard (yd) = 3 feet (ft)
1 mile (mi) = 5,280 feet (ft)

Metric-English
1 kilometer (km) = 0.621 mile (mi)
1 meter (m) = 39.4 inches (in.)
1 inch (in.) = 2.54 centimeters (cm)
1 foot (ft) = 0.305 meter (m)
1 yard (yd) = 0.914 meter (m)

Area

Metric
1 square kilometer (km^2) = 1,000,000 square meters (m^2)
1 square meter (m^2) = 1,000,000 square millimeters (mm^2)
1 hectare (ha) = 10,000 square meters (m^2)
1 hectare (ha) = 0.01 square kilometer (km^2)

English
1 square foot (ft^2) = 144 square inches (in.^{2})
1 square yard (yd^2) = 9 square feet (ft^2)
1 square mile (mi^2) = 27,880,000 square feet (ft^2)
1 acre (ac) = 43,560 square feet (ft^2)

Metric-English
1 hectare (ha) = 2.471 acres (ac)
1 square kilometer (km^2) = 0.386 square mile (mi^2)
1 square meter (m^2) = 1.196 square yards (yd^2)
1 square meter (m^2) = 10.76 square feet (ft^2)
1 square centimeter (cm^2) = 0.155 square inch (in.^{2})

Volume

Metric

1 cubic kilometer (km^3) = 1,000,000 cubic meters (m^3)
1 cubic meter (m^3) = 1,000,000 cubic centimeters (cm^3)
1 liter (L) = 1,000 milliliters (mL) = 1,000 cubic centimeters (cm^3)
1 milliliter (mL) = 0.001 liter (L)
1 milliliter (mL) = 1 cubic centimeter (cm^3)

English

1 gallon (gal) = 4 quarts (qt)
1 quart (qt) = 2 pints (pt)

Metric-English

1 liter (L) = 0.265 gallon (gal)
1 liter (L) = 1.06 quarts (qt)
1 liter (L) = 0.0353 cubic foot (ft^3)
1 cubic meter (m^3) = 35.3 cubic feet (ft^3)
1 cubic meter (m^3) = 0.765 cubic yards (yd^3)
1 cubic kilometer (km^3) = 0.24 cubic mile (mi^3)
1 barrel (bbl) = 159 liters (L)
1 barrel (bbl) = 42 U.S. gallons (gal)

Mass

Metric

1 kilogram (kg) = 1,000 grams (g)
1 gram (g) = 1,000 milligrams (mg)
1 gram (g) = 1,000,000 micrograms (μg)
1 milligram (mg) = 0.001 gram (g)
1 microgram (μg) = 0.000001 gram (g)
1 metric ton (mt) = 1,000 kilograms (kg)

English

1 ton (t) = 2,000 pounds (lb)
1 pound (lb) = 16 ounces (oz)

Metric-English

1 metric ton = 2,200 pounds (lb)
1 kilogram (kg) = 2.20 pounds (lb)
1 pound (lb) = 454 grams (g)
1 gram (g) = 0.035 ounce (oz)

Energy and Power

Metric

1 kilojoule (kJ) = 1,000 joules (J)
1 kilocalorie (kcal) = 1,000 calories (cal)
1 calorie (cal) = 4.184 joules (J)

Metric-English

1 kilojoule (kJ) = 0.949 British thermal unit (Btu)
1 kilojoule (kJ) = 0.000278 kilowatt-hour (kW-h)
1 kilocalorie (kcal) = 3.97 British thermal units (Btu)
1 kilocalorie (kcal) = 0.00116 kilowatt-hour (kW-h)
1 kilowatt-hour (kW-h) = 860 kilocalories (kcal)
1 kilowatt-hour (kW-h) = 3,400 British thermal units (Btu)
1 quad (Q) = 1,050,000,000,000,000 kilojoules (kJ)
1 quad (Q) = 2,930,000,000,000 kilowatt-hours (kW-h)

Approximate crude oil equivalent

1 barrel (bbl) crude oil = 6,000,000 kilojoules (kJ)
1 barrel (bbl) crude oil = 2,000,000 kilocalories (kcal)
1 barrel (bbl) crude oil = 6,000,000 British thermal units (Btu)
1 barrel (bbl) crude oil = 2,000 kilowatt-hours (kW-h)

Approximate natural gas equivalent

1 cubic foot (ft^3) natural gas = 1,000 kilojoules (kJ)
1 cubic foot (ft^3) natural gas = 260 kilocalories (kcal)
1 cubic foot (ft^3) natural gas = 1,000 British thermal units (Btu)
1 cubic foot (ft^3) natural gas = 0.3 kilowatt-hour (kW-h)

Approximate hard coal equivalent

1 ton (t) coal = 20,000,000 kilojoules (kJ)
1 ton (t) coal = 6,000,000 kilocalories (kcal)
1 ton (t) coal = 20,000,000 British thermal units (Btu)
1 ton (t) coal = 6,000 kilowatt-hours (kW-h)

Temperature Conversions

Fahrenheit (°F) to Celsuis (°C):

$$°C = \frac{(°F - 32.0)}{1.80}$$

Celsius (°C) to Fahrenheit (°F):

$$°F = (°C \times 1.80) + 32.0$$

Readings

Chapter 1 Population, Resources, and Pollution: An Overview

Brown, Harrison. 1978. *The Human Future Revisited: The World Predicament and Possible Solutions*. New York: W. W. Norton. Excellent analysis of the interrelated problems of population, resources, pollution, affluence, and weaponry.

Brown, Lester R. 1981. *Building a Sustainable Society*. New York: W. W. Norton. Brilliant analysis of the world's environmental problems and their interrelationships by one of our best multidisciplinary thinkers. Highly recommended.

Brown, Lester R., et al. 1984. *State of the World 1984*. New York: W. W. Norton. Superb overview by the Worldwatch Society.

Callahan, Daniel, ed., 1971. *The American Population Debate*. Garden City, N.Y.: Doubleday. Superb collection of articles on whether the United States is overpopulated.

Commoner, Barry. 1971. *The Closing Circle: Nature, Man and Technology*. New York: Alfred A. Knopf. Well-written presentation of Commoner's view that the misuse of technology is the cause of most pollution. See the critique of this view by Holdren and Ehrlich (1974).

Conservation Foundation. 1982. *State of the Environment 1982*. Washington, D.C.: The Conservation Foundation. Excellent summary. Documents attempts of Reagan administration to undo much of the progress made on environmental problems during the 1970s.

Council on Environmental Quality. 1970–1984. *Annual Reports*. Washington, D.C.: Government Printing Office. Annual summaries of environmental problems and progress. Useful sources of information.

Council of Environmental Quality. 1981. *Environmental Trends*. Excellent presentation of graphs and tables documenting trends in environmental problems in the United States and the world.

Council on Environmental Quality and U.S. Department of State. 1980. *The Global 2000 Report to the President*, Vols. 1–3. Washington, D.C.: Government Printing Office. Outstanding summary of global population, resource, and pollution problems with projections to the year 2000.

Council on Environmental Quality and U.S. Department of State. 1981. *Global Future: Time To Act*. Washington, D.C.: Government Printing Office. Recommendations for action based on *The Global 2000 Report to the President*.

Eckholm, Erik P. 1982. *Down to Earth: Environment and Human Needs*. New York: W. W. Norton. Superb summary of global environmental problems and progress being made on these problems by an outstanding multidisciplinary thinker.

Edberg, Rolf. 1969. *On the Shred of a Cloud*. University: University of Alabama Press. Eloquent and compassionate statement of our problems. An environmental classic.

Gardner, John W. 1970. *The Recovery of Confidence*. New York: W. W. Norton. Moving analysis of hope and how to bring about political change by an important thinker and leader.

Hayes, Denis. 1978. *Repairs, Reuse, Recycling: First Steps Toward a Sustainable Society*. Washington, D.C.: Worldwatch Institute. Very useful summary of the potential for conserving natural resources.

Holdren, John P., and Paul R. Ehrlich. 1974. "Human Population and the Global Environment." *American Scientist*, vol. 62, 282–292. Excellent analysis of the relationships between population size, resource use, and harmful technology and an answer to Commoner's (1971) view that technology is the key factor in producing pollution.

International Institute for Environment and Development. 1982. *The State of India's Environment 1982*. Washington, D.C.: International Institute for Environment and Development. Useful overview of environmental degradation in India.

Kahn, Herman. 1982. *The Coming Boom: Economic, Political, and Social*. New York: Simon & Schuster. Predictions of a rosy future by thinktank futurist who was one of the world's leading technological optimists. Kahn, who died in 1983, considered population, resource, and pollution problems as solved or on the way to being solved.

Meadows, Donella H., et al. 1972. *The Limits to Growth*. New York: Universe Books. Controversial and nontechnical summary of a computer model of the interrelationships between population, food, resource use, economic growth, and pollution (see Enrichment Study 2 for more details).

Murphy, Elaine M. 1983. *The Environment to Come: A Global Summary*. Washington, D.C.: Population Reference Bureau. Superb, concise summary of global population and resource problems. Highly recommended.

Pryde, Philip R. 1983. "The Decade of the Environment in the U.S.S.R.," *Science*, vol. 220, 274–279. Excellent discussion of environmental degradation in the Soviet Union.

Schumacher, E. F. 1973. *Small Is Beautiful: Economics As If People Mattered*. New York: Harper & Row. Eloquent presentation of the need for appropriate technology. Highly recommended.

Simon, Julian L. 1981. *The Ultimate Resource*. Princeton, N.J.: Princeton University Press. Readable presentation of the cornucopian position that economic growth and technology will solve the world's population, resource, and pollution problems. The author makes some good points but bases most of his arguments on the false mathematical idea that all resource supplies are infinite because anything that is infinitely divisible is infinite in quantity—equivalent to saying that since you can divide the money in your bank account into an infinite number of fractions of a cent, you have an infinite amount of money.

Smith, Vaclav. 1984. *The Bad Earth*. New York: Sharpe, Armonk. Useful description of environmental degradation and ecological mismanagement in China.

Tucker, William. 1982. *Progress and Privilege: America in the Age of Environmentalism*.

Garden City, N.Y.: Anchor Press/Double-day. Attacks U.S. environmentalists as being upper-middle-class liberals whose primary concern about the environment is to protect their own wealth and power. This book has been used as intellectual support for the environmental policies of the Reagan administration. He makes some useful points but greatly oversimplifies the diversity of the citizens who support and are active in the environmental movement.

Wattenberg, Ben J. 1984. *The Good News Is the Bad News Is Wrong.* New York: Simon & Schuster. Useful attack on gloom-and-doom pessimism showing how, by most indicators, the average quality of life in the United States has improved since the 1950s.

Chapter 2 Some Matter and Energy Laws

Angrist, S. W., and L. G. Hepler. 1967. *Order and Chaos.* New York: Basic Books. Excellent nontechnical introduction to thermodynamics, emphasizing its fascinating historical development.

Bent, Henry A. 1971. "Haste Makes Waste: Pollution and Entropy." *Chemistry,* vol. 44, 6–15. Excellent and very readable account of the relation between entropy (disorder) and the environmental crisis.

Boulding, Kenneth E. 1964. *The Meaning of the 20th Century.* New York: Harper & Row. Penetrating discussion of the planetary situation by one of our foremost thinkers. See especially Chapters 4, 6, and 7 on the war, population, and entropy traps.

Christensen, John W. 1981. *Energy, Resources, and Environment.* Dubuque, Iowa: Kendall/Hunt. Excellent overview for use at the high school level.

Cook, Earl. 1976. *Man, Energy, Society.* San Francisco: W. H. Freeman. Superb discussion of energy and energy options.

Fowler, John M. 1983. *Energy and the Environment.* 2nd ed. New York: McGraw-Hill. Excellent overview.

Miller, G. Tyler, Jr. 1971. *Energetics, Kinetics and Life: An Ecological Approach.* Belmont, Calif.: Wadsworth. Amplifies and explains the material in Chapter 2 at a slightly higher level.

Odum, Howard T., and Elisabeth C. Odum. 1980. *Energy Basis for Man and Nature.* New York: McGraw-Hill. Outstanding discussion of energy principles and energy options at a somewhat higher level.

Rifkin, Jeremy. 1980. *Entropy: A New World View.* New York: Viking Press. Superb nontechnical description of the need to develop a sustainable earth society based on the second law of thermodynamics.

Steinhart, Carol E., and John S. Steinhart. 1974. *Energy: Source, Use, and Role in Human Affairs.* North Scituate, Mass.: Duxbury Press. Excellent treatment of energy principles and options.

Chapter 3 Ecosystem Structure: What Is an Ecosystem?

Billings, W. D. 1970. *Plants, Man, and the Ecosystem.* 2nd ed. Belmont, Calif.: Wadsworth. See especially the discussion of biomes in Chapter 7.

Clapham, W. B., Jr. 1973. *Natural Ecosystems.* New York: Macmillan. Introduction to ecology at a slightly higher level.

Colinvaux, Paul A. 1973. *Introduction to Ecology.* New York: John Wiley. Excellent basic text using the evolutionary approach.

Colinvaux, Paul A. 1978. *Why Big Fierce Animals Are Rare.* Princeton, N.J.: Princeton University Press. Fascinating and very readable description of major ecological principles. Highly recommended.

Darnell, R. M. 1973. *Ecology and Man.* Dubuque, Iowa: Wm. C. Brown. Excellent simple introduction to ecological principles.

Ehrlich, Paul R., Anne H. Ehrlich, and John P. Holdren. 1977. *Ecoscience: Population, Resources and Environment.* San Francisco: W. H. Freeman. Superb, more detailed text at a higher level.

Emmel, Thomas C. 1973. *An Introduction to Ecology and Population Biology.* New York: W. W. Norton. Another superb introduction.

Gedzelman, Stanley L. 1980. *The Science and Wonders of the Weather.* New York: John Wiley. Superb introduction to climate and weather.

Kormondy, Edward J. 1984. *Concepts of Ecology.* 3rd ed. Englewood Cliffs, N.J.: Prentice-Hall. First-rate introduction at a slightly higher level.

Krebs, Charles J. 1978. *Ecology.* 2nd ed. New York: Harper & Row. Splendid basic text using the evolutionary approach to ecology.

Lehr, Paul E., et al. 1975. *Weather.* New York: Golden Press. Excellent introduction to weather and climate.

Odum, Eugene P. 1983. *Basic Ecology.* Philadelphia: W. B. Saunders. Outstanding textbook by a prominent ecologist.

Richardson, Jonathan L. 1977. *Dimensions of Ecology.* Baltimore: Williams & Wilkins. Excellent brief introductory text.

Rickleffs, Robert E. 1976. *The Economy of Nature.* Portland, Ore.: Chiron Press. Beautifully written introduction to ecology at a slightly higher level.

Smith, Robert L. 1980. *The Ecology of Man: An Ecosystem Approach.* 3rd ed. New York: Harper & Row. Excellent collection of ecological articles with extremely useful introductory commentaries.

Smith, Robert L. 1980. *Ecology and Field Biology.* 3rd ed. New York: Harper & Row. Outstanding basic text in ecology using the ecosystem approach.

Southwick, Charles H. 1976. *Ecology and the Quality of the Environment.* 2nd ed. New York: Van Nostrand Reinhold. Very readable introduction to human ecology.

Sutton, David B., and N. Paul Harmon. 1973. *Ecology: Selected Concepts.* New York: John Wiley. Superb self-study guide for the material in Chapters 3, 4, and 5.

Watt, Kenneth, E. F. 1973. *Principles of Environmental Science.* New York: McGraw-Hill. Excellent discussion of ecological principles at a higher level.

Whittaker, R. H. 1975. *Communities and Ecosystems.* 2nd ed. New York: Macmillan. One of the best discussions of biomes.

Chapter 4 Ecosystem Function: How Do Ecosystems Work?

See the Readings for Chapter 3.

Chapter 5 Changes in Ecosystems: What Can Happen to Ecosystems?

See the Readings for Chapter 3 also.

Ehrenfeld, D. W. 1970. *Biological Conservation.* 2nd ed. New York: John Wiley. Outstanding introduction to conservation of wildlife.

Ehrlich, Paul R. 1980. "Variety Is the Key to Life." *Technology Review,* March-April, pp. 599–668. Important article showing the need for preserving diversity.

Epstein, Samuel S., et al. 1982. *Hazardous Waste in America.* San Francisco: Sierra Club Books. Detailed study of hazardous waste problems, with excellent description of the Love Canal episode.

Farvar, M. Taghi, and John P. Milton, eds. 1972. *The Careless Technology: Ecology and International Development.* Garden City, N.Y.: Natural History Press. Describes and documents numerous cases of ecological backlash.

Gibbs, Lois. 1982. *The Love Canal: My Story*. Albany: State University of New York Press. Very useful description by a former Love Canal area resident who lead the fight by homeowners to have the area condemned as unsafe.

Levine, Adeline G. 1982. *Love Canal: Science, Politics, and People*. Lexington, Mass.: Lexington (Heath). Another useful study by a former area resident.

Odum, Eugene P. 1969. "The Strategy of Ecosystem Development." *Science*, vol. 164, 262–270. Excellent summary of succession.

Stumm, Werner, and Elisabeth Stumm-Zollinger. 1972. "Concepts of Pollution and Its Control." *Technology Review*, October-November, pp. 19–26. Very good introduction to diversity, stability, succession, and the ecological effects of pollution.

Whittaker, Robert H., and George M. Woodwell. 1972. "Evolution of Natural Communities." In John A. Wiens, ed., *Ecosystem Structure and Function*. Corvallis: Oregon State University Press. Good summary of diversity and succession.

Woodwell, G. M. 1970. "Effects of Pollution on the Structure and Physiology of Ecosystems." *Science*, vol. 168, 429–433. Excellent analysis.

Chapter 6 Human Population Dynamics

Bouvier, Leon F. 1976. "On Population Growth." *Intercom*, July, pp. 8–9. Excellent discussion of the misuse of population data.

Bouvier, Leon F. 1980. "American's Baby Boom Generation: The Fateful Bulge." *Population Bulletin*, April, pp. 1–35. Superb discussion of the implications of the baby boom for American society.

Bouvier, Leon F. 1984. "Planet Earth 1984–2034: A Demographic Vision," *Population Bulletin*, vol. 39, no. 1, 1–39. Outstanding overview of future population trends and problems.

Commission on Population Growth and the American Future. 1972. *Population and the American Future*. Washington, D.C.: Government Printing Office. Also available in paperback (Signet, New American Library). Important historical document showing the need for controlling U.S. population growth.

Davis, Kingsley, 1973. "Zero Population Growth: The Goal and Means." *Daedalus*, vol. 102, no. 2, 15–30. Superb analysis of ZPG.

Ehrlich, Paul R., et al. 1977. *Ecoscience: Population, Resources, and Environment*. 3rd ed. San Francisco: W. H. Freeman. Excellent and very comprehensive text on human ecology at a somewhat higher level.

Haupt, Arthur, and Thomas T. Kane. 1978. *The Population Handbook*. Washington, D.C.: Population Reference Bureau. Superb introduction to demographic terms and concepts.

Mauldin, W. Parker. 1980. "Population Trends and Prospects." *Science*, vol. 209, 148–157. Outstanding overview.

Murphy, Elaine M. 1981. "World Population: Toward the Next Century." PRB Teaching Module. Washington: D.C.: Population Reference Bureau. Excellent overview.

Newland, Kathleen. 1981. *Infant Mortality and the Health of Societies*. Washington, D.C.: Worldwatch Institute. Useful overview.

Population Reference Bureau. Annual. *World Population Data Sheet*. Washington, D.C.: Population Reference Bureau. This concise annual summary is the source for most of the population data used in this book.

Population Reference Bureau. 1982. "U.S. Population: Where We Are; Where We're Going." *Population Bulletin*, vol. 37, no. 2, 1–44. Excellent summary.

Rosa, Jean-Jacques, ed. 1982. *The World Crisis in Social Security*. San Francisco: Institute for Contemporary Studies. Excellent overview of this serious problem with proposed solutions.

Salk, Jonas, and Jonathan Salk. 1981. *World Population and Human Values*. New York: Harper & Row. Outstanding presentation of population dynamics.

Trewartha, Glenn T. 1978. *The More Developed Realm: A Geography of Its Population*. New York: Pergamon Press. Excellent geographic analysis.

UNICEF. 1984. *The State of the World's Children*. New York: United Nations. Superb overview.

van der Tak, Jean, et al. 1979. "Our Population Predicament: A New Look." *Population Bulletin*, vol. 34, no. 5, 1–46. Superb overview.

Weller, Robert, and Leon Bouvier. 1981. *Population: Demography and Policy*. New York: St. Martin's Press. Excellent college text at a somewhat higher level.

Chapter 7 Human Population Control

See the Readings for Chapter 6 and Enrichment Study 8 also.

Birdsall, Nancy. 1980. "Population Growth and Poverty in the Developing World." *Population Bulletin*, vol. 35, no. 5, 1–48. One of the best discussions of the relationship between poverty and population growth.

Bouvier, Leon F. 1981. *The Impact of Immigration on U.S. Population Size*. Washington, D.C.: Population Reference Bureau. Excellent analysis.

Brown, Lester T. 1978. *The Twenty-Ninth Day: Accommodating Human Needs and Numbers to the Earth's Resources*. New York: W. W. Norton. Superb discussion of the need to control world population growth.

Brown, Lester T. 1981. *Building a Sustainable Society*. New York: W. W. Norton. An outstanding discussion of the need for population control and the conservation of renewable and nonrenewable resources.

Brown, Lester T. 1984. *State of the World 1984*. New York: W. W. Norton. Superb overview of population trends in Chapter 2.

Callahan, Daniel. 1972. "Ethics and Population Limitation." *Science*, vol. 175, 487–494. Superb analysis of the ethical implications of various population policies.

Cates, Willard, Jr. 1982. "Legal Abortion: The Public Health Record," *Science*, vol. 215, 1586–1590. Useful summary of data for the United States.

Coale, Ansley J. 1983. "Recent Trends in Fertility in Less Developed Countries," *Science*, vol. 221, 828–832. Useful overview.

Connery, John. 1977. *Abortion: The Development of the Roman Catholic Perspective*. Chicago: Loyola University Press. Excellent overview.

Crendson, John. 1983. *The Tarnished Door*. New York: New York Times Books. Excellent overview of U.S. immigration policies and problems.

Davis, Cary, et al. 1983. "U.S. Hispanics: Changing the Face of America," *Population Bulletin*, vol. 38, no. 3, 1–43. Superb overview.

Day, Lincoln H. 1978. "What Will a ZPG Society Be Like?" *Population Bulletin*, vol. 33, no. 3, 1–42. Very useful description of life in a ZPG society.

Gray, Elizabeth Dodson. 1979. *Why the Green Nigger: Remything Genesis*. Wellesley, Mass.: Roundtable Press. Excellent discussion of women's rights and environmental problems.

Hardin, Garrett. 1974. *Mandatory Motherhood: The True Meaning of "Right to Life."* Boston: Beacon Press. Superb discussion of the abortion issue.

Hardin, Garrett. 1978. *Exploring New Ethics for Survival*. 2nd ed. New York: Viking Press. Superb exploration of ethics of population control policies.

Hardin, Garrett. 1982. *Naked Emperors*,

Essays of a Taboo Stalker. San Francisco: William Kaufman. Excellent series of thought-provoking essays on a variety of subjects including overpopulation and abortion.

Jacobsen, Judith. 1983. *Promoting Population Stabilization: Incentives for Small Families.* Washington, D.C.: Worldwatch Institute. Excellent discussion of the use of economic incentives and disincentives to help control population growth.

Jaffe, Frederick S., et al. 1980. *Abortion Politics.* New York: Alan Guttmacher Institute. Excellent balanced approach.

Keely, Charles B. 1982. "Illegal Migration." *Scientific American*, March, pp. 41–47. Excellent analysis.

Keyfitz, Nathan. 1984. "The Population of China," *Scientific American*, vol. 250, no. 2, 38–47. Excellent overview.

Loup, Jacques. 1983. *Can the Third World Survive?* Baltimore: Johns Hopkins University Press. Excellent overview of past and future problems of LDCs with a proposed strategy for the future.

Murphy, Elaine M., and Patricia Cancellier. 1982. *Immigration: Questions and Answers.* Washington, D.C.: Population Reference Bureau. Superb and concise summary of this important issue.

Murphy, Francis X. 1981. "Catholic Perspectives on Population Issues II," *Population Bulletin*, vol. 35, no. 6, 1–43. Superb overview.

NARAL Foundation. 1978. *Legal Abortion: Arguments Pro & Con.* Washington, D.C.: (NARAL). Excellent summary.

Newland, Kathleen. 1977. *Women and Population Growth: Choice Beyond Childbearing.* Washington, D.C.: Worldwatch Institute. Superb discussion of women's roles.

Newland, Kathleen. 1980. *Women, Men, and the Division of Labor.* Washington, D.C.: Worldwatch Institute. Excellent summary.

Oakley, Deborah, and Leslie Corsa. 1979. *Population Planning.* Ann Arbor: University of Michigan Press. Very useful textbook on population issues and population control.

Population Crisis Committee. 1982. "World Abortion Trends." *Population*, no. 9, 1–6. Excellent summary.

Silverman, Anna C., and Arnold Silverman. 1971. *The Case Against Having Children.* New York: David McKay. Excellent discussion of alternatives to motherhood.

Simon, Julian L. 1981. *The Ultimate Resource.* Princeton, N.J.: Princeton University Press. Argues against population control because people are the ultimate resource who will use their creativity and ingenuity to solve the world's population, resource, and pollution problems.

Teitelbaum, Michael S. 1975. "Relevance of Demographic Transition Theory for Developing Countries." *Science*, vol. 188, 420–425. Excellent summary of why the demographic transition may or may not work for today's LDCs.

Tien, H. Yuan. 1983. "China: Demographic Billionaire." *Population Bulletin*, vol. 38, no. 2, 1–42. Excellent summary of China's efforts to control its population.

Tietze, Christopher, and Sarah Lewit. 1977. "Legal Abortion." *Scientific American*, vol. 236, no. 1, 21–27. Excellent summary of the spread of legal abortion throughout the world.

Zero Population Growth. 1977. *The Benefits of Zero Population Growth.* Washington, D.C.: Zero Population Growth. Superb summary.

Chapter 8   Soil Resources

Andrens, W. A. 1973. *A Guide to the Study of Soil Ecology.* Englewood Cliffs, N.J.: Prentice-Hall. Useful description.

Basile, Robert M. 1971. *A Geography of Soils.* Dubuque, Iowa: Wm. C. Brown. Concise review of soil classification and distribution of soil types.

Batie, Sandra S. 1983. *Soil Erosion: Crisis in America's Croplands?* Washington, D.C.: The Conservation Foundation. Useful and objective analysis.

Beasley, R. P. 1972. *Erosion and Sediment Pollution Control.* Ames: Iowa State University Press. Excellent discussion of soil conservation.

Brady, Nyle C. 1974. *The Nature and Properties of Soils.* New York: Macmillan. Excellent introductory text at a slightly higher level.

Brown, Lester R., et al. 1984. *The State of the World 1984.* New York: W. W. Norton. See Chapter 4 for a superb summary of world and U.S. soil erosion.

Dale, Tom, and V. G. Carter. 1955. *Topsoil and Civilization.* Norman: University of Oklahoma Press. Classic work describing soil abuse throughout human history.

Donahue, Roy L., et al. 1971. *Soils: An Introduction to Soils and Plant Growth.* Englewood Cliffs, N.J.: Prentice-Hall. Excellent introductory text.

Hausenbuiller, R. L. 1972. *Soil Science: Principles and Practices.* Dubuque, Iowa: Wm. C. Brown. Another excellent introductory text.

National Academy of Sciences. 1972. *Soils of the Humid Tropics.* Washington, D.C.: National Academy of Sciences. Excellent discussion of the potential use and abuse of tropical soils.

Olson, G. W. 1981. *Soils and the Environment.* New York: Chapman and Hall. Emphasizes use of soil surveys to solve and circumvent environmental problems.

Pritchett, W. L. 1979. *Properties and Management of Forest Soils.* New York: John Wiley A must for those interested in soil ecosystems.

Sanchez, P. A., and S. W. Buol. 1975. "Soils of the Tropics and the World Food Crisis," *Science*, vol. 188, 598–603. Useful description of the potential and limitations for growing more food in the tropics.

Sophen, C. D., and J. V. Baird. 1982. *Soils and Soil Management.* Reston, Va.: Reston Publishing Co. Excellent introductory text that is easy to read but scientifically sound.

Steila, Donald. 1976. *The Geography of Soils.* Englewood Cliffs, N.J.: Prentice-Hall. Easy-to-read and accurate treatment of basic soil properties, soil-forming processes, and spatial distributions of soils.

Chapter 9   Food Resources and World Hunger

Barrons, Keith C. 1981. *Are Pesticides Really Necessary?* Chicago: Regnery Gateway. Excellent presentation of both sides of the pesticide controversy, with emphasis on the benefits of pesticides.

Battie, Sandra S., and Robert G. Healy. 1983. "The Future of American Agriculture." *Scientific American*, vol. 248, no. 2, 44–53. Superb overview.

Berg, Alan. 1981. *Malnourished People: A Policy View.* Washington, D.C.: World Bank. Excellent overview.

Borlaug, Norman E. 1983. "Contributions of Conventional Plant Breeding to Food Production." *Science*, vol. 219, 689–693. Excellent analysis of the green revolution by the father of the movement.

Brewer, Michael. 1981. "The Changing U.S. Farmland Scene." *Population Bulletin*, vol. 36, no. 5, 1–39. Excellent analysis of the pros and cons of conversion of U.S. cropland to nonagricultural uses.

Brown, Joseph E. 1983. *The Return of the Brown Pelican.* Baton Rouge: Louisiana State University Press. Excellent case history of the comeback of this species since the 1972 ban of DDT in the United States.

Brown, Lester R. 1980. *Food or Fuel: New Competition for the World's Cropland.* Washington, D.C.: Worldwatch Institute. Thought-provoking analysis of threats to world food production from running our cars on alcohol or gasohol.

Brown, Lester R. 1981. *Building a Sustainable Society.* New York: W. W. Norton. Outstanding analysis of the limitations and side effects of modern industrialized agriculture with proposals for alternatives.

Brown, Lester R., et al. 1984. *State of the World 1984.* New York: W. W. Norton. Excellent summary of some world food problems and proposed solutions in Chapter 10.

Bull, David. 1982. *A Growing Problem: Pesticides and the Third World Poor.* London: Oxfam. Very useful description of the problems from increased pesticide use in LDCs.

Campbell, Keith D. 1979. *Food for the Future.* Lincoln: University of Nebraska Press. Useful overview of world food problems and possible solutions.

Carson, Rachel. 1962. *Silent Spring.* Boston: Houghton Mifflin. An environmental classic that provided the first major warning about the dangerous side effects of pesticides.

Crosson, Pierre R., and Kenneth D. Frederick. 1977. *The World Food Situation.* Washington, D.C.: Resources for the Future. Excellent overview emphasizing the environmental impact of agriculture.

Dando, William A. 1980. *The Geography of Famine.* New York: John Wiley. Very useful data on the persistent problem of famine throughout many parts of the world.

Dunlap, Thomas R. 1981. *DDT: Scientists, Citizens, and Public Policy.* Princeton, N.J.: Princeton University Press. Excellent discussion of the history of the use of DDT and the problems that led to its banning in the United States.

Eckholm, Erik P. 1976. *Losing Ground: Environmental Stresses and World Food Prospects.* New York: W. W. Norton. Outstanding survey of environmental problems associated with agriculture throughout the world.

Eckholm, Eric P. 1979. *The Dispossessed of the Earth: Land Reform and Sustainable Development.* Washington, D.C.: Worldwatch Institute. Discussion of how land ownership by the wealthy in less developed nations contributes to world poverty and hunger.

Eckholm, Erik P., and Frank Record. 1976. *The Two Faces of Malnutrition.* Washington, D.C.: Worldwatch Institute. Superb summary of the undernutrition of the poor and the overnutrition of the rich.

Fletcher, W. Wendell, and Charles E. Little. 1982. *The American Cropland Crisis.* Bethesda, Md.: American Land Forum. Useful analysis of ways to save U.S. cropland.

General Accounting Office. 1976. *Disincentives to Agricultural Production in Developing Countries.* Washington, D.C.: Government Printing Office. Informative examples of how governments have discouraged food production in LDCs by setting prices either too high or too low.

Gilland, Bernard. 1979. *The Next Seventy Years: Population, Food, and Resources.* Forest Grove, Ore.: ISBS. Excellent overview.

Goldstein, Jerome. 1978. *The Least Is Best Pesticide Strategy.* Emmaus, Pa.: J.G. Press. Excellent discussion of integrated pest management.

Huessy, Peter. 1978. *The Food First Debate.* San Francisco: Institute for Food and Development Policy. Pros and cons of the proposals made by Lappé and Collins (1977).

Jackson, Wes. 1980. *New Roots for Agriculture.* San Francisco: Friends of the Earth. Thought-provoking analysis of problems with modern industrialized agriculture, and proposals for alternatives.

Lappé, Frances M., and Joseph Collins. 1977. *Food First.* Boston: Houghton Mifflin. Provocative discussion of world food problems.

Linburg, Peter R. 1981. *Farming the Waters.* New York: Beaufort Books (Scribner). Excellent overview of aquaculture and mariculture.

Montclair, Susan G. 1977. *How the Other Half Dies: The Real Reasons for World Hunger.* Montclair, N.J.: Allanheld, Osmun. Excellent analysis of the political and economic causes of world hunger, with emphasis on the role played by MDCs.

Morgan, Dan. 1980. *Merchants of Grain.* New York: Penguin Books. Useful political analysis of the major companies controlling the global grain trade.

Murphy, Elaine M. 1984. *Food and Population: A Global Concern.* Washington, D.C.: Population Reference Bureau. Excellent overview.

Pimentel, David, ed. 1980. *Handbook of Energy Utilization in Agriculture.* Boca Raton, Fla.: CRC Press. Excellent source of data.

Pimentel, David, et al. 1980. "Environmental and Social Costs of Pesticides: A Preliminary Assessment." *Oikos,* vol. 34, no. 2, 126–140. Superb overview.

Pimentel, David, and Marcia Pimentel. 1979. *Food, Energy, and Society.* New York: John Wiley. Outstanding discussion of food problems and possible solutions, with emphasis on energy use and food production.

Plucknett, Donald L., and Nigel J. H. Smith. 1982. "Agricultural Research and Third World Food Production." *Science,* vol. 217, 215–219. Excellent summary of positive effects of the green revolution and directions of future research.

Sanchez, Pedro A., et al. 1982. "Amazon Basin Soils: Management for Continuous Crop Production." *Science,* vol. 216, 821–827. Excellent overview of problems and potential of these tropical soils for crop growth.

Reichert, Walt. 1982. "Agriculture's Diminishing Diversity." *Environment,* vol. 24, no. 9, 6–11 and 39–43. Excellent summary of threats from loss of genetic diversity.

Short, R. V. 1984. "Breast Feeding." *Scientific American,* vol. 250, no. 4, 35–41. Excellent overview.

Todd, Nancy J., ed. 1977. *The Book of the New Alchemists.* New York: E. P. Dutton. Description of experiments in developing a decentralized, self-sufficient agricultural system.

United States Department of Agriculture. 1980. *Report and Recommendations on Organic Farming.* Washington, D.C.: U.S. Department of Agriculture. Excellent summary of research.

van den Bosch, Robert. 1978. *The Pesticide Conspiracy.* Garden City, N.Y.: Doubleday. Pest management expert exposes political influence of pesticide companies in preventing widespread use of biological controls and integrated pest management.

van den Bosch, Robert, and Mary L. Flint. 1981. *Introduction to Integrated Pest Management.* New York: Plenum Press. Superb presentation.

World Health Organization. 1981. *Contemporary Patterns of Breast-Feeding.* Geneva: World Health Organization (U.S. distributor, WHO Publications Centre USA, Albany, N.Y.). Useful source of data.

Wortman, Sterling, and R. W. Cummings, Jr. 1978. *To Feed the World: The Challenge and the Strategy.* Baltimore: Johns Hopkins University Press. Optimistic view of how to solve world food problems.

Chapter 10 Land Resources: Wilderness, Parks, Forests, and Rangelands

Allin, Craig W. 1982. *The Politics of Wilderness Preservation.* Westport, Conn.: Greenwood Press. Excellent political history of efforts to preserve wilderness.

Brooks, Paul. 1980. *Speaking for Nature: How Literary Naturalists from Henry Thoreau to Rachel Carson Have Shaped America.* Boston: Houghton Mifflin. Excellent overview.

Brown, Lester R., et al. 1984. *State of the World 1984.* New York: W. W. Norton. See Chapter 5 for an excellent overview of the status of the world's forests and ways to protect them.

Clawson, Marion. 1975. *Forests for Whom and for What?* Baltimore: Johns Hopkins University Press. Excellent discussion of forest uses and policy.

Clawson, Marion. 1983. *The Federal Lands Revisited.* Washington, D.C.: Resources for the Future. Excellent survey of federal land use with suggestions for future policies.

Clepper, H. 1966. *Origins of American Conservation.* New York: Ronald Press. Excellent history of conservation.

Connally, Eugenia, ed. 1982. *National Parks in Crisis.* Washington, D.C.: National Parks and Conservation Association. Very useful collection of articles on problems facing national parks, with recommendations for future policies and actions.

Conservation Foundation. 1982. *State of the Environment 1982.* Washington, D.C.: The Conservation Foundation. Excellent summary of environmental problems with detailed analysis of the environmental policies of the Reagan administration.

Dana, Samuel T., and Sally K. Fairfax. 1980. *Forest and Range Policy: Its Development in the United States.* 2nd ed. New York: McGraw-Hill. Very useful analysis of federal policies affecting these types of land.

Daniel, T. W., et al. 1979. *Principles of Silviculture.* New York: McGraw-Hill. Excellent standard text.

Eckholm, Erik. 1979. *Planning for the Future: Forestry for Human Needs.* Washington, D.C.: Worldwatch Institute. Excellent suggestions for preserving and renewing more of the world's forests.

Eckholm, Erik. 1982. *Down to Earth: Environment and Human Needs.* New York: W. W. Norton. See Chapter 9 for an excellent summary of world deforestation and the global firewood crisis.

Friends of the Earth et al. 1982. *Reagan and Environment.* San Francisco: Friends of the Earth. Excellent summary of the environmental policies of the Reagan administration compiled by 10 major environmental groups.

Graham, Frank. 1971. *Man's Dominion: The Story of Conservation in America.* New York: M. Evans. Outstanding history of conservation.

Hardin, Garrett. 1968. "The Tragedy of the Commons." *Science,* vol. 162, 1243–1248. Classic environmental article describing how land and other resources are abused when they are shared by everyone.

Hendee, John, et al., eds. 1977. *Principles of Wilderness Management.* Washington, D.C.: Government Printing Office. Very useful collection of articles.

Hewett, Charles E., and Thomas E. Hamilton, eds. 1982. *Forests in Demand: Conflicts and Solutions.* Boston: Auburn Publishing House. Very useful discussion of controversies over forest use with recommendations for future policies.

Horowitz, E. C. J. 1974. *Clearcutting.* Washington, D.C.: Acropolis Books. Effective presentation of the case for clearcutting of some species.

Iltis, Hugh H. 1972. "Wilderness: Can Man Do Without?" In David J. Allan and Arthur J. Hanson, eds., *Recycle This Book.* Belmont, Calif.: Wadsworth. An eloquent summary of why we need wilderness.

Jordan, Carl F. 1982. "Amazon Rain Forests," *American Scientist,* vol. 70, July–August, pp. 394–400. Excellent overview of the unique problems of forest management in these ecosystems, with suggestions for new techniques of forest management.

Leopold, Aldo. 1949. *A Sand County Almanac.* New York: Oxford University Press. An environmental classic describing Leopold's ecological land use ethic.

Marsh, George Perkins. 1864. *Man and Nature,* New York: Scribners. An environmental classic considered to be one of the greatest American works on the environment.

Minckler, Leon S. 1980. *Woodland Ecology.* 2nd ed. Syracuse, N.Y.: Syracuse University Press. Superb and readable introduction to the ecological management of forests.

Myers, Norman. 1979. *The Sinking Ark.* New York: Pergamon Press. Excellent discussion of the disappearance of the world's tropical moist forests.

Nash, Roderick. 1968. *The American Environment: Readings in the History of Conservation.* Reading, Mass.: Addison-Wesley. Excellent collection of articles.

Nash, Roderick. 1982. *Wilderness and the American Mind.* 3rd ed. New Haven, Conn.: Yale University Press. Outstanding book on American attitudes toward wilderness and conservation.

National Academy of Sciences. 1980. *Conversion of Tropical Moist Forests.* Washington, D.C.: National Academy of Sciences. Authoritative discussion of the loss of the world's tropical moist forests and what can be done about it.

National Park Service. 1980. *The State of the Parks—1980.* Washington, D.C.: Department of the Interior. Excellent overview.

Olson, Sigurd F. 1969. *The Hidden Forest.* New York: Viking Press. A beautifully illustrated classic that will heighten your powers of observation and appreciation of the beauty and diversity of forest life.

Osborn, Fairfield. 1948. *Our Plundered Planet.* Boston: Little, Brown. An environmental classic that attempted to alert readers to the environmental problems we face today.

Runté, Alfred. 1979. *National Parks: The American Experience.* Lincoln: University of Nebraska Press. Excellent history of the National Park System.

Sax, Joseph. 1980. *Mountains Without Handrails: Reflections on the National Parks.* Ann Arbor: University of Michigan Press. Excellent discussion of the types of recreation the parks should be providing.

Sierra Club. 1982. *Our Public Lands: An Introduction to the Agencies and Issues.* San Francisco: Sierra Club. Excellent overview.

Smith, D. M. 1982. *The Practice of Silviculture.* New York: John Wiley. Excellent standard text.

Spurr, Stephen H., and Buron V. Barnes. 1980. *Forest Ecology.* 3rd ed. New York: Ronald Press. Very good forestry text.

Steen, H. K. 1976. *The U.S. Forest Service: A History.* Seattle: University of Washington Press. Superb history of forest management.

Chapter 11   Wildlife Resources

Allen, Robert L. 1980. *How to Save the World.* London: Kogan Page. Superb presentation of a strategy to preserve more of the world's vanishing wildlife and land ecosystems.

Dasmann, Raymond F. 1981. *Wildlife Biology.* 2nd ed. New York: John Wiley. Excellent text at a higher level.

Eckholm, Erik. 1978. *Disappearing Species: The Social Challenge.* Washington, D.C.: Worldwatch Institute. One of the best overviews of the need for wildlife conservation.

Ehrenfeld, David W. 1970. *Biological Conservation.* New York: Holt, Rinehart & Winston. One of the best introductions to conservation of land and wildlife.

Ehrlich, Paul, and Anne Ehrlich. 1981. *Extinction.* New York: Random House. One of the best treatments of the value of wildlife and the causes of extinction, with suggestions for preventing extinction.

Elton, Charles S. 1958. *The Ecology of Invasions by Plants and Animals.* London: Methuen. An environmental classic on species invasions and introductions.

Fox, Michael W., and Richard K. Morris, eds. 1977. *Animal Liberation and Human Ethics.* New York: Acropolis. Very useful discussion of animal rights.

Gaskin, D. E. 1982. *The Ecology of Whales and Dolphins.* London: Heinemann. Excellent overview.

Hunter, Robert. 1979. *Warriors of the Rainbow: A Chronicle of the Greenpeace Movement.* New York: Holt, Rinehart & Winston. Excellent account of this environmentalist group, which has used commandolike tactics to prevent whaling.

Koopowitz, Harold, and Hilary Kaye. 1983. *Plant Extinctions: A Global Crisis.* Washington, D.C.: Stone Wall Press. Up-to-date summary of this problem with suggestions for preventing plant extinctions.

Laycock, G. 1966. *The Alien Animals.* Garden City, N.Y.: Natural History Press. Basic reference on effects of introducing alien species.

Livingston, John. 1981. *The Fallacy of Wildlife Conservation.* London: McClelland & Stewart, Ltd. Excellent critique of the idea that wildlife resources should be managed by wildlife experts to benefit humans.

Myers, Norman. 1983. *A Wealth of Wild Species: Storehouse for Human Welfare.* Boulder, Colo.: Westview Press. Superb presentation of the value of wild species to humans.

Owen, Oliver S. 1984. *Natural Resource Conservation: An Ecological Approach.* 4th ed. New York: Macmillan. Excellent basic text for the reader wanting more details.

Passmore, John. 1974. *Man's Responsibility for Nature.* New York: Charles Scribner's. Very useful discussion of the inherent rights of species to exist.

Phillips, David, and Hugh Nash, eds. 1981. *The Condor Question: Captive or Forever Free.* San Francisco: Friends of the Earth. Discussion of the controversy over whether the California condor should be saved from extinction by habitat preservation or captive breeding.

Pimentel, David, et al. 1980. "Environmental Quality and Natural Biota." *BioScience,* vol. 30, no. 11, 750–755. Makes a strong case for adding more microorganisms and invertebrates to the endangered species list.

Prance, Ghillean T., and Thomas S. Elias, eds. 1976. *Extinction Is Forever.* New York: Botanical Garden. Excellent collection of articles.

Reagan, Tom, and P. Singer. 1976. *Animal Rights and Human Obligation.* Englewood Cliffs, N.J.: Prentice-Hall. Excellent discussion of this controversial issue.

Roe, Frank G. 1970. *The North American Buffalo.* Toronto: University of Toronto Press. Documented discussion of the rise and fall of the American bison.

Roots, Clive. 1976. *Animal Invaders.* New York: Universe Books. Excellent discussion of good and bad results from introducing species to new areas.

Scheffer, Victor B. 1974. *A Voice for Wildlife.* New York: Charles Scribner's. Excellent overview.

Smith, Robert Leo. 1976. "Ecological Genesis of Endangered Species: The Philosophy of Preservation." *Annual Reviews of Ecology and Systematics,* vol. 7, 33–56. Excellent discussion of how some species are vulnerable to extinction.

Steiner, Stan. 1976. *The Vanishing White Man.* New York: Harper & Row. Excellent discussion of the American Indian philosophy of the sacredness of the earth and all its inhabitants.

Stone, Christopher D. 1975. *Should Trees Have Standing? Toward Legal Rights for Natural Objects.* Los Altos, Calif.: William Kaufman. Useful discussion of the dispute over development at Mineral King, which went to the U.S. Supreme Court.

Trefethen, J. B. 1975. *An American Crusade for Wildlife.* New York: Winchester Press. Excellent history of wildlife conservation in the United States.

Vecsey, C., and R. Venables. 1980. *American Indian Environments.* Syracuse, N.Y.: Syracuse University Press. Good discussion of the ecological wisdom of native American Indians.

Chapter 12   Urban Land Use and Land-Use Planning

Burby, Raymond J., et al. 1976. *New Communities U.S.A.* Lexington, Mass.: Lexington Books. Excellent overview of new towns in the United States.

Butler, Stuart M. 1980. *Enterprise Zones: Pioneering in the City.* Washington, D.C.: The Heritage Foundation. Excellent presentation of the case for encouraging private industry to develop businesses and create jobs in selected declining urban areas.

Brown, David L., and John M. Wardwell, eds. 1980. *New Directions in Urban-Rural Migration: The Population Turnaround in Rural America.* New York: Academic Press. Excellent overview of the metropolitan-to-nonmetropolitan shift.

Brown, Lester R., et al. 1980. *Running on Empty: The Future of the Automobile in an Oil-Short World.* New York: W. W. Norton. Excellent analysis.

Cassidy, Robert. 1980. *Livable Cities. A Grass-Roots Guide to Rebuilding Urban America.* New York: Holt, Rinehart & Winston. Excellent guide to efforts by people to rebuild their own neighborhoods.

Choate, Pat, and Susan Walter. 1981. *America in Ruins: Beyond the Public Works Pork Barrel.* Washington, D.C.: Council on State Planning Agencies. Superb discussion of the deterioration of America's physical plant and suggestions for correcting the problem.

Dantzig, George B., and Thomas L. Saaty. 1973. *Compact City: A Plan for a Liveable Environment.* San Francisco: W. H. Freeman. Outstanding analysis of urban design for a more ecologically sound and self-reliant city.

Detwyler, Thomas R., and Melvin G. Marcus, eds. 1972. *Urbanization and Environment.* North Scituate, Mass.: Duxbury Press. Outstanding introduction to characteristics and problems of urban areas. See especially Chapter 2.

Exline, Christopher H., et al. 1982. *The City: Patterns and Processes in the Urban Ecosystem.* Boulder, Colo: Westview Press. Excellent overview.

Goodman, Percival. 1977. *The Double E.* Garden City, N.Y.: Doubleday. Exciting ideas for the design of small, self-sufficient and ecologically sound cities.

Gruen, Victor. 1964. *The Heart of Our Cities; The Urban Crisis; Diagnosis and Cure.* New York: Simon & Schuster. A classic, eloquent description of how cities can be dynamic and exciting.

Healy, Robert G., and John S. Rosenberg. 1981. *Land Use and the States.* 2nd ed. Baltimore: Johns Hopkins University Press. Excellent overview of land-use policies and in-depth studies of land-use planning and control by several states.

Heller, Alfred, ed. 1972. *The California Tomorrow Plan.* Los Altos, Calif.: William Kaufmann. Superb example of an integrated, ecological land-use plan for a state.

League of Women Voters Education Fund. 1977. *Growth and Land Use: Shaping Future Patterns.* Washington, D.C.: League of Women Voters. Excellent summary of methods for land-use control.

McHarg, Ian L. 1969. *Design with Nature.* Garden City, N.Y.: Natural History Press. A beautifully written and illustrated description of an ecological approach to land-use planning. Also available in paperback from Doubleday.

Meyer, John R., and Jose A. Gomez-Ibañez. 1981. *Autos, Transit, and Cities.* Cambridge, Mass.: Harvard University Press. Excellent analysis of problems and possible solutions.

Morris, David. 1982. *Energy and the Transformation of Urban America.* San Francisco: Sierra Club Books. Excellent discussion of how urban areas, particularly small cities, can take steps toward increased energy efficiency and resource self-reliance.

Mumford, Lewis. 1968. *The Urban Prospect.* New York: Harcourt Brace Jovanovich. An important classic on urban life.

Naisbitt, John. 1982. *Megatrends: Ten New Directions Transforming Our Lives.* New York: Warner Communications. Superb discussion of major national and global trends. See especially Chapter 9 on the North to South and West population shift.

Odum, Eugene P. 1969. "The Strategy of Ecosystem Development." *Science,* vol. 164, 262–270. Classic article on ecological principles and land use.

Owen, Wilfred. 1976. *Transportation in Cities.* Washington, D.C.: Brookings Institution. Summary of urban transportation problems and solutions.

Popper, Frank J. 1981. *The Politics of Land-Use Reform.* Madison: University of Wisconsin Press. Very useful analysis of the political problems associated with attempts at regional, state, and federal land-use planning and control.

Rudofsky, B. 1969. *Streets for People: A Primer for Americans.* Garden City, N.Y.: Doubleday. A classic describing how we should design and use city streets.

Ryn, Sin van der, and Peter Calthorpe. 1982. *Sustainable Communities: A New Design Synthesis for Cities, Suburbs, and Towns.* San Francisco: Sierra Club. Outstanding analysis and suggestions.

Steiner, Frederick. 1980. *Ecological Planning for Farmlands Preservation.* Pullman, Wash.: Student Book Corp., Washington State University. Story of how Whitman County, Washington is preserving farmland using Ian McHarg's ecological planning method.

Stokes, Bruce. 1981. *Global Housing Prospects: The Resource Constraints.* Washington, D.C.: Worldwatch Institute. Excellent analysis of the difficulties and possibilities for providing housing for the world's growing population.

Ward, Barbara. 1976. *The Home of Man.* New York: Norton. Superb discussion of urban problems in LDCs.

Whyte, William H. 1968. *The Last Landscape.* Garden City, N.Y.: Doubleday. Classic analysis of land use and discussion of open space.

Whyte, William H. 1980. *The Social Life of Small Urban Spaces.* Washington, D.C.: Conservation Foundation. Superb analysis of how small urban open spaces should be designed for maximum use by people. These research findings are also discussed in the NOVA TV program "City Spaces, Human Places", originally broadcast on PBS November 29, 1981 and available for classroom use.

Chapter 13   Nonrenewable Mineral Resources

Barnet, Richard J. 1980. *The Lean Years: Politics in an Age of Scarcity.* New York: Simon & Schuster. Superb discussion of the politics and economics of resource use and increasing scarcity.

Barnett, Harold J. 1967. "The Myth of Our Vanishing Resources," *Transactions—Social Sciences & Modern Society,* June, pp. 7–10. Statement of the optimistic view of our resource situation. Compare with the article by Cloud (1975).

Berry, Stephen. 1972. "Recycling, Thermodynamics and Environmental Thrift." *Bulletin of the Atomic Scientists,* May, pp. 8–15. Good discussion of the limits of recycling.

Brown, Lester R., et al. 1984. *State of the World 1984.* New York: W. W. Norton, See Chapter 6 for an excellent overview of recycling.

Chandler, William V. 1983. *Materials Recycling: The Virtue of Necessity.* Washington, D.C.: Worldwatch Institute. Superb overview.

Cloud, Preston E., Jr. 1975. "Mineral Resources Today and Tomorrow." In William W. Murdoch, ed., *Environment: Resources, Pollution and Society.* 2nd ed. Sunderland, Mass.: Sinauer. Superb summary of the neo-Malthusian view. Compare with the works by Barnett (1967), Kahn et al. (1976), Simon (1981), and Smith (1979).

Environmental Protection Agency. 1977. *Fourth Report to Congress: Resource Recovery and Waste Reduction.* Washington, D.C.: Environmental Protection Agency. Excellent summary of solid waste management, recycling, resource recovery, and resource conservation in the United States.

Fischman, Leonard F. 1980. *World Mineral Trends and U.S. Supply Problems.* Washington, D.C.: Resources for the Future. Excellent summary of future availability of U.S. mineral supplies.

Franchot, Peter. 1978. *Bottles and Cans: The Story of the Vermont Deposit Law.* Washington, D.C.: National Wildlife Federation. Excellent summary.

Gabor, D., et al. 1978. *Beyond the Age of Waste.* New York: Pergamon Press. Useful discussion of resource conservation.

Hayes, Denis. 1978. *Repairs, Reuse, Recycling—First Steps Toward a Sustainable Society.* Washington, D.C.: Worldwatch Institute. Splendid overview of resource recovery and conservation.

Kahn, Herman, et al. 1976. *The Next 200 Years: A Scenario for America and the World.* New York: William Morrow. A cornucopian view on mineral supplies.

Lean, Geoffrey. 1978. *Rich World Poor World.* London: Allen & Urwin. Excellent discussion of the need for a new international economic order.

Leontief, Wassily, et al. 1983. *The Future of Nonfuel Minerals in the U.S. and World Economy: 1980-2030.* Lexington, Mass.: Lexington (Heath). Excellent analysis.

Meadows, Donella H., et al. 1972. *The Limits to Growth.* New York: Universe Books. Important and controversial environmental classic giving the results of a computer simulation of the world ecosystem and resource supplies. See Enrichment Study 2 for more details.

National Academy of Sciences. 1975. *Mineral Resources and the Environment.* Washington, D.C.: National Academy of Sciences. Excellent overview of mineral resource problems and recommendations for the future.

Park, Charles F., Jr. 1975. *Earthbound: Minerals, Energy, and Man's Future.* San Francisco: W. H. Freeman. Superb overview emphasizing the neo-Malthusian view.

Purcell, Arthur H. 1980. *The Waste Watchers: A Citizen's Handbook for Conserving Energy.* Garden City, N.Y.: Anchor Press/Doubleday. Superb guide for achieving a low-waste society.

Ridker, Ronald G., and William D. Watson. 1980. *To Choose a Future: Resources and Environmental Consequences of Alternative Growth Paths.* Baltimore: Johns Hopkins University Press. Excellent and fairly optimistic overview.

Seaborg, Glenn T. 1974. "The Recycle Society of Tomorrow." *The Futurist,* June, pp. 108–115. Stirring vision of what a low-waste society would be like.

Simon, Julian L. 1981. *The Ultimate Resource.* Princeton, N.J.: Princeton University Press. Effective presentation of the cornucopian position. Simon makes some good points but many arguments are based on the false ideas that resource supplies are infinite because each supply can be infinitely divided into smaller and smaller amounts, and that energy can be recycled.

Skinner, Brian J. 1976. *Earth Resources.* 2nd ed. Englewood Cliffs, N.J.: Prentice-Hall. Excellent survey of the world's resources.

Smith, V. Kerry. 1979. *Scarcity and Growth Reconsidered.* Baltimore: Johns Hopkins University Press. Excellent analysis of the cornucopian view of world resource supplies.

U.S. Bureau of Mines. 1976. *U.S. Imports of Strategic Materials.* Washington, D.C.: Government Printing Office. Good source of data.

Ward, Barbara. 1979. *Progress for a Small Planet*. New York: W. W. Norton. Superb discussion of the need for a new world economic order.

Chapter 14 Energy Resources: Types, Use, and Concepts

See also Readings for Chapters 15 and 16.

American Physical Society. 1975. *Efficient Use of Energy*. New York: American Institute of Physics. Summary of energy waste and opportunities for energy conservation based on second-law energy efficiencies in the United States.

Bent, Henry A. 1977. "Entropy and the Energy Crisis." *Journal of Science Teaching*, vol. 44, no. 4, 25–29. Readable introduction to implications of the second law of thermodynamics.

Brown, Lester R., et al. 1984. *State of the World: 1984*. New York: W. W. Norton. Excellent overview of oil use and energy trends.

Christensen, John W. 1981. *Energy, Resources, and Environment*. Dubuque, Iowa; Kendall/Hunt. Superb introduction to energy concepts and alternatives for use at the high school level.

Clark, Wilson, and Jake Page. 1981. *Energy, Vulnerability, and War: Alternatives for America*. New York: W. W. Norton. Excellent analysis of vulnerability of centralized U.S. energy system to EMPs from nuclear attack and to cutoffs of imported oil. Based on a study carried out by energy expert Clark for the Department of Defense.

Clarke, Robin. 1977. *Building for Self-Sufficiency*. New York: Universe Books. Use this to see how to prepare for the energy and economic crunch that may come between 1985 and 1995.

Colorado Energy Research Institute. 1976. *Net Energy Analysis: An Energy Balance Study of Fossil Fuel Resources*. Golden, Colo: Colorado Energy Research Institute. Excellent source of data.

Cook, Earl. 1976. *Man, Energy, Society*. San Francisco: W. H. Freeman. Excellent introduction to energy concepts, problems, and alternatives.

Demand and Conservation Panel of the Committee on Nuclear and Alternative Energy Systems, National Academy of Sciences. 1978. "U.S. Energy Demand: Some Low Energy Futures." *Science*, vol. 200, 142–152. Useful analysis showing how the United States could get along with less energy without affecting lifestyles.

Farallones Institute. 1979. *The Integral Urban House: Self-Reliant Living in the City*. San Francisco: Sierra Club Books. Excellent discussion of how to survive in the city.

Flavin, Christopher. 1980. *Energy and Architecture: The Solar and Conservation Potential*. Washington, D.C.: Worldwatch Institute. Excellent summary.

Hayes, Earl T. 1979. "Energy Resources Available to the United States, 1985 to 2000." *Science*, vol. 203, 233–239. Superb overview.

Lovins, Amory B. 1977. *Soft Energy Paths*. Cambridge, Mass.: Ballinger. Superb analysis of energy alternatives. See also Nash (1979).

Lovins, Amory B., and L. Hunter Lovins. 1982. *Brittle Power: Energy Strategy for National Security*. Andover, Mass.: Brick House. Superb analysis of how the present U.S. centralized energy system is highly vulnerable to disruption and how this situation could be corrected by following the soft path.

Lovins, Amory B., and L. Hunter Lovins. 1984. *Energy Unbound: Your Invitation to Energy Abundance*. San Francisco: Sierra Club Books. Outstanding nontechnical version of *Soft Energy Paths*.

Maddox, John. 1975. *Beyond the Energy Crisis: A Global Perspective*. New York: McGraw-Hill. An attack on the environmental approach to energy problems. Optimistic view that we can solve the problems by finding more fossil fuels and using nuclear energy. Compare with Lovins (1977) and Lovins and Lovins (1984).

Nash, Hugh, ed. 1979. *The Energy Controversy: Soft Path Questions and Answers*. San Francisco: Friends of the Earth. Pros and cons of the soft energy path.

National Academy of Sciences. 1980. *Energy in Transition 1985–2010: Final Report of the Committee on Nuclear and Alternative Energy Systems*. Washington, D.C.: National Academy Press. Useful analysis.

Odum, Howard T., and Elisabeth C. Odum. 1981. *Energy Basis for Man and Nature*. 3rd. ed. New York: McGraw-Hill. Superb introduction to energy concepts and alternatives, with emphasis on net useful energy analyses.

Rifkin, Jeremy. 1980. *Entropy: A New World View*. New York: Viking Press. Readable popular account of the sustainable earth approach to energy and society based on the two energy laws.

Sant, Roger W., and Dennis W. Bakke. 1983. *Creating Energy Abundance*. New York: McGraw-Hill. Excellent summary of why saving energy saves money.

Solar Energy Research Institute. 1981. *A New Prosperity: Building a Sustainable Energy Future*. Andover, Mass.: Brick House. Outstanding study showing how more efficient use of energy and greatly expanded use of nonrenewable energy sources could lead to a 25 percent reduction in U.S. energy consumption and virtually eliminate oil imports. This study was funded by the Department of Energy during the last portion of the Carter administration. Its important findings were at first suppressed by the Reagan administration, but later made available to the public by Congress.

Woodwell, G. M. 1974. "Success, Succession and Adam Smith." *BioScience*, vol. 24, no. 2, 81–87. Outstanding overview of the world's energy problems and their ecological implications.

Chapter 15 Nonrenewable Energy Resources: Overall Evaluation

Also see the readings for Chapter 14.

Ackerman, Bruce A., and William T. Hassler. 1981. *Clean Coal/Dirty Air*. New Haven, Conn.: Yale University Press. Excellent discussion of air pollution from coal plants with suggestions for improvement.

Allar, Bruce. 1984. "No More Coal-Smoked Skies?" *Environment*, vol. 26, no. 2, 25–30. Excellent summary of fluidized-bed combustion of coal.

Beckmann, Peter. 1976. *The Health Hazards of Not Going Nuclear*. Boulder, Colo.: Golem Press. Readable, hard-hitting defense of nuclear power.

Brown, Lester R., et al. 1984. *State of the World 1984*. New York: W. W. Norton. See Chapter 7 for excellent overview of the economics of nuclear power.

Browne, Corinne, and Robert Munroe. 1981. *Time Bomb: Understanding the Threat of Nuclear Power*. New York: William Morrow. Excellent overview.

Bupp, Irvin C., and Jean-Claude Derian. 1978. *Light Water: How the Nuclear Dream Dissolved*. New York: Basic Books. Outstanding discussion of why nuclear power is uneconomic.

Caldicott, Helen. 1981. *Nuclear Madness*. New York: Bantam Books. Attack on nuclear power by a physician and leading antinuclear activist.

Cohen, Bernard L. 1983. *Before It's Too Late: A Scientist's Case for Nuclear Power*. New York: Plenum Press. Probably the best available case for nuclear power by an expert.

Cummings, Ronald G., et al. 1979. "Mining Earth's Heat: Hot Dry Rock Geothermal Energy." *Technology Review,* February, pp. 58–78. Very good summary.

Department of Energy. 1980. *Geothermal Energy and Our Environment.* Washington, D.C.: Department of Energy. Superb summary.

Ford, Daniel F. 1983. *Three Mile Island: Thirty Minutes to Meltdown.* New York: Penguin Books. Excellent overview by a nuclear power expert.

Gofman, John W. 1981. *Radiation and Human Health.* San Francisco: Sierra Club Books. An expert's detailed and controversial evaluation of the health effects of exposure to low-level radiation.

Gofman, John W., and Arthur R. Tamplin. 1979. *Poisoned Power: The Case Against Nuclear Power.* 2nd ed. Emmaus, Pa.: Rodale Press. Attack on nuclear power by two prominent nuclear scientists.

Gray, Mike, and Ira Rosen. 1982. *The Warning: Accident at Three Mile Island.* New York: W. W. Norton. Useful description.

Harding, Jim. 1984. "Lights Dim for Nuclear Power," *Not Man Apart,* April, pp. 21–22. Excellent summary of economics of nuclear power in the United States and elsewhere.

Hilgartner, Stephen et al. 1982. *Nukespeak.* San Francisco: Sierra Club Books. Excellent discussion of the history and dangers of nuclear power.

Hippenheimer, T.A. 1984. *The Man-Made Sun: The Quest for Fusion Power.* Boston: Little, Brown. Excellent overview.

Hunt, Charles B. 1984. "Disposal of Radioactive Wastes," *Bulletin of the Atomic Scientists,* April, pp. 44–46. Summary by a prominent geologist of problems associated with geologic disposal of radioactive wastes.

Hurley, Patrick M. 1982. *Living with Nuclear Radiation.* Ann Arbor: University of Michigan Press. Useful evaluation of the risks of exposure to low-level radiation.

Jakimo, Alan, and Irvin C. Bupp. 1978. "Nuclear Waste Disposal: Not in My Backyard." *Technology Review,* March–April, pp. 64–72. Excellent summary.

Kaku, Michio, and Jennifer Trainer. 1982. *Nuclear Power: Both Sides.* New York: W. W. Norton. Useful collection of pro and con essays.

Kemeny, John G. 1980. "Saving American Democracy: The Lessons of Three Mile Island." *Technology Review,* June–July, pp. 65–75. Excellent analysis by the head of the presidential panel that investigated the Three Mile Island nuclear accident.

Kendall, H. W., ed. 1977. *The Risks of Nuclear Power Reactors.* Washington, D.C.: Union of Concerned Scientists. Excellent discussion of problems with nuclear power.

Komanoff, Charles, 1981. *Power Plant Cost Escalation.* New York: Van Nostrand Reinhold. Detailed analysis by an expert of the unfavorable economics of nuclear power.

Kulcinski, G. L., et al. 1979. "Energy for the Long Run: Fission or Fusion." *American Scientist,* vol. 67, 78–89. Superb evaluation of nuclear fusion.

League of Women Voters Education Fund. 1980. *A Nuclear Waste Primer.* Washington D.C.: League of Women Voters. Excellent readable, balanced summary.

League of Women Voters Education Fund. 1982. *A Nuclear Power Primer: Issues for Citizens.* Washington, D.C.: League of Women Voters. Outstanding, readable, balanced summary.

Leon, George de Lucenay. 1982. *Energy Forever: Power for Today and Tomorrow.* New York: Arco Publishing. Excellent nontechnical overview of nonrenewable and renewable energy alternatives.

Lidsky, Lawrence M. 1983. "The Trouble with Fusion." *Technology Review,* October, pp. 32–44. Superb evaluation by one of the world's most prominent nuclear fusion scientists.

Lidsky, Lawrence M. 1984. "The Reactor of the Future," *Technology Review,* February–March, pp. 52–56. Excellent summary by an expert of new and safer designs.

Lindholm, Ulf, and Paul Gnirk. 1982. *Nuclear Waste Disposal: Can We Rely on Bedrock?* New York: Pergamon Press. Useful analysis.

Lipschultz, Ronnie. 1980. *Radioactive Waste: Politics, Technology, and Risk.* Cambridge, Mass.: Ballinger. Useful analysis of this problem.

Lovins, Amory B., and L. Hunter Lovins. 1980. *Energy/War: Breaking the Nuclear Link.* San Francisco: Friends of the Earth. Superb discussion by two experts of the relationship of the development of commercial nuclear power to the proliferation of nuclear weapons.

Lovins, Amory B., and L. Hunter Lovins. 1982. *Brittle Power: Energy Strategy for National Security.* Andover, Mass.; Brick House. Outstanding discussion of how centralized power plants and other hard-path technologies threaten national security.

McCracken, Samuel. 1982. *The War Against the Atom.* New York: Basic Books. Excellent defense of nuclear power.

Martin, Daniel W. 1980. *Three Mile Island: Prologue or Epilogue?* Cambridge, Mass.: Ballinger. Excellent analysis.

Murray, Raymond L. 1982. *Understanding Radioactive Waste.* Columbus, Ohio: Battelle Press. Useful overview by an expert.

National Academy of Sciences. 1980. *The Effects on Populations of Exposure to Low Levels of Ionizing Radiation.* Washington, D.C.: National Academy Press. Controversial report by a team of experts who disagreed widely on the relative effects and risks of exposure to low-level radiation.

O'Banion, Kerry. 1981. "Long-Term Nuclear Options." *Environmental Science & Technology,* vol. 15, no. 10, 1130–1136. Excellent comparison of the environmental effects of nuclear fission breeder reactors and nuclear fusion reactors.

Perry, Harry. 1983. "Coal in the United States: A Status Report." *Science,* vol. 222, no. 4622, 377–394. Excellent overview.

President's Commission on the Accident at Three Mile Island. 1979. *Report of the President's Commission on the Accident at Three Mile Island.* Washington, D.C.: Government Printing Office. Useful analysis of nuclear reactor safety.

Resnikoff, Marvin. 1983. *The Next Nuclear Gamble: Transportation and Storage of Nuclear Waste.* Washington, D.C.: Council on Economic Priorities. Excellent analysis.

Shahinpoor, Mohsen. 1982. "Making Oil from Sand," *Technology Review,* February–March, pp. 49–54. Excellent summary of oil sands.

Shapiro, Fred C. 1981. *Radwaste: A Reporter's Investigation of a Growing Nuclear Menace.* New York: Random House. Excellent overview.

Stephens, Mark. 1980. *Three Mile Island.* New York: Random House. Useful description of this accident.

Sternglass, Ernest J. 1981. *Secret Fallout: Low-Level Radiation from Hiroshima to Three Mile Island.* New York: McGraw-Hill. Controversial evaluation of effects of exposure to low-level radiation by an expert.

United Nations Scientific Committee on Effects of Atomic Radiation (UNSCEAR). 1977. *Sources and Effects of Ionizing Radiation.* New York: United Nations. Evaluation by an international team of experts similar to that by the National Academy of Sciences (1980).

Upton, Arthur C. 1982. "The Biological Effects of Low-Level Ionizing Radiation," *Scientific American,* vol. 246, no. 2, 41–49. Excellent overview.

Weinberg, Alvin M. 1980. "Is Nuclear Energy Necessary?" *Bulletin of the Atomic Scientists,* March, pp. 31–35. Excellent case for nuclear power.

Weinberg, Alvin M., et al. 1979. *Economic and Environmental Impacts of a U.S. Nuclear*

Moratorium, 1985–2010. Cambridge, Mass.: M.I.T. Press. Excellent analysis.

Chapter 16 Renewable Energy Resources: Overall Evaluation

Bockris, J. O. 1980. *Energy Options: Real Economics and the Solar-Hydrogen System.* London: Taylor & Francis. Excellent analysis by an expert on this energy alternative.

Brown, Lester R., and Pamela Shaw. 1982. *Six Steps to a Sustainable Society.* Washington, D.C.: Worldwatch Society. Excellent overview.

Brown, Lester R., et al. 1984. *State of the World 1984.* New York: W. W. Norton. See Chapter 8 for excellent overview of renewable energy resources.

Butti, Ken, and John Perlin. 1980. *A Golden Thread: 2,500 Years of Solar Architecture and Technology.* New York: Cheshire Books. Superb overview.

Calvin, Melvin. 1979. "Petroleum Plantations for Fuels and Materials." *BioScience,* vol. 29, no. 9, 533–538. Nobel Prize-winning chemist discusses his proposal to grow plants that yield petroleum.

Carr, Donald E. 1976. *Energy and the Earth Machine.* New York: W. W. Norton. Readable introduction to energy problems and alternatives.

Center for Science in the Public Interest. 1977. *99 Ways to a Simple Lifestyle.* Garden City, N.Y.: Doubleday. Superb summary of how you can conserve matter and energy.

Charlier, Roger Henri. 1982. *Tidal Energy.* New York: Van Nostrand Reinhold. Excellent description and analysis of this option.

Commoner, Barry. 1983. "A Reporter at Large: Ethanol," *New Yorker,* October 10, pp. 125–140. Excellent overview of ethanol as a biofuel.

Darmstadter, Joel, et al. 1983. *Energy Today and Tomorrow—Living with Uncertainty.* Englewood Cliffs, N.J.: Prentice-Hall. Useful analysis of energy problems and possible solutions.

Duedney, Daniel, and Christopher Flavin. 1983. *Renewable Energy: The Power to Choose.* 1983. New York: W. W. Norton. Probably the best overview of renewable energy resources.

Editorial Research Reports. 1982. *Energy Issues: New Directions and Issues.* Washington, D.C.: Congressional Quarterly. Useful overview.

Energy Conservation Research. 1979. *Energy for Today and Tomorrow.* Malvern, Pa.: Energy Conservation Research. One of the best lists of how to avoid energy waste.

Energy Policy Project. 1974. *A Time to Choose: The Final Report of the Energy Policy Project of the Ford Foundation.* Cambridge, Mass.: Ballinger. Excellent overview by a high-level task force.

Finneran, Kevin. 1983. "Solar Technology: A Whether Report," *Technology Review,* April, pp. 48–59. Excellent overview.

Flavin, Christopher. 1980. *The Future of Synthetic Materials: The Petroleum Connection.* Washington, D.C.: Worldwatch Institute. Explains the importance of using oil to produce petrochemicals and evaluates alternatives.

Flavin, Christopher. 1982. *Electricity from Sunlight: The Future of Photovoltaics.* Washington, D.C.: Worldwatch Institute. Superb overview.

Fowler, John W. 1984. *Energy and the Environment.* 2nd ed. New York: McGraw-Hill. Excellent summary of energy problems and alternatives at a slightly higher level than this text.

Gibbons, John H., and William U. Chandler. 1981. *The Conservation Revolution.* New York: Plenum Press. Excellent and informative overview.

Hayes, Denis. 1977. *Rays of Hope: The Transition to a Post-Petroleum World.* New York: W. W. Norton. Outstanding analysis of energy problems and alternatives.

Hill, Ray. 1980. "Alcohol Fuels—Can They Replace Gasoline?" *Popular Science,* March, pp. 25–34. Very good summary.

Holdren, John P. 1982. "Energy Hazards: What to Measure, What to Compare," *Technology Review,* April, pp. 34–75. Excellent discussion of how to evaluate risks of various energy options by an expert.

Holdren, John P., et al. 1980. "Environmental Aspects of Renewable Energy Sources." In Jack M. Hollander et al., eds., *Annual Review of Energy,* vol. 5. Palo Alto, Calif.: Annual Reviews. Excellent analysis of the environmental impacts of renewable energy alternatives by an expert. Compare this with Inhaber's less favorable estimate (1982) of the impact of these alternatives.

Hollander, Jack M., et al., eds. Annual. *Annual Review of Energy.* Palo Alto, Calif.: Annual Reviews. Excellent series of articles published each year.

Inhaber, Herbert. 1982. *Energy Risk Assessment.* New York: Gordon & Breach. Updating of a controversial 1978 analysis of environmental impacts of energy alternatives indicating that solar, wind, biomass, and other renewable energy options have a more severe impact than most energy options, with nuclear power having the lowest impact. Compare with Holdren et al. (1980).

Kash, Don E., and Robert W. Rycroft. 1984. *U.S. Energy Policy: Crisis and Complacency.* Norman: University of Oklahoma Press. Useful analysis.

Kendall, Henry, and Steven Nadis. 1980. *Energy Strategies: Toward a Solar Future.* Cambridge, Mass.: Ballinger. Splendid analysis of energy alternatives.

Knowles, R. S. 1980. *American's Energy Famine: Its Causes and Cures.* Norman: Oklahoma University Press. Useful analysis.

Mazria, Edward. 1979. *The Passive Solar Energy Book: A Complete Guide to Passive Solar Home, Greenhouse, and Building Design.* Emmaus, Pa.: Rodale Press. One of the best available books on passive solar energy design.

Medsker, Larry. 1982. *Side Effects of Renewable Energy Resources.* New York: National Audubon Society. Excellent summary of environmental effects.

National Academy of Sciences. 1983. *Alcohol Fuels: Options for Developing Countries.* Washington, D.C.: National Academy Press. Useful analysis.

Pimentel, David, et al. 1984. "Environmental and Social Costs of Biomass Energy," *BioScience,* February, pp. 89–93. Excellent overview.

Pryde, Philip R. 1983. *Nonconventional Energy Resources.* New York: Wiley-Interscience. Excellent overview with emphasis on nonrenewable energy resources.

Purcell, Arthur. 1980. *The Waste Watchers: A Citizen's Handbook for Conserving Energy and Resources.* Garden City, N.Y.: Anchor Press/Doubleday. Superb guide.

Ross, Marc H., and Robert H. Williams. 1981. *Our Energy: Regaining Control.* New York: McGraw-Hill. Excellent overview of opportunities for energy conservation.

Sant, Roger W., and Dennis W. Bakke. 1983. *Creating Energy Abundance.* New York: McGraw-Hill. Excellent summary of why saving energy saves money.

Simon, Julian. 1981. *The Ultimate Resource.* Princeton, N.J.: Princeton University Press. Optimistic view by a cornucopian economist who argues that we will always have affordable supplies of energy resources. His view is partially based on the idea that energy can be recycled—ignoring the second law of energy.

Smith, Nigel. 1981. *Wood: An Ancient Fuel with a New Future.* Washington, D.C.: Worldwatch Institute. Outstanding overview.

Stephenson, Richard M. 1982. *Living with Tomorrow: A Factual Look at America's Resources.* New York: Wiley-Interscience. Balanced analysis of the energy and related environmental problems facing the United States.

Stobaugh, Robert, and Daniel Yergin, eds. 1979. *Energy Future: Report of the Energy Project at the Harvard Business School.* New York: Random House. Superb analysis of U.S. energy alternatives.

Underground Space Center, University of Minnesota. 1979. *Earth-Sheltered Housing Design.* Princeton, N.J.: Van Nostrand Reinhold. One of the best sources.

Chapter 17   Water Resources

Ashworth, William. 1982. *Nor Any Drop to Drink.* New York: Summit Books. Outstanding overview of the water crisis in the United States.

Berk, Richard A., et al. 1981. *Water Shortage: Lessons in Conservation from the Great California Drought, 1976–77.* Cambridge, Mass.: Abt Books. Useful overview of water conservation.

Burman, David E. 1982. "The New Pollution: Groundwater Contamination." *Environment*, vol. 24, no. 2, 5–12, 33–36. Excellent overview of this growing problem.

Cousteau, Jacques-Yves, et al. 1981. *The Cousteau Almanac: An Inventory of Life on Our Water Planet.* Garden City, N.Y.: Doubleday. Superb source of information.

Dennis, Harry. 1981. *Water and Power.* San Francisco: Friends of the Earth. Useful discussion of the politics of water in California.

Engelbert, Ernest, and Ann Scheuring. 1982. *California Water.* Berkeley: University of California Press. Useful, fairly technical overview of California's water problems.

Falkenmark, Malin, and Gunnar Lindh. 1974. "The Global Freshwater Circulation—The Most Spectacular of All Desalination Systems." *Ambio*, vol. 3, no. 3–4, 116–122. Superb discussion of the water cycle and present and projected world supplies of fresh water.

Fradkin, Phillip L. 1981. *A River No More: The Colorado and the West,* New York: Alfred A. Knopf. Overview of politics and water resources in the West involving the Colorado river.

Kahrl, William L. 1982. *Water and Power.* Berkeley: University of California Press. Excellent discussion of fight over water supplies for Southern California.

Leopold, L. B. 1974. *Water: A Primer.* San Francisco: W. H. Freeman. Outstanding and easy-to-read introduction to the fundamentals of water resources.

Marx, Wesley. 1977. *Acts of God, Acts of Man.* New York: McCann & Geohegan. Excellent discussion of adverse impacts of building dams for flood control.

Murray, C. R., and E. B. Reeves. 1977. *Estimated Use of Water in the United States in 1975.* U.S. Geological Survey Circular 765. Washington, D.C.: Government Printing Office. Excellent source of data on present and future water use.

Okun, Daniel L. 1975. "Water Management in England: A Regional Model." *Environmental Science and Technology,* vol. 9, no. 10, 918–923. Excellent description of the integrated regional water resource and waste treatment system used in England with great success since 1974.

Pimentel, David, et al. 1982. "Water Resources in Food and Energy Production." *BioScience*, vol. 32, no. 11, 861–867. Excellent analysis and source of data.

Pringle, Laurence. 1982. *Water—The Next Great Resource Battle.* New York: Macmillan. Superb overview of the water crisis in the United States.

Sheaffer, John, and Leonard Stevens. 1983. *Future Water.* New York: William Morrow. Excellent overview of the U.S. water resource problems with suggested solutions.

Sheridan, David. 1981. "The Underwatered West: Overdrawn at the Well." *Environment*, vol. 23, no. 2, 5–13, 30–33. Excellent overview.

Stokes, Bruce. 1983. "Water Shortages: The Next Energy Crisis." *The Futurist*, April, pp. 38–47. Excellent overview.

U.S. Geological Survey. 1984. *Estimated Use of Water in the United States in 1980.* Washington, D.C.: Government Printing Office. Useful source of data.

U.S. Water Resources Council. 1979. *The Nation's Water Resources. 1975–2000.* Vols. 1–4. Washington, D.C.: Government Printing Office. Excellent source of data.

White, Gilbert F. 1971. *Strategies of American Water Management.* Ann Arbor, Mich.: Ann Arbor Paperbacks. Basic reference.

Wolman, Nathaniel, and Gilbert Bonem. 1978. *The Outlook for Water: Quality, Quantity, and National Growth.* Baltimore: Johns Hopkins University Press. Excellent in-depth study of water resources and water pollution in the United States.

Chapter 18   Water Pollution

Bascom, Willard. 1974. "The Disposal of Waste in the Ocean." *Scientific American*, vol. 231, no. 2, 16–25. Argues that with careful control, we can safely dispose of many types of waste in the ocean.

Burmaster, David E. 1982. "The New Pollution: Groundwater Contamination." *Environment*, vol. 24, no. 2, 4–12, 33–36. Excellent overview.

Claus, George, and Karen Bolander. 1977. *Ecological Sanity.* New York: David McKay. Excellent discussion of pollution control.

Council on Environmental Quality. 1978. *Our Nation's Wetlands.* Washington, D.C.: Government Printing Office. Federal interagency task force description of wetlands, the problems they face, and federal policies designed to protect them.

Culliney, John L. 1979. *The Forest of the Sea: Life and Death on the Continental Shelf.* Garden City, N.Y.: Anchor/Doubleday. Superb description.

Davies, J. Clarence, III, and Barbara S. Davies. 1975. *The Politics of Pollution.* 2nd ed. Indianapolis: Pegasus. Excellent account of the political realities (as opposed to the political theory) of pollution control.

Forrestal, Liz. 1975. "Deep Mystery." *Environment*, vol. 17, no. 8, 25–35. Good overview of the problems of injecting wastes into deep underground wells.

Geophysics Research Forum. 1984. *Studies in Geophysics: Groundwater Contamination.* Washington, D.C.: National Academy Press. Excellent overview.

Goldstein, Jerome. 1977. *Sensible Sludge.* Emmaus, Pa.: Rodale Press. Useful overview of how to recycle sludge from waste treatment plants.

Grundlach, Erich R., et al. 1983. "The Fate of *Amoco Cadiz* Oil," *Science*, vol. 221, 122–129. Useful scientific study of the recovery of most marine life within 3 years after this spill.

Hodges, Laurent. 1977. *Environmental Pollution.* 2nd ed. New York: Holt, Rinehart & Winston. See Chapters 8, 9, 10, 11, and 14 for a discussion of water pollution and water pollution control at a slightly higher level than that found in this book.

Keogh, Carol. 1980. *Water Fit to Drink.* Emmaus, Pa.: Rodale Press. Excellent overview of threats to drinking water quality and how individuals can use purifiers or switch water sources to combat such problems.

Ketchum, Bostwick H., et al. 1981. *Ocean Dumping of Industrial Wastes.* New York: Plenum Press. Useful source of technical details on the chemical and biological aspects of ocean dumping.

Lahey, William, and Michael Connor. 1983. "The Case for Ocean Waste Disposal." *Technology Review*, August–September, pp. 61–68. Excellent overview.

Leich, Harold H. 1975. "The Sewerless Society." *Bulletin of the Atomic Scientists*, November, pp. 38–44. How waterless toilets can save money, water, and energy and reduce our need for sewage treatment plants.

Lieber, Harvey. 1975. *Federalism and Clean Waters*. Lexington, Mass.: D. C. Heath. Useful case study of how the Federal Water Pollution Control Act of 1972 came to be and an analysis of its strengths and weaknesses.

Marx, Wesley. 1981. *The Oceans: Our Last Resource*. San Francisco: Sierra Club Books. Excellent discussion of how to preserve the ocean's resources.

National Academy of Sciences. 1983. *Drinking Water and Health*, Vol. 5. Washington, D.C.: National Academy Press. Up-to-date information on the effects on human health of 21 drinking water contaminants.

Pye, Veronica I., and Ruth Patrick. 1983. "Ground Water Contamination in the United States." *Science*, vol. 221, 713–718. Excellent overview.

Ringold, Paul L., and John Clark. 1980. *The Coastal Almanac for 1980—The Year of the Coast*. San Francisco: W. H. Freeman. Useful source of information.

Simon, Anne W. 1978. *The Thin Edge: Coast and Man in Crisis*. New York: Harper & Row. Superb discussion of stresses on estuarine zones and possible solutions.

Stoker, H. S., and Spencer L. Seager. 1976. *Environmental Chemistry: Air and Water Pollution*. 2nd ed. Glenview, Ill.: Scott, Foresman. Excellent summary of air and water pollution at a slightly higher level than that found in this book.

Teal, J., and M. Teal. 1969. *Life and Death of a Salt Marsh*. New York: Ballantine. A classic work on estuaries.

Warren, C. E. 1971. *Biology and Water Pollution Control*. Philadelphia: W. B. Saunders. Excellent introduction at a slightly higher level.

Westman, Walter E. 1972. "Some Basic Issues in Water Pollution Control Legislation." *American Scientist*, November–December, pp. 767–773. Excellent summary of the ecological versus the technological-economic approach to water pollution control.

Woodwell, George M. 1977. "Recycling Sewage Through Plant Communities." *American Scientist*, vol. 65, 556–562. Excellent overview of this natural alternative to expensive waste treatment plants.

World Health Organization. 1981. *Drinking Water and Sanitation 1981–1990: A Way to Health*. Albany, N.Y.: WHO Publications Center. Useful overview of world problems and proposed solutions.

Chapter 19   Air Pollution

American Chemical Society. 1980. *Cleaning Our Environment*. 2nd ed. Washington, D.C.: American Chemical Society. Excellent technical overview of air and water pollution at a slightly higher level.

Berry, James W., et al. 1974. *Chemical Villains: A Biology of Pollution*. St. Louis: C. V. Mosby. Readable summary of the effects of pollutants on living systems.

Boyle, Robert H., and R. Alexander Boyle. 1983. *Acid Rain*. New York: Schocken Books. Excellent overview.

Cowling, Ellis B. 1982. "Acid Precipitation in Historical Perspective," *Environmental Science and Technology*, vol. 16, no. 2, 110A–122A. Useful survey of the literature and awareness of this problem since 1661.

Davies, J. Clarence, III, and Barbara S. Davies. 1975. *The Politics of Pollution*. 2nd ed. Indianapolis: Pegasus. Superb discussion of the politics of air pollution control.

Fennelly, Paul F. 1976. "The Origin and Influence of Airborne Particulates." *American Scientist*, vol. 64, 46–56. Superb overview.

Gold, Michael. 1980. "Indoor Air Pollution." *Science 80*, March–April, pp. 30–33. Excellent overview.

Government Institutes. 1983. *Acid Deposition: Causes and Effects*. Rockville, Md.: Government Institutes. Excellent overview.

Heywood, John, and John Wilkes. 1980. "Is There a Better Automobile Engine?" *Technology Review*, November–December, pp. 19–29. Superb overview of advantages and disadvantages of possible new engines.

Lave, Lester B., and Eugene B. Seskin. 1977. *Air Pollution and Human Health*. Baltimore: Johns Hopkins University Press. Useful source of data.

League of Women Voters Education Fund. 1981. *Blueprint for Clean Air*. Washington, D.C.: League of Women Voters. Excellent description of the Clean Air acts of 1970 and 1977 and suggested changes for the future.

Lundquist, Lennart J. 1980. *The Hare and the Tortoise: Clean Air Policy in the United States*. Ann Arbor: University of Michigan Press. Superb analysis of the politics of air pollution.

Luoma, Jon R. 1984. *Troubled Skies, Troubled Water: The Story of Acid Rain*. New York: Viking Press. Excellent overview.

Lynn, David A. 1976. *Air Pollution—Threat and Response*. Reading, Mass.: Addison-Wesley. Excellent treatment at a slightly higher level.

National Academy of Sciences. 1981. *Indoor Pollutants*. Washington, D.C.: National Academy Press. Excellent summary.

National Academy of Sciences. 1983. *Acid Deposition: Atmospheric Processes in the United States*. Washington, D.C.: National Academy Press. Excellent overview and source of data.

Postel, Sandra. 1984. *Air Pollution, Acid Rain, and the Future of Forests*, Washington, D.C.: Worldwatch Institute. Superb overview.

Waldbott, George L. 1978. *Health Effects of Environmental Pollutants*. 2nd ed. St. Louis: C. V. Mosby. Excellent overview at a slightly higher level. Detailed bibliography.

Ward, Morris A. 1981. "The Clean Air Controversy: Congress Confronts the Issues," *Environment*, vol. 23, no. 6, 8–20, 42–45. Superb summary of proposed changes in the Clean Air acts of 1970 and 1977.

Wark, K., and C. F. Warner. 1981. *Air Pollution: Its Origin and Control*. 2nd ed. New York: Harper & Row. Good updated treatment at a slightly higher level.

Wilson, Richard, et al. 1981. *Health Effects of Fossil Fuel Burning: Assessment and Mitigation*. Cambridge, Mass.: Ballinger. Useful overview and source of data.

Chapter 20   Economics and Environment

Abernathy, William, et al. 1983. *Industrial Renaissance*. New York: Basic Books. Useful description of the decline of American industry.

Andrews, Richard N. L. 1981. "Will Benefit-Cost Analysis Reform Regulations?" *Environmental Science & Technology*, vol. 15, no. 9, 1016–1021. Excellent summary of cost-benefit and cost-effective analysis.

Baram, Michael S. 1980. "Cost-Benefit Analysis: An Inadequate Basis for Health, Safety, and Environmental Regulatory Decisionmaking." *Ecology Law Quarterly*, vol. 8, 473–479. Excellent analysis.

Beckerman, Wilfred. 1974. *Two Cheers for the Affluent Society*. New York: St. Martin's Press. A vigorous defense of the need for an economy based on continued growth. Compare with Daly (1977) and Georgescu-Roegen (1977).

Bluestone, Barry, and Bennett Harrison. 1983. *The Deindustrialization of America*. New York: Basic Books. Useful presentation of the case for reindustrializing America.

Boulding, Kenneth E. 1974. "What Went Wrong, If Anything, Since Copernicus?" *Bulletin of the Atomic Scientists*, January, pp.

17–23. Penetrating analysis of the possible types of equilibrium society.

Bowles, Samuel, et al. 1983. *Beyond the Wasteland*. New York: Anchor Press. Excellent analysis showing how eliminating waste in the American economy would allow continued economic growth without running up against the limits of growth.

Brown, Lester R. 1981. *Building a Sustainable Society*. New York: W. W. Norton. Excellent overview of how interlocking pollution, energy, and resource problems are helping create global economic problems.

Canterberry, E. Ray. 1976. *The Making of Economics*. Belmont, Calif.: Wadsworth. A readable critique of contemporary economic theory. Explains why economics so long ignored issues such as ecology and points the way to a reconstruction of economics on a humanistic base.

Cottrell, Alan. 1978. *Environmental Economics*. New York: Halsted. Good introduction.

Daly, Herman E. 1973. *Toward a Steady-State Economy*. San Francisco: W. H. Freeman. Outstanding analysis.

Daly, Herman E. 1977. *Steady-State Economics*. San Francisco: W. H. Freeman. Superb discussion of a sustainable earth economy and how we can make the transition to such a system.

Daly, Herman E., ed. 1980. *Economics, Ecology, and Ethics*. San Francisco: W. H. Freeman. Superb collection of essays.

Freeman, A. Myrick, III. 1979. *The Benefits of Air and Water Pollution Control: A Review and Synthesis of Recent Estimates*. Washington, D.C.: Council on Environmental Quality. Excellent analysis.

Georgescu-Roegen, Nicholas. 1971. *The Entropy Law and the Economic Process*. Cambridge, Mass.: Harvard University Press. Important advanced work on the relationships between the second law of energy and economics.

Georgescu-Roegen, Nicholas. 1977. "The Steady State and Ecological Salvation: A Thermodynamic Analysis." *BioScience*, vol. 27, no. 4, 266–270. Superb analysis of steady-state and sustainable earth economic systems by one of the world's outstanding economic thinkers. See also his article in Daly, ed. (1980).

Goldsmith, Edward. 1978. *The Stable Society*. Cornwall, England: Wadebridge Press. Useful description of a sustainable earth economy and society.

Hamer, John. 1976. "Pollution Control: Costs and Benefits." *Editorial Research Reports*, vol. 1, no. 8, 147–164. Excellent overview of approaches to pollution control.

Hamrin, Robert D. 1983. *A Renewable Resource Economy*. New York: Praeger. Useful analysis of some aspects of sustainable earth economy.

Hardin, Garrett. 1968. "The Tragedy of the Commons." *Science*, vol. 162, 1243–1248. Classic article describing how common property is ruined by individual actions.

Hawken, Paul. 1983. *The Next Economy*. New York: Holt, Rinehart & Winston. Useful and readable analysis showing how ordinary citizens can buy smart by substituting knowledge for energy.

Hueting, R. 1980. *New Scarcity and Economic Growth*. New York: Oxford University Press. Superb analysis of the interaction of ecology and economics.

Huisingh, Donald, and Vicky Bailey. 1982. *Making Pollution Prevention Pay*. Elmsford, N.Y.: Pergamon Press. Excellent analysis.

Johnson, Warren. 1978. *Muddling Toward Frugality*. San Francisco: Sierra Club Books. Outstanding economic and political analysis of how we might make it to the end of this century.

Kahn, Herman. 1982. *The Coming Boom: Economic, Political, and Social*. New York: Simon & Schuster. Useful projections by a pro-growth technological optimist.

Kasis, Richard, and Richard L. Grossman. 1982. *Fear at Work: Job Blackmail, Labor, and the Environment*. New York: Pilgrim Press. Useful study showing how environmental legislation has created far more jobs than it has eliminated.

League of Women Voters. 1977. "Growth: An Invitation to the Debate." *Current Focus*, no. 146, pp. 1–5. Superb summary of the debate over economic growth.

Mishan, E. J. 1977. *The Economic Growth Debate: An Assessment*. London: Allen & Unwin. Superb analysis.

Naisbitt, John. 1982. *Megatrends: Ten New Directions Transforming Our Lives*. New York: Warner Books. Superb discussion of major trends, economic and other.

Riddel, Robert. 1981. *Ecodevelopment: An Alternative to Growth Imperative Models*. Hampshire, England: Gower Publishing. Useful summary of how LDCs can develop by using ecological principles to become more self-reliant and self-sufficient.

Rifkin, Jeremy. 1980. *Entropy: A New World View*. New York: Viking Press. Important book with a discussion of sustainable earth economics based on the second law of energy.

Royston, Michael G. 1980. "Making Pollution Pay." *Harvard Business Review*, November–December. Excellent summary of how businesses have saved money and made profits through pollution control.

Ruff, Larry E. 1970. "The Economic Common Sense of Pollution." *Public Interest*, Spring, pp. 69–85. Readable introduction to the various economic approaches to pollution control.

Schumacher, E. F. 1973. *Small Is Beautiful: Economics as if People Mattered*. New York: Harper & Row. Important environmental classic describing the need for and the nature of appropriate technology.

Science Council of Canada. 1980. *Entropy and the Economic Process*. Ontario: Science Council of Canada. Useful analysis of relationships between the second law of thermodynamics and economics.

Spencer, Milton H. 1981. *Contemporary Economics*. 4th ed. New York: Worth. Understandable basic text in economics with a discussion of ecology and economics.

Swartzman, Daniel et al., eds. 1982. *Cost-Benefit Analysis and Environmental Regulations: Politics, Ethics, and Methods*. Washington, D.C.: The Conservation Foundation. Useful analysis.

Theobald, Robert. 1970. *The Economics of Abundance*. New York: Pitman. Detailed plan for the transition to a sustainable earth economy and a more just redistribution of wealth.

Walter, Edward. 1981. *The Immorality of Limiting Growth*. Albany: State University of New York Press. Effective presentation of arguments for continuing economic growth.

Woodward, Herbert N. 1977. *Capitalism Can Survive in a No-Growth Economy*. New York: Brookdale. Useful analysis.

Chapter 21   Politics and Environment

Alderson, George, and Everett Sentman. 1979. *How You Can Influence Congress: The Complete Handbook for the Citizen Lobbyist*. New York: Dutton. Superb guide.

Barnet, Richard J. 1980. *The Lean Years: Politics in an Age of Scarcity*. New York: Simon & Schuster. One of the best discussions of politics and the environment.

Caldwell, Lynton K., et al. 1976. *Citizens and the Environment: Case Studies in Popular Action*. Bloomington: Indiana University Press. Outstanding collection of case studies showing what informed and concerned citizens can do.

Cotgrove, Stephen. 1982. *Catastrophe or Cornucopia: The Environment, Politics, and the Future*. New York: John Wiley. Useful overview.

Davies, J. Clarence, III, and Barbara S. Davies. 1975. *The Politics of Pollution.* 2nd ed. Indianapolis: Pegasus. Superb introduction to pollution control by government regulation.

Elgin, Duane S., and Robert A. Bushnell. 1977. "The Limits to Complexity: Are Bureaucracies Becoming Unmanageable?" *The Futurist,* December, pp. 337—349. Excellent analysis.

Falk, Richard A. 1975. *A Study of Future Worlds.* New York: Free Press. Superb detailed plan for achieving world order.

Firestone, David B., and Frank C. Reed. 1983. *Environmental Law for Non-Lawyers.* Woburn, Mass.: Butterworths. Excellent introduction.

Friends of the Earth, et al. 1982. *Ronald Reagan and the American Environment.* Andover, Mass.: Brick House. Detailed analysis by a coalition of major environmental groups of President Reagan's attempts to weaken environmental protection.

Gardner, John W. 1970. *The Recovery of Confidence.* New York: W. W. Norton. A classic describing how to accomplish change.

Gardner, John W. 1972. *In Common Cause.* New York: W. W. Norton. Explains how to bring about political change.

Johnson, Warren. 1978. *Muddling Toward Frugality.* San Francisco: Sierra Club Books. Superb analysis of economics, politics, and environment.

Kennard, Byron. 1982. *Nothing Can Be Done, Everything Is Possible.* Andover, Mass.: Brick House. Superb discussion of bringing about change through networking.

Ophuls, William. 1977. *Ecology and the Politics of Scarcity.* San Francisco: W. H. Freeman. Outstanding book on environment and politics.

Papageorgiou, J. C. 1980. *Management Science and Environmental Problems.* Springfield, Ill.: Charles C. Thomas. Useful overview.

Petulla, Joseph M. 1980. *American Environmentalism: Values, Tactics, and Priorities.* College Station: Texas A & M University Press. Useful historical analysis.

Pirages, Dennis. 1978. *Global Ecopolitics.* North Scituate, Mass.: Duxbury Press. Excellent overview.

Rodgers, William H. 1977. *Environmental Law.* St. Paul, Minn.: West Publishing. Useful, more advanced treatment.

Rosenbaum, Walter A. 1977. *The Politics of Environmental Concern.* 2nd ed. New York: Holt, Rinehart & Winston. Useful discussion of the development of most of our current environmental legislation.

Stone, Christopher D. 1974. *Should Trees Have Standing? Toward Legal Rights for Natural Objects.* Los Altos, Calif.: William Kaufman. Useful discussion.

Tucker, William. 1982. *Progress and Privilege: America in the Age of Environmentalism.* Garden City, N.Y.: Anchor Press/Doubleday. Attacks U.S. environmentalists as elitist liberals whose primary concern about the environment is to protect their own wealth and power. This book has been used as intellectual support for the environmental policies of the Reagan administration. The author makes some good points but greatly oversimplifies environmental problems.

Tarlock, Anthony Dan. 1979. "Environmental Law: What It Is, What It Should Be." *Environmental Science and Technology,* vol. 13, no. 11, 1344–1348. Good summary.

Time magazine (staff report). 1981. "American Renewal." *Time,* February 23, pp. 34–49. Superb in-depth report on governmental reform; includes some of the suggestions given in this chapter.

Ward, Barbara. 1976. *The Home of Man.* New York: W. W. Norton. Superb discussion of how basic needs can be met in all countries within a framework of world order.

Wenner, Lettie M. 1982. *The Environmental Decade in Court.* Bloomington: Indiana University Press. Useful summary of environmental litigation during the 1970s.

Yannacone, V. J., Jr., et al. 1972. *Environmental Rights and Remedies.* San Francisco: Bancroft-Whitney. Classic book on environmental law.

Chapter 22   Environmental Ethics and Hope

Barbour, Ian G., ed. 1973. *Western Man and Environmental Ethics.* Reading, Mass.: Addison-Wesley. Outstanding collection of essays.

Berman, Morris. 1981. *The Reenchantment of the World.* Ithaca, N.Y.: Cornell University Press. Excellent analysis of what is wrong with the Western world view and how it is beginning to break down.

Bodian, Stephan. 1982. "Simple in Means, Rich in Ends: A Conversation with Arne Naess." *The Ten Directions (Zen Center Los Angeles),* Summer–Fall, pp. 7–9. Superb description of the deep ecology movement by the prominent Norwegian philosopher and environmental activist.

Bookchin, Murray. 1982. *The Ecology of Freedom.* Palo Alto, Calif.: Cheshire Books. Excellent discussion of environmental ethics.

Brown, Lester R. 1981. *Building a Sustainable Society.* New York: W. W. Norton. Superb overview of our environmental problem and plans for attaining a sustainable earth society.

Cahn, Robert. 1978. *Footprints on the Planet: A Search for an Environmental Ethic.* New York: Universe Books. Outstanding book on environmental ethics and progress by a former member of the Council on Environmental Quality.

Cailiet, G., et al. 1971. *Everyman's Guide to Ecological Living.* New York: Macmillan. Superb summary of what you can do.

Caldwell, Lynton K., et al. 1976. *Citizens and the Environment: Case Studies of Popular Action.* Bloomington: Indiana University Press. Excellent summary describing what citizens have done to improve the environment.

Callahan, Daniel. 1973. *The Tyranny of Survival.* New York: Macmillan. Magnificent analysis contrasting sustainable earth ethics and spaceship earth ethics.

Callenbach, Ernest. 1975. *Ecotopia.* Berkeley, Calif.: Banyan Tree Books. Stirring vision of what the world could be like if we move to a sustainable earth society.

Callenbach, Ernest. 1981. *Ecotopia Emerging.* Des Plaines, Ill.: Bantam Books. Superb discussion of how a utopian ecological revolution is taking place in northern California.

Capra, Fritjof. 1983. *The Turning Point.* New York: Bantam. Excellent discussion of how we are moving into a new phase of human cultural evolution built around the concepts of deep ecology.

Devall, Bill. 1981. "The Deep Ecology Movement," in J. Donald Hughes and Robert Schults, eds. *Ecological Consciousness.* Washington, D.C.: University Press of America. Excellent summary.

Devall, Bill, ed. 1984. *Voices for Deep Ecology.* Salt Lake City, Utah: Earth First. Excellent collection of writings on deep ecology.

Eckholm, Erik P. 1982. *Down to Earth: Environment and Human Needs.* New York: W. W. Norton. Superb overview of problems and possible solutions.

Ecophilosophy Newsletter. An informal newsletter published irregularly by George Sessions, Department of Philosophy, Sierra College, Rocklin, CA 95677. Excellent way to keep up on the literature and what is happening among deep ecology thinkers.

Ehrenfeld, David. 1978. *The Arrogance of Humanism.* New York: Oxford University Press. Superb discussion of environmental ethics and the dangers of the spaceship earth world view, which views the nonhuman world purely as a means to human ends.

Elder, Frederick. 1970. *Crisis in Eden: A Religious Study of Man and Environment.* Nashville, Tenn.: Abingdon Press. Reply to Lynn White's charge (1967) that Christianity is the culprit. Calls for a theology of nature based on reverence for all life.

Elgin, Duane, and Arnold Mitchell. 1977. "Voluntary Simplicity (3)." *CoEvolution Quarterly,* Summer, pp. 4–27. Superb description of the trend toward sustainable earth life-styles in the United States.

Environmental Ethics Journal, Department of Philosophy, University of Georgia, Athens, GA 30602. Excellent source of research articles.

Fackre, Gabriel. 1971. "Ecology and Theology." *Religion in Life,* vol. 40, 210–224. Superb overview.

Falk, Richard A. 1975. *A Study of Future Worlds.* New York: Free Press. Superb discussion of how to achieve a sustainable earth society.

Fanning, Odum. 1981. *Opportunities in Environmental Careers.* West Bethesda, Md.: Bradley Books. Useful survey of career possibilities and how to plan an educational curriculum for an environmental career.

Foster, Thomas W. 1981. "Amish Society." *Futurist,* December, pp. 33–40. Description of a sustainable earth community that has long existed in America.

Fox, Stephen. 1981. *John Muir and His Legacy: The American Conservation Movement.* Boston: Little, Brown. Superb history of the conservation movement in the United States with emphasis on the continuing struggle between professional conservationists like Gifford Pinchot and more radical deep ecology thinkers like John Muir.

Fritsch, Albert J. 1980. *Environmental Ethics: Choices for Concerned Citizens.* New York: Anchor Books. Outstanding book. Highly recommended.

Fritsch, Albert J., et al. 1977. *99 Ways to a Simple Lifestyle.* Bloomington: Indiana University Press. Read and pass on to others.

Fromm, Eric. 1968. *The Revolution of Hope: Toward a Humanized Technology.* New York: Harper & Row. A classic analysis of hope, going beyond the typical superficial approach.

Gardner, John W. 1970. *The Recovery of Confidence.* New York: W. W. Norton. Another classic showing how hope is the driving force of human action.

Hardin, Garrett. 1977. *The Limits of Altruism: An Ecologist's View of Survival.* Bloomington: Indiana University Press. Superb

and controversial discussion of environmental ethics.

Hayes, Denis. 1980. "The Unfinished Agenda." *Environment,* April, pp. 6–13. Excellent overview of environmental progress since 1970, and challenges for the 1980s.

Heilbroner, Robert L. 1974. *An Inquiry into the Human Prospect.* New York: W. W. Norton. Pessimistic view of our future.

Henderson, Hazel. 1978. *Creating Alternative Futures.* New York: Berkley. Excellent description of exciting experiments and trends that could lead to a sustainable earth society.

Hughes, J. Donald, and Robert Schults, ed. 1981. *Ecological Consciousness.* Washington, D.C.: University Press of America. Excellent collection of essays.

Johnson, Warren. 1978. *Muddling Toward Frugality.* San Francisco: Sierra Club Books. Important and hopeful book showing how we might make it to a sustainable earth society.

Leopold, Aldo. 1949. *A Sand County Almanac.* New York: Oxford University Press. An environmental classic describing Leopold's deep ecology land-use ethic.

Marchant, Carolyn. 1981. "Earthcare: Women and the Environmental Movement." *Environment,* vol. 23, no. 5, 6–13, 38–42. Excellent overview.

Odell, Rice. 1980. *Environmental Awakening: The New Revolution to Protect the Earth.* Cambridge, Mass.: Ballinger. Important book describing environmental progress since 1965.

Partridge, Ernest, ed. 1981. *Responsibilities for Future Generations: Environmental Ethics.* New York: Prometheus Books. Useful collection of articles.

Rifkin, Jeremy. 1980. *Entropy: A New World View.* New York: Viking Press. Important nontechnical overview of the transition to a sustainable earth society based on the second law of energy.

Roszak, Theodore. 1978. *Person/Planet.* Garden City, N.Y.: Doubleday. Stimulating discussion of a low technology, spiritual, ecological utopian vision.

Sessions, George S. 1974. "Anthropocentrism and the Environmental Crisis." *Humbolt Journal of Social Relations,* vol. 2, Fall–Winter, 1–12. Superb overview of our view of the world as a major cause of the environmental crisis.

Sessions, George. 1980. "Shallow and Deep Ecology: A Review of the Philosophical Literature," in J. Donald Hughes and Robert Schults, ed. *Ecological Consciousness.* Washington, D.C.: University Press of America. Outstanding summary of deep ecology.

Soloman, Lawrence. 1978. *The Conserver Society.* Garden City, N.Y.: Doubleday. Excellent discussion of a sustainable earth society.

Stivers, Robert L. 1976. *The Sustainable Society.* Philadelphia: Westminster. Excellent discussion of environmental ethics and a sustainable earth society.

Stokes, Bruce. 1981. *Helping Ourselves: Local Solutions to Global Problems.* New York: W. W. Norton. Superb examples.

Tiger, Lionel. 1979. *Optimism: The Biology of Hope.* New York: Simon & Schuster. Useful antidote for despair.

Valaskakis, Kimon, et al. 1979. *The Conserver Society: A Workable Alternative for the Future.* New York: Harper & Row. Useful description of a sustainable earth society.

White, Lynn, Jr. 1967. "The Historical Roots of Our Ecologic Crisis." *Science,* vol. 155, 1203–1207. Classic and controversial thesis that the root of the ecological crisis lies in the Judeo-Christian tradition.

Wilkinson, Loren, ed. 1980. *Earthkeeping: Christian Stewardship of Natural Resources.* Grand Rapids, Mich.: Erdmans. Useful collection of articles by conservative Christians.

Worster, Donald. 1977. *Nature's Economy: The Roots of Ecology.* San Francisco: Sierra Club Books. Outstanding discussion of why we must work with—not against—nature.

Enrichment Study 1
Human Impact on the Earth

Bennett, Charles F. 1975. *Man and Earth's Ecosystems.* New York: John Wiley. Excellent survey of human impact on the earth with a geographic emphasis.

Bronowski, Jacob, Jr. 1974. *The Ascent of Man.* Boston: Little Brown. Outstanding overview of human cultural change.

Dasmann, Raymond F. 1976. *Environmental Conservation.* 4th ed. New York: John Wiley. Superb overview of past and present human environmental impact on the earth.

Hyams, Edward. 1976. *Soils and Civilization.* New York: Harper & Row. Excellent discussion of the impact of our species on the earth.

Leakey, Richard E. 1981. *The Making of Mankind.* New York: E. P. Dutton. Superb and controversial presentation of human evolution.

Livingston, John A. 1973. *One Cosmic Instant.* Boston: Houghton Mifflin. Highly readable account of human cultural evolution.

Morris, Desmond. 1969. *The Human Zoo.* New York: McGraw-Hill. Interesting and provocative view of human nature.

Mumford, Lewis. 1962. *The Transformations of Man.* New York: Collier. Superb analysis of human cultural change.

Sears, Paul B. 1980. *Deserts on the March.* Norman: University of Oklahoma Press. Probably the best account of how human activities have contributed to the spread of deserts.

Spencer, J. E., and W. L. Thomas. 1977. *Introducing Cultural Geography.* 2nd ed. Excellent account of how human activities have affected the earth's surface and its resources.

Tiger, Lionel, and Robin Fox. 1971. *The Imperial Animal.* New York: Delta. Useful analysis of human behavior.

Enrichment Study 2 The Limits-to-Growth Debate

Boughey, Arthur S. 1976. *Strategy for Survival: An Exploration of the Limits to Further Population and Industrial Growth.* Menlo Park, Calif.: W. A. Benjamin. Excellent introductory text explaining and evaluating computer models.

Boyd, Robert. 1972. "World Dynamics: A Note." *Science,* vol. 177, 516–519. By adding an exponentially growing technology function to the Forrester model, disaster is averted.

Clark, J., and S. Cole. 1975. *Global Simulation Models: A Comparative Survey.* New York: John Wiley. Useful comparison and evaluation of global models.

Cole, H.S.O., et al., eds. 1973. *Models of Doom: A Critique of "The Limits to Growth."* New York: Universe Books. Detailed critical analysis of the Forrester-Meadows world model by a British systems analysis team. See also in this book the reply to their critique by Meadows et al. (pp. 217–240).

Council on Environmental Quality. 1980. *The Global 2000 Report to the President,* vol. 2. Washington, D.C.: Government Printing Office. Useful model with projections of world food, population, land, water, energy, minerals, and pollution problems to the year 2000.

Forrester, Jay W. 1971a. "Counterintuitive Behavior of Social Systems." *Technology Review,* vol. 73, no. 3. Readable summary of results of the first world model.

Forrester, Jay W. 1971b. *World Dynamics.* Cambridge, Mass.: Wright-Allen Press. Detailed description of the first world model.

Kahn, Herman, et al. 1976. *The Next 200 Years: A Scenario for America and the World.* New York: William Morrow. A dazzling example of linear extrapolation by a leading cornucopian. Unfortunately, the assumptions and the reasoning used to arrive at the conclusions generated by this intuitive mental model are not clearly specified.

Meadows, Dennis L., et al. 1974. *The Dynamics of Growth in a Finite World.* Cambridge, Mass.: M.I.T. Press. Detailed technical documentation of the second world model, presented in popularized form as *The Limits to Growth.*

Meadows, Donella H., et al. 1972. *The Limits to Growth.* New York: Universal Books. Popular description of the second world model.

Meadows, Donella et al. 1982. *Groping in the Dark: The First Decade of Global Modeling.* New York: John Wiley. Superb summary and evaluation of the successes and failures of global models developed by various teams since *The Limits to Growth* was published.

Mesarovic, Mihajlo and Eduard Pestel. 1974. *Mankind at the Turning Point.* New York: E. P. Dutton. Popular presentations of a regional model of the world. Compare it with *The Limits to Growth.*

Oltmans, Willem L. 1974. *On Growth.* New York: G. P. Putnam. Useful collection of interviews of 70 of the world's great thinkers in many disciplines on the debate over the Forrester-Meadows model.

Starr, Chauncey, and Richard Rudman. 1973. "Parameters of Technological Growth," *Science,* vol. 182, 358–364. Presentation of the view that technology can grow exponentially and thus avert the problems projected by the Forrester-Meadows and Mesarovic-Pestel models.

Enrichment Study 3 Health and Environmental Effects of Nuclear War

Adams, Ruth, and Susan Culen, eds. 1982. *The Final Epidemic: Physicians and Scientists on Nuclear War.* Chicago: University of Chicago Press. Excellent summary of the effects of nuclear war by physicians and scientists.

Broad, William J. 1983. "The Chaos Factor." *Science 83,* January–February, pp. 41–49. Very useful nontechnical summary of the effect of EMP on the electric power and telecommunications systems of the United States.

Caldicott, Helen. 1979. *Nuclear Madness: What Can You Do?* New York: Bantam Books.

Excellent summary by a physician and early leader of the nuclear freeze movement.

Chivian, Eric, et al., eds. 1982. *Last Aid: The Medical Dimensions of Nuclear War.* San Francisco: W. H. Freeman. Chilling description by health professionals of the medical consequences of nuclear war.

Ehrlich, Anne. 1984. "Nuclear Winter: A Forecast of the Climatic and Biological Effects of Nuclear War," *Bulletin of the Atomic Scientists,* April, pp. 1S–15S. Excellent summary of findings of a 1983 conference of leading atmospheric scientists and biologists.

Ehrlich, Paul R., et al. 1983. "Long-Term Biological Consequences of Nuclear War," *Science,* vol. 222, 1293–1299. Superb analysis by a team of experts.

Grover, Herbert D. 1984. "The Climatic and Biological Consequences of Nuclear War," *Environment,* vol. 26, no. 4, 4–13, 34–38. Outstanding summary.

Hiroshima and Nagasaki. 1981. New York: Basic Books. The most complete description available of the effects of the atomic attack on these two cities written by 34 Japanese physicians, physicists, and social scientists.

Katz, Arthur M. 1982. *Life After Nuclear War.* Cambridge, Mass.: Ballinger. Superb description of the effects of nuclear war.

Lovins, Amory B., and L. Hunter Lovins. 1980. *Energy/War: Breaking the Nuclear Link.* San Francisco: Friends of the Earth. Important book carefully documenting the link between the spread of nuclear power plants and research reactors and the spread of nuclear weapons.

Office of Technology Assessment. 1981. *The Effects of Nuclear War.* Washington, D.C.: Government Printing Office. Very informative and detailed analysis of the effects of nuclear war on the United States and the Soviet Union.

Peterson, Jeannie, and Don Hinrichsen, eds. 1982. *Nuclear War: The Aftermath.* New York: Pergamon Press. Very informative description of the worldwide effects of nuclear war by members of the Royal Swedish Academy of Sciences.

Sartori, Leo. 1983. "When the Bomb Falls." *Bulletin of the Atomic Scientists,* June–July, pp. 40–47. Superb summary of the effects of nuclear war.

Schell, Jonathan. 1982. *The Fate of the Earth.* New York: Alfred A. Knopf. Outstanding attempt to make us think about the unthinkable effects of nuclear war.

Turco R. P. et al. 1983. "Nuclear Winter: Global Consequences of Multiple Nuclear Explosions," *Science,* vol. 222, 1283–1291. Outstanding analysis by a team of experts.

Zuckerman, Solly. 1982. *Nuclear Illusion and*

Reality. New York: Viking Press. Another excellent work describing the horrors of nuclear war.

Enrichment Study 4 Space: High Frontier or Garbage Dump?

Deudney, Daniel. 1982. *Space: The High Frontier in Perspective*. Washington, D. C.: Worldwatch Institute. Superb analysis of human activities in space.

O'Neill, Gerald K. 1978. *The High Frontier: Human Colonies in Space*. 2nd ed. New York: Bantam. Well-thought-out proposal for building self-sufficient colonies in space.

O'Neill, Gerald K. 1982. *2081: A Hopeful View of the Human Future*. New York: Simon & Schuster. Visionary proposals for using space to solve many of the earth's problems.

Enrichment Study 5 Are We Changing the World's Climate?

Allen, Richard. 1980. "The Impact of CO_2 on World Climate." *Environment*, vol. 22, no. 10, 6–38. Excellent overview.

Bolin, Bert. 1977. "The Impact of Production and Use of Energy in Global Climate." In Jack M. Hollander, et al. eds. *Annual Review of Energy*, vol. 2. Palo Alto, Calif.: Annual Reviews. Superb overview of potential effects of human activities on climate.

Bryson, Reid A., and Thomas J. Murray. 1977. *Climates of Hunger: Mankind and the World's Changing Weather*. Madison: University of Wisconsin Press. Excellent summary of the position that the world may be cooling.

Calder, Nigel. 1974. *The Weather Machine: How Our Weather Works and Why It Is Changing*. New York: Viking Press. Readable overview with emphasis on global cooling.

Clark, William C., ed. 1982. *Carbon Dioxide Review 1982*. New York: Oxford University Press. Summary of the CO_2 problem by a group of experts.

Council on Environmental Quality. 1981. *Global Energy Futures and the Carbon Dioxide Problem*. Washington, D.C.: Council on Environmental Quality. Superb overview.

Environmental Protection Agency. 1983. *Can We Delay a Greenhouse Warming?* Washington, D.C.: EPA. Useful evaluation of effects of policies to delay the effects of increasing CO_2 levels.

Gribbin, John. 1982. *Future Weather and the Greenhouse Effect*. New York: Delacorte Press. Useful overview of factors affecting global climate and the greenhouse effect.

Holdren, John P. 1971. "Global Thermal Pollution." In J. P. Holdren and P. R. Ehrlich, eds., *Global Ecology*. New York: Harcourt Brace Jovanovich. Clear summary of the principles and calculations involved in predicting the effects of human heat inputs on climate.

Kellogg, William W., and R. Schware. 1981. *Climate Change and Society: Consequences of Increasing Atmospheric Carbon Dioxide*. Boulder, Colo.: Westview Press. Outstanding overview.

Landsberg, Helmut E., 1981. *The Urban Climate*. New York: Academic Press. Useful overview of research.

Lovins, Amory B., et al. 1981. *Least-Cost Energy: Solving the CO_2 Problem*. Andover, Mass.: Brick House. Excellent summary of how the CO_2 problem could be minimized by a combination of energy conservation and a switch to solar, wind, hydro, biomass, and other forms of renewable energy.

National Academy of Sciences. 1983. *Changing Climate*. Washington, D.C.: National Academy Press. Excellent overview of the CO_2 problem.

Roberts, Walter Orr, and Henry Lansford. 1979. *The Climate Mandate*. San Francisco: W. H. Freeman. Superb discussion of climate and possible climatic effects of human activities.

Rose, David J., et al. 1984. "Reducing the Problem of Global Warming," *Technology Review*, May–June, pp. 49–58. Excellent overview.

Schneider, Stephen H. 1976. *The Genesis Strategy: Climate and Global Survival*. New York: Plenum Press. Outstanding overview of possible effects of human activities on climate, with a detailed plan for action.

Schneider, Stephen H., and Robert S. Chen. 1980. "Carbon Dioxide Warming and Coastline Flooding: Physical Factors and Climatic Impact." In Jack M. Hollander, et al. eds., *Annual Review of Energy*, vol. 5, pp. 107–140. Palo Alto, Calif.: Annual Reviews. One of the best summaries of the CO_2 problem and its possible effects.

Schneider, S. H., and R. S. Londer. 1984. *The Coevolution of Climate and Life*. San Francisco: Sierra Club Books. Excellent overview of possible effects of human activities on global climate.

Woodwell, George M., et al. 1983. "Global Deforestation: Contribution to Atmospheric Carbon Dioxide." *Science*, vol. 222, 1081–1086. Excellent overview of effect of land-clearing activities on CO_2 levels.

Enrichment Study 6 Species Interactions in Ecosystems

See the Readings for Chapter 3.

Schoener, Thomas W. 1982. "The Controversy Over Interspecific Competition." *American Scientist*, vol. 70, 586–595. Excellent summary of the controversy over the relative importance of interspecific competition and predation.

Enrichment Study 7 Environmental Health and Human Disease

Beattie, Edward J. 1980. *Toward the Conquest of Cancer*. New York: Crown Publishers. Superb analysis showing how 40 to 50 percent of cancers can be prevented and about 50 percent can be cured.

Benenson, A. S., ed. 1979. *Control of Communicable Diseases in Man*. 13th ed. Washington, D.C.: American Public Health Association. Basic reference.

Campbell, T. C. 1980. "Chemical Carcinogens and Human Risk Assessment." *Federation Proceedings*, vol. 39, no. 8, 2467–2484. Excellent overview.

Davis, Devra L. 1981. "Cancer in the Workplace: The Case for Prevention," *Environment*, vol. 23, no. 6, 25–37. Excellent overview.

Derr, Patrick, et al. 1981. "Worker/Public Protection: The Double Standard," *Environment*, vol. 23, no. 7, 6–15, 31–36. Useful overview showing how standards for protecting the general public from carcinogens and other hazardous chemicals in the environment are much stricter than those protecting workers.

Doll, Richard, and Richard Petro. 1981. "The Causes of Cancer: Quantitative Estimates of Avoidable Risks of Cancer in America Today," *Journal of the National Cancer Institute*. June. Useful summary of cancer risk factors showing that diet and smoking together account for about 65 percent of all cancer deaths. Their estimate that about 4 percent of cancer deaths are related to occupational exposure is considered to be too low by experts such as Samuel Epstein (1979) and by the authors of a 1978 study conducted jointly by the National Cancer Institute, the National Institute of Environmental Health Sciences, and the National Institute for Occupational Safety and Health.

Eckholm, Erik P. 1977. *The Picture of Health: Environmental Sources of Disease*. New York:

W. W. Norton. Superb overview of environmental health problems throughout the world.

Eckholm, Erik P. 1978. *Cutting Tobacco's Toll*. Washington, D.C.: Worldwatch Institute. Superb overview of smoking problems and possible solutions in the United States and throughout the world.

Epstein, Samuel S. 1979. *The Politics of Cancer*. Garden City, N.Y.: Anchor/Doubleday. Excellent overview of cancer by an expert, with emphasis on occupational exposure to carcinogens.

Goldsmith, Edward. 1980. "The Ecology of Health." *The Ecologist*, vol. 10, nos. 6–7, 225–245. Eloquent summary of an ecological—as opposed to a modern medical—approach to health.

Gorman, James. 1979. *Hazards to Your Health: The Problem of Environmental Disease*. New York: New York Academy of Sciences. Superb overview.

Highland, Joseph, et al. 1980. *Malignant Neglect*. New York: Random House. Excellent discussion of cancer and the environment.

Humphrey, J. H. 1977. "The Challenge of Parasitic Diseases." *Bulletin of the Atomic Scientists*, March, pp. 46–53. Useful overview of tropical diseases.

National Academy of Sciences. 1982. *Diet, Nutrition, and Cancer*. Washington, D.C.: National Academy Press. Authoritative review showing relationships between diet and cancer.

Reif, Arnold E. 1981. "The Causes of Cancer," *American Scientist*, vol. 69, 437–447. Excellent overview.

Richards, Victor. 1978. *Cancer, the Wayward Cell: Its Origins, Nature, and Treatment*. 2nd ed. Los Angeles: University of California Press. Outstanding summary.

Stein, Jane. 1977. "Water for the Wealthy." *Environment*, vol. 19, no. 4, 6–14. Good overview of infectious waterborne diseases.

Enrichment Study 8   Birth Control Methods

Baldwin, Wendy H. 1976. "Adolescent Pregnancy and Childbearing—Growing Concerns for Americans." *Population Bulletin*, vol. 31, no. 2, 1–34. Excellent overview.

Djerassi, Carl. 1980. *The Politics of Contraception*. New York: W. W. Norton. Inside view by an expert of how drug companies and the government see the development of new contraceptive drugs and devices.

Forrest, Jacqueline D., and Stanley K.

Henshaw. 1983. "What U.S. Women Think and Do About Contraception," *Family Planning Perspectives*, vol. 15, no. 4, 157–166. Useful survey of contraceptive use in the United States.

Guttmacher, Alan F. 1970. *Birth Control and Love*. New York: Bantam. Excellent description of birth control methods by a pioneer in the field.

Hatcher, Robert A., et al. 1982. *It's Your Choice*. New York: Irvington Press. Excellent overview of contraceptive methods.

Korenbrot, Carol C. 1980. "New Directions for Contraception." *Technology Review*, November–December, pp. 53–62. Excellent summary of possibilities.

Segal, Sheldon J., and Olivia S. Nordberg. 1977. "Fertility Regulation Technology: Status and Prospects." *Population Bulletin*, vol. 31, no. 6, pp. 1–25. Excellent overview of existing and possible future methods of birth control.

Stokes, Bruce. 1980. *Men and Family Planning*. Washington, D.C.: Worldwatch Institute. Superb discussion of the male's role and responsibilities in preventing unwanted births.

U.S. Office of Technology Assessment. 1982. *World Population and Fertility Planning Technologies: The Next 20 Years*. Washington, D.C.: Government Printing Office. Excellent survey of prospects for development of new contraceptives between 1980 and 2000.

Enrichment Study 9   The Food Additives Controversy

Benarde, Melvin A. 1971. *The Chemicals We Eat*. New York: American Heritage Press. Readable introduction to additives by a prominent health scientist. A moderate view, weighted somewhat toward the food industry.

Chemical and Engineering News staff report. 1977. "Should the Delaney Clause Be Changed? A Debate on Food Additive Safety, Animal Tests, and Cancer," *Chemical and Engineering News*, June 27, pp. 24–46. Informative debate by four experts on the Delaney clause.

Jacobson, Michael F. 1972. *Eater's Digest: The Consumer's Factbook of Food Additives*. Garden City, N.Y.: Doubleday. Outstanding moderate overview. Consult this paperback book to determine which additives you might want to avoid.

Mellinkoff, Sherman H. 1973. "Chemical Intervention," *Scientific American*, vol. 229, no. 3, pp. 102–112. Excellent overview of overuse of drugs and food additives.

National Academy of Sciences. 1982. *The Health Effects of Nitrate, Nitrite, and N-Nitroso Compounds*. Washington, D.C.: National Academy of Sciences. Expert evaluation of this potential problem, with recommendations.

Verrett, Jacqueline, and Jean Carper. 1974. *Eating May Be Hazardous To Your Health*. New York: Simon & Schuster. Excellent overview of the potential dangers of food additives and the problems of consumer protection.

Whelan, Elizabeth M., and Frederick J. Stare. 1983. *The 100% Natural, Purely Organic, Chloresterol-Free, Megavitamin, Low-Carbohydrate Nutrition Hoax*. New York: Atheneum Press. Presentation heavily weighted toward the food industry that debunks concern over the dangers of food additives and pesticides and derides people who grow and eat health foods and use vitamin supplements.

Winter, Ruth A. 1978. *A Consumer's Dictionary of Food Additives*. New York: Crown Publishers. Extremely useful guide to additives, suggesting which ones you may wish to avoid.

Enrichment Study 10   Noise Pollution

Carmen, Richard. 1977. *Our Endangered Hearing*. Emmaus, Pa.: Rodale Press. Excellent overview of noise problems, effects, and possible solutions.

Environmental Protection Agency. 1977. *Toward a National Strategy for Noise Control*. Washington, D.C.: Government Printing Office. Excellent plan for what the United States needs to do. Implementing this plan is the problem.

Environmental Protection Agency. 1978. *Noise: A Health Problem*. Washington, D.C.: Environmental Protection Agency. Good overview of the problems and effects of excessive noise.

Leepson, Marc. 1980. "Noise Control," *Editorial Research Reports*, Feb. 22, pp. 83–96. Excellent overview.

Lipscomb, David M. 1974. *Noise: The Unwanted Sound*. New York: Nelson-Hall. Authoritative review of the health hazards of excessive noise and methods for noise control.

Milne, Anthony. 1979. *Noise Pollution: Impact and Countermeasures*. New York: David Charles. Superb basic reference.

National Academy of Sciences. 1981. *Effects on Human Health from Long-Term Exposures to Noise*. Washington, D.C.: National Academy of Sciences. Excellent overview of research studies on the effects of noise.

Thumann, Albert, and Richard K. Miller. 1976. *Secrets of Noise Control.* Atlanta: Firmont Press. Useful overview with good tips.

Enrichment Study 11 Land, Energy, and Water Resources in the Rocky Mountain Region: A Case Study

Ballard, Steven C., et al. 1982. *Water and Western Energy.* Boulder, Colo.: Westview Press. Excellent analysis.

Harte, John, and Mohammed El-Gasseir. 1978. "Energy and Water." *Science,* vol. 199, 623–634. Superb analysis of the conflict over energy, land, and water.

Rand, Patricia, J., ed. 1982. *Land and Water Issues Related to Energy Development.* Woburn, Mass.: Ann Arbor Science Publishers. Useful analysis.

U.S. Senate. 1976. *Land Use and Energy: A Study of Interrelationships.* Washington, D.C.: Committee on Interior and Insular Affairs. Analysis of land use, water, and energy resources in the Rocky Mountain region.

Enrichment Study 12 Cadmium, Lead, and Mercury in the Environment

D'Itri, Patricia R., and Frank M. D'Itri. 1977. *Mercury Contamination.* New York: John Wiley. Superb summary.

Harrison, R. M., and D. P. H. Laxon. 1981. *Lead Pollution: Causes and Control.* London: Chapman and Hall/Methuen. Excellent overview.

Hiatt, V., and J. E. Huff. 1975. "The Environmental Impact of Cadmium." *International Journal of Environmental Studies,* vol. 7, no. 4, 277–285. Very good overview.

Jenkins, Dale W. 1972. "The Toxic Metals in Your Future—And Your Past." *Smithsonian,* vol. 3, no. 1, 62–69. Superb nontechnical summary.

McCaull, Julian. 1971. "Building a Shorter Life." *Environment,* vol. 13, no. 7, 3–41. Superb review of the cadmium problem.

Montague, Katherine, and Peter Montague. 1976. *No World Without End: The New Threats to Our Biosphere.* New York: G. P. Putnam. Excellent overview of threats from lead, mercury, cadmium, and other toxic metals.

National Academy of Sciences. 1980. *Lead in the Human Environment.* Washington, D.C.: National Academy of Sciences. Authoritative review.

National Science Foundation. 1977. *Lead in the Environment.* Washington, D.C.: National Science Foundation. Authoritative review.

Needleman, Herbert L. 1980. "Lead Exposure and Human Health: Recent Data on an Ancient Problem." *Technology Review,* March–April, pp. 39–45. Excellent overview.

Ratcliffe, J. M. 1981. *Lead in Man and the Environment.* New York: Halsted Press. Excellent technical summary.

Schroeder, Henry A. 1974. *The Poisons Around Us: Toxic Metals in Food, Air, and Water.* Bloomington: Indiana University Press. Superb summary by an expert toxicologist.

Smith, W. Eugene, and Aileen M. Smith. 1975. *Minamata.* New York: Holt, Rinehart & Winston. Well-researched description of methyl mercury poisonings in Japan.

Enrichment Study 13 Solid Waste and Hazardous Wastes

Barnes, Donald. 1983. "An Overview on Dioxin." *EPA Journal,* November, pp. 16–19. Excellent summary by an EPA science advisor.

Barnhart, Benjamin J. 1978. "The Disposal of Hazardous Wastes." *Environmental Science & Technology,* vol. 12, no. 10, 1132–1136. Good overview.

Berry, Stephen R. 1972. "Recycling, Thermodynamics and Environmental Thrift." *Bulletin of the Atomic Scientists,* May, pp. 8–15. Recycling is not always the answer and must be coupled with other approaches.

Bond, Desmond H. 1984. "At-Sea Incineration of Hazardous Wastes." *Environmental Science & Technology,* vol. 18, no.5, 148A–152A. Raises concerns about the risks from using this option.

Brown, Lester R., et al. 1984. *State of the World 1984.* New York: W. W. Norton. Chapter 6 is an excellent summary of recycling.

Brown, Michael. 1979. *Laying Waste: The Poisoning of America by Toxic Wastes.* New York: Pantheon. Critical attack with detailed discussion of the Love Canal disaster.

Chemical and Engineering News staff report. 1983. "Dioxin Report." *Chemical and Engineering News,* June 6, pp. 20–64. Excellent series of articles.

Citizens' Advisory Committee on Environmental Quality. 1976. *A New Look at Recycling Waste Paper.* Washington, D.C.: Citizens' Advisory Committee on Environmental Quality. Excellent discussion of paper recycling problems and possibilities.

Efron, Edith. 1984. *The Apocalyptics.* New York: Simon & Schuster. Contends that concern over hazardous wastes, pollutants, and other toxic and hazardous materials has been overblown and has little or no scientific foundation.

Environmental Protection Agency. 1976. *Decision-Maker's Guide in Solid Waste Management.* Washington, D.C.: Government Printing Office. Superb analysis of advantages and disadvantages for the major methods of solid waste collection, disposal, and high-technology resource recovery.

Environmental Protection Agency. 1977. *Fourth Report to Congress: Resource Recovery and Waste Reduction.* Washington, D.C.: Environmental Protection Agency. Superb analysis of solid waste disposal, high- and low-technology resource recovery, and resource conservation in the United States.

Environmental Protection Agency. 1980. *Damages and Threats Caused by Hazardous Material.* Washington, D.C.: Environmental Protection Agency. Authoritative overview.

Environmental Protection Agency. 1980. *Hazardous Waste Generation and Commercial Hazardous Waste Management Capacity: An Assessment.* Washington, D.C.: Environmental Protection Agency. Useful source of data.

Epstein, Samuel S., et al. 1982. *Hazardous Waste in America.* San Francisco: Sierra Club Books. Superb analysis of the problems, along with suggested solutions.

Franchot, Peter. 1978. *Bottles and Cans: The Story of the Vermont Deposit Law.* Washington, D.C.: National Wildlife Federation. Excellent summary.

General Accounting Office. 1981. *Hazardous Wastes Sites Pose Investigation, Evaluation, Scientific, and Legal Problems.* Washington, D.C.: Government Printing Office.

Hay, Alistair. 1982. *The Chemical Scythe: Lessons of 2,4,5-T and Dioxin.* New York: Plenum Press. Excellent overview.

Hayes, Denis. 1978. *Repairs, Reuse, Recycling—First Steps Toward a Sustainable Society.* Washington, D.C.: Worldwatch Institute. Superb overview of resource recovery and conservation.

Kriebel, David. 1981. "The Dioxins: Toxic and Still Troublesome." *Environment,* January–February, pp. 6–13. Excellent overview.

LaDou, Joseph. 1984. "The Not-So-Clean Business of Making Chips." *Technology Review,* May–June, pp. 24–36. Excellent survey of hazardous waste problem in the microelectronics industry.

League of Women Voters Education Fund. 1981. *A Hazardous Waste Primer.* Washington, D.C.: League of Women Voters. Excellent overview.

Moore, Dennis. 1982. "Recycling: Where Are We Now?" *New Shelter*, February, pp. 56–69. Excellent overview.

Morrell, David, and Christopher Magorian. 1982. *Siting Hazardous Waste Facilities: Local Opposition and the Myth of Preemption.* Cambridge, Mass.: Ballinger. Excellent analysis of the politics of siting.

Nader, Ralph, et al. 1981. *Who's Poisoning America?* San Francisco: Sierra Club Books. Useful description of several case studies.

National Academy of Sciences. 1983. *Transportation of Hazardous Materials: Toward a National Strategy.* Washington, D.C.: National Academy Press. Excellent overview and source of data.

National Academy of Sciences. 1984. *Toxicity Testing: Strategies to Determine Needs and Priorities.* Washington, D.C.: National Academy Press. Study showing that most chemicals in use in the United States have not been tested adequately for toxicity.

Office of Technology Assessment. 1983. *Technologies and Management Strategies for Hazardous Waste Controls.* Washington, D.C.: Government Printing Office. Excellent evaluation.

Purcell, Arthur H. 1980. *The Waste Watchers: A Citizen's Handbook for Conserving Energy and Resources.* Garden City, N.Y.: Anchor Press/Doubleday. Superb guide for achieving a low-waste society.

Randers, Jorgen, and Dennis L. Meadows. 1972. "The Dynamics of Solid Waste." *Technology Review,* March–April, pp. 20–32. Computer simulation of various proposed solutions to the solid waste problem.

Regenstein, Lewis. 1982. *America the Poisoned.* Washington, D.C.: Acropolis Books. Useful description of the hazardous wastes problem.

Rose, David J., et al. 1972. "Physics Looks at Waste Management." *Physics Today,* February, pp. 32–41. Outstanding evaluation of alternative solutions.

Seaborg, Glenn T. 1974. "The Recycle Society of Tomorrow." *The Futurist,* June, pp. 108–115. Readable and stirring vision of what a society based on recycling and resource conservation would be like.

Senkan, Selim M., and Nancy W. Stauffer. 1981. "What To Do with Hazardous Waste?" *Technology Review,* November–December, pp. 34–47. Excellent summary.

Small, W. E. 1971. *Third Pollution: The National Problem of Solid Waste Disposal.* New York: Praeger. Somewhat dated but still a useful analysis of solid waste problems and possible solutions.

Enrichment Study 14 Controlling Eutrophication and Agricultural Water Pollution

Aldrich, S. R. 1972. "Some Effects of Crop Production on Environmental Quality." *BioScience,* vol. 22, no. 2, 90–95. Contains an excellent summary of the contributions of agriculture to water pollution, a response to Commoner's (1971) charges on agricultural pollution, and an appeal for cooperation rather than polarization.

American Society of Agricultural Engineers. 1976. *Managing Livestock Wastes.* St. Joseph, Mo.: American Society of Agricultural Engineers. Very useful summary.

Commoner, Barry. 1971. *The Closing Circle: Nature, Man and Technology.* New York: Alfred A. Knopf. See Chapter 6 on eutrophication and Chapter 5 on the nitrate problem.

Edmondson, W. T. 1973. "Lake Washington." In Charles R. Goldman et al., eds., *Environmental Quality and Water Development.* San Francisco: W. H. Freeman. Excellent summary of this success story by one of its planners.

Edmondson, W. T. 1975. "Fresh Water Pollution." In William W. Murdoch, ed., *Environment: Resources, Pollution and Society.* Sunderland, Mass.: Sinauer. Fine summary of eutrophication by an expert.

Grundy, R. D. 1971. "Strategies for Control of Man-Made Eutrophication." *Environmental Science & Technology,* vol. 5, no. 12, 1184–1190. Excellent overview.

Hasler, Arthur D. 1970. "Man-Induced Eutrophication of Lakes." In S. Fred Singer, ed., *Global Effects of Environmental Pollution.* New York: Springer-Verlag. Superb summary by a prominent limnologist.

Hutchinson, G. Evelyn. 1973. "Eutrophication." *American Scientist,* July, pp. 269–279. Outstanding summary.

Lee, G. Fred, et al. 1978. "Eutrophication of Water Bodies: Insights for an Age-Old Problem." *Environmental Science & Technology,* vol. 12, no. 8, 900–908. Superb overview.

Loehr, Raymond C., ed. 1977. *Food, Fertilizer, and Agricultural Residues.* Ann Arbor, Mich.: Ann Arbor Science Publishers. Excellent series of papers on agricultural pollution, problems, and possible solutions.

Loehr, Raymond C., et al. 1979. *Best Management Practices for Agriculture and Silviculture.* Ann Arbor, Mich.: Ann Arbor Science Publishers. Authoritative source.

Merkel, James A. 1981. *Managing Livestock Wastes.* Westport, Conn.: AVI Publishing. Authoritative source.

Soil Conservation Society of America. 1971. "A Primer of Agricultural Pollution." Reprint from *Journal of Soil Conservation,* March–April. Soil Conservation Society of America, 7515 Northeast Ankeny Road, Ankeny, IA 50021. Readable summary.

Stanford, G., et al. 1970. *Fertilizer Use and Water Quality.* Department of Agriculture, Agricultural Research Service, ARS 41–168. Washington, D.C.: Government Printing Office. Excellent summary of fertilizer problems.

Stoker, H. S., and Spencer L. Seager. 1976. *Environmental Chemistry: Air and Water Pollution.* 2nd ed. Glenview, Ill.: Scott, Foresman. See Chapter 9 for a superb summary of the phosphate detergent problem.

Viets, Frank G., Jr. 1971. "Water Quality in Relation to Farm Use of Fertilizer." *BioScience,* vol. 21, no. 10, 460–467. Basic arguments by a prominent agriculturalist against Commoner's (1971) position.

Wadleigh, C. H., and Clarence S. Britt. 1970. "Issues in Food Production and Clean Water." In T. L. Willrich and G. E. Smith, eds., *Agricultural Practices and Water Pollution.* Ames: Iowa State University Press. Superb introduction to agricultural pollution problems.

Enrichment Study 15   How to Influence Elected Officials

Alderson, George, and Everett Sentman. 1979. *How You Can Influence Congress: The Complete Handbook for the Citizen Lobbyist.* New York: E. P. Dutton. Superb guide.

Gardner, John W. 1972. *In Common Cause.* New York: W. W. Norton. Classic book on citizen political action by the founder of Common Cause, the citizens' lobby.

Green, Mark J., et al. 1972. *Who Runs Congress?* New York: Bantam/Grossman. See especially Chapter 9, "Taking on Congress: A Primer for Citizen Action." An outstanding book.

League of Women Voters. Annual. *When You Write to Washington.* League of Women Voters, 1730 M St., N.W., Washington, D.C. 20005. The best guide on how to write elected officials.

Morris, David, and Karl Hess. 1975. *Neighborhood Power: The New Localism.* Boston: Beacon Press. Excellent guide for local action.

Nader, Ralph, and Donald Ross. 1971. *Action for a Change: A Student's Manual for Public Interest Organizing.* New York: Grossman. How to form a PIRG group.

Peters, Charles. 1980. *How Washington Really Works*. Reading, Mass.: Addison-Wesley. Superb and revealing guide.

Pezzuti, Thomas. 1974. *You Can Fight City Hall and Win*. Los Angeles: Sherbourne Press. Fact-filled guide.

Robertson, James, and John Lewallen, eds. 1975. *The Grass Roots Primer: The Spare Time, Low Cost, At Home Guide to Environmental Action*. New York: Charles Scribner's. Superb guide.

Ross, Donald K. 1973. *A Public Citizen's Action Manual*. New York: Grossman. Superb guide.

Smith, Dorothy. 1979. *In Our Own Interest (A Handbook for the Citizen Lobbyist in State Legislatures)*. Seattle: Madrona. Outstanding handbook.

Glossary

Abiotic   nonliving.

Abyssal zone   bottom zone of the ocean. compare *Bathyal zone, Euphotic zone.*

Acid deposition   combination of wet deposition from the atmosphere of droplets of sulfuric acid and nitric acid dissolved in rain and snow and dry deposition from the atmosphere of particles of sulfate and nitrate salts. These acids and salts are formed when water vapor in the air reacts with the air pollutants sulfur dioxide (SO_2) and nitrogen dioxide (NO_2).

Acid fog   droplets of sulfuric acid and nitric acid mixed with water vapor near the ground.

Acute disease   an infectious disease (such as measles, whooping cough, typhoid fever) that normally lasts for a relatively short time before the victim either recovers or dies.

Aerobic organism   organism that requires oxygen to live.

Aerosols   liquid and solid particles suspended in air.

Age structure (age distribution)   number or percentage of persons at each age level in a population.

Age structure diagram   a horizontal bar graph comparing the proportions of males and females in different age groups in the population.

Air pollution   air that contains one or more chemicals or possesses a physical condition like heat in high enough concentrations to harm humans, other animals, vegetation, or materials.

Air quality standard (AQS)   federally prescribed level of a pollutant in the outside air that should not be exceeded during a specified time in a specified geographical area.

Airshed   a region that shares a common air supply. Because of the nature of air, an airshed is not a precise physical division like a watershed but a political convenience for dealing with air problems that cross municipal and state lines.

Albedo   fraction of the incident light that strikes a surface or body that is reflected from it. A measure of the reflectivity of the earth and its atmosphere.

Alga (algae)   simple one-celled or many-celled plant(s), usually aquatic, capable of carrying on photosynthesis.

Algae bloom   population explosion of algae in surface waters.

Alpha particle   form of radiation consisting of a helium nucleus containing two protons and two neutrons, with no electrons outside the nucleus.

Alveoli   tiny sacs at the end of the bronchiole tubes in the lungs, numbering in the hundreds of millions. Oxygen in the air passes through their walls to combine with hemoglobin in the blood, and carbon dioxide passes from the blood back through the alveoli walls for exhaling.

Ambient air   surrounding outdoor air.

Ambient quality standard (AQS)   maximum level of a specific pollutant allowed by the federal government in the air, water, soil, or food. May vary from region to region depending on conditions. compare *Emission standard.*

Amino acids   basic building block molecules of proteins. A long chain of certain amino acid molecules link together chemically for a specific protein molecule.

Anerobic organism   organism that does not require oxygen to live.

Animal feedlot   confined area where hundreds or thousands of livestock animals are fattened for sale to slaughterhouses and meat processors.

Appropriate (soft) technology   technology that is small, simple, decentralized, and inexpensive, and can preserve meaningful work for people. It conserves matter and energy resources and produces as little pollution as possible. compare *High (hard) technology.*

Aquaculture   growing and harvesting of fish and shellfish in land-based ponds.

Aquifer   permeable layers of underground rock or sand that hold or transmit groundwater below the water table.

Area surface mining   a type of mining in which minerals such as coal and phosphate are removed by cutting deep trenches in flat or rolling terrain.

Artesian well   a water well drilled into a pressurized aquifer where the hydraulic pressure is so great that the water flows freely out of the well without pumping.

Asthma   see *Bronchial asthma.*

Atmosphere   a region of gases and particulate matter extending above the earth's surface.

Atoms   extremely small particles that are the basic building blocks of all matter.

Attractant   sound, light, or sex lure used in pest control to confuse pests so they can't find mates or to draw them into traps containing toxic chemicals.

Autotrophic organism   an organism that uses solar energy to photosynthesize organic food substances and other organic chemicals from carbon dioxide and water. compare *Heterotrophic organism.*

Background radiation   radiation in the environment from naturally radioactive materials and from cosmic rays entering the atmosphere.

Bacteria   smallest living organisms; with fungi, they comprise the decomposer level of the food chain.

Bathyal zone   middle or open-water zone in an ocean below the level of light penetration. compare *Abyssal zone, Euphotic zone.*

Beta particle   swiftly moving electron emitted by a radioactive substance. The isotopes strontium-90 and carbon-14 emit beta particles.

Biocide   any agent that kills living organisms.

Biodegradable   capable of being broken down by bacteria into basic elements

A30

and compounds. Most organic wastes and paper are biodegradable.

Biofuels gas or liquid fuels (such as ethyl alcohol) made from biomass (plants and trees).

Biogas a mixture of methane (CH_4) and carbon dioxide (CO_2) gases produced when anaerobic bacteria break down plants and organic wastes (such as manure).

Biogeochemical cycles mechanisms by which chemicals such as carbon, oxygen, phosphorus, nitrogen, and water are moved through the ecosphere to be renewed over and over again. The three major cycle types are gaseous, sedimentary, and hydrologic.

Biological control pest control that uses natural pedators, parasites, or disease-causing bacteria and viruses (pathogens).

Biological half-life time required for half the amount of a substance (such as a drug or radioactive tracer) to be eliminated from a living organism by excretion, metabolic decomposition, or other natural process.

Biological magnification buildup in concentration of a substance, such as DDT or some radioactive isotopes, in successively higher trophic levels of the food chain or web.

Biological methylation conversion by microorganisms of elemental mercury and inorganic mercury salts into highly toxic methyl mercury. Several other metals also undergo biological methylation.

Biological oxygen demand (BOD) amount of dissolved oxygen gas required for bacterial decomposition of organic wastes in water; usually expressed in terms of the parts per million (ppm) of dissolved oxygen consumed over 5 days at 20°C (68°F) and normal atmospheric pressure.

Biomass total dry weight of all living organisms that can be supported at each trophic level in a food chain; total dry weight of all living organisms in a given area; plant and animal matter that can be used in any form as a source of energy.

Biome a large terrestrial ecosystem characterized by distinctive types of plants and animals and maintained under the climatic conditions of the region.

Biosphere see *Ecosphere.*

Biota all living organisms, both plant and animal, of a region or period.

Biotic living.

Biotic (reproductive) potential the maximum rate at which a population can reproduce given unlimited resources and ideal environmental conditions.

Birth rate number of live births per 1,000 persons in the population at the midpoint of a given year.

Bitumen a black, high-sulfur, tarlike, heavy oil extracted from tar sands and then upgraded to synthetic fuel oil.

Brackish water form of saline water typically found inland that contains 1,000 to 4,000 ppm of dissolved solids. see *Saline water, Salted water, Seawater.*

Breeder reactor nuclear reactor that produces more nuclear fuel than it consumes by converting nonfissionable uranium-238 into fissionable plutonium-239.

Broad-spectrum pesticide chemical that kills organisms besides the target species.

Bronchial asthma a respiratory disease characterized by a narrowing of the bronchial passages and excessive mucus secretion that obstructs the flow of air to the lungs. These conditions bring about recurrent episodes of shortness of breath, prolonged coughing, and difficulty in breathing. compare *Chronic bronchitis.*

Bronchiole tubes tiny ducts or tubes that are subdivisions of the main bronchus tubes and lead to the alveoli.

Bronchus one of the two large tubes entering the lungs, which divide and subdivide into the bronchiole tubes and eventually lead to the alveoli.

Calorie amount of energy required to raise the temperature of 1 gram of water 1°C.

Cancer a group of more than 100 different diseases that strike people of all ages and races; characterized by uncontrolled growth of cells in body tissue.

Carbamates major chemical group of nerve poison pesticides, including Sevin and Zireb.

Carbon monoxide (CO) gaseous molecule containing one atom of carbon and one atom of oxygen; formed by the incomplete combustion of fossil fuels, especially in the internal combustion engine.

Carcinogen a chemical or form of radiation (energy) that directly or indirectly causes a form of cancer.

Carnivore meat-eating organism.

Carrying capacity maximum population that a given ecosystem can support indefinitely under a given set of environmental conditions.

Cellular respiration see *Respiration.*

Channelization strengthening, widening, deepening, clearing, or lining of existing stream channels.

Chemical cycles see *Biogeochemical cycles.*

Chemical energy potential energy stored in chemical bonds that hold atoms or ions in chemical compounds together.

Chemical weathering attack and dissolving of parent rock by exposure to rainwater, surface water, oxygen and other gases in the atmosphere, and compounds secreted by organisms.

Chlorinated hydrocarbon insecticides synthetic, organic nervous system poisons containing chlorine, hydrogen, and carbon. Highly stable and fat soluble, they tend to be recycled through food chains, thereby affecting nontarget organisms. Members include DDT, aldrin, dieldrin, endrin, chlordane, heptachlor, toxaphene, and BHC.

Chronic bronchitis disease characterized by inflammation of the bronchial passages, excessive secretions of mucus, and recurrent coughing. It appears to be aggravated by air pollution, particularly sulfur oxides. compare *Bronchial asthma.*

Chronic disease disease that lasts for a long time (often for life) and that may **(1)** flare up periodically (malaria), **(2)** become progressively worse (cancer), or **(3)** disappear with advancing age (childhood asthma). Chronic diseases may be infectious (malaria, tuberculosis) or noninfectious (cardiovascular disorders, diabetes, hay fever).

Cilia tiny hairs lining the lungs that continually undulate and sweep foreign matter out of the lungs.

Clearcutting removing all trees from a given area in a single cutting.

Climate generalized weather at a given place on earth over a fairly long period.

Climax ecosystem (climax community) a relatively stable stage of ecological succession; a mature ecosystem with a diverse array of species and ecological niches, capable of using energy and cycling critical chemicals more efficiently than simpler, immature ecosystems.

Climax species species that dominates an ecosystem, usually at a mature stage of ecological succession.

Closed system system in which energy but not matter is exchanged between the system and its environment. For all practical purposes, the earth is a closed system. compare *Isolated system, Open system.*

Coal a solid, combustible organic material containing 55 to 90 percent carbon mixed with varying amounts of hydrogen, oxygen, nitrogen, and sulfur compounds.

Coal gasification   a process in which solid coal is converted to either low-heat-content industrial gas or high-heat-content synthetic natural gas (SNG).

Coal liquefaction   a process in which solid coal is converted to synthetic crude oil by the addition of hydrogen (hydrogenation).

Coastal wetlands   shallow shelves that are normally wet or flooded and extend back from the freshwater–saltwater interface. They consist of a complex maze of marshes, bays, lagoons, tidal flats, and mangrove swamps.

Cogeneration   the production of two useful forms of energy from the same process. For example, in a factory steam produced for industrial processes or space heating is run through turbines to generate electricity, which can be used by the industry or sold to power companies.

Coitus interruptus   withdrawal of penis in sexual intercourse before ejaculation.

Combustion   burning. Any very rapid chemical reaction in which heat and light are produced.

Commensalism   a symbiotic relationship between two different species in which one species benefits from the association while the other apparently is neither helped nor harmed. see *Mutualism, Parasitism, Symbiosis.*

Commons   natural resources, especially land, reserved for common use. Many experts in environmental law also treat rivers, lakes, oceans, and the atmosphere as commons.

Community (natural)   populations of different plants and animals living and interacting in a given area at a given time.

Competition (interspecific)   two or more species in the same ecosystem attempting to use the same scarce resources.

Competitive exclusion principle   no two species in the same ecosystem can occupy exactly the same ecological niche indefinitely.

Complete proteins   animal proteins such as meat, fish, eggs, milk, and cheese that can provide humans with all eight essential amino acids.

Composting   breakdown of organic matter in solid waste in the presence of oxygen by aerobic (oxygen-needing) bacteria to produce a humuslike end product, which can be used as a soil conditioner.

Compound   a substance composed of atoms or ions of two or more different elements held together in a fixed ratio by chemical bonds.

Concentration   amount of a chemical or pollutant in a particular volume or weight of air, water, soil, or other medium.

Condom   thin sheath of rubber or animal skin worn tightly over the penis to mechanically prevent sperm from entering vagina.

Consumer   organism that lives off other organisms. Generally divided into primary consumers (herbivores), secondary consumers (carnivores), and microconsumers (decomposers).

Contour farming   plowing and planting along the sloping contours of land in order to reduce soil erosion and conserve water.

Contour surface mining   mining by cutting out a series of contour bands on the side of a hill or mountain. Used primarily for coal. Usually the most destructive form of surface mining.

Control rods   neutron-absorbing rods that are raised or lowered in the core of a nuclear reactor to control the rate of nuclear fission.

Cooling tower   large tower used to transfer the heat in cooling water from a power or industrial plant to the atmosphere either by direct evaporation (wet, or evaporative, cooling tower) or by convection and conduction (dry cooling tower).

Cost-benefit analysis (CBA)   an attempt to compare the pollution control costs and the costs (dollar and otherwise) of pollution damage with the benefits that may occur from pollution control. The goal is to minimize total costs, yet reduce harmful environmental effects to an acceptable level.

Cost effectiveness analysis (CEA) determination of how much it will cost to achieve a benefit from pollution control and comparison of this amount to the cost of obtaining a higher or lower level of the benefit or using some other alternative.

Crop rotation   annual rotation of areas or strips planted with crops such as corn and tobacco that remove large amounts of nitrogen from the soil when harvested with legumes that add nitrogen to the soil or other crops such as oats, barley, or rye.

Crown fire   intensely hot fire that can destroy all vegetation, kill wildlife, and accelerate erosion.

Crude birth rate   see *Birth rate.*

Crude death rate   see *Death rate.*

Crude oil   see *Petroleum.*

Cultural eutrophication   overnourishment of aquatic ecosystems with plant nutrients due to human activities such as agriculture, urbanization, and industrial discharge. see *Eutrophication.*

DDT   *Dichlorodiphenyltrichloroeth-ane,* a chlorinated hydrocarbon that has been widely used as a pesticide.

Death rate   number of deaths per 1,000 persons in the population at the midpoint of a given year.

Decibel (db)   unit used to measure sound power or sound pressure.

Deciduous trees   trees that lose their leaves during part of the year.

Decomposer   bacterium or fungus that causes the chemical disintegration (rot or decay) of organic matter.

Degradable pollutant   pollutant that can be decomposed, removed, or consumed and thus reduced to an acceptable level either by natural processes or by human-engineered processes. Pollutants that are broken down rapidly are called rapidly degraded, or nonpersistent, and those broken down slowly are called slowly degradable, or persistent. compare *Nondegradable pollutant.*

Demographic transition   the transition supposedly brought about by economic development, from a condition of high birth and death rates to substantially lower birth and death rates for a given country or region.

Demography   science of vital and social statistics of populations, such as births, deaths, diseases, and marriages.

Dependency load   ratio of the number of old and young dependents in a population to the work force.

Depletion curve   plot of the supply and production rate of a nonrenewable resource as a function of time. Used to predict when the supply might run out or become scarce. see also *Depletion time.*

Depletion time   the time required to use up a certain fraction (usually 80 percent) of the known or estimated supply of a resource according to various assumed rates of use. see also *Depletion curve.*

Desalination   purification of salt or brackish water by removing the dissolved salts.

Desertification   conversion of productive rangeland into desert through a combination of overgrazing and prolonged drought.

Detritus   dead plant material, bodies of animals, and fecal matter.

Detritus food chain   transfer of energy

from one trophic level to another by decomposers. compare *Grazing food chain*.

Deuterium (hydrogen-2) isotope of the element hydrogen with a nucleus containing one proton and one neutron, thus having a mass number of 2. compare *Tritium*; see also *Heavy water*.

Developed country or nation see *More developed country*.

Developing country or nation see *Less developed country*.

Diaphragm flexible, hemispherical rubber dome inserted into the vagina to fit over the cervix during intercourse to prevent conception.

Dieback see *Population crash*.

Dilation and curettage (D & C) method of abortion in which the cervix is surgically widened and the embryo and placenta are scraped from the walls of the uterus.

Discount factor measure of how much something may be worth in the future compared with what it is worth now.

Disinfection sewage treatment to remove water coloration and to kill disease-carrying bacteria and some (but not all) viruses.

Dissolved oxygen (DO) content amount of oxygen gas (O_2) dissolved in a given quantity of water at a given temperature and atmospheric pressure. It is usually expressed as a concentration in parts per million (ppm) or as a percentage of saturation.

Diversity physical or biological complexity of a system. In many cases it leads to ecosystem stability.

Doubling time time (usually years) that is necessary for a population to double in size.

Douche flushing the vagina with a liquid; ineffective as a method of contraception.

Drainage basin see *Watershed*.

Dredging surface mining of seabeds, primarily for sand and gravel.

Dynamic equilibrium state state in a closed system that is maintained in balance by the dynamic flow of energy through the system and the cycling of critical chemicals within the system.

Dynamic steady state dynamic state of an open system in which the input and output of matter and energy of the system are balanced by a steady flow. Any living organism can be described as an open system in a dynamic steady state.

Ecological efficiency (food chain efficiency) the percent transfer of useful energy from one trophic level to another in a food chain.

Ecological equivalents species that occupy the same or similar ecological niches in similar ecosystems located in different parts of the world. For example, cattle in North America and kangaroos in Australia are grassland grazers.

Ecological niche description of a species' total structural and functional role in an ecosystem.

Ecological succession change in the structure and function of an ecosystem; repeated replacement of one kind of natural community of organisms with a different natural community over time. see *Primary succession, Secondary succession*.

Ecology study of the relationships of living organisms with each other and with their physical and biological environment; study of the structure and function of nature. compare *Human ecology*.

Economic growth rate of increase of an economy's real output or income over time. Frequently expressed as total or per capita GNP over a period of time.

Economics the study of principles and customs that affect the production, consumption, growth, and distribution of material wealth for human needs.

Ecosphere (biosphere) total of all the ecosystems on the planet, along with their interactions; the sphere of air, water, and land in which all life is found.

Ecosystem self-sustaining and self-regulating natural community of organisms interacting with one another and with their environment.

Efficiency see *First-law energy efficiency; Second-law energy efficiency*.

Effluent any substance, particularly a liquid, that enters the environment from a point source. Generally refers to wastewater from a sewage treatment or industrial plant.

Electromagnetic energy radiant energy that can move through a vacuum or through space as waves of oscillating electric and magnetic fields.

Electromagnetic spectrum span of energy ranging from high-energy gamma waves to low-energy radio waves.

Electron fundamental particle found moving around outside the nucleus of an atom. Each electron has one unit of negative charge (-1) and has extremely little mass.

Electrostatic precipitator device for removing particulate matter from smokestack emissions by causing the particles to become electrostatically charged and then attracting them to an oppositely charged plate, where they are precipitated out of the air.

Element chemical such as iron (Fe), sodium (Na), carbon (C), nitrogen (N), and oxygen (O) where distinctly different atoms serve as the 108 basic building blocks of all matter.

Emergency core cooling system (ECCS) system designed to prevent meltdown if the core of a nuclear reactor overheats; the ECCS instantaneously floods the core with large amounts of water.

Emigration the process of leaving one country to take up permanent residence in another.

Emission standard maximum amount of a pollutant that is permitted by the federal government to be discharged from a single polluting source.

Emissivity total amount of degraded heat energy flowing from the earth back into space.

Emphysema see *Pulmonary emphysema*.

Endangered species one having so few individual survivors that the species could soon become extinct in all or part of its region.

Energy ability or capacity to do work or produce a change by pushing or pulling some form of matter.

Energy crisis a shortage or catastrophic price rise for one or more forms of useful energy, or a situation in which energy use is so great that the resultant pollution and environmental degradation threaten human health and welfare.

Energy efficiency the amount of useful energy produced by a source compared to the energy needed to obtain this amount of useful energy.

Energy flow in ecology, the one-way transfer of energy through an ecosystem; more specifically, the way in which energy is converted and expended at each trophic level.

Energy pyramid figure representing the loss or degradation of useful energy at each step in a food chain. About 80 to 90 percent of the energy in each transfer is lost as waste heat, and the resulting shape of the energy levels is that of a pyramid.

Energy quality ability of a form of energy to do useful work. High-quality energy (such as high-temperature heat, fossil fuels, and nuclear fuel) is concentrated, whereas low-quality energy (such as low-temperature heat) is dispersed or diluted.

Entropy   measure of relative disorder or randomness.

Environment   aggregate of external conditions that influence the life of an individual organism or population.

Environmental resistance   all the limiting factors that act together to regulate the maximum allowable size, or carrying capacity, of a population.

EPA   Environmental Protection Agency, the agency responsible for federal efforts to control air and water pollution, radiation and pesticide hazards, ecological research, and solid wastes disposal.

Epilimnion   warm, less dense top layer in a stratified lake. compare *Hypolimnion, Thermocline*.

Essential amino acid   one of the eight chemical building blocks for proteins that cannot be made in the human body and must be included in the diet for good health.

Estuarine zone   area near the coastline that consists of estuaries and coastal salt-water wetlands.

Estuary   thin zone along a coastline where freshwater system(s) and river(s) meet and mix with a salty ocean.

Euphotic zone   surface layer of an ocean, lake, or other body of water through which light can penetrate; thus, the zone of photosynthesis. compare *Abyssal zone, Bathyal zone*.

Eutrophic lake   a lake with a large or excessive supply of plant nutrients (nitrates and phosphates).

Eutrophication (natural)   an excess of plant nutrients from natural erosion and runoff from the land in an aquatic ecosystem supporting a large amount of aquatic life that can deplete the oxygen supply. see also *Cultural eutrophication*.

Evapotranspiration   combination of evaporation and transpiration of water into the atmosphere from living plants and soil.

Evolution   the process by which a population of a species changes its characteristics (genetic makeup) over time.

Exponential growth   geometric growth by doubling; yields a J-shaped curve.

Exponential reserve index   estimated number of years until known world reserves of a nonrenewable resource will be 80 percent depleted if consumed at a rate increasing by a given percentage each year. compare *Static reserve index*.

External cost   cost of production or consumption that must be borne by society, not by the producer.

Externality   external cost or benefit.

Extinction   complete disappearance of a species because of failure to adapt to environmental change.

Family planning   voluntary approach whereby information is provided and contraceptives are distributed to help couples have the number of children they want on the schedule they choose.

Fauna   animal populations of a region.

Fecal coliform bacteria count   number of colonies of fecal coliform bacteria present in a 100-milliliter sample of water. Presence of coliform bacteria in water indicates possible presence of other harmful bacteria from untreated human and animal waste.

Feedback   signal sent back into a self-regulating system to induce system response.

Feedback loop   return to the input of part of the output of a homeostatic system, which is then processed by the system.

Fermentation, anaerobic   process in which carbohydrates are converted in the absence of oxygen to hydrocarbons (such as methane).

Fertile isotopes   isotopes of elements that can be converted by the absorption of fast-moving neutrons into isotopes that will undergo nuclear fission.

Fertilizer   substance that makes the land or soil capable of producing more vegetation or crops.

First energy law   see *First law of thermodynamics*.

First-law energy efficiency   the ratio of the useful work or energy output of a device to the work or energy input that must be supplied to get the output. This ratio is normally multiplied by 100 so that the efficiency can be expressed as a percentage.

First law of thermodynamics (energy)   in any ordinary chemical or physical change, energy is neither created nor destroyed, but merely changed from one form to another. You can't get something for nothing; you can only break even; or, there is no free lunch.

Fissionable isotopes   isotopes of elements that are capable of undergoing nuclear fission.

Floodplain   land next to a river that becomes covered by water when the river overflows its banks.

Flora   plant population of a region.

Fluidized-bed combustion   a process using a flowing stream of hot air to suspend a mixture of powdered coal and limestone so that the coal burns more efficiently. In addition, the limestone removes about 90 to 95 percent of the sulfur in the coal.

Fly ash   small, solid particles of ash and soot generated when coal, oil, or waste materials are burned.

Food additive   a chemical deliberately added to a food, usually to enhance its color, flavor, shelf life, or nutritional characteristics.

Food chain   sequence of transfers of energy in the form of food from organisms in one trophic level to organisms in another trophic level when one organism eats or decomposes another. see *Detritus food chain, Grazing food chain*.

Food contaminant   a substance not deliberately added to food but usually resulting from poor sanitation, improper food processing or storage, or the careless use of compounds such as pesticides and radioactive materials.

Food web   complex, interlocking series of food chains.

Fossil fuel   buried deposits of decayed plants and animals that have been converted to crude oil, coal, natural gas, or heavy oils by exposure to heat and pressure in the earth's crust over hundreds of millions of years.

Freons   chlorofluorocarbon compounds composed of atoms of carbon, chlorine, and fluorine.

Fuel   any substance that can produce heat by being burned or fissioned in a chain reaction, or by undergoing nuclear fusion.

Fuel rod   metal rod containing fissionable isotopes that is inserted into the core of a nuclear reactor.

Fungicide   substance or mixture of substances intended to prevent or kill fungi.

Fungus   simple or complex organism without chlorophyll. The simpler forms are unicellular; the higher forms have branched filaments and complicated life cycles. Examples are molds, yeasts, and mushrooms.

Gamma rays   high-energy electromagnetic waves with very short wavelengths, produced during the disintegration of some radioactive elements. Like x-rays, they readily penetrate body tissues.

Gaseous cycle   a biogeochemical cycle with the atmosphere as the primary reservoir. Examples include the oxygen and nitrogen cycles.

Gasohol   vehicle fuel consisting of a mixture of gasoline and ethyl or methyl alcohol (usually contains 10 to 20 percent alcohol by volume).

Gene pool   total genetic information possessed by a given reproducing population.

Genetic damage   damage by radiation or chemicals to reproductive cells, resulting in mutations that can be passed on to future generations in the form of fetal and infant deaths and physical and mental disabilities.

Genital herpes   sexually transmitted disease caused by the herpes simplex virus 2 (HSV-2).

Genocide   deliberate extermination of all members of a race or nation.

Geometric growth   see *Exponential growth.*

Geothermal energy   heat energy produced when rocks lying below the earth's surface are heated to high temperature by energy from the decay of radioactive elements in the earth and from magma.

Gigawatt (GW)   unit of electrical power equal to one billion watts. see *Watt.*

Gonococcus   bacterium that causes gonorrhea.

Grazing food chain   transfer of energy in the form of food from one organism to another when green plants (producers) are eaten by plant eaters (herbivores), which in turn may be eaten by meat eaters (carnivores). compare *Detritus food chain.*

Green revolution   popular term for the introduction of scientifically bred or selected varieties of a grain (rice, wheat, maize) that, with high enough inputs of fertilizer and water, can give greatly increased yields per area of land planted.

Greenhouse effect   trapping of heat in the atmosphere. Incoming short-wavelength solar radiation penetrates the atmosphere, but the longer-wavelength outgoing radiation is absorbed by water vapor, carbon dioxide, and ozone in the atmosphere and is reradiated to earth, causing a rise in atmospheric temperature.

Gross national product (GNP)   total market value of all goods and services produced in a definite area (usually a nation) during a specific time period (usually a year).

Gross national quality (GNQ)   gross national product (GNP) minus the negative (harmful) products and services. Should be a measure of the items that contribute to the quality of life.

Gross primary productivity   total rate at which green plants convert solar energy by photosynthesis into chemical energy or biomass. see also *Net primary productivity.*

Ground fire   low-level fire that typically burns only undergrowth and occasionally damages fire-sensitive trees.

Groundwater   water that sinks into the soil, where it may be stored for long times in slowly flowing and slowly renewed underground reservoirs.

Growth rate (population)   percentage of increase or decrease of a population. It is the number of births minus the number of deaths per 1,000 population, plus net migration, expressed as a percentage.

Gully reclamation   use of small dams of manure and straw, earth, stone, or concrete to collect silt and gradually fill in channels of eroded soil.

Habitat   place where an organism or community of organisms naturally lives or grows.

Half-life   length of time taken for one-half the atoms in a given amount of a radioactive substance to decay into another isotope. The definition has been extended to refer to biological half-life, or the length of time it takes for half of any substance (such as mercury) in a biological system (such as the brain) to be broken down or excreted.

Hardness (water)   condition caused by dissolved salts of calcium, magnesium, and iron, such as bicarbonates, carbonates, sulfates, chlorides, and nitrates.

Hazardous waste   discarded solid, liquid, or gaseous material that may pose a substantial threat or potential hazard to human health or the environment when improperly handled.

Heat   form of kinetic energy that flows from one body to another as a result of a temperature difference between the two bodies.

Heat island   horizontal pocket of relatively warm air surrounded by cooler air. Often found over city centers and industrial complexes.

Heat pump   device that uses mechanical or electrical energy to transfer heat from a cooler region to a warmer one or vice versa. Heat pumps, air conditioners, and refrigerators work on the same principle.

Heavy metals   group of metallic elements with relatively high atomic weights: mercury, iron, cobalt, cadmium, lead, nickel, zinc, and a number of others.

Heavy oil   a black, high-sulfur, tarlike oil found in deposits of crude oil, tar sands, and oil shale.

Heavy water   water (D_2O) in which all the hydrogen atoms have been replaced by deuterium (D).

Herbicide   chemical that injures or kills plant life by interfering with normal growth.

Herbivore   plant-eating organism.

Herpes simplex virus 2 (HSV-2)   virus that causes the sexually transmitted disease known as genital herpes.

Heterotrophic organism   organism that cannot manufacture its own food and must consume organic food compounds found in other plants and animals. compare *Autotrophic organism.*

High (hard) technology   technology that is complex, centralized, expensive; it tends to replace people with machines, sometimes wastes matter and energy resources, and often produces large amounts of pollution. compare *Appropriate (soft) technology.*

Homeostasis   tendency for a biological system to resist drastic change by maintaining fairly constant internal conditions.

Human ecology   interdisciplinary study of the relations between the human community and its environment. It crosses traditional academic and scientific boundaries and represents an attempt to integrate scientific, behavioral, sociological, political, economic, and ethical functions in human relationships with the environment.

Humus   complex mixture of decaying organic matter and inorganic compounds in the soil that serves as a major source of plant nutrients and increases the soil's capacity to absorb water.

Hydrocarbons   class of organic compounds containing carbon (C) and hydrogen (H). Hydrocarbons often occur as air pollutants from unburned or partially burned gasoline and from evaporation of industrial solvents, especially from refineries. In the presence of sunlight and oxides of nitrogen, they can form photochemical smog.

Hydroelectric plant   electric power plant in which the energy of falling water is used to spin a turbine generator to produce electricity.

Hydrologic cycle   biogeochemical cycle that moves and recycles water in various forms through the ecosphere.

Hydropower electrical energy produced by falling water.

Hydrosphere region that includes all the earth's liquid water (oceans, smaller bodies of fresh water, and underground aquifers), frozen water (polar ice caps, floating ice, and frozen upper layer of soil known as permafrost), and the small amounts of water vapor in the earth's atmosphere.

Hypolimnion bottom layer of cold water in a lake. compare *Epilimnion, Thermocline.*

Hypothetical resources deposits of a resource that can reasonably be expected to exist in areas where deposits have been found in the past. compare *Speculative resources, Undiscovered resources.*

Identified resources specific bodies of mineral-bearing deposits whose existence and location are known. compare *Conditional resources, Reserves.*

Immigration the process of entering one country from another to take up permanent residence.

Incineration the controlled process by which combustible wastes are burned and changed into gases.

Incomplete proteins proteins lacking one or more of the eight essential amino acids.

Industrial smog air pollution, primarily from sulfur oxides and particulates, produced by the burning of coal and oil in households, industries, and power plants.

Infant mortality rate number of deaths of infants under one year of age in a given year per 1,000 births in the same year.

Infectious disease disease resulting from presence of disease-causing organisms or agents, such as bacteria, viruses, and parasitic worms. see also *Non-vector-transmitted infectious disease, Vector-transmitted infectious disease.*

Information feedback information sent back into a homeostatic system so that the system can respond to a new environmental condition.

Inland freshwater wetlands swamps, marshes, and bogs found inland beyond the coastal saltwater wetlands.

Inorganic compounds substances that consist of chemical combinations of two or more elements other than those used to form organic compounds.

Inorganic fertilizer synthetic plant nutrients; examples are ammonium sulfate and calcium nitrate. compare *Organic fertilizer.*

Insecticide substance or mixture of substances intended to prevent, destroy, or repel insects.

Integrated pest management (IPM) combination of natural, biological, chemical, and cultural controls designed for a specific pest problem.

Internal costs costs of production that are directly paid by the user or producer.

Interspecific competition see *Competition.*

Intrauterine device (IUD) small plastic or metal device inserted into the uterus to prevent conception. Very effective.

Inversion see *Thermal inversion.*

Ionizing radiation high-energy radiation that can dislodge one or more electrons from atoms it hits to form charged particles called ions.

Ions species of atoms with either negative or positive electrical charges.

Isolated system system in which neither matter nor energy is exchanged between the system and its environment. compare *Closed system, Open system.*

Isotopes two or more forms of a chemical element that have the same number of protons but different numbers of neutrons in their nuclei.

IUD see *Intrauterine device.*

J-shaped curve curve with the shape of the letter J that depicts exponential or geometric growth (1, 2, 4, 8, 16, 32, . . .).

Kerogen a rubbery, solid mixture of hydrocarbons that is intimately mixed with a limestonelike sedimentary rock. When the rock is heated to high temperatures, the kerogen is vaporized and much of the vapor can be condensed to yield shale oil, which can be refined to give petroleumlike products. see also *Oil shale, Shale oil.*

Kilocalorie (kcal) unit of energy equal to 1,000 calories. see *Calorie.*

Kilowatt (KW) unit of electrical power equal to 1,000 watts. see *Watt.*

Kinetic energy energy that matter has because of its motion and mass.

Kwashiorkor nutritional deficiency (malnutrition) disease that occurs in infants and very young children when they are weaned from mother's milk to a starchy diet that is relatively high in calories but low in protein.

Landfill a land waste disposal site that is located without regard to possible pollution of groundwater and surface water due to runoff and leaching; waste is covered intermittently with a layer of earth to reduce scavenger, aesthetic, disease, and air pollution problems. compare *Open dump, Sanitary landfill, Secured landfill.*

Land-use planning process for deciding the best use of each parcel of land in an area.

Laterite soil found in some tropical areas in which an insoluble concentration of such metals as iron and aluminum is present; soil fertility is generally poor.

Law of conservation of energy see *First law of thermodynamics.*

Law of conservation of matter in any ordinary physical or chemical change, matter is neither created nor destroyed but merely changed from one form to another.

LD-50 (lethal dosage-50 percent) amount of exposure to a toxic chemical that results in the death of half the exposed population.

Leaching extraction or flushing out of dissolved or suspended materials from the soil, solid waste, or another medium by water or other liquids as they percolate down through the medium to groundwater.

Lentic system a nonflowing or standing body of fresh water, such as a lake or pond.

Less developed country (LDC) nation that, compared with more developed countries, typically has **(1)** a low average per capita income, **(2)** a high rate of population growth, **(3)** a large fraction of its labor force employed in agriculture, **(4)** a high level of adult illiteracy, and **(5)** a weak economy and financial base (because only a few items are available for export).

Lifetime cost initial cost plus lifetime operating cost.

Limiting factor factor such as temperature, light, water, or a chemical that limits the existence, growth, abundance, or distribution of an organism.

Limiting factor principle the existence, growth, abundance, or distribution of an organism can be determined by whether the levels of one or more limiting factors go above or below the levels required by the organism.

Limnetic zone open-water surface layer of a lake through which sunlight can penetrate.

Limnology scientific study of physical, chemical, and biological conditions in lakes, ponds, and streams.

Lithosphere region of soil and rock consisting of the earth's crust, a mantle of partially molten rock beneath this crust, and the earth's inner core of molten rock called magma.

Littoral zone area on or near the shore of a body of water.

Lotic system a flowing body of fresh water, such as a river or stream.

Lung cancer the abnormal or runaway growth of cells in the mucous membranes of the bronchial passages.

Macronutrient chemical needed in a relatively large quantity to sustain life in an organism. Carbon, hydrogen, nitrogen, and oxygen are examples.

Magma molten rock material within the earth's interior core.

Magnetohydrodynamic (MHD) generation energy-conversion technique that generates electricity directly from high-temperature ionized gases that are passed through a magnetic field.

Malnutrition condition in which quality of diet is inadequate and an individual's minimum daily requirements (for proteins, fats, vitamins, minerals, and other specific nutrients necessary for good health) are not met.

Malthusian overpopulation result of a tendency for the population size of the world or a given portion of the world to outrun the ability of people to produce or buy food, so that poor health and deaths due to starvation and disease begin to restore the balance between births and deaths. compare *Neo-Malthusian overpopulation*.

Malthusian theory of population the theory of Thomas Malthus that population tends to increase as a geometric progression while food tends to increase as an arithmetic progression. The conclusion is that human beings are destined to misery and poverty unless population growth is controlled.

Marasmus a nutritional deficiency disease that results from a diet low in calories and protein.

Mariculture cultivation of fish and shellfish in estuarine and coastal areas. compare *Aquaculture*.

Mass number the sum of the number of neutrons and protons in the nucleus of an atomic isotope, giving the approximate mass of that isotope.

Mass transit transportation systems (such as buses, trains, and trolleys) that use vehicles that carry large numbers of people.

Matter anything that has mass and occupies space.

Maximum sustained yield maximum rate at which a renewable resource can be used without impairing or damaging its ability to be renewed.

Megalopolis see *Urban region*.

Megawatt (MW) unit of electrical power equal to 1,000 kilowatts, or one million watts. see *Watt*.

Metabolism chemical reactions that keep an organism alive and healthy.

Methyl mercury (CH_3Hg^+) deadly form of mercury that apparently can be formed by microscopic organisms from less harmful elemental mercury and inorganic mercury salts.

Metropolitan area a central city and surrounding suburbs in the United States containing 50,000 or more residents and with an average population density of at least 1,000 persons per square mile.

Microconsumer see *Decomposer*.

Micronutrient chemical that is needed in only a small quantity to sustain life in an organism. Copper, nickel, and at least 20 other chemicals are in this group.

Microorganism generally, any living thing of microscopic size; examples include bacteria, yeasts, simple fungi, some algae, slime molds, and protozoans.

Migration rate difference between the numbers of people leaving and entering a given country or area per 1,000 persons in its population at midyear.

Mineral either a chemical element or a chemical compound (combination of chemical elements) in solid form.

Mineral deposit any natural occurrence of an element or compound in solid form in the lithosphere.

Mineral resource a nonrenewable chemical element or compound in solid form that is used by humans. Mineral resources are classified either as metallic (such as iron and tin) or nonmetallic (such as fossil fuels, sand, and salt).

Minimum tillage farming planting crops by disturbing the soil as little as possible and keeping crop residues and litter on the ground instead of turning them under by plowing.

Moderator substance such as water or graphite used in the core of a nuclear reactor to slow down neutrons so they can cause nuclear fission.

Molecule a chemical combination of two or more atoms of the same chemical element (such as O_2) or different chemical elements (such as H_2O).

Monoculture Cultivation of a single crop (such as maize or cotton) to the exclusion of other crops on a piece of land.

More developed country (MDC) nation that, compared with less developed countries, typically has **(1)** a high average per capita income, **(2)** a low rate of population growth, **(3)** a small fraction of its labor force employed in agriculture, **(4)** a low level of adult illiteracy, and **(5)** a strong economy.

Mortality the death rate.

Multiple use a principle for managing a forest so that it is used for a variety of purposes, including timbering, mining, recreation, grazing, wildlife preservation, and soil and water conservation.

Municipal waste combined residential and commercial waste materials generated in a given municipal area.

Mutagen any substance capable of increasing the rate of genetic mutation of living organisms.

Mutagenic capable of producing harmful genetic mutations.

Mutation process of change in the genetic material that determines the characteristics of a species. Mutations caused by chemical compounds are generally regressive; that is, they produce bizarre, grotesque, or nonviable forms of the parent organism.

Mutualism a symbiotic relationship between two different species that benefits both species. see *Commensalism, Parasitism, Symbiosis*.

Natural community see *Community*.

Natural controls the natural forces that operate to keep populations in check. These include famine, disease, plagues, pestilence, and environmental changes.

Natural eutrophication see *Eutrophication*.

Natural gas natural deposits of gases consisting of 50 to 90 percent methane (a hydrocarbon with the chemical formula CH_4) and small amounts of other, more complex hydrocarbons such as propane (C_3H_8) and butane (C_4H_{10}).

Natural increase (or decrease) difference between the birth rate and death rate in a given population during a given period.

Natural resource see *Resource*.

Natural selection   the mechanism for evolutionary change in which individual organisms in a single population die off over time because they cannot tolerate a new stress and are replaced by individuals whose genetic traits allow them to cope with the stress and to pass these adaptive traits on to their offspring.

Negative feedback   flow of information into a system that causes the system to counteract the effects of an input or change in external conditions. compare *Positive feedback*.

Negative synergy (antagonistic effect) the interaction of two or more factors so that the net effect is less than that resulting from adding their independent effects.

Neo-Malthusian overpopulation   situation in the world or a given country or region in which a relatively small number of people use highly polluting resources so fast that the resulting pollution can threaten the health and survival of human and other species and disrupt the natural processes that cleanse and replenish the air, water, and soil. compare *Malthusian overpopulation*.

Neritic zone   portion of the ocean that includes the estuarine zone and the continental shelf.

Net energy   see *Net useful energy*.

Net migration   in a given population, the difference between the numbers of persons immigrating and migrating during a given period.

Net population change   difference between the total number of live births and the total number of deaths throughout the world or a given part of the world during a specified period (usually a year).

Net primary productivity   rate at which plants produce usuable food or chemical energy (usable biomass). Obtained by subtracting the rate of respiration from the gross primary productivity. see also *Gross primary productivity*.

Net useful energy   total useful energy produced during the lifetime of an entire energy system minus the useful energy used, lost, and wasted in making this useful energy available.

Neutron   elementary particle present in all atomic nuclei (except hydrogen-1). It has a relative mass of one and no electric charge.

Niche   see *Ecological niche*.

Nitrate (NO_3^-)   negatively charged chemical group consisting of one ñitrogen and three oxygen atoms. A major component of some chemical fertilizers.

Nitrite (NO_2^-)   negatively charged chemical group consisting of one nitrogen and two oxygen atoms. It can be poisonous when it combines with hemoglobin in infants.

Nitrogen fixation   process in which bacteria and other soil microorganisms convert atmospheric nitrogen into nitrates, which become available to growing plants.

Nitrogen oxides   air pollutants that consist primarily of nitric oxide (NO) and nitrogen dioxide (NO_2) produced by the reaction of the nitrogen (N_2) and oxygen (O_2) in air at the high temperatures found in internal combustion engines and furnaces.

Nondegradable pollutant   pollutant that is not broken down by natural process; examples are inorganic substances, salts of heavy metals, sediments, some bacteria and viruses, and some synthetic organic chemicals. compare *Degradable pollutant*.

Nongonoccal urethritis   a sexually transmitted disease in men usually caused by the bacterium *Chlamydia trachomatis*.

Noninfectious disease   illness not caused by a disease-causing organism and that, except for genetic diseases, is not transmitted from one person to another. Examples include heart disease, bronchitis, cancer, diabetes, asthma, multiple sclerosis, and hemophilia.

Nonmetropolitan area   a combination of rural areas and other urban places.

Nonpoint source   source of pollution in which wastes are not released at one specific, indentifiable point but from a number of points that are spread out and difficult to identify and control.

Nonrenewable resource   resource that is not replaced by natural processes or for which the rate of replacement is slower than its rate of use. compare *Renewable resource*.

Nonspontaneous process   a process that requires an outside input of energy to occur. compare *Spontaneous process*.

Nonthreshold pollutant   substance or condition harmful to a particular organism at any level or concentration.

Non-vector-transmitted infectious disease   disease that is transmitted from person to person without an intermediate nonhuman live carrier. The transmission usually takes place by (1) close physical contact with infected persons (syphilis, gonorrhea, mononucleosis), (2) contact with water, food, soil, clothing, bedding, or other substance contaminated by fecal material or saliva from infected persons (cholera, typhoid fever), or (3) inhalation of air containing tiny droplets of contaminated fluid, which are expelled when infected persons cough, sneeze, or talk (common cold, influenza).

Nuclear energy   energy released when atomic nuclei undergo fission or fusion.

Nuclear fission   process in which the nucleus of a heavy isotope splits into two or more nuclei of lighter elements, with the release of neutrons and substantial amounts of energy. The most important fissionable materials are uranium-235 and plutonium-239.

Nuclear fusion   process in which the nuclei of two light, nonradioactive isotopes (such as hydrogen isotopes) are forced together at ultrahigh temperatures to form the nucleus of a slightly heavier element (such as helium); the release of substantial amounts of energy accompanies such reactions.

Nucleus   the extremely tiny center of an atom that contains one or more positively charged protons and in most cases one or more neutrons with no electrical charge. The nucleus contains most of an atom's mass.

Nutrient   element or compound that is an essential raw material for organism growth and development. Examples are carbon, oxygen, nitrogen, phosphorus, and the dissolved solids and gases in water.

Nutrition   uptake of materials necessary for good health and survival.

Ocean thermal gradients   temperature difference between warm surface waters and cold bottom waters in an ocean. If the difference is large enough, this storage of solar heat could be tapped as a source of energy.

Oil   see *Petroleum*.

Oil shale   an underground formation of limestonelike sedimentary rock (marlstone) that contains a rubbery, solid mixture of hydrocarbons known as kerogen. see also *Kerogen, Shale oil*.

Oligotrophic lake   a lake with a low supply of plant nutrients.

Omnicide   killing of everyone (probably through global nuclear war).

Omnivore   animal such as a human that can use both plants and other animals as food sources.

OPEC   the Organization of Petroleum Exporting Countries; 13 nations that aim at developing common prices and policies for marketing crude oil extracted within their boundaries.

Open dump   land disposal site where wastes are deposited and left uncovered with little or no regard for control of scavenger, aesthetic, disease, air pollution, or water pollution problems. compare *Landfill, Sanitary landfill, Secured landfill*.

Open pit mining   surface mining of materials (primarily stone, sand, gravel, iron and copper) that creates a large pit.

Open sea (oceanic zone)   the part of an ocean that is beyond the continental shelf.

Open system   system in which energy and matter are exchanged between the system and its environment, for example, a living organism. compare *Closed system, Isolated system*.

Optimum population   level of population that allows most, if not all, of the world's or a region's population to live with reasonable comfort and individual freedom.

Oral contraceptive (the pill)   combination of synthetic female hormones (such as estrogen and progesterone), which are taken once a day (or less frequently with some newer types) to inhibit the release of eggs from the ovaries, thereby preventing conception.

Ore   mineral deposit containing a high enough proportion of an element to permit it to be mined and sold at a profit. compare *Subeconomic resources*.

Organic compounds   molecules that typically contain atoms of the elements carbon and hydrogen; carbon, hydrogen, and oxygen; or carbon, hydrogen, oxygen, and nitrogen.

Organic farming   a method of producing crops and livestock naturally by using organic fertilizer (manure, legumes, composting, crop residues), crop rotation, and natural pest control (good bugs that eat bad bugs, plants that repel bugs, and environmental controls such as crop rotation) instead of using commercial fertilizer and synthetic pesticides and herbicides.

Organic fertilizer   animal manure or other organic material used as a plant nutrient. compare *Inorganic fertilizer*.

Organophosphates   diverse group of nonpersistent synthetic chemical insecticides that act chiefly by breaking down nerve and muscle responses; examples are parathion and Malathion.

Overfishing   harvesting so many fish of a species that there is not enough breeding stock left to repopulate the species for the next year's catch.

Overnutrition   diet so high in calories, saturated (animal) fats, salt, sugar, and processed foods, and so low in vegetables and fruits that the consumer runs high risks of diabetes, hypertension, heart disease,

and other health hazards. compare *Malnutrition*.

Overpopulation   see *Malthusian overpopulation, Neo-Malthusian overpopulation*.

Oxygen-demanding waste   organic water pollutants that are usually degraded by bacteria if there is sufficient dissolved oxygen (DO) in the water. see also *Biological oxygen demand*.

Ozone (O_3)   highly reactive molecule made up of three atoms of oxygen that forms a layer high in the atmosphere. This layer filters out harmful ultraviolet radiation, thus protecting life on earth. Ozone is also formed at the earth's surface as a damaging component of photochemical smog.

Ozone layer   layer of gaseous ozone (O_3) in the upper atmosphere that protects life on earth by filtering out harmful ultraviolet radiation from the sun.

PANs   group of chemicals (photochemical oxidants) known as peroxyacyl nitrates, found in photochemical smog.

Parasitism   a symbiotic relationship between two different species in which one species (the parasite) benefits and the other species (the host) is harmed. see *Commensalism, Mutualism, Symbiosis*.

Paratransit   transit system such as carpools, vanpools, jitneys, and dial-a-ride systems that carry a relatively small number of passengers per vehicular unit.

Particulate matter   solid particles or liquid droplets suspended or carried in the air.

Parts per billion (ppb)   number of parts of a chemical found in one billion parts of a solid, liquid, or gaseous mixture.

Parts per million (ppm)   number of parts of a chemical found in one million parts of a solid, liquid, or gaseous mixutre.

Pathogen   an organism that produces disease.

PCBs (polychlorinated biphenyls)   mixture of at least 50 widely used compounds containing chlorine that can be biologically magnified in the food chain with unknown effects.

Pelvic inflammatory disease (PID)   a sexually transmitted disease in women usually caused by the bacterium *Chlamydia trachomatis*.

Pest   unwanted organism that directly or indirectly interferes with human activities.

Pesticide   any chemical designed to kill

weeds, insects, fungi, rodents, and other organisms that humans consider to be undesirable; examples are chlorinated hydrocarbons, carbamates, and organophosphates.

Petrochemicals   chemicals made from natural gas or petroleum.

Petroleum (crude oil)   gooey, dark greenish-brown, foul-smelling liquid containing a complex mixture of hydrocarbon compounds plus small amounts of oxygen, sulfur, and nitrogen compounds and found in natural underground reservoirs.

pH   numeric value that indicates the relative acidity or alkalinity of a substance on a scale of 0 to 14, with the neutral point at 7.0. Values lower than 7.0 indicate the presence of acids and greater than 7.0 the presence of alkalis (bases).

Photochemical reaction   a chemical reaction activated by light.

Photochemical smog   complex mixture of air pollutants (oxidants) produced in the atmosphere by the reaction of hydrocarbons and nitrogen oxides under the influence of sunlight. Especially harmful photochemical oxidants include ozone (O_3), peroxyacyl nitrates (PANs), and various aldehydes.

Photosynthesis   complex process that occurs in the cells of green plants whereby sunlight is used to combine carbon dioxide (CO_2) and water (H_2O) to produce oxygen (O_2) and simple sugar or food molecules, such as glucose ($C_6H_{12}O_6$).

Photovoltaic cell   device in which radiant (solar) energy is converted directly into electrical energy.

Physical weathering   breaking down of parent rock into bits and pieces by exposure to temperature changes and the physical action of moving ice and water, growing roots, and human activities such as farming and construction.

Phytoplankton   free-floating, mostly microscopic aquatic plants.

Plankton   microscopic floating plant and animal organisms of lakes, rivers, and oceans.

Plasma   "gas" of charged particles (ions) of elements that exists only at such high temperatures (40 million to several billion degrees Celsius) that all electrons are stripped from the atomic nuclei.

Point source   source of pollution that involves discharge of wastes from an identifiable point, such as a smokestack or sewage treatment plant.

Pollution   undesirable change in the physical, chemical, or biological characteristics of the air, water, or land that can harmfully affect the health, survival, or activities of humans or other living organisms.

Population group of individual organisms of the same kind (species) that interbreed and occupy a given area at a given time.

Population crash (dieback) extensive deaths resulting when a population exceeds the ability of the environment to support it.

Population density number of organisms in a particular population per square kilometer or other unit of area.

Population distribution variation of population density over a given country, region, or other area.

Positive feedback information sent back into a homeostatic system that causes the system to change continuously in the same direction; as a result, the system can go out of control. compare *Negative feedback*.

Positive synergy interaction of two or more factors so that the net effect is greater than that resulting from their independent effects.

Potential energy energy stored in an object as a result of its position or the position of its parts.

Power rate at which work is done or energy is expended.

Power tower see *Solar furnace*.

Predation situation in which an organism of one species (the predator) captures and feeds on an organism of another species (the prey).

Predator organism that lives by killing and eating other organisms.

Primary air pollutant chemical that has been added directly to the air and occurs in a harmful concentration. compare *Secondary air pollutant*.

Primary energy source renewable or nonrenewable energy resource used to supplement the direct input of solar energy and used to provide the remaining 1 percent of the energy we use on earth.

Primary succession ecological succession that begins on an area (such as bare rock, lava, or sand) that has never been occupied by a community of organisms.

Primary treatment (of sewage) mechanical treatment in which large solids, like old shoes and sticks of wood, are screened out, and suspended solids in the sewage settle out as sludge. compare *Secondary treatment, Tertiary treatment*.

Primate a mammal of the order Primates, including humans, the apes, monkeys, lemurs, tarsiers, and marmosets.

Prime reproductive age years between ages 20 and 29 during which most women have most of their children. Compare *Reproductive age*.

Producer organism that synthesizes its own organic substances from inorganic substances, such as a plant.

Profundal zone a lake's deep-water region that is not penetrated by sunlight.

Pronatalist refers to cultural attitudes and values that favor motherhood and large families.

Protein-calorie malnutrition combination of undernutrition and malnutrition.

Pulmonary emphysema lung disease in which the alveoli enlarge and lose their elasticity, thus impairing the transfer of oxygen to the blood.

Pyramid of biomass diagram representing the biomass, or total dry weight of all living organisms, that can be supported at each trophic level in a food chain.

Pyramid of numbers diagram representing the number of organisms of a particular type that can be supported at each trophic level from a given input of solar energy at the producer trophic level in a food chain.

Pyrolysis high-temperature decomposition of material in the absence of oxygen.

Radiation propagation of energy through matter and space in the form of fast-moving particles (particulate radiation) or waves (electromagnetic radiation).

Radioactive waste radioactive end products of nuclear power plants, research, medicine, weapons production or other processes involving nuclear reactions.

Radioactivity property of certain chemical elements of spontaneously emitting radiation from unstable atomic nuclei. The emitted radiation may damage organisms. see *Radioisotope*.

Radioisotope isotope of an element whose nuclei are capable of spontaneously emitting at a certain rate radiation in the form of alpha particles, beta particles, or gamma rays to form a different nonradioactive or radioactive isotope.

Range of tolerance the range or span of conditions that must be maintained for an organism to stay alive and grow, develop, and function normally.

Rangeland land on which the vegetation is predominantly grasses, grasslike plants, or shrubs such as sagebrush.

Rate of natural change measure of population change obtained by finding the difference between the birth rate and the death rate.

Rate of population change difference between the birth rate and the death rate plus net migration rate for a particular country or area.

Recycle to collect and treat a resource so it can be used again, as when used glass bottles are collected, melted down, and made into new glass bottles. compare *Reuse*.

Renewable resource resource that potentially cannot be used up because it is constantly or cyclically replenished. Either it comes from an essentially inexhaustible source (such as solar energy), or it can be renewed by natural or human-devised cyclical processes if it is not used faster than it is renewed. compare *Nonrenewable resource*.

Replacement level of fertility fertility rate of 2.11 children per woman (in the United States), which will supply just enough births to replace the parents and compensate for premature deaths, assuming proper age structure and no net effect of migration.

Reproductive age ages 15 to 44, when most women have all their children. compare *Prime reproductive age*.

Reproductive potential see *Biotic potential*.

Reserves amount of a particular resource in known locations that can be extracted at a profit with present technology and prices. compare *Conditional resources, Identified resources*.

Resistant crop variety plant variety that is genetically bred to resist certain insects, fungi, and diseases.

Resource (natural) any form of matter or energy obtained from the environment that meets human needs. see also *Mineral resource, Nonrenewable resource, Renewable resource*.

Resource recovery extraction of useful materials or energy from waste materials. This may involve recycling or conversion into different and sometimes unrelated products or uses. compare *Recycle, Reuse*.

Resources total amount of a particular resource material that exists on earth.

Respiration complex process that occurs in the cells of plants and animals in which food molecules such as glucose ($C_6H_{12}O_6$) combine with oxygen (O_2) and break down into carbon dioxide (CO_2) and water (H_2O), releasing usable energy.

Reuse to use a product over and over again in the same form, as is done with returnable glass bottles, which are washed and refilled. compare *Recycle*.

Rhythm method   method of birth control based on abstention from sexual intercourse during a woman's fertile period.

Runoff   surface water entering rivers, freshwater lakes, or reservoirs.

Rural area   an area in the United States with a population of fewer than 2,500 people.

S-shaped curve   leveling off of an exponential or J-shaped curve.

Saline water   water containing more than 1,000 parts per million (ppm) of dissolved solids of any type. Includes inland brackish water, salted water, and seawater. see *Brackish water, Salted water, Seawater*.

Salinity   amount of dissolved salts in a given volume of water.

Salted water   water having 4,000 to 18,000 parts per million (ppm) of dissolved salts. see *Brackish water, Saline water, Seawater*.

Sanitary landfill   land waste disposal site that is located to minimize water pollution from runoff and leaching; waste is spread in thin layers, compacted, and covered with a fresh layer of soil each day to minimize pest, aesthetic, disease, air pollution, and water pollution problems. compare *Landfill, Open dump, Secured landfill*.

Saprophytic   obtaining food by absorbing the products of organic breakdown and decay.

Saprotrophic organisms   tiny organisms—such as bacteria, fungi, termites, and maggots—that break down complex chemicals in the bodies of dead animals and plants into simpler chemicals.

Scrubber   common antipollution device that uses a liquid spray to remove pollutants from a stream of air.

Seawater   water having 18,000 to 35,000 parts per million (ppm) of dissolved solids. see *Brackish water, Saline water, Salted water.*

Second energy law   see *Second law of thermodynamics*.

Second-law energy efficiency   ratio of the minimum amount of useful energy needed to perform a task in the most efficient way that is theoretically possible to the actual amount of useful energy used to perform the task.

Second law of thermodynamics (law of energy degradation)   **(1)** in all conversions of heat energy to work, some of the energy is degraded to a more dispersed and less useful form, usually heat energy given off at a low temperature to the surroundings, or environment, *or you can't break even in terms of energy quality*; **(2)** any system and its surrounding (environment) as a whole spontaneously tends toward increasing randomness, disorder, or entropy, *or if you think things are mixed up now, just wait*.

Secondary air pollutant   harmful chemical formed in the atmosphere through a chemical reaction among air components. compare *Primary air pollutant*.

Secondary consumer   see *Carnivore*.

Secondary materials   uniformly segregated and processed waste materials from a recycling or resource recovery plant, sold to manufacturers for use in making basic products.

Secondary succession   ecological succession that begins on an area (such as abandoned farmland, a new pond, or land disrupted by fire) that had been occupied by a community of organisms.

Secondary treatment (of sewage)   second step in most waste treatment systems, in which bacteria break down the organic parts of sewage wastes; usually accomplished by bringing the sewage and bacteria together in trickling filters or in the activated sludge process. compare *Primary treatment, Tertiary treatment*.

Secured landfill   a land site for the storage of hazardous solid and liquid wastes, which are normally placed in containers and buried underground in a restricted-access area that is continually monitored. Such landfills are located above geologic strata that are supposed to prevent the leaching of wastes into groundwater. compare *Landfill, Open dump, Sanitary landfill*.

Sediment   soil particles, sand, and minerals washed from the land into aquatic systems as a result of natural and human activities.

Sedimentary cycle   biogeochemical cycle in which materials primarily are moved from land to sea and back again. Examples include the phosphorus and sulfur cycles.

Selection cutting   cutting of mature or diseased trees singly or in small groups to encourage younger trees to grow and to produce an uneven-aged stand with trees of different species, ages, and size.

Septic tank   underground receptacle for wastewater from a home. The bacteria in the sewage decompose the organic wastes, and the sludge settles to the bottom of the tank. The effluent flows out of the tank into the ground through drains.

Shale oil   a low-sulfur, very viscous, petroleumlike liquid, obtained when kerogen in shale oil rock is vaporized at high temperatures and then condensed. Shale oil can be refined to yield petroleum products. see also *Kerogen, Oil shale*.

Shelterwood cutting   removal of all mature trees in an area in a series of cuts over two or three decades.

Silviculture   cultivation of forests.

Single-cell protein (SCP)   form of protein made from oil by the action of microorganisms.

Slash-and-burn agriculture   in many tropical areas, the practice of clearing a patch of forest overgrowth, burning the residue, and planting crops. The patch is abandoned after 2 or 3 years to prevent depletion of soil fertility.

Sludge   solid matter that settles to the bottom of sedimentation tanks in a sewage treatment plant and must be disposed of by digestion or other methods or recycled to the land.

Smog   originally a combination of *fog* and *smoke*; now applied also to the photochemical haze produced by the action of sun and atmosphere on automobile and industrial exhausts. compare *Industrial smog, Photochemical smog*.

Society   group of people living together in a region as a community and sharing the same general living system and cultural benefits.

Soil   complex mixture of small pieces of rock, minerals (inorganic compounds), organic compounds, living organisms, air, and water. It is a dynamic body that is always changing in response to climate, vegetation, local topography, parent rock material, age, and human use and abuse.

Soil erosion   the processes by which soil is removed from one place by forces such as wind, water, waves, glaciers, and construction activity and eventually deposited at some new place.

Soil horizons   horizontal layers that make up a particular type of soil.

Soil profile   cross-sectional view of the horizons in a soil.

Soil structure   the way soil particles clump together in larger lumps and clods.

Soil texture   size of a soil's individual mineral particles and the proportion in which particles of different sizes are found in a soil.

Solar cell   device that converts radiant energy from the sun directly into electrical energy by the photovoltaic process.

Solar collector   device for collecting

radiant energy from the sun and converting it into heat.

Solar energy   direct radiant energy from the sun plus indirect forms of energy—such as wind, falling or flowing water (hydropower), ocean thermal gradients, and biomass—that are produced when solar energy interacts with the earth.

Solar furnace   system for concentrating direct solar energy to produce electricity or high-temperature heat for direct use.

Solar pond   saline body of water in which stored solar energy can be extracted as a result of the temperature difference (thermal gradient) between a layer of saline water on the bottom and a layer of less saline water on top.

Solid waste   any unwanted or discarded material that is not a liquid or a gas.

Spaceship earth   metaphor for the earth as a finite ecosystem in which resources must be husbanded and the ever-changing balance between humans and their environment preserved if life is to survive.

Speciation   splitting of a single species into two different species.

Species   all organisms of a given kind; a group of plants or animals that breed or are bred together but are not bred successfully with organisms outside their group.

Species diversity   ratio between the number of species in a community and the number of individuals in each species. (For example, low diversity occurs when there are few species but many individuals per species.)

Speculative resources   deposits that are thought to be in areas that have not been examined and tested for their presence. compare *Hypothetical resources, Undiscovered resources.*

Spontaneous process   any process that can occur naturally without an outside input of energy, for example, water flowing downhill or heat energy flowing from hot to cold. compare *Nonspontaneous process.*

SST   supersonic transport aircraft that can fly faster than the speed of sound.

Stability   persistence of the structure of a system (such as an ecosystem, community, or organism) over time.

Standard metropolitan statistical area (SMSA)   a central city and surrounding suburbs containing 50,000 or more people with an average population density of at least 1,000 persons per square mile.

Static reserve index   estimated number of years until known world reserves

of a nonrenewable resource will be 80 percent depleted if depletion proceeds at the present annual rate. compare *Exponential reserve index.*

Stationary population   stable population that does not increase or decrease in size.

Steady state   see *Dynamic steady state.*

Strip cropping   planting regular crops and close-growing plants such as hay or nitrogen-fixing legumes in alternating rows or bands.

Strip (surface) mining   mining in which the earth's surface is stripped away.

Subeconomic resources   known supplies of resources that cannot be recovered profitably with present prices and technology. compare *Identified resources, Reserves.*

Subsidence   sinking down of part of the earth's crust due to underground excavation, such as a coal mine.

Subsurface mining   underground extraction of a metal ore or fuel resource such as coal.

Succession   see *Ecological succession.*

Sulfur cycle   transformation of sulfur into different compounds as it passes through the ecosphere.

Sulfur dioxide (SO_2)   heavy, colorless gas that is toxic to plants and can harm humans. It is produced by burning coal and by smelting and other industrial processes.

Sulfur oxides   the common air pollutants sulfur dioxide (SO_2) and sulfur trioxide (SO_3), which are produced when coal or oil containing small amounts of sulfur is burned. Sulfur dioxide can react with oxygen in the air to produce sulfur trioxide, which can react with water vapor to produce sulfuric acid (H_2SO_4).

Sulfuric acid (H_2SO_4)   corrosive acid; often produced from the reaction of sulfur trioxide with water vapor in the air. see *Sulfur oxides.*

Superinsulated house   house that contains massive amounts of insulation, is extremely airtight, typically uses active or passive solar collectors to heat water, and has an air-to-air heat exchanger to prevent buildup of excessive moisture and indoor air pollutants.

Surface mining   the process of removing the overburden of topsoil, subsoil, and other strata to permit the extraction of underlying mineral deposits. see *Area strip mining, Contour strip mining, Dredging, Open pit mining.*

Surface water   water that flows in streams and rivers and in natural lakes, in wetlands, and in reservoirs constructed by humans.

Surroundings (environment)   everything outside a specified system of collection of matter.

Sustained yield   principle for managing a forest in which depletion is avoided by striking a balance between new planting and growing and the amount of wood removed by cutting, pests, disease, and fire.

Symbiosis   interaction in which two different species exist in close physical contact, with one living on or in the other so that both species benefit from the association. see *Commensalism, Mutualism, Parasitism.*

Synergistic effect   result of the interaction of two or more substances or factors that could not have been produced by these factors acting separately. see *Negative synergy, Positive synergy, Synergy.*

Synergy   interaction in which the total effect is greater than or less than the sum of two effects taken independently. **see** *Negative synergy, Positive synergy.*

Synfuels   fuels such as synthetic natural gas (SNG) and synthetic fuel oil produced from coal or sources other than natural gas or crude oil.

System   collection of matter under study.

Tar sands (oil sands)   enormous swamps that contain fine clay and sand mixed with water and highly variable amounts of a black, high-sulfur, molasses-like tar known as heavy oil, or bitumen, which is about 83 percent carbon. The heavy oil can be extracted from the tar sand by heating and flotation, and purified and upgraded to synthetic crude oil.

Temperature   the relative hotness or coldness of a substance. It is a measure of the average kinetic energy of all the atoms and molecules in a sample of matter.

Ten percent rule   only about 10 percent of the chemical energy available at one trophic level is transferred in usuable form to the bodies of the organisms at the next trophic level in a food chain or food web.

Teratogen   substance that, if ingested by a pregnant female, causes malformation of the developing fetus. The drug thalidomide is a powerful teratogen.

Terracing   planting crops on a long,

steep slope that has been converted into a series of broad, level terraces at right angles to the slope of the land.

Territory area that an organism (such as a lion) will defend against intruders of the same species (other lions).

Tertiary treatment (of sewage) removal from wastewater of traces of organic materials and dissolved solids that remain after *primary* and *secondary treatment.*

Tetraethyl lead form of lead added to gasoline to reduce engine knock; considered to be a major source of the lead that is now accumulating in our bodies.

Thermal gradient temperature difference between two areas.

Thermal inversion layer of cool air trapped under a layer of less dense warm air, thus reversing the normal situation. In a prolonged inversion, air pollution may rise to harmful levels.

Thermal pollution an increase in air or water temperature that disturbs the climate or ecology of an area.

Thermocline fairly thin zone in a lake that separates an upper warmer zone (*epilimnion*) from a lower colder zone (*hypolimnion*).

Threshold effect phenomenon in which no effect is observed until a certain level or concentration is attained. see *Threshold pollutant.*

Threshold pollutant substance that is harmful to a particular organism only above a certain concentration, or threshold level.

Time delay lag between the receipt of an information signal or stimulus and the system's making of corrective action by negative feedback.

Tolerance limit point at and beyond which a chemical or physical condition (such as heat) becomes harmful to a living organism.

Total fertility rate (TFR) projection of the average number of children that would be born to each woman if throughout her reproductive years (ages 15 to 44) she were to bear children at the same rate as other women did in each of these years.

Toxic substances substances (chemicals) that can cause serious illness or death.

Trace elements chemical elements needed in very small amounts for good health and survival.

Transpiration direct transfer of water from the leaves of living plants to the atmosphere.

Trickling filter bed of rocks or stones.

Sewage is trickled over the bed so that bacteria can break down the organic wastes. The bacteria collect on the stones through repeated use of the filter.

Tritium (hydrogen-3) isotope of the element hydrogen with a nucleus containing one proton and two neutrons, thus having a mass number of 3. compare *Deuterium.*

Trophic level level where energy in the form of food is transferred from one organism to another in a food chain or food web.

Troposphere the lower layer of the atmosphere, which contains about 95 percent of the earth's air and extends about 8 to 12 kilometers (5 to 7 miles) above the earth's surface.

Ultraviolet (UV) radiation electromagnetic radiation with wavelengths somewhat shorter than those for visible light but longer than those for x-rays.

Undernutrition condition characterized by an insufficient quantity or caloric intake of food to meet an individual's minimum daily energy requirement.

Undiscovered resources resource supplies believed to exist although their specific location, quality, and amount are unknown. see *Hypothetical resources, Speculative resources.*

Upwelling region area adjacent to a continent where ocean bottom waters rich in nutrients are brought to the surface.

Urban area any place with a population of 20,000 or more.

Urban growth increase in size of an urban area.

Urban open space area of land or water in or near an urban area that has a recreational, aesthetic, or ecological function.

Urban region (megalopolis) large zone of metropolitan areas separated only by occasional topographical barriers and containing at least 1 million people.

Urban waste general term used to categorize the entire waste stream from an urban area; sometimes used in contrast to "rural waste."

Urbanization the proportion of the total population concentrated in an urban area.

Vasectomy method of male sterilization in which small sections of the vas tubes are removed, and the tubes are retied. Reversible in some cases.

Vector living organism (usually an insect) that carries an infectious disease from one host (person or animal) to another.

Vector-transmitted infectious disease disease carried from one host to another by a living organism (usually insect), called a vector. Examples include malaria, schistosomiasis, and African sleeping sickness.

Vitamins specific organic compounds required in small amounts for life and good health.

Water cycle see *Hydrologic cycle.*

Water pollution degradation of a body of water by a substance or condition to such a degree that the water fails to meet specified standards or cannot be used for a specific purpose.

Water table level below the earth's surface at which the ground becomes saturated with water.

Waterlogging saturation of soil with irrigation water so the water table rises close to the surface.

Watershed land area from which water drains toward a common watercourse in a natural basin.

Watt unit of power, or rate at which electrical work is done.

Wavelength distance between the crest (or trough) of one wave and that of the next.

Weather day-to-day variation in atmospheric conditions.

Wetland area that is regularly wet or flooded and has a water table that stands at or above the land surface for at least part of the year. Coastal wetlands extend back from estuaries and include salt marshes, tidal basins, marshes, and mangrove swamps. Inland freshwater wetlands consist of swamps, marshes, and bogs.

Whole-tree harvesting use of machines to pull up entire trees from the ground and reduce them to small chips.

Wilderness area where the earth and its community of life have not been seriously disturbed by humans and where humans are only temporary visitors.

Wildlife all undomesticated species of plants and animals on earth.

Windbreaks using rows of trees or hedges to reduce soil erosion on cultivated land exposed to high winds.

X-rays high-energy electromagnetic

radiation emitted when some electrons outside the nucleus of an atom are exposed to a sufficient amount of energy.

Zero population growth (ZPG) state in which the birth rate (plus immigration) equals the death rate (plus emigration) so that population is no longer increasing. Also the name of an important organization dedicated to achieving this goal.

Index

Numbers in boldface type indicate pages where term is defined. Alphabetization is in letter-by-letter mode.
(f) = figure; (t) = table; (n) = footnote; (tn) = table footnote; E = Enrichment Study